DATE DUE

PRINTED IN U.S.A.

*International Encyclopedia of the
Social Sciences, 2nd edition*

International Encyclopedia of the Social Sciences, 2nd edition

VOLUME 4
INEQUALITY, INCOME–MARXISM, BLACK

William A. Darity Jr.
EDITOR IN CHIEF

MACMILLAN REFERENCE USA
A part of Gale, Cengage Learning

GALE
CENGAGE Learning

Detroit • New York • San Francisco • New Haven, Conn • Waterville, Maine • London

International Encyclopedia of the Social Sciences, 2nd edition
William A. Darity Jr., Editor in Chief

LIBRARY OF CONGRESS CATALOGING-IN-PUBLICATION DATA

International encyclopedia of the social sciences / William A. Darity, Jr., editor in chief.—2nd ed. v. cm. Rev. ed. of: International encyclopedia of the social sciences / David L. Sills, editor. c1968–c1991.
   Includes bibliographical references and index.
   ISBN 978-0-02-865965-7 (set hardcover : alk. paper)—ISBN 978-0-02-865966-4 (v. 1 hardcover : alk. paper)—ISBN 978-0-02-865967-1 (v. 2 hardcover : alk. paper)—ISBN 978-0-02-865968-8 (v. 3 hardcover : alk. paper)—ISBN 978-0-02-865969-5 (v. 4 hardcover : alk. paper)—ISBN 978-0-02-865970-1 (v. 5 hardcover : alk. paper)—ISBN 978-0-02-865971-8 (v. 6 hardcover : alk. paper)—ISBN 978-0-02-865972-5 (v. 7 hardcover : alk. paper)—ISBN 978-0-02-865973-2 (v. 8 hardcover : alk. paper)—ISBN 978-0-02-866141-4 (v. 9 hardcover : alk. paper)—ISBN 978-0-02-866117-9 (ebook : alk. paper)
   1. Social sciences—Dictionaries. 2. Social sciences—Encyclopedias. I. Darity, William A., 1953– II. Title: Encyclopedia of the social sciences.
   H40.A2I5 2008
   300.3–dc22

   2007031829

0-02-865965-1 (set)
0-02-865966-X (v. 1)
0-02-865967-8 (v. 2)
0-02-865968-6 (v. 3)
0-02-865969-4 (v. 4)

0-02-865970-8 (v. 5)
0-02-865971-6 (v. 6)
0-02-865972-4 (v. 7)
0-02-865973-2 (v. 8)
0-02-866141-9 (v. 9)

This title is also available as an e-book.
ISBN 978-0-02-866117-9; 0-02-866117-6
Contact your Gale representative for ordering information.

Printed in the United States of America
3 4 5 6 7 8 14 13 12 11 10 09 08

Editorial Board

Contents

I

INEQUALITY, INCOME

Income inequality is an important aspect of the economic and social well-being of a nation. The axiom "the rich are getting richer and the poor are getting poorer" is synonymous with rising income and wealth inequality. Both affluent and poor countries experience some degree of income inequality.

Income inequality rose in the United States between the mid-1970s and early-2000s based on several measures. The United States generally exhibited the highest degree of income inequality of the industrialized OECD (Organization for Economic Cooperation and Development) countries, although research by Peter Gottschalk and Timothy Smeeding (2000) did not discern any universal trend. According to opinion polls by Demos, a U.S. public policy organization, American public opinion toward income inequality tends to shift in response to media reports on excessive executive compensation, corporate downsizing, and the state of the U.S. economy.

Opinions are divided on whether society should be concerned about income inequality. Economists Martin Feldstein and Anne Krueger argue that policymakers should focus on reducing poverty, not inequality. This is because an increase in inequality will occur even though all *income-receiving units* (IRUs) are better off in absolute terms if the incomes of richer IRUs rise by higher proportions than those of their poorer counterparts. An alternative view, articulated by Simon Kuznets (1901–1985) and Kenneth Arrow, winners of the 1971 and 1972 Nobel Prize in Economics, respectively, is that income inequality is an important determinant of aggregate savings and growth, and the perception of unfairness it entails may cause political instability and social conflict.

MEASURING INCOME INEQUALITY

One way of analyzing income inequality trends is to examine the income shares accruing to some segment of the population (e.g., the poorest and richest 10 percent). A falling (rising) income share of the poorest (richest) group indicates rising inequality.

A summary inequality measure is a single number computed from the incomes of several IRUs (individuals, households). This number summarizes the degree of income inequality, with higher values indicating greater inequality.

The *Gini index* or *Gini coefficient*—named after Corrado Gini (1884–1965), the Italian statistician who developed it in 1912—is a popular summary measure. It ranges from zero for *perfect equality* (all IRUs receive identical incomes) to one for *perfect inequality* (one IRU receives all the income). For example, the World Bank (2005) reports the 2000 Gini index for the United States and Canada as 0.38 and 0.33, respectively, indicating that the United States had greater inequality. Such international comparisons are strictly valid if they are based on common definitions of IRUs and income (gross income, net income) and similar geographical coverage (national, urban).

Frank Cowell (1995) provides details (including formulas) of the Gini index and other summary measures. Cowell describes the *generalized entropy* (GE) family, which includes the *mean logarithmic deviation* (GE(0)), *Theil's index* (GE(1)), and *half the squared coefficient of variation* (GE(2)) as special cases, and *Atkinson's measure*.

Atkinson's measure ranges from zero to one and GE from zero to infinity.

There is no single best summary inequality measure. The choice among summary measures is influenced by: (1) computational convenience; (2) satisfaction of desirable properties, including *scale independence* (multiplying all incomes by a constant should not affect inequality), the *Pigou-Dalton transfer principle* (an income transfer from a richer to poorer IRU that does not reverse their ranking should reduce inequality), *anonymity/symmetry* (identities of IRUs are irrelevant), *population independence* (doubling population size by replicating every IRU should not affect inequality), and *decomposability* (total inequality should be conveniently broken down by population subgroups or income components); and (3) the portion of the income distribution to emphasize.

The availability of software for computing inequality measures has rendered computational considerations less important. The Gini index, GE, and Atkinson's measure satisfy scale independence, the transfer principle, anonymity/symmetry, and population independence. The Gini index cannot be conveniently decomposed and is more sensitive to income changes in the middle of the distribution. The sensitivity problem is circumvented by computing a *generalized/extended Gini*, whose formula, like that of Atkinson's measure and GE, incorporates an *inequality aversion parameter* that can be changed to stress different portions of the income distribution. The GE is renowned for its *additive decomposability* (total inequality in a population that is partitioned according to race, gender, or other characteristics is the sum of within-group inequality and between-group inequality).

The degree of income inequality can also be deduced graphically from a *Lorenz curve*. When comparing noncrossing Lorenz curves, the one with greater curvature away from the *perfect equality line* indicates greater inequality. The Gini index is twice the area between the Lorenz curve and the perfect equality line, which may be inaccurate if the Lorenz curve is constructed from data that are grouped into income brackets, as statistical agencies often do.

INCOME INEQUALITY WITHIN AMERICAN SOCIETY AND OTHER OECD COUNTRIES

The Gini index for U.S. household income inequality, reported by the U.S. Census Bureau, increased from 0.397 in 1975 to 0.466 in 2001. Both the GE and Atkinson's measure also increased during this period, indicating rising inequality.

Two factors complicate the analysis of the observed inequality trends. First, the trend may depend on whether a narrow definition of income (market income) or a broader definition that takes into account taxes, social transfers (e.g., child benefits), and noncash benefits (e.g., food stamps) is considered. Rising social transfers may offset an increase in earnings inequality. Second, since summary measures are based on household surveys, researchers should test whether observed inequality changes are statistically significant by computing an appropriate *standard error*. Until the mid-1990s, many practitioners eschewed this issue because of the complexities of most standard error formulas. Advances in computing have facilitated significance tests for inequality changes using the *bootstrap standard error*, as Martin Biewen (2002) has demonstrated.

Economic historian Peter Lindert (2000) has summarized the vast literature explaining the rise in U.S. income inequality. The rise is ascribed to a complex mix of economic and social/demographic factors. Since earnings constitute the largest component of income for most IRUs, explanations of rising inequality in the United States have focused mainly on earnings inequality. They include the weakening of unions, technological changes requiring highly skilled workers, outsourcing of jobs, and immigration. Other explanations include import competition from low-cost countries, government tax and income transfer policies, and the rise in single-parent families. Similar factors have been used to explain inequality trends in other industrialized OECD countries, with variations in the relative importance of the factors.

ECONOMIC GROWTH AND INCOME INEQUALITY

Does economic growth lead to rising inequality? In 1955 Kuznets postulated the existence of an *inverted U-curve* relationship between economic growth and income inequality by tracking the historical experiences of England, Germany, and the United States. This *U-curve hypothesis* contends that the intersectoral shifts associated with the early stages of economic growth exacerbate inequality (the rising portion of the inverted U-curve). At some threshold level, inequality peaks and then falls (the falling portion of the inverted U-curve).

The vast literature on the U-curve hypothesis, reviewed by economist Ravi Kanbur (2000), reveals mixed empirical results. Furthermore, government policy is important in influencing the direction of inequality. Regarding the reverse causation from income inequality to economic growth, empirical evidence by Klaus Deininger and Lyn Squire (1998) reveals that inequality in land distribution is a more important determinant of future growth than income inequality.

INCOME INEQUALITY, RACE, ETHNICITY, WEALTH INEQUALITY, AND INTERGENERATIONAL MOBILITY

It is now widely recognized (e.g., World Bank 2005) that the root cause of persistent earnings and income inequality is unequal opportunities. For example, sustained discrimination in employment or education against a particular racial or ethnic minority group could result in persistently low earnings for the group's members, resulting in an *inequality trap*.

The link between ethnicity and income inequality is convoluted. Economists William Darity and Ashwini Deshpande (2000) articulate how overall inequality could drive interethnic inequality and vice versa. Shelly Lundberg and Richard Startz (1998) explain how community influence and loyalty could shape interethnic inequality even without discrimination. Some have argued that ethnically homogeneous societies should have less inequality since assimilation by ethnic groups is easier and support for income redistribution is more likely. Fractionalization indexes, which measure the probabilities that two randomly selected individuals from a population belong to different ethnic, linguistic, or religious groups, have been used in empirical investigations of the ethnic-diversity income inequality nexus, with mixed results.

The causality between wealth inequality and income inequality may potentially run two ways. On the one hand, those with greater wealth accumulation are more likely to invest and generate higher incomes. On the other hand, those with higher incomes have higher potential to accumulate more wealth.

Are the children of poor parents destined to remain poor? This is the issue of *intergenerational mobility*, the relationship between a person's socioeconomic status and that of his or her parents. The rich are capable of providing their offspring with a better education, increasing their chances of earning higher incomes. Also, the offspring of the rich are likely to inherit greater wealth, which aids the wealth accumulation process for the next generation. Thomas Piketty (2000) has surveyed theoretical and empirical literature on intergenerational mobility. Economists and sociologists measure the degree of intergenerational mobility by computing an *intergenerational elasticity* in income and wealth. Unfortunately, intergenerational elasticity estimates are sensitive to the methodology employed. Irrespective of the exact magnitude, there is no doubt that the level of opportunities allowed by society determines intergenerational mobility.

SEE ALSO *Gini Coefficient; Income; Income Distribution; Inequality, Gender; Inequality, Political; Inequality, Racial; Inequality, Wealth; Interest Rates; Poverty, Indices of; Profits; Rent; Wages*

BIBLIOGRAPHY

Biewen, Martin. 2002. Bootstrap Inference for Inequality, Mobility, and Poverty Measurement. *Journal of Econometrics* 108 (2): 317–342.

Cowell, Frank A. 1995. *Measuring Inequality*. 2nd ed. Wheatsheaf, U.K.: Prentice Hall.

Darity, William, Jr., and Deshpande Ashwini. 2000. Tracing the Divide: Intergroup Disparity Across Countries. *Eastern Economic Journal* 26 (1): 75–85.

Deininger, Klaus, and Lyn Squire. 1998. New Ways of Looking at Old Issues: Inequality and Growth. *Journal of Development Economics* 57 (2): 257–285.

Gottschalk, Peter, and Timothy M. Smeeding. 2000. Empirical Evidence on Income Inequality in Industrialized Countries. In *Handbook of Income Distribution*, eds. Anthony Atkinson and François Bourguignon, 261–307. Amsterdam: Elsevier.

Kanbur, Ravi. 2000. Income Distribution and Development. In *Handbook of Income Distribution*, eds. Anthony Atkinson and François Bourguignon, 791–841. Amsterdam: Elsevier.

Lindert, Peter H. 2000. Three Centuries of Inequality in Britain and America. In *Handbook of Income Distribution*, eds. Anthony Atkinson and Francois Bourguignon, 167–216. Amsterdam: Elsevier.

Lundberg, Shelly, and Richard Startz. 1998. On the Persistence of Racial Inequality. *Journal of Labor Economics* 16 (2): 292–323.

Piketty, Thomas. 2000. Theories of Persistent Inequality and Intergenerational Mobility. In *Handbook of Income Distribution*, eds. Anthony Atkinson and François Bourguignon, 429–476. Amsterdam: Elsevier.

World Bank. 2005. *World Development Report 2006: Equity and Development*. New York: Oxford University Press. http://econ.worldbank.org/.

Tomson Ogwang

INEQUALITY, POLITICAL

Of the disparities among ordinary people in whatever is scarce and valued in a society—economic wherewithal, social respect, public influence, health, freedom—political equality is relevant most especially in democracies. In contrast to authoritarian systems, democracies are based on the expectation that the people are sovereign and that public officials are to be equally accessible and accountable to all. In spite of the egalitarian commitment embodied in the principle of one person, one vote, political equality among ordinary people is not the same thing as equal political power, even in democracies. Those who, by dint of election or appointment, are entrusted with the responsibility for governing—from the prime minister to the city council member—inevitably wield greater political power than others. Instead of equal power, therefore, political equality among citizens would seem to require that they enjoy equal political rights, equal political voice, and equal political responsiveness.

POLITICAL RIGHTS

There is no possibility of political equality without certain rights. The rights intrinsic to what T. H. Marshall calls "civil citizenship" and "political citizenship" provide an essential foundation for political equality (Marshall 1964, chapter IV). Included within civil citizenship are due process of law, with the concomitant right to assert and defend oneself on terms of equality in the courts, and the right to think, speak, and worship freely. Under the umbrella of political citizenship is the right to share in political power, either by acting as a political decision maker or by influencing the choice of such decision makers by voting and otherwise taking part in the processes by which they are chosen. Such rights are not universally shared even in what can be considered to be functioning democracies. Historically, women were everywhere denied the rights necessary for political equality, as were other groups in particular places—for example, African Americans in the American South during the Jim Crow era or native blacks in South Africa during apartheid. Although there are variations across countries, all contemporary democracies abridge the political rights of children and resident aliens. Some add felons and the mentally incompetent to the list.

POLITICAL VOICE

A second requirement for the achievement of political equality is equality of political voice. Political voice refers to the sum total of political inputs that citizens in a democracy use to control who will hold political office and to influence what public officials do. Through their political voice, citizens raise political issues, communicate information about their political interests and concerns, and generate pressure on policymakers to respond to what they hear. Equal political voice requires not that all individuals are equally active, but that aggregate participatory input is representative across all politically relevant groups and categories.

Although the particular mix will vary from polity to polity, citizens in a democracy have a variety of options for the exercise of political voice. They can seek indirect influence through the electoral system by voting or engaging in other efforts to support favored political parties or candidates, or they can seek direct influence through the messages they send to office holders about their politically relevant preferences and needs. They can act individually or collectively. They can undertake mainstream activities, such as joining organizations or contacting public officials, or challenging ones, such as attending protests or demonstrations.

Achieving equality in political voice is much more difficult than achieving equality of political rights. Individual citizens differ in their capacity and desire to take part in politics, and political activities differ in the extent to which the demanded inputs—time, money, or skills—are conducive to broad and representative participation, on the one hand, or to participation by narrower and less representative publics, on the other. In all systems, political voice is skewed, at least to some degree, in the direction of those with high levels of income, occupational status, and especially education. What this implies is that public officials hear an unrepresentative set of messages: They receive disproportionate information about the interests and opinions of, and feel more constrained to respond to, the affluent and well-educated. The extent to which unequal political voice is structured by occupation, education, and income implies, moreover, that disadvantaged groups defined along axes other than social class are also underrepresented politically. In most democracies, the political voice of women is muted, as is, in many polities, the political voice of racial, ethnic, or linguistic minorities. In many cases—for example, African Americans and Latinos in the United States—the inequality in political voice can be explained entirely in terms of socio-economic disadvantage without reference to a group-specific experience or identity. Nevertheless, whether the explanation for the inequality of political voice derives from socio-economic disparities or another aspect of collective experience, the bottom line is that policymakers hear less about the preferences, concerns, and needs of some individuals and some groups.

Although inequalities of political voice are biased in favor of the privileged in all democracies, many factors shape the extent of that socio-economic structuring. For one thing, the rules that govern politics can exacerbate or ameliorate inequalities of political voice. For example, where registration is difficult and electoral turnout is voluntary, as in the United States, the electorate tends to be less representative of the citizenry as a whole than in polities where registration is less demanding or, as in Belgium and Australia, turnout is compulsory. The rules governing campaign finance are also relevant. Free-for-all methods of financing campaigns and a major presence of corporate campaign contributions predispose a polity to inequalities of political voice. In addition, the nature of the institutions that link citizens to policymakers can have an impact on inequalities of political voice. High levels of membership in voluntary associations and the presence of both strong labor unions and a labor or social democratic party, as in the Nordic countries, tend to mute inequalities of political voice. Furthermore, government policies—ranging from free and compulsory education to progressive taxation to the provision of a social safety net—can reduce the socio-economic inequalities among individuals that are associated with inequalities of political voice.

POLITICAL RESPONSIVENESS

Political equality requires not just that citizens speak but that public officials listen. The most complex aspect of political equality, equality of political responsiveness is nearly impossible to measure and highly contested theoretically. Social scientists of a Marxian inclination, along with those who, like Charles E. Lindblom, posit the "privileged position of business," conclude that formidable political resources and control of employment give the corporate sector—corporations and trade and other business associations—the upper hand in any public controversy (Lindblom 1977, chapter 13). That said, there are substantial obstacles to making a systematic empirical assessment of policymakers' responsiveness to various competing forces. Especially since political influence is often exercised behind the scenes or used to shape the political agenda rather than the content of decisions, in any particular policy controversy it is difficult to discern who is exercising power and to whom decision makers are responding. Besides, in aggregating across issues, it is difficult to specify a universe of political controversies to serve as a baseline.

Furthermore, democratic theorists raise concerns about the universal desirability of equal responsiveness. Equal responsiveness in every political conflict would constitute a form of majoritarian democracy that would grant no space for the exercise of independent judgment by political leaders, who may command special information, experience, or insight. Furthermore, it would entail no deference to intensity of preference. That is, an indifferent majority would inevitably prevail over a minority that cares a lot. If such a political configuration were present over and over, that minority would never achieve its proportionate share of political influence. Moreover, if not coupled with equal voice, a pattern of equal responsiveness would give advantage to the noisy over the silent and produce a circumstance far from political equality.

SEE ALSO *Civil Rights; Civil Society; Compulsory Voting; Crony Capitalism; Democracy; Due Process; Exit, Voice, and Loyalty; Gender Gap; Human Rights; Inequality, Gender; Inequality, Income; Inequality, Racial; Inequality, Wealth; Lindblom, Charles; Majoritarianism; Majority Rule; Poverty; Power; Power Elite; Public Rights; Rule of Law; Schattschneider, E. E.; Social Status; Social Structure; Tyranny of the Majority; Voting Schemes; Welfare State*

BIBLIOGRAPHY

Jacobs, Lawrence R., and Theda Skocpol, eds. 2005. *Inequality and American Democracy: What We Know and What We Need to Learn.* New York: Russell Sage.

Lindblom, Charles E. 1977. *Politics and Markets: The World's Political Economic Systems.* New York: Basic Books.

Marshall, T. H. 1964. Citizenship and Social Class. In *Class, Citizenship, and Social Development.* Garden City, NY: Doubleday. (Orig. pub. 1949).

Norris, Pippa. 2002. *Democratic Phoenix: Reinventing Political Activism.* Cambridge, U.K.: Cambridge University Press.

Verba, Sidney, Kay Lehman Schlozman, and Henry E. Brady. 1995. *Voice and Equality: Civic Voluntarism in American Politics.* Cambridge, MA: Harvard University Press.

Kay Lehman Schlozman

INEQUALITY, RACIAL

Social inequality refers to "the condition whereby people have unequal access to valued resources, services, and positions in society" (Kerbo 1983, p. 250). *Racial inequality* in turn can be defined as the limited economic and social opportunities that are distributed along racial lines. Societies where racial inequalities are high are characterized by large disparities among different races and ethnicities in such areas as housing, education, employment income, and health care. While some researchers argue that inequalities exist because of the efforts (or lack of efforts) of individuals, most contemporary scholars agree that persistent racial inequalities are a product of what Eduardo Bonilla-Silva (2001) refers to as a *racialized social system*—a system that reproduces and maintains the status of the dominant group socially, economically, politically, and psychologically. That is, racial inequality implies that access to resources and goods are overwhelmingly denied to people of color because of systemic rather than individual notions of racism. The social system upholds racism and maintains a racialized society.

THEORIES OF RACIAL INEQUALITY

Theories on racial inequality range from individual and cultural explanations that tend to lay blame on the victims (nonwhites) for their social and economic status in society to structural and systemic theories that tend to look beyond the individual to explain why most nonwhites, especially those with darker skin, continue to face discrimination in society. For example, *deficiency theory*, an outdated theory of racial inequality, argues that the economic, political, and social situation of some racial groups is due to some deficiency within the groups themselves. Deficiency theorists point to three causes for these deficiencies: biological, structural, and cultural. Regarding the first, scholars, the vast majority of whom were white, attempted to prove that the cause of racial inequalities stemmed from the biological inferiority of minority groups. Other researchers sought to demonstrate that there were basic flaws in the way minority groups structured their lives that helped to explain racial inequalities. Scholars also argued that racial and ethnic groups' cultural traits and values served as a justification for the inequalities they experienced. The problem with deficiency theories, although still widely espoused by primarily conservative scholars, is their lack of empirical evidence and mostly unsubstantiated claims.

Other theories of racial inequality (e.g., *bias theory*) rely on the assumption that racial inequality is the result of individual prejudice and bias. The main criticism of such theories is that they ignore how societies are often structured along racial lines, which ultimately leads to social, residential, educational, and other forms of segregation. This theoretical framework ignores how racism can continue to operate in a society even when overt prejudices and discriminatory practices are no longer "socially" acceptable.

Structural theories of inequality identify racism within social structures, such as education, institutional policies, laws, and housing and health care practices. Many critical race theorists, such as Derrick Bell, Kimberlé Crenshaw, and Richard Delgado, have written about the importance of understanding why individual prejudices and biases do not fully explain the continuing existence of racism, especially given that many overtly racist policies and laws have long been dismantled. Structural theories tend to focus on how racism is maintained by identifying racist practices in institutions. For example, in the United States such practices as redlining and divestment in poorer neighborhoods result in lower property taxes. Since the quality of public schools is directly tied to property taxes, the schools in socioeconomically disadvantaged neighborhoods tend to have fewer resources compared to schools in more affluent neighborhoods. According to Douglas Massey and Nancy Denton (1993), the United States is a racially and residentially segregated society. African Americans are overrepresented in poor neighborhoods as a result of past and current racist housing practices, such as realtors refusing to sell or rent houses to African Americans in white neighborhoods. As a result African Americans continue to be steered into racially segregated neighborhoods where housing investment is low and social and economic opportunities are few or nonexistent.

Another theoretical framework examines the role of racial hierarchies to explain how different racial and ethnic groups fare compared to whites and to one another. One model, the *black-white model*, has generated major debate among scholars who study race and ethnicity. Joe R. Feagin (2000) and George Yancey (2006) argue that the black-white model is useful because African Americans are the most racially disadvantaged group and have experienced oppression far longer than most minority groups in the United States. Furthermore antiblack racism is one of the most ingrained social institutions in the United States (Feagin 2000). Researchers argue that this model can be applied to other racial and ethnic groups, but they maintain that the bipolar model is still necessary before one can fully understand racial inequality.

Critics of the black-white paradigm argue that it is outdated and does not take into account the demographic changes that have occurred in the United States as a result of increased immigration after the passage of the Immigration and Naturalization Act of 1965, which increased the number of immigrants of color to the United States. Further the black-white model allows only limited understanding of the racialization of nonwhite immigrant groups and their children because the model ignores the different factors associated with the process of racialization (e.g., religion, foreignness, language, citizenship, and gender). Immigrants vary in their experiences in the United States. For example, Asian Americans do not comprise one homogenous group but consist of individuals who come from different countries for a variety of reasons. Their experiences are not uniform but are diverse due to a broad range of factors, such as skin tone, class, reasons for immigrating, and religion, among others. Bonilla-Silva (2006) argues that Chinese Americans, for example, are often considered "honorary" whites, whereas Filipino Americans can be socioeconomically categorized as collective blacks. This is due to a variety of factors, such as skin tone and class status, that are not adequately addressed by the black-white model.

RACIAL INEQUALITY IN SOUTH AFRICA AND BRAZIL

Racial inequality is not an American phenomenon; rather, it is international. South Africa is interesting because of the longevity of the legal system of racial segregation in this industrialized country. Apartheid was a postcolonial system of white supremacy that dominated South Africa. Under this system, all South Africans were racially categorized at birth as *white, Asian, Colored,* or *black.* Economic, political, and legal resources were distributed according to this racial categorization, with South African blacks receiving the fewest resources. Moreover blacks were not permitted to live where they wanted to, and they were forced to carry identification cards at all times, were prohibited from marrying outside of their race, and were denied citizenship in their own land. According to Gay Seidman (1999), South Africa turned toward apartheid rather than follow the pattern of European decolonization because South African blacks continued to provide a source of cheap labor to South African whites.

While the dismantling of apartheid in 1994 led to a concerted effort to democratize South Africa and produce radical changes that would result in racial equality, this proved difficult to achieve because of the extent of racism that apartheid ingrained in the economic, social, and political structures. The dismantling of apartheid did not magically improve the situation for South African blacks. High rates of unemployment and substandard housing, education, and health care continue to plague them due to years of racial oppression and exploitation (Winant and Seidman 2001). The racial inequality that an oppressive and violent system like apartheid leaves behind requires a radical restructuring of social structures. While the post-apartheid South African government is committed to creating an equitable society, it has yet to commit to radical plans for change.

Brazil has also seen racial oppression and inequality due to the impact of colonization by Portugal. In the twentieth century Brazil prided itself on being a "racial democracy" with little racial prejudice. This ideological claim has been tested by many scholars, including Edward Telles and Peter Wade. Between 1890 and 1940 the black Brazilian population decreased from 66 percent of the total population to 34 percent (Paixão 2004). During this period, policies promoting the immigration to Brazil of white Europeans, along with the enactment of a strict penal code against black Brazilians, were implemented in order to rid Brazil of its native black population. In spite of (or perhaps as a result of) this whitening agenda, the Brazilian black population grew to 47 percent of the population between 1940 and 1980 (Paixão 2004). Between the late 1930s and the early 1940s a new ideology emerged in Brazil—a Brazilian national identity where mixed blood was encouraged rather than discouraged. Although this new way of thinking seemed to be a radical shift toward racial equality, it inevitably denied blacks their history and culture and ignored the racial inequality they experienced. Studies indicate that blacks in Brazil continue to face racial discrimination and that, compared to whites, they tend to be paid lower wages and experience higher rates of illiteracy and unemployment.

RACIAL INEQUALITY IN THE UNITED STATES

As in Brazil and South Africa, racial inequality in the United States stems from a long and complex history of racial oppression. The history of racism in the United States is similarly tied to economic exploitation achieved through racial violence and justified through the creation and maintenance of racial hierarchies. The colonization of the United States resulted in the genocide of Native Americans who occupied the land prior to European settlement. White capitalists violently forced African slaves to the Americas for the purpose of unwaged labor, resulting in the economic growth of the United States. Theories

of the racial inferiority of nonwhites—specifically African slaves, Native Americans, and Mexicans but many others as well—were invented to justify their exploitation and the use of violence against them.

Although overt racist policies and laws (e.g., slavery, legal racial segregation) have been dismantled in the United States, their effects remain embedded in social institutions. Quality education is tied to property value, resulting in greater social, political, and economic opportunities for those who live in affluent neighborhoods. In contrast, the overrepresentation of African Americans in poor neighborhoods results in decreased opportunities for upward mobility. Scholars note that the great health disparities between African Americans and white Americans are due to disparities in access to good health care, medical insurance, and preventative care. Low-wage, low-skilled, part-time jobs that do not provide benefits are predominately filled by people of color in the United States, a situation that results in a class of working poor. Racial profiling, along with stricter sentencing for African Americans convicted of crimes, results in their overrepresentation in American prisons and consequently decreased opportunities upon their reentry into mainstream society. Racial inequality continues to exist in the United States because society has been structured around racial lines that provide advantages to whites. Racial inequality endures because it is at home in a "color-blind" society that is ingrained with racist practices that are mostly ignored.

SEE ALSO *Apartheid; Discrimination; Hierarchy; Income Distribution; Inequality, Political; Inequality, Wealth; Jim Crow; Nonwhites; Race; Racialization; Racism; Segregation; Segregation, Residential; Segregation, School; Stratification; Whiteness*

BIBLIOGRAPHY

Bonilla-Silva, Eduardo. 1997. Rethinking Racism: Toward a Structural Interpretation. *American Sociological Review* 62 (3): 465–480.

Bonilla-Silva, Eduardo. 2001. *White Supremacy and Racism in the Post-Civil Rights Era*. Boulder, CO: Lynne Rienner Publishers.

Bonilla-Silva, Eduardo. 2006. *Racism without Racists: Color-Blind Racism and the Persistence of Racial Inequality in the USA*. 2nd ed. Boulder, CO: Rowman and Littlefield.

Conyers, James E. 2002. Racial Inequality: Emphasis on Explanations. *Western Journal of Black Studies* 26 (4): 249–254.

Feagin, Joe R. 2000. *Racist America: Roots, Current Realities, and Future Reparations*. New York: Routledge.

Feagin, Joe R. 2006. *Systemic Racism: A Theory of Oppression*. New York: Routledge.

Gold, Steven. 2004. From Jim Crow to Racial Hegemony: Evolving Explanations of Racial Hierarchy. *Ethnic and Racial Studies* 27 (6): 951–968.

Kerbo, H. R. 1983. *Social Stratification and Inequality.* New York: McGraw Hill Brook.

Massey, Douglas, and Nancy Denton. 1993. *American Apartheid: Segregation and the Making of the Underclass.* Cambridge, MA: Harvard University Press.

Paixão, Marcelo. 2004. Waiting for the Sun: An Account of the (Precarious) Social Situation of the African Descendant Population in Contemporary Brazil. *Journal of Black Studies* 34 (6): 743–765.

Seidman, Gay. 1999. Is South Africa Different? Sociological Comparisons and Theoretical Contributions from the Land of Apartheid. *Annual Review Sociology* 25: 419–440.

Stewart, James. 2004. Globalization, Cities, and Racial Inequality at the Dawn of the Twenty-first Century. *Review of Black Political Economy* 31 (3): 11–32.

Winant, Howard, and Gay Seidman. 2001. South Africa: When the System Has Fallen. In *The World Is a Ghetto: Race and Democracy since World War II,* ed. Howard Winant, 177–218. New York: Basic Books.

Yancey, George. 2006. Racial Justice in a Black/Nonblack Society. In *Mixed Messages: Doing Race in the Color-Blind Era,* ed. David L. Brunsma, 49–62. Boulder, CO: Lynne Rienner Publishers.

Saher Selod
David G. Embrick

INEQUALITY, WEALTH

Wealth represents a stock of accumulated assets; *income* represents a flow of current output. Families not only receive income over the course of a year but also save part of their income in the form of housing, time deposits, stocks, bonds, and the like. Such accumulated savings are referred to as *wealth.* The first part of this entry explains why wealth, like income, has an important bearing on well-being. The second part develops the concept of household wealth and discusses some of the problems inherent in its measurement; the third presents time trends in the inequality of wealth in the United States; and the fourth shows international comparisons of wealth inequality.

WEALTH AND WELL-BEING

Why are we interested in household wealth? Most studies use income as a measure of family well-being. Though certain forms of income are derived from wealth, such as interest from savings accounts and dividends from stocks, income and wealth are by no means identical. Many kinds of income, such as wages and salaries, are not derived from household wealth, and many forms of wealth, such as owner-occupied housing, produce no corresponding income flow.

Moreover family wealth by itself is also a source of well-being, independent of the direct financial income it provides. There are six reasons. First, some assets, such as owner-occupied housing and consumer durables such as automobiles, provide services directly to their owners. Such assets can substitute for money income in satisfying economic needs. Families with the same money income but differing amounts of housing and consumer durables will have different levels of welfare.

Second, wealth is a source of consumption, independent of the direct money income it provides. Many assets can be converted directly into cash and thus provide for immediate consumption needs.

Third, the availability of financial assets can provide liquidity to a family in times of economic stress (such as those occasioned by unemployment, sickness, or family breakup). In this sense wealth is a source of economic security for the family.

Fourth, as the work of Dalton Conley (1999) has shown, wealth is found to affect household behavior over and above income. In particular Conley found that it is necessary to control for wealth in order to understand racial inequality, including differences in school performance and enrollment in the United States.

Fifth, as Seymour Spilerman (2000) argued, wealth-generated income does not require the same trade-offs with leisure as earned income. There is no cost in the form of the foregone alternative use of time in the case of wealth. Moreover, unlike labor earnings, the income flow generated by wealth does not decline with illness or unemployment.

Sixth, large fortunes can be a source of economic and social power that is not directly captured in annual income. Large accumulations of financial and business assets can confer special privileges to their holders. Such large fortunes are often transmitted to succeeding generations, thus creating family "dynasties." In these six ways wealth holdings provide another dimension to household welfare over and above income flows.

WHAT IS HOUSEHOLD WEALTH?

The conventional definition of *household wealth* includes assets and liabilities that have a current market value and that are directly or indirectly marketable. In the Survey of Consumer Finances conducted by the Federal Reserve Board of Washington, D.C., on a triennial basis, marketable wealth (or net worth) is defined as the current value of all marketable assets less the current value of debts. Total assets are the sum of (1) owner-occupied housing; (2) other real estate; (3) cash, demand and time deposits, certificates of deposit (CDs), and money market accounts; (4)

Table 1. Portfolio Composition of U.S. Household Wealth, 2004 (Percentage of gross assets)

Wealth component	
Owner-occupied housing	33.5
Other real estate	11.5
Unincorporated business equity	17.1
Liquid assets	7.3
Pension accounts	11.8
Financial securities	2.1
Corporate stock and mutual funds	11.9
Net equity in personal trusts	2.9
Miscellaneous assets	1.8
Total	100.0
Debt on owner-occupied housing	11.6
All other debt	3.9
Total debt	15.5

SOURCE: Federal Reserve Board, Survey of Consumer Finances, 2004.

financial securities; (5) the cash surrender value of life insurance; (6) pension accounts; (7) corporate stock and mutual funds; (8) unincorporated businesses equity; and (9) trust fund equity. Total liabilities are the sum of (1) mortgage debt and (2) consumer and other debt.

Table 1 presents the portfolio composition for the household sector in the United States in 2004 based on the Survey of Consumer Finances. Owner-occupied housing was the most important household asset, accounting for 33 percent of total assets. Land, rental property, and other real estate held by households made up 12 percent. Unincorporated business equity, which refers to small businesses (such as farms or stores) owned directly by individuals, comprised another 17 percent.

Liquid assets (cash, demand, time and savings deposits, money market funds, CDs, and the cash surrender value of life insurance) comprised 7 percent of total assets. Defined contribution pension accounts, such as individual retirement accounts (IRAs) and Keogh and 401(k) plans, constitute savings like savings accounts but are especially designed to allow workers to save for retirement by providing tax-deferred savings. Pension accounts made up almost 12 percent of household assets. Financial securities, including bonds, notes, and financial securities issued mainly by corporations and the government, are "promissory notes" by which the borrower agrees to pay back the lender a certain amount of money (the principal plus interest) at a certain date. In 2004 they amounted to only 2 percent of total assets.

The next component is corporate stock and mutual funds. A corporate stock certificate issued by a company represents ownership of a certain percentage of the com-

pany's assets. A mutual fund is a package provided by a financial entity, such as a bank, that includes a portfolio of stocks and other financial instruments, such as bonds. Its chief advantage is that it helps diversify the risk associated with individual stock (and bond) movements over time. In 2004 stocks and mutual funds amounted to almost 12 percent of total assets. Personal trusts refer to financial instruments held in a special legal arrangement called a *trust fund*. In a typical trust, the assets are managed by a specially named administrator, and the income earned from the assets is remitted to individual beneficiaries. Trust fund equity comprised only 3 percent of total assets.

On the liability side, the major form of household debt is home mortgages. A mortgage is a loan issued usually by a bank for a period of fifteen to thirty years that is used to finance the purchase of real property. In 2004 mortgage debt comprised 75 percent of total household debt. The remaining 25 percent consisted of other household debt, including automobile and other consumer loans and credit card debt. Total household debt amounted to 16 percent of the value of household assets.

A theme that regularly emerges in the literature on household wealth is that there is no unique concept or definition of wealth that is satisfactory for all purposes. One concept that is broader than marketable wealth is the sum of marketable wealth and consumer durables. Consumer durables, such as automobiles, televisions, and furniture, provide consumption services directly to the household and as such function like "annuities." However, since they are not easily marketed and their resale value typically far understates the value of their consumption services, they are often excluded from marketable wealth. A still broader definition of wealth includes the value of future social security benefits the family may receive upon retirement (social security wealth) as well as the value of retirement benefits from private pension plans (pension wealth). However, even though these funds are a source of future income to families, they are not in the family's direct control and cannot be marketed and are also excluded from marketable wealth.

WEALTH INEQUALITY TRENDS IN THE UNITED STATES

The figures in table 2 show that wealth inequality, after rising steeply between 1983 and 1989, remained virtually unchanged from 1989 to 2004. The share of wealth held by the top 5 percent rose by 2.8 percentage points from 1983 to 1989, that of the top quintile by 2.2 percentage points, and the Gini coefficient (an index that ranges from zero to one, where a higher number indicates greater inequality) increased from 0.80 to 0.83. Between 1989 and 2004 the share of the top 5 percent remained largely unchanged, and the share of the top quintile rose from

Table 2. The Size Distribution of Wealth and Income, 1983–2004

Year	Gini Coefficient	Share of Top 5%	Share of Top 20%
A. Net Worth			
1983	0.799	56.1	81.3
1989	0.832	58.9	83.5
2004	0.829	58.9	84.7
B. Income			
1982	0.480	26.1	51.9
1988	0.521	30.0	55.6
2003	0.540	32.0	57.9

SOURCE: Federal Reserve Board, Survey of Consumer Finances, 1983, 1989, 2004.

83.5 to 84.7 percent. Overall the Gini coefficient fell very slightly, from 0.832 in 1989 to 0.829 in 2004.

The top 5 percent of families (as ranked by income) earned 32 percent of total household income in 2003, and the top 20 percent accounted for 58 percent—large figures but lower than the corresponding wealth shares. The time trend for income inequality was similar to that of wealth inequality. Income inequality increased sharply between 1982 and 1988, with the Gini coefficient rising from 0.48 to 0.52 and the share of the top 5 percent from 26.1 to 30.0 percent. There was then a further but smaller increase of the Gini index by 0.019 points from 1988 to 2003 and of the shares of the top 5 and 20 percent (see Wolff 1998, 2002, 2006 for further details).

Table 3. The Size Distribution of Wealth in Selected Organization for Economic Cooperation and Development Countries, 1983–2001

Year	Gini Coefficient	Wealth Share of Top 10%
A. United States: Wolff (2006)		
1983	0.799	68.2
1989	0.832	70.6
1992	0.823	71.8
1995	0.828	71.8
1998	0.822	71.0
2001	0.826	71.5
B. Canada: Morissette et al. (2006)		
1984	0.691	51.8
1999	0.727	55.7
C. Germany: Hauser and Stein (2006)		
1973	0.748	(NA)
1983	0.701	48.8
1988	0.668	45.0
1993	0.622	40.8
1998	0.640	41.9
D. Italy: Brandolini et al. (2006)		
1989	0.553	40.2
1995	0.573	42.1
2000	0.613	48.5
E. Finland: Jäntti (2006)		
1987	0.470	
1994	0.487	
1998	0.523	

INTERNATIONAL COMPARISONS OF WEALTH INEQUALITY

Wealth inequality is also much higher in the United States than in the other four countries shown in table 3. The Gini coefficient for wealth in the United States in 1998 was 0.82, compared to 0.73 in Canada in 1999, 0.64 in Germany in 1998, 0.61 in Italy in 2000, and 0.52 in Finland in 1998. Similar disparities exist with regard to the share of top wealth holders. In the United States the top 10 percent held 71 percent of all wealth in 1998, compared to a share of 56 percent in Canada in 1999, 42 percent in Germany in 1998, and 49 percent in Italy in 2000. By 2000 or so Finland was by far the most equal of the five countries with comparable data, followed by Italy, Germany, Canada, and then the United States (see Wolff 1987, 1996 for earlier comparisons).

It is also of interest that wealth inequality rose in the United States, Canada, Italy, and Finland, while it declined sharply in Germany. The Gini coefficient rose by 0.027 in the United States between 1983 and 2001, by 0.036 in Canada from 1984 to 1999, and by 0.060 in Italy between 1989 and 2000. In Germany, in contrast, it plummeted by 0.108 from 1973 to 1998 (and by 0.061 from 1983 to 1998).

SEE ALSO *Financial Markets; Gini Coefficient; In Vivo Transfers; Inequality, Income; Inheritance; Wealth*

BIBLIOGRAPHY

Brandolini, Andrea, Luigi Cannari, Giovanni D'Alessio, and Ivan Fatella. 2006. Household Wealth Distribution in Italy in the 1990s. In *International Perspectives on Household Wealth*, ed. Edward N. Wolff, 225–275. Cheltenham, U.K.: Elgar.

Conley, Dalton. 1999. *Being Black, Living in the Red: Race, Wealth, and Social Policy in America.* Berkeley: University of California Press.

Federal Reserve Board. Survey of Consumer Finances: Index. http://www.federalreserve.gov/pubs/oss/oss2/scfindex.html.

Hauser, Richard, and Holger Stein. 2006. Inequality of the Distribution of Personal Wealth in Germany, 1973–98. In *International Perspectives on Household Wealth*, ed. Edward N. Wolff, 195–224. Cheltenham, U.K.: Elgar.

Jäntti, Markus. 2006. Trends in the Distribution of Income and Wealth: Finland 1987–98. In *International Perspectives on Household Wealth*, ed. Edward N. Wolff, 295–326. Cheltenham, U.K.: Elgar.

Morissette, René, Xuelin Zhang, and Marie Drolet. 2006. The Evolution of Wealth Inequality in Canada, 1984–99. In *International Perspectives on Household Wealth*, ed. Edward N. Wolff, 151–192. Cheltenham, U.K.: Elgar.

Spilerman, Seymour. 2000. Wealth and Stratification Processes. *American Review of Sociology* 26: 497–524.

Wolff, Edward N., ed. 1987. *International Comparisons of the Distribution of Household Wealth.* New York: Oxford University Press.

Wolff, Edward N. 1996. International Comparisons of Wealth Inequality. *Review of Income and Wealth* 42 (4): 433–451.

Wolff, Edward N. 1998. Recent Trends in the Size Distribution of Household Wealth. *Journal of Economic Perspectives* 12 (3): 131–150.

Wolff, Edward N. 2002. *Top Heavy: The Increasing Inequality of Wealth in America and What Can Be Done about It.* New York: New Press.

Wolff, Edward N. 2006. Changes in Household Wealth in the 1980s and 1990s in the U.S. In *International Perspectives on Household Wealth*, ed. Edward N. Wolff, 107–150. Cheltenham, U.K.: Elgar.

Edward N. Wolff

INFANT INDUSTRY

Governments in both developed and developing nations regularly apply the concept of *infant industry* to justify protective industrial and trade policy measures. The idea is that temporary support for a new branch of industry (for example, electronics, car manufacturing, or biotechnology) might be needed to help industry to grow and flourish, especially when efficient scales of production and technological skills have not yet been developed. If a young industry were exposed to foreign competition at an early stage, it is argued, it would not be able to survive. Temporary government protection in the form of subsidies, tariffs, or important quotas, then, allows an infant industry to "grow up."

Although Alexander Hamilton (1755–1804), the first secretary of the treasury of the United States, followed this line of reasoning in his *Report on the Subject of Manufactures* (1791), the infant-industry argument is usually attributed to the German economist Friedrich List (1789–1846). In *The National System of Political Economy* ([1841] 1856, p. 378), List argued that the transition of a country's economy from the agricultural to the industrial stage would not occur through the "natural course of things." He recommended, therefore, that the government protect nation-specific manufacturing activities if some countries "outdistanced others in manufactures" (List [1841] 1856, p. 394). List stressed that this promotion of infant industries should build on unique national resources. Moreover, the protection should be temporary; it should stop as the infant industry matures.

International and development economists have related List's infant-industry argument to the theory of comparative advantage. According to this view, countries should concentrate on those economic sectors in which they can produce more efficiently and cheaply than their trading partners. In theoretical terms, infant-industry protection is only legitimized until a potential comparative-advantage sector has become an actual comparative-advantage sector. Thus stated, the infant-industry argument does not conflict with the principle of comparative cost advantage. Economists have also identified other cases in which infant industries might need temporary protection. Countries that lack well-functioning capital-market institutions, such as banks and stock markets, usually have a shortage of venture capital that new industries urgently need to invest and grow. In such a case of market failure, supporting a sector in its early growth phase is justified. Moreover, whenever new industries generate social benefits for which they are not compensated (for example, a biotechnology sector contributing to the improvement of national health care), a government may reward them by offering temporary protection from foreign competition.

In all these cases, an industry should receive public assistance only if it meets two theoretical conditions. The first is that the sector must eventually be able to compete on its own. The second is that the ultimate gains of infant-industry protection for society must be large enough to compensate for the costs incurred during the period of government support. In practice, it is almost impossible to make a proper cost-benefit analysis, which explains why governments generally refer to the infant-industry argument on political rather than theoretical grounds.

MIXED RESULTS

Over the years, the infant-industry argument has persuaded many policymakers all over the globe. Indeed, the argument seems plausible and is theoretically valid under the right set of circumstances. The empirical evidence on the effectiveness of infant-industry protection is inconclusive, however; both developed and developing nations show mixed results. On the one hand, the economic history of some advanced countries suggests that protecting young industries was conducive for industrial development. The United States and Germany, for example, enjoyed high tariffs on manufacturing in the nineteenth century, while Japan benefited from import quotas until the 1970s. On the other hand, there are many examples of industries in North America and Europe (for example, the U.S. computer industry and the Swedish automobile industry) that were infants at one stage but grew and flourished without any government protection. During the 1950s and 1960s, infant-industry promotion in Latin America and Africa often took the form of import substitution, or the replacement of imported goods by products from domestic industries. In countries such as Mexico and Brazil the results of this inward-looking strategy to promote local industrial development were disappointing. In contrast, young industries in East Asian countries such as

Taiwan and South Korea benefited from temporary protection, most likely because these sectors were oriented toward exports. The degree to which a country's economic performance is due to such infant-industry strategies, however, is a matter of ongoing academic debate.

Despite its appeal to common sense, the infant-industry argument is often criticized. The crucial problem is how a government can determine in advance which industries have a potential comparative advantage for the country. In assessing opportunities for industrial growth, the state usually is no better informed than the market. In other words, it is hard for policymakers to "pick winners." Moreover, if a government selects the wrong sector to protect, the costs to society are significant: The infant industry will use the support to expand its capacity but will require continued protection for its survival because no real comparative advantage can be developed. Instead of growing up, the industry will keep producing inefficiently and will become dependent on state assistance. In this case, a policy change is difficult since the infant industry has a vested interest and will fight to stay protected. Telling examples of protective strategies that turned out to be policies of "backing losers" are the British policy toward car manufacturing in the 1970s and the promotion of French microelectronics during the 1980s. In both cases sound economic reasons to stop protection were overridden by political desires to keep the "national champions" alive. Another problem with the infant-industry argument as applied by policymakers follows from historical evidence that countries tend to support similar growth industries during a given period of time. Since the end of the 1990s, for example, most advanced economies have treated their domestic information-technology sector as a growth industry. Hamilton and List, the pioneers of the infant-industry concept, already noted that such a bandwagon effect in industrial policy is inefficient from an economic perspective. After all, national comparative advantage comes from being different, not from doing the same as others do.

SEE ALSO *Absolute and Comparative Advantage; Import Substitution; Protected Markets*

BIBLIOGRAPHY

Baldwin, Robert. 1969. The Case against Infant Industry Tariff Protection. *Journal of Political Economy* 77 (3): 295–305.

Chang, Ha-Joon. 1994. *The Political Economy of Industrial Policy*. New York: St. Martin's Press.

Hamilton, Alexander. 1791. *Report on the Subject of Manufactures*. Philadelphia: Childs and Swaine.

Henderson, William O. 1983. *Friedrich List: Economist and Visionary 1789–1846*. London: F. Cass.

Krugman, Paul R., and Maurice Obstfeld. 2003. *International Economics: Theory and Policy.* 6th ed. Boston: Addison Wesley.

List, Friedrich. [1841] 1856. *The National System of Political Economy.* Trans. G. A. Matile. Philadelphia: J. B. Lippencott.

Gert-Jan Hospers

INFANT MORTALITY

SEE *Morbidity and Mortality.*

INFERENCE, BAYESIAN

Bayesian inference is a collection of statistical methods that are based on a formula devised by the English mathematician Thomas Bayes (1702–1761). Statistical inference is the procedure of drawing conclusions about a population or process based on a sample. Characteristics of a population are known as *parameters*. The distinctive aspect of Bayesian inference is that both parameters and sample data are treated as random quantities, while other approaches regard the parameters as nonrandom. An advantage of the Bayesian approach is that all inferences can be based on probability calculations, whereas non-Bayesian inference often involves subtleties and complexities. One disadvantage of the Bayesian approach is that it requires both a *likelihood function* that defines the random process that generates the data, and a *prior probability distribution* for the parameters. The prior distribution is usually based on a subjective choice, which has been a source of criticism of the Bayesian methodology. From the likelihood and the prior, Bayes's formula gives a *posterior distribution* for the parameters, and all inferences are based on this.

BAYES'S FORMULA

There are two interpretations of the probability of an event *A*, denoted $P(A)$: (1) the long-run proportion of times that the event *A* occurs upon repeated sampling; and (2) a subjective belief in how likely it is that the event *A* will occur. If *A* and *B* are two events, and $P(B) > 0$, then the *conditional probability of A given B* is $P(A|B) = P(AB)/P(B)$, where *AB* denotes the event that both *A* and *B* occur. The frequency interpretation of $P(A|B)$ is the long-run proportion of times that *A* occurs when we restrict attention to outcomes where *B* has occurred. The subjective probability interpretation is that $P(A|B)$ represents the updated belief of how likely it is that *A* will occur if we know *B* has occurred. The simplest version of Bayes's formula is $P(B|A) = P(A|B)P(B)/(P(A|B)P(B) + P(A|\sim B)P(\sim B))$, where $\sim B$ denotes

the complementary event to *B*, that is, the event that *B* does not occur. Thus, starting with the conditional probabilities $P(A|B)$, $P(A|\sim B)$, and the unconditional probability $P(B)$ ($P(\sim B) = 1 - P(B)$ by the laws of probability), we can obtain $P(B|A)$. Most applications require a more advanced version of Bayes's formula.

Consider the "experiment" of flipping a coin. The mathematical model for the coin flip applies to many other problems, such as survey sampling when the subjects are asked to give a "yes" or "no" response. Let θ denote the probability of heads on a single flip, which we assume is the same for all flips. If we also assume that the flips are statistically independent given θ (i.e., the outcome of one flip is not predictable from other flips), then the probability model for the process is determined by θ and the number of flips. Note that θ can be any number between 0 and 1. Let the random variable *X* be the number of heads in *n* flips. Then the probability that *X* takes a value *k* is given by

$$P(X = k|\theta) = C_{n,\,k}\theta^k(1-\theta)^{n-k},\ k = 0,\,1,\,...,\,n.$$

$C_{n,\,k}$ is a binomial coefficient whose exact form is not needed. This probability distribution is called the *binomial distribution.* We will denote $P(X = k|\theta)$ by $f(k|\theta)$, and when we substitute the observed number of heads for *k*, it gives the *likelihood function.*

To complete the Bayesian model we specify a prior distribution for the unknown parameter θ. If we have no belief that one value of θ is more likely than another, then a natural choice for the prior is the uniform distribution on the interval of numbers from 0 to 1. This distribution has a probability density function $g(\theta)$ which is 1 for $0 \leq \theta \leq 1$ and otherwise equals 0, which means that $P(a \leq \theta \leq b) = b - a$ for $0 \leq a < b \leq 1$.

The posterior density of θ given $X = x$ is given by a version of Bayes's formula: $h(\theta|x) = K(x)f(x|\theta)g(\theta)$, where $K(x)^{-1} = \int f(x|\theta)g(\theta)d\theta$ is the area under the curve $f(x|\theta)g(\theta)$ when *x* is fixed at the observed value.

A quarter was flipped $n = 25$ times and $x = 12$ heads were observed. The plot of the posterior density $h(\theta|12)$ is shown in Figure 1. This represents our updated beliefs about θ after observing twelve heads in twenty-five coin flips. For example, there is little chance that $\theta \geq .8$; in fact, $P(\theta \geq .8 \mid X = 12) = 0.000135$, whereas according to the prior distribution, $P(\theta \geq .8) = 0.200000$.

STATISTICAL INFERENCE

There are three general problems in statistical inference. The simplest is *point estimation*: What is our best guess for the true value of the unknown parameter θ? One natural approach is to select the highest point of the posterior density, which is the *posterior mode*. In this example, the posterior mode is $\theta_{Mode} = x/n = 12/25 = 0.48$. The poste-

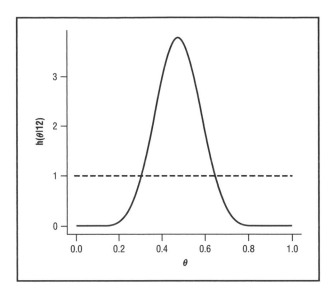

Figure 1: Posterior density for the heads probability ? given 12 heads in 25 coin flips. The dotted line shows the prior density.

rior mode here is also the *maximum likelihood estimate*, which is the estimate most non-Bayesian statisticians would use for this problem. The maximum likelihood estimate would not be the same as the posterior mode if we had used a different prior. The generally preferred Bayesian point estimate is the *posterior mean* : $\theta_{MEAN} = \int \theta\, h(\theta|x)\, d\theta = (x + 1)/(n + 2) = 13/27 = 0.4815$, almost the same as θ_{Mode} here.

The second general problem in statistical inference is interval estimation. We would like to find two numbers $a < b$ such that $P(a < \theta < b\,|X = 12)$ is large, say 0.95. Using a computer package one finds that $P(0.30 < \theta < 0.67|X = 12) = 0.950$. The interval $0.30 < \theta < 0.67$ is known as a *95 percent credibility interval*. A non-Bayesian 95 percent confidence interval is $0.28 < \theta < 0.68$, which is very similar, but the interpretation depends on the subtle notion of "confidence."

The third general statistical inference problem is hypothesis testing: We wish to determine if the observed data support or lend doubt to a statement about the parameter. The Bayesian approach is to calculate the posterior probability that the hypothesis is true. Depending on the value of this posterior probability, we may conclude that the hypothesis is likely to be true, likely to be false, or the result is inconclusive. In our example, we may ask if the coin is biased against heads—that is, is $\theta < 0.50$? We find $P(\theta < 0.50|X = 12) = 0.58$. This probability is not particularly large or small, so we conclude that there is not evidence for a bias for (or against) heads.

Certain problems can arise in Bayesian hypothesis testing. For example, it is natural to ask whether the coin is fair—that is, does $\theta = 0.50$? Because θ is a continuous

random variable, $P(\theta = 0.50|X = 12) = 0$. One can perform an analysis using a prior that allows $P(\theta = 0.50) > 0$, but the conclusions will depend on the prior. A non-Bayesian approach would not reject the hypothesis $\theta = 0.50$ since there is no evidence against it (in fact, $\theta = 0.50$ is in the credible interval).

This coin flip example illustrates the fundamental aspects of Bayesian inference, and some of its pros and cons. Leonard J. Savage (1954) posited a simple set of axioms and argued that all statistical inferences should logically be Bayesian. However, most practical applications of statistics tend to be non-Bayesian. There has been more usage of Bayesian statistics since about 1990 because of increasing computing power and the development of algorithms for approximating posterior distributions.

TECHNICAL NOTES

All computations were performed with the R statistical package, which is available from the Comprehensive R Archive Network. The prior and posterior in the example belong to the family of beta distributions, and the R functions dbeta, pbeta, and qbeta were used in the calculations.

SEE ALSO *Bayes' Theorem; Bayesian Econometrics; Bayesian Statistics; Distribution, Uniform; Inference, Statistical; Maximum Likelihood Regression; Probability Distributions; Randomness; Statistics in the Social Sciences*

BIBLIOGRAPHY

Berger, James O., and José M. Bernardo. 1992. On the Development of the Reference Prior Method. In *Bayesian Statistics 4: Proceedings of the Fourth Valencia International Meeting*, eds. José M. Bernardo, James O. Berger, A. P. Dawid, and A. F. M. Smith, 35–60. London: Oxford University Press.

Berger, James O., and Thomas Sellke. 1987. Testing a Point Null Hypothesis: The Irreconcilability of P Values and Evidence. *Journal of the American Statistical Association* 82: 112–122.

Department of Statistics and Mathematics, Wirtschaftsuniversität Wien (Vienna University of Economics and Business Administration). Comprehensive R Archive Network. http://cran.r-project.org/.

Gelman, Andrew, John B. Carlin, Hal S. Stern, and Donald B. Rubin. 2004. *Bayesian Data Analysis*. 2nd ed. Boca Raton, FL: Chapman and Hall/CRC.

O'Hagan, Anthony, and Jonathan Forster. 2004. *Kendall's Advanced Theory of Statistics*, vol. 2B: *Bayesian Inference*. 2nd ed. London: Arnold.

Savage, Leonard J. [1954] 1972. *The Foundations of Statistics*. 2nd ed. New York: Dover.

Dennis D. Cox

INFERENCE, STATISTICAL

To perform inference, in layman's terms, is to make an educated or informed guess of an unknown quantity of interest given what is known. *Statistical inference*, again in layman's terms, goes one step further, by making an informed guess about the error in our informed guess of the unknown quantity. To the layman, this may be difficult to grasp—if I don't know the truth, how could I possibly know the error in my guess? Indeed, the exact error—that is, the difference between the truth and our guess—can never be known when inference is needed. But when our data set, or more generally, quantitative information, is collected through a probabilistic mechanism—or at least can be approximated or perceived as such—probabilistic calculations and statistical methods allow us to compute the probable error, formally known as the "standard error," of our guess, or more generally, of our guessing method, the so-called "estimator." Such calculations also allow us to compare different estimators, that is, different ways of making informed guesses, which sometimes can lead to the best possible guess, or the most efficient estimation, given a set of (often untestable) assumptions and optimality criteria.

Consider the following semihypothetical example. Mary, from a prestigious university in Europe, is being recruited as a statistics professor by a private U.S. university. Knowing that salaries at U.S. universities tend to be significantly higher than at European universities, Mary needs to figure out how much she should ask for without aiming too low or too high; either mistake could prevent her from receiving the best possible salary. This is a decision problem, because it depends on how much risk Mary is willing to take and many other factors that may or may not be quantifiable. The inference part comes in because, in order to make an informed decision, Mary needs to know something about the possible salary ranges at her new university.

FROM SAMPLE TO POPULATION

As with any statistical inference, Mary knows well that the first important step is to collect relevant data or information. There are publicly available data, such as the annual salary surveys conducted by the American Statistical Association. But these results are too broad for Mary's purposes because the salary setup at Mary's new university might be quite different from many of the universities surveyed. In other words, what Mary needs is a conditional inference, conditional on the specific characteristics that are most relevant to her goal. In Mary's case, the most relevant specifics include (1) the salary range at her new university and (2) the salary for someone with experience and credentials similar to hers.

Unlike at public universities, salary figures for senior faculty at many private universities are kept confidential. Therefore, collecting data is not easy, but in this example, through various efforts Mary obtained $140,000, $142,000, and $153,000 as the salary figures for three of the university's professors with statuses similar to Mary's. Mary's interest is not in this particular sample, but in inferring from this sample an underlying population of possible salaries that have been or could be offered to faculty members who can be viewed approximately as exchangeable with Mary in terms of a set of attributes that are (perceived to be) used for deciding salaries (e.g., research achievements, teaching credentials, years since PhD degree, etc.). This population is neither easy to define nor knowable to most individuals, and certainly not to Mary. Nevertheless, the sample Mary has, however small, tells her something about this population. The question is, what does it tell, and how can it be used in the most efficient way? These are among the core questions for statistical inference.

DEFINING ESTIMAND

But the first and foremost question is what quantity Mary wants to estimate. To put it differently, if Mary knew the entire distribution of the salaries, what features would she be interested in? Formulating such an inference objective, or estimand, is a critical step in any statistical inference, and often it is not as easy as it might first appear. Indeed, in Mary's case it would depend on how "aggressive" she would want to be. Let's say that she settles on the 95th percentile of the salary distribution; she believes that her credentials are sufficient for her to be in the top 5 percent of existing salary range, but it probably would not be an effective strategy to ask for a salary that exceeds everyone else's.

Mary then needs to estimate the 95th percentile using the sample she has. The highest salary in the sample is $153,000, so it appears that any estimate for the 95th percentile should not exceed that limit if all we have is the data. This would indeed be the case if we adopt a pure nonparametric inference approach. The central goal of this approach is very laudable: Making as few assumptions as possible, let the data speak. Unfortunately, there is no free lunch—the less you pay, the less you get. The problem with this approach is that unless one has a sufficient amount of data, there is just not enough "volume" in the data to speak loudly enough so that one could hear useful messages. In the current case, without any other knowledge or making any assumptions, Mary would have no base to infer any figure higher than $153,000 to be a possible estimate for the 95th percentile.

MAKING ASSUMPTIONS

But as a professional statistician, Mary knows better. She knows that she needs to make some distributional assumptions before she can extract nontrivial information out of merely three numbers, and that in general, log-normal distribution is not a terrible assumption for salary figures. That is, histograms of the logarithm of salary figures tend to be shaped like a "bell curve," also known as the Gaussian distribution. This is a tremendous amount of information, because it effectively reduces the "infinitely unknowable" distribution of possible salary figures to only two parameters, the mean and the variance of the log of the salary. Mary can estimate these two parameters using the sample size of three if the three log salary figures (11.849, 11.864, 11.938) she obtained can be regarded as a probabilistic sample. This is a big "if," but for now, let us assume this is approximately true. Then the sample mean 11.884 and sample standard deviation 0.048 provide valid estimates of the unknown true mean μ and true standard deviation σ. Because for the normal distribution $N(\mu, \sigma^2)$ the 95th percentile is $z_{95} = \mu + 1.645\sigma$, Mary's estimate for the 95th percentile for the log salary distribution is $11.884 + 1.645 \times 0.048 = 11.963$. Because the log transformation is strictly monotone, this means that Mary's estimate for the 95th percentile for the salary distribution is $\exp(11.963) = \$156,843$, about 2.5 percent higher than the observed maximal salary of \$153,000!

ASSESSING UNCERTAINTY

With a sample size of three, Mary knows well that there is large uncertainty in estimating the mean μ, as well as in estimating σ. But how do we even measure such error without knowing the true value? This is where the probabilistic calculation comes in, if the sample we have can be regarded as a probabilistic sample. By probabilistic sample, we mean that it is generated by a probabilistic mechanism, such as drawing a lottery. In Mary's case, the sample was clearly not drawn randomly, so we need to make some assumptions. In general, in order for any statistical method to render a meaningful inference conclusion, the sample must be "representative" of the population of interest, or can be perceived as such, or can be corrected as such with the help of additional information. A common assumption to ensure such a "representativeness" is that our data form an independently and identically distributed (i.i.d.) sample of the population of interest. This assumption can be invalidated easily if, for instance, faculty members with higher salaries are less likely to disclose their salaries to Mary. This would be an example of selection bias, or more specifically, a nonresponse bias, a problem typical, rather than exceptional, in opinion polls and other surveys that are the backbone of many social science studies. But if Mary knew how a faculty's response probability is related to the faculty member's salary, then methods do exist for her to correct for such a bias.

Mary does not have such information, nor does she worry too much of the potential bias in her sample. To put it differently, she did her best to collect her data to be "representative," being mindful of the "garbage-in-garbage-out" problem; no statistical analysis method could come to rescue if the data quality is just poor. So she is willing to accept the i.i.d. assumption, or rather, she does not have strong evidence to invalidate it. This is typical with small samples, where model diagnosis, or more generally, assumption checking is not directly feasible using the data alone. But contrary to common belief, just because one does not have enough data to check assumptions, this does not imply one should shy away from making parametric assumptions. Indeed, it is with small samples that the parametric assumptions become most valuable. What one does need to keep in mind when dealing with a small sample is that the inference will be particularly sensitive to the assumptions made, and therefore a sensitivity analysis—that is, checking how the analysis results vary with different assumptions—is particularly necessary.

Under the i.i.d. assumption, we can imagine many possible samples of three drawn randomly from the underlying salary population, and for each of these samples we can calculate the corresponding sample mean and sample standard deviation of the log salary. These sample means and sample standard deviations themselves will have their own distributions. Take the distribution of the sample mean as an example. Under the i.i.d. assumption, standard probability calculations show that the mean of this distribution retains the original mean μ, but its variance is the original variance divided by the sample size n, σ^2/n. This makes good intuitive sense because averaging samples should not alter the mean, but should reduce the variability in approximating the true mean, and the degree of reduction should depend on the sample size: The more we average, the closer we are to the true mean, probabilistically speaking. Furthermore, thanks to the central limit theorem, one of the two most celebrated theorems in probability and statistics (the other is the law of large numbers, which justifies the usefulness of sample mean for estimating population mean, among many other things), often we can approximate the distribution of the sample mean by a normal distribution, even if the underlying distribution for the original data is not normal.

CONSTRUCTING CONFIDENCE INTERVALS

Consequently, we can assess the probable error in the sample mean, as an estimate of the true mean, because we can use the sample standard deviation to estimate σ, which can then be used to form an obvious estimate of the standard error $\sigma/\sqrt{n}$. For Mary's data, this comes out to be $0.048/\sqrt{3} = 0.028$, which is our estimate of the probable error in our estimate of μ, 11.884. In addition, we can use our distributional knowledge to form an interval estimate for μ. Typically, an interval estimator is in an appealing and convenient form of "sample mean $\pm 2 \times$ standard error," which is a 95 percent confidence interval when (1) the distribution of the sample mean is approximately normal; and (2) the sample size, n, is large enough (how large is large enough would depend on problems at hand; in some simple cases, $n = 30$ could be adequate, and in others, even $n = 30,000$ might not be enough). For Mary's data, the assumption (1) holds under the assumption that the log salary is normal, but the assumption (2) clearly does not hold. However, there is an easy remedy, based on a more refined statistical theory. The convenient form still holds as long as one replaces the multiplier 2 by the 97.5th percentile of the t distribution with degrees of freedom $n - 1$. For Mary's data, $n = 3$, so the multiplier is 4.303. Consequently, a 95 percent confidence interval for μ can be obtained as $11.884 + 4.303 \times 0.028 = (11.766, 12.004)$. Translating back to the original salary scale, this implies a 95 percent confidence interval (\$128,541, \$163,407). This interval for the mean is noticeably wider than the original sample range (\$140,000, \$153,000); this is not a paradox, but rather a reflection that with sample size of only three, there is a tremendous uncertainty in our estimates, particularly because of the long tail in the log-normal distribution.

So what is the meaning of this 95 percent confidence interval? Clearly it does not mean that $(11.766, 12.004)$ includes the unknown value μ with 95 percent probability; this interval either covers it or it does not. The 95 percent confidence refers to the fact that among all such intervals computed from all possible samples of the same size, 95 percent of them should cover the true unknown μ, if all the assumptions we made to justify our probabilistic calculations are correct. This is much like when a surgeon quotes a 95 percent success chance for a pending operation; he is transferring the overall (past) success rate associated with this type of surgery—either in general, or by him—into confidence of success for the pending operation.

By the same token, we can construct a confidence interval for σ, and indeed for Mary's estimand, a confidence interval for the 95th percentile $z_{95} = \mu + 1.645\sigma$. These constructions are too involved for the current illustration, but if we ignore the error in estimating σ (we shouldn't if this were a real problem), that is, by pretending $\sigma = 0.048$, then constructing a 95 percent confidence interval for $z_{95} = \mu + 1.65\sigma$ would be the same as for $\mu +$

$1.645 \times 0.048 = \mu + 0.079$, which is $(11.766 + 0.079, 12.004 + 0.079) = (11.845, 12.083)$. Translating back to the original salary scale, this implies that a 95 percent confidence interval for z_{95} would be (\$139,385, \$176,839). The right end point of this interval is about 15 percent higher than the maximal observed salary figure, \$153,000. As Mary's ultimate problem is making a decision, how she should use this knowledge goes beyond the inference analysis. The role of inference, however, is quite clear, because it provides quantitative information that has direct bearing on her decision. For example, Mary's asking salary could be substantially different knowing that the 95th percentile is below \$153,000 or could go above \$170,000.

LIMITATIONS

One central difficulty with statistical inference, which also makes the statistical profession necessary, is that there simply is no "correct" answer: There are infinitely many incorrect answers, a set of conceivable answers, and a few good answers, depending on how many assumptions one is willing to make. Typically, statistical results are only part of a scientific investigation or of decision making, and they should never be taken as "the answer" without carefully considering the assumptions made and the context to which they would be applied. In our example above, the statistical analysis provides Mary with a range of plausible salary figures, but what she actually asks for will depend on more than this analysis. More importantly, this analysis depends heavily on the assumption that the three salary figures are a random sample from the underlying salary distribution, which is assumed to be log-normal. Furthermore, this analysis completely ignored other information that Mary may have, such as the American Statistical Association's annual salary survey. Such information is too broad to be used directly for Mary's purposes (e.g., taking the 95th percentile from the annual survey), but nevertheless it should provide some ballpark figures for Mary to form a general prior impression of what she is going after. This can be done via Bayesian inference, which directly puts a probabilistic distribution on any unknown quantity that is needed for making inference, and then computes the posterior distribution of whatever we are interested in given the data. In Mary's case, this would lead to a distribution for z_{95}, from which she can directly assess the "aggressiveness" of each asking salary figure by measuring how likely it exceeds the actual 95th percentile. For illustration of this more flexible method, see Gelman et al (2004).

SEE ALSO *Classical Statistical Analysis; Degrees of Freedom; Distribution, Normal; Errors, Standard; Inference, Bayesian; Selection Bias; Standard Deviation; Statistics; Statistics in the Social Sciences*

BIBLIOGRAPHY

Casella, George, and Roger L. Berger. 2002. *Statistical Inference.* 2nd ed. Pacific Grove, CA: Thompson Learning.

Cox, D. R. 2006. *Principles of Statistical Inference.* Cambridge, U.K.: Cambridge University Press.

Cox, D. R., and D. V. Hinkley. 1974. *Theoretical Statistics.* London: Chapman and Hall.

Gelman, Andrew, J. B. Carlin, H. S. Stern, and D. B. Rubin. 2004. *Bayesian Data Analysis.* Boca Raton, FL: Chapman and Hall/CRC.

Xiao-Li Meng

INFERENCE, TRAIT
SEE *Trait Inference.*

INFERIORITY COMPLEX

Although Sigmund Freud is best known for his influence on the field of psychology, he was also a renowned teacher. Alfred Adler (1870–1937), a student of Freud, broke from Freud's teachings, criticizing his focus on the sexual. Adler established an approach he called *individual psychology,* which focused on the individual's need for fulfillment and power; he is credited with developing concepts such as birth order, quest for significance, mental life, and a variety of complexes including the *inferiority complex.* Adler suggested that the two needs children have to master are inferiority (or the will for power) and the need for social approval. According to Adler, people are constantly striving to be powerful, and feelings of inferiority (or weakness) often pull them into a consuming state of self-interest. It is important to note that, for Adler, inferiority itself is not negative; rather, it is a normal and even motivating force in life. All humans have some feelings of inferiority and are striving to overcome them. It is when one becomes fully consumed in his or her pursuit of power, or by feelings of inferiority to the point of paralysis, that inferiority becomes a burden. It is at this point that one shifts from having feelings of inferiority to having what Adler called the *inferiority complex.*

Adler initially conceptualized inferiority with regard to what he termed *organ inferiority.* In 1907 Adler wrote *Study of Organ Inferiority and Its Physical Compensation,* in which he theorized that organ inferiority occurred when one bodily organ was significantly weaker than another organ, causing the surrounding organs to compensate for the weakness in the inferior organ and make up for the deficiency in another way. Similarly, Adler suggested that individuals have or perceive that they have areas in which they are deficient—whether physical or psychological. Adler thought that, beginning in childhood, a deep feeling of inferiority is instilled in each individual as a result of the child's physical stature. In contrast to an adult, a child sees himself or herself as inferior in both physical and psychological abilities. However, Adler thought that the degree to which the child feels inferior is largely the result of the child's environment and interpretation of that environment. That is, some children perceive that they have more deficiencies or greater weaknesses because of the challenges they face, the way they interact with the adults in their lives, or the negative messages they get about their abilities. These children come to believe that they are inferior based on their perceptions of themselves and their life, not based on measurable or concrete criteria.

As adults, individuals also perceive areas of deficiency or weakness. These perceived weaknesses may result from life experiences (e.g., receiving a low test score) or from critical statements made by important others (e.g., being called stupid). Regardless of how the perceived deficit is brought to the individual's awareness, once the individual identifies an area perceived to be a weakness, he or she tries to compensate for those feelings of inferiority and achieve power. However, if this compensation does not have the desired result, the individual may become fully focused on the inferiority and develop what Adler called the *inferiority complex.*

According to Adler, the inferiority complex is a neurosis; the individual is fully consumed in their focus on the inferiority. It is a magnification of the normal feelings of inferiority, and results when strivings to overcome inferiority are greatly hindered. Individuals who struggle with feelings of inferiority may rate themselves in some area important to them as a 5 on a scale of 1 to 10, when they would aspire to a 6 or 7. In contrast, those with an inferiority complex may rate themselves as a 2 on a scale of 1 to 10 when they aspire to a 9. Those with an inferiority complex may also believe that there is no hope of ever reaching 9. The perception of one's shortcomings is an important aspect of this complex. That is, it matters more where individuals perceive themselves to be than it does where they actually are.

An individual with an inferiority complex is often overwhelmed, and as a result, the inferiority complex can become as consuming as an ailment or disease. Individuals may become manipulative in order to try to get others to give them the affirmation they are looking for, or they may try to use their deficiencies to get special attention or accommodation for circumstances that they are actually capable of handling or overcoming on their own. Those with inferiority complexes may be self-centered, depressed, incapable of development, compliant, shy, insecure, timid, and cowardly. They may be unable to make decisions for themselves and lack courage to move in any direction unless they are guided by others. Normal feelings of inferiority propel individuals toward solving and overcoming problems. Individuals typically do all they can to improve the situation and rid themselves of the feelings of inferiority. However, individuals with inferiority complexes are prevented from being able to solve or overcome problems. Indeed, Hertha Orgler in *Alfred Adler: The Man and His Work* (1973) wrote that Adler defined the inferiority complex as an "inability to solve life's problems" (p. 56). Adler believed that an inferiority complex, once established in an individual, would be a continued and lasting psychological struggle.

Adler's individual psychology theory is one of the mainstays in psychological thought. However, one controversial aspect of his theory is that it tends to be more conceptual than scientific—that is, it is subjective rather than objective. Further, many of Adler's concepts seem to be based on anecdotal evidence from his own life rather than on evidence integrated as a result of scientific research. There are many other theories that also are difficult to test empirically (e.g., object relations and gestalt), and it is likely that Adler would argue that those were his experiences and that other people could provide anecdotes of their own to corroborate his theories.

BIBLIOGRAPHY

Ansbacher, Heinz, and Rowena Ansbacher. 1956. *The Individual Psychology of Alfred Adler.* New York: Basic Books.

Manaster, Guy, and Raymond Corsini. 1982. *Individual Psychology.* Itasca, IL: Peacock Publishers.

Orgler, Hertha. 1973. *Alfred Adler: The Man and His Work.* London: Sidgwick and Jackson.

Sperber, Manes. 1974. *Masks of Loneliness: Alfred Adler in Perspective.* New York: Macmillan.

Wendy L. Dickinson
Jeffery S. Ashby

INFERTILITY DRUGS, PSYCHOSOCIAL ISSUES

Throughout American history, sociocultural expectations and norms have been that adults of childbearing age should procreate and become parents. This expectation presumes that every couple is able to have children and that they are broken, defective, or flawed if they are not able to conceive. While infertility is a medical problem, a variety of emotional responses are often associated with one's inability to have children. Individuals may begin to struggle with feelings such as anger, stress, disappointment, depression, anxiety, and low self-esteem. These negative emotions, in addition to the often invasive medical procedures associated with trying to become pregnant, can have a significant impact on individuals as well as on their relationships. Advances in assisted reproductive technologies as well as a variety of adoption and surrogacy arrangements now make it possible for some previously infertile individuals and couples to achieve parenthood. However, the psychological and sociocultural issues with regard to using outside interventions to become a parent can be problematic.

It is estimated that infertility affects approximately 6.1 million women and their partners in the United States, about 10 percent of the reproductive-age population (*National Survey of Family Growth, Cycle IV* 1995). Infertility is defined as the inability of a couple to achieve a pregnancy leading to a live birth after one year of regular, unprotected sexual intercourse. Infertility is experienced equally by males and females. Forty percent of infertility is due to what is termed "male factor," 40 percent is due to "female factor," and the remaining 20 percent is shared between the couple. In nearly 90 percent of cases, a clear medical diagnosis is presented to couples after an infertility evaluation. The remaining group, 10 percent, is diagnosed with "idiopathic" or medically unexplained infertility. Even with a clear medial diagnosis of the etiology of infertility, it is estimated that only 30 percent of all couples who receive medical treatment for infertility successfully attain a live birth.

The medical diagnosis of infertility can lead to profound emotional, relational, and sexual distress and social stigma in addition to challenging financial, legal, and medical treatment decisions. The negative feelings and difficult challenges can be profoundly disruptive to a couple or individual's life. In empirical and anecdotal literature, people experiencing infertility often note heightened emotional disturbance (e.g., anger, anxiety, depression, and helplessness), faltering self-esteem, and preoccupation with thoughts about conception. These thoughts and feelings can lead to a disruption in daily functioning as well as changes in sleeping, eating, and moods. Additionally if a diagnosis of infertility is received, there is often little or no societal, cultural, or religious preparation for the impact that is commonly experienced by those struggling to become parents. The duration and intensity of infertility treatment and its failure can increase or exacerbate preexisting mental health issues, intrapersonal and interpersonal concerns (including domestic violence), alcohol and substance use, and workplace challenges. Issues such as pregnancy loss, miscarriage, stillbirth, chemical pregnancies (pregnancy resulting from in vitro fertilization or other reproductive technology, characterized by low levels of HCG and usually miscarriage prior to implantation) may also be experienced by those undergoing infertility treatments and clearly can cause undue stress, anxiety, and health problems as well.

During infertility medical treatments, people often experience a variety of extreme emotional responses as they are faced with repeated high hopes of pregnancy crushed by the failure to conceive month after month. Those undergoing infertility treatment might feel overlooked by medical staff, insensitively managed, or overwhelmed by an array of invasive and expensive procedures. Fertility medications rarely are successfully utilized in isolation and accompany the vast majority of common infertility procedures and assisted reproductive technologies (ART), such as intrauterine insemination (IUI), in vitro fertilization (IVF), egg donation, sperm donation, and embryo donation.

The drugs used to treat infertility work by promoting ovulation (ovulation induction) through stimulating hormones in a woman's brain to prompt multiple eggs to release from the ovaries. Most fertility medications have been safely and effectively utilized for more than thirty years. Common fertility drugs include clomiphene, human menopausal gonadotropins, and bromocriptine. Potential side effects of these medications can include weight gain, hot flashes, mood swings, nausea, breast tenderness, cramping, and ovarian hyperstimulation. Drugs for infertility may result in multiple births, which can be challenging because they increase the likelihood of premature births and babies who may be at higher risk for developmental, social, and psychological complications. Further, conflicting empirical research indicates that women who take ovulation-inducing medications in conjunction with ART might be at increased risk of developing breast, ovarian, or uterine cancers.

As infertility medical technology continues to develop, navigating ethical and legal issues becomes important for both medical and legal policy makers as well as individuals and couples. Increased options for those experiencing infertility continue to be developed. Specialty procedures available through medical treatment include sex selection, screening for genetic anomalies, preimplantation genetic diagnosis (a procedure that can assist couples who have serious genetic disorders such as cystic fibrosis and Tay-Sachs disease), and egg and sperm freezing. While the concept of building a "designer baby" (i.e., one with certain physical or genetic characteristics) tends to get a lot of attention from the media, for most people handling infertility this is a misnomer. The vast majority of people who are trying to conceive simply want to begin or continue building a family in a way that most closely mirrors nonmedical assisted conception.

Infertility medical treatments are typically quite expensive and sometimes financially prohibitive for individuals through private pay. Insurance companies often do not cover infertility treatments, and coverage policies vary by state. Due to the cost of fertility medication and accompanying medical procedures, it is often only the more socially and economically mobile individuals or couples who are able to attempt to undergo medical infertility treatment options in their efforts to have children.

SEE ALSO *Anxiety; Childlessness; Depression, Psychological; Determinism, Genetic; Emotion; Fertility, Human; Medicine; Role Conflict; Self-Esteem; Stigma; Stress*

BIBLIOGRAPHY

Cooper-Hilbert, B. 1998. *Infertility and Involuntary Childlessness: Helping Couples Cope.* New York: Norton.

Daniluk, J. C. 2001. *The Infertility Survival Guide: Everything You Need to Know to Cope with the Challenges While Maintaining Your Sanity, Dignity, and Relationships.* Oakland, CA: New Harbinger Publications.

Jaffe, Janet, Martha Diamond, and David Diamond. 2005. *Understanding and Coping with Infertility: Unsung Lullabies.* New York: St. Martin's.

National Survey of Family Growth, Cycle IV. 1995. Hyattsville, MD: U.S. Department of Health and Human Services, Centers for Disease Control and Prevention, National Center for Health Statistics.

Peoples, Debby, and Harriette Rovner Ferguson. 1998. *Experiencing Infertility: An Essential Resource.* New York: Norton.

Rosen, Allison, and Jay Rosen, eds. 2005. *Frozen Dreams.* Hillsdale, NJ: Analytic.

Wendy L. Dickinson
Jana E. Frances-Fischer

INFIDELITY

Alfred Kinsey's landmark studies of male and female sexuality, beginning in the late 1940s, were the first empirical examinations of infidelity. Following Kinsey, however, little research was done until the 1970s, and it was not for another decade that the first reliable estimates of the prevalence of infidelity were obtained. Thus, research on infidelity, while growing, is still in its nascent phase.

DEFINITIONS AND PREVALENCE

Infidelity is a broad term that encompasses a variety of behaviors. Because of this, social scientists have used innumerable descriptors to more precisely capture the varieties of infidelity (e.g., nonmonogamy, extradyadic involvement, extramarital coitus). Terms fall broadly into two classes: (1) sexual infidelity, which specifies a degree of physical intimacy with someone other than a committed partner; and (2) emotional infidelity, which indicates a channeling of resources such as love, time, and attention toward someone other than one's partner. An additional term, *intimate betrayal*, has been suggested to describe the experience of specific relationship standards and expectations being violated. These terms are not mutually exclusive, and any given extradyadic involvement may include one or all of these aspects of infidelity to varying degrees.

Nationally representative surveys of the American population have focused on the prevalence of sexual intercourse outside of marriage. These studies have found that approximately 22 percent to 25 percent of men and 11 percent to 15 percent of women report at least one instance of extramarital sex while married, though up to 34 percent of men and 19 percent of women in older cohorts reported infidelity. Moreover, these figures almost certainly represent the lower bounds of actual acts of infidelity, as some individuals are unlikely to be candid about such intimate details of their lives. Research using procedures with greater anonymity (e.g., computer assisted self-reporting as opposed to face-to-face interviews) support this conclusion.

CORRELATES AND THEORIES OF INFIDELITY

Gender differences have received more attention than any other correlate of infidelity in the empirical literature. Overall, men are more likely to have an affair, though this finding is strongly dependent on the cohort of the individual. Gender differences are greatest in the baby-boom generation (those born just following World War II [1939–1945]) and reduced in younger cohorts; individuals born during the 1960s and later do not show gender differences in the rate of infidelity. The shrinking gender difference may reflect basic demographic changes, particularly the greater number of women in the workforce, a common place to meet affair partners.

While the overall interest remains low, more men express a desire for infidelity and the active pursuit of an affair relationship. Nonetheless, the majority of both sexes expect sexual monogamy in their marriage relationships. In addition, men's affairs tend to be more sexual and less related to the satisfaction of their marriage as compared to women, while women's affairs tend to be more emotional and described as long-term, loving relationships. It remains unclear how these gendered aspects of infidelity may be shifting with the changing rates of infidelity across generations.

Factors related to infidelity can be organized in terms of their source (i.e., involved partner, spouse, marital relationship, and context). A history of divorce, permissive attitudes toward infidelity, lack of religiosity, being African American, and poor interpersonal connections in the marital relationship have consistently shown a positive association with infidelity for involved partners. Factors related to the spouse of an unfaithful partner remain an interesting but little researched area. In terms of the marital relationship, marital distress, sexual dissatisfaction, imbalances of power, cohabitation prior to marriage, and highly autonomous marital relationships have been linked to infidelity, as has marrying at a young age and the length of the marriage. Some contextual factors include opportunity, travel, income, the availability and willingness of partners, and the individual's perceptions of societal frequency and acceptability of infidelity.

A variety of theories have been put forth to account for infidelity, with evolutionary psychology receiving the most attention. This theory posits that men's desire for sexual variety can be explained by natural selection (i.e., men historically have sought reproductive success by gaining access to a variety of women). As such, men are more bothered than women by sexual infidelity because it threatens this goal. Women, on the other hand, find emotional infidelity more disturbing because it threatens the male's commitment to protecting and providing for a woman and her offspring. Cross-cultural research demonstrates that men consistently both have more affairs and show greater distress due to sexual affairs than women do. However, there is tremendous variability across cultures in the rate of infidelity, underscoring the important influence of cultural and societal factors.

RESPONSES TO INFIDELITY AND THERAPY

Although some therapists have suggested that infidelity may at times be helpful for individuals and couples, the empirical literature strongly supports the negative consequences of infidelity. Extramarital affairs are reliably associated with increased marital distress, conflict, and divorce. When an affair is revealed, the spouse of the person who had the affair is often angry, humiliated, and depressed, and symptoms of post-traumatic stress disorder may be present, such as intrusive thoughts, hypervigilance, and real or imagined images of their spouse with the affair partner. In addition, infidelity can indirectly expose the uninvolved partner to sexually transmitted diseases, including HIV/AIDS. This is a significant risk when the affair relationship involved drugs or alcohol, which in turn reduces the likelihood of safe-sex practices. Research focused on the reactions of the involved spouse have been limited, but there is some evidence that after an affair is revealed he or she experiences increased depressive symptoms, a lower sense of well-being, and greater guilt and shame.

Beyond individual reactions to an affair, there are two broad outcomes for the marital relationship: staying together or getting divorced. Relationship dissolution can be influenced by the nature of the infidelity (e.g., degree and type of involvement, how the affair was discovered), cognitive factors (e.g., attitudes toward infidelity, meaning attached to the affair), and aspects of the marital relationship (e.g., length of marriage, level of commitment, quality and satisfaction with the marriage).

Not surprisingly, marital therapists have described infidelity as one of the most difficult problems to treat—and one of the most damaging for a relationship. In spite of this, there is a paucity of empirical research on marital therapy for infidelity. What research does exist is somewhat optimistic, however. Couples that have experienced an affair and then pursue marital therapy show strong improvements during therapy, including greater marital satisfaction, reduced trauma symptoms, and greater forgiveness in the uninvolved partner. However, it is challenging to generalize these findings to the wide prevalence of infidelity, as only a small number of studies have focused on therapy, and because many couples do not seek therapy after an affair has occurred.

SEE ALSO *Evolutionary Psychology; Marital Conflict; Marriage; Sex and Mating*

BIBLIOGRAPHY

Allen, Elizabeth S., et al. 2005. Intrapersonal, Interpersonal, and Contextual Factors in Engaging in and Responding to Extramarital Involvement. *Clinical Psychology: Science and Practice* 12 (2): 101–130.

Atkins, David C., Donald H. Baucom, and Neil S. Jacobson. 2001. Understanding Infidelity: Correlates in a National Random Sample. *Journal of Family Psychology* 15: 735–749.

Buunk, Bram P., Alois Angleitner, Viktor Oubaid, and David M. Buss. 1996. Sex Differences in Jealousy in Evolutionary and Cultural Perspective: Tests from the Netherlands, Germany, and the United States. *Psychological Science* 7 (6): 359–363.

Gordon, Kristina Coop, Donald H. Baucom, and Douglas K. Snyder. 2004. An Integrative Intervention for Promoting Recovery from Extramarital Affairs. *Journal of Marital and Family Therapy* 30: 1–12.

David C. Atkins
Rebeca A. Marin

INFIDELS

Any society with a more or less coherent cultural boundary tends to have an exclusionary notion of the outside and hence of otherness; the more inclusive the notion of membership, the more intense the notion of an outside.

With the collapse of the ancient world, the problem of otherness became closely associated with the development of the monotheistic and prophetic religions of Judaism, Christianity, and Islam. Because Yahweh was a jealous God, there was a sacred covenant between God and the tribes of Israel, which excluded those who worshipped idols and false gods. In Islam, there is a clear division between the household of the faithful (*dar al-islam*) and the sphere of war (*dar al-harb*). The notion of an external world of infidels is captured in *al-Kafirun*, the title of the 109th *sura* (chapter) of the Qur'an, which opens with, "Say, oh infidels." This Meccan chapter expresses the idea that religion should be freely chosen, stressing the devotion of the Prophet Muhammad (c. 570–632). This division between believers and infidels has, if anything, been reinforced by twentieth-century interpretations of a struggle (*jihad*) against unbelievers—an interpretation fully articulated in the writings of Sayyid Qutb (1906–1966), a radical member of the Egyptian Muslim Brotherhood. Qutb called Muslims to struggle against the darkness or barbarism of the West (*jahiliya*) and to reestablish the true Islam of the early community. Islam also has a definite notion of the dangers of apostasy (*Ridda*). When the Prophet died, many tribesmen assumed that their contract with the Prophet was concluded, but the Apostasy War was fought to maintain the coalition of tribes that formed the political basis of early Islam.

In Christianity, a universalistic orientation that recognized the "other" was contained in Paul's letters to the Galatians and Romans, which rejected circumcision as a condition of salvation. Because the uncircumcised were among the righteous, the message of Jesus had, at least in Pauline theology, a universal significance. However, the church developed a body of theology dealing with the problem of infidelity, making a clear division between the faithful who are baptized and follow the teaching of the church and those who are outside the faith. The term *pagan* connotes both the uncivilized and illiterate who live outside the city (the heathens) and those who live outside the church. *Paganus* stood for "civilian" as opposed to *miles*, "soldier," and hence the Christians of Roman times came to call themselves the *milites* or "soldiers of Christ" who struggle against sin and evil. The modern Salvation Army continues this notion of soldiers of Christ. The idea of an infidel is somewhat different, signifying a distinction between somebody who for whatever reason is ignorant of the Christian message and somebody who has actively rejected the promise of salvation in the life and teaching of Jesus. This notion of infidelity did not become well established in English until the early sixteenth century, when it described active opposition to Christianity on the part of Jews or "Mohammedans," as Muslims were mistakenly called. As a result, *infidel* became a term of opprobrium. The infidel in Catholic doctrine is to be distinguished from *heretic*. While the infidel is somebody who does not believe in the doctrine at all, a heretic is somebody who falls astray from true doctrine by, for example, denying the divinity of Jesus. The problem of the heretic is not one of unbelief so much as rival belief.

Judaism also has a notion of heathens (specifically pagan gentiles) who are called *acum* (an acronym of *Ovdei Cohavim u-Mazzaloth*) or, literally, those who are "star-and-constellation worshippers," or idolaters. Heretical Jews are *minim* or sectarian people, such as the early Christians. The Hebrew term *kofer*, which is cognate with the Arabic *kafir*, is applied to apostate Jews. The various attempts to reform Judaism in the nineteenth and twentieth centuries, such as the Conservative and Orthodox movements, have revived Jewish culture, once more giving greater emphasis to orthodox piety and to the separation of Jews from gentile culture.

The conception of infidelity as a theological condition is therefore peculiar to the Abrahamic religions, which specifically, as a result of strict conformity to monotheism, reject the worship of idols and condemn pagan rites that are designed to placate the gods. Because they claim to be based on a unique revelation and promise of redemption, they have logically and necessarily an exclusive view of the "truth." These religions, especially Christianity and Islam, developed as a result of a strong commitment to evangelism and the conversion of pagans to the true religion. Both Christianity and Islam recognized in their formal teaching that conversion has to be voluntary. In Islam, for example, in verse 256 of *Surat ul Baqara*, the Qur'an states, "There is no compulsion in religion." Roman Catholic doctrine similarly recognizes that conversion must be voluntary, and even the baptism of children cannot take place without consent unless they are in imminent danger of death.

The idea of paganism and infidelity is largely absent from the so-called Asian religions of Confucianism, Buddhism, Hinduism, and Shintoism, which either reject the idea of a single "high God" or tolerate various forms of polytheism and animism. A division between the moral and rational faith of Protestant Christianity and the popular rituals of the non-Christian world, which attempt to placate the gods to secure human prosperity, was developed in Western philosophy in Immanuel Kant's (1724–1804) *Religion within the Boundaries of Mere Reason* (1793). The Enlightenment substituted rational/irrational for the original true believer/infidel distinction. However, this distinction also raises the question as to whether monotheistic traditions are inherently more intolerant of diversity than other religious traditions, and hence legitimize violence against infidels. The New Testament sense that the Jews rejected their savior and crucified him has been regarded as the foundation of anti-Semitism in the medieval and (to a lesser extent) the modern world. Christian and Muslim notions of infidelity are assumed to be the cultural context for crusades and holy wars. In the twenty-first century, religious fundamentalism, dividing the world into true believers and the rest, is associated with the growth of religious nationalism, violence, and terrorism.

SEE ALSO *Animism; Anti-Semitism; Buddhism; Christianity; Heaven; Hell; Islam, Shia and Sunni; Judaism; Monotheism; Polytheism; Religion; Rituals; Supreme Being*

BIBLIOGRAPHY

Johnson, James Turner. 1997. *The Holy War Idea in Western and Islamic Traditions*. University Park: Pennsylvania State University Press.

Kant, Immanuel. [1793] 1998. *Religion within the Boundaries of Mere Reason*. Trans. and eds. Allen Wood and George Di Giovanni. Cambridge, U.K.: Cambridge University Press.

Matar, Nabil I. 1998. *Islam in Britain, 1558–1685*. Cambridge, U.K.: Cambridge University Press.

Vries, Hent de. 2002. *Religion and Violence: Philosophical Perspectives from Kant to Derrida*. Baltimore, MD: Johns Hopkins University Press.

Watt, William Montgomery. 1969. *Islamic Revelation in the Modern World*. Edinburgh: Edinburgh University Press.

Bryan S. Turner

INFLATION

Like many topics in economics, the concept of inflation—defined as an overall increase in the general price level of goods and services measured against a standard level of purchasing power—is subject to considerable disagreements among economists, highlighting the important differences between orthodox and heterodox economics. There are three important areas of disagreements. First, there is no consensus on the possible causes and consequences of inflation, even in a small, open economy. Second, economists disagree on the advantages of fighting inflation; in other words, should inflation-reduction be the primary goal of macroeconomic policy? Finally, economists disagree on the policies to be used to combat inflation. Indeed, in recent years there has been widespread agreement over interest rate–tightening as a way of fighting inflation, but such policies are misplaced, because they produce lower economic activity and higher unemployment.

Inflation is measured by keeping track of the changes in the prices of a number of items within a specific basket of goods and services over a given period of time, ignoring any improvement in quality. There are a number of ways of calculating inflation. For instance, the consumer price index (CPI) measures the changes in the prices of goods and services generally purchased by consumers. It is by far the most commonly used measurement. Other measurements include the gross domestic product (GDP) deflator, which measures inflation over the entire domestic economy.

THE ORTHODOX APPROACH AND INFLATION

For orthodox economists, inflation carries important costs because there are advantages to lower inflation. Among the costs, orthodox economists claim that inflation erodes the value of money, and economic agents are frustrated in making their consumption and saving decisions; it encourages speculative investment to the detriment of productive investment; and it represents hardship for those on limited incomes or on incomes that are not indexed.

Among the benefits of low inflation, orthodox economists point to the ability of economic agents to make better, more informed, long-term decisions given the relative stability of purchasing power. For instance, because inflation is considered to lower the value of money, low inflation restores confidence in money: By reducing future variations in the price level, households can better plan their consumption and saving plans and regain confidence in the future value of money. Economists also claim that low inflation lowers nominal and real interest rates, and therefore produces overall stability of the economic system, as low inflation is self-reinforcing.

In orthodox economics, the principal cause of inflation is excess demand in the goods and/or labor markets, a direct result of scarcity in both markets. Whenever aggregate demand is greater than aggregate supply at any given price, the overall level of prices of goods and services will tend to increase in order to eliminate the excess demand: Inflation is demand-led. This is the necessary consequence of interpreting macroeconomics through the use of aggregate demand (AD; the total demand for goods and services in a national economy) and aggregate supply (AS; the total supply of goods and services in a national economy) analysis, interacting in price-output space. If there is a positive relationship between prices and output, it is because the AS curve is nonhorizontal. In this sense, both output and the price level are the result of AD-AS interaction. This analysis leads to an understanding of the role of prices in orthodox theory as a mechanism that guarantees market clearing.

In fact, irrespective of the specific neoclassical or orthodox approach, excess demand is always a central

focus of inflation. Indeed, for monetarists, the growth of the money supply over and above the growth of output is seen as the principal cause of inflation. In their words, inflation is "always and everywhere a monetary phenomenon" (Friedman 1963). For monetarists, increases in the money supply always precede increases in prices. This results from the belief that the money supply is an exogenously determined quantity, independent of the needs of the economic system. The money supply is simply imposed on the system by the central bank, which can choose at will the growth rate of the money supply. Hence, whenever the central bank is pursuing expansionary policies, it allow the growth rate of the money supply to exceed that of output, resulting in "too much money chasing too few goods," the inevitable result of which is higher price levels. This view is based on the well-known quantity theory of money.

Keynesians, however, although they do not deny the role played by the exogenous money supply, place the emphasis primarily on output, given the relationship between output (unemployment) and inflation as embedded in the Phillips curve, according to which there is a trade-off between unemployment and inflation: Lower unemployment implies higher inflation. In other words, fighting unemployment comes at the cost of higher inflation. As unemployment decreases, wages tend to increase, raising prices in the process.

An obvious question is what then may cause excess demand? The answer lies in expansionary monetary and fiscal policies—in other words, the central bank and the state. In addition to an expansionary monetary policy, inflation arises because governments pursue an expansionary fiscal policy. Inflation arises either because the deficit is financed by printing money, or because an increase in fiscal policy will increase output, spending, and therefore demand for goods and labor.

Given the above discussion, the policy solution to contain inflation is to reduce the pressure on prices by reducing overall demand in the economy. This means limiting the growth of the money supply and reducing fiscal expenditures: Policymakers need to adopt responsible, sound policies. For Keynesians, this implies higher unemployment and lower wages.

THE HETERODOX APPROACH AND INFLATION

For heterodox economists and post-Keynesians in particular, excess demand is not the principal cause of inflation, largely because the economy almost always produces at less than full capacity: There is almost never an excess demand for goods, and similarly, there is but rarely scarcity in the labor market. Post-Keynesians and heterodox economists nonetheless acknowledge that demand may have some influence on prices, but it is considered to be small and indirect. This statement has direct implications for and stands in stark contrast with neoclassical theory. For instance, one of the main consequences is that fiscal spending or excess growth of the money supply cannot be a causal or direct influence on prices and inflation. Indeed, for heterodox economists, money is never a cause of inflation. This is because the money supply is endogenously determined: Excess money cannot exist (Lavoie 1992; Rochon 1999). In other words, the money supply is not determined by the central bank, but rather by the needs of production.

In contrast to orthodox theory, therefore, the principal cause of changes in the price level is increases in the costs of production. In this sense, heterodox economists adopt a cost-push approach to inflation. That said, orthodox economists do not deny the importance of costs in determining changes in the price level, but there are important differences between the orthodox and heterodox approaches. For the former, changes in cost are usually the result of "supply shocks," which occur only occasionally, such as a sudden increase in the price of oil or some unexpected and unforeseen event abroad. For heterodox economists, however, changes in the costs of production are the primary and dominant cause of inflation, and are part of the normal operations of contemporary economic systems.

For heterodox economists, however, inflation is not merely cost-driven, but it is also the result of conflicting claims over the appropriate division of income. Markets are characterized by dynamic interactions between macrogroups, such as workers, firms, and rentiers, each vying to get a larger share of income: Workers want higher wages, firms want higher profits, and rentiers want higher rents. In this sense, inflation is the result of a struggle over the distribution of income. It can arise largely from either a wage-wage spiral or a wage-price spiral, or from the attempt by firms to impose a given rate of return. In this sense, two important features of the heterodox explanation of inflation are collective bargaining and administered prices.

For instance, in formalized conflicting claim models, such as that described by Louis-Philippe Rochon and Mark Setterfield (2007), workers have a target wage share that they consider fair, equitable, or just. And although workers in general want to increase their overall nominal (or real) wages, they also want to maintain their social standing and their wages relative to other workers. If a specific group of workers negotiates higher wages, other groups may also demand higher wages in order to maintain their relative standing in the social order, fuelling the inflationary spiral. In turn, this wage-wage spiral implies higher costs of production for firms, which may try to pass on these costs to consumers through higher prices, which in turn will reduce real wages and lead to possible demand for higher wages in the future.

Moreover, firms may want to increase their standard rate of return to historical levels (Lavoie 1992). Firms may experience lower than normal returns and may want to increase their mark-up in order to bring their rate of return in line with more traditional levels, raising prices in the process. This in turn will lead to lower real wages, and workers may demand higher nominal wages to compensate.

Firms may be able to raise prices because, unlike in neoclassical theory, prices are administered: Firms set prices according to a mark-up over costs of production, not by competitive forces in the economy. In other words, firms will impose a rate of return over and above the normal costs of production, primarily wages and interest costs on debt, because they target a certain margin of profit.

In the end, whether firms or workers succeed in imposing their wills depends on the relative power of workers vis-à-vis firms in the wage bargain, and the relative power of firms in commodity markets. In turn, these powers vary according to the economic cycle or with the market structure. For instance, during periods of growth when unemployment is low, workers have greater power and may be able to demand higher wages. As for firms, brand loyalty, advertising, and the complexity of products give them greater power over prices (Lavoie 1992).

Finally, conflict also arises between firms and rentiers, who also want to increase their share of income. When the central bank increases interest rates, satisfying rentiers, firms may increase their mark-up and prices, and thus lower real wages. This also highlights an indirect conflict between workers and rentiers. For John Smithin (1994), rentiers are at the heart of the conflict. It is in this sense that heterodox economists see the rate of interest as a distributive variable.

The same analysis can be used to analyze deflation, that is a generalized decrease in the overall price level. In a conflicting claims model, one can assume that during periods of high unemployment, when workers are more desperate for work, they would be willing to work at wages lower (lower target wage) than what firms would be willing to offer in an effort to squeeze themselves into the labor market. With these downward pressures on wages, it remains possible for firms to lower prices, although deflation remains a rare phenomenon in contemporary developed economies since World War II, where the general trend on prices has been upward.

Similarly, the cost-plus approach and conflicting-claims model can be used to explain periods of hyperinflation (Camara and Vernengo 2001). For instance, in the case of inter-war Germany, the most probable cause of hyperinflation was the extreme costs of war reparations imposed by the Treaty of Versailles, a collapse of German exports, a depreciation of the currency, and higher prices. One may further assume that workers may resist the resulting important decline in real wages, along the same lines as described earlier. In the end, conflicting claims and distribution are key components of the explanation of both inflation and hyperinflation.

Heterodox economists also stand in contrast with orthodox economists in proposing policy remedies for fighting inflation. Three questions arise. First, should inflation always be the primary target of economic policy? Second, should the central bank be solely responsible for pursuing anti-inflationary policies, as has become the case in recent years? Finally, how can inflation be tamed?

Heterodox economists believe that too much emphasis is placed on fighting inflation, to the detriment of fighting unemployment and growth, which are the central focus of heterodox policy. As excess demand is not a direct contributor to inflation, there is no reason to believe that economic growth necessarily accompanies inflation. Moreover, because money is not seen as the principal cause of inflation, and also because there is only an indirect link between interest rates and inflation, heterodox economists do not see the central bank as the primary institution to fight inflation. In fact, central bank policy exacerbates the inflationary process.

Nevertheless, to fight inflation, heterodox economists propose a two-prong policy. First, we need de-emphasize the role of the central bank by setting the real interest rate at a "fair" level (equal to the growth rate of labor productivity), thereby limiting the influence of the rentier class. Second, we should adopt a permanent price and income policy in order to limit the increase in wages and prices.

SEE ALSO *Aggregate Demand; Class, Rentier; Economics, Keynesian; Economics, Post Keynesian; Excess Demand; Expectations; Macroeconomics; Misery Index; Monetarism; Money; Money, Endogenous; Money, Exogenous; Phillips Curve; Policy, Fiscal; Policy, Monetary; Prices; Quantity Theory of Money; Real Income; Stagflation; Wage and Price Controls; Wages*

BIBLIOGRAPHY

Camara, Alcino, and Matias Vernengo. 2001. The German Balance of Payment School and the Latin American Neo-Structuralists. In *Credit, Interest Rates and the Open Economy: Essays on Horizontalism*, ed. Louis-Philippe Rochon and Matias Vernengo, 143–159. Cheltenham, U.K.: Edward Elgar.

Friedman, Milton. 1963. *Inflation: Causes and Consequences*, New York: Asia Publishing House.

Lavoie, Marc. 1992. *Foundations of Post-Keynesian Economic Analysis*. Aldershot, U.K.: Edward Elgar.

Rochon, Louis-Philippe. 1999. *Credit, Money and Production: An Alternative Post-Keynesian Approach*. Cheltenham, U.K.: Edward Elgar.

Rochon, Louis-Philippe, and Mark Setterfield. 2007. Interest Rates, Income Distribution, and Monetary Policy Dominance: Post-Keynesians and the "Fair" Rate of Interest. http://www.trincoll.edu/~setterfi/Rochon%20Setterfield%20I%20-%20complete%20paper.pdf.

Smithin, John. 1994. *Controversies in Monetary Economics: Ideas, Issues, and Policy*. Aldershot, U.K.: Edward Elgar.

Louis-Philippe Rochon

INFLUENCE

SEE *Social Influence.*

INFLUENCE, PEER

SEE *Peer Influence.*

INFORMAL ECONOMY

All modern states regulate the economy; they also establish what goods and services are not, strictly speaking, part of this formal "economy." *Informal economy* can refer to either or both of these residual spheres. It is therefore useful to discuss the term from the perspective of who uses it and with reference to what kind of society. For some economists a sphere such as the household-based family is not an economic sphere because no finite *transactions* can be observed therein. Sociologists, conversely, use the term to expose a broad array of unrecorded *work*. Thus, besides transactions unregulated by government, they include practices, such as housework, domestic consumption, and caregiving, that fall outside "the economy" as measured by gross domestic product.

PERSPECTIVES ON INFORMAL ECONOMY

Emphasizing "the [low] degree of *rationalization*" of working conditions," the anthropologist Keith Hart (2004, p. 8) first used the term informal economy in 1971 to describe the casual work of the poor in Accra, Ghana (Hart 1973; see also Geertz 1963). While Clifford Geertz and Hart worked from a Weberian understanding of economic *rationality*, the term *informal sector* was picked up by international agencies and development economists in terms of quantitative degrees of scale, productivity, and income. Because the term was used to replace earlier understandings of "developing" societies in terms of "dual economies" (Lewis 1955), its initial usage was confused. Thus relatively independent formal and informal *sectors* now replaced the older notion of modern and traditional sectors of a national economy in which market forces at work in the one were distorted by custom in the other. Development in both formulations was seen to occur as the more dynamic sector expanded to absorb ever larger swaths of the more backward one. The theoretical vagueness of the new term led to criticisms (Bromley and Gerry 1979) that, combined with the empirical failure of these prognoses, led to marginalization of the term until the dawn of the twenty-first century.

Twenty-first century analyses stress the crucial interplay between formal and informal economies in especially two ways. Firstly, there has been a general shift throughout market economies from formal institutions with sharply defined boundaries and functions to those with fuzzy boundaries and highly adaptable functions. As a result some writers prefer the notion informalization *process* rather than use of a set of criteria to distinguish two different spheres of a society (Castells and Portes 1989). Secondly, analysts have increasingly focused on the degree to which different components of the informal economy are crucially linked to the so-called formal economy through putting out to homeworkers and subcontracting to informal workshops, while other components remain relatively less directly linked (Chen 2005).

Interest in the informal economy is widespread among development practitioners and international- and national-level policy makers as well as scholars in the various social sciences. Since it is inconceivable that there would be *no* informal practices in an economy or society, the way one understands such practices is likely to result from the kinds of settings on which one focuses. Among these are developing societies, socialist command regimes and their transformation, welfare regimes, and neoliberal regimes.

SETTINGS OF INFORMAL ECONOMY

A primary concern in the literature on "developing" societies is whether or not the informal economy is a benefit or a handicap. Insofar as a low capital to labor ratio is almost a definitional feature, it can be argued that a large informal economy reduces a country's average productivity; by avoiding start-up and running costs, it also effectively competes with firms paying taxes and legal fees. By contrast, insofar as it is, again almost by definition, the way poor people get by, the informal economy maximizes employment opportunities. In 2000 the Peruvian econo-

mist Hernando de Soto therefore advocated its encouragement through the introduction of a legal code more appropriate to current informal practices. His views, however, remain controversial.

Some commentators argue that these third world informal economies reflect a "weak state" that is unable to regulate uniformly throughout the polity. Prior to 1989 the reverse was the case for the informal economies that flourished under socialist command regimes, whose pervasive and rigid regulatory practices and intentional use of strategic scarcities provided the seedbed for informal practices. These eventually provided important networks that became the basis for resistance and eventual collapse of these regimes. The informal economy that resulted and now pervades the former Soviet bloc (Russia, Hungary, and so on) must be distinguished from socialist command economies that remain in place but have *intentionally* reduced the non-commodified socialist sphere. Here informal economy results from opening up ever larger areas of social interaction to market transactions that are nonetheless inconsistently regulated—China being the most vivid example.

In the "developed" capitalist economies, interest in the growing size of the informal economy has frequently been attributed to the failures of welfare regimes *either* to be comprehensive in their provision of services *or* to stimulate economic dynamism. For some the state was not providing enough welfare, while for others what it did provide was too costly and too inflexible for the changing needs of capitalism. Thus one argument was that informal practices were taken on by people who were not being properly served by the welfare regime, partly as a result of declining formal jobs and partly as the welfare state failed to provide social citizenship to newly arrived immigrants and established visible minorities. The other argument was that high taxes and pervasive regulation drove both workers and firms into informal, semi-legal channels. Nonetheless, while it is common for economists to correlate an expansion in informal activities with the higher taxes and increased labor legislation of welfare regimes, this makes it hard to explain the striking increases in such practices under neoliberal regimes. In partial explanation, while the former was both ideologically and pragmatically set against *informalization*, the latter has encouraged an ideal of "deregulation" positively endorsing decentralization, flexibility, and a "self-regulating" entrepreneurial worker—all supposedly features of informal economy.

ACHIEVING DYNAMISM AND REGULATION

Neither a deregulated economy nor a self-regulating economic actor is a sustainable notion, however. Rather, economies are made up of the regulation of productivity and exchange, one way or the other, so a major challenge is to discover the means by which both dynamism and regulation are achieved. By nature decentralized, informal economies provide a wide range of sites for regulation and dynamism. These include employer-employee micro-enterprises, sites of self-employment, domestic enterprises, and homework. They also include networks of interconnection between these (as well as the formal economy and state agencies) and longitudinal means for social reproduction—among them supply, distribution and credit systems, and culturally specific forms for the transmission of property. All of these—and a multitude of others not mentioned—provide sites for possible regulation, facilitation, and invention. This in turn calls into question use of the word *economy*. As "social" factors are used to regulate market exchanges and appeals to cultural (or "family") belonging are used as a means for regulating labor, the question arises as to whether it is any longer appropriate to refer to the overall phenomenon as an economy at all. There is probably much less distinction between the narrower economists' view of informal economy and the broader sociological one. When one realizes the extent to which a wide range of economic practices are regulated through cultures of intimacy and trust combined with ideologies of male authority and female altruism, one sees how the goals of intensifying productivity and even controlling quality expand to embrace a wide range of *social* practices and relationships.

Like other residual terms, the notion of informal economy will continue to be used to sum up what are in fact hugely varied practices. Insofar as these account for as much as one-half to two-thirds of nonagricultural employment in developing countries and one-quarter in the United States (International Labour Organization 2002), social scientists are challenged to cease conceptualizing these practices as pathological versions of a supposedly "normal" formal economy and instead develop concepts appropriate to a world that has always existed and yet has just begun to command the attention it deserves (Davis 2006).

SEE ALSO *Development Economics; Dual Economy; Economic Growth; Gross Domestic Product; Lewis, W. Arthur; Modernization; Rationality; Regulation; Tradition; Weber, Max*

BIBLIOGRAPHY

Bromley, Ray, and Chris Gerry, eds. 1979. *Casual Work and Poverty in Third World Cities*. Chichester, U.K.: Wiley.

Castells, Manuel, and Alejandro Portes. 1989. World Underneath: The Origins, Dynamics, and Effects of the Informal Economy. In *The Informal Economy: Studies in Advanced and Less Developed Countries*, eds. Alejandro Portes, Manuel Castells, and Lauren A. Benton. Baltimore, MD: Johns Hopkins University Press.

Chen, M. A. 2005. Rethinking the Informal Economy: Linkages with the Formal Economy and the Formal Regulatory Environment. EGDI-WIDER, United Nations University Research Paper #2005/10 1-28.

Davis, Mike. 2006. *Planet of Slums*. London: Verso.

De Soto, Hernando. 2000. *The Mystery of Capital: Why Capitalism Triumphs in the West and Fails Everywhere Else*. New York: Basic Books.

Fernández-Kelly, Patricia, and Jon Shefner, eds. 2006. *Out of the Shadows: Political Action and the Informal Economy in Latin America*. University Park: Pennsylvania State University Press.

Geertz, Clifford. 1963. *Peddlers and Princes: Social Change and Economic Modernization in Two Indonesian Towns*. Chicago: University of Chicago Press.

Hart, Keith. 1973. Informal Income Opportunities and Urban Employment in Ghana. *Journal of Modern African Studies* 11 (1): 61–89

Hart, Keith. 2004. Formal Bureaucracy and the Emergent Forms of the Informal Economy. Paper presented at the EGDI-WIDER, United Nations University, conference Unlocking Human Potential, September 17–18, 2004, Helsinki. http://www.thememorybank.co.uk/papers/forms.

International Labour Organization. 2002. *Women and Men in the Informal Economy: A Statistical Picture*. Geneva: International Labour Office, Employment Sector.

Lewis, W. Arthur. 1955. *The Theory of Economic Growth*. Homewood, IL: R. D. Irwin.

Smart, Alan, and Josephine Smart, eds. 2005. *Petty Capitalists and Globalization: Flexibility, Entrepreneurship, and Economic Development*. Albany: State University of New York Press.

Stark, David, and László Bruszt. 1998. *Postsocialist Pathways: Transforming Politics and Property in East Central Europe*. Cambridge, U.K.: Cambridge University Press.

Zhang, Li. 2001. *Strangers in the City: Reconfigurations of Space, Power, and Social Networks within China's Floating Population*. Stanford, CA: Stanford University Press.

Gavin Smith

INFORMAL SECTOR

SEE *Informal Economy.*

INFORMATION, ASYMMETRIC

Asymmetric information exists when one participant in trade knows something that the other participant does not know about the quality of the particular good or service they are trading. This violates one assumption of perfect competition—"perfect information" (when market participants have all the information relevant to goods' and services' quality and price). The canonical example is the market for used cars (Akerlof 1970): The seller knows her attention to the car's maintenance, but the buyer's evaluation of the car's value is limited to the features he can observe and his knowledge of the average quality of this type of car. In this case, the seller has more information about the product's quality, but there are also markets in which the buyer has more information. When buying health insurance, for example, the buyer knows his own eating, drinking, and smoking habits, and the seller (the insurer) does not have as clear a picture of the buyer's quality of health.

The concern of the economist or policy maker is that this asymmetry can lead to market failure: The asymmetric knowledge causes less trade between buyers and sellers than would be optimal for society; in the extreme case, only low-quality goods or services are traded. In this case of complete market failure, high quality goods are not sold: Used-car buyers assume (correctly) that only owners of "lemons" want to sell their cars, and insurance companies assume (correctly) that only less healthy individuals desire insurance. Like other market failures, asymmetric information corrupts the price mechanism: If the buyer lacks information (used cars), the market price will be too low for higher-quality exchange; if the seller lacks information (health insurance), the market price will be too high for higher-quality exchange.

Consider a numerical example in the case of used cars to make these ideas concrete. There are two types: high quality cars valued at $15,000 and low quality cars valued at $10,000. These values, common to both buyer and seller, indicate the utility gained from owning a car. If 10 percent of the cars are low quality, then the prospective buyer could assume with 90 percent probability that he is buying a high-quality car and will offer to pay $(0.90)(\$15,000) + (0.10)(\$10,000) = \$14,500$ or less. But at this price, only the owners of low-quality cars will be willing to sell. As a result, buyers and sellers expect only low-quality cars to be available on the market, and those cars sell for $10,000. Sellers of the low-quality cars know who they are, but the buyers do not. This phenomenon explains why a new car loses so much of its value as soon as it is driven off the dealer's lot.

A similar example illustrating the case of health insurance would show that there is less incentive for the high-quality (healthy) types to buy insurance, which drives up the price of insurance. Only the customers with poor health and higher willingness to pay are served because the insurer cannot sufficiently differentiate between the high- and low-quality types, but the buyers know their own quality of health. Of course, these extreme examples sel-

dom occur because buyers and sellers find ways to mitigate the asymmetric information, as described below.

The similarity between outcomes under imperfect information and some other types of market failure is the existence of a "free rider." The buyers (in the case of health insurance) or sellers (in the case of used cars) of the lower quality goods are "free riding" on the reputation of the higher quality goods. The increased incentive for low quality goods and services to be traded is known as "adverse selection." This is also related to, but different from, the concept of "moral hazard." The distinction between the two is one of timing: Moral hazard describes the incentive, once an individual has health insurance, to behave more recklessly because he no longer faces the full financial impact of addressing medical conditions brought on by his poor health habits.

Asymmetric information is not simply a lack of information. Even though each piece of fruit at the grocery, for example, may hide some information from the buyer, it is hidden from the seller, too, and the market price can reflect this chance of selling and buying poor-quality fruit. We are also not focused directly on some advantage held by the seller of a low-quality car, or an advantage held by an unhealthy purchaser of insurance. The market failure is simply the lack of a market for high-quality goods. If there were perfect information in the market for used cars, for example, then there would be two car markets, one for trading high quality and one for trading low quality.

There are various solutions to this market failure, but they often have their own drawbacks. Experts may provide the inadequately informed party with improved information, but this also increases the transaction cost—and if there is any remaining unknown information, high-quality goods are still difficult to sell. A physical examination may reveal a health insurance buyer's health to potential insurers. Regulations may require a minimum quality (of cars or physicians, for example) or certification exams (for electricians or plumbers, for example), but this barrier to entry may provide the regulated group with market power. Quality regulations may also inhibit the provision of lower-quality goods and services for which a market (with lower prices) would otherwise exist (with perfect information).

Could the high-quality agents simply state that they have the high-quality product or characteristics? If this statement, or "signal," is costly for those with a low-quality product or service, then such a solution is feasible. For example, offering warranties is expensive for those selling low-quality cars, but not for those selling high-quality cars. (This solution may face moral hazard problems, as mentioned above.) Likewise, a college degree need not prepare the student for her intended profession in order to be useful (Spence 1973a; Stiglitz 1975), as long as it is difficult to obtain for those students valued by potential employers. The degree could simply serve as a signal to employers that this student is bright or a hard worker, qualities that would otherwise be difficult for a potential employer to observe before hiring her. Further, the time and effort involved in courting a prospective spouse may also "signal" the love and commitment that would otherwise be difficult to observe before entering into marriage (Spence 1973b).

Another possible market solution is to provide the low-quality types an incentive to reveal themselves through the available contracts (Rothschild and Stiglitz 1976). In the case of health care, insurers provide contracts with lower deductibles that can be chosen by those less-healthy buyers willing to pay a higher premium. Healthy buyers pay lower premiums but a higher deductible, benefiting from their lower likelihood of illness.

SEE ALSO *Adverse Selection; Collective Action; Free Rider; Market Economy; Markets; Moral Hazard; Regulation; Risk; Signals; Uncertainty*

BIBLIOGRAPHY

Akerlof, George A. 1970. The Market for "Lemons": Quality Uncertainty and the Market Mechanism. *The Quarterly Journal of Economics* 84 (3): 488–500.

Rothschild, Michael, and Joseph Stiglitz. 1976. Equilibrium in Competitive Insurance Markets: An Essay on the Economics of Imperfect Information. *The Quarterly Journal of Economics* 90 (4): 629–649.

Spence, Michael. 1973a. Job Market Signaling. *The Quarterly Journal of Economics* 87 (3): 355–374.

Spence, Michael. 1973b. Time and Communication in Economic and Social Interaction. *The Quarterly Journal of Economics* 87 (4): 651–660.

Stiglitz, Joseph E. 1975. The Theory of "Screening," Education, and the Distribution of Income. *The American Economic Review* 65 (3): 283–300.

Christopher S. Ruebeck

INFORMATION, ECONOMICS OF

The primary sources of the tremendous growth of modern economies are technologies (including sociopolitical ones), and these are applications of systems of information. For entrepreneurs, information is a valuable but often costly commodity. Hence for political and business executives and managers, so-called inside information, that is, information that is known to business managers and public policy executives but not to the general public, presents constant temptation for illegal trading.

The absence of information influences markets, especially through the troublesome use of public ignorance, not to mention ignorance of information about technological innovations. The paradigm case for this is Adolf Von Bayer's discovery of synthetic indigo in 1880, which famously and tragically ruined Indian farmers who grew the indigo plant in ignorance of the innovation. Less drastic but more spectacular was the fall of the price of shares of telephone companies, once deemed gilt-edged, due first to deregulation and then to the advent of Internet telephony; both were made possible by new technologies. The economic value of innovations creates incentives for secrecy regarding them. Patent laws were designed to discourage this secrecy; their success depends on their success as disincentives.

The most important innovation in retail trade was the replacement of haggling with price-fixing, which entails sellers publicizing information about the minimum price they would settle for. Initially motivated by moral considerations, it proved efficient and prevailed in competitive markets. The theoretical basis for it came from Adam Smith (1776), who deemed competition to be the best incentive for efficiency (Smith 1776, bk. 1, chap. 7). He refuted there (Smith 1776, bk. 1, chap. 1) the popular idea of trade as players outguessing one another in a zero-sum game (that is, one player's gain is another's loss). Because free exchange rests on expectation of improvement, all parties to it are partners. Trade is not zero-sum game: Specialization raises productivity and imposes trade. Smith's major recommendation was to cancel protective import duties that protect the inefficient. In contrast, partial equilibrium theory (Marshall 1890), which is the bread and butter of traditional economics, incorporates the assumption that markets are perfectly competitive—that is to say, free of friction. They suffer no constraints, allow free entry, offer perfect knowledge of all relevant information, and incur no transaction costs. As this assumption is obviously false, economic advisers can easily blame friction for the failure of their forecasts. This is an excuse, the right for which is available only to those who begin with informing their clients of it. Lionel Robbins in 1932 stressed that this makes their economic forecasts sheer speculations, unlike the ones based on generalizations about observed regularities. This then resembles the distinction that Frank Knight (1921) and John M. Keynes (1921, chap. 26) made between risk and uncertainty. Unlike uncertainty, risk assessments rest on regularly observed probabilities. What information then can we have on the probabilities that affect markets? This is a vast field, as friction is blamed for so many aspects of the market untreated by the standard models yet given to statistical studies, including changes of tastes, unemployment, market fluctuations, money markets, and even markets for innovations.

The earliest studies of imperfect competition were the models for monopolistic competition (Chamberlain 1933; Robinson 1933). Friction can be viewed as space-time dependent monopoly (and often also vice versa). Kenneth Arrow and Gerard Debreu (1954) offered an economic-equilibrium model that allowed for friction, including information asymmetry, the asymmetry being in one partner to any given transaction having more relevant information than the other. They ascribed to each transaction space-time coordinates and its own characteristics, thus allowing for a diversity of market situations that permit the study of transitions from one market situation to another, including improved information systems and innovations. Particular commodities, such as second-hand cars and risky investments, invite the misuse of information asymmetry, which is troublesome. By contract, ignorance of prices of fairly standard commodities is far less troublesome. Where asymmetry is harmful, as in real estate deals, prospective customers usually examine matters more carefully. The literature shuns the study of the most blatant information asymmetry, namely that of experts. A partial remedy for this is the use of a second opinion, and this is why insurers support it. There is also the matter of conflict of interest, conspicuous in the cases of accountants who examine the books of their clients and of teachers whose grading of their students is inevitably also grading themselves (Flexner 1910). In medicine, informed consent, though legally required, is seldom practiced. To improve matters it should apply not only in treatment of disease but also in diagnosis and from the very first meeting, so that patients will be able to acquire vital information from their physicians (Laor and Agassi 1990).

Information on probabilities helps determine insurance rates. Competition should force the insurance to render premiums fair. Yet all projections are imperfect. Catastrophic deviations from estimates force those who rely on these estimates into bankruptcy. The network of insurance systems that safeguards any subsystem from collapse raises the likelihood of collapse of the whole system, however. For as the saying goes, there is no insurance against epidemics. And the epidemics may be due to some information, misinformation, or even disinformation.

The most valuable information concerns the outcome of tests of theories on valuable matters. Before daring to apply a theory, one must test it to prevent causing too much harm. Information leading to tests of theories is harder to come by in the human sciences than in the natural sciences. It is hard to test even educational theories in experimental classes because conducting tests in classes may be dangerous for the pupils. The same holds true for medical information, and this is why its procurement requires certain precautions guided by the Helsinki Accord and similar constraints. There is nothing to inform the seekers of information regarding education, even though its importance for global politics is all too obvious. Milton Friedman estimated that returns from investment in education are highest and explained the reluctance of entrepreneurs to invest in education as a lack of information (Friedman and Kuznets 1945).

The absence of elementary information forces social researchers to resort to complex theoretical and testing techniques, including systems dynamics. This technique employs systems theory, which is the beneficial suggestion that it is often possible to simplify assumptions about complex systems in diverse ways and obtain different sets of test models. In systems dynamics study is centered on inflow and outflow of certain inventory items in system with feedback loops. These studies are simply too complex to study empirically and often even mathematically. Efforts to apply this to markets are still too hard to evaluate.

In the meantime, entrepreneurs insure themselves as best they can against being pushed out of the market by surprising new technologies. Even marginal investments in small laboratories that function as conduits of new information—habitually useless—have often saved firms from collapse.

This brings a new aspect of information to the fore: How does it flow? This question is basic for the information-transfer technologies that now are growing rapidly. Claude E. Shannon (1949) developed information theory to deal with technical questions, such as how much distortion can a telephone cause without the loss of the ability to identify the voice of a speaker? To be applicable to all sorts of information conduction, Shannon examined signal transfer over channels and distortions as the difference between the message in the source and in the target and asked in the abstract, what characterizes the information that is essential? Unusual information is clearly rare, and Shannon equated information with improbability. (Newer studies improve upon this assumption.) Shannon noted that redundant information helps restore a distorted message. Assuming that no message transfer is perfect, he suggested that with no redundancy a message will be lost with the slightest distortion. Hence the often cited advice to be brief must be qualified. The simplest redundancy is repetition; it helps avoid some distortion. All this holds for signals, not for information proper. Information theory deals with the former and is unable to deal with the latter. The treatment of information as signals was a bold step, and it is central to all computerized systems, including the information highway. Thus a computer spell-checker program spots a rare combination of letters and suggests that it is possibly a misspelled word; if misspelling transforms a word to a common word, then the spell-checker program can only spot it by examining not the word but the sentence. This gets increasingly complicated, and no spell-checker program is perfect.

The rise of information technology is the outcome of a few developments, beginning with the wish to increase mathematical rigor in response to George Berkeley's criticism of the calculus (Wisdom 1953), the wish to develop logic as a formal system, and the wish to combine logic and mathematics. All this informed the transition from calculators to computers. Information theory was the peak of this process. The hope to see the brain as a computer must fail, as computers are blind to meanings, but much insight developed this way, leading to exciting developments in brain science, computer science, and even perception theory, all of which have breathtaking applications. The greatest boon to the economy, however, is the rise of the Internet, as is manifest from the tremendous new knowledge industries and the enormous markets for them.

SEE ALSO *Arrow, Kenneth J.; Competition; Debreu, Gerard; Drucker, Peter; General Equilibrium; Information, Asymmetric; Keynes, John Maynard; Microsoft; Partial Equilibrium; Robinson, Joan; Smith, Adam; Tâtonnement*

BIBLIOGRAPHY

Arrow, Kenneth J., and Gerard Debreu. 1954. Existence of a Competitive Equilibrium for a Competitive Economy. *Econometrica* 22 (3): 265–90.

Chamberlain, Edward H. 1933. *Theory of Monopolistic Competition.* Cambridge, MA: Harvard University Press.

Flexner, Abraham. 1910. *Medical Education in the United States and Canada: A Report to the Carnegie Foundation for the Advancement of Teaching.* New York: Carnegie Foundation for the Advancement of Teaching.

Friedman, Milton, and Simon Kuznets. 1945. *Income from Independent Professional Practice.* New York: National Bureau of Economic Research.

Keynes, John Maynard. 1921. *A Treatise on Probability.* London: Macmillan.

Kirkwood, Craig W. System Dynamics Methods: A Quick Introduction. Arizona State University System Dynamics Resource Page, August 1, 2001. http://www.public.asu.edu/~kirkwood/sysdyn/SDIntro/SDIntro.htm.

Knight, Frank H. 1921. *Risk, Uncertainty, and Profit.* Boston: Houghton Mifflin.

Laor, Nathaniel, and Joseph Agassi. 1990. *Diagnosis: Philosophical and Medical Perspectives.* Dordrecht, Netherlands: Kluwer.

Marshall, Alfred. 1890. *The Principles of Economics.* London, Macmillan.

Robbins, Lionel. 1935. *Essay on the Nature and Significance of Economic Science.* London: Macmillan.

Robinson, Joan. 1933. *Economics of Imperfect Competition.* London: Macmillan.

Shannon, Claude E. 1949. The Mathematical Theory of Communication. In *The Mathematical Theory of Communication,* ed. Claude E. Shannon and Warren Weaver. Urbana: University of Illinois Press.

Smith, Adam. 1776. *An Inquiry into the Nature and Causes of the Wealth of Nations.* London: Strahan and Cadell.

Wisdom, John O. 1953. Berkeley's Criticism of the Infinitesimal. *British Journal for the Philosophy of Science* 4: 22–25.

Joseph Agassi

INFORMATION CRITERIA

SEE *Model Selection Tests.*

INFORMATION ECONOMY

SEE *Knowledge Society.*

INFORMATION PROCESSING

SEE *Reinforcement Theories.*

INFORMATION SOCIETY

SEE *Knowledge Society.*

INFORMED CONSENT

The term *research* refers to a systematic investigation designed to develop or contribute to generalizable knowledge by testing and proving or disproving specific hypotheses. The knowledge gained through research may be important as a basis for the formulation of social policy or the improvement of practice in medicine, education, social services, or other areas. Research may produce information as the result of experimentation that involves introducing some new variable (e.g., a test drug or method of treatment) into the situation and seeing what difference, if any, that new variable makes. Alternatively, research may entail gathering data and drawing conclusions by observing things happening naturally (i.e., a natural experiment). In both the experimental and observational methods, research may involve using human beings as participants who serve as the sources of data from which the generalizable conclusions are drawn. Especially when human participants are involved, research must be conducted in an ethical manner, including assurances that the participants have given *informed consent* for their involvement.

Principles regarding the proper conduct of research involving human participants have been incorporated into over thirty different international guidelines and ethical codes. The first of these was the Nuremberg Code, adopted in 1947 for Nazi war-crime trials in which defendant physicians tried to justify their horrible actions as scientific experiments. Subsequent ones were spurred on by various scandals involving the mistreatment of human subjects, such as the forty-year Tuskegee (Non-Treatment of) Syphilis Study, the deliberate hepatitis infection of residents at Willowbrook (New York) state hospital between 1956 and 1971, and injection of live cancer cells into patients in 1963 at the Jewish Chronic Disease Hospital in Brooklyn, New York. In the United States, Congress in 1974 enacted the National Research Act, establishing the National Commission for the Protection of Human Subjects in Biomedical and Behavioral Research (popularly referred to as the *Belmont Commission*). In 1981 regulations embodying some of the Belmont Commission's recommendations were issued by the federal Department of Health and Human Services (DHHS, but at the time called the Department of Health, Education, and Welfare). These regulations have been adopted by other federal agencies as a *Common Rule* to protect human participants in any research protocol those agencies sponsor. Also, any research concerning the testing of investigational drugs or medical devices is regulated simultaneously by the federal Food and Drug Administration (FDA).

Research to which these regulations apply must be reviewed and approved by an interdisciplinary Institutional Review Board (IRB) and is subject to continuing IRB oversight. Conducting a research protocol without IRB approval or over IRB objection subjects the investigator and sponsoring institution to the loss of any future government funding for the conduct of research.

For any proposed research protocol, the IRB must ensure (among other things) that informed consent will be obtained from each potential participant. Potential participants must be informed of the following:

1. the purposes of the research, its expected duration, and the procedures involved;

2. anticipated risks or discomforts, as well as benefits, of participation and all reasonable alternatives to participation in the research protocol;

3. the extent to which research records will be kept confidential;

4. the availability of any compensation and/or treatment for research-related injuries;

5. the right not to participate and to discontinue participation at any time without penalty.

The IRB also must ensure that participants' informed consent is appropriately documented.

The IRB must police the requirement that no human subject is involved in research unless ethically sufficient informed consent has been obtained and the prospective participant has had the chance, without coercion or undue influence (i.e., voluntarily), to really consider whether or not to participate. The regulatory provisions for informed consent in research are basically a codification and extension of the common law (i.e., the judge-made law that evolves on a case-by-case basis) in the diagnostic and therapeutic setting. Under the common law, valid consent requires that the individual's agreement be voluntary, informed, and given by a person with adequate cognitive and emotional capacity. Individual IRBs are themselves monitored by the Office for Human Research Protections within DHHS.

Some states have enacted their own, additional laws, which vary quite a bit, concerning conditions for protection of research subjects. Moreover, private civil malpractice lawsuits may be brought by an individual participant against researchers and protocol sponsors for violation of common law standards regarding the obtaining of informed consent or other deviations from the acceptable standard of care under the circumstances.

Ethical researchers owe a heightened obligation to make certain that meaningful informed consent has been obtained for research involving especially vulnerable participants, particularly when the research consists of risky experimental interventions. Especially vulnerable persons in this context include persons with mental disabilities that impair decision-making capacity, prisoners, children, and pregnant women. Racial factors must also be taken into account when considering the need for special protections for vulnerable groups, because it has been common historically for researchers to both take undue advantage of members of racial minority groups by including them disproportionately in very risky studies, and to deny them the potential benefits of research participation by unfairly excluding them from certain studies. When a potential research participant is unable to give valid voluntary, informed consent personally, a surrogate acting on behalf of the person's best interests may act as decision-maker.

BIBLIOGRAPHY

Coleman, Carl H., Jerry A. Menikoff, Jesse A. Goldner, and Nancy N. Dubler. 2005. *The Ethics and Regulation of Research with Human Subjects.* Newark, NJ: Matthew Bender.

DeRenzo, Evan G., and Joel Moss. 2006. *Writing Clinical Research Protocols: Ethical Considerations.* Burlington, MA: Elsevier.

Noah, Barbara A. 2003. The Participation of Underrepresented Minorities in Clinical Research. *American Journal of Law and Medicine* 29 (2–3): 221–245.

Title 45, *Code of Federal Regulations*, Part 46: Protection of Human Subjects. 2003. Washington, DC: U.S. Government Printing Office.

Marshall B. Kapp

INGRATIATION

Ingratiation refers to behaviors that one enacts in order to be liked by another person. There are many tactics to accomplish this. First, we can show interest in another person by asking questions, paying attention, and singling out the person to make him or her feel special. Second, we can do favors or help or assist a person. Third, we may show support and loyalty. Fourth, we can smile and be friendly, cheerful, and positive. Fifth, we can directly express admiration by flattering people and telling them what we like or admire about them. Sixth, we can create sympathy by talking about things we have in common with someone.

Any behavior that potentially has the effect of enhancing one's likeability and that is enacted for this reason can be seen as an instance of ingratiation. So, the same behavior (e.g., helping a friend to study for an exam) can be an instance of ingratiation (if you want to borrow the friend's car later on) or not (if you are just being helpful), depending on the motive.

Different research paradigms have been used to study how people ingratiate themselves and what the effects are. For instance, when looking at the ingratiator's part, the researcher may instruct participants interacting with someone to make the other person like them, and then examine how they behave. Looking at the target's end, the researcher may expose participants to an ingratiating actor and examine if they like this person or are easily influenced by him or her, compared with control conditions (e.g., a noningratiating actor, or participants observing the same behavioral episode directed at someone else).

In his seminal book on ingratiation, Edward Jones (1964) noted that the goal of ingratiation is typically instrumental: We ingratiate ourselves to people because we want to influence their behavior in some way (e.g., get a date, borrow money, get a raise, get a good grade). Thus, ingratiation is a strategy for social influence, and it is typically used quite a lot by salespeople. Because people generally want something from people who have more power or status, the typical example of ingratiation is a lower-status person flattering a higher-status person. This type of ingratiation is recognized very easily by observers because the dependence of the ingratiator alerts them to the possibility of ulterior motives.

During the era of slavery this instrumental motive for ingratiation occurred among black slaves who acted in a subservient manner, expressing agreement with white authority figures (called *tomming*, after the character Uncle Tom from the book *Uncle Tom's Cabin*) in order to receive more lenient treatment (e.g., less physically demanding duties) in the hope that eventually they might be watched less closely and be able to escape. Similarly, in a work environment an ambitious employee may act very servile and conforming with respect to superiors in order to be liked and perceived as unthreatening by them, so that eventually he or she can usurp a superior's position. In instances like these, as in cases of toadying, the ingratiator is quite aware of his or her goals and the best possible ways to achieve them, and he or she may even have a long-term plan that is carried out with great sophistication.

Often, though, when people ingratiate themselves they are not aware of it. Many instances of ingratiation are unconscious, so people probably ingratiate a lot more than they think. Also, the target of the ingratiation is very often not aware of what is going on; whereas observers tend to quickly notice when ingratiation occurs, targets of ingratiation are less suspicious. So, the effects of ingratiation are generally as intended: The target likes the ingratiator, and is more inclined to do favors for the ingratiator. The ingratiator may not be aware of his own insincerity either, and may get away with the feeling that he and the target get along very well. E. E. Jones called this the "autistic conspiracy": Both ingratiator and target are not fully aware of the hidden agenda in their interaction (the ingratiator who wants something; the target who is happy to be flattered, satisfying his or her self-enhancement motive), and they simply feel good because they both get what they want. Neither of them is very motivated to look more critically at the interaction.

In addition to instrumental motives (i.e., influencing others' behavior), there are other motives for ingratiation as well. It smoothens social interaction, as when we don't tell people everything we think (e.g., a colleague has a terrible new hairdo). Also, if we get along well with people, they will like us and respond favorably to us, which in turn is good for our self-esteem.

SEE ALSO *Hierarchy; Jones, Edward Ellsworth; Patronage; Social Relations; Stratification; Uncle Tom*

BIBLIOGRAPHY

Gordon, R. A. 1996. Impact of Ingratiation on Judgments and Evaluations: A Meta-Analytic Investigation. *Journal of Personality and Social Psychology*, 71: 54–70.

Jones, E. E. 1964. *Ingratiation.* New York: Appleton-Century-Crofts.

Vonk, Roos. 2002. Self-Serving Interpretations of Flattery: Why Ingratiation Works. *Journal of Personality and Social Psychology* 82: 515–525.

Roos Vonk

INHERITANCE

Pride and Prejudice opens with the proclamation that it is well known that a man with a fortune is in want of a wife (Austen 1991, p. 1). This satirical remark conveys a theme that is illuminated elsewhere in the text: In nineteenth-century Britain, having an inheritance made a man an attractive marriage prospect. While the advantages that inheritances convey to the individuals who receive them may vary across time and across societies, benefits exist. The nature of these benefits and the motives of the givers are two issues that have been discussed extensively in the social sciences literature.

An inheritance can be described as funds or assets that an individual receives from another person at the latter's time of death. Accordingly, they are monies that individuals come to possess not through their effort in the marketplace, but through their relationships to other people, typically older family members and most often parents.

CONTROVERSIES AND CRITICAL ISSUES

One hotly contested debate about inheritances concerns the extent to which differences in the propensity to inherit and in the amounts inherited contribute to the observed differences in the amount of wealth that different individuals have. This is an important question because it has bearing on the validity of a popular economic theory of saving. Economists' life-cycle hypothesis attributes an individual's wealth at any point in time to the process of saving, arguing that individuals compile savings by spending less than they consume early in life so that they will have funds to turn to during retirement. According to this theory, it is an individual's earnings, age, and other demographic variables that determine the amount of wealth that the individual has. The receipt of an inheritance provides another potential source of wealth, however, and empirical research suggests that its effects may be significant. During the 1980s Franco Modigliani (1988) and

Laurence Kotlikoff and Lawrence Summers (1981) offered estimates of the magnitude of funds that U.S. adult children received from their parents. Modigliani put the sum at about 20 percent of the total wealth that individuals possess, while Kotlikoff and Summers argued that the amount was much higher (almost 80 percent). These data are illustrative because of the historical significance of the debate between these three authors. The debate laid the foundation for additional research on inheritances. Moreover, studies that have been conducted since this time routinely provide estimates of the magnitude of wealth transfers across the generations that lie within the range laid down in the Modigliani and Kotlikoff-Summers debate.

A second debate focuses on the motivations of those who give money to others. With this shift in focus comes a change in language. The term *bequest* is generally used to describe funds that one leaves to others when one dies, while the term *inheritance* is reserved for characterizing the funds after they have been received. The debate about bequests asks why people leave them. From a theoretical standpoint bequests can be either planned or accidental. Individuals may make deliberate decisions to leave money to their offspring, or bequests may be given simply because individuals who have accumulated substantial wealth that they plan to spend during retirement die before they finish consuming this wealth, thereby unintentionally leaving something for their offspring to inherit.

When a bequest is planned, theory suggests that there are numerous reasons that parents may choose to leave a bequest (Masson and Pestieau 1997). Some scholars argue that they might be used as a device for disciplining children—that parents can use the promise of a bequest and the associated threat of disinheriting their offspring as ways to force members of the younger generation to devote attention to their elders. Other scholars argue that bequests are given for purely altruistic reasons, stating that wealthy parents who have led comfortable lifestyles may leave bequests simply to ensure that their children also can have comfortable lifestyles or to guarantee that the children are protected against misfortune. Because it is hard to test the theories about motives directly, it is not possible to know exactly how many families use bequests as a disciplining device or how many intentionally leave bequests.

A final controversy surrounds the effects that inheritances have on individuals and on society. Because individuals who are wealthy have advantages that individuals who are poor do not, many social scientists argue that inheritances and other intergenerational transfers may have a negative effect of perpetuating inequalities in society. Proponents of this view note that the ability to leave one's wealth to one's children allows children from wealthy, comfortable backgrounds to be ensured of being fairly wealthy and comfortable themselves, while children in families where parents are too poor to have a pool of savings to leave at their time of death have no choice but to finance all their needs through their own earnings. Sociologists Melvin L. Oliver and Thomas M. Shapiro have been influential in laying out these arguments and in providing qualitative evidence from interviews with individuals who received inheritances that helps researchers understand the processes through which inheritances can perpetuate inequality (Oliver and Shapiro 1995; Shapiro 2004). Studies based on large national data sets containing information from families throughout the United States provide corroborating evidence suggesting that inheritances contribute to racial inequality (Menchik and Jianakoplos 1997).

POLICY IMPLICATIONS

A discussion of inheritance would be remiss without some mention of policy. One question many societies face is whether to tax inheritances. Naysayers often argue that taxing inheritances is inappropriate because it hampers families' ability to transfer family businesses from one generation to the next. Others argue that given the privilege that inherited wealth conveys, limiting the amount of funds that can be transferred is consistent with ideals of equal opportunity and making it on one's own. The theoretical debate about bequest motives also has implications for policy. If most bequests are accidental, taxing inheritances should not substantially alter saving behavior. However, if people are motivated to accumulate wealth for the expressed purpose of being able to leave it to their offspring at death, tax policies that reduce the amount that can be transferred after death might reduce saving. How inheritances affect the incentive to work is another important policy issue. The receipt of an inheritance can reduce individuals' willingness to work (Holtz-Eakin, Joulfaian, and Rosen 1993). This may provide a justification for policies designed to limit inheritances, much in the same way that there was popular support to reform welfare in the United States due to concerns about its effect on work incentives during the 1990s.

SEE ALSO *Inequality, Wealth; Wealth*

BIBLIOGRAPHY

Austen, Jane. 1991. *Pride and Prejudice.* New York: Knopf.

Holtz-Eakin, Douglas, David Joulfaian, and Harvey Rosen. 1993. The Carnegie Conjecture: Some Empirical Evidence. *Quarterly Journal of Economics* 108, no. 2: 413–435.

Kotlikoff, Laurence, and Lawrence Summers. 1981. The Role of Intergenerational Transfers in Aggregate Capital Accumulation. *Journal of Political Economy* 89, no. 4: 706–732.

Masson, André, and Pierre Pestieau. 1997. Bequest Motives and Models of Inheritance: A Survey of the Literature. In *Is Inheritance Legitimate? Ethical and Economic Aspects of Wealth Transfers*, ed. Guido Erreygers and Toon Vandevelde. New York: Springer.

Menchik, Paul, and Nancy Jianakoplos. 1997. Black-White Wealth Inequality: Is Inheritance the Reason? *Economic Inquiry* 35, no. 2: 428–442.

Modigliani, Franco. 1988. Measuring the Contribution of Intergenerational Transfers to Total Wealth: Conceptual Issues and Empirical Findings. In *Modelling the Accumulation and Distribution of Wealth*, ed. Denis Kessler and André Masson. Oxford: Clarendon.

Oliver, Melvin L., and Thomas M. Shapiro. 1995. *Black Wealth/White Wealth: A New Perspective on Racial Inequality.* New York: Routledge.

Shapiro, Thomas M. 2004. *The Hidden Cost of Being African American: How Wealth Perpetuates Inequality.* New York: Oxford University Press.

Ngina Chiteji

INHERITANCE TAX

An inheritance tax is a tax on funds or assets that an individual receives from someone else when the latter dies. Most European countries levy their taxes on bequests from deceased individuals using this type of tax. This is not the only way that a government can tax transfers made from one generation to the next, however. The United States has an estate tax, meaning that the tax assessed by the government is levied on the entire estate before the estate is subdivided among heirs. The difference is more than semantic. Most countries have marginal tax rates that rise as individual income and wealth rise. With an estate tax, a $50,000 estate left to ten heirs will be taxed at the rate that applies for sums of $50,000. With an inheritance tax, each of the ten individuals receiving a share of the estate would be taxed on the $5,000 that they receive. If their marginal tax rate is low, their after-tax proceeds could be much higher than their share of a $50,000 estate that was taxed at a high rate.

In most European and North American societies, policies toward taxing transfers that elders leave their offspring at death have their roots in a pre-industrial, agricultural form of social and economic organization, where land represented the primary form in which wealth was held and social convention dictated that it was important to make sure that a family's estate remained intact as it was passed from one generation to the next (Delong 2003). As countries modernized, attitudes toward transfers changed, and tax policy evolved simultaneously. For example, the nineteenth century was a period in U.S. history in which the economy was rapidly expanding and land was plentiful.

Accordingly, J. Bradford Delong (2003) notes that Americans began to view inherited wealth with suspicion during this period, asserting instead that to be rich one was supposed to have earned his or her riches through thrift and industry. The shift in attitudes helped to create conditions that allowed for the passage of the first estate tax in 1916, and the tax rates actually have been quite high throughout time, indicating that there have been periods in history in which Americans did not view taxing intergenerational transfers as inappropriate or controversial. For example, during the New Deal era the marginal tax rate on large estates was set at 70 percent (p. 50). However, by the 1990s U.S. attitudes had changed and legislation was passed to phase the estate tax down to zero by 2011.

Why is taxing inheritances or estates so controversial? As with any tax there are trade-offs to contemplate when assessing the likely merits of the tax. Opponents argue that the tax makes it difficult to transfer a family business from one generation to the next, although policymakers presumably can prevent this outcome by setting an exemption for "small" estates. A second potential cause for concern exists because economic theory suggests that taxing estates or inheritances might reduce individuals' propensity to save. If individuals save because of a bequest motive, one expects them to save less during their lifetime if they fear their savings will be taxed by the government rather than being passed on fully to their heirs. However, the ability to receive an inheritance can also distort behavior. Theory suggests that individuals who receive an inheritance have incentives to reduce their work effort. This distortion to a labor-supply decision provides an argument for levying a tax on inheritances or estates.

SEE ALSO *Inequality, Wealth; Inheritance; Wealth*

BIBLIOGRAPHY

Delong, J. Bradford. 2003. A History of Bequests in the United States. In *Death and Dollars: The Role of Gifts and Bequests in America*, ed. Alicia H. Munnell and Annika Sunden. Washington, DC: Brookings Institution.

Gates, William H., Sr., and Chuck Collins. 2003. *Wealth and Our Commonwealth: Why America Should Tax Accumulated Fortunes*. Boston: Beacon.

Pestieau, Pierre. 2003. The Role of Gift and Estate Transfers in the United States and Europe. In *Death and Dollars: The Role of Gifts and Bequests in America*, ed. Alicia H. Munnell and Annika Sunden. Washington, DC: Brookings Institution.

Vandevelde, Toon. 1997. Inheritance Taxation, Equal Opportunities, and the Desire of Immortality. In *Is Inheritance Legitimate? Ethical and Economic Aspects of Wealth Transfers*, ed. Guido Erreygers and Toon Vandevelde. New York: Springer.

Ngina Chiteji

INIKORI, JOSEPH
1941–

Historian Joseph E. Inikori was born in Nigeria's Delta state in 1941. He obtained his undergraduate degree in 1967 from the University of Ibadan, where he embarked on a PhD program in 1968. A special arrangement allowed Inikori to study at the London School of Economics from 1969 to 1971 under the direction of A. H. John (1915–1978), a preeminent scholar of the early modern English economy. Inikori obtained his PhD in history there in 1973.

After a brief stint as an assistant lecturer at the University of Ibadan (1972–1973), Inikori was appointed lecturer at Ahmadu Bello University in Zaria, Nigeria, in 1973. In October 1981 he was promoted to the post of professor of history and subsequently became chair of the History Department. During this period, Inikori received two prestigious fellowships to English universities: he was named a visiting fellow at the London School of Economics (1974–1975) and he won the John Cadbury Fellowship at the University of Birmingham (1980). In 1989 Inikori became a professor of history and associate director of the Frederick Douglass Institute (1989–1998) at the University of Rochester in New York after serving there for a year as a visiting professor. In 2001 Inikori became the University of Rochester's director of graduate studies, in which capacity he was pivotal in the creation of the doctoral program in global history.

Inikori's research has been essential to the growth of scholarship on the Atlantic slave trade. International interest in quantifying the Atlantic slave trade erupted after the appearance of Philip Curtin's *The Atlantic Slave Trade: A Census* (1969), a groundbreaking work presenting a systematic estimate of the trade that was significantly lower than most previous estimates. Using newly discovered evidence in British customs records in a 1976 article, Inikori was one of the first scholars to revise Curtin's estimate upward. Publishing numerous articles and presenting papers at many conferences, Inikori has made an invaluable contribution to the literature on quantifying the slave trade.

Inikori has also examined the economic aspects of the slave trade, particularly its market structure, profit levels, hazards, and financial relationships. All of Inikori's works on this subject revolve around the central factor informing his multifarious research—the preoccupation with placing the Atlantic slave trade in its proper context in the development of the global economy. Inikori's analysis assigns a major role to the slave trade in the development of Africa's economic backwardness before 1850. In addition, Inikori has explored what he sees as the central role of diasporic Africans in the Americas during the Industrial Revolution in England, an argument first articulated in

Eric Williams's *Capitalism and Slavery* (1944). Inikori's various journal articles and conference papers have put forth the thesis that export markets throughout the Atlantic, markets generated through the labor of enslaved Africans, were crucial to the industrialization process in England. More than thirty years of scholarship culminated in the publication of *Africans and the Industrial Revolution in England: A Study in International Trade and Economic Development* (2002), a massive work drawing on classical trade theory and economic development analysis that focuses on the role of diasporic Africans in the Americas in fueling the growth of multilateral Atlantic trade between 1500 and 1850.

SEE ALSO *African Diaspora; Slave Trade*

BIBLIOGRAPHY

Curtin, Philip. 1969. *The Atlantic Slave Trade: A Census.* Madison: University of Wisconsin Press.

Inikori, Joseph. 2002. *Africans and the Industrial Revolution in England: A Study in International Trade and Economic Development.* Cambridge, U.K.: Cambridge University Press.

Williams, Eric. 1944. *Capitalism and Slavery.* Chapel Hill: University of North Carolina Press.

Joseph Avitable

INITIAL PUBLIC OFFERING (IPO)

An initial public offering (IPO) is the first ("initial") sale of equity to the public by a private company, usually through investment banks. The private company thereby becomes a public company (it "goes public").

The purpose of an IPO is to raise a substantial amount of equity capital and create a public market for company shares to be traded on stock exchanges. The funds raised can be used to finance various projects, such as the expansion of manufacturing, marketing, and research and development (R&D) activities. If a company needs to raise a large sum that cannot be financed by private investors, such as venture capitalists or banks, then an IPO might be the best, albeit a costly, way to obtain the necessary funds (the *pecking-order theory*). The number of IPOs has fluctuated over time, but in some years, it has exceeded six hundred. According to Jay Ritter and Ivo Welch (2002), there were over six thousand IPOs during the 1980–2001 period, raising (in gross) $488 billion (in 2001 dollars). After the collapse of the dot.com bubble in 2000, the number of IPOs declined, but increased to 179 in 2004.

Once public, firms have direct access to the capital markets, enabling them to raise more capital by issuing additional stock in a secondary offering (a *seasoned equity offering*). Public companies can also more easily raise funds privately.

Some insiders participate in the IPO by selling part of their shareholdings to receive possibly a substantial amount of cash and to diversity their portfolios. This can also be an exit point for many venture capitalists. Insiders can also sell their shares at later dates to convert their equity into cash.

An IPO is an expensive way to finance in three aspects: (1) the fees and expenses; (2) the change in ownership structure; and (3) the disclosure requirements. The underwriting fees (underwriting *discount* or *gross spread*) alone in the United States amounted to 7 percent of the gross proceeds for 90 percent of the IPOs in the late 1990s, although the figures are lower in other countries (Chen and Ritter 2000). By going public, the previous owners (e.g., founders and venture capitalists) sell a slice of their company to dilute their ownership stake, which may reduce their ability to control the enterprise.

Firms must supply detailed information to the potential investors at the time of the IPO (in the registration statement, including a preliminary prospectus—commonly called a *red herring*—and the final prospectus). This requires costly preparation of reports, as well as possible disclosure of strategic and sensitive information to competitors. Subsequently, firms operating in the United States are required as public companies to file quarterly and annual reports with the Securities and Exchange Commission (less frequently in some countries).

Most IPOs are offered to the public through an *underwriting syndicate*, consisting of a number of underwriters who agree to purchase the shares from the issuer to sell to investors (best effort or firm commitment). The lead underwriter usually sets the basic terms and structure of the offering, including the allocation of the shares and the offering price. Syndicate members do not necessarily receive equal allocations of securities for sale to their clients. Most underwriters target institutional or wealthy investors in IPO allocations, since they are able to buy large blocks of IPO shares, assume the financial risk, and hold the investment for the long term. Since "hot" IPOs are in high demand, underwriters usually offer those shares to their most valued clients.

IPO companies tend to be young and small companies that lack a long-established record of profitable operation. The median age (from the year of founding) of IPO firms is seven years (Ritter 2006). Roughly one-third of IPO firms reported losses in their IPO prospectuses before going public, although being profitable used to be standard (Ritter and Welch 2002). Ritter (2006) reports that

34.3 percent of IPOs are technology companies, of which 60.6 percent were backed by venture capitalists (compared to 39.9 percent of all IPO companies) for the 1980–2003 period. Therefore, investors purchasing stock in IPOs generally must be prepared to accept large risks for the possibility of large returns.

It is often observed that IPO shares open at a slightly higher price and close at a substantially higher price than the offering price at the end of the first of day of trading (providing a significant return to the IPO participants with the allocated shares). This phenomenon is referred to as IPO *underpricing* or *leaving money on the table* and is observed not only in the United States, but also in other countries. A price run-up on the first day occurs when the demand exceeds the supply (the IPO is "hot" or the offering is underpriced).

The first-day return averaged 18.8 percent (the average daily market return is 0.05 percent) during the two decades prior to 2001. It decreased with the collapse of the bubble, but is still substantial at 12.1 percent. Although the first-day return is typically positive, IPOs have in general underperformed in the long run both in terms of stock returns and financial accounting results. Ritter and Welch (2002) report that the average three-year buy-and-hold returns (from the closing price of the first day) of IPOs underperformed by 23.4 percent (compared to the CRSP [Center for Research in Security Prices] value-weighted market index) and by 5.1 percent (compared to seasoned companies with the same market capitalization and book to market ratio). Smaller firms (in terms of sales prior to an IPO) appear to do much worse. Underpricing and poor long-run performance do not appear to be related in a systematic manner, however. Why do firms leave so much money on the table? Why do so many IPOs underperform? These questions are important subjects of academic inquiry in finance.

The academic accounting literature documents that many IPO firms engage in earnings management through an aggressive use of (discretionary) accruals to inflate reported earnings around the time of the IPO. Long-run underperformance is more pronounced for firms with more aggressive discretionary accruals (Teoh et al. 1998). Some IPO firms in R&D-intensive industries reduce R&D expenditures below the optimal level to increase reported earnings (Darrough and Rangan 2005). These findings suggest that some managers try and sometimes succeed to influence the perception of investors of IPO firms by manipulating accounting numbers.

BIBLIOGRAPHY

Chen, Hsuan-Chi, and Jay Ritter. 2000. The Seven Percent Solution. *Journal of Finance* 55 (3): 1105–1131.

Darrough, Masako, and Srinivasan Rangan. 2005. Do Insiders Manipulate Earnings When They Sell Their Shares in Initial Public Offerings? *Journal of Accounting Research* 43 (1): 1–33.

Ritter, Jay, and Ivo Welch. 2002. A Review of IPO Activity, Pricing, and Allocation. *Journal of Finance* 57 (4): 1795–1828.

Ritter, Jay 2006. Some Factoids about the 2005 IPO Market. Working Paper. http://bear.cba.ufl.edu/ritter.

Teoh, Siew Hong, Ivo Welch, and T. J. Wong. 1998. Earnings Management and the Long-Run Market Performance of Initial Public Offerings. *Journal of Finance* 53 (6): 1935–1974.

Masako N. Darrough

INITIATION RITES

SEE *Rites of Passage.*

INITIATIVE

An *initiative* (also known as a *popular initiative*) is a type of direct democracy (along with the *referendum* and the *recall*) in which citizens participate directly in governance, rather than indirectly by voting in elections. Initiatives allow citizens to propose a measure—either a statute or a constitutional amendment—by filing a petition with a specified number of valid signatures from registered voters. The measure is then subject to an up or down vote in the next election. The initiative is available in twenty-four states, about half of all U.S. cities, and in nations such as Ireland and Switzerland.

The initiative has existed in the United States since colonial times. It gained considerable popularity during the Progressive Era, when 83 percent of all states to adopt the initiative (20 of 24) did so between 1898 and 1918. Its emergence was closely tied to western populism, with 71 percent of initiative states (17 of 24) lying west of the Mississippi River.

The initiative was called upon frequently in the 1910s and 1920s, but its use slipped into a period of relative dormancy during the Great Depression. It recaptured the public's imagination again in 1978 with the passage of Proposition 13 in California, a controversial measure that cut the state's property taxes in half. The political success of Proposition 13 spurred conservative interest groups and legislators to pursue tax-slashing measures in numerous other states, such as Oregon, Nevada, and Florida.

Proponents of initiatives argue that they provide a practical means for citizens to get results on issues that their elected leaders fail to address. They also claim that initiatives help to educate citizens about public policy and the democratic process. Critics point out, however, that the initiative may empower special interests at the expense of the general public. While narrow economic interests rarely have the resources to mount successful initiative campaigns independently, well-organized citizens' groups may be able win passage of new laws at the expense of minorities, the poor, and other disadvantaged populations.

Beyond their direct effects on public policy through the creation of new laws, initiatives have myriad indirect effects on citizens, interest groups, and political parties. For citizens, they help to stimulate voter turnout, cultivate civic engagement, and enhance trust in government. Interest groups may threaten to propose an initiative if the legislature does not do its bidding on a particular subject, thus enhancing the influence of such groups in policy matters. Political parties may invoke ballot initiatives as a means to achieve broader electoral objectives. For example, during the 2004 presidential election, Republican Party officials proposed initiatives banning same-sex marriage in critical swing states as part of an effort to promote voter turnout among conservatives sympathetic to President George W. Bush. Although survey evidence suggests that the marriage initiatives may not have had the effect that Republicans intended in 2004, their continued use in the 2006 midterm elections indicates that political parties now see polarizing ballot initiatives as a staple in their electoral strategies.

The debate over whether the initiative is beneficial or detrimental to democracy is unlikely to abate in the foreseeable future. While it is unclear which specific interests are most advantaged or disadvantaged by the initiative's existence, it is clear that savvy political actors will continue to invent ways to co-opt initiatives to advance their goals.

SEE ALSO *Ballots; Democracy; Democracy, Representative and Participatory; Interest Groups and Interests; Progressives; Referendum; Voting*

BIBLIOGRAPHY

Boehmke, Frederick J. 2005. *The Indirect Effect of Direct Legislation: How Institutions Shape Interest Group Systems.* Columbus: Ohio State University Press.

Cronin, Thomas E. 1989. *Direct Democracy: The Politics of Initiative, Referendum, and Recall.* Cambridge, MA: Harvard University Press.

Gerber, Elisabeth R. 1999. *The Populist Paradox: Interest Group Influence and the Promise of Direct Legislation.* Princeton, NJ: Princeton University Press.

Matsusaka, John G. 2004. *For the Many Or the Few: The Initiative, Public Policy, and American Democracy.* Chicago: University of Chicago Press.

Smith, Daniel A., and Caroline J. Tolbert. 2004. *Educated by Initiative: The Effects of Direct Democracy on Citizens and Political Organizations in the American States.* Ann Arbor: University of Michigan Press.

Smith, Daniel A., Matthew DeSantis, and Jason Kassel. 2006. Same-Sex Marriage Ballot Measures and the 2004 Presidential Election. *State and Local Government Review* 38 (2): 78–91.

Michael T. Heaney

INKBLOT TEST

SEE *Rorschach Test.*

INPUT-OUTPUT MATRIX

An input-output matrix, A, is a square table with elements a_{ij}, representing the amount of input i required per unit of output j. A column of the matrix depicts the inputs needed for the production of a specific output and, therefore, can be considered a technique. The matrix is a constellation of techniques. For example, if $A = \begin{pmatrix} 0 & 1/3 \\ 1/2 & 0 \end{pmatrix}$, then the technique for product 1 is $\begin{pmatrix} 0 \\ 1/2 \end{pmatrix}$ (1/2 a unit of input 2 per unit of output 1), while the technique for product 2 is $\begin{pmatrix} 1/3 \\ 0 \end{pmatrix}$ (1/3 a unit of input 1 per unit of output 2).

If the list of inputs is complete, including factor inputs, the input-output matrix also contains "techniques" for the production of the factor services. In 1936, in the first input-output study, the Russian-born American economist Wasily Leontief (1906–1999) presented consumption coefficients for the "production" of labor services. This case is the so-called closed input-output model. If only produced inputs enter the input-output matrix, one speaks of the open input-output model.

The basic equation of the open model is the material balance, $x = Ax + y$, where x is the vector of gross outputs, Ax the vector of intermediate inputs, and y is the vector of net outputs. The latter comprises the commodity components of household and government consumption, investment, and net exports. The material balance can be solved to determine the gross outputs, x, that are required to sustain the production of alternative bills of final demands, y. The solution is obtained by applying the so-called Leontief inverse, $(1 - A)^{-1} = 1 + A + A^2 + \dots$, to the equation: $x = (1 - A)^{-1} y = y + Ay + A^2 y + \dots$. The total output equals the final demand itself plus the direct input requirements given by the input-output matrix plus the indirect requirements. For $A = \begin{pmatrix} 0 & 1/3 \\ 1/2 & 0 \end{pmatrix}$, we have $(I - A)^{-1} = \begin{pmatrix} 1.2 & 0.4 \\ 0.6 & 1.2 \end{pmatrix}$. The first application was the U.S. World War II (1939–1945) effort.

The second equation of the open model is the financial balance, $p = pA + v$, where p is the row vector of prices, pA the row vector of material unit costs, and v the row vector of value-added coefficients, representing the factor costs per unit of output of each product. The financial balance can be solved to trace the effects of changes in the factor costs (such as wages, rental rates, and taxes) on all the commodity prices. The solution is $p = v + vA + vA^2 + \dots$. Price equals unit factor costs plus the unit factor costs of the direct input requirements plus the unit factor costs of the indirect input requirements.

A simple but important application is the national income identity. Simple manipulation of the two equations yields the identity $py = vx$. On the left-hand side is the value of the net output of the economy or the national product, and on the right-hand side is the value added generated in the production of the gross outputs or the national income. The identity between the national product and income cannot be disaggregated. For example, business services belong to intermediate demand, and hence do not constitute a component of the national product. Their production, however, contributes to national income. If one neglects that the national product must be based on the net output of the economy, one makes the mistake of double counting.

Roughly speaking, an input-output matrix details the average input requirements for the various products, and reductions in input-output coefficients represent productivity gains. The most important source of such reductions is technical change, but input-output coefficients may also be reduced by eliminating waste or by efficiency change. The third source of productivity growth is a composition effect. If relatively efficient firms gain market share, the input-output coefficients of the industry will fall.

Some confusion surrounds the dimensions of an input-output matrix. Some practitioners (including Leontief) consider these to be products, others consider them industries, and still others think of "sectors," a concept that supposedly integrates products and industries. To clarify, one must consider the statistical roots of an input-output matrix. These are an input matrix or use table $U = (u_{ij})_{i=1,\dots,m; j=1,\dots,n}$ and an output matrix or make table $V = (v_{ij})_{i=1,\dots,m; j=1,\dots,n}$. Here m is the number of products and n is the number of activities (firms or industries). The first column of the use table depicts the inputs of the first activity (typically agriculture) and the

first column of the make table depicts the outputs of that activity. The question is how to construct an input-output matrix on the basis of an input and an output matrix.

The United Nations (1993) advocates the so-called commodity technology model. In the case of square tables (with an equal number of products and industries), this amounts to taking the product of the input matrix and the inverse of the output matrix. However natural, this construction is troublesome. A complication is that the consequent input-output matrix may have negative cells, due to the presence of secondary products. (The off-diagonal entries in the output table create negative elements in the inverse.) In the case of rectangular tables (with more firms than products), the commodity technology model stipulates that the input-output coefficients are the regression coefficients in the equation where the inputs are regressed on the outputs.

To circumvent the problem of negatives and to distinguish between average requirements and best practices, modern input-output analysis works directly with the input and output matrices, without constructing input-output matrices. The gross output variable, x, is replaced by an activity vector, s. (If the first component is 1.01, this means that agriculture produces an additional 1 percent.) In the material balance, intermediate demand, Ax, is replaced by Us, and gross output x by Vs. In short, by working directly with the input and output matrices one can calculate activity levels that sustain alternative bills of final demands without addressing the complications that surround the construction of an input-output matrix (ten Raa 2005).

The logic of input-output analysis can be extended from production to income distribution. Households consume products (the inputs) and provide factor services (the outputs). Social accounting matrices treat different types of households (e.g., rural and urban) as separate "industries." Just as a product row of a use table depicts the distribution of output across industries, a factor-income row of a social-accounting matrix depicts the distribution of factor incomes across households and other income institutions.

SEE ALSO *Fixed Coefficients Production Function; Leontief, Wassily; Social Accounting Matrix*

BIBLIOGRAPHY

Leontief, Wassily. 1936. Quantitative Input and Output Relations in the Economic System of the United States. *The Review of Economics and Statistics* 18 (3): 105–125.

ten Raa, Thijs. 2005. *The Economics of Input-Output Analysis.* Cambridge, U.K.: Cambridge University Press.

United Nations Statistics Division. 1993. *Revised System of National Accounts.* Studies in Methods, Series F, No. 2, Rev. 4. New York: United Nations.

Thijs ten Raa

INQUISITION

SEE *Roman Catholic Church.*

INSTITUTIONAL INVESTORS

SEE *Investors, Institutional.*

INSTITUTIONAL REVIEW BOARD

In the United States, all academic institutions and other entities that receive federal government funding and that conduct research involving human subjects must maintain an institutional review board (also known as an internal review board, or IRB) to oversee the adherence to federal regulations that govern research using human subjects. These boards are committees of professional researchers and administrators who screen research proposals with the intent of enforcing the federal regulations covering research on human subjects. The primary intent of these regulations is to protect human subjects from potential physical or mental harm that may result from participating in a research project.

All research projects that employ human subjects, from medical drug trials to social behavior surveys, must be reviewed by the host institution's IRB to ensure that federal regulations are met within the proposed research design. Before proceeding with a project, researchers must receive approval, or in some special cases an exemption, from their local IRB. All research projects involving human subjects or employing data collected from people are subject to federal regulations, regardless of the source of financial support for the project. Since institutions found violating human subject regulations may be forced to forfeit all federal funding, the IRB is a critical component of any research university's governance structure.

HISTORICAL BACKGROUND

The global movement to safeguard and protect human subjects can be traced back to the aftermath of World War II (1939–1945) and the war trials held in Nuremberg, Germany, when the world learned of the atrocious medical experiments conducted on prisoners interned in Nazi concentration camps. The Allies developed what came to be known as the Nuremberg Code to assist the military tribunal in judging the Nazis' conduct. This code outlined the basic tenets that became the foundation of the ethics that govern research on human subjects. From the subjects' perspective, these tenets include: (1) the ability to voluntarily participate or withdraw from participation; (2)

the freedom from coercion to participate; and (3) the right to be informed of all potential risks and benefits of participation. Furthermore, the code's provisions require that researchers be professionally qualified for the specific type of research in question, that they use appropriate research designs, and that they seek to minimize the risk of potential harm to human subjects.

Throughout the 1950s and 1960s, numerous medical associations and national governments around the world passed declarations and endorsements of professional codes of conduct based on the Nuremberg Code. In the United States, this occurred when the National Institutes of Health issued its Policies for the Protection of Human Subjects in 1966. In 1974 the Department of Health, Education, and Welfare raised these policies to regulatory status and introduced IRBs as a mechanism for institutions to ensure the protection of human subjects through regulatory compliance.

The American codification of rules designed to protect human subjects in the 1960s and 1970s was spurred on by two high-profile cases that employed procedures that many considered to be unethical. In 1963 Yale psychologist Stanley Milgram (1933–1984) published the results of a study on obedience to authority in which one human subject was asked to deliver electrical shocks of increasing voltage to another person who was secretly collaborating with the experimenter. Even though the shocks were fictitious, the screams and pleas of the collaborator led the subject to believe that they were real. Ironically, Milgram's motivation for the study was the psychology behind the Nazi atrocities. In 1972 the press revealed that the U.S. Public Health Service was conducting a decades-long clinical study of the effects of syphilis using a sample of several hundred, mostly poor, African Americans living near Tuskegee, Alabama. While some subjects were given proper treatment, others were not informed of their diagnosis and were prevented from receiving treatment from other health-care providers. The primary goal of the Tuskegee study was to determine how, over extended periods of time, syphilis affects the human body and eventually kills. Not only did many human subjects in this experiment die from nontreatment, but the disease was also spread to the spouses and children of the untreated participants. The Tuskegee researchers did not receive the informed consent of the subjects and did not disclose the risks of participation to them and their families. Once it became public, the study was terminated and the remaining subjects were given proper medical care. Eventually, in 1997, President Bill Clinton issued a formal apology on behalf of the U.S. government.

The passage of the National Research Act (1974) established the National Commission for the Protection of Human Subjects of Biomedical and Behavioral

Research. This commission's 1979 report, commonly referred to as the Belmont Report (named after the Smithsonian Institution's Belmont Conference Center, where the commission met) served as the basis for the subsequent revisions to the federal regulations, which eventually evolved into the current Federal Policy for the Protection of Human Subjects (Code of Federal Regulations, Title 45, Part 46). As of 2005, sixteen federal departments and agencies that support or conduct human subjects research had adopted this policy, which is sometimes called the Common Rule.

REGULATORY PRINCIPLES AND PRACTICES

Three general ethical principles outlined in the Belmont Report serve as the basis for the rules outlined in the Common Rule: (1) respect—honor for the personal dignity, autonomy, and the right to privacy of individuals; (2) beneficence—the obligation to minimize the risks of potential harm to human subjects while seeking to maximize the benefits of research to humanity; and (3) justice—ensuring that the benefits and costs of research on human subjects are distributed equitably. These principles guide the regulatory rules overseen by IRBs in the daily practice of academic research. For example, the requirement to obtain informed consent is derived from the principle of respect; the requirement to explicitly weigh potential risks against potential benefits is derived from the principle of beneficence; and the requirement to recruit human subjects fairly is derived from the principle of justice.

For an experimental project involving human subjects to fall under the regulations of the Common Rule, it must be classified as research. Specifically, the Common Rule defines *research* as "a systematic investigation, including research development, testing and evaluation, designed to develop or contribute to generalizable knowledge." Projects that fail to meet this definition of research are exempt from the regulations. In some cases, local IRBs have exempted whole classes of academic exercises, most notably oral history projects, from their oversight. However, individual researchers are not at liberty to make an exemption determination on their own; only an IRB is allowed to review a proposed project and to determine if it meets the Common Rule's definition of research.

The technological revolution of the late twentieth and early twenty-first centuries spawned a resurgence in advocacy for the protection of privacy and individual rights. This was a contributing factor to what some saw as a tightened enforcement of Common Rule regulations by local IRBs, which were also being forced to respond to several high-profile cases of careless procedures during medical drug trials. As a result, many social scientists and educators discovered that their institutions wanted to make a closer examination of their research practices and procedures. The additional scrutiny and accompanying paperwork resulted in public complaints about the regulatory burdens imposed by the IRB system.

Some social scientists claim that the human subjects regulations are overly burdensome and have a stifling effect on the research climate. They say this is particularly true for survey-based research projects where the potential for personal harm to human subjects is either negligible or nonexistent. To date there is little compelling empirical evidence that the IRB system has significantly reduced the level of research using human subjects. However, most social scientists will agree that the enforcement of Common Rule regulations by IRBs does protect human subjects from highly risky experimental research practices. Given this, it is likely that the IRB system will remain entrenched in the governance of American academic research institutions for the foreseeable future.

SEE ALSO *Experiments, Human; Experiments, Shock; Marriage, Interracial; Milgram, Stanley; Tuskegee Syphilis Study*

BIBLIOGRAPHY

Levine, Robert J. 1986. *Ethics and Regulation of Clinical Research.* 2nd ed. Baltimore, MD: Urban & Schwarzenberg.

Sieber, Joan E. 1992. *Planning Ethically Responsible Research: A Guide for Students and Internal Review Boards.* Newbury Park, CA: Sage.

U.S. Department of Health and Human Services: Office for Human Research Protections. 2005. Code of Federal Regulations: Title 45, Public Welfare; Part 46, Protection of Human Subjects (Common Rule). http://www.hhs.gov/ohrp/humansubjects/guidance/45cfr46.htm.

U.S. Department of Health, Education, and Welfare: National Commission for the Protection of Human Subjects of Biomedical and Behavioral Research. 1979. *The Belmont Report: Ethical Principles and Guidelines for the Protection of Human Subjects of Research.* http://www.hhs.gov/ohrp/humansubjects/guidance/belmont.htm.

Paul W. Grimes

INSTITUTIONAL REVOLUTIONARY PARTY

SEE *Partido Revolucionario Institucional.*

INSTITUTIONALISM

The institutional approach to the economy had its genesis in the work of Thorstein Veblen, whose *The Theory of the Leisure Class* (1899) introduced the term *conspicuous consumption* into popular lexicon. A defining characteristic of Veblen's approach was the dichotomy between the dynamic forces of technology and the static forces of institutions. This conflict was played out in a modern business economy where the technological potential to produce goods was impeded by the demand of business enterprise that goods be sold profitably.

The terms *institutionalism* and *institutional economics* were coined in 1919 by Walton Hamilton. In an article in the *American Economic Review*, he presented the case that institutional economics was *economic theory*. This was true, Hamilton argued, because only institutional economics provided a unified approach to economic problems. Further, it rejected a laissez-faire view of the world and emphasized the role of institutions and the process of economic change. Finally, institutional economics understood the importance of habit and rejected the "pleasure and pain" of the utilitarian view of human behavior. For the next decade and a half, institutionalism gained important adherents in academia, many of whom subsequently rose to prominent policymaking positions in government.

As Yuval Yonay documented in *The Struggle over the Soul of Economics* (1998), institutional economics was on the rise in the interwar period and appeared poised to be a significant force in American economics. There were the labor studies of John R. Commons and his students at the University of Wisconsin. Veblen's student, Wesley Clair Mitchell, was the first director of the National Bureau of Economic Research. His pioneering work on business cycles was based on Veblen's *The Theory of Business Enterprise* (1904). Mitchell's student, Simon Kuznets, was instrumental in developing national income accounting. Yet another institutionalist, Morris Copeland, a student of J. M. Clark's, developed the flow of funds accounting, which in the 2000s is regularly reported by the Federal Reserve System and links the financial balance sheet with national income accounting.

Idle machines and hungry people in the 1930s were a glaring illustration of the conflict between making money and making goods. Many important institutionalists such as Rexford Guy Tugwell, an original member of Roosevelt's Brain Trust, were involved in the economic policy changes of the New Deal era. Adolf Berle and Gardiner Means, whose *The Modern Corporation and Private Property* (1932) had provided an understanding of the implications of the separation of ownership and control in the modern firm, were also institutionalists in the administration.

THE TEXAS SCHOOL

The most significant concentration of institutional economists in the United States in the post–World War II period, other than Commons' Wisconsin school of institutionalism, was at the University of Texas (UT) at Austin. The leading figure in the Texas School was Clarence Edwin Ayres, a philosopher turned economist who was greatly influenced by Veblen and John Dewey. The department included other figures who shared a common methodological tool (the Veblenian dichotomy) and were in agreement on economic policy; each was a strong personality, and collectively they sought to disseminate their view of the world. Though the institutionalist tradition remained at UT until the 1980s, the peak period of influence was undoubtedly in the 1950s. Another war, this time the U.S. intervention in Vietnam, divided the department and hastened the demise of institutionalism at UT.

OUT WITH THE OLD, IN WITH THE NEW

Some have viewed institutionalism as a story outside the mainstream of economics. However, as Yonay showed, the story of the rise and fall of institutionalism is intricately tied with changes in society and the evolution of the mainstream of economics. Just as the changes of World War I and the Russian Revolution provided a context for the rise of institutionalism, it was the aftermath of the Great Depression and World War II that resulted in its decline. Within the economics profession, institutionalism was swept away by mathematics, econometrics, and Keynesian economics. By 1956 a roundtable at the annual meetings of the American Economic Association pronounced the end of institutionalism. For the next three decades, institutionalism existed in the underworld of economics. Institutionalists were pushed toward, or willingly embraced, the view that they were outside the mainstream. This tended to marginalize the institutional economists that followed Veblen.

In 1985 Martin Bronfenbrenner published an article in the *American Economic Review* (*AER*) in which he stated that institutionalism had been pushed into "minority status although not into complete obscurity" (Bronfenbrenner 1985, p. 20). Attempts to respond to Bronfenbrenner were rebuffed by the editors of the *AER*. It was not until 1998 that there was again an AEA session on institutionalism, but this time it was the "new" institutionalism of Ronald Coase, Douglas North, and Oliver Williamson. This also rekindled an interest in the "original" institutional economics. The editors of the *Journal of Economic Literature* invited a paper on the institutional economics of Veblen and Commons.

The relationship between old and new institutionalism is an uneasy one. On the one hand, many of the new institutionalists view the Veblen-Commons-Ayres tradition to be one that is anti-theory—meaning anti-neoclassical theory. On the other hand, the old institutionalists view the new institutionalism as still wedded to outmoded views of technological change, human behavior, and the market mechanism. Despite differences that some see as significant, there is little doubt that the new institutionalism represents a recognition of the limitations of textbook economics and the validity of the concerns raised by Veblen and his followers.

THE IMPACT OF INSTITUTIONALISM

If one considers Hamilton's 1919 definition of institutional economics, it seems evident that the mainstream of economics has come a long way toward becoming institutional economics. This evolution has occurred mostly without the direct input of original institutional economists. The mainstream has sought a unified explanation through the microeconomic foundations of macroeconomics. Today neoclassical economics has recognized through the analysis of noncompetitive market structures that perfect competition does not prevail. Even the theory of contestable markets is a move beyond the stale concept of perfect competition. Virtually all economists now accept that institutions matter. Neoclassical economics has developed sophisticated economic dynamics and evolutionary game theory. The work of Herbert Simon on satisficing and bounded rationality is a recognition that the atomistic, hedonistic man of neoclassical economics is not valid, and instead humans, though they may seek their own self-interest, are constrained from doing so precisely because they have limited capacity for rational behavior.

Though there is a basic similarity between the old and the new institutionalism, the essential difference hinges on whether one believes that there is an invisible hand that guides the creation of efficient institutions or whether it is all a matter of habit, technological change, and path dependency. The new institutionalists tend to emphasize the progressive aspects of institutions, while the old institutionalists see institutions as holding back technology. A balance between these views would seem to be the most realistic view of how society evolves over time.

As Ron Stanfield explained, the bottom line is that economics has advanced. It is becoming more realistic in the face of technological and institutional change in society (Stanfield 1999, pp. 252–253). It would seem that there is now a real possibility that Hamilton's claim will be realized in the twenty-first century: institutional economics is economic theory.

SEE ALSO *Economics; Economics, Institutional; Stratification*

BIBLIOGRAPHY

Bronfenbrenner, Martin. 1985. Early American Leaders—Institutional and Critical Traditions. *American Economic Review* 75 (6): 13–28.

Hamilton, Walton. 1919. The Institutional Approach to Economic Theory. *American Economic Review, Supplement* 9 (1): 309–318.

Hodgson, Geoffrey. 1998. The Approach of Institutional Economics. *Journal of Economic Literature* 36 (1): 166–192.

North, Douglas C. 1990. *Institutions, Institutional Change and Economic Performance.* Cambridge, U.K.: Cambridge University Press.

Phillips, R. J., ed. 1995. *Economic Mavericks: The Texas Institutionalists.* Greenwich, CT.: JAI Press.

Stanfield, James Ronald. 1999. The Scope, Method, and Significance of Original Institutional Economics. *Journal of Economic Issues* 33 (2): 230–55.

Yonay, Yuval. 1998. *The Struggle over the Soul of Economics: Institutionalist and Neoclassical Economists in America Between the Wars.* Princeton, NJ: Princeton University Press.

Ronnie J. Phillips

INSTRUMENTAL VARIABLES REGRESSION

In regression analysis social scientists use data to understand relationships among the people, institutions, and conditions represented by the measurements contained in the data's variables. These observations of the variables, along with some assumptions about the relationships, are used to test hypotheses generated by the model. The method of instrumental variables (IV) estimation addresses a particular difficulty encountered in ordinary least squares (OLS) regression: One or more of our explanatory variables may be "endogenous." Consider either the simple regression model with observations $i = 1, \ldots, n$, of variables x and y,

$$y_i = \beta_0 + \beta_1 x_i + \epsilon_i, \qquad (1)$$

or the multiple regression model analogue with additional explanatory variables (without loss of generality, one additional variable)

$$y_i = \beta_0 + \beta_1 x_{1,i} + \beta_2 x_{2,i} + \epsilon_i. \qquad (2)$$

The goal of regression analysis (using OLS, IV, or other methods) is to estimate the values of the β parameters and thus the relationship between x and y and, in the process, calculate values for each observation's error, ε_i, as well. IV estimation can improve our interpretation of this relationship as causation rather than simply correlation. IV estimation attempts to address the concern that correlation between x and ε confounds the causation running from x to y. There are several reasons to suspect this "endogeneity," the correlation between the error and an explanatory variable.

First, the explanatory variable(s) and the dependent variable may be determined simultaneously—there may be feedback from the dependent variable to the explanatory variable. For example, when estimating the demand curve, x is a good's price, and y is the quantity of that good purchased. The observed quantity is an equilibrium quantity, which is jointly determined with price. Higher prices are associated with larger error terms. Due to the law of supply, a deviation of price above the demand curve induces a deviation of quantity to the right of the demand curve, which would bias OLS regression to measure a weaker relationship than actually exists. In fact the earliest known application of IV estimation was Philip Wright's (1928) study of the butter and flaxseed markets.

Second, there may be an omitted variable that is correlated with both the explanatory and explained variables. IV methods are often associated with labor economics, where the return to education may be of interest: the effect of another year of education (x) on a person's future earnings (y). Ability is an omitted variable in this regression—either because it is unmeasured or because it is difficult to measure accurately. The estimate of β may be biased if individuals who are more likely to pursue additional education also have more innate ability that is rewarded in the labor market by higher wages. The correlation between education on wages calculated by OLS would be larger than the correlation holding ability constant.

Third, an explanatory variable may be measured with error. Because an explanatory variable's (x's) measurement error is part of the regression's unobserved error (ε), larger errors are associated with larger values of the explanatory variable, and thus x is endogenous. The importance of this bias will be affected by the size of the measurement errors relative to other error components.

Although Wright (1928) is recognized as the first appearance of the method of instrumental variables, there is some controversy as to the actual author of the technique—it may have been Philip Wright's son Sewall. James Stock and Francesco Trebbi (2003) confirm that Philip deserves the credit. Olav Reiersøl (1941) was the first to use the term *instrumental variables* when the method was "rediscovered" decades after the Wrights did their work (Reiersøl 1945; Geary 1949). The Cowles Commission (Christ 1994) and Trygve Haavelmo (1944) pursued issues of model identification, to which IV techniques are linked. The development of two-stage least squares (Theil 1953; Basmann 1957; Theil 1958) was an important step in computational feasibility and statistical efficiency for equations with multiple endogenous variables and instruments. In the early twenty-first century the discussion of instrumental variable estimation's merits and faults continues (Angrist and Krueger 2001; Rosenzweig and Wolpin 2000), even in the popular press (Hilsenrath 2005; Whitehouse 2007).

REGRESSION TECHNIQUES

OLS regression estimates β in equation (1) by calculating the covariance of each side of the equation with x. Taking that covariance on each side of (1) produces the equation

$$\mathrm{cov}(x, y) = \beta\,\mathrm{cov}(x, x) + \mathrm{cov}(x, \epsilon). \qquad (3)$$

If x and ε are uncorrelated, so that $\mathrm{cov}(x, \varepsilon) = 0$, then we can estimate $\beta = \mathrm{cov}(x, y)/\mathrm{cov}(x, x)$ from (3), and this also produces estimates of each observation's ε_i. Without the population-level assumption of zero correlation between the explanatory variable and the equation errors, we do not have enough information to "identify" both the β and ε_i values.

IV regression addresses the problem of $\mathrm{cov}(x, \varepsilon) \neq 0$ by assuming that the correlation between ε and another variable z, the "instrumental variable," is zero: $\mathrm{cov}(z, \varepsilon) = 0$. Taking the covariance between this instrumental variable and our equation (1) (replacing x in the first terms of equation (3)) produces

$$\mathrm{cov}(z, y) = \beta\mathrm{cov}(z, x) + \mathrm{cov}(z, \varepsilon)$$

which can be solved for $\beta = \mathrm{cov}(z, y)/\mathrm{cov}(z, x)$, as long as $\mathrm{cov}(z, \varepsilon) = 0$. Note that we do not replace x entirely in the equation; we are still investigating the relationship between x and y, not that between z and y. In fact the condition that z and ε be uncorrelated implies that there is no relationship between z and y other than through the relationship between z and x. This solution for β also shows mathematically why it is important that $\mathrm{cov}(z, x) \neq 0$.

The two important assumptions of IV are reflected by the connection between the instrument(s) z and x and the lack of any other connection between the instrument(s) and the dependent variable. The first assumption can be checked: The instrumental variable z must be correlated with the endogenous explanatory variable x. The second assumption relies on our knowledge of the social phenomenon under study. The only effect of the instrument z on the dependent variable y is through the explanatory variable x, so that there is no correlation between the instrument and the error ε in equation (1). Because we do not actually know the true value of the error, we cannot fully test this second assumption. Although we can test the first assumption statistically, it too should be supported by our understanding of the underlying theory and relationships. Finally, IV estimates are consistent but biased, which indicates that large samples are necessary.

Using multiple regression to estimate equation (2) requires calculation of a column vector β. Each observation can now be expressed as a row vector, resulting in the matrix X containing all observations' explanatory variables and the column vector Y containing all observations' dependent variable, $Y = X\beta + \varepsilon$. OLS calculates β as $(X'X)^{-1}X'Y$, again requiring zero correlation between the error ε and any of the explanatory x variables. The IV method instead calculates β using a row vector of instrumental variables, collected over all estimates in the matrix Z, as $(Z'X)^{-1}Z'Y$.

Returning to the examples, instrumental variables addresses each of them as follows. First, in the estimation of a demand curve, an instrument (z) for price is the cost of production: It is correlated with the price that buyers pay (x), but it is not correlated with quantity demanded (y). Second, a particularly well-known instrument for years of education is Joshua Angrist and Alan Krueger's (1991) quarter of birth, which is explained in more detail below. Quarter of birth is unlikely to have a direct effect on future earnings, but if a child is born close to the cutoff date, he or she will start school either substantially earlier or substantially later than other children but will still be required to remain in school through age sixteen. Thus some children are required to have up to one year of additional education. Third, if the dependent variable is measured with error, we can use another measure of the dependent variable as an instrument, so long as the two measures' errors are not correlated.

The method most often used to implement IV is two-stage least squares (2SLS); it efficiently takes advantage of multiple instruments in addition to multiple explanatory variables (both endogenous and exogenous), as in equation (2). We can use the relative efficiency of IV and OLS to test for endogeneity with a Hausman (1978) test, and we can use "extra" instrumental variables to test their exogeneity.

SHORTCOMINGS OF THE INSTRUMENTAL VARIABLES METHOD

Before considering the drawbacks to the instrumental variables method, note that we are only concerned with the issue of endogenous variables if causality is an important part of the analysis. If the goal is only to describe statistical relationships in the data, IV estimation is not necessary (Moffitt 2003a).

We could also imagine that the omitted variable bias could be addressed by choosing participants randomly, avoiding the need to use IV methods, yet this is typically difficult in the social sciences. Although there have been some innovative public policy experiments (Moffitt 2003b) and field experiments (Smith 2002), many important questions in the social sciences require natural experiment methods, of which IV is an important part.

An important drawback to the method of instrumental variables is low correlation between the instrument(s) and an endogenous variable. The explanatory power of the regression is limited as a result. Not only are standard errors large, but a lack of variation in the instrument will translate into a limit on the range of behaviors that we can understand from the IV regression. We can return once more to our three categories of endogeneity and their associated examples. First, we learn about the demand curve only to the extent that changes in the supply curve reveal it. The portions of the demand curve that are not explored by changes in supply are no longer part of the estimation. Second, Angrist and Krueger (1991) estimated the return to education by instrumenting for education by quarter of birth. The combination of compulsory starting dates and compulsory schooling through the age of sixteen means that students born in different seasons may have up to a year's difference in compulsory education. Yet when instrumenting years of education by birth date, the regression estimate now has little relevance to those students who continue on to college, for example, because entrance to college is not determined by age but by high school graduation and performance in high school. Compulsory schooling does not affect the education decision of these people. Third, errors in measurement require an alternate measurement technique that covers a range of values similar to the measurement technique of interest.

Various authors also highlight the lack of specific theory in many instrumental variable studies. Mark Rosenzweig and Kenneth Wolpin (2000) carefully review many results from the labor economics literature, describing the theoretical assumptions implied by those studies' use of IV estimation. They argue that implicit assumptions are made whether the practitioners employing IV realize it or not. In either case, what these critiques call for is an improved understanding of the people, institutions, and conditions that are interacting as we study them. With better understanding we can improve our ability to generate relevant testable hypotheses about the actors' decisions and their connections to the conditions and institutions they face.

SEE ALSO *Least Squares, Ordinary; Least Squares, Three-Stage; Least Squares, Two-Stage; Regression; Regression Analysis; Simultaneous Equation Bias*

BIBLIOGRAPHY

Angrist, Joshua D., and Alan B. Krueger. 1991. Does Compulsory School Attendance Affect Schooling and Earnings? *Quarterly Journal of Economics* 106 (4): 979–1014.

Angrist, Joshua D., and Alan B. Krueger. 2001. Instrumental Variables and the Search for Identification: From Supply and Demand to Natural Experiments. *Journal of Economic Perspectives* 15 (4): 69–85.

Basmann, Robert L. 1957. A Generalized Classical Method of Linear Estimation of Coefficients in a Structural Equation. *Econometrica* 25: 77–83.

Christ, Carl F. 1994. The Cowles Commission's Contributions to Econometrics at Chicago, 1939–1955. *Journal of Economic Literature* 32 (1): 30–59.

Geary, Robert C. 1949. Determination of Linear Relations between Systematic Parts of Variables with Errors of Observation the Variances of Which Are Unknown. *Econometrica* 17 (1): 30–58.

Haavelmo, Trygve. 1944. The Probability Approach to Econometrics. *Econometrica* 12 (Suppl): 1–118.

Hausman, Jerry A. 1978. Specification Tests in Econometrics. *Econometrica* 46: 1251–1271.

Hilsenrath, Jon E. 2005. Novel Way to Assess School Competition Stirs Academic Row. *Wall Street Journal*, October 24.

Moffitt, Robert. 2003a. Causal Analysis in Population Research: An Economist's Perspective. *Population and Development Review* 29 (3): 448–458.

Moffitt, Robert. 2003b. The Negative Income Tax and the Evolution of U.S. Welfare Policy. *Journal of Economic Perspectives* 17 (3): 119–140.

Reiersøl, Olav. 1941. Confluence Analysis by Means of Lag Moments and Other Methods of Confluence Analysis. *Econometrica* 9 (1): 1–24.

Reiersøl, Olav. 1945. Confluence Analysis by Means of Instrumental Sets of Variables. *Arkiv for Mathematik Asstronomi och Fysik* 32: 1–119.

Rosenzweig, Mark R., and Kenneth I. Wolpin. 2000. Natural "Natural Experiments" in Economics. *Journal of Economic Literature* 38 (4): 827–874.

Smith, Vernon L. 2002. Method in Experiment: Rhetoric and Reality. *Experimental Economics* 5 (2): 91–132.

Stock, James H., and Francesco Trebbi. 2003. Retrospectives: Who Invented Instrumental Variable Regression? *Journal of Economic Perspectives* 17 (3): 177–194.

Theil, Henri. 1953. *Repeated Least Squares Applied to Complete Equation Systems*. Mimeo. The Hague, Netherlands: Central Planning Bureau.

Theil, Henri. 1958. *Economic Forecasts and Policy*. Amsterdam: North-Holland.

Whitehouse, Mark. 2007. Is an Economist Qualified to Solve Puzzle of Autism? *Wall Street Journal*, February 27.

Wright, Philip G. 1928. *The Tariff on Animal and Vegetable Oils*. New York: Macmillan.

Christopher S. Ruebeck

INSTRUMENTALISM
SEE *Theory.*

INSULATING FACTORS
SEE *Stress-Buffering Model.*

INSURANCE

Risk is ubiquitous in the world and is generally considered a burden. Risk management, the art of coping with this onus, takes several forms: (1) doing nothing, or bearing the burden; (2) avoiding the risk, which includes reducing or quitting the risky activity; (3) spending resources to reduce the risk's implication or probability, such as self-insurance; (4) hedging; and (5) transferring the burden to someone else, which is insurance. Some risks, like individual and group extinction, are so important that one could study history as the theme of risk management or view culture and social institutions like marriage and state, as evolving in response to the challenge of risks. Risk management is not special to humans—for example, ants spend effort and hoard excessive food, a form of self-insurance that humans parallel by precautionary saving—but insurance is a human invention.

Insurance is a transaction that transfers a specified risk to another party for a fee, called a "premium." In return the insurer provides the insured with a promise of indemnification (insurance company payment for damages) should the specified event occur. The specified events vary widely and comprise the different lines of the insurance industry: marine, property, vehicle, liability, life, and health, but the basic structure is the same. The amount of indemnification may be event-dependent (small or large fire) or fixed (life). In life insurance the event specified is either death or longevity. Insurance is both a consumption good consumed by households and an intermediate input purchased by firms. In property insurance the business is split about equally between households and firms. As can be gleaned from a cross-section as in Table 1, insurance is growing faster than national product, suggesting that it is a luxury good (income elasticity larger than one) and a "super normal" input. It may imply that adequate development of the insurance industry is vital for economic development and growth. By providing assets whose value is contingent on a given random state of nature, insurance helps make the market more complete and therefore more efficient. Without insurance availability some useful transactions and investments would be curtailed or thwarted.

Gross premium as percent of GDP	Total	Life	Non-Life
Japan	13.2	10.0	3.2
US	10.6	5.2	5.4
European Union	9.2	6.0	3.3
Poland	2.9	1.0	1.9
Turkey	1.5	0.3	1.3

SOURCE: OECD Insurance Statistics Yearbook, 2002.

Table 1

The demand for insurance is theoretically explained by risk aversion. A risk-averse person faced with a probability p of loss D, like a house that may burn, is willing to insure against that risk even at a premium higher than the mean damage pD. Firms demand insurance to placate their risk-averse owners and other parties, like customers, suppliers, employees, and lenders, thereby securing better contract terms with them.

Insurance differs from gambling by some of its fundamentals designed to restrain devious incentives. The purchaser must have "insurable interest," that is interest in the well-being of the insured asset (owner, mortgage lender). Other than in the case of life insurance, indemnification must be bounded by the value of the asset, including by double coverage. In return for indemnification, the insured surrenders to the insurer subrogation of all his relevant legal rights to claim from other parties. Still, the insurance market is burdened by fraud and by imperfections like adverse selection, where the firm cannot completely ascertain the risk of each customer thereby charging a premium that attracts the bad risks more than the good, and by moral hazard, where after the insurance transaction the insured may wish to increase his or her risk.

The supply side raises two puzzles. First, what is the relative advantage of the insurer in bearing risks over its clients? Second, if indeed it has some such relative advantage, why does it seek to insure itself by purchasing reinsurance? Reinsurance is a transaction where an insurer buys insurance from another insurer thereby transferring, or ceding, some of its risks and business to others. The remainder is called retention. Reinsurance is a global industry with some large specialized firms.

The production of insurance can be done in two distinct modes: mutual and capital-backed. A mutual is an association of members-customers who barter in insurance and pledge to indemnify each other if damaged. This insurance is backed by members' commitments and capital. It must be a natural and intuitive arrangement since it goes back to antiquity. Second-century CE agreements among boat or donkey owners are legally analyzed in the Talmud.

Even a two-person mutual is advantageous. If each one has total property W and faces an independent risk of losing value D (like a house by fire) with probability p the advantage of such a mutual is:

$$[p^2U(W-D) + 2p(1-p)U(W-D/2) + (1-p)^2 U(W)] -$$
$$pU(W-D) + (1-p)U(W) = \qquad (1)$$
$$p(1-p)\{[U(W-D/2) - U(W-D)] - [U(W) - U(W-D/2)]\} > 0$$

The first line in (1) is the expected utility of each person in the 2-member fire-mutual, while the second line is his expected utility bearing the risk alone. The inequality follows from the concavity of the utility function that is implied by risk aversion.

The agreement improves with any additional member. The attractiveness of an n-member mutual may be explained by the expediency of (risky) portfolio diversification. Instead of holding one risky asset valued D, the agreement affords the member to hold the risk of n small assets, each valued D/n, which is always better for a risk-averse. In (1) the two fire events were assumed independent. Partial positive dependence leaves the inequality intact but reduces the advantage. Most mutuals collect a provisionary premium upfront and reassess members after risks' realization, collecting more or refunding some.

However the main mode of insurance provision nowadays is by a stock company where insurance is backed by equity capital. Such production dates to the fourteenth-century marine transaction that combined banking and insurance. In such maritime loans the lender would finance a trade transaction but waive the loan if the vessel is lost. It appeared in two variants regarding the collateral: bottomry (the vessel) and respondentia (the cargo). While in a mutual the number of owners-partners must vary jointly with that of the insureds, in the stock firm the two are independent.

OPERATION

Assume schematically an insurance firm that sells only one type of policy against the risk of, say, fire, which occurs independently with the same known probability p of total loss D for each customer. Let V be the firm's capital before any insurance transaction, serving as a cushion to enhance the value of its policies-promises. Suppose n such policies are sold at price $s + c$ where cn covers the cost of running the business. Usually s would exceed pD, the expected loss (and indemnification), and the balance is a safety factor that goes to profit and tax. The revenue ns is called unearned reserve because it is designated for probable coming claims. As time elapses the uncertainty regarding the year's fires is gradually cleared, more and more of the reserve becomes earned reserve, owned by the firm and part of its annual profit and of V. The firm's funds $V + ns$ are meanwhile invested and bear a random rate of return *r* thereby generating a major part of its profits. The number of fires that occur is a random variable *k*. If the two random variables happen to have realizations *R* and *K*, then the firm's net worth at the year end is $(V + ns)(1 + R) - KD$. If it is negative, the firm's future promises are worthless so it is declared insolvent and ceases operation.

The risk of failure is real and troubling. In the United States during the 1990s approximately 70 firms, or 0.8 percent of all insurance firms, failed within a year. The condition $(V + ns)(1 + r) - KD < 0$ points out the reasons for failure: low *V*; low premia *s*; low *R*; large *K*. The dependence of the ex-ante probability of failure $\text{Prob}((V + ns)(1 + r) - KD < 0)$ on the magnitude of *n* is less clear-cut. Conventional wisdom attributes the relative advantage of the stock insurance firm in bearing risk to the multitude of clients and the law of large numbers. However, whether the numbers (*n*) in insurance are large enough to warrant this explanation is an empirical question. According to the 1963 work of Paul A. Samuelson, the advantage of the insurance firm lies in the multitude of its owners. Spreading a given risk over many bearing shoulders (stockholders) tends to evaporate its burden. In 1970 Kenneth J. Arrow and Robert C. Lind analyzed a large risky public project, where the risk was spread over the population, and demonstrated it for a single risk. This result explains the advantage that governments may have in insuring against catastrophic losses. It does not address the issue faced by the insurance industry of insuring against multiple risks. In this light, reinsurance is a handy mechanism to spread risks.

BUSINESS CYCLE

The insurance industry manifests a peculiar business cycle of its own. In times of hard market, prices are high and yet insurance is hard to get as firms offer only constrained extent of coverage and carefully select the clients. The result is high profits and rise in surpluses. That by itself may lead to the opposite, soft market, as the high surplus warrants more business and risk taking so prices go down to attract more and necessarily lower-grade customers. Profits go down, equities are depleted, and the cycle repeats itself.

INNOVATIONS

Since the 1990s a rise in world catastrophes like earthquakes, hurricanes, and terrorist activities drained world insurance surplus and constrained the industry's production capacity. In response financial innovations were introduced as substitutes for equity capital. The simplest is catastrophe bonds. An insurer issues such a bond, and the repayment of the interest and/or the principal is made contingent on a specified event like the catastrophe cost (for the insurer, for the region, or for the world) not exceeding a predetermined number. It shifts some of the risk from shareholders to bond holders and is a modern resurrection of the Middle Ages' maritime loan-cum-insurance. More complicated instruments are call and put options whose strike price is some catastrophe number.

REGULATION

All over the world, insurance industries are regulated. The raison d'etre of regulation is the risk of insurers' insolvency. Such occurrence would disrupt the economy, prevent gains from trade in risk-bearing, and cause personal loss and suffering to consumers. Although insurers themselves would suffer in case of insolvency, they can not be fully counted on to take steps to avoid it because of several market imperfections. First, because of the limited liability of a stock company, stockholders would not have to bear, in case of insolvency, its full cost but lose at most their equity. That weakens stockholders' incentives to avoid excessive risk. Second, moral hazard and agency problems develop. After issuing policies purchased under presentation of a certain risk level, the insurer may wish to assume more risk because part of its cost is borne by the insured policyholders. Regulators issue guidelines regarding the extent of underwriting, prices, and investment policy. They monitor the business and upon detecting signs of trouble intervene by issuing various directives.

SEE ALSO *Adverse Selection; Business Cycles, Real; Gambling; Insurance Industry; Moral Hazard; Regulation*

BIBLIOGRAPHY

Arrow, Kenneth J., and Robert C. Lind. 1970. Uncertainty and the Evaluation of Public Investment Decisions. *American Economic Review* 60: 364–378.

Dionne, Georges, ed. 2000. *Handbook of Insurance*. Norwell, MA: Kluwer.

Samuelson, Paul A. 1966. Risk and Uncertainty: A Fallacy of Large Numbers. In *Collected Scientific Papers of Paul A. Samuelson*, ed. Joseph E. Stiglitz. Cambridge, MA: MIT Press.

Winter, Ralph A. 1991. Solvency Regulation and the Property-Liability Insurance Cycle. *Economic Inquiry* 29: 458–471.

Yuval Shilony

INSURANCE INDUSTRY

Contracts transferring risk have been in existence since at least the time of ancient Babylon. The growth of a large-scale insurance industry dedicated to regularizing and facilitating transactions dates, however, from the growth of transoceanic shipping in the seventeenth century as well as the growth of mathematical and computational sophistication needed to support mass transfers of risk. The industry has grown to one of the world's largest and in the twenty-first century comprises a ubiquitous and central component of life in developed nations, with written premiums surpassing $3.4 trillion in 2005.

Insurance—as a contract that often overcomes impediments to trade created by risk and that, of necessity, often requires significant agglomerations of corporate wealth—has long been an instrument of social success and social disgrace. It has unquestionably permitted the development of modern capitalism by stabilizing large concentrations of property or, in the case of life insurance, the preservation of family wealth with reduced regard for the longevity of particular family members. On the other hand, it was critical to the development of industrial-era slavery by permitting those involved in human trafficking to diversify the significant risks involved. It has often fueled and ameliorated the planet's environmental woes by permitting various industries to thrive notwithstanding the oft-materializing risk of environmental harm they create, though it has also provided a major source of capital from which those injuries can be at least partly redressed. It has increased safety in fields such as fire prevention, building codes, and vehicle safety by providing a relatively centralized repository of information on risk and significant motivation for its reduction. And it has unquestionably transformed the legal system in many jurisdictions by providing otherwise unavailable large sources of wealth to vindicate rights formally created by those jurisdictions.

The modern insurance industry is divided into three parts: (1) a life and health insurance segment; (2) a property/casualty segment; and (3) a financial management segment involving reinsurance and various forms of excess insurance. While many companies engage in all parts of the industry, often through various subsidiaries, others specialize in only segments and subsegments of the market consistent with their skills in marketing, assessing risks, processing claims, and coping with regulatory impediments. The life and health industry generally assesses the health trajectories of prospective insureds. Private health insurance is used in the United States to defray the significant cost of medicine and is often (though decreasingly) offered by employers as a tax-advantaged prerequisite. It also frequently serves there as a buying agent, negotiating in advance for lower prices for medical services on behalf of its insureds. In nations with broader government-provided health care, health insurance nonetheless often functions as a supplemental vehicle for transferring the risk associated with procedures the government plan does not cover or as to which government-provided care is thought inadequate. Life insurance offers payment to reduce the risk of premature death or,

in the case of annuities, offers a stream of income to offset the risk of living longer than expected. It also frequently permits a tax-advantaged form of investment.

The property and casualty insurance insures individuals and businesses from direct and indirect losses due to fire, various forms of natural disaster, and other "perils." Casualty insurance transfers the risk of the insured encountering various legal obligations, such as an obligation to pay damages in a lawsuit or to perform on a contract. Major forms of casualty insurance include liability insurance, suretyships, and marine insurance. Large segments of the legal services industry assist casualty insurers in defense of claims against their insureds.

ECONOMIC CHALLENGES

Much of the modern insurance contract represents an effort to address four economic challenges inherent in virtually any attempt to transfer risk. Reducing this process into words often makes many insurance contracts extremely complex and forbidding documents, as insurers use various shorthands and jargon to compress complex concepts. The first challenge, moral hazard, is the proclivity of people with insurance to increase the level of insured risk they encounter beyond what otherwise would be the case. Insurers control moral hazard through such means as making the insurance incomplete through deductibles that reduce by a fixed or formula amount an insurer's otherwise obligation to pay a claim. The insurer likewise controls moral hazard through various exclusions and conditions that limit its obligations unless the insured adheres to various behavioral norms thought to reduce risk. These control mechanisms may make contract administration more costly, however, and can lead to dispute when the provisions involved are ambiguous or surprising to the insured.

The second challenge, adverse selection, is the proclivity of insureds that accurately perceive themselves as having a higher risk of loss than would be imagined by the insurer to purchase insurance disproportionately. Insurers attempt to curb adverse selection through tighter "underwriting," the examination of prospective insureds before contract formation is complete, through insistence on legal systems that condition the insurer's payment obligations on various forms of information transfer from insured to insurer, and through conditions and exclusions that prevent risk transfer in situations where the information needed by the insurer or the proper interpretation of that information would prove too costly for the particular insurer. Adverse selection potentially poses great hazards to the insurance industry, particularly where prospective insureds harbor secret information about their own level of risk. Various insurance systems have entered "death spirals" when they were unable to control adverse selection.

A third issue is that of systematic risk. Insurance works best when the risks are independent of one another and insurers can thus depend on the unbreakable "law of large numbers" to assure their profitability. When insurers encounter correlated risks, such as those posed when insuring a large number of homes in an area of seismic activity or hurricane risk or, potentially, terrorism risk, they thus either enter the market only with great caution or deploy various risk spreading and aggregation mechanisms such as reinsurance or catastrophe bonds that reduce systematic risk. These mechanisms are capable of succeeding because, while the risk that a home in the vicinity of one volcano will be destroyed from an eruption is correlated with destruction to a neighboring home, an insurance system that pooled both of their risks with those of homeowners near other seismically uncorrelated volcanoes would effectively create somewhat larger but still uncorrelated risks as to which the law of large numbers would more closely apply. The increased globalization of the insurance industry, coupled with the growth of institutions such as reinsurance, has greatly assisted with this problem.

Finally, there is simply the matter of insurers keeping their promises. Particularly in cases of life insurance or various "toxic tort" claims such as asbestosis or other environmental harms, the time between payment of premium and an insurer's obligation to pay on a claim may span decades. Moreover, individual policyholders or smaller businesses are often at a severe disadvantage in resolving disputes with large, sophisticated, and experienced insurers and generally have difficulty banding together to attain their common interests. Insurers thus must be forced by governments to be particularly prudent with their investments and to be responsible in the way they handle claims. Doctrines such as "contra proferentem," "reasonable expectations," "good faith," and "intelligibility" often play significant roles in this latter effort, though the greater ability to provide information in the modern age may result in a larger role for regulation via ratings and reputation.

INTERMEDIARIES

Critical to the operation of the insurance industry are various intermediaries who bridge information gaps between consumer and insurer. Agents, who may work for insurers or groups of insurers, attempt to fit existing insurance products to the needs of potential insurance consumers. Brokers, or independents as they are sometimes called, serve as expert shoppers, assisting businesses of varying sophistication in the purchase of complex and often coordinated packages of insurance products. These intermediaries often permit prospective insureds to access insurance products offered by insurers in other states or nations that would otherwise be unavailable. Often, the law imposes on these intermediaries duties of diligence in assessing the fit between the insured's needs and the products offered, the solvency of a proposed insurer, and in accurately transmitting information related to the risk posed by the insured.

REGULATION

Insurance tends to be a highly regulated industry. This is so in part because insurers have tremendous powers over the lives and fortunes of the individuals and businesses they insure (or refuse to insure) and in part because of their close resemblance to other large financial service industry players such as banks, whose ability to fulfill promises in times of need serves a vital social purpose. Because of the ability of insureds to cancel their insurance in most circumstances without severe financial penalty or to decline to renew their policies at relatively frequent intervals, insurance companies, like banks and other financial institutions, can lose capital rapidly. This fact means that even hints of trouble can precipitate a financial collapse with attendant financial and social ripples. Traditional insurance regulation attempts to reduce this risk through various forms of auditing, investment controls, government-sponsored backstop insurance and mechanisms to facilitate quiet recapitalization or merger of troubled insurers. In common law nations such as the United States and Commonwealth nations, courts have also been extremely important and influential in regulating insurers through the development of precedents regarding contract formation and interpretation.

In the United States, insurance regulation is conducted largely at the state level as a result of the 1868 decision of *Paul v. Virginia* and the substantial reconfirmation of that decision through the 1946 McCarran-Ferguson Act. There has, however, been an increasing role for the federal government, particularly in health insurance and, to a perhaps growing extent, in providing a backstop for insurance against terrorism. The McCarran-Ferguson Act generally displaces federal law regulating insurance, at least when a state is vigorously regulating the same subject, and specifically displaces most federal competition (antitrust) laws. The weakened role of competition law is said to foster healthy exchanges of information amongst insurers regarding risk and, on occasion, to regularize pricing in ways different than which would be achieved through competition.

In Europe, insurance is likewise subject to dual control, at the traditional national level and, increasingly since 1973, through directives from the European Community. Integration of these often disparate bodies of law and the various cultures and norms of these markets has been a significant challenge of the recent decades.

FUTURE PROSPECTS

The insurance industry faces new challenges in the years ahead. The industry will need to penetrate developing economic markets and adapt to local risks, regulation, and customs. As technology increases the ability to predict the future, risk pools may become more heterogeneous than they are presently perceived. Thus, unless long range contracting can be accomplished prior to the time prediction proves possible, or unless governments intervene with compulsory pooling mechanisms, insurance may become more difficult and more expensive for some groups to attain. Insurers will likely be called on to take heightened responsibility for the discrimination they foster through various rating practices that depend sometimes on accurate if unflattering information and sometimes on informational proxies that may neither be fair nor particularly accurate. Privacy issues likewise will concern the insurance industry. As large aggregators of data, insurers will come under increasing pressure to develop codes of conduct relating to the assimilation and dissemination of information. Cultural or religious barriers to insurance are likely to come under pressure as various segments of the globe develop more mature forms of capitalism; and, indeed, the growth of "takaful," mutual insurance that complies with Islamic limitations on purchase of commercial insurance, are symptoms of both this adaptation and expansion of the insurance industry. Finally, the industry will likely wish to develop mechanisms for handling new risks. Global climate change potentially poses significant risk to the insurance industry, which may grow in its advocacy for measures designed to reduce the impact of adverse weather conditions.

SEE ALSO *Adverse Selection; Global Warming; Industry; Moral Hazard; Risk; Slavery; Uncertainty*

BIBLIOGRAPHY

Abraham, Kenneth S. 1986. *Distributing Risk: Insurance, Legal Theory, and Public Policy.* New Haven, CT: Yale University Press.

Chandler, Seth J. 2000. Insurance Regulation. In *Encyclopedia of Law and Economics*, ed. Boudewijn Bouckaert. Cheltenham, U.K.: Edward Elgar Publishing.

Clarke, Malcolm A. 2005. *Policies and Perceptions of Insurance Law in the Twenty-First Century.* New York: Oxford University Press.

Hodgin, R. W. 1987. *Insurance Intermediaries and the Law.* London: Lloyd's of London Press.

Jackson, Howell E. 1999. Regulation in a Multi-Sectored Financial Services Industry: An Exploratory Essay. *Washington University Law Quarterly* 76: 319–397.

Muller-Reichart, Matthias. 2005. The EU Insurance Industry: Are We Heading for an Ideal Single Financial Services Market? *Geneva Papers on Risk and Insurance: Issues and Practice* 30 (2): 285–295.

Rejda, George E. 2005. *Principles of Risk Management and Insurance.* 9th ed. London and Boston: Addison Wesley.

Thomas, Heather. 2004. *The Regulation of Insurance Brokers and Intermediaries.* London: Butterworths.

Seth J. Chandler

INTEGRATED PUBLIC USE MICRODATA SERIES

Integrated Public Use Microdata Series (IPUMS) refers to three distinct collections of individual-level data. IPUMS-USA is a coherent individual-level national database describing the characteristics of 100 million Americans in fifteen decennial census years spanning the period from 1850 through 2000. IPUMS-International includes data from 47 censuses of 13 countries, and new data are being added regularly. IPUMS-CPS provides annual data from the March demographic supplement of the Current Population Survey for the period from 1962 to 2006.

IPUMS contains information about both individuals and households in a hierarchical structure, so researchers can construct new variables based on information from multiple household members. Because it is microdata as opposed to summary aggregate data, IPUMS allows researchers to create tabulations tailored to particular research questions and to carry out individual-level multivariate analyses. Among key research areas that can be studied using the IPUMS are economic development, poverty and inequality, industrial and occupational structure, household and family composition, the household economy, female labor force participation, employment patterns, population growth, urbanization, internal migration, immigration, nuptiality, fertility, and education.

The database includes comprehensive hypertext documentation—the equivalent of over 10,000 pages of text—including detailed analyses of the comparability of every variable across every census year. Both the database and the documentation are distributed through an on-line data access system at http://ipums.org, which provides powerful extraction and search capabilities to allow easy access to both metadata and microdata. The National Science Foundation and the National Institutes of Health fund the project, so all data and documentation are available to researchers without cost.

IPUMS-USA is the oldest and best known of the three data series. It combines nationally representative probability samples produced by the Census Bureau for the period since 1940 with new high-precision historical samples produced at the University of Minnesota and elsewhere. By putting all the samples in a common format, imposing con-

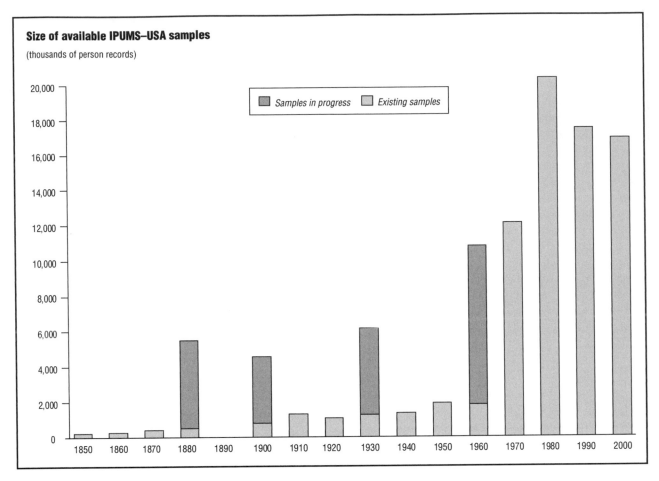

Size of available IPUMS–USA samples

(thousands of person records)

Table 1

sistent variable coding, and carefully documenting changes in variables over time, IPUMS is designed to facilitate the use of the census samples as a time series.

The sizes of IPUMS-USA samples are shown in Table 1. The only census year missing from the series is 1890, which was destroyed by fire. From 1970 onward, available samples include at least six percent of the population, and census years prior to 1970 cover approximately one percent of the population. Because the population grew rapidly in the nineteenth and twentieth centuries, the older 1 percent samples are considerably smaller than recent ones.

The large samples available for recent census years have proven valuable for study of small population subgroups, ranging from same-sex couples to the grandchildren of immigrants. In many instances, the large samples also permit the use of innovative methods; to take just one example, these files have allowed demographers to carry out multilevel contextual analyses by making it feasible to assess the characteristics of small geographic areas. Accordingly, projects are underway to create larger samples for the earlier census years. As shown in Table 1, higher-density samples are in preparation for the 1880, 1900, 1930, and 1960 census years.

IPUMS-USA is designed to encourage analyses that incorporate multiple census years for the study of change over time. The census has always contained certain core questions that are generally comparable over the entire time span of the database. Other questions have come and gone. Table 1 describes many of the subject areas covered by the census since 1850 (many of these topics correspond to multiple variables in the database). In general, the IPUMS samples include all the census questions available in each year, but for the period from 1940 onward, some detail is suppressed in order to preserve respondent confidentiality. In particular, geographic detail is far superior in the pre-1940 samples. In fact, the samples for the period prior to 1940 include the names and addresses of the respondents. On the other hand, topics such as income, educational attainment, and migration have only been covered by the census for the last six decades of the twentieth century. All IPUMS samples also include a common set of constructed variables to allow easy data manipula-

Availability of select IPUMS-USA subject areas, 1850–2000

	1850	1860	1870	1880	1900	1910	1920	1930	1940	1950	1960	1970	1980	1990	2000
Household record															
State	X	X	X	X	X	X	X	X	X	X	X	X	X	X	X
County	X	X	X	X	X	X	X	X	—	—	—	—	—	—	X
County group/microdata area	—	—	—	—	—	—	—	—	—	—	P	X	X	X	X
State economic area	X	X	X	X	X	X	X	X	X	X	P	—	—	—	—
Metropolitan area	X	X	X	X	X	X	X	X	X	X	—	X	X	X	X
City	X	X	X	X	X	X	X	X	X	X	—	—	X	X	X
Size of place	X	X	X	X	X	X	X	X	X	X	—	—	X	X	X
Urban/rural status	X	X	X	X	X	X	X	—	—	—	X	X	X	X	X
Farm	X	X	X	X	X	X	X	X	X	X	X	X	X	X	X
Ownership of dwelling	—	—	—	—	X	X	X	X	—	—	X	X	X	X	X
Mortgage status	—	—	—	—	X	X	X	—	—	—	—	—	X	X	X
Value of house or property	—	—	—	—	—	—	—	—	X	X	X	X	X	X	X
Monthly rent	—	—	—	—	—	—	—	—	X	X	X	X	X	X	X
Total family income	—	—	—	—	—	—	—	—	—	X	X	X	X	X	X
Person record															
Relationship to household head	—	—	—	X	X	X	X	X	X	X	X	X	X	X	X
Age	X	X	X	X	X	X	X	X	X	X	X	X	X	X	X
Sex	X	X	X	X	X	X	X	X	X	X	X	X	X	X	X
Race	X	X	X	X	X	X	X	X	X	X	X	X	X	X	X
Marital status	—	—	—	X	X	X	X	X	X	X	X	X	X	X	X
Age at first marriage	—	—	—	—	—	—	—	—	X	—	X	X	X	—	—
Duration of marriage	—	—	—	—	X	X	—	—	X	—	—	—	—	—	—
Times married	—	—	—	—	—	—	X	—	X	X	X	X	X	—	—
Children ever born	—	—	—	—	X	X	—	—	X	X	X	X	X	X	—
Birthplace	X	X	X	X	X	X	X	X	X	X	X	X	X	X	X
Parents' birthplaces	—	—	—	X	X	X	X	X	X	X	X	X	—	—	—
Ancestry	—	—	—	—	—	—	—	—	—	—	—	—	X	X	X
Years in the United States	—	—	—	—	X	X	X	X	X	—	—	X	X	X	X
Mother tongue	—	—	—	—	—	X	X	X	—	—	X	X	—	—	—
Language spoken	—	—	—	—	X	X	X	X	—	—	—	—	X	X	X
School attendance	X	X	X	X	X	X	X	X	X	X	X	X	X	X	X
Educational attainment	—	—	—	—	—	—	—	—	X	X	X	X	X	X	X
Literacy	X	X	X	X	X	X	X	X	—	—	—	—	—	—	—
Employment status	—	—	—	—	—	—	X	—	X	X	X	X	X	X	X
Occupation	X	X	X	X	X	X	X	X	X	X	X	X	X	X	X
Industry	—	—	—	—	—	X	X	X	X	X	X	X	X	X	X
Class of worker	—	—	—	—	—	—	X	X	X	X	X	X	X	X	X
Weeks worked last year	—	—	—	—	—	—	—	—	X	X	X	X	X	X	X
Weeks unemployed	—	—	—	X	X	X	—	—	X	X	—	—	—	—	—
Total personal income	—	—	—	—	—	—	—	—	—	X	X	X	X	X	X
Wage and salary income	—	—	—	—	—	—	—	—	X	X	X	X	X	X	X
Value of personal or real estate	X	X	X	—	—	—	—	—	—	—	—	—	—	—	—
Migration status	—	—	—	—	—	—	—	—	X	X	X	X	X	X	X
Veteran status	—	—	—	—	—	X	—	X	X	X	X	X	X	X	X
Surname similarity code	X	X	X	X	X	X	X	X	X	X	—	—	—	—	—
Name	X	X	X	X	X	X	X	X	—	—	—	—	—	—	—

Note: X = available in that census year; P = available in a future data release.

Table 2

tion. Most important among these is a set of family interrelationship variables that have proven broadly useful in the construction of consistent family composition and own-child fertility measures.

In 2010 the scope of the U.S. census will be sharply reduced. The Census Bureau plans to eliminate the detailed long-form census questionnaire, and the census will include only a few basic inquiries such as age, sex, race, and relationship of each person to the householder. Information about such topics as income, education, housing, migration, or disability will instead be provided by the American Community Survey (ACS). With virtually the same questions as the Census 2000 long form questionnaire, the ACS provides data on three million households each year. The ACS has released an annual public use microdata file since 2000, and IPUMS has incorporated these samples. For most purposes, ACS samples are closely comparable to those from censuses, so the shift from census to surveys introduces only minor discontinuities to the data series.

IPUMS—International samples

Available 6/2006

Brazil	1970, 1980, 1991, 2000
Chile	1960, 1970, 1982, 1992, 2002
China	1982
Colombia	1964, 1973, 1985, 1993
Costa Rica	1963, 1973, 1984, 2000
Ecuador	1962, 1974, 1982, 1990, 2001
France	1962, 1968, 1975, 1982, 1990
Kenya	1989, 1999
Mexico	1960, 1970, 1990, 2000
South Africa	1996, 2001
United States	1960, 1970, 1980, 1990, 2000
Vietnam	1989, 1999
Venezuela	1971, 1981, 1990

Samples in progress

Argentina	1970, 1980, 1991, 2001
Armenia	2000
Austria	1971, 1981, 1991, 2001
Belarus	1999
Bolivia	1976, 1992, 2001
Cambodia	1998
Canada	1971, 1981, 1991
Czech Rep.	1991, 2001
Dominican R.	1960, 1970, 1981
El Salvador	1992
Egypt	1986, 1996
Fiji	1966, 1986, 1996
France	1999
Greece	1971, 1981, 1991, 2001
Guatemala	1973, 1981
Honduras	1961, 1974, 1988
Hungary	1970, 1980, 1990, 2001
Indonesia	1971, 1980, 1990, 1995
Iraq	1997
Israel	1961, 1972, 1983, 1995
Italy	1981, 1991
Madagascar	1993

Table 3

Researchers who require annual data for the preceding four decades can turn to IPUMS-CPS, which provides a coherent version of the widely used U.S. population survey produced by the Bureau of Labor Statistics. The CPS includes virtually all the subject areas covered by the decennial census and the ACS, but provides much greater detail in certain areas, such as health insurance coverage.

The IPUMS-International project is extending the IPUMS paradigm to approximately fifty countries around the world. Large quantities of machine-readable microdata survive from census enumerations since the 1950s, but few of them are available to researchers and most are at risk of becoming unreadable. The first goals of the IPUMS-International project are to preserve machine-readable census microdata files wherever possible and to obtain permission to disseminate anonymized samples of the data to researchers. Then—just like the original IPUMS project—researchers convert the data into consistent format, supply comprehensive documentation, and make microdata and documentation available through a

Web-based data dissemination system. Table 2 summarizes current and planned IPUMS-International data releases. The project began releasing data in 2003, and with information on 143 million persons, by June 2006 it already exceeded the scale of IPUMS-USA. The project has concluded agreements to preserve and disseminate data from some 200 censuses in 71 countries; negotiations with most of the other major countries of the world are underway. Information on the IPUMS-International release schedule is available at http://ipums.org.

BIBLIOGRAPHY

Integrated Public Use Microdata Series. Minnesota Population Center. http://ipums.org.

Ruggles, Steven. 2006. *The Minnesota Population Center Data Integration Projects: Challenges of Harmonizing Census Microdata Across Time and Place.* 2005 Proceedings of the American Statistical Association, Government Statistics Section. Alexandria, VA: American Statistical Association.

Ruggles, Steven, et al. 2003. IPUMS-International. *Historical Methods* 36 (2): 60–65.

Ruggles, Steven, et al. 2003. IPUMS Redesign. *Historical Methods* 36 (1): 9–21.

Steven Ruggles

INTEGRATION

Integration is the process by which individuals and groups come to interact freely and equally in society without regard to distinctions of skin color. In a completely racially integrated society, no systemic or institutional discrimination exists against the members of any racial group. Even if economic and cultural differences exist, these do not decrease access to employment, housing, politics, health, public services, and recreation for any racial group. Integration has both formal and substantive dimensions. Formal integration is based on principles, laws, and symbols that represent equality and nondiscrimination. Substantive integration involves the implementation (or actualization) of integration laws and is reflected in the significant and sustained incorporation of minority groups into the economic, political, and social institutions of the larger society.

By contrast, *segregation* describes a situation in which members of different racial groups rarely come into contact with one another or interact as social equals. Under segregation, separation along racial lines applies to nearly all aspects of life and those contacts between racial groups that do occur are socially controlled. Social distance is reflected in a "color line" that clearly demarcates dominant and subordinate groups. Segregation may vary from de jure forms, which are overt, formal, and written into law, to de facto forms that are covert coded, and informal and exist independently of the law. In the United States, "Jim Crow" de jure segregation was dominant from the end of Reconstruction up until the early 1960s. In the North and West, however, de facto segregation based on custom and institutional discrimination was more prevalent.

Desegregation is the legal remedy used to bring about reforms in previously segregated institutions (Clark 1953, p. 2). While desegregation is often associated with "racial balance" and "racial mixing," and is necessary for the achievement of integration, it alone is not sufficient to bring about racial integration. First, while desegregation meets the expectations of formal integration in that it follows the "letter of the law," it does not meet those requirements of substantive integration that come closer to the "spirit of the law." Formal integration places the burden of integrating on the disadvantaged group and is commonly accomplished through "token" efforts. Secondly, desegregation does not necessitate that people in the reformed institutions interact freely and equally and without discrimination. Resegregation can occur with desegregation. For example, efforts to desegregate schools may result in "white flight" or the establishment of different tracks in schools, with disadvantaged racial groups disproportionately assigned to lower tracks. Third, the implementation of desegregation tends to be uneven and is influenced by the history, culture, and politics of different regions and communities and the salience of local color lines.

INTEGRATION POLICY RATIONALES AND IMPLEMENTATION

Racial segregation existed as both the "spirit" and "letter" of the law in the United States from the end of Reconstruction through the early post–World War II years. In 1896 the landmark Supreme Court case *Plessy v. Ferguson* declared racial segregation constitutional so long as public facilities were "separate but equal." The development of a system of "Jim Crow" segregation, built on dominant American beliefs in white supremacy, was socially reproduced in institutions, organizations, and daily folkways and mores. Discrimination restricted most black Americans that remained in the South to farm, domestic, and unskilled labor, and disproportionately subjected them to involuntary servitude in the form of convict labor. Indentured jobs and union membership were mostly closed to blacks, and when blacks were hired they were often used as strikebreakers. Blacks also suffered economic discrimination when it came to securing land, credit, and public relief and social welfare. The disenfranchisement of most blacks from voting and jury selection occurred as a consequence of violence, lynching, intimidation, "white-only" primaries, and poll taxes. Segregation and discrimination also extended to public schools, libraries, churches, recreational facilities, transportation, and other public accommodations.

Rationales for integrationist policy eventually emerged in response to sociopolitical changes brought about by World War II and the cold war, and as a result of the growing struggle for racial equality. As the United States entered World War II and the moral and ideological imperatives of fighting against German fascism and Nazi racial doctrines became increasingly evident, American leaders turned to inclusive egalitarian values to justify the war. Black leaders, black newspapers, and civil rights organizations called for a "Double V" Campaign—for victory against both fascism abroad and racism at home. The large-scale military and economic mobilization of the United States during World War II and the early years of the cold war involved a significant number of black Americans, both in the military and in civilian society. Black Americans struggled against the segregation and discrimination that continued during wartime, as evidenced by A. Phillip Randolph's March on Washington Movement (1941), which sought to end discrimination in defense industries, and by a campaign that threatened to mount civil disobedience protests against the segregation of the armed forces (1948). President Franklin D. Roosevelt's signing of Executive Order 8802 (1941), which prohibited discrimination in industries receiving federal defense contracts, and President Harry Truman's signing of Executive Order 9981 (1948), which integrated the armed forces, represented victories for these protest movements and provided precedents for substantive economic integration (Bennett 2003).

In the postwar period, the cold war between the United States and the Soviet Union and the international struggle to win the allegiance of newly independent nonwhite nations in Asia, Africa, and the Americas led to the articulation of enlarged moral and ideological imperatives favorable to racial equality. The convergence between these imperatives and the continuing struggles of black Americans and civil rights organizations against segregation and discrimination resulted in Supreme Court decisions and federal policies fostering integration (Klinkner 1999; Klarman 2004). Justifications for integration and desegregation policies also derived from practical considerations. By the cold war years, the cost of maintaining "separate but equal" schools and other facilities in the South had mounted substantially and was becoming increasingly impractical. "Equalization" strategies that were successfully used by the National Association for the Advancement of Colored People (NAACP) during the 1930s and 1940s forced many Southern districts that wanted to maintain legal segregation to duplicate services and overspend on resources (McNeil 1983).

Those seeking to develop rationales for the implementation of integrationist policies were forced to consider two competing models of governance. A strong and centralized federal government with the ability to enact and forcefully implement civil rights laws was viewed as necessary by a coalition of liberal politicians and civil rights organizations who believed that only such a force could undo the historic and continuing effects of segregation and discrimination. It was recognized that reforms in segregation laws would open up the opportunity structure and improve the social and economic status of black Americans (Myrdal 1944; Clark 1953). Another, older conception of how racial justice might be achieved argued for reliance on local governments (i.e., "states rights"), and emphasized that states and local areas, rather than the federal government, should determine the appropriateness of laws concerning the functioning of institutions, including the color line. This conservative and segregationist coalition argued that only when the local folkways and mores had accepted the imperatives of racial equality should integration and desegregation occur.

The landmark Supreme Court decision *Brown v. Board of Education* (1954) illustrates the attempt to balance these competing conceptions of governance and, in effect, to reconcile integration and segregation. The Supreme Court's invalidation of the "separate but equal" doctrine with respect to school segregation provided arguments that formally initiated school desegregation. With respect to implementation, however, the Supreme Court ordered no immediate remedy and deferred reargument until the following year (1955). The Supreme Court endorsed a "gradual transition" to desegregation ("with all deliberate speed") that took local conditions into account and was sensitive to the "flexibility" of traditional principles of equitableness. The justices reasoned that immediate desegregation was unenforceable, impractical, and would lead to violence and school closures. President Eisenhower and the Justice Department supported a decentralized approach that would allow district court judges to return to the case and reargue it with limited guidance. By contrast, civil rights organizations such as the NAACP had urged complete and immediate desegregation (Klarman 2004).

Justification for integrationist policies also derived from the convergence between cold war domestic politics of the "Great Society" and the heightened mobilization of the civil rights movement during the early 1960s. The sustained mobilization of local organizing committees and movement organizations such as the NAACP, the Southern Christian Leadership Council, the Congress of Racial Equality, and the Student Nonviolent Coordinating Committee, along with the organized and sometimes violent resistance of local white institutional actors and communities, brought to America's consciousness the contradiction between democratic ideals and continued segregation and discrimination. The enactment and implementation of integrationist policies signified that the goals of the civil rights movement were legitimate and had been met—and that it was thus no longer necessary to mobilize demonstrations and protests. Minimalist conceptions of integration emphasized the principle of each individual being judged only by the "content of their character" and not by racial, ethnic, or religious distinctions.

The integration policies enacted during the 1960s comprised the most sweeping civil rights legislation in American history. The Civil Rights Act of 1964 was designed to target and prohibit all aspects of discrimination: voter discrimination (Titles I and VIII), public accommodation discrimination (Title II), public facilities segregation (Title III), segregation of educational facilities (Title IV), and employment discrimination (Title VII). It also mandated Civil Rights Commission investigations (Title IV) and established various federally assisted programs (Title VI). Resistance in several Southern states to ending voter discrimination was met head on by the mobilization of civil rights organizations, which resulted in the passage of the Voting Rights Act of 1965. This allowed federal registrars to take over the voter registration process in areas where past discrimination existed and oversee the polls on elections. The passage of the Civil Rights Act of 1968, which prohibited discrimination in housing, followed the assassination of Martin Luther King Jr.

Implementation of nondiscrimination policies depended on the voluntary actions of private-sector corporations, businesses, and firms, on public-sector bureaucracies and agencies, and on federal enforcement agencies such as the Equal Employment Opportunity Commission (EEOC) and the Office of Federal Contract Compliance Program (OFCCP). The policy of prohibiting racial discrimination in the employment practices of businesses that hold contracts with the government was formally strengthened with President John Kennedy's issuing of Executive Order 1375, which established an obligation on the part of federal contractors not only to refrain from discrimination but also to undertake "affirmative action" to ensure that equal employment principles are followed. The implementation of affirmative action as governmental policy took root under President Richard Nixon's administration as the "Philadelphia Plan." The government's motivation for pursuing the Philadelphia Plan was largely political, as the policy was designed to drive a wedge between the civil rights community and organized labor (Klinkner 1999, p. 294). As affirmative action evolved it came to encompass various programs and measures to improve the educational, employment, and business opportunities of racial minorities, women, and other socially disadvantaged groups.

INTEGRATION: A DREAM FULFILLED OR DEFERRED?

Integration affirmed the principles of democracy and equality and sought the progressive inclusion of black Americans into the institutions and organizations of American society. As with nondiscrimination policies, the implementation of integration policies depended in practice on the voluntary actions of private-sector corporations and businesses, on public-sector bureaucracies, and on federal enforcement agencies. At the same time, federal court decisions mandating school desegregation were constrained by cautious gradualism, the persistence of localism and "states rights" governance, and high levels of racial segregation in the largest cities, where blacks were increasingly living. Federal integration policies had their most immediate impact in the South, where there was a history of de jure segregation.

While the effects of integration were immediately evident in the desegregation of public accommodations and the extension of voting rights, these advances did not translate into economic integration (or economic rights). After 1965 Martin Luther King increasingly emphasized the goal of achieving economic equality, which, he argued, would derive from: (1) the refocusing of macroeconomic policy from military-industrial spending and the Vietnam War to domestic economic spending and the poor; (2) improving black economic competitiveness through education and training; and (3) blacks leveraging their buying power by boycotting specific goods and services (King 1968). King's opposition to the Vietnam War and his support for the Memphis garbage-workers strike and the Poor People's Campaign were intertwined with his advocacy of economic rights. Since the late 1960s, civil rights organizations have followed King's lead by embracing affirmative action, "set-asides," "moral covenant" policies, and minority franchises (Walker 1998).

That integration was a dream deferred was made evident by the Kerner Commission's report, which warned that America was increasingly becoming two societies: one black, and living in the central cities; the other white, and living in the suburbs (National Advisory Commission on Civil Disorders, 1968). Integration's inability to address the social and economic conditions of the black masses and continuing conflicts between blacks and whites over education, jobs, housing, and the police led to the emergence of separatist and nationalist movements during the 1960s. Malcolm X, a national spokesman for the Nation of Islam, argued that black nationalism and separatism, rather than integration, were necessary for black empowerment and social improvement. Within segregated com-

munities and ghettos, blacks were challenged to develop a sense of history, social consciousness, and solidarity and to support black institutions and organizations that would enable freedom and self-determination (Breitman 1990). The emergence of the black power movement signaled the fact that instead of embracing integration, blacks were increasingly "closing ranks" and seeking to control political and other institutions in black communities. At the same time that it criticized integration and black liberal coalitions, the black power movement introduced the concept of institutional racism to identify the complex intersection between institutional actions, cultural beliefs, and policies that contribute to the subordination of blacks (Carmichael and Hamilton 1967).

While federal policies of integration and desegregation began to reshape race relations in the South, in the North and West there was much less recognition on the part of white Americans that racism, discrimination, and segregation existed.

THE PERSISTENCE OF RACIAL SEGREGATION AND RESEGREGATION

The introduction of federal programs intended to foster integration was largely initiated during the cold war years of the 1960s. During the post–civil rights years of the 1970s, 1980s, and 1990s, the declining significance of cold war ideological and moral imperatives and of New Deal coalitions in national Democratic Party politics was accompanied by the rise of increasingly conservative political and social movements urging resistance to integration and racial equality. While the universal principles of integration were widely embraced, programs to implement integration and desegregation were frequently resisted (Schuman, Steeh, Bobo, and Krysan 1997).

The retreat from racial equality and the dismantling of programs intended to foster desegregation and integration have taken several forms. First, institutions such as the Supreme Court have retreated from strong interpretations of school desegregation, minority "set-asides," and affirmative action. At the same time, federal agencies such as the EEOC and the Fair Employment Practices Committee have been weakened by diminished funding. Second, in policy discussions and popular discourse affirmative action and integration programs are being redefined as "reverse discrimination." Although affirmative action applies to protected classes defined not only by race, but also by gender, age, and disability, and although enforcement of gender-based affirmative action largely surpass race-based enforcement, the discourse of "reverse discrimination" largely relates to the politics of racial resentment. Third, white Americans' perceptions and beliefs concerning race-based economic inequality are more likely to emphasize individualistic explanations than structural or systemic explanations (Kluegel and Smith 1986; Kluegel 1990).

Despite important civil rights reforms such as *Brown v. Board of Education* (1954), the Civil Rights Act of 1964, the Voting Rights Act of 1965, the Fair Housing Act of 1968, and affirmative action, racial segregation continues to socially structure housing, education, the workforce, and other social institutions and organizations. Racial segregation remains a widespread social relationship, practice, and symbol of racial and ethnic inequality in American society. Continued patterns of segregation experienced by racial minority groups symbolize and actualize the lower social status of these groups in the social hierarchy and their limited access to opportunities and resources connected to the American Dream.

During the post–civil rights years, high levels of black segregation have continued despite small but steady decreases in segregation in those metropolitan areas with the largest black populations. Sociologists use a "segregation index" to measure the degree of segregation, ranging from 0 for full integration to 100 for complete segregation. In 2000 the average black-white segregation index in U.S. metropolitan areas was 65, and in the Northeast and Midwest it was 74 (Iceland, Weinberg, and Steinmetz 2002). Based on a multidimensional construct of segregation with five dimensions of spatial variability—evenness, isolation, clustering, and concentration—and scores of at least 60 on four of the five dimensions, twenty metropolitan areas were identified as "hypersegregated." Together, these contained roughly eleven million black Americans (in 1990) and constituted 36 percent of the entire U.S. black population (Massey and Denton 1993).

Hispanic segregation in metropolitan areas has been more moderate, with average scores ranging from 46 to 55 (between 1970 and 1990) (Denton and Massey 1988), and Asian segregation has been relatively lower than both black and Hispanic levels (averaging from 36 to 44 between 1970 and 1990) (Massey 2001, pp. 407–409). One of the most salient features of segregation is the concentration of blacks in central cities and whites in suburbs.

Racial segregation tends to be socially reproduced across institutional contexts. Individuals in racial groups who are segregated in one institutional area—whether in housing, education, employment, criminal justice, or informal social interactions—are also likely to have mostly segregated experiences in other institutional environments.

The persistence of internal segregation in schools derives from institutional relationships and public policies. High levels of residential segregation are associated with commensurate levels of racial segregation in schools. Although school segregation decreased between 1968 and 1980 as a result of judicial enforcement, during the 1980s and 1990s governmental inaction and deregulation of mechanisms to desegregate schools led to increasing resegregation. In many school districts where court-mandated desegregation has ended, there has been a major increase in segregation (Orfield and Lee 2004). Levels of school segregation have been higher in the Northeast and Midwest than in the South and West (Orfield 2001). The abandonment of desegregation as public policy has mirrored the rise in national politics of the assumption that segregation and racial inequality are historic problems that have already been addressed. Contemporary movements to expand educational choice, through publicly funded vouchers that enable students to attend private schools, are occurring in a context in which the civil rights afforded by the *Brown* decision are being derailed.

Racial minorities who attend racially segregated urban schools are less likely to take college preparatory courses and attend college than those in more integrated and suburban schools. Teacher assignment practices reinforce inequality, because the least proficient teachers tend to be assigned to the least desirable schools, which are often in minority neighborhoods. Yet even in more integrated schools, minorities experience disadvantage due to lower expectations on the part of teachers and placement in lower tracks.

During the post–civil rights years, continued improvements were made in high school graduation rates across racial groups, which was reflected in a narrowing of the racial gap. Although actual and percentage levels of college graduation increased for all groups during the 1990s, there has been a growing racial gap in college attendance rates between whites and blacks and between non-Hispanic whites and Hispanics (Blank 2001, pp. 25–26). Recent efforts in higher education to increase academic standards and eliminate affirmative action have come at the expense of continued movement toward racial equality and educational opportunity.

Continuing racial segregation and discrimination has affected wealth accumulation, earned incomes, and employment chances across racial groups. Racial differences in wealth, which reflect intergenerational wealth and current asset ownership, are more extreme than income differences. Wealth differences are reflected in differences in levels of home ownership, which are not merely the result of income differences but rather a product of the historical legacy of residential segregation, Federal Housing Authority and Veterans Administration policies, and redlining. Blacks are rejected for home loans 60 percent more often than whites with the same income level, black families pay more in mortgage interest than white families, and the valuing of homes and equity is color-coded by segregation (Oliver and Shapiro 1995).

Segregation in labor markets, which are associated with different formal and informal social networks, is reflected in higher rates of unemployment and joblessness among racial minorities. Unemployment rates for both blacks and Hispanics have remained roughly twice the white unemployment rate. Among the factors contributing to high joblessness rates are *selective recruitment* and *statistical discrimination*, employer practices that reduce access to jobs for inner city applicants. These may involve limiting recruitment to selective neighborhoods, avoiding the placement of ads in central city newspapers, passing over applicants from black public schools, and subjective tests of job productivity (Wilson 1996, pp. 133–136).

Segregation and deprivation among blacks have been accompanied by criminal justice policies with impacts that are highly differentiated by race. "Racial profiling" by law enforcement associates particular racial and ethnic characteristics with dangers, risks, and threats. The federal Anti-Drug Abuse Act of 1988 prescribes the same mandatory-minimum sentence for 50 grams of crack cocaine (a form of the drug more likely to be used by low-income blacks) as it does for 5,000 grams of powdered cocaine (a form more likely to be used by high-income whites) (Blumenstein 2001, p. 26). An individual caught possessing only 1 to 5 grams of crack cocaine is subject to a mandatory minimum sentence of five years in prison. Crack cocaine is the only drug for which there exists a mandatory minimum sentence for the first offense (Kennedy 2001, p. 15). More than 30 percent of black high school dropouts will go to prison at some time in their lives, compared to 10 percent of white male high school dropouts (Patillo, Weiman, and Western 2004). Among black males in their twenties, 30 percent were under the control of the criminal justice system—prison, jail, probation, or parole (Mauer 1990).

When U.S. integration policies were first adopted, race-based discrimination was officially recognized and black-white relationships were the primary focus of formal and substantive integration. Through the 1960s, the federal government and its civil rights agencies were expected to end legal segregation and discrimination. By the post–civil rights years, the goals of integration had expanded into a policy of diversity, which policymakers struggled to implement. While civil rights organizations have emphasized that integration programs should be sustainable and relatively enduring considering the long history of slavery and segregation, there is a growing tendency among politicians to view integration as a set of transitional programs that have "run their course" and are no longer necessary. New patterns of integration emphasize formal integration and are based on the principle of "colorblindness," which argues that people should be treated as individuals and not as members of groups. By asserting that race does not matter, colorblindness as a principle and social policy denies the reality of continued discrimination. At the beginning of the twenty-first century, racial segregation and institutional discrimination persist in the United States despite the emergence of a colorblind society.

INTEGRATION IN CROSS-NATIONAL CONTEXTS

The philosophical bases for the adoption and implementation of integration policies in the United States may have been informed by similar attempts to promote racial and ethnic integration in other societies such as India, Brazil, Britain, and France. Integration policies in these countries have varied with respect to their emphasis on either formal or substantive integration, their articulation of race and racial discrimination (as distinct from ethnic and class discrimination), the role of the government and government agencies, and the demographic characteristics of racially and ethnically subordinate groups. Differences also exist regarding the question of whether such programs should be viewed as transitional or long-term.

India's integration policy, the "reservation system," grew out of the larger Indian struggles for home rule and independence, which had as one of their goals the elimination of the caste system. The Indian caste system, which existed for more than 2,500 years (up until 1947), was a status hierarchy and occupational stratification system with religious, color-based, and regional dimensions. Under the country's constitution, the "reservation system" sets aside a proportion of all government jobs, seats in educational institutions with government funding, and electoral constituencies for persons from "scheduled castes," "scheduled tribes," and "other backward classes" (Deshpande 2005, p. 10). Because Indian integration policies are based on the constitution, they cannot be legally challenged. National minority status, rather than racial status, is the basis of assignment to one of the protected classes. Unlike the United States, integration is based completely on voluntary efforts. Greatest resistance to the integration of the "untouchables" has come from the highest castes, which are highly represented in the decision-making positions of government. Critics of India's integration have emphasized that the poorest and outcast "scheduled castes" and "schedule tribes" are greatly outnumbered by the "other backward classes" and that the "quota system" has selected from the more privileged members of these underclasses and not the poorest. At the same time, many of the slots made available by the quota system go unfilled due to low levels of education, training, and preparation among low-caste groups (Sowell 2004).

Brazil's integration policies have been constrained by a national ideology that views the country as a "racial democracy," a self-perception supported by the absence of legalized racial segregation, substantial miscegenation and interracialism, and a constitutional provision of equality before the law. Until recently, race as an official category did not exist and public discussions of the "racial question" were officially prohibited. The ideology of "racial democracy," which maintains that race does not matter, is intricately combined with an informal system of discrimination and a social hierarchy of color (or "pigmentocracy"), in which lighter skin is associated with greater prestige and economic status and darker skin is associated with lower prestige and poverty. Under the dominant cultural belief system, African ancestry or blackness was defined by the European elites as anti-Brazilian. Relatedly, among blacks the notion of a color-blind "racial democracy" has undermined the legitimacy of organized struggle and the development of collective consciousness, self-help, and uplift. During World War II and the postwar years, any possibilities of integration in Brazil were further thwarted by two major periods of authoritarian rule (1937–1945 and 1964–1985) (Nascimento and Nascimento 2001).

More recently, Afro-Brazilian activists have struggled to have the "racial question" recognized as a national issue and have demanded the articulation of specific public policies addressing racism. At the same time, the number of Afro-Brazilians elected to political office and in other positions of power has increased, though it is still very far from proportionate. Also, racism is increasingly coming to be viewed as a question of human rights. In the late 1990s, President Fernando Henrique Cardoso publicly denounced racism and began to introduce affirmative action programs for Brazilians of African descent. The government of President Luiz Inácio Lula da Silva (2002–present) created the Special Ministry to Promote Racial Equality and state universities in Rio de Janeiro, Bahia, and Minas Gerais began the policy of reserving vacancies for blacks and public school students. The Brazilian Congress has also introduced bills that mandate quotas for all public universities, government services, and television shows. The implementation of affirmative action policies in the universities has derived from the convergence of Afro-Brazilian struggles and new governmental policies.

In Britain and France, official recognition of race, ethnicity, and discrimination was virtually absent until after World War II. In both countries, the large-scale influx of immigrants from former colonies in the Southern Hemisphere led to a perceived need for integration policies.

British integration policies grew out of legislation that was initially designed to restrict immigration and depoliticize race. In response to the growth of West Indian and East Indian immigrant populations, in 1964 the Labor-dominated British government enacted legislation that both restricted immigration and encouraged integration (Bleich 2003, pp. 65–66). Four years later, a progressive coalition brought about the enactment of the more comprehensive 1968 Race Relations Act, which made discrimination on racial grounds unlawful in housing, employment, training, education, and the provision of goods, facilities, and services. This legislation established an administrative agency for race-related issues, structured access into British institutions, and widened protections against racism. Paralleling developments in the United States, the 1968 Act reframed issues of integration as issues of access. The British Parliament expanded the definition of discrimination from direct intentional discrimination to indirect discrimination, whether intentional or not, and laid out a soft form of affirmative action known as *positive action* (Bleich 2003, pp. 101–102). The Race Relations Amendment (2000) extended the coverage of the 1976 Act to all public institutions, with only a few limited exceptions. Since the 1976 Race Relations Act, movement toward increased access has been constrained by institutional changes—such as decentralization, which saw political power shift to the judiciary, local jurisdictions, and the bureaucracy—and, beginning in the 1980s, by a succession of conservative-led British governments that were not receptive to "race-conscious" policies addressing indirect discrimination.

France's antidiscrimination policies derived from French memories of Nazism, anti-Semitic newspapers, and speeches by far-right demagogues. Protections against unequal access to employment and services were negligible. Focused largely on formal integration and "expressive racism," French integration legislation introduced in 1972 criminalized racial defamation and the provocation of racial hatred against groups or individuals; outlawed discrimination in hiring, firing, and the provision of goods and services; and enabled the government to disband groups that seek to promote racism. Protections against unequal access to employment and services remain negligible (Bleich 2003, pp. 139–141).

French legislation conceived of discrimination as based on religion or ethnic or national origin—but not on race. France has a "colorblind" code that omits the word *race*. The government collects no census data relating to race and ethnicity, and in 1978 it banned race-based statistics. There is no public- or private-sector use of racial or ethnic data to estimate the status of minorities (Bleich 2003, p. 141). Although the immigration of North and West Africans has continued, and immigrants in France experience substantial economic inequality and segregation, structural discrimination and unequal access are not recognized in France's integration policy.

SEE ALSO *Affirmative Action; Anti-Semitism; Apartheid; Assimilation; Black Nationalism;* Brown v. Board of Education, *1954; Caste; Caste, Anthropology of; Civil Rights Movement, U.S.; Crowding Hypothesis; Desegregation; Discrimination, Racial; Education, Unequal; Ethnocentrism; Ghetto; Great Society, The; Immigration; Jim Crow; Jingoism; Kerner Commission Report; Nation of Islam; Nazism; Quotas; Race-Blind Policies; Race-Conscious Policies; Racism; Segregation; Segregation, Residential; Segregation, School; Separate-but-Equal; Separatism; Voting Rights Act*

BIBLIOGRAPHY

Bennett, Lerone, Jr. 2003. *Before the Mayflower: A History of Black America.* 7th ed. Chicago: Johnson Publishing Company.

Blank, Rebecca M. 2001. An Overview of Trends in Social and Economic Well-Being, by Race. In *America Becoming: Racial Trends and Their Consequences*, vol. 1, eds. Neil J. Smelser, William Julius Wilson, and Faith Mitchell, 21–39. Washington, DC: National Academy Press.

Blumenstein, Alfred. 2001. Race and Criminal Justice. In *America Becoming: Racial Trends and Their Consequences*, vol. 2, eds. Neil J. Smelser, William Julius Wilson, and Faith Mitchell, 21–31. Washington, DC: National Academy Press.

Breitman, George, ed. 1990. *Malcolm X Speaks: Selected Speeches and Statements.* New York: Grove Weidenfeld.

Carmichael, Stokely, and Charles V. Hamilton. 1967. *Black Power: The Politics of Liberation in America.* New York: Random House.

Clark, Kenneth B. 1953. Desegregation: An Appraisal of the Evidence. *Journal of Social Issues* 9 (4): 2–76.

Denton, Nancy, and Douglas Massey. 1988. Residential Segregation of Blacks, Hispanics, and Asians by Socioeconomic Status and Gender. *Social Science Quarterly* 69 (4): 797–817.

Iceland, John, Daniel H. Weinberg, and Erika Steinmetz. 2002. Racial and Ethnic Segregation in the United States, 1980–2000. U.S. Census Bureau Special Report Series CENSR-3. Washington, DC: U.S. Census Bureau.

Kennedy, Randall. 2001. Racial Trends in the Administration of Justice. In *American Becoming: Racial Trends and Their Consequences*, vol. 2, eds. Neil J. Smelser, William Julius Wilson, and Faith Mitchell, 1–20. Washington, DC: National Academy Press.

King, Martin Luther, Jr. 1968. *Where Do We Go from Here: Chaos or Community?* Boston: Beacon Press.

Klarman, Michael J. 2004. *From Jim Crow to Civil Rights: The Supreme Court and the Struggle for Racial Equality.* New York: Oxford University Press.

Klinkner, Phillip A., with Rogers M. Smith. 1999. *The Unsteady March: The Rise and Decline of Racial Equality in America.* Chicago: University of Chicago Press.

Kluegel, James R. 1990. Trends in Whites' Explanations of the Black-White Gap in Socioeconomic Status, 1977–1989. *American Sociological Review* 55 (4): 512–525.

Kluegel, James R., and Elliot Smith. 1986. *Beliefs about Inequality: Americans' Views of What Is and What Ought to Be.* New York: Aldine de Gruyter.

Massey, Douglas S. 2001. Residential Segregation and Neighborhood Conditions in U.S. Metropolitan Areas. In *America Becoming: Racial Trends and Their Consequences*, vol. 1, eds. Neil J. Smelser, William Julius Wilson, and Faith Mitchell, 391–434. Washington, DC: National Academy Press.

Massey, Douglas S., and Nancy A. Denton. 1993. *American Apartheid: Segregation and the Making of the Underclass.* Cambridge, MA: Harvard University Press.

McNeil, Genna Rae. 1983. *Groundwork: Charles Hamilton Houston and the Struggle for Civil Rights.* Philadelphia: University of Pennsylvania Press.

Myrdal, Gunnar, with Richard Sterner and Arnold Rose. 1944. *An American Dilemma: The Negro Problem and Modern Democracy.* New York: Harper & Row.

National Advisory Commission on Civil Disorders. 1968. *Report of the National Advisory Commission on Civil Disorders.* New York: Bantam Books.

Oliver, Melvin L., and Thomas M. Shapiro. 1995. *Black Wealth/White Wealth: A New Perspective on Racial Inequality.* New York: Routledge.

Orfield, Gary. 2001. Schools More Separate: Consequences of a Decade of Resegregation. Cambridge, MA: Civil Rights Project, Harvard University.

Patillo, Mary, David Weiman, and Bruce Western, eds. 2004. *Imprisoning America: The Social Effects of Mass Incarceration.* New York: Russell Sage Foundation.

Schuman, Howard, Charlotte Steeh, Lawrence D. Bobo, and Maria Krysan. 1997. *Racial Attitudes in America: Trends and Interpretations.* Rev. ed. Cambridge, MA: Harvard University Press.

Sowell, Thomas. 2004. *Affirmative Action around the World: An Empirical Study.* New Haven, CT: Yale University Press.

Walker, Juliet E. K. 1998. *The History of Black Business in America: Capitalism, Race, and Entrepreneurship.* New York: Macmillan.

Wilson, William Julius. 1996. *When Work Disappears: The World of the New Urban Poor.* New York: Alfred A. Knopf.

Frank Harold Wilson

INTELLECTUAL PROPERTY

SEE *Property.*

INTELLECTUALISM, ANTI-

It is difficult to define *anti-intellectualism* with precision. In the simplest sense, the term expresses enmity against the life and works of the mind and adherence to allegedly unmediated practicality. Still, it is hasty to assume that this resentment of the intellect pertains to actions or practices devoid of intelligence. The name silences a basic contradiction. Anti-intellectualism refers to a certain tendency or mentality, therefore a specific state of mind, that paradoxically refuses to recognize the capacity and value of the mind.

It would be misguided to take anti-intellectualism at its word and determine that it consists of unexamined sentiment, pious faith, common sense, or unmitigated pragmatism. Anti-intellectual discourses deployed against ideas and values thereby pronounced dangerous are themselves propelled by a whole complex of ideas. However—and here lies the contradiction—these ideas must remain strictly unacknowledged; their presence and exercise must be denied. In this respect, there is something ideological about anti-intellectualism, or perhaps it is more accurate to say that anti-intellectualism is likely to adhere to the primacy of an ideological, rather than critical, relation to the world. This can be said despite the claim that in certain instances of modern history, under the banner of populist egalitarianism, anti-intellectualism was deployed in order to break down various ideologies of privilege.

Given anti-intellectualism's paradoxical conditions—whether we examine it as an idea, an attitude, or a historical phenomenon—it is most productive to trace its multiple and fluctuating reference frames rather than to insist, in anti-intellectual fashion perhaps, on its self-evident nature. As a departure point, we may take anti-intellectualism to consist of whatever discourse subverts conditions that enable intellectual life to flourish: an open horizon of interrogation, a plurality of sources of knowledge, the right to dissent, the freedom to challenge certainties and authorities, the capacity to pursue independent research and investigation. The means of subversion is to foster instead a climate of dogmatism and conformity, often driven by narrow and politically expedient aims, that enforces a closed system of thoughts and beliefs exercised throughout the social sphere, though often concentrated in the realms of religion, education, and mass culture. Anti-intellectualism triumphs when such conditions strangle not only the terms of intellectual life but also the very essence of democratic existence.

Anti-intellectualism in the United States should be considered "older than national identity itself," as Richard Hofstadter succinctly put it in his *Anti-intellectualism in American Life* (1963), which remains the consummate treatment of the subject. Published a few months before the assassination of President John F. Kennedy, at a time of tremendous intellectual optimism in U.S. politics and obviously unwitting of its imminent collapse, Hofstadter's book sought to theorize the conditions that produced McCarthyism—one of the gravest instances of American anti-intellectualism—by thinking backward, in broad historical terms, in order to elucidate a phenomenon with deep roots in American society.

Certainly, the anti-intellectualism that brought Dwight Eisenhower to power in 1952 against Adlai Stevenson (in whose name the term *egghead* achieved popular usage) could be seen as a replay, in another historical register, of the same attitude that brought Andrew Jackson to power against the privileged and bookish easterner John Quincy Adams. What became known as the Jacksonian Era (1824–1840) is traditionally considered to be a period of emancipatory democratization in U.S. history, and yet this is when the down-home posturing of David ("Davy") Crockett in the corridors of the U.S. Congress, his vulgar and contemptuous response to the American Enlightenment tradition, elevated him to what by today's standards would be a mass-cultural icon.

The anti-intellectualism exemplified by Crockett and many Jacksonians, which led to the "decline of the gentleman" in the American social imagination (Hofstadter 1963), does not automatically dispel the genuine argument that the Jacksonian Era signified real democratic expansion. Conversely, however, any argument henceforth about the processes of social democratization in the United States cannot avoid being tainted by suspicion of anti-intellectualism, a tradition that has repeatedly marked U.S. history by, if nothing else, driving the country into periods of self-imposed denial of the surrounding world, with disastrous social, political, and cultural consequences.

This early historical instance is a good example of how the study of anti-intellectualism might produce an equivocal assessment. For the Jacksonians, anti-intellectualism was an explicit platform against established class privilege, represented by the rich, powerful, and highly educated old New England families. In this respect, it served as means for upward mobility, as a weapon in a classic case of class warfare, whereby the intrinsic intellect or "know-how" of less educated folk—one might say, the entrepreneurial capacity (or autodidact practical intelligence) of the unprivileged bourgeoisie—was celebrated as the only genuinely American way of being. This is to say that the proponents of anti-intellectualism in the Jacksonian Era were not uneducated farmers or workers; they were educated middle-class men who sought (and got) a piece of the pie of privilege in the name of expanding the range of opportunity for the uneducated and the unprivileged (farmers or workers). Jackson's people were great populist propagandists. In this sense, they managed to portray the Jackson-Adams presidential race as a contest of the representative of *vita activa* versus the representative of *vita contemplativa*, considering the latter to be too weak for the task of the presidency. The outcome of this contest legitimized a social and political imagination that drew its authority precisely from defying the Union's Enlightenment foundations, revering them as mere constitutional legacy while disregarding them in real life.

Conversely, one may just as easily argue that the Enlightenment tradition is only one strain of American foundation, obviously linked to the revolutionary politics that brought to this society a national existence. The other strain, less directly political but nonetheless profoundly social, is the morality of Christian Protestantism, particularly the pietist and Puritan strains of the early colonists. This aspect animated a certain imaginary in which communities formed by subsequent waves of immigration, even when not necessarily Puritan or even Protestant in a general sense, found solace and identification. It is this imaginary of Christian moral authority and Puritan work ethic, and not the Enlightenment imaginary of the nation's intellectual founders, that mobilized Western expansion and immigrant assimilation. This imaginary is constitutively anti-intellectual because it is essentially moralist and, more specifically, religious in its moralism. As one strain of a bifurcated social-imaginary foundation, anti-intellectualism is thus fundamental in American society, even if it is not consistently dominant in the public sphere.

Certainly, the contemporary emergence into political power by the Christian Right, with its explicit religious and moral fundamentalism, is but one more manifestation in a long history of evangelical participation in the American anti-intellectual tradition. The incessant drive to displace Darwinian theories of evolution from the high-school science curriculum in favor of creationism is an obvious such instance, signaling a profound reversal of a matter considered resolved in the 1925 Scopes trial. But equally obvious are the attempts to strong-arm court appointments at all levels of the justice system, where the actual stakes ultimately reside in a battle for an open framework of discussion and argument over interpretation of the law according to predetermined ideological principles that regard the institution of law not as a human enterprise and endeavor but an indication of the word of God written in stone. The current alliance between Christian evangelists and neoconservative ideologues at the highest levels of U.S. government elucidates the deceptive anti-intellectualism of the latter. Although the so-called neocons are all highly educated men, many of them with academic careers, they nonetheless espouse a vision of American society where plurality of views, open interpretation, interrogation of received knowledge, and,

of course, dissent—the cornerstone of democracy—are rendered null and void.

Not surprisingly, the avowed enemies of contemporary anti-intellectualism reside in education and in media, two domains of enormous influence in matters of formation, cultivation, and refinement of democratic consciousness. But this current development has its roots in the Right's reaction to the United States' post-Vietnam conditions, particularly the fact that the student movement and an independent press played the most crucial role in the demise of the Nixon administration. Since the 1980s, U.S. social services and civil liberties have confronted the most orchestrated onslaught of government-based anti-intellectualism to such an extent that, for example, the "dumbing-down of American universities" turned from a slogan to a reality that is now statistically confirmed. With public primary and secondary schooling driven to bankruptcy due to fiscal restructuring that relegated education the lowest priority, the whole function of university education (anchored to its definitional demands for higher learning) is thus incapacitated. Although one surely finds anti-intellectual strains within academic ranks, of greatest concern regarding society's future is the increasing anti-intellectualism of the student population. This is manifested on campuses in myriad ways, from objections to types of courses and course materials to demands for uncritical expressions of opinion in the classroom in the name of objectivity or so-called balanced accounts.

American youth, however, cannot be blamed for what is de facto the "dumbing-down" of an entire country, which is most visible in the extraordinary manipulation and spectacular vulgarity that characterize contemporary media. Although there was a time one could count on investigative reporting to expose social and political injustice, thus restoring the democratic capacity of ordinary citizens, in the early twenty-first century one sees journalists, embedded in the political status quo, who merely seek to outdo each other in showmanship, quick and empty sloganeering, and allegedly bottom-line pronouncements. It is this talent for catchy slogans and cheap bravado that marks the ideological reversal of certain once-upon-a-time scions of the intellectual Left, such as David Horowitz and Christopher Hitchens, who now gloat on the front lines of neoconservative platforms. However we might judge whether and to what extent their politics (one way or another) were ever genuine, what accounts for their new conservative prominence is their blatant anti-intellectualism. In addition to narcissistic posturing in the media, the need to push the reporting of events through the news-item assembly line with the greatest possible speed, in the service of higher viewer ratings, feeds the anti-intellectualism that conceived of embedded journalism in the first place. It is certainly no surprise that American academics and intellectuals of great stature are nowhere to be seen in the mass media. They are effectively censored, not merely because of their independent views but also because of their refusal to speak in advertising slogans, because their language has been rendered incompatible with the media's current production values.

It must be said, however, that responsibility for the charge that intellectuals are out of touch with the people because they speak a language that no one understands, a charge espoused so effectively by the agents of anti-intellectualism, rests on the shoulders of intellectuals themselves. Indeed, the best way to resist anti-intellectualism is by cultivating an intellectual life that: (1) does not let the attraction to concentrated and detailed knowledge become an endeavor of uncommunicative specialization; and (2) does not let the pleasure in concentrated and expert research get in the way of active participation in the public sphere of ideas and practices. In effect, anti-intellectualism will have no opposition from which to draw its menacing energy if the distinction between *vita activa* and *vita contemplativa* is rendered irrelevant.

SEE ALSO *Ideology; Intellectuals, Public*

BIBLIOGRAPHY

Bromwich, David. 1996. Anti-intellectualism. *Raritan* 16: 18–27.

Claussen, Dane S. 2004. *Anti-intellectualism in American Media.* New York: Peter Lang.

Hofstadter, Richard. 1963. *Anti-intellectualism in American Life.* New York: Knopf.

Sacks, Peter. 1996. *Generation X Goes to College.* Chicago: Open Court.

Schlag, Pierre. 1995. Anti-intellectualism. *Cardozo Law Review* 16: 1111–1120.

Washburn, Katherine, and John F. Thornton, eds. 1996. *Dumbing Down: Essays on the Strip Mining of American Culture.* New York: Norton.

Stathis Gourgouris

INTELLECTUALS, ORGANIC

Rejecting the very idea of the disinterested scholar, Antonio Gramsci (1891–1937) in *The Prison Notebooks* (pp. 3–23) argues that all intellectual activity arises from specific socioeconomic circumstances. In fact, each sector of society yields its own variety of organizers, creators, mediators, and contemplators, whom Gramsci labels "organic intellectuals." In so arguing, Gramsci recasts some of the key notions of modern political thought: hegemony, civil society, class difference, and the national-

popular. More recently, Gramsci's organic intellectual has served as a key concept within, or in opposition to, structuralist and poststructuralist theory, including postcolonial studies (Edward Said), subaltern studies (Renajit Guha), cultural studies (Stuart Hall, David Lloyd, Paul Thomas, Grant Farred), ethnic studies (George Lipsitz), post-Marxist thought (Jacques Rancière), and critical pedagogy (Henry Giroux, Michael Apple).

Gramsci introduces his notion, first, by insisting that education does not emerge from but actually creates the political foundations of the state; and second, by contesting existing views on traditional intellectuals. Typically seen as bearers of universal reason and general truths, such intellectuals in fact originate from the ecclesiastics qua the organic intellectuals of the aristocracy, and later take their place as subjects and agents of a particular historical block: the bourgeoisie. That the elite scholar is actually organic to a class, historical development, and social circumstance (points that Giroux and Apple emphasize) indicates as well that the division between the educated and uneducated, the cultured and uncultured, is not natural or necessary but contingent: a result of specific intellectual activity, whose true, if unspoken purpose, is to produce and reproduce these oppositions.

As to the working-class intellectual, Gramsci focuses upon the way in which the hegemonic state induces the consent of this group through the channels of an increasingly uniform civil society: the schools, the media, the Church, and so on. Gramsci's well-known *Prison Notebook* assertion that "all men are intellectuals" lies here (p. 3). Because assent on the part of the oppressed or working class turns on a nonviolent, *rational* acceptance of official discourses and edicts, intellect and reason are conditions even of that subjugation. The point, though, proves double-edged: If intelligence is the requisite of the worker's or peasant's suppression, the capitalist state cannot *not* risk generating the alternative interventions that upset its order, even though its goal (homogeneity, consensus) depends, precisely, on the eradication of those alternatives. And when the state confronts another reason and the reason of the other it is forced to swallow them repeatedly: Devour an exterior, unfamiliar, deleterious intellectual legitimacy—as opposed to an irrational or wild outside, which the state can always cast as hazardous, and thus annihilate in the name of right—into its common sense, transforming itself into a dynamic process of assimilation, transmutation, and becoming.

None of this means that organic intellectuals sprout, like plants, from the material ground into which they are born. They are contingently, not essentially, bound to a class base. The organic is not the natural. In fact, in order to realize themselves, organic intellectuals must venture into alien arenas, including if not especially the realm (the metropolis) of universal reason, represented by the state. Intellectual activity is a perpetual outing. For example, manual laborers such as metalworkers must familiarize themselves with state edicts, disconnected from their daily labor, if they are to initiate an effective legal appeal for improved lathes, that is, for better safety conditions. Likewise, the attorneys who handle the appeal must, through communication with workers, attain detailed practical and technological knowledge of the lathe, possibly altering their daily contacts, the texts that they study, the library where they conduct the research, and the vocabulary of their briefs to do so. Unplanned constellations, leading to unintended though not accidental (for they are products of work) interventions, surface as the various classes and/or types convene: Out of a congregation of lawyers and manual laborers concerned with worker well-being emerges a non-class-based women's collective seeking state-sponsored child care. Such cross-professional encounters, moreover, generate novel jargons and idiolects. These both permit the diverse sectors to communicate and represent potential foundations for future expertises and experts, for new tasks grounded organically in the invented vernaculars and emergent gatherings.

Traditional education, Gramsci argues, involves the repetition, delivery, accumulation, coordination, and control of existing as well as new ideas. It both manufactures and casts as inevitable, as a matter of common sense, a current "state of affairs" whose base is class difference. Indeed, as the officialdom is naturalized, it need not even be taught: The commonsensical, by definition, goes without saying, thereby without teaching. The aim of public state education, it would seem, is its own obsolescence, as well as the obsolescence of the alterity that education oftentimes generates. Conversely, organic intellectuals, charged by Gramsci with the boosting of education via its revolutionary overhaul, forge the idioms that link, coming between and disrupting this accretion of familiar signifiers, and of the status quo that they represent. Class *difference* resurfaces through these connections and articulations as class *relations*: relative, contingent, and precarious, like class itself. Because they are neither inside nor outside (but between) the established fields of meaning, these relational formulations materialize beyond sense and nonsense, effecting a demand for interpretation and intelligibility, that is, for thought. Who will meet the challenge, broach and articulate the uncommon sense—the organic intellectual who could deploy it for novel activity, for the renovation of the social field itself, or the traditional intellectual who will either appropriate or eradicate it in the name of greater hegemonic expansion? Because, by logic, either could, the class struggle is traversed through and through by these questions of education, knowledge, and creativity.

The responsibility of the organic intellectual, then, is less to insert newly legitimized knowledges into the aggregate of thought, hence to displace the extant field, than to disclose the fact that current conditions do not go without saying. The class injustices that sustain the state are not present by nature; therefore, they can be altered. Leftist politics remains conceivable. Organic intellectuals are not working-class heroes but, as Gramsci put it in the *Prison Notebooks*, forgers of the bond between the *homo faber* and *homo sapiens* (p. 4), making and saying, practice and theory. Effecting the suspension of the common sense, they cut through, gnaw away from within, relay and relate the provisional nature of the capitalist state, which cannot stand without clear class oppositions, the very oppositions that the organic intellectual's labor calls into question.

Interestingly, recent scholarship that recurs to Gramsci's notion often departs fruitfully from the Italian philosopher's conceptualization—in part due to Gramsci's class- and state-based foundation, and in part due to the new interest in cultural difference and identity. Often focusing on transnational, largely cultural uprisings (examples include the civil rights movements in North America and the Caribbean, and Pan-African unrest) these studies tend to employ as their models activists, poets, and scholars such as Frantz Fanon and C. R. L. James—figures who demonstrate the way in which the organic intellectual, when recast, can play and indeed have played major roles in actual, contemporary insurgencies.

SEE ALSO *Communism; Gramsci, Antonio*

BIBLIOGRAPHY

Apple, Michael. 2004. *Ideology and Curriculum*. 3rd ed. London: Taylor and Francis.

Farred, Grant. 2003. *What's My Name? Black Vernacular Intellectuals*. Minneapolis: University Press of Minnesota.

Giroux, Henry A. 2004. *Border Crossings: Cultural Workers and the Politics of Education*. London: Taylor and Francis.

Gramsci, Antonio. 1971. The Intellectuals. In *Selections from the Prison Notebooks*, trans. and ed. Quintin Hoare and Geoffrey Nowell Smith, 3–23. New York: International Publishers.

Guha, Renajit. 1999. *Elementary Aspects of Peasant Insurgency in Colonial India*. Durham, NC: Duke University Press.

Hall, Stuart. 1992. Cultural Studies and Its Theoretical Legacies. In *Cultural Studies*, ed. Lawrence Grossberg, Cary Nelson, and Paula Treichler, 277–294. London: Routledge.

Lipsitz, George. 1995. *In the Struggle: Ivory Perry and the Culture of Opposition*. Philadelphia: Temple University Press.

Lloyd, David, and Thomas, Paul. 1998. *Culture and the State*. New York: Routledge.

Rancière, Jacques. 1989. *The Nights of Labor*. Trans. John Drury. Philadelphia: Temple University Press.

Said, Edward. 2002. *Reflections on Exile and Other Essays*. Cambridge, MA: Harvard University Press.

Brett Levinson

INTELLECTUALS, PUBLIC

The term *public intellectual* has no meaning outside of an American context. Nowhere in the European tradition, for example, does one find references to this term because, strictly speaking, it is redundant. Intellectuals are distinguished from scholars or scientists because their role is necessarily public. They may indeed be scholars and scientists, academics and specialists in a particular discipline, and they may also be writers or artists, but they become intellectuals when the knowledge and learning they represent goes beyond the strict domain that gives them authority. Intellectuals achieve this status when their learned experience, their capacity for inquiry, interpretation, and speculation, is trained upon problems that concern the society to which they belong and, in the global epoch, problems that concern humanity and the planet as a whole.

That "public intellectuals" emerge into the English language as a specifically American idiom is indicative of a historical framework and tradition where anti-intellectualism carries a deeply imbedded and formidable legacy. Still, the term has a short history; it belongs to the latter half of the twentieth century. No one would think of identifying Thomas Jefferson (1743–1826), Benjamin Franklin (1706–1790), or Thomas Paine (1737–1809) as public intellectuals, though they were obviously intellectuals of great stature and public figures of enormous renown and influence. Though eighteenth-century scholars agree that Enlightenment ideas flourished politically because they coincided with (perhaps even had a hand in bringing about) the first vestiges of a veritable mass culture and the public sphere it demands, it is nonetheless a mark of the considerable alienation of intellectual life from politics in America that public intellectuals have become necessary as a specifically designated category since the Vietnam War. The term's redundancy raises questions in both directions: (1) What is the public (or even, is there a public?) that renders the role of intellectuals meaningful, and (2) of what must the role of the intellectual consist in order to merit (and achieve) a public?

The term *intellectual* itself is entirely modern, emerging during the great public debates in France over the Dreyfus affair (1894–1899). The elements of that specific historical conjuncture—the fact that citizens of learning engaged over a political issue (which, moreover, touched on fundamentals of national character)—cannot be maneuvered. It is not enough for intellectuals to apply themselves to the work of the intellect, or even to engage the world intellectually. It seems inevitable that intellectuals carry a political significance, that intellectual work is acknowledged as a domain of acts and practices that pertains to the political demands and conditions of the world they inhabit. It comes as no surprise then that the ques-

tion of the role of the intellectual is one of the most debated issues in the Marxist tradition, with Antonio Gramsci's (1891–1937) famous theorization of intellectual positions having served as a departure point for subsequent theorizations even outside the Marxist canon. It is precisely because the role of the intellectual has assumed a political significance since the term was invented—in other words, that intellectuals achieve meaning only within the parameters of the *polis*—that the newer term, *public intellectuals*, inheres a redundancy.

Nonetheless, the current usage defines a particular object and deserves specific focus, as if the explicit insistence on the word *public* bears a need at the core for bringing attention to a lack. Only a society that develops a public sphere in which intellectuals are marginalized develops a need for the category of public intellectual. The marginalization of intellectuals in America is not ideologically driven, despite the grand tradition of anti-intellectualism. The causes are complex, but two factors must be specifically accentuated. First, there are real social-historical changes affecting the base of American politics since the 1950s, most important of which is the shift in the demography of political constituencies from the cosmopolitan urban centers to vast expanses of newly constructed suburban social landscapes. In the matter that concerns us here, this shift coincides with an increase in the ranks of college professionals across the country, simultaneous with a gravely rapid expansion in academic specialization. Second, the unprecedented development in mass media and communication technology in the so-called information age inevitably decenters both the authority and the dissemination of knowledge, producing instead multiple points of active and direct access (Internet technology) as well as passive reception of information (television and the entertainment industry—which, in recent years, have, in economic terms at least, merged into one). This disables the effect of old intellectual centers (New York being the most celebrated), where people of learning and the world of publishing and print media were at one time organically intertwined, driving one side to retreat behind academic walls and the other to alliance with the media forces of mass entertainment culture. These new realities have given rise to a widely evoked lament for the decline of American intellectual culture.

Though such laments have historical merit, they cannot, by definition, escape the shackles of nostalgia. Under contemporary conditions, intellectuals were forced to figure new ways to participate in the proliferation of authoritative knowledge, indeed to find the proper language to engage with the contentious field of public exchange without submitting to the streamlining of ideas and the sloganeering that satisfied the commercial demands of the mass media. This necessarily produces a broader profile of knowledge than the one accounting for top reputation in a discipline, as is the case, for example, with Noam Chomsky, who as a linguist developed an entirely new field of linguistics, yet as a public intellectual distinguished himself as a political commentator. Incidentally, it is worth noting that a 2005 Internet poll—keeping in mind all caveats over the accuracy of Internet polling—showed Chomsky to be the world's most recognized intellectual, even though his reputation in the United States, by virtue of his politics, is much maligned. His is a case where a public intellectual achieves both stature and reputation outside his society; Chomsky's public sphere is not so much American society but the world at large.

Yet, the Chomsky phenomenon confirms that a public intellectual must create a public, not merely conform to the parameters of the established public sphere around him. In fact, in this era of great conformism to public opinion produced, disseminated, and controlled by mass media through the voice of alleged experts, a public intellectual becomes precisely the figure who interrogates the self-confirmation and unexamined repetition of expertise, a figure whose life consists of raising critical questions "in the quest for new uncertainties" (1963, p. 16), as Richard Hofstadter (1916–1970) so memorably put it. No one, however, has made a bolder and more farseeing description of the public intellectual's task than Edward Said (1935–2003): "This role has an edge to it, and cannot be played without a sense of being someone whose place it is publicly to raise embarrassing questions, to confront orthodoxy and dogma (rather than to produce them), to be someone who cannot be co-opted by governments or corporations, and whose raison d'être is to represent all these people and issues that are routinely forgotten or swept under the rug" (1994, p. 11). Said is exemplary, in this respect, because his global activist profile never compromised his intransigence or his rigor as a writer and a thinker, who was, moreover, unique in making the intellectual as such a subject of critical reflection.

Said adds a crucial dimension to the complex portrait of the public intellectual in America, which is usually overlooked or not quite articulated. In conversation with the classic 1927 book by Julien Benda (1867–1956), a French rationalist conservative who decried the political irresponsibility of intellectuals whom he dubbed "clerics," Said emphasized the quintessentially secular humanist task of the public intellectual. Even in the most committed activist practices, an intellectual's relation to the public must necessarily resist any sort of metaphysical or aestheticist investment. A public intellectual conceives this task neither as a prophet crying in the wilderness, in some sort of radical vanguard bearing a torch, nor as an ascetically restrained ethicist, advocating the integrity of a desiring public from the humble position of service to wisdom. The task is rather to foster a public, and indeed a public that reveres questioning authorities and identi-ties, that shares the pleasure of disclosure, and in the end finds self-affirmation in dissent, in exercising its autonomy in the real social and political sphere.

There is, in other words, an intimate relation between whatever produces the need for public intellectuals and whatever cultivates the need, even in the darkest of times, for a real democratic politics—which must always be a politics of citizens unswayed by the pronouncements of experts, a politics of critique, self-authorization, and self-enfranchisement. Regardless of how they may articulate their personal politics, public intellectuals, by definition, must be engaged in democratic criticism, which must be uncompromising in its suspicion of pronounced authority and yet never nihilist. A public with democratic consciousness must be first and foremost a skeptical public, but nonetheless, a public committed to a vision of a future, an emancipated future. In the early twenty-first century world, where political stakes are graver than ever and political consciousness is in a state of questionable vitality, an intellectual public—however it is to be constituted—would best embody Gramsci's inimitable call for "pessimism of the intellect and optimism of the will."

SEE ALSO *Intellectualism, Anti-*

BIBLIOGRAPHY

Benda, Julien. 1928. *The Treason of the Intellectuals.* Trans. Richard Aldington. New York: Morrow.

Bender, Thomas. 1993. *Intellect and Public Life: Essays on the Social History of Academic Intellectuals in the United States.* Baltimore, MD: Johns Hopkins University Press.

Gramsci, Antonio. 1971. The Intellectuals. In *Selections from the Prison Notebooks of Antonio Gramsci,* eds. and trans. Quintin Hoare and Geoffrey Nowell Smith, 2–23. New York: International Publishers.

Hofstadter, Richard. 1963. *Anti-intellectualism in American Life.* New York: Knopf.

Jacoby, Russell. 1987. *The Last Intellectuals: American Culture in the Age of Academe.* New York: Basic Books.

Michael, John. 2000. *Anxious Intellects: Academic Professionals, Public Intellectuals, and Enlightenment Values.* Durham, NC: Duke University Press.

Posner, Richard A. 2001. *Public Intellectuals: A Study of Decline.* Cambridge, MA: Harvard University Press.

Robbins, Bruce. 1993. *Secular Vocations: Intellectuals, Professionalism, Culture.* London: Verso.

Rorty, Richard. 1998. *Achieving Our Country: Leftist Thought in Twentieth-Century America.* Cambridge, MA: Harvard University Press.

Said, Edward W. 1994. *Representations of the Intellectual.* New York: Pantheon.

Said, Edward W. 2004. *Humanism and Democratic Criticism.* New York: Columbia University Press.

Stathis Gourgouris

INTELLECTUALS, VERNACULAR

As a concept that pertains to language, the vernacular has a history that dates back centuries. The concept of the vernacular intellectual is, however, of much more recent vintage. It first entered the lexicon in 2003 with Grant Farred's work, *What's My Name? Black Vernacular Intellectuals*. Farred's term *vernacular intellectual* derives from a critique of Antonio Gramsci's (1891–1937) notion of traditional and organic intellectuals; in his famously democratic pronouncement, "all men are intellectuals," Gramsci distinguishes between traditional and organic intellectuals (Gramsci 1972, p. 13). The former are those trained primarily as ecclesiastics, initially rooted within the medieval church; the latter are those who locate themselves more firmly within the political apparatuses of their society—thinkers organic to their class, their political party, or the state bureaucracy.

The vernacular intellectual represents a reconsideration of the category *intellectual*. It is premised on the critical expansion of the category in that it proposes that the work of thinking assumes many guises and cannot be restricted to the formally educated classes. According to this reconception, the vernacular intellectual is an individual whose interventions into how a society thinks about itself—its politics, race, justice—are significant in part because of the person's identity and position. The vernacular intellectual represents a form of critical social engagement that demonstrates the intellectuality, or thought processes, of subaltern life.

The vernacular figure redefines who is understood to be an intellectual, challenging the restriction of the term *intellectual* to those trained by conventional intellectual means—accredited by the university system, by café or soirée society, or by political parties. This means that the vernacular intellectual may not be widely known, or not known at all, to wider society. This is because the vernacular intellectual generally emerges from the ranks of the subaltern classes and speaks the language of those constituencies, articulating a politics that is often, but not always, incommensurable with that of dominant society. The vernacular intellectual is not necessarily a figure who espouses a radical politics. The issue of language, including how the vernacular intellectual speaks and his or her vocabulary, metaphors, and idioms, is thus critical to the construction of the vernacular intellectual.

Cultural figures such as the boxer Muhammad Ali (b. 1942), the reggae singer Bob Marley (1945–1981), the singer Grace Jones (b. 1952), the rhythm and blues singer James Brown (c. 1933–2006), and the tennis player Martina Navratilova (b. 1956) all represent, in their different articulations, the vernacular intellectual. They speak particular truths to power: about race, anti-colonialism, poverty, oppression, sexuality, and subaltern pleasure. The vernacular is, therefore, most audible in popular culture: in the music, the articulations of sportspersons, and popular expressions.

When Muhammad Ali famously declared in 1966, "I ain't got no quarrel with them Viet Cong," he was doing considerably more than making public his own refusal to be drafted into the U.S. military. Through this statement, Ali simultaneously critiqued America's internal racism and its international imperialism and linked one to the other, demonstrating how the vernacular intellectual can make interventions into the public sphere in a highly idiomatic yet resonant language. The vernacular intellectual is, in essence, that cultural figure who addresses the political but whose critiques are almost never recognized as the work of an intellectual.

SEE ALSO *Ali, Muhammad (USA); Anticolonial Movements; Bureaucracy; Credentialism; Gramsci, Antonio; Imperialism; Intellectuals, Organic; Racism; Resistance; Vietnam War*

BIBLIOGRAPHY

Farred, Grant. 2003. *What's My Name?: Black Vernacular Intellectuals*. Minneapolis: University of Minnesota Press.

Gramsci, Antonio. 1972. *Selections from the Prison Notebooks of Antonio Gramsci*, ed. and trans. Quintin Hoare and Geoffrey Nowell Smith. New York: International Publishers.

Grant Farred

INTELLIGENCE

Intelligence is defined as the capacity for learning, reasoning, understanding, and similar forms of mental activity. This definition implies that the concept of intelligence is both multifaceted (i.e., reflective of many aspects of mental ability) and implicative of differences among people (i.e., reflective of degrees of capacity, ability, or aptitude among individuals). Yet this definition does not necessarily relate directly to the definition of intelligence used by scientists. In fact there is no consensus on the definition of intelligence among professionals who study it (e.g., psychologists, educators, computer scientists).

MULTIPLE DEFINITIONS

There have been multiple attempts to define intelligence. These definitions can be broadly classified into five large groups: (1) consensus definitions, (2) operational definitions, (3) task-based or psychometric definitions, (4) process-based definitions, and (5) domain definitions.

"Consensus definitions" of intelligence are typically associated with attempts of researchers in the field to consolidate a variety of points of view and produce, collectively, a comprehensive common definition. In this regard two symposia that brought together researchers in the field are important. The first symposium, which took place in 1921 under the title "Intelligence and Its Measurement: A Symposium," focused on the abilities to learn and adapt to the environment. However, the definitions of these abilities varied. For example, the American psychologist Lewis Terman emphasized abstract thinking, whereas another American psychologist, Edward Thorndike, stressed the importance of providing good responses to questions. The second symposium, which took place in 1986, brought together a new generation of intelligence researchers (e.g., Douglas Detterman, Ulric Neisser, Robert Sternberg). By then the field of intelligence had developed markedly, having produced hundreds of research articles and books. The resulting consensus definition kept the reference to learning and adaptive abilities but expanded to include many other abilities, including meta-cognitive abilities.

Although there is still no single consensus definition of intelligence, based on the discussions at these symposia, multiple other meetings, and in the press a broad definition of intelligence includes references to lower-level processes, such as perception and attention, and higher-level processes, such as problem solving, reasoning, and decision making, with regard to learning and demonstrating adaptive behaviors in problem situations. These lower- and higher-level processes are typically referred to in two dimensions: quality and speed. Quality refers to efficacy or lack of errors, and speed refers to time while learning or solving a problem. Intelligence implies the presence of no or few errors and high speed in all processes.

"Operational definitions" of intelligence are closely linked to the concept of intelligence testing. Intelligence testing was conceived of and developed by the French psychologists Alfred Binet and Théodore Simon, who first used such a test to identify learning-impaired Parisian children in the early 1900s. The "invention" was welcomed by psychologists around the world, especially in the United States, and resulted in the development of innumerable tests of intelligence. To reflect the wealth of the research and the differential power of intelligence tests in describing individual differences, the American psychologist Edwin Boring noted in 1923 that intelligence was simply what intelligence tests test. Although obviously circular in nature, this definition of intelligence is still powerful. Researchers and practitioners often use the common metric of IQ (intelligence quotient), even though IQ typically reflects many different theoretical positions when generated by different tests of intelligence. For example, the first tests of intelligence by Binet were primarily based on sensory processes; David Wechsler's tests (which exist in three versions spanning infancy, childhood, and adulthood) measure primary judgment skills. Then there are theory-based tests, such as the tests of Raymond Cattell, which are based on the theory of crystallized (i.e., acquired and learned over the total life span) and fluid (i.e., transformable to novel materials, situations, and tasks) intelligence, and such modern tests of intelligence as the Cognitive Assessment System (by Jack Naglieri and Jagannath Prasad Das) or K-ABC (by Alan and Nadeen Kaufman), which are both based on the theories of the Soviet neuropsychologist Alexander Luria. Yet as long as a test can generate an IQ, it is assumed to measure intelligence.

"Task-based or psychometric" definitions of intelligence are associated with ideas of defining intelligence through tasks that, by agreement among researchers, call for intelligence. One of the first proponents of task-based definitions of intelligence was the American psychologist Charles Spearman (1863–1945). In the early 1900s Spearman proposed that intelligence includes a so-called general (g-, or mental energy) factor and task-specific factors. The g-factor can explain the observation that indicators of performance on all intelligence tasks tend to correlate with each other (e.g., doing well on one task typically suggests strong performance on other tasks as well), whereas task-specific factors can explain why these correlations are not perfect (e.g., the performance indicators will differ on tasks that involve reading versus arithmetic). Spearman's work had a tremendous impact on the field of intelligence: Students and followers include Cattell, Wechsler, Anne Anastasi, Detterman, Arthur Jensen, and many others. Spearman's work also had opponents. For example, Thorndike argued for three forms of intelligence: abstract, mechanical, and social. Similarly Louis Thurstone argued that several primary mental abilities form intelligence (verbal comprehension, word fluency, number facility, spatial visualization, associative memory, perceptual speed, and reasoning). In an attempt to reconcile the theories of Spearman and Thurstone, Cattell proposed a hierarchical theory of intelligence in which lower-level abilities form two higher-order factors, fluid (reasoning with novel stimuli) and crystallized (reasoning with acquired knowledge) intelligence, which in turn contribute to the g-factor. Another opponent of Spearman's was Joy Paul Guilford, who, developing Thurstone's ideas, stated that intelligence can be represented by 150 abilities that result from different combinations of operations (e.g., cognition and memory), content (e.g., figural and symbolic), and products (e.g., unit and class).

"Process-based" definitions of intelligence are linked to theories that are not test or task based but, rather, capture processes involved in intelligence across tasks, domains, and tests. For example, the so-called triarchic theory of Robert Sternberg postulates three fundamental processes underlying intelligence: (1) analytical processes, which reflect judgment of a quality of an argument; (2) practical processes, which indicate skills of adaptation to situations or environment; and (3) creative processes, which capture skills of generating new knowledge and practices. Each of these types of processes is "constructed" from three different components: (a) knowledge acquisition components, (b) performance components, and (c) metacognitive components. These componential processes can manifest themselves in any area of human functioning.

"Domain-based" definitions of intelligence are typically associated with domains of expertise. For example, Howard Gardner postulates eight dimensions of intelligence. These dimensions, to a various degree, are present in all people and are recruited when particular types of tasks are performed or in particular domains of expertise. Specifically these intelligences are (1) bodily-kinesthetic, in which sportsmen excel; (2) musical, demonstrated to a high degree by musicians; (3) interpersonal, characteristic of philosophers; (4) intrapersonal, common among politicians; (5) logical-mathematical, possessed by mathematicians; (6) naturalistic, demonstrated by scientists; (7) verbal-linguistic, characteristic of writers; and (8) visual-spatial, necessary at high levels for engineers. Another example of domain-based definitions of intelligence is the theory of emotional intelligence (developed by Peter Salovey, John Mayer, and Daniel Goleman). This theory specifies intelligence in the domain of emotional functioning as the ability to perceive, appraise, express, access, generate, and regulate emotions and feelings.

DEVELOPMENT OF INTELLIGENCE

The concept of IQ was developed by psychologists and statisticians in such a way that the distribution of scores remains relatively constant over a life span. IQs are compared across people, not within an individual, and are characterized by a population mean of 100 and a standard deviation of 15. Yet intelligence changes developmentally, and these changes occur in a number of ways. It is obvious that the intelligence of a one-year-old cannot be compared with the intelligence of a fifty-year-old, although their IQs can be compared. There are many developmental theories, for example those of Jean Piaget (1896–1980), that demonstrate that children reason in ways distinctly different from adults. Thus if a person had an IQ score of 110 at age one and has an IQ score of 110 at age fifty, this person's "texture" of intelligence has changed, but his or her relative position among peers has remained constant. A few relevant observations should be noted. First, early childhood intelligence is not a good predictor of level of intelligence later in life. Second, intel-

ligence tends to vary across a person's life span, with a gradual increase toward middle age adulthood and a graduate decline in older ages. Third, it has been reported that in the developed world, intelligence tended to increase during the twentieth century (often called the Flynn effect), but it has appeared to stabilize or even decrease in the twenty-first century.

ETIOLOGY OF INTELLIGENCE

Individuals in the general population differ in their intelligence. Differences are captured by assessments of intelligence, which include both standardized tests (e.g., K-ABC) and experimental tasks (e.g., computerized tasks administered to register reaction time in response to particular stimuli). To identify the sources of these individual differences, researchers investigate the etiology (i.e., origin) of intelligence.

The etiology of intelligence is typically formulated in psychology as a question of nature and nurture: Does intelligence stem from genes (i.e., nature) or environments (i.e., nurture)? This question can be traced back to ancient times, where it was initially formulated as an "either/or" dilemma. In the early twenty-first century, however, there is a consensus that both hereditary and environmental factors play substantial and complementary roles in the development of intelligence. Two statistical coefficients are typically used to express the contributions of both genes and environments: "heritability," which shows the amount of variation in intelligence among individuals attributable to genes, and "environmentality," which captures the variation in intelligence attributable to environment. Both coefficients are relevant only at the level of population analyses and cannot be applied to individuals. Exciting tasks in early twenty-first century research pertain to the identification of specific genes and environments that underlie differences in intelligence. For example, it has been shown that variants in such genes as COMT (a gene responsible for the production of catechol-O-methyl transferase, an enzyme involved in the breakdown of major neurotransmitters) and BDNF (a gene responsible for the production of brain-derived neurotrophic factor, a protein involved in the biochemistry of neuronal survival, growth, and differentiation) are associated with individual differences in cognitive functioning and intelligence. It has also been shown that specific environments, such as impoverished or enriched with certain micronutrients (e.g., iodine), lead to individual differences in intellectual functioning. It is important to realize that neither genes nor environment have a deterministic impact on intelligence. The influence of both types of etiological factors, both additive and interactive, is probabilistic and takes place through the brain. Specifically there is a body of research that establishes evidence regarding which structures and pathways of the brain are associated with solving intellectual tasks and how patterns of brain activation vary among people and in different experimental conditions (e.g., sleep depleted versus deprived).

Although the majority of experts agree on the importance of both genes and environment in the etiology of intelligence, there are still leftovers of the raucous debate of the early 1990s related to the arguments put forth in *The Bell Curve*. Written by the psychologist Richard Herrnstein and the geneticist Charles Murray, *The Bell Curve* claimed IQ is hereditary and, as such, the single determinant of a person's life outcomes. That and similar debates indicate that the concept of intelligence remains a point of disagreement with the capacity to raise charged social issues.

The concept of intelligence is viewed by some as a social construct developed to capture individual differences in cognitive functioning and as such has no "permanent" definition or understanding; both vary with the change of societal context. Thus yet another disagreement in the literature on intelligence pertains to the debate of a "social" versus "real" phenomenon. Those who argue that the concept of intelligence is a social construct suggest it was invented by the privileged classes to maintain their privilege. Those who argue that the concept of intelligence is based on the latent ability truly differentiating people maintain it is a helpful differentiating and predictive concept that has value in decisions pertaining to education and job placement.

GROUP DIFFERENCES IN INTELLIGENCE

Four types of differences are typically discussed in the study of intelligence: sex differences, ethnic and racial differences, cultural differences, and differences in conditions (i.e., intelligence in deaf and hard of hearing versus in hearing people). Males and females tend to demonstrate equivalent or comparable average scores on tests of intelligence. Yet although there are no differences in performance when performance indices are averaged across tasks, there are differences on specific tasks as well as differences in variability and range. Specifically males tend to score higher on spatial and visual tasks, among others, requiring memory, motor tasks involving aiming, and certain tasks requiring mathematical skills. Females tend to score higher on tasks requiring phonological and semantic processing, verbal production and comprehension, and fine motor skills. Broadly speaking, males demonstrate advantages in spatial reasoning, and females demonstrate advantages in verbal reasoning, but this generalized statement can be challenged by the presence and absence of sex differences on other tasks. As of the early

twenty-first century there is no consensus on the profile, stability, and nature of sex differences in intelligence.

Another source of group differences in intelligence is variation in performance among different ethnic and racial groups. Group differences are typically seen on standardized tests of intelligence, especially those that rely heavily on *g*-theories. The differences among ethnic and racial groups demonstrate the underperformance of Hispanic Americans, Native Americans, and African Americans as compared with Asian and white Americans (of a variety of ethnic backgrounds). The differences are asystematic, meaning that the profiles of differences vary for different tasks. In other words, there is no systematic differentiation of profiles of abilities among the ethnic or racial groups. It is of special interest that the ethnic gap appears to be smaller or closed when testing is conducted using tasks from process- or domain-based theories of intelligences.

Similarly people in different cultural groups around the world demonstrate varied performances on intelligence tasks. Moreover definitions of intelligence vary across cultures as well. Thus what is considered to be "intelligent" behavior among the Luo people of Kenya is different from that of Yup'ik people of Alaska. A number of researchers have studied so-called implicit theories of intelligence—ideas about intelligence conceived by laypeople. It turns out that definitions of intelligence in the East and the West, for example, are quite different, with Eastern cultures emphasizing more social-emotional components of intelligence and Western cultures emphasizing information-processing aspects of intelligence.

Another source of group differences is the difference among people with special needs. For example, deaf people tend to score lower on tests of intelligence that call for verbal skills, but their performance on tests of spatial reasoning is similar to hearing individuals. Blind people score lower on spatial tasks (when administered in Braille), but their scores are average on verbal tasks. Thus characteristics of biological development (i.e., hormonal differences), acculturation, education, and various other peculiarities of development can all be related to group differences in intelligence. At this point there is no definitive answer to why these group differences exist.

SEE ALSO *Cognition; Intelligence, Social; IQ Controversy; Memory; Multiple Intelligences Theory; Nature vs. Nurture; Psychology; Psychometrics*

BIBLIOGRAPHY

Cianciolo, Anna T., and Robert J. Sternberg. 2004. *Intelligence: A Brief History*. Malden, MA: Blackwell.

Deary, Ian J. 2000. *Looking down on Human Intelligence: From Psychometrics to the Brain*. Oxford: Oxford University Press.

Mackintosh, N. J. 1998. *IQ and Human Intelligence.* Oxford: Oxford University Press.

Sternberg, Robert J., ed. 2000. *Handbook of Intelligence.* New York: Cambridge University Press.

Sternberg, Robert J., ed. 2004. *International Handbook of Intelligence.* New York: Cambridge University Press.

Elena L. Grigorenko

INTELLIGENCE, ADAPTIVE

SEE *Intelligence, Social.*

INTELLIGENCE, EMOTIONAL

SEE *Multiple Intelligences Theory; Intelligence, Social.*

INTELLIGENCE, SOCIAL

The term "social intelligence" is typically associated with the conception of intelligence developed by Edward Thorndike (1874–1949), a distinguished animal psychologist and a recognized founder of connectionism, a movement within the cognitive sciences attempting to explain human abilities and cognitive skills as complex emergent functions arising from the recruiting of simple elements (i.e., neurons and neuronal groups) into complex networks (i.e., neuronal networks). In the early twentieth century, Thorndike separated three types of intelligence: (1) abstract (capturing what tests of intelligence measure); (2) mechanical (related to visualizing relationships among objects and understanding how the physical world works); and (3) social intelligence (reflective of the degree of success in functioning in interpersonal situations). The notion of social intelligence was further developed in the 1920s and 1930s and referred primarily to the ability of getting along with people, but also to the ability to decode, understand, and manipulate the moods of others. In addition, during the 1920s and 1930s the first tests of social intelligence were developed. The George Washington Social Intelligence Test included, for example, tests of Judgment in Social Situations, Memory for Names and Face, Observation of Human Behavior, and Sense of Humor. Yet, the concept of testing for social intelligence was not uniformly accepted: Psychologist David Wechsler, for example, argued that social intelli-

gence is a manifestation of general intelligence in its application to social situations.

After a number of empirical studies failed to show construct validity of the social intelligence concept as it was measured at the beginning of the twentieth century, work on social intelligence slowed down substantially. It was not until psychologist Joy Paul Guilford developed a representation of social intelligence through various abilities in the domain of behavioral operations (i.e., all behavioral-psychological acts) in the late 1960s that interest in the "essence" of the construct resurfaced. But the concept of social intelligence was defined differently, through a number of terms, such as behavioral or social cognition (by Maureen O'Sullivan), social competence (by Martin Ford and Marie Tisak), intra- and interpersonal intelligence (by Howard Gardner), practical intelligence (by Robert Sternberg), emotional intelligence, and dimensions of personality (by Hans Eysenck). Although in modern day there is great interest in the concept of social intelligence, there is no consensus definition and no unity with regard to assessment approaches. Another source of support for the importance of the concept of social intelligence is associated with implicit studies of intelligence. In this research, people are typically asked to generate a list of traits relevant to intelligent behavior. Of interest is the observation that in the majority of all such studies, the dimension of social competence inevitably comes up as an important component of intelligent behavior.

In the late 1980s, psychologists John Kihlstrom and Nancy Cantor systematized the literature on cognition, intelligence, and personality. Kihlstrom and Cantor derived the definition of social intelligence as a person's knowledge and expertise concerning oneself and the surrounding social world, and determinant of an individual's approach to solving problems of social life. They proposed to classify social knowledge into two categories: (1) declarative social knowledge including abstract concepts and specific memories, which can be subdivided into context-free semantic and context-dependent episodic memories; and (2) procedural knowledge including rules and skills (cognitive and motor), which are necessary for the translation of declarative knowledge into action. Examples of sets of declarative social knowledge are social concepts of personalities, situations and groups, and individuals' autobiographic memory. Examples of sets of procedural social knowledge are interpretive rules for understanding, processing, and representing social experience, such as establishing social causality; making inferences about other people's behaviors, emotions, and feelings; judging likeability; implying trust; inducing and deducing responsibility; managing cognitive dissonance; and formulating and testing social hypotheses. According to Cantor and Kihlstrom, social intelligence is evoked when a person is faced with the need to solve problems of social life, in particular when faced with life tasks, current concerns, or personal projects. These problems can either be formulated by people themselves or imposed on them from outside. Using this definition, social intelligence can be judged quantitatively (i.e., high or low) only through the eyes of the beholder, that is, from the point of view of the person whose life is in play.

Stephen Greenspan includes social intelligence, along with practical intelligence, in his model of adaptive intelligence. In turn, adaptive intelligence, together with physical competence and socioemotional adaptation, are dimensions of personal competence. This view of social intelligence implies that it consists of three components: (1) social sensitivity (captured in social role-taking and making social inferences); (2) social insight (manifested by comprehending social situations, generating social–psychological insights, and forming ethical and moral judgments); and (3) social communication (evoked in carrying out social communication and social problem solving). This conceptualization of intelligence is important in establishing levels of mental competencies. The main argument here is that mental retardation in human societies should be defined not only based on general levels of intelligence, but also on indicators of adaptive functioning, of which social intelligence is viewed to be a major portion.

In the late twentieth and early twenty-first centuries, work on social intelligence became closely linked to research on autism. It has been argued that one of the main deficits in autism and other disorders on the autism spectrum is a lack of proper development of social intelligence or expertise in dealing with people. This line of work on social intelligence is related to the "theory of mind," which typically refers to a specific cognitive capacity to understand that others have beliefs, desires, and intentions that are different from one's own.

Another line of research that uses the concept of social intelligence is linked to the work on artificial intelligence (AI), which is the capacity of a digital computer or computer-controlled robot device to perform tasks commonly associated with higher intellectual processes characteristic of humans, such as the ability to reason, discover meaning, generalize, and learn from past experience. The foundation of this link is in the realization that although computers can be programmed successfully to carry out effectively and proficiently some complex analytical tasks (e.g., simulating human capabilities for problem solving), there are still no computer systems that match human flexibility in navigating the breadth of tasks encountered in everyday life. Through its connection with AI, social intelligence is also studied in game theory (i.e., the investigation and modeling of decision-making by multiple players attempting to maximize their return), action selection (i.e., the

investigation and modeling of performing a choice between multiple parallel, competing, conflicting and overlapping goals), swarm intelligence paradigm (i.e., the investigation and modeling of complex emergent intelligent networks), and many other fields of applied mathematics, computer science, economics, and evolution.

SEE ALSO *Cognition; Computers: Science and Society; Game Theory; Intelligence; Multiple Intelligences Theory; Personality; Theory of Mind*

BIBLIOGRAPHY

Baron-Cohen, Simon. 1995. *Mindblindness: An Essay on Autism and Theory of Mind.* Cambridge, MA: MIT Press.

Gardner, Howard. 1993. *Multiple Intelligences: The Theory in Practice.* New York: Basic Books.

Goleman, Daniel. 1995. *Emotional Intelligence.* New York: Bantam.

Greenspan, Stanley I. 1997. *The Growth of the Mind: And the Endangered Origins of Intelligence.* New York: Addison-Wesley.

Kihlstrom, John, and Nancy Canton. 2000. Social Intelligence. In *Handbook of Intelligence*, ed. Robert J. Sternberg. New York: Cambridge University Press.

Salovey, P., and J. D. Mayer. 1990. Emotional Intelligence. *Imagination, Cognition, and Personality* 9: 185–211.

Sternberg, Robert J. 1996. *Successful Intelligence: How Practical and Creative Intelligence Determine Success in Life.* New York: Simon & Schuster.

Thorndike, Edward L. 1920. Intelligence and Its Use. *Harper's Magazine*, 140: 227–235.

Elena L. Grigorenko

INTELLIGENT DESIGN
SEE *Creationism.*

INTERACTIONISM
SEE *Role Theory.*

INTERACTIONISM, SYMBOLIC

Symbolic interactionism is centrally but not exclusively concerned with the interpretive study of urban life. The American sociologist Herbert Blumer coined the term *symbolic interactionism* in 1937, initially using it to refer to the study of the symbols and meanings that operate within specific social groups. He also emphasized the importance of the ideas of Charles Horton Cooley. Thirty-two years later Blumer published *Symbolic Interaction*, a book that clarifies the central ideas of the perspective, emphasizes that the origins of the approach are found in George Herbert Mead's work (rather than in Cooley's), and advocates the use of an eclectic set of qualitative methods without completely ruling out quantification. Blumer's interpretation of and extension to Mead's work also connected symbolic interactionism to the empirical interests of the Chicago school of sociology, the first major body of works specializing in urban sociology that arose during the 1920s and 1930s.

Symbolic interactionism has also retained its initial connection to the Progressive politics of the early-twentieth-century United States that were favored by many of the sociologists in Chicago during this time. Blumer's 1969 formulation of symbolic interactionism stresses three premises and six root images. The three premises are: (1) "human beings act toward things on the basis of the meanings that the things have for them"; (2) meanings are derived from social interaction and group life; and (3) "these meanings are handled in, and modified through, an interpretive process used by the person in dealing with the things he [or she] encounters" (1969, p. 2). The six root images stress that social life is a group activity that is structured by layers of meaning. These meanings are incorporated into any group's understanding of physical, social, and abstract objects. Group members initially learn these meanings through childhood socialization processes and, over time, each group member develops a sense of self through both role taking and the internalization of the group into his or her own identity. This activity is not a mechanical process: People remake their social worlds collaboratively and Blumer stressed that symbolic interactionists must be aware of the fact that although social interaction is regulated, routinized, and therefore stable, it is not fixed.

Blumer believed that symbolic interactionism was an alternative to three rival approaches: mainstream sociological research with its emphasis on quantification and variable analysis; the structural functionalism of Talcott Parsons; and psychoanalysis. Contemporary sociologists, notably Gary Alan Fine in his 1993 work and David Maines in 2001, argue that the symbolic interactionist perspective has been incorporated into mainstream sociology. However, according to Maines, this incorporation is not widely acknowledged and has therefore produced a fault line that runs through the discipline. Fine argued that the contemporary relationship between symbolic interactionism and contemporary sociology is unclear because symbolic interactionism has simultaneously been "fragmented, expanded, incorporated, and adopted" by sociologists of very different persuasions. In Fine's view,

symbolic interactionists themselves have become "intellectually promiscuous" (1993, p. 64).

In 1954 Manford Kuhn and his associates quantified traditional interactionist concerns, thus paving the way for contemporary quantitative studies of self and identity, notably by Peter Burke and Sheldon Stryker, both in 1980. Symbolic interactionists have also explored theoretical intersections, not only to structural functionalism and psychoanalysis, but also to semiotics, feminism, poststructuralism, and other traditions of thought. The journal *Symbolic Interaction* is a major resource for those interested in this perspective.

SEE ALSO *Blumer, Herbert; Groups; Mead, George Herbert; Parsons, Talcott; Sociology*

BIBLIOGRAPHY

Blumer, Herbert. 1937. Social Psychology. In *Man and Society*. Ed. Emerson Schmidt. New York: Prentice Hall.

Blumer, Herbert. 1969. *Symbolic Interactionism*. Englewood Cliffs, NJ: Prentice Hall.

Burke, Peter. 1980. The Self: Measurement Implications from a Symbolic Interactionist Perspective. *Social Psychology Quarterly* 43: 18–29.

Denzin, Norman. 1992. *Symbolic Interactionism and Cultural Studies*. Oxford: Blackwell.

Fine, Gary Alan. 1993. The Sad Demise, Mysterious Disappearance and Glorious Triumph of Symbolic Interactionism. *Annual Review of Sociology* 19: 61–87.

Kuhn, Manford, and T. McPartland. 1954. An Empirical Investigation of Self-Attitudes. *American Sociological Review* 19: 68–77.

Maines, David. 2001. *The Faultline of Consciousness: A View of Interactionism in Sociology*. New York: Aldine de Gruyter.

Manning, Philip. 2005. *Freud and American Sociology*. Cambridge, U.K.: Polity Press.

Stryker, Sheldon. 1980. *Symbolic Interactionism: A Social Structural Version*. Reading, MA: Cummings.

Turner, Jonathan. 1974. Parsons as a Symbolic Interactionist: A Comparison of Action and Interaction Theory. *Sociological Inquiry* 4: 283–294.

Wiley, Norbert. 1994. *The Semiotic Self*. Chicago: University of Chicago Press.

Philip Manning

INTERDISCIPLINARY RESEARCH

SEE *Research, Trans-disciplinary.*

INTEREST, NATURAL RATE OF

Economists frequently refer to the interest rate the economy will tend toward under an equilibrium with price stability as the "natural" rate of interest. This equilibrium occurs in the long run, after any existing business cycles have played out. The natural rate of interest surfaced more than a century ago in the work of Swedish economist Knut Wicksell (1851–1926), though its prominence in mainstream economic thought has waxed and waned at different periods in time. Since the 1970s, the natural rate has taken a more central role in the study of monetary economics and is seen as one of the key ingredients in determining monetary policy.

One way to think about the natural rate of interest comes from the Keynesian IS-LM model of the macroeconomy. In this model, the interest rate adjusts to equate savings and borrowing decisions across the entire economy. Savings is determined by the level of output and there exists a rate of interest that clears the savings market for every level of output. The natural rate of interest is the interest rate where output is equal to potential output, with potential output defined as the level that results under full employment.

Figure 1 shows that the natural rate of interest is determined by the intersection of potential output and the IS curve. At the intersection, real GDP (gross domestic product) equals potential GDP, and the real interest rate equals the natural rate of interest. The IS curve represents all interest rate and output combinations that clear the savings market. This curve shows that output decreases as the real interest rate rises. This is due to the negative relationship between investment, a major component in aggregate demand, and the real rate of interest.

Yet another, more modern way of describing the natural rate of interest comes from the neoclassical growth model originally outlined in the works of Frank Ramsey (1903–1930), David Cass, and Tjalling Koopmans (1910–1985). In this model, households choose investment and consumption through time in order to maximize lifetime utility. The natural rate of interest in this model can be thought of as the rate that clears the capital market when the economy is growing at its natural steady rate. This rate turns out to depend inversely on the amount by which households value future consumption. If households value future consumption relatively less, then the natural rate of interest will be higher in order to compensate households that save and therefore give up current consumption in favor of future consumption.

In the United States and many other countries, the short-term interest rate is the primary monetary policy instrument. In particular, U.S. central bankers use the federal funds rate, the rate at which banks borrow from

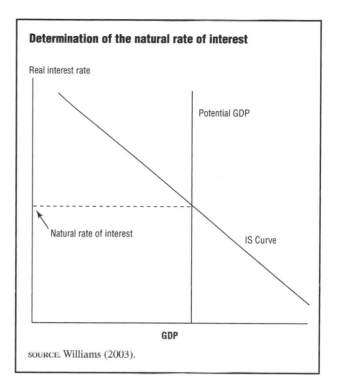

Figure 1

each other, as a tool to move interest rates and therefore the economy. As the main goals of monetary policy include price stability and output stabilization, the natural rate of interest provides an obvious benchmark for interest rate targeting. By setting the federal funds rate equal to the natural rate plus an inflation target (which could be zero), a bank is essentially trying to achieve the outcome resulting under an ideal economy. Interest rates above the natural rate tend to lower inflation, while rates below are expected to increase inflation.

Interestingly, John Maynard Keynes (1883–1946) ultimately objected to the idea of a natural rate of interest. He believed that this rate depended on the level of employment in the economy. Thus, there were several possible natural rates of interest, each associated with a different level of unemployment. Keynes preferred this idea of a "neutral rate of interest," which describes the unique interest rate that equates savings and investment at full employment.

MEASURING THE NATURAL RATE

One of the major drawbacks in using the natural rate of interest is the inability to accurately observe or calculate it. Since the natural rate of interest can change due to persistent changes in aggregate supply or demand or even changes in the projections of federal government budget deficits, it is often hard to pin down. In addition, changes in potential GDP can affect the natural rate of interest. Thus, measuring the natural rate of interest is not straightforward, and estimation techniques must be used. If the natural rate were actually constant over time, it could be estimated by averaging past real interest rates. Various methods have been implemented to account for the changing nature of the natural rate of interest.

Some methods involve weighting the data on past real interest rates differently. For example, one simple way would be to compute averages of past values of the interest rate while putting more weight on more recent data. Despite the differential weighting, this simple method does not work well during periods of large increases or decreases in inflation—when the real interest deviates substantially from the natural rate.

More sophisticated economic models have been used to measure the natural rate of interest. These include estimating the location of the slope of the IS curve and potential output to obtain estimates of interest rates. An important statistical technique known as the Kalman filter is used in some economic models to estimate the natural rate of interest. It works by adjusting the estimate of the natural rate based on how far off the model's prediction of output is from actual output. If actual output is higher than the prediction from the model, one possible explanation is that monetary policy was more expansionary than expected, which implies that the difference between the real federal funds rate and the natural rate of interest is more negative than expected. The estimate of the natural rate then increases by an amount proportional to the prediction error. This method allows for changes in the natural rate. The estimate of the natural rate by Thomas Laubach and John C. Williams (2003) using the Kalman filter technique was 3 percent in 2002, which is not far from the average of the historical federal funds rates. However, the estimate has varied from 1 percent in the 1990s to over 5 percent in the 1960s.

Despite its intuitive appeal, monetary policy analysis involving the natural rate of interest has serious drawbacks. There is no single agreed-upon method of estimating the natural rate, and estimates can be sensitive to the statistical method used to measure it. Nonetheless, the natural rate of interest is still an important concept for evaluating monetary policy, and central banks continue to devote attention to developing and improving estimation strategies.

SEE ALSO *Interest Rates; IS-LM Model; Neoclassical Growth Model; Policy, Monetary*

BIBLIOGRAPHY

Cass, David. 1965. Optimum Growth in an Aggregative Model of Capital Accumulation. *Review of Economic Studies* 32: 233–240.

Keynes, John Maynard. 1936. *The General Theory of Employment, Interest and Money.* London: Macmillan.

Koopmans, Tjalling C. 1965. On the Concept of Optimal Economic Growth. In *The Econometric Approach to Development Planning,* 225–300. Amsterdam: Elsevier.

Laubach, Thomas, and John C. Williams. 2003. Measuring the Natural Rate of Interest. *The Review of Economics and Statistics* 85 (4): 1063–1070.

Ramsey, Frank. 1928. A Mathematical Theory of Saving. *Economic Journal* 38: 543–559.

Wicksell, Knut. [1898] 1936. *Interest and Prices (Geldzins and Güterpreise): A Study of the Causes Regulating the Value of Money.* Trans. R. F. Kahn. London: Macmillan.

Williams, John C. 2003. The Natural Rate of Interest. *Federal Reserve Bank of San Francisco Economic Letter,* 2003–2032.

Betty T. Tao

INTEREST, NEUTRAL RATE OF

The *neutral rate of interest* is, in modern parlance, the short-term interest rate that minimizes the gap between the actual and the potential output of the economy while keeping inflation close to zero. At that interest-rate level money is considered to be neutral in the sense that monetary policy does not exert any distinct influence on economic activity other than fulfilling its primary tasks of preserving a stable value of money and safeguarding the financial system.

The concept of the neutral rate of interest provides a benchmark for modern central banking in accordance with the core model of the new neoclassical synthesis, the mainstream framework for macroeconomic policy analysis that has replaced the IS-LM model. The new synthesis is based on the concept of a natural rate of output, which is the potential output that would be realized in an equilibrium with flexible wages and prices. The corresponding natural rate of interest keeps the output gap at a minimum. In an environment with sticky wages and prices this can be achieved only if inflation is minimized, such that the stickiness does not matter. Hence the term natural rate of interest is often used as synonymous with the neutral rate. Michael Woodford's key contribution to the new synthesis, his *Interest and Prices* (2003), is a prominent example (though it has few explicit references to neutrality).

However, caveats and objections have been raised, both to defining the neutral rate of interest in terms of inflation and output gap minimization, and to equating the neutral rate with the natural rate. The most relevant objections can be traced back to the very origin of neutral-rate concepts in Knut Wicksell's *Interest and Prices.*

There is a certain rate of interest on loans which is neutral in respect to commodity prices, and tends neither to raise nor to lower them. This is necessarily the same as the rate of interest which would be determined by supply and demand if no use were made of money and all lending were effected in the form of real capital goods. It comes to much the same thing to describe it as the current value of the natural rate of interest on capital (1898, p. 102).

Wicksell's definition of neutral and natural rates of interest comprises three characteristics: price-level stability, capital market equilibrium, and the correspondence of barter lending to monetary equilibrium. The first characteristic implies zero inflation. The second characteristic requires that real investment (demand) equals saving (supply). The third characteristic is the claim that credit relations in monetary economies can be studied as if they were credit relations in economies where transactions are made in kind (*in natura*, hence the expression "natural rate"). A fourth characteristic, also contained in Wicksell's *Interest and Prices*, is the proposition that market systems tend to gravitate toward the natural rate of interest. As the representative monetary rate of interest converges on the natural rate, it becomes neutral with respect to the level and structure of real economic activity. This proposition is at the core of postulates of the (long-run) neutrality of money and has become a defining criterion for modern natural-rate concepts (such as the natural rate of unemployment).

In the early 1930s two followers of Wicksell, Erik Lindahl and Gunnar Myrdal, demonstrated that, in nonstationary monetary economies with more than one good, the expected rate of return on real investment cannot be determined independently of the monetary loan rate of interest. Hence they rejected the third characteristic of Wicksell's definition. Lindahl, Myrdal, and August Friedrich Hayek also argued that the absence of inflation does not necessarily imply that the underlying rate of interest is neutral. Interest-rate gaps, that is, discrepancies between loan rates and the rates of return to real investment, could lead to investment activities that change the capital stock, and hence the structure and level of the production, in such a way that the price level remains unchanged. Conversely, as Lindahl pointed out, a "neutral rate of interest does not necessarily imply an unchanged price level, but rather such a development of prices as is in accordance with the expectations of the public" (1930, p. 252). Wicksell's first characteristic of the neutral rate and key ingredient of its modern definition was thus put into doubt. On the base of all these arguments, Lindahl and Myrdal (though not Hayek) refuted Wicksell's fourth characteristic, the gravitational force of the natural rate. They argued that the equilibrium rate of return to real

investment is influenced by past monetary policy through the latter's effect on market rates of interest and capital valuation. Thus money is not automatically neutral.

The only characteristic of Wicksell's neutral-rate concept that survived the scrutiny of Lindahl and Myrdal was the criterion of capital market equilibrium in the sense of planned investment equalling planned saving. Even this criterion came under attack when the English economist John Maynard Keynes published his *The General Theory of Employment, Interest and Money* (1936). In Keynes' system, as in the conventional IS-LM framework that was subsequently developed from it, the market rate of interest does not coordinate investment with saving ex ante, but saving adjusts to investment ex post, through the latter's multiplier effect on income. Saving thus equals investment at different levels of interest and income, and Keynes concluded that there is no unique "natural" or equilibrium rate of interest. The only rate of interest that is "unique and significant ... must be the rate which we might term the neutral rate of interest, namely, the natural rate ... which is consistent with full employment" (1936, p. 243). More strictly defined, the neutral rate of the interest is the rate that "prevails in equilibrium when output and employment are such that the elasticity of employment as a whole is zero" (p. 243). Whether a zero elasticity of employment is identical with potential output, and whether the latter can be described by the natural rate of unemployment has been a matter of much dispute ever since the debates about the Phillips Curve, the suggestion of a trade-off between inflation and unemployment, started in the 1960s. That the old caveats concerning the neutral rate of interest are ignored in its modern definitions is not necessarily a sign of scientific progress. It is largely due to a shift toward models of intertemporal general equilibrium in terms of continuous optimization of representative agents. Such modelling strategies simply have no room for the problems in the coordination of investment and saving decisions that were at the heart of older debates about the neutral rate of interest.

SEE ALSO *Employment; Full Employment; Inflation; Interest, Natural Rate of; Interest, Own Rate of; Interest Rates; Involuntary Unemployment; Keynes, John Maynard; Phillips Curve; Unemployment*

BIBLIOGRAPHY

Hayek, Friedrich A. 1931. *Prices and Production.* London: Routledge, Kegan & Paul.

Keynes, John. 1936. *The General Theory of Employment, Interest and Money.* London: Macmillan.

Lindahl, Erik. 1930. *Studies in the Theory of Money and Capital.* Trans. Tor Ferholm. London: Allen & Unwin, 1939.

Myrdal, Gunnar. 1931. *Monetary Equilibrium*. Trans. R.B. Bryce and N. Stolper. London: William Hodge & Company, 1939.

Wicksell, Knut. 1898. *Interest and Prices: A Study of the Causes Regulating the Value of Money*. Trans. Richard F. Kahn. London: Macmillan, 1936.

Woodford, Michael. 2003. *Interest and Prices: Foundations of a Theory of Monetary Policy*. Princeton, NJ: Princeton University Press.

Hans-Michael Trautwein

INTEREST, OWN RATE OF

The concept of own rates of interest can be traced back to Irving Fisher's *Appreciation and Interest* (1896, pp. 8ff.). It was then revived and extended by Piero Sraffa (1932) to the determination of "commodity rates of interest" on all durable assets in his critique of Friedrich August Hayek's *Prices and Production* (1931), and subsequently taken up by John Maynard Keynes in chapter 17, "The Essential Properties of Interest and Money," in his *General Theory of Employment, Interest and Money* (1936). There Keynes used the concept to demonstrate that the rate of interest on money plays a crucial role in setting a limit to production below full employment.

Keynes used Sraffa's notion that for every durable commodity there is a rate of interest for it in terms of itself, as, for example, a cotton rate of interest or a wheat rate of interest. Three components enter into the own-rate of interest of assets: a physical yield or output q, a carrying cost c, and its liquidity-premium l. Thus $q_i - c_i + l_i$ is the own-rate of interest ρ_i of any commodity i, with q, c, and l measured in terms of itself as the standard. These commodity rates of interest may differ between commodities, just as interest rates are likely to differ between different currency areas. For purposes of comparison, these commodity rates must be converted into a common standard of value (*numéraire*), usually money. Furthermore, one has to consider the expected rate of appreciation or depreciation of the price of a commodity $\delta_{i,t}$ in terms of money, determined on spot and forward markets. If, for example, the spot price of 100 quarters of wheat is p_t, the forward price in θ periods $p_{t+\theta}$, and the money rate of interest (the own-rate of interest on money) for θ periods $i_{t,\theta}$, then the own rate of interest of wheat between t and $t + \theta$ equals $\rho_{t,\theta} = \dfrac{(1+i_{t,\theta})p_t - p_{t+\theta}}{p_{t+\theta}} = \dfrac{(1+i_{t,\theta})p_t}{p_{t+\theta}} - 1$.

If the spot price of wheat is £100, the forward price for delivery in a year hence £107, and the money rate of interest 5 percent per annum, then the wheat rate of interest is about −2 percent per year (see Keynes 1936, p. 223).

According to Keynes, the own rate of interest of any commodity i in terms of money thus can be written as

$$i_{i,t} = \rho_i + \delta_i = q_i - c_i + l_i + \delta_i + \rho_i\delta_i.$$

The difference between the wheat rate of interest and the money rate of interest indicates that the market for wheat is not in long-run equilibrium. Although at any moment in time there might exist as many "natural" rates of interest as there are commodities, they would not be "equilibrium" rates, as has been emphasized by Sraffa in his critique of Hayek. It is only in equilibrium that the spot and the (discounted) forward price for all commodities coincide and that "all the 'natural' or commodity rates are equal to one another, and to the money rate" (Sraffa 1932, p. 50), which is regarded by Sraffa as the normal rate of interest for the economy as the whole.

The latter concept has no meaning in modern general equilibrium theory of the Arrow-Debreu type, in which a complete break with the classical concern with long-period equilibria has taken place. Commodities are specified not only in physical terms, but also with regard to their date of availability. The set of intertemporal equilibrium prices consists of prices paid on current markets for commodities to be traded at a future date. Although there is some technical similarity in the calculation of own rates of interest with a multiplicity of these rates in intertemporal equilibrium, there remains the crucial difference that the concept of a long-run equilibrium, in which all rates of interest are equal in terms of the standard of value and equal to the own rate of interest of that numéraire, is missing.

In contrast to modern general equilibrium theory, there are no complete future markets in Keynes's economics. In his *General Theory* Keynes came to the conclusion that in the long run, the economy may end up in an unemployment equilibrium, and that, in absence of rigid money wages, it is the level of the money rate of interest that rules the roost and creates a barrier to full employment. The reasons are to be found in three essential properties of money: (1) (near) zero elasticity of production, which makes it scarce because it cannot be produced privately; (2) (near) zero elasticity of substitution, a potential bottomless sink for purchasing power when money demand increases; and (3) a yield of nil with negligible carrying costs while comprising a substantial liquidity premium. This opens the way for the "liquidity trap" as the decisive cause for the money rate of interest to fall inadequately. Keynes used Sraffa's ideas in his analysis of the determination of the volume of investment. However, it is doubtful whether Keynes fully understood Sraffa's arguments (Kurz 2000). This is reflected in Keynes's ambiguous use of a short-run rate of interest and a long-run equilibrium rate of interest, and in the fact that his schedule of marginal efficiency of capital cannot be independent of the rate of interest (Barens and Caspari 1997).

SEE ALSO *Arrow-Debreu Model; Carrying Cost; General Equilibrium; Keynes, John Maynard; Liquidity; Liquidity Premium; Liquidity Trap; Long Period Analysis; Sraffa, Piero; Yield*

BIBLIOGRAPHY

Barens, Ingo, and Volker Caspari. 1997. Own-Rates of Interest and Their Relevance for the Existence of Underemployment Equilibrium Positions. In *A "Second Edition" of the General Theory*, Vol. 1, eds. Geoffrey C. Harcourt and Peter A. Riach, 283–303. London and New York: Routledge.

Fisher, Irving. 1896. *Appreciation and Interest*. New York: Macmillan.

Hayek, Friedrich A. 1931. *Prices and Production*. London: Routledge and Kegan Paul.

Keynes, John Maynard. 1936. *The General Theory of Employment, Interest and Money*. London: Macmillan.

Kurz, Heinz D. 2000. The Hayek-Keynes-Sraffa Controversy Reconsidered. In *Critical Essays on Piero Sraffa's Legacy in Economics*, ed. Heinz D. Kurz, 257–301. Cambridge, U.K.: Cambridge University Press.

Sraffa, Piero. 1932. Dr. Hayek on Money and Capital. *Economic Journal* 42 (1): 42–53.

Harald Hagemann

INTEREST, PUBLIC

SEE *Public Interest.*

INTEREST, REAL RATE OF

The *real rate of interest* is the money rate adjusted for the loss, due to inflation, of the purchasing power of the amount lent. In short, the real rate of interest is equal to the money rate of interest less the rate of inflation. This statement is often called the *Fisher equation* after Irving Fisher (1867–1947), an American economist who developed it in a series of publications in the first thirty years of the twentieth century. Looking back at interest rates and inflation at the end of a period, it is possible to use statistics to calculate how the real rate of interest behaved over that period. However, what is of major interest in economics is what decision makers think real interest is going to be in the future period relevant to the decision being made. Thus, in economics, as opposed to economic history, the size of the real rate of interest is something people think will hold in the future. It cannot be measured precisely. However, if at the end of a period the Fisher equation has not held, either the inflation rate was

not what was expected at the beginning of the period or people did not fully take inflation into account and suffered, at least to some extent, from what is called *money illusion*. This latter view was the one held by Fisher himself. In his 1930 book *The Theory of Interest*, he argued that the relationship between the real rate of interest, the money rate, and inflation was a long-run relationship that only held when the rate of inflation did not change much over a long period. He thought that when the rate of inflation fluctuated, the rate of interest adjusted to some extent but not by enough to compensate fully, or even largely, for the changes in the rate of inflation; Fisher squarely blamed money illusion for this.

Although the real rate of interest is normally defined by the Fisher equation, it has a large role to play in economic theory apart from any relationship between inflation and interest rates. The dominant school in economics holds that the real rate of interest is the price that brings into equality the demand and supply of savings. The demand for savings comes partly from those who want to obtain income in the future either by investing in physical capital goods or by increasing their ability and skills. Demand also comes from those who wish to consume more now, relative to their income in the future. The supply of savings comes from those who wish to consume more in the future, relative to income, than now, those who are saving to buy a capital good in the future, and those who have borrowed in the past and are paying off loans. Overall, these various components of demand and supply depend on things that only change slowly, such as demographics, the rate of productivity change, institutions, and culture. When the underlying demand for savings equals the underlying supply of savings and there is no tendency for the rate of inflation to change, the real rate of interest is called the *equilibrium real rate of interest*. It is this rate that economists often have in mind when they are discussing real interest rates. It sums up for the community overall the degree to which future benefits and costs are discounted compared to those in the present. Depending on the context, this is called the *rate of time preference* or the *social discount rate*.

Modern economic theory assumes that money illusion is unimportant, that the economy moves quickly to a position of equilibrium, and that in equilibrium the real interest rate is stable. Taken together, these three propositions suggest that the real interest rate is less volatile than the money interest rate. However, empirical studies suggest that this is not the case and that, when the rate of inflation varies, the money interest rate adjusts less than it should if the above three propositions are correct. Given that it is the expected rate of inflation when decisions are made that is relevant, the key issue in these studies is how to measure expected inflation. Some studies use survey data. Others assume a variety of mechanisms by which peoples' expectations are formed and use statistical techniques to measure the expectations, determined from the past data that formed expectations. Generally these studies show that, assuming a relatively stable real interest rate, the Fisher equation does not hold. Various ingenious propositions have been put forward to explain this, but the weight of the evidence confirms Fisher's view that money illusion has a significant role to play in the operation of the economy.

The real rate of interest is an important concept in economic theory. However, because this theory largely ignores money illusion, its relevance to economic policy is greatly reduced.

SEE ALSO *Expectations; Fisher, Irving; Inflation; Interest, Natural Rate of; Interest Rates; Interest Rates, Nominal; Investment; Money; Money Illusion; Policy, Monetary*

BIBLIOGRAPHY

Fisher, Irving. 1930. *The Theory of Interest: As Determined by Impatience to Spend Income and Opportunity to Invest* (Pts. I and II). London: Macmillan.

Summers, Lawrence H. 1983. The Nonadjustment of Nominal Interest Rates: A Study of the Fisher Effect. In *Macroeconomics, Prices, and Quantities: Essays in Memory of Arthur M. Okun*, ed. James Tobin, 201–240. Washington, DC: Brookings Institution.

J. W. Nevile

INTEREST GROUPS AND INTERESTS

In every democratic society, a plethora of interest groups seeks to influence public policy. Groups representing businesses, consumers, environmental causes, and a wide range of other concerns flock in the halls of power. Interest groups can, on the one hand, be seen as contributing positively to democratic processes by allowing different parties to state their case before government. On the other hand, they may be described as unduly affecting public policy on behalf of special interests. No matter which side of this ambivalence is emphasized, the role of such groups must be of great concern to those interested in understanding politics. Among the topics attracting particular attention are the questions of how groups attract and maintain members and how groups influence public policy.

Interest groups are conventionally defined as organizations seeking to influence public policy. They are distinguished from political parties in that they do not seek election to public office. Apart from this common ground, there are different opinions as to exactly which organizations should be categorized as interest groups. Notably, some authors include individual businesses, government institutions, as well as other types of organizations that make policy-related appeals to government. Others restrict the term to membership organizations, but accept that group members might be individuals, firms, or even other interest groups. In an attempt to clear up this confusion, Grant Jordan and his collaborators (2004) have suggested reserving the terms *interest group* or *pressure group* for organizations with members, while letting the term *pressure participant* refer to the wider spectrum of politically active organizations.

In discussions of interest groups, it is often fruitful to distinguish between different types of groups. Various ways of subdividing the universe of interest groups have been suggested, but among the most persistently used is the distinction between *special interest groups* and *public interest groups*. Special interest groups or *sectional groups* represent specific sectors of society, while public interest groups act for various causes. The latter are also referred to with the terms *cause groups, idealistic groups*, and *citizen groups*. This category encompasses both groups working for specific short-term goals and groups acting for more general causes, such as environmental protection or human rights. Whereas sectional groups typically recruit their members within the sector they represent, public interest groups are at least theoretically open to anyone supportive of group goals.

The classical approach within the study of interest groups is *pluralism*. Writing in the 1950s and 1960s, authors such as David Truman (1913–2003) attached great importance to groups. Pluralists portray groups as competing for influence in a relatively open political system. While resources are not seen as equally distributed among groups, it is asserted that no group is able to be consistently dominant. According to pluralists, new groups will mobilize almost automatically, provided their interests are sufficiently threatened, and these groups will counteract the influence of existing groups. Even though pluralism has come under attack from many quarters, it remains an important frame of reference in the interest group literature.

Among the important blows to pluralism was E. E. Schattschneider's (1892–1971) ascertainment that: "The flaw in the pluralist heaven is that the heavenly chorus sings with a strong upper-class accent" (Schattschneider 1960, p. 35). Contrary to the pluralist notion of a fairly balanced group system, Schattschneider and the scholars following in his footsteps documented that the interest group system is heavily biased in favor of business interests. The most influential attack on pluralism directly targeted the assumption of automatic group mobilization. In *The Logic of Collective Action* (1965), the economist Mancur Olson (1932–1998) argued that rational self-interested individuals will not act to achieve their group interests. According to Olson, interest groups typically work to achieve public goods. It is in the nature of such goods that nonmembers cannot be excluded from consuming the good if the group is successful in providing it. If a business group is successful in obtaining business-friendly regulation of an industry, all firms in the industry will benefit. Furthermore, in large groups the contribution of one member does not make a difference in regard to whether a group will achieve its goals or not. Every potential member would therefore be better off by saving their membership dues than by joining the group. According to this logic, it is surprising that interest groups exist at all.

Following Olson's seminal work, much attention has been devoted to discussing how interest groups come into existence. Olson himself pointed out that interest groups might recruit members by offering selective incentives, such as cheap insurance or free magazines. Other authors have argued that groups offer their members a variety of benefits ranging from material goods over social relations to the good feelings arising from contributing to a cause one believes in. Further, the importance of entrepreneurs or patrons—private or governmental—investing in the creation of groups has been emphasized. Although numerous factors helping the creation and maintenance of groups have been identified, it is highly unlikely that the existing universe of interest groups reflects a perfect mobilization of all groups and concerns.

Once established, interest groups become active in influencing politics. In these efforts, they use different strategies. Groups can rely on *insider strategies*, where public decision makers are targeted directly, or they can engage in *outsider strategies*, where the media and citizen mobilizations are used to exert pressure on policymakers. In the U.S. literature, much effort has gone into studying the lobbying of Congress, whereas Europeans have focused more on the interaction between interest groups and the bureaucracy. Among other factors, this difference reflects cross-national variation in the importance of different lobbying activities. Apart from cross-national factors, the choice of strategy also depends on group type and on factors related to the issue at hand.

An important question in regard to interest groups is whether the political process can best be described as relatively open to different types of groups or as characterized by structured interaction by certain groups and public decision makers. In the United States, authors such as Theodore J. Lowi in *The End of Liberalism* (1969) pointed to the close interaction between interest groups and government agencies and the resulting accommodation of interest group demands—according to Lowi working to the detriment of liberal democracy. In Europe, many countries were even described as *corporatist*, indicating that the integration of interest groups into public decision making was a crucial element of the political system. Although stated in other terms, the literatures on iron triangles, policy subsystems, and policy communities share common ground with corporatism in emphasizing how policy processes are often much more structured and less open than the pluralists assumed. While this debate has attracted much scholarly attention, there is now widespread agreement that most societies exhibit both characteristics corresponding to the pluralist notion of competition between interest groups and more structured patterns of interaction between groups and government. The challenge is therefore to account for the causes and consequences of variation in the role of interest groups.

SEE ALSO *Associations, Voluntary; Campaigning; Collective Action; Free Rider; Lobbying; Organizations; Public Policy*

BIBLIOGRAPHY

Baumgartner, Frank R., and Beth L. Leech. 1998. *Basic Interests: The Importance of Groups in Politics and in Political Science.* Princeton, NJ: Princeton University Press.

Jordan, Grant, Darren Halpin, and William Maloney. 2004. Defining Interests: Disambiguation and the Need for New Distinctions? *British Journal of Politics and International Relations* 6 (2): 195–212.

Lowi, Theodore J. 1969. *The End of Liberalism: Ideology, Policy, and the Crisis of Public Authority.* New York: Norton.

Olson, Mancur. 1965. *The Logic of Collective Action: Public Goods and the Theory of Groups.* Cambridge, MA: Harvard University Press.

Schattschneider, E. E. 1960. *The Semisovereign People: A Realist's View of Democracy in America.* New York: Holt, Rinehart, and Winston.

Schmitter, Philippe. 1974. Still the Century of Corporatism? *Review of Politics* 36: 85–131.

Truman, David. 1951. *The Governmental Process: Political Interests and Public Opinion.* New York: Knopf.

Walker, Jack L., Jr. 1991. *Mobilizing Interest Groups in America: Patrons, Professions, and Social Movements.* Ann Arbor: University of Michigan Press.

Anne Binderkrantz

INTEREST RATES

In everyday language, *interest* is the payment, made by the borrower of a sum of money to the lender, that is in addition to the repayment of the amount borrowed. The *rate of interest* is the price of loans, a critical economic variable. However, its importance extends beyond economics. Payment of interest has been a major issue in ethics, and the Jewish, Christian, and Islamic religions have all had, at least for long periods of their history, outright prohibitions on demanding interest when making loans. The dominant nature of interest varies according to the culture of the society in which it is set. For example, loans made to people who are in need and face severe hardship if they cannot get a loan are an essentially different type of transaction from loans that are made to an entrepreneur to finance business operations that are confidently expected to be profitable. This entry will concentrate on the nature and role of interest in modern market economics.

In technical economic language, *interest* is a payment for the use of capital, with the *rate of interest* the price paid for this use. Except in some specialized contexts, interest is a financial variable paid for the use of financial capital or money. Economists often talk of the rate of interest. In practice there is not one rate of interest but many, and the form of the transaction can vary from the usual. For example, one way in which banks borrow is by selling bank bills, or a promise to pay the holder of the bill a stated amount at a stated date in future. The difference between the amount paid for a bank bill and the amount the bank pays back on maturity is the interest on the loan to the bank. Also, of course, interest rates can be on loans of any length of time. Loans from overnight to ten years are common, but some are indefinite, with no commitment ever to repay the money. In addition to the amount paid for the use of capital, interest rates often incorporate a risk premium to compensate the lender for bearing the risk that the capital may not be repaid promptly or at all. The risk of most national governments defaulting is practically zero, so the interest rate they pay can be taken as a measure of the pure interest part of an interest rate.

INTEREST AND PROFITS

Since the interest rate is a financial variable, one would expect that interest rates are determined by the demand for, and supply of, loans and other financial assets. However, at least since the work of Adam Smith (1723–1790) in the late eighteenth century, the dominant view among economists has been that interest rates will tend toward a figure determined by profits. In equilibrium—that is, in a situation where there is no tendency to change—the rate of interest is equal to the rate of profit on the use of new physical capital goods. Hence, despite disturbances caused by purely financial factors, interest rates are largely determined by nonfinancial or real factors.

The modern form of the theory underlying this process is based on the work of Swedish economist Knut Wicksell (1851–1926). In his pathbreaking book *Interest*

and Prices (1898), Wicksell was concerned with explaining trends in prices. Wicksell calls the interest rate fixed by financial markets the *money rate of interest*, and the interest rate determined by real factors the *natural rate of interest*. He starts with a situation in which the money rate is equal to the natural rate. Wicksell then assumes an increase in the natural rate due, say, to a new innovation increasing the productivity of capital goods. The money rate is assumed to remain unchanged. Since the new capital goods are more productive and the interest costs are unchanged, profits will increase, leading to an increased demand for new capital goods in the next period.

Like most other economists of his time, Wicksell thought that the economy was always more or less in a state where there was full employment of both labor and capital. Hence, an increased demand for new capital goods will raise their prices. The incomes of those supplying capital goods will increase, and they will spend more on consumer goods, raising the prices of consumer goods. The money rate of interest has not changed, so it is still profitable to borrow to cover any higher prices of inputs, and the whole process will continue until the banking system raises interest rates to the extent required to make the money rate equal to the natural rate. The reverse process occurs if the money rate is greater than the natural rate and causes falling prices. In both cases, equilibrium is only reached when the money rate of interest changes to be equal to the natural rate, which itself is equal to the profit rate on new capital goods.

This analysis of how a divergence between the natural and money rates of interest causes cumulative movements in prices can be adapted to explain changes in the rate of inflation from some rate widely accepted as normal. It can even include relaxation of the assumption of full employment, as long as any lapses are temporary and are automatically removed by the functioning of the economy. In this analysis, interest is the price that equates the supply of funds from net savings with the demand for funds for investment in new capital goods.

INTEREST AND MONEY

John Maynard Keynes's (1883–1946) enormously influential *General Theory of Employment, Interest, and Money* (1936), among other things, turned the focus of interest rate theory onto financial markets. In contrast to Wicksell's analysis, Keynes focused attention on why people want to hold money rather than other financial assets such as bonds. The reason for holding money is that it is completely liquid. One can use it immediately. Keynes listed three reasons for desiring liquidity. One is the *transaction motive*: to make easy both commercial and personal exchanges. Another is the *precautionary motive*: to have the ability to respond immediately to unforeseen future needs.

The last reason is the *speculative motive*: to try and make a profit by guessing or knowing the future better than the market as a whole. Keynes thought that the major influence on interest rates in the short run was that arising from speculation on the level of future interest rates.

Not surprisingly, given the institutional arrangements of his time, Keynes thought that the volume of money in a country was determined by the central bank. This supply of money, together with the demand for money, especially that resulting from liquidity preference, determined the rate of interest. Today, institutional arrangements are very different. The ability of financial markets to create money is determined by the demand for money, with external constraints much less important. Central banks now rely on more direct ways of influencing interest rates, mainly using changes in the interest rate they charge banks who borrow from them. Nevertheless, Keynes's emphasis on monetary factors and the allocation of assets remains important.

Fitting together the two theories by using monetary factors to explain interest rates in the short run and real influences to explain interest rates in the longer run does justice to neither theory. In both cases, the determination of the rate of interest is an integral part of the bigger whole. Keynesian economists deny the proposition that the economy trends strongly toward the full-employment position, which is a crucial part of the theory in the Wicksellian tradition. If the Keynesian view is correct and there can be continuing equilibrium at less than full employment, then causation will run more from interest rates determined in financial markets to real variables like output and capital productivity than the reverse. The different theories have very different implications for monetary policy.

INTEREST RATES AS A LINK WITH THE FUTURE

Irrespective of how it is determined, the interest rate has a crucial role to play in the allocation of new capital goods. Businesspeople will only buy new capital goods if the expected profit rate on those goods is equal to or greater than the rate of interest. The rate of interest sets the hurdle that determines which of the myriad ways in which new capital can be used are realized. Thus, the interest rate determines now what types of new capital goods there will be in the future, when the output these capital goods help to produce comes on the market.

So far this entry has not discussed the situation where the money borrowed is used to buy consumer goods, rather than capital goods. Here too the interest rate has a role to play in linking the present and the future. A person may borrow to increase current consumption because future income is expected to be greater than present income or future needs to be less than present needs. Alternatively, the borrower may give more weight to consumption in the present than to consumption in the future. The price of consuming more now is given by the interest rate. Generally, the higher the interest rate the less consumption is shifted from the future to the present, though the strength of the relationship may not be strong and for many individuals the desire to consume now may result in future consumption being discounted enough to outweigh any likely rate of interest.

Interest rates can also play a role in decisions about government expenditures and other policies, such as a tariff on imports of a particular commodity or the introduction of restrictions on logging. Cost-benefit analysis can be used to evaluate policy decisions, taking into account wider social criteria and not only narrow economic benefits and costs. There are many technical problems in estimating the various costs and benefits of a particular policy change. The one that is relevant here arises because many costs and benefits will occur in the future. In many cases, more of the costs occur in the near future compared to the benefits, so the choice of the interest rate used to discount future flows of costs and benefits has a major effect on the result. Some argue that the after-tax interest return on risk-free government bonds less the rate of inflation should be used in such analyses. Others argue that, because this is a market rate of interest, it incorporates a higher rate of discounting the future than is appropriate for a social discount rate.

MONETARY POLICY

The precise way monetary policy operates depends on the institutional arrangements of financial markets, but there is now widespread agreement that the immediate target of monetary policy is the level of interest rates. The dominant view among economists is that the underlying objective of monetary policy should be to contain inflation, often to keep it in a publicly announced target range. In Wicksellian terms, the objective is to keep the money rate close to the natural rate.

Orthodoxy also allows that, when employment is markedly below full employment, monetary policy can help hasten the return to full employment. Keynesian economists hold that, in the absence of policies to prevent it, a market economy can remain well below the full-employment level indefinitely. For them, monetary policy has a part to play in restoring full employment.

In countries with floating exchange rates, monetary policy may also be used to support the exchange rate. A freely floating exchange rate, where transactions are not constrained by any controls on capital transactions, is a very flexible price, responding quickly to changes in supply and demand. In the modern global economy, the vast majority of foreign exchange transactions are investments in financial markets where the returns are high. The return to investing foreign funds in a country is the rate of interest obtained in the country plus the expected appreciation of the country's currency in foreign exchange markets (or less any expected depreciation). Thus, other things being equal, a rise in interest rates will lead to a higher exchange rate or prevent or reduce a fall in exchange rates if depreciation is expected. There have been clear examples of countries raising interest rates to very high levels to prevent a disastrous fall in exchange rates. Behind the scenes, use of monetary policy to support the exchange rate may be more widespread.

In the traditional story, interest rate changes affect inflation and economic activity through their influence on investment in new capital goods. The implication is that this investment is made by businesses. In fact, an interest rate change usually has a stronger direct effect on residential construction by households. It may also affect credit card usage and other forms of household debt.

A second way a change in interest rates can influence the economy is its effect on bank assets. The value of existing financial assets goes down when interest rates rise. When the values of banks' assets fall, banks are less willing to lend, and a slight or a serious credit squeeze occurs. Many economists think that the availability of credit is more important than the level of the interest rate in transmitting the effects of changes in monetary policy.

The exchange rate also has a part to play in transmitting the effects of changes in the rate of interest. If interest rates rise, the value of a country's currency will rise on foreign exchange markets. This will make imports cheaper and reduce the return to exports. The low prices for imports will help restrain inflation, and the lower returns in exporting and import-competing industries will discourage investment in these industries.

The exchange rate also has a major influence on the efficacy of monetary policy, especially in the case of small countries with many economic links to the outside world. If the exchange rate is fixed and expected to stay fixed at its current value, monetary policy relies on capital controls to stop people borrowing in foreign countries. Consequently, monetary policy is usually not effective.

On the other hand, if a country has a freely floating exchange rate, problems arise if a major depreciation of the value of its currency is expected in financial markets. In this situation, monetary policy may have to ignore its usual goals and focus solely on supporting the exchange rate.

More generally, globalization has reduced the efficacy of monetary policy. For example, if rising interest rates reduce the availability of credit from domestic sources, this will be offset to some extent by the willingness of foreigners to lend. The biggest problem is probably the risk

that policy aimed at expanding economic activity by reducing interest rates may lead to expectations of a depreciation in the value of a country's currency. Some depreciation is usually helpful in these circumstances, but a large depreciation can have a serious impact, especially on the distribution of income. The desire to avoid such an impact may hamstring monetary policy in some circumstances. Nevertheless, the general view is that governments still have considerable freedom in domestic macroeconomic management, but since the efficacy of monetary policy has been reduced significantly, more reliance may have to be placed on other policies.

A different aspect of the operation of monetary policy has attracted considerable attention: its effect on the relationship between short-term and long-term interest rates. This relationship is usually called the *term structure* of interest rates or the *yield curve*. Central bank operations directly influence short-term interest rates. When the actions of the central bank raise short-term interest rates, longer-term rates may not rise much, since the rises at the short-term end of the market are often considered temporary and liable to be reversed when policy changes. Normally, interest rates rise as the term of the loan lengthens, probably due to increased uncertainty about the level of interest rates in the more distant future. Thus the yield curve slopes upward as the loan lengthens. For the reasons given above, tight monetary policy can flatten, or even invert, the yield curve. Many studies have documented a historical relationship linking a flat or inverted yield curve with a recession somewhat later. Interest has arisen in using the yield curve to predict the level of activity in the genuinely unknown future, but this is a much more difficult exercise.

SEE ALSO *Balance of Payments; Cambridge Capital Controversy; Central Banks; Cost-Benefit Analysis; Currency; Economics, Keynesian; Exchange Rates; Interest, Natural Rate of; Interest, Neutral Rate of; Interest, Own Rate of; Interest, Real Rate of; Interest Rates, Nominal; Keynes, John Maynard; Liquidity; Macroeconomics; Policy, Monetary; Profitability; Recession; Solow, Robert M.; Taylor, Lance; Yield Curve*

BIBLIOGRAPHY

Chick, Victoria. 1983. *Macroeconomics after Keynes: A Reconsideration of the General Theory* (chaps. 9–11). Oxford: Philip Allan.

Keynes, John Maynard. 1936. *The General Theory of Employment, Interest, and Money* (chaps. 13–15). London: Macmillan.

Kriesler, Peter, and J. W. Nevile. 2003. Macroeconomic Impacts of Globalization. In *Growth and Development in the Global*

Economy, ed. Harry Bloch, 173–189. Cheltenham, U.K.: Elgar.

Macfarlane, Ian, and Glenn Stevens. 1989. Overview: Monetary Policy and the Economy. In *Studies in Money and Credit*, eds. Ian Macfarlane and Glenn Stevens. Sydney: Reserve Bank of Australia.

Solow, Robert M. 1997. Is there a Core of Usable Macroeconomics We Should All Believe In? *American Economic Review* 87: 230–232.

Taylor, Lance. 2004. *Reconstructing Macroeconomics: Structuralist Proposals and Critiques of the Mainstream* (chaps. 3 and 10). Cambridge, MA: Harvard University Press.

Wicksell, Knut. [1898] 1936. *Interest and Prices (Geldzins and Güterpreise): A Study of the Causes Regulating the Value of Money*. Trans. R. F. Kahn. New York: A. M. Kelly.

J. W. Nevile

INTEREST RATES, NOMINAL

The *nominal rate of interest* is the rate (usually per year) stated as the interest rate paid. If a lender charges fees of one sort or another, then the nominal rate is less than the actual rate of interest, where *interest* is defined as the price of the loan. Also, when interest is paid more than once a year, the nominal rate is less than the actual rate of interest received. For example, if money is lent at 8 percent for a year with the interest paid quarterly, 2 percent of the amount lent will be paid each quarter. Sometimes, the interest is compounded, that is, not paid but added to the principal amount and interest paid on the interest. In this case, the actual rate of interest received is approximately 8.24 percent. However, even if the interest is paid quarterly, the lender has the use of the money received and could lend it to another borrower, so that effectively the rate of interest is the same as when interest is compounded.

In many circumstances, the greatest weakness in using the nominal rate of interest in decision making is that it does not take into account the loss of purchasing power due to inflation. Thus, if in the example above there is 3 percent inflation over the year, after allowing for the loss of purchasing power the lender only receives as interest 5.24 percent of the amount lent. This figure is known as the *real rate of interest* and the difference between it and the nominal rate is called the *inflation tax*. If the loan is to the government, the inflation tax is indeed a tax. If it is to a person or institution in the private sector, it equally represents a transfer of real income from the lender to the borrower. Moreover, even if those participating in financial markets took into account the inflation tax and the rate of interest adjusted accordingly, all of the interest that the lender would receive would be subject to income tax, although part of it is not income but compensation for the loss of the purchasing power of the amount lent. It is possible to overcome to some extent these deficiencies in the nominal rate of interest by indexing the amount lent to a measure of the inflation rate, but this is not usually done.

In economic theory, the rate of interest used is usually, either implicitly or explicitly, the real rate of interest. It is assumed that the inflation tax is quickly taken into account by borrowers and lenders, and that the nominal rate of interest rises and falls more or less equally with the rate of inflation. The amounts lent and borrowed and the real incomes of lenders and borrowers are not changed, at least if the effects of income taxes are ignored. The use of the nominal rate of interest in contracts in the real world is mainly considered by theorists in the context of the effects of the taxation system on peoples' decisions. However, in the world of this economic theory, not only does everything happen quickly, there is also perfect knowledge. In the real world, neither of these conditions holds. Empirical research shows that nominal rates do not usually adjust quickly and fully when the rate of inflation changes. Nominal rates do rise and fall with inflation to some extent, but often slowly and rarely to the full extent, at least for decades. Sometimes a rise in interest rates may even come before the rise in inflation rates. Raising interest rates is the principal weapon central banks use to combat inflation, which is usually their most important concern. The lags in monetary policy are notoriously long, and central banks sometimes make a preemptive rise in interest rates when they expect a rise in inflation. When the inflation rate is falling, the reverse could occur. However, because of their great concern about inflation, central banks are often quicker to raise rates than to reduce them.

The use of the nominal rate of interest causes inefficiencies in the operation of the economy by subsidizing borrowers at the expense of lenders. Its use in monetary policy may have undesirable consequences for the distribution of income. If the rate of inflation is stable and relatively low, these consequences are small, but the more these two conditions are broken, the more important are the consequences of using the nominal rate of interest.

SEE ALSO *Central Banks; Equity Markets; Federal Reserve System, U.S.; Inflation; Interest Rates; Interest, Real Rate of; Money; Policy, Monetary; Stock Exchanges*

BIBLIOGRAPHY

Eichenbaum, Martin. 1997. Some Thoughts on Practical Stabilization Policy. *American Economic Review* 87 (2): 236–239.

Fisher, Irving. 1930. *The Theory of Interest: As Determined by Impatience to Spend Income and Opportunity to Invest* (chap. 2). London: Macmillan.

J. W. Nevile

INTERGENERATIONAL TRANSMISSION

In the social sciences, *intergenerational transmission* refers to the transfer of economic or social status across generations. These cross-generational transfers occur through a variety of means, including the inheritance of occupational status, educational attainment, earnings, and wealth. In a society marked by significant levels of intergenerational transmission, there will be a corresponding persistence in economic and social stratification, and a child's socioeconomic outcome will be highly predictable. While immobility is not necessarily synonymous with inequality, intergenerational transmissions can generate unequal opportunities for children born into the society. Thus, the presence of intergenerational transmissions has strong implications for public policy, and many scholars have made efforts to improve the knowledge of how and to what extent these transfers exist.

RESEARCH ON LEVELS OF INTERGENERATIONAL MOBILITY

A central question in the analysis of social mobility and stratification is the extent to which advantages and disadvantages are passed from generation to generation. There is a rich history of scholarship attempting to quantify the level of intergenerational transmissions. In the 1950s sociologists improved both local data collection and mobility scales, and began to assemble intergenerational mobility tables to examine inflow and outflow percentages among different occupational classes. These classes were oftentimes highly aggregated, making it difficult to arrive at substantial conclusions on intergeneration mobility. Methodologies improved significantly in the 1960s, with the introduction of the socioeconomic index (SEI), a set of scores for occupational categories that allowed researchers to apply continuous data analysis techniques to occupational groups. In 1967 Peter Blau and Otis Dudley Duncan (creator of the SEI) published a groundbreaking work, *The American Occupational Structure*. In it, Blau and Duncan introduced their model of the "process of stratification," which allowed for the multivariate testing of direct and indirect effects (such as education and family background) on the earnings of children. In isolating the effects of various factors on a child's occupational status, Blau and Duncan found that the ratio of education effects to father's occupation effects on a son's current occupation is approximately 2.9 to 1, suggesting that achievement tends to be far more important than ascription in occupational outcomes.

Many scholars from around the world began to apply status-attainment models to their own intergenerational transmission analyses in the 1970s. As methodological improvements continued to be made, including the transition from multivariate linear regressions to loglinear models, a growing consensus developed that intergenerational mobility was at high levels in industrial countries. Specifically, in several Western European countries and the United States, researchers in the 1970s and 1980s consistently found intergenerational elasticity coefficients of 0.20 to 0.25 (which implies that only 20 to 25 percent of earnings gaps between groups would remain after one generation). In a 1988 address, American Economic Association president Gary Becker's comments reflected widespread sentiments at the time: "In every country with data that I have seen … earnings strongly regress to the mean[;] … low earnings as well as high earnings are not strongly transmitted from fathers to sons."

Yet the common belief that intergenerational mobility levels were high in industrial countries would change dramatically in the late 1980s and early 1990s. Regarding the United States, specifically, recent results for elasticity coefficients suggest that intergeneration mobility is more limited than previously thought. Gary Solon (1989) argued that the low correlation between a parent and child's socioeconomic indicators was due to selection biases and poor data measurement in previous studies. By using an entire dataset from the Panel Study on Income Dynamics (as opposed to the numerous data omissions typical of previous research) and using a five-year average of fathers' earnings data in lieu of the standard one-year data (to better represent lifetime earnings), Solon (1992) discovered that intergenerational elasticity coefficients rose significantly from 0.21 to 0.41. Using data from the National Longitudinal Survey, David Zimmerman (1992) arrived at a similar conclusion, and in combination these two studies provided compelling evidence that after methodological corrections, intergenerational mobility was more limited than previously thought.

Many scholars have since tried to replicate and expand on Solon and Zimmerman's original findings, and most have arrived at an intergeneration elasticity of about 0.4 or higher for the United States. Bhashkar Mazumder (2005) argued that the usage of five-year averages on fathers' earnings is flawed because data from such a short period of time can still reflect the effects of temporary shocks, which tend to be correlated in time. Mazumder is able to average fathers' earnings over sixteen years using social security earnings histories, and finds that the intergenerational elasticity between a father and a child's earnings is dramatically higher at 0.6. By contrast, researchers in other industrialized countries have typically found intergenerational elasticity coefficients that are less than in the United States. It is important, however, to note the difficulty of cross-country coefficient comparisons, because variations in earnings measures, age ranges, and other important study characteristics can be misinterpreted as differences between countries. Taking this issue into account, it appears that Sweden, Canada, and Finland enjoy more mobility than the United States, whereas Britain and France may be slightly worse. "American exceptionalism"—the perception that the United States is a uniquely mobile country—is largely discredited as a myth.

RESEARCH ON HOW INTERGENERATIONAL TRANSMISSIONS OCCUR

Scholarly evidence suggests that intergenerational mobility is highly limited, particularly in the United States, but why it is limited and how these outcomes are transmitted across generations is not clear. One theory that has garnered much attention is the human capital explanation, developed by Gary Becker and Nigel Tomes (1979, 1986). Becker and Tomes argue that the human capital acquired by children greatly affects their earnings outcomes, and that this capital is greatly affected by investment choices made by "utility-maximizing" families. Given a limited set of resources (time, income), parents will continue investing available resources in a child until their expected rate of return (determined by a child's ability and earnings potential) is no better than the market rate of return on investments (i.e., interest rates). Some implications of this theory are as follows: (1) Given unlimited resources, the levels of investment in a child will be determined by the child's ability; (2) the presence of credit constraints (in low-income families) will lead to reductions in child earnings and less intergenerational mobility. Several findings support the Becker-Tomes framework, most notably the evidence from cross-country comparisons suggesting that countries with high levels of educational subsidies (and therefore lower levels of credit constraints) tend to be associated with more intergenerational income mobility. However, as previously mentioned, cross-country comparisons are difficult given the variety of alternative explanations for differences, and it should be noted that the overall evidence on the human capital investment explanation is mixed.

A second economic explanation for the persistence in intergeneration immobility is the transfer of wealth in the form of inheritances. This explanation has received little attention due to the lack of panel data on respondents who have reached the age at which bequests are typically passed on. In studying the death records of wealthy Connecticut residents and their children, Paul Menchik (1979) found an intergenerational elasticity of 0.69 between child and parent wealth at death. This finding suggests that inheritances are highly important for the upper end of the income distribution. However, scholars have largely dismissed wealth as a major factor in overall intergenerational persistence of outcomes simply because most families do not pass along substantial inheritances. For example, according to Casey Mulligan (1997) only 2 to 4 percent of estates passed on from deaths in the United States between 1960 and 1995 were subject to inheritance taxes.

Several other avenues of intergenerational transfer deserve mention as alternative explanations of immobility, despite having received minimal scholarly attention. George Borjas (1992) alludes to the possibility of "neighborhood effects" in his assessment of the impact of parent and ethnic group successes on the wage rates and occupational statuses of first- and second-generation Americans (excluding African Americans and Native Americans). His results suggest that ethnic group effects are at least as high as parent effects on the economic successes of these immigrant children. While Borjas does not attempt to explain what underlies these group effects, several possibilities exist, including discrimination, cultural effects on behavior and personality, and unequal access to information.

If discrimination is in fact a significant explanation for intergenerational immobility, this poses a considerable challenge to a society's claim to be a meritocracy. Indeed, scholarship since *The American Occupational Structure* has acknowledged the unique difficulties faced by African Americans in achieving economic and social mobility. Using data from the Panel Study on Income Dynamics, Tom Hertz (2005) finds a 25 to 30 percent difference in income between the adult income of blacks and whites who grew up in households with identical long-run average incomes, even when parental levels of education were taken into account. But is this due to discrimination, or other potentially confounding factors? For example, Dalton Conley (1999) asserts that it is not race that matters in the intergenerational transmission of poverty, but rather parental assets or the class status that is typically associated with race in America. Alternatively, Thomas Sowell (1981) argues that cultural deficiencies, not market-based discrimination, explain intergroup differences in economic success. By contrast, William Darity et al. (2002) have provided some evidence that despite sharing cultural backgrounds, black Latinos suffer discriminatory wage deficiencies relative to other Latinos, indicating that "color" matters. Overall, controversy continues over the interpretation of racial and ethnic differences. Further analysis is required to determine the extent to which a "legacy of race" is reflected in economic outcomes.

While the evidence is not definitive, research suggests that levels of economic mobility across generations are low, especially in the United States. Explanations for this persistence are inconclusive, although several possibilities, including human capital, wealth, group effects, and discrimination, have received some attention. Samuel Bowles and Herbert Gintis (2002) attempt to provide a comparison of some possible causal channels of intergenerational status transmissions in the United States, and conclude that wealth, race, and schooling are important, whereas IQ and genetics are not. Though the authors acknowledge that much of the transmission process remains unclear (at least two-fifths is still unexplained in their work), their analysis serves as a model for future research. Experts hope that continued efforts in this direction will result in a better sense of how intergenerational transmissions occur, and perhaps how social inequality can be rectified.

SEE ALSO *Achievement Gap, Racial; Discrimination; Human Capital; Inheritance*

BIBLIOGRAPHY

Becker, Gary S. 1988. Family Economics and Macro Behavior. *American Economic Review* 78 (1): 1–13.

Becker, Gary S., and Nigel Tomes. 1986. Human Capital and the Rise and Fall of Families. *Journal of Labor Economics* 4 (3): S1–S39.

Blau, Peter M., and Otis D. Duncan. 1967. *The American Occupational Structure.* New York: Wiley.

Borjas, George. 1992. Ethnic Capital and Intergenerational Mobility. *The Quarterly Journal of Economics* 107 (1): 123–150.

Bowles, Samuel, and Herbert Gintis. 2002. The Inheritance of Inequality. *Journal of Economic Perspectives* 16 (3): 3–30.

Conley, Dalton. 1999. *Being Black, Living in the Red: Race, Wealth, and Social Policy in America.* Berkeley: University of California Press.

Darity, William A., Darrick Hamilton, and Jason Dietrich. 2002. Passing on Blackness: Latinos, Race and Labor Market Outcomes. *Applied Economics Letters* 9 (13): 847–853.

Ganzeboom, Harry B. G., Donald J. Treiman, and Wout C. Ultee. 1991. Comparative Intergenerational Stratification Research: Three Generations and Beyond. *Annual Review of Sociology* 17: 277–302.

Hertz, Tom. 2005. Rags, Riches, and Race: The Intergenerational Economic Mobility of Black and White Families in the United States. In *Unequal Chances: Family Background and Economic Success*, ed. Samuel Bowles, Herbert Gintis, and Melissa Osborne Groves, 165–191. New York: Russell Sage Foundation; Princeton, NJ: Princeton University Press.

Mazumder, Bhashkar. 2005. Fortunate Sons: New Estimates of Intergenerational Mobility in the United States Using Social Security Earnings Data. *Review of Economics and Statistics* 82 (2): 235–255.

Menchik, Paul. 1979. Inter-Generational Transmission of Inequality: An Empirical Study of Wealth Mobility. *Economica* 46: 349–362.

Mulligan, Casey. 1997. *Parental Priorities and Economic Inequality.* Chicago: University of Chicago Press.

Solon, Gary. 1989. Biases in the Estimation of Intergeneration Earnings Correlations. *The Review of Economics and Statistics* 71 (1): 172–174.

Solon, Gary. 1992. Intergenerational Income Mobility in the United States. *American Economic Review* 82 (3): 393–408.

Solon, Gary. 2002. Cross-Country Differences in Intergenerational Earnings Mobility. *Journal of Economic Perspectives* 16 (3): 59–66.

Sowell, Thomas. 1981. *Ethnic America.* New York: Basic Books.

Zimmerman, David J. 1992. Regression towards Mediocrity in Economic Stature. *The American Economic Review* 82 (3): 409-429.

Jeffrey K. Lee

INTERGROUP RELATIONS

The study of intergroup relations has long been a staple in social science research and in particular, social psychology. More recent work has tried to determine when contact between groups is likely to result in positive outcomes (Lee et al. 2004). Events such as the 9/11 Al-Qaeda terrorist attacks in the United States, the 1994 Rwandan massacre of Tutsis, and the ongoing conflicts between Sunni and Shia Muslims in Iraq are all examples of intergroup relations gone awry.

Social psychologist Gordon Allport (1897–1967) is credited with having produced the earliest and most comprehensive research on intergroup relations. His book, *The Nature of Prejudice* (1954), has provided a foundation for the study of intergroup relations since the mid-1950s. Since that time, a great deal of research in social psychology has improved our understanding of intergroup relationships, and in particular the conditions most likely to give rise to positive contact between groups (e.g., Amir 1969; Lee et al. 2004). For example, it is now well established that dramatic shifts in population and immigration policies, technological advancements, and economic volatility, as well as the overthrow of existing political regimes, can alter the nature of relations between groups—for better and for worse.

Intergroup relations are influenced by the *social identities* and perceptions of groups that individual group members hold. Furthermore, the quality of intergroup relations influences group members' group identities. Thus, there is a circular aspect to group identity processes and the quality of intergroup relations. One influences and is influenced by the other.

The potential problem for intergroup relations lies in the overarching tendency human beings have for *social categorization*. Because of the perceptual tendency to divide the world into separate categories (i.e., social categorization), identification with one group rather than another is almost inevitable. People engage in social categorization to bring order to a seemingly endless array of stimuli (e.g., other people) that they encounter. Thus, the process of designating someone as a member of one's own group (i.e., the in-group) or not (i.e., a member of an out-group) is one that occurs almost automatically. When intergroup relations are harmonious, members of different groups will be less apt to emphasize differences between in-groups and out-groups. However, when there is conflict, identification with one's group becomes stronger, out-group differences are accentuated, and intergroup conflict increases.

According to researchers Henri Tajfel and John Turner, the tendency toward social categorization is all the more problematic if, as they suggest, people are generally motivated to enhance their self-esteem by identifying with certain social groups. According to *social identity theory* (Tajfel and Turner 1986), people are able to enhance their self-esteem by identifying with groups that they perceive to be superior to out-groups. This theory has been used most widely as an explanation for prejudice. *Prejudice* generally refers to negative attitudes toward members of a group that is based solely on the fact that they are members of that group. Individuals who harbor prejudice for members of a group usually have negative impressions about each of the group's members and tend to perceive the group members as being more similar to one another than is actually the case.

Early studies of prejudice revealed unabashed pronouncements of bigoted sentiment (LaPiere 1934; Pettigrew 1969; Hyman and Sheatsley 1956/1964). More recent work demonstrates that prejudiced attitudes in the United States have declined and become subtler. For example, whites express less prejudice toward blacks today because they are indeed less prejudiced than earlier generations, and also because it is socially unacceptable to appear prejudiced. This latter point is an important one because a large volume of research involving the use of subtle measures can detect the continuing presence of negative sentiment for members of various out-groups (e.g., Banaji and Bhasker 2000; Bargh and Chartrand 1999; Dovidio et al. 1997). Taken together, legislation, normative social pressure, and fears about retaliation have attenuated expressions of prejudice.

Though less sanguine, many contemporary social psychologists who study prejudice contend that what has replaced "old-fashioned" prejudice is a newer, more insidious form of prejudice called *modern racism* (McConahay

et al. 1981). This form of prejudice involves the deliberate concealment of prejudiced attitudes except when in the presence of like-minded others. It is expressed in terms of opposition to race-related issues such as affirmative action and interracial marriage. The modern racist is one who attributes his or her prejudiced attitudes to reasons other than prejudice. Social psychologists have developed unobtrusive measures to assess this more contemporary form of prejudice (e.g., the Implicit Association Test).

Prejudice is usually accompanied by stereotypes. *Stereotypes* are cognitive structures that contain information about a person (group, place, or thing). Stereotypes influence the extent to which specific information is attended to, encoded, and subsequently retrieved. In short, stereotypes influence the processing of social information. Stereotypes are functional in that they permit the conservation of cognitive resources. By stereotyping, people are able to avoid engaging in effortful processing of social information. However, the problem with relying on these heuristics is that they neglect the variability that exists among people. When we stereotype others we ignore their individuality and impose limitations upon them. Not surprisingly, the quality and extent of intergroup relations is influenced by people's stereotypes and the prejudice they have toward out-group members. In the context of intergroup relations, less is definitely better (i.e., less stereotyping and prejudice is associated with more positive intergroup relations). Those who study intergroup relations have tended to focus upon the negative outcomes of intergroup relations, including prejudice and discrimination.

Discrimination represents a behavioral manifestation of prejudice. It involves unjustified behavior toward a group or its members simply because of their membership in that group. As is the case with outright expressions of prejudice, civil rights legislation and social normative pressure have effectively reduced blatant forms of discrimination in recent years in the United States and in other countries (Swim et al. 1995). Nevertheless, instances of discrimination continue to be unearthed and in some cases hotly contested. For example, according to Fred Pincus (2000), unchecked discrimination in the Los Angeles Police Department and criminal justice system resulted in the 1992 beating of Rodney King. The leadership of the Los Angeles Police Department condoned antiblack behaviors, and the assault on King was symptomatic of an atmosphere that supported discriminatory behavior toward black citizens. Moreover, when the defense requested a change of venue and the trial was moved to a conservative, predominantly white community, an all-white jury acquitted the officers. This is a clear example of discrimination at the institutional level.

Institutional discrimination usually refers to the way that an institution or an organization systematically or repeatedly treats people differently because of their race (or sex). This refers to the effect of practices and policies that may at times be carried out without conscious regard to race, but which has the net effect of having an adverse impact upon a group of a people. Individuals need not be personally prejudiced for institutional discrimination to be present.

The study of intergroup relations and its correlates (i.e., social identity, stereotypes, prejudice, and discrimination) continues to be a fruitful area of inquiry for researchers and policymakers. People around the world belong to many different types of groups, and groups often exert powerful influences upon individual group members and other groups. Recent and continuing world events underscore the importance of research aimed at explicating the conditions most likely to produce favorable intergroup relations.

SEE ALSO *Al-Qaeda; Contact Hypothesis; Discrimination; Economics; Economics, Stratification; Ethnocentrism; Genocide; Groups; Identity; Other, The; Prejudice; Racism; September 11, 2001; Social Categorization; Social Identification; Social Psychology; Stereotypes; Stratification*

BIBLIOGRAPHY

Allport, Gordon. 1954. *The Nature of Prejudice*. Reading, MA: Addison-Wesley.

Amir, Yehuda. 1969. Contact Hypothesis Ethnic Relations. *Psychological Bulletin* 71 (5): 319–342.

Banaji, Mahzarin R., and R. Bhaskar. 2000. Implicit Stereotypes and Memory: The Bounded Rationality of Social Beliefs. In *Memory, Brain, and Belief*, eds. Daniel L. Schacter and Elaine Scarry, 139–175. Cambridge, MA: Harvard University Press.

Bargh, John A., and Tanya L. Chartrand. 1999. The Unbearable Automaticity of Being. *American Psychologist* 54: 462–479.

Dovidio, John, Kerry Kawakami, Craig Johnson, et al. 1997. On the Nature of Prejudice: Automatic and Controlled Processes. *Journal of Experimental Social Psychology* 33 (5): 510–540.

Hyman, Herbert H., and Paul B. Sheatsley. 1956/1964. Attitudes Toward Desegregation. *Scientific American* 195 (6): 35–39, and 211 (1): 16–23.

LaPiere, Richard T. 1934. Attitude and Actions. *Social Forces* 13: 230–237.

Lee, Yueh-ting, Clark McCauley, Fathali Moghaddam, and Stephen Worchel. 2004. *The Psychology of Ethnic and Cultural Conflict*. Westport, CT: Praeger.

McConahay, John B., Betty B. Hardee, and Valerie Batts. 1981. Has Racism Declined in America? It Depends on Who Is Asking and What Is Asked. *Journal of Conflict Resolution* 25: 563–579.

Pettigrew, Thomas F. 1969. Racially Separate or Together? *Journal of Social Issues* 2: 43–69.

Pincus, Fred L. 2000. Discrimination Comes in Many Forms: Individual, Institutional, and Structural. In *Readings for Diversity and Social Justice: An Anthology on Racism, Sexism, Anti-Semitism, Heterosexism, Classism, and Ableism*, eds. Maurianne Adams, Warren Blumenfeld, Rosie Castañeda, et al., 31–34. New York: Routledge.

Swim, Janet K., Kathryn J. Aikin, Wayne S. Hall, and Barbara A. Hunter. 1995. Sexism and Racism: Old-fashioned and Modern Prejudices. *Journal of Personality and Social Psychology* 68: 199–214.

Tajfel, Henri, and John C. Turner. 1986. The Social Identity Theory of Intergroup Behavior. In *Psychology of Intergroup Relations*, eds. Stephen Worchel and William G. Austin, 7–24. 2nd ed. Chicago: Nelson-Hall.

Kellina Craig-Henderson

INTERNATIONAL BANK FOR RECONSTRUCION AND DEVELOPMENT

SEE *World Bank, The.*

INTERNATIONAL COVENANT ON CIVIL AND POLITICAL RIGHTS

SEE *Civil Liberties.*

INTERNATIONAL ECONOMIC ORDER

The term *international economic order* refers to the set of proscribed rules, norms, and procedures that regulate the cross-border exchange of goods, services, and capital. While economists have persistently preached the virtues of an open economy since David Ricardo (1772–1823), leaders have been warier because of a combination of ideological concerns, domestic politics, and realpolitik.

At present, the idea of an international economic order seems inextricably linked to multilateralism. However, in the century prior to 1945, almost all of the global economic rules were established at the bilateral or unilateral level. The opening of the global economy to trade in the mid-1800s was due to the Cobden-Chevalier Treaty (1860) between France and Great Britain, and the decision to extend most-favored nation trading status to new trading partners (Stein 1984; Lazer 1999). As for capital markets, the gold standard was a creation of British hegemony; its large domestic market and deep capital markets compelled other countries to operate by the Bank of England's rules (Eichengreen 1996).

These arrangements were temporarily suspended during World War I (1914–1918), and then disintegrated after 1930. The British tried to sustain the pre-war order, but their economic power had waned, and the United States refused to act as a supporter of the system (Lake 1983). The interwar economic system was characterized by high tariffs and beggar-thy-neighbor policies, in which countries engaged in competitive devaluations of their currency as a means to improve their balance of trade (Kindleberger 1973).

During and after World War II (1939–1945), the United States was bound and determined to foster an international economic order that would prevent the high tariff barriers and beggar-thy-neighbor policies of the 1930s. This included a global trading system to ensure that all participating members received nondiscriminatory treatment in traded goods. To aid in trade expansion, the United States also pressed for currencies to be fixed in value relative to the dollar, which in turn could be exchanged for gold. Great Britain was reluctant to accede to this kind of regime, because it undermined the British system of imperial preferences, threatened currency runs on the war-torn European economies, and potentially constrained the autonomy of domestic policymakers.

In 1944 a conference in Bretton Woods, New Hampshire, hammered out a compromise that John Gerard Ruggie (1982) famously labeled "embedded liberalism." The world trading system was opened, and exchange rates would be fixed. Governments, however, were still given significant policy leeway to ensure full employment policies at home.

To ensure the stability of the system, the United States endorsed and funded the creation of international financial institutions (IFIs) to monitor and enforce the international economic order. The International Monetary Fund (IMF) was designed to prevent a balance-of-payments crisis among the participating countries. The World Bank was intended to help the European economies recover from the war. In contrast to the one-country/one-vote principle of other international organizations, decision-making power in the IFIs was weighted by economic size.

The third leg of the international economic order was to be the International Trade Organization (ITO). However, the proposed institution was never created due to the U.S. Senate's failure to ratify the Havana Charter. As a result, the General Agreement on Tariffs and Trade (GATT)—originally designed as an interim facility until the ITO came into existence—became the international regime governing trade.

The GATT was considered to be a weaker institution compared to the IFIs. Despite this gap in institutional strength, however, the trade regime yielded significant results. Between 1950 and 1970, merchandise trade levels grew at twice the rate of the global economy. In contrast, Bretton Woods was short-lived; western European countries did not make their currencies convertible until 1958, and the United States unilaterally ended the fixed exchange rate portion of the Bretton Woods agreement in 1971. At crisis junctures, the United States acted outside the IFIs to promote its stated interests, deploying greater resources in the process. In the late 1940s, for example, the resources committed to the Marshall Plan dwarfed those of the World Bank. In the mid-1990s, the United States provided its own financing to bail Mexico out of its financial crisis.

The failure of the IFIs to fulfill their intended functions was also due to the economic contradictions contained within Bretton Woods. As capital controls were removed, it became next to impossible for countries to maintain the "unholy trinity" of fixed exchange rates, open capital markets, and monetary policy autonomy (Cohen 1993). The United States also ran into the "Triffin Dilemma"—it was incapable of simultaneously increasing international liquidity while pledging to keep the dollar convertible into gold.

The collapse of Bretton Woods in 1971, the rise of the third world in the form of the Group of Seventy-Seven (G-77), and the oil shocks of the 1970s led to a bifurcated, contested international economic order. To handle exchange rates, the Group of Seven (G-7) countries (Canada, France, Germany, Italy, Japan, the United Kingdom, and the United States) supplanted the IFIs. This ad hoc arrangement proved moderately successful over the next two decades in managing the floating exchange rate system among the G-7. The IFIs found themselves bereft of their original purpose at the same time that developing countries were hit by the oil crises of the 1970s. These institutions increasingly focused their resources toward the developing world. The debt crisis of the 1980s ensured that many developing countries needed the imprimatur of the IFIs in order to secure external financing. The IMF in particular exploited the conditionality of loans to developing countries in order to affect national macroeconomic policies.

The growing reliance on official financial flows came as an important shift in economic ideas was taking place. The IFIs moved away from promoting Keynesianism and toward more neoclassical policies of balanced budgets, trade liberalization, and low inflation.

At the same time, the newly sovereign nations of the third world began to contest the market-friendly rules that underpinned embedded liberalism. A slow decline in commodity prices caused worsening terms of trade in the developing world in the 1970s, and led governments to be suspicious of the vicissitudes of market forces. Inspired by the success of the Organization of Petroleum Exporting Countries (OPEC) cartel in increasing the price of oil, these countries proposed a "new international economic order" (NIEO; Cox 1979) in the 1974 United Nations General Assembly. The NIEO included several initiatives, including orderly market arrangements to stabilize commodity prices, institutionalized forms of technology transfer, and changes in trade rules to allow the third world greater access to Organization for Economic Cooperation and Development (OECD) markets while protecting their home markets from foreign competition and the presence of multinational corporations. All of these requests were resisted by the advanced industrialized states, and the structure of IFI voting guaranteed a veto by the G-7 countries in those venues (Krasner 1985). With the debt crisis of the early 1980s, third world solidarity on the NIEO collapsed, with little achieved beyond a modest increase in UN development funds.

The end of the cold war and the rise of economic globalization expanded the assigned tasks of the IFIs to include everything from advising transition economies, to establishing common financial codes and standards, to promoting democracy, to combating corruption. The leverage of the IFIs in these issue areas, however, has been limited to countries that cannot borrow from private capital markets.

The GATT morphed into the World Trade Organization (WTO) in 1995. Although the WTO has stronger enforcement mechanisms, the rising influence of developing countries like China, India, and Brazil has threatened to paralyze its ability to expand trade further. A partial response to the gridlock within the WTO has been a proliferation of regional and bilateral trade agreements outside the WTO's purview.

At the start of the twenty-first century, the international economic order remains relatively open for trade and finance, though there are no clear rules for migration. Increasingly, the focus of international economic negotiations has shifted to questions about business and social regulation (Braithwaite and Drahos 1999; Slaughter 2004). As China begins to challenge the United States as the economic hegemon, the stability of the current system will soon be open to question.

SEE ALSO *General Agreement on Tariffs and Trade; Globalization, Social and Economic Aspects of; International Monetary Fund; Internationalism; World Bank; World Trade Organization*

BIBLIOGRAPHY

Braithwaite, John, and Peter Drahos. 1999. *Global Business Regulation.* Cambridge, U.K.: Cambridge University Press.

Cohen, Benjamin J. 1993. The Triad and the Unholy Trinity: Problems of International Monetary Cooperation. In *Pacific Economic Relations in the 1990s: Cooperation or Conflict,* eds. Richard Higgott, Richard Leaver, and John Ravenhill, 133–158. New York: Allen and Unwin.

Cox, Robert W. 1979. Ideologies and the New International Economic Order: Reflections on Some Recent Literature. *International Organization* 33 (2): 257–302.

Drezner, Daniel W. 2007. *All Politics Is Global: Explaining International Regulatory Regimes.* Princeton, NJ: Princeton University Press.

Eichengreen, Barry. 1996. *Globalizing Capital: A History of the International Monetary System.* Princeton, NJ: Princeton University Press.

Kindleberger, Charles. 1973. *The World in Depression, 1929–1939.* Berkeley: University of California Press.

Krasner, Stephen D. 1985. *Structural Conflict: The Third World against Global Liberalism.* Berkeley: University of California Press.

Lake, David, 1983. International Economic Structures and American Foreign Economic Policy, 1887–1934. *World Politics* 35 (4): 517–543.

Lazer, David. 1999. The Free Trade Epidemic of the 1860s and Other Outbreaks of Economic Discrimination. *World Politics* 51: 447–483.

Ruggie, John Gerard. 1982. International Regimes, Transactions, and Change: Embedded Liberalism in the Postwar Economic Order. *International Organization* 36 (2): 379–415

Slaughter, Anne-Marie. 2004. *A New World Order.* Princeton, NJ: Princeton University Press.

Stein, Arthur. 1984. The Hegemon's Dilemma: Great Britain, the United States, and the International Economic Order. *International Organization* 38 (2): 355–386.

Daniel W. Drezner

INTERNATIONAL LABOR ORGANIZATION

SEE *Gender and Development; Sweatshops.*

INTERNATIONAL LAW

SEE *Internationalism.*

INTERNATIONAL MONETARY FUND

The International Monetary Fund (IMF) originated at a United Nations (UN) conference in Bretton Woods, New Hampshire, in July 1944. The IMF is thus known as a Bretton Woods institution. The forty-five governments represented at that conference decided to build an institution to facilitate economic cooperation. They hoped the existence of such an institution would help countries avoid a recurrence of the disastrous, self-interested economic policies that led to the Great Depression that began in the United States around 1929 and spread throughout the world. The principal architects of the IMF were the British economist John Maynard Keynes (1883–1946), the author of *The General Theory of Employment, Interest, and Money* (1936), a work that revolutionized economic theory, and the chief international economist at the U.S. Treasury Department, Harry Dexter White (1892–1948). The IMF actually came into existence in December 1945 when the first twenty-nine countries signed its Articles of Agreement. The goals of the IMF were to encourage international monetary cooperation, remove foreign-exchange restrictions, stabilize exchange rates, and facilitate a multilateral payments system between member countries.

The IMF acts as an umpire in the international market and takes action to ensure the stability of the world's financial system. Its main role in its first years was to supervise the newly established fixed exchange-rate system initiated in Bretton Woods. After the collapse of the fixed exchange rate in February 1973 and the adoption of flexible exchange rates, the IMF became more involved with member countries' economic policies by providing advice. In the 1980s the IMF had to confront the problem of mounting foreign debt in developing countries. In the 1990s the IMF addressed the transition of former socialist countries to market capitalism, and more recently it had to assist countries facing currency crises.

The main goal of the IMF is to promote a healthy world economy. The organization's responsibilities include: (1) promoting international monetary cooperation; (2) facilitating the expansion and balanced growth of international trade; (3) promoting exchange-rate stability; (4) assisting in the establishment of a multilateral system of payments; (5) fostering economic growth and high levels of employment; and (6) providing temporary financial assistance to countries experiencing balance-of-payments problems. The IMF also strives to reduce poverty in countries around the globe, independently and in collaboration with the World Bank and other international organizations.

The IMF had 184 member countries in 2007. With the exception of North Korea, Cuba, Liechtenstein, Andorra, Monaco, Tuvalu, and Nauru, all UN member states are members of the IMF or are represented by other member states. The IMF is headquartered in Washington, D.C., with an international staff of more than 2,500. As of March 2006, the IMF's total quotas were $308 billion, with loans outstanding of $34 billion to seventy-five countries, of which $6 billion to fifty-six countries was on concessional terms.

The IMF is financed by quota subscriptions, the share of each member in the IMF's total funds. The quota allocated to each IMF member determines that country's voting power, the amount of gold or international currency or its own currency that the country initially subscribes, and its access to various borrowing facilities. A large quota offers an IMF member prestige and borrowing power because a large initial subscription provides liability to extend credit to countries that need to borrow. National quotas are periodically revised.

The IMF strives to prevent economic crises by encouraging countries to adopt what IMF directors perceive to be appropriate economic policies. The organization meets these objectives primarily through surveillance, technical assistance, and lending. Surveillance is the regular policy advice that the IMF offers once a year to each of its members. The fund conducts an in-depth analysis of each member country's economic state of affairs. Members usually allow the publication of their IMF evaluation, supplying the information to the public. Technical assistance and training are offered, mostly free of charge, to help member countries strengthen their capacity to design and implement effective policies. Technical assistance is also offered in several economic areas, including fiscal policy, monetary and exchange-rate policies, banking, financial system supervision and regulation, and statistical collection and analysis. Financial assistance is available to help member countries correct balance-of-payments problems. Countries under financial distress are required to develop a policy program supported by IMF financing, and continued financial support is conditional on the effective implementation of the program.

Major controversies surround the role and practices of the IMF in the world economy, especially concerning the conditionality of financial support, which is provided only if recipient countries implement IMF-approved economic reforms. Indeed, in a world of mostly floating exchange rates, in contrast to the fixed exchange rates in existence when the IMF was established, it is even questionable why this institution remains in existence. The IMF has received extensive criticism from people representing the entire political spectrum, including grassroots protestors and activists objecting to IMF policies in countries subjected to "structural adjustment." Even the Austrian economist Friedrich Hayek (1899–1992) was deeply troubled by the global "statism" practiced by the

IMF. IMF policies are implemented under the principle of "one-size-fits-all" (Stiglitz 2002, p. 141). Jeffrey Sachs, the economic advisor who encouraged transitioning economies to implement shock therapy programs, argued that "the International Monetary Fund's view, all too often, is … based on a misunderstanding of what its own role should be" (1994, p. 504).

The principles behind IMF policies are based on what John Williamson (1990) referred to as the "Washington Consensus." *Washington*, for Williamson, encompassed the World Bank and the U.S. Treasury, in addition to the IMF. Williamson identified ten policy instruments for which Washington-based institutions could muster a reasonable degree of consensus, and he summarized the content of the Washington Consensus as macroeconomic prudence, outward orientation, domestic liberalization, and free market policies. The Washington Consensus, as the set of economic policies implemented by the administrations of U.S. president Ronald Reagan (1911–2004) and British prime minister Margaret Thatcher, has been labeled a "neoliberal manifesto." The program involves devaluation of the exchange rate, liberalization of markets where prices are regulated, privatization of public sector enterprises, contraction of public sector expenditure, and the implementation of restrictive monetary policy. There is an obvious hostility to inflation, which is strongly influenced by the effect of inflation on foreign investors (Payer 1974, p. 37). The IMF imposes these economic policies on countries in financial distress that request assistance through conditionality. Countries facing a crisis often have little alternative but to accept the terms stipulated by the IMF in order to receive assistance. Thus IMF financial support of a government program concurrently ensures obedient behavior (Payer 1974, p. 31).

Proponents of the IMF's conditionality policy argue that the fund should not give money away for free. The IMF is a financial institution, and, like any financial institution, when it lends out money it requires borrowers to guarantee the loan that they have signed by accepting IMF-approved policies. Proponents insist that it is reasonable to stipulate that further financial support will only be released after the successful implementation of reforms. At the same time, it is not clear whether the policies enforced by the IMF have been successful. Lance Taylor argues that "a fair assessment would say that the outcomes of orthodox packages ranged to moderately successful to disastrous" (1988, p. 147). Nevertheless, the success or failure of IMF programs should not be measured by monetary criteria alone; qualitative criteria, such as socioeconomic improvements and social reforms, should also be considered in any evaluation of the IMF (Körner et al. 1986, p. 4).

SEE ALSO *World Bank, The*

BIBLIOGRAPHY

Dell, Sidney. 1986. The History of the IMF. *World Development* 14 (9) 1203–1212.

Keynes, John Maynard. 1936. *The General Theory of Employment, Interest, and Money.* London: Macmillan.

Körner, Peter, Gero Maass, Thomas Siebold, and Rainer Tetzlaff. 1986. *The IMF and the Debt Crisis: A Guide to the Third World's Dilemma.* Trans. Paul Knight. London: Zed.

Payer, Cheryl. 1974. *The Debt Trap: The IMF and the Third World.* Harmondsworth, U.K.: Penguin.

Sachs, Jeffrey. 1994. Life in the Economic Emergency Room. In *The Political Economy of Policy Reform,* ed. John Williamson, 503–523. Washington, DC: Institute for International Economics.

Stiglitz, Joseph. 2002. *Globalization and its Discontents.* New York: Norton.

Taylor, Lance. 1988. *Varieties of Stabilization Experience: Towards Sensible Macroeconomics in the Third World.* New York: Oxford University Press.

Williamson, John. 1990. What Washington Means by Policy Reform. In *Latin American Adjustment: How Much Has Happened?* ed. John Williamson, 7–20. Washington, DC: Institute for International Economics.

Aristidis Bitzenis
John Marangos

INTERNATIONAL NONGOVERNMENTAL ORGANIZATIONS (INGOs)

International nongovernmental organizations (INGOs) are not-for-profit voluntary associations operating at the international, transnational, or global level, with members or participants from many countries. They bring together like-minded individuals or associations of individuals to conduct a wide variety of activities across virtually all social domains, from astronomy to football to plant biology to zoo management. Although the best-known INGOs focus on human rights (for example, Amnesty International), the environment (Friends of the Earth), disaster relief (the Red Cross), and the like, most INGOs are found in scientific, technical, business and industry, medical, and professional domains. Sizable numbers are also active in domains such as sports and recreation, development, education, women's rights, and many others. As of 2006, more than 7,000 "conventional" INGOs were in operation, along with about 20,000 internationally oriented nongovernmental organizations of more limited scope (Union of International Associations 2006).

ORIGINS AND EXPANSION

The earliest modern INGOs appeared toward the middle of the nineteenth century. Examples include the British and Foreign Anti-Slavery Society (founded in 1839), the World's Evangelical Alliance (1846), and the Verein Deutscher Eisenbahnverwaltungen (an association of German railroad companies, 1846). By the 1860s and 1870s new INGOs had been founded in many domains such as ophthalmology, labor, geodesy, international law, dentistry, hotel management, and so on. Hundreds of INGOs were in operation by 1900, and the first compilation of information about INGOs, the initial *Annuaire de la vie internationale*, listed 374 active organizations in 1909. Many hundreds more, across an expanding range of domains, appeared in the interwar period. Since the postwar period of rapid globalization INGO organizing has soared, with more than a hundred new organizations forming each year.

In the *Yearbook of International Organizations*, the successor to *Annuaire de la vie internationale* and the definitive source of information about INGOs, conventional INGOs are defined as (1) federations of INGOs whose members are themselves large INGOs, such as the International Scientific Union and the World Federation of Trade Unions; (2) "universal" INGOs, with members in at least sixty countries or at least thirty countries on several continents (e.g., International Union Against Cancer, Education International); (3) "intercontinental" INGOs, with members in many countries on at least two continents (e.g., American Association of Port Authorities, Suzuki Association of the Americas); and (4) "regional" INGOs, with members in many countries in one continent or region (e.g., European Association for Machine Translation, Pan African Organization for Sustainable Development). A more inclusive set of INGOs includes organizations of many different types—foundations, research centers, aid and relief organizations, advocacy groups, and so on—that are internationally oriented but are based in or operate from only one or a few countries.

Active conventional INGOs increased from 374 in 1909 to 841 in 1940, to more than 3,000 in 1972, and to more than 7,300 in 2005, with the total for INGOs of all types exceeding 27,000 in 2005 (Union of International Associations 1948–). INGO growth has been almost exponential in recent decades. The world wars interrupted INGO formation, but after each war voluntary international nongovernmental organizing immediately recovered. Most of the early INGOs were universal in scope, welcoming members from anywhere in the world and defining their goals in worldwide terms—seeking to organize, for example, all the world's chemical engineers, literary critics, rubber producers, or science librarians. After World War II regional INGOs began to appear in large numbers (Boli and Thomas 1999). The regions at issue include not only geographical areas such as Africa or Latin America, but also cultural regions (e.g., francophone countries or the Islamic world), ecological regions (tropical forest or alpine areas), and so on. In many cases, regional organizations have arisen within the aegis of universal (global) INGOs. For example, the International Organization for Standardization promoted the creation of regional technical standards bodies for Africa, Asia, and other geographical regions, whereas the International Society for Photogrammetry and Remote Sensing has encouraged the participation of relevant regional organizations (Asian, African, Pan American, South Pacific) as associates in its global endeavors.

Most INGOs founded before World War I were based in Europe or the more developed former European colonies, and INGO participation has always been higher among citizens of developed Western countries than elsewhere. However, in the postwar period the citizens of less developed, non-Western, and non-Christian countries have rapidly increased their participation in and founding of INGOs. This greater inclusiveness has increased dissension and conflict within INGOs, particularly with respect to issues of importance to members from poorer countries. For example, global women's organizations have found it difficult to grapple with issues such as veiling and female genital cutting because some non-Western women's groups embrace such practices and reject Western criticisms of them. Similarly, INGO members from outside the West often insist that social and economic rights—clean water, adequate food, basic health care—are more important than the civil and political rights that are usually championed by their Western human rights counterparts.

INGO OPERATIONS AND ACTIVITIES

INGOs are a highly disparate group of transnational organizations engaged in most arenas of human activity. As nonprofit voluntary associations, they rely primarily on donations, member fees, and voluntary labor for their operations. Their goals and activities are neither economic nor political in the usual sense. Instead, they are mostly concerned with information, communication, and practical projects to organize global domains or effect global change (Boli and Thomas 1999). Many are rule-making bodies; for example, some 200 international sports federations make worldwide rules for their respective sports, and hundreds of professional associations make global rules regarding the ethical norms that apply to their members. Some INGOs seek to solve social problems or improve living conditions; others aim to improve technology, advance knowledge, create global standards, protect threatened peoples or species, or induce states, businesses, and individuals to abide by specific norms and principles. Such activities are typical of civil society organizations at the national level, and INGOs are often seen as the core of an increasingly active global civil society (Anheier et al. 2001–) that helps temper the power struggles of states and reduce the excesses of large corporations (Florini 2000). Unlike states or corporations, most INGOs focus on the promotion of public goods and the welfare of others. Only a portion of INGOs (a quarter to a third of the total), most of which are business and industry associations, act mainly to promote the interests of their members.

A striking trend in recent decades is the increasing interconnectedness of INGOs. Empowered by advanced communication systems, especially the Internet, INGOs frequently associate in loose networks and coalitions, particularly when tackling broad global problems such as environmental degradation, poverty, human rights violations, and related issues. A prominent example is the International Campaign to Ban Landmines, a coalition of more than 1,400 INGOs that convinced states to establish the 1997 treaty outlawing the manufacture, sale, or use of antipersonnel mines. Many INGOs are only "virtual" organizations with small staffs supported by tiny budgets, serving as information clearinghouses to help coordinate other INGOs' efforts. The most common targets of these networks and coalitions are major intergovernmental organizations (IGOs) such as the International Monetary Fund (IMF) and the World Trade Organization (WTO), which are taken to task for promoting neoliberal capitalist policies without regard for social, environmental, and cultural concerns. Large corporations are also frequent targets. INGOs insist that businesses must consider the "triple bottom line" that adds social and environmental concerns to the traditional focus on profit.

Although INGOs that criticize large companies or global governance organizations such as the IMF and WTO often have antagonistic relationships with their targets, cooperative relationships between INGOs and IGOs are increasingly common (Willets 1996). More than 2,000 INGOs have formal consultative status with the United Nations Economic and Social Council and many organizations work with UN agencies on disaster relief, development, education, health, agriculture, and other issues. INGOs are also heavily involved in the operations of technical and regulatory IGOs such as the International Telecommunication Union and the International Civil Aviation Authority. Both conflict and cooperation characterize INGO/IGO relationships at major world summits sponsored by the United Nations on matters such as the environment, human rights, and women's issues. At these summits INGOs gather in the thousands as the voices of global civil society speaking to states about their policies and programs, and conflicts over principles and practicalities are endemic. As increasingly professionalized and expert organizations, however, INGOs are emerging as accepted partners in these global governance fora (Charnovitz 1997).

CRITICISMS OF INGOS

Because INGOs focus unwelcome attention on the behavior of powerful states, corporations, and intergovernmental organizations, they themselves are subject to attack by their targets. Critics question INGO accountability, representativeness, and transparency. They argue that, unlike political leaders, INGOs are not accountable to identifiable constituencies and their members may not belong to the groups they claim to represent; unlike democratic institutions, INGOs are not entirely open about their internal operations. Critics also charge that INGOs promote irresponsible or unrealistic economic, social, and environmental policies. INGOs respond by invoking broadly legitimated world-cultural principles, standards, and norms as sources of their authority to justify both themselves and their criticisms of powerful global actors. At issue is a global struggle for legitimacy in which INGOs continue to have the edge because they are relatively disinterested and nonpartisan.

Criticism has been especially acute since 2000 regarding large development INGOs operating in the less developed countries. Both the intended beneficiaries of development aid and outside observers take development INGOs to task for numerous failings: inadequate knowledge of the cultures and societies where they operate, reliance on abstract measures of improvement that poorly reflect local realities, insufficient autonomy from donors (especially the official development assistance agencies of powerful Western states), excessive professionalization that raises barriers between INGO officials and local NGO workers, and piecemeal specialization that misses the interconnectedness of local needs and problems. Development INGOs are caught in a double bind: If they act primarily as funders and facilitators of development projects, critics deem their efforts distant, unengaged, and superficial; if they become deeply immersed in local power and stratification structures, critics accuse them of imperialistic meddling. In either mode, they may be castigated for promoting "developmentalism"—that is, projects, policies, and forms of development that exacerbate existing inequalities and exploitation while serving the economic and political interests of Western countries. Some of the most telling critiques have come from within the development sector itself. Many development INGOs have taken such criticism to heart, searching for better ways of engaging with and relying on the peoples they intend to help, but satisfactory improvements are not easily generated and controversy remains endemic and ubiquitous.

Most INGOs, however, are neither subject to criticism nor involved in clashes of ideology, politics, or legitimacy. They operate in relative obscurity, organizing their specialized domains with considerable autonomy and exercising remarkably effective authority at the global and regional levels.

SEE ALSO *Foundations, Charitable*

BIBLIOGRAPHY

Anheier, Helmut, Marlies Glasius, and Mary Kaldor, eds. 2001–. *Global Civil Society Annual Yearbook.* Oxford: Oxford University Press.

Boli, John, and George M. Thomas, eds. 1999. *Constructing World Culture: International Nongovernmental Organizations Since 1875.* Stanford, CA: Stanford University Press.

Charnovitz, Steve. 1997. Two Centuries of Participation: NGOs and International Governance. *Michigan Journal of International Law* 18 (2): 183–286.

Florini, Ann, ed. 2000. *The Third Force: The Rise of Transnational Civil Society.* Washington, DC: Brookings Institution Press.

Union of International Associations. 1948–. *Yearbook of International Organizations.* Munich, Germany: Author. 1st ed. 1909.

Willetts, Peter, ed. 1996. *The Conscience of the World: The Influence of Non-governmental Organizations in the UN System.* Washington, DC: Brookings Institution Press.

John Boli

INTERNATIONAL RELATIONS

International relations (IR) is the study of relationships among the actors of international politics. Such actors include nation-states, international organizations, nongovernmental organizations, and multinational corporations. The field is also sometimes called *international politics, international studies,* or *international affairs.* In the United States, IR is a branch of political science, while it is considered its own interdisciplinary field in the European and British academy. What makes IR unique from other forms of political analysis is that international politics is characterized by anarchy—or the absence of any authority superior to the nation-state. Sovereign states are thus the primary, though not the sole, important actors in the international system, because historically states are the organizations with the legitimate authority to use force within their geographically recognized areas.

APPROACHES TO IR THEORY

IR theorists do not all share the same epistemology (ways of knowing) or methodology (analyzing what they know) for approaching the puzzles of world politics. There are generally three epistemological perspectives in the field of IR. A plurality of IR scholars are *positivists*, and assert that the only way to know something about the world is to approach it scientifically, by producing models that approximate the reality of international politics. These models are tested with facts in order to predict the future behavior of international actors. *Interpretivists* disagree with this approach, in that they do not aim to predict the behavior of international actors, but to interpret and understand the motives behind that behavior. Interpretivists see a world of intersubjective understandings and ideas to be interpreted rather than used for prediction. *Post-positivists* think that both interpretation and causal analysis is inappropriate, and that the theories and models developed by IR theorists could instead be used to control global populations. Post-positivists seek to emancipate oppressed groups by deconstructing the relationships and concepts taken for granted in world politics to reveal how they are not "natural" but forms of power and discipline.

Epistemology influences the methodology various scholars use. For instance, most (but not all) positivists use quantitative, statistical techniques to test their models, whereas interpretivists and post-positivists use qualitative techniques (such as discourse analysis or process tracing) to illustrate their arguments.

There are several theoretical approaches in IR, as well as substantive subfields of study, as noted below.

Realism Realist IR theorists argue that the condition of anarchy in international politics results in one motivation for state action—survival. Because power helps states ensure their own survival, state interests are defined in terms of power. This means that cooperation among states will be rare, and plans to overcome such tension will ultimately fail. Classical realists like Hans Morgenthau (1946), John Herz, Raymond Aron, and E. H. Carr conceptualized power in a variety of ways—both materially (the military, the economy, geography) and strategically (diplomacy, prestige). While much of the defining literature of classical realism was produced in the immediate decades after World War II (1939–1945), later scholars such as Anthony Lang, Richard Ned Lebow, and Michael C. Williams (2004) resurrected the critical nature of classical realist work.

Liberalism Liberalism assumes that while states operate within anarchy and are primarily self-interested, this self-interest leads to cooperation rather than conflict. Institutional liberalism posits that international organizations and regimes facilitate cooperation by reducing uncertainty among states and increasing transparency. Economic or commercial liberalism asserts that open trading systems make cooperation more likely because the benefits of trade outweigh the costs of going to war. Political liberalism assesses the likelihood of cooperation or conflict based upon the nature of a country's political system. Political liberalism has developed into a separate research program known as *democratic peace theory*, which posits that democratic countries are less likely to go to war with one another because of the structural and cultural nature of democratic decision-making. Liberalism is often termed *idealism*, but this label is inaccurate in that all IR perspectives focus upon certain ideals over others. Yet liberalism is an admittedly more optimistic view of international politics than most other perspectives.

English School (Grotian or International Society) The English school has been a viable approach to the study of IR theory since the late 1950s and early 1960s. Representatives of this school include Herbert Butterfield, Hedley Bull, Adam Watson, R. J. Vincent, Martin Wight, and more recently Barry Buzan, Timothy Dunne, Robert Jackson, Nicholas Wheeler, and Barak Mendelsohn. The name *English school* refers to the location where many of the founders of the school first congregated—the London School of Economics. These scholars acknowledge the role that material forces play in international politics, but also how rules, principles, and ideas augment these material forces. Thus, while states cannot escape anarchy in their calculations with other states, certain "rules" of membership govern state relations. Therefore, international politics resembles an anarchical society where sovereignty as a principle is usually respected because states value order to ensure their survival (see Bull 2002).

Constructivism Constructivism is a sociological approach to social relations, rather than a specific theory of international politics. IR constructivists see the relations and patterns of nation-states and nonstate actors as socially constructed, or made up of intersubjectively shared ideas. Constructivists explore the manner in which identities, discourse, and rules shape and are shaped by states. They claim that states seek to do more than survive in a condition of anarchy; states also seek to socialize with other nation-states. Because ideas are intersubjectively shared among states, ideas can change and thus so can the interests of nation-states. This does not mean, however, that constructivists deny the importance of conflict. IR constructivists include such mainstream scholars as Alexander Wendt, Martha Finnemore, and Michael Barnett, as well as critical theorists such as Nicholas Onuf (1989) and Friedrich Kratochwil (1989).

Neorealism and Neoliberalism Neorealism (sometimes termed *structural realism*) and neoliberalism both represent attempts to develop classical realism and liberalism into scientific theories of international politics to make them more amenable to causal analysis. The defining publications—for neorealism, *Theory of International Politics* (1979) by Kenneth Waltz; for neoliberalism, *Power and Interdependence* (1977) by Robert Keohane and Joseph Nye—both attempted to develop systemic analyses of international politics. Both neorealists and neoliberals argue that states are units that act rationally to survive in a realm of anarchy, and such a universal motive produces regular behavior that can be predicted through hypothesis testing and theoretical development similar to that found in the physical sciences. The principal disagreement between the two approaches is whether states are concerned with relative gains (i.e., how a state performs relative to other states) or absolute gains.

Foreign Policy Analysis Foreign policy analysis seeks to understand the ways in which foreign policies are enacted by individuals or small groups of decision makers. International politics, from this perspective, is grounded in decisions made by leaders and elites. This subfield of IR borrows heavily from other disciplines in social science—most notably psychology. Much of this work views elites as having, for various reasons, imperfect rational capabilities, and thus attempts to make intelligible how individuals interpret incoming information and produce decisions that result in varied and sometimes disastrous outcomes. Although much foreign policy analysis focuses on individuals, it also accommodates the influence of domestic political entities (such as parties and coalitions) and bureaucracies on the foreign policy decisions made by elites. Scholars who have shaped this approach include Richard Snyder, James Rosenau, Harold and Margaret Sprout, Margaret Hermann, Charles Hermann, Richard Herrmann, Stephen Walker, and Martha Cottam.

CRITICAL THEORY

Critical theorists seek to challenge the core concepts and "commonsense" or prevailing wisdoms of mainstream IR approaches. Such theorists posit that mainstream approaches are "problem-solving theories" that through predictive analysis seek to form solutions to the most prevalent puzzles of international politics. Critical theory, on the other hand, is meant to develop an understanding of how theories and assumptions in IR are formed in the first place—and to reveal how some of these assumptions (like the "permanence" of nation-states) might instead be responsible for much of the suffering that occurs in international politics. Several forms of critical theory are discussed below.

Poststructuralism Poststructuralism draws on the social theory of philosophers like Jacques Derrida and Michel Foucault to reveal how forces and power operate in subtle ways. Poststructuralists problematize even the idea that history is connected in any meaningful way. Notable IR post-structuralists include Richard Ashley, David Campbell, and James Der Derian.

Neo-Marxist and Gramscian Theory World-systems theory and dependency theory are forms of what is known as neo-Marxist IR. Such perspectives focus less upon states and more upon the forces of capital and production in the international economic system. Gramscian perspectives (derived from the work of early twentieth-century Italian Marxist Antonio Gramsci), defined by Robert Cox (1981) and Stephen Gill, have focused upon the ways in which social relationships work in conjunction with market forces to produce certain processes and patterns evident in the international economy. It is not enough, Gramscian scholars posit, for the forces of capital to create the inequality that exists in international politics. It is also necessary for individuals and groups to believe in the market itself—and thus such internalization (ideas plus materials) makes change much more difficult and inequality more permanent.

Feminism Feminist IR is a subset of feminist social theory. As a form of critical theory, it challenges the mainstream assumptions of IR. For instance, feminist IR scholars such as J. Ann Tickner (1992), Spike Peterson, Elizabeth Hutchings, Christine Sylvester, and Cynthia Enloe have explored the masculine assumptions (war, aggressive behavior, etc.) that underpin how the nation-state is conceptualized in IR theory.

SUBFIELDS OF INTERNATIONAL RELATIONS

All these perspectives, to varying degrees, encompass important subfields in IR. *Security studies*, also known as *international security*, focuses on threats to states and the state system that stem from the environment, health (such as pandemics like HIV-AIDS), nuclear weapons, and transnational terrorist organizations. Certain scholars in this subfield use formal modeling and game theory to understand the strategic patterns of state behavior. *Civil society studies* focuses upon the manner in which nongovernmental organizations influence the state system. Another normative turn in IR theory has produced vibrant work on *international ethics*. Much of this work focuses upon phenomena such as humanitarian intervention, human rights doctrines, just war theory, genocide and ethnic conflict, and economic deprivation. The field of *international political economy* examines the relation-

ships between nation-states and the international market, as well as how multinational corporations use the global economy to further their material goals. And *international law* remains an important subfield of interest for IR scholars. For instance, many constructivists and English school theorists have used the development of international laws to demonstrate their arguments regarding the presence of identity communities or an international society.

SEE ALSO *Constructivism; Just War; Liberalism; Nation; Neoliberalism; Nongovernmental Organizations (NGOs); Peace; Positivism; Poststructuralism; Realism; World-System*

BIBLIOGRAPHY

Bull, Hedley. [1977] 2002. *The Anarchical Society: A Study of Order in World Politics.* 3rd ed. New York: Columbia University Press.

Cox, Robert. 1981. Social Forces, States, and World Orders: Beyond International Relations Theory. *Millennium: Journal of International Studies* 10 (2): 126–155.

Keohane, Robert O., and Joseph S. Nye Jr. [1977] 2000. *Power and Interdependence.* 3rd ed. New York: Longman.

Kratochwil, Friedrich V. 1989. *Rules, Norms, and Decisions on the Conditions of Practical and Legal Reasoning in International Relations and Domestic Affairs.* Cambridge, U.K.: Cambridge University Press.

Morgenthau, Hans. [1946] 1978. *Politics Among Nations: The Struggle for Power and Peace.* 6th ed. New York: Knopf.

Onuf, Nicholas 1989. *World of Our Making: Rules and Rule in Social Theory and International Relations.* Columbia: University of South Carolina Press.

Tickner, J. Ann 1992. *Gender in International Relations: Feminist Perspectives on Achieving Global Security.* New York: Columbia University Press.

Waltz, Kenneth N. 1979. *Theory of International Politics.* Reading, MA: Addison-Wesley.

Williams, Michael C. 2004. *The Realist Tradition and the Limits of International Relations.* Cambridge, U.K.: Cambridge University Press.

Brent J. Steele

INTERNATIONAL RORSCHACH SOCIETY

SEE *Rorschach Test.*

INTERNATIONALISM

Internationalism has a series of overlapping meanings, all of which revolve around an attempt to regulate political life at the global level in the hopes of constructing a more peaceful order. Its most common meaning is that of a political ideology that advocates greater cooperation among nation-states in the pursuit of peace through the creation of international law and institutions. It is closely associated with international organizations such as the League of Nations and the United Nations (UN), although it is not synonymous with these organizations.

Internationalism is also a U.S. foreign policy doctrine that advocates working through international organizations. Obviously related to the first definition of internationalism, this foreign policy idea is based upon the assumption that working through such organization is beneficial to U.S. national interests, and will additionally benefit the global community.

Internationalism is also a form of cooperation advocated by socialists that assumes the eventual disappearance of the nation-state. For some, this would come only through a revolutionary process; for others it would be a gradual reformation of the international system.

Each of these forms of internationalism is premised on the assumption that peace will result only from programmatic attempts at organizing international affairs. It is thus primarily a liberal ideology, although some suggest there can be a conservative version of it as well (Holbraad 2003). The overriding goal, however, is the promotion of peace through alignment of what might otherwise be conflicting interests.

IDEATIONAL HISTORY

As an idea, internationalism arose from the collapse of a European, Christian institutional order (Ishay 1995). As the Christian ethicopolitical order came under strain as a result of the rise of Protestantism, the Renaissance, and then the Enlightenment, political philosophers turned toward natural law as a means by which to construct a peaceful international system. An important part of this move was the recognition that allegiance to and obligations toward political communities are not necessarily wrong, but that such allegiances and obligations need to be modified by a larger set of rules and norms that might govern relations among those communities. One of the first attempts to construct such an order came from Hugo Grotius (1583–1645), a Dutch theologian and philosopher who helped create modern international law by linking older natural theories to an emerging Renaissance interest in the historical practice of political communities. Grotius's famous *The Rights of War and Peace* (1625) proposed a theoretical foundation for governing war that reformulated the "just war" tradition and launched modern international law.

The nineteenth century saw the emergence of positivist international law, which kept the same internationalist agenda but turned to different sources for its justifications (Nardin 1998). International law became the primary focus of attempts to promote internationalism, with its insistence that states remain the central agents and its attempts to limit their ability to launch war (Koskenniemi 2002). Internationalism as a political project arose from these legal attempts to align an unwillingness to give up on the nation-state with a desire for peace.

Internationalism was also an important idea among philosophers. Immanuel Kant famously argued for methods by which the international community could avoid war (Ishay 1995). Kant's proposal for a republican peace pact has been the foundation both of the democratic peace thesis and for internationalism. Kant argued that as more states became republics, their citizens would demand more cooperation (1795). This located internationalism within the nation, something that others sought to do during the Enlightenment and romantic periods.

A very different type of internationalism arose from the philosophy of Karl Marx. Marx's argument that the decay of capitalism would result in the construction of communism was meant to apply not just to specific states but also to the human condition more broadly. Lenin took Marx's ideas to a more specifically international level in his work on imperialism. These ideas were taken up by both revolutionary socialists, who argued that active attempts to overturn the nation-state and its bourgeois foundations were necessary, and reform-oriented socialists, who believed that cooperation through various international fora would lead to the collapse of the capitalist order.

INSTITUTIONAL HISTORY

These ideas, particularly those in the realm of international law, became more concrete at the end of the nineteenth and in the early twentieth centuries. Prior to and particularly after World War I, proponents of greater international institutional arrangements to ensure peace published a number of works (Navari 2000, Jones 2002). With the end of World War I, proposals for international institutions to moderate war came to fruition with the League of Nations. For some internationalists, the League was a concrete expression of their views, but for others it was too weak to create a truly internationalist sentiment. The failure of the United States to join the League and the abandonment of its tenets by Germany, Italy, and then Japan eviscerated it, and World War II finally forced the collapse of the League.

The end of World War II saw a resurgence of internationalism, particularly in the United States. Leading the way to the creation of a new international institution, the Americans agreed to host the newly created United Nations. Once again, some internationalists were enthusiastic about the new institution, but others found it wanting. The creation of the World Federalist League was an attempt to push the U.S. public, and the wider international community, toward greater forms of cooperation. Functionalists argued that as international affairs became more complex, there would be greater need for cooperation among nations.

Coupled with the creation of the United Nations, international law exploded in the post–World War II era. The International Law Commission, a body of international lawyers exploring important issues, pushed various issues forward on the international agenda, with some becoming treaties that led to new international organizations such as the International Criminal Court. As decolonization progressed the UN General Assembly soon grew beyond its few members and passed numerous nonbinding resolutions. After the end of the cold war the UN Security Council aggressively expanded its reach, producing not just binding resolutions but also more regulations to govern wider aspects of international life.

RELATED IDEAS

Internationalism needs to be kept separate from two related but distinct terms: *cosmopolitanism* and *globalization*. Cosmopolitanism finds its roots in antiquity, with Stoic philosophers from ancient Greece and Cicero in Rome arguing for the consideration of all persons as equal (Hayden 2006). If all were truly "citizens of the world," war and strife for the purposes of empire or monarchical advancement were pointless. This sentiment resurfaced in various religious traditions, with Christianity and Islam both arguing for a broadly understood universal community, albeit one founded on their particular religious tenets. Cosmopolitan thinking intersected with internationalism during the Enlightenment, but internationalists such as Immanuel Kant and Jean-Jacques Rousseau did not see much point in abandoning the nation-state. Instead, they thought that republican forms of cooperation, in which states agreed to limit their sovereignty for purposes of greater cooperation, were preferable to the destruction of those states in the name of a larger international community.

Cosmopolitanism has been revived with globalization, a process by which the international economic and cultural sphere becomes more unified and interdependent. Especially among analytic philosophers interested in global justice, cosmopolitan ideas have great resonance. Again, though, internationalists find some of these proposals at odds with the current power structure of the international system, in which great powers would be loathe to abandon their position in a formally anarchic, but practically hierarchic system.

Internationalism differs from proposals for a world government, against which it was largely posited in the late nineteenth and early twentieth centuries. Worried that a world government would lead to an oppressive and unwieldy bureaucracy, internationalists hoped to keep the nation-state as a foundation, but to moderate its aggressive elements through various institutional arrangements.

Finally, within the American polity, internationalism reflects a support for a foreign policy orientation toward international institutions. Although some international economic institutions—for example, the World Trade Organization, the International Monetary Foundation, and the World Bank—are widely accepted by the U.S. foreign policy elite, the United Nations continues to generate strong debate. Neoconservatives and libertarians find the constraints imposed by the UN on the ability of the United States to run its own affairs unconscionable, whereas many Democrats and centrist Republicans find the UN and its promise of multilateralism the only real option in a world so interconnected and conflictual. Especially as U.S. power is stretched to its limits in places such as Iraq, the benefits of internationalism as a foreign policy strategy will become more influential. For those who believe in the values of the Enlightenment, such a move would be most welcome, returning the United States to its role as a leading proponent of Enlightenment theory and practice.

SEE ALSO *Cosmopolitanism; Enlightenment; Globalization, Social and Economic Aspects of; Government, World; International Economic Order; International Monetary Fund; League of Nations; Lenin, Vladimir Ilitch; Libertarianism; Marx, Karl; Peace; Transnationalism; United Nations; World War II*

BIBLIOGRAPHY

Grotius, Hugo. [1625] 2003. *The Rights of War and Peace*, ed. Richard Tuck, from the edition by Jean Barbeyrac. Indianapolis, IN: Liberty Fund.

Hayden, Patrick. 2006. *Cosmopolitan Global Politics*. Aldershot, U.K.: Ashgate.

Holbraad, Carsten. 2003. *Internationalism and Nationalism in European Political Thought*. New York: Palgrave.

Ishay, Michelene. 1995. *Internationalism and Its Betrayal*. Minneapolis: University of Minnesota Press.

Jones, Dorothy. 2002. *Toward a Just World: The Critical Years in the Search for International Justice*. Chicago: University of Chicago Press.

Kant, Immanuel. [1795] 1991. Perpetual Peace: A Philosophical Sketch. In *Political Writings*, ed. Hans Reiss, trans. H. B. Nisbett. Cambridge, U.K.: Cambridge University Press.

Koskenniemi, Martii. 2002. *The Gentle Civilizer of Nations: The Rise and Fall of International Law, 1870–1960*. Cambridge, U.K.: Cambridge University Press.

Nardin, Terry. 1998. Legal Positivism as a Theory of International Society. In *International Society: Diverse Ethical Perspectives*, ed. David Mapel and Terry Nardin, 17–35. Princeton, NJ: Princeton University Press.

Navari, Cornelia. 2000. *Internationalism and the State in the 20th Century*. London: Routledge.

Anthony F. Lang Jr.

INTERNET

The Internet is a vast global system of interconnected technical networks made up of heterogeneous information and communication technologies. It is also a social and economic assemblage that allows diverse forms of communication, creativity, and cultural exchange at a scope and scale unknown before the late twentieth century.

The terms *Internet* and *net* are often used when discussing the social implications of new information technologies, such as the creation of new communal bonds across great distances or new forms of wealth and inequality. Such a usage is imprecise: The Internet is distinct from the applications and technologies that are built upon it, such as e-mail, the World Wide Web, online gaming, file-sharing networks, and e-commerce and e-governance initiatives. There are also many networks that are or were once distinct from the Internet, such as mobile telephone networks and electronic financial networks.

Stated more precisely, the Internet is an infrastructural substrate that possesses innovative social, cultural, and economic features allowing creativity (or innovation) based on openness and a particular standardization process. It is a necessary, but not a sufficient, condition for many of the social and cultural implications often attributed to it. Understanding the particularity of the Internet can be key to differentiating its implications and potential impact on society from the impacts of "information technology" and computers more generally.

HISTORY AND STRUCTURE OF THE INTERNET

The Internet developed through military, university, corporate, and amateur user innovations occurring more or less constantly beginning in the late 1960s. Despite its complexity, it is unlike familiar complex technical objects—for example, a jumbo jetliner—that are designed, tested, and refined by a strict hierarchy of experts who attempt to possess a complete overview of the object and its final state. By contrast, the Internet has been subject to innovation, experimentation, and refinement by a much less well-defined collective of diverse users with wide-ranging goals and interests.

In 1968 the Internet was known as the ARPAnet, named for its principal funding agency, the U.S. Department of Defense Advanced Research Projects Agency (ARPA). It was a small but extensive research project organized by the Information Processing Techniques Office at ARPA that focused on advanced concepts in computing, specifically graphics, time-sharing, and networking. The primary goal of the network was to allow separate administratively bounded resources (computers and software at particular geographical sites) to be shared across those boundaries, without forcing standardization across all of them. The participants were primarily university researchers in computer and engineering departments. Separate experiments in networking, both corporate and academic, were also under way during this period, such as the creation of "Ethernet" by Robert Metcalfe at Xerox PARC and the X.25 network protocols standardized by the International Telecommunications Union.

By 1978 the ARPAnet had grown to encompass dozens of universities and military research sites in the United States. At this point the project leaders at ARPA recognized a need for a specific kind of standardization to keep the network feasible, namely a common operating system and networking software that could run on all of the diverse hardware connected to the network. Based on its widespread adoption in the 1970s, the UNIX operating system was chosen by ARPA as one official platform for the Internet. UNIX was known for its portability (ability to be installed on different kinds of hardware) and extensibility (ease with which new components could be added to the core system). Bill Joy (who later cofounded Sun Microsystems) is credited with the first widespread implementation of the Internet Protocol (IP) software in a UNIX operating system, a version known as Berkeley Systems Distribution (BSD).

The Internet officially began (in name and in practice) in 1983, the date set by an ad hoc group of engineers known as the Network Working Group (NWG) as the deadline for all connected computers to begin using the Transmission Control Protocol and Internet Protocol (TCP/IP) protocols. These protocols were originally designed in 1973 and consistently improved over the ensuing ten years, but only in 1983 did they become the protocols that would define the Internet. At roughly the same time, ARPA and the Department of Defense split the existing ARPAnet in two, keeping "Milnet" for sensitive military use and leaving ARPAnet for research purposes and for civilian uses.

From 1983 to 1993, in addition to being a research network, the Internet became an underground, subcultural phenomenon, familiar to amateur computer enthusiasts, university students and faculty, and "hackers." The Internet's glamour was largely associated with the arcane nature of interaction it demanded—largely text-based, and demanding access to and knowledge of the UNIX operating system. Thus, owners of the more widespread personal computers made by IBM and Apple were largely excluded from the Internet (though a number of other similar networks such as Bulletin Board Services, BITNet, and FidoNET existed for PC users).

A very large number of amateur computer enthusiasts discovered the Internet during this period, either through university courses or through friends, and there are many user-initiated innovations that date to this period, ranging from games (e.g., MUDs, or Multi-User Dungeons) to programming and scripting languages (e.g., Perl, created by Larry Wall) to precursors of the World Wide Web (e.g., WAIS, Archie, and Gopher). During this period, the network was overseen and funded by the National Science Foundation, which invested heavily in improving the basic infrastructure of fiberoptic "backbones" in the United States in 1988. The oversight and management of the Internet was commercialized in 1995, with the backing of the presidential administration of Bill Clinton.

In 1993 the World Wide Web (originally designed by Tim Berners-Lee at CERN in Switzerland) and the graphical Mosaic Web Browser (created by the National Center for Supercomputing Applications at the University of Illinois) brought the Internet to a much larger audience. Between 1993 and 2000 the "dot-com" boom drove the transformation of the Internet from an underground research phenomena to a nearly ubiquitous and essential technology with far-reaching effects. Commercial investment in infrastructure and in "web presence" saw explosive growth; new modes of interaction and communication (e.g., e-mail, Internet messaging, and mailing lists) proliferated; Uniform Resource Locators (URLs, such as www.britannica.com) became a common (and highly valued) feature of advertisements and corporate identity; and artists, scientists, citizens, and others took up the challenge of both using and understanding the new medium.

PROTOCOLS AND THE INTERNET STANDARDS PROCESS

The core technical components of the Internet are standardized protocols, not hardware or software, strictly speaking—though obviously it would not have spread so extensively without the innovations in microelectronics, the continual enhancement of telecommunications infrastructures around the globe, and the growth in ownership and use of personal computers over the last twenty years. Protocols make the "inter" in the Internet possible by allowing a huge number of nonoverlapping and incompatible networks to become compatible and to route data across all of them.

The key protocols, known as TCP/IP, were designed in 1973 by Vint Cerf and Robert Kahn. Other key protocols, such as the Domain Name System (DNS) and User Datagram Protocol (UDP), came later. These protocols have to be implemented in software (such as in the UNIX operating system described above) to allow computers to interconnect. They are essentially standards with which hardware and software implementations must comply in order for any type of hardware or software to connect to the Internet and communicate with any other hardware and software that does the same. They can best be understood as a kind of technical Esperanto.

The Internet protocols differ from traditional standards because of the unconventional social process by which they are developed, validated, and improved. The Internet protocols are elaborated in a set of openly available documents known as Requests for Comments (RFCs), which are maintained by a loose federation of engineers called the Internet Engineering Task Force (IETF, the successor to the Network Working Group). The IETF is an organization open to individuals (unlike large standards organizations that typically accept only national or corporate representatives) that distributes RFCs free of charge and encourages members to implement protocols and to improve them based on their experiences and users' responses. The improved protocol then may be released for further implementation.

This "positive feedback loop" differs from most "consensus-oriented" standardization processes (e.g., those of international organizations such as ISO, the International Organization for Standardization) that seek to achieve a final and complete state before encouraging implementations. The relative ease with which one piece of software can be replaced with another is a key reason for this difference. During the 1970s and 1980s this system served the Internet well, allowing it to develop quickly, according to the needs of its users. By the 1990s, however, the scale of the Internet made innovation a slower and more difficult procedure—a fact that is most clearly demonstrated by the comparatively glacial speed with which the next generation of the Internet protocol (known as IP Version 6) has been implemented.

Ultimately, the IETF style of standardization process has become a common cultural reference point of engineers and expert users of the Internet, and has been applied not only to the Internet, but also to the production of applications and tools that rely on the Internet. The result is a starkly different mode of innovation and sharing that is best exemplified by the growth and success of so-called "free software" or "open-source software." Many of the core applications that are widely used on the Internet are developed in this fashion (famous examples include the Linux operating system kernel and the Apache Web Server).

CULTURAL, SOCIAL, AND ECONOMIC IMPLICATIONS OF THE INTERNET

As a result of the unusual development process and the nature of the protocols, it has been relatively easy for the Internet to advance around the globe and to connect heterogeneous equipment in diverse settings, wherever there are willing and enthusiastic users with sufficient technical know-how. The major impediment to doing so is the reliability (or mere existence) of preexisting infrastructural components such as working energy and telecommunications infrastructures. Between 1968 and 1993 this expansion was not conducted at a national or state level, but by individuals and organizations who saw local benefit in expanding access to the global network. If a university computer science department could afford to devote some resources to computers dedicated to routing traffic and connections, then all the researchers in a department could join the network without needing permission from any centralized state authority. It was not until the late 1990s that Internet governance became an issue that concerned governments and citizens around the world. In particular, the creation of the Internet Corporation for Assigned Names and Numbers (ICANN) has been the locus of fractious dispute, especially in international arenas. ICANN's narrow role is to assign IP numbers (e.g., 192.168.0.1) and the names they map to (e.g., www.wikipedia.org), but it has been perceived, rightly or wrongly, as an instrument of U.S. control over the Internet.

With each expansion of the Internet, issues of privacy, security, and organizational (or national) authority have become more pressing. At its outset the Internet protocols sought to prioritize control within administrative boundaries, leaving rules governing use to the local network owners. Such a scheme obviated the need for a central authority that determined global rules about access, public/private boundaries, and priority of use. With the advent of widespread commercial access, however, such local control has been severely diluted, and the possibility for individual mischief (e.g., identity theft, spam, and other privacy violations) has increased with increasing accessibility.

On the one hand, increased commercial access means a decline in local organized authority over parts of the Internet in favor of control of large segments by Internet Service Providers (ISPs) and telecommunications/cable corporations. On the other hand, as the basic infrastructure of the Internet has spread, so have the practices and norms that were developed in concert with the technology—including everything from the proper way to configure a router, to norms of proper etiquette on mailing lists and for e-mail. Applications built on top of the Internet have often adopted such norms and modes of use, and promoted a culture of innovation, of "hacking" (someone who creates new software by employing a series of modifications that exploit or extend existing code or resources, with good or bad connotations depending on the context), and of communal sharing of software, protocols, and tools.

It is thus important to realize that although most users do not experience the Internet directly, the development of the particular forms of innovation and openness that characterize the Internet also characterize the more familiar applications built on top of it, due to the propagation of these norms and modes of engineering. There is often, therefore, a significant difference between innovations that owe their genesis to the Internet and those developed in the personal computer industry, the so-called "proprietary" software industry, and in distinct commercial network infrastructures (e.g., the SABRE system for airline reservations, or the MOST network for credit card transactions). The particularity of the Internet leads to different implications and potential impact on society than the impacts of "information technology" or computers more generally.

DIGITAL MUSIC, FILM, AND INTELLECTUAL PROPERTY

One of the most widely discussed and experienced implications of the Internet is the effect on the culture industries, especially music and film. As with previous media (e.g., video and audio cassette recorders), it is the intersection of technology and intellectual property that is responsible for the controversy. Largely due to its "openness," the Internet creates the possibility for low-cost and extremely broad and fast distribution of cultural materials, from online books to digital music and film. At the same time, it also creates the possibility for broad and fast violation of intellectual property rights—rights that have been strengthened considerably by the copyright act of 1976 and the Digital Millennium Copyright Act (1998).

The result is a cultural battle over the meaning of "sharing" music and movies, and the degree to which such sharing is criminal. The debates have been polarized between a "war on piracy" on the one hand (with widely varying figures concerning the economic losses), and "consumer freedom" on the other—rights to copy, share, and trade purchased music. The cultural implication of this war is a tension among the entertainment industry, the artists and musicians, and the consumers of music and film. Because the openness of the Internet makes it easier than ever for artists to distribute their work, many see a potential for direct remuneration, and cheaper and more immediate access for consumers. The entertainment industry, by contrast, argues that it provides more services and quality—not to mention more funding and capital—and that it creates jobs and contributes to a growing economy. In both cases, the investments are protected primarily by the mechanism of intellectual property law, and are easily diluted by illicit copying and distribution. And yet, it is unclear where to draw a line between legitimate sharing (which might also be a form of marketing) and illegitimate sharing ("piracy," according to the industry).

THE DIGITAL DIVIDE

A key question about the Internet is that of social equity and access. The term *digital divide* has been used primarily to indicate the differential in individual access to the Internet, or in computer literacy, between rich and poor, or between developed and developing nations. A great deal of research has gone into understanding inequality of access to the Internet, and estimates of both differential access and the rate of the spread of access have varied extremely widely, depending on methodology. It is, however, clear from the statistics that between 1996 and 2005 the rate of growth in usage has been consistently greater than 100 percent in almost all regions of the globe at some times, and in some places it has reached annual growth rates of 500 percent or more. Aside from the conclusion that the growth in access to the Internet has been fantastically rapid, there are few sure facts about differential access.

There are, however, a number of more refined questions that researchers have begun investigating: Is the quantity or rate of growth in access to the Internet larger or smaller than in the case of other media (e.g., television, print, and radio)? Are there significant differences within groups with access (e.g., class, race, or national differences in quality of access)? Does access actually enhance or change a person's life chances or opportunities?

The implication of a digital divide (whether between nations and regions, or within them) primarily concerns the quality of information and the ability of individuals to use it to better their life chances. In local terms, this can affect development issues broadly (e.g., access to markets and government, democratic deliberation and participation, and access to education and employment opportunities); in global terms, differential access can affect the subjective understandings of issues ranging from religious intolerance to global warming and environmental issues to global geopolitics. Digital divides might also differ based on the political situation—such as in the case of the Chinese government's attempt to censor access to politicized information, which in turn can affect the fate of cross-border investment and trade.

SEE ALSO *Information, Economics of; Media; Microelectronics Industry; Property Rights, Intellectual*

BIBLIOGRAPHY

Abbate, Janet. 1999. *Inventing the Internet*. Cambridge, MA: MIT Press.

Castells, Manuel. 2001. *The Internet Galaxy: Reflections on the Internet, Business, and Society*. Oxford: Oxford University Press.

DiMaggio, Paul, Eszter Hargittai, Coral Celeste, and Steven Shafer. 2004. Digital Inequality: From Unequal Access to Differentiated Use. In *Social Inequality*, ed. Kathryn Neckerman, 355–400. New York: Russell Sage Foundation.

International Telecommunication Union. ICT Indicators. http://www.itu.int/ITU-D/ict/.

Meuller, Milton. 2004. *Ruling the Root: Internet Governance and the Taming of Cyberspace*. Cambridge, MA: MIT Press.

National Telecommunications and Information Administration. A Nation Online: Entering the Broadband Era. http://www.ntia.doc.gov/reports/anol/index.html.

Norberg, Arthur L., and Judy E. O'Neill. 1996. *Transforming Computer Technology: Information Processing for the Pentagon, 1962–1986*. Baltimore: Johns Hopkins University Press.

Pew Internet and American Life Project. http://www.pewinternet.org.

Schmidt, Susanne K., and Raymund Werle. 1997. *Coordinating Technology: Studies in the International Standardization of Telecommunications*. Cambridge, MA: MIT Press.

Waldrop, M. Mitchell. 2001. *The Dream Machine: JCR Licklider and the Revolution That Made Computing Personal*. New York: Viking Penguin.

Weber, Steven. 2004. *The Success of Open Source*. Cambridge, MA: Harvard University Press.

Christopher M. Kelty

INTERNET, IMPACT ON POLITICS

Since the mid-1990s a new force has emerged to reshape modern society—the Internet. One aspect of society that the Internet has changed significantly is politics. In politics, the Internet has produced three types of change. The first is the way that politicians reach the voting public. Previously, politicians could only reach the public using the established media (television, radio, or newspapers and magazines) or by meeting people on the street. This is no longer the case. The second change produced by the Internet relates to the participation of the average citizen in political processes. People used to be limited to voting, sit-ins, strikes, public gatherings, letter writing, and similar types of activities, but since the advent of the Internet, many new activities have developed. The third change caused by the Internet is the creation of a whole new group of participants in the political process. Before the Internet was available, the only private groups that were politically active were either very large, very specialized, or both; the Internet has enabled small, local groups to also participate in politics.

Politicians and their staffs can use the Internet to maintain contact with supporters and to gather new supporters. Chat rooms, blogs, and email updates are the preferred resources for maintaining contact with supporters. These allow supporters to form a community and to receive the latest news about a candidate directly. The process of drawing new supporters relies on World Wide Web (WWW) sites maintained by the candidate and his or her staff. Politicians may also gain support through blogs maintained by people not officially affiliated with the candidate, as well as through email briefs to bloggers and traditional media, search engines, and general information sources such as Wikipedia. The Internet is sufficiently important in political campaigns that by the time of the 2004 U.S. presidential election, major candidates maintained staff positions dedicated to Internet campaigning.

The ability of politicians to reach their constituents does have some drawbacks. Political opponents can employ the same technologies to undermine candidacies, as happened to Barack Obama in the presidential campaign at the end of 2006 with the release of information about his attendance at a Muslim school. In the beginning of 2007, John Edwards illustrated that candidates are also capable of damaging their own campaigns when attempting to employ blogs. Both of these incidents spread over the Internet with incredible speed. Some organizations form explicitly to use the Internet politically against politicians, as with Moveon.org's actions against President George W. Bush, while others such as PoliticsNow.com arise to inform voters. Just like organizations, individual reporters from independents like the Drudge Report to mainstream reporters from *The Washington Post* or *The New York Times* have used the Internet to present various positions.

During elections, private citizens can use the Internet to show support for preferred candidates by using the candidates' Web sites directly (including making online donations) or by visiting general sites, through which they may take part in opinion polls or contribute to blog commentary. Supporters may also visit private Internet sites supporting a candidate or even sites run by interest groups that support a slate of candidates. Although Internet voting has not yet been employed on a large scale, Arizona has experimented with limited Internet voting as far back as 2000. Beyond election-related activities, citizens can use the Internet to engage in the political process in many new ways. The U.S. Congress and some state legislatures post proposed and enacted legislation on the Internet. Interested citizens can then email a representative or sen-

ator. Some state, county, and even city governments provide Web broadcasts (webcasts) of meetings. Many big-city police departments maintain Web sites with law enforcement information and crime reports.

This information allows interested citizens to follow government activity and react quickly when appropriate. Usually, citizens communicate about politics using Web sites, email, and text messaging (also called instant messaging or IM). There have been a number of instances when people used Internet resources to come together quickly to pressure a government. For example, the Internet allowed people to organize for a large protest in the Philippines in early 2001 that forced President Joseph Estrada from power. In such cases, instant messaging can be used to gather large numbers of people so rapidly that law enforcement is too slow to respond. Such gatherings, known as *flash mobs*, have been known to force change in governments. Flash mobs were used by protestors during the 1999 World Trade Organization meeting in Seattle, Washington, and overwhelmed local law enforcement.

Small local groups are also able to use the Internet for political purposes. It was once necessary for groups to establish either size or significant specialization before they could influence national or international politics. The Internet has allowed smaller, more localized groups to combine their influence, tap public opinion, and take a role in both national and international politics. For example, the leaders of various organizations within the militia movement in the United States have used the Internet to connect with each other, organize jointly, disseminate propaganda, and trade techniques since the late 1990s. Examples of such efforts in other countries include the Mexican Zapatista movement, whose leaders used the Internet to garner international awareness of their situation and apply international pressure on the Mexican government during the mid- to late 1990s. Activists involved in the world environmental movement used the Internet during the June 1992 United Nations Conference on Environment and Development in Rio de Janeiro, a meeting known informally as the Earth Summit, to coordinate the activities of numerous disparate groups. During the 1992 Rio sessions, these groups organized and presented their positions to delegates using the Internet. As a result of these Internet-based efforts across national borders by small political-interest groups, the opinions of these groups were taken into account and included in the resulting international treaty. Although activities at the Rio sessions predate the Internet's arrival into mainstream political activity, it showed the potential of the then newly-emerging technology and helped to promote the early use of the Internet. Although the Internet was not sufficiently widespread for groups to reach public audiences, the environmental groups used email to communicate with technophiles in other groups and to coordinate activities. The capacity of the Internet to influence closed totalitarian societies remains unclear, but its impact on open societies is generally accepted.

From the perspective of politicians, individual citizens, or interest groups, the Internet has changed the way in which people participate in politics by allowing them to break free from historical limitations. In the case of private citizens and small interest groups, the Internet has allowed both to gain access to the political process and political powers in a manner not previously available. The role of the Internet on politics is still developing, and research on its impact is underway.

SEE ALSO *Internet; Politics*

BIBLIOGRAPHY

Anderson, David M., and Michael Cornfeld, eds. 2003. *The Civic Web: Online Politics and Democratic Values.* Lanham, MD: Rowman and Littlefield.

Davis, Richard. 2005. *Politics Online: Blogs, Chatrooms, and Discussion Groups in American Democracy.* New York: Routledge.

Deibert, Ronald J. 1997. *Parchment, Printing, and Hypermedia: Communication in World Order Transformation.* New York: Columbia University Press.

Franda, Marcus. 2002. *Launching into Cyberspace: Internet Development and Politics in Five World Regions.* Boulder, CO: Lynne Rienner.

Kalathil, Shanthi, and Taylor C. Boas. 2003. *Open Networks, Closed Regimes: The Impact of the Internet on Authoritarian Rule.* Washington, DC: Carnegie Endowment for International Peace.

Norris, Pippa. 2001. *Digital Divide: Civic Engagement, Information Poverty, and the Internet Worldwide.* New York: Cambridge University Press.

Potter, Evan H., ed. 2002. *Cyber-Diplomacy: Managing Foreign Policy in the Twenty-first Century.* Montreal: McGill-Queen's University Press.

Rheingold, Howard. 2002. *Smart Mobs: The Next Social Revolution.* Cambridge, MA: Perseus.

Shane, Peter M., ed. 2004. *Democracy Online: The Prospects for Political Renewal through the Internet.* New York: Routledge.

Sunstein, Cass. 2001. *Republic.com.* Princeton, NJ: Princeton University Press.

David B. Conklin

INTERNET BUBBLE

A bubble is an unsustainable increase in the price of an asset type driven by the expectation of further price increases rather than fundamental characteristics. Bubbles are a concern of social science since they result from individual calculations about the behavior of others in society.

Indeed, in his 1721 poem about the first price escalation for which the term bubble was widely used, Jonathan Swift linked the British South Sea Bubble to the "madness of the crowd" denying the fundamentals: "But as a Guinnea will not pass / At Market for a Farthing more / Shewn through a multiplying Glass / Than what it allways did before" (1958, p. 255).

During a bubble, the downplaying of fundamental analysis leaves little to counterbalance the momentum of the rising price and the solidifying of interests in its preservation. Lower-quality assets rise along with higher-quality assets when fundamental characteristics are less distinguished. As suggested by John Stuart Mill in *Principles of Political Economy* (1848), assessing price becomes even more difficult when money is borrowed: "Some accident, which excites expectations of rising prices … a generally reckless and adventurous feeling prevails, which disposes people to give as well as take credit more largely than at other times, and give it to persons not entitled to it" (1899, p. 47). The most vexing feature of a bubble was captured by Alan Greenspan, the chairman of the Federal Reserve Board, when he testified in April 2000 at a Senate Banking Committee hearing that a bubble cannot be definitively identified until after the fact. The benefit of hindsight suggests that there was an Internet stock bubble as Greenspan spoke.

The Internet Bubble was set against the backdrop of rapid growth in Internet use. The 1991 invention of the World Wide Web and the 1994 release of the Netscape browser transformed a text interface into a more accessible graphical interface that propelled Internet use from about 10 percent of Americans in 1995 to 50 percent by 2000. This growth held the promise of making money and a boom of investment capital flowed into Internet enterprises, commonly referred to as "dot.coms."

One way to generate investment dollars was by issuing stock in an Internet-related company. Upon issue, Internet stocks often experienced a dramatic rise in price. Multifold increases in price on the day of issue were common. The success of early Internet stock issues prompted additional offerings. Prices for Internet stocks continued to soar in the late 1990s.

The broad expectation of increasing Internet stock prices reduced concern for the fundamental characteristics of the individual companies whose stock price was increasing. Many of the dot.coms had never made a profit. Companies operated under the assumption that if they could generate a sizable user base by giving away their product or Web site content, they would eventually figure out how to make money. Traditional standards of longevity and profitability before issuing a stock gave way in a climate of high valuations for even fundamentally weak business models. The number of potential stock buyers increased with the advent of online trading in which the Internet itself reduced transaction costs for buying stocks. Many stock buyers were encouraged to borrow based on expected price increases. Investment clubs and day traders proliferated. The expectation of rising prices was strong, but not sustainable. Lacking strength in the fundamentals, Internet stocks could not avoid the ultimate spiral downward when owners began selling to take profits and later to reduce losses.

The significant presence of Internet-related companies on the Nasdaq Stock Market makes it an appropriate place for identifying the contours of the Internet Bubble. Nasdaq closing values reveal a thirty-month period in which the composite index tripled and then returned. The Nasdaq closed at 1639.19 on October 20, 1998, reached 3000 for the first time on November 3, 1999, and peaked at 5048.62 on March 10, 2000. On the decline, it had closed below 3000 by November 13, 2000, and was at 1638.80 on April 4, 2001. The deflated bubble left Internet stock values at a tiny percentage of their highs and dotted the landscape with failed companies.

The massive shift of wealth during the Internet Bubble produced winners and losers. A variety of advantages, including access to the initial offering price and reserved shares, meant that those on the inside of stock offerings were more likely to be winners than were ordinary buyers. One clear winner was Internet innovation, which was facilitated by the large amounts of capital that went to enterprises during the Internet Bubble.

SEE ALSO *Bubbles; Great Tulip Mania, The; Internet; Technological Progress, Economic Growth; Telecommunications Industry*

BIBLIOGRAPHY

Ip, Greg, Susan Pulliam, Scott Thurm, and Ruth Simon. 2000. The Color Green: The Internet Bubble Broke Records, Rules and Bank Accounts; Wall Street and Allies Built $1.4 Trillion Monument to Fast-Money Madness. *Wall Street Journal*, July 14.

Mill, John Stuart. 1899. *Principles of Political Economy with Some of Their Applications to Social Philosophy*. Vol. 2. New York: Colonial Press. (Orig. pub. 1848).

Swift, Jonathan. 1958. The Bubble. In *The Poems of Jonathan Swift*. Vol. 1, ed. Harold Williams. London: Oxford University Press. (Orig. pub. 1721).

Robert J. Klotz

INTERNMENT, JAPANESE AMERICAN

SEE *Incarceration, Japanese American.*

INTERRACIAL MARRIAGE

SEE *Marriage, Interracial.*

INTERRACIAL SEX

SEE *Sex, Interracial.*

INTERROGATION

Interrogation is a process that seeks to obtain information by questioning (usually direct questioning) from a person often described as either a suspect or a source. Interrogation may be conducted for a number of reasons, most commonly in pursuit of a criminal investigation or to collect intelligence concerning foreign states, terrorist groups, or other persons considered to be actual or potential threats to national security. Interrogation raises a variety of legal and ethical issues that turn upon the techniques employed. But a practical issue common to all methods of interrogation concerns the efficacy of the method deployed. This depends, in part, on the ability of the interrogator (or the interrogator's associates) to detect deception. However, it is not possible to conduct a legitimate empirical study assessing the comparative efficacy of aggressive and nonaggressive interrogation tactics. Such a study would violate accepted norms of research ethics, not to mention numerous domestic and international legal provisions. For this reason, claims of relative efficacy tend to rest on sporadic anecdotal evidence.

METHODS OF INTERROGATION

Interrogation techniques range from so-called rapport-building—which often uses conversation to gain the trust and confidence of the suspect or source—to physical or mental torture that leaves the victim with permanent physical or mental scars. Between these two extremes are a number of aggressive tactics, such as stress positions, sleep deprivation, prolonged isolation, and exposure to temperature extremes. These techniques—particularly when used in combination—often constitute cruel, inhuman, or degrading treatment in violation of international law as well as domestic legal norms. In some cases, aggressive tactics may constitute physical or mental torture, despite the absence of permanent physical injury or psychological damage. Although interrogational torture has been used (and is still used) throughout the world, public statements of experienced interrogators tend to eschew torture on the grounds that it yields unreliable results.

This is because, under pressure, suspects tend to say what they think their interrogators want to hear.

Often suspects will confess in the hope that this will ease the pressure imposed by interrogators. These are sometimes called *pressured-compliant confessions* (Gudjonsson 2003). Sometimes persistent pressured interrogation leads suspects to doubt their own recollections, particularly in the face of apparently confident assertions by interrogators that the suspect is guilty of a crime. There have been a number of well-documented cases in which false confessions—and, as a result, criminal convictions—were obtained following the use of high pressure interrogation tactics. One of the best-known examples, given international prominence by the Oscar-nominated film *In the Name of the Father* (dir. Jim Sheridan, 1993), is the case of the so-called Guildford Four. It arose out of a devastating bombing campaign conducted by the Irish Republican Army on mainland Britain in 1974. Convictions were secured largely on the basis of purported confessions, despite the defendants' claims that they had been threatened and assaulted while in custody. The convictions were not overturned until 1989, after the defendants had spent fifteen years in prison. In 2005 the British prime minister, Tony Blair, apologized to the Guildford Four and said that they deserved to be "completely and publicly exonerated."

Interrogators have long been interested in using pharmacological agents to overcome resistance to interrogation. In the 1950s and 1960s, the U.S. Central Intelligence Agency (CIA) ran a program known by the codename MKULTRA, established in response to reports of alleged Soviet, Chinese, and North Korean mind-control techniques. (These reports were given some credence when thirty-six American airmen shot down in the Korean War falsely confessed to a vast plot to bomb civilian targets.) The MKULTRA program involved experiments (many of which were carried out on unwitting subjects) using psychoactive drugs such as LSD and mescaline in an attempt to control or influence human behavior. Other drugs reportedly used, either in experiments or during actual counterintelligence interrogations, include scopolamine, sodium pentothal, and sodium amytal. However, there is little evidence that any so-called truth serum has ever lived up to its name or its legend in popular culture. It has been alleged that, after the terror attacks in the United States on September 11, 2001, the CIA took a renewed interest in using drugs as interrogation aids. It has also been reported that the CIA used drugs prior to interrogating (among others) Khalid Sheikh Mohammed, a senior Al-Qaeda operative who is alleged to have been the architect of the 9/11 attacks and who was captured by the United States in 2003.

LIE DETECTION

There are a variety of approaches to detecting deception in interrogation. They include analysis of verbal and nonverbal behavioral cues, analysis of the content of interrogation responses, and measurement of the physiological responses to questioning. Empirical research indicates that most people (including many professional interrogators) are unable to detect deception from demeanor. Several studies have demonstrated that accuracy is generally close to chance. However, a very small number of people have proven exceptionally prodigious in their ability to detect deception. According to psychologist Paul Ekman, these people are able to detect lies by observing *microexpressions*, fleeting movements of dozens of facial muscles. (Ekman has catalogued these microexpressions and taught others to recognize them [Ekman 2004].) Another approach, *content-based criteria analysis*, scrutinizes the contents of statements for potential evidence of truthfulness, such as superfluous detail and spontaneous self-correction.

Advances in technology often seem to promise simpler methods for detecting deception, but they usually fail to deliver. The polygraph (the so-called lie detector) relies on physiological manifestations of anxiety—changes in skin conductance, heart rate, and respiration—in order to flag deception. It is therefore not effective when the subject is a sociopath or has learned to suppress these manifestations. In addition, anxiety about being tested makes the polygraph "intrinsically susceptible to producing erroneous results" (National Research Council 2003, p. 2). A number of universities and private companies—some of which are reported to have substantial U.S. government funding—are trying to develop and promote technologies such as functional magnetic resonance imaging (fMRI), electroencephalography (EEG), and infrared spectroscopy in order to detect deception by monitoring brain activity. Since the publication of a scientific paper on fMRI-based lie detection in early 2002 (Langleben at al. 2002), there has been considerable interest in the use of fMRI in particular. Despite concerns about the artificiality of such laboratory studies and their limited application in real-world scenarios, there are reports that fMRI may have already been used in counterterrorism interrogations. Some commentators have argued that fMRI has the potential to make interrogation more humane. However, false positives create further risk of mistreatment and abuse, particularly if there is undue confidence in the ability of the new technology to screen terrorists from a pool of suspects. On the other hand, if new brain imaging technologies ultimately meet their proponents' expectations, their impact on privacy and so-called cognitive liberty will need to be addressed.

CRIMINAL INTERROGATION AND INVESTIGATIVE INTERVIEWING

A popular approach to criminal interrogation in the United States is known as the *Reid Technique*, named after the late president of John E. Reid & Associates, a corporation that provides interrogation training to both public and private sectors in the United States. The Reid Technique is a nine-step process designed for use on "suspects whose guilt seems definite or reasonably certain" (Inbau et al. 2001). It commences with direct confrontation of the suspect by the investigator—who states that the suspect is considered guilty of the offense—and is intended to lead to a formal confession. Proponents of the technique advocate the use of deception, including props such as a large file containing blank sheets of paper, to create the impression that the investigator already has incriminating evidence. At various stages, the investigator evaluates the suspect's verbal and nonverbal responses. If the suspect listens attentively when he is offered a motive for the crime and a potential moral excuse, this may be taken as an indication of guilt. But if he reacts with resentment, it may be considered an indication of innocence. Critics of this approach claim that it rests on the assumption that the only method of solving many criminal investigations is by obtaining a confession from the perpetrator. They also challenge the need to use trickery, deceit, and psychological manipulation, including techniques that the general public would ordinarily consider unethical (Gudjonsson 2003).

There is considerable variation—even among Western democracies—in the legal rights accorded to suspects who are interrogated in the course of a criminal investigation. In the United States, before suspects in police custody are interrogated, they must be informed that they have the right to remain silent, that anything they say can and will be used in evidence against them, that they have the right to an attorney, and that if they cannot afford an attorney, one will be appointed for them. This is often described as the *Miranda warning* (while the rights themselves are referred to as *Miranda rights*) after the decision of the U.S. Supreme Court in *Miranda v. Arizona* (1966). That case made clear the necessity for the warning in order to implement and protect the privilege against self-incrimination (or the right not to be compelled to incriminate oneself) enshrined in the Fifth Amendment to the U.S. Constitution. If, following a Miranda warning, the suspect refuses to talk, the prosecution will not be permitted to comment at trial on the suspect's silence. A statement obtained by police without a Miranda warning cannot be relied upon by the prosecution in order to make its case at trial, unless the defendant contradicts that statement in his oral testimony—in which case, the statement may be used to impeach the defendant, that is, to undermine his credibility as a witness.

The Supreme Court has also made clear that suspects should not be "threatened, tricked, or cajoled into a waiver" of their Miranda rights. However, empirical studies suggest that in at least 80 percent of cases suspects do waive their rights and make a statement to the police. This may be due in part to strategies adopted by police interrogators—such as deemphasizing the importance of the Miranda warning by reading it in a monotonous voice or trying to persuade the suspect that he is being offered a good opportunity to tell his story and that the interrogator is trying to help him. These strategies will not invalidate the suspect's waiver of the Miranda rights if, taking into account all the circumstances, the court concludes that the waiver was "voluntary and intelligent."

INTERROGATION AND THE COLLECTION OF INTELLIGENCE

The laws of war—in particular, the provisions of the Third Geneva Convention of 1949—impose strict limits on the questioning of prisoners of war. Strictly speaking, prisoners of war are only required to state their name, rank, and serial number. They must not be subjected to physical and mental torture or "any other form of coercion," and they must be protected against "acts of violence or intimidation and against insults." If prisoners of war refuse to answer questions during interrogation, they "may not be threatened, insulted, or exposed to any unpleasant or disadvantageous treatment of any kind." Similar protections are also provided for civilian detainees by the Fourth Geneva Convention of 1949. The laws of war do not, however, prohibit positive inducements or incentives for responsiveness to questioning. International human rights law—which applies both in war and in times of peace—also prohibits torture and cruel, inhuman, and degrading treatment and positively requires the humane treatment of detainees.

Prior to the terrorist attacks in the United States on September 11, 2001, official U.S. Army interrogation policy and practice reflected these international norms. Army *Field Manual 34-52* (1992) on interrogation states that the laws of war and U.S. policy "expressly prohibit acts of violence or intimidation, including physical or mental torture, threats, insults, or exposure to inhumane treatment as a means of or aid to interrogation." It also states that the "use of torture and other illegal methods is a poor technique that yields unreliable results, may damage subsequent collection efforts, and can induce the source to say what he thinks the interrogator wants to hear." After 9/11, when further attacks were anticipated and feared, more aggressive interrogation techniques were formally authorized and adopted at U.S. detention facilities in Afghanistan, Iraq, and Guantánamo Bay, Cuba. Techniques used included sleep deprivation, stress positions, prolonged isolation, and exposure to temperature extremes. (Controversially, U.S. Army psychiatrists and psychologists—attached to military intelligence and acting as behavioral science consultants—were tasked with advising interrogators as to the most effective approach for individual detainees.) Such tactics were formally justified on a number of legal grounds, among them that terrorists were not subject to the protections of the Geneva Conventions and that the international human rights obligations of the United States did not prohibit cruel, inhuman, and degrading treatment of aliens detained abroad. (It was the latter claim that the U.S. Congress intended to rebut when it passed the so-called McCain Amendment to the Defense Appropriations Bill at the end of 2005.) The U.S. government has claimed that the use of more aggressive interrogation techniques has procured valuable intelligence, but this has not been independently verified.

The publication of photographs in 2004 recording the abuse of detainees by U.S. soldiers at Abu Ghraib prison in Iraq triggered public debate in the United States and abroad about the proper limits of interrogation. These debates were further fuelled by revelations that the CIA was interrogating detainees at secret locations in eastern Europe and elsewhere (called *black sites*, whose existence President George W. Bush subsequently confirmed) and that the United States had handed detainees over to nations known to torture suspects (a practice described as *extraordinary rendition*).

In a landmark decision in June 2006, the U.S. Supreme Court held that suspected Al-Qaeda detainees are entitled to the basic protections found in Common Article 3 of the Geneva Conventions (*Hamdan v. Rumsfeld* 2006). At a minimum, they must be treated humanely, and protected from cruel, inhuman, and degrading treatment and from outrages on personal dignity. A few weeks later the army published a new field manual on interrogation, *Field Manual 2-22.3* (2006), which prohibits interrogation tactics such as "waterboarding" (a procedure designed to simulate the experience of drowning), the hooding of detainees, and the use of barking dogs. However, this manual does not apply to detainees in the custody of the CIA, and concerns about the continuing use of aggressive interrogation tactics were fueled by two further developments.

After President Bush criticized the provisions of Common Article 3 of the Geneva Conventions for being "too vague," Congress passed the Military Commissions Act of 2006, which purports to give the president the authority to "interpret the meaning and application of the Geneva Conventions" (Sec. 6(a)(3)). When the president signed the act into law, he noted that it would "allow the Central Intelligence Agency to continue its program for questioning key terrorist leaders and operatives" (Bush 2006). Just days later, while lawyers and commentators were debating the effect of the act on permissible interrogation strategies, Vice President Richard Cheney sparked further controversy. When asked in a radio interview if "a dunk in water is a no-brainer if it can save lives," Mr. Cheney replied, "it's a no-brainer for me" (Eggen 2006, p. A2). He also expressed agreement with the view that the debate over interrogation techniques was "a little silly" (Eggen 2006, p. A2).

SEE ALSO *Human Rights; Torture*

BIBLIOGRAPHY

Bond, Charles F., Jr., and Bella M. DePaulo. 2006. Accuracy of Deception Judgments. *Personality and Social Psychology Review* 10 (3): 214–234.

Bowden, Mark. 2003. The Dark Art of Interrogation. *Atlantic Monthly*. 292 (3): 51–76.

Bush, George W. 2006. *President Bush Signs Military Commissions Act of 2006.* http://www.whitehouse.gov/news/releases/2006/10/20061017-1.html.

Central Intelligence Agency. 1963. *Kubark Counterintelligence Interrogation.* http://www.gwu.edu/~nsarchiv/NSAEBB/NSAEBB27/01-01.htm.

Department of the Army. 1992. *Field Manual 34-52: Intelligence Interrogation.* Washington, DC: Author. http://www.fas.org/irp/doddir/army/fm34-52.pdf.

Department of the Army. 2006. *Field Manual 2-22.3 (FM 34-52): Human Intelligence Collector Operations.* Washington, DC: Author.

Eggen, Dan. 2006. Cheney Defends "Dunk in the Water" Remark. *Washington Post,* October 28: A02.

Ekman, Paul. 2004. Microexpression Training Tools (METT) and Subtle Expression Training Tools (SETT). http://www.paulekman.com.

Gudjonsson, Gisli H. 2003. *The Psychology of Interrogations and Confessions: A Handbook.* Chichester, U.K.: Wiley.

Hamdan v. Rumsfeld, 126 S.Ct. 2749 (2006). http://caselaw.lp.findlaw.com/scripts/getcase.pl?court=US&vol=000&invol=05-184.

Inbau, Fred E., John E. Reid, Joseph P. Buckley, and Brian C. Jayne. 2001. *Criminal Interrogation and Confessions.* 4th ed. Gaithersburg, MD: Aspen.

International Committee of the Red Cross, International Humanitarian Law: Treaties and Documents. http://www.icrc.org/ihl.nsf/CONVPRES?OpenView.

Langleben D. D., et al. 2002. Brain Activity During Simulated Deception: An Event-Related Functional Magnetic Resonance Study. *Neuroimage* 15 (3): 727–732.

Mackey, Chris, and Greg Miller. 2004. *The Interrogators: Inside the Secret War Against Al Qaeda.* New York: Little, Brown.

Margulies, Joseph. 2006. The More Subtle Kind of Torment. *Washington Post,* October 2: A19.

Marks, Jonathan H. 2005. Doctors of Interrogation. *Hastings Center Report.* 35 (4): 17–22.

McCoy, Alfred. 2006. *A Question of Torture: CIA Interrogation from the Cold War to the War on Terror.* New York: Henry Holt.

Military Commissions Act of 2006. 2006. Washington, DC: Government Printing Office. http://frwebgate.access.gpo.gov/cgi-bin/getdoc.cgi?dbname=109_cong_bills&docid=f:s3930enr.txt.pdf.

Miranda v. Arizona, 384 U.S. 436 (1966). http://caselaw.lp.findlaw.com/cgi-bin/getcase.pl?court=US&vol=384&invol=436.

Moreno, Jonathan D. 2006. *Mind Wars: Brain Research and National Defense.* New York: Dana Press.

National Research Council: Committee to Review the Scientific Evidence on the Polygraph. 2003. *The Polygraph and Lie Detection.* Washington, DC: National Academies Press.

Persaud, Raj. 2005. Deception Special: The Truth about Lies. *New Scientist* 2510: 28–31.

Society of Professional Journalists. Geneva Conventions: A Reference Guide. http://www.genevaconventions.org/.

Thaman, Stephen C. 2001. Miranda in Comparative Law. *Saint Louis University Law Journal* 45: 581–624.

Thompson, Sean Kevin. 2005. The Legality of the Use of Psychiatric Neuroimaging in Intelligence Interrogation. *Cornell Law Review* 90 (6): 1601–1637.

Toliver, Raymond T., and Hanns Joachim Scharff. 1978. *The Interrogator: The Story of Hanns Scharff, Luftwaffe's Master Interrogator.* Fallbrook, CA: Aero.

Vrij, Aldert. 2000. *Detecting Lies and Deceit: The Psychology of Lying and the Implications for Professional Practice.* New York: Wiley.

White, Welsh S. 2001. *Miranda's Waning Protections: Police Interrogation Practices after Dickerson.* Ann Arbor: University of Michigan Press.

Williamson, Tom, ed. 2005. *Investigative Interviewing: Rights, Research, and Regulation.* Devon, U.K.: Willan

Wolpe, Paul Root, Kenneth R. Foster, and Daniel D. Langleben. 2005. Emerging Neurotechnologies for Lie-Detection: Promises and Perils. *American Journal of Bioethics* 5 (2): 39–49.

Jonathan H. Marks

INTERROLE CONFLICT

SEE *Role Conflict*.

INTERSECTIONALITY

The premise of intersectionality theory, first articulated by feminists of color, is that social differentiation is achieved through complex interactions between markers of difference such as gender, race, and class. In order to comprehend how an individual's access to social, political, and economic institutions is differentially experienced, it is necessary to analyze how markers of difference intersect and interact.

In the 1970s feminist theory could be divided into different perspectives based on the identification of the root of women's oppression. Liberal feminists identified unequal access to existing economic and political systems, whereas radical feminists named patriarchy, the control of women by men, as the key oppressive system. Marxist and socialist feminists, following the writings of Karl Marx and Frederick Engels, believed that capitalism was the main determinant of women's oppression. Socialist feminists engaged in active debates on the relationship between class and gender oppression, some arguing that women constituted a sexual class that functioned within the capitalist framework. Others, such as Betsy Hartmann, posited a dual-systems theory or a capitalist patriarchy in which patriarchy was viewed as a system of oppression anchored in material conditions (e.g., the institution of marriage, property ownership) acting alongside the relations of class. Issues of race and sexuality were largely absent from these debates.

Although second-wave feminists challenged traditional scholarship for positioning the experiences of men as universal, black feminists and lesbians critiqued these feminists for excluding issues of race and sexuality from feminist analysis, thus falsely universalizing the experiences of middle-class heterosexual white women. In the late 1970s only a few authors, mostly women of color, were writing about gender, race, and class as interconnected systems of oppression. The Combahee River Collective, a group of black feminist activists from Boston, is widely credited for first theorizing the interconnections between gender, race, class, and sexuality. In "A Black Feminist Statement" (1983) they outline how they view gender, race, class, and sexuality as connected: "We are actively committed to struggling against racial, sexual, heterosexual and class oppression, and see as our particular task the development of integrated analysis and practice based upon the fact that the major systems of oppression are interlocking. The synthesis of these oppressions creates the conditions of our lives" (p. 210). An intersectional approach complicates analyses of power relations that give priority to one element of identity.

Although intersectionality theory emerged in the 1970s, its roots can be traced back to a speech delivered by Sojourner Truth (c. 1797–1883), a black woman who had been a slave, at the 1851 Women's Rights Conference in Akron, Ohio. In this passage, she articulates how her identity is shaped not only by her gender, but also by her race and class: "That man over there says that women need to be helped into carriages, and lifted over ditches, and to have the best place everywhere. Nobody ever helps me into carriages, or over mud puddles, or gives me any best place. And ain't I a woman?" (Painter 1996, p. 165). According to Avtar Brah and Ann Phoenix (2004), "Sojourner Truth's identity claims are thus relational, constructed in relation to white women and all men and clearly demonstrate that what we call 'identities' are not objects but processes constituted in and through power relations" (p. 77).

In the early twenty-first century, intersectionality theory received wide support from social science researchers. Many researchers adopted intersectionality theory in their development of research questions, methodologies, and analysis. Some researchers who used this approach framed the intersections of gender, race, and class as additive so that a black woman would be seen as facing a "double jeopardy" due to the combined impact of gender and racial inequality. Elizabeth Spelman (1988) argued that treating interlocking systems of oppression as additive implies that processes of gender, race, and class are separate entities, and it ignores how these factors interact to shape lived experience. Intersectionality approaches the concepts of gender, race, and class as social constructions that vary across geography and time; markers of difference are not viewed as static traits, but as processes that are (re)produced in the daily actions of people.

Both qualitative and quantitative researchers have taken up intersectionality theory in their investigations into the workings of social reality, although qualitative approaches have far outnumbered quantitative studies. Marlene Kim (2002) applied an intersectionality framework to her quantitative investigation of how gender and race processes affect the wages of women in the United States. Her research indicates that black women face a "race penalty" in that when all factors are considered, they earn 7 percent less than white women in the same industries. Feminist economists Rose M. Brewer, Cecelia A. Conrad, and Mary C. King (2002) point out that there are many challenges of applying an intersectionality framework to the empirical investigation of social differentiation: "Even as we increasingly understand the mutually constitutive nature of color, caste, race, gender, and class, analytically, as categories of analysis and identity, the project remains difficult" (p. 5). Quantitative research studies tend to address issues of gender independent of race or class.

An important quantitative research project was conducted by Leslie McCall (2001), who analyzes the impact of gender, race, and class on wage inequality in four U.S. cities with different local economic contexts: Detroit, Miami, St. Louis, and Dallas. By combining an analysis of case-study and large-scale survey data, McCall demonstrates that gender and racial inequality have different consequences in different contexts; in some instances, a decrease in gender inequality is accompanied by an increase in racial inequality between women. She identifies *configurations of inequality* as a term to describe the shifting interactions between gender, race, and class. These configurations "reveal that in no local economy are all types of wage inequality systematically and simultaneously lower or higher; complex interactions of various dimensions of inequality are the norm" (p. 6). Her analysis is an important development in understanding the relationship between relations of gender, race, and class.

Researchers who use intersectionality theory present a more sophisticated, nuanced understanding of the workings of power relations. Susan Stanford Friedman (1995) proposed a framework of "relational positionality" that acknowledges how "the flow of power in multiple systems of domination is not always unidirectional. Victims can also be victimizers; agents of change can also be complicit, depending on the particular axis of power one considers" (p. 18). Sherene Razack (1998) argues that "it is vitally important to explore in a historical and site-specific way the meaning of race, economic status, class, disability, sexuality, and gender as they come together to structure women in different and shifting positions of power and privilege" (p. 12). The research of intersectionality theorists makes an important contribution to the social sciences; it is now considered incomplete scholarship in women's studies or cultural studies for a researcher to undertake an analysis of gender relations without consideration of how race and class relations are also implicated.

SEE ALSO *Capitalism; Ethnic Conflict; Ethnic Enclave; Ethnicity; Feminism; Gender; Identity; Immigration; Inequality, Gender; Inequality, Racial; Liberalism; Nationalism and Nationality; Power; Race; Racism; Social Movements; Truth, Sojourner; Women; Women's Movement*

BIBLIOGRAPHY

Brah, Avtar, and Ann Phoenix. 2004. Ain't I a Woman? Revisiting Intersectionality. *Journal of International Women's Studies* 5 (3): 75–86.

Brewer, Rose M., Cecelia A. Conrad, and Mary C. King. 2002. The Complexities and Potential of Theorizing Gender, Caste, Race, and Class. *Feminist Economics* 8 (2): 3–18.

Combahee River Collective. 1983. A Black Feminist Statement. In *This Bridge Called My Back: Writings by Radical Women of Color*, eds. Cherrie Moraga and Gloria Anzaldua, 210–219. New York: Kitchen Table: Women of Color Press.

Friedman, Susan Stanford. 1995. Beyond White and Other: Relationality and Narratives of Race in Feminist Discourse. *Signs* 21 (1): 1–21.

Kim, Marlene. 2002. Has the Race Penalty for Black Women Disappeared in the United States? *Feminist Economics* 8 (2): 115–124.

McCall, Leslie. 2001. *Complex Inequality: Gender, Class, and Race in the New Economy.* New York: Routledge.

Painter, Nell Irvin. 1996. *Sojourner Truth: A Life, a Symbol.* New York: W. H. Norton.

Razack, Sherene H. 1998. *Looking White People in the Eye: Gender, Race, and Culture in Courtrooms and Classrooms.* Toronto: University of Toronto Press.

Spelman, Elizabeth. 1988. *Inessential Woman: Problems of Exclusion in Feminist Thought.* Boston: Beacon Press.

Bonnie Slade

INTERSTATE COMMERCE COMMISSION

SEE *Progressive Movement.*

INTERSUBJECTIVITY

In its most general sense of that which occurs between or exists among conscious human actors, *intersubjectivity* is little more than a synonym for "the social." As used by social scientists, however, *intersubjectivity* usually denotes some set of relations, meanings, structures, practices, experiences, or phenomena evident in human life that cannot be reduced to or comprehended entirely in terms of either subjectivity (concerning psychological states of individual actors) or objectivity (concerning brute empirical facts about the objective world). In this sense, the concept is usually intended to overcome an unproductive oscillation between methodological subjectivism and objectivism. The concept is especially predominant in social theories and theories of the self.

Although German idealist philosophers Johann Fichte (1762–1814) and G. W. F. Hegel (1770–1831) stressed the importance of intersubjectivity, the concept became influential in the twentieth century through the work of American social psychologist George Herbert Mead (1863–1931). Mead claimed that the development of cognitive, moral, and emotional capacities in human individuals is only possible to the extent that they take part in symbolically mediated interactions with other persons. For Mead, then, ontogenesis is essentially and irreducibly intersubjective. He also put forward a social theory explaining how social norms, shared meanings, and systems of morality arise from and concretize the gen-

eral structures of reciprocal perspective-taking required for symbolic interaction. In short, he argued that intersubjectivity—understood specifically in terms of linguistically mediated, reflexively grasped social action—furnishes the key to understanding mind, self, and society.

Although the work of Martin Heidegger (1889–1976) and Ludwig Wittgenstein (1889–1951) was often more directly inspirational, Mead's bold claim that self and society are irreducibly intersubjective has been rearticulated and supported by many distinct subsequent intersubjectivist approaches. Action theory, symbolic interactionism, lifeworld phenomenology, hermeneutic analysis, conversational analysis, ethnomethodology, social constructivism, dialogism, discourse theory, recognition theory, and objects relations theory all take intersubjectivity as central and irreducible. For example, Erving Goffman (1922–1982) insisted that we need a microanalysis of face-to-face interactions in order to properly understand the interpersonal interpretation, negotiation, and improvisation that constitute a society's interaction order. While macro- and mesostructural phenomena may be important in setting the basic terms of interaction, social order according to Goffman is inexplicable without central reference to agents' interpretations and strategies in actively developing their own action performances in everyday, interpersonal contexts. Harold Garfinkel and other ethnomethodologists likewise insist that social order is only possible because of the strongly normative character of a society's particular everyday interaction patterns and norms.

Widely diverse social theorists influenced by phenomenology also center their analyses in intersubjective phenomena and structures. Most prominently, Alfred Schutz (1899–1959) sought to show how the lifeworld of persons—the mostly taken-for-granted knowledge, know-how, competences, norms, and behavioral patterns that are shared throughout a society—delimits and makes possible individual action and interaction. In particular, he sought to analyze the way in which the constitutive structures of any lifeworld shape social meanings and personal experiences, by attending to the lifeworld's spatiotemporal, intentional, semantic, and role typifying and systematizing dimensions. Other theories analyze different aspects of the lifeworld: how experience and knowledge is embodied (Maurice Merleau-Ponty), the intersubjective construction of both social and natural reality (Peter Berger and Thomas Luckmann), the social construction of mind and mental concepts (Jeff Coulter), and the social power and inequalities involved in symbolic capital (Pierre Bourdieu). Finally, Jürgen Habermas emphasizes the linguistic basis of the lifeworld, constructing a theory of society in terms of the variety of types of communicative interaction, the pragmatic presuppositions of using language in order to achieve shared understandings and action coordinations with others, and the role of communicative interaction for integrating society. While acknowledging that some types of social integration function independently of communicative action—paradigmatically economic and bureaucratic systems—Habermas claims that intersubjective communication is fundamental in, and irreplaceable for, human social life.

Diverse prominent theories of the self are united in supporting Mead's claim that the self is developed and structured intersubjectively. Martin Buber's (1878–1965) distinction between the different interpersonal attitudes involved in the I-Thou stance and the I-It stance leads to the insight that the development and maintenance of an integral sense of personal identity is fundamentally bound up with the capacity to interact with others from a performative attitude, rather than an objectivating one. Mead's claim is also developed in diverse theories of the self: Habermas's account of interactive competence and rational accountability, Axel Honneth's and Charles Taylor's theories of interpersonal recognition and identity development, Daniel Stern's elucidation of the interpersonal world of infants, and psychoanalytic object-relations theories stressing the dependence of the ego on affective interpersonal bonds between self and significant others.

SEE ALSO *Bourdieu, Pierre; Goffman, Erving; Habermas, Jürgen; Mead, George Herbert; Other, The*

BIBLIOGRAPHY

Benjamin, Jessica. 1988. *The Bonds of Love: Psychoanalysis, Feminism, and the Problem of Domination.* New York: Pantheon.

Berger, Peter L., and Thomas Luckmann. 1966. *The Social Construction of Reality: A Treatise in the Sociology of Knowledge.* Garden City, NY: Doubleday.

Bourdieu, Pierre. 1990. *The Logic of Practice.* Trans. R. Nice. Stanford, CA: Stanford University Press.

Buber, Martin. 1958. *I and Thou.* 2nd ed. Trans. Ronald G. Smith. New York: Scribner.

Coulter, Jeff. 1989. *Mind in Action.* Atlantic Highlands, NJ: Humanities Press.

Garfinkel, Harold. 1967. *Studies in Ethnomethodology.* Englewood Cliffs, NJ: Prentice-Hall.

Goffman, Erving. 1959. *The Presentation of Self in Everyday Life.* Garden City, NY: Doubleday.

Goffman, Erving. 1983. The Interaction Order. *American Sociological Review* 48 (1): 1–17.

Habermas, Jürgen. 1984. *Reason and the Rationalization of Society.* Trans. Thomas McCarthy. Vol. 1 of *The Theory of Communicative Action.* Boston: Beacon.

Habermas, Jürgen. 1992. Individuation through Socialization: On George Herbert Mead's Theory of Subjectivity. In *Postmetaphysical Thinking: Philosophical Essays.* Trans. William Mark Hohengarten, 149–204. Cambridge, MA: MIT Press.

Honneth, Axel. 1995. *The Struggle for Recognition: The Moral Grammar of Social Conflicts.* Trans. Joel Anderson. Cambridge, MA: Polity.

Merleau-Ponty, Maurice. 1964. The Child's Relations with Others. In *The Primacy of Perception, and Other Essays on Phenomenological Psychology, the Philosophy of Art, History, and Politics,* ed. James M. Edie, 96–155. Evanston, IL: Northwestern University Press.

Schutz, Alfred. 1962. *The Problem of Social Reality,* ed. Maurice Natanson. Vol. 1 of *Collected Papers.* The Hague, Netherlands: Martinus Nijhoff.

Schutz, Alfred. 1962. *Studies in Phenomenological Philosophy,* ed. I. Schutz. Vol. 3 of *Collected Papers.* The Hague, Netherlands: Martinus Nijhoff.

Schutz, Alfred. 1962. *Studies in Social Theory,* ed. Arvid Brodersen. Vol. 2 of *Collected Papers.* The Hague, Netherlands: Martinus Nijhoff.

Stern, Daniel N. 1985. *The Interpersonal World of the Infant: A View from Psychoanalysis and Developmental Psychology.* New York: Basic Books.

Taylor, Charles. 1989. *Sources of the Self: The Making of the Modern Identity.* Cambridge, MA: Harvard University Press.

Winnicott, Donald Woods. 1964. *The Child, the Family, and the Outside World.* Harmondsworth, U.K.: Penguin.

Christopher F. Zurn

INTERTEMPORAL SUBSTITUTION
SEE *Elasticity; Time Preference.*

INTERVENTIONS, SOCIAL POLICY

Social policy interventions include policies affecting the social conditions under which people live. Social policy aims to improve human welfare and to meet human needs. Many policies that are ostensibly economic, such as cash assistance to the poor, fall under the rubric of social policy interventions because they have a direct impact on the social conditions under which people live and are aimed at improving human welfare and meeting human needs. Social policies may also regulate and govern human behavior in such areas as sexuality and morality. Policies that involve access to abortion or laws governing marriage and divorce therefore fall within the sphere of social policy interventions.

Between the 1880s and the 1920s, many European countries instituted pension and social insurance programs for industrial workers and needy individuals. These programs became comprehensive social welfare systems in the 1950s to 1960s. Early U.S. social policy involved the most inclusive system of public education in the industrializing world, as well as generous benefits to elderly veterans and their families. The United States also instituted social benefits for women and their children. The Social Security Act of 1935 created a basic framework for U.S. social policy interventions that is still in place today. In the 1960s, in conjunction with the war on poverty, major new programs of public assistance were established in the United States.

Among comparably developed countries, the United States has the highest level of economic inequality and the lowest level of cash assistance to the poor. With noncash assistance added, the United States falls in the middle. Cash benefits require trust that recipients will spend the extra income on expenditures the public deems worthy. Noncash public assistance programs pay directly for those expenditures deemed worthy, such as food in the case of the Food Stamp Program or health care in the case of Medicaid.

EXAMPLES OF SOCIAL POLICY INTERVENTIONS

A broad set of public assistance or antipoverty programs exists in the United States; these programs constitute a fundamental social policy intervention. The four largest components of U.S. public assistance include: the Food Stamp Program; Medicaid; Aid to Families with Dependent Children (AFDC), replaced in 1996 with the Temporary Assistance to Needy Families (TANF) block grant; and the Earned Income Tax Credit (EITC).

The Food Stamp Program is a nationally provided program. It is the only public assistance program available to all poor people, whether or not they have children. The Food Stamp Program is the first line of defense against hunger in the United States. Food stamp recipients spend their benefits to buy eligible food in authorized retail stores. As family income increases, food stamp benefits decline. Therefore, recipients who live in states that provide less in the way of cash assistance to the poor receive more in food stamps.

Medicaid, established in 1965, pays for health-care costs among eligible low-income groups. The program is run by the states, with certain mandates from the federal government. Like all health-care costs, Medicaid costs have substantially increased over the 1980s, 1990s, and early 2000s. This is mostly due to increased costs for long-term care among the elderly and disabled, as well as the fact that the benefits expanded in the 1980s to include all poor children. Medicaid is the most costly of U.S. public assistance programs.

Aid to Families with Dependent Children (AFDC), commonly known as *welfare*, provides cash assistance to poor families with children. An individual receives the highest level of assistance from AFDC when she or he has the least income; in fact, for every extra dollar in income the recipient earns, a dollar is lost in benefits. In many cases, the economic reality of AFDC recipients' lives means that neither welfare nor low-wage work gives them enough income to meet their families' expenses. Moreover, inflation has steadily eroded the real value of AFDC benefits over the years. AFDC is a controversial social policy intervention, primarily due to changing views regarding the primary recipient population—single mothers. In 1996 Congress passed the Personal Responsibility and Work Opportunity Reconciliation Act, which implemented fundamental changes in the design and funding of public assistance programs in the United States, particularly AFDC. AFDC was abolished and replaced with a program called Temporary Assistance to Needy Families. States were expected to replace their AFDC programs with new programs of their own; federal mandates include work requirements for recipients and limited time periods for benefits.

The federal Earned Income Tax Credit (EITC) is another large and growing public assistance program. EITC is a refundable tax credit that reduces or eliminates the taxes that low-income working people pay. The program frequently operates as a wage subsidy for low-income workers. People who work, earn low wages, and have children are eligible to receive EITC. In contrast to AFDC, since EITC pays nothing for people who are not working, it provides an incentive to work, assuming that recipients understand how EITC operates. The rationale underlying this intervention is that employment alone is insufficient to bring people out of poverty. By the early 2000s, EITC had become one of the largest antipoverty tools in the United States.

Another example of an important, albeit controversial, social policy intervention is *affirmative action*. Affirmative action is a policy or program whose stated goal is to redress past or present discrimination through active measures to ensure equal opportunity, generally to higher education and employment. The stated goal of affirmative action is to counteract discrimination sufficiently such that the power elite reflect the demographics of society at large, at which point such a strategy will no longer be necessary. Groups who are targeted for affirmative action are characterized by race, gender, ethnicity, or disability status.

Proponents of affirmative action generally advocate it either as a means to address past discrimination or to enhance racial, ethnic, gender, or other diversity. Proponents argue that the simple adoption of meritocratic principles of race blindness or gender blindness will not suffice to change the situation for several reasons: (1) Discriminatory practices of the past preclude the acquisition of "merit" by limiting access to educational opportunities and job experiences; (2) ostensible measures of "merit" may be biased toward the same groups who are already empowered; and (3) regardless of overt principles, people already in positions of power are likely to hire people they already know or people from similar backgrounds. Opponents claim that affirmative action: (1) acts as a new form of discrimination and benefits privileged individuals within minority racial groups (such as middle- to upper-class blacks) at the expense of disenfranchised individuals within majority racial groups (such as poor whites); (2) increases racial tension and creates a stigma such that all minority groups within a college or employment setting are perceived as having received special treatment; and (3) creates a skill "mismatch" (i.e., individuals who are less qualified than their peers are admitted into more rigorous programs in which they cannot adequately perform).

EVALUATION OF THE EFFECTS OF SOCIAL POLICY INTERVENTIONS

A central issue in the evaluation of social policy interventions is how the outcome of interest is defined. Many Americans contend that because high poverty rates continue to exist in the United States, antipoverty programs must be ineffective. However, many public assistance programs have accomplished exactly what they were intended to accomplish. Most of the antipoverty programs were not designed to eliminate poverty, but to provide assistance to needy families. For example, the Food Stamp Program has improved nutrition among the poor, and Medicaid has increased access to medical care and contributed to improvements in the health of the poor. The combined impact of these programs has also improved the health of pregnant women and reduced low birth weights among infants born to low-income mothers.

Studies have found that while cash assistance for the poor does not do much to decrease the overall poverty rate in the United States, such assistance provides more cash income to families than they would have otherwise, making them less poor. In the absence of welfare benefits, individuals work more on average, but do not earn as much money as they would receive or did receive from welfare. Moreover, earnings of less-educated U.S. workers have stagnated or fallen since about the 1970s, such that employment is not necessarily effective in combating poverty.

Affirmative action is another example of a controversial social policy that provokes intense debate regarding its effects. The evidence suggests that affirmative action has had a major impact on the representation of minorities in university admissions and employment, even if the overall numbers of redistributed positions is small. Replacement of affirmative action programs based on race and gender with class-based practices is likely to reduce the presence of minorities on college campuses while doing little to improve the overall position of white males. There is some evidence that the performance of students admitted to colleges and universities with the aid of affirmative action lags behind that of students admitted without such aid. However, there may be an overall benefit to more diversity on campuses. Moreover, minority students benefit greatly in the labor market from having attended college. Nevertheless, affirmative action programs remain under intense challenge.

Serious evaluation of any social policy intervention requires some sort of comparison group. A comparison group provides a means of evaluating the counterfactual, that is, what would have happened to program recipients in the absence of participation in the program. A randomized experiment where one group is assigned to receive the benefits of a program while another group receives no such benefits is typically considered the best way to deduce causation. However, most programs, particularly nationwide entitlement programs, provide limited opportunities for randomized experiments.

SEE ALSO *Affirmative Action; Experiments, Human; Gautreaux Residential Mobility Program; Natural Experiments; Negative Income Tax Experiment; Poverty; Public Health; Public Policy; Welfare State*

BIBLIOGRAPHY

Black, Rebecca. 1997. *It Takes a Nation: A New Agenda for Fighting Poverty.* Princeton, NJ: Princeton University Press.

Freeman, Richard. 1997. *When Earnings Diverge: Causes, Consequences, and Cures for the New Inequality in the U.S.* Washington, DC: National Policy Association.

Holzer, Harry J., and David Neumark. 2006. Affirmative Action: What Do We Know? *Journal of Policy Analysis and Management* 25 (2): 463–490.

Neckerman, Kathryn, ed. 2004. *Social Inequality.* New York: Russell Sage Foundation.

Skocpol, Theda. 1995. *Social Policy in the United States: Future Possibilities in Historical Perspective.* Princeton, NJ: Princeton University Press.

Jennie E. Brand

INTERVENTIONS, SOCIAL SKILLS

Social relationships among individuals account for much of what is studied in the social sciences. Considerable research supports the essential role of social relationships in behavioral, emotional, and academic/vocational well-being, showing that relationships with others directly impact self-esteem, daily functioning, and life success. Positive relationships foster positive well-being while problematic relationships result in poorer functioning. In keeping with these findings, the goal of social skills interventions (SSI) is to train individuals in specific skills and strategies that foster positive relationships.

One of the first theorists to propose that social relations with peers have a lasting impact on future intimate relationships as well as on personality development was Harry Stack Sullivan. In his seminal book *The Interpersonal Theory of Psychiatry* (1953), Sullivan postulated that childhood friendships, or "chumships," play a causal role in children's understanding of social rules and social roles. This belief system then determines interpersonal actions and reactions throughout adolescence and adulthood. Correspondingly, though SSI have been applied across the life span, they are most frequently practiced and studied with children during the elementary school years.

Generally, learning theory is the theoretical basis of SSI through which individuals are taught specific social skills and given opportunities to practice in a structured fashion. The assumption in SSI work is that factors within the individual are largely responsible for the quality of one's social relationships; if those factors are changed, then changes in social relationships will follow. Thus, the focus of SSI is on the individual, rather than the environment or other external contributing factors. However, conducting SSI within a group setting is considered an important ingredient for effecting change. In a group, individuals are able to learn and practice skills within a social context of same-aged peers. However, the group setting is more structured and safe than real-life peer settings, so fear of rejection and teasing is decreased and willingness to try new social behaviors is increased and supported. The social interactions within the group are also observed by group leaders who can then intervene when problems emerge and reinforce positive changes as they occur. The group leader serves as a coach, providing constructive criticism, alternative suggestions, and positive reinforcement.

Behavioral skills have traditionally been the mainstay of SSI. How to control impulses, how to cooperate with others, and how to initiate contact with others are basic behavioral skills taught through most SSI. In the 1980s social scientists began to recognize the mutual impact of thought, emotion, and behavior, and increasingly incorporated cognitive and emotional skills into SSI. Cognitive skill training focuses on helping individuals identify, challenge, and restructure maladaptive thought patterns. Negative social experiences, such as being bullied, tend to engender negative expectations for future social encounters. Testing negative assumptions and managing their influence on behavior is a core social-cognitive skill taught through SSI. Emotional skill training focuses on building self-awareness of how one feels in the moment and learning to manage those emotions. SSI help individuals recognize when emotions, such as anger or hurt, are short-circuiting social skills so they can control those emotions before acting.

SSI are appropriate for anyone who experiences social difficulties, such as isolation, rejection, or bullying. However, certain groups are at higher risk for social problems and, therefore, benefit particularly from SSI. Aggressive individuals experience high levels of conflict that are closely linked with negative relationships. Persons with attention deficit hyperactivity disorder (ADHD) exhibit increased activity level and impulsivity that are seen as intrusive and disruptive by peers. Individuals with developmental disorders, such as autism, or learning or physical disabilities stand out as different from peers and are more likely to display immature, awkward social behaviors that foster peer victimization and rejection. Finally, persons with emotional difficulties, such as depression or anxiety, are likely to withdraw from social interactions and experience isolation.

Research on SSI is intended to establish the effectiveness of intervention and better understand the mechanisms of change. A large literature exists evaluating the efficacy of different SSI with different populations and ages. A thorough review of interventions with school-age children was conducted by Mark Greenberg and colleagues in 2001. Overall, support for SSI for improving social competence and relationships has been found, although effect sizes tend to be moderate. SSI are most effective when: (1) cognitive and emotional skill training are included rather than behavioral skills alone; (2) training occurs over a longer period; (3) multiple components are used to bridge home, school, and clinical settings; and (4) training emphasizes both strengths and weaknesses of the individual.

BIBLIOGRAPHY

Greenberg, Mark T., Celene Domitrovich, and Brian Bumbarger. 2001. The Prevention of Mental Disorders in School-Aged Children: Current State of the Field. *Prevention & Treatment* 4: 1–67.

Parker, Jeff G., Ken H. Rubin, Joe M. Price, and Melissa E. DeRosier. 1995. Peer Relationships, Child Development and Adjustment: A Developmental Psychopathology Perspective. In *Developmental Psychopathology: Risk, Disorder, and Adaptation*, Vol. 2, ed. Dante Cicchetti and Donald J. Cohen, 96–161. New York: Wiley.

Sullivan, Harry Stack. 1953. *The Interpersonal Theory of Psychiatry*. New York: Norton.

Melissa E. DeRosier

INTERWAR YEARS

The interwar years (1919–1938) pose a challenging puzzle for students of globalization: Why did the prolonged period of relative peace and prosperity in Europe, from 1815 to 1914, give way to world war, economic collapse, and the rise of fascism and socialism?

The interwar period began with the Paris Peace Conference and the Treaty of Versailles, which formally ended World War I—the "Great War"—in 1919. The war destroyed the Westphalian System under which elites of government colluded to channel the fate of Europe's empires and colonial subjects. The Treaty of Versailles humiliated Germany and imposed burdensome reparation payments. The war also saddled with national debts the other defeated Central Powers (Austria-Hungary and the Ottoman Empire) and the victorious Allies (France, Russia, Britain, Italy, and the United States).

This period witnessed efforts to construct a self-regulating global market, the rise of the human rights framework, and the emergence of new international political bodies, all of which ultimately failed, but which left lasting impacts on the economic, social, and political landscape of the twentieth century. Internationalists, who rejected policies of economic and political isolationism, pursued global peace through two mechanisms: the creation of the League of Nations and the restoration of the gold standard.

With the Westphalian balance of power in ruins, the U.S. president Woodrow Wilson promoted the League of Nations as the primary body for a new style of international relations. However, the League of Nations, which first met in November 1920, initially represented only forty-two nations. Germany, Russia, and the United States were notably absent. Embarrassingly for Wilson, the United States voted in 1919 against membership in the League, and the United States never joined. Although it refused to participate in international political bodies such as the League, the United States remained involved in the economic affairs of Europe. Throughout the 1920s the United States insisted upon repayment of the loans made to Britain and France during the war. France and Britain in turn insisted that Germany repay to them the enormous reparations agreed to at Versailles. But the strain on the German economy threatened to disrupt the German political and economic order and weaken European stability in general. The Dawes Plan in 1924 and the Young Plan in 1929 both refinanced international loans to Germany. But toward the end of 1929, the New York stock market boom had absorbed all available funds for foreign investment, which placed severe pressure on a German economy that had become dependent on this flow.

Other internationalists promoted a return to the gold standard. Conventional wisdom held that banknotes had value only if they represented gold. Between the 1870s and until the start of World War I, a transnational network of elites embracing market liberalism created a financial mechanism called the gold standard to extend the scope of markets internationally by enabling people in different countries with different currencies to freely engage in transactions with each other. The idea was to create a mechanism for global self-regulation by imposing a gold standard that relied on three rules: First, set the value of any nation's currency in relation to a fixed amount of gold and commit to buying and selling gold at that price; second, base the domestic money supply on the quantity of gold that your nation is holding in its reserves, so that circulating currency will be backed by gold; and third, give residents maximum freedom to engage in international economic transactions. However, efforts to restore the gold standard and an open world economy after World War I failed to reestablish the stability of the prewar period. The openness of the international economy only served to transmit deflationary pressures from one country to another after 1929, and acted as an obstacle to national recovery programs in the early 1930s.

In the United States, the Federal Reserve Board refused to manage the economy according to the gold standard. It instead acted to neutralize the expansionary effects of large gold imports into the United States from Europe, preventing a domestic price rise while placing an even greater burden of adjustment on European economies already facing severe economic problems. Despite the United States' contributions to the structural weakness of the interwar gold standard, it was not until the Great Depression that internationalists abandoned their experiment with restoring the gold standard. Germany, under the Nazis, built up a structure of exchange controls to close their economy off from the rest of the world, and U.S. president Franklin D. Roosevelt began institutionalizing his more protectionist New Deal policies.

More enduring signs of cultural transnationalism during this period were expressed in the form of jazz music, which was popularized initially in rapidly urbanizing North America but soon traveled to, and became localized within, Paris, as well as to more distant places such as Japan and China. Indeed, the interwar years are frequently referred to as "the Jazz Age," and the music became an important symbol of an emerging aesthetic of modernism, and cultural modernity more generally.

Despite earnest international efforts to construct institutions to secure global peace, and some signs of cultural transnationalism, conflict within nations was widespread and laid the groundwork for another descent into total war. In 1917 the Bolsheviks established a single-party dictatorship under the leadership of Vladimir Lenin after seizing power in the Russian Revolution. After Lenin's death in 1924, Joseph Stalin abandoned Lenin's economic policy for a totalitarian system of central planning. When the better-off peasants (*kulaks*) rebelled in 1929 to 1930, Stalin initiated a reign of terror that killed three million people.

In the United States rapid demobilization and the lack of price controls sparked inflation and unemployment, which intensified competition for jobs among the working class. In 1919 more than twenty race riots erupted in cities across the country. White workers violently protested returning black soldiers' demand for equal rights to employment. Americans watched their stock market roar in the 1920s, only to suffer the Great Depression in the 1930s.

In China the Manchu Dynasty fell in 1911, leaving local warlords to tax their populations. In the 1920s Mao Zedong cofounded the Chinese Communist Party, and the nationalist organization Guomindang (GMD) became a mass party under the leadership of Chiang Kai-shek. By 1931 the GMD had defeated most of the warlords, confined the Communists to one rural region in the south, and gained nominal control of most of the country. Chinese peasants, hard hit by the Great Depression, helped Mao launch a comeback. Chiang was forced to contend with this Communist threat at the same time that he was battling Japanese encroachments on, and (in 1937) invasion of, Chinese territory.

Nationalism also grew in the Middle East during the collapse of the Ottoman Empire. During World War I the British had heavily sponsored Arab nationalist thought and ideology to challenge the Ottoman Empire. However, Britain's secret Sykes-Picot Agreement with France divided the eastern Arab lands between the two imperial powers, and Arab nationalism became the basis for an important anticolonial movement.

In Italy political tensions between fascist "black shirts" and Communist "red shirts" brought the country to the brink of civil war. The fascist leader Benito Mussolini took power, later became one of Hitler's most important allies, and provided support for the fascist cause, fueling Spain's civil war. In 1936 Spanish military nationalists under General Francisco Franco's leadership declared their intention to overthrow the government that replaced the monarchy. The stage was now set for World War II (1939–1945).

SEE ALSO *Arabs; Bolshevism; Collectivism; Communism; Fascism; Federal Reserve System, U.S.; Franco, Francisco; Gold Standard; Great Depression; Hitler, Adolf; Jazz; League of Nations; Lenin, Vladimir Ilitch; Mao Zedong; Mussolini, Benito; Ottoman Empire; Palestinians; Riots; Russian Revolution; Socialism; Spanish Civil War; Stalin, Joseph; Totalitarianism;* *Union of Soviet Socialist Republics; Wilson, Woodrow; World War I; World War II; Zionism*

BIBLIOGRAPHY

Atkins, E. Taylor. 2001. *Blue Nippon: Authenticating Jazz in Japan.* Durham, NC: Duke University Press.

Block, Fred L. 1977. *The Origins of International Economic Disorder: A Study of United States International Monetary Policy from World War II to the Present.* Berkeley: University of California Press.

Dray, Philip. 2002. *At the Hands of Persons Unknown: The Lynching of Black America.* New York: Random House.

Foran, John. 2005. *Taking Power: On the Origins of Third World Revolutions.* New York: Cambridge University Press.

Humphreys, R. Stephen. 2005. *Between Memory and Desire: The Middle East in a Troubled Age.* Berkeley: University of California Press.

Jackson, Jeffrey H. 2003. *Making Jazz French: Music and Modern Life in Interwar Paris.* Durham, NC: Duke University Press.

Jones, Andrew F. 2001. *Yellow Music: Media Culture and Colonial Modernity in the Chinese Jazz Age.* Durham, NC: Duke University Press.

Lauren, Paul Gordon. 2003. *The Evolution of International Human Rights: Visions Seen.* 2nd ed. Philadelphia: University of Pennsylvania Press.

Polanyi, Karl. [1944] 2001. *The Great Transformation: The Political and Economic Origins of Our Time.* 2nd Beacon paper ed. Boston: Beacon Press.

John G. Dale

INTIFADA, THE

The Arabic term *intifada*—"the act of shaking-off"—was coined by Palestinians to refer to the Palestinian uprising of December 9, 1987, conjuring the image of shaking off the shackles of twenty years of Israeli occupation in the Gaza Strip, the West Bank, and East Jerusalem. The event that sparked the Palestinian uprising occurred in the refugee camp of Jabalya in Gaza on December 8, 1987, when an Israeli truck ran into two vans transporting Palestinian workers, killing four and injuring seven. At the funeral of three of the men in Jabalya refugee camp, which drew more than six thousand people from the Gaza Strip, the crowd protested the killings in a spontaneous demonstration that targeted the army outpost in the camp. The Israeli military used live ammunition, tear gas, beatings, and arrests to suppress the demonstrators, and in the process killed twenty-year-old Hatem Al-Sisi, who became the uprising's first martyr. Simultaneously, clashes between Palestinian youths and Israeli soldiers spread rapidly to the rest of the occupied Palestinian territories.

The intifada represented both a departure from as well as a reproduction of prior forms of Palestinian resistance against the Israeli occupation since 1967. The Palestinian repertoire of resistance up to 1987 had consisted of sporadic cycles of spontaneous demonstrations, strikes, and sit-ins, usually violently suppressed by the Israeli military and often resulting in Palestinian deaths. Those deaths were mourned in elaborate, mass-attended funerals that often ended in street protests, which were met by further Israeli military punishments, including the closing of universities, the bulldozing of Palestinian homes and olive trees, and the detention without trials and deportation of the activists. The difference with the intifada was that although it was initially spontaneous, it quickly became an organized and sustained popular resistance with a clear agenda of ending the Israeli occupation and demanding Palestinian self-determination. A broad strategy was articulated by its local leaders, the Unified National Leadership of the Uprising (UNLU), an underground umbrella coalition of the main Palestinian political factions in the occupied territories. The UNLU periodically published leaflets to inform the public and coordinate resistance activities in various parts of the territories; the Palestine Liberation Organization (PLO), stationed in Tunis, lent its support. Posing as an alternative to the UNLU, the Muslim Brotherhood mobilized a militant wing, Hamas, and joined the uprising, issuing its own leaflets that incorporated an Islamic ideology into the struggle.

The main aim of the uprising was to denormalize life under the Israeli occupation while increasing the cost of the occupation on Israel by using civil disobedience and protests. The UNLU leaflets urged Palestinians to strikes and peaceful protests (armed struggle by the civilian Palestinian population under occupation was rejected, and when it occurred, was limited); to stop paying taxes (which led to the tax rebellion in the town of Beit Sahour in the West Bank); and to boycott Israeli products, work in Israel, and all posts connected to Israeli administration of the territories.

The uprising was a decentralized movement involving coordination between the underground leadership and the "people's committees" that sprang up in the refugee camps and the villages of the territories and organized local initiatives. The mass-based structure of the uprising was possible only because people's committees had already been in place since the 1970s as part of Palestinian institution building to counteract the deteriorating conditions under occupation. When Palestinians realized in the 1970s that a speedy reversal of the occupation was not in sight, they focused on surviving on their occupied land, awaiting liberation from the external Palestinian national movement, and applied the term *steadfastness* to the process. In the absence of municipalities, they mobilized volunteer work committees, including medical relief committees that provided preventive medical care to the camps and villages and women's work committees that offered income-generating projects and support for prisoners' families. These and other groups formed the basis for sustaining the uprising and its goal of delinking from the occupation by meeting civil needs, from health to agriculture.

The Israeli response was repression, curfews, labor control through border control, and general movement restrictions. The repressive and often violent tactics supported by the Israeli defense minister Yitzhak Rabin (1922–1995) in January 1988 translated into high Palestinian casualties and detention rates. Between 1988 and 1990, one in twenty-two Palestinian children was either killed or injured, according to the Israeli human rights organization B'Tselem. By the time of the signing of the Oslo Accords in September 1993 between the PLO and Israel, the intifada had already waned, and casualties topped 1,500.

The uprising made visible the Palestinians as a people struggling against Israeli occupation through the images of the stone throwers—previously their plight had been coded under the "Arab-Israeli conflict"—and made it difficult for Israel to continue the occupation as before. Moreover, the uprising realized Palestinian will to be represented solely by the PLO (Jordan halted its administrative responsibility for the West Bank in July 1988). The Palestine National Council session in Algiers in November 1988 issued a Declaration of Independence of Palestine, making Jerusalem its capital. Shortly afterward, Yasser Arafat (1929–2004) promised future, formal recognition of Israel and Palestine's readiness for territorial concessions in the United Nations General Assembly address in December 1988.

Although Palestinians greeted the arrival of the Palestinian Authority in Gaza in 1994 as a symbol of the triumph of their intifada, their hopes for an independent state were not realized. Israel retained military and economic controls over Gaza's borders, air and sea routes, international relations, and overall security even after its disengagement, and more than half of the West Bank remained under Israeli control in 2000, with additional areas under Israeli security control. Palestinian living standards continued to deteriorate, falling to pre–intifada levels, as the Israeli policy of border closure since March 1993 placed Gazans in a prison-like situation with limited work options, mostly in the inflated Palestinian security forces.

A second widespread uprising broke out in reaction to events on September 28, 2000, when the controversial Israeli politician Ariel Sharon (b. 1928) made a provocative visit to Al-Aqsa mosque in East Jerusalem, deploying thousands of security forces to seal off the area. The uprising of December 9, 1987, came to be referred to as the "first intifada" and the September 28, 2000, uprising came to be referred to as the "second intifada," or the "Al-Aqsa intifada."

By 2000 the Palestinian Authority was present in parts of the territories and more of the Palestinian population was armed, so during the second intifada there was greater focus on armed struggle and greater use of full military force by Israel, which constructs the intifada as a war between states. The Palestinian Authority is caught in a double bind: Israel expects them to contain the armed struggle, but at the same time they must maintain legitimacy among Palestinians, and this perpetuates not only the uprising but also internal Palestinian confrontation, with increased hardships for daily life for Palestinians.

SEE ALSO *Arab-Israeli War of 1967; Arabs; Arafat, Yasir; Civil Disobedience; Palestine Liberation Organization (PLO); Palestinian Authority; Palestinians; Peace Process; Protest*

BIBLIOGRAPHY

Al-Haq. 1990. *Punishing a Nation: Israeli Human Rights Violations during the Palestinian Uprising, December 1987–December 1988.* Boston: South End Press.

Carey, Roane, ed. 2001. *The New Intifada: Resisting Israel's Apartheid.* New York: Verso.

Farsoun, Samih. 1997. Palestinian Resistance to Israeli Occupation: The Intifada. In *Palestine and the Palestinians*, 213–252. Boulder, CO: Westview Press.

Heacock, Roger, and Jamal Nassar, eds. 1990. *Intifada: Palestine at the Cross Roads.* New York: Praeger.

Mary Hovsepian

INTIMACY
SEE *Friendship.*

INTRAROLE CONFLICT
SEE *Role Conflict.*

INTUITIVE CRITERION
SEE *Screening and Signaling Games.*

INUIT

The Inuit make their homes in Chukotka, Alaska, Arctic Canada and Labrador, and Greenland, and are one of the several indigenous peoples of the Circumpolar North. The name *Inuit* (singular, *Inuk*) has political as well as cultural and linguistic connotations. It means "the people" in Inuktitut, the language of the Inuit in Greenland and the central and eastern Canadian Arctic. Since the late 1970s the term has become the political designation for all of the peoples once known as Eskimos. The term *Eskimo* remains correct for archaeologically known populations.

Numbering approximately 150,000 people in 2006, contemporary Inuit are diverse in lifestyle, cultural practices, language, and economic and social circumstances. Within the broad political category Inuit, there are four major cultural divisions: Siberian Yupik, Alutiiq, Alaskan Yup'ik, and Inuit. Those who call themselves Inuit make additional regional, language, and cultural distinctions such that those in north Alaska are known as Iñupiat, while Inuit in Canada differentiate among Inuvialuit, Inuinnait, and Inuit. Greenlanders sometimes refer to themselves as Inuit, but also use the regional and cultural designations of Kalaallit, Inughuit, and Iit. While these contemporary distinctions have some basis in cultural, linguistic, and regional difference, the current divisions are also a result of colonial and administrative histories that reified some differences and denied others.

CULTURAL ORIGINS

Linguistic, cultural, and archaeological data indicate that the Inuit populations are related to the indigenous peoples of Siberia, and Inuit cultures most likely have their origins in Siberia or Central Asia. Archaeological evidence suggests that the ancestors of contemporary Inuit peoples moved across the Bering Strait in several waves, and probably in small groups, as early as 5000 BCE. These hunting peoples spread out across the North American Arctic, where they depended on both land and marine animals. Around 1,500 years ago, the maritime-adapted peoples in southwest Alaska began spreading north, establishing themselves as whale hunters in north Alaska. Contemporary Iñupiat are their descendants. Some of these northern Alaskans moved eastward into the Arctic Archipelago and Greenland during a warming period around 800 to 1000 CE, and are the ancestors of the contemporary Inuit of Canada and Greenland. The Thule Eskimos, as they are known, either replaced or absorbed the Eskimo cultures that had preceded them.

There are similarities as well as differences between the various Inuit peoples. The similarities, which are most striking in terms of language and traditional cosmological beliefs, are clearly due to the relatively recent geographic divergence between groups. Linguists distinguish at least two closely related languages, Inuktitut and Yupiaq, each with several distinct but mutually intelligible dialects. Inuit cosmology attributed a life force to all aspects of the natural world. Humans, in order to survive and prosper, attended to numerous taboos and engaged in morally correct behavior. Animals were said to give themselves to those hunters who were respectful, modest, and generous. Souls of the dead, both human and animal, returned to the world of the living in new bodies. Alaskan Yupiit (plural of Yup'ik), for example, celebrated a Bladder Festival each winter in which the souls of the sea mammals killed that year were feasted and then returned to the sea where they would be reborn. The recycling of souls is also reflected in human naming practices, which bestow the name, and thus the soul, of a recently deceased person upon a newborn infant. This tradition of naming children continues, and many contemporary Inuit contend that the name/soul chooses the child rather than being chosen for the child.

The differences between the various Inuit peoples, in contrast, are superficial and generally reflect differences in material circumstances rather than distinctions in life ways and social values. Many of the differences result from variation in the natural environment across Inuit lands, which encompass a number of ecosystems and climatic conditions. At the southern margin, Alutiit (plural of Alutiiq) and Yupiit lived in subarctic boreal forest zones, built sod houses in permanent winter villages, and had economic security provided by dependable stocks of fish and sea mammals. Farther north, Iñupiat reliance on bowhead whales enabled them to establish semipermanent villages of up to five hundred people. Large numbers of people living together and cooperating in subsistence whaling demanded a fairly formal political organization. Iñupiat were led by male *umialiit* (singular, *umialik*, literally, "boat owners") and their wives, who organized and directed whale hunting activities and later distributed the proceeds of the hunt. The Iit, who live along the narrow rocky coastline of eastern Greenland, in contrast, led a precarious existence and occupied multifamily longhouses of stone and sod.

Only Inuit in the central and eastern Canadian Arctic lived in domed snowhouses and hunted seals at breathing holes. This stereotype of Inuit life was true for them only during midwinter and early spring. They and Inuit elsewhere depended upon seasonally variable marine and terrestrial animals for food, clothing, and tools. All Inuit peoples in the various regions and ecosystems adapted their communities and developed sophisticated technologies in order to survive and prosper.

COLONIAL EXPERIENCES

Inuit in Greenland, and possibly those in Labrador and on Baffin Island, had some contacts with the Norse colonists in the tenth century. In 1576 English explorer Martin Frobisher (c. 1535–1594) encountered Inuit at Baffin Island while searching for a northwest passage to Asia. His

was the first of numerous, sometimes sustained European encounters with modern Inuit. It was only in the early eighteenth century that Europeans successfully colonized Inuit lands. The Danes, hoping to restore contact with the lost Norse, established a colony on the west coast of Greenland in 1721. A few years later Russians, having already established trading colonies in Chukotka, began exploring and settling Alutiiq regions of Alaska. Both established trading monopolies and sought to convert Inuit to Christianity and to make them into reliable suppliers of fur and other renewable resources.

Inuit in other parts of the Arctic, though not directly subjected to colonizing settlers, experienced the disruptive influence of whalers, traders, prospectors, and missionaries. The purchase by the United States of Alaska from Russia in 1867 and Canada's acquisition of British Arctic territories in 1870 and 1880 set the stage for those nations to administer Inuit lands and peoples. For the most part, however, both nations left the day-to-day administration to missionaries and traders. Inuit in both nations received the education, health care, and other public services provided to citizens of modern nation-states only after World War II (1939–1945).

Since the 1950s there have been dramatic changes in the social and material life of Inuit in all four nations. Some of the changes resulting from economic modernization and government administration have had positive consequences. Still, Inuit in all four nations have also suffered forced relocations, the imposition of alien cultural values and economic systems, and the reorganization of domestic and community life.

CONTEMPORARY CONCERNS

Today Inuit struggle to participate as citizens of modern nations while retaining a degree of cultural self-determination. There are concerns regarding resource development, economic and food security, education, language retention, health, and climate change. Greenlanders have succeeded in institutionalizing their language as the everyday vernacular of work and government, while the Siberian Yupik language is nearly extinct. The language situation in Alaska and Canada is mixed. Inuit have been required to adopt the political institutions and structures of their various nations. In all regions but Siberia, Inuit constitute a majority of the population in their traditional lands. Thus, they are able to maintain a measure of control over resource development, education, and other public services. This situation is recent. Struggles over resource development reached a climax in the 1970s and were catalysts for the settlement of aboriginal land claims in Alaska and Canada.

Hunting and the management of wildlife are also salient issues for contemporary Inuit. Although all Inuit live in modern communities, and many work for wages, they have retained a cultural identification with hunting. Having access to and eating traditional foods continues to be socially, emotionally, and culturally valued. This traditional activity appears to be threatened by global climate change, which has created unstable, unpredictable, and dangerous weather conditions in the Arctic and threatens the survival of many animal species. The Inuit Circumpolar Conference, a nongovernmental organization representing Inuit in international affairs, has taken on climate change as its central focus and has argued that global climate change must be considered a human rights issue.

BIBLIOGRAPHY

Bodenhorn, Barbara. 1990. "I'm Not the Great Hunter, My Wife Is": Iñupiat Models of Gender. *Etudes/Inuit/Studies* 14 (1–2): 55–74.

Briggs, Jean L. 1970. *Never in Anger: Portrait of an Eskimo Family.* Cambridge, MA: Harvard University Press.

Damas, David, ed. 1984. *Handbook of North American Indians.* Vol. 5: *Arctic.* Washington, DC: Smithsonian Institution.

Fienup-Riordan, Ann. 2000. *Hunting Tradition in a Changing World: Yup'ik Lives in Alaska Today.* New Brunswick, NJ: Rutgers University Press.

McGhee, Robert. 2005. *The Last Imaginary Place: A Human History of the Arctic World.* Oxford: Oxford University Press.

Stern, Pamela R. 2004. *Historical Dictionary of the Inuit.* Lanham, MD: Scarecrow.

Pamela R. Stern

INVENTORIES

Inventories are sets of goods and materials held available to cover immediate or future needs. Inventories can be goods and materials for sale after some processing or as they are, or they can be goods (like fixtures, supplies, furniture, or equipment) that are not for sale but are nevertheless kept by organizations, manufacturers, and service providers.

In business, inventories are assets that are used in the productive process and transformed to realize sales of the final products the market demands. They may be classified in three major categories: raw materials, work in process, and finished goods.

Inventories of raw materials are the collections of items used to begin the production process of a firm. They could be materials from agricultural, forest, or mining operations, or they could be the finished goods of another company. For example, a computer microchip could be the final product of a firm that manufactures microchips and a raw material for a firm that manufactures personal computers. Work-in-process inventories exist and are created in all the stages of the production process from the moment raw materials are received to the stage just before the production of the final goods ready for sale. An inventory of final goods represents the last stage of the production process. It is a collection of items that are ready to be sold to customers, having been inspected for quality to meet certain standards.

Inventories are acquired based on a production schedule and a sales forecast to determine the target level of inventories in each category. If the inventory level is too high, the company faces an unnecessarily high cost of carrying inventories. If the level is too low, the firm might not have enough materials for its production process and risks losing sales and dissatisfying its clients by not meeting their demand. The management of a company must therefore determine how much inventory it should carry by evaluating the costs with the production requirements and customer demand.

COMPOSITION OF INVENTORIES

The composition of a firm's inventories depends on several factors. Raw-materials inventories depend on the plans and schedules of production, the seasonality of sales, the available technology, the level of confidence toward the various suppliers for the on-time delivery of the needed goods, and several other factors. The level of work-in-process inventories depends on the type of the finished goods to be made ready for sale and the complexity of the production process. The level of finished-goods inventories depends on external factors, such as the expectations of the consumers and other market forces.

Inventories in business have certain financial characteristics that can be divided into three categories. First, they are part of the current assets on a firm's balance sheet and in most cases can be converted into cash during a period of one year. (There is an exception in some specialized industries in which the conversion might take longer.) Second, they are the least liquid of the current assets. This means that in companies with high variability in sales and production processes, it is more difficult to liquidate the company's inventories when needed unless they are sold at a discount, or less than their true value. Third, during the various inventory stages beginning with the purchase of raw-materials inventories until the realized sales of finished-goods inventories, there exist certain time lags that can have a positive or a negative effect for the firm. These are:

Manufacturing lag: The inventories that are bought by the company from its suppliers are usually raw materials. The payment for these inventories is usually made on credit. The credit period usually is longer than one month, while other operating expenses of the firm, such as labor and wages, must be paid within a month. Furthermore, the firm can have the needed inventories available before it covers its obligations to its suppliers. Hence the firm has a type of financing for the goods it has obtained without any financial cost. This lag has a positive effect for the company.

Stockage lag: When the finished goods inventories are ready to be sold, in most cases they are not sold immediately and therefore do not create cash inflows. However, there are many cash outflows for the payment of labor, the payment of suppliers, and other expenses of the production process. This delay in selling the inventories and creating cash inflows to meet the realized cash outflows has a cost to the firm in reducing the firm's liquidity.

Sales lag: Even when sales are realized for the finished-goods inventories, they could be on credit and not cash sales, creating accounts receivable for the firm that sells the inventory. These accounts receivable could take up to a year to be paid and generate cash inflows. This type of cost is called the cost of maintaining or creating accounts receivable.

A company keeps inventories for the reasons of transaction, safety, and arbitrage. For the purpose of transactions, a firm keeps inventories of all types to have raw materials to work with and to have finished goods to sell in order to minimize or eliminate the risk of stock outs, (the risk of not having enough inventories of a certain type needed in the production process, so production will not stop or be delayed) or total depletion of inventory and to make financial transactions. If it keeps large amounts of inventories, the cost of investing in inventories rises, but the likelihood of stock outs falls. For the purpose of safety in meeting product demand, a firm must keep a high enough level of inventories to meet the demand for its products. For the purpose of arbitrage, a firm might keep a high level of inventories to take advantage of situations where prices are expected to increase. A firm that has bought or produced inventories at a low cost may profit by selling them later at higher prices. Furthermore, by purchasing higher amounts of raw materials, a firm can take advantage of possible discounts offered by its suppliers due to the larger quantities ordered.

CATEGORIES OF COSTS

A company might consider four major categories of costs before making significant decisions regarding inventories. The first category is carrying, or holding, costs. This category relates to the keeping of inventories and can be distinguished into the following specific types of carrying costs:

Storage and handling costs: A firm needs to store its inventories in specific locations it owns or rents. This involves rental costs or the opportunity costs of using the storage areas rather than renting them to others along with the labor expenses of moving, storing, cleaning, distributing, reporting, securing, and generally handling the inventories.

Destruction or theft costs: Once a firm stores its inventories in specific locations, it needs to protect them from theft or destruction from those outside or inside the company.

Security costs: Both the inventories and their storage locations have to be secured from fires, floods, accidents, and other natural catastrophes, usually through a purchased security or insurance program.

Age costs: Certain categories of inventories, such as medicine, food, and computer products, have an expiration date beyond which they become obsolete and unfit for sale. The cost of keeping inventory beyond its expiration date is the age cost.

The second cost category is the ordering costs, which concern the placement of orders to the firm's suppliers. Each order that is received by a supplier has costs for the invoice to be issued and paid, for the transportation of the goods, for their quality inspection once the goods arrive, and so on. If a firm reduces the number of orders it places (making fewer but larger orders instead), it also reduces the total ordering costs of its inventories and becomes more profitable.

The third category is the opportunity costs, which are related to the amount of funds invested in inventories. If a large amount of funds is tied up in inventories, the firm loses opportunities it might have had to invest its finances instead in more profitable opportunities. Furthermore, if inventories are financed by borrowed funds, this carries interest costs that the firm has to pay back, thereby reducing its profitability.

The fourth category is the stock out costs or the costs associated with keeping too low an inventory or depleting an inventory. This can cause breaks and delays in the production of the finished goods, with negative consequences for the firm. It will have dissatisfied clients and customers, it might lose sales, it might have to pay fees for delaying its products' delivery, and it will damage its reputation. According to Geoff Relph and Peter Barrar (2003), there is also an opposite type of cost to stock out costs: that of having too much inventory, or overage. They suggest that firms should formally plan overage since an effective control of overage will enhance the company's profitability by minimizing the investment in inventories.

Certain factors affect the level of inventories a firm should carry to be profitable and efficient. These include:

the required materials for each stage in the production process;

the sales forecast;

seasonal or cyclical factors that characterize the firm's sales during a year; and

changes in technology that may render the finished-goods inventories obsolete.

INVENTORY MANAGEMENT

Inventory-management techniques aim to reduce the total inventory costs by holding and ordering inventories in the most efficient ways. They are covered extensively in special courses of production management. Inventory management also has economic consequences for a business and affects the value of the firm, so it is also studied from a financial point of view. The most common inventory management techniques follow.

The ABC system separates inventories into the categories A, B, and C according to their importance and nature so the total cost of inventory control can be reduced. The most valuable inventories are in category A, while the least important ones are category C.

The economic ordering quantity (EOQ) system uses a simple mathematical model to determine the ideal quantity of each order of inventories that will reduce the total ordering and carrying costs.

The system of reorder point is based on the EOQ model and shows the quantity of inventories that should be on hand when an order is placed to keep the total inventory costs at a minimum.

The automated system of inventory control is used by firms that have many products and determines the optimal quantities to be ordered based on the EOQ. It is a dynamic system that is easily adjusted depending on a company's needs.

The just-in-time inventory system is a system first introduced in Japan that minimizes the level of inventories a firm carries and the investment in them by achieving a perfect coordination between the ordering and receiving of necessary inventories at each stage of the production process. Hence no inventory stocks are created,

and the inventory costs are kept at a minimum. The disadvantage of this system is that if the coordination is interrupted between the product suppliers and the customers' orders, the costs can be high.

NATIONAL CYCLES

Inventories also play an important role in national accounts. Some short-term macroeconomic fluctuations are attributed to the inventory cycle. Goods held as inventories are considered an investment and are counted for the year produced, not the year sold. Although inventories are a small portion of the overall investment sector, all the inventories from all the businesses in one economy constitute a critical component of the gross domestic product (GDP).

If the economy is moving toward a recession period, an undesired accumulation of inventories is a negative signal. Leading up to a recession, consumers have less liquidity and reduce their purchases. This leads to fewer sales of goods and services, which causes inventories of finished goods to increase. As inventories pile up, businesses reduce their production of goods to keep costs low. Since there is less productive activity, fewer employees are needed, and firms lay off staff to further reduce costs. Unemployment rises, output falls, GDP growth falls, and the economy goes into a recession. The idea that a recession might be caused by low product demand was introduced as early as 1889 by Albert Frederick Mummery and J. A. Hobson in their book *The Physiology of Industry* and upset the neoclassical economists. However, the British economist John Maynard Keynes (1936) praised Mummery and Hobson for their "heresy," as Keynes called their proposition. Mummery and Hobson further proposed that too much saving has a negative effect in the economy since it leads to underconsumption. Lower levels of consumption will mean less demand for goods and services, which will cause the piling up of inventories in the immediate future and eventually will lead to lower production output, more unemployment, and a decrease of the GDP.

Conversely, an undesired or unexpected decrease in business inventories means that the demand for goods is greater than the one predicted by the firms, and the existing inventories become depleted quickly. Businesses reorder more inventories, hire more employees, and increase production to meet the increased demand and realize higher sales. As this phenomenon occurs throughout the economy, the unemployment rate falls, and the economic output rises, resulting in an increase in economic growth as measured by the GNP.

In addition, with more jobs, less unemployment, and higher output, income also increases and contributes further to a rise in the demand for goods and services. Higher demand, though, leads to higher prices. The level of prices goes up, creating demand-pull inflation. As demand for more labor rises, wages increase, which will further increase the rate of inflation.

Inventories can thus be considered a leading indicator of business cycles. Changes in the variable of business inventories can lead to changes in the future condition of the economy and economic growth. Economic analysts therefore monitor the aggregate levels of business inventories for potential changes in future economic growth.

SEE ALSO *Business Cycles, Real; Depression, Economic; Economic Crises; Expectations; National Income Accounts; Recession*

BIBLIOGRAPHY

Blinder, Alan S. 1981. Inventories and the Structure of Macro Models. *American Economic Review* 71 (2): 11–16.

Blinder, Alan S. 1982. Inventories and Sticky Prices: More on the Microfoundations of Macroeconomics. *American Economic Review* 72 (3): 334–348.

Blinder, Alan S., and Louis John Maccini. 1991. The Resurgence of Inventory Research: What Have We Learned? *Journal of Economics Surveys* 5 (4): 291–328.

Brigham, E. F. 1992. *Fundamentals of Financial Management.* 6th ed. Orlando, FL: Dryden.

Fisher, Jonas D. M., and Andreas Hornstein. 2000. Inventory Policies in General Equilibrium. *Review of Economic Studies* 67 (1): 117–145.

Irvine, F. Owen, Jr. 1981. Merchant Wholesaler Inventory Investment and the Cost of Capital. *American Economic Review* 71 (2): 23–29.

Keynes, John Maynard. 1936. *General Theory of Employment, Interest, and Money.* London: Macmillan.

Mummery, Albert Frederick, and J. A. Hobson. 1889. *The Physiology of Industry: Being an Exposure of Certain Fallacies in Existing Theories of Economics.* London: J. Murray.

Relph, Geoff, and Peter Barrar. 2003. Overage Inventory: How Does It Occur and Why Is It Important? *International Journal of Production Economics* 81–82 (1): 163–171.

Katerina Lyroudi

INVENTORY OF FATHER INVOLVEMENT

SEE *Fatherhood.*

INVERSE MATRIX

The concept of *inverse matrix* is somewhat analogous to that of the *reciprocal* of a number. If *a* is a nonzero number, then $1/a$ is its reciprocal. The fraction $1/a$ is often written as a^{-1}. Aside from the fact that only nonzero numbers have reciprocals, the key property of a nonzero number and its reciprocal is that their product is 1, that is, $a \cdot a^{-1} = 1$. This makes a^{-1} the *multiplicative inverse* of the nonzero number *a*.

Only nonsingular square matrices *A* have inverses. (A square matrix is *nonsingular* if and only if its determinant is nonzero.) When *A* is nonsingular, its inverse, denoted A^{-1}, is unique and has the key property that $A \cdot A^{-1} = I = A^{-1} \cdot A$, where *I* denotes the $n \times n$ *identity matrix*. The determinant of a square matrix *A* (of any order) is a single scalar (number), say $a = \det(A)$. If this number is nonzero, the matrix is nonsingular, and accordingly has a reciprocal. Moreover, when $\det(A) \neq 0$, the inverse of *A* exists and its determinant is the reciprocal of $\det(A)$. That is, $\det(A^{-1}) = (\det(A))^{-1}$.

A tiny example will illustrate these concepts, albeit somewhat too simplistically. Let

$$A = \begin{bmatrix} a_{11} & a_{12} \\ a_{21} & a_{22} \end{bmatrix}.$$

Then, the determinant of *A* is the number

$$\det(A) = a_{11}a_{22} - a_{12}a_{21}.$$

If $\det(A) \neq 0$, then

$$A^{-1} = \frac{1}{\det(A)} \cdot \begin{bmatrix} a_{22} & -a_{12} \\ -a_{21} & a_{11} \end{bmatrix}.$$

As a check, one can see that

$$A^{-1} \cdot A = \frac{1}{\det(A)} \cdot \begin{bmatrix} a_{22} & -a_{12} \\ -a_{21} & a_{11} \end{bmatrix} \cdot \begin{bmatrix} a_{11} & a_{12} \\ a_{21} & a_{22} \end{bmatrix} = \begin{bmatrix} 1 & 0 \\ 0 & 1 \end{bmatrix}.$$

This formula for the inverse of a 2×2 matrix is useful for hand calculations, but its generalization to matrices of larger order is far more difficult conceptually and computationally. Indeed, the formula is

$$A^{-1} = \frac{1}{\det(A)} \operatorname{adj}(A),$$

where $\operatorname{adj}(A)$ is the so-called *adjoint* (or *adjugate*) of *A*. The adjoint of *A* is the "transposed matrix of cofactors" of *A*, that is, the matrix *B* with elements $b_{ij} = (-1)^{i+j} \det(A(j|i))$.

One way to carry out the inversion of a nonsingular matrix *A* is to consider the matrix equation $A \cdot X = I$, where *X* stands for A^{-1}. If *A* is $n \times n$, then this equation can be viewed as a set of *n* separate equations of the form $Ax = b$ where *x* is successively taken as the *j*th column of unknown matrix *X* and *b* is taken as the *j*th column of *I* ($j = 1, \ldots, n$). These equations can then be solved by Cramer's rule.

The concept of the inverse of a matrix is of great theoretical value, but as may be appreciated from the above discussion, its computation can be problematic, just from the standpoint of sheer labor, not to mention issues of numerical reliability. Fortunately, there are circumstances in which it is not necessary to know the inverse of an $n \times n$ matrix A in order to solve an equation like $Ax = b$. One such circumstance is where the nonsingular matrix A is lower (or upper) triangular and all its diagonal elements are nonzero. In the case of lower triangular matrices, this means (i) $a_{ii} \neq 0$ for all $i = 1, \ldots, n$, (ii) $a_{ij} = 0$ for all $i = 1, \ldots, n - 1$ and $j > i$. Thus, for instance

$$A = \begin{bmatrix} 4 & 0 & 0 \\ 3 & -1 & 0 \\ 2 & 1 & 5 \end{bmatrix}$$

is lower triangular; the fact that its diagonal elements 4, −1, and 5 are all nonzero makes this triangular matrix nonsingular. When A is nonsingular and lower triangular, solving the equation $Ax = b$ is done by starting with the top equation $a_{11}x_1 = b_1$ and solving it for x_1. In particular, $x_1 = b_1/a_{11}$. This value is substituted into all the remaining equations. Then the process is repeated for the next equation. It gives $x_2 = [b_2 - a_{21}(b_1/a_{11})]a_{22}$. This sort of process is repeated until the last component of x is computed. This technique is called *forward substitution*. There is an analogous procedure called *back substitution* for nonsingular upper triangular matrices. Transforming a system of linear equations to triangular form makes its solution fairly uncomplicated.

Matrix inversion is thought by some to be a methodological cornerstone of regression analysis. The desire to invert a matrix typically arises in solving the normal equations generated by applying the method of ordinary least squares (OLS) to the estimation of parameters in a linear regression model. It might be postulated that the linear relationship

$$Y = \beta_1 + \beta_2 X_2 + \cdots + \beta_k X_k \tag{1}$$

holds for some set of parameters $\beta_1, \ldots, \beta_k$. To determine these unknown parameters, one runs a set of, say, n experiments by first choosing values $X_{i2}, \ldots, X_{ik}$ and then recording the outcome Y_i for $i = 2, \ldots, n$. In doing so, one uses an error term U_i for the ith experiment. This is needed because for a specific set of parameter values (estimates), there may be no solution to the set of simultaneous equations induced by (1). Thus, one writes

$$Y_i = \beta_1 + \beta_2 X_{i2} + \cdots + \beta_k X_{ik} + U_i, \qquad i = 1, 2, \ldots, n. \tag{2}$$

The OLS method seeks values of $\beta_1, \ldots, \beta_k$ that minimize the sum of the squares errors, that is $\sum_{i=1}^{n} U_i^2$. With

$$Y = \begin{bmatrix} Y_1 \\ \vdots \\ Y_n \end{bmatrix}, \quad X = \begin{bmatrix} 1 & X_{12} & \cdots & X_{1k} \\ \vdots & \vdots & & \vdots \\ 1 & X_{n2} & \cdots & X_{nk} \end{bmatrix}, \quad \text{and } \beta = \begin{bmatrix} \beta_1 \\ \vdots \\ \beta_k \end{bmatrix},$$

this leads to the OLS problem of minimizing $Y'Y - 2Y'X\beta + \beta'X'X\beta$. The first-order necessary and sufficient conditions for the minimizing vector β are the so-called *normal equations* $X'X\beta = X'Y$.

If the matrix $X'X$ is nonsingular, then

$$\beta = (X'X)^{-1}X'Y. \tag{3}$$

Care needs to be taken in solving the normal equations. It can happen that $X'X$ is singular. In that case, its inverse does not exist. Yet even when $X'X$ is invertible, it is not always advisable to solve for β as in (3). For numerical reasons, this is particularly so when the order of the matrix is very large.

SEE ALSO *Determinants; Hessian Matrix; Jacobian Matrix; Matrix Algebra; Regression Analysis*

BIBLIOGRAPHY

Marcus, Marvin, and Henryk Minc. 1964. *A Survey of Matrix Theory and Matrix Inequalities.* Boston: Allyn and Bacon.

Strang, Gilbert. 1976. *Linear Algebra and its Applications.* New York: Academic Press.

Richard W. Cottle

INVESTMENT

There are three contexts of investment relevant to the social sciences. First, there is the authoritative investment of endowing a person with social and institutional authority, power, or privilege. Second, a financial investment consists of the production or purchase of an asset in order to obtain its yield, such as interest from bonds. Financial investments involve the exchange of one paper asset (money) for another asset—for example, stocks, bonds, and real estate. Third, an economic investment is the production of some new asset (new plant and equipment, expansion of inventories, new residential construction, reputation) or the creation of new laboring ability (human capital).

The methods of authoritative investing are delegation, inheritance, and usurpation. In a democracy, authoritative investment endows officials with authority in accord with the rules of elections and appointments to office. That authority vests the officials with power and privilege as legally delegated to them from the people, as ultimate sovereignty rests with the people. In a kingdom, royal authority is usually handed down by inheritance, and inheritance also invests heirs with titles to private property. In a dictatorship, the chief of state invests himself or herself with ruling power, and criminals too vest themselves with power over their victims, such as when they illegitimately take property from their victims.

In finance and economics, investing is distinct from speculation. Speculators buy assets with the expectation of gaining due to shifts in supply and demand. Speculators buy shares of stock in a silver mining company if they expect the demand for the metal to increase. Investors buy the stock in order to obtain the dividends from the profits of the firm. The purchase can, of course, include both investment and speculation.

The yields of financial investments include interest, dividends, rentals, capital gains, and business profits. Dividends are a share of corporate profits from stocks or a mutual fund, while interest is obtained from loaned funds, such as bonds and savings accounts. Capital gains occur when an asset sells for a higher price than its initial price of purchase. The return to an investment can also be in the form of the retained earnings or profits of a corporation.

ECONOMIC INVESTMENT

Economic investment consists in the production of capital goods and the enhancement of human capital, the education, skills, and training obtained by workers. A capital good can be intangible, such as when a company invests in advertising in order to create goodwill and reputation capital. Human capital includes relationships with other persons, which is more specifically referred to as social capital. A person also invests in human capital to be a better consumer, such as learning music appreciation to enjoy symphonic music, which is more specifically referred to as cultural capital.

The inputs of production are classified as three "factors," land, labor, and capital goods. *Land* means natural resources, existing prior to and apart from human action and its products. The purchase of land is a financial but not an economic investment. *Capital goods*, such as buildings, machines, and inventory, are products whose value is not yet consumed. Improvements to a site, such as clearing and leveling the surface, are included in capital goods.

A bond is a loan of funds to a borrower who pays interest for the duration or term and returns the funds when the bond matures. The bond might be used by the seller to produce capital goods, but the bonds are not in themselves produced goods and so are not an economic investment.

Technology is embedded in both capital goods and in human capital. If there is no change in technology, investments eventually have diminishing returns. Given a fixed area of land, fertilizer can increase the yield of a crop, but

as more and more fertilizer is added, the extra amount of fertilizer provides a reduced amount of extra yield. If one keeps adding fertilizer, eventually the *marginal product* or extra yield becomes zero and then negative—too many cooks spoil the broth.

An increase in the amount of a variable input eventually yields diminishing returns when some other input is fixed. However, there can initially be increasing returns from more investment if there are network effects that increase the value of each good. For example, if fax machines are more widespread, then a machine has higher usefulness because it can send and receive messages from more units. Capital goods can also complement other investments so that there are at first increasing returns. But such increasing returns themselves eventually diminish. Much of the historic increase in productivity has come not just from an increase in the stock of capital goods but from better technology. There are no diminishing returns to better technology.

Both capital goods and human capital depreciate; they lose economic value due to "wear and tear" as well as from obsolescence and uncertainty. Gross investment is the total amount of production of capital goods and human capital, while net investment equals gross investment minus depreciation. In national income or output accounts, typically only investments in capital goods are included in the investment category in calculating gross and net domestic product.

EFFICIENT FINANCIAL MARKETS

The purpose of investment is to maximize future consumption, thus to obtain the greatest increase in future yields. The optimal investment has the highest risk-adjusted rate of return. *Risk* means the possibility of loss with a known probability. *Uncertainty* means the possibility of change with no known probability. The optimal investment has the greatest net present value, the value at present of a stream of future income minus the initial outlay and other costs, discounted by the relevant interest rate.

Even though subject to large fluctuations, financial markets tend to be rather efficient, meaning that the prices of financial assets encompass the known public information about the asset, the relevant industry, and the economy. The seller is pessimistic, believing the price will fall, and the buyer is optimistic, believing the price will rise. The price is the midpoint between the pessimists and the optimists. On the average, one who buys the stock will do no better than the market average. In fact even most professional financial managers and advisers have not performed better than market averages in the long run.

The concept of efficient markets does not imply that prices are perfect reflections of future earnings and economic conditions but rather that it is not likely that one will systematically profit from market timing or stock picking. It does imply, however, that riskier assets will normally have a higher return to compensate for the greater possibility of loss or of the greater fluctuations that make the price at some future date less predictable.

The theory of efficient markets for financial investments is called *modern portfolio theory* (MPT). It prescribes that an investor should seek no more than to match the averages of the various sectors of financial markets. However, the relevant knowledge has to be utilized by some investors or speculators in order to set the efficient price in the first place. Research into companies, industries, and the economies must offer some reward, and in an efficient market this reward would be commensurate with other gains.

Efficient markets also do not preclude some financial analysts from having insights and analysis superior to those of others in some types of markets and economic conditions. Not only is there great uncertainty about future economic variables, such as inflation and interest rates, but there is also a lack of consensus about many aspects of economic theory, such as business cycles.

SAVINGS AND INVESTMENT

Savings equal income minus consumption. In economics, *consumption* means the using up of economic value, like fire consuming wood. *Production* means the creation of economic value. The consumption of a house consists in its depreciation. The purchase of a car has the same economic characteristics; the car is an investment, and its consumption is the depreciation. From the economic point of view, all goods that one buys are investments until they are consumed, although in national income accounts, outlays other than for a house are counted as consumption.

Savings are either invested or kept in money. Few people normally hoard large amounts of cash, so ordinarily people save money in a financial institution, such as a bank or a money market fund. These institutions in turn loan out their money. Money borrowed for consumption offsets some of the money saved, and the rest is spent for investment. Thus in general the net savings of households is either invested or kept as money in the banking system. Banks are legally required to have a small portion of their deposits held in reserve, and they loan out the excess reserves.

Investment comes from savings, but the amounts households plan to save do not necessarily equal the amounts that investors seek to borrow. If investors seek to borrow more than what is available from savings, then the market rate of interest will rise, reducing the amount of intended borrowing while increasing the amount of savings. If the supply of savings increases, then interest rates

fall as bankers seek to loan out the excess reserves. The market rate of interest thus has an important role in the economy: it equilibrates savings and investment so that the quantity of loanable funds supplied by savings equals the quantity demanded for investment by borrowers.

The total savings in the economy also includes government savings, government revenues minus government spending. A government deficit that is used for consumption creates negative savings, a reduction in national savings. Government bonds can compete with corporate bonds, raising interest rates and "crowding out" private investment that would have taken place unless the funds are borrowed from abroad or private savings increase. Unless the deficit spending is used for productive investments, such as infrastructure, the government deficit can burden future generations by reducing private investment and also by making future taxpayers pay interest on debt that does not benefit the present generation.

INVESTMENT AND THE BUSINESS CYCLE

Investment fluctuates much more than consumption. Major changes in investment drive the business cycle as recessions occur after a large decline in investment. Investment declines because entrepreneurs expect lower profits, and profits usually decline either because costs have gone up or because the demand for goods is expected to fall. In some economic models, the *accelerator principle* asserts that investment depends on the annual increase in output and the capital needed to produce the increase. The more fundamental explanation is that savings, interest rates, and expectations about the future determine the amount and the mix of investment.

Lower real interest rates induce more investment in fixed capital goods, such as real estate construction. When the monetary authority expands credit by injecting money into the banking system, the interest rate is lowered as the banks seek to lend out the extra money. Later, to prevent excessive inflation, the monetary authority then reduces the rate of money growth, and interest rates go back up. Investments profitable at the previous lower interest rates are no longer profitable, reducing investment and also wasting capital that would have been better invested in goods with a faster turnover.

Meanwhile the lowered rate of interest also makes it attractive to invest and speculate in real estate. Much of the benefit of economic growth is soaked up by higher rentals and land values due to the fixed supply of land and implicit subsidy to land values from public works not financed from the generated rents.

Speculative demand adds to the demand for use, pulling up real estate prices. At the peak of the boom, higher interest rates plus higher real estate costs diminish profits, and industries such as construction slow down. The diminishing investment reduces demand for other goods, and the economy falls into a recession. Real estate prices and interest rates then fall, and the reduced costs eventually lead entrepreneurs to invest again, and then the economy recovers.

TAXATION, REGULATION, AND INVESTMENT

Income taxes reduce investment by taxing the interest, dividends, profits, and capital gains from savings, enterprise, and investment. The effect is more severe when, as in the United States, the income tax is on nominal gains and nominal depreciation, ignoring inflation, thus taxing the principal as well as the gain. This excess burden has been recognized by providing for tax sheltered savings, such as individual retirement accounts (IRAs), by lower tax rates on capital gains, and by investment credits for businesses. Nevertheless, much of investment remains subject to taxation. Sales and value-added taxes have similar excess burdens. Some economists advocate shifting public revenues to pollution charges, user fees, and rents of natural resources to avoid excess burdens on investment in both capital goods and human capital.

Regulations can enhance markets, such as when they prevent fraud, but they also impose costs similar to taxation. Excessive restrictions and reporting costs can create a deadweight loss similar to taxation, a reduction of investment not offset by social benefits.

SEE ALSO *Finance; Macroeconomics*

BIBLIOGRAPHY

Elton, Edwin J., Martin Gurber, Stephen Brown, and William Goetzman. 2006. *Modern Portfolio Theory and Investment Analysis.* 7th ed. Hoboken, NJ: John Wiley.

Haugen, Robert A. 2001. *Modern Investment Theory.* 5th ed. Upper Saddle River, NJ: Prentice Hall.

Fred Foldvary

INVESTMENT BANKING

SEE *Banking.*

INVESTORS

The term *investor* is widely used not only by economics and finance academics and professionals, but also by ordinary people. An investor is an individual or an organiza-

tion that makes an *investment.* The term *investment* itself is interpreted differently by the common public and finance professionals on the one hand, and by academic and professional economists on the other.

INVESTMENT IN ECONOMICS LITERATURE

In economics, *investment* refers to resources used to increase capital stock. The items included are expenditure on:

1. Plants (machines) and equipments.
2. Structures (factories, office building, etc.).
3. Inventories (of finished and unfinished goods).
4. New residential houses.

Moreover, the above items must be the result of *current* production. Suppose, for example, that General Motors (GM) spends $20 million in 2007 to build a new automotive factory to produce cars based on alternative fuel. GM will be considered by economists to have invested $20 million in 2007. This investment will add to the capital stock (the accumulated value of all capital: plants, equipment, buildings, factories, etc.) owned by GM at the end of 2006. However, if GM buys in 2007 a factory that Ford had utilized through 2006, economists will not consider the transfer of the automotive factory as investment from the nation's point of view. This is because the factory Ford sold is not new—it is not the result of production in 2007. The purchase of the Ford factory by GM merely reflects a change in ownership of existing capital. Similarly, if you buy a five-year-old mansion for $7.5 million, it is not considered investment by economists, but buying a new mansion will be counted as investment.

Notice that even long-lasting new things that consumers buy are not counted in investment, except for new houses. Suppose you spend $150,000 to buy a new seaworthy boat, and $90,000 to buy a new condominium. The condominium will be counted as investment, but not the boat (which is actually more expensive). The boat is considered a consumption item, not an investment item. However, if a business had bought the same new boat to operate a sightseeing tour, it would be considered an investment item.

Economists also distinguish between *net* and *gross* investment. This distinction is necessitated by the fact that there is a wear and tear of capital stock as it is used in the production process—that is, the capital stock *depreciates.* Thus, investment that includes depreciation is called *gross* investment, and after the value of *depreciation* is subtracted from the *gross* investment, the resulting amount is the *net* investment. The nation's capital stock during any year rises by the extent of net investment. The part of current income that consumers do not consume is called *saving*. It is this saving that largely finances investment by businesses, and leads to an increase in the capital stock of the nation. The widely used term *capitalism* is based on the notion of an economic system that is based on ownership of capital.

INVESTMENT IN FINANCE LITERATURE AND ORDINARY USE

The use of the term *investment* in finance and by ordinary people refers to buying an asset. The asset can be a financial instrument, commonly called a *security* (such as stocks, bonds, and a certificate of deposit or CD) or a real object (such as real estate, gold, and paintings).

To understand the notion of an investor, one should look at the various types of investments that he or she could invest in. The choice of the investment vehicle by an investor indicates how much *risk* the investor is willing to take. The following describes the major categories of investment or assets.

Equity or *stocks* represent ownership in a company or business. If you own 10 percent of GM stocks, you literally own 10 percent of GM. Equities constitute a major asset class. Stocks are considered risky in the sense that you can lose money if their value falls or if the company goes bankrupt. Stock investors of Enron, a U.S. public corporation that went bankrupt in 2001, were left with stocks that were worthless. Ownership of stocks can change frequently—they are traded on stock exchanges or computer-linked systems.

Bonds are the second most prominent asset class. A bond, also called a *debt security*, represents a loan made by an investor to a borrower. Normally, a bond has a maturity period of one to thirty years. The maturity period of a bond indicates in how many years the loan is due to be repaid. Thus, an investor holding a ten-year GM bond will receive periodic interest payments (usually twice a year) from GM and will receive the principal amount loaned at the end of the ten-year period. There is risk associated with bonds as well, because the borrower may be unable to pay interest and the principal on time or not at all. This is called *default risk*. If a company goes bankrupt, the bondholders as lenders have claims on the company's assets. The company's assets when sold may provide to the bond investors, say, fifty cents for every dollar lent. Stockholders, being owners, do not get anything at all in this case. Two major entities provide default-risk ratings in the United States: Moody's and Standard & Poor's. Bonds issued by the U.S. Treasury are considered default-risk free.

Money market instruments are the third important asset class. They are also debt instruments like bonds, except that the maturity period is one year or less. Because fewer things can go wrong in a year, a money market instrument is less risky than stocks or bonds. In fact, the money market is a way for an investor to hold cash (a liquid or cashlike asset). By investing in money market instruments, an investor has a relatively riskless asset, while still earning some interest income.

In addition to the preceding three widely utilized assets, there are other assets that an investor may choose to invest in. These include (among others): real estate (ownership of land or buildings); foreign exchange or currency (U.S. dollars, yen, euros, etc.); commodities (precious metals, crude oil, soybeans, etc.); derivatives (such as options and futures—these financial instruments are derived from or based on other financial securities); and works of art or other collectibles.

To distinguish between the notion of investment as used in finance and economics, investment in items such as plants and equipment is called simply *investment*, whereas investment in financial securities is called *portfolio investment*.

The choice of security indicates the extent of risk an investor is willing to take—the greater the risk, the greater the expected return on the investment. A risk-averse investor tries to diversify within an asset class or across asset classes.

RELATED TERMS IN USE

One will encounter a large number of terms in the context of discussing an investor or an investment. The following provides a nonexhaustive list of terms that have not been mentioned above: individual investors (including trusts on behalf of individuals, and umbrella companies formed to pool investment funds from two or more investors), angel investor (an affluent person who provides capital for a business start-up), amateur investor (often indicating an individual who invests blindly or is influenced by romantic notions rather than hard facts), venture capital funds (which provide start-up capital in lieu of a share of the business), financial intermediaries, banks, mutual funds, pension funds, hedge funds, insurance companies, investment banks, investment trusts (such as real-estate investment trusts), and regulatory institutions (such as the U.S. Securities and Exchange Commission or SEC).

SEE ALSO *Equity Markets; Finance; Financial Markets; Investment; Investors, Institutional; Risk; Stock Exchanges*

BIBLIOGRAPHY

Froyen, Richard T. 2005. *Macroeconomics: Theories and Policies*. 8th ed. Upper Saddle River, NJ: Pearson/Prentice Hall.

Mishkin, Frederic S. 2007. *The Economics of Money, Banking, and Financial Markets*. 8th ed. Boston: Pearson/Addison Wesley.

Mittra, Sid. 2005. *Practicing Financial Planning for Professionals.* 9th ed. Rochester, MI: RH Publishing.

Saunders, Anthony, and Marcia Millon Cornett. 2007. *Financial Markets and Institutions: An Introduction to the Risk Management Approach.* 3rd ed. Boston: McGraw-Hill/Irwin.

Anandi P. Sahu

INVESTORS, INSTITUTIONAL

Institutional investors are professional fiduciary entities managing investment portfolios on behalf of their clients as well as for their own proprietary accounts. The major groups include mutual funds, independent investment advisors, banks, insurance companies, foundations, endowments, pension funds, and, more recently, hedge funds.

Mutual funds are traditional investment companies managing investment portfolios for funds' shareholders. Independent investment advisors are typically associated with large diversified financial institutions (e.g., Lehman Brothers, Bear Stearns) and can invest for their own proprietary accounts as well as manage portfolios for their clients (such as wealthy individuals, pension funds, endowments, etc.). Investments managed by banks are mostly limited to trusts and some pension funds. Insurance companies invest primarily in fixed-income securities. University endowments and charitable foundations are mostly concerned with capital preservation and often outsource all or most of their investment portfolios to professional money managers (e.g., independent investment advisors). Hedge funds are mostly unregulated investment vehicles, which are restricted to qualified wealthy investors and are not required to register with the Securities and Exchange Commission or to report their ownership positions.

Since the 1950s, institutional investing has played an increasingly important role in global financial markets. Professional investors and money managers of the twenty-first century have control over a significantly larger asset base than their colleagues thirty or forty years ago. According to quarterly institutional filings with the Securities and Exchange Commission (Form 13F), both the number of institutional entities and aggregate assets under their management experienced tremendous growth during the second half of the twentieth century. According to Paul Gompers and Andrew Metrick (2001), reported U.S. holdings of large institutional investors (excluding hedge funds) grew from $375 billion in 1980 to $3.98 trillion in 1996. Institutional ownership of the U.S. equity markets grew from less than 10 percent in

1950 (estimated by Friedman 1996) to 27.6 percent in 1980 and to over 61.2 percent in 2005. According to the Conference Board, in 2005 large U.S. institutions controlled over $24 trillion in assets (excluding hedge funds). Independent investment advisors have experienced the greatest growth of all institutions. In 1997 there were roughly six times more independent investment advisors than in 1983 (1,128 versus 195). Most recently, hedge funds outpaced other types of institutions in number of entities, which skyrocketed from about 530 in 1990 to over 7,000 in 2007 (excluding funds of funds), and it is estimated that in 2007 hedge funds controlled between $1.5 to $2.0 trillion assets under management worldwide.

The growth in institutional investments can partially be attributed to the worldwide proliferation of public and private pension plans (e.g., Government Pension Investment in Japan, ABP in Netherlands, CalPERS in the United States) and tax-deferred retirement savings plans (e.g., 401(k), 403(b), IRA). Large institutional investors became active advocates of shareholder interests and corporate monitors (Hartzell and Starks 2003). Blockholders and other large owners play an increasingly important role in corporate governance as well as proxy battles. While some institutional investors are very independent in their voting decisions (e.g., CalPERS), others often rely on recommendations of Institutional Shareholder Services.

For their professional management, institutions earned a reputation of "smart money." In fact, some institutional investors appear to be able to predict future negative events, such as class-action shareholder litigation (Barabanov et al. 2007) and may also benefit through informed trading at the expense of less-sophisticated individual investors. For example, institutions capture postearnings announcement drift in stock prices (Cohen et al. 2002), participate less frequently in lower-quality seasoned equity offerings (Gibson et al. 2004), select stronger initial public offerings (Field and Lowry 2005), do a better job interpreting both analyst recommendations (Mikhail et al. 2005) and earnings announcements (Ali et al. 2004), and do not trade as often as individuals on misleading "pro forma" earnings (Bhattacharya et al. 2005). Sergey Barabanov and colleagues (2007) show that information advantage of institutional investors stems mostly from their skills in analyzing public quantitative information. Unlike some individuals, institutions seem to refrain from trading on illegal insider information.

Good performance of institutional portfolios is driven by institutions with a short-term performance focus, such as independent investment advisors and mutual funds (e.g., Barabanov and McNamara 2007), whose compensation is based primarily on performance relative to their peers and respective benchmarks. Unlike institutions with a long-term focus (banks, insurance companies, foundations, and endowments), short-horizon institutions possess private information about long-term earnings, which is reflected in short-term prices (Ke et al. 2006). Mutual funds and independent investment advisors are typically more aggressive than banks, insurance companies, and endowments. Consequently, mutual fund managers often choose to invest in relatively risky securities with high levels of ownership turnover (Bennett et al. 2003). While 77 percent of mutual fund managers have been found to be return momentum traders (Grinblatt et al. 1995), bank-managed trusts and pension funds, in contrast, are typically more conservative in their investment policies and do not strongly pursue potentially destabilizing trading behavior such as herding (mass buying or selling of a particular asset) or momentum trading (e.g., Lakonishok et al. 1992). Because they are subject to the American Bankers Association's Model Prudent Man Investment Act and the American Law Institute's Restatement of Trusts, managers of bank trusts and bank-managed pension funds are personally liable and aim to ensure that their investments are considered prudent by courts should any litigation arise (Longstreth 1986; Del Guercio 1996). Insurance companies invest only a small portion of their assets in equities and prefer low volatility of returns (Badrinath et al. 1996). Endowment managers display conservative behavior as they typically do not have performance incentives for high relative returns, but may suffer highly negative publicity in the case of poor performance (Brown 1999).

Historically, institutions preferred to invest in large capitalization companies with better visibility and transparency of earnings, revenues, and management, wider analyst coverage, and low transaction costs (e.g., Gompers and Metrick 2001; Falkenstein 1996; O'Brien and Bhushan 1990). With increasing competition among professional money managers, institutional preferences have shifted toward smaller stocks, where they can achieve more benefits from their informational advantage (Bennett et al. 2003), as well as new asset classes (e.g., private equity, venture capital, hedge funds) and developing and emerging markets.

Institutional participation enhances market liquidity, efficiency, transparency, and corporate governance both in developed and emerging markets. The information acquisition activities of institutional investors, for example, stimulate the speed of adjustment to new information (Sias and Starks 1997) and reduce information asymmetries between insiders and capital markets (Szewczyk et al. 1992). Even though aggregate institutional ownership data provides evidence of institutional herding and momentum trading, this behavior appears to be exhibited less by institutions than by individuals and is attributed mostly to trading by mutual funds and independent

investment advisors. Overall, institutional investors help mitigate potential instabilities in financial markets by facilitating efficient allocation of resources through transfers of risks and access to capital.

SEE ALSO *Equity Markets; Financial Markets; Herd Behavior; Information, Asymmetric; Initial Public Offering (IPO); Investment; Investors; Risk; Stock Exchanges; Transparency; Uncertainty*

BIBLIOGRAPHY

Ali, Ashiq, Cindy Durtschi, Baruch Lev, and Mark Trombley. 2004. Changes in Institutional Ownership and Subsequent Earnings Announcement Abnormal Returns. *Journal of Accounting, Auditing, and Finance* 20: 221–248.

Badrinath, S. G., Jayant R. Kale, and Harley E. Ryan. 1996. Characteristics of Common Stock Holdings of Insurance Companies. *Journal of Risk and Insurance* 63: 49–77.

Barabanov, Sergey, and Michael J. McNamara. 2007. Institutional Ownership, Bid-Ask Spreads, and Returns on NASDAQ Stocks. Working Paper, University of Saint Thomas and Washington State University.

Barabanov, Sergey, Onem Ozocak, Harry J. Turtle, and Thomas J. Walker. 2007. Institutional Investors and Shareholder Litigation. *Financial Management* Forthcoming.

Bennett, James, Richard Sias, and Laura Starks. 2003. Greener Pastures and the Impact of Dynamic Institutional Preferences. *Review of Financial Studies* 16: 1203–1238.

Bhattacharya, Nilabhra, Ervin Black, Theodore Christensen, and Richard Mergenthaler. 2007. Who Trades on Pro Forma Earnings Information? *Accounting Review* 82 (3): 581–619.

Brown, William. 1999. University Endowments: Investment Strategies and Performance. *Financial Practice and Education* 9: 61–69.

Cohen, Randolph, Paul Gompers, and Tuomo Vuolteenaho. 2002. Who Underreacts to Cash-Flow News? Evidence from Trading between Individuals and Institutions. *Journal of Financial Economics* 66: 409–462.

Conference Board. 2007. U.S. Institutional Investors Continue to Boost Ownership of U.S. Corporations. http://www.conference-board.org.

Del Guercio, Diane G. 1996. The Distorting Effect of the Prudent-Man Laws on Institutional Equity Investments. *Journal of Financial Economics* 40 (1): 31–62.

Falkenstein, Erik. 1996. Preferences for Stock Characteristics as Revealed by Mutual Fund Portfolio Holdings. *Journal of Finance* 51: 111–136.

Field, Laura, and Michelle Lowry. 2005. Institutional versus Individual Investment in IPOs: The Importance of Firm Fundamentals. Working Paper, Pennsylvania State University.

Friedman, Benjamin. 1996. Economic Implications of Changing Share Ownership. *Journal of Portfolio Management* 2: 59–70.

Gibson, Scott, Assem Safieddine, and Ramana Sonti. 2004. Smart Investments by Smart Money: Evidence from Seasoned Equity Offerings. *Journal of Financial Economics* 72: 581–604.

Gompers, Paul, and Andrew Metrick. 2001. Institutional Investors and Equity Prices. *Quarterly Journal of Economics* 116: 229–259.

Grinblatt, Mark, Sheridan Titman, and Russ Wermers. 1995. Momentum Investment Strategies, Portfolio Performance, and Herding: A Study of Mutual Fund Behavior. *American Economic Review* 85: 1088–1105.

Hartzell, Jay, and Laura Starks. 2003. Institutional Investors and Executive Compensation. *Journal of Finance* 58: 2351–2374.

Ke, Bin, Santhosh Ramalingegowda, and Yong Yu. 2006. The Effect of Investment Horizon on Institutional Investors' Incentives to Acquire Private Information on Long-Term Earnings. Working Paper, Pennsylvania State University.

Lakonishok, Josef, Andrei Shleifer, and Robert Vishny. 1992. The Impact of Institutional Trading on Stock Prices. *Journal of Financial Economics* 32: 23–43.

Longstreth, Bevis. 1986. *Modern Investment Management and the Prudent Man Rule*. New York: Oxford University Press.

Mikhail, Michael, Beverly Walther, and Richard Willis. 2005. When Security Analysts Talk, Who Listens? Working Paper, Duke University and Northwestern University.

O'Brien, Patricia, and Ravi Bhushan. 1990. Analyst Following and Institutional Ownership. *Journal of Accounting Research* 28 (suppl.): 55–76.

Sias, Richard, and Laura Starks. 1997. Return Autocorrelation and Institutional Investors. *Journal of Financial Economics* 46: 103–131.

Szewczyk, Samuel, George Tsetsekos, and Raj Varma. 1992. Institutional Ownership and the Liquidity of Common Stock Offerings. *The Financial Review* 27: 211–226.

Sergey S. Barabanov

INVISIBLE HAND

SEE *Cantillon, Richard; Smith, Adam.*

INVOLUNTARY UNEMPLOYMENT

Unemployment is a labor-market state in which a person is without a job and is actively looking for work. There is nothing, however, in this definition to suggest whether the person is unemployed voluntarily or involuntarily. Prior to the publication of John Maynard Keynes's *General Theory of Employment, Interest, and Money* in 1936, mainstream economists within the "classical" (or, more correctly, the "neoclassical") tradition categorized unemployment into two major types, both relating to the supply side of the labor market. Unemployment could be conceived as a short-term *equilibrium* phenomenon arising from the choice of workers to participate in the labor market and engage *voluntarily* in job search—a situation in which individuals could find themselves temporarily "between jobs" and in a state of "frictional unemployment." On the other hand, unemployment was also construed as a *disequilibrium* phenomenon arising from the existence of institutional barriers in the labor market, such as trade unions, government fiscal and monetary policy, and the market power of firms, which were presumed to prevent the downward adjustment of real wages to shortfalls in labor demand. In this latter case, individual workers could be said to be *involuntarily* "off their labor supply function" because of labor-market imperfections. If only wages could be left to adjust freely to fluctuations in labor demand and supply, it was believed that competition would clear the labor market and result in a state of equilibrium at full employment compatible with the presence of only voluntary and/or frictional unemployment. From this orthodox analysis, it ensues that the existence of job scarcity in the labor market could never be a long-term phenomenon, unless institutional forces persist to prevent market clearance.

Keynes challenged this particular conception of the labor market. While recognizing the existence of frictional unemployment, he questioned the neoclassical view of unemployment as a supply-side phenomenon resulting from wage rigidity. For Keynes, the labor market cannot be analyzed in isolation but, instead, is itself dependent on conditions in the overall product market. Through derived demand for labor, it is the state of aggregate effective demand for goods and services in the economy that ultimately sets the constraint on the level of employment, and not the lack of a mechanism of competitive downward wage adjustment in the labor market that generates unemployment. Furthermore, even the most unlikely situation, where workers accept a reduction of their money wage, would not necessarily guarantee a reduction of their real wage. Indeed, Keynes argued that because of the negative feedback effect on current and expected future sales proceeds, a cut in wages could only make matters worse and result in even higher (rather than lower) unemployment.

Keynes dubbed this type of unemployment endemic to a demand-constrained economy stuck in a state of underemployment equilibrium—"involuntary unemployment." In chapter 2 of the *General Theory*, Keynes provides a test for the existence of involuntary unemployment:

> *Men are involuntarily unemployed if, in the event of a small rise in the price of wage-goods relatively to the money wage, both the aggregate supply of labour willing to work for the current money-wage and the aggregate demand for it at that wage would be greater than the existing volume of employment.* (Keynes 1936, p. 15, emphasis in original)

In short, if the gap between labor demand and supply persists with a fall in the real wage (brought about by a rise in prices), individual job seekers would be considered by Keynes to be in a situation of involuntary unemployment—a state associated with a nonzero elasticity of employment and output with respect to changes in aggregate demand (Darity and Young 1997, p. 26). In highlighting a particular causal sequence—going from changes in prices (for a given money wage) to a fall in real wages—he asserted that the fundamental cause of involuntary unemployment is job scarcity and the inadequacy of existing demand, not workers' obstinacy in resisting a cut in their real wage, as maintained by neoclassical economists.

Soon after the publication of the *General Theory*, numerous economists began to reinterpret Keynes's analysis. Influenced by Keynes's own empirical recognition of the stickiness of money wages in chapter 2 of the *General Theory* and the assumption of the money-wage unit as a mere historical datum, beginning with Franco Modigliani (1918–2003) in 1944 writers began to postulate a labor-supply function that is perfectly elastic up to full employment at a historically given money wage. Consequently, they began to explain involuntary unemployment as the result of workers' resistance to money wage adjustment because of irrational behavior (sometimes referred to as "money illusion"). A whole generation of Keynesian economists, such as Modigliani and James Tobin (1918–2002), from the 1940s to the 1960s built macroeconomic models to explain unemployment on the basis of this static wage rigidity assumption, despite the fact that Keynes himself had rejected wage stickiness as an explanation of involuntary unemployment. In the early post–World War II (1939–1945) years, however, there emerged a related, yet competing strand of thought, commencing in 1948 with the work of Don Patinkin (1922–1995), who reinterpreted a state of involuntary unemployment as a dynamic disequilibrium due not to exogenous wage fixity but to the sluggish adjustment of wages to labor market pressures. By the late 1960s and early 1970s this work had given rise to the so-called disequilibrium theory of involuntary unemployment, associated with such writers as Robert Clower, Robert J. Barro and Herschel I. Grossman, and Edmond Malinvaud. Whether framed in an equilibrium (static) or disequilibrium (dynamic) setting, in both strands of analysis the cause of involuntary unemployment was the lack of adequate downward adjustment of wages and prices to shortfalls in aggregate effective demand.

During the 1970s and 1980s both of these approaches quickly succumbed to the criticisms of Milton Friedman, Robert E. Lucas, and the new classical economists because of problems of logical inconsistency and insufficient microeconomic grounding. According to the monetarists and the new classical economists, one cannot develop theories of the economy that assume rational behavior for an economic agent in the product market (say, as consumer) but irrational behavior as supplier of labor services in the labor market, as the earlier Keynesian writers had surmised. Moreover, because of their assumption of continual market clearance, new classical economists easily eschewed the sluggishness argument of the disequilibrium theorists. Hence, new classical economists such as Lucas were able to conclude that it was not possible, "… even in principle, to classify individual unemployed people as either voluntary or involuntary unemployed …" (Lucas 1981, p. 243).

Despite the attempt of new classical economists to purge involuntary unemployment from the vocabulary of modern macroeconomics, the concept of involuntary unemployment has shown resilience in the hands of both New Keynesian and post-Keynesian economists over the last two decades. Numerous New Keynesian models have been developed within a choice-theoretic microeconomic framework compatible with neoclassical theory. Particularly noteworthy is the abundant literature on implicit contracts and on efficiency wages that reconcile wage rigidity and involuntary unemployment and now see the existence of the latter as a Pareto-efficient solution in the labor market (see Davidson 1990). In contrast, post-Keynesian models that follow more closely Keynes's original insights emphasize the macroeconomic basis of their theories of involuntary unemployment in which wage rigidity plays no role, even though some are founded on microeconomic foundations of Marshallian pedigree (see Davidson 1994, chapter 11).

The notion of involuntary unemployment is at the core of Keynesian theory. Ever since the publication of Keynes's *General Theory* more than seventy years ago, this concept has been plagued with controversy and has remained a wedge that separates those who believe that a capitalist economy is prone to systemic instabilities, as reflected in the existence of periodic recessions accompanied by mass unemployment, from those who believe in the strength of the self-correcting forces in market economies, in which actual unemployment is conceived as a mere short-term transitional phenomenon gravitating around some stable, long-term "natural" rate of unemployment. Although today one could find some strong Keynesian sympathizers who might even be prepared to do away with the concept of involuntary unemployment because of conceptual difficulties and refer, instead, to some less controversial notions of underemployment (see De Vroey 2004), the former concept still remains very deeply ingrained in the professional vocabulary of many contemporary economists.

SEE ALSO *Employment; Keynes, John Maynard; Unemployment; Voluntary Unemployment*

BIBLIOGRAPHY

Darity, William, Jr., and Warren Young. 1997. On Rewriting Chapter 2 of *The General Theory*. In *A "Second Edition" of* The General Theory, vol. 1, eds. G. Colin Harcourt and Peter Andrew Riach, 20–27. London and New York: Routledge.

Davidson, Carl. 1990. *Recent Developments in the Theory of Involuntary Unemployment.* Kalamazoo, MI: W. E. Upjohn Institute for Employment Research.

Davidson, Paul. 1994. *Post-Keynesian Macroeconomic Theory: A Foundation for Successful Economic Policies for the Twenty-First Century.* Aldershot, U.K.: Edward Elgar.

De Vroey, Michel. 2004. *Involuntary Unemployment: The Elusive Quest for a Theory.* London and New York: Routledge.

Keynes, John Maynard. 1936. *The General Theory of Employment, Interest, and Money.* London: Macmillan.

Lucas, Robert E., Jr. 1981. Unemployment Policy. In *Studies in Business Cycle Theory*, ed. Robert E. Lucas, Jr., 240–247. Cambridge, MA: MIT Press.

Mario Seccareccia

IQ CONTROVERSY

Four issues dominate debate about IQ: how intelligence should be defined and measured; genetic versus environmental factors; group differences; and the degree to which IQ stratifies individuals and groups by class and occupation.

INTELLIGENCE DEFINED AND MEASURED

Science suggests a distinction between pre-theory and post-theory definitions. The transition from classical to modern astronomy marked a shift from one pre-theory concept to another, that is, from the notion that planetary motions should be reduced to circles to the notion of forces that are a function of mass and distance. The latter notion was more fruitful but had no advantage over the former in terms of clarity or quantification. Adding those attributes is the job of competing theories, each of which transforms the broad pre-theory concept into a post-theory concept. René Descartes said the sun turned on its axis and created a whirlpool; Isaac Newton said the sun attracted the planets in proportion to its mass and inversely as the distance squared; Albert Einstein said the sun warps space (and time) in its vicinity, and the planets follow the path of the resulting curved space. All accepted that they should pay attention to mass and space, but none thought that this concept should hand them specificity and measurability—that was their job.

Arthur Jensen (1998) gave up using the word *intelligence* because it lacked the specificity and measurability of his theory-embedded concept of *g*. He was asking a pre-theory concept to exhibit the characteristics that only a post-theory concept can have. In fact the architects of IQ tests have a perfectly satisfactory pre-theory concept to guide them: Intelligence is greater the greater the speed and quality of learning (where all have an equal chance and are positively disposed); and intelligence involves solving problems and therefore requires not only on-the-spot acuity but also working memory, information processing, a reasonable vocabulary, a reasonable fund of general information, basic numeracy, and so forth. IQ tests such as the Wechsler Intelligence Scale for Children (WISC) incorporate this notion of intelligence with subtests (Vocabulary, Information, and Coding), whose names betray their origins.

This concept was formulated in modern industrial societies. Those assessing intelligence in other social contexts should consult the Piagetian anthropologists. Some theorists recommend a broader concept. Robert Sternberg (1988) says we need not only analytic skills but also creativity and the practical intelligence to deal with problems such as a difficult coworker. Howard Gardner (1993) adds musical talent and athletic ability to the list of "intelligences." Daniel Goleman (1995) includes the character traits, such as empathy, temperance, and self-esteem, needed to solve "human" problems.

In response we need only amplify the pre-theory concept to make it plain that "speed and quality of learning" and "problem-solving skills" must be broad enough to allow various thinkers and students of various cultures to evidence just what skills and traits are relevant to socially valued problem solving. These empirical questions will not be settled by debate about whether we have an "adequate" definition of intelligence.

GENES VERSUS ENVIRONMENT

Twin studies show that genes are powerful and environment weak in affecting individual differences in intelligence. Massive IQ gains over time (average IQ has risen as much as 20 points in a single generation) suggest environmental factors of enormous potency. To resolve this paradox, we must distinguish between the dynamics of individual differences within a cohort and trends between cohorts.

As an example, John and Joe are identical twins separated at birth. Identical genes make them both taller and quicker than average. John goes to school in one city, plays basketball a bit better on the playground, catches the eye of the grade school coach, plays on a team, and goes on to play in high school, where he gets really professional coaching. Joe goes to a different school, in a city 100 miles away. However, precisely because his genes are identical to John's, precisely because he is taller and quicker than average to the same degree, he is likely to have a similar life history. In contrast, Mark and Allen are separated twins whose identical genes make them both a bit shorter and stodgier than average. They too have similar basketball life histories, except in their case both play little, develop few skills, and become mainly spectators.

Turning to IQ, one child is born with a slightly better brain than another. Which of them will tend to like school, be encouraged, start haunting the library, get into top-stream classes, and attend a university? And if that child has a separated identical twin who has much the same academic history, what will account for their similar adult IQs? Not identical genes alone—the ability of those identical genes to co-opt environments of similar quality will be the missing piece of the puzzle.

Between generations, the effect of environment is hugely potent because persistent environmental factors seize control of a powerful instrument that multiplies their effects. With the invention of television, basketball got a mass audience, and the pay of professional players soared. Wider and keener participation raised the general skill level, and that higher average performance fed back into play. Those who learned to shoot baskets with either hand became the best—and then they became the norm—which meant you had to be able to pass with either hand to excel—and then that became the norm—and so forth. In other words, rising average performance became a potent causal factor in its own right, and there was a huge escalation of basketball skills in a single generation.

As for IQ, after the Industrial Revolution, when a grade school education became the norm, middle-class aspirations dictated a high school diploma. When a high school diploma became the norm, people wanted a university education. Economic progress created new expectations about hands-on parenting, highly paid professional jobs in which we are expected to think for ourselves, and more cognitively demanding leisure activities. No one wants to seem deficient as a parent, unsuited for promotion, or boring as a companion. Everyone responds by enhancing his or her performance, which pushes the average higher, so all respond to that new average, which pushes the average higher still.

The paradox is resolved. Within a generation, genetic differences use feedback processes to magnify IQ differences between individuals. Between generations, environmental trends use feedback processes to escalate mean IQ over time. It all depends on whose hand is on the throttle.

This has implications for interventions designed to raise IQ, which must be persistent, or the tendency of genes to match environmental quality will slowly erode their effects. However, genes do not pin each of us to a place on the IQ hierarchy. Similarly people can improve on their physical endowment for running. Either circumstances force you to train throughout life, or you develop a love for running and train without compulsion. There will be some who beat me even though I train more than they do, but I can run rings around every couch potato within twenty years of my age.

GROUP IQ DIFFERENCES

Factor analysis suggests two sorts of IQ differences: differences between racial or ethnic groups, and differences between groups separated by social trends over time. Often subjects take a whole battery of IQ tests; for example, the ten subtests of the WISC measure cognitive skills ranging from information, vocabulary, and arithmetic to coding, solving puzzles, and seeing what concepts have in common. Subjects who do better than average on one tend to do better than average on all. Factor analysis measures this tendency and calls the result the "*g* factor." Above-average subjects open up a wider gap over the average person on some tasks than on others, and these tend to be more cognitively complex. So cognitively complex tasks have higher "*g* loadings" than simple tasks, such as rote memorization. This is why Jensen thinks *g* a good measure of intelligence. It identifies those tasks on which intelligent people tend to do best. Some people excel to an unusual degree on verbal, or mathematical, or spatial tasks, and factor analysis also measures these tendencies and calls them "subordinate factors."

American whites outscore blacks by 5 to 17 IQ points, and the gap increases from ages five to twenty-five. The subtest differences are factor invariant, that is, the racial score gaps tend to mimic the *g* loadings. Indeed there is a tendency for the gaps to widen the higher the *g* loading. However, when a generation outscores the last by 9 to 20 points, subtest differences are wildly at variance with factor loadings. The Vocabulary and Similarities subtests are close for *g* loadings, and yet the latter shows a 24-point gain compared to a 2-point gain.

Another sports analogy: Factor analysis of the ten events of the decathlon produces a *g* because at a given time and place, someone who is superior on one is better on all. Different events get various *g* loadings because superior athletes perform further above average on some than others. The 1,500 meters has a low loading because endurance is not very necessary in the other events. The 100 meters, the hurdles, and the high jump all have large and similar loadings. However, over time social priorities change. People become obsessed with the 100 meters (which determines the "world's fastest human"). Over thirty years, performance escalates by a full standard deviation (SD) in the 100 meters, half an SD in the hurdles, and not at all in the high jump. The trends do not mimic the relative *g* loadings of the "subtests." After thirty years, we do another factor analysis, and lo and behold, *g* is still there. Although average performance has risen "eccentrically" on various events, superior performers still do better than average on all ten events and are about the same degree above average on various events as they were thirty years before.

Athletic coaches lament that everyone prefers the 100 meters and do not take other events seriously. They point out that sprint speed may be highly correlated with high jump performance, but past a certain point it is actually counterproductive—if you hurl yourself at the bar at maximum speed, your forward momentum cannot be converted into upward lift, and you will time your jump badly. They are not surprised that increased sprint speed has made some contribution to the hurdles, because speed between the hurdles is important. But it is only half the story: You have to control your speed so that you take the same number of steps between hurdles and always jump off the same foot.

In the WISC subtests the *g* factor was a bad guide to which real-world cognitive skills are merely correlated and which are functionally related. Assume that science has engendered a sea change. Once we used logic primarily with concrete referents: All toadstools are poisonous; that is a toadstool, therefore it is poisonous. Now we use logic with the abstract categories provided by science: Only mammals bear their young alive; rabbits and dogs both bear their young alive; therefore they are both mammals. This would bring huge gains over time on the similarities subtest, which demands that we classify in terms of abstractions.

But on subtests that sample the core vocabulary and information of everyday life, this causal factor would not trigger large gains. Indeed changing social priorities might include both a more scientific outlook and less time for reading, in which case huge gains on the Similarities subtest would be accompanied by losses on the Vocabulary and Information subtests. Real-world functional skills would assert their autonomy from one another and from the straitjacket of factor loadings. IQ differences are not factor invariant, but they are not trivial. They just have a different real-world significance.

When blacks gained 5.5 IQ points on whites between 1970 and 2000, the gains were not *g* gains. Gains on various subtests did not tally with their *g* loadings. Despite this, the 2000 IQ gap between the races was still a *g* gap and had diminished by 5.13 points, largely because the difference in *g* loadings on WISC subtests are small. If further environmental progress eliminates the black-white IQ gap, blacks will probably match whites for *g* as well as for IQ.

Debate about whether the black-white IQ gap is genetic or environmental has shifted. It used to cite the work of Klaus Eyferth, who found that the offspring of black American soldiers in Germany had no IQ deficit; Sandra Scarr, Richard Weinberg, and Irwin Waldman (1993), who found that black children adopted by white parents show only small gains at maturity; and Jensen (1998), who emphasized that the racial gap was a *g* gap. Now the black loss of ground on whites with age is central. After all, the gap is only 4.6 points at age four (perhaps 1 point at nine months). If the decline with age were arrested, that would be that. Few would argue that the races enjoy complete environmental equality at present. Adherents of environment and genes both believe they can supply the causes of the decline.

STRATIFICATION BY IQ

There are IQ thresholds for various occupations. Someone with an IQ below 100 is unlikely to qualify as a professional, manager, or technician.

Blacks and whites have similar thresholds. Therefore as long as their IQ gap persists, only the top one-sixth of blacks will qualify for jobs open to the top one-half of whites. Chinese Americans develop a character structure such that they can qualify for these occupations with an IQ threshold of 93. They also capitalize more effectively on the pool of those who score above this threshold, and as a group they behave as if they had a bonus of 20 IQ points. Despite similar IQs, females outperform males academically. At age seventeen, the girl's median for written composition is at the boy's 75th percentile. The girl's median for reading is at the boy's 67th percentile. Female advantage in academic achievement does not translate into a better occupational profile because of larger investment in child rearing.

Measures of self-discipline, such as saving money, are better predictors of grades than is IQ. Noncognitive factors, such as self-esteem and the degree of control people feel they have over their fates, are as important as cognitive skills in predicting not only wages and productivity but also teenage pregnancy, smoking, marijuana use, and criminal behavior. When black women are matched with white women with the same IQs, the black women are about three times as likely to be single parents, have been on welfare, and be in poverty. They suffer from a marriage market in which for every 100 black women of marriageable age, there are only 57 black men in steady work.

Some predict a nightmarish scenario. As industrial societies equalize opportunity and environments, only talent will count, and because genes drive individual differences in talent, good genes will go to the top and we will have a caste system based on "merit." The least successful will become a permanent underclass. Because this scenario assumes people driven by wealth and status, it seems problematic that such people will finance the equalization of environments. If an underclass does develop, their children will hardly profit from equal environments and opportunities. A meritocracy that engendered an underclass would be inherently unstable. Social stratification by genes or IQ is unlikely to make a radical break with the past.

SEE ALSO *Determinism; Determinism, Biological; Determinism, Genetic; Flynn Effect; Heredity; Intelligence; Meritocracy; Nature vs. Nurture; Science; Stratification; Twin Studies; Underclass*

BIBLIOGRAPHY

Flynn, James R. 1980. *Race, IQ, and Jensen.* London: Routledge.

Flynn, James R. 1991. *Asian Americans: Achievement beyond IQ.* Hillsdale, NJ: Erlbaum.

Flynn, James R. 2007. *What Is Intelligence? Beyond the Flynn Effect.* New York: Cambridge University Press.

Gardner, Howard. 1993. *Multiple Intelligences: The Theory in Practice.* New York: Basic Books.

Goleman, Daniel P. 1995. *Emotional Intelligence.* New York: Bantam.

Gottfredson, Linda S. 2003. *g*, Jobs, and Life. In *The Scientific Study of General Intelligence: Tribute to Arthur R. Jensen*, ed. H. Nyborg, 293–342. New York: Pergamon.

Hallpike, Christopher R. 1979. *The Foundations of Primitive Thought.* Oxford: Clarendon.

Heckman, James J., Jora Stixrud, and Sergio Urzua. 2006. The Effects of Cognitive and Non-Cognitive Abilities on Labor Market Outcomes and Social Behavior. *Journal of Labor Economics* 24: 411–482.

Herrnstein, Richard J., and Charles Murray. 1994. *The Bell Curve: Intelligence and Class in American Life.* New York: Free Press.

Jensen, Arthur R. 1998. *The g Factor: The Science of Mental Ability.* Westport, CT: Praeger.

Scarr, Sandra, Richard Weinberg, and Irwin Waldman. 1993. IQ Correlations in Transracial Adoptive Families. *Intelligence* 17: 541–555.

Sternberg, Robert J. 1988. *The Triarchic Mind: A New Theory of Human Intelligence.* New York: Penguin.

James R. Flynn

IRA

SEE *Irish Republican Army.*

IRAN-CONTRA AFFAIR

The Iran-Contra affair is a political scandal that occurred during the second term of Ronald Reagan's (1911–2004) presidency. The scandal encompassed two secret programs coordinated by the National Security Council: (1) the sale of arms to Iran in contravention of U.S. policy and without congressional approval; and (2) the diversion of the proceeds from the weapons sales to support the activities of the anticommunist Contra rebels in Nicaragua, in violation of the 1982 Boland Amendment ban on military aid.

In October 1986 the government of Nicaragua shot down an American cargo plane carrying military supplies to Contra forces and captured an American employee of the Central Intelligence Agency. One month later, a Lebanese news magazine, *Ash-Shiraa*, revealed a secret program for the sale and transfer of military weapons to Iran in exchange for the release of U.S. hostages being held in Lebanon. Iran, at war with Iraq for six years and in need of American-made military equipment, purchased weapons in exchange for securing the release of American hostages. In response to these reports, President Reagan denied on national television that any arms had been traded to Iran, but one week later he admitted the Iranian arms transfer occurred.

It was quickly discovered that the United States had begun negotiating with Iran in secret, while the country was allegedly neutral in the Iran-Iraq War and maintained a policy against trading for hostages. In early 1986 Reagan's first national security adviser, Robert McFarlane, and his successor, Admiral John Poindexter, shipped weapons, including surface-to-air and antitank missiles, from Israel to Iran's revolutionary government without congressional approval, diverting the proceeds from the sales to the Contras, who sought to overthrow the Sandinista government in Nicaragua. Reagan's attorney general, Edwin Meese, was directed to investigate the arms sales and requested the appointment of an independent counsel. In December 1986 Lawrence E. Walsh was appointed to investigate the weapon sales and the process by which the proceeds were diverted to the Contras.

In December 1986 President Reagan appointed former Republican senator John Tower (1925–1991) to investigate the Iran-Contra affair and issue a report on the actions of the National Security Council. The *Tower Commission Report* found Poindexter responsible for authorizing the illegal sale of arms to Iran in exchange for the release of the U.S. hostages, as well as for the diversion of the profits to support the Contras. The report also named Marine colonel Oliver North as the main negotiator. Both the sale of weapons to Iran and the funding of the Contras were found to be in violation of Congress, particularly the Boland Amendment and the 1976 Arms Export Control Act. The report faulted President Reagan for not properly supervising his subordinates and stated that ultimate responsibility for the events were the president's alone.

Poindexter and North were found guilty of obstruction of Congress, while Defense Secretary Caspar Weinberger (1917–2006) was indicted for withholding information from the independent council. The convictions of Poindexter and North were later overturned on appeal. In 1992, following his electoral defeat to William Jefferson Clinton, President George H. W. Bush, who had served as vice president during the Iran-Contra scandal, issued presidential pardons to all who had been indicted.

SEE ALSO *Iran-Iraq War; Reagan, Ronald*

BIBLIOGRAPHY

Office of the Independent Counsel for Iran/Contra Matters (Lawrence E. Walsh, independent counsel). 1993. *Final Report of the Independent Counsel for Iran/Contra Matters.* 3 vols. Washington, DC: U.S. Government Printing Office.

President's Special Review Board (John Tower, chairman). 1987. *Tower Commission Report: The Full Text of the President's Special Review Board.* New York: Bantam.

Reagan, Ronald. 1986. Address to the Nation on the Iran Arms and Contra Aid Controversy, November 13. Ronald Reagan Presidential Library. http://www.reagan.utexas.edu/archives/speeches/1986/111386c.htm.

James E. Freeman

IRAN-IRAQ WAR

Since its establishment in 1921, Iraq has had a precarious relationship with its eastern neighbor, Iran. The sources of contention between the two countries involved border demarcation and the desire of both states to prevent the other's hegemonic aspirations in the Persian Gulf. However, the tensions did not result in armed conflict until Iraqi president Saddam Hussein decided to invade Iran in 1980.

Until the 1970s, both countries had been militarily and economically weak. This mutual weakness sustained a delicate balance that made open conflict undesirable to both sides. However, the rise of Iran as a regional power under Mohammad Reza Shah (1919–1980) in the 1970s undermined this balance. The Algiers Agreement of 1975 resulted in the reversal of a 1937 boundary treaty that had been preferable to Iraq. Iraq agreed to a less favorable border demarcation in exchange for Iran's withdrawal of support from the Kurdish insurgency in northern Iraq.

The relationship between Iran and Iraq entered a new phase with the Iranian Revolution of 1979. While the revolution severely hampered the military capabilities of Iran, it greatly increased the Iraqi perception of the Iranian threat. Fearful of the destabilizing impact of the Iranian Revolution to his rule, Saddam decided to preemptively strike on

September 22, 1980. The immediate goal of the Iraqi invasion was to reverse the terms of the 1975 agreement; the strategic goal was the containment of the "Islamic threat."

Although Iraq was successful in the initial phases of the war, Iran managed to recover the Iraqi occupied territory by 1982. Yet repeated Iranian attempts to make inroads into Iraqi territory were unsuccessful, and Iraq repeatedly used chemical weapons against Iran. The war continued until 1988, when it became clear to Iran's clerical leaders that they could not achieve any decisive breakthroughs. A cease-fire was agreed on August 20, 1988, after Iran accepted United Nations Security Council Resolution 598 of 1987. The war resulted in no major border changes.

American policies during the war were driven by the goal of containing the new Iranian regime, which had threatened American hegemony in the Middle East. Consequently, official U.S. neutrality during the war was accompanied by policies that aimed to prevent a complete Iranian victory. The U.S. Navy engaged in skirmishes with Iranian forces in the Persian Gulf, and an Iranian passenger aircraft was shot down by a U.S. cruiser on July 3, 1988. However, at the same time, the United States was covertly supplying arms to Iran in an effort to free U.S. hostages in Lebanon and to finance Nicaraguan guerrillas.

Although the "Islamic threat" was contained, the war resulted in the consolidation of the authoritarian Islamic regime in Iran. With the exception of Libya and Syria, almost all Arab countries tacitly or actively supported Iraq during the war in an effort to thwart the prospect of Iranian hegemony. In the aftermath of the war, however, Iraq emerged as a major regional power with a strong military force, a development that led to the Iraqi invasion of Kuwait on August 2, 1990.

SEE ALSO *Destabilization; Diplomacy; Fundamentalism, Islamic; Hussein, Saddam; Iran-Contra Affair; Iranian Revolution; Khomeini, Ayatollah Ruhollah; Stability, Political; United Nations*

BIBLIOGRAPHY

Karsh, Efraim. 1990. Geopolitical Determinism: The Origins of the Iran-Iraq War. *Middle East Journal* 44 (2): 256–268.

Khadduri, Majid. 1988. *The Gulf War: The Origins and Implications of the Iraq-Iran Conflict.* New York: Oxford University Press.

Gunes Murat Tezcur

IRANIAN REVOLUTION

A revolution is a mass movement that aims to establish a new political regime by violently transforming the existing government. The Iranian Revolution of 1978–1979 violently ended the monarchy of Shah Mohammed Reza Pahlavi (1919–1980) and replaced it with an Islamic republic, the theocracy of Ayatollah Ruhollah Khomeini (1901–1989). The shah's reign had been briefly interrupted between 1951 and 1953 with the interlude of Prime Minister Mohammed Mossadeq (1881–1967).

BACKGROUND

The shah's rule began on September 16, 1941, and witnessed twenty-four different prime ministers heading over forty cabinets. In 1951 Iranian nationalist Mohammed Mossadeq rose to power and amassed enough support to oust the shah. He presided over the establishment of the National Front, composed of divergent forces with similar goals. Mossadeq forced oil nationalization through parliament, which provoked boycott by European powers. Shah supporters and the U.S. administration perceived him as too far to the political left. A 1953 coup restored the shah's central authority. Alarmed over Mossadeq's leftist backing in nationalizing the oil company, numerous clergy and the *bazaaris* (those who make their livelihoods in the bazaars), among some others, supported the shah in regaining power. They welcomed the U.S. Central Intelligence Agency's (CIA's) pivotal involvement in the coup.

The shah aimed to lead his country towards a great civilization, which he asserted to have pre-Islamic, Aryan roots. This insulted Iran's devout Shi'is. Shi'ism, a branch of Islam that began as an opposition party, was the official state religion. Approximately ninety percent of the population was Shi'i. The shah's monarchy was based on the constitution of 1906 and 1907. Guided by U.S. and Israeli intelligence officers, he established the National Intelligence and Security Organization (SAVAK) in 1957. It became the government's strong arm and scrutinized allegedly suspicious organizations, such as labor unions, peasant organizations, student groups, guilds, and mosques. SAVAK's tactics instilled pervasive fear of consequences for criticizing the regime or of disagreeing with its policies. Suspects were imprisoned, stories of torture circulated underground, and censorship laws prevailed.

The shah's vision for Iran included a modernization program modeled after the West. In 1961 he ordered the government to implement a land law that limited the amount of land anyone could hold. Nevertheless, the Pahlavis continued to be one of the largest landowning families. The law elicited opposition predominantly from landowners, the clergy, and the resurgent National Front, culminating in riots at the University of Tehran. The peasants' economic position generally worsened as a result of the law's policies. Land reform also had economic consequences for religious institutions that relied on a network of exchange. In 1963 the shah inaugurated a six-point program, the White Revolution, to reshape Iran's eco-

nomic, political, and social life. Numerous Iranians saw the measures as being imposed on Iran by the United States in order to bolster the shah's power and wealth while expanding U.S. dominance in the region. A religious uprising and a bloody counter-revolution resulted. In this context, Ruhollah Khomeini, bearing the title *ayatollah*, or man of God, became an emergent leader in opposition to the shah. His opposition ultimately landed Khomeini in exile in Iraq, from where he sent taped edicts and sermons to his followers.

The shah sought to develop an industrial base with an influx of foreign contractors and corporations. Some of these invested directly. In 1976 Iran was the fourth largest oil exporter in the world, and in 1977 its economy ranked fifteenth in the noncommunist world. A quantum jump in oil revenues created problems of absorbing those funds into the economic development process, resulting in dramatic increases in spending. Iran entered into a cycle of inflation, greater income inequality, corruption, and growing dependence on the West to help resolve increasing disparities. Peasants displaced to cities by land reform had to cater to thousands of Westerners for economic survival while also being confronted by the impressions Western culture had made in the cities. They found solace in the mosques, where they heard the taped sermons of Khomeini.

THE REVOLUTION HEATS UP

These massive cultural and structural changes, monitored by SAVAK, destabilized Iran's social order. With the exception of the administration of U.S. president Jimmy Carter, which demanded the observance of human rights and restricted the availability of military equipment, the United States supported the shah's rule. Accommodating Carter's human rights demands, the shah relaxed his grip over the country in 1977, but the experiment failed. Instead of dialogue at the negotiating table, a series of demonstrations in the streets ensued. Khomeini continued his attacks against the shah.

On January 9, 1978 students and clergy in Qom, Iran, protested Carter's visit to the country as well as a libelous story about Khomeini in the state press. This began a cycle of escalating violence as demonstrations became more massive and frequent. The shah declared martial law and banned demonstrations, which only provoked his opponents further. The infamous September 8 Black Friday resulted when the Iranian military responded to the public unrest and killed several hundred demonstrators in Tehran. Increasingly alienated Iranians took to the streets and hundreds were killed daily. Iran's allies abroad distanced themselves. During the holy month of Muharram, on December 12, several million demonstrated against the shah in Tehran. The military disintegrated and the regime crumbled.

The revolution saw an eclectic alliance of secular and religious factions, including intellectuals, students, workers, peasants, bazaar merchants, trades people, and clergy. They coalesced around the Ayatollah Khomeini, who symbolized identity, stability, and social justice. In contrast to the shah, supporters perceived Khomeini as leading a simple life, refusing to compromise with foreign powers. All of the revolutionaries wanted to end the shah's rule. They differed on their vision for the type of government for Iran, but the theocratic republic prevailed. The shah was forced from the throne and left Iran on January 16, 1979, and Khomeini returned from exile on February 1.

EFFECTS

With its platform of social justice and autonomy, the Iranian Shi'i theocracy had a potentially destabilizing effect on neighboring countries with Shi'i populations. Worried over Iran's call to oppose corruption and foreign influence, particularly U.S. and Soviet policies, neighboring governments feared internal social unrest. Iran supported developing African nations, Cuba, and the Palestine Liberation Organization (PLO), among others. Iraq, with its Shi'i majority in numbers, but minority in terms of access to power, felt particularly threatened and invaded Iran in 1980. The invasion was an effort to preempt a possible Shi'i attempt to gain political power and overthrow the Sunni-controlled government of Iraq's president, Saddam Hussein. Thus began a costly and bloody eight-year war between Iran and Iraq, in which Iraq was largely supported by the United States and most Arab regimes. The war had an unanticipated consequence: Iranians with previously divergent views banned together behind their government in the face of this external threat. This development reinforced the outcome of the revolution. At the same time, as it united Iranian hard-liners and moderates even more against the United States, it influenced the nature of the future relationship between the two countries.

SEE ALSO *Dictatorship; Fundamentalism, Islamic; Iran-Iraq War; Revolution*

BIBLIOGRAPHY

Abrahamian, Ervand. 1982. *Iran between Two Revolutions.* Princeton, NJ: Princeton University Press.

Area Handbook of Iran. 1978. *Iran: A Country Study.* 3rd ed. Ed. Richard F. Nyrop. Foreign Area Studies. Washington DC: The American University.

Esposito, John L., ed. 1990. *The Iranian Revolution: Its Global Impact.* Gainesville: University Presses of Florida.

Fischer, Michael M. J. 1980. *Iran: From Religious Dispute to Revolution.* Cambridge, MA: Harvard University Press.

Brigitte U. Neary

IRAQ-U.S. WAR

Years of tension between the United States and Iraq led in March 2003 to a direct invasion of Iraq by an American-led coalition. Iraq's Ba'th Party government, headed by Saddam Hussein (1937–2006), was quickly overthrown, but years of instability followed as a variety of Iraqi groups, and some foreigners, fought against the American occupying forces and against the new Iraqi government the United States sponsored.

TENSION: 1991–2001

In the first Gulf War, in 1991, a coalition led by the United States drove Iraqi forces out of Kuwait and destroyed much of the Iraqi military, but major coalition ground units went only a modest distance into southern Iraq; they did not attempt to enter any city.

Hussein, and most key leaders of his government and of the Ba'th Party, were Arabs belonging to the Sunni branch of Islam. Sunni Arabs made up about one-fifth of Iraq's population; they lived mostly in central and western Iraq. Another fifth were Kurds, who lived overwhelmingly in the north. Arabs belonging to the Shiite branch of Islam made up a majority of the population; they were especially strong in the south. Most of the Kurds were Sunni, but when people spoke of "the Sunnis" in Iraq, they almost always meant just the Sunni Arabs, not the Kurds.

Immediately after the 1991 war, there were revolts by both Shiite Arabs in the south and Kurds in the north. The government put down the Shiite rebellion with great brutality, but international intervention helped the Kurds achieve de facto autonomy in a large region of northern Iraq, called Kurdistan.

Iraq grudgingly accepted United Nations Security Council resolutions under which it was to eliminate, under international supervision, all nuclear, chemical, and biological weapons ("weapons of mass destruction" or WMDs). Hussein believed at first that he could conceal Iraq's extensive WMD programs and stockpiles from UN inspectors, but the inspectors proved more effective than he had expected. He then disposed of most of his prohibited weapons and programs, keeping no more than he could reasonably hope to conceal from the inspectors. Years of cat-and-mouse games followed. Late in 1998 the United States and Britain launched strikes using aircraft and cruise missiles to punish Hussein for his refusal to cooperate with the inspection process. The inspectors withdrew from Iraq before these strikes, and did not return afterward.

Iraq remained under severe economic sanctions, originally imposed late in 1990 after the Iraqi invasion of Kuwait. The effect of these was moderated only somewhat by the "oil-for-food" program after 1996. The Iraqi economy remained crippled, and the Iraqi armed forces remained far below their 1990 strength for lack of funding. U.S. aircraft patrolled large "no-fly zones" where the Iraqis were forbidden to operate military aircraft. The patrol aircraft frequently bombed antiaircraft guns, surface-to-air missiles, and radars when the Iraqis fired on aircraft or seemed about to do so.

TOWARD A SECOND WAR: 2001–2003

After the Afghanistan-based terrorist organization Al-Qaeda attacked the United States on September 11, 2001, President George W. Bush quickly began thinking of invading Iraq. Senior administration officials believed that significant links existed between the Iraqi government and Al-Qaeda. In June 2002 they increased the frequency of U.S. air strikes in southern Iraq. These continued to be officially explained as responses to attacks and threats against aircraft patrolling the no-fly zones. But, in fact, the United States was systematically destroying Iraqi air-defense systems.

The U.S. Congress authorized the use of force against Iraq on October 10, 2002, but the UN Security Council was reluctant to go so far. Security Council Resolution 1441, passed on November 8, offered Iraq "a final opportunity to comply with its disarmament obligations," with a reminder that the Security Council "has repeatedly warned Iraq that it will face serious consequences as a result of its continued violations of its obligations." The United States expected, after a short interval, to obtain a second resolution stating that Iraq had missed its final opportunity, and authorizing force. But Iraq allowed the UN weapons inspectors to return before the end of 2002, and gave them cooperation that was, while not perfect, far better than at any time in the 1990s. In early 2003 the United States was arguing, with evidence that later turned out to have been mostly inaccurate, that Iraq's WMD programs and stockpiles were so large and diversified as to constitute a major threat, justifying military action. But it was difficult to reconcile these American claims with the failure of UN inspectors to find any WMDs, despite searching in the places where American officials told them to search.

The U.S. government responded by attacking the credibility of the inspectors. But French Foreign Minister Dominique de Villepin and his allies, who argued that there was no immediate need for war, drew increasing support from the members of the Security Council. President Bush decided to go to war without UN authorization, as head of a "coalition of the willing."

THE INVASION OF IRAQ: MARCH–APRIL 2003

Early on March 20, 2003, the United States tried to kill Saddam Hussein and his two sons using aircraft and Tomahawk cruise missiles. The ground invasion of Iraq, coming from Kuwait, began a few hours later. The number of troops involved was surprisingly small. American leaders were so confident of Iraq's weakness that, for an invasion aimed at taking the whole country, they used a force far smaller than the one they had sent in 1991 to accomplish much more limited goals.

A primarily British force occupied the extreme southeast, around the city of Basra. American troops took the main body of Iraq. Marine units, on the right wing, crossed the Euphrates River at Nasiriyah; the heaviest American losses of the campaign were in that city. Most of the Marines proceeded north, crossed the Tigris River, and then turned west toward the capital, Baghdad. Army units, on the left wing, went west across the deserts south of the Euphrates until they were south or even a little southwest of Baghdad, then turned north and finally came at Baghdad from the southwest.

Iraqi air defenses had been so weakened by months of American air strikes that U.S. helicopter gunships and fixed-wing aircraft were able to operate in comparative safety in large areas of Iraq. They devastated Iraqi military units in the path of the American ground forces, especially the larger units with heavier weapons. What remained of the Iraqi forces were no match for American ground forces. And the Americans moved so fast that the Iraqis had little opportunity to draw lessons from the defeat of one unit that could enable another to do better.

The speed with which the Americans advanced would have made them vulnerable to ambushes, and attacks on their supply lines, by competent and innovative enemy forces. They encountered few such forces. The Iraqi units that were willing to fight—that did not just fade away—mostly placed themselves unimaginatively in the path of the American juggernaut, and were crushed by it. The first unpleasant surprise for the Americans was a paramilitary organization, the Fedayeen Saddam. But the surprise was that the Fedayeen Saddam fought at all. They did not fight with great skill, they did not have heavy weapons, and they did not inflict heavy casualties on the Americans. Another surprise was more ominous. On March 29 a suicide bomber driving a taxi killed four U.S. troops at a checkpoint. Another suicide bomber killed three Americans on April 3.

Small groups of American forces went into northern Iraq by air, seizing some positions themselves and helping Kurdish forces, the *peshmerga*, to seize others. The United States had hoped to send in a much larger force through Turkey, but the Turks had refused permission.

American bombing of the Iraqi air-defense system before the nominal opening of the war had been effective, and the tactical air strikes that supported the ground invasion were very successful. American strategic bombing during the war was less so. The "shock and awe" bombing of conspicuous government buildings and palaces in central Baghdad, on March 21, did not have the hoped-for psychological effect.

The American forces went more than half the distance from Kuwait to Baghdad in a week, paused for a few days to allow supplies to catch up with the front of the advance and to clear Iraqi forces away from their supply lines, and then resumed their advance. U.S. Army troops had full control of Baghdad's main airport, west of the city, by April 5. On that day, a task force of tanks and other tracked vehicles made an armed reconnaissance patrol, a "thunder run," going deep into Baghdad from the south and then departing to the west. One American was killed, but American forces killed an estimated eight hundred to one thousand Iraqi soldiers. Two days later the same task force and two others made a second thunder run. This time they went to the heart of the city, occupying, among other sites, two of Hussein's palaces beside the Tigris, and remained there. The Iraqis were unable to dislodge them on April 7 and 8, and meanwhile other Army units were entering the city from the northwest. U.S. Marines were coming from the southeast. During the night of April 8 to 9, Iraqi leaders, recognizing that they had lost the struggle for Baghdad, went into hiding. Their government ceased to function as a government, though some of their soldiers continued to resist the Americans.

Looting began in parts of Baghdad on April 7. It reached disastrous levels on April 9. There were not nearly enough American troops to restore order, and they did not at first even make much of an attempt; few thought of the maintenance of order as their responsibility.

RECONSTRUCTION AND RESISTANCE

The United States had done little to prepare for the occupation of Iraq. Apparently it was believed that once Saddam Hussein was gone, a new government, with exiled leaders such as the secular Shiite Ahmad Chalabi playing key roles, could be created with little further American effort. When this did not happen, Paul Bremer was sent in May 2003 to head a new body, the Coalition Provisional Authority, which ruled Iraq until mid-2004. An "Iraqi Governing Council" was established in July 2003 but was not given much authority.

An insurgency made up primarily of Sunni Arabs emerged gradually out of the background of general lawlessness that followed the war. Its diverse elements often cooperated, but had no overall command. First, there were the surviving elements of the Ba'th Party. When the government collapsed in April 2003, leaders and officers going into hiding took with them considerable funds, some of which they used to finance the insurgency. The Americans at first overestimated the importance of the Ba'th leaders, and hoped that the capture of Hussein in December 2003 would seriously weaken the insurgency, but there was not much effect. (Hussein's execution in December 2006 seemed, if anything, to inflame the insurgency further.)

Groups rooted in local communities and tribes formed the great mass of the insurgency. Many felt a nationalist hostility toward foreign occupiers. Many resented the way the Americans had reduced the power of the Sunni Arabs, traditionally the dominant force in Iraq, by empowering the Shiite majority and the Kurds. Many were angry with the number of Iraqis the Americans had killed, about the way troops searched Iraqi homes at night, looking for weapons and hauling off suspects in handcuffs and hoods, and so forth.

Finally, there were foreign fighters from many countries. The most important of these were very similar to Al-Qaeda and eventually began calling themselves "Al-Qaeda in Mesopotamia." They were led by a Jordanian, Abu Musab al-Zarqawi, until his death in June 2006. They thought of Iraq as one front in a broader struggle directed both against the United States and against corrupt secular governments in the Muslim world. They are believed to have been responsible for most of the spectacular suicide bombings in Iraq, killing large numbers of people, including many Shiite civilians, and trying to trigger a civil war of Sunnis against Shiites.

The coalition headed by the United States had a substantial number of British troops and smaller numbers of troops from other nations, but these were overwhelmingly in areas of southern Iraq that were predominantly Shiite. It was the Americans who faced the Sunni Arab insurgency.

The violence had become a major problem by August 2003, and it grew thereafter. By early 2004 numerous towns were under insurgent control. In April, when the United States assaulted Fallujah, west of Baghdad, it became apparent that taking Fallujah would require so much firepower as to destroy much of the city. The Americans backed off, and Fallujah remained under insurgent control until it was finally taken in a bloody battle that indeed destroyed much of the city in November 2004.

At times, the coalition faced a dangerous widening of the insurgency into the Shiite community. A radical young Shiite cleric, Moqtada al-Sadr, wanted Iraq to have a religiously based government similar to that of Iran. His militia, the Mahdi (Mehdi) Army, clashed with American forces on a serious scale in April 2004, and again in August.

On June 28, 2004, the United States officially granted sovereignty to an Iraqi government headed by Prime Minister Ayad Allawi, a secular Shiite. In January 2005 elections were held for a national assembly. An alliance of religiously oriented Shiites, presided over but not openly led by Ayatollah Ali al-Sistani, the most respected religious leader in Iraq, won a majority of the seats. A constitution was then written, and an election under the new constitution was held in December 2005. Many more Sunni Arabs voted in this election than had voted in January. It was hoped that this development would lead many of those who had supported the insurgency to shift their efforts toward participation in peaceful political processes. But this did not quickly occur.

In the second half of 2004, the United States significantly expanded its efforts to train Iraqi military and security forces. By the second half of 2005, Iraqi forces were having a clear and substantial impact, establishing, for example, a reasonable level of security on the notorious highway linking the city of Baghdad with its airport. But there was increasing concern about the extent to which some elements of the security forces, especially the police, were being infiltrated by and becoming tools of the militias of Sadr and other religiously oriented Shiite leaders.

For a long time, the Shiites showed remarkable restraint, not retaliating indiscriminately for Sunni insurgents' murders of Shiite civilians. But in February 2006 insurgents blew up the Golden Mosque in Samarra, one of the holiest Shiite shrines in Iraq, and the Shiites exploded in rage. Soon Shiite "death squads" were abducting, torturing, and murdering Sunnis by the thousands, and Sunnis were doing the same to Shiites in a cycle of revenge killings, mainly in Baghdad and nearby cities, that produced higher death tolls than the ongoing struggle pitting the insurgency against coalition and government forces. Militants on each side carried out ethnic cleansing, driving members of the other group out of mixed neighborhoods. The United States blamed Shiite militias, especially the Mahdi Army, for the worst of the violence. But Prime Minister Nuri al-Maliki was politically allied with Moqtada al-Sadr and other militia leaders; he often resisted American efforts to crack down on the militias.

U.S. Secretary of Defense Donald Rumsfeld was determined to use as few American military personnel as possible in the occupation of Iraq, and he long downplayed the magnitude of the problems there. Critics argued that the American force in Iraq was too small to accomplish its mission. But as the violence escalated, political support for the war effort declined in the United States. Critics of government policy increasingly spoke of setting a timetable for withdrawal of the forces the United States already had in Iraq, rather than sending more.

Rumsfeld resigned at the end of 2006, and top American officials spoke more openly than ever before about the need for a change of policy. In January 2007 President Bush announced that Prime Minister al-Maliki had committed himself to a real crackdown on violent militias, regardless of sect. Bush also announced that he was sending more than 21,000 additional American troops to Iraq, most of them to Baghdad, to support Iraqi government efforts to restore order. Few in the American public or the Congress had much faith that this new effort would succeed, though as of spring 2007 violence in and around Baghdad decreased significantly.

SEE ALSO *Al-Qaeda; Arabs; Bush, George W.; Counterterrorism; Gulf War of 1991; Hussein, Saddam; Islam, Shia and Sunni; Petroleum Industry; September 11, 2001; Terrorism; War; Weapons of Mass Destruction*

BIBLIOGRAPHY

Diamond, Larry. 2005. *Squandered Victory: The American Occupation and the Bungled Effort to Bring Democracy to Iraq.* New York: Times Books/Holt.

Fick, Nathaniel. 2005. *One Bullet Away: The Making of a Marine Officer.* Boston: Houghton Mifflin.

Fontenot, Gregory, E. J. Degen, and David Tohn. 2005. *On Point: The United States Army in Operation Iraqi Freedom.* Annapolis, MD: Naval Institute Press.

Gordon, Michael, and Bernard E. Trainor. 2006. *Cobra II: The Inside Story of the Invasion and Occupation of Iraq.* New York: Pantheon.

Packer, George. 2005. *The Assassins' Gate: America in Iraq.* New York: Farrar, Straus and Giroux.

Reynolds, Nicholas E. 2005. *Basrah, Baghdad, and Beyond: The U.S. Marine Corps in the Second Iraq War.* Annapolis, MD: Naval Institute Press.

Ricks, Thomas E. 2006. *Fiasco: The American Military Adventure in Iraq.* New York: Penguin.

Woodward, Bob. 2004. *Plan of Attack.* New York: Simon & Schuster.

Zucchino, David. 2004. *Thunder Run: The Armored Strike to Capture Baghdad.* New York: Grove.

Edwin E. Moise

IRISH REPUBLICAN ARMY

The term *Irish Republican Army* was first used during the Fenian raids in Canada during the 1860s. Today the term is used in concert with the outbreaks of violence throughout Ireland, and especially in Northern Ireland, called the *Troubles.* The Irish Republican Army has a much longer history than that begun in the late 1960s and early 1970s, having been instrumental in the Easter Uprising in 1916. The *Troubles* refers to the sectarian conflict in Ireland (especially Northern Ireland) that began in the late 1960s.

The immediate postfamine years in Ireland were a period of escalating unrest between the Irish and their English occupiers. In 1916 the conflicts came to a head when a group of charismatic Irish began a revolt in Dublin. The focal point of the revolt was the General Post Office, now a shrine to their efforts, but the entire city, especially the area in and around O'Connell Street and Parnell Square, was involved in the violent armed conflict. In the end, the leaders of the revolt were arrested, put in Kilmainham Gaol, and many were executed. In the aftermath of the uprising and their executions, Michael Collins (1890–1922) and others organized guerrilla forces against the English Black and Tans. These forces became known as the Irish Volunteers.

In 1919 the Dáil Éireann or First Dáil (the government of Ireland) recognized the Irish Volunteers as the Irish Republican Army (IRA), and they in turn fought the Irish War of Independence from 1919 to 1921 against the English. At the signing of the Anglo-Irish Treaty in 1921, the IRA split into protreaty forces (which became known as the Old IRA, government forces, or regulars) and antitreaty forces (Republicans or irregulars). The antitreaty forces continued to use the name Irish Republican Army. In 1922 the two sides entered into the Irish Civil War, with the regulars led by Michael Collins on the side of the new Irish Free State, which still recognized England, and the Republicans led by Liam Lynch (1893–1923) refusing to recognize the new state or the partitioning of Northern Ireland. Collins was later assassinated by IRA members for his participation in the Civil War and support of the Free State government.

Éamon de Valera (1882–1975), a member of the antitreaty group Sinn Féin, eventually came to power as leader of the Fianna Fáil Party, currently the largest political party in Ireland. The IRA remained active in the Republic until the 1960s, when it split again to become the Official IRA (OIRA) and the Provisional IRA (PIRA). The Provisionals were most active in Northern Ireland and split with the Official IRA due to what they recognized as the OIRA's lack of protection for nationalist communities in the North. This split came in 1969 as violence between sectarian communities and Republican and Unionist groups began to escalate. This is often recognized as a conflict between Catholics and Protestants in the North, but the underlying reasons remain tension between Unionists (those who support English rule) and Republicans (those who support unity with the Republic of Ireland and devolution from England).

Bloody Sunday, a violent clash between protesters and British and Northern Irish troops in Derry in 1972, was a flashpoint in the sectarian conflicts. Troops opened fire upon the crowd of protesters killing thirteen, all of whom were unarmed. There are conflicting reports from those present that suggest either a gun was fired from the protesters' side toward the troops or that the troops were commanded to fire on the agitated crowd. In the days and months that followed, extreme violence in the form of shootings, bombings, murders, and arson engulfed the North. The PIRA carried out many of the killings and are suspected to be the perpetrators of specific acts of violence carried out against the Royal Ulster Constabulary (RUC) and the British army, among them the bombings of police stations and barracks and the targeting of pubs frequented by the RUC and the army. They are also accused of a number of attacks in Dublin and throughout the United Kingdom. In over thirty years of violence in Northern Ireland, more than three thousand people have died as a result of the conflict.

Since the mid-1990s, a process of political devolution has been under way in Northern Ireland. The peace process, as it is known, has been opposed by many, including the Real IRA, a splinter group of the PIRA that broke ranks in 1997. The Real IRA, considered to be a paramilitary group, has held out against the decommissioning of weapons as proposed in the Hume-Adams report. In 1993 the Hume-Adams initiative agreed to by John Hume, leader of the SDLP (the North's nationalist party) and Gerry Adams was a directive to begin an IRA cease-fire and to include Sinn Féin in the peace talks. This in turn led to a series of cease-fires and began the peace process. Sinn Féin, led by Gerry Adams, entered the Dáil Éireann and now participates in the political decision-making process.

SEE ALSO *Peace Process; Revolution*

BIBLIOGRAPHY

Behan, Brendan. 1965. *Confessions of an Irish Rebel.* London: Hutchinson.

Coogan, Tim Pat. 2002. *The IRA.* Rev. ed. London: Palgrave Macmillan.

Coogan, Tim Pat. 2002. *The Troubles: Ireland's Ordeal and the Search for Peace.* London: Palgrave Macmillan.

English, Richard. 2003. *Armed Struggle: The History of the IRA.* Oxford: Oxford University Press.

Moloney, Ed. 2002. *A Secret History of the IRA.* New York: Norton.

Toolis, Kevin. 1995. *Rebel Hearts: Journeys within the IRA's Soul.* London: Picador.

Kelli Ann Costa

IRON CURTAIN

The term *iron curtain* was coined by the British author and suffragette Ethel Snowden in her book *Through Bolshevik Russia* (1920). In her very early and negative critique of the Bolshevik form of communism, this British feminist referred to the iron curtain simply as the contemporary geographical border of Bolshevik Russia in 1919 ('We were behind the 'iron curtain' at last'). At the end of the Nazi regime in Germany the minister of propaganda, Joseph Goebbels, used the term in a journal article and several times in his private diary in February 1945, and the minister of finance, Lutz Graf Schwerin von Krosigk, used it in a radio broadcast on May 2, 1945. Both Nazi leaders argued that the Soviet Army is occupying one country after the other, lowering an iron curtain immediately afterward on these occupied countries in order to commit war crimes, without being observed and controlled by the outside world. During the last months of the Third Reich, both ministers regarded the iron curtain as a moving part of the ongoing occupation process by Soviet troops within the territorial scope of the Yalta agreements from 1943. This analogy with an iron curtain in a theater (Goebbels was in charge of German theaters and culture) in this usage of the notion refers to the fact that events behind the theater curtain are not visible by the audience and somehow cut off from outside observation. The British prime minister Winston S. Churchill used the term in a diplomatic telegram to President Harry S. Truman in May 1945, and in a public speech in the British Parliament on August 16, 1945, but the term was not popularized until the following year, with Churchill's speech at Westminster College in Fulton, Missouri, on March 5, 1946:

> From Stettin in the Baltic to Trieste in the Adriatic an iron curtain has descended across the Continent. Behind that line lie all the capitals of the ancient states of Central and Eastern Europe, Warsaw, Berlin, Prague, Vienna, Budapest, Belgrade, Bucharest and Sofia; all these famous cities and the populations around them lie in what I must call the Soviet sphere, all are subject, in one form or another, not only to Soviet influence but also to a very high and in some cases increasing measure of control from Moscow. (Cannadine 1990, pp. 303–304)

The iron curtain refers to the boundary that divided Europe politically and militarily from the end of World War II until the end of the cold war. Geographically, the borderline ran from Estonia in the north to Yugoslavia in the south. Churchill's famous 1946 address, which is sometimes referred to as the "Iron Curtain Speech," is regarded as marking the commencement of the cold war between the democratic Western world and the Communist Eastern bloc with the Soviet Union as its political center. Between 1946 and 1989, the existence of this symbolic boundary forced many Central and East European countries to join the Communist bloc under the control of the Soviet Union. These countries—Bulgaria, Czechoslovakia, East Germany, Hungary, Poland, Romania, and (until the 1960s) Albania—were labeled "Iron Curtain countries."

The iron curtain was manned and defended militarily against the West by the Warsaw Pact, which combined the Soviet Red Army and troops from the new Communist one-party states after the end of World War II. It also served as a wall to prevent citizens of Eastern bloc countries from migrating west. In Berlin, the section of the iron curtain dividing West from East Germany took the form of the Berlin Wall, a long concrete wall separating Berlin into democratic and Communist parts; many East Germans lost their lives trying to escape over the wall to the West. In other areas, the iron curtain was constructed of nearly impenetrable steel fencing, creating a long and narrow strip of no-man's-land of untouched wildlife.

The iron curtain was finally lifted on June 27, 1989, at the border between Austria and Hungary by the foreign ministers Gyula Horn (Hungary) and Alois Mock (Austria), forty-three years after Churchill's historic speech. This first crack in the long border between the free world and the Communist world was the beginning of the final collapse of communism in November and December 1989, and the first sign of the fall of the Soviet Union in 1991. The fall of the iron curtain coincided with the end of the cold war, signifying the end of a crucial and dramatic period of European and world history.

SEE ALSO *Berlin Wall; Churchill, Winston; Cold War; Communism; Democracy; Diplomacy; International Relations; Union of Soviet Socialist Republics*

BIBLIOGRAPHY

Cannadine, David, ed. 1990. *The Speeches of Winston Churchill.* London: Penguin.

Harbutt, Fraser J. 1989. *The Iron Curtain: Churchill, America, and the Origins of the Cold War.* New York: Oxford University Press.

Muller, James W. 1999. *Churchill's "Iron Curtain" Speech Fifty Years Later.* Columbia: University of Missouri Press.

Rose, Brian. 2004. *The Lost Border: The Landscape of the Iron Curtain.* Princeton, NJ: Princeton Architectural Press.

Snowden, Ethel. 1920. *Through Bolshevik Russia.* London: Cassell.

Wright, Patrick. 2007. *Iron Curtain: From Stage to Cold War.* New York: Oxford University Press.

Christian W. Haerpfer

IRON INDUSTRY

SEE *Steel Industry.*

IRON LAW OF OLIGARCHY

SEE *Oligarchy, Iron Law of.*

IROQUOIS

The Iroquois were a Native North American confederacy of five nations whose aboriginal territory included much of upstate New York. The Iroquois thought of this territory as a longhouse, a rectangular multifamily dwelling with a door at each end and a series of hearths in the aisle that ran the length of the dwelling. Each of the five Iroquois nations occupied one of the five fireplaces in this metaphorical longhouse. From east to west these were the Mohawk, the Oneida, the Onondaga, the Cayuga, and the Seneca. As the western-most nation in the Iroquois longhouse, the Senecas were considered the "Doorkeepers of the Confederacy" and the Mohawks are often styled the "Keepers of the Eastern Door." Iroquois refer to themselves as *Haudenosaunee* (with variant spellings) meaning, roughly, "people of the longhouse," a designation many contemporary Haudenosaunee prefer. *Iroquois* was the name utilized by the French; the English usually referred to the confederacy as the Five (later, Six) Nations.

At the time of contact with Europeans the Iroquois lived in large villages consisting of elm-bark longhouses, each housing a number of families. Surrounding the village were fields in which the women planted the "three sisters"—corn, beans, and squash. These crops were the staples of Iroquois diet.

Each of the Iroquois nations was divided into exogamous matrilineal clans. The Wolf, Bear, and Turtle clans were found in all five nations; five or six additional clans were found among the Onondagas, Cayugas, and Senecas. The clans were further divided into matrilineages, each headed by a senior female, the lineage matron. Some of these lineage matrons enjoyed considerable political power. The Iroquois Confederacy Council consisted of fifty positions, each hereditary within a matrilineage. The lineage matron appointed a male member of her matrilineage to that position and had the right to depose him if he proved negligent or incompetent in that role.

Dean Snow estimated the Iroquois population as almost 22,000 in 1630, prior to their first experience of smallpox (Snow 1994, p. 110). Diseases introduced to North America from Europe took a terrible toll in Iroquoia, but these population losses were to some degree offset by the Iroquois practice of adopting war captives and incorporating refugee populations. One refugee group, the Tuscarora, arrived in the 1720s, and after their arrival the confederacy was often known to the English as the Six Nations.

Initially the Iroquois established a strong trading relationship with the Dutch colony of New Netherland. The Iroquois quickly adopted elements of European culture such as brass kettles and steel axes and knives. These economic and political ties continued after the English replaced the Dutch as governors of the colony, having renamed it New York.

Occupying a highly strategic position between the English colonies on the Atlantic Coast and the French in Canada, the Iroquois usually maintained neutrality between the two colonial powers. On occasion Mohawks took the field as allies to the British whereas the Senecas, close to the French trading post at Niagara, sometimes fought beside the French. There were several Mohawk colonies on the St. Lawrence River established by converts to Catholicism who were persuaded by their Jesuit priests to migrate to a locale remote from English influences. These people, from the founding of their communities in the 1670s, consistently fought as allies to the French.

By the outbreak of the American Revolution the Iroquois had largely abandoned the multifamily bark longhouses and were living in smaller houses, often log cabins. The Mohawks had converted to the Church of England. The Oneida were heavily influenced by the New England missionary Samuel Kirkland (1741–1808). Those nations farther to the west were not yet Christian, but their towns closely resembled those of the non-Indian inhabitants of the frontier.

The American Revolution divided the Iroquois Confederacy. The Oneidas and Tuscaroras aided the supporters of the Continental Congress; Mohawks, Cayugas, and Senecas (and later the Onondagas) fought as allies to the British. The treaty that ended that conflict in 1783 made no provisions for the Indian allies of the Crown, and Britain surrendered all interests in the Iroquois homeland south of Lake Ontario. Many Iroquois moved north of the new American border to lands secured for them by Quebec governor Frederick Haldimand. These lands included the Tyendinaga Mohawk Reserve (or Territory) on the Bay of Quinté and the Six Nations Reserve on the Grand River, both in what is now Ontario. The latter was settled predominantly by Mohawks, Cayugas, and Onondagas. Most of the Senecas remained in New York State, and a series of treaties (Fort Stanwix [1784], Canandaigua [1794], and Big Tree [1797]) established several reservations, of which Allegany, Cattaraugus, Oil Spring, and Tonawanda remain in Seneca hands. The

Onondaga Nation retains territory near Syracuse, New York, but Cayuga and Oneida lands in New York were purchased through treaties of questionable legality with the State of New York. The larger portion of the Oneidas migrated to lands secured in Wisconsin and Ontario early in the nineteenth century.

In 1799 a Seneca, Handsome Lake (1735–1815), experienced a vision that led him to preach a message of both nativism and reform that established the contemporary practice of traditional Iroquois (or Longhouse) religion. Anthony F. C. Wallace's ethnohistorical analysis of these events formed the basis of anthropological understanding of revitalization movements (Wallace 1970).

In the 1840s Lewis H. Morgan pursued personal contacts, particularly through a bilingual Seneca youth, Ely S. Parker, among the Tonawanda Senecas to compile what has been touted as the first ethnographic monograph describing a Native North American culture (Morgan 1851).

Any estimate of current Iroquois population is subject to error, but a compilation of numbers of those formally enrolled in various Iroquois communities between 1990 and 2000 states that 16,829 are enrolled in New York Iroquois communities, 42,857 belong to communities in Ontario, 10,831 are enrolled in Quebec Iroquois bands, 11,000 belong to the Wisconsin Oneida community, and 2,460 belong to a Seneca-Cayuga group that resides in Oklahoma (Lex and Abler 2004, p. 744).

Some Iroquois communities have pursued land claims for nearly two centuries (see Vecsey and Starna 1988), seeking the return or compensation for lands felt to be fraudulently taken. These claims have led to violent clashes with authorities, as at Ganienkeh in northern New York in the 1970s and at Kanesatake outside Montreal in 1990. Legalized gambling and other economic activities have also deeply divided many communities, creating internal conflicts that have led in some cases to violence, arson, and even deaths.

SEE ALSO *Native Americans*

BIBLIOGRAPHY

Fenton, William N. 1998. *The Great Law and the Longhouse: A Political History of the Iroquois Confederacy.* Norman: University of Oklahoma Press.

Lex, Barbara, and Thomas S. Abler. 2004. Iroquois. In *Encyclopedia of Medical Anthropology: Health and Illness in the World's Cultures*, eds. Carol R. Ember and Melvin Ember, 743–754. New York: Kluwer Academic/Plenum.

Morgan, Lewis H. 1851. *League of the Ho-dé-no-sau-nee or Iroquois.* Rochester, NY: Sage.

Parker, Arthur C. 1968. *Parker on the Iroquois*, ed. William N. Fenton. Syracuse, NY: Syracuse University Press.

Shimony, Annemarie Anrod. 1994. *Conservatism among the Iroquois at the Six Nations Reserve.* Syracuse, NY: Syracuse University Press.

Snow, Dean. 1994. *The Iroquois.* Oxford, U.K.: Blackwell.

Vecsey, Christopher, and William A. Starna, eds. 1988. *Iroquois Land Claims.* Syracuse, NY: Syracuse University Press.

Wallace, Anthony F. C. 1970. *Death and Rebirth of the Seneca.* New York: Knopf.

Thomas S. Abler

IRREDENTISM

SEE *Nationalism and Nationality.*

IRRIGATION

Irrigation refers to techniques for augmenting the moisture content of soil to grow crops. These techniques have played an important role in intensifying agriculture, increasing production, and improving the productivity of land and labor. Early civilizations in China, Egypt, Mesopotamia, Peru, and India relied on them to support large and complex populations. One of the earliest and most successful large-scale hydraulic works was the Dujiangyan irrigation project built in the third century BCE in southwest China's Sichuan Province. The project was designed to simultaneously solve the problem of the incessant flooding of the Minjiang River, a tributary of the Yangtze River, in the summer, and provide water during the winter when it was beset with drought. Working without a dam, the river was divided by a long bank in the middle, with the inner river serving as a channel for delivering water for irrigation and the outer river used as a floodway. This enabled the delivery of water during the dry season and the return of excess water during the winter to the mainstream of the Minjiang River. A weir made of bamboo cages filled with stones balanced the channel's inflow. The project fed a grid of irrigation canals watering 160,000 hectares of arable land in the Chengdu Plain.

Many ancient large-scale irrigation systems were accompanied by elaborate, complex, social organization. Descriptions of these systems in the nineteenth century intrigued the social theorists Karl Marx (1818–1883) and Max Weber (1864–1920). Marx's idea of the Asiatic mode of production, based largely on irrigation-based societies in China, included state control and collection of rents, a despotic political system, and societal organization obtained through religion, rather than economics and exchange. Village life, rather than cities, circumscribed the social spheres of people. Weber, in contrast, drew attention to the peculiar "hydraulic-bureaucratic official-state" in China and India. Although flawed due to limits in the data then available, these constructs were quite influential in the subsequent development of social theory.

Karl Wittfogel, inspired by the writings of Weber, revisited the materials and proposed in *Oriental Despotism* (1957) that large-scale waterworks required centralized direction, bureaucratic organization, and disciplined armies. He distinguished such "hydraulic societies" from smaller-scale "hydroagricultural societies" relying on less provident water sources in regions where geographical features hydraulically compartmentalized the countryside. Wittfogel's hydraulic society thesis generated various criticisms, of which the most telling were examples of locally controlled and managed irrigation in societies where irrigation authority was formally centralized. More recently, Donald Worster in *Rivers of Empire* (1985) reinvigorated the discussion of large-scale irrigation, arguing that Wittfogel's hydraulic societies take a somewhat different form in the modern world. In his analysis of river-based irrigation in the western United States he finds parallels between the archaic centralized regimes of ancient hydraulic societies and the centralized state agencies of the Bureau of Reclamation and the Army Corps of Engineers.

IRRIGATION TECHNIQUES

The motivation for irrigation stems from the difficulties of farming in arid and semiarid areas of the world beset with insufficient or unreliable precipitation. Where precipitation is insufficient, irrigation may be the only way farmers can supply moisture for growing crops. In areas with sufficient, but otherwise unreliable, precipitation, it can provide insurance against crop failure. And in lands with adequate moisture, irrigation can be used to grow water-intensive subsistence crops such as rice, or high-value market crops such as sugar beets or beans.

Irrigators commonly draw on gravity to move surface water from a source through canals and furrows to fields and to store water in reservoirs and cisterns. Techniques to move surface water run the gamut from simple and unsophisticated counterbalanced poles mounted with buckets to complex, labor-intensive feats of engineering such as large-scale dams and canal systems. Surface-water irrigation often works in concert with the control and manipulation of floodwater. In one frequent form, as soon as the flood in a perennial river reaches a sufficient level, inundation canals start to flow and water is led over fields. In another, recession irrigation, a rising perennial river overflows its banks and inundates the plains alongside the river. Crops are grown on the rising or receding flow or on the residual moisture.

In spate irrigation, found throughout semiarid environments of the Middle East, North Africa, East Africa,

West Asia, and parts of Latin America, seasonal water is used as a source. Seasonal floods are contained in mountain catchments or diverted from riverbeds and spread over large areas. Seasonal floodwater may last only a few hours or a few days, and sophisticated local knowledge is required to organize and manage the accumulation and distribution of the floodwater. Spate irrigation is associated with low returns to labor, great variability in productivity between good and bad years, and a high degree of social organization. Its uncertainty restricts its appeal to only the very poorest.

In areas with high water tables or surface depressions, human or animal energy has been used to raise groundwater for irrigation. Gravity usually has only limited potential in this regard. One exception is the complex "horizontal wells" that tapped subterranean aquifers through filtration galleries in the ancient Middle East (*qanats*), and the Andes (*puquios*). In the nineteenth century pumps driven initially by steam, and later by electricity and gasoline or diesel, were adopted to irrigate with groundwater from shallow aquifers and deep groundwater basins. The availability of small, portable, inexpensive, submersible pumps in the late twentieth century expanded groundwater irrigation dramatically. In groundwater-rich spate-irrigated areas, hydraulic infrastructure has been neglected and land use intensified through perennial cropping.

The adoption of industrial irrigation altered significantly the scale, impact, and productivity of agriculture, and its reliance on inanimate mechanical converters of energy, especially fossil fuels. Irrigation played a key role in the Green Revolution of the 1960s, helping to ensure the high yields of "miracle seeds." It remains instrumental in realizing the potential of genetic engineering and precision agriculture, the application of space-age technologies to tailor soil and crop management to local conditions. Two techniques now in widespread use include drip irrigation, relying on emitters to release carefully calibrated amounts of water, and sprinkler irrigation, with relatively permanent or portable sprinkler systems.

Despite new and more efficient irrigation technologies, today's demands for water produced by the Green Revolution, population growth, urbanization, and industrialization outstrip supply. Scarcity of water provokes conflicts in many areas of the world; they are endemic in the Middle East over access to the water of the Euphrates, Jordan, and Nile Rivers. At the heart of the Arab-Israeli conflict is the allocation to Israel, Jordan, the Palestinian Territories, and Syria of the water of the Jordan River, its tributaries, coastal rivers, and two aquifer systems.

SUCCESSES AND FAILURES

Although many regions in China, Egypt, Mesopotamia, and India have enjoyed continuous and sustainable irrigation for centuries, it has not always been an unmitigated success. Archaeological and historical research has uncovered significant evidence of cases of agrarian collapse due to environmental degradation and mismanagement. Poorly managed surface-water irrigation can lead to the excessive buildup of salts, exacerbated by shallow soils, water with relatively high salt content, aridity, and high water tables. For example, the Aral Sea, located in inland Central Asia, has been shrinking since the 1960s as the U.S.S.R. diverted the rivers that feed it for irrigation.

Often, inadequate drainage is at the root of the irrigation failures. Drainage does not always have to be a problem, however. Some societies have devised techniques for draining heavily waterlogged soils to levels sufficient to support intensive agriculture. Raised-bed agriculture in Lake Titicaca of southern Peru and Bolivia achieved levels of productivity comparable to irrigated land.

In the industrial era, irrigation has increased the risks of ground- and surface-water pollution from the intensive use of pesticides and nitrate fertilizers. Groundwater extraction poses an additional problem; it is much more difficult to regulate than surface-water irrigation and in many regions of the world, overpumping has contributed to the drying up of aquifers and groundwater basins.

SEE ALSO *Development, Rural*

BIBLIOGRAPHY

Glick, Thomas. 1970. *Irrigation and Society in Medieval Valencia.* Cambridge, MA: Harvard University Press.

Mabry, Jonathan B., ed. 1996. *Canals and Communities.* Tucson: University of Arizona Press.

Watson, Andrew M. 1983. *Agricultural Innovations in the Early Islamic World.* Cambridge, U.K.: Cambridge University Press.

Wittfogel, Karl. 1957. *Oriental Despotism.* New Haven, CT: Yale University Press.

Worster, Donald. 1985. *Rivers of Empire: Water, Aridity, and the Growth of the American West.* New York: Pantheon Books.

David W. Guillet

ISHI

SEE *Kroeber, Alfred Louis.*

ISLAM, NATION OF

SEE *Nation of Islam.*

ISLAM, SHIA AND SUNNI

Islam was born in the Arabian Peninsula in the seventh century CE, a time when the peninsula was populated by nomadic tribes, as well as settled agriculturalists and merchants. There was no central authority beyond a scattering of tribal leaders, most of them devoted to polytheistic religions.

The Prophet Muhammad was born around 570 CE, in Mecca. His family came from a poor branch (the Banu Hashim) of the leading Meccan tribe (the Quraysh). His father died before he was born and his mother died when he was a child; he was brought up by his grandfather and uncle. As a young man, Muhammad worked as the business manager of a wealthy widow named Khadijah (d. 619). He was dubbed "the trustworthy" for his business dealings and was thoroughly respected. He married Khadijah, who was his senior, when he was in his twenties. They had four daughters who married into eminent families. Little more is known about his early life before his "call" at age forty.

Like other young men in Mecca, Muhammad made solitary retreats into the nearby mountains. He was known to have become contemplative about leading a pure and honest life. On one of these occasions, he had a vision in which the angel Gabriel commanded him to recite God's message which is now encapsulated in the Qu'ran, Sura 96, verses 1–5. According to the *hadith*, a collection of the Prophet's sayings and actions, Muhammad was terrified by his vision. He is supposed to have wondered whether he was going mad, and he was physically affected by these thoughts, which he knew were not his own; this manifestation has been compared to an epileptic seizure.

Muhammad was reassured by his early supporters, including his wife, his cousin Ali ibn Abi Talib (599–661), and his close friends Abu Bakr (c. 573–634) and Uthman ibn Affan (d. 656), that he was not losing his mind. In 613 Muhammad began preaching in the streets of Mecca. His monotheistic message offended leading members of the dominant Quraysh, and he was scorned, derided, and attacked. One of his persecutors, Umar ibn al-Khattab (c. 586–644), later became a convert.

In 619 Muhammad's wife and uncle died, and his position in Mecca became precarious. He began to look for support outside of Mecca, and was encouraged by exchanges with people from Medina (about 250 miles north of Mecca), a town with a population of émigré Jews. In 622 he moved to Medina in the so-called *hijrah* (migration), and, around this time, he gave his movement a political identity, formulating the ideal of a community of religious believers, known as the *ummah*.

In Medina, Muhammad came into contact with Christians as well as Jews and soon became a leader in the community. In 624 he began to ambush the caravans of Meccan traders in an attempt to economically and psychologically undermine the prestige of the Quraysh clan. The Meccans responded by sending an army against Muhammad and his followers, who, though seriously outnumbered, were victorious. Muhammad led an expedition into Syria, and his military prowess won him the support of Bedouin tribesmen. In 627 the Quraysh again were unsuccessful in their attempts to suppress Muhammad and his followers. In 630 Muhammad returned to Mecca as the leader of a united Arabian Peninsula. He died in 632.

After Muhammad's death, his followers expanded throughout the Mediterranean basin and into the east. In the west, their expansion was checked by the Frankish ruler Charles Martel (c. 688–741) at the Battle of Tours in 732.

Muhammad's death precipitated a crisis among his followers. The community was in danger of crumbling, and it was only through the vigorous efforts of his successor, Abu Bakr, that it survived. Abu Bakr kept the Arabs unified by pursuing an expansionist policy, invading Syria and Iraq. When Abu Bakr died, he was succeeded by Umar, who continued the expansion, taking Egypt and Syria, and overthrowing the Persian Empire. Umar's conquests were culturally important in that they bought a refined civilization within the Muslim orbit.

When Umar died in 644, the succession was contested. The two main candidates were Uthman and Ali. The electors chose Uthman. Uthman's reign began with an initial period of calm followed by corruption and lawlessness. He was asked to abdicate his position by the son of the first caliph Muhammad Abi Bakr, who reportedly was part of a group of men from Egypt who seized Uthman's house and murdered him. After Uthman's death, Ali took control, but a civil war broke out between him and Uthman's cousin, Muawiya ibn Abu Sufyan (d. 680), the governor of Syria. In 661 Ali was murdered by Ibn Muljam of the Kharijites (secessionists), one of the earliest sects of Islam that contested the validity of the caliphate, and the line of "right-guided" caliphs (community leaders) ended. Muawiya inaugurated a new dynasty (the Umayyad caliphate), centered in Damascus.

The civil war precipitated the first split in Islam. A minority group, known as *Shiites*, became differentiated from the majority (later to be known as *Sunnis*) in their belief that the descendants of Ali had a special claim to authority. Many Shiites assert that they are linked by blood to the Prophet through a series of holy men. In subsequent centuries, further splits developed within Shia Islam.

The Umayyads continued the holy war, spreading into North Africa, Spain, and France. Their success resulted from the weakness of the Byzantine Empire and the Latin West, the bureaucratic skills of the Umayyad caliphs, and the fact that the Germanic Goths and Vandals had trouble adapting to a settled way of life. In the 740s the Umayyad dynasty gave way to the Abbasid line, and the center of Islam moved from Damascus to Baghdad.

THE BASIC RELIGIOUS TENETS

Muslims of all sects share several basic principles. At the center are two main doctrines: (1) there is one God; and (2) the righteous are required to submit to God. Etymologically, *Islam* means "submission to God" and *Muslim* means "one who has submitted." A *Muslim* then, is someone who adheres to Islam by accepting and committing to the teachings of the Qu'ran and the Prophet Muhammad. In time, the term *Islam* came to signify more than just a tradition of faith; it is also used to refer to entire peoples, cultures, and nation-states.

Submission involves the five pillars of the faith:

1. Confession of faith: "There is no God but God, and Muhammad is his Prophet." Muhammad is regarded as the last and greatest in a line of prophets, including Abraham, Moses, and Jesus.

2. Prayers. Muslims offer prayers five times daily, preceded by ritual purification.

3. Almsgiving. One must give a minimum of one-fortieth of one's income for the benefit of the poor and the underprivileged in the community; the righteous give more. The Qu'ran repeatedly urges fairness and generosity.

4. Fasting. In the month of Ramadan, nothing may be eaten or drunk between sunrise and sunset (allowances are made for the sick, pregnant women, and travelers). Ramadan marks the month that the Qu'ran was revealed to Muhammad.

5. Pilgrimage to Mecca. The pilgrimage to Mecca involves visiting the site at which Abraham is supposed to have placed a sacred rock. The pilgrimage connects Islam not only with the source of Judaism and Christianity, but also with Arab traditions that precede Islam.

All of the pillars, with the exception of almsgiving (*zakat*), are matters of ritual. *Zakat* concerns everyday behavior. The Qu'ran is much concerned with directing the *actions* of the faithful. It insists again and again on honesty and justice in daily life.

There may be a sixth pillar—*jihad*. According to some interpretations of the Qu'ran, Muslims must spread the word of Allah and contend with nonbelievers. This interpretation is controversial, and some have described *jihad* to mean holy war. The concept of jihad is as old as Islam but may be manipulated. In the Qu'ran, it is discussed as a personal struggle (in terms of faith, belief, and virtue). This has been interpreted as a larger struggle against non-believers.

All Muslims have in common a belief in the scripture. This is particularly important in understanding and approaching Islam as a discursive or textual (rather than oral) tradition, as argued by Talal Asad (1986).

SUNNISM

The branch of Islam known as Sunnism was already defined as distinct from Shiism in the eighth century. Sunnis represent nine-tenths of the total world Muslim population. Taking a cue from Marshall Hodgson (1974), one should not consider Sunnism to be mainstream Islam, nor the normative depiction of what is considered Islamic orthodoxy to be represented by Sunnism, with Shiism standing for heterodoxy. Sunnism, as it has been shaped since shortly after the birth of Islam, should be considered a sect of Islam. The followers of this sect are referred to as the "men of the sunnah" (established practice) and the *jama'ah* (Muslim community). The term is an acknowledgment of the religious power of Muhammad's companions, and does not refer to the bloodline of Ali and his family. By this definition, *Sunnism* encompasses the majority of the Muslim community.

During the eighth century, Sunnis strove to continue the tradition of the Prophet's daily practices as expressed in the hadith. By the ninth century, Sunni Islam had become well established through schools of law and seminaries known as *madrasahs*. Sunnis acknowledged the Qu'ran, the hadith, and the *sharia* (Islamic law) as the basic principles of Islam. The Umayyad caliphate endeavored to establish a belief system that would not differentiate Muslims based on creed or set a specific standard for what it is to be a Muslim.

For Sunni Muslims, Islam became institutionalized in four schools of law: (1) the Maliki school in North Africa; (2) the Hanafi school, dominant in South Asia, Central Asia, Turkey, Egypt, Syria, Jordan, and Iraq; (3) the Shafii school, established in Egypt and Southeast Asia; and (4) the Hanbali school in Saudi Arabia. Though distinct in approach, all four schools agreed on the basic principles of the faith.

SUFISM

Literally, the term *Sufism* refers to the woolen clothing worn by adherents. Sufism dates back to the beginning of Islam when companions of the Prophet sought an ascetic and monastic lifestyle. A strong relationship with God is important to Sufis, who retreat inward while striving to become closer to God and gain a better understanding of Islam. The earliest Sufi master (*pir*) was Hasan al-Basri (d. 728), a hadith scholar who taught fear of God. Sufism began to take shape among Sunnis in Kufa at the same time that Shiism and Sunnism were developing. In these early years, most Sufis were Sunni. However, Sufis developed strong ties to Shiite thought and practice, especially the idea of the imam as infallible and a belief in the imam's close, esoteric, and mystical relationship with God.

The concept of a community led by an exalted leader with divine ordinance is central in Sufism, as are spirituality and a personal relationship with God. Sufi forms of worship also differ from those of Sunni and Shiite practice. Sufis attend weekly meetings at a place of worship (*khanaqah, tekke,* or *zawiyah*) and perform *dhikr*, which is the union with God through constant repetition of his name. These meetings vary among each Sufi order.

Sufism grew from a small movement in the eighth and ninth centuries to become an important aspect of Islamic civilization. It was particularly important in spreading Islam to South Asia and Southeast Asia. Most Sufi masters lived by example, but a few actually developed schools of thought. Al-Junayd (d. 910), founder of the school of Baghdad, was the first Sufi Muslim to develop a comprehensive system of Sufi thought. Al-Hallaj (d. 923), founder of the school of Khurasan, became a martyr among Sufis after he was executed by the Abassid caliph for heresy for proclaiming, "I am *haqq*" (truth, here meaning God).

By the twelfth century, Sufi orders had begun to develop global followings. Some orders later became politically active (especially in Turkey during the 1920s when they were threatened by Kemal Atatürk [1881–1938]). Others shunned material life and took vows of chastity and purity, all in order to bring them closer to God and truth.

SHIISM

The term *Shia* refers to followers of Ali. There are several sects within Shiism: the Alids, who believe in Ali as leader of the Muslim community (followers are few and spread throughout the globe but can be found largely in Syria); the Zaydis, followers of Zayd (d. 738), a brother of the fifth imam who established a dynasty in Yemen that lasted until the 1960s; the Ismailis or Seveners, considered by many to be militant because of their establishment during the tenth through twelfth centuries of the Fatimid dynasty in Syria and Egypt; and the Twelvers, the largest of the Shiite groups, found mostly in Iran, Iraq, and Lebanon.

The most important event in Shiite history is the Battle of Karbala (680). The governor of Syria and Uthman's cousin, Muawiya urged the Muslim community to accept his son Yazid as the leader of the community. Some of the older families refused to accept Yazid and urged Ali's second son, Husayn, to rebel in the city of Kufah in present-day Iraq. Husayn, the Prophet's grandson, was belied by the people of Kufah who showed their support for Yazid. Husayn and his small army, which included his family, did not surrender and were pushed out to the desert near the city of Karbala. They were murdered at this famous battle. After this battle, the Shia considered themselves distinct from the Sunnis. The battle also led to the institutionalization of Shiite rituals that commemorate Imam Husayn's martyrdom, a holiday called Ashura that is held on the tenth of the Islamic month of Muharram. Spectacular passion plays are set each year reenacting Husayn's martyrdom, leading to what Hodgson called "the piety of protest" and an idealization of martyrdom. Some Shia groups do not participate in such commemorations of the Battle of Karbala.

After the death of Muhammad in 632, Muslims rallied around Ali, who was regarded as the Prophet's successor. However, the first three caliphs questioned Ali's succession. The first caliph, Abu Bakr, by establishing the caliphate, stripped the Prophet's family of its special privileges, an act that challenged the ascendancy of blood over community (*ummah*). Thus, the caliph's position as head of the community was established shortly after the death of Muhammad.

The second caliphate, headed by Umar, was established in 634 after the death of Abu Bakr. Before his death, Umar urged six men to choose a new caliph. Uthman was chosen and became the third caliph in 644. However, some Muslims considered Uthman to be corrupt and ineffective. According to some sources, Ali began to express disapproval of Uthman's reign and with his followers formed a party of dissent—the Shia. Thus, the rift between Sunni and Shia developed during the third caliphate. Ali had support in KuFa (in present-day Iraq), and he established his governance there. Muawiya decided to avenge his cousin Uthman's death. Muawiya questioned Ali's role in his cousin's death because Ali initially refused to avenge his death, preferring to end the bloodshed instead of seeking revenge. What followed were a series of skirmishes and arbitration that led to Muawiya raising a successful army and gaining territory, while Ali lost support, the caliphate, and ultimately his life to kharijites, or seceders. Kharijites are the earliest sect of Islam, who opposed many of the caliphate's governance.

The Umayyad caliphate, led by Muawiya, sought power after the death of Ali by signing a peace treaty with his son Hasan (625–670), Muawiya, in turn, promised the safety of the followers of Ali. After Muawiya's death in 680, his son Yazid (c. 645–683) was named his successor, an event that is considered the first dynastic succession in Islamic history. Yazid's first order of business was to establish unity and allegiance to the Umayyad caliphate. He called on Husayn to give his allegiance to the governor of Medina, but Husayn refused, an act that prompted oppositional movements against Yazid in other cities. Having discovered that his legitimacy as caliph was being questioned by some prominent families in Medina, Yazid decided to crush Husayn and his small army. After Husayn refused to surrender, Yazid's forces isolated him in the desert near Karbala, where he was killed in battle in 680. That event, along with Ali's death, confirmed the role of Shiites as protesters to tyranny and established power.

For Shia Islam, authority lies in the figure of Ali as imam and caliph, and allegiance and loyalty to Ali and his descendents became a guiding principal. Thus the imamate system is the single most important theological and political aspect of Shiism. Shiites developed their own hadith based on Ali's *Nahj al-Balaghah* (Path of Eloquence); for Shiites, these missives, aphorisms, and sayings of Ali remain words to live by. Shiism also developed its own school of law—the Jafari school, named after the sixth imam, Jafar al-Sadiq (c. 702–765), who established the principle of *nass*. Nass refers to a special power to gain a deep understanding of the Qu'ran and hadith, as well as the power to pass this knowledge on to the succeeding imam. It is common in Shiism to view the imam as *masum*, an innocent, flawless leader of knowledge concerning religious truth.

Ali's line of descendents ended with the twelfth imam, Imam-i Zaman (born in 689, and believe to be still alive in occultation) who was referred to as the *mahdi*, or the messiah, a crucial fact about the imamate system within Shiism. The twelfth imam is believed to have left the earthly world only to return to restore the true faith and to establish justice and a kingdom of God on earth. This view is markedly different from what the majority of Sunni Muslims believe. Sunnis believe strongly in the strength of tradition (hadith) and the agreement of jurists on all matters, as opposed to belief in the piety of Ali and his descendents.

SEE ALSO *Heaven; Hell; Mecca; Monotheism; Muhammad; Religion*

BIBLIOGRAPHY

Asad, Talal. 1986. *The Idea of an Anthropology of Islam.* Washington, DC: Georgetown University Center for Contemporary Arab Studies.

Brown, Daniel. 1996. *Rethinking Tradition in Modern Islamic Thought.* Cambridge, U.K.: Cambridge University Press.

Crone, Patricia, and Martin Hinds. 1986. *God's Caliph: Religious Authority in the First Centuries of Islam.* Cambridge, U.K.: Cambridge University Press.

Donner, Fred. 1998. *Narratives of Islamic Origins: The Beginnings of Islamic Historical Writing.* Princeton, NJ: Darwin.

Hodgson, Marshall. 1974. *The Venture of Islam: Conscience and History in a World Civilization.* Chicago: University of Chicago Press.

Rahman, Fazlur. 2000. *Revival and Reform in Islam: A Study of Islamic Fundamentalism,* ed. Ebrahim Mossa. Oxford: Oneworld.

Narges Erami

ISLAM, SHIITE

SEE *Islam, Shia and Sunni.*

ISLAMIC ECONOMICS

SEE *Economics, Islamic.*

ISLAMIC SOCIALISM

SEE *Socialism, Islamic.*

IS-LM MODEL

Macroeconomics is a subfield of economic theory that is concerned with the study of economies as a whole. It bears on aggregate variables and is geared toward providing policy advice. The IS-LM model was the prevailing macroeconomic model from the 1950s to the 1970s.

FROM KEYNES TO HICKS

The origin of the IS-LM model is to be found in *The General Theory of Employment, Interest, and Money* (1936) by John Maynard Keynes (1883–1946). This book was written in the aftermath of the Great Depression of the 1930s, a time of great disarray, with unemployment reaching peak levels while no remedy seemed to be available to fix the ailing economic system. The general confusion did not spare academic economists, who were torn between their expertise and their gut instincts. According to economic theory, unemployment must have been caused by real wages being too high, so decreasing them should be the remedy. Yet the economists' instincts told them that this was untrue, and the remedy lay in state-induced demand activation. Keynes's book aimed at solving this contradiction by providing a theoretical basis for the economists' gut feelings. The proposed path was to generalize Marshallian theory, which was exclusively concerned with partial equilibrium analysis, so as to enable it to address issues related to interdependency across markets. Keynes's hunch was that unemployment was due to deficient aggregate demand, the cause of which had its roots in the money market or finance.

Keynes's book was kaleidoscopic, mingling several threads of reasoning. Its central message was clarified when three young economists—James Meade (1907–1995), Roy Harrod (1900–1978), and John Hicks (1904–1989)—presented their interpretations of Keynes's book at the European meeting of the Econometric Society in Oxford in September 1936 (see Young [1987] for a vivid account of the event). Of the three papers, Hicks's (1937) came to prominence. It contained the first version of what was to become the IS-LM model. Hicks succeeded in transforming Keynes's convoluted reasoning into a simple system of simultaneous equations comprehensible to working economists. Hicks's paper also included an ingenious graph, allowing the outcome of two distinct markets to be represented in one simple two-dimensional diagram. At the time, Hicks could not have imagined the success his model would later encounter. In effect, it became the organizing theoretical apparatus of the emerging discipline of macroeconomics, in spite of the fact that its ability to capture the central message of the *General Theory* has been questioned by several interpreters of Keynes's work. Hicks's original diagram is shown in Figure 1.

This diagram resembles the Marshallian scissorlike representation of the matching of supply and demand in a given market, but its content is totally different. First, it

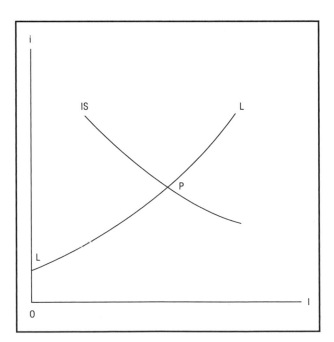

Figure 1

docs not relate to a single market. Second, the two functions it displays are not supply and demand. Instead, it sets the interest rate on the vertical axis, and the aggregate nominal income on the horizontal axis. The downward-sloping IS curve is the combination of income (I, to become Y in the subsequent literature) and the interest rate (r), for which investment (a function of interest rates) and saving (a function of income) are equal. It is assumed that investment varies inversely with the rate of interest and that saving increases with income. Higher income implies higher saving. As a result, in order for investment to equal saving, the rate of interest must be lower. This explains the inverse relationship between income and the interest rate. The upward-sloping LL curve represents the combination of income and the interest rate that keeps the demand for and the supply of money equal. In the money market, a given supply of money faces a demand for money, which is a function of income and the interest rate. As income increases, the transaction demand for money increases. The other component of the demand for money is *liquidity preference*. Holding money entails the opportunity cost of foregoing interest on bonds. Hence, the higher the interest rate, the lower this second component of the demand for money. Assuming a fixed supply of money, an increase in income involves a higher transaction demand for money. In order for the total demand for and supply of money to match, the liquidity preference part of the total demand must decrease. This requires a higher interest rate. Hence the upward slope of the LL curve.

Hicks located the essential difference between Keynes and the classical economists in the shape of the LL curve. According to Hicks, Keynes's system becomes "completely out of touch with the classical world" (1937, p. 154) whenever the LL curve exhibits a horizontal section with the IS and the LL curves intersecting on this section. In this situation, which came to be called the *liquidity trap*, monetary expansion—unlike fiscal policy—is unable to increase employment.

FROM HICKS'S IS-LL MODEL TO THE TEXTBOOK IS-LM MODEL

Hicks's model was not to become the canonical IS-LM model. Franco Modigliani (1918–2003) was the economist responsible for the transition from the Hicks's model to the IS-LM formulation (Modigliani 1944). Another influential economist in this move was Alvin Hansen (1887–1975) (1949, 1953). While dismissing the role of liquidity preference, Modigliani argued that a Keynesian outcome was sure to arise whenever two factors were jointly present: a particular shape of the labor supply curve (supposed to capture the sociological elements that affected the labor supply) and some form of money disturbance, in particular, an insufficient quantity of money. In this recasting, the classical and the Keynesian submodels become more sharply opposed than they had been in Hicks's original paper (see De Vroey 2000). The classical model now featured flexible wages and generalized market clearing, the Keynesian model's downward-rigid wages, and (possibly) involuntary unemployment. According to Modigliani, the Keynesian model is characterized less by a lack of investment than by a maladjustment between the quantity of money and the money wage, the latter being too high relative to the quantity of money. The proper remedy for this situation is an increase in the money supply.

For some twenty-five years after the end of World War II (1939–1945), the IS-LM model dominated macroeconomics. By degrees, standard textbooks adopted the IS-LM model as their framework. It was enriched in various ways by the consideration of open economies, the integration of the Phillips curve, and attempts at giving microfoundations to the consumption function, portfolio decisions, and investment schedules. The success of the IS-LM model can also be explained by its adaptability to econometric modeling.

As the model became more dominant theoretically, it lost its Keynesian character with respect to practical policy issues. That is, non-Keynesians could simply state that only its classical variant was valid, its Keynesian variant being flawed by its ad hoc assumption of rigid wages. Thus, friends and foes of Keynes alike could use the model to promote or refute Keynesian policy prescriptions.

There are several reasons for the success of the IS-LM model. First, it made Keynes's theory tractable. Second, it provided a simplified account of interdependency across markets, allowing the interrelationships between fundamental macroeconomic variables such as income, interest rate, saving, investment, and the supply and demand for money to be studied. Third, the model prompts interesting comparative statics exercises. For example, an increase in the propensity to invest shifts the IS curve to the right, and an increase in the money supply moves the LM curve to the right. Fourth and finally, it has proven to be resilient in the face of criticism.

THE DEMISE OF THE IS-LM MODEL

In the 1970s the dominance of the IS-LM model was strongly challenged as part of a broader offensive against Keynesian theory led by new classical economists, such as Robert E. Lucas and Thomas Sargent. The model's demise accompanied the dethroning of Keynesian macroeconomics, centered on the study of unemployment, and its replacement by dynamic stochastic Walrasian macroeconomics in which the issue of unemployment has only a minor place.

Flaws in the IS-LM model that had until then been overlooked were now fully exposed: the sloppy microfoundations of the model, its lack of consideration for expectations, its lack of connection with long-period analysis, and the inability of macroeconometric models to guide the choice between alternative economic policies.

However, the IS-LM model lives on. While no longer central to the graduate training of most macroeconomists or to cutting-edge macroeconomic research, it continues to be a mainstay of undergraduate textbooks, finds wide application in areas of applied macroeconomics away from the front lines of macroeconomic theory, and lies at the conceptual core of most governmental and commercial macroeconometric models.

SEE ALSO *Hicks, John R.; Keynes, John Maynard; Macroeconomics; Mundell-Fleming Model*

BIBLIOGRAPHY

De Vroey, Michel. 2000. IS-LM "à la Hicks" versus IS-LM "à la Modigliani." *History of Political Economy* 32: 293–316.

Hansen, Alvin. 1949. *Monetary Theory and Fiscal Policy.* New York: McGraw-Hill.

Hansen, Alvin. 1953. *A Guide to Keynes.* New York: McGraw-Hill.

Hicks, John. 1937. Mr. Keynes and the "Classics." *Econometrica* 5: 147–159.

Keynes, John Maynard. 1936. *The General Theory of Employment, Interest, and Money.* London: Macmillan.

Modigliani, Franco. 1944. Liquidity Preference and the Theory of Interest and Money. *Econometrica* 12: 44–88.

Young, Warren. 1987. *Interpreting Mr. Keynes: The IS-LM Enigma.* London: Polity.

Michel De Vroey

IS-LM-BP MODEL

SEE *Mundell-Fleming Model.*

ISOLATIONISM

Isolationism can be defined as a state's deliberate policy of extensive withdrawal and seclusion from some forms of interaction in the international system. Notable examples include the economic isolationism of Japan and China before the nineteenth century and the cultural isolationism of China and the Soviet Union in parts of the twentieth century. In the U.S. context, isolationism has constituted one of the principle foreign policy grand strategies from the founding of the country up to the present day.

EARLY U.S. ISOLATIONISM

From the United States' inception, isolationists such as George Washington have argued for the benefits of avoiding wars and "entangling alliances" with other great powers at all costs. Military commitments and involvement in the affairs of such states bleed the country of its prosperity. Precious money is wasted on armaments that often antagonize foreign nations. Democratic principles are sometimes suspended and sacrificed in the effort to fight wars. And the United States is unnecessarily distracted from more pressing objectives. "Keep the ships at home," said Thomas Jefferson (1743–1826), "and we will have fewer reasons to fight." It was such philosophies that helped keep the United States out of war with European states for most of the eighteenth and nineteenth centuries. Apart from the United States' relatively minor involvement in the Napoleonic Wars against France from 1798 to 1801, the only war that was fought with a European power was the War of 1812 against the British. Isolationist policies freed America to focus on territorial expansionism in North America, interventionism in Asia and Latin America, and economic activism throughout the globe.

While it is true that U.S. isolationism was assisted by its geographic separation from Europe by the Atlantic Ocean, as Walter Lippman describes in *U.S. Foreign Policy: Shield of the Republic* (1943), U.S. security during most of the nineteenth century was safeguarded more through a shrewd, unwritten 1823 alliance with Great Britain and the British-led balance of power in Europe than through its geography. Because of Britain's naval dominance of the approaches from Europe to the Western Hemisphere, Britain was the only force that in theory posed a significant threat to the United States. From the perspective of the British, such an alliance had the advantages of freeing much of its navy to police more critical regions than the Western Hemisphere and to preserve its dominion of Canada from U.S. messianic visions of continental annexation.

When the British-led European balance of power unraveled at the end of the nineteenth century, isolationists nevertheless persisted with the false assumption that the United States was still secure. To avoid a creeping U.S. allegiance to any side in Europe, Congress enacted the Neutrality Acts of 1934 and 1936, which forbade the sale of war matériel to belligerent states. German efforts to dominate Europe during World Wars I and II and Soviet expansionism after World War II nevertheless shattered the illusion of geographic invulnerability. U.S. leaders realized that a single power, such as Germany or the Soviet Union, or a hostile alliance of powers, in control of most of Eurasian military and industrial power, could pose a potentially superior threat. Therefore, the possibility of an unfriendly balance of power against the United States justified a policy of military "preponderance" rather than isolationism (Layne 1997, pp. 88–97).

COLD WAR

When the cold war became the dominant focus of U.S. policymakers, isolationism returned as one among a number of realist strategies, including containment and rollback, which were designed to secure U.S. interests when faced with a menacing Soviet Union. Proponents of cold war isolationism, such as Robert A. Tucker (1972), departed from some of the traditional isolationist arguments. Tucker conceded that isolationism had previously failed to take into account the necessity of having allies. Allies tipped the world balance of power in the United States' favor by helping to preclude the emergence of a threatening Eurasian hegemon.

Tucker (1972), however, argued that with nuclear weapons powerful allies in Western Europe or elsewhere were no longer necessary. The threat of mutually assured nuclear destruction made concerns about a balance of power irrelevant. Even if the Soviet Union were to somehow conquer Western Europe, Soviet control of the European military-industrial complexes would do little to add to the existing threat posed by a Soviet nuclear first-strike from submarine-based nuclear missiles. In the new nuclear-armed world, the United States was safe from direct Soviet threat because of the deterrent effect of an assured U.S. nuclear counterstrike, not by whether U.S. allies were safe.

Furthermore, it was argued that an isolationist foreign policy is completely compatible with fulfilling an activist U.S. economic agenda abroad since market forces provide the incentives for trade rather than alliances or physical control. For example, even hostile states will be eager over the long run to sell their oil and other goods to the United States—let alone friendly and developed states—whose economies frequently have more to lose through a loss of U.S. trade than the U.S. economic colossus has with respect to them. And with the complete withdrawal of U.S. military commitments from Asia and Europe, those regions will be physically secure from an economically devastating attack, because states such as Germany and Japan would acquire their own nuclear capabilities.

POST–COLD WAR

While the term *isolationism* may not be so popular today, the assumptions, goals, and remedies that the isolationist concept provides continue to be attractive to many. Modern-day versions of isolationist foreign policy are variously referred to as "disengagement," "benign detachment," "policy of restraint," "offshore balancing," and "Jeffersonian policy." Post–cold war isolationists build on the aforementioned cold war arguments. They continue to stress the great costs and dangers of a forwardly engaged military with bases and troops across the globe. Such militarism, they argue, incites terrorism, creates incentives for nuclear proliferation, needlessly wastes money when the United States would be secure anyway, and tends to "turn allies into neutrals and neutrals into enemies" (Gholz, Press, and Sapolsky 1997, p. 37). Like their predecessors, modern isolationists nevertheless agree with limited military engagement. They are in favor of a strong (although significantly reduced) military to fight piracy, defend the homeland, and to ensure the safety of commerce. They believe in maintaining a considerable nuclear deterrent. And they support firm U.S. retaliation in the event of attack. Isolationists, however, continue to be criticized. Critics are uncomfortable with trusting other states to a multipolar balance of power based on nuclear weapons. As the Cuban missile crisis showed, brinksmanship and near misses are still possible even with nuclear weapons. Still, others criticize the isolationists for being immoral and irresponsible in their strong reluctance to forcefully prevent wars, humanitarian emergencies, and genocide. They are also criticized for being careless in protecting U.S. economic interests abroad in the event of future regional conflicts.

SEE ALSO *Public Policy*

BIBLIOGRAPHY

Art, Robert J. 2003. *A Grand Strategy for America*. Ithaca, NY: Cornell University Press.

Bandow, Doug. 1994. Keeping the Troops and the Money at Home. *Current History* 93, no. 579: 8–13.

Fensterwald, Bernard. 1958. The Anatomy of American "Isolationism" and Expansionism. Part I. *Journal of Conflict Resolution* 2, no. 2: 111–139.

Gholz, Eugene, Daryl G. Press, and Harvey M. Sapolsky. 1997. Come Home, America: The Strategy of Restraint in the Face of Temptation. *International Security* 21, no. 45–48.

Layne, Christopher. 1997. From Preponderance to Offshore Balancing: America's Future Grand Strategy. *International Security* 22, no. 1: 5–48.

Lippmann, Walter. 1943. *U.S. Foreign Policy: Shield of the Republic*. Boston: Little, Brown.

Mead, Walter Russell. 2001. *Special Providence: American Foreign Policy and How It Changed the World*. New York: Knopf.

Nordlinger, Eric A. 1995. *Isolationism Reconfigured: American Foreign Policy for a New Century*. Princeton, NJ: Princeton University Press.

Posen, Barry R., and Andrew L. Ross. 1995. Competing Visions for U.S. Grand Strategies. In *Strategy and Force Planning*, ed. Strategy and Force Planning Faculty, 115–134. Newport, RI: Naval War College Press.

Ravenal, Earl. 1991. The Case for Adjustment. *Foreign Policy* 81: 3–19.

Tucker, Robert W. 1972. *A New Isolationism: Threat or Promise?* New York: Universe.

David A. Rezvani

ITEM RESPONSE THEORY
SEE *Psychometrics.*

J

JACOBIAN MATRIX

The Jacobian matrix was developed by Carl Gustav Jacob Jacobi (1804–1851), a German Jewish mathematician. The Jacobian is a matrix whose entries are first-order partial derivatives defined as

$$\begin{matrix} \partial y_1 / \partial x_1 & \supset & \partial y_1 / \partial x_n \\ \vdots & \ddots & \vdots \\ \partial y_m / \partial x_1 & \supset & \partial y_m / \partial x_n, \end{matrix}$$

where the function is given by m real-valued component functions, $y_1(x_1, \ldots, x_n), \ldots, y_m(x_1, \ldots, x_n)$, continuous (smooth with no breaks or gaps) and differentiable (the derivative must exist at the point being evaluated). If $m = n$, then the Jacobian matrix is a square matrix. This matrix is denoted by $J_F(x_1, \ldots, x_n)$.

The interesting concept about the Jacobian is its determinant: Jacobian determinant, $|J|$. The analysis of the $|J|$ permits one to characterize the behavior of the function around a given point, which has uses in the social sciences.

First, $|J|$ is used to test functional dependence, linear and nonlinear, of a set of equations. If $|J| = 0$, the equations are functionally dependent. If $|J| > 0$, the equations are functionally independent. Note $|J|$ does not determine the functional relationship, linear or nonlinear. Second, if $|J|$ at a given point is different from zero, the function is invertible near that point, that is, an inverse function exists. Then the Jacobian determinant in conjunction with the implicit function theorem can be used to identify changes in an endogenous variable, which may be a choice or optimization variable, as an exogenous variable changes.

Unlike the Hessian matrix, the Jacobian can be used to analyze constrained-optimization problems. However, like the Hessian, calculating the $|J|$ becomes laborious as the dimensions of the matrix increase. In addition, the Jacobian is difficult to use with a nonlinear optimization problem, which produces a Jacobian matrix with elements that may not be constant.

SEE ALSO *Inverse Matrix; Matrix Algebra*

BIBLIOGRAPHY

Chiang, Alpha C., and Kevin Wainwright. 2005. *Fundamental Methods of Mathematical Economics*. 4th ed. Boston: McGraw-Hill/Irwin.

Dowling, Edward T. 2001. *Schaum's Outline of Theory and Problems of Introduction to Mathematical Economics*. 3rd ed. Boston: McGraw-Hill.

Fuente, Angel de la. 2000. *Mathematical Methods and Models for Economists*. New York: Cambridge University Press.

Jehle, Geoffrey A., and Philip J. Reny. 2001. *Advanced Microeconomic Theory*. 2nd ed. Boston: Addison-Wesley.

MacTutor History of Mathematics Archive. University of St. Andrews, Scotland. http://www-groups.dcs.st-and.ac.uk/~history/.

Silbergberg, Eugene, and Wing Suen. 2001. *The Structure of Economics: A Mathematical Analysis*. 3rd ed. Boston: McGraw-Hill/Irwin.

Simon, P. Carl, and Lawrence Blume. 1994. *Mathematics for Economists*. New York: Norton.

Varian, Hal R. 1992. *Microeconomic Analysis*. 3rd ed. New York: Norton.

Rhonda V. Sharpe
Idrissa A. Boly

JACOBINISM

The Jacobins, founded in 1789 by the Breton deputies to the National Assembly, were the most famous and powerful of the political clubs or societies of the French Revolution. Their official name was the Society of the Friends of the Constitution. They derived their popular name from the house on the Rue St. Jacques where they met in Paris. The bloodiest excesses of the Reign of Terror (1793–1794) can be attributed to their influence and activities. Jacobinism came to denote rabble-rousing radicalism.

Some of the most famous figures of the revolution, most notably Maximilien Robespierre (1758–1794), were members of this society. Many of its leaders served in prominent posts in the Directory of Public Safety that, following the overthrow of the monarchy, ruled France from 1793 to 1794. At first, only deputies, liberal aristocrats, and well-off bourgeois could afford to belong. However, after the reduction of its subscription rates, its ranks were open to the less well off: writers, small shopkeepers, and artisans. The expansion of its membership brought in members with more radical antimonarchical and anticlerical views.

Political clubs grew in popularity as the church and guilds declined. Hundreds of organizations similar to the Jacobin clubs were established from the 1780s to the reign of Napoleon Bonaparte (r. 1804–1815) when they were abolished. They performed many of the functions of a modern political party or party caucus where citizens could meet to discuss public issues, devise strategies, hear speakers, and send delegations to the National Assembly to lobby or threaten.

The mother club in Paris spawned a network of approximately 5,500 Jacobin "cells" in the provinces. These clubs served a variety of roles and functions. They were foremost agents for propaganda-disseminating newspapers, pamphlets, and circulars. As quasi-official units of government, the clubs promoted civic improvement. They held rallies and revolutionary festivals to arouse revolutionary passion and honor the heroes of the revolution. They also raised funds to assist the widows and orphans of victims of revolutionary wars and helped members find jobs. In addition, the clubs operated a spy network to keep an eye on local authorities and émigrés, refractory priests, and other suspected persons. During the Reign of Terror the Jacobins were especially vigilant denouncing persons and purging administrators suspected of antirevolutionary sympathies. Similar to the Communist Party under Vladimir Ilitch Lenin, they were the ideological and organizational heart of the revolution. Their highly centralized organization was held together by their implacable faith in equality and the revolution.

The Jacobins championed republican government, the rule of the people, the abolition of the hereditary aristocracy, popular education, separation of church and state, and universal manhood suffrage. Convinced that the unequal distribution of private goods would lead to political inequality, Robespierre favored fixed limits on the accumulation of wealth. Envisioning a nation of small property owners, however, he opposed the demand of the more radical *Enragés* for the nationalization of all property. The Jacobins, in their bourgeois phase, believed in laissez-faire economic policies and a qualified right to private property that would exclude émigrés and priests.

All people were created equal, they believed, because they are naturally good and virtuous. Tradition, custom, and religion were condemned as impediments to the attainment of universal equality. Social inequality would be eliminated by the spread of education and enlightened reason. Confident of their personal virtue, the Jacobins condemned their opponents as not only wrong but also evil. Moreover, this "band of the elect" felt obligated to root out political heresies and blasphemies.

As historian Crane Brinton (1961) points out, the Jacobins were mostly prosperous middle-class people who became religious fanatics. After the ascendancy of Robespierre, Jacobinism was transformed into a kind of quasi-religious cult. Robespierre saw himself as the prophet of a new civic religion. He envisioned a spiritual republic, a Republic of Virtue, rooted in "holy Equality and the sacred Rights of Man." Under his leadership a totalitarian dictatorship was created through the Committee of Public Safety. His religion of virtue would bring a new moral world and the regeneration of humanity. This creed also provided a moral justification for the Terror. Purity became a political fetish. Anyone who did not enthusiastically embrace the new faith was suspected of harboring antirevolutionary opinions and summarily condemned to the guillotine.

The end for the Jacobins came swiftly. As Robespierre's power grew, his popularity waned. The members of the National Convention, fearing that a new purge would be directed at them, declared him and his associates to be outlaws on July 27, 1794, and had them guillotined the following day. With the fall of Robespierre came the fall of the Jacobins.

The spirit of Jacobin ideas continued in a somewhat altered form in the Directory and later in the Revolution of 1848 and the Paris Commune of 1871. Some of the ideas of the Jacobins persist as a radical opposition to European and North American civilization. They gained a small victory in the Americas when their slogans of "liberty and equality" inspired the 1791 slave revolt in the French West India colony of San Domingo. Called "black Jacobins" by the black Marxist historian, C. L. R. James

(1938), Toussaint Louverture (1746–1803) and his followers successfully fought for the French Republic against the British, forcing them to withdraw from Haiti in 1798. In the early twenty-first century, some critics of American foreign policy believe that the neoconservative quest for global hegemony in the name of "human rights," "democracy," "freedom," "equality," and "capitalism" represents an extension of the Jacobin imagination.

SEE ALSO *French Revolution; Left and Right*

BIBLIOGRAPHY

Brinton, Crane. 1961. *The Jacobins: An Essay in the New History.* New York: Russell and Russell.

James, C. L. R. 1963. *The Black Jacobins.* New York: Vintage.

Matrat, Jean. 1975. *Robespierre: Or, the Tyranny of the Majority.* Trans. Alan Kendall, with Felix Brenner. New York: Scribner's.

Ryn, Claes G. 2003. *America the Virtuous: The Crisis of Democracy and the Quest for Empire.* New Brunswick, NJ: Transaction.

Schama, Simon. 1989. *Citizens: A Chronicle of the French Revolution.* New York: Knopf.

W. Wesley McDonald

JACOBS, JANE
1916–2006

Jane Jacobs was an original American social thinker whose books challenged mainstream views on urban planning and socioeconomic development. Devoid of any professional training, she used her own observations to develop an evolutionary perspective on cities, economy, and society. Jacobs was against social engineering, one-size-fits-all strategies, and big plans; instead, she stressed the importance of the human measure, diversity, and small-scale initiatives for development.

On May 4, 1916, Jacobs was born as Jane Butzner in Scranton, Pennsylvania, where her father was a family doctor. Shortly after graduating from high school she went to New York City and accepted all kinds of writing jobs. In the periods when she was unemployed, Jacobs took long city walks that gave her a notion of what was going on in urban and business life. In 1944 she married the architect Robert Jacobs, with whom she had three children. From 1952 to 1962 Jacobs worked as an associate editor of *Architectural Forum;* thereafter she was regularly involved in neighborhood activism to oppose urban renewal in New York. In 1969 Jacobs moved with her family to Toronto, where she lived and wrote until her death on April 25, 2006.

Jacobs's most significant works can be divided in two periods. In the first phase (Jacobs Mark I) she published three books on cities. In *The Death and Life of Great American Cities* (1961) Jacobs portrayed urban life as a "sidewalk ballet" that is served best by diverse, mixed, and densely populated neighborhoods with short building blocks. In *The Economy of Cities* (1969) and *Cities and the Wealth of Nations* (1984) Jacobs used urban history and archaeology to show that cities always have been the driving force behind economic development. In the second phase (Jacobs Mark II) Jacobs shifted her attention to socioeconomic issues. *Systems of Survival* (1992) focused on the moral differences between people working in commerce ("traders") and politics ("guardians"), whereas *The Nature of Economies* (2000) dealt with the similarities between the economy and the ecosystem ("biomimicry"); both books were written in the form of a dialogue between fictional New Yorkers. In her last book, *Dark Age Ahead* (2004), Jacobs warned that the decay of fundamental societal pillars (e.g., family and education) might lead to the deterioration of western civilization.

Undoubtedly, *The Death and Life of Great American Cities* was Jacobs's most influential work. Her strong critique that traditional urban renewal policy only destroyed communities shocked planners and established Jacobs's reputation as a radical thinker. Her writing style has been called "urban montage" (like snapshots of real city life) and thus is often dismissed as unscientific. Indeed, her analyses are rather anecdotal, unsystematic, and subjective, but that is exactly where their power lies: Unhindered by mainstream thinking, Jacobs could approach urban and socioeconomic issues in a relatively unbiased manner. Therefore it is not so much for the scientific analysis that Jane Jacobs's books still deserve a wide read, but for the provocative and original insights they provide.

BIBLIOGRAPHY

PRIMARY WORKS

Jacobs, Jane. 1961. *The Death and Life of Great American Cities.* New York: Vintage.

Jacobs, Jane. 1969. *The Economy of Cities.* New York: Random House.

Jacobs, Jane. 1984. *Cities and the Wealth of Nations.* New York: Random House.

Jacobs, Jane. 1992. *Systems of Survival: A Dialogue on the Moral Foundations of Commerce and Politics.* New York: Random House.

Jacobs, Jane. 2000. *The Nature of Economies.* New York: Random House.

Jacobs, Jane. 2004. *Dark Age Ahead.* Toronto: Random House.

SECONDARY WORKS

Allen, Max, ed. 1997. *Ideas That Matter: The Worlds of Jane Jacobs.* Owen Sound: Ginger Press.

Alexiou, Alice Sparberg. 2006. *Jane Jacobs: Urban Visionary.* Toronto: Harper Collins Publishers.

Hospers, Gert-Jan. 2006. Jane Jacobs: Her Life and Work. *European Planning Studies* 14: 723-732.

Gert-Jan Hospers

JAINISM

Currently numbering only about 4.2 million (according to the 2001 census of India), the Jains are an ancient religious community of India. They are basically an urban community, and their largest numbers are found in the Indian states of Gujarat, Karnataka, Madhya Pradesh, Maharashtra, and Rajasthan. Trade is the traditional occupation of Jains, and they are extremely prominent among India's merchants, especially in the country's north and west. Contrary to stereotype, not all Jains are rich traders, but many are, with the result that Jains have achieved a degree of economic and political influence in modern India disproportionate to their relative smallness as a community.

The Jains themselves believe their religion to be eternal and thus uncreated. They maintain that it is merely rediscovered by omniscient teachers known as *Tirthankaras* (fordmakers) or *Jinas* (victors), that it is something that has already occurred, and will continue to occur an infinity of times, because time itself is beginningless and endless. Modern scholarship, however, traces the origin of Jainism to Lord Mahavira, a genuine historical figure whom Jains consider to be the most recent of the *Tirthankaras* to have appeared in our region of the universe. Mahavira's date and place of birth are not certain, although tradition maintains that he was born in 599 B.C.E. in a city called Kundagrama in the Ganges basin near modern-day Patna. It is possible that Mahavira was influenced by the teachings of an earlier figure named Parshva, the only other *Tirthankara* considered a historical figure by scholars.

Mahavira lived and taught during a period of rapid social change and urbanization in which the Vedic orthodoxy promoted by the Brahman priesthood of those days faced powerful challenges. Wandering ascetics were preaching new religions that devalued Vedic ritualism and emphasized instead the centrality of the individual salvation seeker who renounces the world. Of the nonorthodox traditions that emerged at that time, only two survive as living religions, Jainism and Buddhism, and of these, only Jainism survived in India. As did the other dissenting traditions, Jainism seems to have found special favor among newly emerging urban classes, especially the urban nobility and the merchant class. Merchants (as well as wander-

ing mendicants) played a key role in the spread of Jainism from the Ganges basin to other regions, and royal patronage was an important factor in establishing Jainism in the south.

A major disagreement emerged early in Jainism's history over the question of whether Jain monks should wear clothing, and the dispute crystallized into a schism in the fifth century C.E. Monks and nuns belonging to the Shvetambara ("white clad") sect wear white garments; monks (not nuns) belonging to the sect known as Digambara ("space clad") are nude. The divide between the Digambaras and Shvetambaras has been deep and lasting, and is the principal sectarian divide in Jainism today, with further subsectarian divisions on either side. The Digambaras are especially prominent in South India, with the Shvetambaras strongest in the northwestern states of Gujarat and Rajasthan.

The Jains maintain that the cosmos contains an infinite number of souls (*jivas*) that do not perish when the body dies, but are reborn in other bodies. Each soul recycles unceasingly, finding rebirth—as determined by its behavior in life—as humans, denizens of hell, deities, animals and plants, and even as primitive life forms inhabiting inanimate objects and substances. The cosmos is a vast structure with multiple heavens above and hells below, separated by a small zone where human life is found. Even the gods in the heavens, however, are caught in the same cycle of death and rebirth as all of the other creatures of the cosmos. Indeed, the Jains maintain that because the cosmos was uncreated and will never cease to be, all souls have already inhabited all possible bodies an infinite number of times, and will do so an infinite number of times to come unless liberated from the cycle, which is the ultimate goal of Jain religious life.

The Jains say that *karma* is the cause of the soul's bondage to the cycle of death and rebirth. In contrast to other Indic traditions, the Jains consider karma to be an actual material substance that accumulates as an encrustation on the soul as a result of its actions. To attain liberation, therefore, one must bring the accumulation of additional karmic material to a stop and rid one's soul of past accumulations. Because violent action is a potent cause of karmic influx, nonviolence (*ahimsa*) is a key strategy in the pursuit of liberation and is the foundation of Jain ethics. However, the attainment of liberation also requires the eradication of already accreted karmic matter. Ascetic practice, for which the Jains are justly famous, is said to "burn away" karmic accumulations, and is a conspicuous feature of Jain life. Once liberated, the soul rises to the apex of the cosmos, where it remains for all eternity in a state of isolated and omniscient bliss.

Jain tradition divides the Jain social order into four components: laymen and laywomen and monks and nuns. The monks and nuns constitute a small and peripatetic mendicant elite, and although all Jains are supposed to aspire to liberation, the mendicants are viewed as more directly on liberation's path than are the laity. The mendicants' daily conduct is governed by five "great vows" (*mahavratas*): (1) nonviolence (*ahimsa*), (2) truthfulness, (3) not stealing, (4) celibacy, and (5) nonpossession. All five vows leave a deep imprint on mendicant life, but especially notable are the first and fifth. The vow of nonviolence is the foundation for much of the distinctive character of Jain mendicants' day-to-day life, which is organized around the need to avoid violence even to microscopic forms of life. For example, they carry special brooms with which to clear living things from surfaces on which they intend to sit or lie, and in some subsects wear masks over their mouths to prevent their hot breath from harming microscopic life forms in the air. The vow of nonpossession cements the lay and mendicant communities into a single social order by ensuring that the mendicants are totally dependent on the laity for their most basic needs, including nourishment, which must be sought from lay households on a daily basis.

Although Jainism was once a proselytizing religion, recruitment today is by birth, and most Jains belong to merchant castes that are Jain or partly Jain in composition. Lay religious life centers on support of mendicants, ascetic practices (especially fasting), observance of Jain calendrical rites, and—in those subsects that permit it—worship of the *Tirthankaras'* images in temples. By comparison with the mendicants, the requirement of nonviolence is relaxed for laity, but there are normative minima applying to all lay Jains, and of these, strict vegetarianism is the most essential. Laity do the work of the world and support the mendicant elite, with the result that the mendicants are insulated from the negative effects of the violence that is an inevitable requirement of making a living, food preparation, and simply living in the workaday world. Laymen and laywomen, in turn, benefit from the mendicants' teaching and from the worldly and spiritual rewards of the merit generated by supporting them.

SEE ALSO *Hinduism; Religion*

BIBLIOGRAPHY

Babb, Lawrence A. 1996. *Absent Lord: Ascetics and Kings in a Jain Ritual Culture.* Berkeley: University of California Press.

Cort, John E. 2001. *Jains in the World: Religious Values and Ideology in India.* New York: Oxford University Press.

Dundas, Paul. 2002. *The Jains.* 2nd ed. London: Routledge.

Jaini, Padmanabh S. 1979. *The Jaina Path of Purification.* Berkeley: University of California Press.

Lawrence A. Babb

JAJMANI MATRIX

In two papers published in 1991 and 2004, James G. Scoville analyzed the traditional Indian caste system using a matrix algebra format. Matrix algebra provides a simple way of expressing and analyzing large sets of equations involving numerous variables.

In these papers, Scoville employed a conceptual device called the Jajmani matrix. This matrix, denoted J, has as its elements the flows of goods or services produced by a household of one caste to households of other castes (as well as to itself). Thus, a farming household provides foodstuffs to the carpenter household based on a reciprocal flow of carpentry services; a barber provides haircuts to the washerman based on a reciprocal flow of laundry services. In practice, these transactions are highly complex, but J abstracts from all that complexity and measures (in theory) flows between typical households.

The system of reciprocal flows described is called the jajman system, from the Hindi word for patron. Hence the descriptive adjective is applied to the matrix: *Jajmani.*

The conceptual utility of the Jajmani matrix is to serve as a key tool in a social accounting framework for the exchange relations associated with the occupational hierarchy of the Hindu caste system. These output and income flows are built into an essentially classical economic model of the traditional Indian caste system. This accounting framework shows the flow of goods and services to a particular caste; one can then compare those flows with some vector of basic needs to see if those needs are met. If there is a surplus, a classical economist might expect that caste's population to grow; a shortfall would cause that caste's population to shrink. The mechanism by which caste populations adjust to surpluses or shortages compared to needs is argued to be through changes of marriage rules (age of marriage, number of children, widow remarriage practices). Scoville found some support for the predicted population effects in Indian Census data, and outlined these findings in his 2004 paper.

SEE ALSO *Caste; Hierarchy; Inequality, Political; Stratification*

BIBLIOGRAPHY

Scoville, James G. 1991. Toward a Model of a Caste Labor Market. In *Status Influences in Third World Labor Markets: Caste, Gender and Custom,* ed. James G. Scoville. Berlin: Walter de Gruyter.

Scoville, James G. 2004. Discarding Facts: The Economics of Caste. *Review of Development Economics* 7 (August): 3.

James G. Scoville

JAMES, C. L. R.
1901–1989

Cyril Lionel Robert James was born and raised in Trinidad but spent most of his adult life in Britain and the United States. A gifted essayist and speaker, he wrote with great insight on Shakespeare, Melville, Hegel, Athenian democracy, slavery, the Soviet Union, black nationalism, calypso, and cricket. His novel *Minty Alley* (1936) signaled the emergence of a West Indian literary voice, while *Beyond a Boundary* (1963) fused autobiography, sports history, and area studies. He penned a critical study of Soviet foreign policy, *World Revolution 1917–1936: The Rise and Fall of the Communist International* (1937), followed by *The Black Jacobins: Toussaint L'Ouverture and the San Domingo Revolution* (1938), which brought a comparative perspective to the study of the French and Haitian revolutions. James explored U.S. culture and history in *American Civilization* (1950), and lauded a major novelist in *Mariners, Renegades, and Castaways: Herman Melville and the World We Live In* (1953). In *Modern Politics* (1960), he applied Enlightenment ideals to West Indian conditions, while *Party Politics in the West Indies* (1962) leveled a blistering critique of Trinidad's independence movement. James wrote on West Africa in *Kwame Nkrumah and the Ghana Revolution* (1977). In his final years, he oversaw the publication of three volumes of selected writings, a single-volume reader, and a collection of essays on cricket. In 1988 he was awarded the Trinity Cross, Trinidad and Tobago's highest national honor.

C. L. R. James embraced Marxism in the mid-1930s, while living in England. He threw himself into political activity and was widely known on the Left for his simultaneous advocacy of socialism and Pan-Africanism. Prior to leaving for the United States in 1938, James edited a Trotskyist newspaper, *Fight*, and the journal of the International African Service Bureau, *International African Opinion*. In the United States in the 1940s he collaborated with a small circle of co-thinkers, the Johnson-Forest Tendency, which staked out an independent radical praxis that characterized the Soviet Union as "state capitalist" and emphasized the creative role of blacks, women, young people, and workers in the making of a "new society." ("Johnson" was the "party name" for C. L. R. James, while "Forest" was Raya Dunayevskaya, a Russian-born intellectual.) The group produced boldly argued texts on topics ranging from the 1956 Hungarian uprising to Marx's early writings. While the tendency never numbered more than one hundred members, its ideas prefigured certain New Left positions of the 1960s and 1970s.

James was apprehended by the U.S. immigration authorities in 1952 and expelled the following year. After that, he mainly resided in Britain, although he traveled widely in continental Europe, Africa, and the Caribbean. In the late 1950s and early 1960s he spent nearly four years in Trinidad, playing a high-profile role in the transition to independence. For eighteen months he edited the newspaper of the People's National Movement (PNM), at the invitation of his old friend and former pupil, Eric Williams, whose landmark *Capitalism and Slavery* (1944) drew on *The Black Jacobins* and benefited from James's comments on successive drafts. James's relationship with Williams and other PNM leaders soured as a result of differences over foreign relations and party-building. James left Trinidad on the eve of formal independence, and when he returned in 1965, Williams placed him under house arrest as a dangerous subversive. After his release, James founded the Workers and Farmers Party (WFP) as an electoral challenge to Williams's rule. The WFP performed poorly in the 1966 elections, and James flew back to Britain.

Since the mid-1990s, there has been an outpouring of scholarship on James's life and work. Some scholars have focused on retrieving biographical information, and making available unpublished or neglected writings, while others have explored James's contributions to literary criticism, scholarship on Hegel, cultural studies, and postcolonial studies. A number of authors have emphasized his role as an observer of cultural and historical change; others have focused on his relationship to left politics and historical materialism. Along with Antonio Gramsci, James offers an example of a twentieth-century Marxist whose reputation has risen after the collapse of Soviet Communism. The fact that his name is embedded in the West Indian cultural firmament speaks to the multifaceted character of his complex legacy. There are few modern writers of note who ranged as widely and creatively as C. L. R. James did across the humanities and social sciences.

SEE ALSO *Black Nationalism; Caribbean, The; Haitian Revolution; Marxism*

BIBLIOGRAPHY

Buhle, Paul. 1989. *C. L. R. James: The Artist as Revolutionary.* London: Verso.

Cudjoe, Selwyn R., and William E. Cain, eds. 1995. *C. L. R. James: His Intellectual Legacies.* Amherst: University of Massachusetts Press.

Grimshaw, Anna, ed. 1992. *The C. L. R. James Reader.* Oxford: Blackwell.

Worcester, Kent. 1996. *C. L. R. James: A Political Biography.* Albany: State University of New York Press.

Kenton W. Worcester

JAMES, SHERMAN

SEE *John Henryism.*

JAMES, WILLIAM
1842–1910

William James was born in New York City on January 11, 1842, and died in Chocurua, New Hampshire, on August 26, 1910. He was one of the most important and influential American thinkers of the late nineteenth century and early twentieth century and is particularly known for his contributions to the growth of psychology as a scientific field of study and to the school of philosophy known as pragmatism.

CONTRIBUTIONS TO PSYCHOLOGY

James came from a distinguished family. His father, Henry James Sr. (1811–1882), was a philosopher and author in his own right and a close friend of Ralph Waldo Emerson (1803–1882). His younger brother, Henry James Jr. (1843–1916), became a highly regarded novelist and literary figure. In his early years William James experienced a crisis in deciding on a career. He briefly studied art and painting but was convinced by his father to pursue scientific studies instead. While attending Harvard Medical School in the mid-1860s, James spent a year traveling and studying in Germany, and it was during this time that he was exposed to the research being done in that country on the relationship between physiology and psychology, a direction that would lay the groundwork for the emergence of psychology as a scientific discipline.

After returning to Harvard and completing his medical degree, James joined the Harvard faculty in the early 1870s. He served first as an instructor of anatomy and physiology, and then in 1875 began offering a course in psychology based on the ideas he had encountered in Germany. In the same year he established at Boylston Hall one of the first experimental laboratories for psychological research. Among his important early contributions to the field of psychology was his formulation, simultaneous with that of the Danish psychologist Carl Lange (1834–1900), of the James-Lange theory of emotion, which argues that emotion follows, rather than precedes, physiological stimulus. He continued to focus on the study of psychology throughout the 1880s and in 1890 published his great, two-volume work *The Principles of Psychology.* The work, which had taken him twelve years to write, gained him an international reputation and stands as a landmark in the development of psychology as a scientific field of study.

JAMES AND PRAGMATISM

James's approach to psychology was based on what he later called (in the preface to *The Will to Believe,* 1897) "radical empiricism." In this view, human consciousness resembles a flowing stream of undifferentiated objects or data out of which the mind selects specific items, by virtue of personal interest or need, on which to focus its attention. This theory of the mind, and especially its epistemological implications, led James increasingly to the study of philosophy, in which he first offered courses at Harvard in the 1880s, and in particular to the philosophical ideas of pragmatism.

During his earliest days as a teacher at Harvard, James had been part of a group known as the Metaphysical Club that included among its members Charles Sanders Peirce (1839–1914), considered to be the founder of pragmatic philosophy. After the publication of *Principles of Psychology* in 1890, as James turned more to the investigation of philosophical and epistemological questions in his work, Peirce's ideas influenced his direction. The root assumption of pragmatic epistemology is that theoretical ideas ought to be judged in terms of their practical consequences—if some real benefit accrues from holding a particular idea, then it is valuable; if there is no discernable benefit, it can be discarded. In this view, truth should never be viewed as wholly complete or absolute, because one must be prepared to adjust it to accommodate new information and new understandings.

Although James's best-known discussion of pragmatism appears in the essay collection *Pragmatism: A New Name for Some Old Ways of Thinking* (1907), an earlier collection, *The Will to Believe, and Other Essays in Popular Philosophy* (1897), also offers a good expression of his thought. As these titles suggest, James was by no means strictly an academic philosopher but instead sought to make his ideas accessible to a general audience. To this end his essays, often written originally as public lectures, are both interesting and highly readable, and he demonstrates a particular skill in using examples drawn from everyday life. In one of his best known short essays, "What Pragmatism Means" (in *Pragmatism*), he begins with a story about a group of individuals on a camping trip arguing over the position of a squirrel on a tree and then uses this incident as a way to discuss the pragmatic approach to truth. James also felt strongly that philosophy ought to address the significant social and moral issues of the times. In his essay "The Moral Equivalent of War," based on a talk he gave at Stanford University in 1906, James argued for a form of organized national service that anticipated the Civilian Conservation Corps in the 1930s as well as later programs such as VISTA and AmeriCorps.

Pragmatism is sometimes seen as a philosophy that destroys any hope of discovering absolute truth and that leads, through its emphasis on "usefulness" as a primary criterion for establishing truth, to moral relativism. James to some degree anticipated these concerns in his work. Pragmatic epistemology, in his view, remains open to the introduction of new information, especially information resulting from new scientific discoveries, and his application of pragmatic principles to the questions of ethics and even to religion led him to hold highly traditional views on both. In essays such as "The Will to Believe" and "Reflex Action and Theism" (in *The Will to Believe*) and "Pragmatism and Religion" (in *Pragmatism*) he set forth the reasons for believing in a theistic God. In fact the study of religion was a matter of considerable importance to James, and his wide-ranging study of religious experience, *The Varieties of Religious Experience* (1902), made a significant contribution to the study of comparative religion.

JAMES'S LONG-TERM SIGNIFICANCE

James's ideas were extremely significant. They influenced a generation of thinkers who followed him, most notably the great philosopher-educator John Dewey (1859–1952), and they played a role in forming the underlying mind-set—of social experimentation and reform—that characterized the Progressive (1900–1917) and New Deal (1933–1939) periods in U.S. history.

SEE ALSO *Emotion; Empiricism; Epistemology; Functionalism; National Service Programs; New Deal, The; Philosophy; Pragmatism; Progressive Movement; Psychology; Religion; Stream of Consciousness; Theory of Mind*

BIBLIOGRAPHY

PRIMARY WORKS

James, William. 1890. *The Principles of Psychology.* 2 vols. New York: Henry Holt.

James, William. 1897. *The Will to Believe, and Other Essays in Popular Philosophy.* New York: Longmans, Green.

James, William. 1902. *The Varieties of Religious Experience: A Study in Human Nature.* New York: Modern Library.

James, William. 1907. *Pragmatism: A New Name for Some Old Ways of Thinking.* New York: Longmans, Green.

SECONDARY WORKS

Corkin, George. 1990. *William James, Public Philosopher.* Baltimore, MD: Johns Hopkins University Press.

Crunden, Robert M. 1994. From Anti-Social Darwinism to Pragmatism, 1865–1917. In *A Brief History of American Culture,* vol. 8, 144–158. New York: Paragon House.

Donnelly, Margaret E., ed. 1992. *Reinterpreting the Legacy of William James.* Washington, DC: American Psychological Association.

Putnam, Ruth Anna, ed. 1997. *The Cambridge Companion to William James.* Cambridge, U.K.: Cambridge University Press.

Simon, Linda. 1998. *Genuine Reality: A Life of William James.* New York: Harcourt Brace.

Scott Wright

JANATA PARTY

India's Janata Party grew out of the tumultuous political conditions of the 1970s. Following India's military success in East Pakistan in 1971, leading to the independence of Bangladesh, the architect of this victory, Prime Minister Indira Gandhi (1917–1984), led the Congress Party to an overwhelming political victory in the March 1971 national elections. The Congress Party gained two-thirds of the seats in the lower house of parliament, the Lok Sabha. Thereafter, there were accusations of political corruption against Gandhi, arising initially from the charge that she had illegally used the state's political machinery and funds to conduct her election campaign in Allahabad, Uttar Pradesh. When, in 1974, the Allahabad supreme court ruled that she had violated the law, several opposition groups led by Jaya Prakash Narayan (1902–1979) demanded her resignation as prime minister. Widespread demonstrations against Gandhi occurred amidst labor strikes, a slow economy, and public discontent.

Led by Narayan, the head of an opposition socialist party, a group of parties that included the Bharatiya Jan Sangh (BJS), the Bharatiya Lok Dal (BLD), the Rashtriya Swayamsevak Sangh (RSS), and the breakaway Congress Party of Morarji Desai (1896–1995) joined together to form a new party called the Janata Party (the "Peoples Party"). Gandhi's Congress Party was defeated in 1977 by the newly formed Janata Party, ushering in the first non-Congress government of India. Morarji Desai, a former Congress Party finance minister, became the first Janata prime minister. The Janata Party held 270 out of 539 electoral seats in the Lok Sabha. (The total number of seats in the Lok Sabha is 542, including reserved nonelected seats for minorities and backward castes.) Desai's two rivals for leadership, Charan Singh (1902–1987) and Jagjivan Ram (1908–1986), became his deputy prime ministers. The leader of the BJS, Atal Bihari Vajpayee, became the minister for external affairs. H. M. Patel became the finance minister, and Lal Krishna Advani became the minister for information and broadcasting. Neelam Sanjiva Reddy (1913–1996), a Janata leader, was elected president of India in 1977 upon the death of the incumbent, Fakhruddin Ahmed (1905–1977), thus completing the Janata hold over India's political cabinet and presidency.

The Desai administration lasted from 1977 to 1979, when various splits emerged in the Janata government. The BJS and the RSS wings broke away from the Janata coalition, and the BLD also threatened to leave.

With sufficient coalition partners under the Janata political banner, Charan Singh was sworn in as the new prime minister in June 1979 as leader of the BLD and the new Janata (socialist). But his government did not have a majority in the Lok Sabha, and needed the support of the Congress Party to maintain a majority vote in parliament. Indira Gandhi initially promised to support Singh, but later withdrew the offer, leaving Singh unable to form a government. The Lok Sabha was dissolved and President Reddy called for new elections in January 1980.

Indira Gandhi's Congress Party was swept back into power by an overwhelming majority in 1980. After her assassination in 1984, her son Rajiv Gandhi (1944–1991) became prime minister and achieved a commanding victory in the elections of 1985. However, in the 1989 elections, Rajiv Gandhi's Congress Party was defeated under circumstances similar to those Indira Gandhi had faced. Once again, the Janata-BLD coalition, led this time by V. P. Singh, took power with a narrow majority. The Singh Janata government fell in 1991. Since then, several groups have called themselves the Janata Party or variations of that name. By 2007 the party was most closely identified with the group led by Subramaniam Swamy.

SEE ALSO *Communalism; Congress Party, India; Gandhi, Indira; Political Parties*

BIBLIOGRAPHY

Baxter, Craig, Yogendra Malik, Charles Kennedy, and Robert Oberst. 2002. *Government and Politics in South Asia.* 5th ed. Boulder, CO: Westview.

Norton, James. 2003. *Global Studies: India and South Asia.* 6th ed. New York: McGraw-Hill Dushkin.

Thomas, Raju G. C. 1996. *Democracy, Security, and Development in India.* New York: St. Martin's Press.

Warshaw, Steven, and C. David Bromwell. 1994. *India Emerges: A Concise History of India from Its Origin to the Present.* Berkeley, CA: Diablo.

Raju G. C. Thomas

JANE CROW

SEE *Jim Crow.*

JANOWITZ, MORRIS
1919–1988

The sociologist and political scientist Morris Janowitz was born on October 22, 1919, in Paterson, New Jersey, the son of an immigrant family from eastern Europe. He attended Paterson East Side High School, and in 1937 he enrolled at Washington Square College of New York University, where he came under the influence of the political scientist Bruce Lannes Smith and the philosopher Sydney Hook. He graduated with a degree in economics four years later.

After college, Janowitz worked briefly for Harold Lasswell, who was heading the Experimental Division for the Study of War Time Communications at the Library of Congress. He then went to work for Attorney General Francis Biddle at the Department of Justice Special War Policies Unit. In 1943 he was drafted to serve in the armed forces. He was assigned to the Office of Strategic Services (OSS) in London, and then moved to the General Headquarters (GHQ) of the Allied Expeditionary Forces. He worked on mass communication, morale, and propaganda before being sent to Compiègne, France, where he directed interviews of German POWs. This experience fed his calling as a social scientist, as well as his awareness about issues he would always consider important, such as the inescapability of collective violence and the fabric of social control. The experience also provided data for seminal coauthored papers, including the classic 1948 article, written with Edward Shils, about the effects of primary groups on cohesion and fighting capabilities in the Wehrmacht.

After being discharged, Janowitz was employed briefly as an intelligence analyst for the U.S. State Department. But the advice of friends such as Edward Shils and his own attraction to a stimulating and distinguished academic environment led Janowitz to enroll at the University of Chicago in 1946. He became a lecturer in sociology the following year, and in 1948 he obtained a doctoral degree with his thesis *Mobility, Subjective Deprivation, and Ethnic Hostility.* It was also at Chicago that he formed close associations with Bruno Bettelheim, William Ogburn, Quincy Wright, Lloyd Fallers, and Edward Shils.

Early in 1951, the same year he married Gayle Shulenberger, Janowitz went to the University of Michigan, where he became full professor in 1957. He returned to the University of Chicago in 1961, where he stayed till his premature death on November 7, 1988. Between 1967 and 1972 he chaired the Sociology Department, helping to restore the prestige it had enjoyed in the past.

The centrality of the themes Janowitz dealt with and the depth and originality of his thinking gave his scholarship an exceptional quality and made him a major figure in American social sciences. In addition, the variety of his interests is astonishing. He explored issues such as social stratifications, mass communication, propaganda, race and ethnic prejudice, collective action, voting behavior, and the institutional use of armed force (an issue to which he drew other social scientists). His work cut across numerous fields of the social sciences, from psycho-sociology to international relations, and from urban studies to comparative politics. The list of his publications is indeed impressive. Many of his books are now considered to be classic reference works. Among them are *The Dynamics of Prejudice* (1950, with Bruno Bettelheim), *Community Press in an Urban Setting* (1952), *The Professional Soldier* (1960), *Institution Building in Urban Education* (1969), *The Social Control of the Welfare State* (1976), *The Last Half-Century* (1978), and *The Reconstruction of Patriotism* (1983). His major edited pieces include *The New Military* (1964b), *Reader in Public Opinion and Communication* (1966, with Bernard Berelson), and *Civil-Military Relations* (1981). Some of his leading articles have been republished in collections such as *Political Conflict* (1970) and *Military Conflict* (1975). These works offer a system of innovative hypotheses, each having a value of its own, at the same time addressing the larger, all-encompassing issues and problematics in the social sciences, giving coherence and logic to the whole. His hypotheses about the modern military—for example, his developments on the changing format of military institutions, comparative models of civil-military relations, or the "constabulary use" of force in contemporary international relation—are illustrative in this regard, for they served both to define the perimeter of a new field of social science inquiry and to orient research on the subject.

One of these central concerns Janowitz touched upon was how the organization and the regulation of societies—never more than an ensemble of loosely aggregated institutions—operate in an orderly manner, especially in constantly changing environments, and especially when subjected to the disruptive forces of modernization. In other words, how can social control, which helps to mitigate self-interest in favor of common values, be maintained, when coercion and socialization have only a limited effect? To grasp such an all-encompassing issue, Janowitz—who considered grand theories inadequate as they postulate more social coherence than in reality—favored an institutional perspective that underlines interorganizational linkages and reciprocations, which, in some circumstances, can be negative, leading to "fragmentation" or "disarticulation," as with contemporary extended welfare states, for example, affected by lower social cohesion, weakened citizenship, and fragile political

legitimacy. At the same time, his analysis is multileveled and shows a preoccupation with micro-macro interactions, without which the complexity of modern society cannot be understood. These include the links between primary groups and larger structures, as well as the formation of social personality, a concept derived from W. I. Thomas to refer to enduring predispositions externalizing the psychic and "which carry over from one interpersonal and social setting to the next."

Pragmatism was Janowitz's intellectual standpoint. He was directed to it by Sydney Hook, as well as by his own reading of John Dewey and his familiarity with the outlooks and methods of the Chicago school of sociology. A pragmatic approach provided him with intellectual direction, informed him with the thematic centrality of his sociological concern, and gave him the theoretical and methodological unity his work demonstrates. It also fashioned his career conceptions and his ideas on the social role of a scholar, rejecting on the one hand the "engineering" posture essentially concerned with applied research, and on the other hand the ivory tower style of pursuit of knowledge. He always argued that the social sciences should contribute to the alleviations of social strains, the maintenance of democracy, and effective citizenship by offering the public as well as decision makers reasoned evaluations of problems and possible solutions and policies. He was thus a fervent advocate of the "Enlightenment model." In this regard, he considered himself a "citizen sociologist," and his conception of institution building highlights his belief in the public calling of social scientists. He was concerned with searching for renewed forms of social control to cope with fragmented social systems, such as an enhanced civic consciousness, which could emerge from converging reforms aimed at enlarging the professional outlook of the military, education, and justice.

This high sense of responsibility, together with his conception of the academic profession, led him to devise means, both institutional and material, to support, encourage, and expand research. Thus, in 1960 he founded the Inter-University Seminar on Armed Forces and Society, as well as the organization's quarterly *Armed Forces and Society*, a leading interdisciplinary journal that has given a strong impetus to the social science study of the military and armed conflict. Similarly his editing of the *Heritage of Sociology* series offered the academic community important comments and analyses about classical sociological works, beginning with the Chicago school. His challenging teaching and thesis direction are remembered by many who now occupy a prominent place on the academic scene in America and elsewhere.

SEE ALSO *Bettelheim, Bruno; Civil-Military Relation; Lasswell, Harold; Militarism; Military; Military*

Regimes; Organization Theory; Organizations; Pragmatism; Prejudice; Selective Service

BIBLIOGRAPHY

PRIMARY WORKS

Janowitz, Morris. 1948. Cohesion and Disintegration in the Wehrmacht in World War II. (With Edward Shils). *Public Opinion Quarterly* 12: 280–315.

Janowitz, Morris. 1952. *Community Press in an Urban Setting: The Social Elements of Urbanism.* Glencoe, IL: The Free Press.

Janowitz, Morris. 1959. *Sociology and the Military Establishment.* New York: Russell Sage Foundation. (Revised with Roger Little in 1965, 3rd edition published in 1974.)

Janowitz, Morris. 1960. *The Professional Soldier: A Social and Political Portrait.* New York: Free Press. (Expanded edition in 1971, 3rd edition in 1975.)

Janowitz, Morris. 1964a. *The Military in the Political Development of New Nations.* Chicago: University of Chicago Press. (Re-edited in 1977 as *Military Institutions and Coercion in the Developing Nations.*)

Janowitz, Morris. 1964b. *The New Military: Changing Patterns of Organization.* (Edited volume). New York, Russell Sage Foundation.

Janowitz, Morris. 1969. *Institution Building in Urban Education.* New York: Russell Sage Foundation.

Janowitz, Morris, ed. 1970. *Political Conflict: Essays in Political Sociology.* Chicago: Quadrangle Books.

Janowitz, Morris, ed. 1975. *Military Conflict: Essays in the Institutional Analysis of War and Peace.* Beverly Hills, CA: Sage Publications.

Janowitz, Morris. 1976. *The Social Control of the Welfare State.* New York: Elsevier.

Janowitz, Morris. 1978. *The Last Half-Century. Societal Change and Politics in America.* Chicago: University of Chicago Press.

Janowitz, Morris, ed. 1981. *Civil-Military Relation. Regional Perspectives.* Beverly Hills, CA: Sage Publications.

Janowitz, Morris. 1983. *The Reconstruction of Patriotism: Education for Civic Consciousness.* Chicago: University of Chicago Press.

Janowitz, Morris, ed., with Bernard Berelson. 1966. *Reader in Public Opinion and Communication.* 2nd ed. New York: Free Press.

Janowitz, Morris, with Bruno Bettelheim. 1950. *The Dynamics of Prejudice: A Psychological and Sociological Study of Veterans.* New York: Harper and Row.

SECONDARY WORKS

Burk, James. 1991. Introduction: A Pragmatic Sociology. In *Morris Janowitz: On Social Organization and Social Control,* 1–56. Chicago: University of Chicago Press.

Burk, James. 1993. Morris Janowitz and the Origins of Social Research on Armed Forces and Society. *Armed Forces and Society,* 19 (2): 167–186.

Martin, Michel Louis. 1984. Of Arms and the Man: A Short Intellectual History of Morris Janowitz's Contribution to the Sociology of the Military. In *The Military, Militarism, and the Polity: Essays in Honor of Morris Janowitz,* eds. Michel Louis Martin and Ellen Stern MacCrate, 1–31. New York: Free Press.

Shils, Edward. 1990. Biographical Memoir: Morris Janowitz. In *Yearbook of the American Philosophical Society 1989,* 201–207. Philadelphia, PA: American Philosophical Society.

Smith, Denis. 1988. *The Chicago School: A Liberal Critique of Capitalism.* London: Macmillan.

Suttles, Gerald D. 1985. A Tribute to Morris Janowitz. In *The Challenge of Social Control: Citizenship and Institution Building in Modern Society—Essays in Honor of Morris Janowitz,* eds. Gerald Suttles and Mayer N. Zald, 13–19. Norwood, NJ: Ablex Publishing.

Michel Louis Martin

JAPANESE AMERICAN INCARCERATION

SEE *Incarceration, Japanese American.*

JAPANESE AMERICAN INTERNMENT

SEE *Incarceration, Japanese American.*

JAPANESE AMERICANS

There may well be no other group that simultaneously represents and challenges the meaning of such terms as *American dream, model minority,* or *reparations.* These terms are essential to debates about immigration policies, racial politics, and economic opportunities in the United States. Like other immigrant groups, Japanese Americans (*Nikkei*) embody the struggles, contradictions, and possibilities that are inherent in the promise of a new life in America. And like other nonwhite groups in the United States, the attempts of Japanese Americans to take advantage of what American life promised were met with racism. And like many other U.S. minority groups, racial or not, Japanese Americans have faced an enormous amount of overt and covert discrimination throughout their history. It is here, at the crossroads of U.S. immigration history, racial politics, civil rights struggles, and ideas about economic success, that Japanese Americans, past and present, stand out most starkly.

A MODEL MINORITY

There is no question that Japanese Americans, who began to come to the United States and Hawaii in the late nineteenth century as laborers in the vegetable and sugarcane fields of the Pacific and Western coastal states, could be collectively called an immigrant success story. As the first waves of men arrived, eventually followed by their wives and children, they immediately began to encounter blatant discrimination and exploitation from employers and neighbors, as well as from local, state, and federal governments. They were not alone. The first Japanese immigrants entered the United States at a time when xenophobia, racist nativism, jingoism, and labor struggles helped to create the realities of hardship and survival that give credibility to every American immigration success story. The first Japanese immigrants faced a configuration of the Asiatic Exclusion League, formed in 1908; the Alien Land Laws, passed in 1913 and 1922; the 1922 U.S. Supreme court ruling declaring Japanese ineligible to become naturalized citizens (*Ozawa v. United States*); the bloody strikebreaking and lockouts in the Hawaiian cane fields during the 1920s and 1930s; and in 1942 the signing of Executive Order 9066, which began the forced removal and incarceration of Japanese Americans during World War II (1939–1945).

When comparing this first generation (*Issei*) and their children (*Nisei*) to today's fourth (*Yonsei*) and fifth (*Gosei*) generations, it is not difficult to see why Japanese Americans are considered to be a model minority. The differences between the first and subsequent generations are obvious. And because of the internment of Japanese Americans during World War II, the comparison of the earliest Japanese immigrants to Japanese Americans living in the early twenty-first century is remarkable, and emotionally charged for many. This increasingly multiracial and multiethnic group of descendants, as well as a large number of people who do not claim Japanese ancestry, looks to the history of Japanese people in the United States as representing the best and the worst of what going to America for a better life has meant.

It is not just that Japanese men and women, through their diligence and hard work, laid the framework, both economically and culturally, for their descendants to achieve increasing success with each new generation. That story is part of the immigrant history for many American ethnic groups. Japanese Americans stand out because their history includes the experience of internment, and not only surviving but thriving after being released. As a group, they not only prospered in the postwar years, with a long list of notable and famous Japanese Americans, but they were able to mobilize and achieve redress and reparations in 1988 against a great deal of opposition from the U.S. government. But, like all immigrant histories, the Japanese American success story demands a closer look in order to understand the realities, as well as the images, that give it power and appeal.

Academic research on Japanese Americans has tended to focus on three subjects—the Issei generation, World War II (including internment and Nisei military service), and the redress movement of the 1980s. There are multiple ways of interpreting these episodes, and many stories that remain untold. As interest in the Japanese success story has increased, an attempt to build upon existing understandings and analyses of the varieties of Japanese American histories has unfolded, and with it a desire to expand the ways that Japanese Americans, as individuals and as a group, are seen as part of U.S. history. This effort has cut across disciplinary boundaries and generated a great deal of exciting and often controversial work.

Some scholars have challenged assumptions about who the men and women were that left Japan and what they brought with them as they faced a system of anti-Japanese laws and sentiment in the United States. The assumption that they came with no skills and little education and were able to achieve middle-class status in one (or less than one) generation encourages a look at culture and not economics for an explanation. This is especially important when Japanese Americans are set in stark contrast to other nonwhite and ostensibly nonachieving groups in the United States. Economist Masao Suzuki (2002) makes it clear that the story of Japanese Americans is much more complex than commonly imagined. Focusing on the large out-migration of Japanese back to Japan during the 1920s (the majority of immigrants left) and the ways that the Gentlemen's Agreement of 1908 regulated and thus changed the type of Japanese immigrant coming to the United States from Japan (the earliest Issei were unskilled farmers; later Issei came with more education and skills), Suzuki argues that the Japanese American immigration story demands contextualization. He argues that lateral mobility, not upward mobility, and selective immigration must be stressed when considering which Japanese Americans achieved economic success, and how they did so. Arguments like this challenge other widely held interpretations that focus on Japanese cultural values by calling attention to the gendered, classed, generational, and regional realities of Japanese Americans before World War II.

INTERNMENT

When President Franklin D. Roosevelt (1882–1945) signed Executive Order 9066 in February, 1942, he did more than direct the removal of more than 120,000 Japanese Americans to desolate areas in the U.S. mainland interior. He helped to create one of the most symbolic moments in both U.S. and Japanese American history.

The internment of Japanese Americans, like the Holocaust, the Great Migration, and the Trail of Tears, is a deservedly major event in U.S. history. Today, the internment is written about widely. This was not always the case, as the subject was not generally discussed in textbooks or in popular culture until the 1980s. This was due, in part, to the decision by many Japanese Americans, though not all, to downplay this injustice.

The removal and four-year incarceration of Japanese Americans led to more than economic hardship and emotional suffering. As they were rounded up and sent to assembly centers in California, Oregon, and Washington with little more than what they could carry—many Issei men were sent to federal prisons without trials or evidence—the meaning of *Japanese American* began to change. Most were American citizens and minors who were taken to places where their alleged allegiance to Japan would not be a threat to the U.S. war effort. And although such accounts of injustice factor into the ways that internment is useful in arguing that Japanese Americans were a model minority, the incarceration and eventual relocation of Japanese Americans helped to create a generation of Nisei who would never forget the racial injustice that they and their relatives faced during the war. In places like Tule Lake in California and Rowher, Arkansas, some Japanese Americans looked out from behind barbed wire in armed camps and began to rethink what it would mean to be Japanese in postwar America.

Some young Japanese men joined the U.S. military and won numerous medals during the war in an effort to prove their loyalty and make things easier for their relatives. Others, known as the No-No Boys, refused to pledge allegiance or serve in the U.S. military and thus were sent to jail. After the war, some moved as far away from their old lives and the internment camps as possible, creating large postwar Japanese populations in cities like Chicago, where they and their families became part of a new fabric of race, class, and civil rights struggles. During this period, the model minority and success labels began to be applied to Japanese Americans. Yet Japanese American responses to the incarceration indicate that there is a multiplicity of ways that their history can be conceived, both within and outside of the model minority and Japanese American success story images.

REPARATIONS

Beginning in 1970 and ending with the Civil Liberties Act of 1988, the struggles of Japanese Americans to achieve recognition and a token payment for what happened to them during World War II mark yet another moment where the contradictions of the Japanese American immigrant success story are laid bare. There were differing opinions on how to achieve redress, and, as the only racial or ethnic group to be granted an apology and cash settlement from the federal government, this hard-earned victory also helped cast Japanese Americans as a favored minority. As other minority groups, such as African Americans and Native Americans, continue to work for their own reparations, the Japanese American success is held up by a variety of interests who are either demanding or suppressing calls for further reparations acts. What is perhaps most interesting with regard to future claims by other groups was the way that the Japanese American redress initiative was cast—it was about citizenship, not race. Today, the Japanese American Citizen's League (JACL) continues to frame itself as an organization committed to preventing a recurrence of the civil rights violations that led to the internment. The JACL has, for example, been a loud voice in post-9/11 debates over national security. The images and realities that Japanese Americans embody continue to be of major importance to how life in the United States is imagined and lived.

SEE ALSO *African Americans; Citizenship; Discrimination; Immigrants, Asian; Incarceration, Japanese American; Migration; Mobility, Lateral; Model Minority; Native Americans; Race; Racism; Reparations; Whites; World War II*

BIBLIOGRAPHY

Asakawa, Gil. 2004. *Being Japanese American: A JA Sourcebook for Nikkei, Hapa … and their Friends*. Berkeley, CA: Stone Bridge.

Kashima, Tetsuden. 2004. *Judgment without Trial: Japanese American Imprisonment during World War II*. Seattle: University of Washington Press.

Okihiro, Gary Y. 1992. *Cane Fires: The Anti-Japanese Movement in Hawaii, 1865–1945*. Philadelphia: Temple University Press.

Okubo, Miné. [1946] 1983. *Citizen 13660*. Seattle: University of Washington Press.

Suzuki, Masao. 2002. Selective Immigration and Ethnic Economic Achievement: Japanese Americans before World War II. *Explorations in Economic History* 39 (3): 254–281.

Takaki, Ronald. 2000. *Iron Cages: Race and Culture in 19th-Century America*. Rev. ed. New York: Oxford University Press.

Yamamoto, Eric, Margaret Chon, Carol Izumi, et al., eds. 2001. *Race, Rights, and Reparation: Law and the Japanese American Internment*. Gaithersburg, MD: Aspen.

Jacalyn D. Harden

JAPAN, INC.

SEE *Orientalism; Xenophobia.*

JAZZ

Jazz is a uniquely American style of music that developed in the early twentieth century in urban areas of the United States. As it grew in popularity and influence, jazz served as a means of bringing young people together. It has always created and sustained artistic subcultures, which have produced new and increasingly sophisticated artistry. As a pervasive and influential musical style, jazz has at times been a great social leveler and unifier. It has melded black and white citizens in a love of fast, rhythmic music, which was first proliferated through radio and the recording industry. Jazz became the basis for most social dance music and also provided one of the first opportunities for public integration.

Jazz first emerged in the black cultures of New Orleans from the mixed influences of ragtime (songs with a syncopated rhythm), blues, and the band music played at New Orleans funerals. The term *jazz* or *jass* derives from a Creole word that means both African dance and copulation. The term *jazz* referring to peppy dance music first appeared in a March 1913 edition of the *San Francisco Bulletin*, an appearance that indicates jazz's rapid spread as a popular musical genre as well as its connection to dancing and nightlife. Developed by such innovative musicians as Buddy Bolden (1877–1931) in New Orleans in the first decade of the twentieth century, jazz had moved west, east, and north to Chicago by 1919. Spread by such New Orleans jazz groups and performers as King Oliver (1885–1938) and his Creole Jazz Band and Jelly Roll Morton (1890–1941), jazz first became popular in the nightclub cultures of big cities. King Oliver's band in Chicago was soon joined by a young Louis Armstrong (1901–1971), who pioneered the rapid rhythmic jazz style called *hot jazz*. White musicians such as Bix Beiderbecke (1903–1931), Jack Teagarden (1905–1964), and Joe Venuti (1903–1978) began to copy the jazz style of New Orleans bands, and soon jazz was an American national phenomenon, appealing to sophisticates and young audiences around the country.

Jazz evolved simultaneously in the 1920s in New Orleans, Chicago, and Kansas City, performed by both black and white ensembles and orchestras. As it developed from its Dixieland forms, jazz styles ranged from the hot jazz of Louis Armstrong to the "symphonic" jazz of Paul Whiteman's (1890–1967) band. Hot jazz, one of the first influential developments of jazz, featured a strong soloist whose variations on the melody and driving momentum were accompanied by an expert ensemble of five or seven players. The idea of soloists playing in relation to backup ensembles also worked easily with larger bands, which began to form in the 1920s.

Fletcher Henderson (1897–1952) and Duke Ellington (1899–1974) established black jazz orchestras that began performing at prominent nightclubs in Chicago and New York. Henderson employed some of the most accomplished jazz musicians of his time, including Armstrong and saxophonist Coleman Hawkins (1904–1969). Ellington, who began as a piano player, established another orchestra, noted for its sophistication in its long-running appearance at New York's Cotton Club. Paul Whiteman, a successful white California orchestra leader, adapted jazz for his larger dance orchestra, which became the most popular band of the 1920s. Whiteman was interested in distinguishing a high art jazz as represented by George Gershwin's (1898–1937) *Rhapsody in Blue* (1924, which Whiteman had commissioned for his orchestra) from what he thought of as the cruder jazz of such white jazz ensembles as the Original Dixieland Jazz Band. The Original Dixieland Jazz Band, booked into New York in 1917, was one of the first successful jazz groups.

Live band appearances and a booming recording industry increased jazz's audience, as did Prohibition, which paradoxically made nightlife even more fashionable. Associated with nightclubs and nightlife, jazz became attractively exotic both in the United States and in Europe. Popular jazz bands traveled widely, playing at all kinds of venues from dancehalls and nightclubs to restaurants. The rapidly growing record industry quickly became interested in jazz performers. Such artists as Louis Armstrong, Jelly Roll Morton, Paul Whiteman, Benny Goodman (1909–1986), Duke Ellington, Fletcher Henderson, and others made records that reached audiences who did not venture into city nightlife.

The Great Depression, however, took its toll on smaller and less successful jazz bands, black bands more than white bands. With the advent of *swing* music, many white bands could continue to prosper, but many black bands had more difficulty finding large audiences. They were less commercially successful in general, since most black orchestras did not have the mainstream connections and recording contracts of white bands. In addition, Jim Crow segregation laws kept black orchestras separate from white orchestras. For these reasons, many black jazz musicians went to Europe in the 1920s and 1930s, where they were welcomed. Coleman Hawkins and clarinetist Sidney Bechet (1897–1959) both played in Europe, where audiences were captivated by the erotic suggestiveness of jazz.

Swing, a jazz-inflected dance music, developed in the 1930s and was hugely popular during World War II (1939–1945). Swing jazz was designed for larger musical groups. It continued hot jazz's back-and-forth between a solo player and the supporting ensemble, but it framed and balanced the solo with a more structured accompaniment, which often involved a musical battle between various sections of the band. Swing developed gradually, but

Benny Goodman's August 21, 1935, performance at the Palomar Ballroom in Los Angeles is often considered swing's debut. Its popularity established swing as a dance music and style that cut across classes and races. Swing bands—known as *Big Bands*—also employed band singers, many of whom became hugely popular in their own right. Frank Sinatra (1915–1998), for example, caused riots during his appearances with the Tommy Dorsey Band, while Bing Crosby (1903–1977), Ella Fitzgerald (1917–1996), Billie Holiday (1915–1959), Doris Day, and Rosemary Clooney (1928–2002) all became stars in their own right.

Female singers, especially Fitzgerald and Sarah Vaughn (1924–1990), had a larger part in the evolution of jazz than most women did. Since its inception, innovations in jazz seemed to come mainly from those who played wind instruments—trumpet players Louis Armstrong, Dizzy Gillespie (1917–1993), and Miles Davis (1926–1991); saxophonists Charlie Parker (1920–1955) and John Coltrane (1926–1967); and clarinetist Benny Goodman. Players of other instruments, such as piano, drums, bass, and guitar, though enjoying roles as soloists, were primarily responsible for maintaining the driving rhythm of jazz pieces. Until they became prominent as jazz vocalists, women musicians seemed to have little role as jazz artists or innovators. Although they occasionally played in jazz groups, women musicians were most often pianists, such as Louis Armstrong's wife, Lillian Hardin (1898–1971). The introduction of female vocalists whose role was increasingly like that of other featured wind instruments broadened the dimensions of jazz. *Scat* singing, or singing nonsense syllables, which had been used earlier by Ethel Waters (1900–1977), Edith Wilson (1896–1981), and Louis Armstrong, made the voice sound more like a jazz instrument. Melodic voice improvisation developed by such women vocalists as Adelaide Hall (1904–1993), Ivie Anderson (1905–1949), and most notably Fitzgerald made the voice an instrument and an important part of the jazz repertoire. Vocalist Billie Holiday added her own brand of blues inflected improvisation, phrasing like a wind player and injecting fun and suggestiveness into the music. In the 1940s two other vocalists, Dinah Washington (1924–1963) and Sarah Vaughn, added their own imprimatur to jazz: Washington imported a powerful clarity from gospel music, and Vaughn further developed the voice as an instrument in the context of bebop.

The popularity of swing music beginning in the 1930s also enabled bands to cross color lines. Before swing, bands mostly played to audiences of their own race, but with swing, white audiences began to follow black bands as well. In the mid-1930s, Benny Goodman integrated his jazz ensemble, working with Teddy Wilson (1912–1986), a pianist, and Lionel Hampton (1908–

2002), a vibraphonist. Because jazz musicians knew, admired, and even borrowed one another's work, jazz ensembles were among the first integrated public performance groups.

Swing also helped moor up the national mood both during both the Depression and the Second World War. Armed Services Radio broadcast swing music to soldiers. Although musicians and record companies were at a standoff over musicians' royalties for airplay in 1942, a special V-Disc program produced records for the use of the military.

After the war, many musicians who had begun their careers in swing bands—including Charlie Parker and Dizzy Gillespie—began exploring a more frenetic small-ensemble form of jazz known as *bop*. With such younger artists as Miles Davis and Art Blakey (1919–1990), bop developed as a more hard-driving, difficult jazz characterized by the prominence of soloists who played rapid complex improvisations in business suits. Bop was primarily the bailiwick of black musicians, who were rescuing the form from the pleasant popularity of swing and who would, with their development of *hard bop* or *bebop* and *cool jazz*, turn jazz into something more intellectual, difficult, and soulful. These later forms became a connoisseur's jazz, played again in smaller clubs and establishing jazz artists as the avant-garde of music. Such *beat* artists as Jack Kerouac (1922–1969) extolled bop jazz as representing an expression of soul that beat writers wished to emulate by breaking down traditional forms.

Despite its often improvisational character, jazz benefited from a number of talented composers. Instrumentalists such as Bix Beiderbecke, Louis Armstrong, Dizzy Gillespie, Charles Mingus (1922–1979), Miles Davis, Horace Silver, Thelonious Monk (1917–1982), Sun Ra (1914–1993), Wayne Shorter, and Randy Weston contributed to the growing body of jazz music, as did Duke Ellington and his collaborator Billy Strayhorn (1915–1967). Ellington and Strayhorn, both pianists, forged a productive association, writing Ellington's theme song, "Take the 'A' Train" (1941), as well as other well-known favorites played by the Ellington orchestra. More recently, other composers have continued jazz's evolution, including Jeff Wains and Wynton Marsalis.

Jazz had also long incorporated a broader base of musical styles and influences, so even as it became cool and increasingly sophisticated, it also dipped again and again into a variety of sources, renewing itself and extending its influence into more popular musical forms. As Dizzy Gillespie developed bop, he also infused his music with Afro-Cuban jazz rhythms and musicians. Chano Pozo (1915–1948), a Cuban percussionist, joined Gillespie's band in 1947, and the addition of Pozo and a wide array of Latin percussion instruments, such as the congas, bongos, timbales, and claves, produced complex and rapidly moving pieces. Latin musicians such as trumpet player Arturo Sandoval also joined Gillespie. In the 1950s Puerto Rican percussionist Tito Puente (1923–2000) and Cuban musicians Chico O'Farrill (1921–2001) and Chucho Valdés played Latin mambo in New York, influencing both big band and jazz ensemble sounds. In the early 1960s Brazilian jazz, called *bossa nova*, emerged in the United States. João Gilberto and Antonio Carlos Jobim (1927–1994) brought the style to the United States, and their work was taken up by saxophonist Stan Getz (1927–1991). Miles Davis worked with Brazilian drummer Airto Moreira, and in the 1990s Roy Hargrove incorporated Afro-Cuban elements in his Crisol project. The influence of Latin rhythms and styles enlarged the appeal of jazz, making it more joyous and rhythmic, and via such forms as bossa nova, linking it to more mainstream styles.

As jazz became more esoteric, it became more sophisticated than popular. Although it continued to influence the styles of newer music, such as rock and roll, its audience shrank to those who could appreciate its difficulties, and jazz no longer played as direct a role in the evolution of popular music. It retained its links to nightclubs, but lost its aura of carefree joy. Jazz musicians of the 1950s, 1960s, and 1970s became associated with the innovations and countercultural sentiments of the beats. Some, such as pianist Dave Brubeck and saxophonist Paul Desmond (1924–1977), became campus favorites, touring with their jazz quartet around Midwest college campuses in the 1950s. In its links to countercultural art and lifestyles, as well as to a more intellectual milieu, jazz also became associated with civil rights efforts, Black Nationalism, and other radical movements of the 1960s and 1970s. Although jazz musicians (like many performers) had long been linked to drugs and less-than-suburban lifestyles, as drugs became an openly rebellious facet of the hippie and youth movements of the 1970s, they became a part of the myth of jazz as well.

At the same time, jazz also became more academic and respectable as a high culture phenomenon. Music conservatories and universities began offering courses in jazz history and composition and training jazz musicians. Such renowned institutions as the Berklee College of Music in Boston, the Juilliard School in New York City, and the Eastman School of Music in Rochester, New York, as well as numerous universities in the United States and throughout the world, train jazz musicians.

Jazz of the later twentieth century continued to develop multiple styles—free jazz, soul jazz, jazz-rock fusion—that represented attempts to reclaim jazz as a specifically black musical tradition, even though jazz continued to be an integrated effort. Jazz groups again

became smaller ensembles and their work became more experimental and aimed at appreciative listeners rather than at dancing. Jazz clubs developed in larger cities; the clubs attract audiences of jazz lovers but not nearly the kind of widespread adulation given to swing. In the 1990s Wynton Marsalis and his brother Branford Marsalis led a renaissance in the widespread popularity of jazz. Wynton Marsalis, a classically trained trumpet player, won Grammy Awards in both classical and jazz categories. More important perhaps was his energetic advocacy of jazz as a central genre of American music. Collaborating with documentary filmmaker Ken Burns, Wynton Marsalis contributed his own more conservative perspective to Burns's twenty-hour documentary, *Jazz* (2001). Some musicians, such as Miles Davis, thought that Marsalis's ideas of a pure jazz were too conservative, but Marsalis has certainly been responsible for the revival of jazz as an important musical form.

As it has throughout its history, jazz continues to find talented and innovative musicians who continue to reinvent and redefine jazz. Becoming increasingly international and opening slightly to greater participation by women musicians, jazz continues to influence developing musical styles, but its mixture of styles, its contributions to racial integration, and its establishment of a uniquely American form as a central influential musical tradition already form its legacy.

SEE ALSO *Music, Psychology of; Popular Music; World Music*

BIBLIOGRAPHY

Erenberg, Lewis. 1998. *Swingin' the Dream: Big Band Jazz and the Rebirth of American Culture.* Chicago: University of Chicago Press.

Giddings, Gary. 1998. *Visions of Jazz: The First Century.* New York: Oxford University Press.

Shack, William. 2001. *Harlem in Montmartre: A Paris Jazz Story between the Great Wars.* Berkeley: University of California Press.

Shipton, Alyn. 2001. *A New History of Jazz.* London: Continuum.

Szwed, John. 2000. *Jazz 101: The Complete Guide to Learning and Loving Jazz.* New York: Hyperion.

Ward, Geoffrey C., and Ken Burns. 2000. *Jazz: A History of America's Music.* New York: Knopf.

Judith Roof

JAZZ AGE

SEE *Interwar Years.*

J-CURVE

A country's trade balance is defined as the difference between the amount it exports and the amount it imports. When the value of imports exceeds that of exports, the trade balance is said to be in a deficit position. One policy to improve a deficit situation is devaluation; that is, lowering the value of one currency in terms of another currency. By devaluing its currency, a country makes its exports cheaper in terms of foreign currency and its imports more expensive in terms of domestic currency, leading to an increase in export volume and a decrease in import volume. The expansion in exports and retardation of imports are expected to improve the trade deficit. However, for several reasons, after devaluation the trade balance often worsens before improving. Since this pattern of movement of the trade balance over time subsequent to devaluation resembles the letter *J*, economists have termed it the J-Curve phenomenon.

Several factors contribute to the J-Curve effect. First, at the time of devaluation, commodities in transit are priced at the old exchange rate. If the trade balance had been deteriorating before devaluation, it will continue to deteriorate after devaluation. Only after the passage of some time when new prices begin to prevail at the new exchange rate will the trade balance improve. Second, at the time of devaluation a country could experience a rapid increase in its economic activity, leading to economic growth. Since a growing economy consumes more of not only domestically produced goods but also of imported goods, its imports could rise substantially. The increase in imports may offset any favorable effects of devaluation, resulting in a short-run deterioration of the trade balance. Finally, devaluation is expected to increase the volume of exports and reduce the volume of imports. However, the adjustment of export and import volumes to a change in the exchange rate may occur with some time delay or adjustment lags. For example, there may be lags in delivery time, lags in replacing inventories, and lags in adjusting the production process.

The J-Curve effect was first observed in 1973 by Stephen Magee when the U.S. trade balance deteriorated in 1972 despite devaluation of the dollar in 1971. One question researchers have raised is how long it takes for the trade balance to experience an improvement after devaluation. In an effort to provide an answer to this question, in 1985 Mohsen Bahmani-Oskooee was the first to introduce a method of testing the J-Curve phenomenon by directly relating the trade balance to the exchange rate in addition to other determinants. Early studies employed aggregate trade data (i.e., export and import data between one country and the rest of the world) to test the phenomenon. Generally, these studies provided mixed results and were criticized as suffering from aggregation bias. To over-

come the problem, a second group of studies concentrated on the trade between one country and each of its major trading partners, a disaggregation at the bilateral level. This group was able to discover more evidence in support of the J-Curve. A few studies in the last decade have disaggregated the trade data further by investigating the response of trade flows to exchange rate changes at the commodity level. These studies show that the phenomenon could be commodity specific.

Recent advances in time-series analysis have helped researchers to modify the definition of the J-Curve as a short-run deterioration of the trade balance and a long-run improvement. This definition extends the original definition of the J-Curve and is in line with more recent advances in econometric modeling such as error-correction and cointegration techniques. Generally, the error-correction specification of any model tests the short-run dynamics while cointegration tests the long-run effects. The modified definition and application of modern techniques generally provide strong support for the phenomenon.

SEE ALSO *Beggar-Thy-Neighbor; Currency Devaluation and Revaluation; Exchange Rates*

BIBLIOGRAPHY

Bahmani-Oskooee, Mohsen. 1985. Devaluation and the J-Curve: Some Evidence from LDCs. *Review of Economics and Statistics* LXVII (3): 500–504.

Bahmani-Oskooee, Mohsen, and Artatrana Ratha. 2004. The J-Curve: A Literature Review. *Applied Economics* 36 (July): 1377–1398.

Magee, Stephen P. 1973. Currency Contracts, Pass-Through, and Devaluation. *Brookings Papers on Economic Activity* 1: 303–325.

Mohsen Bahmani-Oskooee

JEFFERSON, THOMAS
1743–1826

Thomas Jefferson's interests and pursuits presaged many substantive and methodological concerns of the modern social sciences. Jefferson exemplified the spirit of the Enlightenment—that great, diverse intellectual movement that dominated Atlantic civilization from the late seventeenth century to the dawn of the nineteenth century. The sorting and synthesizing habits characteristic of Enlightenment thought formed the core of his thinking. Not just intellectual curiosity spurred Jefferson, however. The challenges posed by the American Revolution (1775–1783)—creating a new nation, defining its form of government and politics, and shaping the kind of nation that the United States would become and the kind of people it would have—lent practical urgency to Jefferson's investigations of the natural, social, and political world.

Jefferson was born in Shadwell, Virginia, on April 13, 1743, the son of a gentleman planter determined to secure the best possible education for his son. At the College of William and Mary, Jefferson found his two mentors. Professor William Small (1734–1775) introduced Jefferson to Enlightenment thought and the study of natural philosophy (his era's term for science), and the attorney George Wythe (1726–1806) inspired Jefferson to join the bar. Wythe supervised Jefferson's legal training, insisting that he not only master the law but see it as a learned profession. Under Wythe's tutelage, Jefferson situated his legal knowledge within a wide and deep classical, historical, and philosophical education. Though his legal practice lasted less than a decade, his legal training continued to shape his work as a politician and a scientific and political thinker.

Jefferson's lifelong commitment to public service began with his election in 1768 to the Virginia legislature. Jefferson watched with anxiety the growing dispute between Great Britain and its North American colonies over the scope of British power to tax the colonists and legislate for them. In 1774 Jefferson drafted a set of instructions for the Virginia delegation to the First Continental Congress. His draft, judged too radical, nonetheless appeared as a pamphlet, *A Summary View of the Rights of British America*. Jefferson's eloquence and cogency won him acclaim, but his willingness to lecture King George III (1738–1820) on his duty to his American subjects provoked hostility in London.

In 1775 Jefferson was named a Virginia delegate to the Second Continental Congress. Though he rarely took the floor, he won his colleagues' respect by his ability as a draftsman to synthesize their clashing views. His ultimate challenge came when, in June 1776, Congress named him to a committee, with John Adams (1735–1826), Benjamin Franklin (1706–1790), Robert R. Livingston (1746–1813), and Roger Sherman (1721–1793), to draft a declaration of independence; the committee assigned the task to Jefferson. Jefferson always preferred his draft to Congress's version, complaining that Congress had ruined his work by cutting key portions of his argument, including a passage blaming George III for the American institution of chattel slavery; by contrast, most historians maintain that Congress's edits improved the document's cogency and force. The Declaration of Independence has three parts: (1) a preamble invoking Lockean social-contract theory to lay the intellectual groundwork for the Americans' assertion of the right of revolution; (2) an indictment of George III for violating the unwritten

English constitution as the Americans understood it, thus dissolving Americans' obligations to remain loyal to him; and (3) a closing incorporating the congressional resolution declaring independence. The Declaration looks backward, tying off the constitutional argument with Great Britain, and forward, delineating the core principles of an independent America. Further, the eloquent preamble of the Declaration inspired democratic revolutions for generations thereafter.

Recognizing that independence required legitimate government, Congress authorized the thirteen colonies to frame new constitutions. For Jefferson, new-modeling constitutions and laws was integral to creating a good American society. Sweeping away such vestiges of feudalism as primogeniture (a system of inheritance naming the oldest son sole heir) and entail (a system of land ownership allowing the original owner to restrict transfer of his lands to heirs of his family) would, he thought, advance the cause of democracy and republican government. The resulting society would be a true republic committed to the ideals of the Revolution.

For these reasons, when he returned to Virginia, Jefferson focused his energies on legal reform. With his mentor George Wythe and Wythe's rival Edmund Pendleton (1721–1803), Jefferson launched a project to revise the state's laws. Their 1779 report included such pathbreaking proposals as Jefferson's "Bill for Establishing Religious Freedom," his "Bill for Proportioning Crimes and Punishments," and his "Bill for Establishment of a System of Public Education." This compilation crystallized Jefferson's vision of the good society, forming his political agenda for Virginia for the rest of his life. The legislature, however, tabled the report. In the 1780s, Jefferson's ally, James Madison (1751–1836), spearheaded efforts to enact some of the report's bills, including the 1786 Act for Establishing Religious Freedom.

Two of the three key measures of Jefferson's lawmaking had to do with the life of the mind and individual liberty; all three embodied his devotion to Enlightenment ideals. Arguing that any alliance between church and state was dangerous to individual liberty and the health of the political realm, Jefferson insisted on strict separation of church and state, denying government any power to direct what citizens should believe or do in matters of religious belief and observance. Jefferson's proposed system of public education embodied his view that an informed citizenry was essential to the success of republican government. Finally, his measure for proportioning crimes and punishments reflected the profound influence of Marquis Cesare di Beccaria's (1738–1794) *Treatise on Crimes and Punishments* (1764), in particular Beccaria's commitment to humanizing law and setting aside old, barbarous punishments as inconsistent with a modern, just legal system.

In 1779 the legislature elected Jefferson governor of Virginia—a post with many responsibilities but little power. Jefferson served two one-year terms, but in 1781 his governorship's closing weeks, when he faced a British invasion of Virginia, provoked criticism souring him on public life, and he decided to retire. One incident of his governorship has lasting significance for his role in the social sciences. François de Barbé-Marbois (1745–1837), a French diplomat, sent the governors of all thirteen states a questionnaire about each state's geography, history, resources, people, and laws. Jefferson restructured this list of queries and made it the skeleton of his only full-length book, *Notes on the State of Virginia*, which occupied him, on and off, for the next six years. It distracted him from his sorrows after his wife's sudden death in 1782, and it gave him an intellectual focus while he returned to public life, first as a delegate to the Confederation Congress and then as American minister to France (1784–1789).

Published privately in Paris in 1785 and in a revised form in London in 1787, *Notes on the State of Virginia* embodied the spirit of the Enlightenment. It gave Jefferson the chance to advocate some of his cherished ideas, such as the need for religious liberty and separation of church and state, the excellence and desirability of republican government, and his love for his native land, which he promoted as a welcoming refuge from the corruptions of the Old World and a model of what a good society could be. Jefferson offered a powerful defense of America against the strictures of such European thinkers as the Comte de Buffon (1707–1788), who argued that nature and humanity degenerated in the New World. In particular, Jefferson defended Native American peoples against charges that they were lesser beings than Europeans, foreshadowing his lifelong interest in ethnography. At the same time, *Notes* presents Jefferson's agonized struggles with the issue of slavery. Jefferson, himself a slaveowner, wrote eloquently about slavery's injustice but offered a tortured case for slavery based on his claim that people of African descent were inferior to Europeans in intellect, morals, and physical beauty, and thus could not be trusted with liberty. Though such thinkers as Immanuel Kant (1724–1804) and David Hume (1711–1776) had voiced racist views of Africans, these were casual asides. By contrast, Jefferson expounded a defense of slavery based on what later generations would call "racial science."

While Jefferson was in France, he began a sexual relationship with his slave Sally Hemings (1773–1835), a daughter of Betty Hemings (1735–1807), who had been both the slave and the mistress of Jefferson's father-in-law. (Thus, Sally was half-sister to Jefferson's wife, Martha

Wayles Skelton Jefferson [1748–1782].) The teenaged Sally Hemings came to France with Jefferson's younger daughter, Maria Jefferson (1778–1804), whom he had summoned to live with him and his older daughter, Martha (1772–1836). According to Sally Hemings's son Madison Hemings (1805–1877), the two became lovers in France, and Sally extracted from Jefferson a promise that if she returned with him to Monticello, he would free all her children. The liaison continued for more than two decades. When Jefferson died, the only slaves that he freed were children of Sally Hemings and others connected with the Hemings family.

During Jefferson's presidency, James Thomson Callender (1758–1803), a muckraking journalist furious that Jefferson had not rewarded his support with a government job, revealed the Jefferson-Hemings liaison in the *Richmond Enquirer*. Jefferson's allies, family, and most biographers rejected the accusation as a political smear. In 1997, however, Professor Annette Gordon-Reed of New York Law School reexamined the evidence and the controversy's history, challenging assumptions that influenced previous scholars (such as "black people lie, white people tell the truth" and "slaves lie, slaveowners tell the truth"). Her rigorous assessment convincingly showed that the Jefferson-Hemings liaison was more probable than not. In 1998 a DNA analysis of evidence from descendants of Eston Hemings (1808–c.1853) and descendants of Jefferson's uncle Field Jefferson (1702–1765) found a match indicating that a male member of Jefferson's family was the father of Eston Hemings. That finding, combined with Gordon-Reed's analysis of the historical evidence and the discovery that every time Sally Hemings gave birth Jefferson was in the vicinity nine months before the delivery, reversed the scholarly consensus from rejection to acceptance of the liaison between Jefferson and Hemings.

While he served as American minister to France, Jefferson became a mentor to such French politicians as Lafayette (1757–1834) and Mirabeau (1715–1789). Indeed, in 1789 Jefferson was an informal adviser to the drafting of the French Declaration of the Rights of Man. He also traveled widely in Europe; his travel diaries and letters reveal him to be an astute observer of society and politics. His letters' recurring themes include his contrast of European corruption with American innocence. His approval of the French Revolution (1789–1799)—though its excesses horrified many of his friends, such as John and Abigail Adams (1744–1818) and William Short (1759–1849)—was rooted in his conviction of the horrifying injustices perpetuated by the *ancien régime* and his belief that revolutionary violence was not too high a price to pay to end those abuses.

In late 1789 Jefferson returned to America for a leave of absence. Instead, he accepted President George

Washington's (1732–1799) offer of the post of secretary of state in the new government under the Constitution. When Jefferson took office in May 1790, still in the grip of his impressions of Europe, he was horrified by what he found. In his eyes, Americans were falling under the spell of corrupting doctrines from Great Britain privileging commerce and speculation, undermining his vision of an honest agrarian republic of yeoman farmers. These realizations caused Jefferson to become increasingly doctrinaire and rigid.

The fiscal policies of Treasury Secretary Alexander Hamilton (1755–1804) formed the first flashpoint of contention, followed by clashing views about America's relations with the revolutionary French Republic. Unlike Jefferson, the prophet of agrarian democracy, Hamilton argued for a national economic system in which agriculture, trade and commerce, and manufacturing would form the three pillars of a healthy and prosperous nation. Hamilton also favored a vigorous national government—which Jefferson saw as a threat to American liberty. Finally, Jefferson hailed the French Revolution as the first salvo of a worldwide democratic revolution that he hoped would reshape the world, whereas Hamilton saw it as a threat to stability, religion, property, and good order—the props of a stable republic.

Until Jefferson stepped down from Washington's cabinet at the end of 1793, and for a decade thereafter, his epic political and constitutional battles with Hamilton helped to define key polarities of American politics—strict versus broad interpretation of the Constitution, agrarianism versus commerce and trade and industry, and decentralized versus centralized government. In response to what he saw as Hamilton's threat to liberty, republican government, and the success of the American Revolution, Jefferson and Madison helped lay the groundwork for partisan politics under the Constitution. Frustrated and exhausted by partisan battles, Jefferson retired in 1793, not returning to politics until his election as vice president in 1796, under his old friend and political adversary, President John Adams.

The Adams presidency was plagued by strife over the French Revolution and the wars convulsing Europe. Facing the quasi-war with France (1798–1800), the Adams administration rammed through Congress laws restricting rights of aliens and defining federal power to punish criticism of the government. Jefferson and Madison covertly penned two sets of resolutions against these measures that the Kentucky (Jefferson) and Virginia (Madison) legislatures adopted. These resolutions argued that the federal laws were unconstitutional and that the states had varying means to resist unconstitutional federal laws, helping to fuel generations of controversy over the

nature of the American union and the powers of the federal government over the states.

In 1801, after an electoral deadlock that threatened to shake the government to its foundations, Thomas Jefferson was sworn in as the nation's third president. With the support of solid Republican majorities in Congress, Jefferson set out to undo what he viewed as Federalist corruption of American principles, outlining in his inaugural address his approach to American government: "a wise and frugal government" overseeing a union of states that would keep its distance from the wars convulsing Europe.

When Jefferson took office, access to the Mississippi River was a key political and diplomatic issue. Determined to secure that access and American claims to the trans-Mississippi West, Jefferson devised a combined scientific and military expedition, blending the goal of scientific research into the geography, flora, fauna, and native peoples of the region with the equally important goal of assertion of American power. At the same time, he sent American diplomats to Paris to find a means to acquire the vital port of New Orleans. By good fortune and deft diplomacy, these diplomats secured from France the entire Louisiana Territory, including New Orleans. Jefferson then set in motion his plans for the expedition, to be commanded by captains Meriwether Lewis (1774–1809) and William Clark (1770–1838). Jefferson's confidential instructions to Lewis set an ambitious research agenda and became a model for all later American expeditions of science and discovery. The Lewis and Clark expedition ranks with the Louisiana Purchase among the greatest achievements of Jefferson's presidency.

Jefferson's first term was notably successful, in great measure because he could control the development of events; his second was less so, as increasingly he had to react to events beyond his control in the international realm. Seeking to end European hostilities threatening American shipping, Jefferson imposed an embargo on the warring nations, hoping to use American economic power to coerce Britain and France to make peace. The policy backfired, forcing Jefferson to adopt ever-more draconian enforcement measures, creating the very model of a strong central government that he had so long opposed. It was with relief that he retired from the presidency in 1809.

Jefferson's life followed a pattern of ventures into public life followed by retreats into retirement at his home, Monticello. In the early 1770s, Jefferson leveled a hilltop inherited from his father and began to build a house, deriving its design from the works of the Italian architect Andrea Palladio (1508–1580), himself strongly influenced by classical models. Not only did Palladio please Jefferson's aesthetic sense, his work echoed Jefferson's belief that classical architecture fostered values associated with the Athenian democracy and the Roman Republic. For a decade, Jefferson worked to make Monticello a model of classical refinement. When in 1789 he returned from France, he recast his plans for Monticello; from 1793 to the early 1820s he undertook a massive program of pulling down and building up—a plan interrupted by his service as vice president, continued in fits and starts during his presidency, and resumed after his retirement in 1809. In this period, Monticello acquired its present form—a house designed to appear from outside as a single story, with a low dome and porticos on both fronts. Monticello also was a stage set where Jefferson could welcome visitors as the sage of Monticello.

Monticello is only one of Jefferson's architectural achievements. The second example is the Virginia capitol, which he modeled on the Maison Carrée at Nîmes, France. The third example is Jefferson's country home, the octagonal Poplar Forest, completed in 1809, which was his refuge from the pressure of visitors at Monticello. With the University of Virginia, these projects were pivotal in popularizing classical ideas and ideals of architecture in the United States.

The former president became a figure of interest for the hundreds of travelers and fellow-citizens who hoped to meet him. He also dealt with a massive correspondence, "drudging at the writing-table" (as he told John Adams, with whom he resumed friendship in 1812). Jefferson used his letters to explore issues of democracy and republican government that had preoccupied him since the Revolution. He argued that laws and constitutions must change with changing times and circumstances and that each generation ought to be able to make its own laws and create its own government without being held hostage by the work of previous generations. Dearest to his heart was his idea that society and government should be divided into wards or hundreds, which would form counties, which would form states linked together in a union of shared affection, sentiments, and interests and needing only a weak government to superintend foreign relations. Jefferson was not a rigorous political theorist, however, and never produced a sustained work of political philosophy.

Jefferson devoted his last years to two great endeavors in the social sciences. Building on the work of his friend, the chemist and theologian Reverend Joseph Priestley (1733–1804), he prepared a short book for his own use, *The Life and Morals of Jesus of Nazareth*, removing from the Gospels what he deemed false and fraudulent material attributable to "priestcraft." Published for the first time in 1804 by Congress, this book, a pioneering example of historical criticism of the Bible, has acquired the (mistaken) title *The Jefferson Bible*.

Closest to Jefferson's heart, and in many ways his last great struggle, was his campaign to create a new university

for Virginia, not allied with any religious sect or denomination. It was the capstone of his plan of a system of public education, but he now realized that the university was all that he would have a chance to create. At Jefferson's urging, the Virginia legislature created a commission that he would chair. He wrote its report, shepherded it through the legislature, and began to design the University of Virginia. He picked the professors, defined the curriculum, laid out the campus, and designed all the buildings. When it opened in 1825, with Jefferson as its first rector, it was the culmination of his life's work.

Jefferson died on July 4, 1826, the fiftieth anniversary of the adoption of the Declaration of Independence, at the age of eighty-three. A few hours after he died, his friend and fellow signer of the Declaration of Independence, John Adams, died at the age of ninety. The coincidence of these deaths seemed to their fellow citizens an event of almost biblical proportions, as if the almighty had called the two patriarchs to heaven to honor their political labors.

In his epitaph, drafted in the last months of his life, Jefferson codified his legacy: "Author of the Declaration of Independence and of the Virginia Statute for Religious Freedom, and Father of the University of Virginia." This summation distilled his commitment to the revolution of ideas that reshaped the world in the late eighteenth century. In addition, these achievements helped to shape a world in which the social sciences could evolve into powerful tools by which human beings could come to understand their world and reshape it for the better. And yet, Jefferson's life and thought also show the dangers as well as the hopes of uncritically relying on the social sciences to make the world anew.

SEE ALSO *American Revolution; Americanism; Constitution, U.S.; Declaration of Independence, U.S.; Education, USA; Enlightenment; Ethnography; Hume, David; Kant, Immanuel; Presidency, The; Republicanism; Slavery; Washington, George*

BIBLIOGRAPHY

Adams, John, Abigail Adams, and Thomas Jefferson. 1959. *The Adams-Jefferson Letters*. Ed. Lester J. Cappon. Chapel Hill: University of North Carolina Press for the Institute of Early American History and Culture.

Bedini, Silvio A. 1990. *Thomas Jefferson: Statesman of Science*. New York: Macmillan.

Bernstein, R. B. 2003. *Thomas Jefferson*. New York: Oxford University Press.

Gordon-Reed, Annette. 1997. *Thomas Jefferson and Sally Hemings: An American Controversy*. Charlottesville: University Press of Virginia.

Jefferson, Thomas. [1787] 1955. *Notes on the State of Virginia*. Ed. William Peden. Chapel Hill: University of North

Carolina Press for the Institute of Early American History and Culture.

Jefferson, Thomas. 1984. *Writings.* Ed. Merrill D. Peterson. New York: Library of America.

Jordan, Winthrop D. 1968. *White over Black: American Attitudes toward the Negro, 1550–1812.* Chapel Hill: University of North Carolina Press for the Institute of Early American History and Culture.

McLaughlin, Jack. 1987. *Jefferson and Monticello: The Biography of a Builder.* New York: Holt.

Onuf, Peter S., ed. 1993. *Jeffersonian Legacies.* Charlottesville: University Press of Virginia.

Onuf, Peter S. 2000. *Jefferson's Empire: The Language of American Nationhood.* Charlottesville: University Press of Virginia.

Onuf, Peter S. 2007. *The Mind of Thomas Jefferson.* Charlottesville: University of Virginia Press.

Peterson, Merrill D. 1970. *Thomas Jefferson and the New Nation: A Biography.* New York: Oxford University Press.

R. B. Bernstein

JENCKS, CHRISTOPHER
1936–

Christopher Jencks is among the most widely respected and influential social scientists in the United States. His career has been driven by an interest in economic opportunity and the welfare of individuals at the bottom of the income distribution. Following a brief tenure as a high school teacher, Jencks entered the social policy world in the early 1960s as a self-described "journalist and political activist," working at *The New Republic* and the Institute for Policy Studies, a left-leaning Washington, D.C., think tank. The public impact of the "Coleman Report" (Coleman et al. 1966) impressed Jencks with the power of fact-based social science research to influence public attitudes. He subsequently began a distinguished academic career marked by an adherence to data-driven conclusions that challenge the preconceptions of all ideological perspectives.

He joined the faculty of the Harvard Graduate School of Education's newly formed Center for Educational Policy Research in the late 1960s, where he and his collaborators produced *Inequality: A Reassessment of the Effect of Family and Schooling in America* (1972) and *Who Gets Ahead? The Determinants of Economic Success in America* (1979). *Inequality* challenged the received wisdom that equalizing educational opportunities would eliminate economic inequality by showing, not uncontroversially, that while both schools and family background have sizable effects on economic success, they still explain only a modest fraction of the total variation in income.

Who Gets Ahead? argues for the importance of cognitive skills and personality, though it also highlights the roles of family background and schooling. The findings in these volumes catalyzed much subsequent research on the causes of economic inequality and on policies to reduce inequality.

In his influential 1992 book, *Rethinking Social Policy*, Jencks focuses on a set of policy issues that had risen to prominence in the preceding decade—including affirmative action, welfare, and the "underclass." His measured analyses aim to both illuminate and temper debates over those controversial issues by, as he writes, "unbundl[ing] the empirical and moral assumptions that traditional ideologies tie together" (Jencks 1992, p. 21). For example, while the nature versus nurture debate polarizes individuals on opposite ends of the political spectrum, Jencks argues that the question is neither completely resolvable—since the two interact—nor necessarily relevant to deciding what policy choices are best for dealing with poverty and inequality. Jencks's research has also challenged the validity of income-based measures of poverty, instead arguing for increased government efforts to directly track material hardship. His ensuing policy recommendations regarding the safety net emphasize both the importance of the responsibilities of society to its members and those of individuals to the collective.

The Homeless (1994) attributes the rise in the number of homeless people in the United States during the 1980s to the deinstitutionalization of the mentally ill, the crack-cocaine epidemic, the rise in long-term joblessness, the decline in the value of welfare benefits, the decline in marriage among women with children, and the decline in the availability of cheap "skid row" housing. It also proposes a series of policies aimed at different groups within the homeless population.

Jencks returned to the potential of human capital policies to reduce inequality in his edited volume (with Meredith Phillips), *The Black-White Test Score Gap* (1998). Contrary to his prior assertions that human capital policies would have little effect on reducing inequality, he argues that "reducing the test score gap is probably both necessary and sufficient for substantially reducing racial inequality in educational attainment and earnings" (Jencks and Phillips 1998, p. 4). This new conclusion is warranted because "the world has changed" (p. 4).

In addition to his empirically based analyses, Jencks has contributed to philosophical perspectives on the meaning of equal opportunity. Seemingly all political groups in the United States support the ideal of equal opportunity. In his essay, "Whom Must We Treat Equally for Educational Opportunity to be Equal" (1988), Jencks shows that the apparent consensus is due to the multiple meanings attached to the term. While equal opportunity's popularity is largely due to its pliancy, Jencks laments that this impreciseness ultimately renders it of little use as a guide to policy.

After a career focused on the causes of inequality, Jencks turned his attention to its consequences for social outcomes such as family structure, educational attainment, and civic engagement. Jencks is known for his clear, penetrating writing style, and he frequently publishes in nonacademic venues such as *The New York Review of Books* and *The American Prospect,* where he serves on the editorial board. His numerous awards and honors include four book awards and memberships in the National Academy of Sciences, the American Philosophical Society, and the American Academy of Political and Social Science. Jencks has been the Malcolm Wiener Professor of Social Policy at Harvard University's Kennedy School of Government since 1998.

SEE ALSO *Affirmative Action; Class; Education, USA; Equal Opportunity; Family; Homelessness; Human Capital; Income Distribution; Inequality, Income; Poverty; Upward Mobility; Welfare*

BIBLIOGRAPHY

Coleman, James S., Ernest Q. Campbell, Carol F. Hobson, et al. 1966. *Equality of Educational Opportunity.* Washington, DC: National Center for Educational Statistics.

Jencks, Christopher. 1988. Whom Must We Treat Equally for Educational Opportunity to Be Equal? *Ethics* 98: 518–533.

Jencks, Christopher. 1992. *Rethinking Social Policy: Race, Poverty, and the Underclass.* Cambridge, MA: Harvard University Press.

Jencks, Christopher. 1994. *The Homeless.* Cambridge, MA: Harvard University Press.

Jencks, Christopher, Susan Bartlett, Mary Corcoran, et al. 1979. *Who Gets Ahead? The Determinants of Economic Success in America.* New York: Basic Books.

Jencks, Christopher, and Susan E. Mayer. 1989. Poverty and the Distribution of Material Hardship. *The Journal of Human Resources* 24: 88–114.

Jencks, Christopher, and Paul Peterson, eds. 1991. *The Urban Underclass.* Washington, DC: Brookings Institution.

Jencks, Christopher, and Meredith Phillips, eds. 1998. *The Black-White Test Score Gap.* Washington, DC: Brookings Institution.

Jencks, Christopher, and David Riesman. 1968. *The Academic Revolution.* New York: Doubleday.

Jencks, Christopher, Marshall Smith, Henry Acland, et al. 1972. *Inequality: A Reassessment of the Effect of Family and Schooling in America.* New York: Basic Books.

Andrew Clarkwest
David J. Harding

JENKINS ACTIVITY SURVEY
SEE *Personality, Type A/Type B.*

JENSEN, ARTHUR
SEE *Race and Psychology.*

JERVIS, ROBERT
1940–

Robert L. Jervis, the Adlai E. Stevenson Professor of International Politics at Columbia University since 1980 and president of the American Political Science Association (2000–2001), has been a leading figure in academic research on war, peace, and diplomacy. His theories explain how misperceptions, unintended consequences, and competitive dilemmas often confound the efforts of political leaders and strategists to escape from the insecurities of international competition.

The Logic of Images in International Relations (1970) introduced the distinction between *signals* and *indices* in strategic bargaining, later referred to as "cheap talk" and "costly signals." *Perception and Misperception in International Politics* (1976) assessed the applicability of a wide range of psychological propositions to the study of deterrence failures, conflict spirals, intelligence failures, strategic assessments, and diplomatic judgments and misjudgments. The central message is that perception is theory-driven, that decision makers tend to see what they expect to see, and that these expectations are often driven by stereotyped lessons of history, analogies, or routine scripts that provide short cuts in making assessments under uncertainty. Jervis examines common perceptual biases, such as the cognitive shortcuts that lead actors to overestimate the extent to which their opponents intend the harmful consequences of their actions and underestimate the extent to which those actions are a reaction to the observers' own initiatives.

Jervis's most cited article, "Cooperation Under the Security Dilemma" (1978), draws on Jean-Jacques Rousseau's (1712–1778) parable of the stag hunt and the prisoner's dilemma game to show how states seeking only to defend the status quo can end up fighting due to the fears engendered by the situation of anarchy. Jervis defines a *security dilemma* as a situation in which any state's efforts to increase its security necessarily decreases the security of others. In this situation, one side's efforts to escape its insecurity through an arms buildup or through the conquest of strategic territory will inevitably trigger similar behavior by other security-conscious actors. Both strategic circumstances and the whole array of perceptual biases discussed in Jervis's earlier work shape behavior under the security dilemma. Offensive military technology and barrier-free geography heighten vulnerability to attack and thus intensify the security dilemma. Strategists and political leaders often misestimate the ease of attacking or defending, misperceive the balance between offensive and defensive incentives, and err in their judgment of the likelihood that the other "stag hunters" will defect from cooperation.

Applying these ideas to the problem of nuclear deterrence, Jervis explained why nuclear war-fighting is a delusion and how a stable balance of terror relaxes the security dilemma. While building on earlier theories of deterrence, Jervis added important new insights by drawing on new ideas from cognitive psychology. For example, psychologists have found that most people are risk-averse when faced with the chance to grab gains, but are more risk-acceptant in forestalling losses. Thus, Jervis reasoned that the side defending the status quo, and in particular the side defending its vital interests, should be more willing to run the shared risk of mutual annihilation. If so, the nuclear stalemate ought to make threats to change the status quo less credible and consequently should ease the security dilemma. In 1990 Jervis's *The Meaning of the Nuclear Revolution* (1989) won the Grawemeyer Award for the book with the Best Ideas for Improving World Order.

Jervis received his BA from Oberlin College in 1962 and his PhD from the University of California, Berkeley, in 1968. He also taught at the University of California, Los Angeles (1974–1980), and Harvard University (1968–1974).

SEE ALSO *American Political Science Association; Conflict; Cooperation; Deterrence; Deterrence, Mutual; Diplomacy; International Relations; National Security; Risk; Risk Neutrality; Risk Takers; Strategic Behavior; Strategic Games; Weaponry, Nuclear*

BIBLIOGRAPHY

Jervis, Robert. 1968. Hypotheses on Misperception. *World Politics* 20 (3): 454–479.

Jervis, Robert. 1970. *The Logic of Images in International Relations.* Princeton, NJ: Princeton University Press.

Jervis, Robert. 1976. *Perception and Misperception in International Politics.* Princeton, NJ: Princeton University Press.

Jervis, Robert. 1978. Cooperation Under the Security Dilemma. *World Politics* 30 (2): 167–214.

Jervis, Robert. 1979–1980. Why Nuclear Superiority Doesn't Matter. *Political Science Quarterly* 94 (4): 617–633.

Jervis, Robert. 1984. *The Illogic of American Nuclear Strategy.* Ithaca, NY: Cornell University Press.

Jervis, Robert. 1985. From Balance to Concert: A Study in International Security Cooperation. *World Politics* 38 (1): 58–79.

Jervis, Robert. 1989a. *The Meaning of the Nuclear Revolution: Statecraft and the Prospect of Armageddon.* Ithaca, NY: Cornell University Press.

Jervis, Robert. 1989b. Rational Deterrence: Theory and Evidence. *World Politics* 41 (2): 183–207.

Jervis, Robert. 1991. Domino Beliefs and Strategic Behavior. In *Dominoes and Bandwagons: Strategic Beliefs and Superpower Competition in the Eurasian Rimland,* eds. Robert Jervis and Jack Snyder, 20–50. New York: Oxford University Press.

Jervis, Robert. 1993. International Primacy: Is the Game Worth the Candle? *International Security* 17 (4): 52–67.

Jervis, Robert. 1997. *System Effects: Complexity in Political and Social Life.* Princeton, NJ: Princeton University Press.

Jervis, Robert. 1998. Realism in the Study of World Politics. *International Organization* 52 (4): 971–991.

Jervis, Robert. 2005. *American Foreign Policy in a New Era.* New York: Routledge.

Jervis, Robert, Richard Ned Lebow, and Janice Stein. 1985. *Psychology and Deterrence.* Baltimore, MD: Johns Hopkins University Press.

Jack Snyder

JESUS CHRIST

Jesus of Nazareth, one of the most influential humans in history, lives on as Jesus Christ. One-third of the human race, almost 2 billion people, identify with his name, calling themselves Christians. He is influential and believers identify with him because most of them see him as not merely human but as divine, whether as "Son of God" or in some other way uniquely bearing divine nature. Beyond the circle of believers as well as within it, many admire him, cite him, and seek to apply his teachings—especially about love—in human affairs apart from what most Christians claim about his divine character or his deity.

This fame and acclaim are astonishing, given the humbleness of his circumstances, the obscurity of origins and details about his life, and the arguments from the beginning about the meaning of his ministry and his character as being both human and divine. As for the circumstances, he was born to Mary, a young woman of Nazareth in Galilee, probably from four to six years "before Christ." That confusing calendar reference results from adjustments in chronology made in more modern times. The period found Israel, which was conceived—also by Jesus—to be God's special people, under the rule of

Romans, to whom they grudgingly paid taxes and against whom there were occasional revolts. Jesus himself came to be regarded as suspicious both by Jewish authorities in religion and in their relations to the Roman rulers as well as to the Romans themselves. In the mixture of loyalties and disloyalties, Jesus was executed by crucifixion. His dispersed followers regathered instantly, convinced that he was risen from the dead and that many among them had "seen the Lord" after his death. Forty days later they witnessed his Ascension and adored him as one who, in the words of the best-known Christian creed, "sits at the right-hand of his Father" in heaven and as invisible ruler of the world.

THE GOSPEL ACCOUNTS OF JESUS

Historians know this information not because a single Roman or Jewish historian left a record of any sort before Jesus' death, but because stories cherished by Jesus' immediate followers, quotations of his sayings and parables, and ponderings of the meaning of his divine and human character inspired his followers, or disciples, to produce four documents called "gospels," which were transmissions of "good news" about him. Three of them, called Matthew, Mark, and Luke, were edited into the forms contained in the modern Bible, probably a generation after his death. The authors or editors of these had slightly different intentions, depending upon whether they wanted to attract Jewish or Gentile readers, or for some other purpose. Yet, for all their variations and despite some conflicts in their accounts, overall they present a coherent portrait. The Fourth Gospel, called John, may have come around the end of the first century of the Common Era, and includes more reflection on the meaning of Jesus' words and works. In the centuries that followed, numbers of other "gospels" appeared. While some of them have advocates in the twenty-first century, none of them were accepted into the canon, the authorized collection called the New Testament that was approved by church leaders in the second and third centuries.

THE REFLECTION OF JESUS IN THE LETTERS OF PAUL

Before the gospels appeared, however, reflection on Jesus, now called "the Christ," which meant "the anointed one of God" who had been foreseen and promised in the Hebrew Scriptures—the "Messiah" whom devout Jews still await—was developed and spread most notably by Saul of Tarsus, called Paul the Apostle after his own conversion. In his letters collected in the New Testament and in stories within the book of Acts, which can be seen as "Volume Two" after Luke's Gospel as "Volume One," Paul describes himself as a persecutor of Christian believers until he had an ecstatic experience of Jesus, who called

him to a new vocation. Paul's letters make very few references to the life of Jesus as it is described in the Gospels, but they concentrate on the meaning of his death and resurrection. In such writings Jesus is no longer the rabbi, healer, and wonder-worker of Nazareth so much as the risen and exalted Lord of all creation. Through faith in the divine grace God gave to believers in Jesus the crucified and self-sacrificial Savior from sin and divine condemnation, these believers are gathered as a kind of mystical "Body of Christ" and are to be raised from the dead as he was.

The understandings of who Jesus was were vastly diverse. President Thomas Jefferson, almost eighteen hundred years after Jesus' death, despised the assertions and beliefs about Jesus the miracle-maker and exalted divine Lord. Like so many other advocates of the Enlightenment in his century and many admirers of Jesus in the twenty-first century, he wanted to rescue Jesus from the priests and to see him as the greatest exemplar of love and teacher of justice. At the opposite extreme there have been through all of Christian history movements that can be classified as "docetic," for in their vision Jesus only *appeared* to be a mortal. Attempts to reconcile the extremes, represented already in the first Christian centuries by those who stressed his "human nature" versus those who overstressed the divine nature, became the preoccupying agenda item for a series of church councils, whose influence extended from the fourth century into modern times and into Christian discourse and teaching on all continents.

THE SPREAD OF WITNESS TO JESUS

As for these councils: According to the book of Acts and the New Testament letters of Paul, Jewish religious authorities in Jerusalem and Roman rulers there and elsewhere began to persecute followers of Jesus. Some saw them as subversive of Jewish temple practices and others as threats to Roman rule throughout the Empire. Very soon after Jesus' death and resurrection, according to the book of Acts, a witness named Stephen was stoned to death in Jerusalem. According to tradition, in 64 CE both Paul and a leading disciple named Peter were executed in Rome. While many followers of Jesus in these times were basically nonpolitical, they refused to engage in simple acts of what to them looked like betrayals of Jesus, such as offering a pinch of incense on the emperor's shrine, the emperors then being conceived themselves as somehow divine.

The boldness of the apostles, as early articulators and witnesses were called, and then the readiness of their followers to face whatever the authorities threatened because of their faith in Jesus, only added luster to his reputation and served to attract ever more followers. By the second century followers of Jesus, called not "Jesusians" or "Jesusists" but "Christians," were spreading north and east beyond Antioch into present-day Syria and through Asia Minor, present-day Turkey. Early strongholds of belief in Jesus were in northern Africa, where notable "church fathers" held sway. In both Asia and Africa some followers took the call of Jesus to mean denial of the pleasures of the world, and went to the desert and other remote places, there in isolation of community to become monks. They pioneered in a practice that through the twenty centuries had led to special devotion to Jesus and self-sacrifice in his honor and following his commands.

Those commands, however, took their impetus from Gospel records that embody and impart some apparently contradictory impulses and commands. On one hand, the Gospel writers remember Jesus calling for drastic self-renunciation. Followers were to deny themselves, take up their cross—a reference to the mode of his death by crucifixion—and even to desert their families and familial obligations.

On the other hand, and just as emphatically, the Gospel writers depict Jesus as enjoying life and teaching others to do the same. His special form of discourse was in parables, short stories that usually included a kind of overturning of conventional ways of looking at reality. It has been said that one will not understand these preserved parables without recognizing that they turn everything topsy-turvy. The proud and powerful and respectable will be dumped and debased, while the humble and weak and outcast will be privileged in what Jesus announced as "the Kingdom of God." Kingdom of God did not mean an early reign, since the Gospels have him saying that his kingdom was not of this world, but instead focused on the sovereign saving activity of God manifested in Jesus who was in their midst. So "the last will be first" and the first last; no one could enter the kingdom, he had said, unless they changed and became "like a little child;" the lost sheep matters more than those at home in the flock. More shockingly, Jesus favored the company at table of prostitutes, the hated tax collectors, and others seen as marginal or outcast by respectable people.

JESUS ON JUSTICE AND LOVE

The Gospel portraits show Jesus as both an announcer of God's justice and imparter of God's love. As for justice, a series of sayings preserved as the Sermon on the Mount or, in another gospel, the Sermon on the Plain, called for radical adherence to the call of God to effect justice in the world. The discourse combines such stern language with words of blessing and comfort, sayings followers have cherished through the centuries. These announce that "blessed are" the peacemakers and those who hunger and thirst after righteousness.

It is not likely that Jesus would have remained such a powerful and attractive force to all conditions and sorts of people, from those in royal courts to those falsely imprisoned or abandoned by others, were it not for the Gospels' portraits and preserved sayings about love. Jesus in these accounts showed extreme devotion to the law of God, also as it was believed to be condensed in the Ten Commandments and in many other laws preserved in the Hebrew Scriptures and declared as applicable in Jesus' own time. He was even more extreme in declaring that this Law of God had its limits in the face of human need. He saw the value of the Sabbath, the divinely commanded day of rest, yet when his disciples were desperately hungry he allowed them to prepare grain for food, and when someone needed healing, he healed, scorning those who invoked the Law of God over the call to love. He was particularly confrontational when he faced religious authorities that overlooked human need in the name of their interpretations of divine commands. When asked to summarize all the commandments he drew them down to two: the love of God and the love of neighbors, or others. Every serious return to the teachings of Jesus focuses on both the seriousness of his demands for justice and the abundance of his calls to love, the love that followers saw in his giving of himself to death.

JESUS IN PRAYER AND DOCTRINE

To believing Christians in all cultures, Jesus is not merely an historical figure, written about and admired after twenty centuries. Most of them regard him as a living presence. The Gospels hear him saying that when two or three followers are gathered in his name, he is there among them, so they regularly worship in his name. Some pray *to* him, but the main interest for Christians is to pray *through* him, following his word that they are to approach God, the one he called "Abba," an endearing word for "Father," in his name. Catholic Christianity in many denominational forms is sacramental, and its adherents believe that Jesus is especially present among them in the sacred meal described in the Gospels as occurring first the night before he was killed and which he commanded that they should repeat.

Second, Jesus has been present in visual representations. No one knows what he looked like, and in all societies and cultures artists portray him as an ideal figure in their own. In the Eastern Orthodox churches he appears in very formal guise in icons. In Latin (in Europe, in Spanish cultures; in the Western Hemisphere, in Latin American cultures), he is usually portrayed as a whipped, bleeding sufferer on the cross. In other cultures he is domesticated and portrayed as a kind of bourgeois comforter of children and quiet teacher.

Third, Jesus lives on in doctrine or dogma. While the gospels show him uninterested in abstractions and distant from formulations, it was natural that as Hebrew-speaking Jewish followers of Jesus moved into the larger culture today called "Greco-Roman"—the Gospels about Jesus and other speakers of Aramaic and Hebrew were themselves written in common Greek—teachers found it important to define how Jesus differed from others for whom divine claims were made. They had to show how he related to his divine Father and, since the New Testament writings made much of this, to the Holy Spirit. In the early church councils leaders combined Hebrew biblical testimony and simple stories with Greek philosophical themes. They had to show how to make sense in their world of their belief that the human Jesus was also the exalted Lord. They were pressed to show to Jews and others that and how they were monotheists, believers in one God, and not in two or, with the Holy Spirit, in three. Out of this grew the doctrine of the divine Trinity, in which Jesus is "of one being" with the Father and is also a true human.

JESUS IN SOCIETY AND POLITICS

Those interested in the social sciences—history, sociology, and political science—may be aware of the other three modes but they also study how devotion to Jesus inspires ethical response among those who want to be numbered as his followers. They pay attention to the movements and church bodies that exist because of the desire by believers to respond to his calls and promises. In his name leaders helped guide the persecuted believers to situations of power. After Constantine in the fourth century, both in the Roman West and the "Constatinopolitan" East, Jesus, as represented by bishops and other church leaders, shared earthly power with emperors and magistrates. The name of Jesus was invoked by his followers against their and, they believed, his enemies. His cross appeared on the banners of Crusaders who more than a thousand years after Jesus carried on campaigns against those who occupied lands in which he lived or sites devoted to worship of him and to his memory. In both the Christian West and East, both sides invoked his blessing on their troops and, when victorious, credited him, however all these military doings seemed to have departed from the humble portrait of one who called them to be peacemakers.

No portrait of Jesus and invocation of his memory would be fair, however, did one not notice that more than the warrior, Jesus remains the peacemaker and bears the image of the healer. He called disciples to treat the homeless, the hungry, the imprisoned, and the ill, as if they were treating him—or even *because* they were treating him, as

he lived in people of need. In prayers and hymns his name lives on as someone to be relied on and invoked by those who are troubled, ill, or dying. If these invocations seem far removed from those that see him as a ruler through representatives on Earth, as the leader of "Christian soldiers, marching as to war," the anticipations of both are present in the writings of Paul, the portraits of the Gospel, and the many efforts through the ages by believers to come to terms with someone they believe is obviously human and, in faith, adored and often followed as divine.

SEE ALSO *Christianity; Fundamentalism, Christian; Liberation Theology; Religion*

BIBLIOGRAPHY

Pelikan, Jaroslav. 1985. *Jesus through the Centuries.* New Haven, CT: Yale University Press.

Martin E. Marty

JEWISH DIASPORA

Diasporas in general and the Jewish Diaspora in particular are very important complex sociopolitical entities that are playing a growing role in most states worldwide, as well as in regional, international and transnational politics. The diaspora phenomenon, including the Jewish Diaspora, is an expanding field of study.

Many people worldwide, including scholars—especially those adhering to the instrumentalist and constructivist approaches to the origins and development of ethnic groups, nations, and diasporas—consider the Jewish Diaspora as a modern or even a postmodern phenomenon. While it is true that the period since the mid-nineteenth century has seen a marked change in the entire diasporic phenomenon—including the Jewish Diaspora—the Jewish Diaspora, like other ancient diasporas, has maintained many of its "old" characteristics.

THE HISTORY OF THE JEWISH DIASPORA

The Jewish Diaspora was established as a result of both voluntary and forced migrations of Jews out of their ancient homeland—Eretz Israel (the Land of Israel). Later, Jews were either exiled from their host countries (such as Spain and England in the Middle Ages and Middle Eastern states in the twentieth century) or voluntarily migrated to secondary and tertiary host countries. The forced and voluntary migrations that resulted in the establishment of the Diaspora began much earlier than what has been regarded as the "official" date of the

Diaspora's establishment, that is, the creation of the Jewish Diaspora in Babylon.

Return movements of Hebrews from Egypt (the Exodus) and other Middle Eastern countries to the Land of Israel have occurred throughout antiquity and the Middle Ages. Nevertheless, Jewish communities continued to exist in these countries after such return migrations. Hence, a Jewish Diaspora has persisted since antiquity.

The expulsion of the Israelites by the Assyrians and of the Judeans by the Babylonians only added new larger groups to the already-existing Jewish diasporic communities in various parts of the Middle East. This means that after the initial establishment of the Jewish diasporic entities in Egypt and Syria, new Jewish diasporic entities were established in various parts of the Middle East and Asia Minor and later in the Balkans. The Babylonian Jewish Diaspora served as a model because the Jews created there an "autonomous diasporic sociopolitical system," in which the Diaspora, rather than the devastated homeland, became the national center and played the crucial role in the nation's persistence, cultural development, and political influence.

The establishments of the Greek Empire and later the Roman Empire, both of which controlled vast territories, facilitated both the permanent settlement of Jews and the establishment of communities in various parts of these empires and the communication between the various dispersed Jewish communities.

This expansionist trend continued during most of the Middle Ages. The Jewish Diaspora spread from the eastern Middle East, Greece, and Rome to North Africa, Europe, and Asia. Later, partly voluntarily and partly because of anti-Semitism, anti-Jewishness, and hatred, Jews migrated and established diasporic entities in South and Latin America, and then they moved to the United States, Canada, Australia, and South Africa. In fact, the center did not shift back to the homeland even when the regional geopolitical situation changed.

MORE RECENT DEVELOPMENTS

The Zionist Movement, which advocated the return to Palestine and the establishment of a Jewish independent state there, was established toward the end of the nineteenth century and during the early twentieth century. Because of growing temptations of assimilation and of integration into democratizing and secularizing host lands, on the one hand, and because of persecution, anti-Semitism, and pogroms, on the other hand, the most urgent problem then facing Jewry was how to prevent defection of individuals and groups from Judaism and from membership in the Diaspora's communities. Thus, already at that historical juncture, the problem was how to

ensure continuity and enhance the readiness of Jews to identify as such, as a basis for a solidarity that could enable Jewish diasporic joint action.

Partly because of the Diaspora's geographic dispersion and partly because of ideological pluralism among Diaspora Jews, it was difficult to reach consensus about the preferable strategy for the nation's survival and persistence. Hence, during the late nineteenth and early twentieth centuries there emerged various approaches to these questions, and virtually all shades of strategies gained adherents. These included assimilation, integration, participation in class struggle (namely, adopting the socialist and social-democratic solutions), cultural and political autonomy, and corporatism, the latter of which meant formal representation of the Jewish community vis-à-vis host governments, such as in Great Britain.

During this period, the main new facet was the birth of the separatist Zionist movement's strategy, which called for the Jews' return to Palestine and the reestablishment there of their own sovereign state.

Prior to World War II (1939–1945), the emerging but small Zionist movement faced tough intranational competition with other Jewish movements that had emerged in the Diaspora. Actually, prior to the emergence of Nazism and World War II, Zionism was a marginal movement in world Jewry, and its strategy did not attract the majority of Jews. The impact of that war, especially the painful realization of the full scope of the Holocaust and its disastrous consequences, created the right backdrop for a breakthrough by the Zionist movement. Many Diaspora Jews realized that the Zionist strategy was not only feasible but also an appealing solution to the problem of Jewish survival and national revival. Though the situation was ripe for the implementation of the Zionist strategy, membership in and support of the Zionist movement was still rather limited.

DEBATES ABOUT FUNDAMENTALS

The efforts to form consensus around the Zionist solution generated many delicate questions about central issues, some of which are still debated in the early twenty-first century. Among these, an important issue has been what should be the relations between the Zionists and other Jewish groups that opted for other strategies. Another unsolved issue revolves around reconciling the various elements in the national identity and perceptions. Because this fundamental question has not been solved, the issues of the principles that determine Israeli citizenship, and consequently the relations between Israel and certain segments in the Diaspora, have remained unsolved.

An additional debate about essentials that has not been concluded concerns the centrality of Israel versus the autonomy of diasporic communities. In two large and strong diasporic communities—the U.S. and French communities—strong inclinations toward cultural and political self-sufficiency and freedom of action have emerged vis-à-vis Israel. Connected to these trends, new attitudes have emerged concerning certain practical issues, such as loyalty to Israel versus host countries, and Israel's "right" to influence Diaspora leaders and members in order to increase support for its endeavors.

Furthermore, there was and there still is no consensus between Diaspora and Israeli leaders concerning the role of the Diaspora in the establishment of the Israeli state. In the wake of World War II, this historical act was promoted and actually implemented by leaders and parties adopting an ideology that emphasized the predominance of the Yishuv (the Jewish community in Palestine) in the Jewish nation.

After the Holocaust, when the Jews still constituted a stateless diaspora, large segments in various Jewish communities adopted an exceptionally supportive strategy toward the Jewish state. Later this strategy changed. In most Western democracies, where Jewish communities have been able to act relatively freely, these entities have adopted a communal strategy. Essentially, this strategy means not only moderate social, political, and economic behavior, but it also has determined the nature of the organizations the Diaspora operates. On a spectrum of strategies that runs from an assimilationist poll, on the one hand, to a return to the homeland, on the other hand, the communal strategy is regarded as one that poses major threats neither to the host countries nor to the members of the Diaspora. By adopting this strategy the Diaspora members implicitly pronounce that they accept the main social, political, and economic rules of the game in the host countries and that only under extreme circumstances would they adopt dual loyalties. When fully implemented, this pattern diminishes potential and actual controversies and clashes between the Diaspora and its host lands.

THE EFFECTS OF THE ESTABLISHMENT OF THE STATE OF ISRAEL

The establishment of Israel in 1948 marked a fundamental change in the position of the Jewish Diaspora. Whereas prior to its establishment the Jews constituted a "classical stateless diaspora," afterward the Jews dwelling outside Israel should be regarded as a "classical state-based diaspora." Since 1948 the Jewish Diaspora has shown great similarity to other classical diasporas whose connections are with independent homelands.

After the establishment of Israel a new group joined the classical Jewish Diaspora—Israeli emigrants. Most of these Israelis emigrated to and settled in various host countries as a result of voluntary decisions, and therefore they also hardly regard their situation as exilic.

The Land of Israel is a crucial element in the ethno-national-religious identity of Diaspora Jews. Throughout history the collective memories of the homeland remained vivid in the hearts and minds of Diaspora Jews. The spiritual and emotional ties of Jews, though not all Jews, to the ancient homeland contributed to a sense of national solidarity. Later this solidarity also served as a basis for various activities on behalf of that segment of the nation that dwelled in the homeland. Such support peaked in the wake of the establishment of modern Israel, and still later during and after the 1967 and 1973 wars. Since then general support for the Jewish state has been declining.

Similar to the situation with all other diasporas, the Jews form a majority only in Israel, and only small minorities in all their host countries. In fact, the majority of the nation dwells outside the homeland—most of them in relative security, economic prosperity, and cultural bloom. These facts and Israel's problematic security situation have raised the issue of the location of the national center, and of its corollary, the question of peripheriality in this nation. During the first two decades after the establishment of Israel it seemed as if the Diaspora recognized the new nation-state as the main Jewish center, and its policies and actions determined developments in the Diaspora.

By the early twenty-first century, there were at the least four major Jewish centers—the American, French, Russian, and Israeli. Among these centers there is implicit and explicit, continuous tacit competition about predominance in the entire nation.

In most of the host countries, especially the United States, Canada, Great Britain, France, Australia, Mexico, and Peru, there are relatively large groups of core Jews who have well integrated into these societies, political systems, and economies. These Jews—most of whom were in their forties and fifties in the early twenty-first century—obtained an academic education and became affluent. Many of the members of these well-integrated groups are in high-tech fields, academia, and other professional occupations, such as journalism, medicine, banking, insurance, and law. Some of them belong to the richer segments in these countries, but most of the members of these groups belong to the middle and upper-middle class. The main reasons for these achievements are: Jews' determination to continue to survive and overcome actual and perceived difficulties in their host lands, their painful memories of historical deprivation and persecution, family and communal support and encouragement, a strong emphasis on education within their families and communities (education being a precondition for economic success), and the existence of Jewish communal and international networks and systems of communication.

There are, however, still many Jews permanently residing in the above-mentioned and other host lands, such as east and central European and some Latin and South American countries. These Jews are typically older and belong to lower income groups or to the working class. These poorer Jews need support from their host governments and their Jewish communities. This last factor affects the allocation of the resources that are at the disposal of the various Jewish diasporic communities. When the political and economic conditions in such host lands become more difficult, such Jews get support from the wealthier Jewish communities. This has been the case, for example, with the Jewish refugees created by World War II, with Jews in Middle Eastern and North African countries until the 1950s, and, more recently, with Ethiopian Jews.

By the early twenty-first century, the return of Jews to countries where they were persecuted and from which they were expelled had also become apparent. The "return" of Jews to host countries such as Germany, Spain, and Austria, shows that Israel is not regarded as the undisputed national center. Moreover, the majority of Diaspora Jews has stayed and will be staying in their host countries.

Despite persecution and migration to secondary and tertiary host countries, on the one hand, and acceptance by host societies and governments that result in assimilation or full integration, on the other hand, in various host countries a Diaspora core is maintained. These cores of devout Jews maintain their ethnonational and religious identity and resist assimilation or full integration.

In the past, the religious element in the Jewish identity was essential for the entire nation. Since World War II, however, this element has lost some of its significance. Though religious Jews claim that they constitute the main barrier against a sweeping assimilation that would result in the disappearance of Jewry, the ethnonational factor now serves as the basis for the continuous existence of many Jewish communities all over the world.

THE COMPARATIVE PERSPECTIVE

Because of its origins, endurance, and attachment to its ancient homeland, it is not surprising that the Jewish Diaspora has been considered an imperishable "classical," "archetypal," and "mobilized" diaspora. Some observers, however, are pessimistic about its future survival. The gist of the pessimists' argument is that the new pluralism, multiculturalism, and tolerance toward the "others," which prevail in the more democratic host countries, speed up the assimilatory tendencies that demographically decimate world Jewry.

This diaspora should now be regarded as an ethnonational–religious state–linked diaspora that is similar to other older and newer existing diasporas. In fact, the Jewish Diaspora fits a collective profile of ethnonational diasporas (Cohen 1997; Sheffer 2006). As applied to the Jewish case, the profile includes a number of elements.

As has been shown in the historical analysis above, the Jewish Diaspora was created as a result of voluntary and forced migration out of its homeland—Eretz Israel—and out of other host countries, and eventually as a result of its members' permanent settlement in host countries. This diaspora has remained a rather small minority in all its host lands; after permanently settling in their host lands, the Diaspora's members have maintained their ethnonational identity. This identity is buttressed by strong religious beliefs. The identity of this entity's members is based on a combination of nonessentialist-primordial, psychological, and instrumental factors. The nonessentialist-primordial factors include the idea of common ancestry, biological connections, a common historical language, collective historical memories—among which the twentieth-century Holocaust is important—a discernable degree of national solidarity, a deeply rooted connection to the ancient homeland, and similar patterns of collective behavior. This identity is also based on instrumental factors concerning various benefits that derive from being members of the Diaspora. The strategy of many Jewish diasporic entities is communalist and is implemented through multiple organizations and active trans-state networks that protect and promote the diaspora's political and economic interests. Another element of the profile is that most members of the Diaspora do not regard their existence in their host countries as exilic.

On the basis of such identity and identification, a sense of solidarity emerged and has been sustained. Such solidarity has facilitated continuous connections between the elites and active members on the grassroots level, which pertain to the cultural, social, economic, and political matters of the entire entity. In turn, these constitute determining factors in the relations among Jewish diasporans, their host countries, their homeland, their brethren in other host lands, and other international actors.

All the above-mentioned factors serve as the bases for organization and collective action. An essential purpose of these organizations and activities is to ensure the Diaspora's capability to survive and to promote its interests in host lands and in the homeland, as well as to maintain cultural, social, economic, and political connections with the homeland and with other segments of the same nation.

Wherever and whenever they are free to choose, Jewish diasporans tend to adopt distinct strategies concerning their existence in their host lands and with their homeland. Generally, core members of the Jewish Diaspora adopt the communalist strategy, which is intended to ensure integration, rather than assimilation, in the host countries. This strategy, coupled with the wish to maintain contacts with the homeland determines the nature of the organizations that the Diaspora establishes, and also leads them to establish elaborate and labyrinthine trans-state networks.

The establishment of the Diaspora's organizations, including the trans-state networks, and their subsequent activities, raises complex issues of loyalty. To avoid and prevent undesirable clashes between the Diaspora and its host societies and governments concerning the laws of the land and the norms of the dominant segments in the host societies, the Diaspora's members usually accept these norms and comply with the laws. Nevertheless, during certain periods, especially when the homeland or the host country finds themselves in the midst of crises, or when the Diaspora encounters severe difficulties, certain segments in the host societies develop negative attitudes about the Diaspora's disloyalty. On certain occasions, such tensions and clashes lead to the homeland's intervention on behalf of its Diaspora or meddling in its affairs.

As noted above, despite certain pessimistic predictions of the demise of this ancient diaspora, all indicators show that like other similar diasporas, the Jewish Diaspora will continue to exist and even prosper.

SEE ALSO *Anti-Semitism; Assimilation; Citizenship; Communalism; Ethnicity; Holocaust, The; Jews; Judaism; Migration; Pogroms; Socialism; Statelessness; Zionism*

BIBLIOGRAPHY

Boyarin, Daniel, and Jonathan Boyarin. 2003. Diaspora: Generation and the Ground of Jewish Diaspora. In *Theorizing Diaspora: A Reader*, eds. Jana Evans Braziel and Anita Mannur, 85–118. Oxford: Blackwell.

Braziel, Jana Evans, and Anita Mannur, eds. 2003. *Theorizing Diaspora: A Reader*. Oxford: Blackwell.

Cohen, Robin. 1997. *Global Diasporas: An Introduction*. London: UCL Press.

Kellas, James G. 1991. *The Politics of Nationalism and Ethnicity*. New York: St. Martin's Press.

Safran, William. 2005. The Jewish Diaspora in a Comparative and Theoretical Perspective. *Israel Studies* 10 (1): 36–60.

Sheffer, Gabriel. 2005. Is the Jewish Diaspora Unique? Reflections on the Diaspora's Current Situation. *Israel Studies* 10 (1): 1–35.

Sheffer, Gabriel. 2006. *Diaspora Politics: At Home Abroad*. Cambridge, U.K.: Cambridge University Press.

Vertovec, Steven. 1997. Three Meanings of "Diaspora," Exemplified among South Asian Religions. *Diaspora* 6 (3): 277–299.

Gabriel (Gabi) Sheffer

JEWS

According to the Torah, the history of the Jewish people begins with a call to the patriarch Abraham to abandon his ancestors' idol worship and to "Get thee out from thy country … unto the land that I will show thee" (Gen. 22:1). Jewish history and identity, as recounted within the people's own tradition, thus begin with a command, a renunciation, and a departure. The Torah also recounts the earliest Jewish generations' experience of exile in Egypt, followed by the miraculous deliverance, return, and reconquest of that divinely promised land. However, current archaeological consensus is unable to agree on confirmation of key moments in the biblical account.

The name *Jew* and its various cognates (e.g., French *Juif*, German *Jude*, Arabic *yahud*) all stem from the name *Judah*, the ancient kingdom that shared the name of one of the twelve sons of the biblical patriarch Jacob. Other names for the group are *Hebrew* (generally referring to the ancient period, but also the name of the main ethnic language) and *Israel* (a name of Jacob in the Bible and also the name of the second ancient Jewish kingdom).

REASONS FOR AND LOCATIONS OF THE ORIGINAL DIASPORA

Jews are known simultaneously for their lasting devotion to their homeland (Israel, Zion, Palestine, or simply "the Land") between the eastern shore of the Mediterranean and the Jordan River, and for their long endurance in conditions of diaspora or exile. The main historical exiles of ancient Jewry followed the destruction in 586 BCE, by the Babylonians, of the ritual center in Jerusalem known today as the First Temple, and then the destruction in 70 CE, by the Romans, of the Second Temple. However, Jewish *diaspora*—the existence of stable and persistent Jewish communities outside the historical homeland— long predates the loss of the ritual center and of Jewish sovereignty. The ancient Jewish community of Alexandria, with its rich Hellenic culture and regular remission of tribute to Jerusalem, is only the most dramatic example of such a pre-exilic diaspora.

Babylonia quickly became a key and powerful center of ancient Jewish life, throughout the entire Second Temple period and beyond. In the wake of the Roman exile, groups of religious leaders collectively known to current scholarship as "the Rabbis" devoted generations to the elaboration and transmission of the Oral Torah, eventually redacted into the texts known as the Mishnah, and in the commentaries on the Mishnah known respectively as the Babylonian Talmud and the Jerusalem or "Palestinian" Talmud. Rabbinic Judaism was a minority formation in its earliest centuries (outnumbered by what is broadly known as Hellenic Judaism and by other rival formations, eventually including its only surviving rival, known as Karaite Judaism). Despite continuing sentimental attachment to the ancient homeland, the Babylonian Talmud retained far more central authority than its Jerusalem rival. The Rabbinic models of scriptural interpretation, legal adaptation, and substitution of prayer for Temple ritual came to serve as the fundamental template for Jewish communal life throughout various diasporas until the modern period.

BASIC RELIGIOUS BELIEFS AND PRACTICES

The notion of "chosenness" is understood in Jewish tradition in terms of obligation and reward. The Book of Deuteronomy recounts the Hebrew nation's reaffirmation of God's original covenant with Abraham; the people will keep God's "statutes" and "commandments" and "ordinances," and God will in turn keep them as "His own treasure" (*am segula*) (Deut. 26:16–18). Various examples of the literary genre of commentary known as *midrash* recount God's prior offer of the Torah to other nations, each of which is unable to accept one of its major premises and thus refuses to enter into the divine covenant.

Though this deity is sometimes referred to as "the God of our ancestors" or "the God of Israel," the biblical narrative—and especially the Prophetic writings—reflect the conviction that, as the creator of all being and of all humanity, this divinity's sphere of power and interest is not limited to one nation or territory. Moreover, in sharp contrast to some other national epics, the origin of the people in human history is separated from the original creation of the earth and its creatures. Accordingly, Jewish tradition and rhetoric view the non-Jewish "other" through a range of metaphorical frameworks: as "cousins," descended through a mythic genealogy from the common human ancestors Adam and Eve; as instruments of a divine plan centrally dependent on the covenant and on the Jews' always inadequate performance thereof; and occasionally as creatures equally precious in the sight of God: "Are ye not as the children of the Ethiopians unto Me, saith the Lord?" (Amos 9:7).

At the ideological plane, diaspora Jewish life has been played out in this continuing and productive tension between ethnocentrism and universalism. The synagogue, wherever it is, becomes a form of *mikdash me'at*, a "miniature" substitute for the lost Temple in Jerusalem. The study of the forms of Temple worship and recitation of the order of sacrifices both recall ancient sovereignty and give form to dreams of messianic restoration. The study of sacred texts transcends mere recitation through a chain of commentaries that both preserve understandings and distort them to make the authorities fit new circumstances. The Rabbinic academies (*yeshivot*) of ancient Babylonia come to serve as models for the new academies in eastern

Europe devoted to the defense and reinvention of Talmud study in response to modern forms of knowledge and inquiry.

Practice—the meticulous and highly rationalized observance of positive commandments and prohibitions—is central to the conduct of a traditionally Jewish life. Laws of separation and purity (such as dietary limitations, bans on the mixing of certain species in agriculture, and menstrual taboos) both help to order the social world and sustain the larger lifeworld separation distinguishing Jews from non-Jews. During the period of Jewish sovereignty, many of these laws served to underscore the special sacredness of the land itself. In diaspora, their function in preventing the dissolution of the Jews as a kin and ideological group become more salient.

Jewish law and custom are all highly androcentric, though not univocally so. They are heteronormative, though they do not reflect the gender structures of the post-Enlightenment European bourgeoisie, from the perspective of which the Rabbinic ideal of the quiet, studious, "tent-dwelling" Jacob may even seem effeminate (see Boyarin 2004). Men under traditional Jewish law exclusively enjoy various rights and powers, such as serving as witnesses, as members of prayer quorums, and as the initiators of divorce. Apologetic accounts stress the key role of women in the family, but at various points women in Jewish communities have also held important economic roles, and the Talmud also makes clear the rights of women as property holders and contracting parties in ancient Babylonia.

Since the Prophetic response to the nation's demoralization in the wake of the first and second exiles, the messianic promise of ultimate redemption and restoration—sometimes accompanied by visions of universal peace and well-being—has been a core tenet of Jewish belief, ritual, and culture. Messianism has also been a central motivating theme of the powerful and continuing tradition of Jewish mysticism, which has sometimes coexisted with and sometimes contended with Rabbinic textualism. Some leading scholars have argued that Jewish messianism is distinctly characterized by the expectation of the advent of the messiah as a historical and public event, over and against ideologies of individual redemption.

JEWISHNESS AND ITS OTHERS

Since earliest times, and including periods of state sovereignty, the Jewish collective has often found itself either a client of or in conflict with larger powers. Much Prophetic discourse turns on the geopolitical dilemma of choosing between loyalty to the rival empires of Assyria and Egypt. The biblical narrative of enslavement and deliverance turns on an image of the Egyptians as heartless and unworthy emperors. The destruction of the Second Temple resulted in large part from Jewish resistance to incorporation within the Roman provincial administrative system. Christianity was an outgrowth of certain messianic trends among Jews, and there has been growing scholarly acknowledgment in recent years not only of the significance of Jesus' Jewishness, but the continued Jewishness of many of the first "Christians," including Paul. Yet Christianity became radically distinguished from, and powerfully opposed to, Judaism and Jewishness once it became the state religion of the Roman Empire. Similarly, Islam arose in Arabia in a social milieu where Jews were a prominent part of the mix, yet the rejection of Muhammad's (c. 570–632) message by the local Jewish community gave rise to strains in Islam that are at best ambivalent toward Jews and at worst overtly hostile.

ENGAGEMENT IN WORLD CIVILIZATION

Jewish communities eventually spread (or were established by conversion) throughout the circum-Mediterranean region, Central Asia, and eastern and western Europe. With the exception of sub-Saharan Africa and much of East Asia (there were smaller Jewish communities for centuries in India and China), Jews were thus found throughout the Old World. Throughout the medieval and early modern periods, Jews played prominent roles in the world system of trade and communication that stretched from the Atlantic coast of Europe through the Mediterranean and into Asia, and for centuries, Jewish communities were concentrated in Islamic lands, ranging from Iberia through North Africa and the Middle East. Yet that world system was unstable, and Crusader anti-Muslim zeal sometimes spilled over into murderous anti-Jewish violence.

During the High Middle Ages, in a complex process tied to the formation of nascent nation-states, long-established Jewish communities were forced out of various parts of western Europe; many of their number migrated to regions in eastern Europe that were then being colonized by Christian nobility, peasants, and clergy. More than a century of forced conversions and persecutions culminated in the expulsion of Jews from Iberia at the end of the fifteenth century. While this ended centuries of fruitful and conflicted multireligious contact that had produced Jewish luminaries such as Moses Maimonides (1135–1204), Abraham Ibn Ezra (1092–1167), and Solomon Ibn Gabirol (c. 1021–1058), it also gave rise to new, flourishing, and influential communities across the Ottoman Empire, known as Sephardim and speaking the Judeo-Spanish language of Ladino. However, a dramatic rise in the Jewish population of eastern Europe during the nineteenth century radically shifted the "center of gravity" of Jewish communities in the modern period.

THREATS AND SOLUTIONS TO EXISTENCE IN MODERNITY

Modern European nationalism, the rise of democratic citizenship, and Enlightenment ideologies of individual autonomy and of freedom of conscience all presented both dangers and opportunities for Jews and Jewishness. Distinctive legal status—both limitations and protections—for Jews began to crumble. In western Europe, the National Assembly during the French Revolution of 1789 heralded the abolition of autonomous Jewish communities with the famous phrase, "To the Jews as a nation, nothing; to Jews as individuals, everything." In modernizing Germany, Jews were prominent in literature, science, and the arts, though they continued to suffer social and institutional discrimination. In the Russian Empire, "the prisonhouse of nations," Jewish communities faced a bewildering and inconsistent sequence and array of liberalizing gestures, increasing restrictions on settlement and occupations, and forced assimilation in the guise of modernization. Individual Jews and Jewish movements (notably the Jewish Workers' Bund in Russia, Poland, and Lithuania) were prominent in socialist and revolutionary efforts to overthrow the czarist regime. Jews were full participants in colonial, democratic, and capitalist ventures in the New World, and the United States became a center of Jewish population and creativity.

Perhaps fueled by the dramatic encounter between traditional Jewish communities and the new bourgeois sphere, thinkers of Jewish origin such as Karl Marx (1818–1883), Sigmund Freud (1856–1939), and Émile Durkheim (1858–1917) were pioneers in the reflexive articulation of modernity's self-understanding, while Jewish writers, scientists, and musicians likewise made disproportionate contributions to modern culture. The *haskalah* or "Jewish enlightenment" stimulated a new, secular Hebrew literature, as well as a modern Yiddish literature, much of which has stood the test of generations as a commentary both on the limitations of tradition and on the frequently empty pretensions of the new.

Yet Jewishness and the Jews were frequently seen as a "problem" for Western modernity, whether because their potential loyalty and capacity for absorption as fellow citizens of secular nation-states was in question, or because the organizing logic of those nation-states rested in unacknowledged ways on assumptions of their constituents' shared Christian heritage. One reaction was the crystallization of Zionism as the Jews' own modern nationalist movement, which eventually took material form in the effort to convince Jews to migrate to Palestine and to create the infrastructure for Jewish state sovereignty there to be renewed after nearly two millennia. Zionism bears in turn a complex relation to traditional Jewishness, rejecting as neurotic substitutions much of the diasporic forms of Jewish life, while mobilizing the memory and longing for the lost homeland that have nourished Jewish sensibilities in exile.

Political engagement by Jews in liberal and socialist struggles throughout the West helped fuel the modern anti-Semitic movement. Anti-Semitism was itself a reactionary response to the rapid pace of social and economic change, paradoxically bolstered by modern theories of biologically determined and hence immutable racial characteristics. During the 1930s, a time when Western economy and society were simultaneously resisting workers' revolution and reeling from catastrophic disruption to the capitalist economy, Jews were irrationally but opportunistically tarred as the bête noire of the imagined "Aryan" race. The consequent call to eliminate the Jews, originally a demand for expulsion, was transformed in the course of World War II (1939–1945) into an active program of genocide. There were an estimated 18,000,000 Jews at the beginning of that war; by its end, a third of them had been slaughtered.

PRESENT SITUATION

The map of the Jewish world has been dramatically reshaped in past centuries, as a result of genocide, assimilation, migration, nation-building, and renewal. The Jews of the world are far less widely dispersed than they once were, and much has been lost. The State of Israel explicitly defines itself as a Jewish state, yet along with a significant Arab minority, its population includes numbers of immigrants whose "Jewish" status according to religious law has been hotly debated. Moreover, Israel and its Jewish population continue to face vital issues of cultural and political integration into the Middle East.

Along with Israel, the United States holds by far the world's largest Jewish population, and American Jews are generally considered well integrated. Markers of Jewish identity and culture are readily present and celebrated in media and popular culture. Those concerned with Jewish continuity worry about high rates of intermarriage among moderately affiliated Jews. There is an extraordinary range of options for expression of religious Judaism, for the explicit linkage of Jewishness to other nonmajoritarian identities, and for the preservation and reinvention of secular Jewish culture. Meanwhile, traditionalist religious communities have enjoyed a resurgence, experiencing high birthrates and close to universal retention of young people within their communities.

Outside of Israel and the United States, France retains the largest Jewish population, largely comprising North African immigrants and their descendants. French

Jewry today stands as a test case for the continued viability of Jewish and indeed of minority communities more generally in contemporary western Europe, and some see its future as clouded by the appearance of a "new anti-Semitism" there. Significant Jewish populations also are found in the countries of the former Soviet Union, in Canada, in the United Kingdom, and in Argentina.

SEE ALSO *Anti-Semitism; Assimilation; Christianity; Enlightenment; Ethnocentrism; Gender; Genocide; Heteronormativity; Holocaust, The; Islam, Shia and Sunni; Jewish Diaspora; Judaism; Migration; Modernism; Modernization; Nation of Islam; Nationalism and Nationality; Religion; Reparations; Supreme Being; Zionism*

BIBLIOGRAPHY

Biale, David, ed. 2002. *Cultures of the Jews: A New History.* New York: Schocken.

Boyarin, Daniel. 2004. *Border Lines: The Partition of Judaeo-Christianity.* Philadelphia: University of Pennsylvania Press.

Gerber, Jane. 1992. *The Jews of Spain: A History of the Sephardic Experience.* New York: Free Press.

Gilman, Sander. 1986. *Jewish Self-Hatred: Anti-Semitism and the Hidden Language of the Jews.* Baltimore, MD: Johns Hopkins University Press.

Gruen, Erich. 2002. *Diaspora: Jews amidst Greeks and Romans.* Cambridge, MA: Harvard University Press.

Mendes-Flohr, Paul, and Jehuda Reinharz, eds. 1995. *The Jew in the Modern World: A Documentary History.* 2nd ed. New York: Oxford University Press.

Moore, Deborah Dash, and S. Ilan Troen, eds. 2001. *Divergent Jewish Cultures: Israel and America.* New Haven, CT: Yale University Press.

Scholem, Gershom. 1971. *The Messianic Idea in Judaism and Other Essays on Jewish Spirituality.* New York: Schocken.

Urbach, Efraim. 1979. *The Sages: Their Concepts and Beliefs.* 2nd ed. Trans. Israel Abrahams. Jerusalem: Magnes.

Weinreich, Max. 1980. *History of the Yiddish Language.* Trans. Shlomo Noble, with Joshua Fishman. Chicago: University of Chicago Press.

Jonathan Boyarin

JIHAD

Jihad is an Arabic term meaning, as a noun, "struggle" or, as a verb, "to exert effort" toward a goal. The primary associations of the term are religious, specifically with reference to Islam. The Qur'an exhorts believers to struggle "in the path of God" or "to make God's cause succeed" (8:39). Such struggle involves all of one's power and resources, as one seeks to "command right and forbid wrong." Under certain circumstances, jihad is identified with *qital*, meaning "fighting" or "killing"; indeed, in Islamic juridical discourse, this association is prevalent, so that in some contexts, jihad can be translated as "armed struggle." In some contemporary writing by Muslims, the broader meaning of the term as "moral struggle" is stressed, and military associations are downplayed. Overall, it is best to keep in mind that the term occurs in connection with a view by which human responsibility is a matter of striving to bring all of life into a pattern of relationships consistent with God's will. In some circumstances, the means appropriate to this struggle are military; in others, not.

Stories by which Muslims interpret the Qur'anic "verses on fighting" illustrate this way of construing the meanings of jihad. According to traditional dating, Muhammad's call to prophecy occurred in the year 610 CE, and by 612 he began to preach or to "call" others to Islam. A small band of "companions" gathered around him. They met with hostility, even persecution from the people of Mecca, the Prophet's home city. In this context, some of the companions urged the use of force, by way of retaliation for wrongs done to the believers, and to deter further persecution. Muhammad resisted, indicating that God's orders only allowed him to preach.

By the year 622 (the year 1, in the Islamic calendar), things had changed. In that year, Muhammad received God's order to immigrate to Medina, a city to the north. He also received permission to fight, specifically in terms of God's provision for the protection of believers (Qur'an 22:39–40). Once in Medina, Muhammad functioned as head of state and military commander, all the while continuing to preach. Verses of the Qur'an that Muslims number among the "Medinan" texts indicate a growing sense that military action is not only permitted, but necessary, and finally obligatory in the campaign to establish a "zone of security" for the Islamic community. In his Farewell Sermon (630), Muhammad declared that "Arabia is now solidly for Islam," meaning that the various tribes were now under Islamic governance.

In the years following Muhammad's death, jihad came to be associated with the efforts of Muslims to extend the benefits of Islamic governance to people and territories beyond Arabia. A series of conquests "opened" most of the Middle East, and much of North Africa and Asia, to the influence of Islam. In this connection, the religious specialists called *"ulama"* developed a set of "judgments pertaining to jihad" that function as an Islamic "just war tradition." Thus, jihad, in the sense of legitimate war, must be commanded by the officials of an Islamic state. It should be fought for the cause of God, meaning the expansion, establishment, or defense of Islamic territory. And it should be fought with right intention, in the sense of avoiding undue aggression. Fighters should avoid

directly targeting noncombatants and, according to some authorities, they should further avoid the use of weapons or tactics that might bring about unacceptable levels of "indirect" damage to civilian life. The rules governing jihad were developed and recognized by specialists associated with the majority (Sunni) and minority (Shia) versions of Islam, though the latter insisted that jihad could only be authorized by a divinely authorized Imam or leader, the implication being that most wars fought in the name of Islam did not really qualify.

In the nineteenth and twentieth centuries, jihad came to be associated with Muslim resistance to European and North American imperialism. Some argued for military resistance, others for education designed to make Muslim economies competitive. Important examples of military jihad include uprisings led by Uthman Dan Fodio (1754–1817) in Nigeria and Muhammad Ahmad al-Mahdi (1884–1885) in Sudan. As for the educational approach, the development of Aligarh Muslim University in India by Sayyid Ahmad Khan (1817–1898) and the campaign for educational reform in Egypt led by Muhammad 'Abduh (1849–1905) are particularly worthy of mention.

More recently, jihad has come to be associated with the program of certain groups (called *jihadis*) who hold that armed force is a necessary means for Muslims to resist the encroachment of a "Zionist-Crusader alliance" by which a variety of false or idolatrous practices are being foisted upon humanity. These practices, which include democratic politics, free market capitalism, and the equality of men and women, are held to violate divine law. Various declarations issued by the leaders of Al-Qaeda and like-minded groups suggest that the spread of these practices constitutes a kind of emergency condition for Muslims, and that in such a condition, fighting becomes an obligation for every Muslim. In contrast with the historic "judgments pertaining to armed struggle," this contemporary jihad involves fighting without authorization by established heads of state. According to many *jihadis*, the new jihad may also be conducted without regard to distinctions between civilian and military targets. Such points are controversial, with the large majority of Muslims condemning such tactics as violations of Islamic tradition, even while expressing sympathy for some of the causes *jihadis* cite as motivation, viz., the rights of Palestinians, resistance to "undue influence" by the United States and others in the internal affairs of historically Muslim countries, and the desire for effective and legitimate government in Muslim lands.

SEE ALSO *Fundamentalism, Islamic; Islam, Shia and Sunni*

BIBLIOGRAPHY

Abou El Fadl, Khaled. 2001. *Rebellion and Violence in Islamic Law.* Cambridge, U.K., and New York: Cambridge University Press.

Benjamin, Daniel, and Steven Simon. 2003. *The Age of Sacred Terror.* New York: Random House.

Cook, Michael. 2000. *Commanding Right and Forbidding Wrong in Islamic Thought.* Cambridge, U.K., and New York: Cambridge University Press.

Enayat, Hamid. 1982. *Modern Islamic Political Thought.* Austin: University of Texas Press.

Hourani, Albert. 1983. *Arabic Thought in the Liberal Age, 1798–1939.* 2nd ed. Cambridge, U.K., and New York: Cambridge University Press.

Johnson, James T., and John Kelsay, eds. 1990. *Cross, Crescent, and Sword: The Justification and Limitation of War in Western and Islamic Tradition.* New York: Greenwood.

Kelsay, John. 1993. *Islam and War: A Study in Comparative Ethics.* Louisville, KY: Westminster/John Knox Press.

Kelsay, John, and James T. Johnson, eds. 1991. *Just War and Jihad: Historical and Theoretical Perspectives on War and Peace in Western and Islamic Traditions.* New York: Greenwood.

Peters, Rudolph. 1996. *Jihad in Classical and Modern Islam.* Princeton, NJ: Princeton University Press.

John Kelsay

JIM CROW

Jim Crow was the colloquial term for forms of systematic discrimination employed by whites against African Americans from the second half of the nineteenth century through the first half of the twentieth. The expression insinuates the legal components of the color line (e.g., Jim Crow laws), but also encompasses the cultural and symbolic conventions of hierarchical race relations.

OVERVIEW

The roots of Jim Crow lay deep in the American landscape of slavery. Despite its jocular allusion to a persona, Jim Crow articulated ideologies of black inferiority, which, wrapped in racist rhetoric, signified white supremacy, the control of virtually every aspect of black public life, and access to black private life. As shorthand for the malice of race relations in America, Jim Crow lived out a "strange career," the historian C. Vann Woodward (1908–1999) wrote. "Jim Crow … did not assign the subordinate group to a fixed status in society. [It was] constantly pushing the Negro further down" (Woodward [1955] 2002, p. 108).

The scholar W. E. B. Du Bois (1868–1963) used the term "the veil" in reference to the barrier separating blacks and whites. Penetrable but immovable, the veil provided African Americans with a view outward, while limiting the ability of whites to see into black society. "Within and without the somber veil of color," Du Bois wrote of black life in *The Souls of Black Folk* (1903), "vast social forces have been at work,—efforts for human betterment, movements toward disintegration and despair, tragedies and comedies in social and economic life, and a swaying and lifting and sinking of human hearts which have made this land a land of mingled sorrow and joy, of change and excitement and unrest" (pp. 181–182). Behind the veil, then, African Americans engaged in the discourse and action of daily life, often unconcerned with white life. Here, they forged lively communities, built strong institutions, and nurtured generations of activists who took part in the long civil rights movement to "destroy Jim Crow."

As a period of history, the "Jim Crow era" can be set off by two significant decisions made by the U.S. Supreme Court, each determining the constitutionality of racial segregation. On one end, *Homer Plessy v. John H. Ferguson* 163 U.S. 537 (1896) sanctioned racial segregation and discrimination with the doctrine of "separate but equal," arguing that the Fourteenth Amendment "could not have been intended to abolish distinctions based upon color, or to enforce social, as distinguished from political equality, or a commingling of the two races upon terms unsatisfactory to either." On the other end of a timeline, *Oliver Brown, et al. v. Board of Education of Topeka, et al.* 387 U.S. 483 (1954) outlawed racial segregation in public schools arguing that "separate educational facilities are inherently unequal." *Brown* opened the door to question and to challenge other forms of racial inequity.

THE HISTORY OF JIM CROW

Jim Crow far exceeds the temporal markers of Supreme Court decisions, reaching back to the mid-nineteenth century and beyond the modern civil rights movement. Moreover, although Jim Crow is associated mostly with the intractable South, similar patterns, indeed its cultural origins, can be found in the North. The term was being used by the mid-nineteenth century by African Americans and abolitionists to describe the unfair practice of directing black passengers to separate substandard railroad cars. *Jimcrow* or *jimcrowing* referred to the injustice of segregating blacks to lesser facilities.

The term *Jim Crow* originated in American popular culture, specifically in a stage performance, a mocking imitation of a black plantation slave by Thomas Dartmouth "Daddy" Rice (1808–1860), a white entertainer. In the tradition of minstrelsy, Rice blackened his face with burned cork or black wax, wore ragged clothes as a costume, shuffled as he danced, and sang:

Come listen all you galls and boys I's jist from
Tuckyhoe,
I'm going to sing a little song, my name's Jim
Crow,
Weel about and turn about and do jis so,
Eb'ry time I weel about I jump Jim Crow.

A popular little ditty, "Jump Jim Crow" was a center-piece of an emerging American popular culture. Popularized, the character Jim Crow and his stage counterpart Zip Coon—an urban dandy from the North—caricatured African Americans as foolish, dim, lazy, sneaky, incompetent, untrustworthy, dishonorable, and without the strength of character required to be an American citizen and white. These degrading stereotypes, infused by distortion and propaganda, provided a substantial base on which to create a rationale for slavery: that African Americans required close supervision, and that only under the control of whites could such people be restrained.

Jim Crow entered a new phase after the Civil War (1861–1865) with enactment of the Black Codes. At the end of the war, in the political chaos that followed Abraham Lincoln's death in 1865, Confederates claimed southern legislatures and passed laws that restricted the freedom of freedpeople. Replicating slavery in all ways except name, the Black Codes required blacks to accept unfavorable work contracts, limited their mobility, and denied them citizenship rights. As traditional powers collapsed at the beginning of Reconstruction, African Americans claimed and exercised the citizenship rights guaranteed by the Thirteenth, Fourteenth, and Fifteenth amendments. Southern whites viewed this new societal arrangement as a corruption of race and gender relations that historically favored white males.

At the end of Reconstruction, when power returned to white southerners, distorted descriptions of Reconstruction governments signified whites' resentment for their losses and provided the tinder for racial fires to burn through the turn of the century. Referring to black political participation as "Negro rule" or "Negro domination," and distorting the work of Reconstruction legislatures as corrupt and immoral, white politicians determined that black power would neither continue nor return. By the end of the nineteenth century, every southern state and community had forged a set of constitutional amendments, legislation, or legal maneuvers to disfranchise African American men by force of law and intimidation. Almost every school was racially segregated and disparate in condition. Consistently, blacks were employed in the most difficult jobs for the lowest of wages.

As the color line itself solidified at the turn of the nineteenth century, Jim Crow imposed on black people clear tactical disadvantages: restricted economic possibilities, narrow educational opportunities, inadequate hous-ing options, high rates of death and disablement, persistent unemployment, and unrelenting poverty. Inasmuch as Jim Crow represented the race problem described by Gunnar Myrdal (1898–1987) in his 1944 treatise *The American Dilemma*, it was Jim Crow that created the race quandary; whites constructed the obstacles African Americans confronted, while also blaming them for their conditions, denying them access to the resources of problem solving, and daring them—under threat of violence—to complain, protest, or advance.

Jim Crow laws segregated not only public venues but also restaurants, restrooms, hospitals, churches, libraries, schoolbooks, waiting rooms, housing, prisons, cemeteries, and asylums. Customary signs noting "colored" and "white" or "white only" marked off the southern landscape, dividing public conveyances, public accommodations, and birth, residence, and death. Purportedly equal, these circumstances usually were unequal. Laws regulated not only segregation but also social relations. In most states, blacks and whites could not marry by law, or socialize by custom. According to a Maryland law, "all marriages between a white person and a negro, or between a white person and a person of negro descent, to the third generation, inclusive … are forever prohibited, and shall be void." Blacks and whites could not compete against each other, whether at checkers or college sports. A Mississippi law read, "any person guilty of printing, publishing or circulating matter urging or presenting arguments in favor of social equality or of intermarriage between whites and negroes, shall be guilty of a misdemeanor."

ENFORCEMENT

Jim Crow could be fluid, amorphous, and nuanced. Because the laws and practices of Jim Crow varied from place to place, the scheme was confusing, and African Americans were careful to learn the racial etiquette of the locales to which they traveled. In addition, different groups of African Americans, rural and urban, women and men, and people of varying classes, experienced Jim Crow in different ways. Inasmuch as women and men faced differential limitations of Jim Crow, civil rights and women's movement activist Pauli Murray (1910–1985) coined the term *Jane Crow* to describe sex discrimination against women, and race and sex discrimination against black women. African Americans could not always unify against Jim Crow because segregation could benefit some to the detriment of others. Black colleges thrived, for example, but most segregated public elementary and secondary schools struggled with inadequate resources to prepare students for higher education.

Finally, protests or challenges to Jim Crow often proved futile, given law enforcement's complicity in the structure. From emancipation to the turn of the century, the Ku Klux Klan operated as a paramilitary arm of the Democratic Party in the South. The Klan, nightriders, red shirts, and other white terrorists intimidated African Americans with personal attacks, school burnings, and lynchings. African Americans rarely served as policemen, sheriffs, or deputies before the late 1940s. During the 1950s and 1960s, the connections between municipal and state governments, law enforcement, and racial violence were well known by officials and citizens alike. White officers were known to harass black people, disrupt black neighborhoods, and assault black women. Arrested for inflated charges, denied satisfactory counsel, and serving harsh sentences, African Americans were further disadvantaged in the courtroom. Rarely did they receive good counsel, nor could they serve on juries. When black lawyers could appear in the courtroom to argue cases, white judges and juries rarely listened. All-white juries decided against black defendants, even in the most obvious cases of innocence, but rarely convicted white defendants, despite evidence of guilt. African Americans—including the innocent—suffered the harsher punishments of extended jail time, forced farm labor, and peonage. Even women could be placed on the chain gangs working the roads and tracks across the South.

Extralegally, Jim Crow justice was rough. According to the National Association for the Advancement of Colored People (NAACP), between 1889 and 1918 over 2,500 African Americans were lynched: captured and viciously murdered by mobs. Ostensibly, accusations of rape provided the reason for lynching, yet rarely were these cases validated. A form of social control and vengeance, lynching followed when a black person stepped out of line, did not demonstrate enough deference, acted out of antagonism, committed assault or manslaughter as self-defense, or spoke out of turn. Through the first half of the twentieth century, furthermore, riots flared as an expression of white antagonism, among them the Wilmington Riot of 1898, the Atlanta Riot of 1906, the East Saint Louis Riot of 1917, and the Tulsa Riot of 1921. In each of these and other conflagrations, whites expressed their racial rage by entering black neighborhoods to assault men, women, and children, and by burning down homes, schools, and churches. African American veterans in uniform also were targets of random attack, subject to vengeance for wearing a symbol of American citizenship.

AFRICAN AMERICANS AND JIM CROW

For these reasons, Jim Crow presented a formidable opponent—one that could divide its victims against themselves. Numerous leaders stepped forward to speak to the quandary of race relations. Booker T. Washington (1856–1915) advised black men to shift their focus from electoral politics to economics, to take up the trades, farming, and domestic and service work in order to build character and capital. While Washington supported industrial education, Du Bois recommended that the most talented of black folk be trained in the liberal arts so that they could emerge as leaders of the race. Ida B. Wells-Barnett (1862–1931), a fearless antilynching campaigner, took up the mantle of agitation, advising African Americans to protect themselves and to leave the South altogether.

The question of migration as a form of protest dominated black discourse and action after emancipation, and as the century turned, a trickle of black southerners, mostly women, began to leave the land for the cities of the South and the North. They laid the groundwork for what was later called the Great Migration, when millions of African Americans left the brutalities of the South for the possibilities of the North. Black migrations were fueled by several factors. African Americans hoped to escape the tyranny of the South, especially economic oppression. The importunate character of sharecropping pressed families to give up the land for the city. There, however, they found new sets of barriers to employment or improved living conditions. Nevertheless, as the war economies expanded and European immigration slowed, African Americans found employment in the industries and the trades. Black people also migrated to find personal freedom not available to them in the South. African American women, for example, migrated to escape the persistent danger of public sexual assault by white and private assault by black men. As migrants within the South, women also laid the foundations upon which black southern communities were built, and it is here that the war against Jim Crow took place.

In urban areas, African Americans upbuilt communities from small settlements of freedpeople into dynamic neighborhoods of homes, institutions, and organizations. Although segregated, schools instilled a sense of race pride and responsibility in children. Churches served multiple roles, as community, political, and recreational spaces. Teachers, professors, undertakers, doctors, lawyers, and nurses served to uplift the black community. Held in high esteem, they presented not only models to emulate, but also a daily reminder of black accomplishment despite Jim Crow. National organizations like the NAACP, the National Negro Business League (NNBL), and black fraternities and sororities all functioned to improve the quality of life for African Americans. Founding segregated YWCAs, YMCAs, Boy's Clubs, Boy Scouts, and Girl Scouts, adult African Americans supervised the development of young people with an eye toward the demands of citizenship. Indeed, although historians have called the early years of Jim Crow "the Nadir," the lowest point in African American history, the period also was the zenith of the black press, black business, black church organizations, and the black women's club movement as African Americans set about the work of race progress.

Still, the disadvantages of Jim Crow far outweighed the advantages, and beginning in the 1930s, African Americans took up a number of civil rights crusades. The NAACP, for example, began the battle against educational inequality, with the support of local branches. Local communities also engaged in "don't-buy-where-you-can't-work" campaigns, denying their dollars to businesses that did not employ black people. Veterans returned from a war against racism expecting to be accorded citizenship rights commensurate with their sacrifices. Turned back at the courthouses, they launched voting rights campaigns. By the 1940s, several events signaled that the demise of Jim Crow had begun. In Texas, the Supreme Court decision in *Smith v. Allwright, Election Judge, et al.* 312 U. S. 649 (1944) ended the all-white primary, opening the southern electoral process to black voters. In 1948 President Harry Truman (1913–2003) signed Executive Order 9981, desegregating the armed forces. Finally, the Supreme Court decision in *Brown v. Board of Education* sounded the end of constitutionally sanctioned Jim Crow in public schools, making way for African Americans to demand the integration of all public facilities and accommodations.

Just as Jim Crow was not a strictly definable historical period, the struggle against it was protracted. Using forms of direct action, nonviolent protests, and demonstrations, civil rights activists of the 1950s and 1960s were determined to break the back of Jim Crow, and they were successful, at least as far as the legal arena was concerned. Inasmuch as Jim Crow was a milieu that permeated culture and ideology historically, the struggle against American apartheid continues.

SEE ALSO *Apartheid;* Bamboozled*; Black Face;* Brown v. Board of Education, *1954;* Brown v. Board of Education, *1955; Civil Rights; Civil Rights Movement, U.S.; Discrimination; Discrimination, Racial; Ku Klux Klan; Lynchings; Minstrelsy; Race Relations; Racism; Segregation; Separate-but-Equal; Stereotypes; Truman, Harry S.; Tulsa Riot; Voting Rights Act; White Supremacy; Whiteness; Wilmington Riot of 1898*

BIBLIOGRAPHY

Chafe, William H., Raymond Gavins, Robert Korstad, et al. 2001. *Remembering Jim Crow: African Americans Tell about Life in the Segregated South.* New York: New Press.

Du Bois, W. E. B. 1903. *The Souls of Black Folk.* 2nd ed. Chicago: A. C. McClurg.

Gilmore, Glenda. 1996. *Gender and Jim Crow: Women and the Politics of White Supremacy in North Carolina, 1896–1920.* Chapel Hill: University of North Carolina Press.

Klarman, Michael J. 2004. *From Jim Crow to Civil Rights: The Supreme Court and the Struggle for Racial Equality.* New York: Oxford University Press.

Litwack, Leon. 1998. *Trouble in Mind: Black Southerners in the Age of Jim Crow.* New York: Knopf.

Williamson, Joel. 1984. *The Crucible of Race: Black-White Relations in the American South since Emancipation.* New York: Oxford University Press.

Woodward, C. Vann. [1955] 2002. *The Strange Career of Jim Crow.* New York: Oxford University Press.

Leslie Brown

JINGOISM

The term *jingoism* dates from the late 1870s. The jingoes, so termed after a music-hall song, were vociferous supporters of a strong British foreign policy in the Near East. *Jingoism* subsequently came to define any foreign policy in support of national interests that took its cue from public opinion. For social scientists, jingoism stands as one of the manifestations of nationalism in the Western world in the half-century leading up to World War I (1914–1918).

In the spring of 1877, Russia went to war with Turkey. The Conservative British government, led by Benjamin Disraeli (1804–1881), was concerned that Constantinople might fall to the Russians and that this would endanger the security of British routes to its Indian empire. Neutrality was declared, but conditional on the safeguarding of British interests. Toward the end of the year, it seemed as if these interests might be threatened, and the possibility loomed that Britain would become involved in a reprise of the Crimean War of the 1850s. A strong peace campaign urged the government not to get involved in the war, and for some weeks it seemed to carry all before it. But then, in January 1878, the peace meetings began to be broken up by supporters of a strong policy. The changing mood of the public was evident also in popular entertainment. G. W. Hunt (c. 1830–1904) wrote and composed a song to reflect and express the views of those who wanted the government to stand firm in the face of the Russian advance. It played on a deep-rooted Russophobia in Britain, one verse going:

> The 'Dogs of War' are loose, and the rugged
> Russian Bear,
> Full bent on blood and robbery, has crawled
> out of his lair,
> It seems a thrashing now and then will never
> help to tame

That brute, and so he's bent upon the 'same old game.'

Sung by G. H. Macdermott (c. 1845–1901) in London, and then on a provincial tour, the song became a popular hit, its rousing chorus giving the jingoes their name:

We don't want to fight,
But by Jingo if we do
We've got the ships, we've got the men, we've got the money too.
We won't let the Russians get to Constantinople.

Thoroughly alarmed at the changing mood of the public, and at the violent breakup of their meetings, the advocates of peace described their opponents as *jingoes*, "the new tribe of music-hall patriots who sing the jingo song."

From that moment on, through the late nineteenth and early twentieth centuries, *jingoism* was a term used by opponents of an assertive foreign policy. Moderate Conservatives as well as Liberals and socialists were alarmed at what they saw as the undue influence on policymaking of raucous public opinion. It was not that there had not previously been virulent antiforeign sentiment, against the Spanish in the early modern period, and against the French in the eighteenth and early nineteenth centuries. A fear of Russia itself had deep roots. What was new, and what distinguished jingoism from these earlier manifestations, was that it coincided in time with Britain becoming increasingly democratic. Most urban working-class men had become entitled to vote in 1867, and this was extended to those living in rural areas in 1884. The worry of the elite classes, whatever their politics, was that an undereducated electorate, swayed by a cheap popular press and music-hall songs, would exercise an undue influence on the conduct of foreign policy.

Lord Derby (1826–1893), who had been Disraeli's foreign secretary in 1878 but lost his job when Disraeli gave way to the jingoes, complained in 1882 that the leading idea of jingoism seemed to be "that no State can be in a healthy condition that is not occasionally pitching into its neighbour." Lord Salisbury (1830–1903), Conservative prime minister for much of the late nineteenth century, argued in 1897 that an arbitration system "would be an invaluable bulwark to defend the Minister from the jingoes." The most extended attack on jingoism came from the Liberal publicist J. A. Hobson (1858–1940), whose *The Psychology of Jingoism* (1901) was prompted by the renewed breakup of peace meetings during the South African War of 1899 to 1902. Hobson explained jingoism by linking together the fashionable psychology that was alarmed by the "herd instinct" of the populations of the large cities of the modern world and the growth of the popular press, which seemed to pander to the worst instincts of these urban masses.

Detailed research on those who might be called active jingoes—those who tried to break up peace meetings—suggests that they were often associated with other right-wing populist causes such as fair trade (to keep out foreign imports) and opposition to immigration. Medical students, hardly typical of an undereducated urban mass, featured prominently in the rowdy meetings. Many jingoes had links with the Conservative Party. Although the party leaders were often distinctly lukewarm about jingoism, there is much evidence that, as in the 1900 general election where the South African war was the dominant issue, Conservatives gained by their association with an assertive foreign policy. More generally, a nationalistic foreign policy appealed to the growing lower middle class of clerks and shopkeepers who may have been trying to overcome their anxiety about their status by affirming loyalty to the nation.

Jingoism as a word crossed the Atlantic, its use particularly prevalent in the 1890s. In 1896 the *Nation* in New York referred to "Jingoish ideas of America's past and future," and in 1898 President William McKinley (1843–1901) was reported to have said that he "will not be jingoed into war." But whether or not the word *jingo* was used, all Western countries were familiar with the phenomenon prior to World War I. In France, *chauvinism* was the equivalent of *jingoism*.

The experience of World War I put an end to the more overt assertions of national aggression. There were people who continued to hold views similar to the jingoes, but they were more on the fringe. The right-wing nationalism of the 1920s and 1930s came in the even more alarming form of fascism. After World War II (1939–1945), critics of British foreign policy or public opinion sometimes blamed jingoism, for example, for the war over the Falkland Islands in the 1980s. But as a permanent presence on the political scene, jingoism had a lifespan of some forty years preceding World War I.

SEE ALSO *Boer War; Conservative Party (Britain); Elites; Ethnocentrism; Foreign Policy; Herd Behavior; Imperialism; Militarism; Nationalism and Nationality; Nativism; Patriotism; Right Wing; World War I; World War II*

BIBLIOGRAPHY

Cunningham, Hugh. 1971. Jingoism in 1877–1878. *Victorian Studies* 14 (4): 429–453.

Porter, Bernard. 2004. *The Absent-Minded Imperialists: Empire, Society, and Culture in Britain.* Oxford: Oxford University Press.

Price, Richard N. 1977. Society, Status, and Jingoism: The Social Roots of Lower Middle Class Patriotism, 1870–1900. In *The Lower Middle Class in Britain, 1870–1914,* ed. Geoffrey Crossick, 89–112. London: Croom Helm.

Readman, Paul. 2001. The Conservative Party, Patriotism, and British Politics: The Case of the General Election of 1900. *Journal of British Studies* 40 (1): 107–145.

Hugh Cunningham

JINNAH, MOHAMMED ALI
1876–1948

Mohammed Ali Jinnah was born in 1876 in Karachi, then a small port town on the western coast of British India. A bright and ambitious young boy, he soon found his way to London and joined Lincoln's Inn, one of the best-known legal institutions in England. Jinnah acquired many things from British culture, perhaps most important of all, a sense of respect for the law.

On returning to India, Jinnah set up practice in Bombay and soon made a mark on society as a prominent leader. He became a passionate nationalist for the freedom of India and for unity between the two major communities of South Asia—Hindus and Muslims. He was called the "ambassador of Hindu-Muslim unity" by Gopal Krishna Gokhale (1866–1915), the distinguished Hindu leader. In 1918 Jinnah fell in love with and married Ruttie, who was half his age, and they had one child, a daughter called Dina.

In the 1920s the politics of India was changing dramatically. Mohandas Gandhi (1869–1948) and Jawaharlal Nehru (1889–1964) emerged as superstars to lead the Indian National Congress. The main Muslim party, the Muslim League, could not field anyone of their stature. Uncomfortable with what he saw as the emergence of communal politics, Jinnah was finding it difficult to place himself.

When Ruttie died in 1929, Jinnah left India to practice law in London. In the meantime, the Muslims of India became alarmed at the growth of what they saw as Hindu communalism in politics and the vulnerability of Muslims. Several delegations visited Jinnah and asked him to return to India and lead the Muslims.

Jinnah was persuaded to return and by the late 1930s galvanized the Muslims into a political force. He changed the way he dressed and even his arguments to reflect a more Islamic identity. In a historic Muslim League session in 1940 in Lahore, Jinnah introduced the idea of Pakistan, a defined political entity for the Muslims of India. Jinnah then led a full-scale campaign to create Pakistan in the face of vigorous opposition from the Indian National Congress and, initially, from the British.

In August 1947 Pakistan was carved out of the Muslim dominated areas of the northwest of India and the province of Bengal in the east. Although Jinnah had warned against it, Lord Louis Mountbatten (1900–1979), the viceroy, ensured that the two major provinces of India, the Punjab and Bengal, were cut in half. This division plunged the subcontinent into a bloodbath as some fifteen million people escaped communal rioting to migrate to the new homelands—Hindus and Sikhs escaping from Pakistan to India, and Muslims from India going to Pakistan. It is estimated that about two million people died in the communal frenzy that summer.

Jinnah became the first governor-general of the independent state of Pakistan, which was then the largest Muslim nation on earth. But the moment of triumph was darkened for Jinnah by the scale of the death and destruction. Depicted as a cold and formal man, Jinnah could not control his emotions at the scale of the tragedies unfolding around him. In speech after speech, he talked of the "harrowing accounts of the terrible happenings" and his "deep distress and heavy heart." Fatima Jinnah, his sister and constant companion, wrote of Jinnah's emotional condition in the last months of his life. "As he discussed with me these mass killings at the breakfast table, his eyes were often moist with tears. The sufferings of Muslim refugees that trekked from India into Pakistan, which to them had been the Promised Land, depressed him" (Jinnah 1987, p. 11).

In the midst of the chaos, Jinnah set up an entirely new government based in Karachi. His first two speeches to the Constituent Assembly in August that year clearly outlined his vision of a modern Muslim state: while inspired by the principles of Islam, the rights of everyone were to be respected. Jinnah specifically mentioned the freedom that non-Muslims would enjoy in Pakistan. He condemned nepotism and corruption in the strongest terms.

Already ill, Jinnah was now physically and emotionally exhausted. He spent several months in Ziarat, a hill station in Baluchistan, in the hope of recovering his health. In September 1948 Jinnah died in Karachi.

Pakistanis saw Jinnah as a leader who gave them their own homeland against impossible odds, and they called him the *Quaid-e-Azam*, or the great leader. Alan Campbell Johnson (1913–1998), a key official of Lord Mountbatten, described Jinnah thus: "Here indeed is Pakistan's King Emperor, Archbishop of Canterbury, Speaker and Prime Minister concentrated into one formidable Quaid-e-Azam" (Mitchell 1997). Jinnah's grand mausoleum in Karachi is a main attraction for foreigners and Pakistanis alike.

With the triumph of Jinnah's life, there were also great tragedies that still haunt South Asia. One of these is the unresolved dispute over the large and important state of Kashmir. Pakistan has advocated that a plebiscite be held so that Kashmiris can decide their own fate. Its mainly Muslim population and contiguous territory to Pakistan have led Pakistanis to believe that Kashmir should have become part of Pakistan in 1947. However, its Hindu ruler opted for India. Pakistanis suspected that the friendship between the Mountbattens and Nehru, the first prime minister of India, was responsible for this injustice. Three wars have been fought between India and Pakistan over Kashmir, and now that both countries are nuclear powers, the region has been described by President Bill Clinton as the most dangerous place in the world.

Jinnah's life shows the importance of personal relationships in politics. While Jinnah was comfortable dealing with such contemporaries as Gandhi and Motilal Nehru (1861–1931), father of Jawaharlal, there was little rapport between him and the Mountbattens or their friend Jawaharlal Nehru. They, in turn, saw him as a figure from the past and spoke unkindly of him. Jinnah's relationship with B. R. Ambedkar (1891–1956), the leader of the Dalit—or those once called the "untouchable" caste—is surprisingly neglected. Jinnah and Ambedkar came to represent the two important minority groups of India—the Muslims and the Dalit. Both were suspicious of Gandhi's identification with mainstream Hinduism and warned against *Ram Raj*, or the rule of upper-caste Hindus who used Lord Ram as a symbol of Hindu revivalism. Ambedkar was supportive of the idea of Pakistan, but he did point out the problems its creation would pose for Hindus and Muslims in general. While Jinnah appreciated Ambedkar's criticism of Hinduism, he was also aware of Ambedkar's vitriolic criticism of some of the social practices of Indian Muslims. The tactical alliance between the Muslims and the Dalit that could have altered the shape of Indian politics thus never took place.

Considering the scale of his achievement, it is not surprising that Jinnah remains a subject of discussion and debate. Historians continue to interpret his position on the creation of Pakistan. For some, the Pakistan movement was the logical outcome of the politics and social ideas of the first half of the twentieth century (Ahmed 1997; Wolpert 1984, 2006). Others have argued that Jinnah was using the demand for Pakistan as a bargaining chip to improve the position of the Muslim minority in India (Jalal 1985). Jinnah would have thus resolved the contradiction between a demand for a separate Muslim state and the need for a strategy that would safeguard the interests of all Indian Muslims. No one, however, can deny that Jinnah did what few have done in history: almost single-handedly, he created a nation.

SEE ALSO *Ambedkar, B. R.; Caste; Caste, Anthropology of; Decolonization; Gandhi, Mohandas K.; Islam, Shia and Sunni; Muslims; Nation-State; Nehru, Jawaharlal; Partition; Secession*

BIBLIOGRAPHY

Ahmed, Akbar S. 1997. *Jinnah, Pakistan, and Islamic Identity: The Search for Saladin*. London: Routledge.

Jalal, Ayesha. 1985. *The Sole Spokesman: Jinnah, the Muslim League, and the Demand for Pakistan*. Cambridge, U.K.: Cambridge University Press.

Jinnah, Fatima. 1987. *My Brother*. Karachi: Quaid-i-Azam Academy.

Mitchell, Christopher. 1997. *Mr. Jinnah, the Making of Pakistan*. London: Café Productions.

Wolpert, Stanley. 1984. *Jinnah of Pakistan*. New York: Oxford University Press.

Wolpert, Stanley. 2006. *Shameful Flight: The Last Years of the British Empire in India*. New York: Oxford University Press.

Akbar S. Ahmed

JOB GUARANTEE

A job-guarantee program is one in which government promises to make a job available to any qualifying individual who is ready and willing to work. Qualifications required of participants could specify age range (e.g., teens), gender, family status (e.g., heads of households), family income (e.g., below poverty line), educational attainment (e.g., high school dropouts), residency (e.g., rural), and so on. The most general program—sometimes called an *employer of last resort* (ELR) program—would provide a universal job guarantee by which government promises to provide a job to anyone legally entitled to work.

Many job-guarantee supporters see employment not only as an economic condition, but also as a right. L. Randall Wray and Mathew Forstater (2004) justify the right to work as a fundamental prerequisite for social justice in any society in which income from work is an important determinant of access to resources. Philip Harvey (1989) and John Burgess and William F. Mitchell (1998) argue for the right to work on the basis that it is a fundamental human (or natural) right. Such treatments find support in modern legal proclamations such as the United Nations Universal Declaration of Human Rights, the U.S. Employment Act of 1946, and the Full Employment Act of 1978. Amartya Sen (1999) supports the right to work on the basis that the economic and social costs of unemployment are staggering, with far-reaching consequences beyond the single dimension of a loss of income (see also Rawls 1971). William Vickrey identified unemployment with "cruel vandalism," outlining the social and economic inequities of unemployment and devising strategies for its solution (Forstater and Tcherneva 2004). A key proposition of such arguments is that no capitalist society has ever managed to operate at anything approaching true full employment on a consistent basis. Further, the burden of joblessness is borne unequally, concentrated among groups that already face other disadvantages: racial and ethnic minorities, immigrants, younger and older individuals, women, people with disabilities, and those with lower educational attainment. For these reasons, government should and must play a role in providing jobs to achieve social justice.

There are different versions of the job-guarantee program. Harvey proposed to provide to anyone unable to find work a public sector job with pay approximating a "market wage"; more highly skilled workers would receive higher pay (1989). Argentina's Jefes program (examined below) targets heads of households only, offering a uniform basic payment for what is essentially half-time work. In another model, initially proposed by Hyman Minsky (1965) and developed further at the Center for Full Employment and Price Stability, University of Missouri—Kansas City, and independently at the Centre of Full Employment and Equity, University of Newcastle, Australia, the federal government provides funding for a job-creation program that offers a uniform hourly wage with a package of benefits (Wray 1998; Burgess and Mitchell 1998). The program could provide for part-time and seasonal work as well as other flexible working conditions as desired by the workers. The package of benefits would be subject to congressional approval, but it could include health care, child care, payment of Social Security taxes, and usual vacation and sick leave. The wage would also be set by Congress and fixed until Congress approved a rate increase, much as the minimum wage is currently legislated. The perceived advantage of the uniform basic wage is that it would limit competition with other employers because they could attract workers out of the ELR program by offering them a wage slightly above the program wage. Since the basic wage is held constant, it will not go up in competition with private employers, to try to bid workers away from them.

Proponents of a universal job-guarantee program operated by the federal government argue that no other means exists to ensure that everyone who wants to work is able to obtain a job. Advantages include poverty reduction, amelioration of many social ills associated with

chronic unemployment (such as health problems, spousal abuse and family breakups, drug abuse, crime), and enhanced skills from training on the job. Such a program would improve working conditions in the private sector because employees would have the option of moving into the ELR program; hence, private sector employers would have to offer a wage and benefit package and working conditions at least as good as those offered by the ELR program. The informal sector would shrink as workers become integrated into formal employment, gaining access to protection provided by labor laws. There would be some reduction of racial or gender discrimination because unfairly treated workers would have the ELR option, although, of course, an ELR program by itself cannot end discrimination. Still, it has long been recognized that full employment is an important tool in the fight for equality (Darity 1999). Mathew Forstater has emphasized how an ELR program could be used to increase economic flexibility and to improve the environment, as projects can be directed to mitigate ecological problems (1999).

In addition, some supporters emphasize that an ELR program with a uniform basic wage helps to promote economic and price stability by acting as an automatic stabilizer as employment in the program grows in recession and shrinks in economic expansion, counteracting private sector employment fluctuations. The federal government budget becomes more counter-cyclical because its spending on the ELR program likewise grows in recession and falls in expansion. Furthermore, the uniform basic wage reduces both inflationary pressure in a boom and deflationary pressure in a bust. In a boom, private employers can recruit from the ELR pool of workers, paying a premium over the ELR wage. The ELR pool acts like a "reserve army" of the employed, dampening wage pressures as private employment grows. In recession, workers downsized by private employers can work at the ELR wage, which puts a floor to how low wages and income can go.

Critics argue that a job guarantee would be inflationary, and they point to a version of a Phillips Curve approach, according to which lower unemployment necessarily means higher inflation (Sawyer 2003). Some argue that an ELR program would reduce the incentive to work, raising private sector costs because of increased shirking, because workers would no longer fear job loss; in fact, workers might be emboldened to ask for greater wage increases. Some argue that an ELR program would be so big that it would be impossible to manage; some fear corruption; others argue that it would be impossible to find useful things for ELR workers to do; still others argue that it would be difficult to discipline ELR workers. It has been argued that a national job guarantee would be too expensive, causing the budget deficit to grow to unsustainable levels, and that higher employment would worsen trade deficits (Aspromourgous 2000; King 2001). (See Mitchell and Wray 2005 for responses to all of these critiques.)

There have been many job-creation programs implemented around the world, both narrowly targeted and broad-based. The United States' New Deal of the 1930s contained several moderately inclusive programs, including the Civilian Conservation Corps and the Works Progress Administration. Sweden developed broad-based employment programs that virtually guaranteed access to jobs, until government began to retrench in the 1970s (Ginsburg 1983). In the aftermath of its economic crisis that came with the collapse of its currency board in December 2001, Argentina created *Plan Jefes y Jefas* in April 2002, which guaranteed jobs for poor heads of households (Tcherneva and Wray 2005). The program successfully created two million new jobs that provided not only employment and income for poor families, but also needed services and free goods to poor neighborhoods. More recently, India passed the National Rural Employment Guarantee Act (2005), which commits the government to providing employment in a public-works project to any adult living in a rural area. The job must be provided within fifteen days of the applicant's registration, and must provide employment for a minimum of 100 days per year (Hirway 2006). These real-world experiments provide fertile ground for testing the claims on both sides of the job-guarantee debate.

BIBLIOGRAPHY

Aspromourgos, Tony. 2000. Is an Employer-of-Last-Resort Policy Sustainable? A Review Article. *Review of Political Economy* 12 (2): 141–155.

Burgess, John, and William F. Mitchell. 1998. Unemployment Human Rights and Full Employment Policy in Australia. *Globalization, Human Rights, and Civil Society*, ed. Melinda Jones and Peter Kreisler, 112–130. Sydney: Prospect Press.

Darity, William, Jr. 1999. Who Loses from Unemployment. *Journal of Economic Issues* 33 (2): 491–496.

Forstater, Mathew. 1999. Full Employment and Economic Flexibility. *Economic and Labour Relations Review* 11: 69–88.

Forstater, Mathew, and Pavlina R. Tcherneva, eds. 2004. *Full Employment and Price Stability: The Macroeconomic Vision of William S. Vickrey.* Cheltenham, U.K.: Edward Elgar.

Ginsburg, Helen. 1983. *Full Employment and Public Policy: The United States and Sweden.* Lanham, MD: Lexington Books.

Harvey, Philip. 1989. *Securing the Right to Employment: Social Welfare Policy and the Unemployed in the United States.* Princeton, NJ: Princeton University Press.

Hirway, Indira. 2006. Enhancing Livelihood Security through the National Employment Guarantee Act: Toward Effective Implementation of the Act. Levy Economics Institute Working Paper 437 (January). http://www.levy.org/default.asp?view=publications_view&pubID=108fd5fff36.

King, John E. 2001. The Last Resort? Some Critical Reflections on ELR. *Journal of Economic and Social Policy* 5 (2): 72–76.

Minsky, Hyman P. 1965. The Role of Employment Policy. In *Poverty in America*, ed. Margaret S. Gordon, 175–200. San Francisco: Chandler.

Mitchell, William F., and L. Randall Wray. 2005. In Defense of Employer of Last Resort: A Response to Malcolm Sawyer. *Journal of Economic Issues* 39 (1): 235–245.

Rawls, John. 1971. *Theory of Justice.* Cambridge, MA: Harvard University Press.

Sawyer, Malcolm. 2003. Employer of Last Resort: Could It Deliver Full Employment and Price Stability? *Journal of Economic Issues* 37 (4): 881–908.

Sen, Amartya. 1999. *Development as Freedom.* New York: Knopf.

Tcherneva, Pavlina, and L. Randall Wray. 2005. Gender and the Job Guarantee: The Impact of Argentina's Jefes Program on Female Heads of Poor Households. Center for Full Employment and Price Stability Working Paper 50 (December). http://www.cfeps.org.

Wray, L. Randall. 1998. *Understanding Modern Money: The Key to Full Employment and Price Stability.* Cheltenham, U.K.: Edward Elgar.

Wray, L. Randall, and Mathew Forstater. 2004. Full Employment and Economic Justice. In *The Institutionalist Tradition in Labor Economics*, ed. Dell Champlin and Janet Knoedler, 253–272. Armonk: NY: M.E. Sharpe.

L. Randall Wray

JOHANSON, DONALD
1943–

Donald Carl Johanson was born in Chicago, Illinois, on June 28, 1943. He earned a BA from the University of Illinois, Urbana-Champaign, in 1966 and an MA and a PhD from the University of Chicago's Anthropology Department in 1970 and 1974, respectively. Johanson wrote his doctoral thesis on variability in the dentitions of bonobos and chimpanzee subspecies, chiefly under the guidance of Albert A. Dahlberg, the founder of U.S. dental anthropology. Before getting his doctorate, Johanson worked variously on archaeological projects in Iowa and Illinois, as a research assistant in a dental anthropological study on Kodiak Island, Alaska, and as a research assistant to F. Clark Howell with the Omo Research Expedition to the Lower Omo Basin, Ethiopia (1970–1971).

In 1972 Johanson joined the International Afar Research Expedition to Ethiopia's Afar Depression, where the following year he found four Pliocene hominid fossils, consisting of femoral fragments and a knee joint (A.L. 129-1), that clearly indicated bipedal posture. Initially, Johanson thought that more than one species was represented, but when the sample was greatly augmented by the discovery in 1974 of a notable portion of a skeleton (AL-288-1, dubbed "Lucy"), and a large collection of remains of hominids at locality 333 (dubbed "the first family") in 1975–1977, he came to believe that the findings represented a variable single species, *Australopithecus afarensis*, which lived between 3 and nearly 4 million years ago. Furthermore, he concluded that contemporaneous specimens from 3.5-million-year-old deposits at Laetoli, Tanzania, discovered by a team led by Mary Leakey, were also *Australopithecus afarensis*. Johanson's use of one of the Laetoli mandibles (LH-4) as the type specimen for *Australopithecus afarensis* and his negative comments about Richard, Mary, and Louis Leakey and other professional colleagues in *Lucy: The Beginnings of Humankind* (1981) and *Lucy's Child: The Discovery of a Human Ancestor* (1989) and on the lecture circuit detracted from his overall scientific credibility among some peers. Nonetheless, Johanson stands as the foremost U.S. contributor to the hominid fossil record during the 1970s, the 1980s, and the early 1990s.

Beginning in 1972 Johanson served as a curator of anthropology, then of physical anthropology, at the Cleveland Museum of Natural History and was on the faculties of Case Western University in Cleveland, Ohio, and Kent State University in Kent, Ohio. In 1981 he founded the Institute of Human Origins (IHO) in Berkeley, California. In 1998 the IHO relocated to the University of Arizona, where Johanson continues as director and occupies the Virginia M. Ullman Chair in Human Origins. He and his colleagues at IHO have continued to augment knowledge and understanding of human development via empirical paleoanthropological data from the field, educational television films—most notably, *Lucy in Disguise* (1980), *The First Family* (1980), and *In Search of Human Origins* (1994)—public lectures, presentations at scientific meetings, and publications. Johanson has also trained many doctoral and postdoctoral students, some of whom are from Ethiopia and other nations where hominid fossils are found.

SEE ALSO *Anthropology; Archaeology; Leakey, Richard; Primates*

BIBLIOGRAPHY

Johanson, Donald, and Maitland Armstrong Edey. 1981. *Lucy: The Beginnings of Humankind.* New York: Simon and Schuster.

Johanson, Donald, and James Shreeve. 1989. *Lucy's Child: The Discovery of a Human Ancestor.* New York: Morrow.

Kalb, Jon. 2001. *Adventures in the Bones Trade: The Race to Discover Human Ancestors in Ethiopia's Afar Depression.* New York: Copernicus Books.

Swisher, Carl C., III, Garniss H. Curtis, and Roger Lewin. 2000. *Java Man: How Two Geologists' Dramatic Discoveries Changed Our Understanding of the Evolutionary Path to Modern Humans.* New York: Scribner's.

Tuttle, Russell H. 2002. Paleoanthropology Read in Tooth and Nail. *Reviews in Anthropology* 31 (2): 103–128.

Russell H. Tuttle

JOHN HENRYISM

John Henryism (JH), a psychological construct formally proposed in 1983 by Sherman James and colleagues (James et al. 1983), is defined as a "strong behavioral predisposition to cope actively with psychosocial environmental stressors" (James 1994, p. 163). JH is characterized by three factors: (1) efficacious mental and physical vigor; (2) a strong commitment to hard work; and (3) a single-minded determination to succeed. James and colleagues hypothesized that for persons lacking sufficient socioeconomic resources, active coping (i.e., sustained cognitive and emotional engagement—in other words, prolonged determination to succeed) with persistent psychosocial and environmental stressors may increase the risk of negative health outcomes.

JH takes its name and is inspired in part by the story of John Henry, the fabled "steel-driving man." According to legend, John Henry was an uneducated black steel driver who participated in a competition with a mechanical steam-powered drill. Though he rallied the physical strength needed to win the competition, he died soon after from overwhelming mental and physical fatigue. For James, the story of John Henry was a metaphor for the empirical literature that links active coping with psychosocial stress to dysregulation of the sympathetic nervous system (which may heighten blood pressure and hypertension risk).

James and his colleagues conducted a number of cross-sectional investigations of the JH hypothesis in then-rural North Carolina. The initial 1983 study of 132 working-class black men aged seventeen to sixty years demonstrated that black men with low education and high JH had higher mean diastolic blood pressure than other subgroups, though the difference was not statistically significant. However, in their 1984 follow-up study, James and his colleagues found a significant interaction between JH and perceived job success in the prediction of diastolic blood pressure among 112 black male workers. In 1987, James et al. recruited a sample of 820 black and white men and women aged twenty-one to fifty years, and found that blacks with high JH and low socioeconomic status (SES) were almost three times as likely to be hypertensive, compared to blacks of high socioeconomic position; no similar relationship was found among whites.

James's group focused their 1992 study on a much larger sample of African Americans from an eastern North Carolina county that was more urbanized and socioeconomically diverse than the areas in their previous studies. When the traditional JH hypothesis—high JH and low SES constitutes risk—was not supported, James posited that high JH should only be deleterious for those of lower SES who also have high levels of perceived stress. Indeed, post hoc analyses revealed significantly elevated blood pressure levels among those with high JH and low SES, but only for those who also reported high levels of perceived stress.

In addition to James's early work, a number of other studies have investigated the JH hypothesis in sociodemographically diverse samples, with a wide array of health outcomes. Results from these studies have been mixed. For example, Lynda Wright and colleagues (1996) demonstrated that high JH scores were associated with higher resting blood pressure, higher total peripheral resistance, and lower cardiac index among 173 healthy white and black children aged ten to seventeen. William Wiist and John Flack (1992) found that high JH, low SES participants were significantly more likely to have higher cholesterol levels (> 240 mg/dl). In a sample of 600 African American men and women, William Dressler and colleagues (1998) found an interaction between gender and John Henryism such that for men, higher JH was associated with increased systolic blood pressure and hypertension risk, whereas elevated JH was associated with lower blood pressure and hypertension risk among women.

Despite these and other positive findings, a number of studies have failed to support the traditional JH hypothesis. To illustrate, Linda Jackson and Lucile Adams-Campbell (1994), found no JH effect on blood pressure among urban black college students. A study of 658 Nigerian civil servants yielded a nonsignificant trend for higher blood pressure among those with high levels of both JH and socioeconomic status (Markovic et al. 1998). Anita Fernander and colleagues (2005) found that participants with low education who had low JH reported higher nicotine dependence scores, compared to any other subgroup. Finally, Vence Bonham and colleagues (2004) found that better self-reported physical health among a sample of high socioeconomic-position African American men was marginally associated with high John Henryism.

Methodological inconsistencies as well as differences in the sociodemographic composition of study samples may partly explain these mixed findings. For example, although JH originally was thought to constitute risk in the context of lower socioeconomic position, a number of studies have studied JH as an independent risk factor (i.e., without modeling the JH x SES interaction). Most stud-ies investigating JH independently have shown no association with the studied health outcomes. Certainly, there is controversy regarding the most appropriate measures of SES, though there is consensus that the definition varies by population. A wide variety of socioeconomic indicators have been studied in association with JH, but no clear pattern has emerged. A largely unresolved issue concerns whether JH is most predictive in specifically socially disadvantaged populations, or whether it is more widely occurring.

Those researching the JH construct have examined a range of health outcomes, but have been primarily focused on cardiovascular parameters (particularly blood pressure). Other outcomes with positive findings include cholesterol, cigarette smoking, pain susceptibility, and stress-related illness. JH research has been conducted with various samples (e.g., older populations, high school and college students, clinical samples) of various racial-ethnic, socioeconomic, and geographic composition. Though support for the JH hypothesis was originally found among populations in the American southeast, the construct has been widely investigated in a range of populations throughout the United States and in European and African countries, and in both urban and rural settings. A growing area of JH research concerns the role of JH in predicting the adoption of adverse health behaviors (including smoking, alcohol dependence, and stress-related eating). A new body of work uses JH in the clinical realm to learn more about the health effects of high-effort coping among those with chronic illness. A recent study has estimated the proportion of JH behaviors that are inherited (Whitfield et al. 2006). The JH literature proposes a novel and compelling hypothesis for understanding the promotion of disparities in a number of key health outcomes. The body of evidence investigating JH is replete with areas for additional inquiry, thus ensuring that JH research will continue.

SEE ALSO *Anxiety; Disease; Hypertension; Inequality, Racial; Stress*

BIBLIOGRAPHY

Bennett, Gary G., Marcellus M. Merritt, John J. Sollers, et al. 2004. Stress, Coping, and Health Outcomes among African-Americans: A Review of the JH Hypothesis. *Psychology and Health* 19 (3): 369–383.

Bonham, Vence L., Sherrill L. Sellers, and Harold W. Neighbors. 2004. John Henryism and Self-Reported Physical Health among High-Socioeconomic Status African American Men. *American Journal of Public Health* 94 (5): 737–738.

Dressler, William W., James R. Bindon, and Yasmin H. Neggers. 1998. John Henryism, Gender, and Arterial Blood Pressure in an African American Community. *Psychosomatic Medicine* 60 (5): 620–624.

Fernander, Anita F., Christi A. Patten, Darrell R. Schroeder, et al. 2005. Exploring the Association of John Henry Active Coping and Education on Smoking Behavior and Nicotine Dependence among Blacks in the USA. *Social Science and Medicine* 60 (3): 491–500.

Jackson, Linda A., and Lucile L. Adams-Campbell. 1994. John Henryism and Blood Pressure in Black College Students. *Journal of Behavioral Medicine* 17 (1): 69–79.

James, Sherman A. 1994. John Henryism and the Health of African-Americans. *Culture, Medicine, and Psychiatry* 18 (2): 163–182.

James, Sherman A., Sue A. Hartnett, and William D. Kalsbeek. 1983. John Henryism and Blood Pressure Differences among Black Men. *Journal of Behavioral Medicine* 6 (3): 259–278.

James, Sherman A., Nora L. Keenan, David S. Strogatz, et al. 1992. Socioeconomic Status, John Henryism, and Blood Pressure in Black Adults. The Pitt County Study. *American Journal of Epidemiology* 135 (1): 59–67.

Markovic, Nina, Clareann H. Bunker, Flora A. M. Ukoli, et al. 1998. John Henryism and Blood Pressure among Nigerian Civil Servants. *Journal of Epidemiology and Community Health* 52 (3): 186–190.

Whitfield, Keith E., Dwayne T. Brandon, Elwood Robinson, et al. 2006. Sources of Variability in John Henryism. *Journal of the National Medical Association* 98 (4): 641–647.

Wiist, William H., and John M. Flack. 1992. A Test of the John Henryism Hypothesis: Cholesterol and Blood Pressure. *Journal of Behavioral Medicine* 15 (1): 15–29.

Wright, Lynda Brown, Frank A. Treiber, Harry Davis, et al. 1996. Relationship of John Henryism to Cardiovascular Functioning at Rest and During Stress in Youth. *Annals of Behavioral Medicine* 18 (3): 146–150.

Gary G. Bennett
Dustin T. Duncan

JOHNSON, LYNDON B.
1908–1973

As thirty-sixth president of the United States, Lyndon Baines Johnson presided over one of the most turbulent periods in American history. His administration's confrontations with both severe domestic turmoil and international conflict highlight the potential and constraints of the modern presidency.

Johnson was born in Stonewall, a poor rural outpost located on the Pedernales River in central Texas. His political education began at an early age, as his paternal grandfather regaled his progeny with stories of his participation in the Populist movement of the late nineteenth century, while Johnson's father was active in state and local politics and served in the Texas state legislature during Johnson's youth.

Still, while politics played an important role in Johnson's life in childhood, it was during his attendance at Southwest Texas State Teachers College in San Marcos that Johnson developed the attitudes and qualities that would suffuse his political career. Upon his arrival at the college, he quickly set about the task of studying the school's internal dynamics and used the information he garnered to place himself close to its centers of power, a pattern he repeated several times during his participation in national politics. It was also at this juncture that Johnson articulated—in a series of editorials in the college newspaper—much of the philosophy that guided his political activities and approach to government later on.

After graduation, Johnson took a high school teaching position in Houston. Shortly thereafter, however, Johnson began to dabble with increasing seriousness in national politics, first as campaign manager for a Texas state legislator and then as a staffer for a newly elected member of the U.S. Congress. This latter position finally brought Johnson to Washington, D.C., where he remained for much of the duration of his political career. And as he had done in San Marcos, Johnson devoted his time to unearthing the sources of influence in the federal legislature and, armed with that knowledge, maneuvering himself as close to its power center as possible.

Johnson entered elective politics in 1937, when he was sent to Congress in a special election in Texas's Tenth District. He served in the House of Representatives until his 1948 election to the Senate, where he rose quickly through the Democratic Party ranks to become Senate minority leader in 1953 and majority leader in 1955. It was in these roles that Johnson's political career reached its zenith. Perhaps most notably, it was in these leadership roles that he perfected what quickly came to be known as "the Johnson treatment": a repertoire of psychological appeals and talking points that Johnson employed to enforce party discipline and more generally coax and strong-arm recalcitrant colleagues to rally around his legislative agenda.

The Senate leadership roles thus presented an ideal platform for Johnson to exploit the deep understanding of legislative power he had cultivated during his congressional career. As a Texan who brought to politics both pragmatism and a keen awareness of the possibilities for using the power of government to address social problems, Johnson was pivotally poised to mediate between the congressional Democratic Party's liberal and southern factions. In many ways, therefore, being Senate majority leader offered Johnson the opportunity to exert substantial influence over the course of national politics and public policy.

Nevertheless, Johnson left the Senate in 1961 to serve as President John F. Kennedy's vice president until

November 22, 1963, when Kennedy was assassinated during a political tour in Dallas, Texas. Johnson was sworn in as president that same afternoon and served out the remaining year of Kennedy's term. Then in November 1964 he was elected president in his own right in a landslide victory against the Republican Party's ultraconservative candidate, Barry Goldwater.

The hallmark of Johnson's presidency was the Great Society program, which, as he described it in his commencement address at the University of Michigan in 1964, sought to "enrich and elevate our national life, and to advance the quality of our American civilization" (Johnson 1965, p. 704). Specific initiatives included the declaration of a War on Poverty; the introduction of various laws aimed at improving education, Social Security, health care, and the environment; and the creation of Head Start, the Job Corps, and the National Endowment for the Arts and the Humanities. Civil rights also figured prominently in Johnson's domestic agenda. One of his first acts as president was to fulfill the Kennedy administration's promise to support an antisegregation bill by working tirelessly to secure passage of the omnibus Civil Rights Act of 1964. A dramatic wave of protests in Alabama the following winter led him to champion ratification of the Voting Rights Act of 1965. And although Congress failed to enact the civil rights legislation he introduced in 1966 and 1967, Martin Luther King Jr.'s assassination created favorable conditions for Johnson to push through a Fair Housing Act in 1968.

In foreign policy, Johnson was preoccupied primarily with the United States' protracted postwar effort to contain communism, in which the Vietnam War played a particularly prominent role. This conflict, which pitted North Vietnam and the Viet Cong against the southern Army of the Republic of Vietnam, began prior to Johnson's accession to the presidency. Nevertheless, his administration was responsible for the sizable escalation of U.S. involvement in the struggle. Johnson's war policies faced considerable opposition on the domestic front, especially from draft-age college students. This unrest contributed to Johnson's decision to retire from politics rather than run for a second term in 1968.

The legacy of Johnson's presidency is mixed. His ambitious agenda had many significant implications for the subsequent dynamics and practice of American politics, particularly with regard to the scope of domestic policy and federal-state relations. Nevertheless, the difficulties he faced in negotiating the highly charged social and political atmosphere of the late 1960s cast doubt on the possibility of effective presidential leadership and inaugurated an era of distrust in government.

SEE ALSO *Civil Rights Movement, U.S.; Great Society, The; Kennedy, John F.; Marshall, Thurgood; Presidency, The; Vietnam War; Voting Rights Act*

BIBLIOGRAPHY

Caro, Robert A. 1982–2002. *The Years of Lyndon Johnson.* 3 vols. New York: Knopf.

Dallek, Robert. 1998. *Flawed Giant: Lyndon Johnson and His Times, 1961–1973.* New York and Oxford: Oxford University Press.

Johnson, Lyndon B. 1965. *Public Papers of the Presidents of the United States: Lyndon B. Johnson, 1963–64,* Vol. 1. Washington, DC: Government Printing Office.

Johnson, Lyndon B. 1971. *The Vantage Point: Perspectives of the Presidency, 1963–1969.* New York: Holt, Rinehart, and Winston.

Milkis, Sidney M., and Jerome Mileur, eds. 2005. *The Great Society and the High Tide of Liberalism.* Amherst: University of Massachusetts Press.

Shamira M. Gelbman

JONES, EDWARD ELLSWORTH
1926–1993

The American social psychologist Edward Ellsworth Jones earned his AB (1949) and PhD (1953) from Harvard University, both under the direction of Jerome Bruner. He held professorial appointments at Duke University from 1953 to 1977, and was the Stuart Professor of Psychology at Princeton University from 1977 until his untimely death in 1993.

Social psychologists had been interested in the accuracy of interpersonal judgments from the field's inception, but in the 1950s seminal figures such as Solomon Asch and Fritz Heider sparked a new interest in understanding the cognitive processes by which such judgments were made. Heider in particular suggested that ordinary people think of behavior as a product of an actor's enduring dispositions and the situation within which that behavior unfolds, and that a small set of inferential rules allows them to determine to which of these variables an actor's behavior should be attributed on any occasion.

Jones offered social psychology its first formal model of these attributional rules (Jones and Davis 1965). His correspondent inference theory, along with some likeminded theories (e.g., those outlined in Bem 1967, Kelley 1967, and Schachter and Singer 1962), created a sea change in social psychology, and by the early 1970s attribution theory had replaced cognitive dissonance theory as the field's premiere theoretical engine. (A full history of attribution theory can be found in Gilbert 1998).

One prediction of correspondent inference theory was that rational observers should not infer dispositions from actions that are performed under extreme duress. But in his experimental work, Jones found that observers do, in fact, infer dispositions under these circumstances (Jones and Harris 1967), and much of his research in the following decades was devoted to exploring the causes and consequences of this "correspondence bias," or "fundamental attribution error." His discovery and analysis of this important and robust phenomenon set the stage for the explosion of research in social psychology on biases in human inference that took place in the 1980s.

Having established that observers tend to make a particular kind of mistake when drawing inferences about others, Jones suggested that observers make precisely the opposite mistake when drawing inferences about themselves (Jones and Nisbett 1971). He argued that people tend to think of their own actions as having been controlled by situational forces, but tend to think of others' actions as expressions of the other's enduring beliefs, desires, and propensities. His analysis of this "actor-observer effect" implicated perceptual and cognitive factors rather than emotional or motivational factors as the primary sources of what was often a self-serving pattern of inferences, and in so doing, it pioneered a new style of explanation in social psychology.

Jones also argued that if people use attributional rules to draw inferences about others, then they can use these same rules to manipulate the inferences that others draw about them. For example, ingratiation is a tactic by which actors attempt to make observers like them, and Jones's early analysis of this phenomenon (Jones 1964) laid the groundwork for his later, more general work on strategic self-presentation (Jones and Pittman 1982). His work on self-handicapping (Berglas and Jones 1978) showed that people sometimes use these tactics to deceive themselves. He summarized much of his thinking on these and other issues in his final book, *Interpersonal Perception* (1990).

Jones won virtually all the major awards his field could offer, including the American Psychological Association's Distinguished Scientific Contribution Award in 1977. He was an influential and productive social psychologist who combined a deep insight into human affairs with an unflagging commitment to clear theorizing and experimental investigation. In a half-century of careful and inspiring work, he built a significant part of the foundation on which modern social psychology rests.

SEE ALSO *Attribution; Ingratiation; Self-Presentation*

BIBLIOGRAPHY

PRIMARY WORKS

Berglas, Steven, and Edward E. Jones. 1978. Drug Choice as a Self-handicapping Strategy in Response to Noncontingent Success. *Journal of Personality and Social Psychology* 36 (4): 405–417.

Jones, Edward E. 1964. *Ingratiation*. New York: Appleton-Century-Crofts.

Jones, Edward E. 1990. *Interpersonal Perception*. New York: W. H. Freeman.

Jones, Edward E., and Keith E. Davis. 1965. From Acts to Dispositions: The Attribution Process in Person Perception. In *Advances in Experimental Social Psychology*, Vol. 2, ed. Leonard Berkowitz, 219–266. New York: Academic Press.

Jones, Edward E., and Victor A. Harris. 1967. The Attribution of Attitudes. *Journal of Experimental Social Psychology* 3: 1–24.

Jones, Edward E., and Richard E. Nisbett. 1971. The Actor and the Observer: Divergent Perceptions of the Causes of Behavior. In *Attribution: Perceiving the Causes of Behavior*, ed. Edward E. Jones, David E. Kanouse, Harold H. Kelley, et al., 77–94. Morristown, NJ: General Learning Press.

Jones, Edward E., and Thane S. Pittman. 1982. Toward a General Theory of Strategic Self-presentation. In *Psychological Perspectives on the Self*, Vol. 1, ed. Jerry Suls, 231–260. Hillsdale, NJ: Erlbaum.

SECONDARY WORKS

Bem, Daryl J. 1967. Self-perception: An Alternative Interpretation of Cognitive Dissonance Phenomena. *Psychological Review* 74: 183–200.

Gilbert, Daniel T. 1998. Ordinary Personalogy. In *Handbook of Social Psychology*, 4th ed., Vol. 2, ed. Daniel T. Gilbert, Susan T. Fiske, and Gardner Lindzey, 89–150. New York: McGraw Hill.

Kelley, Harold H. 1967. Attribution Theory in Social Psychology. In *Nebraska Symposium on Motivation*, Vol. 15, ed. David Levine, 192–238. Lincoln: University of Nebraska Press.

Schachter, Stanley, and Jerome Singer. 1962. Cognitive, Social, and Physiological Determinants of Emotional State. *Psychological Review* 69: 379–399.

Daniel Gilbert

JOURNALISM

Journalism is the gathering, writing, editing, photographing, or broadcasting of information through newspapers, magazines, radio, television, or the Internet by any news organization as a business. Just as journalism reports day-to-day news and current affairs, its attributes change with the times. Journalism's history is closely associated with democracy and business. Not only does journalism derive its financial strength and power from mass audiences purchasing the product, but it also attains its political strength by swaying the masses. Thus while many may decry the commercialization of information, the mark of success, whether financial or political, is seen in the number of people who access that information and therefore support the endeavor. It is described as the lifeblood of democracy. The intersection between politics and journalism has important and fundamental effects on the stability and legitimacy of democratic regimes.

EARLY JOURNALISM

Newsletters contained news that was written for merchants, businesspeople, and politicians during the seventeenth century. The newsletters exchanged sporadic information about friends abroad or in other colonies between people with common interests. This created an organized circulation, which eventually led to the development of the newspaper.

Pamphlets were published papers that dealt with public questions, while ballads were accounts written in verse. These were distributed in public houses, coffeehouses, and taverns. Such information was printed on broadsides, meaning it was printed on one side of a single sheet. These sheets were sold on the street for a few pence.

Journalism's popularity and influence in the political process emerged at about the same time as the European discovery and colonization of North America. Johannes Gutenberg (1400–1467) created the first moveable type press in 1455, yet it was not until Christopher Columbus (1451–1506) sailed from Spain in 1492 that the printing press was popularized in Europe. Columbus wrote many letters describing his discoveries of the "Indies." In 1620, around the time the *Mayflower* landed at Plymouth, the first "coranto," or pioneer newspapers, appeared for sale in the streets of London. The first printing press was imported to America in 1639. Over the next forty years, journalism became established in England with the first newspaper, the *Weekly Newes*.

In England, the popularization of such materials represented the first clash between government and journalism, with authors and importers of imported books being subject to censorship and harsh prosecutions as well as other impediments, such as high taxes. Undeterred by those punishments, the business of journalism grew. It is estimated that between 1640 and the restoration of the monarchy in 1660, more than 30,000 political pamphlets and newspapers were issued. The beginnings of journalism also coincided with the rise of political parties in England. Political groups realized that if they could get endorsements from newsletters and pamphlets, their interests would be more easily disseminated to the public.

This eventually led to the partisan press in both the United Kingdom and America.

The first continuous American newspaper began publishing in Boston on April 24, 1704. It was founded by the city's postmaster, John Campbell, and was called the *Boston News-Letter*. It carried news from London journals and focused on English politics and foreign wars. Local content was limited to the arrival of ships, deaths, sermons, political appointments, storms, crimes, and misadventures.

The modern newspaper progressed over the next 200 years, evolving from the broadsheets and pamphlets to weekly sheets and eventually the daily press. Notable figures in the early days of newspapers include Benjamin Franklin (1706–1790), who, with his brother James, published the *New England Courant*. Seeking new sales, Franklin established the publishing tradition of letters to the editor. Initially Franklin himself wrote letters under pseudonyms to create controversy and arouse interest in his own editorials. The first daily newspapers tended to be highly partisan. This partisan press eventually was replaced by the penny press.

Economies of scale figure prominently in the evolution of newspapers. As presses became larger, the need for greater capital also increased. Those with the most capital were able to secure larger presses and larger audiences, thereby pushing out of business the small, independent producers and creating larger, more standardized formats. The larger scale of the modern newspaper helped develop the craft and techniques of journalism. Tenants of modern journalism are objectivity, the inverted pyramid, and other conventions of standardized writing. The formatting of news in specific ways, such as the inverted pyramid, means that the most important information, the five Ws (who, what, when, where, and why), are placed at the start of the story. This allows readers to find the most important facts quickly. It also means that if the story has to be edited because of space limitations, the last paragraphs are easily cut without losing the main story elements and without the need to rewrite the story.

In addition to movable type, other advances occurred in the creation of the newspaper that influenced the way in which news is reported. The stereotype was invented in 1725 by the Scottish goldsmith William Ged (1690–1749). This consisted of a printing plate of a whole page of type cast in a single mold. These stereotypes were mass produced and were thin enough to be sent through the mails. Large presses purchased the stereotype and sent it to various newspapers. Subscribing newspapers could simply take the stereotype of the news or of cartoons and reproduce them for local readers. The stereotype proved to be so successful that by 1877 nearly eight out of ten newspapers in America provided their readers the same political cartoon more cheaply than they could write and set their own. The term *stereotype* is now used to describe how ideas and public opinion were formed through a consistent message, often one that is simplistic and erroneous.

NEWSWIRES, THE PENNY PRESS, AND YELLOW JOURNALISM

As competition increased, so did the need to be the first to break the news. Many technological advances in the nineteenth century facilitated news-gathering competition. These included the steamship, the railroad, and the magazine telegraph. The telegraph proved to be the most efficient means of conveying information over long distances, and the newspaper helped to popularize and ensure its success. While the telegraph was a boon for the speed of news, it was also expensive.

The first newswire, Agence Havas, was started in 1835 by Charles-Louis Havas (1783–1858), considered the father of the press agency. Havas translated material from abroad for the French national press. In 1940 the company was taken over by the state and renamed Agence Française de Presse (AFP). Twelve years later the first North American press agency was created, starting with an agreement between the publishers of the *Journal of Commerce* and the *New York Herald.* In 1848 the Associated Press (AP) was founded at a meeting of ten men representing six New York newspaper publishers. They pooled their efforts in collecting international news. Horace Greeley (1811–1872), the founding editor of the *New York Tribune,* was also a founder of the AP. Having a news wire license would mean a great deal to future newspaper barons because it would ensure their success against competitors who did not have access to the wire. By October 1851 the German-born Paul Julius Reuter (1816–1899) was transmitting stock market quotes between London and Paris over the Calais-Dover cable. His agency, which eventually became known as Reuters, extended its service to the whole British press and to other European countries. Other news wires that emerged were the United Press Association, set up by E. W. Scripps (1854–1926), U.S. Newswire, and Bloomberg, whose focus remains business news. Most countries have some form of newswire service. Newswires helped move newspapers away from partisan declarations. To be a successful news agency, one had to have many subscribing newspapers. The ability to get the story meant stripping the copy of its editorial content and focusing on the facts.

As newspapers became more powerful, their partisan nature extended their impact. Journalism was said to be so powerful that it could elect presidents as well as ruin political careers. One figure who changed the power structure of the partisan press was Joseph Pulitzer (1847–1911), whose career in publishing began inauspiciously with his

account of being taken in as a scam artist, written for the *Westliche Post,* a German-language paper in St. Louis, Missouri. After establishing himself, he purchased the *St. Louis Post-Dispatch* at auction for $2,500 (Brian 2001, p. 31). Pulitzer had an inherent sense of social justice, which he brought to his paper. His editorial position was that the *St. Louis Post-Dispatch* would not be a tool of partisan politics. Denis Brian (2001) noted Pulitzer's pledge: that the paper "opposes all frauds and shams wherever and whatever they are, will advocate principles and ideas rather than prejudices and partisanships" (Brian 2001, p. 32).

Pulitzer is also associated with yellow journalism. Once the *St. Louis Post-Dispatch* was an established and successful paper, he moved to New York and purchased the *New York World.* Within a few years, he took a derelict paper and made it one of the most profitable newspapers in the most competitive U.S. market. To do this he made the paper affordable, cutting the price to 2 cents an issue, and focused on stories that attracted the mass public. Much of this centered on reporting crime and scandal. Later William Randolph Hearst (1863–1951), who admired Pulitzer's business acumen, copied his success and launched the *New York Journal* to compete against the *World.* The competition for readers between the two New York papers culminated in the dueling Sunday supplements containing the Yellow Kid cartoons, the first cartoons published in color. The *New York Press* editor Ervin Wardman dubbed this competition "yellow journalism," and the phrase soon became a metaphor for any kind of salacious reporting.

Yellow journalism is the reporting of scandal, divorce, and crime alongside sports. Yellow journalism also refers to false reports, faking of news or interviews, and heavy use of graphic pictures. The battle between Hearst and Pulitzer raged with misleading headlines and each accusing the other of false reports. While the era of yellow journalism reigned from 1892 to 1914, many of its features still linger in contemporary journalism: big headlines, the use of pictures to present information, and the colored comic Sunday supplement.

Despite being associated with the worst of journalism, Pulitzer is also associated with its best. His penchant for accuracy, brevity, and persistence became hallmarks of journalism. While at the time of his death Pulitzer's estate was in excess of $18 million, he remained interested in the common good. His core journalistic credo was that journalism should never worry about the profits of the owners but rather about telling the truth and uncovering injustice. To this end he provided $2 million for the creation of the Columbia School of Journalism, which opened on September 30, 1912, just under a year after Pulitzer's death.

While journalism had been big business for some time, the height of its power began at the end of the nineteenth century. As the investment in presses became larger, so did the business of journalism and the realization that more money could be made if one owned several small papers rather than one large paper. The person who pioneered this type of capital investment in newspapers was E. W. Scripps, who purchased established papers rather than start new ones. He would choose a city with 50,000 to 100,000 in population and purchase a paper already in operation. Most every year from 1893 until his death, he added nearly a half dozen papers to his holdings. In 1926 the Scripps chain owned thirty-four papers. Hearst too amassed a newspaper empire. The difference was that Hearst established himself in the largest American cities. By the end of 1922 Hearst owned twenty daily papers and eleven Sunday papers in thirteen markets. At his peak Hearst had bought or established forty-two daily papers.

MODERN INNOVATIONS: RADIO, TELEVISION, CABLE, AND THE INTERNET

Newspaper journalism began to wane in popularity as other communication technologies emerged. Radio had a unique ability to transmit wire information directly to the public. This challenged newspapers, which feared they would lose their influence. Initial attempts by newspapers to prevent radio from taking over journalism included blocking radio from receiving newswire stories. Nonetheless, there was little to prevent radio stations from reading the news from competing newspapers. When limiting information to radio did not work, newspapers tried to discredit radio journalism by claiming that radio could not uphold the ideals of objectivity, could not provide public service, or was bad for democracy. All these issues were resolved when AP lifted its ban on radio in 1939, allowing radio to compete with newspapers.

Just as radio challenged and changed the nature of journalism, so too did television news. Not only was information equally available, but television news provided better pictures than newspapers with the timeliness of radio. The focus on images in television news changed the nature of journalism, with images reigning paramount over content. From 1950 to the 1980s television news was the most popular means by which the public received information on current events. Television's success was in part due to the ease of receiving the information as well as the visual nature of the medium.

The American networks created bureaus in countries around the world and furnished firsthand accounts of history unfolding. While newspapers were severely challenged by radio, both radio and television eventually lost part of their audience. While newspapers declined, they still maintain significant readership. Radio journalism has

suffered the most and is used less frequently than other forms of journalism.

Despite the technical innovations of getting the message out, the period between the 1920s and 1970s saw journalists become more routinized and codified in their presentation of material. Journalism schools were created, and the occupation of journalist was elevated from a technical or trade occupation—one that was also low paying—to a profession characterized by higher education, social status, and eventually pay.

As journalism became more standardized, so too were complaints of perceived bias in the media. Those who supported more government intervention in the economy argued that because journalism is a big business, it focuses on protecting the elites and avoiding stories that might embarrass advertisers. Others, those who supported less government, charged that because journalists were becoming more educated, their views were more in keeping with left-wing intellectuals. At the height of the cold war Senator Joseph McCarthy (1908–1957) led the charge by accusing many prominent journalists (as well as entertainers) of being Communist sympathizers. In particular he took issue with the popular former war correspondent and radio and television journalist Edward R. Murrow (1908–1965) as evidence. Murrow fought back, exposing McCarthy's false accusations and setting the standard for hard-hitting investigative journalism. His documentary on McCarthy is considered the most famous ever broadcast, and it signaled the end of McCarthyism. When one considers that television news was still in its infancy, with relatively few people having direct access to television, and that it was a program not promoted by the network, it spoke to the potential impact of the medium. That impact was developed during the 1960s and 1970s with domestic events such as race relations and the assassinations of President John F. Kennedy, civil rights leader Martin Luther King Jr., and Senator Robert Kennedy. All these events were given heightened sense of crisis and immediacy in part because television news was able to provide the pictures to go along with the information.

In addition to broadcasting local events in North America as well as Europe, television news could provide pictures from faraway places such as Africa and Southeast Asia. Walter Lippmann's 1922 depiction of "the world outside and the pictures in our heads" (Lippmann 1922, p. 1) was never more true than with television news broadcasting images from faraway places.

Walter Cronkite, the managing editor and anchor of CBS News from 1962 to 1981, was a trusted and well-respected journalist in part because he maintained the CBS News policy of independent, nonpartisan reporting. Some argue that it was not the continuing pictures and stories of the war from Vietnam that changed the majority view on the conflict but the fact that Cronkite, a former World War II (1939–1945) correspondent, stepped aside from the neutral anchor to present his opinion on the war.

That legacy continued and culminated with the *Washington Post*'s reporting of a break-in in the Watergate complex in Washington, D.C., in 1972. Relatively junior reporters Bob Woodward and Carl Bernstein are credited with investigating the story in a series of newspaper articles that revealed that the break-in was linked to the Republican Party, whose officials were seeking information about the Democratic Party. President Richard Nixon eventually resigned rather than face impeachment. While many point to the Watergate reporting as the high-water mark for investigative journalism, others argue that the role of journalism in bringing down the president is more myth than fact. Edward Jay Epstein, for example, argues that Woodward and Bernstein were only slightly ahead of the prosecutors and relied on leaked information from the prosecutor's case. As such, Epstein argues, the information would have come out anyway. It was not Woodward and Bernstein who uncovered the link between the burglars and the White House and traced the illegal activities to the Nixon campaign, it was the FBI. Epstein charges that Woodward and Bernstein "systematically ignored or minimized" the work of law enforcement officials to "focus on those parts" of the story "that were leaked to them" (as quoted in Feldstein 2004, p. 3).

Nixon aide Howard Dean states that the role of the journalists in the Watergate story was not investigative reporting but keeping the story alive long enough to legitimize law enforcement agents who were doing the investigation. The media coverage and subsequent frenzy is what kept the Watergate story in the public eye. The press coverage also helped to keep the public's interest alive during the televised hearings about the scandal. Ultimately, however, the business of journalism is sustained by the routine gathering of news rather than by investigative journalism. While television became dominant in news gathering and dissemination, the investigative model is ultimately time consuming and expensive. The day-to-day news business is focused on feeding the news cycle with short, easily digested information. As a result investigative articles are more rare than routine.

Only with the emergence of cable news networks did network television news begin its decline. Despite the pressures from other communications technologies, public opinion surveys indicate that local television news remains the most frequent source of information, followed by local newspapers.

Cable news networks challenged traditional television news in several ways. First, providing one service on cable was significantly cheaper than having to supply stations in every market. These savings allowed cable networks such as CNN to establish more bureaus around the world at a time when network television news had to close down bureaus or cut staff. The twenty-four-hour format gave CNN an advantage on stories with great public interest, such as the 1991 Gulf War. CNN not only changed the way international news is covered but also increased interest in and the scope of international affairs on public policy. Thus it is seen as a catalyst for Western governments to intervene in humanitarian crises, subsequently dubbed the "CNN effect." The extent to which governments react to media coverage of suffering people is debatable, but the public's awareness of humanitarian crises are much more extensive as a result of the twenty-four-hour news format. By shifting the focus from local topics to international issues, the focus of the public has become more globalized.

The popularization of the Internet has blurred the lines of journalism and public comment. The Internet not only allows for on-demand news, which traditional media have adopted, but it also allows for individuals not normally considered journalists to present their interpretations of current affairs. The Web log, or blog, is a Web site on which individuals write their views on any subject. Blogs have been associated with breaking publication bans, providing critical commentary on accepted journalistic stories, and popularizing certain political interests. Just as challenges to newspapers were discredited as not being proper journalism, traditional journalists also question and try to discredit blogs. The current definition of journalism disavows blog writers in that they do not typically write for commercial interests. The Washington Press Gallery, for example, limits membership by stipulating that to qualify as a journalist, one must be employed by "a periodical that is published for profit and is supported chiefly by advertising or by subscription" (United States House of Representatives, Periodical Press Gallery, Rules and Regulations).

SEE ALSO *Democracy; Internet; Media; Medium Is the Message; Radio Talk Shows; Television; Watergate*

BIBLIOGRAPHY

Barton, Gina. 2002. What Is a Jour-na-list? *Quill Magazine*, (May): 10–13.

Brian, Denis. 2001. *Pulitzer: A Life*. New York: Wiley.

Carey, James, W. 1974. The Problem of Journalism History. *Journalism History* 1 (1): 3–5, 27.

Dizard, Wilson, Jr. 2000. *Old Media, New Media: Mass Communications in the Information Age*. 3rd ed. New York: Longman.

Feldstein, Mark. 2004. Watergate Revisited. *American Journalism Review*, August–September. www.ajr.org/Article.asp?id=3735.

Gramling, Oliver. 1940. *AP: The Story of News.* Port Washington, NY: Kennikat.

Jackaway, Gwenyth. 1995. *Media at War: Radio's Challenge to the Newspapers, 1924–1939.* Westport, CT: Praeger.

Lippmann, Walter. 1922. *Public Opinion.* New York: Harcourt, Brace.

Mott, Frank Luther. 1962. *American Journalism: A History: 1690–1960.* 3rd ed. New York: Macmillan.

Oreskes, Michael. 2000. News: A Bit Hard to Define. *Harvard International Journal of Press/Politics* 5 (3): 102–104.

Payne, George Henry. 1920. *History of Journalism in the United States.* New York and London: Appleton.

Robinson, Piers. 2002. *The CNN Effect: The Myth of News, Foreign Policy, and Intervention.* London and New York: Routledge.

Saad, Lydia. 2007. Local TV Is No. 1 Source of News for Americans: Network and Cable News Viewership Down. Gallup Poll, January 5. http://www.galluppoll.com.

Sperber, A. M. 1998. *Murrow: His Life and Times.* New York: Fordham University Press.

United States House of Representatives. Periodical Press Gallery, Rules and Regulations. http://periodical.house.gov/rules.shtml.

Lydia Miljan

JOURNALS, PROFESSIONAL

There are several means to disseminate ideas, results, experiments, criticism, and discoveries in the sciences and humanities. The most often used are professional journals, books, working papers, technical reports, pamphlets, and presentations at academic conferences. Professional journals are the main means of communication because the majority of journals use the referee or peer-review system for papers submitted for publication. The referee system aims at selecting the best papers and achieving the greatest objectivity possible. In addition, journals provide a fast and efficient way to spread the latest developments in a field of study. They also serve as a forum for discussion, which is essential for the advance of knowledge.

Publications in academic journals are used to rank departments and scholars. Publications are one of the key instruments used to assess the quantity and quality of scholars and departments through objective criteria, a method in line with the belief that scholars and academic institutions should be evaluated on the basis of merit. The ranking of departments and scholars requires a list of journals that are themselves ranked according to their importance. Rankings of journals are based on the relative impact of the papers published. Generally, the impact of a journal is captured by the number of citations to its articles in other journals (Liebowitz and Palmer 1984). An alternative approach to ranking journals is to survey members of the relevant profession (Malouin and Outreville 1987).

Due to the increase in specialization among and within many branches of the sciences and humanities, the number of specialized journals is increasing. Rajeev Goel and João Faria (2007) showed, in a differential game between editors and authors, that the launching of new journals generates greater competition among editors, enhancing research quality. Another consequence of specialization can be observed in economics, where there has been a fall in the importance of general journals relative to specialized journals (Faria 2002a). In addition, new academic journals have been established as a result of the publication congestion in existing journals. This congestion results from the increasing difficulty of producing high-reputation journals, causing a rise in rejection rates and a time delay between submission, acceptance, and final publication of papers. Glenn Ellison (2002) argues that in economics this slowdown is due to an increasing tendency among journals to require that papers be extensively revised prior to acceptance.

Professional journals are part of the publishing business and thus are subject to market forces. The main agent behind the market performance of academic journals is the publisher. In most cases, a publisher with a good reputation, experience, and penetration in the academic market can make a difference in the performance of an academic journal. In economics, commercial publishers have gained a substantial market share. They have been successful in creating new journals, as well as taking over top journals formerly published by nonprofit organizations, such as professional associations and university presses.

One consequence of the increasing role of commercial publishers in the production of professional journals is a rise in prices. David Rosenbaum and Meng Hua Ye (1997) produced evidence that commercial publishers engage in price discrimination between individual and library subscribers, showing that library prices rise faster than individual subscribers' prices. Owen Phillips and Lori Phillips (2002) showed that library prices are two to ten times higher than private prices. Nathan Berg (2002) proposed that university libraries, in order to cope with journal-price inflation, pick a threshold level of quality of academic journals below which no subscriptions are ordered.

Plagiarism, rhetorical conventions, and editorial favoritism are among the potential problems that plague professional journals. The majority of the 117 editors of economic journals surveyed by Walter Enders and Gary

Hoover (2004) considered the use of several unattributed sentences to constitute plagiarism. Eighty-three of the 117 editors said that they had seen no cases of plagiarism in a typical year. Of the remainder, twenty-eight editors reported a collective total of forty-two occurrences of plagiarism in an average year. The key findings of Enders and Hoover are that editors tend to rely on copyright law to protect themselves from plagiarism; they are not likely to publicize an instance of plagiarism; and the majority of editors favor a code of ethics enumerating various forms of plagiarism and the appropriate penalties.

Technological innovations change the research tools and may affect the way professionals present their findings. Rhetorical conventions become a problem for journals when professionals put more importance on the presentation of their work than on its content (see McCloskey 1991). Anecdotal evidence suggests, at least in economics, that technical knowledge, such as sophisticated mathematics and econometric techniques, increases the chances for publication. One possible reason lies in the fact that technical knowledge decreases the opportunity cost for a contributor who has acquired the minimal technical expertise demanded by the journal (Wallis and Dollery 1993); in addition, technical knowledge makes it easier for a referee to evaluate an article. As stressed by Bruno Frey (2001), the emphasis on formalism may lead to a disregard for relevance and originality.

Editorial favoritism is a serious problem for professional journals because it can be a significant source of bias in the evolution of knowledge. The bias is mainly reflected in the choice of topics, research techniques, and literature. Editors and referees may choose to publish a paper not because of its content but because of the author's network of connections or his or her views. David Laband and Michael Piette (1994) point out that editorial favoritism generates sizable wealth redistributions among members of the scientific community, providing strong incentives for authors to attempt to influence their chances of publication and citation. Of course, academic networks facilitate the circulation of ideas and personal contacts, which are essential to fostering the advance of knowledge (Faria 2002b). In the same vein, editors, following Thomas Kuhn (1962), may be interested in defending the prevalence of and reinforcing a given paradigm. However, in spite of the difficulty in investigating the fundamentals of editorial bias (Medoff 2004), the possibility of its occurrence raises a red flag on the dangers of exogenous factors interfering with the process of knowledge formation.

SEE ALSO *Citations*

BIBLIOGRAPHY

Berg, Nathan. 2002. Coping with Journal-Price Inflation: Leading Policy Proposals and the Quality-Spectrum. *Economics Bulletin* 4 (14): 1–7.

Ellison, Glenn. 2002. The Slowdown of the Economics Publishing Process. *Journal of Political Economy* 110: 947–993.

Enders, Walter, and Gary A. Hoover. 2004. Whose Line Is It? Plagiarism in Economics. *Journal of Economic Literature* 42: 487–493.

Faria, João R. 2002a. An Analysis of Rankings of Economic Journals. *Brazilian Journal of Business Economics* 2: 95–117.

Faria, João R. 2002b. Scientific, Business, and Political Networks in Academia. *Research in Economics* 56: 187–198.

Frey, Bruno. 2001. Why Economists Disregard Economic Methodology. *Journal of Economic Methodology* 8: S. 41–47.

Kuhn, Thomas S. 1962. *The Structure of Scientific Revolutions*. Chicago: University of Chicago Press.

Laband, David N., and Michael J. Piette. 1994. Favoritism versus Search for Good Papers: Empirical Evidence Regarding the Behavior of Journal Editors. *Journal of Political Economy* 102: 194–203.

Liebowitz, Stan J., and John P. Palmer. 1984. Assessing the Relative Impacts of Economic Journals. *Journal of Economic Literature* 22: 77–88.

Malouin, Jean-Louis, and J.-Francois Outreville. 1987. The Relative Impact of Economics Journals: A Cross-Country Survey and Comparison. *Journal of Economics and Business* 39 (3): 267–277.

McCloskey, Donald N. 1991. Mere Style in Economics Journals, 1920 to the Present. *Economic Notes* 20: 135–158.

Medoff, Marshall H. 2004. An Analysis of Parochialism at the JPE and QJE. Unpublished manuscript.

Phillips, Owen R., and Lori J. Phillips. 2002. The Market for Academic Journals. *Applied Economics* 34: 39–48.

Rosenbaum, David I., and Meng Hua Ye. 1997. Price Discrimination and Economics Journals. *Applied Economics* 29: 1611–1618.

Wallis, J. L., and B. E. Dollery. 1993. The Economics of Economics: A Model of Research Discourse. *Australian Economic Papers* 32: 175–183.

João Ricardo Faria

JUÁREZ, BENITO
1806–1872

In twentieth-century Mexico, no name was used more frequently to name streets, public buildings, and towns than that of Benito Juárez. A Zapotec Indian lawyer from the southern state of Oaxaca, Juárez stood at the helm of the liberal, reformist republican project during the bloody nineteenth-century civil war against the conservatives, which became a struggle against a monarchical regime supported by French military intervention (1858–1867). He then presided over the restoration of the republic and governed, until his death, under the heavy criticism of the opposition in Congress and an exceptionally free press. One of nineteenth-century Mexico's ablest politicians, he became, within a generation of his death, one of the nationalist imagination's most enduring symbols. His life story opens a window on the complex workings of politics in nineteenth-century Mexico at a critical juncture, and the recurrent reconstruction of his image as a national symbol offers clues to the transformations of Mexican political culture.

Juárez left the monolingual Zapotec community of San Pablo Guelatao as a twelve-year-old who spoke little Spanish (he would later be able to read Latin, English, and French) to join his sister, a house servant, in the state capital city of Oaxaca. He studied law at the city's seminary and then at its secular, modern Institute of Arts and Sciences. In a state where liberalism had a broader, more popular appeal than in other regions, Juárez entered politics early and gained experience at all levels of government. He was a member of the Oaxaca city council and of the local and then the federal Congress. He was also a judge, prosecutor, secretary of state, and governor. Nevertheless, his promising political career was interrupted, like that of many young politicians in the provinces, by the dictatorship, from 1853 to 1855, of military strongman Antonio López de Santa Anna (1794–1876), which sought to put an end to representative politics and state autonomy. Juárez was exiled and ended up in New Orleans, Louisiana, where his perspectives were broadened and his political vision sharpened through contacts with more sophisticated Mexican radicals like Melchor Ocampo, Ponciano Arriaga, and José María Mata.

The fall of Santa Anna brought about a new era in Mexican politics that was known as the Reform (1855–1867). Despite differences among them, the young provincial liberals who arrived on the national stage in 1855—among whom Juárez would cut an elder-statesman figure—were committed to modernizing Mexico through the restoration of federalism, the strengthening of the national government, and the destruction of those "vices" that were the legacy of colonial times: corporate privilege, which denied equality before the law; corporate ownership of land, which made for a sluggish economy; and the overwhelming power of the Church. Their project was given expression in the 1857 constitution, which prevailed after ten years of armed struggle. The first conflict (1858–1860) was against the conservatives, who feared that the constitution's attack on the Church and religion would tear apart the deteriorated social and moral fabric of Mexican society. The struggle next included

Napoléon III's army, who joined the conservative cause and sought to establish a French-sponsored empire led by Austrian archduke Maximilian, who served as emperor of Mexico from 1864 to 1867. Unlike the four constitutions that preceded it, that of 1857 provided a stable, if not always heeded, juridical framework over the course of half a century.

Juárez, as minister of justice, drafted the 1855 law that put an end to ecclesiastical and military judicial privilege in civil suits. Although he did not participate in the design of the constitution, having been reelected governor of his home state, it became his touchstone and source of legitimacy as he assumed the presidency in 1858 after a conservative coup d'etat. When the coup set up a government that abrogated the constitution in the nation's capital, Juárez set up the constitutional government in Veracruz. The country was effectively divided in two. For Juárez, the constitution stood for putting the rule of law above petty rivalries, politically convenient shortcuts, and regional interests. The Reform laws promulgated by Juárez in 1859 and 1860 greatly diminished the power of the Church by nationalizing ecclesiastical wealth, shutting down religious orders, establishing a civil registry, and formalizing religious freedom. It was his insistence on adherence to the constitution that consolidated his legitimate leadership as a civilian president over the military. It provided the principles through which he tried to solve one of the national government's most pervasive problems since independence: its recurrent altercations with the states, particularly over men and money. On the other hand, he did not consider constitutional principle a strict mandate for government action. Like all presidents who governed under the 1857 law, he repeatedly asked Congress for emergency powers. In 1865, when his presidential period ran out, he refused to step down, alleging that the war made holding new elections impossible. When in 1867 he tried and failed to amend the constitution, he appealed directly to the electorate instead of following the constitutionally mandated process for reform.

After leading the country in what was then called the second war of independence, Juárez won two contested reelections, carried by a political machine that relied on the federal bureaucracy. He died as president in 1872, having secured the principle of constitutional rule; until 1917, challenges to political authority were articulated in defense of the constitution, never again against it. But if the constitution was consecrated as a national symbol and as the structure for political struggle, it failed to set up the mechanics for some crucial aspects of government, particularly for the transmission of power through elections. This is attested by the two rebellions led by Porfirio Díaz (1830–1915), one called the Plan de la Noria in 1871, the other called the Plan de Tuxtepec in 1876. Additionally, the Reform's disentitlement of communal lands and the nationalization of Church wealth did not bring about the prosperous nation of farmers that the liberals envisioned, but often the concentration of land ownership and the discontent of Indian communities.

Juárez's performance as a politician and statesman was controversial. Nevertheless, his transformation into an icon preceded his death: In the 1860s, other Latin American countries hailed him as a symbol of successful resistance to European imperialism. Once dead, Juárez, as Charles Weeks writes in his book *The Juárez Myth in Mexico* (1987, p. 42), "was far more valuable to all" as a particularly powerful and pliable symbol. In the 1890s orthodox liberals, despairing of Porfirio Díaz's authoritarian ways and his rapprochement to the Church, upheld Juárez as a symbol of true liberalism betrayed. Díaz ably took this banner away from them by claiming to be Juárez's true heir and throwing the weight and resources of government behind the *juarista* cult. In 1904 Francisco Bulnes (1847–1924), a prominent Porfirian politician, wrote a scathing critique of Juárez's actions during the French intervention and of the nationalist narrative that he believed was reducing history to hagiography. He unleashed a furious reaction from both Porfirian intellectuals and their opposition, and his criticism of Juárez was taken as an attack on the nation.

The Bulnes controversy sets the tone for the use and abuse of Juárez's figure as a source of legitimacy throughout the twentieth century as the self-proclaimed revolutionary state took up the mantle of nineteenth-century liberalism. References to Juárez in official rhetoric have been inevitable, especially from the mid-1940s, with the consolidation of civilian government and with the increasing importance of stability and economic growth over reform. He has personified administrative honesty, the secular state (despite his moderation and good relations with the Church in Oaxaca), strict adherence to law (although he violated the letter of the constitution), the defense of national sovereignty (although he authorized the signing of the unfavorable McLane-Ocampo treaty with the United States in 1859), and indigenism (even though he did not speak of "Indian rights" and repressed Che Gorio Melendre's movement to defend community resources in Juchitán in 1850). To the opposition right, on the contrary, he has been the embodiment of treachery to the true (Catholic) nation. Allusions to Juárez, then, are not meant to refer to historical experience or to policy content; they intend to draw the line between good and evil, patriotism and treason. Juárez has arguably been more important for what he has represented than for what he did.

SEE ALSO *Mexican Revolution (1910–1920); Revolutions, Latin American*

BIBLIOGRAPHY

Bulnes, Francisco. 1904. *El verdadero Juárez y la verdad sobre la intervención y el imperio.* Paris, Mexico City: Viuda de Charles Bouret.

Hamnett, Brian R. 1994. *Juárez.* London, New York: Longman.

Roeder, Ralph. 1947. *Juárez and His Mexico.* New York: Viking Press.

Sierra, Justo. 1969. *The Political Evolution of the Mexican People.* Trans. Charles Ramsdell. Austin: University of Texas Press.

Weeks, Charles A. 1987. *The Juárez Myth in Mexico.* Tuscaloosa: University of Alabama Press.

Erika Pani

JUDAISM

Judaism is the religion founded upon the Hebrew Scriptures, or "Old Testament," which is viewed as an exhaustive account of God's will for humanity. Judaism is the oldest of the three monotheist religions—the others being Christianity and Islam. The Hebrew scriptures first took shape around 450 BCE with the assembling of the Torah ("instruction"), which recorded the revelation of God to Moses at Mount Sinai. The Torah is composed of the Five Books of Moses: Genesis, Exodus, Leviticus, Numbers, and Deuteronomy. The sacred Scripture also encompasses the Prophets: Joshua, Judges, Samuel, and Kings, Isaiah, Jeremiah, and Ezekiel, and the twelve minor prophets; as well as the Writings: Psalms, Proverbs, Job, Ecclesiastes, Lamentations, Song of Songs, Ruth, Esther, Daniel, Chronicles, and Ezra-Nehemiah.

The Torah and the Prophets tell twin stories of exile from Paradise—one concerned with humanity as a whole, the other with Israel, the people of the Torah. Adam and Eve, representing humanity, lose Paradise—the Garden of Eden—because of their rebellion against God. The people of Israel likewise lose their paradise—the Land of Israel—because of their disregard of God's will as revealed in the Torah. Israel had acquired the Promised Land in fulfillment of God's covenant with Israel's founders, Abraham and Sarah, and their descendants. In 722 BCE, however, the northern kingdom of Israel fell to the Assyrians and was incorporated into Assyria, and in 586 BCE the southern kingdom of Judea fell to the Babylonians, who destroyed the Temple of Jerusalem. Following this, the Jews went into exile in Babylonia (present-day Iraq). In the later sixth century BCE the Babylonians were conquered by the Persians, who in 530 permitted the exiled Judeans to return to Jerusalem and rebuild the Temple there on Mount Zion. Some did just that. Then, around 450 BCE the scribe Ezra, in cooperation with the Temple priests, promulgated the Torah of Moses as the law for Israel.

The Torah portrays Israel's exile as the consequence of rebellion and its return as its reward for repentance, and sets forth the rules that Israel must keep if it is to retain paradise in the Land of Israel. The parallel narratives—the stories of Adam and Eve and their counterpart, the people of Israel—part ways with the return to Zion, for whereas Israel could repent and reform, Adam, representing the rest of humanity, without the Torah could do nothing to regain Paradise.

THEOLOGY OF JUDAISM

The theology of Judaism is set forth by the rabbis of the first six centuries CE in their readings of Scripture. These readings took place in dialogue with a set of documents that record the oral traditions that had been passed on via a chain of masters and disciples stretching back to Moses and up to the early centuries of the Common Era. The first of these documents recoding oral tradition is the Mishnah (ca. 200 CE), a law code that both amplifies the laws of Scripture and sets forth laws that take up topics not treated by Scripture. A collection of supplements, the Tosefta (ca. 300 CE), and two commentaries to the Mishnah, the Talmud of the Land of Israel (ca. 400 CE) and the Talmud of Babylonia (ca. 600 CE), augmented the laws of Scripture as systematized in the Mishnah's topical expositions. The same rabbis produced commentaries on Scripture, called Midrashim: among others, Genesis Rabbah (ca. 400), on Genesis; Mekhilta Attributed to Rabbi Ishmael (ca. 300), on Exodus; Leviticus Rabbah (ca. 450), on Leviticus; and Sifré to Numbers and Sifré to Deuteronomy, on Numbers and Deuteronomy, respectively.

The monotheism of Judaic theology as set forth in Scripture and oral tradition contrasts strongly with the polytheism prevalent at the time of Judaism's foundation. For a religion of numerous gods, life's problems have many causes; for a religion of only one God, there is only one cause. To explain why life is seldom fair and often unpredictable, polytheism identifies multiple causes, one god per anomaly. Diverse gods do diverse things, so it stands to reason that the outcomes of their actions conflict. Monotheism by its nature explains many things in a single way. One God rules all and everywhere. Life is meant to be fair, and just rules are supposed to describe what is ordinary, all in the name of that one-and-only God. Thus, in Judaic monotheism a simple logic governs, to limit ways of making sense of things. But that logic contains its own dialectics. If one true God has done everything, then, because he is God all-powerful and omniscient, all things are credited to, and blamed on,

him. In that case he can be either good or bad, just or unjust—but not both.

Jewish theology attempts to systematically reveal the justice of the one-and-only God of all creation. God is not only God but also good. The Torah pictures a world order based on God's justice and equity. Judaism finds its dynamic in the struggle between God's plan for creation—to create a perfect world of justice—and man's will. That dialectic is embodied in a single paradigm: the story of Paradise lost and regained.

Four key sets of beliefs characterize the theology of Judaism:

1. God formed creation in accord with a plan, which the Torah reveals. The facts of nature and society set forth in that plan conform to a pattern of reason based on justice and together constitute God's world order. Private life as much as public order conforms to the principle that God rules justly in a creation of perfection. Those who possess the Torah—namely, Israel—know God and those who do not—the gentiles—reject him in favor of idols. What happens to these two sectors of humanity, respectively, corresponds to their relationship with God. Israel in the present age is subordinate to the nations, because God has designated the gentiles as the medium for penalizing Israel for its rebellion— meaning that Israel's subordination and exile is intended to provoke repentance.

2. The perfection of creation, realized in the rule of exact justice, is signified by the timelessness of the world of human affairs, and its conformity to a few enduring paradigms that transcend change. Perfection is further embodied in the unchanging relationships of the social commonwealth, which assure that scarce resources, once allocated, remain unchanged. Further indications of perfection lie in the complementarity of the components of creation, and in the correspondence between God and man, who was created in God's image.

3. Israel's condition, public and personal, constitutes flaws in creation. What disrupts perfection is the sole power capable of standing on its own against God: man's will. What man controls and God cannot coerce is man's capacity to form intention and therefore choose either arrogantly to defy, or humbly to love, God. Because man defies God, the sin that results from man's rebellion flaws creation and disrupts world order. As with Adam and Eve's exile from Eden, the act of arrogant rebellion leads to humanity's flawed condition. God retains the power to encourage repentance through punishing man's arrogance. In mercy, moreover, God exercises

the power to respond to repentance with forgiveness—that is, a change of attitude bringing about a change in man's condition. Because man also has the power to initiate the process of reconciliation with God through repentance—an act of humility—man may restore the perfection of that order his arrogance has marred.

4. God ultimately will restore that perfection that embodied his plan for creation. In the process of restoration, death—which exists because of sin—will die, the dead will be raised and judged for their deeds, and most, having been justified, will go on to eternal life in the world to come. The paradigm of man restored to Eden is realized in Israel's return to the Land of Israel. In that world or age to come, idolaters will perish, and the remaining portion of humanity, comprising Israel, will know the one, true God and spend eternity in his light.

JUDAISM AND PHILOSOPHY: MEDIEVAL RATIONALISM

The theology of Judaic monotheism set forth by the rabbis of the first six centuries CE was subsequently amplified by philosophers and mystics. Judaic intellectuals in the Islamic world, from the advent of the Prophet Muhammad in the seventh century CE, faced the challenge posed by Muslim rationalism and philosophical rigor. The task at hand was to reconcile and accommodate Torah and the philosophical form of science.

That is why alongside the study of Torah—meaning the Babylonian Talmud and later codes, commentaries, and rabbinical court decisions—a different sort of intellectual-religious life flourished in Judaism. This was the study of the Torah-tradition through the instruments of reason and the discipline of philosophy: the quest for generalization, a critical sifting of evidence, and, above all, the attempt to find harmony between the generalizations of the Torah and the scientific principles of Aristotle. For example, how can the scriptural notion that God changes his mind be harmonized with the Aristotelian principle that change indicates imperfection, and how can the belief that miracles interrupt the course of nature be reconciled with the philosophical principle that laws of nature are immutable? If God is arbitrary, then God is no philosopher. But for Judaic, Christian, and Islamic theology, God is the source of all truth, whether revealed in nature or in scripture.

The Judaic philosopher had to cope with problems imposed not only by the Torah's conflict with philosophy, but also by the anomalous situation of the Jews themselves. For instance, what was the meaning of the unfortunate history of the Jews? How was philosophy to account reasonably for the homelessness of God's people, who were well aware that they lived as a minority among powerful, prosperous majorities—Christian or Muslim? If the Torah were true, why did different revelations claiming to be based upon it—and to complete it—flourish, while the people of Torah suffered? Why, indeed, ought one to remain a Jew, when every day one was confronted by the success of the daughter religions? Conversion was always a possibility—an inviting one even under the best of circumstances—for a member of a despised minority.

The search was complicated by the formidable appeal of Greek philosophy to medieval Christian and Islamic civilizations, two cultures in which Judaism was practiced. Its rationalism, openness, and search for pure knowledge challenged all revelations. Philosophy called into question all assertions based not on reason, but on appeals to a source of truth not universally recognized. Specific propositions of faith and the assertions of holy books had to be measured against the results of reason. Belief in mysterious divine plans conflicted with claims for the limitless capacity of human reason. It seemed, therefore, that reason stood in opposition to revelation, and free inquiry could not be relied on to lead to the synagogue, church, or mosque. Faith *or* reason—this seemed to be the choice.

For the Jews, moreover, the very substance of faith—in a personal, highly anthropomorphic God who exhibited traits of character not always in conformity with humanity's highest ideals and who in rabbinic hands looked much like the rabbi himself—posed a formidable obstacle. The obvious contradictions between belief in free will and belief in divine providence further enriched classical philosophical conundrums. Is God all-knowing? Then how can people be held responsible for what they do? Is God perfect? Then how can he change his mind or set aside his laws to forgive people? No theologian in such a cosmopolitan, rational age could begin with an assertion of a double truth or a private, relative one. The notion that something could be true for one party and not for another, or that faith and reason were equally valid and yet contradictory were ideas that had little appeal.

JUDAISM AND THE OTHER MONOTHEISTIC RELIGIONS

From the time of the Roman emperor Constantine, who in the fourth century declared Christianity legal and whose heirs made it the religion of the Roman Empire, to the nineteenth century, Jewry in Christendom had sustained itself as a recognized and ordinarily tolerated minority. The contradictory doctrines of Christianity—which saw Jews as Christ-killers to be punished, and as witnesses to be kept alive and ultimately converted at the second coming of Christ—held together in an uneasy balance. Official policy—keep the Jews alive, but do not reward their disloyalty—accounts for the Jews' survival in some of the Christian realms, particularly those on the frontiers of Christian Europe, south and east. The pluralistic character of some multiethnic societies explains the welcome accorded Jewish entrepreneurs in certain territories, including Spain before 1492, and Norman England, Lithuania, Poland, Russia, and Ukraine in the early centuries of their development.

The rabbinic system, for its part, had addressed the agenda of Christianity and for long centuries had given answers that, for Israel, proved self-evidently valid. Judaism had answered the question made urgent by Christianity's triumph: What is Israel in the divine plan? This it did by appeal to the sanctification of Israel and its future salvation. Normative Judaism had taken shape in response to the challenge of Christianity. So long as in Christian lands Christianity defined the issues, Judaism would flourish without effective competition within Jewry, absorbing and accommodating new ideas. The same was true of Islamic lands and the character of Judaism in the Muslim world.

JUDAISM AND MODERNITY

In modern times, faced with the political changes brought about by the American Constitution of 1787 and the French Revolution of 1789, Jews in western Europe and the United States aspired to rights possessed by the majority population: citizenship, equality before the law. But an urgent question emerged: How could and why should one be *both* Jewish *and* German or Jewish and French or Jewish and British? (The issue was conceived in terms of the categories of religion and nationality; that is, Jews were Jewish by religion and German by nationality. In the late-twentieth-century United States the issue would be conceived in terms of religion and ethnicity; thus, one could be both Christian and ethnically Jewish.) From the earliest decades of the nineteenth century, new Judaisms took shape, dealing with this and other urgent questions. They offered explanations of how a Jew could be not solely an Israelite but also something—anything—else. To do so, people had to identify a neutral realm in the life of individuals and consequently of the community, a realm left untouched by the processes of sanctification leading to salvation, which had for so long made Jews into "Israel," the community of Judaism. Each of these Judaisms claimed to continue in linear succession the Judaism that had flourished for so long, to develop it incrementally, and so to connect, through the long past, to Sinai. But in fact, each one responded to contemporary issues deemed urgent among one or another group of Jews.

THE REFORM, ORTHODOX, AND CONSERVATIVE JUDAIC RELIGIOUS SYSTEMS

Three main new Judaisms took shape between 1800 and 1850. The first to emerge was Reform Judaism, which developed in the early part of the nineteenth century. Reform Judaism made changes in liturgy, then in doctrine and in the Jewish way of life. More significantly, perhaps, it recognized the legitimacy of making changes and regarded change as reform—hence its name.

Second to develop was Orthodox Judaism, which achieved its first systematic expression in the middle of the nineteenth century. A reaction to Reform Judaism, Orthodox Judaism was in many ways continuous with traditional Judaism, but in other ways it was as selective in its adoption of elements of traditional Judaism as was Reform Judaism. Orthodox Judaism denied the validity of change, and held that Judaism lies beyond history; it is the work of God, and constitutes a set of facts of the same order as the facts of nature. Hence change is not reform, and Reform Judaism is not Judaism. But, at the same time, Orthodox Judaism affirmed that one could devote time to science as well as Torah-study, an accommodation with contemporary culture different only in degree from the Reform compromise.

Third in line and somewhat after Orthodox Judaism came positive Historical Judaism, known in America as Conservative Judaism, which occupied a middle position between the two other new Judaisms. This Judaism maintained that change *could* become reform, but only in accordance with the principles by which legitimate change may be separated from illegitimate change. Conservative Judaism would discover those principles through historical study. In an age in which historical facts were taken to represent theological truths, the historicism of Conservative Judaism gave it compelling weight. Positivism and dependence on history to validate theological conviction would serve Conservative Judaism poorly later on, however, when the discoveries of archaeologists called into doubt principal parts of the scriptural narrative.

SEE ALSO *Jews*

BIBLIOGRAPHY

Baron, Salo Wittmayer. 1952–1993. *A Social and Religious History of the Jews.* 2nd rev. ed. 18 vols. New York: Columbia University Press.

Ben-Sasson, Haim Hillel, ed. 1976. *A History of the Jewish People.* Cambridge, MA: Harvard University Press.

Finkelstein, Louis, ed. 1966. *The Jews: Their History, Culture, and Religion.* 3rd ed. Philadelphia: Jewish Publication Society of America.

Heschel, Abraham Joshua. 1987. *God in Search of Man: A Philosophy of Judaism.* Northvale, NJ: Jason Aronson.

Neusner, Jacob. 1987. *The Enchantments of Judaism: Rites of Transformation from Birth through Death.* New York: Basic Books. Reprint, Lanham, MD: University Press of America, 2005.

Neusner, Jacob. 2003. *The Way of Torah: An Introduction to Judaism.* 7th ed. Belmont, CA: Wadsworth/Thomson.

Schwarz, Leo W., ed. 1956. *Great Ages and Ideas of the Jewish People.* New York: Random House.

Jacob Neusner

JUDICIAL REVIEW

Judicial review is the legal principle that recognizes the power of courts to declare an act of Congress or the president unconstitutional. This power was most firmly established in the 1803 U.S. Supreme Court case of *Marbury v. Madison*. In a larger sense, the case exemplifies the uncertainties of litigation and how law evolves in a democratic form of government. It was the uncertainty embedded in litigation that prompted Supreme Court Justice Oliver Wendell Holmes (1841–1945) to declare that the object of the law is prediction when he stated that: "the prophecies of what the courts will do in fact, and nothing more pretentious are what I mean by the law" (1897, p. 461). In the American judicial system, what courts will do in fact about legal controversies brought before them will necessarily differ and possibly evolve from one case to another depending upon the facts and circumstances surrounding each case. Although the Framers conceived of the judiciary as the "least dangerous branch" insofar as the constitutional rights of the people are concerned, many now believe that this claim no longer rings true because they see the Supreme Court as the most powerful of the three stations of constitutional power in U.S. government. For the most part, the Court owes its current power and high status to the principle of judicial review.

The story of the origin of modern judicial review started in earnest with the presidential election of 1800 between the incumbent president John Adams (1735–1826) and the challenger Thomas Jefferson (1743–1826). That contest produced no clear winner after all Electoral College votes were counted. In that situation, the U.S. Constitution requires the House of Representatives to settle the election by choosing the president and vice president. During the month of February 1801, after much debate in Congress, Thomas Jefferson was selected president and Aaron Burr (1756–1836) vice president. Because the Federalist Party (the modern-day Democratic Party) had lost control of Congress and the presidency, the out-

going president, John Adams, proposed and Congress approved the Circuit Court Act of 1801, which authorized six new circuit courts and several district courts to accommodate the new states of Kentucky, Tennessee, and Vermont. This bill guaranteed the Federalists temporary control over the judiciary. During his final six months in office, John Adams submitted well over two hundred nominations to Congress, with sixteen judgeships approved by the Senate during his last two weeks in office.

One of the most important developments that took place during this transition period was that Federalist Oliver Ellsworth (1795–1800) resigned his position as chief justice of the Supreme Court, giving Adams an opportunity to name a Federalist successor. Adams immediately turned to former Chief Justice John Jay (1745–1829), who had resigned to become the governor of New York. Jay refused to return to the center chair. Then Adams turned to his secretary of state, John Marshall (1755–1835). Marshall accepted the appointment and was quickly confirmed by the Senate in January 1801 while he was still serving as secretary of state.

In addition to the Circuit Court Act, the Federalist Congress enacted the Organic Act, authorizing the president to appoint forty-two justices of the peace in the District of Columbia. The men Adams chose to fill these positions were called "midnight appointees," and virtually all were Federalists. It is noteworthy that this seemingly trivial act would set the stage for the most dramatic event that led to the Court's decision in *Marbury v. Madison*, the case that firmly established the doctrine of judicial review.

During the last days of John Adams's administration, there was a sudden rush to clean house in preparation for the new administration's arrival. As a result, Secretary of State John Marshall neglected to deliver some of the commissions for justice of the peace. If he had not neglected this duty, the ensuing controversy would have been avoided. One of these commissions belonged to William Marbury, a resident of the District of Columbia. When the new administration assumed power, Thomas Jefferson was displeased with his predecessor's blatant effort to pack the judiciary with Federalist loyalists. Therefore, he ordered his secretary of state, James Madison (1751–1836), not to deliver the commissions. Determined to obtain their commissions, Marbury and three others went directly to the Supreme Court. They invoked the Court's original jurisdiction powers and requested a writ of mandamus, which is an order that would require a government official (in this case, the secretary of state) to perform a government function (e.g., deliver the commissions). The case was placed on the Court's docket for the 1802 term. But while the case was pending, the new Republican majority in Congress decided to eliminate the entire 1802 Supreme Court term out of anger toward the actions of a lame-duck president, and so the decision in *Marbury v. Madison* was postponed until February 24, 1803.

This case presented John Marshall and the Supreme Court with a daunting predicament. Should the Supreme Court issue the writ of mandamus? What if the writ were issued and President Jefferson (through his secretary of state) refused to honor it? These were important questions requiring careful deliberation. Certainly the potential institutional consequences for the Supreme Court could be disastrous if the Court made the wrong choice. The balance of power in the government would be dramatically altered and the Court would suffer further diminished influence in the current and future affairs of government. Worse still, Jefferson and subsequent presidents could play fast and loose with the Constitution by assuming an inherit authority to act as they pleased without the watchful eye of the Court.

One can think of this case as a game of strategy. Both the Court and the president had real choices to make and each choice presented a real consequence. Since the Supreme Court had to make a decision after receiving the case, it got to move first in the game. The Court had to decide whether to issue the writ or not. If the Court chose to issue the writ, President Jefferson would probably choose not to honor it, precipitating a constitutional crisis. In this outcome, the Court would be severely weakened since it would lack the power to enforce its own decisions. If Jefferson honored the writ, however, that choice would be viewed as an embarrassing defeat for him and his administration. His power of persuasion would be damaged. Neither of these two possible scenarios—the Court's choices or the president's—sounded promising.

If, on the other hand, the Supreme Court failed to issue the writ, it would be viewed as weak by members of the Federalist Party in Congress and Marshall's reputation within the party would be severely tarnished. The remaining decisional choice was for the Court to declare the law authorizing William Marbury's legal request unconstitutional. The Court settled for this option, thereby avoiding a constitutional confrontation with the president. By declaring a federal law null and void for the first time, the Supreme Court firmly ushered in judicial review and sent a clear message that it stood ready to assert itself as an independent and coequal branch of the federal government. Historians of the Marbury affair consider the Court's decision something of sheer genius, although by all practical purposes it is possible that both the Supreme Court and the president were merely reacting rationally based upon information available to them.

How did John Marshall and the Supreme Court reach that decision? Analysis of the opinion suggests that the Court addressed three interrelated questions raised in the case. First, was William Marbury legally entitled to the commission? The Court answered yes, noting that the commission was indeed signed by the president; hence the appointment was made and it was completed when the secretary of state affixed a seal of the United States. Marbury therefore suffered a legal injury and as a matter of right was entitled to the commission. Second, did the law afford Marbury a remedy for his claim? Yes. Failing to offer Marbury an appropriate remedy would amount to a plain violation of his right under the Constitution. Finally, was that remedy a mandamus issued by the Supreme Court? The Court said no. Even though the Judiciary Act of 1789 authorized the Court to issue a writ of mandamus to "persons holding office, under the authority of the United States," the Court lacked the proper jurisdiction to issue a writ of mandamus because Section 13 of that Act provides an unconstitutional grant of original powers to the Supreme Court. Article III of the U.S. Constitution specifies in full the original jurisdiction powers of the Supreme Court. To alter that constitutional grant of power requires a constitutional amendment, not a congressional statute.

Judged under proper standards of ethical behavior, it seems that Marshall should have exempted himself from participating in this case since his own absent-mindedness precipitated the conflict in the first place. Although the law creating the vacancies for justice of the peace was later repealed by the anti-Federalist Congress, its legacy has lived and will continue to live on for generations to come.

The significance of *Marbury v. Madison* is that it declared an act of Congress unconstitutional, thereby affirming judicial review and independence. But the idea of judicial review itself was neither new nor born in that case. For instance, in 1795, eight years before the *Marbury* decision came down, there was a glimpse of the Court's thinking on the issue of judicial review in the case of *Van Horne's Lessee v. Dorrance*. In that case, Justice William Paterson (1745–1806) explained that in the American form of government, the "Constitution is the sun of the political system, around which all Legislative, Executive, and Judicial bodies must revolve. Whatever may be the case in other countries, yet in this there can be no doubt, that every act of the Legislature, repugnant to the Constitution, is absolutely void" (*The Supreme Court of the United States* 1992, p. 18). It was the principle elegantly expressed by Justice Paterson that *Marbury v. Madison* confirmed and later institutionalized as the most wide-ranging grant of power to the American judiciary.

Since Marbury's decision came down, the Supreme Court has relied on its power of judicial review to redefine the institutional relationships between the three branches of government, as well as the power-sharing relationships between the states and federal government. Most observers think judicial review has been a success. And this can be seen in part by the adoption of judicial review by emerging and even well-established democracies. In 2004, for example, an independent judiciary with the power of judicial review in Ukraine nullified a widely perceived fraudulent presidential election. In South Africa, Ecuador, and many other young democracies, judicial review has been adopted as an institutional reform to bring about a sense of permanence and stability to their governments. Clearly, these countries have seen the benefits of judicial review in the United States and other established democracies, such as Germany, Japan, and Spain.

SEE ALSO *Activism, Judicial; Bill of Rights, U.S.; Electoral College; Judiciary; Supreme Court, U.S.*

BIBLIOGRAPHY

Clinton, Robert Lowry. 1994. Game Theory, Legal History, and the Origins of Judicial Review: A Revisionist Analysis of *Marbury v. Madison. American Journal of Political Science* 38: 285–302.

Epstein, Lee, and Thomas G. Walker. 2004. *Constitutional Law for a Changing America: Rights, Liberties, and Justice.* 5th ed. Washington DC: CQ Press.

Haskins, George L., and Herbert Johnson. 1981. *Foundations of Power: John Marshall, 1801–1815.* New York: Macmillan.

Holmes, Oliver Wendell. 1897. The Path of the Law. *Harvard Law Review* 10: 457.

The Supreme Court of the United States: Its Beginnings and its Justices, 1790–1991. 1992. Washington, DC: Commission on the Bicentennial of the United States Constitution.

Isaac Unah

JUDICIARY

The judiciary is the branch of government charged with resolving, or adjudicating, disputes between citizens, between other government institutions, and between the government and its people. Judicial power may extend to three separate functions: (1) administering the criminal justice system by determining when a violation of the criminal law has occurred and declaring the appropriate sanction for that violation; (2) administering the civil justice system by resolving disputes, enforcing contractual obligations, and protecting property rights; and (3) exercising judicial review of legislative enactments to ensure that new laws comport with constitutional requirements.

The disputes resolved by judicial entities—often called *courts* or *tribunals*—are referred to as *cases.* Courts may rest the authority to resolve a case in a single official, who may be called a *magistrate,* a *judge,* or a *justice.* In the alternative, some courts, called *collegial courts,* place decision-making authority in a group. In a collegial court, a group of judges will hear a single case and will collectively be responsible for adjudicating its outcome.

The scope of a court's authority is its *jurisdiction.* Jurisdiction may be defined geographically, with a judicial entity having authority over a particular city, state, or region. In the alternative—or additionally—a court's jurisdiction may be defined by subject matter. For example, a court may have authority only over issues of intellectual property or only over issues of criminal law; such a court would be a court of limited jurisdiction, as opposed to a court of general jurisdiction.

Finally, a court's jurisdiction may be *original* or *appellate* in nature. A court's original jurisdiction extends to those cases it hears before any other court. In contrast, a court's appellate jurisdiction extends to cases in which it is reviewing the decision of another court. The notion of appellate jurisdiction presupposes a hierarchical judicial system.

For example, in the United States, each state has its own judicial system, and the federal government has a separate—more appropriately, a parallel—judicial system. The federal judiciary is hierarchical: federal district courts, which have original jurisdiction in most disputes, have jurisdiction over a set geographic territory, no larger than a state; U.S. circuit courts of appeals, which function as intermediate appellate courts, also have jurisdiction over a set geographic territory, usually a group of contiguous states; and the U.S. Supreme Court is a single judicial body that has jurisdiction over the entire nation.

The U.S. Supreme Court primarily exercises appellate jurisdiction, reviewing decisions of lower federal courts and state high courts; a citizen involved in a dispute with his neighbor cannot go directly to the U.S. Supreme Court but, rather, can only appeal to the U.S. Supreme Court after attempting to obtain a favorable verdict from at least one lower court, and usually several. The U.S. Constitution, however, carves out a few types of cases, such as cases involving foreign officials, over which the Supreme Court has original jurisdiction; accordingly, such a case could begin and end in the Supreme Court, with no other judicial body ever rendering a decision.

COMMON PRINCIPLES

Although judicial systems vary significantly from nation to nation—and even sometimes from jurisdiction to jurisdiction within a single nation—there are a few aspirational characteristics that most judicial bodies share. Among these ideals are objectivity and institutional independence.

Objectivity The *rule of law* is a cornerstone of government legitimacy, particularly in democratic states. The judiciary is the voice of the law, and in a just society the application of the law is not affected by favoritism or bias. Accordingly, an ideal judicial system is objective.

Judicial officials are expected to leave their personal preferences out of their decision making, and institutional rules are often designed to eliminate or minimize the possibility, even the appearance, that judges are motivated by anything other than the law. In an effort to expose potential bias, judges frequently must disclose their financial records, and in systems where judges are elected, rules relating to campaign contributions may be especially stringent. Many judicial systems provide rules against *ex parte communication*—communication about a case with one party or attorney to which the other party or attorney is not privy—and rules against the judge discussing the case with the public or media before an official decision has been rendered. Ultimately, the goal of all of these rules is to eliminate any personal interest in the outcome of the case and to limit the ability of outside parties to sway the judge's position.

Of course, like every government institution, the judiciary is composed of human beings who cannot leave their humanity at the door. Most judges have studied the law, perhaps worked as attorneys or held other public office, and are generally well-informed individuals. It would be bizarre to expect that they do not have opinions about legal issues, judicial philosophy, and public policy. Moreover, it would be unreasonable to expect that judges can compartmentalize their own opinions to such an extent that they have no effect whatsoever on their judicial decisions.

Studies of judicial behavior, primarily of justices on the U.S. Supreme Court, have persuasively demonstrated that judicial decisions are affected to some extent by ideological concerns. Specifically, to the extent that Supreme Court justices disagree about the outcome of a particular case—an indication that the law is not entirely clear—there are predictable patterns of agreement between the justices and predictable patterns of voting that correspond, roughly, to liberal and conservative viewpoints. There is considerable debate about the conditions under which and the degree to which ideology colors judicial decision-making, but it is generally accepted that ideology is a factor. Indeed, decisions about selecting and electing judges in the United States are highly politically charged because it is generally understood that judges bring their individuality to the task of judging and are not, rather, automatons rigidly applying the law.

Institutional Independence To protect the rule of law, judicial officials must be objective; the influence of their personal preferences, biases, and interests on their decisions should be minimal. Yet it is not enough to constrain the members of the judiciary; they must also be protected from threats of reprisal from unpopular decisions. Thus, another common ideal for judicial institutions is that they enjoy institutional independence.

Referring to a government institution as a judiciary generally distinguishes it from a legislature (a deliberative body that develops laws and policies) or an executive (the individual or individuals charged with carrying out the will of the government). The judicial power, however, is not always severed from the legislative and executive powers. For example, the biblical King Solomon was renowned for his ability to resolve disputes, and in the English feudal system of the Middle Ages, landowners adjudicated disputes among their tenants. Similarly, many Native American tribes traditionally vested the authority to resolve disputes and impose criminal sanctions in the tribal council, a body that also possessed legislative and executive powers. Such intermingling of political responsibility and judicial responsibility is generally considered suboptimal because it often means that the individuals exercising judicial authority are subject to political pressures that may taint their judicial decisions.

Even when the judicial power resides in a formally separate institution—a judiciary—the relationship between the judiciary and other institutions of government may impair the ability of the judiciary to uphold the rule of law. Judges who rely on other government actors to secure their wages, to maintain their staffs and their facilities, and even to keep their jobs are understandably vulnerable to political pressures. Freeing the judiciary from these sources of dependence, specifically by institutional arrangements that make it difficult if not impossible for other government institutions to undermine the judiciary's ability to function, advances judicial independence.

While it is easier to insulate the judiciary from public pressure, the separation of the judiciary from electoral influence poses more philosophical problems for democratic states, particularly when the judiciary exercises judicial review. The notion of a government entity that is not answerable to the public effectively exercising a veto over legislative acts runs counter to the idea of majority rule; for precisely that reason, some states opt to select judges through popular elections or allow the public to remove unpopular judges through recall elections.

Advocates of judicial independence argue, in response, that the judiciary provides a critical check on majoritarian government, protecting enduring political values and the interests of political minorities from fleeting political passions or minority tyranny. Proponents of judicial independence suggest appointing judges based on merit, for life tenure or for a fixed, nonrenewable term.

Even when institutional arrangements maximize judicial independence, the interplay between the judiciary and more political forces is apparent. For example, members of the U.S. federal judiciary are appointed by the president but must be confirmed by the Senate, and they enjoy life tenure. Still, historically, the federal courts have shown deference to political sentiment. The U.S. Supreme Court seemed to abandon principle to political pressure when it upheld the constitutionality of the Japanese internment during World War II (1939–1945) and when it shifted its position on economic liberty to allow adoption of the New Deal policies of Franklin D. Roosevelt (1882–1945). Even when the Supreme Court made the politically unpopular move of ordering the desegregation of public schools, the Court's concern for public opinion was apparent; Chief Justice Earl Warren (1891–1974) carefully crafted his opinion in *Brown v. Board of Education* (1954) to ensure a unanimous Court, and the Court waited a year after declaring segregated schools unconstitutional before issuing the opinion ordering desegregation. In other words, even when the Supreme Court uses its independence, it often attempts to make concessions for public opinion.

VARIATION IN JUDICIAL SYSTEMS

While most judicial systems share a common purpose and certain common ideals, there is tremendous variation in the structure and function of judicial systems when viewed in comparative perspective. The rest of this article will focus on some of the key dimensions along which judicial systems vary.

Criminal Justice: Inquisitorial and Adversarial Systems

The judiciary often bears primary responsibility for the administration of criminal justice: adjudicating guilt and assessing sanctions for the violation of criminal laws. Criminal justice systems and, more specifically, the role of courts in those systems, may be *adversarial* or *inquisitorial*; these terms define endpoints on a continuum, with most judicial systems blending elements of both adversarial and inquisitorial procedures.

In a purely adversarial system, prosecutorial and adjudicating powers are completely separated. A prosecuting authority makes the decision to charge a citizen with a crime, gathers evidence of guilt, and argues on behalf of the state. The role of the judiciary is limited to receiving evidence from both the prosecutor and the accused, weighing that evidence, and adjudicating guilt. Thus the party adjudicating guilt and innocence hears both sides of the story, presented as cohesive wholes, in relatively quick succession.

In contrast, in a purely inquisitorial system, both prosecutorial and adjudicating authority are vested in a single institution. In an inquisitorial system, the same individual or institution will be responsible for charging a citizen with a crime and for determining whether the cit-

izen is guilty. Judicial officials in inquisitorial systems gather evidence and directly question witnesses. The danger of an inquisitorial system is that during the course of investigation, the judicial authority will become committed to a particular theory or belief and that subsequent, countervailing evidence will not be accorded sufficient weight. In other words, inquisitorial systems create a real risk that prosecutorial zeal and momentum will cloud the ultimate determination of guilt.

Civil Justice: Common Law and Civil Law Systems

The role of the judiciary in the administration of civil justice—the resolution of disputes between private parties—varies considerably between *common law* countries and *civil law* countries. Common law countries are, generally, England and its former colonies, while the civil law tradition has its origins in France.

The common law tradition is premised on the notion that law, as a body of community norms, derives as much from custom and usage as from government edicts. In common law countries, a significant portion of the law is developed by the judiciary through the process of resolving disputes. When confronted with a new dispute, courts will look at past similar disputes—what we call *precedent*—for guidance. In this incremental fashion, building resolution upon resolution, a body of judge-made common law is created.

In the civil law tradition, the role of the judiciary is considerably more limited. Codified law is far more detailed and governs every aspect of social intercourse. The role of the judiciary is limited to interpreting those laws that have been enacted by the legislative branch of government.

Judicial Review: American and European Models

One dimension along which we can differentiate types of judicial systems is the manner in which they exercise *judicial review*. Judicial review is the process of evaluating new legislative enactments and executive policies to ensure that they are consistent with constitutional requirements. There are two principal models of judicial review: the European model and the American model.

The European model is characterized by a division between ordinary courts, which are typically hierarchical systems for addressing basic civil and criminal matters, and a constitutional court, which is a single court of limited jurisdiction devoted solely to the business of ruling on the constitutionality of legislative acts. France, Portugal, Germany, and Russia all have a constitutional court system. In these countries, when the legislature passes a new law, it may be challenged directly in the constitutional court. In some countries, such as France, the challenge must come from a state actor. In others, such as Germany, even ordinary citizens may allege a constitutional violation.

The American system is considerably less efficient. The American judicial system is unified: there is a single, hierarchical federal court system—with trial courts, intermediate appellate courts, and a Supreme Court—that handles civil matters, criminal matters, and constitutional questions. Challenges to the constitutionality of legislative enactments must work their way through the complete hierarchy, a long and burdensome process. What's more, the challenges must arise in the context of an actual case or controversy rather than as a simple allegation of unconstitutionality.

To illustrate, imagine a law forbidding the distribution of pamphlets critical of the government. In a country with a European system of constitutional courts, an individual who believes the law violates the country's constitution would address this argument directly to the constitutional court; the constitutional court would rule up or down on the issue of constitutionality, and the dispute would be over. In an American-model country, however, an individual who believes the law is unconstitutional would have to create a case—likely by breaking the law, enduring arrest, and then challenging the constitutionality of the law during the course of his or her criminal trial. The challenge may need to be repeated in the trial court, one or more appellate courts, and finally the U.S. Supreme Court.

SEE ALSO *Activism, Judicial; Bill of Rights, U.S.; Jurisprudence; Supreme Court, U.S.*

BIBLIOGRAPHY

Abraham, Henry J. 1998. *The Judicial Process: An Introductory Analysis of the Courts of the United States, England, and France.* 7th ed. New York: Oxford University Press.

Baum, Lawrence. 2001. *American Courts: Process and Policy.* 5th ed. New York: Houghton Mifflin.

Jacob, Herbert, Erhard Blankenburg, Herbert M. Kritzer, and Doris Marie Provine. 1996. *Courts, Law, and Politics in Comparative Perspective.* New Haven, CT: Yale University Press.

Segal, Jeffrey A., and Harold J. Spaeth. 2002. *The Supreme Court and the Attitudinal Model Revisited.* Cambridge, U.K.: Cambridge University Press.

Stone-Sweet, Alec. 2000. *Governing with Judges: Constitutional Politics in Europe.* New York: Oxford University Press.

Tate, C. Neal, and Torbjörn Vallinder, eds. 1995. *The Global Expansion of Judicial Power.* New York: New York University Press.

Wendy L. Watson

JUNG, CARL
1875–1961

Carl Gustav Jung was born in Kesswyl, Switzerland, on July 26, 1875. Jung was a self-described lonely and isolated son of an emotionally troubled mother and a poor but extremely well-read country pastor. A gifted student, Jung originally wanted to be an archaeologist. Due to limited financial resources, Jung was forced to attend the University of Basel, which did not offer courses in archaeology, and he studied medicine with the intention of becoming a surgeon. Jung switched to psychiatry to pursue his interests in dreams, fantasies, the occult, theology, and archaeology. Upon graduation Jung received an appointment to the Burgholzli Mental Hospital in Zurich where, from 1900 to 1909, he studied the nature of schizophrenia and developed into a world authority on abnormal behavior.

Jung was an early supporter of the psychotherapist Sigmund Freud (1856–1939) because of their shared interest in the unconscious. When the International Psychoanalytic Association was formed in 1910, Jung became its first president at the request of Freud. However, growing theoretical differences between them, especially over the importance of libido (i.e., sexual energy) and the nature of the unconscious resulted in Jung's resignation from the group only four years later. The two men never met or spoke to each other again.

From 1913 to 1917, while Jung was experiencing serious emotional difficulties in his life and even contemplating suicide, he engaged in an extensive self-analysis. The outcome of his self-analysis produced some of Jung's most original theoretical concepts, which he continued to develop over the next sixty years as Jung established himself as one of the most noted psychological and eclectic thinkers of the twentieth century. For example, Jung was extremely well read in theology, anthropology, archaeology, psychology, ancient texts, the occult, mythology, and psychiatry. He studied psychological adjustment in selected groups of individuals around the world (e.g., Navajo Indians, native tribes in Africa); and participated in archaeological and anthropological expeditions in a variety of cultures (e.g., Egypt, Sudan, India), while incorporating his diverse knowledge and experience into his theory of personality and psychotherapeutic applications in an attempt to verify his ideas. Jung died on June 6, 1961, in Zurich at the age of 85. He was an active and productive researcher and writer his entire life, with a collection of works totaling twenty volumes.

FREUDIAN VERSUS JUNGIAN TRADITIONS

Although initially a strong supporter of Freud and his ideas, Jung's eventual disagreement with some of the cornerstones of Freud's theory resulted in the termination of their professional relationship and personal friendship. A principal source of disagreement was with Freud's concept of libido. Freud's conceptualized libido as primarily the source of sexual energy that served to created a state of emotional tension that the individual was driven to decrease, forming the basis of the two primary motivating sources of behavior—life instinct (i.e., creation of tension) and death instinct (i.e., the reduction of tension). In direct contrast, and much to Freud's disagreement, Jung de-emphasized the importance of the libido as a source of sexual energy. Jung described libido as a more generalized life energy source that served to motivate the individual to seek a sense of personal balance within the psyche in a number of different ways, including socially, intellectually, emotionally, spiritually, and creatively.

This point of disagreement regarding the nature and role of libido helped to create the distinction between the Freudian and Jungian traditions in psychology. The Freudian tradition is characterized by the presence of intrapsychic conflict and the creation and reduction of psychic tension. The Jungian tradition, referred to as "analytical psychology," is characterized by the seeking of intrapsychic harmony and the balanced expression of the separate aspects of the self.

THE STRUCTURE OF THE MIND AND ITS CONTENTS

Another significant source of disagreement between Freud and Jung was their contrasting views of the structure of the mind and the nature of unconsciousness. In comparison to Freud, Jung's view of the structural nature of personality reflected a redefined and expanded view of the mind, especially the unconscious mind, which Jung believed to be much deeper and wider in the scope of its content than Freud. The "conscious ego" is the center of conscious awareness of the self. The major functions of the conscious ego are to make individuals aware of their internal processes (e.g., thoughts or feelings of pain) and the external world (e.g., surrounding noises) at a level of awareness necessary for daily functioning.

Directly next to the conscious ego and below conscious awareness, Jung proposed the "personal unconscious" region of the mind. The contents of the personal unconscious include all thoughts, memories, and experiences that are momentarily not being thought about and/or repressed because they are too emotionally threatening. The most important elements in the personal unconscious are what Jung described as "complexes." A complex is a collection of thoughts, feelings, attitudes, and memories that center around a particular concept. The more elements attached to the complex, the greater its influence on the individual. If the complex becomes too strong it can become pathological, serving to create a sense of imbalance in the individual's personality, such as a power complex associated with a dictatorial leader.

While the personal unconscious is unique to each individual, the collective unconscious was the region of the unconscious mind believed by Jung to be shared by all people. Jung conceptualized the collective unconscious as being "transpersonal" in nature. The transpersonal nature of the collective unconscious reflected Jung's view that there is a region of the unconscious mind containing a collection of general wisdom that is shared by all people, has developed over time, and is passed from generation to generation across the ages. The principal function of this wisdom is to predispose individuals to respond to certain external situations in a given manner. For example, anytime a group of individuals gets together, there is a natural tendency or predisposition for them to establish a social order.

The most significant of these predispositions or images in the collective unconscious are referred to as "archetypes." Archetypes are universal thoughts, symbols, or images having a large amount of emotion attached to them. Their special status comes from the importance they have gained across the many generations and the significant role they play in day-to-day living. Another concept Jung used to illustrate the universal connectedness of the collective unconscious was the principle of "synchronicity." Jung used synchronicity to explain the occurrence of two meaningful events that do not appear to have any physical cause-and-effect sequence, such as dreaming of a distant relative's death and then receiving news a week later that the relative had died on the same day you had the dream.

While there are a variety of archetypes, there are four archetypes that play a significant role in the establishment of a balanced personality: the persona; animus/anima; shadow; and self. The "persona" is an archetype that develops over time as a result of the tendency of people to adopt the social roles and norms that go along with living with other people. From the Latin word meaning "mask," the persona reflects what might be defined as a person's public personality (e.g., being courteous in public). However, attaching too much emotion and importance to the persona can result in the individual losing contact with his or her true feelings and identity, which can then become dictated by others (e.g., an individual with a shallow and conforming personality). Jung believed that individuals were psychologically bisexual in nature in that each individual possesses characteristic features and tendencies of the opposite sex that are represented by the archetypes of the animus and anima. The "animus" is the masculine aspect of females, such as being aggressive. The "anima" is the feminine aspect of males, such as being nurturing. The well-developed personality contains both masculine and feminine characteristics. The "shadow" represents the dark and primitive side of personality. Like the id developed by Freud, the shadow represents all of the instinctive and impulsive aspects of personality typically repressed in the unconscious regions of the mind and kept out of the public personality.

The "self," the most significant archetype, is that element of the personality predisposing the individual to unite all other aspects of the personality. The development of the self as an archetype reflects the desire by people across generations to seek unity and harmony. Within the individual, the self is the motivating force seeking to achieve unity and harmony between all the private and public, masculine and feminine, and conscious and unconscious aspects of the individual. Failure on the part of the self to achieve this sense of unity and balance can result in the overdevelopment of one aspect of the personality at the expense of all others.

JUNG'S PERSONALITY TYPES

According to Jung there are two general types of personality attitudes by which individuals orient themselves toward their environment: extraversion and introversion. The "extraversion" attitude is an outward orientation in which psychic energy is invested in events and objects in the external environment (e.g., preference for group activities). The "introverted" attitude reflects an inward orientation in which psychic energy is invested in internal and personal experiences (e.g., preference for spending time alone). While Jung believed that both types of attitudes are present within each personality, he thought that in each person one attitude is expressed more at the conscious level than the other.

Besides the two basic attitudes of personality, Jung also proposed the existence of four functions of personality. Each function is characterized by a specific orientation for understanding the events and experiences in the environment.

- The "sensation function" involves relating to the world through the senses.

- The "thinking function" refers to the tendency to relate to the world through ideas and intellect.

- The "feeling function" concerns reacting to the world on the basis of the emotional quality of one's experiences with it.

- The "intuition function" goes beyond all other conscious functions and relies on a deeper, more internal sense of understanding.

As with the two attitude types, Jung assumed that each personality possesses all four functions, but one is often expressed at a predominant, conscious level at the expense of the others.

The technique of personality assessment most closely identified with Jungian principles is the Myers-Briggs Type Indicator (MBTI). The MBTI is a self-report instrument using objective criteria (i.e., standardized response and scoring procedures) based on Jung's type theory and designed to assess how variations in the expression of the two attitudes and four functions result in differences in the way individuals use perception and judgment as general orientations to their experiences when taking in information and making decisions. The utility of the MBTI can be seen in its use in a variety of areas, including literary criticism, career-counseling, organizational consulting, design of information technology, academic advising, and the health care industry.

THE NATURE OF MENTAL HEATH AND ANALYTICAL PSYCHOTHERAPY

Mental health was represented by Jung as a balanced expression of the various archetypes. Jung proposed that well-adjusted individuals learn to incorporate private aspects of their personality into the persona and express them consciously in socially acceptable forms. The developmental concept of "individuation" is used to describe the process by which individuals become aware of the different aspects of their personality at both the conscious and unconscious level, and expend mental energy to develop and express them in a meaningful way. The development of "neuroses" is a result of the individual failing to achieve a sense of integration, resulting in the projection of the underrepresented aspects of the self (e.g., connectedness with others) on to others (e.g., blaming a spouse for not being affectionate), which serves to foster maladaptive interpersonal social relationships. The development of "psychosis" is a result of extreme and prolonged repression of underrepresented aspects of the self, resulting in the aspects exploding into the individual's psyche in the form of drastic shifts away from the conscious, public persona (e.g., massive retreat into the unconscious mind and away from reality, as is with schizophrenia).

Based on Freud's technique of psychoanalysis, Jung's form of therapy is referred to as "analytical psychotherapy" and is characterized by a greater emphasis in the unconscious and the reestablishing of psychological balance within the individual. One method used to investigate the unconscious was the word association test. The test, which Jung invented, was used principally to help identify the client's problematic complexes. A problematic complex is characterized by the overinvestment of mental and emotional energy into one aspect of an individual's personality (e.g., obsession with work) at the expense of other aspects of the individual's personality (e.g., neglecting one's family).

Going beyond the identification of problematic complexes, Jung analyzed dreams to explore the archetypes of clients using a technique referred to as the "method of amplification," which he also developed. In this method the client not only reports what is going on in the dream but also expands on the details as if actually a part of the dream (e.g., describing how it feels to be free and very powerful, as represented by a sports car as a symbol of the self in the dream). To facilitate this process, Jung used the dream series method, which involved amplifying and analyzing a series of dreams for the repeated occurrence of particular archetype symbols (e.g., the self appearing as the sun or a tall building). He also used the method of active imagination in which the client is asked to imagine having an interaction with the significant archetypes identified during treatment (e.g., talking to a "mechanic/therapist" about making the "car/self" perform more effectively).

JUNG'S RELATIONSHIPS WITH NAZISM

In 1933 as Adolf Hitler came to power, the German Medical Society of Psychotherapy was reorganized based on National Socialistic principles in an attempt to remove its Jewish members. An International General Medical Society for Psychotherapy was organized in Germany and permitted individual membership, including Jewish members, and national societies, including the German Society. Jung was elected the International Society's first president in 1933 and served until 1939. Jung also served as the chief editor of *Zentralblatt für Psychotherapie und ihre Grenzgebiete*, a journal that eventually published an article promoting Hitler's *Mein Kampf* as required reading for all psychoanalysts. Jung's affiliation with this Nazi-dominated International Society led to accusations that Jung was a Nazi sympathizer. Jung maintained that his involvement with the International Society was an indirect attempt to make it possible for Jewish practitioners to maintain their professional involvement and help preserve psychoanalysis, which the Nazis viewed as a "Jewish science." It should be noted that Jung resigned from the International Society for Psychotherapy toward the end of World War II (1939–1945), had public supporters who were Jewish, was blacklisted by the Nazis, and had his works suppressed in Germany and other occupied countries by the Nazis.

Despite Jung's novel contributions to the study of personality and psychotherapy, the acceptance of Jung's ideas has been limited by the vague definitions of his principal concepts (e.g., the collective unconscious, archetypes, synchronicity), which made his concepts difficult to test empirically by the traditional scientific methods. Given the difficulty in quantitative testing, Jung's ideas have been more popular and influential in the more qualitative areas of scholarship, such as the humanities (e.g., literary criticism, mythology, and symbolism) and humanistic social sciences (e.g., anthropology and qualitative sociology) than the quantitative areas associated with postmodern experimental psychology and psychiatric medical research.

SEE ALSO *Freud, Sigmund; Hitler, Adolf; Nazism; Personality; Psychology; Psychotherapy*

BIBLIOGRAPHY

Douglas, C. 2000. Analytical psychotherapy. In *Current Psychotherapies*, 6th ed., eds. Raymond J. Corsini and Danny Wedding, 99–132. Itasca, IL: Peacock Publishers.

Ellenberger, Henri F. 1970. *The Discovery of the Unconscious: The History and Evolution of Dynamic Psychiatry*. New York: Basic Books, Inc.

Hall, Calvin S., and Vernon J. Nordby. 1973. *A Primer of Jungian Psychology*. New York: New American Library.

Jung, Carl G. 1961. *Memories, Dreams, and Reflections*. New York: Random House.

Myers, Isabel B., Mary H. McCaulley, Naomi L. Quenk, and Allen L. Hammer. 1998. MBTI *Manual: A Guide to the Development and Use of the Myers-Briggs Type Indicator*. Palo Alto: Consulting Psychological Press.

Storr, Anthony 1991. *Jung*. New York: Routledge.

Bernardo J. Carducci

JURISPRUDENCE

The term *jurisprudence* refers generally to the science or study of law and encompasses any effort to define, describe, or conceptualize the nature of the law. In practice, such efforts vary dramatically in scope and focus. Broadly speaking, jurisprudential efforts can be divided into two types: applied jurisprudence and the philosophy of law.

APPLIED JURISPRUDENCE

Applied, or empirical, jurisprudence is the study of the nature and development of the law through its actual practice. In other words, the endeavor of applied jurisprudence is to examine judicial decisions in which rules of law are applied to actual cases and conflicts, and from that application infer something about the nature of the law being applied. For example, one might look at a series of U.S. Supreme Court decisions that apply the establishment clause of the First Amendment to actual conflicts and, from those decisions, develop an understanding of what the establishment clause means and how it might be applied to other, hypothetical situations. This understanding and the judicial decisions giving rise to it would be known, collectively, as *establishment clause jurisprudence*.

Applied jurisprudence is particularly important in common law legal systems—primarily in England and its former colonies. *Black's Law Dictionary* defines common law as "the body of law derived from judicial decisions, rather than from statutes or constitutions" (1999, p. 270). Common law systems are based on the idea that law derives primarily from custom or usage. In a common law system, the basis or grounds on which a court resolves a dispute comes from past decisions of the court; those past decisions are called *precedents*. Statutes and other codified laws may alter or supersede common law principles, but common law principles are used to interpret statutes, and traditional common law principles fill the interstices between codified laws.

In common law systems, legal norms develop incrementally over time, with judicial decisions announcing or explaining the law only when necessary to resolve the particular dispute before it. Anticipating how the law will be applied to a new factual scenario necessarily requires assimilating a large number of judicial decisions and analogizing to the new fact pattern. As a result, the endeavor of applied jurisprudence—looking at judicial decisions and, from them, discerning the nature of the law—is an integral part of the practice of law in common law countries.

PHILOSOPHY OF LAW

The term *jurisprudence* also refers to the philosophy of law, which is concerned not with the law of a particular state or country but with the nature of law more generally. The philosophy of law is concerned with the origin of law, the difference between law and other social norms, the difference between legal systems and other institutions, and the legitimacy of laws and legal systems. Some philosophical inquiries focus on what the law is, and these inquiries form the basis of *analytic jurisprudence*. Other philosophical inquiries focus on what the law should be, and these inquiries form the basis of *normative jurisprudence*.

Analytic jurisprudence addresses questions about what the law is: What do we mean by the term *law*? How do we come to understand the law? What differentiates laws from other norms and institutions? What is the rela-

tionship between the law and other concepts, such as power and morality?

Perhaps the most significant and fundamental issue in the context of analytic jurisprudence is the debate between natural law theorists and legal positivists. Put very simply, natural law theorists assert that law derives from a higher order, imposed by God or nature and adducible by reason; law exists independently of states and sovereigns, and law is inseparable from morality. A state may articulate a rule and use its coercive power to enforce that rule, but the rule is not genuinely law unless it conforms with some standard of what is right, moral, or just. Although philosophical writings dating back to Aristotle (384–322 BCE) reflect the theory of natural law, its most prominent champion in the twentieth and early twenty-first centuries is the Australian legal scholar John Finnis.

In contrast to natural law, legal positivism views law as a purely social construct and asserts that the law is what the sovereign declares it to be; the question of whether a law is good or right is distinct from the question of whether it is, in fact, a law. Some of the most notable proponents of legal positivism include the British jurist John Austin (1790–1859) and the British scholar H. L. A. Hart (1907–1992).

Legal interpretivism presents a conceptual alternative to both natural and positive theories of law. The interpretivist approach argues that law is not a fixed concept at all, but the result of legal practice. Rules articulated by the state must be interpreted, and their interpretation by legal practitioners is necessarily informed by those practitioners' moral beliefs. Thus, law does not derive from morality but is shaped by it. The interpretivist approach is most often associated with the American legal scholar Ronald Dworkin.

Whereas analytic jurisprudence seeks to describe law and legal systems objectively and, in some circumstances, to address the relationship between law and morality, normative jurisprudence addresses the moral questions raised by legal problems: When should the rights of one person be compromised to protect the rights of another? Is a state justified in restricting an individual's liberty to protect that individual by, for example, requiring the use of automobile seatbelts or prohibiting suicide? Why and how should violations of the law be punished?

Normative jurisprudential debates frequently invoke religious arguments and overlap with political philosophy. For example, one of the most enduring questions of normative jurisprudence is whether a state is ever justified in imposing capital punishment. Both the popular and scholarly dialogues on the issue frequently involve arguments based on religious teachings. Similarly, in the United States, the capital punishment debate is sometimes framed as a political question: As the ultimate restriction on liberty, is capital punishment consistent with liberal democratic values?

SEE ALSO *Judicial Review; Judiciary; Law*

BIBLIOGRAPHY

Coleman, Jules, and Scott Shapiro, eds. 2002. *The Oxford Handbook of Jurisprudence and Philosophy of Law.* New York: Oxford University Press.

Dworkin, Ronald. 1986. *Law's Empire.* Cambridge, MA: Harvard University Press.

Finnis, John. 1980. *Natural Law and Natural Rights.* New York: Oxford University Press.

Garner, Bryan A., ed. 1999. *Black's Law Dictionary.* 7th ed. St. Paul, MN: West Group.

Hart, H. L. A. 1961. *The Concept of Law.* New York: Oxford University Press.

Wendy L. Watson

JURORS, DEATH-QUALIFIED

In a process unique to criminal law in the United States, jurors in capital trials are subjected to a process known as "death qualification." Since 1976 all criminal trials for which the death penalty is a possible sentence have been held in two different phases (producing what is known as a "bifurcated trial"): a guilt-determination phase, followed by a penalty phase if the defendant is found guilty of a capital crime. The rationale for death qualification is that justice in capital cases cannot be properly administered if jurors' views about the death penalty are so strong that they prevent impartial decision making. So, during the voir dire jury-selection process, the prosecution and defense lawyers have an opportunity to "death-qualify" potential jurors by questioning them about their views regarding the death penalty.

Contemporary death qualification under the Supreme Court decision in *Wainwright v. Witt* (1984) eliminates potential jurors if they believe that their ability to function as a juror in a capital case would be impaired because of their views on the death penalty. This standard differs notably from that established previously by *Witherspoon v. Illinois* (1968), which excluded only those jurors who indicated such a strong opposition to the death penalty that they would not consider voting for a guilty verdict if there was even a possibility that a death sentence would be ordered.

Criticism of the death-qualification process has focused on two basic arguments: (1) that the process is unreliable, and (2) that the process creates systematic bias

among the pool of eligible jurors such that they are predisposed toward guilty verdicts during the penalty phase. Research in this area generally has relied upon mock-juror and mock-jury studies in a social-psychological tradition, although sometimes researchers have been able to question jury-pool members and jurors who have served in actual capital cases.

A mock-juror study conducted by Ronald Dillehay and Marla Sandys (1996) suggested that the current *Witt* standard for excluding jurors in death penalty trials is unreliable, eliminating those who would ultimately be able to perform adequately as capital jurors and failing to identify some potential jurors known as "automatic death penalty" jurors who would always vote for the death penalty if a defendant had been convicted of murder. In addition, the death-qualification process itself may cause jurors to believe that the defendant is guilty and that a penalty of death is expected. Social science research also suggests that the death-qualification process may increase the likelihood of guilty verdicts during the first stage of bifurcated trials.

BIBLIOGRAPHY

Dillehay, Ronald C., and Marla R. Sandys. 1996. Life Under *Wainwright v. Witt:* Juror Dispositions and Death Qualifications. *Law and Human Behavior* 20: 147–165.

Marc W. Patry

JURY SELECTION

The jury system is the cornerstone of the common law legal system, the legal system shared by England and most of its former colonies. The common law legal system is premised on the notion that legal norms develop through common practice rather than formal rules; juries—groups of people lacking formal legal training who are brought in to adjudicate disputes—provide the perspective of the community, a common rather than formal perspective. Because juries are essential to the common law legal tradition, their selection and composition affect the very heart of common law systems of justice. Jury selection systems vary from jurisdiction to jurisdiction, but the goal of all such systems is to convene juries that are representative of the broader community and that are unbiased.

Jury selection begins with the process of identifying those people who are eligible to serve. A list of potential jurors may be constructed from voter registration lists, drivers' license and state identification lists, or other official rosters of citizens. The goal of a representative jury is best achieved with a comprehensive list of potential jurors;

using voter registration lists as a source of potential jurors, for example, may result in a jury pool that underrepresents certain demographic groups, such as the poor and young adults.

From the list of potential jurors, a jury pool is randomly selected. In smaller jurisdictions, where the need for a jury is rare, a jury pool may only be selected when the need arises. In most jurisdictions, however, jury pools are convened as a regular matter. From a single jury pool, multiple juries will be selected over the course of the pool's service (which may range from a single day to several weeks to several months).

Individuals who receive a summons to appear for jury duty—to be a part of the jury pool—are generally asked to complete a short list of questions. Based on their answers, jurors may be disqualified—deemed ineligible to serve. Citizens may be disqualified for jury service because of a lack of language proficiency, mental or emotional disturbance, or a criminal record or pending criminal charges. Historically, in the United States, citizens were disqualified from jury service on the basis or their race or gender, but the U.S. Supreme Court has determined that such disqualifications are inconsistent with the equal protection clause of the Fourteenth Amendment to the Constitution.

Some potential jurors, while not disqualified, are nevertheless excused from jury service. In other words, while they may serve, they are not legally obligated to serve. Members of certain professions—doctors, teachers, lawyers, military personnel, and small business owners— as well as individuals whose physical condition would make jury service difficult, may be excused.

When a particular jury is needed for a particular case, names are randomly selected from the jury pool. These individuals—called *venirepersons*—are subjected to more detailed questioning by the attorneys and judge involved with the case. This questioning process is known as *voir dire*. The purpose of voir dire is to identify particular biases a juror might have that would affect his or her ability to be objective in resolving the case: knowledge of the parties to the case, witnesses, or attorneys; exposure to prejudicial media coverage about the case; past experiences that might color the juror's judgment; or even biases against certain groups of people.

On the basis of the venirepersons' answers to questions during voir dire, attorneys may challenge their ability to serve on the case. Specifically, attorneys may use two types of challenges: *challenges for cause* and *peremptory challenges*. In a challenge for cause, the attorney requests that the judge strike the potential juror because of some obvious bias. For example, in cases involving the death penalty in the United States, the prosecuting authority is entitled to a jury of individuals who are not opposed to capital punishment; such a jury is said to be *death-qualified*. If, during the course of voir dire, a venireperson expressed opposition to the death penalty, the prosecuting attorney could challenge that venireperson for cause.

Attorneys can use peremptory challenges to strike jurors who are not clearly biased. Peremptory challenges give attorneys the opportunity to strike jurors whose answers do not necessarily reflect bias but whose demeanor or background raise concerns for the attorney. Attorneys use questions about the types of television shows jurors watch, the books they read, their hobbies, and even the bumper stickers on their cars to develop profiles of potential jurors and to expose unspoken biases. While there is no limit to the number of potential jurors who may be struck for cause, each party to a case has a fixed number of peremptory challenges and, once they are exhausted, may not exercise any more.

Peremptory challenges are controversial. In England, peremptory challenges are not allowed. In the United States, peremptory challenges are allowed, but they cannot be used to eliminate jurors on the basis of race or gender, and there is considerable variation in how the process is implemented. Specifically, some jurisdictions use a *sequential system*, while others use what is called a *struck system*.

In a sequential system, the number of venirepersons empanelled equals the number of individuals needed for the jury, so that when a party uses a peremptory challenge to strike a venireperson, that party has no idea what the replacement venireperson will be like. A party may use its last peremptory challenge to strike a venireperson only to find that the replacement venireperson is even less desirable. In a struck system, however, the number of venirepersons chosen equals the number of jurors required plus the total number of peremptory challenges the parties may exercise. Thus, a party may use its peremptory challenges to eliminate the least desirable of a known set of potential jurors.

Once both parties have passed the jury panel for cause—concluded that everyone who remains is capable of serving impartially—and have exercised all of the peremptory challenges they choose to use, the remaining venirepersons are issued an oath of service and become the jury. While no jury is perfectly representative and some personal bias is unavoidable, the iterative process of random selection and careful screening increase the likelihood of a jury that reflects community values and common sense in legal decision making.

SEE ALSO *Judiciary; Jurors, Death-Qualified*

BIBLIOGRAPHY

Abramson, Jeffrey. 1994. *We the Jury: The Jury System and the Ideal of Democracy.* New York: Basic Books.

Hans, Valerie P., and Neil Vidmar. 1986. *Judging the Jury.* New York: Plenum.

Hastie, Reid, Steven D. Penrod, and Nancy Pennington. 1983. *Inside the Jury.* Cambridge, MA: Harvard University Press.

Vidmar, Neil, ed. 2000. *World Jury Systems.* New York: Oxford University Press.

Wendy L. Watson

JUST WAR

"Just war" principles seek to transform war and peace into moral questions, to move international relations beyond the "realist" conception classically expressed in *The Peloponnesian War* by the fifth-century BCE Greek historian Thucydides. A realist conceives of wars as a normal if undesirable fact of international relations, a matter of irreconcilable national interests or policies in which the "royal prerogative," the authority to decide for war or for peace, is an inherent sovereign power of governments. The realist is dubious about the contention that, in a world order still characterized by anarchy, war can be reconceived at its root as a moral matter, although moral considerations can certainly be compelling in one way or another. To a realist, wars have occurred in history because, as the French philosopher Jean-Jacques Rousseau (1712–1778) said, there is nothing adequate to stop them. To a just war advocate, on the other hand, realism is far from irrelevant, but it is only the beginning of civilizing, that is, justifying and limiting humankind's most damaging activity.

But just war principles are not at all the same as pacifism. Just war theorists argue that all war is in some sense evil, yet some wars are justified. A universal presumption against war, let alone a national policy of nonviolence, would be not only self-destructive but immoral because sometimes war is both necessary and right, particularly wars of self-defense against aggression.

CRITERIA FOR A "JUST WAR"

A just war is a right use of force founded in the moral responsibility of a government for the political community as a whole. In just war thinking, the "Westphalian system" launched in 1648 was based on a great mistake. This system refers to the modern international order consisting of sovereign nation-states, established by the European Treaty of Westphalia in 1648. Sovereignty was defined in purely procedural terms, implying that whoever successfully controls a territory should be accepted internationally as sovereign in it. The result was that, until quite recently, dictators used the legal principle of national sovereignty as a shield to protect themselves while tyrannizing their own people. Just war principles attempt to inject the concept of sovereignty with substantive moral meaning.

The just war idea has roots in ancient Israel and was first conceptualized in Catholic tradition by Augustine (354–430 CE), the bishop of Hippo, in *The City of God.* The Italian natural law philosopher Thomas Aquinas (1225–1274) gave the classic statement of just war principles in *Summa Theologica.* According to Thomas Aquinas, a just war is defined by two sets of criteria: whether the cause is just (*jus ad bellum*) and whether the methods of combat are just (*jus in bello*). Just war is thus an issue of both means and ends: A just war may be fought unjustly and vice versa. While the principles are fairly clear (although not entirely without ambiguity), controversy is inevitable in judging any particular case, a theme particularly well developed in the work of the influential American just war theorist Michael Walzer (2000).

Walzer argued that a just cause for war exists if five criteria are met. (1) The intention must be right, meaning a war must be waged either in self-defense against aggression or it must be an international intervention to aid another people victimized by egregious aggression. Since World War I (1914–1918), certain states (especially the United States) and international organizations (the United Nations, the North Atlantic Treaty Organization [NATO], and the European Union) have invoked a right to intervention on moral and humanitarian, as well as realist, terms. Since the 1990s, the international community, in the United Nations and outside it, has begun to codify not only a right to intervene but also a duty to do so—a "responsibility to protect" peoples in danger, a duty to reverse grave violations of human rights. (2) The decision to go to war must be made by a duly constituted sovereign, that is, a legitimate authority. (3) War must be a last resort, the *ultima ratio*, undertaken only after all diplomatic means have failed. (4) There must be a reasonable probability of success, the reason being to avoid futile damage. (5) The good to be achieved must clearly outweigh the harm to be done, the intrinsic evil aspect of even a just war.

In terms of the means of combat, a war is considered just if it meets two conditions. The principle of "discrimination" must be respected, that is, distinguishing insofar as possible between combatants and civilians, and strictly limiting the "double effect" or "collateral damage" of killing innocents while fighting. In addition, the principle of "proportionality" must be respected, meaning that damage inflicted must bear some reasonable relationship to the original aggression.

In retrospect, the catastrophic world wars and genocides of the twentieth century paradoxically emphasized both the continued relevance of realist international-relations thinking and the desirability of moving toward just war principles. For example, the Geneva Conventions on protection of prisoners of war and the prohibition of torture may be considered just war treaties. The Holocaust, the atomic bombings of the Japanese cities of Hiroshima and Nagasaki, and the firebombing of German and Japanese cities during World War II (1939–1945) have led to a widespread conclusion that genocide or the use of weapons of mass destruction can never be justified.

The American-led Gulf War of 1991 to reverse Saddam Hussein's invasion and annexation of Kuwait, the European-American intervention in the Balkan wars of the 1990s, and the post–September 11, 2001, war in Afghanistan all were fought as just wars, that is, moral campaigns larger than the evident interest of the international community in reestablishing peace and security. There may be serious argument about whether or not any particular war is a just war (for example the American-led invasion of Iraq in 2003 to overthrow Saddam Hussein's regime). But at the beginning of the twenty-first century it is evident that moral arguments about goals and methods of war are increasingly relevant in the real world of international relations, as opposed to realist Westphalian-type declarations of national interest or policy. This is fundamental moral progress, even as it is obvious that prudence remains the statesperson's necessary virtue.

"JUST WAR" AND TERRORISM

The new age of global-scale terrorist attacks has obvious relevance for just war thinking. On the other hand, evaluating the justice of terrorist campaigns, although it may seem simple, is no easy matter. Judgments are not intuitive and the results are a matter of sharp dispute in world politics in the early twenty-first century. While it is insufficient simply to say that "one man's terrorist is another man's freedom fighter," distinctions can and must be made in the real world or else it is too easy to end up in a situation in which might, or the most effective propaganda, makes right. Gradually, as with other aspects of international law, such as outlawing torture and genocide, increasing consensus about terrorism across different kinds of states, cultures, religions, and world regions may emerge. One example of international agreement on a definition of terrorism is found in the 2004 United Nations report, "A More Secure World."

Terrorist acts are a tactical means of waging war. In just war terms, terrorism is illegitimate and unjust in itself, no matter how much sympathy this form of fighting may inspire in a civilian population. However, it is important to remember that terrorist groups are unaffected by this, since they reject the customary international laws of war as such, invoking their own, usually religious conception of just war ends and means. Terrorist groups, especially the new phenomenon of global terrorist networks, willfully defy the principle of discrimination by intentionally targeting civilians on a wide scale in an attempt to instill destabilizing fear in governments and populations. There is a sharp difference, at least in principle, between the intentional killing of innocents and military action that kills or wounds civilians in spite of genuine attempts to limit such damage, generally called *collateral damage*. In just war theory, intentions are fundamental, and the fallacy of moral equivalence—that is, civilians killed are civilians killed, no matter what the circumstance—must be avoided.

On the other hand, the concept of collateral damage can be dangerous because it can become overly expansive. For example, in spite of rigorous attempts to limit the killing of civilians in certain ways, a given state's overall military campaign against terrorism may involve collateral damage on such a scale, with a more or less hidden intent to terrorize a population and turn it against erstwhile popular terrorist groups (themselves fighting with unjust means), that the military campaign itself becomes state-sponsored terrorism. In other words, terrorism may be a weapon of duly constituted, sovereign authority.

Furthermore, a terrorist group may in fact be fighting for a just cause—for example, it may be a military wing of a national liberation movement seeking national sovereignty and independence against a colonialist foreign power, or one or both sides in a civil war. Success of a terrorist campaign in such a case will not be military victory; rather, its goal will be to demoralize the adversary's military or political leadership or its home population to the extent that a negotiated compromise or even total withdrawal may result. In such a case, a terrorist campaign that historically was only one aspect of a successful struggle for national independence may be remembered differently than it would have been had the struggle been lost.

In any case, however, terrorist acts on any side remain in and of themselves unjust and illegitimate. It is wrong to take any innocent person's life, whether or not it can be claimed that a just end is being served. It is a fallacy to contend flatly that "just war trumps unjust means." At the same time, just war judgments must somehow recognize a situation in which a rebellion's use of only just means will leave a population more or less defenseless against an even more unjust power—whether the latter is its own government or an outside power. In such a case, agreement might be reachable by saying that, as with war itself, all terrorism is evil but it is always justifiable to choose the lesser evil.

Altogether, just war principles are not—far from it—a single unified doctrine that will easily unite the world politically or could be easily codified in international law. They represent moral guidelines, extending long-established, basically pragmatic, realist laws of war. They constitute a broad set of standards continuing a secular struggle to justify war in human terms and to limit its damage, against which individual cases can be argued and measured. Again, just war thinking does not envisage the abolition of war, because sometimes war is not only necessary but right.

Perhaps the appropriate conclusion at this point is to say that just war thinking is simultaneously a beginning and a hope, above all if, as increasing numbers of thoughtful people agree, war is a cultural phenomenon rather than human fate. Cultural practices may evolve in response to circumstances. In any case, realism and prudence will remain, at least for some time, the necessary foundations of international policy in a world order still characterized by anarchy.

SEE ALSO *Civil Wars; Law; Terrorism; Terrorists; War*

BIBLIOGRAPHY

Elshtain, Jean Bethke, ed. 1992. *Just War Theory*. New York: New York University Press.

Johnson, James Turner. 2005. Just War, As It Was, and Is. *First Things* 149 (2005): 14–24.

Walzer, Michael. 2000. *Just and Unjust Wars: A Moral Argument with Historical Illustrations*. 3rd ed. New York: Basic Books.

Ronald Tiersky

JUSTICE

Justice is a moral quality of individuals and of institutions, whereby they give equality of respect to persons and strive to preserve the rights of all. Along with wisdom, courage, and moderation, justice was considered by ancient Greek as well as medieval Christian and Islamic thinkers to be a cardinal virtue. In the *Republic,* Plato (c. 427–347 BCE) portrays justice as the right ordering of the parts of the individual soul and the groups of persons in the city. Aristotle (384–322 BCE) devoted a central chapter of the *Nicomachean Ethics* to the virtue of justice. He distinguished between *general justice,* which is the complete exercise of all the virtues in one's treatment of other persons, and *special justice,* which is both the fair distribution of honors, wealth, and other goods, and fairness in the exchange of goods. Later tradition followed Aristotle by distinguishing between *distributive* justice (justice in the allotment of commonly held goods) and *commutative* justice (justice in exchange and in rectification of injuries). Distributive justice is governed, for Aristotle, by equality, but not by identical treatment for all. If "the people involved are not equal, they will not [justly] receive equal shares" (Aristotle 1985, p. 123). Whether one is wealthy, of good birth, or virtuous are among the factors that are believed by different people to affect one's just share of common goods, according to Aristotle.

Medieval philosophers followed the Greeks in defining justice as part of the *natural law*, those laws governing human actions that are founded in reason, in the human need to live in societies, and ultimately in a divine ordering of the universe.

MODERN ACCOUNTS OF JUSTICE

Modern political philosophy, although still sometimes using the language of natural law theories, transposed the discussion of justice into a *social contract* framework of thought. The English philosopher Thomas Hobbes (1588–1679) argued in *Leviathan* (1651) that prior to the establishment of a government, people lived in a *state of nature*, a state of war in which their lives and property were utterly insecure. In the state of nature, justice and injustice did not exist: "Therefore before the names of just, and unjust can have place, there must be some coercive power, to compel men equally to the performance of their covenants, by the terror of some punishment" (Hobbes [1651] 1962, p. 113). Justice, for Hobbes, has its ground in self-preservation and self-interest. John Locke (1632–1704) argued in the *Second Treatise of Government* (1690) that even in the state of nature people have a natural right to life, liberty, and property. The rulers, once the commonwealth is established, are obligated, according to Locke, to preserve these natural rights of individuals. Thus justice, for Locke, predates the establishment of the government and places some constraints upon the actions of those in power.

JUSTICE AND UTILITARIANISM

Utilitarian philosophy, resting as it does on the principle that the rightness of actions and of social institutions depends on the degree to which they promote human happiness, has often been charged with disregarding justice. Because the happiness of the greatest number could, at least in theory, result from unjustly depriving a minority of their rights or even of their lives, utilitarianism is often accused of failing to account for intuitive and traditional judgments about justice toward individuals. In defense of utilitarianism, John Stuart Mill (1806–1873) argued in *Utilitarianism* (1863) that the claims of justice, including individual rights to life, liberty, and property, as well as the right of individuals to be dealt with truthfully and impartially, are fully compatible with utilitarianism. Because there can be no security for anyone unless each is treated justly, Mill argued, justice is the foundation of any society that seeks to promote the general happiness. Mill acknowledged widespread disagreement over such issues as whether those with greater talents or skills should be rewarded better than those without and whether taxes should be assessed based on the ability to pay or as an equal share.

A number of questions emerge from the foregoing sketch of historical views of justice: Should justice be considered a social convention or does it have a basis in natural or divine law? To what extent does justice, which demands that everyone be treated in some sense equally, admit that different treatment is appropriate in different cases? What are the differences (e.g., of individual merit or of need) that appropriately lead to differences in treatment?

RAWLS'S THEORY OF JUSTICE

The American philosopher John Rawls (1921–2002) was the twentieth century's most influential thinker concerning these questions. In *A Theory of Justice* (1971), Rawls argued that justice is at its basis a matter of fairness. Justice, for Rawls, is "the first virtue of social institutions, as truth is of systems of thought" (Rawls [1971] 1999, p. 3). Rawls's theory advocates a form of *procedural justice*, meaning that justice results from following a fair procedure, where there is no separate measure of what a just outcome would be. In the tradition of social contract theory, Rawls describes a hypothetical "original position" in which free and equal parties agree to the principles of justice by which society will be governed. To ensure fairness, the choice is made behind a "veil of ignorance" in which each of the contracting parties is denied knowledge of certain facts about themselves. None of them knows "his place in society, his class position or social status, nor does anyone know his fortune in the distribution of natural assets and abilities, his intelligence, strength, and the like" (p. 11). The parties are ignorant of their gender, and they do not know to what generation they belong. They know that when the veil is lifted they will have some conception of the good, that their notions of the good life will require some measure of resources to carry them out, and that those resources will be somewhat scarce.

Once the agents of the original position have been presented with a variety of available conceptions of justice, Rawls argues that they would adopt what he calls the two principles of justice. "First: each person is to have an equal right to the most extensive scheme of equal basic liberties compatible with a similar scheme of liberties for others. Second: social and economic inequalities are to be arranged so that they are both (a) reasonably expected to be to everyone's advantage, and (b) attached to positions and offices open to all" (Rawls [1971] 1999, p. 53). Rawls gives priority to the first of these principles, such that basic liberties "can be restricted only for the sake of liberty" (p. 266). He refines the second principle (termed "the difference principle") to say that inequalities are to be "to the greatest benefit of the least advantaged" (p. 266). As a result of adopting these principles of justice, Rawls defends a liberal constitutional democracy in which the government protects basic liberties and oversees the just distribution of resources. The principles of justice led Rawls, in his 2001 book *Justice as Fairness: A Restatement,* to criticize welfare and laissez-faire capitalism, as well as state socialism having a "command economy," in favor of "property-owning democracy" and "liberal socialism" (Rawls 2001, p. 138).

In his 1993 book *Political Liberalism*, Rawls argues that the principles of justice are subject to an *overlapping consensus,* that is, that they are acceptable from the perspective of many different philosophical or religious systems of thought. In this way, Rawls advances the discussion of the principles of justice without requiring a decision on whether justice is ultimately a matter of social convention or of natural or divine law.

Though not a strict *egalitarian* (for he allows inequalities as long as they are to the advantage of the least well-off), Rawls views as unjust any distribution of goods that serves only to better the conditions of those possessing greater natural or social advantages than others. It is important to note that, for Rawls, individual endowments such as talent, wealth, and social standing are arbitrary gifts of fortune rather than individual possessions or entitlements. The "difference principle" ensures that those who possess such advantages will not be able to translate them into a greater share of society's goods at the expense of those who are less advantaged. Thus, on the question of whether merit, need, or some other criterion should become the basis for the distribution of social goods, Rawls asks that we remember that what appears to be an individual's "merit" is generally the result of luck rather than desert.

OBJECTIONS TO RAWLS'S THEORY

Rawls's work has been widely praised and criticized. Communitarian critics, such as Michael Sandel, have objected that the parties in the original position are artificially deprived of the knowledge that membership in a particular community is essential to their identities, leading to an overly individualistic account of justice. Libertarians, including Robert Nozick (1938–2002), viewed Rawls's principles as leading to infringements of individual liberty because of Rawls's willingness to redistribute social goods that were initially obtained through what libertarians view as legitimate means (e.g., not obtained through deceit or coercion). Advocates of Catholic social teaching, along with other religiously oriented thinkers, have objected that Rawls's thought relegates religious belief to the private sphere, thereby denying the important role of religious faith in the promotion of social justice. The feminist political thinker Susan Moller Okin (1946–2004) argued that Rawls overlooked the need for justice within families. Advocates of *capability ethics*, including Amartya Sen and Martha Nussbaum, criticized Rawls for stressing the equal distribution of goods without noting the differing degrees to which society enhances or undermines individuals' capacities to make use of those goods. (Nussbaum has, in her own work, extended the discussion of justice to include questions of justice toward the disabled, toward nonhuman animals, and across international boundaries.) Despite these and other objections, Rawls's theory, with its powerful defense of individual rights and its attention to the claims of the disadvantaged, continues to exert a commanding influence on contemporary ethical and political thought.

SEE ALSO *Democracy; Egalitarianism; Equality; Justice, Distributive; Locke, John; Rawls, John; Social Contract; Utilitarianism*

BIBLIOGRAPHY

Aristotle. 1985. *Nicomachean Ethics.* Trans. Terence Irwin. Indianapolis, IN: Hackett.

Hobbes, Thomas. [1651] 1962. *Leviathan, or the Matter, Form, and Power of a Commonwealth Ecclesiastical and Civil*, ed. Michael Oakeshott. New York: Collier.

Locke, John. [1690] 1980. *Second Treatise of Government*, ed. C. B. Macpherson. Indianapolis, IN: Hackett.

Mill, John Stuart. [1863] 2002. *Utilitarianism*, 2nd ed., ed. George Sher. Indianapolis, IN: Hackett.

Rawls, John. [1971] 1999. *A Theory of Justice*, rev. ed. Cambridge, MA: Belknap.

Rawls, John. 1993. *Political Liberalism.* New York: Columbia University Press.

Rawls, John. 2001. *Justice as Fairness: A Restatement*, ed. Erin Kelly. Cambridge, MA: Belknap.

Paulette Kidder

JUSTICE, DISTRIBUTIVE

Distributive justice refers to a process whereby a society allocates certain rewards and resources to persons based on a moral belief or set of moral beliefs. Once a typical fea-

ture of envisioned social utopias, ranging from a late medieval scheme of Thomas More (1478–1535) to the more modern experiments of thinker-activists like Robert Dale Owen (1801–1877), allocation became linked to modern theories of justice with the rise of bourgeois democracies. Jeremy Bentham's (1748–1832) liberal utilitarian creed of the greatest good for the greatest number was contrasted in the nineteenth century with oppositional calls by radical thinkers from anarchist, socialist, and communist movements for a collectivist justice based on some form of economic leveling or allocation to each according to his or her needs.

The call for distributive justice found its expression in the transformation of Western bourgeois democracies into social democracies, along with the development of a postrevolutionary form of state socialism in the Soviet Union. The first consisted of state-centered provision of various forms of universal insurance, as well as of a full range of social and human services, and was financed typically by more progressive income and inheritance taxes. Greater equity, but not broad-based economic equality, resulted. Scandinavian countries, notably Sweden, had the greatest success in reducing income and wealth differences. The Soviet Union achieved much greater equity, though the creation of a nomenclature consisting of party officials and state bureaucrats did great damage toward attempts to achieve absolute economic equality.

Since the 1970s with the decline of Communist regimes and a general retreat from socialist/reformist thinking, there has been a return of more liberal calls for greater economic and social equity. They possess a twofold and somewhat contradictory character. First, they are decidedly more individualist and libertarian in their concerns. Modern philosophers in the Anglo-American tradition, such as John Rawls (1921–2002), stress the need to provide individuals with adequate resources for fulfilling lives—*equality of opportunity*, in a phrase. The leveling process, contrary to utilitarian and generally socialist aims, is clearly curtailed in this tradition by the desire to protect individual liberty and the freedom of choice in the economic transactions of civil society. Ronald Dworkin argues for an *equality of outcomes*, insofar, however, as persons are prudent and responsibly choose forms of insurance that could be offered by a state to compensate persons from potential or real harms.

Simultaneously, distributive justice has acquired a distinctly collective sociological character. The modern study of invidious distinctions ranging from class and caste to status, and the differences among persons thereby, have created a more radical theory of justice based upon the elimination of economic and social inequalities arising from membership in disadvantaged classes based upon income, wealth, race, gender, sexuality, and disability.

Empirical social science has provided extensive documentation that has been used by judiciaries, legislators, public administrators, and policy formulators to construct a variety of remedies, ranging once more from providing equality of opportunity to the more demanding requirement of equality of outcomes. The latter often requires limiting the freedom of others more privileged in some sense and of transferring resources to members of disadvantaged classes in amounts equal to or greater than amounts available to those not suffering from the disadvantage(s) under review.

More recently, economist and philosopher Amartya Sen has sought to join concerns for the well-being of individuals with the disadvantages they acquire as members of a discriminated class. Every individual, Sen argues, is an assemblage of specific capabilities. To provide equality of opportunity, interventions need to provide resources that strengthen an individual's capabilities to function in a manner she finds conducive to her well-being. Her freedom of choice is preserved, along with her desire to live her particular life. To get resources to individuals with discernible capability deficits, Sen argues strongly that resources must be targeted to specific kinds of persons rather than simply added to a society's macroeconomic mix. Hence, the individuality of deficits is matched with ameliorative social programs based upon the realization that deficits can be identical, person to person. Gender inequality, for instance, commonly affects certain women who could be grouped into a class, while this same class could differ from other women with another provenance.

This shift in the concept of distributive justice from universal entitlement to individual capabilities in the 1990s has had an enormous influence on social policy. International assistance to poor countries by the World Bank, rich countries, and nongovernmental organizations has been redirected from capital-intensive infrastructure projects to expenditures on public health and basic education, as well as gender-related remedies founded on the widespread recognition that women's capabilities are sorely damaged by discrimination worldwide. In rich countries, the focus on individual capability deficits has led to a restructuring of income support programs that seek to hold individuals more responsible for their own development.

The calls for more equitable forms of distributive justice have stimulated a variety of opposition responses. The first might be termed a *naturalist* response. Persons are composed of innate differences in a variety of aptitudes that cannot be overcome by programs of distributive justice. Even if persons are compensated in ways that provide each with economic equality, natural differences will express themselves in the original cohort or in their progeny to re-create natural differences in aptitude once more.

Charles Murray and Richard Herrnstein (1930–1994) argue that differences in intelligence lead to the formation of an elite based upon their superior abilities, and subaltern status for those less fortunate. A second, less genetically based version posits that subaltern groups form destructive ways of life that greatly diminish their chances for well-being. This position is typically referred to as the *culture-of-poverty* argument.

A second response bears a long and distinguished genealogy, and viewed from this end of the telescope is a profoundly sociological account of the origins and development of society. There are several sources. Thomas Hobbes (1588–1679) argues that the very equality between persons in the original state of society creates a drive for aggrandizement on a person's part, if only to protect one from the envy and finally aggression of another. A state thus becomes necessary to protect each from all. John Locke (1632–1704) held a more congenial view of humankind, believing that persons were self-possessed and cognizant of their own needs and wants. The products of their toil, Locke argued, were theirs. The acquisition of property, however, provided them with a place for amicable exchange but also of legal defense against others in an organized society. Money creates a fetter in this otherwise peaceable kingdom, requiring that a civil government adjudicate fairly the disputes that arise between persons, especially as they become more unequal.

Both the more punitive motivations of Hobbes and the more genial motivations of Locke contribute to a modern, minimalist view of the state whose justice consists of ensuring fairness in the exchanges of individuals. Often called the *night watchman state* theory, its principal exponent in modern discourse is Robert Nozick (1938–2002). The job of the state, on Nozick's view, is to repel national invaders and enforce contracts. As humans are their own property and not that of others, they are entitled to whatever property they acquire through their efforts—in fact, as much as they can acquire so long as they do not destroy the property of others or that of the commons. The state guarantees free markets in property, capital, and labor. Justice is no longer connected with distribution, but instead associated with equitable rules applied in the marketplaces of society.

This broad view has been used to support free-market-based economic and social policy. In the social sciences, it underlies the increased resort to so-called *rational choice* theory, whereby individuals are taken a priori to be rational, and create society via interactions on their own behalf. However, from this same premise, this notion that the self-interested person is a rational person can be severed from a purely means-ends rationality and applied to assumptions about the strength of greed, network, and group ties in orienting action.

This position also affected the nature of the social scientific investigation of inequality. Considering the broad endorsement of a kind of first-order naturalness to unequal social existence, investigators from the functionalist tradition in the postwar period produced descriptive paradigms of economic and social inequality in modern societies, and between rich and poor societies, that abjured comment on the moral and political dimensions of their studies. Their fundamental premise was that societal development necessitated an increasing division of labor, and inequality was its inevitable—and valuable—result.

A strong critical and highly politicized movement developed across the social sciences to combat what was seen as this received view. As a consequence, normative theorizing about inequality and the value of forms of distributive justice now constitute themselves as the normal conditions of discourse.

SEE ALSO *Choice in Economics; Culture of Poverty; Egalitarianism; Equal Opportunity; Equality; Ethics; Hobbes, Thomas; Inegalitarianism; Inequality, Gender; Inequality, Political; Inequality, Racial; Locke, John; Philosophy; Rationality; Rawls, John; Sen, Amartya Kumar; Socialism; Welfare Economics*

BIBLIOGRAPHY

Becker, Gary. 1971. *The Economics of Discrimination.* Chicago: University of Chicago Press.

Bendix, Reinhard, and Seymour Martin Lipset. 1966. *Class, Status, and Power: Social Stratification in Comparative Perspective.* 2nd ed. New York: Free Press.

Blim, Michael. 2005. *Equality and Economy: The Global Challenge.* Walnut Creek, CA: AltaMira.

Dworkin, Ronald. 2000. *Sovereign Virtue: The Theory and Practice of Equality.* Cambridge, MA: Harvard University Press.

Friedman, Milton. [1962] 2002. *Capitalism and Freedom.* Chicago: University of Chicago Press.

Giddens, Anthony. 1998. *The Third Way: The Renewal of Social Democracy.* Cambridge, U.K.: Polity.

Hobbes, Thomas. [1651] 1962. *Leviathan: On the Matter, Forme, and Power of a Commonwealth Ecclesiasticall and Civil.* New York: Collier.

Hobsbawm, Eric. 1987. *The Age of Empire, 1875–1914.* New York: Pantheon.

Horowitz, Irving, ed. 1964. *The Anarchists.* New York: Dell.

Locke, John. [1679–1680] 1963. *Two Treatises of Government.* Cambridge, U.K.: Cambridge University Press.

Mills, C. Wright. 1959. *The Sociological Imagination.* New York: Oxford University Press.

Mills, C. Wright. 1962. *The Marxists.* New York: Dell.

Murray, Charles, and Richard Herrnstein, 1996. *The Bell Curve: Intelligence and Class Structure in American Life.* New York: Free Press.

Nozick, Robert. [1974] 2001. *Anarchy, State, and Utopia.* Malden, MA: Blackwell.

Nussbaum, Martha. 1999. *Sex and Social Justice.* New York: Oxford University Press.

O'Connor, Alice. 2002. *Poverty Knowledge: Social Science, Social Policy and the Poor in Twentieth Century United States History.* Princeton, NJ: Princeton University Press.

Rawls, John, 1971. *A Theory of Justice.* Cambridge, MA: Harvard University Press.

Sachs, Jeffrey. 2005. *The End of Poverty: Economic Possibilities for Our Time.* New York: Penguin.

Sen, Amartya. 1992. *Inequality Reexamined.* Cambridge, MA: Harvard University Press.

Sen, Amartya. 1999. *Development as Freedom.* New York: Alfred Knopf.

Michael Blim

JUSTICE, SOCIAL

There are two important types of justice. *Procedural justice,* a primary goal of Western law, focuses upon using and implementing decisions according to fair processes. *Substantive justice,* on the other hand, reflects the content of the result of procedural justice and often is concerned with deeper issues of equity. Procedural justice can be viewed in terms of whether the process of punishment appears *objectively* fair to outside observers, while substantive justice can be interpreted in terms of whether a punishment *subjectively* is perceived as fair by the participants inside the process. Theories on justice and equity, and the implementation of these ideals, are usually found in philosophical literature. Justice as a concept typically is presented as universal and transcendent rather than as grounded in a social reality that has a particular historical and comparative context. Most of the dominant theories focus on the normative goal of what justice should be rather than studying how justice is defined by societies in specific places and at particular times. These concepts increasingly are used and imposed via hegemony (Gramsci 1971); that is, they are often exported through processes of cultural imperialism (Fanon 1967).

ENTITLEMENT AND UTILITARIAN VIEWS OF JUSTICE

The entitlement or libertarian view of the American philosopher Robert Nozick (1938–2002), the utilitarianism of John Stuart Mill (1806–1873), John Locke's (1632–1704) concept of consensual constitutional government, and the social contract of Immanuel Kant (1724–1804) via the American philosopher John Rawls (1921–2002) represent some of the more popular Western theories of justice. Justice from these perspectives often serves as a source of legitimation for the development and use of law. Justice from an entitlement perspective emphasizes the importance of private property and individual freedom in juxtaposition to the increasingly controlling role of the state. Entitlement stresses the importance of liberty and efficient economic relations—whereby liberty is posited as more crucial than equality. As a transfer of property, however, such a system of social relations has not been realized in practice. Specifically, its assumptions about fairness in acquisition and transfer not only have proved unworkable, they are a central part of the allegiance to entitlement for the privileged and typically reproduce or increase inequity in class and community relations. When put into action, entitlement theory has placed efficiency before equity, and greater inequality has ensued.

Justice from a utilitarian point of view following Mills's demands that society provide the greatest utility or happiness to the greatest number, the majority. A dominant part of this theory requires that people treat each other equally, yet equity can be sacrificed for the greatest utility or happiness. However, as Rawls argues, natural endowments should not determine material outcomes, although this theory of merit, too, can be revised in light of what most benefits the common good. More problematic is how the majority often has been defined—for example, Aristotle's (384–322 BCE) exclusion of slaves in ancient Greece, and the exclusion of indigenous peoples in many modern nation-states. In the Western tradition, the "majority" typically is defined as those who support, implicitly or explicitly, the Western liberal project and the narrow meaning of rational "man" and are uncritical of technological development. Following the current standards of most international organizations, however, the majority of the population in the world consists of "minorities."

Rawls's social-contract metaphor presents the idea of a veil of ignorance to correct such inequities. Behind this veil, individuals make decisions about fair and equitable resource allocations. The role of conventional policymaking in implementing the contract reveals, however, consistent allegiances to uncritical plans of development promoting, once again, efficiency over equality. Policymakers and planners often do not serve the interests of justice because they or their political authorities serve their own interests at the expense of others. Rawls's justice principle—that development for some is justified only if it benefits all—becomes circumvented.

The problems mentioned above can be addressed by deriving principles of justice from a particular historical and comparative context. Justice can be examined within social relations and material conditions that are specific and concrete. In this context, justice can become an important tool for analyzing change, "development," and the use of law. Legal equality, for example, is an abstract ideal that often has been employed as a metaphor for justice. From the Western perspective on liberalism, in the United States in the eighteenth century, for example, the individual was defined as autonomous, the fundamental unit of society. Rather than viewed as subjects, individuals were defined as citizens who were born equal and free. This definition excluded the majority. Under the declaration that all "men" are created equal, women, poor men, and slaves were ignored. Legal equality for women, poor men, and slaves did not become a fact until the twentieth century. Legal equality, therefore, far from being a reality, can be viewed as a metaphor that emerges from specific, historical conditions.

As the twentieth century progressed, the modern nation-state legitimated its control and expanded its jurisdiction by deconstructing indigenous solidarity, experiential education, and family and community welfare as it constructed national citizenship, formal education, and limited forms of government welfare for individuals. Concepts of *nation-state* and *citizen* were presented as major sources of solidarity and identity, emphasizing an abstract concept of nationalism. Formal education was proclaimed as superior to experiential learning. The nation-state centralized welfare amid claims of its progressive care, yet modern forms of state welfare usually have created varying levels of stigma for recipients.

THE NEED FOR COMPARATIVE AND HISTORICAL ANALYSIS OF JUSTICE

Justice, then, is a useful concept when one examines how it is constructed in different social and political settings and explores how it is used as a source of legitimation for the development and use of rules such as law (Lauderdale 1997). The study of justice should include an analysis of the fair distribution of benefits and burdens, including rights, obligations, deserts, and needs. This manner of studying justice also differentiates between short- and long-term impacts of change, and may identify well-intentioned suggestions for change that may result in unfortunate consequences. The comparative and historical analysis of theories and practices of justice is a relevant alternative to most perspectives on what justice should be. A commitment to addressing the injustices committed in the past by making the lives of people who have suffered those injustices more secure, peaceful, and prosperous may benefit those people who have (directly or indirectly) benefited from historical injustices (Thompson 2002).

A comparative and historical analysis of justice also considers the crucial role of noneconomic factors, such as religious beliefs and ideology, which people sometimes privilege over the goals of Western development. Liberation theology, for example, appeared as a religious social movement in reaction to the binding ties between the elites and the Catholic Church, which exacerbated obvious inequities, especially those of land use and ownership (Gutiérrez 1988). The theology began not with theory but with the realities of injustice experienced by the peasants and indigenous people of Latin America. It calls for individuals, communities, and corporate entities to be involved in extricating themselves from serving the interests of the elites of society and instead to work on behalf of the marginal with the goal of establishing solidarity and equity. Working with the oppressed is presented as a pragmatic prescription to fight poverty and oppression and to liberate people here and now. From such a perspective, justice is revealed as a structural phenomenon, and the dynamics of the world market system, promoted in tandem with liberal democratic principles, are shown to be unjust.

Such approaches to justice stress the development of peoples and not economies, emphasizing the conditions under which economic and political dependency works against community determination and autonomy. The perspective, then, is about whether certain kinds of growth can really solve the problems at hand. The dominance of capital or economic interests as the developing principle is seen as contradicting the ethical principle that workers and labor must be given priority in development of an economy based upon justice. Here, there is a principle that there must be an ethics of means as well as ends. The scholasticism found in many ethnocentric theories of justice based on Western philosophy can benefit from analyses of where perceptions of justice emerge.

Theories of justice based solely on abstract and universalistic criteria have been unable to respond to people throughout the world who are experiencing the presence of injustice in the form of poverty, landlessness, dispossession, political and religious oppression, and genocide. Philosophical formulas of justice are inadequate without systematic explications of the sources of injustice, including, at least: (1) an analysis of how participants are excluded from the creation of justice-related agendas, as well as decision making regarding policy agendas; (2) the continued exposure of exploitation in labor relations; (3)

an examination of the factors leading to the erosion of communities, collective identity, and the right to sovereignty; and (4) the long-term cost to nature (including humans) when justice is defined as separate and subservient to humans.

Diversity cannot be denounced as deviance. Society cannot fail to acknowledge the dialectical nature of the conflict between totalization and particularism, corporate monoculture and bioregional diversity, and abstract universalism and collective indigenous identity. Time (historical setting) and place (comparative setting) have proven that traditional assumptions about the implementation of fairness and equality are inadequate, especially for those individuals who exist at the margins of globalization. A workable theory of justice not only must acknowledge and extend foundational theories, but also must critically evaluate those theories so as not to neglect the fundamental connection.

SEE ALSO *Democracy; Egalitarianism; Equality; Justice, Distributive; Locke, John; Rawls, John; Social Contract; Utilitarianism*

BIBLIOGRAPHY

Fanon, Frantz. 1967. *Black Skin, White Masks.* Trans. Charles Lam Markmann. New York: Grove.

Gramsci, Antonio. 1971. *Selections from the Prison Notebooks of Antonio Gramsci.* Trans. and eds. Quintin Hoare and Geoffrey Nowell Smith. London: Lawrence and Wishart.

Gutiérrez, Gustavo. 1988. *A Theology of Liberation: History, Politics, and Salvation,* rev. ed. Trans. and eds. Caridad Inda and John Eagleson. Maryknoll, NY: Orbis.

Lauderdale, Pat. 1997. Indigenous North American Jurisprudence. *International Journal of Comparative Sociology* 38: 131–148.

Thompson, Joanna. 2002. *Taking Responsibility for the Past: Reparation and Historical Injustice.* Cambridge, U.K: Polity; Malden, MA: Blackwell.

Pat Lauderdale

JUSTIFICATION, SELF-
SEE *Self-Justification.*

K

KAHN, RICHARD F.
1905–1989

British economist Richard Ferdinand Kahn, fellow of King's College Cambridge (from 1930) and professor of economics at the University of Cambridge (from 1951), was John Maynard Keynes's (1883–1946) favorite pupil and closest collaborator during the writing of Keynes's *General Theory* (1936). Kahn became Keynes's literary executor and remained the torchbearer of Keynesian theory and policy throughout his life (Pasinetti 1987). Kahn first graduated in 1927 in natural sciences, then switched to economics and was awarded first-class honors in the 1928 Economics Tripos (courses and examinations leading to the Cambridge B.A.). In the following year and a half, he wrote a dissertation on *The Economics of the Short Period* (1989), which secured him a fellowship at King's College. Kahn's dissertation remained unpublished for fifty years, but it contained the essentials of the economics of imperfect competition, which would be refined and extended by Joan Robinson (1903–1983) in her 1933 book, *The Economics of Imperfect Competition*, as well as the short-period method, which came to form the mold in which the *General Theory* was cast (Marcuzzo 1994).

Kahn is best known for his discovery of one of the ingredients of the Keynesian revolution, namely, the principle of the multiplier. By this is meant the relation between the increase in any component part of the exogenous aggregate expenditure and the increase in income and employment whenever there are idle resources in the economy, such as undercapacity utilization of plant and machinery and unemployment of labor. In its simple form, it can be stated as follows: if c is the fraction of any increase in income that individuals decide to consume, an increase of, say, \$1 in expenditure will generate an increase in income equal to $\$1/(1-c)$.

Kahn presented his result in the midst of the controversy over public investment as a means to fight unemployment; the idea was to show that an increase in public expenditure would be effective in increasing total employment, contrary to the view held at the time that it would simply "crowd out" private employment (Kahn 1931). Its main implication, which is central to Keynesian macroeconomics, is that it is the level of investment that determines savings and not the other way around, as pre-Keynesian economic theories had it.

Besides playing a leading role in the discussions that paved the way to the *General Theory*, Kahn contributed to extending and clarifying some of its concepts and tools of analysis. His evidence to the Radcliffe Committee on the Working of the Monetary System (Kahn 1959a, 1959b) and his work on the liquidity preference (Kahn 1954) are landmarks in the Keynesian view of monetary theory and policy (Dardi 1994). He also contributed to the understanding of the so-called wage-spiral, built into the process of wage negotiation, in causing inflation (Kahn 1976), and, last but not least, left his mark on the post-Keynesian theory of growth and income distribution (Kahn 1959c).

BIBLIOGRAPHY

PRIMARY WORKS

Kahn, Richard F. 1931. The Relation of Home Investment to Unemployment. *Economic Journal* 41: 173–198.

Kahn, Richard F. 1954. Some Notes on Liquidity Preference. *Manchester School of Economic and Social Studies* 22: 229–257.

Kahn, Richard F. 1959a. *Memorandum of Evidence.* In Radcliffe Committee on the Working of the Monetary System: *Principal Memoranda of Evidence*, 138–146. London: HMSO.

Kahn, Richard F. 1959b. *Evidence.* To the Radcliffe Committee, Q. 10938–11024. In Radcliffe Committee on the Working of the Monetary System: *Minutes of Evidence*, 739–746. London: HMSO.

Kahn, Richard F. 1959c. Exercises in the Analysis of Growth. *Oxford Economic Papers* 11: 143–156.

Kahn, Richard F. 1976. Inflation: A Keynesian View. *Scottish Journal of Political Economy* 23: 11–16.

Kahn, Richard F. 1989. *The Economics of the Short Period.* London: Macmillan.

SECONDARY WORKS

Dardi, Marco. 1994. Kahn's Theory of Liquidity Preference and Monetary Policy. *Cambridge Journal of Economics* 18: 91–106.

Marcuzzo, Maria Cristina. 1994. R. F. Kahn and Imperfect Competition. *Cambridge Journal of Economics* 18: 25–40.

Pasinetti, Luigi. 1987. Kahn, R. F. In *The New Palgrave: A Dictionary of Economics*, eds. John Eatwell, Murray Milgate, and Peter Newman, 1–3. London, Macmillan.

Maria Christina Marcuzzo

KAHNEMAN, DANIEL

SEE *Rationality.*

KALDOR'S LAW

SEE *Verdoorn's Law.*

KALECKI, MICHAŁ
1899–1970

The Polish economist Michał Kalecki was born in 1899 in Lodz and died in Warsaw in April 1970. His academic training was in engineering, and he was self-taught in economics, influenced by writers such as Karl Marx (1818–1883) and Rosa Luxemburg (1870–1919). He obtained his first quasi-academic employment in 1929 at the Research Institute of Business Cycles and Prices in Warsaw. A Rockefeller Foundation fellowship allowed him in 1936 to study abroad in Sweden and then England, where he remained for the next ten years, including employment during World War II (1939–1945) at the Oxford University Institute of Statistics. After working for the International Labour Office in Montreal in 1945 and 1946, Kalecki was appointed deputy director of a section of the economics department of the United Nations Secretariat in New York at the end of 1946. He resigned from the United Nations in 1954 in response to the appointment of a board of directors to exercise control over the World Economic Report, which was seen as resulting from American involvement in the work of the United Nations. Kalecki returned to Poland in 1955, where he was heavily involved in the debates over the role of decentralization and workers' councils, the speed of industrialization, and the relative size of consumption and investment. In the last decade of his life, Kalecki was heavily involved with problems of economic development.

Kalecki discovered a range of ideas on the importance of effective demand and the role of investment similar to those discovered by John Maynard Keynes (1883–1946), and Kalecki can claim priority of publication (1933 for Kalecki versus 1936 for Keynes). While there are similarities between Kalecki and Keynes, there are also differences—for example, over the determinants of investment and the perception of the economy as competitive or oligopolistic (on the relationship between Kalecki and Keynes, see Sawyer 1985, chap. 9). The school of thought known as *post-Keynesianism* has been strongly influenced by the work of Kalecki, and many of the ideas current there can be traced back to Kalecki (King 1996 and 2002, chap. 2). Kalecki was influenced by Marx and Marxist writers but would not have described himself as a Marxist (Sawyer 1985, chap. 8).

A key element in Kalecki's work was the idea that the level of economic activity would be determined by the level of aggregate demand, and that investment decisions were a particularly significant element in the determination of the level of demand. Any decision to increase investment expenditure can only come to fruition if finance is available and provided through the banking system. Actual investment expenditure generates a corresponding amount of savings. Kalecki argued that savings were undertaken predominantly out of profits, and he often assumed as a first approximation that workers did not save, and hence investment expenditure in aggregate determined the volume of profits. As Kalecki wrote, "capitalists as a class gain exactly as much as they invest or consume, and if—in a closed system—they ceased to construct and consume they could not make any money at all" (Kalecki 1990, p. 79). The assumption that wages are spent and the view that capitalists' expenditure determines their income was reflected in an aphorism that was ascribed by Joan Robinson to Kalecki—"the workers spend what they get, and capitalists get what they spend"

(Robinson 1966, p. 341)—though it cannot be found in the writings of Kalecki. There is also a reverse direction of causation at the level of the enterprise, whereby the profitability of the enterprise will influence its investment decisions. Profits provide internal finance for investment, and the present level of profits influences expectation on future profits.

Kalecki saw capitalism as oligopolistic and monopolistic, and he dismissed the notion of perfect competition as a "dangerous myth." His approach to pricing put forward the idea of the "degree of monopoly," which expresses the notion that the market power that an enterprise possesses will strongly influence the markup of its price over its (production) costs. The extent of market power depends on such factors as the dominance of the enterprise in its market, the barriers to entry into the industry, and so on. The degree of monopoly leads to a theory of the distribution of income and of the determination of real wages. At the level of the enterprise, the degree of monopoly sets the price-cost ratio; from this, the ratio of profits to sales can be derived. Further derivation and then aggregation indicates that the share of profits in national income depends on the average degree of monopoly and on the cost of imports. Since wages are a major component of costs, the degree of monopoly has a major impact on the real product wage. Kalecki thus advanced a distinctive theory of the distribution of income between wages and profits, and the view that a firm's pricing behavior, rather than events in the labor market, set the real wage.

The phenomenon of the business cycle was central to Kalecki's economic analysis of capitalism, and his discovery of the importance of aggregate demand for the level of economic activity was undertaken in the context of cyclical fluctuations. Kalecki viewed "the determination of investment decisions by, broadly speaking, the level and the rate of change of economic activity" as the pièce de résistance of economics (Kalecki 1968, p. 263). The central feature of Kalecki's explanation of the business cycle is the influence of investment on economic activity and hence the determinants of investment. Kalecki distinguished between the decision to invest and the placing of orders for investment, with a significant lag between investment orders and actual investment. Investment orders depend on profits, and profits are generated by actual investment.

Kalecki also postulated that investment is negatively influenced by the size of the capital stock. Combining these elements, Kalecki arrived at a mixed differential-difference equation (Kalecki 1990, pp. 82–83), for which there may be many solutions. Kalecki sought to establish that there is one solution for which the amplitude remains constant. "This case is especially important because it cor-responds roughly to the real course of the business cycle" (Kalecki 1990, p. 87). He then argued that, with that condition satisfied, the other parameters of the model are such that a regular cycle of around ten years would be generated, which conforms with the general pattern of the time of a cycle of the order of eight to twelve years in length. The mixed differential-difference equation was the basis of Kalecki's attempt to generate a self-perpetuating cycle, which was later to be resolved through the notion of *limit cycles*.

Another important ingredient of his approach is summarized in the oft-quoted statement that "the long-run trend is but a slowly changing component of a chain of short-period situations; it has no independent entity" (Kalecki 1968, p. 263). This can be interpreted as undermining the predominant equilibrium approach to economic analysis whereby there is a long-period equilibrium around which the economy fluctuates or toward which the economy tends and which is unaffected by the short-period movements of the economy.

The discoveries of Keynes and Kalecki in the 1930s on the principle of effective demand and the associated idea that governments could (and should) manipulate their budget stance to generate high levels of employment (rather than aim for a balanced budget) seemed to open the way for the achievement of permanent full employment in capitalist economies. Kalecki raised many doubts about the possibilities of achieving prolonged full employment in a laissez-faire capitalist economy, most notably the resistance by business to prolonged full employment arising from a loss of "discipline in the factories."

SEE ALSO *Economics, Post Keynesian*

BIBLIOGRAPHY

Kalecki, Michał. 1933. *Proba teorii koniunktury*. Warsaw: Institute of Research on Business Cycles and Prices. Available in English as chapter 1 of *Selected Essays on the Dynamics of the Capitalist Economy, 1933–1970*. 1971. Cambridge, U.K.: Cambridge University Press.

Kalecki, Michał. 1968. Trend and the Business Cycle. *Economic Journal* 78: 263–276.

Kalecki, Michał. 1990. *Capitalism: Business Cycles and Full Employment*. Vol. 1 of *Collected Works of Michał Kalecki*. Ed. Jerzy Osiatyński. Oxford: Clarendon Press.

Keynes, John Maynard. 1936. *General Theory of Employment, Money, and Interest*. London: Macmillan.

King, J. E., ed. 1996. *An Alternative Macroeconomic Theory: The Kaleckian Model and Post-Keynesian Economics*. Boston: Kluwer.

King, J. E. 2002. *A History of Post Keynesian Economics since 1936*. Aldershot, U.K.: Edward Elgar.

Robinson, Joan. 1966. Kalecki and Keynes. In *Problems of Economic Dynamics and Planning: Essays in Honour of Michał Kalecki*, ed. P. A. Baran, 335–341. Oxford: Pergamon.

Sawyer, Malcolm. 1985. *The Economics of Michał Kalecki.* Basingstoke, U.K.: Macmillan.

Sawyer, Malcolm, ed. 1999. *The Legacy of Michał Kalecki.* 2 vols. Aldershot, U.K.: Edward Elgar.

Malcolm Sawyer

KANT, IMMANUEL
1724–1804

Immanuel Kant was born in 1724 in Konigsberg, Prussia (now Kalingrad, Russia). He contributed to metaphysics, epistemology, ethics, and political philosophy. He lived most of his life in Konigsberg, where he died in 1804. He lived long enough to see the early stages of the French Revolution, which he initially welcomed because of its emphasis on both liberty and equality.

Kant's philosophy emphasized the reconciliation of disparate themes and theories. In human nature he tried to reconcile the demands of heteronomy and autonomy. The latter has two distinct meanings: one ethical, the second metaphysical. In epistemology he tried to reconcile the competing claims of the rationalists—who emphasized a priori knowledge, primarily mathematics—with those of the empiricists, who claimed that all knowledge is based on experience. David Hume's skeptical development of empiricist philosophy, Kant said, "interrupted my dogmatic slumber" (Kant [1783] 1953, p. 9). Humean skepticism threatened both traditional theism and the recently triumphant Newtonian science.

KANT'S COPERNICAN REVOLUTION

Kant wanted to defend religion from skeptical arguments and Newtonian science from a similar type of skepticism. He also defended a libertarian theory of human nature from the new determinism that many saw as implicit in Newtonian physics. This is the problem of *heteronomy* and *autonomy.* The former is the view that even human behavior is controlled by the same laws as the rest of the universe, implying that free will is an illusion. The latter is the view that not all human actions are dependent on (or deducible from) the laws of nature.

Kant's theory of knowledge was based on a complex theory of categories of the mind that we have a priori (prior to, and independently of, experience) and that we apply to experience. Without it we could not have any coherent experience. It constitutes a third way of knowledge between a priori mathematical and logical concepts and those based on experience. It is *synthetic* a priori knowledge. Just as Copernicus reversed the roles of the sun and earth, so Kant reversed the role of thought and experience: We impose our mental categories on the world, not vice versa.

Kant argued that these concepts applied only to the world of experience and could not apply to metaphysical problems such as God, freedom, and immortality. He produced a complex critique of the three traditional theistic proofs (ontological, teleological, and cosmological) but also argued that reason could not disprove God's existence, and then offered pragmatic proofs for such a belief. Kant's *Religion within the Limits of Reason Alone* ([1787] 1960) was an attempt to replace religion based on revelation or fideism.

MORAL AND POLITICAL PHILOSOPHY

Kant's moral philosophy was based on an ethical interpretation of autonomy culminating in his categorical imperative(s) and his proto-liberal political philosophy of freedom. The categorical imperative has two versions: "I ought never to act except in such a way that I can also will that my maxim should become a universal law" ([1797] 1964, p. 70) and the somewhat clearer, "act in such a way that you always treat … the person of any other, never simply as a means but always … as an end" ([1797] 1964, p. 96). The best interpretation of this is: "Don't use people as if they were tools or machines; they are persons with independent wills and desires of their own." Because Kant assumed that people have conflicting wills and desires, he asserted that legislators must pass laws that protect everyone equally. Kantian equality is purely formal, meaning that laws must protect everyone equally, but he permitted massive material inequality, based on differences in everyone's "talent, industry, and good fortune" ("Two Essays on Right" [1797] in Phelps 1973). Kant denied that there could be a principle of welfare or happiness, inferring from this that neither morality nor legislation could be based on experience

Kant distinguished between perfect and imperfect duties. The former are based on the putative rights of others; the latter are not. Therefore, although animals do not have rights, we should not be cruel to them. Charity to the poor is another imperfect duty.

Despite the cosmopolitan character of his categorical imperative and political philosophy, Kant seemed to absorb from Hume an uncritical racism, especially concerning Africans. There are two ways in which one might defend either Kant or Hume. One would be the historicist argument, that we cannot judge people from different times and places by our contemporary standards. The other is to downplay the significance of these views in either philosopher in their overall philosophy. The latter is the more promising route because the eighteenth century was allegedly the age of Reason and Enlightenment. It also was the age in which slavery was first attacked on a widespread basis, leading to its eventual abolition in most of the world. Jeremy Bentham (1748–1832) argued for decent treatment for blacks, for animals, and (albeit secretly) for homosexuals, on the grounds that the key issue was not "Can they reason?" but "Can they suffer"? In addition, racism seems to conflict logically with Kant's cosmopolitanism.

Kant's greatest influence on the twentieth century may have involved his proposals for perpetual peace via a League of Nations. He also had great faith in republican governments to promote such peace better than monarchies would. In 1784 he wrote "What Is Enlightenment?" The basic idea was a willingness to dare to think for ourselves. His idea of autonomy, however, should not be confused with a "do your own thing" mentality: Instead, it meant that the laws we impose on ourselves are based on logically impeccable arguments.

SEE ALSO *Autonomy; Bentham, Jeremy; Enlightenment; Epistemology; Ethics; Hermeneutics; Hume, David; League of Nations; Philosophy; Racism; Religion; Slavery*

BIBLIOGRAPHY

Kant, Immanuel. [1781] 1902. *Critique of Pure Reason.* New York: Collier.

Kant, Immanuel. [1783] 1953. *Prolegomena to Any Future Metaphysics.* Manchester, U.K.: Manchester University Press.

Kant, Immanuel. [1785; 1784] 1959. *Groundwork of the Metaphysics of Morals, and an Answer to the Question: What Is Enlightenment?* Indianapolis, IN: Bobbs-Merrill

Kant, Immanuel. [1787] 1960. *Religion within the Limits of Reason Alone.* Trans. with intro. and notes Theodore M. Greene and Hoyt H. Hudson. New York: Harper and Row.

Kant, Immanuel. [1788] 1956. *Critique of Practical Reason.* Indianapolis, IN: Bobbs-Merrill.

Kant, Immanuel. [1790] 1964. *Critique of Judgement.* New York: Hafner.

Kant, Immanuel. [1797] 1964. *Groundwork of the Metaphysics of Morals.* New York: Harper and Row.

Kant, Immanuel. 1963. *On History,* ed. with intro Lewis White Beck; trans. Lewis White Beck, Robert E. Anchor, and Emil L. Fackenheim. Indianapolis, IN: Bobbs-Merrill.

Phelps, Edmund, ed. 1973. *Economic Justice: Selected Readings.* Middlesex, U.K.: Penguin.

Calvin Hayes

KARIEL, HENRY S.
1924–2004

Henry S. Kariel was one of the most influential postmodern political scientists of the latter half of the twentieth century and a significant critic of the fundamental concept of pluralism in American politics. Born in Plauen, Germany, on July 7, 1924, Kariel earned his doctorate in political science at the University of California at Berkeley and served primarily on the faculty of the University of Hawaii at Honolulu. Kariel's scholarship vaulted him to the forefront of the "antipluralist" movement that attempted to interpret and describe the political and social unrest of the 1960s and 1970s. He proposed a new methodology of political science rooted in the identification of citizens at the political margins. This was a concerted effort to expand democracy by transforming the disaffected into willing and vital participants within the political process at the expense of the traditional pluralistic tradition.

Kariel was heavily influenced by German philosopher Friedrich Nietzsche (1844–1900), who argued that it was impossible for human beings to attain final knowledge of the political and social realms. Kariel's political science was informed by this brand of postmodern relativism, and he posited that a consistent relativism recognized the claims and ends of all people, rather than those of a pluralistic elite. Established truths were no longer true, especially in rapidly changing social conditions. In this view, what the individual believes to be real is subjective, and the political scientist must therefore question established systems and truths in an effort to understand and make sense of new directions, as well as help create a more direct democracy that serves the needs of all.

Kariel viewed the student protests against the Vietnam War on college campuses, the riots in urban ghettos, governmental scandals, and the general backlash against the pluralistic reliance upon trusted institutions that often characterized the late 1960s and 1970s as evidence of the decline of pluralism and the onset of a new political dichotomy, one that legitimately questioned the authority of government while demanding an egalitarian society. As opposed to the general disturbance among citizens and more conservative academics that such events caused, Kariel and many critics of liberal pluralism saw not wanton violence or decadent protest, but rather a controlled effort aimed at forging a new political and social reality. He thus urged the adoption of "a suspension of the empirical" and looking beyond traditional data-gathering to define and explain new political theory.

While Kariel claimed to not repudiate constitutionalism, his approach was criticized for contradicting the fundamental ideology of constitutionalism. The essential critique of Kariel posited that while the citizenry's flexibility and freedom to act politically are indeed a part of the pluralistic tradition, the sovereign power to govern is limited by the people's own creation—the Constitution. In addition, critics charged that antipluralists such as Kariel failed to explain how a society in which everything was politicized would guarantee equitable results. In addition, despite the difficulties of the late 1960s and the demoralizing resignation of President Richard M. Nixon in 1974, citizens were unlikely to abandon the authority vested in governmental institutions in favor of the unknown dynamic for which Kariel argued. Kariel died in Hawaii on July 8, 2004.

SEE ALSO *Constitutionalism; Constitutions; Critical Theory; Elite Theory; Freedom; Nietzsche, Friedrich; Pluralism; Political Science; Postmodernism; Power; Sovereignty; Vietnam War*

BIBLIOGRAPHY

PRIMARY WORKS

Kariel, Henry S. 1961. *The Decline of American Pluralism.* Stanford, CA: Stanford University Press.

Kariel, Henry S. 1964. *In Search of Authority: Twentieth-Century Political Thought.* New York: Free Press.

Kariel, Henry S. 1966. *The Promise of Politics.* Englewood Cliffs: Prentice-Hall.

Kariel, Henry S. 1969. *Open Systems: Arenas for Political Action.* Itasca, IL: F. E. Peacock.

Kariel, Henry S. 1989. *The Desperate Politics of Postmodernism.* Amherst: University of Massachusetts Press.

SECONDARY WORKS

Belz, Herman. 1972. Changing Conceptions of Constitutionalism in the Era of World War II and the Cold War. *Journal of American History* 59 (3): 640–669.

Lowi, Theodore J. 1969. *The End of Liberalism: Ideology, Policy, and the Crisis of Public Authority.* New York: Norton.

Norton, Anne. 1990. Response to Henry S. Kariel. *Political Theory* 18 (2): 273–279.

Tugwell, Rexford G. 1970. Constitution for a United Republics of America. *The Center Magazine* III (November/December), 24–25.

Matthew May

KARMA

SEE *Reincarnation.*

KARUSH-KUHN-TUCKER CONDITIONS

SEE *Maximization; Programming, Linear and Nonlinear.*

KAUNDA, KENNETH
1924–

The decolonization decade of the 1960s in Africa produced not only a bevy of territorial successor states, but a crowd of would-be "fathers" of new countries. Most remembered, perhaps, are Kwame Nkrumah (1909–1972) of Ghana, Julius Nyerere (1922–1999) of Tanzania, and Félix Houphouët-Boigny (1905–1993) of Côte d'Ivoire. In the same class, but perhaps less memorable for indiscernible reasons, is Kenneth David Kaunda, who was prime minister and first president of Zambia (formerly Northern Rhodesia) in Central Africa. Kaunda stayed in office for twenty-seven years, peacefully handing over power to an elected successor in 1991. With his country prey to the powerful and white supremacist neighbor, South Africa, painfully dependent on the one major natural resource, copper, and threatened by ethnic strife, Kaunda proved unable to transcend his country's underdevelopment and vulnerability to division, nevertheless accomplishing the daunting feats of maintaining independence and national integration.

Similar to other emergent civic leaders of his generation, Kaunda was educated in mission schools (his father was a missionary), became a teacher, served on a local council, and plunged into nationalist politics. In 1950 he was secretary of his branch of the Northern Rhodesia African Congress; by 1953 he was secretary-general of the African National Congress (ANC). He served a brief term in prison for a political offense, visited Britain as a guest of the anticolonialist Labour Party, and broke with the ANC in 1958. The politics of the era was dominated by the Southern Rhodesian whites and the British government's attempt to form a Central African Federation. Resistance to federation resulted in another prison term for Kaunda and then to the formation of the United National Independence Party (UNIP) that delivered independence in 1964 to an ultimately unfederated Northern Rhodesia.

Kaunda's leadership received popular approval, achieving renewal every five years—in 1988 with 95 percent of the vote—until an ignominious defeat in 1991 in an internationally observed contest. In keeping with the political trend of the era, Zambia banned opposition parties in 1968, became a one-party state in 1972, and declared an official ideology called *Zambia Humanism,* which reflected the "African socialist" fad of the times, as represented by Nkrumah's *Consciencism* and Nyerere's *Ujamaa.* Like these two well-known African figures, Kaunda published an autobiography (1962), a volume of speeches (1966), and a guide to his own thinking, *Humanism in Zambia and a Guide to Its Implementation* (1968).

Kaunda's successor, Frederick Chiluba, treated the country's founder-president rather shabbily in the post-election period, first attempting to deport him as a "noncitizen" (Kaunda's father was born in Malawi), then getting the country's constitution amended to prevent Kaunda from entering the elections of 1996. After accusations of sponsoring a failed coup attempt in 1997, Kaunda retired from politics, devoted himself to good works and his passion for ballroom dancing, and assumed the post of African president-in-residence at Boston University (2002–2004).

Kaunda's achievements ultimately remain mixed. His writings come across as more diffuse than his contemporaries Nkrumah and Nyerere, although no one doubts Kaunda's personal integrity. His efforts to negotiate with South African president John Vorster (1915–1983) exposed him to charges of naiveté, although Kaunda was steadfast in providing sanctuary to the (South African) African National Congress in its exile. While avoiding a successful coup—characteristic of West African states in the 1960s and 1970s—Kaunda continually faced sectional and ethnic tensions in the country, despite single-party rule in the 1970s.

As to economic development, Zambia lurched through several programs of rural development and state-led strategies, piling up huge international debts. With copper and cobalt providing 95 percent of the country's foreign exchange, dramatic drops in international prices from the mid-1970s caused great economic pain, stirring massive opposition among mineworkers, whose union formed the basis of political opposition that ultimately produced the person who ousted Kaunda, Frederick Chiluba.

Kaunda sought help from the World Bank and the International Monetary Fund in the 1980s. One immediate consequence was the fateful maize-meal riots on Zambia's Copperbelt in December 1986. The Zambian government backtracked; the World Bank and Western governments withheld funds; and inflation, black markets, and internal unrest all ensued. The June 1990 university student protests led to more riots, an announced coup, dancing in the streets, Kaunda contradicting himself on a referendum, and finally a restoration of multiparty government. By 1991 the major opposition party, the Movement for Multiparty Democracy, swept parliamentary voting and retired Kaunda as president with less than 20 percent of the ballots. Kaunda's message to his successor included a final contribution to democratic government: "Well, congratulations, you have won… I stand ready to assist you, if you should need my services. For the time being, God bless and goodbye."

SEE ALSO *African National Congress; Anticolonial Movements; Decolonization; Developing Countries; Labour Party (Britain); Liberation Movements; Neocolonialism; Nkrumah, Kwame; Nyerere, Julius; Socialism, African*

BIBLIOGRAPHY

Kaunda, Kenneth. 1962. *Zambia Shall be Free: An Autobiography.* London: Heinemann.

Kaunda, Kenneth D. 1968. *Humanism in Zambia and a Guide to Its Implementation.* Lusaka: Zambia Information Services.

Legum, Colin, ed. 1966. *Zambia, Independence and Beyond: The Speeches of Kenneth Kaunda.* London: Nelson.

Macpherson, Fergus. 1974. *Kenneth Kaunda of Zambia: The Times and the Man.* Lusaka, Zambia: Oxford University Press.

Harvey Glickman

KAUTSKY, KARL

SEE *Imperialism.*

KEFAUVER, ESTES
1903–1963

Carey Estes Kefauver was born to Phredonia Estes and Cooke Kefauver July 26, 1903 on a farm near Madisonville, Tennessee. His older brother, Robert, and younger sisters, Nancy and Leonora, rounded out his family. Following a career in law and service in the U.S. House of Representatives (1939–1949) and the U.S. Senate (1949–1963), Kefauver died in Washington, D.C. August 10, 1963. Kefauver attended local public schools, and then entered the University of Tennessee, where he participated in various extracurricular activities. He earned a BA in 1924 but had already begun to study law. After brief service as a teacher and coach in Arkansas, Kefauver entered Yale Law School and was granted an LLB *cum laude* in 1927. He had previously passed the Tennessee bar examination, so Kefauver moved to Chattanooga and joined first a practice set up by his cousins and later another firm, where he became a junior partner in 1930. Civic affairs, work with the Tennessee Valley Authority (TVA), and representation of a local newspaper promoting government reform led Kefauver into political activism, and in 1936 he was narrowly defeated in a state senate bid.

In 1939 Kefauver was appointed state finance and taxation commissioner, served briefly, returned to his law practice, then entered a special election for Tennessee's third congressional district (Chattanooga) seat upon the incumbent's death. Kefauver won, and was reelected four times; in 1948 he sought a U.S. Senate seat and won a plurality victory in the Democratic primary over the incumbent and a third candidate sponsored by Tennessee's "Boss" Crump. He was reelected in 1954 and 1960, and in intervening years pursued the Democratic presidential nomination. In 1952 President Harry S. Truman and other party leaders offset Kefauver's surprising string of primary victories and delivered the nomination to Illinois governor Adlai Stevenson; the 1956 rematch also produced a Stevenson nomination, but Kefauver's withdrawal in favor of Stevenson late in the campaign encouraged Stevenson to allow convention delegates to select his running mate. Kefauver was nominated, but the Democratic ticket was again defeated in the election, by Dwight Eisenhower.

Kefauver's presidential efforts grew out of his work chairing the Senate's Special Committee to Investigate Organized Crime in Interstate Commerce during the Eighty-first and Eighty-second Congresses. While a congressman, Kefauver had supported Presidents Roosevelt and Truman, the TVA, and government reform and antitrust policy; he sponsored the modern presidential succession statute and supported abolition of the poll tax. Kefauver's involvement in a House investigation of judicial corruption, as well as his personal ambition, underscored by encouragement of some newspaper executives, caused him to see opportunity in a Senate study of organized crime. Events overcame the Democratic Senate leadership's reluctance, and internal Senate politics led to Kefauver's selection as chair when the committee was authorized in May 1950.

The committee held hearings in several cities and began to attract attention as witnesses helped to build a case that criminal elements had developed a national organization substantially rooted in illegal gambling and protected from law-enforcement efforts through bribery and the efforts of friends in useful offices. Public interest in the investigation grew with the publicizing of the connections between racketeers and various public officials, as well as several prominent political organizations; it flourished as hearings first in New Orleans and subsequently in other cities were televised. Committee proceedings were less popular, however, in the White House and in Democratic Senate Majority Leader Scott Lucas's office, as they suggested ties between the Kansas City Democratic organization (President Truman's home base) and gangsters and between Cook County, Illinois, Democrats (Lucas's base) and criminal elements. Kefauver refused to defer study of them, which probably led to Lucas's defeat in his 1950 reelection bid and Truman's opposition to Kefauver's 1952 Democratic presidential nomination

quest. The committee's work bore legislative fruit only after the Kennedy administration took office, but several states defeated legalized gambling, and a number of cities established crime commissions in the immediate wake of its reports.

Kefauver had married Nancy Paterson Pigott, Scottish-born daughter of American expatriates and an aspiring artist, in 1935. Daughter Eleanor was born to the couple in 1941, and when other children did not quickly follow, they adopted six-week-old David in 1946. Diane was then born in 1947, and Gail completed the family upon her birth in 1950.

Kefauver fell ill during the summer of 1963 and was diagnosed as having an aortal aneurism; it burst before remedial measures could be taken, and he died at Bethesda Naval Hospital. He was buried in the family cemetery in Madisonville, Tennessee.

SEE ALSO *Congress, U.S.; Crime and Criminology; Mafia, The*

BIBLIOGRAPHY

Fontenay, Charles L. 1980. *Estes Kefauver: A Biography.* Knoxville: University of Tennessee Press.

Gorman, Joseph Bruce. 1971. *Kefauver: A Political Biography.* New York: Oxford University Press.

Moore, William Howard. 1974. *The Kefauver Committee and the Politics of Crime, 1950–1952.* Columbia: University of Missouri Press.

James F. Sheffield Jr.

KELLEY, HAROLD
1921–2003

Harold Harding Kelley's field of study, social psychology, has been defined variously as the study of attitudes, of groups, or of the ways mental representations shape social behavior and person perception. Hal Kelley contributed to all of these aspects of his field.

Kelley was among the young scholars, including Morton Deutsch (born 1920), Stanley Schachter (1922–1997), and John Thibaut (1917–1986), drawn to the Research Center for Group Dynamics established by Kurt Lewin (1890–1947) at the Massachusetts Institute of Technology (MIT). Kelley's (1950) dissertation research at MIT asked: Do people "key" on particular social information? He found that when a person was described by a list of adjectives, others' attitudes toward that person were especially affected by whether the word *warm* or *cold* appeared in the list. Kelley's interest in person perception was evident again approximately fifteen years later when he coined the term *attribution theory.*

Kelley's true forte was not empirical research, however; it was theorizing. In his academic appointment at Yale University in the early 1950s, Kelley collaborated with a leading attitude researcher, Carl Hovland (1912–1961), and Irving Janis (1918–1990) to review and synthesize theory and research concerning communication and persuasion.

But it was with John Thibaut, while at the University of Minnesota and later the University of California at Los Angeles, that Kelley developed a prominent theory concerning interpersonal influence in groups. The theory focused on interdependence in the simplest social group—the *dyad* (two-person "group"). *Interdependence* implies that the dyad members can benefit or harm one another, and the theory identified bases of mutual influence stemming from patterns of interdependence. *Reflexive control* constitutes the extent to which dyad members control their own outcomes independent of the other's actions; *fate control* is the extent to which individuals control the other's outcomes irrespective of the other's actions; and *behavior control* concerns the extent to which both members of the dyad gain or lose based on the configuration of their actions. For example, when mutual cooperative action is particularly beneficial, or competition is harmful, there is an incentive for each to coordinate with the other's actions, yielding mutual behavior control.

Although the best-known precursors to this theory, by George Homans (1910–1989) and Peter Blau (1918–2002), are labeled *exchange* theories, Kelley rejected this label in favor of *interdependence* theory, because exchange of rewards is just one solution to some of the problems posed by particular interdependence structures. For example, people can reevaluate outcomes or develop sequences of actions (described by *transition lists*) that are more complex than simple exchange.

Kelley probably is best known for work on attribution theory. He proposed that laypeople can be systematic processors of social information, implicitly arraying information in what came to be known as *Kelley's cube.* This ANOVA model distinguished three types of information that people can use to analyze the causes of others' (or their own) behavior. For example, when a person *uniquely* (i.e., low on the *consensus* dimension of the information cube) and *consistently* chooses to play backgammon but not, say, chess or checkers (yielding *distinctiveness* of game-playing behavior), the behavior is attributable to something internal to the person (e.g., a strong preference), and not external (e.g., social convention). Later, Kelley described alternate attribution processes involving cognitive schemas. Hundreds of subsequent studies of

attribution, conducted over the next decade, were reviewed by Kelley and John Michela (1980).

In the 1980s and 1990s Kelley helped to build a community of researchers of close relationships (e.g., marriages). One outgrowth, *An Atlas of Interpersonal Situations* (2003), may be seen as a step in the direction of Kelley's vision that social psychology should develop very general principles—paralleling chemistry's periodic table, for example—and steer clear of demonstrations of counterintuitive social phenomena that often dominate the field but are neither cumulative nor rich.

Harold Kelley received numerous awards for his contributions, from social psychology societies and from the broader scientific community, as when he was elected to the U.S. National Academy of Sciences.

SEE ALSO *Blau, Peter M.; Communication; Cooperation; Intergroup Relations; Persuasion; Schachter, Stanley; Social Psychology*

BIBLIOGRAPHY

Hovland, Carl I., Irving L. Janis, and Harold H. Kelley. 1953. *Communication and Persuasion: Psychological Studies of Opinion Change.* New Haven, CT: Yale University Press.

Kelley, Harold H. 1950. The Warm-Cold Variable in First Impressions of Persons. *Journal of Personality* 18: 431–439.

Kelley, Harold H., and John L. Michela. 1980. Attribution Theory and Research. *Annual Review of Psychology* 31: 457–501.

Kelley, Harold H., John G. Holmes, Norbert L. Kerr, et al. 2003. *An Atlas of Interpersonal Situations.* Cambridge, U.K.: Cambridge University Press.

Raven, Bertram, Albert Pepitone, and John G. Holmes. 2003. Harold H. Kelley, 1921–2003. *American Psychologist* 58: 806–807.

Thibaut, John W., and Harold H. Kelley. 1959. *The Social Psychology of Groups.* New York: Wiley.

John L. Michela

KENNEDY, JOHN F.
1917–1963

John Fitzgerald "Jack" Kennedy, the thirty-fifth president of the United States, was born May 29, 1917, in Brookline, Massachusetts, and was assassinated in Dallas, Texas, on November 22, 1963. Jack was the son of Joseph Patrick Kennedy (1888–1969) and Rose Fitzgerald (1890–1995); both grandfathers, Patrick Joseph Kennedy (1858–1929) and John F. "Honey Fitz" Fitzgerald (1863–1950), had been politically prominent in Boston. Jack's father was determined to see his first born, Joseph

Patrick Jr., elected president, but Navy pilot Joe Jr.'s death in 1944 caused Joe to transfer his political dreams to Jack.

Jack was an indifferent student at day schools, then in a Catholic boarding school, and finally at Choate, a preparatory school in Connecticut that Joe Jr. was attending. Fellow seniors named Jack "most likely to succeed," and he graduated in the middle of his class. Joe Jr.'s shadow led Jack to attend Princeton University rather than Harvard, but poor health, which plagued his entire life, soon forced him to withdraw. He entered Harvard in 1936 and continued to perform modestly as a student, but public affairs then captured Jack's attention. He registered for a heavy academic load in the fall of 1937 so that he might travel to Europe in early 1938 to research an honors thesis on contemporary politics. That paper reviewed Great Britain's prewar policies toward Germany and was published in 1940 as *Why England Slept*; it proved unexpectedly popular in an America unnerved by world events.

War approached, and Kennedy attempted to enter officer candidate schools, but failed the physical examinations. Joe Kennedy Sr., the U.S. ambassador to Great Britain in the late 1930s, arranged through his former naval attaché for Jack to enter the U.S. Navy in late 1941. Kennedy was trained to operate patrol-torpedo boats and was sent to the Pacific, where his boat (*PT-109*) was rammed by a Japanese destroyer in August 1943. Jack led survivors to a nearby island, directed successful efforts to attract a rescue, and later returned to duty, but physical maladies caused his return to the states and his eventual retirement from the Navy.

Joe Kennedy enthusiastically supported Jack's race for the eleventh Massachusetts congressional district seat in 1946, and after three terms in the U.S. House of Representatives Jack successfully challenged incumbent Henry Cabot Lodge Jr. (1902–1985) for a U.S. Senate seat. Kennedy's bid for the 1956 Democratic vice-presidential nomination fell just short, and immediately following Dwight D. Eisenhower's (1890–1969) reelection he mounted a campaign for the 1960 Democratic presidential nomination. Kennedy's Catholicism was inevitably an issue, but he defused it by asserting the principle of church-state separation. He won the nomination, then defeated the Republican candidate, Richard Nixon (1913–1994), by 120,000 popular votes; the electoral vote was not so close (303–219).

Jack, his wife Jacqueline Bouvier Kennedy (1929–1994), and their young children presented active, sophisticated, optimistic faces to the country. In accepting his party's nomination, Kennedy had described a "New Frontier" of possibilities for the nation, and his inaugural speech built on that vision. The White House became "Camelot" after the romantic stage version of King Arthur's reign; the Kennedys were admired as royalty, and it was sometimes suggested that a Kennedy dynasty had begun wherein Jack would be succeeded first by his brother Robert (1925–1968) and then by their younger brother Edward (b. 1932).

Cold War issues hounded the Kennedy presidency, however. A 1961 invasion of Cuba, a Soviet client, at the Bay of Pigs by CIA-sponsored Cuban exiles failed, and it was soon followed by East Germany's provocative construction of a wall isolating western sectors of Berlin. In 1962 U.S. intelligence efforts revealed that the Soviet Union was basing offensive missiles and long-range bombers in Cuba. Kennedy mobilized the military, authorized complaints in the United Nations Security Council, and ordered the Navy to "quarantine" Cuba to prevent receipt of more weapons. Diplomacy and U.S. willingness to resort to military action caused removal of the arsenal. This incident provided the most dangerous moment of the Cold War.

The "space race" gave Kennedy another means of challenging the Soviets, one that was also infused with domestic policy. Soviet satellites and manned orbital flights embarrassed the United States. Initial American efforts were spectacular failures, but science advisors concluded that a manned moon landing was feasible. Convinced that gaining the upper hand in space would enhance U.S. prestige abroad, restore American confidence, and open doors to technological and economic advances, Kennedy committed the United States to a safe manned flight to the moon and back by the close of the 1960s. His vision was fulfilled in July 1969.

The civil rights movement posed different domestic policy problems. Kennedy had telephoned the wife of Reverend Martin Luther King Jr. (1929–1968) when King was imprisoned during the election campaign; this encouraged many to expect Kennedy to champion civil rights. His administration proved less than they hoped, although it made some efforts to extend voting rights and to reduce employment discrimination. But activists known as "freedom riders," who were testing Kennedy's promise to end public-transportation segregation, were violently attacked in Alabama, and the University of Mississippi was awkwardly integrated, causing a deadly riot. Kennedy proposed a sweeping civil rights bill during the summer of 1963, but Congress acted only when Kennedy's successor, Lyndon Johnson (1908–1973), promoted the bill as a memorial to the slain president.

In November 1963 Kennedy traveled to Texas to end bickering among Democrats there. As his limousine approached downtown Dallas, gunshots fatally wounded him. A government commission headed by Chief Justice Earl Warren (1891–1974) later blamed Lee Harvey Oswald (1939–1963) for the act as a solitary assassin, but conspiracy theories abounded. Robert Kennedy and President Johnson were suspicious of the CIA, American mobsters, and Cuban operatives, and Johnson himself was suspected of involvement by some. Oswald's murder as he was being transferred between jails only two days after Kennedy's shooting further fueled misgivings that persisted for decades. Gerald Posner's 1993 book *Case Closed* best refuted conspiracy advocates.

Kennedy was survived by Jacqueline, who later remarried, was again widowed, and died in 1994 of cancer; daughter Caroline, who became a writer, attorney, wife, and mother of three Kennedy grandchildren; and son John Jr., who perished in a 1999 private-plane crash. Another son, Patrick Bouvier Kennedy, had been born prematurely and died within days in August 1963.

Had Kennedy not been murdered, health problems may have prematurely ended his presidency; some suggest that scandals resulting from his dealings with gangsters and a succession of female acquaintances would have brought down his administration. The Vietnam War may have ended sooner under Kennedy's leadership, but that may have delayed the eventual Soviet collapse and slowed establishment of Chinese-American relations. Civil rights legislation may have been slower and more limited, and America's baby boomers may have become more constructively active and less cynical and distrustful. The more positive vision suggests that a "normal" Kennedy presidency could have forestalled many of the political traumas that later plagued the United States, along with the personal, combative political style that they engendered.

SEE ALSO *Bay of Pigs; Civil Rights Movement, U.S.; Cuban Missile Crisis; Johnson, Lyndon B.; Presidency, The*

BIBLIOGRAPHY

Allison, Graham T., and Philip Zelikow. 1999. *Essence of Decision: Explaining the Cuban Missile Crisis.* 2nd ed. New York: Longman.

Branch, Taylor. 1988. *Parting the Waters: America in the King Years, 1954–63.* New York: Simon and Schuster.

Dallek, Robert. 2003. *An Unfinished Life: John F. Kennedy, 1917–1963.* Boston: Little, Brown.

Kennedy, Robert F. 1969. *Thirteen Days: A Memoir of the Cuban Missile Crisis.* New York: Norton.

O'Donnell, Kenneth P., and David F. Powers. 1972. *"Johnny, We Hardly Knew Ye": Memories of John Fitzgerald Kennedy.* Boston: Little, Brown.

Posner, Gerald. 1993. *Case Closed. Lee Harvey Oswald and the Assassination of JFK.* New York: Random House.

President's Commission on the Assassination of President Kennedy (Warren Commission). 1964. Report. Washington, DC: U.S. Government Printing Office. http://www.archives.gov/research/jfk/warren-commission-report/index.html.

Public Papers of the Presidents of the United States: John F. Kennedy, 1961–1963. 1962–1964. Washington, DC: U.S. Government Printing Office.

James F. Sheffield Jr.

KENYATTA, JOMO
1893–1978

Jomo Kenyatta, also known as Mzee Jomo Kenyatta, is considered the founding father of the independent nation of Kenya. He became Kenya's first prime minister (1963–1964) and first president (1964–1978). Acknowledged as a fascinating and courageous leader, his controversial life began when he was born to Muigai and Wambui as a member of the Kikuyu people. His birth name was Kamau wa Ngengi. His parents died while he was a young boy, and he spent time in his youth working with his grandfather, who was a medicine man steeped in the Kikuyu tradition. Kenyatta married his first wife, Grace Wahu, in 1920. They had two children, a daughter and a son.

Kenyatta entered local politics in 1924 when he joined the Kikuyu Central Association (KCA). He created and began to edit a monthly journal for the KCA known as *Muigwithania* (The Reconciler) in 1928. Much of the writing in this journal was focused on cultural nationalism, unity, and moral ethnicity for the Kikuyu people. He also focused heavily on campaigning for land reform, ownership rights, and political rights for African people. The KCA sent Kenyatta to London to lobby for Kikuyu rights, and in 1931 he enrolled in Woodbrooke Quaker College in Birmingham, England. He later attended the Comintern School in Moscow, then returned to London to study at the University College London and the London School of Economics (LSE). He focused on social anthropology and economics, and published his LSE thesis in 1938 as his first book, *Facing Mount Kenya*, an ethnography of the Kikuyu people penned under the name Jomo Kenyatta. He was briefly married to Edna Clarke during this period, and she gave birth to his son in 1943.

In England, Kenyatta had many friends and associates, and formed the Pan-African Federation with Kwame Nkrumah (1909–1972) in 1946. He then returned to his homeland and became the principle of Kenya Teacher's College and president of the Kenya African Union (KAU). Upon his return to Kenya, he married Grace Wanjiku in 1946. She died in childbirth in 1950 after giving birth to a daughter. The following year, he married his fourth wife, Ngina Kenyatta, to whom he would remain married for the rest of his life. They had four children together.

On October 20, 1952, Kenyatta was arrested by the British government and charged with being a manager and member of the society of Mau Mau. The Mau Mau revolution was a lengthy battle of the Kikuyu people against British control. Kenyatta denied any participation and countered that he spoke out against the Mau Mau because they were not working with the KAU. After a lengthy trial in 1953, Kenyatta was convicted and imprisoned for six years in Lokitaung, a region in northwestern Kenya. He was later sent into exile. While in exile, he was elected president in absentia of the Kenya African National Union, which later joined with the Kenya African Democratic Union to become one party. Kenyatta was released by the British government, and returned to government in 1961. He was instrumental in forming a parliamentary body, instituting a new constitution, and creating the republic of Kenya. Kenyatta is heralded as a great leader. He was also a noted author, publishing numerous books and pamphlets, including *My People of Kikuyu and the Life of Chief Wangombe* (1944), *Suffering without Bitterness* (1968, a biography), *Kenya: The Land of Conflict* (1971), and *The Challenge of Uhuru: The Progress of Kenya, 1968 to 1970* (1971). He died in his sleep in Mombasa in 1978.

SEE ALSO *Anticolonial Movements; Kimathi, Dedan; Mau Mau; Nkrumah, Kwame; Pan-African Congresses*

BIBLIOGRAPHY

Berman, Bruce J., and John M. Lonsdale. 1998. The Labors of Muigwithania: Jomo Kenyatta as Author, 1928–45. *Research in African Literatures* 29 (1): 16–27.

Branch, Daniel, and Nicholas Cheeseman. 2006. The Politics of Control in Kenya: Understanding the Bureaucratic-executive State, 1952–78. *Review of African Political Economy* 107: 11–31.

Kenya: Landslide for Kenyatta. 1963. *New Republic* 148 (23): 8.

Kenyatta, Jomo. 1968. *Suffering without Bitterness: The Founding of the Kenya Nation*. Nairobi, Kenya: East African Publishing House.

Kijua Sanders-McMurtry

KEOHANE, ROBERT
1941–

Robert Owen Keohane is an American political scientist and an expert in international relations. He is most well known for his insistence on the importance of international institutions in shaping state behavior. Keohane challenged the stress of many political scientists on unitary actors and on the conflictual tendencies of anarchy; he simultaneously shifted the focus of the discipline away from security studies and toward economic policies and relationships.

In turning to economic policy in his early work in the 1970s, Keohane saw that this arena involved the interaction of political actors within states in behaviors that cut across states. This observation challenged the unitary actor assumption, a key element of the "realist" school, which treats states as unitary wholes, preoccupied primarily with the problem of national security, which is seen largely in military terms. The concepts of "transnational relations" and "complex interdependence," which Keohane developed with political scientist Joseph Nye, replaced the unitary actors with networks of firms and interest groups operating within and across borders, and offering conflicting pressure on decision makers to define "national interest." Keohane argued that national governments are players in a policy arena, but their control is by no means exclusive, nor total. Regimes (a mixture of norms and institutions cutting across states) shape state behavior and policy outcomes.

Keohane and Nye pointed out the decline of force as the exclusive issue area, the importance of international regimes, and the fragmentation of authority in each state and thus in their interactions. From 1974 to 1980, Keohane served as editor of *International Organization*, a scholarly journal on international affairs, and transformed it from a largely descriptive and evaluative publication into a significant vehicle for social science and peer-reviewed research.

In the 1980s Keohane shifted his attention away from the fragmented, national-actor arena of domestic politics toward a debate on the international system with the political scientist Kenneth Waltz. Whereas Waltz theorized that anarchy was the root of conflict, because the logic of self-help created a security dilemma (in protecting oneself, one antagonizes others), Keohane argued that cooperation could take place among units in anarchy under the right conditions. According to Keohane, international institutions could solve the problems of coordination and information that inhibit cooperation. These institutions would not be supranational—that is, they do not impose rules from above, but arise out of voluntary participation.

Drawing on research in game theory and institutional economics, Keohane argued that institutions make it easier to share information, reduce transaction costs, facilitate bargains across issue areas, provide mechanisms for dispute resolution, and supply processes for making decisions. Institutions can increase cooperation even without coercive power. Institutions may increase iteration—that is, the number of interactions among units—thus generating a positive cycle of cooperation. The debate between Keohane's neoliberal institutionalism and Waltz's neorealism structured the field for many years.

Three lines of inquiry challenged the centrality of the Keohane-Waltz debate. First, the domestic politics school, whose members generally were sympathetic to Keohane's critique of Waltz, complained that by moving the debate toward system arguments—cooperation versus conflict by unitary states under anarchy—the domestic political elements of international politics were being neglected. These writers wanted to continue the disaggregation of the unitary state, which Keohane had begun to do in the 1970s, by exploring the role of domestic politics in shaping how states defined their position in the world. A state's position in the international system is open to rival interpretations. The issue of whether a state wants to cooperate turns on domestic politics, on whether there is support at home for international cooperation, and on whether the supporters are able to prevail in policy debates.

The second line of inquiry, forwarded by constructivists and sociological theorists, complained that both Keohane and Waltz neglected nonrationalist and nonmaterial aspects of the interaction of units. Keohane accepted, after all, Waltz's assumption that states were utility maximizers. What he disputed was what maximization under anarchy led to; under the right conditions, according to Keohane, it led to cooperation, not the inevitability of conflict. But neither Keohane nor Waltz paid much attention to such aspects as culture, ideas, values, the internalization of norms, the constitutive elements of identity, and the tissue of human exchanges and cultures, which structure interaction.

A third line of inquiry, advanced largely by security specialists, attacked Keohane's emphasis on institutions, on the way these operate, and on the neglect of security issues, generally and in relation to the functioning of institutions. Some specialists in this camp are realists who agree rather more with Waltz, while others disagree on agenda, the evaluation of interests, the actual prospects for cooperation, and the implications for public policy.

Keohane was born in Chicago in 1941. He earned a bachelor's degree from Shimer College in Mount Carroll, Illinois, in 1961, and a Ph.D. from Harvard University in Cambridge, Massachusetts, in 1966. Keohane's distinguished teaching career began at Swarthmore College in Pennsylvania in 1965. He then taught at Stanford University in California (1973–1981), Brandeis University in Massachusetts (1981–1985), Harvard University (1985–1996), and Duke University in North Carolina (1996–2004). In 2005 Keohane became professor of international affairs at the Woodrow Wilson School of Public and International Affairs at Princeton University

in New Jersey. In 2005 Keohane was elected to the National Academy of Sciences, an unusual honor for a political scientist.

SEE ALSO *International Relations; Waltz, Kenneth*

BIBLIOGRAPHY

PRIMARY WORKS

Keohane, Robert O. 1984. *After Hegemony: Cooperation and Discord in the World Political Economy.* Princeton, NJ: Princeton University Press.

Keohane, Robert O., ed. 1986. *Neorealism and Its Critics.* New York: Columbia University Press.

Keohane, Robert O., and Joseph S. Nye. 1977. *Power and Interdependence: World Politics in Transition.* Boston: Little, Brown.

Keohane, Robert O., Peter J. Katzenstein, and Stephen D. Krasner, eds. 1999. *Exploration and Contestation in the Study of World Politics.* Cambridge, MA: MIT Press.

Keohane, Robert O., Judith L. Goldstein, Miles Kahler, and Anne-Marie Slaughter. 2000. Introduction: Legalization and World Politics. *International Organization* 54 (3): 385–399.

Keohane, Robert O., Gary King, and Sidney Verba. 1994. *Designing Social Inquiry: Scientific Inference in Qualitative Research.* Princeton, NJ: Princeton University Press.

SECONDARY WORKS

Waltz, Kenneth N. 1979. *Theory of International Politics.* Boston: McGraw Hill.

Peter Gourevitch

KERNER COMMISSION REPORT

From 1965 through 1968, a total of 329 racial disturbances erupted in 257 U.S. cities, causing 300 deaths and millions of dollars in property damage. In summer 1967 rioting broke out in several cities, causing 84 deaths and an estimated $75 to $100 million in property damage. Federal troops had to be brought in to quell the disorder. In Detroit alone, in 1967 43 people died and 1,383 buildings were burned. Alarmed, on July 28, 1967, President Lyndon Johnson created the National Advisory Commission on Civil Disorders, commonly known as the "Kerner Commission" after its chairman, Otto J. Kerner Jr., the governor of Illinois, to investigate the causes of the civil disturbances and to provide recommendations for the future.

The other members of the bipartisan commission appointed by President Johnson included John Lindsay, the mayor of New York; Senator Fred R. Harris,

Democrat of Oklahoma; Representatives James C. Corman, Democrat of California, and William M. McCulloch, Republican of Ohio; I. W. Abel, president of the United Steelworkers of America; Roy Wilkins, director of the National Association for the Advancement of Colored People; Senator Edward W. Brooke, Republican of Massachusetts; Charles B. Thornton, chairman of Litton Industries, Inc.; Katherine Graham Peden, Kentucky's commissioner of commerce; and police chief Herbert Jenkins of Atlanta. A large staff headed by David Ginsburg, a Washington, D.C., lawyer, was drawn from the liberal establishment that had supported the civil rights movement. The 426-page report, issued on February 28, 1968, quickly became a best seller, selling more than 2 million copies, and influenced thinking on race relations in the United States for the forthcoming decade.

President Johnson suspected that a political conspiracy was responsible for encouraging black urban militants to incite racial uprisings. But the commission found no evidence of a political conspiracy; instead, it blamed the racial upheavals on the frustrations and grievances of inner-city blacks, which were caused by persistent economic deprivation and racial discrimination. The most frequently quoted sentence from the report warned that the United States was "moving toward two societies, one black, and one white—separate and unequal" (National Advisory Commission on Civil Disorders 1968a, p. 1) The problems of racial discrimination, poverty, high unemployment, poor schools, inadequate schools, poor health care, and police bias and brutality were cited as major contributing factors to the United States' racial apartheid. Unless these problems were remedied, the report predicted, the racial divide in the United States would widen. The commission called for sweeping reforms: a large increase in federal aid to cities, a federal jobs program, a system of income supplementation, and an increase in the minimum wage.

None of the proposals were implemented during the Johnson administration, and they were largely ignored after the election of President Richard M. Nixon in 1968. Martin Luther King Jr. hailed the report as a "physician's warning of approaching death, with a prescription for life." (Report of the Select Committee on Assassinations, U.S. House of Representatives 1979, pp. 356-357.) Critics, though, argued that by blaming the problems of the black community on white racism, the report spawned an enduring sense of black victimization and hopelessness.

SEE ALSO *Black Power; Civil Rights; Civil Rights Movement, U.S.; Discrimination; Discrimination, Racial; Integration; Johnson, Lyndon B.; Nixon,*

Richard M.; Policing, Biased; Race; Race Relations; Race Riots, United States

BIBLIOGRAPHY

Lipsky, Michael, and David J. Olsen. 1977. *Commission Politics: The Processing of Racial Crisis in America.* New Brunswick, NJ: Transaction Books.

Meranto, Philip, ed. 1970. The Kerner Report Revisited. *Institute of Illinois Bulletin* 67 (121).

National Advisory Commission on Civil Disorders. 1968a. *Report of the Commission on Civil Disorders.* New York: Dutton.

National Advisory Commission on Civil Disorders. 1968b. *Supplemental Studies for The National Advisory Commission on Civil Disorders.* Washington, DC: U.S. Government Printing Office.

W. Wesley McDonald

KEY, V. O., JR.
1908–1963

V. O. Key Jr., one of the United States' greatest political scientists, pioneered the study of elections, political parties, and public opinion, and left a remarkable collection of books and articles despite a career cut short at age fifty-five. His *Southern Politics in State and Nation* (1949) analyzed in penetrating fashion the confusing, little-understood political arrangements of the one-party Democratic South using innovative, intelligible techniques of electoral analysis. Noting that in "its grand outlines, the politics of the South revolves around the position of the Negro" (1949, p. 5), Key went on to show that the big losers in the region's odd political system were "those who have less," of both races.

Likewise, his masterful *Public Opinion and American Democracy* (1961) offered invaluable theoretical insights into the elusive role of public attitudes in the governing process, elucidating the all-important linkage between what governments do and what the people think. "If a democracy tends toward indecision, decay, and disaster, the responsibility rests [with its political leaders], not in the mass of the people" (1961, p. 558), he concluded.

Key grew up in the West Texas town of Lamesa, where his father was a prominent lawyer. After earning a BA and MA at the University of Texas, he studied at the University of Chicago from 1930 to 1934 under Charles Merriam, an advocate of a "new science of politics," earning his PhD in 1934. After two years of teaching at UCLA and a year each working for the Social Science Research Council in Chicago and the National Resources Planning

Board in Washington, D.C., Key assumed his first long-term faculty position, at Johns Hopkins University in 1939. There he immediately launched into writing his influential, path-breaking textbook *Politics, Parties, and Pressure Groups*, which appeared in 1942 and went through five editions. His colleagues hailed the book; Charles Beard wrote to the author that his "bully" book "gleams with humor well concealed" (quoted in Lucker 2001, p. 49). Key made political power the book's central theme, telling the publisher in his 1939 proposal that "all of what we call political phenomenon can be interpreted" around this concept, adding: "By imaginative treatment, these dry-as-dust matters could perhaps be made, if not to sparkle, at least gleam" (quoted in Lucker 2001, pp. 43–44). Therein lies an element of Key's success: He matched insightful analysis with an engaging writing style.

Key remained at Johns Hopkins University for a decade, broken only by wartime service at the Bureau of the Budget. Yale University lured him away in 1949, but two years later he moved to Harvard, where he operated at the pinnacle of his discipline for the last twelve years of his life. In the *Journal of Politics* in February 1955 he published his most famous article, "A Theory of Critical Elections," which called attention to a type of election "in which the decisive results of the voting reveal a sharp alteration of the pre-existing cleavage within the electorate" (p. 4). The article gave birth to an enduring subfield—the study of electoral realignments.

Always at the forefront of his discipline, Key mastered the new techniques of survey research in the late 1950s, taking up residence at the University of Michigan to work with the National Election Studies, then in their infancy. "To speak with precision of public opinion," he asserted at the outset of his resulting 1961 book, *Public Opinion and American Democracy*, "is a task not unlike coming to grips with the Holy Ghost" (p. 8). But in 550 well-crafted pages, Key captured the elusive topic, locating it firmly within the political process.

At the time of Key's death in 1963, he was at work on a massive study of the voting process. Using Key's incomplete manuscript, his student Milton C. Cummings published *The Responsible Electorate* in 1966. The central theme of this slim volume is that voters exhibit an impressive amount of rationality in light of the choices they face, a notion still widely quoted using Key's apt phrasing: "Voters are not fools." If he had lived to complete the work himself, there is no doubt he would have produced a weighty study comparable to his last classic, *Public Opinion and American Democracy*.

SEE ALSO *Democracy; Elections; Interest Groups and Interests; Merriam, Charles Edward, Jr.; Political Science; Politics, Southern; Public Opinion; Race and Political Science; Rationality; Survey; Voting Patterns*

BIBLIOGRAPHY

Key, V. O., Jr. 1942. *Politics, Parties, and Pressure Groups.* New York: Thomas Y. Crowell.

Key, V. O., Jr. 1949. *Southern Politics in State and Nation.* New York: Knopf.

Key, V. O., Jr. 1955. A Theory of Critical Elections. *Journal of Politics* 17 (1): 3–18.

Key, V. O., Jr. 1961. *Public Opinion and American Democracy.* New York: Knopf.

Key, V. O., Jr., and Milton C. Cummings. 1966. *The Responsible Electorate: Rationality in Presidential Voting.* Cambridge, MA: Belknap Press.

Lamis, Alexander P., and Nathan Goldman. 1987. V. O. Key's Southern Politics: The Writing of a Classic. *Georgia Historical Quarterly* 71 (2): 261–285.

Lucker, Andrew M. 2001. *V. O. Key, Jr.: The Quintessential Political Scientist.* New York: Peter Lang.

Alexander P. Lamis

KEYNES, JOHN MAYNARD
1883–1946

The doyen of Cambridge economists, bursar of King's College, and eventual Baron Keynes of Tilton, John Maynard Keynes was a leading member of the Bloomsbury Group, an astute collector of the writings of Isaac Newton (1642–1727), a long-time editor of the *Economic Journal*, a U.K. government policy advisor of significant magnitude, and the main instigator of a revolution in economic theory that created an approach *(Keynesianism)* that came to dominate Western economic discourse from the end of World War II (1939–1945) until the mid-1970s.

Keynes was undoubtedly the most famous and influential economist of the mid-twentieth century. His 1936 book *The General Theory of Employment, Interest, and Money* is often cited as the single most important book in economic theory published in the interwar period, and it could reasonably be said to have created modern macroeconomics. One graphical representation of the economy that came out of this book—IS-LM analysis—became a staple of textbook economics for many years to come, even though it was later shown not to originate from Keynes's work alone, but from one individual's particular interpretation of it. Keynes's interventionist proposals for helping to regulate the aggregate level of employment through demand management remained in use in various forms for decades after World War II, and his policy advice on financing both World War I (1914–1918) and World War II was crucial to enabling Allied victories on both occasions. Some of his pithy aphorisms, such as "in the long run we are all dead," have become legendary.

Despite his undoubted great influence on economics, his legacy is highly controversial. Criticized from the right for advocating inflationary financing, and from the left for attempting to rescue capitalism rather than replace it, the demise of Keynesianism as the dominant force in mainstream economics is usually dated to the mid-1970s, when inflation combined with high unemployment to produce stagflation, something that Keynes had not predicted. Despite such unforeseen developments, his influence still remained active through a number of heterodox approaches to the subject, such as *post-Keynesian* economics and even *new Keynesianism*. Like all truly great intellectuals, fresh interpretations of his work are periodically presented, and neglected aspects of it are continually rediscovered.

BIOGRAPHY

Maynard Keynes (as he was known to his friends) was the son of John Neville Keynes (1852–1949), also a well-known economist and the author of *The Scope and Method of Political Economy* (1891). Maynard Keynes experienced an elite education at Eton and then studied at King's College Cambridge, where he was appointed to a lectureship in economics after a period working in the British Civil Service. He was soon involved in providing policy advice on financial affairs in India, which then developed into governmental service in the U.K. Treasury regarding the financing of World War I. He was the main Treasury representative at the signing of the Peace Treaty at Versailles, and after the war he strongly criticized the level of the reparations demands made on Germany. In the early 1920s, he argued that Britain should not return to the prewar gold standard system, and if it did, it should not be at prewar parity. In both these instances, his advice was ignored, but in retrospect his judgment has appeared correct to many commentators. By the end of the 1920s, Keynes was supporting David Lloyd George's (1863–1945) call for a program of government-funded economic expansion of around 2.5 percent of national income per year, in order to cure persistent unemployment.

In addition to his economic works, Keynes published *A Treatise on Probability* (1921), which provided a critique of the frequency conception of probability then in vogue. Instead of this approach, Keynes favored a logical conception in which probability was seen as being relative to human knowledge, rather than being taken as a given fact

of nature. He also published various essays on political matters and even some biographical sketches. In an essay on his early beliefs, he stressed the significance of the British philosopher G. E. Moore's (1873–1958) *Principia Ethica* (1903) to the formation of his general attitudes. Keynes had interpreted Moore as applying logical analysis to such areas as feelings, sense-data, and morality, and he later described such an approach as "sweeter air by far" than Sigmund Freud (1856–1939) or Karl Marx (1818–1883). During World War II, Keynes again successfully served in the U.K. Treasury, where he coordinated his activities closely with the U.S. government. He died in 1946, a year after the war ended.

ECONOMIC THEORY

Keynes is best known for introducing into the vocabulary of economists concepts such as the marginal efficiency of capital, liquidity preference, effective demand, the multiplier, and the propensity to consume. He also developed more rigorous definitions of the basic elements of economic analysis, such as income, savings, and investment. However, it is important to realize that Keynes was not working in isolation; instead he actively participated in debates that occurred throughout the 1920s and 1930s among British economists such as D. H. Robertson (1890–1963), Richard F. Kahn (1905–1989), R. G. Hawtrey (1879–1975), and Joan Robinson (1903–1983). Consequently, what precisely is taken to constitute the "Keynesian revolution" in economics is an essentially disputed topic. Keynes himself emphasized that the revolution was directed against the classical theory of employment, but his account of this theory through the work of the economist A. C. Pigou (1877–1959) was itself controversial. Keynes argued that the classical approach only allowed for the existence of frictional and voluntary unemployment, and denied the possibility of involuntary unemployment. Given the context of the Great Depression of the 1930s, Keynes implied that this approach was unrealistic, and set about showing how capitalism could generate significant levels of involuntary unemployment when certain conditions were met.

Keynes presented effective demand (aggregate demand backed by money) as the key concept of his general theory. He asserted that the volume of total employment was determined by the interrelation of aggregate supply and aggregate demand. As opposed to the classical doctrine, in which supply was said to create its own demand (Say's Law), Keynes suggested that in reality an increase in supply did not necessarily lead to a corresponding increase in demand. This was because when employment increased, aggregate real income also increased. However, due to the psychological factors involved (the propensity to consume), when income increased so also did consumption, but (crucially) by not as much as income. In order to cover this deficit, an increase in investment sufficient to absorb the excess was required, but there was no guarantee that the necessary level of increased investment would naturally follow. Keynes outlined that the amount of investment was actually dependent on the inducement to invest, which in turn was determined by the relation between the marginal efficiency of capital and interest rates.

Keynes defined the marginal efficiency of capital as being equal to the interest rate that would make the present value of the future returns from a capital good equal to its supply price, and hence it depended on expected returns. Keynes further outlined how the marginal efficiency of capital declined as investment in any particular capital good increased. Given this declining schedule and with any given rate of interest, there was no reason to assume that actual investment would correspond to the amount required to cover the deficit between increased income and consumption. Thus the level of effective demand required to ensure full employment was not necessarily created by the self-adjusting mechanisms of a market economy. Put another way, the economic system did not automatically generate full employment.

To explain the unusual duration of the Great Depression, Keynes suggested that in the 1930s the marginal efficiency of capital was actually much lower than it had been in the nineteenth century, and hence the rate of interest that would generate higher employment levels was unacceptable to many owners of accumulated wealth. To explain the heightened amplitude of depressions, Keynes christened the ratio between an increment of investment and increased income the *investment multiplier*, and suggested that a multiplier greater than unity accounted for how relatively small fluctuations in investment could generate much larger fluctuations in employment. Keynes concluded from this analysis that investment was promoted by low rates of interest and that this would be facilitated by the disappearance of the rentier class within capitalism.

The "Keynesian revolution" was not only directed against classical economists, but also against Keynes's earlier approach, which had preached adherence to the framework provided by the Cambridge version of the quantity theory of money. In this respect it is necessary to consider Keynes's major works in economics published prior to *The General Theory*. His first book was *Indian Currency and Finance* (1913), which provided an analysis of the operation of the gold-exchange standard. This was followed by *The Economic Consequences of the Peace* (1919), an attack on the terms of the Versailles Peace Treaty, and a *Tract on Monetary Reform* (1923), dealing with the problems of postwar inflation. These books,

although undoubtedly important in practical terms, were less significant in terms of providing innovations in pure theory. The *Treatise on Money* (1930) was Keynes's most significant work in economic theory prior to *The General Theory*. Here Keynes emphasized the importance of the behavior of the banking system to understanding fluctuations; by controlling credit, banks necessarily controlled aggregate expenditure. Booms and slumps were thus the result of the oscillation of the terms of credit about their equilibrium position, defined as occurring when savings equaled investment. Disequilibrium was possible in this model as international influences adversely affected the domestic banking system, causing the terms of credit to move above or below their equilibrium level at any given time. The difference between this type of analysis of trade cycles and that given in *The General Theory* was significant; in the latter, emphasis was transferred away from monetary factors to psychological propensities and expectations of future yields on investment goods.

THE CONSEQUENCES OF KEYNES

Keynes's new economics, brilliant though it undoubtedly was, was not without flaws. The abstract concepts that Keynes deployed with such aplomb were sometimes ambiguous, and his use of them produced much ongoing debate. Milton Friedman's *A Theory of the Consumption Function* (1957) was devoted to empirically investigating Keynes's psychological rule of increased savings (in percentage terms) as income rose. Friedman concluded that Keynes was mistaken in his presentation of the nature of the propensity to consume, as the ratio between income and savings was the same for all levels of income, but depended on other factors, such as interest rates and the ratio of wealth to income. Friedman later led the monetarist counterrevolution against the Keynesian approach. There was also a question over how "general" Keynes's *General Theory* actually was. Since it was designed in part to explain the historical circumstances of the 1930s, was its relevance limited only to the interwar period?

Despite such ambiguities, the impact of *The General Theory* on Western economics immediately after 1936 was so great that it swept aside the valuable contributions of contemporary economists like Joseph Schumpeter (1883–1950), whose monumental work *Business Cycles* (1939) found little direct resonance in the West due, at least in part, to the phenomenal success of Keynes's book. Keynes also became involved in a debate over the importance of the new econometric methodology (as developed by the Dutch economist Jan Tinbergen [1903–1994]) to economic analysis. Keynes was highly critical of the extensive use of mathematical models in economics being promoted by the econometricians, but his reservations were quickly swept aside. Ironically, it was the success of the

Keynesian IS-LM model that added some impetus to the drive for econometric modeling.

The Keynesian system was for many years after World War II hailed by the Left as proof of the inadequacies of capitalism as an economic system and the necessity of increased state control of the commanding heights of the economy. Keynes himself saw his work as a means of improving the internal mechanics of the free-market system, and he criticized state socialism as inefficient and as too restrictive of individual freedoms. Keynes traveled to the USSR on a number of occasions, but he found the fanatical zeal of the Bolsheviks toward Marx's *Capital* to be incomprehensible. He declared support for significant inequalities of wealth and income, but not to such a degree that it would impede the entrepreneurial function. Yet he disputed the argument that enlightened self-interest always operated in the public interest, and he saw an important role for the directive intelligence of society organized as a whole exercising some control over private business.

Given the level of his fame and the degree of his policy influence, Keynes's private life and general views have come under some scrutiny. Early in his life he had intimate relationships with male suitors (such as Duncan Grant [1885–1978], the Bloomsbury painter), but he went on to marry a Russian ballerina in 1925, his "conversion" to heterosexuality being the cause of some friction between members of the Bloomsbury set. He has been accused of "soft" anti-Semitism and also of not realizing the full consequences of his policies of war finance for less developed countries like Russia. Despite such criticism, Keynes's status as one of the most important economists since Adam Smith (1723–1790) remains unshaken, and his legacy of bringing greater sophistication to economic theory is an enduring one. It seems unlikely that any individual economist could replicate Keynes's pervasive influence over the subject in the future.

SEE ALSO *Absolute Income Hypothesis; Consumption Function; Economics, Keynesian; Economics, New Keynesian; Economics, Post Keynesian; Interest, Neutral Rate of; Macroeconomics; Policy, Fiscal; Policy, Monetary; Unemployment; Voluntary Unemployment*

BIBLIOGRAPHY

Barnett, Vincent. 2001. Calling Up the Reserves: Keynes, Tugan-Baranovsky, and Russian War Finance. *Europe-Asia Studies* 53 (1): 151–169.

Clarke, Peter. 1988. *The Keynesian Revolution in the Making, 1924–1936*. Oxford: Clarendon Press.

Friedman, Milton. 1957. *A Theory of the Consumption Function*. Princeton, NJ: Princeton University Press.

Hicks, J. R. 1937. Mr. Keynes and the "Classics": A Suggested Interpretation. *Econometrica* 5 (2): 147–159.

Keynes, John Maynard. 1921. *A Treatise on Probability*. London: Macmillan.

Keynes, John Maynard. 1930. *Treatise on Money*. London: Macmillan.

Keynes, John Maynard. 1936. *The General Theory of Employment, Interest, and Money*. London: Macmillan.

Laidler, David. 1999. *Fabricating the Keynesian Revolution: Studies of the Inter-War Literature on Money, the Cycle, and Unemployment*. Cambridge, U.K.: Cambridge University Press.

Skidelsky, Robert. 1992. *John Maynard Keynes: The Economist as Saviour, 1920–1937*. London: Macmillan.

Vincent Barnett

KHALDŪN, IBN

SEE *Ibn Khaldūn.*

KHMER ROUGE

The Khmer Rouge (Cambodian for "Red Khmer") was a Communist regime that ruled Cambodia from April 1975 to January 1979. The group, led by Pol Pot, was formally the Communist Party of Kampuchea. In trying to reach its ambitious agricultural production goals and to protect itself against opposition, the regime worked large numbers of people to death and slaughtered its perceived opponents. Characterized by extreme brutality, the regime was responsible for the deaths through slaughter, starvation, overwork, and disease of 1 to 1.7 million Cambodians of a pre-1975 population of 7 or 8 million.

Under the Khmer Rouge, the cities were emptied; industry virtually halted; money, markets, and religion extinguished; and the entire populace sent out to agricultural labor camps in the countryside. Despite the regime's notional commitment to creating a classless society, in practice, people were divided into "base people," those who had been under the Khmer Rouge before April 1975 and "new people," those who came under the regime's control only with the final victory. New people suffered particularly in the austere rural labor conditions. Food was inadequate, the work schedule was harsh, and medical facilities and medicine were almost nonexistent. Gradually, the family unit was broken up; from 1977 dining was communalized.

The regime slaughtered officials from the old regime, intellectuals (which included teachers), Buddhist monks, and uncovered "enemies." The *Santebal* internal security service kept meticulous records of the tortures and executions in which it engaged, Phnom Penh's S-21/Tuol Sleng facility being the pinnacle of the regime's torture camps. Failures to achieve the regime's unrealistic economic goals were blamed on internal and external conspirators. Confessions of sabotage were wrung from Cambodians who were forced to name their accomplices, drawing more innocents into the regime's web of terror. Cambodia's numerous mass grave sites have come to be known as the Killing Fields.

Khmer Rouge thought placed particular attention to the idea of Khmer purity. Non-Khmer Cambodians of Vietnamese, Cham (Muslim), or Chinese descent faced particular threats. The young were considered especially pure by the Khmer Rouge, as they had not been tainted by the attitudes of the past (*Pol Pot's Little Red Book* cites the following Khmer Rouge slogan: "Clay is molded while it is soft"). Society was supposed to start afresh from the "year zero."

Heavily influenced by the ideas of Mao Zedong of China, Cambodia's Communist leaders believed they could substitute human willpower for other economic inputs, thus carrying out a "super great leap forward" and revolutionizing agricultural production. The need to continually write one's autobiography and correct errors of thought were also borrowed from the Chinese Communists. Self-reliance was a core value and, with the exception of supporter China, the regime was effectively closed to the outside world.

In 1979, the Khmer Rouge was ousted from power by a Vietnamese invasion. The regime's remnants fled to the Thai border and continued to control territory and followers into the 1990s. A United Nations (UN)–organized election in 1993 marginalized the group, which boycotted the polls. By 1996–1997, primarily through defections to the new government, the Khmer Rouge was virtually nonexistent. A show trial of Pol Pot was held in the Khmer Rouge–controlled zone of Cambodia in 1997, and the former leader was put under house arrest. He died in April 1998. In conjunction with the UN, Cambodia agreed in 2003 to set up a mixed Cambodian/international tribunal to bring remaining top Khmer Rouge leaders to justice for their crimes while in power, including Ta Mok, known as "the Butcher," and Comrade Duch, the head of the S-21 camp.

SEE ALSO *Communism; Genocide; Killing Fields; Military Regimes; Pol Pot; Underclass; United Nations*

BIBLIOGRAPHY

Chanda, Nayan. 1986. *Brother Enemy: The War after the War.* New York: Collier.

Chandler, David. 1999. *Brother Number One: A Political Biography of Pol Pot.* Boulder, CO: Westview.

Chandler, David. 1999. *Voices from S-21: Terror and History in Pol Pot's Secret Prison.* Berkeley: University of California Press.

Kiernan, Ben. 1985. *How Pol Pot Came to Power: Colonialism, Nationalism, and Communism in Cambodia, 1930–1975.* London: Verso.

Kiernan, Ben. 1996. *The Pol Pot Regime: Race, Power, and Genocide under the Khmer Rouge, 1975–1979.* New Haven, CT: Yale University Press.

Locard, Henri. 2004. *Pol Pot's Little Red Book: The Sayings of Angkar.* Chiang Mai, Thailand: Silkworm Books.

Ponchaud, Francois. 1978. *Cambodia: Year Zero.* New York: Holt Rinehart and Winston.

Schanberg, Sidney. 1980. *The Death and Life of Dith Pran.* New York: Penguin.

Shawcross, William. 1979. *Sideshow: Kissinger, Nixon, and the Destruction of Cambodia.* New York: Simon & Schuster.

Paige Johnson Tan

KHOMEINI, AYATOLLAH RUHOLLAH
1902–1989

Ayatollah Ruhollah Khomeini was the leader of the Islamic Revolution in Iran. He was born on September 24, 1902, in the western Iranian town of Khomein to a clerical family. His father Mustafa was murdered by bandits when Khomeini was five months old. His older brother Sayyid Murtaza (later known as Ayatollah Pasandida) assumed responsibility for Khomeini's education after their mother died in 1918.

At nineteen, Khomeini traveled to nearby Arak, where he studied religion under Ayatollah Abd al-Karim Ha'iri, a well-known Islamic scholar. Khomeini followed Ha'iri to the Fayzieh *madrasa* (religious college) in Qom the following year, where Khomeini distinguished himself in ethics and religious philosophy. Upon completing his education, Khomeini taught Islamic philosophy and jurisprudence. After Ha'iri's death in 1937, he became an assistant to Ayatollah Husayn Boroujerdi, one of the leading Shi'ite authorities of the day. Khomeini's residence in Qom coincided with the rise of Reza Shah, who curtailed the influence of the clergy as he centralized authority.

In 1932 he married the daughter of a prominent Tehran cleric and had seven children, five of whom survived infancy. Both sons died under mysterious circumstances—his eldest son Mustafa in Najaf in 1977 and his youngest son Ahmad died in Tehran in 1995.

Khomeini published his first tract on spiritual philosophy at age twenty-seven. His reputation as a teacher of *fiqh* (Islamic jurisprudence) grew throughout the 1940s and 1950s. He published his first major book, *Kashf al-*

Asrar ("Secrets Revealed"), in 1944, to refute an influential antireligious pamphlet published several years before.

Khomeini catapulted to the national stage in 1962 after he publicly opposed a government reform package that included land reform, women's suffrage, and a provision which would allow the religious minority Baha'is to seek office. He was a master of rhetoric and coalesced an opposition including traditional clergy, nationalists, and the poor. After Khomeini denounced the Iranian government on June 5, 1963, the shah ordered his arrest, but he was soon released because of popular pressure. After two more arrests, on November 4, 1964, the shah exiled Khomeini to Turkey from where he made his way to Najaf.

It was during his Iraqi exile that, in 1970, Khomeini wrote *Hukumat-i Islami* (Islamic government) that outlined his theory of *vilayat-i faqih* (guardianship of the jurists) in which he countered the traditional Shi'ite opposition to direct clerical rule. Khomeini's followers smuggled many of his sermons into Iran by audiocassette.

Protests erupted on January 7, 1978, after a state-controlled newspaper questioned Khomeini's sexuality and patriotism. Police fired onto the crowds, beginning a cycle of escalating demonstrations. In October 1978, Khomeini flew to France where he received Iranian visitors and the Western press. The shah fled Iran on January 16, 1979. On February 1, 1979, Khomeini returned to Iran and, two months later, declared the Islamic Republic. As supreme leader (*rahbar*) and against the backdrop of the U.S. hostage crisis and Iran-Iraq War, he launched a cultural revolution and consolidated his power in a series of bloody purges. Khomeini died on June 4, 1989.

SEE ALSO *Fundamentalism; Fundamentalism, Islamic; Iranian Revolution; Iran-Iraq War; Religion*

BIBLIOGRAPHY

Khomeini, Ruhollah. 1981. *Islam and Revolution: Writing and Declarations,* trans. Hamid Algar. London: Routledge and Kegan Paul.

Moin, Baqer. 1999. *Khomeini: Life of the Ayatollah.* London: I. B. Tauris.

Michael Rubin

KHRUSHCHEV, NIKITA
1894–1971

Nikita Sergeyevich Khrushchev, born into an illiterate peasant family in Kalinovka, Russia, rose through the Communist Party ranks to become the third leader of the Soviet Union. An activist from his teenage years, and a political commissar with the Bolshevik forces during the Russian Civil War, Khrushchev joined the Communist Party of the Soviet Union in 1918. After studying at Kharkov University, he undertook a series of political assignments, which gained the attention of top party leaders in the Ukraine (see Smith 1992). In 1931 Khrushchev moved to Moscow, where he served as secretary of the Bauman district party organization. He became first secretary of the Moscow party organization in 1935.

By 1938 Khrushchev had become a member of the Politburo and went on to serve as first secretary in the Ukraine, where he oversaw the Ukrainian party organization's purges. He fought in World War II (1939–1945) and afterward became chairman of the Ukrainian Council of Ministers. Other notable positions held by Khrushchev include first secretary of the Moscow City Party Committee (1949), member of the Central Committee Secretariat responsible for supervising party affairs in the various republics, and full member of the Presidium, which well situated him for ascension to the Communist Party's top leadership after the death of Joseph Stalin in 1953. Khrushchev almost immediately espoused a plan for reforming the economy and stimulating agricultural output. For example, the Virgin Lands program called for plowing up virgin prairie lands in the Caucasus regions, Siberia, and the Volga Basin, and planting corn to use as feed to expand beef production. The plan, a dismal failure, coupled with other failures and leadership challenges, had an impact on Khrushchev's popularity (see Breslauer 1982).

In 1956 Khrushchev launched a de-Stalinization campaign as a means to shore up his popularity, but it also enhanced the rule of law in Soviet society. The de-Stalinization campaign called attention to a series of Stalinist abuses and breaches of power that included establishing a personality cult, orchestrating purges that terrorized innocent people, and violating the Leninist principle of collective leadership. Khrushchev's campaign and reforms also yielded unintended results, as exemplified by the burst of artistic creativity, strikes, demonstrations, and political reform efforts in Eastern Europe. This aside, he also sought to reduce the Soviet Union's isolation in the world.

Khrushchev was the first Soviet leader to advocate "peaceful coexistence" with the West, and the first Soviet leader to visit the United States. In 1959 he met with President Dwight D. Eisenhower (1890–1969) at Camp David, traveled to Iowa to learn about hybrid corn, and toured IBM and Disneyland. The path to improved relations was, however, short-circuited by the 1960 U-2 affair, the 1961 U.S.–sponsored Bay of Pigs invasion, and the 1962 Cuban missile crisis. Interestingly, Khrushchev's public persona, as exemplified by heated exchanges with Richard Nixon (1913–1994) during the so-called kitchen debate in 1959, his shoe-banging demonstration at the United Nations in 1960, and communications with John F. Kennedy (1917–1963) during the Cuban missile crisis, most likely contributed to his downfall and banishment from Soviet politics.

SEE ALSO *Communism; Cuban Missile Crisis; Eisenhower, Dwight D.; Kennedy, John F.; Nixon, Richard M.; Stalin, Joseph; Stalinism; Union of Soviet Socialist Republics; United Nations*

BIBLIOGRAPHY

Breslauer, George W. 1982. *Khrushchev and Brezhnev as Leaders: Building Authority in Soviet Politics.* Boston: Allen and Unwin.

Fainsod, Merle. 1953. *How Russia Is Ruled.* Cambridge, MA: Harvard University Press.

Nogee, Joseph L., and Robert H. Donaldson. 1992. *Soviet Foreign Policy Since World War II.* New York: Macmillan.

Smith, Gordon B. 1992. *Soviet Politics: Struggling with Change.* 2nd ed. New York: St. Martin's Press.

Kathie Stromile Golden

KILLING FIELDS

Killing Fields, the term for Cambodia's mass grave sites, has become synonymous with the country's Khmer Rouge regime that ruled Cambodia from 1975 to 1979. In trying to reach its ambitious agricultural production goals and to protect itself against opposition, the regime worked large numbers of people to death and slaughtered its perceived opponents, resulting in the deaths of between 1 and 1.7 million individuals of a pre-1975 population of 7 to 8 million.

Agricultural production was key to the Khmer Rouge's plans for Cambodia's transformation. The entire population was transferred to state-run farms where food was inadequate, medical attention sparse, and working conditions harsh. The population was exhorted to produce the unrealistic quantity of "three tons [of rice] per hectare." Many of those who died under the Khmer Rouge died from overwork. Failure to work hard enough or "feigning" illness could transform one into a perceived enemy of the regime, and the regime resolutely hunted its enemies.

Reasons for torture and execution included expressing doubts about the government; having a prerevolutionary past as an intellectual, professional, teacher, or servant of the old regime; or growing one's own food. The Khmer Rouge also gorged on its own with frequent brutal purges within the Khmer Rouge ranks. Soldiers, fellow workers, even one's own children were encouraged to report on one's incorrect thoughts or actions. The Khmer Rouge did little to engage in re-education of those found to have erred. Interrogation involved torture meant to elicit confessions of wrong-doing, thus proving the party's correctness in arresting the person; death came during torture or soon thereafter. Fewer than ten persons are known to have survived the regime's most notorious torture camp, S-21 in Phnom Penh.

It was from the S-21/Tuol Sleng facility that victims were taken to Cambodia's most well-known killing field site at Choeung Ek, nine miles outside the capital, where victims were killed by blunt-force trauma (a rifle butt or farm implement to the base of the head), stabbing/hacking, or shooting. In the early twenty-first century, at Choeung Ek, a stupa (Buddhist shrine) of human skulls and a map of the country made of skulls and other bones remind visitors of the horror once meted out there. Almost 9,000 sets of remains have been excavated from the Choeung Ek grounds. Many more bodies remain buried, though, as tens of graves at the site have been left undisturbed.

The regime crumbled in 1979 due to a Vietnamese invasion, after which S-21 was transformed into the Tuol Sleng Museum of Genocide. Following a United Nations (UN)–brokered peace plan in 1991 and elections in 1993, the Khmer Rouge was gradually sidelined. In conjunction with the United Nations, Cambodia agreed in 2003 to set up a mixed Cambodian/international tribunal to bring remaining top Khmer Rouge leaders to justice for their crimes while in power.

SEE ALSO *Communism; Genocide; Khmer Rouge; Military Regimes; Pol Pot; Underclass; United Nations*

BIBLIOGRAPHY

Chanda, Nayan. 1986. *Brother Enemy: The War after the War.* New York: Collier.

Chandler, David. 1999. *Brother Number One: A Political Biography of Pol Pot.* Boulder, CO: Westview.

Chandler, David. 1999. *Voices from S-21: Terror and History in Pol Pot's Secret Prison.* Berkeley: University of California Press.

Documentation Center of Cambodia. http://www.dccam.org.

Kiernan, Ben. 1985. *How Pol Pot Came to Power: Colonialism, Nationalism, and Communism in Cambodia, 1930–1975.* London: Verso.

Kiernan, Ben. 1996. *The Pol Pot Regime: Race, Power, and Genocide under the Khmer Rouge, 1975–1979.* New Haven, CT: Yale University Press.

Locard, Henri. 2004. *Pol Pot's Little Red Book: The Sayings of Angkar.* Chiang Mai, Thailand: Silkworm Books.

Schanberg, Sidney. 1980. *The Death and Life of Dith Pran.* New York: Penguin.

Shawcross, William. 1979. *Sideshow: Kissinger, Nixon, and the Destruction of Cambodia.* New York: Simon & Schuster.

Paige Johnson Tan

KIMATHI, DEDAN
1920–1957

Dedan Kimathi (also known as Kimathi wa Waciuri) was an important member of Kenya's militant nationalist group, the Mau Mau. He became notorious as the elusive "general." Born in 1920 in the village of Thegenge in the Tetu Division of the Central Nyeri district in Kenya, Kimathi began his formal education at the age of fifteen when he enrolled at the local elementary school, Karunaini. He funded his education by collecting seeds for the forestry department. He later entered the Tumutumu CMS School, but could not complete his secondary education due to a lack of funds. In 1941 Kimathi enlisted in the army to help prosecute World War II (1939–1945), but he was discharged three years later for misconduct. In 1946 he became a member of the Kenyan African Union (KAU), a political organization established to fight British colonialism. In 1949 he returned to teach briefly at his former elementary school, but quit within two years.

In 1950 Kimathi embraced radical politics when he subscribed to the oath of the Mau Mau, the group demanding freedom and the return of Kenyan land from the British. Kimathi became one of the most prominent of the three dominant leaders of Mau Mau's Land and Freedom Armies, with oversight functions for the Aberdare forest. In 1952 he was elected the local branch secretary of the KAU in the Ol' Kalou and Thomson's Falls area. He was arrested the same year when he was implicated in a murder, but he escaped from police detention with the help of a sympathizer. The following year he created the Kenya Defense Council to coordinate guerrilla activities, and moved to the Nyandarua forest, which served as the operational base of his army. Besides the armed struggle, he toured the forest and towns attempting to inspire people to join his group. Kimathi soon developed skills as a strategist and became an accomplished master of disguises. In addition, he became a skillful writer, penning letters to the colonial authorities and to friendly and unfriendly chiefs, as well as articles that were published in newspapers. Due to the activities of the Mau Mau, the colonial regime was forced to declare a state of emergency in 1952.

In 1956 Kimathi was captured with Wambui, his "forest wife," and sentenced to death. He was hanged on February 18, 1957, at Nairobi Prison and was buried in a mass grave. Despite attempts by British propagandists to label him a dangerous and elusive terrorist, Kimathi became a folk hero among the people of Kenya. After independence, several towns in Kenya named buildings or streets after him. A statue was also dedicated to him in Nairobi in December 2006. Kimathi's life has inspired several literary and historical works, including *The Trial of Dedan Kimathi* (1976) by Ngugi wa Thiong'o and Micere Mugo, and *L'inafferrabile Mau Mau* (The Elusive Mau Mau, 1957), a novel by Ottavio Sestero. Kimathi also lives on in the history, legends, and music of ordinary Kenyans.

SEE ALSO *Anticolonial Movements; Decolonization; Kenyatta, Jomo; Mau Mau*

BIBLIOGRAPHY

Anderson, David M., 2005. *Histories of the Hanged: The Dirty War in Kenya and the End of Empire.* New York: Norton.

Barnett, Donald L., and Karari Njama. 1966. *Mau Mau from Within: Autobiography and Analysis of Kenya's Peasant Revolt.* London: MacGibbon & Kee.

Maughan-Brown, David. 1985. *Land, Freedom, and Fiction: History and Ideology in Kenya.* London. Zed.

Olutayo C. Adesina

KIN SELECTION
SEE *Sociobiology.*

KINDLEBERGER, CHARLES POOR
1910–1993

Charles Kindelberger's career unfolded in three distinct phases: public service; university teaching; and postretirement scholarship. A native New Yorker, he entered Columbia University's doctoral program in 1932 near the bottom of the Great Depression. His first employers were the U.S. Treasury and the Federal Reserve. As World War II approached, he moved to the Bank for International Settlements in Switzerland, returning to Washington in 1940. After Pearl Harbor, he served with the Office of Strategic Services (OSS) and the U.S. Army in Europe. An unpretentious man of Kantian moral standards, he was overjoyed to have played an important role at the State Department in establishing the Marshall Plan for

European Recovery. Kindleberger moved to the Massachusetts Institute of Technology in 1948, where he remained until he retired in 1976. In response to the warmth, wit, and wisdom he showered on students and colleagues alike, he was universally known as "Charlie" or "cpk."

Kindleberger enjoyed contrasting his expertise in old-fashioned "literary economics" with the more-circumscribed "technical economics" practiced by his colleagues and graduate students. The belief that he could help government policymakers avoid a repeat of signal economic disasters served as the cornerstone of his sixty-year professional life.

Unlike most of his contemporaries, Kindleberger made his mark through books, words, and index cards rather than with articles, equations, and datasets. His curiosity, energy, and vision overspread not only the page limits enforced by journal editors, but the narrow taxonomy of problem areas and research paradigms recognized in modern economics.

His teaching and research in international economics embraced the idea that nations, exchange-rate regimes, and technologies had ineluctable life cycles. His efforts to document these cycles spilled increasingly into what he teasingly renamed "historical economics."

The transition became clear in 1964 with the publication of *Economic Growth in France and Britain: 1851–1950*, but reached full flower only after his retirement. Kindleberger saw himself not as doing history, but as using "historical episodes to test economic models for their generality" (Kindleberger 1990, p. 3). His research method was to read everything he could find on a subject and then to turn what he had learned into a coherent explanation of things. The eclectic syntheticizations this method produced challenged the methodological foundations of both financial history (*The World in Depression, 1929–1939*, 1973) and mainstream finance (*Manias, Panics, and Crashes: A History of Financial Crises*, 1978).

Both books portray financial institutions and markets as so volatile and prone to crisis that they must be stabilized by government. *The World in Depression, 1929–1939* developed the thesis that the instability of national economies between the wars was a global problem that was enabled to spread by the absence of a dominant nation-state (a "hegemon") willing and able to act as an international lender of last resort. *Manias, Panics, and Crashes* sought to refute the widely held hypothesis that participants in financial markets process information rationally.

These studies stand out from Kindleberger's other twenty-eight books in the size, heat, and durability of the controversies they produced. On one side of the debate, opponents in political science and finance dispute the empirical applicability of his models of irrational actors and breakdown-prone markets and institutions. Many of these critics see government action as more likely to spawn or exacerbate institutional and market failures than to prevent or mitigate them. On the other side, Kindleberger attracted many followers and is remembered as a founding father of the fields of hegemonic stability and behavioral finance. He spent his last years energetically preparing new editions that answered specific critics and applied his models to additional episodes.

BIBLIOGRAPHY

PRIMARY WORKS

Kindleberger, Charles Poor. 1964. *Economic Growth in France and Britain: 1851–1950*. Cambridge, MA: Harvard University Press.

Kindleberger, Charles Poor. [1973] 1986. *The World in Depression, 1929–1939*. London: Allen Lane.

Kindleberger, Charles Poor. [1978] 2001. *Manias, Panics, and Crashes: A History of Financial Crises*. 4th ed. New York: John Wiley.

Kindleberger, Charles Poor. 1990. *Historical Economics: Art or Science*. Berkeley: University of California Press.

Edward J. Kane

KINDNESS

SEE *Altruism.*

KING, MARTIN LUTHER, JR.
1929–1968

Martin Luther King Jr. was a Baptist minister and iconic leader of the U.S. civil rights movement. Famous for advocating nonviolent resistance to racial oppression, he led numerous demonstrations, boycotts, and voter registration drives from the mid-1950s until his death by assassination in 1968. King was fueled by a strong religious faith, believing that Christian love could function as a powerful agent for social change.

Both his maternal grandfather, A. D. Williams, and his father, Martin Luther King, were Baptist ministers and leaders of Ebenezer Baptist Church in Atlanta, Georgia. King carried on the family tradition, becoming an ordained Baptist minister at the age of eighteen. After completing a sociology degree from Morehouse College, a historically black institution in Atlanta, King attended racially integrated Crozer Theological Seminary in Pennsylvania, graduating as valedictorian of his class in 1951. He then continued his training at Boston University, earning a doctorate in systematic theology in 1955.

It was while immersed in his graduate studies that King first encountered Mohandas Gandhi's philosophy of nonviolent resistance. King combined Gandhi's belief that nonviolence was not only the most ethical but also the most effective form of social protest with his own rigorous training in Christian theology, claiming, "Christ furnished the spirit and motivation, while Gandhi furnished the method" (King 1958, p. 85). Nonviolent protest as King described it was "nonagressive physically but dynamically aggressive spiritually," seeking the "friendship and understanding" of one's opponent (King 1957, p. 166).

On June 18, 1953, King married Coretta Scott, then a student at the New England Conservatory of Music. The marriage produced four children. In 1954 the couple moved to Montgomery, Alabama, where King became pastor of the Dexter Street Baptist Church.

EMERGENCE AS A CIVIL RIGHTS LEADER

Shortly after moving to Montgomery, King was catapulted into the growing civil rights movement. On December 1, 1955, local civil rights activist Rosa Parks (1913–2005) was arrested after she refused to give up her seat to a white passenger on a segregated city bus. The local black community organized a bus boycott to protest Parks's arrest and elected King as leader of the Montgomery Improvement Association, an organization created to support the boycott. Under King's leadership, the black community responded nonviolently to white intimidation and violence and sustained the boycott for over a year. In 1956 the Supreme Court ruled segregated seating on buses unconstitutional. King chronicled his involvement in the boycott in his powerful 1958 memoir *Stride toward Freedom.*

After the success in Montgomery, King and a group of black ministers formed the Southern Christian Leadership Conference (SCLC) in 1957. King was elected leader of this new organization, which was designed to support various civil rights activities.

The SCLC was not the only civil rights organization operating in the United States at this time, but King and his followers were key players in many of the most memorable showdowns between civil rights activists and the forces of white supremacy. In 1963 the SCLC joined Reverend Fred Shuttlesworth in a campaign to end segregation in Birmingham, Alabama. Defying a court injunction forbidding protest activities, King was arrested on

April 12, 1963. While in prison he penned his famous "Letter from Birmingham Jail," eloquently defending civil disobedience and urging religious leaders to enlist in the struggle for civil rights.

Local Birmingham officials, shamed by national media coverage of police attacking unarmed protestors with fire hoses and police dogs, reluctantly agreed to many of the activists' demands. However, white resistance did not immediately abate. On September 15, 1963, in a particularly gruesome display of violence, the Ku Klux Klan bombed the Sixteenth Street Baptist Church, killing four young African American girls.

The SCLC and other civil rights advocates met similarly mixed results elsewhere, winning concessions but drawing violent reprisals from white supremacists. The SCLC was involved in many demonstrations including campaigns in Albany, Georgia, and Selma, Alabama. The federal government eventually responded to the problem of racial inequality by passing important civil rights legislation. The Civil Rights Act of 1964 outlawed discrimination in public facilities and in employment, and the Voting Rights Act of 1965 effectively put an end to disenfranchisement on the basis of race.

INTERNATIONAL FAME

King quickly became the most visible face of the civil rights struggle, capturing media attention wherever he went. On several occasions he met with President John F. Kennedy and later with President Lyndon B. Johnson. In 1963 he was named *Time* magazine's "man of the year," and in 1964 he was awarded the Nobel Peace Prize. During the 1963 March on Washington for Jobs and Freedom, he delivered his sonorous "I Have a Dream" speech, one of the most memorable examples of American oratory in the twentieth century.

Due in part to growing resentment over King's fame, tensions developed between the SCLC and other civil rights organizations. The National Association for the Advancement of Colored People (NAACP) focused on fighting white supremacy through litigation rather than through the direct-action campaigns favored by the SCLC, causing tactical disagreements between members of the respective groups. Leaders of all the major civil rights organizations vied with one another and with King for media coverage and for opportunities to shape the direction of the movement. Roy Wilkins, executive secretary of the NAACP, was no exception. After NAACP field secretary Medgar Evers's death by assassination on June 11, 1963, Wilkins became resentful of King's efforts to raise funds in honor of the slain man, demanding instead that memorial contributions be sent exclusively to the NAACP. Despite these pressures, King remained an ardent supporter of Wilkins and of the venerable civil rights organization he represented.

Similarly, many members of the Student Nonviolent Coordinating Committee (SNCC) offered powerful critiques of King. Some resented the media's depiction of King as the predominant leader of the movement, referring to King in jest as "De Lawd." Weary of being jailed and beaten, many young activists grew increasingly skeptical of King's dedication to nonviolent resistance. Others began to embrace black nationalism rather than King's integrationist vision for the United States. King remained receptive to criticism, and these profound disagreements did not stand in the way of warm, personal relationships between King and many SNCC members, including Stokely Carmichael (1941–1998), the radical black nationalist who was elected to the chairmanship of SNCC in 1966.

Malcolm X (1925–1965), the charismatic minister of the Nation of Islam and later, founder of the Organization of Afro-American Unity, was critical of nonviolent resistance, a tactic he regarded as cowardly. Malcolm was particularly outspoken in his criticisms of King, labeling him a "traitor to the Negro people." King was stung by Malcolm's condemnation, but the pair shared a well-publicized handshake on Capitol Hill on March 26, 1964. Although he continued to repudiate nonviolent resistance, Malcolm later sought ways to cooperate with King and other civil rights leaders. However, King rebuffed Malcolm's efforts, certain that his fiery rhetoric and failure to embrace nonviolence would "reap nothing but grief."

King was also a prominent target of the FBI director, J. Edgar Hoover (1895–1972). Hoover used wiretaps, spread false rumors, and planted infiltrators in an attempt to disrupt the movement and to tarnish the reputation of King and other leaders.

CHANGING DIRECTIONS

Throughout his life, King remained committed to the principal of nonviolent resistance, but his thinking did not become static. He listened thoughtfully to criticism and responded to the changing times. In 1965 he expanded the scope of his activism by speaking out against the Vietnam War. Increasingly, King began to focus on class issues, seeking ways to improve the lives of the underprivileged, regardless of race. In 1967 the SCLC began planning a Poor People's Campaign designed to protest economic inequality through nonviolent direct action.

In 1968 King's struggle for economic justice brought him to Memphis, Tennessee, to support striking sanitation workers. While there he gave what was to be his final address, "I've Been to the Mountaintop." The recipient of frequent death threats, King long knew that his civil rights activism might cost him his life. That night he prophetically told his audience, "I might not get there with you … [but] we, as a people, will get to the Promised Land." The next day, April 4, 1968, while standing on the balcony outside his hotel room, King was shot and killed by a sniper.

White supremacist James Earl Ray (1928–1998) was arrested for King's murder. In order to avoid the death penalty, Ray made a plea bargain and confessed to the killing. However, Ray almost immediately recanted his confession, claiming that he was framed. In 1997 Ray convinced King's son Dexter Scott King of his innocence, but Tennessee authorities refused to grant Ray, who died in prison in 1998, a new trial. King's death has been the subject of many conspiracy theories, some involving the federal government in the plot to kill King.

Today King's vision of interracial harmony has gained widespread acceptance among many Americans. However, his radical critique of economic inequality in the United States is less widely remembered. In 1983 Congress voted to establish a national holiday in his honor, enshrining King among the nation's pantheon of heroes.

SEE ALSO *Black Power; Civil Disobedience; Civil Rights; Civil Rights Movement, U.S.; Malcolm X; Passive Resistance*

BIBLIOGRAPHY

Branch, Taylor. 1988. *Parting the Waters: America in the King Years, 1954–63.* New York: Simon and Schuster.

Branch, Taylor. 1998. *Pillar of Fire: America in the King Years, 1963–65.* New York: Simon and Schuster.

Branch, Taylor. 2006. *At Canaan's Edge: America in the King Years, 1965–68.* New York: Simon and Schuster.

Burns, Stewart. 2004. *To the Mountaintop: Martin Luther King, Jr.'s Sacred Mission to Save America, 1955–1968.* New York: HarperCollins.

Carson, Clayborne. 1998. *The Autobiography of Martin Luther King, Jr.* New York: Warner Books.

Garrow, David. 1986. *Bearing the Cross: Martin Luther King, Jr. and the Southern Christian Leadership Conference.* New York: William Marrow.

King, Martin Luther, Jr. 1957. Nonviolence and Racial Justice. *Christian Century*, February 6: 165–167.

King, Martin Luther, Jr. 1958. *Stride toward Freedom: The Montgomery Story.* New York: Harper and Row.

Jennifer Jensen Wallach

KINSEY, ALFRED
1894–1956

No figure in twentieth-century American sexuality is more influential, controversial, or misunderstood than

Alfred Charles Kinsey. Kinsey was born on June 23, 1894, in Hoboken, New Jersey, a product of working-class Protestant culture. Throughout his life, Kinsey struggled with the contradictions of a profoundly moralistic attitude toward sexuality and faith, a love of nature and the Boy Scouts, and a zealous commitment to purge sexual education of its religiosity and moralism. Following a doctor of science degree from Harvard University (1919), Kinsey became a highly respected entomologist and naturalist, with an unshakable belief in science and a fascination with sex. His research was undertaken primarily at Indiana University beginning in 1920, where he eventually founded the Kinsey Institute (1946) and conducted the largest survey study of American sexuality, unsurpassed until the 1990s.

Kinsey's work represented a scientific reaction to Sigmund Freud's (1856–1939) popular developmental sexuality and the sexual "psychopath" laws that sprang from its medical model. Kinsey famously created a population-based questionnaire emphasizing the diversity of sexuality and the collection of representative numbers of individual interviews to understand sexual behavior across the course of life. Even homosexuality was, for Kinsey, a variation of the norm, and unlike Freud, Kinsey believed that it was better to express, rather than sublimate, these desires. Culture was largely an impediment to sexuality in his model, however, since he believed that culture and religion undermined sexual desire and pleasure, resulting in "unnecessary" sexual taboos.

Between the late 1930s and 1950s, Kinsey and colleagues collected more than 5,300 male sexual histories and 5,940 female histories, many actually conducted by Kinsey, subsequently published in two books: *Sexual Behavior in the Human Male* (1948) and *Sexual Behavior in the Human Female* (1953). Demonstrating that Americans' beliefs were at odds with "reality," Kinsey showed that masturbation, homosexuality, and premarital and extramarital sexual relations for men and women were far more common than previously believed. The famous "Kinsey scale" of heterosexual to homosexual, based upon seven kinds of preference, countered the conventions of male/female, heterosexual/homosexual binaries. The methodology was criticized for its white male bias, behavioralism, lack of African American sample, and overrepresentation of homosexuals. Although Kinsey sometimes interviewed the same person at two different times, he always used only the most recent interview score, which was aggregated into the general sample, thus militating against the sense of dynamic change across the life course of individuals (Herdt 1990).

Politically attacked from its inception, Kinsey's research facilitated social progress in attitudes and laws regarding American sexuality, particularly on issues sur-

rounding the frequency of female sexual pleasure and masturbation, the normalization of homosexuality, and sexual expression outside of marriage. Such cultural changes, of course, represented challenges to gender and familial stereotypes and cold war ideologies. Historians have argued that Kinsey's empirical data—such as, for example, the finding that 37 percent of all American males had had some homosexual experience—was significant in changing sexual attitudes, perhaps laying the groundwork for second-wave feminism, the sexual revolution, and the gay and lesbian social movement. By compelling a different understanding of the world in which they were growing up, individuals who came of age under the influence of the Kinsey reports in the media and popular culture of the late 1950s and early 1960s greeted sexuality through the lens of changing norms about masturbation, female sexuality, and homosexuality. The absolute influence of taboos and laws was to some extent mediated by a growing idea of cultural relativism and social constructionism in universities. Armed with new knowledge and data that laid the foundation for social advocacy in society and the university, second-wave feminism and the gay and lesbian movement began the push toward greater tolerance for new gender roles and sexual diversity in America. In subsequent decades, the roots of these changes in Kinsey's works were sometimes eclipsed, but a rash of new biographies and filmic studies suggests a renewed appreciation for the pivotal role of this seminal thinker in American sexuality.

SEE ALSO *Hite, Shere; Sexuality*

BIBLIOGRAPHY

Gathorne-Hardy, Jonathan. 2000. *Sex, the Measure of All Things: A Life of Alfred C. Kinsey*. Bloomington: Indiana University Press.

Herdt, Gilbert. 1990. Developmental Continuity as a Dimension of Sexual Orientation Across Cultures. In *Homosexuality/Heterosexuality: Concepts of Sexual Orientation*, ed. David McWhirter, June M. Reinisch, and Stephanie Sanders, 208–238. New York: Oxford University Press.

Kinsey, Alfred C., Wardell B. Pomeroy, and Clyde E. Martin. 1948. *Sexual Behavior in the Human Male*. Philadelphia: Saunders.

Kinsey, Alfred C., Wardell B. Pomeroy, Clyde E. Martin, and Paul H. Gebhardt. 1953. *Sexual Behavior in the Human Female*. Philadelphia: Saunders.

Robinson, Paul. 1976. *The Modernization of Sex: Havelock Ellis, Alfred Kinsey, William Masters, and Virginia Johnson*. New York: Harper and Row.

Gilbert Herdt

KINSEY REPORT
SEE *Kinsey, Alfred.*

KINSHIP

Kinship refers to relationships among individuals and groups that are based on descent or marriage. The study of kinship covers how different cultures conceptualize these relationships, the linguistic terms by which they distinguish and classify kin, marriage rules and practices, and the social, political, economic, religious, and symbolic uses that human societies make of kinship. Kinship is a human universal, found in all societies, although the cross-cultural variation in all these aspects of kinship is significant.

Anthropologists use a particular set of symbols to represent kinship relations, see Figure 1. These symbols are used to construct kinship diagrams for many different purposes. For example, they can be used to represent an individual's genealogy as in Figure 2, which shows a male (called "ego" and shaded in the diagram) in relation to an array of relatives. This diagram also shows that ego's four grandparents are deceased and that while many of ego's relatives are married, his mother's brother is divorced and his mother's brother's son is unmarried but has a sexual relationship with a partner.

The diagram labels ego's kin with English terms that follow the Eskimo terminology system (named after the Inuit, who were once called Eskimos). Other terminology

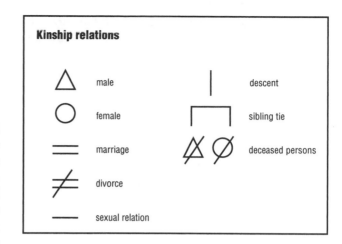

Figure 1

systems classify kin differently. For example, in the Hawaiian system, ego calls all female kin of his parent's generation (mother, mother's sister, and father's sister) by the same term he or she uses for mother. Worldwide, there are only a few major types of kinship terminology systems.

As with kinship terminology systems, societies vary in how they trace descent and how they use it to form important groups. Some societies follow unilineal descent, meaning that they trace membership in descent groups through one gender only. Unilineal descent may be either patrilineal (tracing descent only through males) or matrilineal (tracing descent only through females). In patrilineal descent, both male and female children inherit

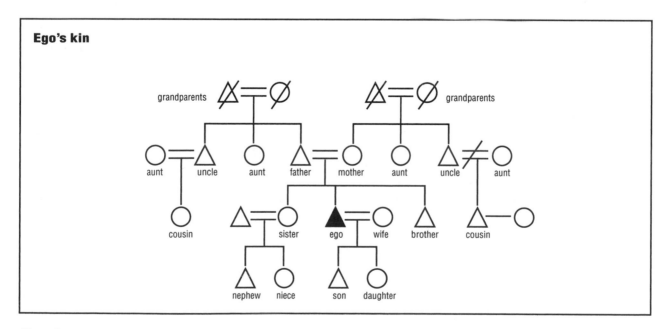

Figure 2

affiliation with their father's descent group, but only males pass on membership to their children. Chinese societies show examples of patrilineal descent. In the matrilineal case, male and female children are members of their mother's descent group, but only females pass on this membership to their children. The Navajo Native Americans are an example of a matrilineal group. Unilineal societies trace descent through one gender only, but in virtually all societies individuals trace many other ties of kinship bilaterally, or through both parents.

Other societies trace descent cognatically, or through both males and females. All descendants of a founding ancestor may be members of the descent group. An example is the Kwaio of the Solomon Islands, where cognatic descent groups control territory and their members have rights to use this land. Most people of Europe and North America perceive descent cognatically but do not use this principle of decent to form significant groups.

Worldwide, patrilineal descent is the most common, covering an estimated 44 percent of world cultures. Societies tracing descent through both genders account for another 36 percent, whereas matrilineal descent covers about 15 percent of world cultures. Another rare descent type accounts for the final 5 percent.

Many societies with unilineal or cognatic descent use these descent principles to form important groups such as lineages and clans. Lineages are kin groupings in which members are cognizant of the paths through which they trace common descent. Clans are kin groups in which the exact routes by which people trace common descent are not known or considered: Individuals simply know their clan affiliations by inheriting a clan name from a parent. Some societies have both clans and lineages, in which case the lineages are subdivisions of the clans. The founding ancestors of clans are often considered to be mythological animals, plants, or special objects. Many clans have origin myths about how they were created from such mythological forces.

In many societies descent reckoning thus links individuals and groups together into larger kinship units in such a way that descent is a fundamental framework for the social and political organization of a people. In some societies descent groups are extremely important and powerful. They can be large corporations, owning property and other resources in common and transmitting rights to such property over the generations. Often descent groups are interwoven with religion, where, for example, members worship their ancestors in common.

One of the ways in which descent groups are important in the lives of individuals is that descent group membership specifies whom one may or may not marry. Very often descent groups are exogamous, that is, marriage is forbidden within them. In these cases, descent groups may arrange marriages with outside groups as a means of forging important social and political alliances with them. In other cases, descent group endogamy, or marriage within the group, is permitted or encouraged; for example, a man in a patrilineal system may be allowed or encouraged to marry his father's brother's daughter (or a father's father's brother's son's daughter). One consequence of descent group endogamy is that the wealth that both brides and grooms may inherit can be kept within the descent group.

Like notions of descent, the institution of marriage is found in all human cultures. Marriage may either be monogamous (two people, usually a man and a woman, are united in marriage), polygynous (a man is married to more than one woman at the same time), or polyandrous (a woman is married to more than one man at the same time). Monogamous marriages are the most common worldwide. Many societies permit polygyny, but in these, polygynous unions may account for only a fraction of all marriages. Polyandry is rare, but is found among some Tibetan populations and a few other groups.

Along with relationships of descent and marriage, anthropologists have studied how societies construct so-called "fictive" kinship, that is, kin-like relationships locally understood to be apart from standard kinship. Examples include adopted children, ritual siblings such as "blood brothers," and godparents. These kinds of relationships are found worldwide.

The study of family relationships is important in many social sciences, but kinship studies developed as a particularly significant specialty within the discipline of anthropology. Beginning in the late nineteenth century, the work of Lewis Henry Morgan (1818–1881) in the United States brought kinship into the fold of the discipline. Morgan focused on kinship terminology systems and interpreted them as reflecting earlier levels or stages of peoples' cultural evolution. This evolutionary perspective of Morgan and others was discredited by later anthropologists, but ever since Morgan, kinship study has continued to reflect the currents of the broader theoretical perspectives within anthropology.

By the 1970s anthropology had accumulated a considerable body of kinship data worldwide. But by this time also, some anthropologists contended that anthropological concepts of kinship had grown too rigid, that they did not quite fit with the way local peoples themselves were conceptualizing their own kinship. In this context, David Schneider in the United States and Rodney Needham in England charged that anthropological kinship was seriously flawed. Schneider in particular pointed out that anthropological concepts of kinship were rooted in notions of biological procreation, reflecting "kinship" as understood in the particular cultural framework of the

Western world. However, other cultures often construct "kinship" relationships on other bases, such as common residence or food sharing. In other words, the anthropological concept of kinship had been an ethnocentric imposition of Western cultural constructs on other cultures.

With this critique, kinship in anthropology suffered a twenty-year decline, although it was kept alive within feminist anthropology, where it was studied in relation to gender. By this time a shift in kinship studies was evident. Over the first half of the twentieth century anthropologists studied kinship primarily as a key to peoples' social, political, and economic structures, often drawing comparisons among cultures. Through the 1980s, by contrast, kinship studies were conducted from within each culture separately, in terms of purely local categories and cultural meanings.

Kinship not only survived in anthropology, but, beginning in the 1990s, it revived. Influencing this revival was Janet Carsten, who sought to broaden the concept of kinship to make it cross-culturally valid. The work of Carsten and others also reflected another trend: the view of kinship as process. Their research demonstrated that in many societies kinship statuses or ties are not set once and for all by acts of birth, but rather emerge, strengthen, or fade through the process of human interactions, for example, the giving and receiving of food. Kinship studies of this period also incorporated the idea of kinship as choice. In the United States and Europe, for example, studies of gay or lesbian families, as well as studies of "blended" families consisting of stepparents and stepsiblings, have shown that meaningful kinship construction can be as much a matter of choice and commitment as biological connection.

In the opening decades of the twenty-first century the central question of kinship studies became not so much "How do kinship systems work?" but rather, "How do people work cultural constructions of kinship?" How do individual human actors confirm, challenge, or change these constructions? With this emphasis kinship studies focused on a wide variety of topics, including the impact on kinship constructions of the new reproductive technologies and new family forms, and the intersection of kinship with political struggles and transformations.

SEE ALSO *Family*

BIBLIOGRAPHY

Carsten, Janet. 1995. The Substance of Kinship and the Heat of the Hearth: Feeding, Personhood, and Relatedness Among Malays in Pulau Langkawi. *American Ethnologist* 22: 223–241.

Fox, Robin. 1989. *Kinship and Marriage: An Anthropological Perspective.* Cambridge, U.K.: Cambridge University Press.

Parkin, Robert. 1997. *Kinship: An Introduction to Basic Concepts.* Oxford: Blackwell Publishers.

Pasternak, Burton, Carol R. Ember, and Melvin Ember. 1997. *Sex, Gender, and Kinship: A Cross-Cultural Perspective.* Upper Saddle River, NJ: Prentice Hall.

Schneider, David M. 1984. *A Critique of the Study of Kinship.* Ann Arbor: University of Michigan Press.

Stone, Linda. 2006. *Kinship and Gender: An Introduction.* 3rd ed. Boulder, CO: Westview Press.

Linda Stone

KINSHIP, EVOLUTIONARY THEORY OF

Altruistic behavior—"self-sacrificial behavior performed for the benefit of others" (Wilson 1975, p. 578)—has long been a paradox for evolutionary theorists, because natural selection favors traits that contribute to the reproductive success ("individual fitness") of those who possess or perform them. Hence, altruism, which by definition contributes to the reproductive success of competitions at the expense of performers, ought not to evolve by natural selection. Yet it is widespread in nature. The sterile worker castes in bees, ants, and wasps provide prime examples (Wilson 1975). In 1964 William Hamilton, a graduate student at the University of London, saw that biological altruism can evolve, even though it reduces the individual reproductive success of the help's donor, if it aids the donor's genetic kin, some of whom inherit the helping allele from a common ancestor of the donor and recipient.

Consider C, the cost to a donor of a helping act, and B, the benefit of the act to a recipient. Hamilton's statement can be expressed as $Br_1 > Cr_2$ where r_1 equals the probability that the recipient's offspring has a copy of a helping allele inherited from a common ancestor of the donor and recipient, such as a parent or grandparent; and r_2 equals the probability that the donor's own offspring would have a copy of the same helping allele inherited from a common ancestor, such as a parent or grandparent. These probabilities are called "genetic correlations" or "coefficients of relatedness" between individuals.

As an example, consider a donor who inherited a helping allele from his mother for giving up one offspring to help a half-sibling produce three additional offspring. This allele was inherited via the common parent of the half siblings, their mother. When an organism reproduces, only one of each pair of chromosomes is passed to its gamete (Mendel's law of segregation), which unites with a gamete from another individual to produce the zygote that grows into an adult. Therefore, the probability that any particular allele at a locus on a chromosome in a parent is passed on to its offspring is 0.5. There are two gamete-producing reproductive events between the donor and any of his or her three *additional* half nieces or nephews produced *because* of the help: One produces the half-sibling that is being helped; the other produces each of the three offspring of the half-sibling who is being helped (the half-nieces and half-nephews of the donor) *because* of the help. Therefore, there is a 0.5 × 0.5 = 0.25 chance that any one of them inherits a copy of the helping allele possessed by the donor, their uncle or aunt. Putting these numbers into the above equation produces 3(0.25) > 1(0.50); 0.75 > 0.50.

Hence, natural selection can favor the evolution of psychological mechanisms for producing helping behaviors directed to genetic relatives. Note that both sides of the equation refer to changes in the helper's reproductive success *because* of helping acts. The right side, Cr_2, indicates the direct reproductive cost to the donor through offspring not produced, whereas the left side, Br_1, indicates the indirect reproductive benefits to the donor through *additional* offspring—a genetic relative produced *because* of the help. This reasoning leads to replacing the concept of individual fitness with the concept of "inclusive fitness," the reproductive success of an individual adjusted by the help it gives and receives from genetic relatives. *Kin selection* refers to natural selection acting via inclusive fitness rather than via individual fitness. Finally, note that those desiring an evolutionary explanation for "true altruism," in which a donor receives no benefit for a helping act, will not find it in Hamilton's equation.

Hamilton's paper (1964) is one of the most important scientific papers of the twentieth century. First, it enables evolutionary explanations for a wide range of social interactions in organisms (Alcock 2005; Wilson 1975) and humans (Burnstein 2005; Buss 2004). Second, it shifted the focus in evolutionary thinking from the reproduction of individuals to the replication of genes. Albert Einstein gave us relativity theory when he imagined how the universe would look if he were riding on a beam of light; Hamilton gave us a new way of thinking about evolution when he imagined how natural selection would seem to work if he were riding on a gene as it crossed generations.

SEE ALSO *Altruism; Darwin, Charles; Evolutionary Psychology; Hamilton's Rule; Natural Selection; Sociobiology*

BIBLIOGRAPHY

Alcock, John. 2005. *Animal Behavior: An Evolutionary Approach.* 8th ed. Sunderland, MA: Sinauer Associates.

Burnstein, Eugene. 2005. Altruism and Genetic Relatedness. In *The Handbook of Evolutionary Psychology*, ed. David M. Buss, 528–551. Hoboken, NJ: Wiley.

Buss, David M. 2004. *Evolutionary Psychology: The New Science of the Mind.* 2nd ed. New York: Pearson.

Hamilton, William D. 1964. The Genetical Evolution of Social Behavior, I and II. *Journal of Theoretical Biology* 7: 1–52.

Wilson, E. O. 1975. *Sociobiology: The New Synthesis.* Cambridge, MA: Harvard University Press.

Charles Crawford

KISSINGER, HENRY
1923–

Henry Kissinger is a political scientist who served as national security adviser (1969–1975) and secretary of state (1973–1977) during the presidencies of Richard M. Nixon (1913–1994) and Gerald R. Ford (1913–2006).

Born Heinz Alfred Kissinger on May 27, 1923 in Fürth, Germany, Kissinger and his family escaped Nazi persecution by immigrating to New York City in 1938. Kissinger joined the U.S. army during World War II, and later earned his BA, MA, and PhD in government at Harvard University. After joining the Harvard faculty, in 1955 and 1956 Kissinger served as director of a study group set up by the Council on Foreign Relations to analyze the influence of nuclear arms on international relations. Although he served as a consultant to the Democratic administrations of John F. Kennedy (1917–1963) and Lyndon B. Johnson (1908–1973), Kissinger tried but failed to secure a major, influential position under either Kennedy or Johnson. Generally indifferent to party affiliations, Kissinger also served as a foreign and defense policy adviser to Governor Nelson A. Rockefeller of New York (1908–1979), a liberal Republican with presidential ambitions during the 1960s.

Partly because Kissinger was identified with the Rockefeller faction of the Republican Party, President Richard M. Nixon appointed Kissinger national security adviser in 1969. Kissinger perceived the United States to be experiencing a period of relative decline in its international power during the 1970s. He believed that U.S. foreign policy needed to adapt to this relative decline by practicing "power politics," or the politics of "realism," by reducing its ideological hostility and distrust of the Soviet Union and mainland China and protecting U.S. interests through the creation and maintenance of a balance of power and spheres of influence among major world powers. Kissinger had studied and developed the ideas of "realism" in international relations since he was a student at Harvard. His application of "realism" in Nixon's and Ford's foreign and defense policies was evident in the gradual U.S. military withdrawal from Vietnam, the negotiation and signing of the Strategic Arms Limitation Treaty (SALT) with the Soviet Union in 1972, and Nixon's diplomatic visit to Communist China in 1972. For their efforts in negotiating and securing a peace treaty to end the Vietnam War, Kissinger and Le Duc Tho, a North Vietnamese diplomat, received the Nobel Peace Prize in 1973.

Kissinger, however, found the practice of "power politics" to be more difficult in the Middle East. Oil-producing nations in the Middle East imposed an embargo on oil exports to the United States, and U.S.-Soviet relations were strained because of U.S. support of Israel during the Yom Kippur War of 1973. Nonetheless, Kissinger's diplomacy helped to achieve cease-fire agreements between Israel and Egypt and Israel and Syria. During the 1976 presidential election, Kissinger's "realism" was criticized by Democratic presidential nominee Jimmy Carter (b. 1924) for neglecting human rights and lacking a moral purpose.

After leaving the Ford administration in 1977, Kissinger headed an international consulting firm, lectured, wrote his memoirs, and occasionally advised Presidents Ronald W. Reagan (1911–2004) and George H. W. Bush (b. 1924) on foreign policy. In 1983 Seymour Hersh, an American journalist, published *The Price of Power*, in which he implicated Kissinger in several controversial decisions of Nixon's foreign policy such as the 1970 invasion of Cambodia, the massive U.S. bombing of North Vietnam in 1972, and the 1973 overthrow of President Salvador Allende of Chile. During the 1990s more national security documents and other government sources pertaining to Kissinger's roles as national security adviser and secretary of state were made available to researchers. Using some of these primary sources, Christopher Hitchens, a British journalist, published *The Trial of Henry Kissinger* (2001), denouncing Kissinger as a war criminal. In particular, Hitchens argued that Kissinger's influence on U.S. foreign policy prolonged the Vietnam War, violated human rights and international law, and contributed to politically motivated mass murders in Chile, Cambodia, East Timor, and elsewhere.

Kissinger refused to publicly comment on Hitchens's book. He continued to lecture, write, and manage his consulting firm, Kissinger and Associates. He briefly served as chairman of the 9/11 Commission in 2002, but resigned after Democrats claimed that there were conflicts of interest between his chairmanship and consulting firm.

SEE ALSO *Diplomacy; Nixon, Richard M.; Nobel Peace Prize; Realism, Political; Union of Soviet Socialist Republics; Vietnam War*

BIBLIOGRAPHY

PRIMARY WORKS

Kissinger, Henry. 1979. *White House Years.* Boston: Little, Brown.

SECONDARY WORKS

Hanhimaki, Jussi. 2004. *The Flawed Architect: Henry Kissinger and American Foreign Policy.* New York: Oxford University Press.

Hersh, Seymour. 1983. *The Price of Power: Kissinger in the Nixon White House.* New York: Summit.

Hitchens, Christopher. 2001. *The Trial of Henry Kissinger.* London: Verso.

Isaacson, Walter. 1982. *Kissinger.* New York: Simon and Schuster.

Sean J. Savage

KITCHEN DEBATE

SEE *Khrushchev, Nikita; Nixon, Richard M.*

KITCHIN CYCLE

SEE *Business Cycles, Real.*

KLEIN, LAWRENCE
1920–

Lawrence R. Klein was born in Omaha, Nebraska, in 1920, graduated from the University of California at Berkeley in 1942, and went on to receive in 1944 the first PhD awarded by a Department of Economics at MIT that was, like himself, at the very beginning of a long and eminent career. Klein's first post was a three-year stint as research associate of the Cowles Commission at the University of Chicago; Cowles was then strongly oriented to econometrics, and was certainly an important influence on Klein's early research interests. In 1949 he migrated to teaching and research posts at the University of Michigan. He was driven from Ann Arbor, and from the United States, by the McCarthy witch hunt, and went in 1954 to the Institute of Statistics at Oxford. In 1958 he became professor of economics at the University of Pennsylvania, then University Professor and Benjamin Franklin Professor, until his formal retirement in 1991.

Klein's long and distinguished career led to an enormous list of articles, many books, thirty or more honorary degrees, a series of visiting professorships, the presidency of the Econometric Society in 1960 and the American Economic Association in 1977, the John Bates Clark Medal of the American Economic Association in 1959, and the Alfred Nobel Memorial Prize in Economic Sciences in 1980. It is safe to say that what honors were available, he has had.

Beginning with the publication of *Economic Fluctuations in the United States, 1921–1941* (1950), Klein succeeded the Dutch economist Jan Tinbergen (1903–1994) as the preeminent macroeconometric model builder in the United States and the world. With a series of coauthors, he produced a larger and improved model of the United States in 1955 and a model of the United Kingdom in 1961, participated in the Brookings quarterly econometric model of the United States (1965, 1969, 1975), and was the guiding force in the Wharton model of the United States (1967, 1968). From its start in 1968, Klein led a large group of participants in Project LINK, a systematic effort to link together, through explicit trade and capital flows, as many national econometric models as could be mustered. In his eightieth year, Klein was actively engaged in the econometric modeling of the Chinese economy.

His first macroeconometric models were Keynesian in inspiration, drawing on *The Keynesian Revolution* (1947, based on his PhD thesis). They were primarily models of aggregate demand. Later versions began to add a supply side and a model of inflation. In view of later controversies in academic macroeconomics, it is useful to note that one of Klein's earliest articles (1946) was on "Macroeconomics and the Theory of Rational Behavior." In those days, attention to "microfoundations" amounted to asking if this or that macro-equation could arise from the approximate aggregation of the behavior of rational agents. That still seems more sensible than the current tendency to a much more literal interpretation that leads to the casual acceptance of extreme assumptions for no better reason.

From the beginning, Klein was motivated by the possibility that empirical macromodels could be used to guide fiscal and monetary policy, and to estimate the effects of other policy measures. Sixty years later, the technique is still highly imperfect. But nothing better has been found in practice; and central banks, government agencies, and international agencies all over the world maintain and use econometric models that are direct descendants of Klein's lifework.

BIBLIOGRAPHY

PRIMARY WORKS

Klein, Lawrence. 1946. Macroeconomics and the Theory of Rational Behavior. *Econometrica* 14: 93–108.

Klein, Lawrence. 1950. *Economic Fluctuations in the United States, 1921–1941.* New York: Wiley.

Klein, Lawrence. [1947] 1966. *The Keynesian Revolution.* 2nd ed. New York: Macmillan.

Klein, Lawrence. 1976. Five-Year Experience of Linking National Econometric Models and of Forecasting International Trade. In *Quantitative Studies of International Economic Relations*, ed. Herbert Glejser. Amsterdam: North-Holland.

Klein, Lawrence, R. James Ball, Arthur Hazlewood, and Peter Vandome. 1961. *An Econometric Model of the United Kingdom.* Oxford: Blackwell.

Klein, Lawrence, James Duesenberry, Gary Fromm, and Edwin Kuh, eds. 1965. *The Brookings Quarterly Econometric Model of the United States.* Chicago: Rand McNally.

Klein, Lawrence, and Michael K. Evans. 1968. *The Wharton Econometric Forecasting Model.* 2nd ed. Philadelphia: Wharton School of Finance and Commerce.

Klein, Lawrence, and Arthur S. Goldberger. 1955. *An Econometric Model of the United States, 1929–1952.* Amsterdam: North Holland.

Klein, Lawrence, and Shinichi Ichimura, eds. 2000. *Econometric Modeling of China.* Singapore: World Scientific.

Robert M. Solow

KNESSET, THE

The Knesset is the unicameral parliament of the State of Israel, and as such it is the country's highest legislative body. There are 120 members of Knesset (MK), who are elected to four-year terms in office. In addition to passing legislation, the Knesset also appoints Israel's president—a largely symbolic position—and the state comptroller. In addition, the Knesset has the authority to dissolve itself by simple majority, which would result in the holding of new elections and the formation of a new government. The Knesset meets in Jerusalem, the capital of Israel. When the State of Israel was initially established in May 1948, the Knesset sat in Tel Aviv. It moved to Jerusalem in December 1949 and has remained there ever since.

Because Israel does not have a written constitution, the rules and regulations governing how the Knesset functions—and even its establishment—are laid down in Israel's Basic Laws. According to "Basic Law: The Knesset," article 4, elections for the Knesset are to be "general, country-wide, direct, equal, secret, and proportional" (Government of Israel 2004). Israel has universal suffrage for all citizens aged eighteen and over, and all citizens are eligible to vote in these elections. In this respect, elections for the Knesset are viewed as general elections, as opposed to elections for municipal officers. With respect to the elections being "country-wide," for the purposes of

Knesset elections, the entire country is considered one district. There are not separate electoral districts based on geographic region for distribution of Knesset seats.

Numerous parties participate in Israeli politics and are represented in the Knesset. According to the 1992 Parties Law, a *party* is defined as "a group of persons who joined together in order to promote in a legal way political or social objectives and to express them in the Knesset by their representatives." Parties can be established by registering the signatures of one hundred adult Israeli citizens who are residents of Israel. However, a party is prohibited from registering or competing in the electoral-legislative process if one of the following four conditions is found to be present in its "objectives or actions": (1) it rejects the existence of Israel as a Jewish and democratic state; (2) it encourages racism; (3) it supports the armed struggle against the State of Israel by either terrorist organizations or enemy states; and (4) it is believed that the party will be used "for illegal activities."

In order to gain entry to the Knesset, a party must obtain 2 percent of the votes cast in the election. Since the entire country is one "district" for the purpose of Knesset elections, parties must receive 2 percent of all votes cast throughout the country in order to be represented in the Knesset. The division of seats in the Knesset is based on a system of proportional representation. The number of seats that each party receives in the chamber is proportional to the number of votes it receives in the election, once the 2 percent threshold has been passed. Previously, the threshold had been as low as 1 or 1.5 percent, but it was raised to 2 percent in 2003. Individuals are elected to the Knesset based on what are known as *closed party lists*. In other words, when an Israeli citizen votes in a Knesset election, he or she votes for a particular party, not for an individual representative. Different parties choose their slate of representatives in different ways, but the individual voter does not get to select individual representatives on election day.

As a result of this system, no party has ever received the necessary majority (sixty-one seats) to form a government on its own. In this respect, Israeli governments have always comprised multiple parties, or, in other words, they are coalition governments. Occasionally, parties have been able to form "minority" governments (a coalition of fewer than sixty-one seats) with the support of Arab parties that vote with the government but are not formal members of the coalition. At the same time, the relatively low threshold necessary to gain entry into the Knesset has also resulted in the proliferation of numerous small parties into the Knesset and in the Israeli political system as a whole. There are parties representing all different groups of Israeli society, ranging from religious to secular, right wing to socialist, and parties that specifically represent

Arab citizens. Generally, however, Israeli politics has been dominated by large left-leaning parties (e.g., Labor and its predecessors) and right-leaning parties (e.g., Likud and its predecessors), with smaller parties and religious parties floating between the larger parties to create the government coalitions.

As the parliament, the Knesset is responsible for writing and passing legislation. Bills must pass three readings before they are signed into law. There is no process of judicial review. However, existing legislation may be amended or canceled by the passage of a new bill. Additionally, there is no authority that has power to veto legislation that is passed by the Knesset. While the Knesset has supreme legislative authority, in matters concerning "personal status," such as marriage, divorce, or burial, it is the various religious denominations that set the rules, based on their own religious laws. In other words, the Jewish authorities regulate marriage and divorce for Jewish citizens, the Muslim religious authorities do the same for Muslim citizens, and the Christian religious authorities for Christian citizens.

As a parliamentary system, the prime minister is usually the head of the largest party in the Knesset. However, in an attempt to create more stability in the Knesset and the governments, between May 1996 and March 2001 the prime minister was directly elected separately from the rest of the Knesset. The election did not have the intended consequences, however, and many argued that the "reform" was a resounding failure. The direct election provision was quickly repealed, and the prime minister is again the head of the largest party in the Knesset.

SEE ALSO *Parliaments and Parliamentary Systems*

BIBLIOGRAPHY

Government of Israel. 2003. The Knesset at Work: Legislation. http://www.knesset.gov.il/description/eng/eng_work_mel2.htm.

Government of Israel. 2004. The Knesset in the Government System: The Electoral System in Israel. http://www.knesset.gov.il/description/eng/eng_mimshal_beh.htm.

Peretz, Don, and Gideon Doron. 1997. *The Government and Politics of Israel.* 3rd ed. Boulder, CO: Westview.

Rachel Bzostek

KNOWLEDGE

If someone asks, "What is knowledge?" science seems a likely answer. Its impact is enormous, and its method is logical and rigorous, immunized from personal bias, and based on repeatable experiments revealing predictable facts of the universe. But can one live by science alone? One should not overlook the "who-why" question: "Who wants to know, and why?" The twenty-first-century economy seems even more dependent on knowledge than when the extracting and producing industries were dominant and natural science seemed all one needed to know. Now the economy comprises "knowledge workers," information technology, intellectual property, collaborative networks—to say nothing of laws, customs, culture, and the other aspects of social life—so it is probably even more important to understand what the term *knowledge* means.

The study of knowledge is *epistemology*, a type of philosophizing that differs from metaphysics, logic, aesthetics, or ethics. From Plato (427–347 BCE) one learns that knowledge is "justified true belief." When one believes something to be true, the burden of demonstrating it as knowledge rather than mere opinion falls on how it is justified or "warranted." In René Descartes's (1596–1650) time, "full justification" was taken to mean that a statement was certain beyond doubt. Knowing that the senses can be deceived, Descartes attacked our knowing with radical doubt. He argued that only our own thinking is unmediated by the senses, so our only certainty is the mind's certainty of itself. This positioning of reasoning cut through millennia of muddled debate and established knowledge as the antithesis of doubt, rather than the achievement of certainty. But epistemology has struggled ever since with the damage done: a loss of innocence spawning a plurality of epistemologies, each defining doubt and knowledge differently. We shall look at knowledge through this multi-epistemic prism, focusing on doubt and outlining the types of knowledge emerging, and conclude with their integration. Rather than merely list the knowledge types spoken of today (explicit, tacit, social, individual, practical, emotional, etc.), our analysis proposes a framework for their mutual constitution.

Descartes presumed that thinking should be logical; operating correctly, the mind is computer-like. This view sets emotion, also unmediated by the senses, in opposition to cold reason, dismissing emotion from knowing. Second, with both sense-data and emotion dismissed, there can be no knowledge of the world beyond the mind's computations—for example, of the physical world in which the brain seemingly exists. So what can be known is of no relevance to our world, and what is certain is so because it is tautologous, like a mathematical proof. Given these assumptions, this conclusion is inescapable. Knowledge is also individual, private, within the mind, and detached from the interests, discourses, and activities of our fellows, denying Francis Bacon's (1561–1626) maxim that "knowledge is power."

Logicality is powerful justification, but alone it demands too much. Scientific knowledge is a compromise between logic and other warrants that allows knowledge of the world beyond Cartesian tautology without demanding certainty. Instead of entirely removing doubt, science treats doubt as pervasive, a condition to be managed. Reaching beyond the mind, all doubt-managing, as opposed to doubt-rejecting, epistemologies take off from assumptions about what and where we are—thinking, memorizing, observing, experiencing, and so forth—though each person orders these differently. For most people, science is a variation on realism and embraces, for instance, positivism and critical realism. Realisms presume a logical and observable reality "out there," independent of our observing. All knowledge is of this reality. Sense-data is prioritized over what we think, over opinion. Science aspires to the facts of this reality, though, afflicted by doubt, we know our impressions are conjectures, never certainties.

In contrast to realism, idealist or interpretive epistemologies like phenomenology bring us closer to Descartes, prioritizing the mind over assumptions about reality. They presume we can never know reality's essence, and this is not our target; indeed our senses may be incapable of capturing it. All we can know is experience and our senses' impact on our thinking. This becomes ordered as we lay mental maps or meaning systems over our experience, capturing it as knowledge. We make this our knowledge of the world, rather than our imaginings, by using it to predict our experience. We may structure it as causal relationships, but, as David Hume (1711–1776) argued, we impose such causality; we cannot observe it at work. Knowledge as meaning takes us a step back from immediate sense-data about the objects that comprise the world and into generalizations, relations, associations, covering laws, and so forth. Though epistemologically distinct, facts and covering laws are both representations of the world. Facts make the stronger claim, purporting to describe the world as it really is, but covering laws may be more useful, describing relations or forces between the factlike objects comprising the world.

All epistemologies seek justified truth-yielding links between our thinking and the world beyond the mind, which obviously includes our brains and bodies. Each epistemology adopts different strategies to manage the doubt involved. Naive realism, for instance, proposes that the mind is in intimate contact with nature; things are what they seem to be and doubt does not enter. Knowledge is individual. Justified true belief differs, for it moves knowledge beyond the privacy of the mind, presupposing its capture in a shared language whose construction and interpretation is knowing. Scientific knowledge is intersubjective, beyond the individual, and necessarily contextualized to a specific society and located in its discursive spaces and activities—book-learning statements in libraries or at conferences, for instance.

Statements can be conjectural, as Albert Einstein's (1879–1955) were, to be tested later, or they can be empirical, based on past experience of the world. Our hypothesizing and experimentation integrates our thinking and observing, and doubt is managed through science's intersubjective processes, supported by open discourse, multiple experiments, statistical analysis, and criticism. Disputes about whether or not this process manages doubt adequately comprise the philosophy of science (Curd and Cover 1998). Some argue that experimental confirmations raise confidence in our conjectures. Karl Popper (1902–1994), in contrast, sought falsification, seeing logical asymmetry between verification and rejection. This is an error. Rejection depends on observation theory too, so experimentation merely compares science's confidence in the theorizing behind the hypothesis and the observation. As neither is free of doubt, the outcome remains logically ambiguous.

The methods of science can generate knowledge of the entities comprising society, as well as of the objects and relationships comprising nature. Thus realist sociology and psychology are warrantable companions to realist physics, chemistry, and biology, but who-why questions loom larger as we move from the natural to the social sciences. In pragmatist epistemologies, the usefulness of knowledge becomes the truth criterion. Representational correctness gives way to utility or "cash value." Pragmatism is a flavor of realism in that it takes the world's existence for granted, though this world is social, technological, and political, rather than that of the natural scientist. Jürgen Habermas integrated pragmatism with our presumed common rationality to locate knowledge in the intersubjective discourse of the democratic "ideal speech situation," where knowledge is consensual and directed toward our interests, such as changing the lived world (Habermas 2003).

Reintroducing peoples' interests inclines us to think reflexively of ourselves as knowing. Given doubt and a pragmatic point of view, it may be more useful to know why someone acted as they did than to know the facts of the situation they faced. Two things are going on here. First, as an actor's knowledge is never free of doubt, there is a crucial difference between the facts and the actor's perception of them. Instead of knowing the causes that move people as objects, we seek the actor's perceptions and explanation of the situation. But this admits heterogeneity, for we know with all the force of *cogito ergo sum*, that people and their knowing differ. Second, doubt is transformed into the necessity to choose. Since reality cannot speak to us directly, we choose how to attend to and interpret the world. This choice transforms the relationship between the actor and the actor's knowledge, for this is now more than a representation to be applied through rational decision making; it is shaped by the actor's values

and intentions, and so by his or her emotions. Doubt and emotion become integral parts of our agency and interest in changing the world. When things are certain, our actions are wholly determined; we have no options, no way of manifesting ourselves in the world. Thus doubt, emotion, variety, and diversity challenge our notions of knowledge as universal.

Science works hard for universality, and, given doubt, agreement across the community of scientists becomes a proxy for objectivity and truth, seemingly limiting the impact of emotion. But the relativism implicit in perception raises subjective doubt, not so much separating the mind from the thing known as separating people, in their knowing, from each other and undercutting the idea of knowledge as intersubjective and shared. Once admitted, intersubjective doubt needs to be managed if we are to escape epistemological anarchy and the conclusion that knowledge is whatever one wishes it to be. The openness of scientific discourse seeks convergence, or at least some form of epistemological democracy. Rejecting naive realism or a "correspondence theory" of knowledge can lead to the universal consensuality of Habermas or, within a discipline, a Kuhnian paradigm that presumes that right-thinking scientists are in broad agreement. This "social constructionist" discourse institutionalizes scientific knowledge or, rather, manages doubt and emotion in institutionalized ways (Gergen 1994). Historical studies like Thomas Kuhn's (1922–1996), or those of sociologists of knowledge like Karl Mannheim (1893–1947) and Robert K. Merton (1910–2003), suggest that socially constructed knowledge may change sharply and unpredictably, like an ecology, and that the politics and clashing interests of the group may shape both its changes and what the group defines as knowledge. Power penetrates the discourse and process of justification.

Thus far this entry has touched on three principal modes of justification: reality, social agreement, and utility. All such post-Enlightenment epistemologies embrace reason and empiricism and stand against the transcendentalism that preceded them, when, perhaps, holy books or the Delphic oracle were the warrants for knowledge. These epistemologies also presuppose constancy of situation, reflecting the realist's assumption of nature's invariance. Will what was useful yesterday be useful tomorrow? Just as we know we differ, so we know situations change. Absent doubt, of course, we would be at that Archimedean fulcrum of equilibrium and truth from where we would understand change as the world's dynamic, just as we understand a clock in spite of its moving hands. But the phenomenological drift contradicted the idea of knowledge as just about the world "out there," turning us toward the notion of knowledge as more about ourselves and our agentic choices. Just as we become what we eat, we become what we choose to know. Knowledge is us, and this is clear for today's knowledge-intensive professional. But if by *us* we mean only what we think, we fall into the chasm of relativism that terrorizes all epistemologies. Social conformance might save us, implying that we become a member of a society or a profession as and because we share its body of knowledge. But knowledge's susceptibility to power and history makes us cautious. Is there a more justifiable basis for justification? Pragmatism's usefulness criterion seems a good way to go, but it is tricky to establish ahead of the action to be evaluated. Still, it brings justification back to us and our intentions.

Given doubt, and not finding definitive invariance in nature or social reality, we presume it in ourselves. Only then can our knowing be carried from one instance to another. This takes us back to the model of humans on which our epistemology stands. But as we probe our agency, we find imagination as well as rationality. Doubt attacks reasoning, interfering with computation and action; the computer freezes, yet we act anyway. John Locke (1632–1704) attributed this to "judgment," our native facility to arrive at conclusions in the absence of certain knowledge, that is, under conditions of doubt. To this point, what we might mean by "not-knowledge" has been dismissed as emotion or as falsified or undiscovered knowledge. Lockean judgment, on the other hand, implies forms of knowing beyond that captured in language. This suggests two things. First, as we negotiate the lived world we draw on these extra-linguistic forms of knowing. Second, knowing is no longer the application of knowledge abstracted and brought into the reasoning process; it is more intimately wrapped into the immediacy of living. Knowing is more than representing. It includes dealing with the unrepresented aspects of being in the world. Our knowing becomes who we are, integrating a complex of memorized facts and meanings, our ability to compute, and our ability to imagine as doubt intrudes and memory or reason fail. We redefine knowledge as our identity as we engage in effective practice.

The search for objectivity is also the observer's search for a vantage point outside and abstracted from the practice of living. Knowledge is what is left behind as the observer withdraws. In contrast, the phenomenological attitude ultimately draws us into the world, suggesting an engagement and intimacy of practice that generates a different kind of knowledge—the actor's epistemology proposed, for example, by Edmund Husserl (1859–1938) and Martin Heidegger (1889–1976). As we consider the action of the imagination as it deals with the experience of doubt, we move toward constructivist views, the idea that the only world we can know is the one we ourselves have constructed, that knowledge itself is a construction, a set of tools for dealing with living in the world. The critique must be equally applied to our assumptions about our-

selves. While senses, reason, and imagination may be necessary conditions for consciousness and agency, they are not sufficient. Our sense of ourselves is also a construction of these components and, penetrated again by doubt, we never know ourselves with certainty or completely.

Following the work of Michel Polanyi (1891–1976), it has become common to use the description "tacit" to point to this extralinguistic form of knowing, covering both the ability to act under conditions of doubt and, reflexively, to bridge the gap between our sense of identity and our doubting self-knowledge. What we mean by knowledge must cover both what is known explicitly, justified true belief about the natural, social and psychological entities comprising our world, and what we know tacitly, only evident in our ability to act and sustain our identity living under the normal conditions of doubt and uncertainty. Constructivist epistemologies, such as Ernst von Glasersfeld's (1995), show that constructing the world also sets its boundaries, the limits to what can be known about what we might refer to as the context of our situated knowledge. Ludwig Wittgenstein (1889–1951), who considered all truth to be carried in language, saw practice as giving language meaning. If individuals are the only agents, then constructivism is individual. But others see knowledge and agency as intersubjective and see groups, organizations, and societies as agentic, suggesting social or collective constructionism (Nelson and Winter 1982). So to the previous modes of justification—reality, social consensus, and utility—we can add efficient practice and identity. Practice is a complex—either the deductive application of reason and explicit knowledge, or the constructive application of our judgment or imagination that indicates our tacit knowledge. The pragmatist's utility criterion turns out to be far from project evaluation, performed from a point outside the practice itself. On the contrary, the constructivist view presupposes the instant-by-instant co-construction of meaning, context, and identity.

This multi-epistemic snapshot summarizes our different types of knowledge: realism suggests knowledge as data about the world "out there"; cognition focuses on the explicit systems of meaning we impose on our experience; while the immediacy of phenomenalism focuses us on various forms of practice, individual and collective, and the distinction between reasoning and imagining. Mnemonically we can distinguish *knowledge-as-data* from *knowledge-as-meaning* and *knowledge-as-practice*. In the same way that knowing embraces both what is known, memorized, and recoverable for abstract computation, it also includes the self-based judgment to cope with doubt. Practice embraces both the execution of rational plans and the recursive co-construction of self and context. Emotion is an aspect of that response, and emotional knowledge comes from observing the construction of self and being able, pragmatically, to apply that to the agentic process (Nussbaum 2001).

Today's knowledge-intensive lives entail integrating our knowing across these distinctions, imaginatively coping with the disjunctions and distinctions entering our thinking with our epistemology-originating assumptions. Integration comes into sight as we appreciate that each type of knowledge presumes the other. There can be no mind without the brain, no knowledge without the mind, no meaning or living without practice, no data without meaning, and so forth. Each mode of justification entails the others. To grasp today's meaning of "knowledge" we must first admit the multiple epistemologies spawned by Cartesian doubt while realizing our ability to traverse the void of doubt between them by deploying our native creativity to construct life's seeming coherence. Knowing harnesses our imagination and reason to our senses, memory, and language as we reach out agentically to our fellows. From this vantage point, our knowing is part of our consciousness and identity, but all of a piece, embracing knower and known, as each epistemology reflects its unique axiomatic emphasis as an analytic tool, disparate elements in our doubt-pervaded toolkit.

SEE ALSO *Cognition; Cognitive Dissonance; Collective Wisdom; Epistemology; Ideology; Information, Economics of; Intelligence; Intelligence, Social; Journalism; Knowledge Society; Knowledge, Diffusion of; Science; Social Cognition*

BIBLIOGRAPHY

Curd, Martin, and J. A. Cover, eds. 1998. *Philosophy of Science: The Central Issues.* New York: Norton.

Eden, Colin, and J. C. Spender, eds. 1998. *Managerial and Organizational Cognition: Theory, Methods, and Research.* Thousand Oaks, CA: Sage.

Gergen, Kenneth J. 1994. *Toward Transformation in Social Knowledge.* 2nd ed. New York: Sage.

Habermas, Jürgen. 2003. *Truth and Justification.* Trans. and ed. Barbara Fultner. Cambridge, MA: MIT Press.

Marr, Bernard, and J. C. Spender. 2004. Measuring Knowledge Assets: Implications of the Knowledge Economy for Performance Measurement. *Measuring Business Excellence* 8 (1): 18–27.

Nelson, Richard R., and Sidney G. Winter. 1982. *An Evolutionary Theory of Economic Change.* Cambridge MA: Belknap.

Nussbaum, Martha C. 2001. *Upheavals of Thought: The Intelligence of Emotions.* Cambridge, U.K.: Cambridge University Press.

Spender, J. C. 1989. *Industry Recipes: An Enquiry into the Nature and Sources of Managerial Judgement.* Oxford: Blackwell.

Spender, J. C. 2001. Management's Options in the Knowledge Economy. *Business/Higher Education Round Table News* 11: 10–12.

Spender, J. C. 2002. Knowledge Management, Uncertainty, and the Emerging Theory of the Firm. In *The Strategic Management of Intellectual Capital and Organizational Knowledge,* eds. Chun Wei Choo and Nick Bontis, 149–162. New York: Oxford University Press.

Spender, J. C. 2003. Exploring Uncertainty and Emotion in the Knowledge-based Theory of the Firm. *Information Technology and People* 16 (3): 266–288.

Spender, J. C. 2003. Knowledge Fields: Some Post 9/11 Thoughts about the Knowledge-based Theory of the Firm. In *Handbook on Knowledge Management,* ed. Clyde Holsapple, 59–71. Berlin: Springer-Verlag.

Spender, J. C. 2003. Multidimensional Theorizing: Some Methodological Comments about John Dunning's Eclectic Approach. In *Extending the Eclectic Paradigm in International Business: Essays in Honor of John Dunning,* ed. Peter Gray, 181–195. Northampton, MA: Elgar.

Spender, J. C. 2004. Knowing, Managing, and Learning. In *Essential Readings in Organizational Learning,* eds. Christopher Grey and Elena Antonacopoulou, 137–152. London: Sage.

Spender, J. C. 2005. An Overview: What's New and Important about Knowledge Management? Building New Bridges between Managers and Academics. In *Managing Knowledge: An Essential Reader,* eds. Steve Little and Tim Ray, 127–154. 2nd ed. Thousand Oaks, CA: Sage.

Spender, J. C. 2005. Speaking about Management Education: Some History of the Search for Academic Legitimacy and the Ownership and Control of Management Knowledge. *Management Decision* 43 (10): 1282–1292.

Spender, J. C. 2006. Getting Value from Knowledge Management. *TQM Magazine* 18 (3): 238–254.

Spender, J. C., and Hugo Kijne, eds. 1996. *Scientific Management: Frederick Winslow Taylor's Gift to the World?* Boston: Kluwer.

Spender, J. C., and Bernard Marr. 2005. A Knowledge-Based Approach to Human Capital. In *Perspectives on Intellectual Capital,* ed. Bernard Marr, 183–195. Boston: Elsevier.

von Glasersfeld, Ernst. 1995. *Radical Constructivism: A Way of Knowing and Learning.* London: Falmer.

J. C. Spender

KNOWLEDGE, DIFFUSION OF

Diffusion suggests a drop of color in water, spreading until uniformly distributed. Knowledge, such as the cause of a disease, can diffuse until "everybody knows." Diffusion is less specific than communication, and seems driven by the inherent tendency for the differentials between knowledge and ignorance to disappear, just as heat differences decay and entropy rises. But managing diffusion may be very different. Instead of knowledge moving under its own impulse, seeking equilibrium, knowledge needs to be "pushed" or "pulled." It may be "sticky," as if in a frictional medium; pressure is required to make knowledge flow. At other times, knowledge seems "slippery," and one struggles to prevent leakage. Knowledge is inherently diffusible because of its nonrivalrousness, there being no loss of knowledge by those who already have it as it is diffused to others who do not.

Stickiness and slipperiness seem inherent properties of different types of knowledge. But diffusion may be more shaped by the relationship between the knowledge being moved and the context or medium through which it is moving. Stickiness implies antipathy, whereas slipperiness implies a mutuality of context, a readiness to take up and move the knowledge along, as when rumors fly. Contexts can be local, as when one department resists sharing knowledge with another, or broad, as when new political ideas spread like wildfire.

The heterogeneity of diffusion contexts is explored in network theory. Early research reflected communications technology and distinguished "star" or "radial" networks from "wheel" and more complex interconnections. Recent research focuses on social systems and social capital, when the context of knowledge flow is shaped by political, social, or economic power, or by interconnectedness (centrality). Horizontal and vertical knowledge diffusion imply transfer between equals versus transfer between those with different social power or degrees of centrality. "Small world" or "scale-free" structures are particularly interesting, suggesting people are closer and knowledge flows more rapid than were social networks randomly connected (Watts 2003).

But people ignore questions like "what is knowledge?" and "what flows?" (Ryle 1949). Knowledge cannot be understood simply in contrast to ignorance, for that would require a person to know ignorance too. Knowledge is revealed by contrasting types of knowledge. The explicit/tacit distinction is often invoked to "explain" stickiness (e.g., Szulanski 1996; Boisot 1998), presuming a normal context is sympathetic to explicit messages but less so to tacit knowledge. Yet in other contexts, explicit knowledge may be sticky and resisted, and tacit knowledge slippery. The explicit message "smoking kills" is well known, but apparently not in ways that greatly affect the behavior of smokers. Child abuse is often based on cycles of slippery tacit knowledge-diffusion that seem difficult to break. In short, analyses of the diffusion of the "knowledges" shaping human behavior must consider both the heterogeneity of the modes of knowing and of the contexts of that knowing. Thus the analysis of knowledge diffusion calls up epistemological assumptions about human beings and the world to be known, and their interaction.

For many, knowledge is about gathering data about the world "out there." Data can be diffused or moved so long as the underlying notion of that world is shared and stable. Knowledge-as-data contrasts with knowledge-as-meaning, the lens that is put over data to make sense of it, to make it accessible to analysis. Meaning is about people rather than the world of facts, and diffusing it is different from diffusing data that fits within a shared meaning system. Language can only inform those who already speak it, and Ludwig Wittgenstein (1889–1951) argued that practice is the key to meaning. Data and meaning are mutually supporting and are tied together in information. Both are mental and imply stepping back and reflecting on one's experience of the world. But practice, in contrast, is in the world and the instant. Tacit knowledge is important because it draws attention to this third type of knowledge, knowledge-as-practice, which lies beyond data plus meaning.

Diffusing data means helping the receiver distinguish, within an agreed field of possibilities, the noted from the unnoted. But to diffuse meaning, you rely on receivers to add something of their own construction; you can only send data to another. Even more creative, to diffuse your practice, you rely on receivers to cope with the unique moment and context of their activity and construct practices that emulate yours. Thus practice is always embedded in its context and cannot be transferred to another. Diffusion means creating a new practice, guided rather than determined by prior practice.

BIBLIOGRAPHY

Boisot, Max H. 1998. *Knowledge Assets: Securing Competitive Advantage in the Information Economy.* Oxford: Oxford University Press.

Ryle, Gilbert. 1949. *The Concept of Mind.* London: Hutchinson.

Szulanski, Gabriel. 1996. Exploring Internal Stickiness: Impediments to the Transfer of Best Practice within the Firm. *Strategic Management Journal* 17 (Winter): 27–43. Special issue: *Knowledge and the Firm.*

Watts, Duncan J. 2003. *Six Degrees: The Science of a Connected Age.* New York: Norton.

J. C. Spender

KNOWLEDGE ECONOMY

SEE *Knowledge Society.*

KNOWLEDGE, GROUP

SEE *Collective Wisdom.*

KNOWLEDGE SOCIETY

The term *knowledge society* refers to a society in which the creation, dissemination, and utilization of information and knowledge has become the most important factor of production. In such a society, *knowledge assets* (also called *intellectual capital*) are the most powerful producer of wealth, sidelining the importance of land, the volume of labor, and physical or financial capital.

The term *knowledge society* has several meanings. First, it is used by social scientists to describe and analyze the transformation toward so-called postindustrial society. Second, it is used to refer to a normative vision that nations or companies should aspire to fulfill. Third, it is used as a metaphor, rather than a clear-cut concept, under which various topics are examined. In many cases, the distinction among these three usages is blurred, and it is not clear whether the author using the term is putting forward an analysis of current trends, is forecasting changes, or is proposing a strategy that should be followed.

Although the term is frequently evoked, it is rarely defined and explored in a systematic way. However, the key characteristics of a knowledge society can be outlined as follows: (1) the mass and polycentric production, transmission, and application of knowledge is dominant; (2) the price of most commodities is determined by the knowledge needed for their development and sale rather than by the raw material and physical labor that is needed to produce them; (3) a large portion of the population attains higher education; (4) a vast majority of the population have access to information and communication technologies and to the Internet; (5) a large portion of the labor force are *knowledge workers* who need a high degree of education and experience to perform their job well; (6) both individuals and the state invest heavily in education and research and development; and (7) organizations are forced to innovate continually.

EVOLUTION OF SOCIETAL DEVELOPMENT

All societies have rested on knowledge, and knowledge has always played an important role in the rise of prosperity and social well-being. Why then should we speak of this emerging type of society as a "knowledge society"? It is useful to contrast a knowledge society with previous types of human society that were based upon the dominant mode of production and the most common source of livelihood.

In a *hunting and gathering society*, the earliest societal type, people gained their livelihood from hunting, trapping, fishing, and gathering edible plants growing in the wild. About 8000 BCE, some hunting and gathering groups began raising domesticated animals and cultivating fixed plots of land. This domestication revolution led to the advent of *horticultural* and *pastoral societies*. A pastoral society is a society in which the primary means of subsistence is domesticated livestock, whereas in horticultural societies the primary means of subsistence is the cultivation of crops using hand tools. Many societies were pastoral and horticultural at the same time. The replacement of horticulture by agriculture is associated with the invention of the plow in about 3000 BCE in Mesopotamia and Egypt. This process, sometimes called the *agricultural revolution*, made large-scale agricultural production possible and led to the development of *agrarian societies*. The agricultural revolution had such a profound impact on society that many people call this era the "dawn of civilization." During this period, not only the plow, but also the wheel, writing, and numbers were invented. Nevertheless, in an agrarian society, land and livestock were the key resources.

Agrarian societies, in which most of the population was directly engaged in the production of food, began to be replaced by a new societal type around 1750 at the dawn of the Industrial Revolution. *Industrial Revolution* is a shorthand term for a complex set of technological innovations that led to a dramatic change in the nature of production in which machines replaced tools and inanimate power resources (such as steam and electricity) replaced human or animal power. Productivity and wealth creation in an *industrial society* is based upon the mechanized manufacturing of goods, or, more specifically, upon the extensive and organized use of machines in factories. In an industrial economy, physical assets such as steel, factories, and railroads are the key factors of production. A large majority of the employed population works in factories and offices (while the proportion of the population engaged in agriculture rapidly declines). In addition, people are geographically concentrated. Because most jobs can be found in towns and cities, people move to cities, and industrial society becomes highly urbanized.

THEORIES OF POSTINDUSTRIAL SOCIETIES

Since the 1960s, many authors have suggested that we are entering into a type of society beyond the industrial era altogether. The first comprehensive description of the so-called *postindustrial society* was provided by Daniel Bell (1973). According to Bell, service occupations grow at the expense of those producing material goods, and white-collar workers come to outnumber blue-collar workers employed in factories. Work in services generally requires more knowledge and intellectual ability than work in industrial occupations. Bell also argued that theoretical knowledge is the main strategic resource of society, and those who are concerned with its creation and distribution (scientists and professionals of all kinds) become the leading social group, replacing industrialists and entrepreneurs.

Some scholars have challenged Bell's ideas. First, his theory rests upon the now-obsolete distinction between primary (agriculture, mining, fishing, and forestry), secondary (industry), and tertiary (services) economic sectors. In contrast to Bell's assumption, the manufacturing sector is not declining in terms of its contribution to overall economic performance and growth. The term *postindustrial* is thus misleading because "industry" is neither disappearing nor losing its importance. Both within the agricultural and industrial sector, significant transformations are taking place: Even agriculture and industry are becoming more knowledge-intensive, and thus more productive. In contrast, many jobs in services are in fact blue-collar (such as a gas-station attendant), while many white-collar positions involve very little specialized knowledge.

Terms such as *information society* or *network society* have been proposed to replace *postindustrial society*. Such terms attempt to capture the unprecedented development and use of information and communication technologies and the fact that information generation, processing, and transmission have become the fundamental sources of productivity and power (Castells 1996). These concepts, however, have been criticized as too narrow and too oriented toward technology. Critics argue that technology is merely useless "hardware" if not accompanied by "software"—the knowledge, work, and creativity of people who actually understand, make sense of, and apply the information available. Consequently, from the late 1990s the broader concept of *knowledge society* came to be preferred (Stehr 1994).

CONSEQUENCES OF KNOWLEDGE SOCIETY

Empirical data reveals that some countries (especially Scandinavian and western European countries, as well as Japan, the United States, Canada, and Australia) have moved toward becoming truly knowledge-driven societies (World Bank 1998; United Nations 2005). Many other countries remain in an industrial age, while others are still essentially agrarian. Why is this so? If knowledge is considered the most productive factor, why are not all societies knowledge-based or at least heading in that direction? And how can industrial and agrarian societies become knowledge societies?

In principle, knowledge is a nonrival and nonexcludable public good: one person's use of a particular piece of knowledge does not preclude the use of that same knowledge by others, and when a piece of knowledge is already in the public domain, it is difficult for the knowledge creator to prevent others from using it. In reality, knowledge, in contrast to information, cannot be easily acquired and applied. First, only so-called explicit knowledge can be easily transferred across time and space. Large portions of

knowledge—tacit knowledge—reside in people's minds, can be accessed on a first-person basis only, and take time to develop. Second, the effective creation and application of knowledge depends upon the broader context—culture, institutions, and governance. Knowledge must be integrated into an effective system of research institutions, innovation-driven enterprises, universities, and other establishments. Third, because knowledge is considered the key factor of production and is expensive to create, rich countries have broadened the protection of intellectual property rights (especially patents), and thus have increased the amount of knowledge that is secured and monopolized.

These factors contribute to an unequal distribution of knowledge across and within countries, a situation known as the *knowledge gap*. Indicators used to evaluate the development of knowledge society (such as educational attainment, investment in research and development, and Internet access) seem to show that the knowledge gap has been widening, because knowledge produces further knowledge in an ever-increasing rate, and this in turn increases productivity. It is risky for a country or company to rely largely on unskilled labor and natural resource–based goods. Countries, companies, and people who do not invest sufficiently in education and new technologies for acquiring and disseminating knowledge will find it increasingly difficult to catch up to those who did invest. Yet, investment in education and new technologies is not enough; it is also necessary to create appropriate conditions to foster innovation, creativity, and cooperation. Otherwise, negative consequences, such as *brain drain* (the emigration of one country's highly educated people to other countries offering better economic and social opportunity), can be expected.

SOCIAL STRATIFICATION IN KNOWLEDGE SOCIETY

What will be the class structure of knowledge society? Who will become richer and who poorer? According to Robert Reich (1991), there is a three-tiered workforce in the most advanced economies. At the bottom are workers who offer personal services; in the middle are production workers in factories or offices performing simple, repetitive tasks; and at the top are *symbolic analysts* who solve, identify, and broker problems by manipulating symbols. Symbolic analysts include research scientists, engineers, lawyers, and consultants of various types, but also publishers, writers, editors, journalists, or musicians. Reich predicted that advances in technology and globalization would widen the gaps in income and opportunity between these tiers.

While symbolic analysts are globally in great demand and their income is thus steadily increasing, production workers in advanced economies could be easily replaced by routine producers in other nations, which results in the disappearance of available routine jobs. Similarly, Peter Drucker (1994) and others speak of *knowledge workers*, that is, a newly emerging dominant group being employed in professions that require formal education and theoretical knowledge, as well as a different approach to work—qualifications that the industrial worker does not possess and is poorly equipped to acquire. Drucker also warned, though without details, against a potential new class conflict between the highly productive minority of knowledge workers and the majority of people who make their living traditionally. Though the future of knowledge and nonknowledge workers remains to be seen, even now there is empirical evidence that in advanced economies the number of jobs that demand only low cognitive skills is declining and that high-level skills and knowledge are substantial determinants of earnings (OECD 2000).

If knowledge workers are the leading social class economically, do they also dominate in a political and cultural sense? Who possesses control and power in a knowledge society? Can a knowledge society devolve into an Orwellian totalitarian society, where one social group is able to dominate other groups through its possession of knowledge and information? Authors disagree on this. According to Zbigniew Brzezinski (1970), we are entering into a "technetronic society," where scientific and technical elites will seize control of the essential flow of information; their claim to political power would rest on allegedly superior scientific know-how. Similarly, Alvin Gouldner (1979) forecasts the rise of a so-called "new class"—as opposed to the "old moneyed class"—that is composed of intellectuals and technical intelligentsia. This class will be bonded by similar education, culture, and language codes that facilitate solidarity between class members and enable collective political action. This "culture of critical discourse," as Gouldner terms the essential unifying attribute of this new class, functions as more than the group's common ideology; it is its instrument of domination and control and the source of its growing power.

In contrast, Nico Stehr (2002) argues that knowledge-based occupations do not and cannot form a social class because they are found in all sectors of the economy and their job description and interests are very diverse. Moreover, in decentralized and pluralistic democracies like the United States, all policymaking actors try to legitimize their claims using knowledge and information, and for this reason they employ various experts and consultants. In turn, it is difficult to enforce any claim solely on the basis of knowledge. Although those with scientific knowledge have a high social standing, they are often questioned. The consequence is a fragile society where controlling, planning, and predicting social conditions becomes more and more difficult and where the power of formerly monolithic institutions, such as the state, the church, and the military, declines.

The basic difference between Gouldner and Stehr is an assumption of knowledge distribution and its attributes. While Gouldner believes that knowledge can be concentrated in relatively few hands, Stehr assumes that knowledge is widely dispersed, that there are various types of knowledge and they are rapidly changing. Empirical studies seem to support Stehr's view. Though the number of experts has grown rapidly since World War II (1939–1945), they have limited influence on policymaking, except on issues of narrowly technical interest (Brint 1994).

CONCLUSION

If *knowledge society* is to be a useful term, it must be taken critically and further elaborated. There are several problems with its usage. First, it does not (and cannot) capture all aspects of modern postindustrial societies. It simply states that knowledge is the most important productive factor. Yet, any type of economic determinism should be avoided. There can be different types of knowledge societies, with different value structures, life styles, and even political systems. Similarly, modern societies can be given many other labels, such as risk society, consumption society, and so on. Second, *knowledge* is too broad a term and should be carefully decomposed and defined in any analysis or strategy. Third, attaining a knowledge society is not ensured but must be actively supported. Fourth, there is no clear-cut threshold from which societies become knowledge societies. It is more about processes (knowledge production, learning, innovation, and creativity) than about fulfilling static objectives.

SEE ALSO *Globalization, Social and Economic Aspects of; Knowledge*

BIBLIOGRAPHY

Bell, Daniel. 1973. *The Coming of Post-Industrial Society: A Venture in Social Forecasting.* New York: Basic Books.

Brint, Steven. 1994. *In an Age of Experts: The Changing Role of Professionals in Politics and Public Life.* Princeton, NJ: Princeton University Press.

Brzezinski, Zbigniew. 1970. *Between Two Ages: America's Role in the Technetronic Era.* New York: Viking.

Castells, Manuel. 1996. *The Rise of Network Society.* Vol. 1 of *The Information Age.* Oxford: Blackwell.

David, A. Paul, and Dominique Foray. 2002. An Introduction to the Economy of the Knowledge Society. *International Social Science Journal* 54: 9–24.

Drucker, Peter. 1994. The Age of Social Transformation. *The Atlantic Monthly* 274 (5): 53–80.

Drucker, Peter. 2001. The Next Society. *The Economist.* November 3.

Gouldner, Alvin Ward. 1979. *The Future of Intellectuals and the Rise of the New Class.* London: Macmillan.

Organization for Economic Cooperation and Development (OECD). 2000. *Literacy in the Information Age: Final Report of the International Adult Literacy Survey.* Paris: Author.

Reich, Robert B. 1991. *The Work of Nations: Preparing Ourselves for 21st-Century Capitalism.* New York: Knopf.

Stehr, Nico. 1994. *Knowledge Societies.* London: Sage.

Stehr, Nico. 2002. *Knowledge and Economic Conduct: The Social Foundations of the Modern Economy.* Toronto: University of Toronto Press.

Stewart, Thomas A. 2001. *The Wealth of Knowledge: Intellectual Capital and the Twenty-first Century Organization.* New York: Currency.

United Nations, Department of Economic and Social Affairs, Division for Public Administration and Development Management. 2005. *Understanding Knowledge Societies: In Twenty Questions and Answers with the Index of Knowledge Societies.* New York: United Nations.

World Bank. 1998. *Knowledge for Development: World Development Report 1998/99.* New York: Oxford University Press.

Arnost Vesely

KOHLBERG, LAWRENCE
1927–1987

The psychologist and educator Lawrence Kohlberg proposed a cognitive-developmental theory of morality that dominated the fields of moral psychology and moral education for over two decades until the mid-1990s. Though born of a wealthy family in New York, he chose to identify himself with the oppressed, helping to smuggle Jews through the British blockade of Palestine after World War II (1939–1945). He viewed his theory of moral development as a response to Nazi Germany and the Holocaust. Despite the pervasive reliance of everyday decision-making on notions of right and wrong, good and bad, that constitute the domain of moral psychology, little empirical research had actually been done on the subject. At the time Kohlberg completed his dissertation in 1958, moral psychology in North America was dominated by theories that portrayed people as either caught in a conflict between powerful self-interest and social convention (Freudian psychoanalysis) or passively molded by social norms (behaviorism). In Freud's account, morality was at best something to be endured in order for people to live cooperatively. On the assumption of cultural relativity, there were no morally justifiable grounds upon which to judge Hitler's actions as wrong.

It was in Kohlberg's seminal work *From Is to Ought: How to Commit the Naturalistic Fallacy and Get Away with It* (1971) that he acknowledged self-interest, cultural embeddedness, and cultural relativity (the "is"), and at the same time saw within the process of cognitive development the grounds for validating a formally more adequate and universal morality (the moral "ought"). (The "naturalistic fallacy" of the book's title refers to the invalid derivation of the moral good from the facts of how the world is.) Extending the earlier work of Jean Piaget, he proposed three broad and universal levels of moral development that proceeded from primary self-interest (level 1: preconventional morality), to embeddedness within social norms and structures (level 2: conventional morality), to the highest level of developmental maturity (level 3: postconventional or principled morality). Each of the three levels was further divided into two stages. Nature would point the way, so to speak, in differentiating higher-stage morality from more conventional views on morality, and moral development was described as proceeding through an invariant and irreversible stage sequence.

Each successive stage of moral development was made possible by increases in perspective-taking ability, with the highest, principled level taking into account the perspectives of all individuals in a moral conflict (i.e., a universal perspective). Level 3: stage 5 (the social-contract legalistic orientation) includes a number of moral principles commonly found in philosophy and professional codes of ethics. Ideal societies are those that are founded upon: (1) a free and willing participation in a common agreement (or contract) to live together in a law-structured society, (2) respect for individual rights, and (3) a utilitarian analysis of consequences to society for one's actions. Stage 6 (the universal ethical principle orientation) was Kohlberg's vision of ideal moral reasoning, where self-chosen, abstract moral principles of universal justice were viewed as transcending social convention and law.

To investigate moral reasoning within Kohlberg's model, research participants are asked to discuss hypothetical dilemmas that place values into conflict (e.g., life versus law). In the most famous of these dilemmas, the protagonist Heinz considers stealing an unaffordable drug that would cure his terminally ill wife. Heinz has explored every option but comes up financially short. Should Heinz obey the law or steal the drug to save his wife's life? For scoring purposes, the decision to steal or not steal the drug is not as important as the stage of reasoning used to reflect upon the life-versus-law conflict the story imposes. Using this procedure, a considerable body of longitudinal and cross-cultural research has confirmed that individuals do progress through Kohlberg's stages in the proposed invariant sequence (stages 1, 2, 3, etc.).

Despite the far-reaching theoretical and practical influence of Kohlberg's model within psychology, education, and even correctional settings, the model has not been without its strong critics. The theory has been alleged to be biased against women and non-Western cultures who were said to reason in "lower level," social conventional terms (Gilligan 1982; Shweder 1994). Even in Western culture, few individuals reason about moral dilemmas in "high level," post-conventional terms. The most recent version of the scoring manual has removed the highest level (stage 6) reasoning altogether—not a small deletion given that stage 6 defined the stage sequence as a theory of justice reasoning. Although many of the criticisms have been addressed, the model seems to have lost its conceptual hold within the field. In comparison with earlier published reviews of moral psychology that celebrated the legacy of Kohlberg, more recent reviews emphasize the very social, relationship, and emotional-personality factors that he sought to exclude from the moral domain. Nonetheless, his work remains an important foundation within the field.

SEE ALSO *Morality; Piaget, Jean*

BIBLIOGRAPHY

Gilligan, Carol. 1982. *In a Different Voice: Psychological Theory and Women's Development.* Cambridge, MA: Harvard University Press.

Killen, Melanie, and Judith Smetana, eds. 2006. *Handbook of Moral Development.* Mahwah, NJ: Erlbaum.

Kohlberg, Lawrence. 1981. *The Philosophy of Moral Development.* Vol. 1 of *Essays on Moral Development.* San Francisco: Harper and Row.

Kohlberg, Lawrence. 1984. *The Psychology of Moral Development.* Vol. 2 of *Essays on Moral Development.* San Francisco: Harper and Row.

Shweder, R. 1994. Liberalism as Destiny. In *Moral Development: A Compendium,* Vol. 4, *The Great Justice Debate*, ed. Bill Puka, 71–74. New York: Garland.

Karl H. Hennig

KONDRATIEF, NIKOLAI

SEE *Russian Economics.*

KONDRATIEF WAVE

SEE *Long Waves.*

KONDRATIEV, NIKOLAI

SEE *Russian Economics.*

KOOPMANS, TJALLING
1910–1985

Tjalling Charles Koopmans, who shared the 1975 Nobel Memorial Prize in Economic Sciences with Leonid Kantorovich (1912–1986), was born in Graveland, the Netherlands. Koopmans studied mathematics and physics at the University of Utrecht (MA, 1933, publishing a paper on quantum mechanics) and mathematical statistics at the University of Leiden (PhD, 1936). His pioneering dissertation introduced concepts developed by R. A. Fisher (1890–1962) and by Jerzy Neyman (1894–1981) and Egon Pearson (1895–1980) in probability theory and statistical inference into econometrics, which he published in English (Koopmans 1937). He studied economics and econometrics with Jan Tinbergen (1903–1994) at the University of Amsterdam in 1934 and for five months with Ragnar Frisch (1895–1973) in Oslo. At Frisch's request, Koopmans lectured in Oslo about statistical inference, but Frisch did not accept the case for using probability models in econometrics put forward by Koopmans and by Frisch's student Trygve Haavelmo (1911–1999). Koopmans took over Tinbergen's classes at the Rotterdam School of Economics in 1937 when Tinbergen moved to Geneva to conduct his League of Nations study on statistical testing of business cycle theories. Koopmans then took Tinbergen's place in Geneva upon Tinbergen's return in 1939. Koopmans moved to the United States in 1940 (eventually taking U.S. citizenship), where he was employed as a research assistant at Princeton, an instructor in statistics at New York University, an economist with a Philadelphia insurance company, and from 1942 a statistician for the British Merchant Shipping Mission in Washington, D.C., analyzing optimal routing of ships.

In 1944 Koopmans became a research associate with the Cowles Commission for Research in Economics at the University of Chicago, where he was also associate professor of economics from 1946 (full professor from 1948). He succeeded Jacob Marschak (1898–1977) as Cowles research director in 1948 and became president of the Econometric Society in 1950. While in Chicago, building upon his and Haavelmo's dissertations, Koopmans led the development of the Cowles Commission approach to the identification and estimation of simultaneous-equations econometric models, including full-information maximum likelihood (FIML) estimation, stressing that simultaneous-equations methods are better asymptotically (that is, as sample size approaches infinity) than single-equation least-squares estimation (Koopmans 1950; Koopmans and

Hood 1953). Another pioneering Cowles monograph edited by Koopmans (1951) applied linear programming methods to the analysis of production and allocation. This work was the basis for his sharing the Nobel Prize with Kantorovich, who had conducted parallel research in the Soviet Union. George Dantzig (1914–2005), another pioneer of linear programming (and a contributor to Koopmans [1951]), did not share the prize, presumably because he was a mathematician rather than an economist. Koopmans anonymously donated to a research institute associated with Dantzig what would have been Dantzig's share of the prize money, a fact not revealed until after Koopmans died.

In 1947 Koopmans sharply criticized the empirical business cycle research of Arthur F. Burns (1904–1987) and Wesley Mitchell (1874–1948) of the National Bureau of Economic Research as "Measurement without Theory," and he urged that empirical economists use formal economic theory as the starting point for explicit, structurally identified models (Hendry and Morgan [1995] reprint Koopmans's review article, together with his subsequent exchange with Rutledge Vining). This methodological controversy worsened relations between the Cowles Commission and other University of Chicago economists, especially Milton Friedman (1912–2006), once Burns's doctoral student, who insisted that Mitchell's approach was also a valid form of economic theorizing. When Koopmans was scheduled to go on sabbatical (to write his *Three Essays on the State of Economic Science*), James Tobin (1918–2002) of Yale was invited to succeed him as Cowles research director. When Tobin declined to leave Yale, the Cowles Commission (including Koopmans) moved to Yale in 1955 as the Cowles Foundation for Research in Economics. Koopmans, a professor of economics at Yale from 1955 until his retirement in 1981, succeeded Tobin as director of the Cowles Foundation from 1961 to 1967.

Following his critique of NBER methodology, Koopmans's *Three Essays* (1957), his most widely read work, offered a positive statement of his own methodology. The first essay argued that the use of more fundamental methodological tools reveals the common logical structure of economic theories of diverse origin. The second urged "a clearer separation, in the construction of economic knowledge, between reasoning and recognition of facts, for the better protection of both" (Koopmans 1957, p. viii). The concluding essay speculated on the future interaction between tools of analysis and choice of problems in economics. Koopmans's later research concentrated on the normative analysis of optimal economic growth and on the incorporation of exhaustible natural resources into growth theory (Koopmans 1970–1985; Gordon et al. 1987; Werin and Jungenfelt 1976, Pt. II).

SEE ALSO *Frisch, Ragnar; League of Nations; Linear Systems; Maximum Likelihood Regression; Mitchell, Wesley Clair; Programming, Linear and Non-Linear; Simultaneous Equation Bias; Tinbergen, Jan; Tobin, James*

BIBLIOGRAPHY

PRIMARY WORKS

Koopmans, Tjalling C. 1937. *Linear Regression Analysis of Economic Time Series.* Haarlem, Netherlands: De Erven Bohn.

Koopmans, Tjalling C. 1947. Measurement without Theory. *Review of Economic Statistics* 29 (3): 161–172.

Koopmans, Tjalling C., ed. 1950. *Statistical Inference in Dynamic Economic Models.* New York: Wiley.

Koopmans, Tjalling C., ed. 1951. *Activity Analysis of Production and Allocation.* New York: Wiley.

Koopmans, Tjalling C. 1957. *Three Essays on the State of Economic Science.* New York: McGraw-Hill.

Koopmans, Tjalling C. 1970–1985. *The Scientific Papers of Tjalling C. Koopmans.* Vol. 1, Berlin: Springer-Verlag. Vol. 2, Cambridge, MA: MIT Press.

Koopmans, Tjalling C., and William C. Hoods, eds. 1953. *Studies in Econometric Method.* New York: Wiley.

SECONDARY WORKS

Gordon, Robert B., Tjalling C. Koopmans, William D. Norhaus, and B. J. Skinner. 1987. *Toward a New Iron Age? Quantitative Modeling of Resource Exhaustion.* Cambridge, MA: Harvard University Press.

Hendry, David, and Mary Morgan, eds. 1995. *Foundations of Econometric Analysis.* Cambridge, U.K.: Cambridge University Press.

Scarf, Herbert E. 1995. Tjalling Charles Koopmans, 1910–1985. *National Academy of Sciences Biographical Memoirs* 67: 1–31.

Werin, Lars, and Karl G. Jungenfelt. 1976. Tjalling Koopmans' Contribution to Economics. I: Activity Analysis, Methodology and Econometrics. II: Koopmans and the Recent Development of Growth Theory. *Scandinavian Journal of Economics* 78: 81–102.

Robert W. Dimand

KOREAN AMERICANS

SEE *Immigrants, Asian.*

KOREAN WAR

On June 25, 1950, North Korea's invasion of South Korea transformed a civil conflict under way since the end of World War II (1939–1945) into a conventional war. In

April 1945, U.S. president Harry S. Truman (1884–1972) abandoned a trusteeship plan for the restoration of Korea's sovereignty after forty years of Japanese colonial rule. His quest for unilateral U.S. occupation, after an atomic attack forced Japan's prompt surrender, ended when the Soviet Union entered the Pacific war, resulting in the last-minute decision to divide Korea at the 38th parallel into zones of occupation. The failure of negotiations to reunite Korea led to the creation in 1948 of an authoritarian government under Syngman Rhee (1875–1965) in the south and a Communist regime under Kim Il Sung (1912–1994) in the north. Both Koreas were obsessed with reunification, resulting in major military clashes at the parallel during the summer of 1949. Washington and Moscow, however, opposed their clients' plans for invasion until April 1950, when Kim persuaded Soviet premier Joseph Stalin (1879–1953) that an offensive would spark an internal uprising and bring swift conquest of the peninsula.

At first, Truman hoped that South Korea could defend itself with U.S. air support and more military equipment, actions that the United Nations endorsed in resolutions calling for a ceasefire and assistance for South Korea. Commitment of U.S. ground forces came after General Douglas MacArthur (1880–1964), the U.S. occupation commander in Japan, visited the front and advised that the South Koreans could not halt the advance. Overconfident U.S. soldiers would sustain defeat as well, retreating to the Pusan Perimeter, a rectangular area in the southeast corner of the peninsula. On September 15, MacArthur staged a risky amphibious landing at Inchon behind enemy lines that sent Communist forces fleeing back into North Korea. Mao Zedong (1893–1976), leader of the People's Republic of China (PRC), viewed the U.S.–South Korean reunification offensive that followed as a threat to China's security and prestige. In late November, Chinese "volunteers" attacked en masse. After a chaotic retreat, UN forces counterattacked in February 1951 and moved the line of battle just north of the parallel. MacArthur wanted to widen the war to China, but Truman instead sought a ceasefire and then relieved the general for publicly ridiculing this policy. By June 1951, fighting had reached a stalemate.

Negotiations to end the war began in July 1951, but, after steady progress toward a truce, stalemated in May 1952 over the issue of repatriation of prisoners of war. Peace came because of Stalin's death in March 1953 rather than a U.S. threat to use nuclear weapons against China. An armistice in July ended a brutal war that killed nearly three million combatants and Korean civilians. Almost as destructive was the conflict's impact on world affairs. Still divided, Korea would remain a source of tension threatening regional peace. Sino-American relations were poisoned for twenty years, especially after the United States persuaded the United Nations to condemn the PRC for

aggression in Korea. For Japan, Korea not only ignited economic recovery, but led to treaties restoring sovereignty and establishing a security alliance with the United States. Hailed as an example of collective security, the war instead severely strained relations between the United States and its allies, not least because it ensured the survival of odious regimes on Taiwan and in South Korea. Most important, the Korean conflict intensified the cold war, motivating huge increases in U.S. defense spending, the rearmament of West Germany, and the militarization of the North Atlantic Treaty Organization.

SEE ALSO *Cold War; Communism; Mao Zedong; North Atlantic Treaty Organization; Partition; Truman, Harry S.; Union of Soviet Socialist Republics; United Nations*

BIBLIOGRAPHY

Cumings, Bruce. 1981–1990. *The Origins of the Korean War.* 2 vols. Princeton, NJ: Princeton University Press.

Goncharov, Sergei N., John W. Lewis, and Xue Litai. 1993. *Uncertain Partners: Stalin, Mao, and the Korean War.* Stanford, CA: Stanford University Press.

Stueck, William. 1995. *The Korean War: An International History.* Princeton, NJ: Princeton University Press.

James I. Matray

KOYCK LAGS
SEE *Lags, Distributed.*

KREPS, DAVID
SEE *Screening and Signaling Games.*

KRISTOL, IRVING
SEE *Neoconservatism.*

KROEBER, ALFRED LOUIS
1876–1960

Alfred Louis Kroeber earned the second PhD awarded in anthropology in North America, and is regarded as a founder of the modern discipline. He was born in

Hoboken, New Jersey to well-to-do German-speaking parents. Although his family is often described as Protestant, Kroeber attended the Ethical Culture School, which though officially nonsectarian was associated with a secular humanist strand of Judaism. He studied English at Columbia College, switching to anthropology after meeting the charismatic and forceful Franz Boas. His twenty-eight-page dissertation "Decorative Symbolism of the Arapaho" (1901) was an analysis of specimens he collected for the American Museum of Natural History. Kroeber spent his academic career in California, where he established the Department of Anthropology at the University of California at Berkeley and directed what became the Museum of Anthropology there. He retired in 1946, but remained active in the field until his death.

Kroeber married twice. His first wife, Henrietta Rothschild, died in 1913 of tuberculosis. He married Theodora Kracaw Brown in 1926, and adopted her sons, Theodore and Clifton, from an earlier marriage. Theodora and Alfred had two more children, Ursula and Karl. The Kroebers were an academic and literary family. Theodora published many books, including *Ishi in Two Worlds* (1961), a biography of a California Indian. Alfred Kroeber's relationship to Ishi has recently become a controversial subject addressed in *Ishi in Three Centuries* (2003), a collection of scholarly articles edited by sons Karl, a professor of literature, and Clifton, a historian. Kroeber's daughter is the science fiction and fantasy writer Ursula K. LeGuin.

Alfred Kroeber regarded anthropology as a method for doing history. His academic research and writings addressed two broad concerns: theorizing the nature of culture, and delineating the boundaries of and patterns within specific cultures. In the case of the latter, this can be appreciated in his archaeological investigations in Nazca, Peru, through which he contributed to the archaeological concept of seriation, or relative dating, by observing stylistic changes over time. Cultural boundaries figured into his work on the culture area concept published in *Cultural and Natural Areas of Native North America* (1939), whereas patterns within cultures was the subject of his much criticized *Configurations of Culture Growth* (1944). In both works he developed typologies of cultures based on compilations of traits. For Kroeber, a culture was something analogous to grammar: Both were composed of unconscious mental rules or patterns that could be discerned and described.

Perhaps Kroeber's most controversial idea concerned his concept of culture generally. In a 1917 article published in *American Anthropologist* he described culture as "superorganic," an entity that existed apart from and independent of individuals. It was not inherited, only transmitted socially. In other words, culture caused culture.

One corollary of this was that individuals and individual variation were inconsequential to describing specific cultures. The trouble with this position is that it ignores the context in which people, the culture bearers, live. The problem is illustrated in a story told by the late George Foster, a founder of medical anthropology and one of Kroeber's students at Berkeley in the 1930s. As a young graduate student Foster was expected to learn how to collect ethnographic data by interviewing an elderly member of a northern California Indian tribe, a man who had been Kroeber's informant many years earlier. As required, Foster traveled to northern California and conducted a series of interviews about "Native culture" with the old man. Finally, the elder told Foster he would have to stop the interviews as he was becoming exhausted from reading Kroeber's *Handbook of the Indians of California* (1925) every evening in order to have something to tell Foster each day.

Kroeber's understanding of culture as monolithic also informed his relationship with the Native California man known as Ishi (c.1860–1916). Ishi was the sole survivor of a group of northern California Indians hunted, harassed, and dislocated by white ranchers and other settlers. In 1911, alone and starving, Ishi came into the town of Oroville, where he was jailed and then turned over to Kroeber's Department of Anthropology. Kroeber, like others in that era, believed Ishi to be the "last wild Indian," and therefore to be in possession of culture uncontaminated by "civilization." Kroeber arranged for Ishi to live and to be a living exhibit at the University of California museum. Kroeber also arranged for his academic colleagues, T. T. Waterman and Edward Sapir, to "work" with Ishi to record his culture and language. The story of Ishi's life in San Francisco is well told in a film made for public television, *Ishi, The Last Yahi* (1992). Ishi died of tuberculosis while Kroeber was in Europe, and despite Kroeber's supposed directive to the contrary, his body was autopsied "for science." Kroeber himself sent Ishi's brain to the National Museum of Natural History of the Smithsonian Institution. The whereabouts of Ishi's brain and Kroeber's role during Ishi's last years of life became a controversy in 1999. Eventually, the brain was removed from the museum and was buried with Ishi's cremated remains in northern California in 2000.

Kroeber's actions and his academic work show him clearly as a man of his time. Despite theoretical and methodological shortcomings now apparent in his work, Kroeber rightly deserves recognition for his contributions to the discipline of anthropology: He published more than 600 scholarly articles and books; along with Boas, he is responsible for institutionalizing anthropology as a university-based discipline; and most significantly, he established culture as the primary object of North American anthropological inquiry, where it remains a productive subject for social theory.

SEE ALSO *Anthropology; Boas, Franz; Culture; Ethnography; Jews; Le Guin, Ursula K.; Native Americans*

BIBLIOGRAPHY

PRIMARY WORKS

Kroeber, A. L. 1901. Decorative Symbolism of the Arapaho. *American Anthropologist* 3: 308-336.

Kroeber, A. L. 1917. The Superorganic. *American Anthropologist* 19: 163–213.

Kroeber, A. L. 1925. *Handbook of the Indians of California.* Washington, DC: Government Printing Office.

Kroeber, A. L. 1939. *Cultural and Natural Areas of Native North America.* Berkeley: University of California Press.

Kroeber, A. L. 1944. *Configurations of Culture Growth.* Berkeley: University of California Press.

SECONDARY WORKS

Kroeber, Theodora. 1961. *Ishi in Two Worlds.* Berkeley: University of California Press.

Kroeber, Karl, and Clifton Kroeber, eds. 2003. *Ishi in Three Centuries.* Lincoln: University of Nebraska Press.

Pamela Stern

KSHATRIYAS

The word *Kshatriya* (from the Sanskrit *kṣatra,* meaning "power") refers to the military and administrative subdivisions of South Asian society that arose by the first millennium BCE and those who claim descent from them. It is the second of four *varṇa*s (commonly known as *castes*) in an idealized Hindu social order. Despite shifting political configurations under and after colonialism, the designation *Kshatriya* remains potent as a status marker in the Indian Subcontinent and, to a lesser degree, Southeast Asia due to its prestigious ritual entitlements and literary associations.

Although the word itself is not used, the earliest reference to Kshatriyas as a ruling class appears in the *Rig Veda* (c. 1000 BCE), a sacred text whose codification was roughly contemporaneous with the ostensively occupational stratification of society in what is now Pakistan and northern India. Shortly thereafter, Vedic commentaries assigned differing sacrificial obligations, food prohibitions, greetings, funeral practices, and so on to each of the four *varṇa*s. Kshatriyas were, for example, polygamous and allowed meat and alcohol. However, recorded instances of intermarriage and occasional upward mobil-

ity between Brahmans and Kshatriyas of this period illustrate an early fluidity, as well as a tendency to group these two higher *varṇa*s together in relation to everyone else (Anand 1985).

Endogamy and Commensality prohibitions had probably taken hold by around the sixth century BCE, when Brahmans and Kshatriyas began to share competing claims to the top of the status hierarchy. The frame-stories of the philosophical *Upanishads* feature Brahmans at the feet of Kshatriya gurus, while the scriptures of the Kshatriya-founded Buddhist and Jain faiths contain references to and arguments for Kshatriya supremacy.

Brahmanical rejoinders appear in the Indian epics *Ramayana* and *Mahabharata* and in treatises on law and statecraft compiled in the early centuries of the Common Era. The literary record balances valorization of archetypical Kshatriyas such as Rama, the ideal king, with insistence on the superiority of Brahmans and the traditional separation of powers. Much of the conflict in the latter of the two epics, the *Mahabharata,* stems from the reluctance of Kshatriya characters to fulfill their royal or martial duties. This is explicitly argued in the *Bhagavad Gita,* where the god Krishna, himself a Kshatriya, teaches that "heroism, fiery energy, resolve, skill, refusal to retreat in battle, charity, and majesty in conduct" are qualities intrinsic to Kshatriyas, who either act accordingly or incur sin (Miller 1986, p.149). Furthermore, the epics narrate tensions between Brahmans and Kshatriyas in the story of the semidivine axe-wielding Brahman Parashurama's extermination of the world's Kshatriyas. This myth enabled claims, particularly in south India, that true Kshatriyas no longer exist.

A textual tradition that took shape around the same time as the epics concerned itself with the science of *dharma* (law, duty). In addition to a battery of distinctive ritual prescriptions and provisions for succession and alternate sources of income (trading, farming, or banking) under extenuating circumstances, the sustained reflections on the Kshatriya *varṇa* found in these sources interrogate the relationship between the Kshatriya *varṇa* and kingship. An impetus for this debate, which continued into the seventeenth century, was the rise of non-Kshatriyas to political sovereignty. A variety of positions emerged in response, with "only Kshatriyas are rightfully kings" on one end of the spectrum and "whoever rules is king" on the other (Pollock 2005). In practice, further slippage seems to have occurred such that even Muslim rulers could be considered Kshatriyas through matrimonial alliances (Alam 2004).

Varṇa was the primary category employed in the early censuses of the British Raj, which showed marked regional variation in the distribution and social position of the numerous subcastes (*jāti*) anachronistically labeled

Kshatriyas and Allied Castes. While well represented in the north and northwest, Kshatriyas were fewer, poorer, and less educated in eastern and especially southern India, where some Kshatriya subcastes are now considered "backward" and eligible for quotas in the public sector under the Indian constitution (Dirks 2001). Nonetheless, numerous clerical, merchant, and agriculturalist groups around the country, viewing the census reports as opportunities to bolster their reputation, representation, and local rights, formed caste associations to lobby the state for recognition as Kshatriyas. The claims of groups that allowed widow-remarriage or dined with their purported inferiors were denied, but their desire to become known as Kshatriyas and the later use of the Kshatriya ideal to inspire bravery and patriotism by Aurobindo Ghose (1872–1950) and other Indian nationalist leaders highlights the category's cultural capital (Varma 1904).

In 2003 American scholar James Laine's biographical study *Shivaji: Hindu King in Islamic India* provoked heated and at points violent controversy in part by questioning the Kshatriya pedigree of the seventeenth-century hero. Although Oxford University Press withdrew the book from publication in Indian and issued an apology, activists in Pune, Maharastra, assaulted local scholars known to have assisted Lane and severely vandalized the Bhandarkar Oriental Research, where Laine conducted much of his research. Soon thereafter, the state of Maharashtra banned the book and filed slander charges against Laine; all of which indicates that the Kshatriya *varṇa* remains extremely powerful, at least as an idea.

SEE ALSO *Brahmins; Buddhism; Caste; Caste, Anthropology of; Dalits; Hierarchy; Hinduism; Jainism; Stratification; Sudras; Vaisyas*

BIBLIOGRAPHY

Alam, Muzaffar. 2004. *The Languages of Political Islam: India, 1200–1800.* Chicago: University of Chicago Press.

Anand, Shanta. 1985. *Kṣhatriyas in Ancient India: A Socio-economic and Religious Study.* Delhi: Atma Ram.

Davis, Richard. 2004. Review: *Shivaji: Hindu King in Islamic India. Journal of the American Academy of Religion* 72 (4): 1045–1050.

Dirks, Nicholas B. 2001. *Castes of Mind: Colonialism and the Making of Modern India.* Princeton, NJ: Princeton University Press.

Dumont, Louis. 1980. *Homo Hierarchicus: The Caste System and Its Implications.* Rev. English ed. Trans. Mark Sainsbury, Louis Dumont, and Basia Gulati. Chicago: University of Chicago Press.

Hopkins, Edward Washburn. 1889. The Social and Military Position of the Ruling Caste in Ancient India, as Represented by the Sanskrit Epic. *Journal of the American Oriental Society* 13: 57–376.

Karashima, Noboru, ed. 1999. *Kingship in Indian History.* New Delhi: Manohar.

Laine, James W. 2003. *Shivaji: Hindu King in Islamic India.* New York: Oxford University Press.

Miller, Barbara Stoler, trans. 1986. *The Bhagavad-Gita: Krishna's Counsel in Time of War.* New York: Bantam Books.

Pollock, Sheldon. 2005. *The Ends of Man at the End of Premodernity.* Amsterdam: Royal Netherlands Academy of Arts and Sciences.

Richards, John F., ed. 1998. *Kingship and Authority in South Asia.* Delhi and New York: Oxford University Press.

Shah, Ghanshyam. 1975. *Caste Association and Political Process in Gujarat: A Study of Gujarat Kshatriya Sabha.* Bombay: Popular Prakashan.

Somjee A. H. 1981. Social Cohesion and Political Clientilism among the Kshatriyas of Gujarat. *Asian Survey* 21 (9): 1000–1010.

Varma, Kumar Cheda Singh. 1904. *Kshatriyas and Would-Be Kshatriyas: A Consideration of the Claims of Certain Hindu Castes to Rank with the Rajputs, the Descendants of the Ancient Kshatriyas.* Allahabad, India: Pioneer Press.

Joel Bordeaux

KUHN, THOMAS
1922–1996

Thomas Kuhn was the author of five works in the history of science, of which the most influential, *The Structure of Scientific Revolutions*, explores the character of scientific change. On its appearance in 1962 it became the central document for attacks on the logical empiricist account of science as the progressive accumulation of objective knowledge controlled by experimental and observational methods. Though Kuhn regretted and rejected the radical interpretation of this book, this interpretation was natural and served as the starting point for one side in a generation-long "culture war" between exponents and detractors of science's claim to objectivity.

Kuhn's ostensible topic was scientific change, how the broadest theories replace one another during periods of scientific revolution. Among the most important of these was the shift from Aristotelian physics to Newtonian mechanics, from phlogiston chemistry to Lavoisier's theories of reduction and oxidation, from nonevolutionary biology to Darwinism, and from Newtonian mechanics to relativistic and quantum mechanics. Periods of revolutionary change in science alternate with periods of what Kuhn called "normal science," during which the direction, methods, instruments, and problems that scientists face are all fixed by what he called "a paradigm" (the term has gone into common usage). Paradigms are more than just equations, laws, statements encapsulated in the chapters of a textbook. The paradigm of Newtonian mechanics was not just Newton's laws of motion, it was also the model or picture of the universe as a deterministic clockwork in which the fundamental properties of things were their position and momentum from which all the rest of their behavior could eventually be derived when Newtonian science was completed. The Newtonian paradigm also included apparatus, a methodology, indeed an entire metaphysics. Paradigms drive normal science, and normal science dictates the direction of scientific progress by determining what counts as science altogether.

During normal science, three sorts of empirical enquiries flourish: redetermining previously established observational claims to greater degrees of precision; the establishment of facts without significance themselves but which vindicate the paradigm; experiments undertaken to solve problems to which the paradigm draws one's attention. Failure to accomplish any of these three aims reflects on the scientist attempting them, not the paradigm employed.

Naturally, some disciplines are, as Kuhn put it, in "pre-paradigm" states, as evinced for example by the lack of textbook uniformity. These disciplines are ones, like many of the social sciences, where the lack of commonality among the textbooks reveals the absence of consensus on a paradigm. At some points in the histories of each of the mature sciences, a ruling paradigm emerged. But it could not have done so owing to its correctness or empirical warrant. Apparently, its ascendancy must have a social explanation.

According to Kuhn, once established, the paradigm determined the outcome of empirical inquiry. It is not empirical inquiry that determines the paradigms scientists embrace. Independent of paradigms there are no empirical facts to observe. To illustrate and support this claim Kuhn cited evidence from psychological experiments about optical illusions, gestalt-switches, expectation-effects, and the unnoticed theoretical commitments of many apparently observational words we incautiously suppose to be untainted by presuppositions about the world. Here was Kuhn's most forceful direct attack on the theoretical/observational distinction that underwrites logical empiricism's account of scientific knowledge.

As normal science progresses, its puzzles succumb to what Kuhn called "the articulation" of the paradigm. A small number of puzzles continue to be recalcitrant: phenomena that the paradigm cannot explain, or phenomena the paradigm leads us to expect but that do not turn up, discrepancies in the data beyond the margins of error, or major incompatibilities with other paradigms. In each case, there is within normal science a rational explanation for these anomalies; and eventually further work turns an anomaly into a solved puzzle. Revolutions occur when an anomaly resists solution long enough to produce a crisis. As more scientists attach paramount importance to the problem, the entire discipline's research program begins to be focused around the unsolved anomaly. At some point a (usually younger) scientist formulates a new paradigm, which turns the anomaly into a solved puzzle. But revolutionaries are not behaving in the most demonstrably rational way; nor are their (usually elderly) establishment opponents who defend the ruling paradigm against their approach acting irrationally.

During these periods of competition between old and new paradigms, nothing between them can be settled by observation or experiment. Often there is little or no difference between the competing paradigms when it comes to predictive accuracy, and often the new paradigm fails to solve puzzles solved in the old one. A new paradigm disagrees radically with its predecessor. Sometimes new paradigms are advanced by scientists who do not realize their incompatibility with ruling ones. But the new paradigm must be radically different from its predecessor just insofar as it can treat as a mere puzzle what the previous one found an increasingly embarrassing recalcitrant anomaly. Paradigms are so all encompassing, and the difference between paradigms is so radical, that Kuhn wrote that scientists embracing differing paradigms find themselves literally in different worlds. Paradigms are, in Kuhn's words, "incommensurable" with one another, in the sense of not being translatable one into the other, as poems in one language are untranslatable into another. And this sort of radical incommensurability underwrites the further claim that paradigms do not improve on one another, and that therefore science does not cumulate in the direction of successive approximation to the truth. Thus the history of science is like the history of art, literature, religion, politics, or culture, a story of changes, but not over the long haul a story of "progress."

Because a new paradigm is literally a change in worldview, and at least figuratively a change in the world in which the scientist lives, it is often too great a shift for well-established scientists. These scientists, wedded to the old paradigm, will not just resist the shift to the new one, they will be unable to make the shift; what is more, their refusal will be rationally defensible. Or at any rate, arguments against their view will be question-begging because they will presume a new paradigm they do not accept. What is more, there is, recall, no neutral ground on which competing paradigms can be compared. When allegiance is transferred from one paradigm to another, the process is more like a religious conversion than a rational belief shift supported by relevant evidence. Old paradigms fade away as their exponents die off, leaving the proponents of the new paradigm in command of the field.

Progress is to be found in science, according to Kuhn, but like progress in evolution, it is always a matter of increasing local adaptation. In one of the last pages of his book Kuhn wrote, "We may, to be more precise, have to relinquish the notion, explicit or implicit, that changes of paradigm carry scientists and those who learn from them closer and closer to the truth" (1962, p.170).

The consequences of this account for skepticism about science's epistemic status were evident to Kuhn. He spent much of his career after the appearance of *The Structure of Scientific Revolutions* trying to reconcile its account of scientific change with the objectivity and cumulation of scientific knowledge.

BIBLIOGRAPHY

PRIMARY WORKS

Kuhn, Thomas. 1962. *The Structure of Scientific Revolutions.* Chicago: University of Chicago Press.

Kuhn, Thomas. 1977. *The Essential Tension: Selected Studies in Scientific Tradition and Change.* Chicago: University of Chicago Press.

Alex Rosenberg

KUHN-TUCKER CONDITIONS

SEE *Maximization; Programming, Linear and Nonlinear.*

KU KLUX KLAN

Founded in Pulaski, Tennessee, in the spring of 1866 by six former Confederate soldiers, the Ku Klux Klan quickly emerged as an antiblack and anti-Republican force in the South. Following the passage by Congress of the Reconstruction Acts in 1867, Klansmen began a reign of terror, abusing, intimidating, assaulting, and sometimes murdering those who sought to create a true democracy in the former slave states. Riding across the countryside in white (and black) robes, they burned churches, schools, and the homes of former slaves and their white sympathizers.

In his fine study of the topic, Allen Trelease (1971) described this first Klan as a "conspiracy" among many whites in the Democratic Party to subdue their rivals, but historians have pointed out the lack of communication between Klan members in different states and locales during this period. Even if there was no conspiracy, there was large-scale participation. One estimate noted that in Alabama alone there were ten thousand Klan members. In

1870 and 1871, however, President Ulysses S. Grant (1822–1885) signed into law what were called the Force Acts, giving the federal government authority to protect freedmen and Republicans. The Force Acts drove the Klan underground, and the racial and political violence that occurred in subsequent years was mostly caused by white vigilante groups.

The second Klan, founded by William Joseph Simmons (1880–1945) at Stone Mountain, Georgia, in 1915, expanded the geographical reach and organizational purpose of the group. The second Klan acquired immediate legitimacy with the almost simultaneous release of D. W. Griffith's sympathetic and successful motion picture, *Birth of a Nation* (1915), based on Thomas Dixon Jr.'s novel *The Clansman* (1905). By the 1920s, Klan rallies, complete with cross burnings, were being held in the South, Southwest, and north-central states. The city where perhaps the largest Klan rally in American history occurred was Kokomo, Indiana, on July 4, 1923, when about 100,000 Klansmen and Klanswomen gathered to celebrate the inauguration of a new Grand Wizard. The second Klan stood against foreigners, Jews, blacks, and Catholics, proclaiming "Native, white, Protestant supremacy." In this movement to create an all-white society, the Imperial Wizard of the Invisible Empire, as the head of the Klan was called, explained: "We know that we are right in the same sense that a good Christian knows that he has been saved and that Christ lives" (Mann 1968, p. 129). With a national organization and national distribution of regalia, the new message of hate attracted a large membership, estimated at several million. It was this incarnation of the Klan that neither the U.S. government nor state and county agencies, including law enforcement departments, were able to curb or drive to cover. The Great Depression of the 1930s, however, decimated its ranks. With poverty, hunger, and unemployment among millions of Americans during the Great Depression of the 1930s, the Klan's membership declined precipitously.

Following World War II (1939–1945), several Klan organizations emerged in various sections of the country. Klan members fought against the civil rights movement in the South and were responsible for bombings, burnings, and murders in Alabama, Mississippi, and other states. In response to this violence, the Southern Poverty Law Center, a small civil rights law firm, was founded in 1971 in Montgomery, Alabama. Today, the center is internationally known for its tolerance education programs, its legal victories against white supremacists, and its tracking of hate groups. More recently, some Klansmen, including David Duke, have gained celebrity status by appearing on television talk shows. Throughout its history, however, the Ku Klux Klan has been a secret, terrorist organization dedicated to promoting white supremacy in the United States.

SEE ALSO *Racism; White Supremacy*

BIBLIOGRAPHY

Chalmers, David M. 1965. *Hooded Americanism: The History of the Ku Klux Klan.* New York: Doubleday.

Mann, Arthur, comp. 1968. *Immigrants in American Life.* Boston: Houghton Mifflin.

Trelease, Allen. 1971. *White Terror: The Ku Klux Klan Conspiracy and Southern Reconstruction.* New York: Harper.

Loren Schweninger

KURTOSIS

SEE *Descriptive Statistics.*

KUZNETS' CURVE

SEE *Kuznets Hypothesis.*

KUZNETS HYPOTHESIS

During the twentieth century, economists began analyzing the growth and development of economies to determine their welfare-improving effects on citizens. One of the ways these effects have been measured is by calculating the impact of economic growth on a country's income distribution. Simon Kuznets (1901–1985) was the first economist to attempt to do this. Kuznets (1955) conducted a study into the evolution of the distribution of personal income from 1870 to the 1950s and found that the relative distribution of pretax income in the United States, Germany, and England had been gradually moving toward equality. Per capita income in these countries had been increasing over the entire period, but at some point the share of the lower-income group began increasing more rapidly than that of the higher-income groups. The developed countries saw increasing income inequality with growth, then experienced decreasing income inequality. In developing countries, however, income inequality had been increasing along with increases in per capita income.

Economic theory suggests that a higher income share among a country's wealthy will lead to increased savings, thus increased wealth. Economic growth also usually leads to an increase in industrialization and urbanization, with an increasing disparity in income between rural and urban sectors. These trends suggest that there should be increased inequality with economic growth. Therefore, the trend toward income equality for these developed economies was a puzzle to Kuznets.

W. A. Lewis's (1954) dual economy model provides some explanation. According to Lewis, an economy starts with unlimited supplies of labor in its agricultural sector. As the economy develops, it creates another more industrialized sector—a manufacturing sector. This change causes a movement of labor from the agricultural sector to the new sector, and leads to worsening income inequality as the new sector enjoys better returns. However, increased movement of labor across the two sectors will, in the long run, reach a turning point, causing incomes in the agricultural sector to improve and leading to greater income equality.

Another plausible explanation for the effect of development on income inequality is its effect on education and the production of human capital. At the initial stages of development, only the rich may be able to afford education, augmenting their skills and thus their income. This will increase income inequality. However, as per capita income increases and more people are able to afford education, the income of the poor will converge with that of the rich.

THE INVERTED-U HYPOTHESIS

The inverted-U hypothesis paradigm originated from Kuznets's initial observation of the growth and distribution of income inequality in the United States, Germany, and England. Some economists argue that this theorem can be applied to all economies, and they have been using empirical evidence to prove this theorem and to determine the causal roots of this process. To be able to successfully test this theorem, however, long-term income distribution data is required. The lack of such data has led to many creative means of testing and to a lack of consensus among economists on how the hypothesis works and what happens when there is increasing per capita growth.

Felix Paukert (1973) used cross-sectional data of countries (although he acknowledged the need for long-term data) and found a tendency toward equality among developed countries, as evidenced by an increase in the share of income of the bottom 60 percent. Among developing countries, however, there is a tendency toward inequality, although Paukert was unable to offer definitive conclusions due to the lack of data in the sample. He therefore analyzed a cross section of forty-three countries and found a Gini ratio of 0.467 among developing countries and 0.392 among developed countries. Since the Gini ratio measures inequality of a distribution ranging from 0 to 1, where 0 corresponds to perfect equality (everyone has the same income) and 1 corresponds to perfect inequality (all but one person has zero income), Paukert's findings suggest that developed countries have moved toward greater equality relative to developing countries.

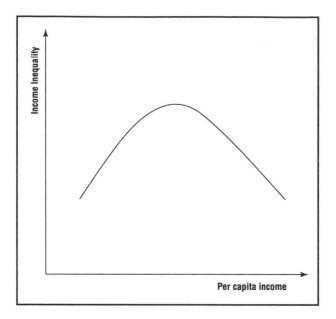

Figure 1

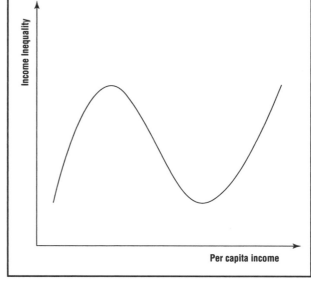

Figure 2

Montek Ahluwalia (1976) followed up on the work of Paukert and determined the relationship between income inequality and per capita growth rate using cross-country data. His sample included sixty countries—forty developing countries, fourteen developed countries, and six socialist countries. Ahluwalia's results showed that an inverted U-shape could be fitted onto the countries at various stages of development and income inequality. However, the slope of the fitted curve changed when he looked at the sample of developing countries. These results were, however, obtained by controlling for socialist countries, because their policies tend to move countries toward development. Ahluwalia suggested that these results may be "stylized facts" for which an explanation may not be possible.

The use of cross-country regressions with countries at different stages of development is not an effective method for testing the Kuznets hypothesis. This method assumes that the turn from increasing to decreasing income inequality happens around the same level of per capita income for all countries. It also assumes homogeneity across countries. Ashwani Saith (1983) questioned whether the empirical work done to confirm the U-hypothesis is in vain. There exists diversity between countries that cannot be accounted for by controlling for whether a country is socialist or developing. A logical way to test the hypothesis may be a time series analysis for individual economies or simultaneous equations on all countries. Nonavailability of the necessary data has kept this project from being undertaken.

THE S-CURVE

Income inequality began increasing in the late 1960s and early 1970s in the United States, England, and Germany, creating yet another puzzle for economists. Rati Ram's (1991) time series study of U.S. data on income inequality from 1947 to 1987 showed that income inequality followed more of a U-shaped pattern than an inverted-U. His data do not include the earlier period of increasing income inequality. This finding has led to the S-curve hypothesis, which implies that with growth in per capita income, an economy will begin to experience increasing and then decreasing income inequality, and after a period of adjustments, income inequality will begin to rise again. Other economists have argued that the inverted-U is just repeating itself, and thus we should expect to see another period of declining inequality. However, the why and when remain unanswered.

John List and Craig Gallet (1999) analyzed data from seventy-one countries for the 1961–1992 period to test this hypothesis, and found that countries could be placed along all the turns of an S-curve. For example, third-world and developed countries are located on the upward-sloping portion of the curve, while emerging economies are located on the downward-sloping portion. Unfortunately, in addition to covering only a short time period, their data did not include all years for all countries. What they ultimately prove is the relationship between per capita income and income inequality in the world. They fail to address historical change in inequality with changes in per capita income.

Romie Tribble (1999) associated the turn from decreasing income inequality to increasing income inequality with another change in the important sector that affects economic growth. The first turning point in the S-curve can be attributed to economies moving from an agricultural to a manufacturing sector. The second turning point occurs when the service sector becomes dominant, a development characterized by increasing returns to education, thus leading to economic growth. Using U.S. data from 1947 to 1990, Tribble proved that the S-curve fit the data. The shifts in the sectors matched the years considered, but he was unable to test this finding. If his analysis is correct, it implies that some developing countries that never build up their manufacturing sector and seemingly move directly from an agricultural sector to a dominant service sector may never experience a period of decreasing income inequality.

THE CURRENT STATE OF INCOME INEQUALITY

An example of whether Kuznets's hypothesis can be translated to other developing countries can be found in the economic growth of Asian countries, especially the "tigers." The four big East Asian tigers—Singapore, Taiwan, Hong Kong, and South Korea—achieved high growth rates between the 1960s and the 1990s through export-driven economies. They were able to maintain this growth rate by an increasing shift to the manufacturing sector, industrialization, and improvements in education. However, armed with the experiences of developed nations, these economies offered protection for their agricultural sector in the form of better property rights and subsidies. A graph of income inequalities as measured by the Gini-coefficient over this period shows Hong Kong with a U-shaped curve, and its minimum inequality occurring in 1980 at a Gini of 0.39. Taiwan experienced declining income inequality up to the 1980s, and its Gini of about 0.29 remained fairly constant thereafter. Singapore and South Korea's income inequality also appears to have remained fairly constant over the time period (data obtained from the UNU/WIDER World Inequality Database, Version 2.0, developed from the Deininger and Squire [1996] dataset).

Income inequality has been increasing in most countries, with the worst increases occurring in developing countries. Countries that should be experiencing decreasing inequality according to the inverted-U hypothesis do not experience it. Increases in cross-country trade, factor mobility, and the ease of capital movement across nations have led to increased globalization. Growth in per capita income could thus be occurring in a nation, but its benefits may not be realized by its population.

CONCLUDING REMARKS

Empirical work done on the Kuznets hypothesis generally begins with an assumption about what the relationship between growth and inequality should be, leading to an estimation technique that confirms the assumption. Growth in per capita income cannot fully explain changes in income inequality. Economic growth does not in itself change the income of the poor; rather, it presents opportunities for improving the population's welfare through the policies adopted in a country. Analyzing this relationship requires a better understanding of these policies and their effects.

Another complication in this analysis is the reverse effects that income inequality could have on economic growth. Economists have theorized that more money in the hands of the rich would lead to increased investments and thus growth in the nation. However, isolating the effects of economic growth could prove daunting.

SEE ALSO *Inequality, Income*

BIBLIOGRAPHY

Ahluwalia, Montek S. 1976. Inequality, Poverty, and Development. *Journal of Development Economics* 3 (4): 307–342.

Deininger, Klaus, and Lyn Squire. 1996. A New Data Set Measuring Income Inequality. *World Bank Economic Review* 10 (3): 565–591.

Kuznets, Simon. Economic Growth and Income Inequality. 1955. *The American Economic Review* 45 (1): 1–28.

Lewis, W. A. 1954. Economic Development with Unlimited Supplies of Labour. *Manchester School* 22: 139–191.

List, John A., and Craig A. Gallet. 1999. The Kuznets Curve: What Happens After the Inverted-U? *Review of Development Economics* 3 (2): 200–206.

Paukert, Felix. 1973. Income Distribution at Different Levels of Development: A Survey of Evidence. *International Labour Review* 108 (2/3): 97–125.

Ram, Rati. 1991. Kuznets's Inverted-U Hypothesis: Evidence from a Highly Developed Country. *Southern Economic Journal* 57 (4): 1112–1123.

Saith, Ashwani. 1983. Development and Distribution: A Critique of the Cross-Country U-Hypothesis. *Journal of Development Economics* 13 (3): 367–382.

Tribble, Romie, Jr. 1999. A Restatement of the S-Curve Hypothesis. *Review of Development Economics* 3 (2): 207–214.

United Nations University: World Institute for Development Economics Research. June 2005. UNU/WIDER World Income Inequality Database, Version 2.0a. http://www.wider.unu.edu/wiid/wiid.htm.

Frimpomaa Ampaw

L

LABAN, RUDOLF VON

SEE *Dance.*

LABANOTATION

SEE *Dance.*

LABELING THEORY

According to the French sociologist Émile Durkheim, the broad themes of labeling theory are located in the definition of crime as necessarily relative. Other antecedents of the explicit theory include Erving Goffman's stigma, Robert K. Merton's discussions of innovators, rebels, and conformers, Frank Tannenbaum's wonder at the actual normalcy of much delinquent behavior, and Edwin M. Lemert's distinction between primary and secondary deviance. The theme of social conflict over the decision of what to label as deviant is at the heart of this concept, and scholars emphasize it repeatedly. Further, John Hagan's work asserts that labeling theory is fundamentally concerned with the effect of the label in the process of creating the deviant career.

The work of identifying the deviant and the importance of the deviant's label has primarily focused on crime and illness, both mental and physical, although Goffman's general concern with stigma and spoiled identities includes attention to understanding minority identities as deviant. After acknowledging the power and consequences of the label, several authors discuss the tools people use to achieve, contest, hide, or discard these labels. In his research, William Chambliss focused on the importance of visibility in the labeling of deviants as in part a function of economic inequality. The expertise of appropriate demeanor when confronted with authorities to whom one is visible is also crucial. Others tools include reinforcement/intervention, identity transformation and reintegration, selective concealment, and negotiation and fighting back.

Although prolific in symbolic interactionist and micro-level approaches, historical analyses of the labeling process look to structural, macro-level processes, such as the change in label from serf to vagrant, and the implications of the "new" phenomenon of middle-class delinquency, understood in part as a function of a failure to label due to structural positions of particular deviants and the "informal handling and preferential treatment" they thus receive (Vaz 1967, p. 1). While not necessarily using labeling theory terminology, the law and society perspective incorporates the idea that what the law does is label and create insiders and outsiders. As well, in general social structural terms, the importance of the moral entrepreneur in re-labeling in social change efforts, such as the Marijuana Tax Act or the civil rights movement, is important.

Critiques of the theory have focused on its assumption of an overly reactive individual. Sethard Fisher argued that labeling theory improperly weighted the label, and did not pay sufficient attention to choice, opportunity, or "common pre-existing characteristics" that might lead one to commit a deviant act (1972, p. 83). This involves a focus on the preexisting in terms of an actual deviant labeling process vis-à-vis a particular instance of behavior, but it is perhaps too narrow a focus. Labeling as a perspective may be understood to encompass attention to the interaction of a host of labels, social positions, or roles. In this early set of critiques, Hagan also posited "psychological difference" as one such preexisting difference that labeling theory does not attend to with enough rigor. However, research does support that preexisting differences such as class, race, and gender are among the prime concerns of the perspective, even if psychological differences per se are not.

Hagan's late-twentieth-century work introduced the Power-Control theory, which emphasizes inherent power relations in determining delinquent actions and what is considered deviant; for example, "the class structure of the family plays a significant role in explaining the social distribution of delinquent behavior through the social reproduction of gender relations" (1988, p. 146). This is an explicit acknowledgement of the problem of failing to live up to a variety of labels (e.g., girl, middle-class, white). However, this position does not seem to acknowledge that interaction across "vertical, hierarchical lines of power" has indeed been the major theme of labeling theory. For example, "[P]ower usually brings preferential symbolism" (1988 p. 2) seems to be another way to say, "In the eyes of the police and school officials, a boy who drinks in an alley and stands intoxicated on a street corner is committing a more serious offense than a boy who drinks to inebriation in a nightclub or a tavern and drives around afterwards in a car" (Chambliss 1973, p. 10). "What distinguishes a structural criminology is its attention to instrumental and symbolic uses of power, both in relation to criminal behavior and in the study of reactions to this behavior" (Hogan 1988, p. 2), is not unlike Nancy J. Herman's argument—albeit in the lifeworld of the ex-crazy—on such negotiations of power. Thus, the newer perspectives of critical criminology and structural criminology are in many ways permutations of the general themes of the labeling perspective: "rules are the product of someone's initiative" and "duties are imposed upon us that we have not expressly wished. Yet it is through a voluntary act that they arose" (Becker 1963, p. 147; Durkheim 1982, p. 174). In other words, members of society must negotiate over their labels, even if they do so from within unequal positions of social power.

SEE ALSO *Deviance*

BIBLIOGRAPHY

Becker, Howard S. 1963. *The Outsiders.* New York: Free Press.

Chambliss, William. 1964. A Sociological Analysis of the Laws of Vagrancy. *Social Problems* 12 (1): 67–77.

Chambliss, William. 1973. The Saints and the Roughnecks. *Society* 11 (2): 4–31.

Durkheim, Émile. 1982. *The Rules of the Sociological Method.* Trans. W. D. Halls. New York: Free Press. (Orig. pub. 1896).

Fisher, Sethard. 1972. Stigma and Deviant Careers in School. *Social Problems* 20 (1): 78–83.

Goffman, Erving. 1959. The Moral Career of the Mental Patient. *Psychiatry* 22 (2): 123–142.

Goffman, Erving. 1961. *Asylums.* Garden City, NY: Doubleday.

Goffman, Erving. 1963. *Stigma: Notes on the Management of a Spoiled Identity.* Englewood Cliffs, NJ: Prentice Hall.

Hagan, John. 1973. Labeling and Social Deviance: A Case Study in the "Sociology of the Interesting." *Social Problems* 20 (4): 447–458.

Hagan, John. 1988. *Structural Criminology.* New Brunswick, NJ: Rutgers University Press.

Hagan, John. 1994. *Crime and Disrepute.* Thousand Oaks, CA: Pine Forge Press.

Herman, Nancy J. 1993. Return to Sender: Reintegrative Stigma-Management Strategies of Ex-Psychiatric Patients. *Journal of Contemporary Ethnography* 22 (3): 295–330.

Lazarus-Black, Mindie. 1994. *Legitimate Acts and Illegal Encounters: Law and Society in Antigua and Barbuda.* Washington and London: Smithsonian Institution Press.

Lemert, Edwin M. 1951. *Social Pathology.* New York: McGraw-Hill.

Kitsuse, John I. 1964. Societal Reaction to Deviant Behavior: Problems of Theory and Method. In *The Other Side: Perspectives on Deviance,* ed. Howard S. Becker. New York: Free Press of Glencoe.

Marshall, Gordon. 1998. *Oxford Dictionary of Sociology.* Oxford: Oxford University Press.

Merton, Robert K. 1938. Social Structure and Anomie. *American Sociological Review* 3 (5): 672–682.

Tannenbaum, Frank. 1951. *Crime and the Community.* New York: McGraw-Hill.

Vaz, Edmund W., ed. 1967. *Middle-Class Juvenile Delinquency.* New York: Harper and Row Publishers.

Sarah N. Gatson

LABOR

Labor is one of the three primary factors of production, next to capital and land. However, different from the other two, labor deals with the work of humans rather than money or the property it can rent or buy. Being part of labor requires thus that one is paid for one's labor services.

The provision of labor was seen by the French sociologist Émile Durkheim (1858–1917) as part of the identification of a worker with society or part of the struggle of the personality with society. The laborer as the member of a class—the working class—is also a recurring theme in sociology. Two classical expositions come from the political philosopher Karl Marx (1818–1883), who offers a historical analysis of class struggle, and the sociologist Max

Weber (1864–1920), who uses class more as a classification of stratification. The reward of wages in the context of labor, especially its share of the entire production process encompassing all factors of production, also mirrors the importance and power of the class within society.

ANCIENT LABOR TO INDUSTRIALIZATION

Ancient labor markets, especially in ancient Greece and Rome, were based on agriculture and manufacturing. Both relied heavily on slave labor, which provided both skilled and unskilled labor.

In medieval times, the common agricultural laborer, or peasant, produced for self-sufficiency, and there was little exchange economy. Labor was dependent on the aristocrats, who were the landowners. The feudal landlords granted protection and the right to use the land in exchange for taxes that included labor services, which is commonly called bondage. This hierarchy from lord to serf was common from higher to lower aristocracy and from aristocrats to peasants. Extortion of both goods and labor services were enforced not only by the aristocracy's ownership of the land, but also by their executive and judicial power.

Manufacturing, which was usually strong in the free cities (i.e., those not under the rule of an aristocrat), was in the hands of guilds whose members organized themselves to protect their interests. Workers had to learn a craft by going through the apprenticeship as journeyman, and they depended on their guild master both financially and also professionally as the guild masters decided upon elevation to the master level. While labor was in this sense not free, moving to the free cities to become a craftsman allowed one to free oneself from aristocratic rule.

Factory work forms the core process of industrialization, moving away from small-scale production at home and toward large-scale, specialized production. This specialization process is described with the example of the pin factory by the Scottish economist Adam Smith (1723–1790):

> [I]n the way in which this business is now carried on, not only the whole work is a peculiar trade, but it is divided into a number of branches, of which the greater part are likewise peculiar trades. One man draws out the wire, another straights it, a third cuts it, a fourth points it, a fifth grinds it at the top for receiving the head; to make the head requires two or three distinct operations; to put it on, is a peculiar business, to whiten the pins is another; it is even a trade by itself to put them into the paper; and the important business of making a pin is, in this manner, divided into about eighteen distinct operations, which, in some manufactures, are all performed by distinct hands. (Smith 1776, p. 15)

While Smith understood the importance of specialization, in his time the impact of machines was probably still underestimated. Mechanization using the steam engine in the eighteenth century led to a higher productivity of factory work, which is commonly seen as the breakthrough in the process of industrialization.

Smith did provide the intellectual underpinning of the capitalist model in which the pursuit of self-interest under free competition leads to higher wealth for society. His influential work was even used in English courts to prohibit union activities, as the unionization of labor was seen as a hindrance to free competition.

Together, mechanization and specialization led to a certain alienation of the laborer toward the production process. Labor became, next to capital, a true factor of modern production. During the period of industrialization, peasant workers moved away from agricultural work and toward that of unskilled labor in the newly established manufacturing plants. These laborers were no longer dependent on landowners but became wage workers, forming the working class. The process of industrialization was a long one. Exploitation of the workers was the norm rather than the exception as sufficient labor arrived from the ranks of agricultural workers. Edward P. Thompson, in "The Moral Economy of the English Crowd in the Eighteenth Century" (1971), writes of the formative years from 1780 to 1832 in England. He describes in detail the life and the movements of the English working class of that time. It was through the struggle of the workers that the notion of a working class evolved, which was necessary to develop labor organization.

It took about a century for wage labor to become the norm in the nineteenth century as increasingly more workers were employed, replacing work on the land with work in the newly established factories. The movement from larger workshops to mechanized industries took two centuries, from the late eighteenth century into the early twentieth century. Industrialization commenced in England and was started in continental Europe several decades later, starting with Flanders, France, and later in Germany, Switzerland, and some southern European countries.

LABOR ORGANIZATION

Labor organization commenced in Europe in the eighteenth century, first within an urban setting or within factories, solely to perform the social functions of exchange and insurance against illness. National organization arose in Europe in the late nineteenth century. It was the skilled worker, at a level between owner and unskilled labor, who participated in the organization of labor in unions. Labor organization was not at first a reaction to hardship. In fact, the living standards of workers, unionized or not, were steadily rising throughout Europe from 1850 to 1900.

The history of unions in the United States started in the nineteenth century. In the turbulent decades from 1870 to 1890 the groundwork for organized labor was laid. The National Labor Union (NLU), founded in 1866, was the first federation of unions, followed by the Knights of Labor in 1869. The latter disintegrated after the Haymarket Riot on May 1, 1886, in Chicago in which unions unsuccessfully demanded the eight-hour working day.

The American Federation of Labor (AFL), founded in 1886, organized mainly skilled workers, while the more radical Industrial Workers of the World (IWW), founded in 1905, provided a federation for unskilled labor. The membership in the IWW declined with the Palmer Raids (1918–1921), named for Alexander Mitchell Palmer, the U.S. attorney general after World War I who led the government attack on the radical left during the "Red Scare" period.

Unions in the United States did not become a political factor in those years. This has been attributed to several reasons: The U.S. political system was fragmented between states and the federal level, and it discouraged worker movements. Furthermore, employers' associations reacted very strongly against the labor organizations. Janet Currie and Joseph Ferrie argue in the *Journal of Economic History* (2000) that despite some legislative changes in favor of the laborer, unions refrained from a national political influence and instead sought to negotiate on a company level.

This changed after the Great Depression and especially under the New Deal programs of President Franklin D. Roosevelt. The labor movement was strengthened, and the government found its role in brokering agreements between businesses and labor unions. The government's aims were to provide some assistance to poor and unemployed workers and to establish the rights of labor unions, which culminated in the Wagner Act.

During the 1930s, the Congress of Industrial Organizations (CIO) organized industrial workers who were part of the emerging large-scale corporations. This represented a movement from crafts-based unionism toward industry unions. The CIO argued that crafts-based unionism was no longer suitable to many industries in which several crafts were undertaken, thus artificially dividing the unionized workers within a firm. One union organized within the CIO was the United Auto Workers (UAW). The CIO split off from the AFL to form its own entity in 1938. After World War II (1939–1945), as most differences were settled, the two combined into the AFL-CIO, under which most unions are aligned.

NEW MODES OF PRODUCTION, LABOR SAVINGS, AND GLOBALIZATION

The 1960s marked the beginning of steady decline in union membership. After the economically strong years following World War II, workers faced increasingly more plant shutdowns. During the 1970s the fear of mechanization and the displacement of men by machines was a recurring theme. In the 1980s cheaper foreign labor began replacing domestic labor. This was most explicit within the automobile industry, in which European and especially Japanese manufacturers provided fierce competition against the American car manufacturers. Under this pressure, union power eroded over time. The fear of globalization was amplified during the negotiations about the North American Free Trade Agreement, which opened up the markets of Mexico, Canada, and the United States in 1994. The opponents feared U.S. workplaces being moved to Mexico, with cheaper labor and lower working standards. In consecutive years, intensifying trade and the outsourcing of labor-intensive industries, especially to Asian countries, weakened the union even more.

This increasing globalization was anticipated in Robert Reich's book *The Work of Nations* (1991). His main theme is that the division of workers into skilled and unskilled occupations is extended to a threefold partition into routine producers, in-person service providers (services that have to be provided person to person), and knowledge workers. The last type is rather broad as it includes some people who are usually not considered part of labor, such as entrepreneurs. It is this last type of worker for whom Reich foresees the best prospects, while the routine producers in particular will be replaced either by foreign competition or machines. The in-person service workers are somewhat protected from foreign competition as they require the physical availability of labor.

While the traditional struggle between the capitalist class (the providers of capital) and the labor class seems outdated, Stanley Aronowitz argues in *How Class Works* (2003) that labor still struggles over institutional arrangements such as working hours, overtime pay, and working conditions. These social movements are in essence class struggles over the division of power between capital and labor. In the United States capital is still the decisive element, argues Aronowitz, as the workers did not unite the aims of the different groups (immigrants versus native, black versus white, male versus female), but Aronowitz argues labor should still strive to unite as a force in order to strongly support its common goals.

U.S. FEDERAL LABOR LAW

Labor law reflects the struggle and achievement of labor in a nation. In the United States, the following legal developments show the evolution of current laws. While not intended to forbid the labor unions, the Sherman Antitrust Act of 1890 was used for many years to hinder union work. Its unspecific nature prohibiting "combinations in restraint of trade" allowed its use against combined, unionized demands from workers. The Clayton Antitrust Act, Section 6 (1914), remedies this shortcoming as it explicitly exempts labor unions. The National Labor Relations Act, or the Wagner Act (1935), allowed union representation and established the National Labor Relations Board. It allowed for collective bargaining and strikes to enforce demands. However, the Wagner Act does not encompass all workers; agricultural workers, for example, are excluded.

The Fair Labor Standards Act (1938) enacts minimum wages and overtime pay, and it abolishes oppressive child labor. While it originally included many exemptions, over time several of those have been eliminated so the act covers all blue-collar workers while excluding supervisory functions.

During World War II, the Fair Employment Act (1941) was introduced, prohibiting racial discrimination. Initially it was intended only for the national defense industry, but it was later extended to encompass all labor relations and to prohibit many forms of discrimination in the workplace.

The Taft-Hartley Act (1947), or Labor-Management Relations Act, and the Labor Management Reporting and Disclosure Act (1959) amended the National Labor Relations Act to restrict union power. The acts prohibit unfair labor practices by unions, which were previously only prohibited for employers. Unions were no longer allowed to influence the employers in their allocation of work to different plants. Secondary boycotts—for example, the refusal to handle the goods of non-unionized companies—were also prohibited. Closed-shop agreements—that only union labor could be hired by employers—were also outlawed.

LABOR INSTITUTIONS

The International Labor Organization (ILO) was created in 1919. There were several reasons for the establishment of such an organization. Its primary concern, a humanitarian one, was for the welfare of the worker. Numerous workers in many different countries had to work under exploitative circumstances, threatening their life, health, and family life. A second purpose was to integrate the growing working class into the political process and thereby to avoid social unrest or revolutions that could impede international peace. This aim is also found in the constitution of the ILO, as peace can only be achieved along with social justice. An economic motivation for the establishment of the ILO was concern over the cost of upholding humanitarian working standards. It was generally agreed that international standards for working conditions would avoid a race to the bottom—that is, a competition among nations over low labor costs, to the detriment of the workers. The organization of the ILO is tripartite. Each member country has two representatives of the government, one of the employers' associations, and one of the labor unions.

In 1926 the ILO introduced a supervisory system to control the implementation and enforcement of its standards. This was an important step toward a more functional organization that went beyond discussing pressing issues. The United States, which was involved in several aspects of the founding and establishment of the ILO, became a member in 1934. One of the main steps forward was the Declaration of Philadelphia, adopted in 1944, which introduced freedom of association for workers. In 1969, the ILO was awarded the Nobel Peace Prize.

The U.S. Department of Labor is the governmental organization responsible for labor in relation to occupational safety, wage and hour standards, unemployment insurance benefits, reemployment services, and labor statistics. On the national level, the Bureau of Labor Statistics is the principal organization within the United States to provide statistical information and research for the government. While it is part of the Department of Labor, it serves as an independent statistical agency and provides labor market statistics as well as occupational forecasts. Other countries have organizations that have similar goals, albeit often less extensive ones.

SEE ALSO *Agricultural Industry; Capitalism; Class Conflict; Division of Labor; Factories; Factory System; Industrialization; Industry; Labor Force Participation; Labor Market; Labor Supply; Labor Union; Management; Productivity; Smith, Adam; Thompson, Edward P.; Unions; Work; Work Day; Work Week*

BIBLIOGRAPHY

Aronowitz, Stanley. 2003. *How Class Works: Power and Social Movement*. New Haven, CT: Yale University Press.

Berger, Stefan, and David Broughton, eds. 1995. *The Force of Labour: The Western European Labour Movement and the Working Class in the Twentieth Century*. Oxford: Berg Publishers.

Commons, John R., David J. Saposs, Helen L. Sumner, et al. 1918–1936. *History of Labour in the United States*. New York: Macmillan.

Currie, Janet, and Joseph P. Ferrie. 2000. The Law and Labor Strife in the U.S., 1881–1894. *Journal of Economic History* 60: 42–66.

Durkheim, Émile. 1984. *The Division of Labor in Society*. Trans. W. D. Halls. New York: Free Press.

Geary, Dick. 1981. *European Labour Protest, 1848–1939*. New York: St. Martin's Press.

Henderson, W. O. 1954. *Britain and Industrial Europe, 1750–1870: Studies in British Influence on the Industrial Revolution in Western Europe*. Liverpool, U.K.: Liverpool University Press.

Marx, Karl. [1867–1894] 1971. *Das Kapital*. Vols. 1–3. London: Lawrence & Wishart.

Reich, Robert B. 1991. *The Work of Nations: Preparing Ourselves for 21st-Century Capitalism*. New York: Alfred A. Knopf.

Smith, Adam. [1776] 1904. *An Inquiry into the Nature and Causes of the Wealth of Nations*. 5th ed. London: Methuen and Co.

Thompson, Edward P. 1971. The Moral Economy of the English Crowd in the Eighteenth Century. *Past and Present* 50 (1): 76–136.

Weber, Max. [1922] 1978. *Economy and Society: An Outline of Interpretive Sociology*. Berkeley: University of California Press.

Ben Kriechel

LABOR, MARGINAL PRODUCT OF

Consider a firm producing a homogeneous output y employing labor l and other n factors of production: x_1, x_2, ..., x_n. The change in output resulting from the addition of one extra unit of labor, with the other inputs being held constant, is called the marginal, or physical, product of labor (MPL). Formally, assuming that the technology of the firm is described by the production function $y = f(l, x_1, x_2, ..., x_n)$, MPL is expressed as follows:

$$MPL = \frac{\Delta y}{\Delta l} \quad (\text{given } x_1, x_2, ...x_n)$$

Broadly speaking, the concept of MPL describes the ratio of change in output stemming from a small, or "marginal," increase in the use of labor. Moreover, modern neoclassical production theory assumes that labor (and the other inputs it is combined with) can be employed at a continuous level (a realistic assumption labor is measured in "labor time"), and that the production function is continuous, with continuous first derivatives. The marginal product of labor can then be rigorously expressed by the first partial derivative of f with respect to l:

$$MPL = \frac{\partial f(l, x_1, x_2, ...x_n)}{\partial l}$$

Although the same name is generally given to the two definitions reported above—and what follows will con-

form to this general use—it would be more appropriate to call the former (the discrete case) the "marginal product of labor," while the latter (the continuous case) would be more appropriately defined as the "marginal *productivity* of labor." These definitions may be easily extended to the case of joint production, that is, when a firm, for a given combination of inputs, produces more than one output (the so-called multiproduct firm).

THE MARGINAL PRODUCT OF LABOR AND THE DISTRIBUTION OF INCOME

The concept of MPL has a central place in marginal productivity theory, since at the very core of this approach is the understanding that in a competitive market the remuneration of each productive factor should be equal to its marginal contribution to production. A direct implication is that as the relative prices of factors change, the proportion in which they are employed will change as well, in order to reestablish equality between marginal product and input prices. This is known as the *principle of variation*. With respect to labor (p and w are, respectively, the unit prices of output and labor), profit maximization requires that, at equilibrium, the real wage should be equal to MPL: $\frac{\Delta y}{\Delta l} = \frac{w}{p}$. This can also be written as $p\frac{\Delta y}{\Delta l} = w$ (the second order condition for a maximum is guaranteed by the assumption that MPL is, at least to a certain level of l on, a decreasing function of l). The equation $p\frac{\Delta y}{\Delta l}$ represents *the value of the marginal product of labor* (VMPL) and its schedule below the maximum of the *value of average product of labor* (VAPL $= p\frac{y}{l}$) represents the short-run firm's demand curve for labor. If the firm operates in a noncompetitive market for its product, profit maximization requires that MPL × MR = w, where MR is the marginal revenue generated by an extra unit of output (in perfect competition MR = p). MPL × MR is called *the marginal revenue product*, and in this case its schedule (below the maximum of VAPL) represents the short-run firm's demand curve for labor (a deeper analysis of these matters may be found in any standard microeconomic text).

THE LAW OF VARIABLE PROPORTIONS AND THE LAW OF DIMINISHING PRODUCT

Consider, for the sake of simplicity, a "canonical" short-run production function: $y = f(K_0, l) = F(l)$, where l (as before) is labor, y is the output of the firm, and K_0 is a fixed given amount of another input that is conventionally defined as "capital" (or better services of a "capital good"). Neoclassical production theory admits various possibilities concerning the variation of MPL as l changes. According to the *law of variable proportions,* as the firm increases the use of labor, holding K constant at a given level (K_0), the output will first increase at an increasing rate up to a point, say $l = l^*$, and thereafter increase at a decreasing rate, depicting a *S*-shaped production function. This law expresses the idea that, for given input prices, there is an optimal employment ratio of K and l in correspondence of each quantity of output produced, but since capital is an indivisible input the firm cannot use less capital than K_0. Consequently, the first increments of l will cause y to increase at an increasing rate, since the addition of further units of labor leads to a more "favorable" proportion between l and K_0. However, successive additions of labor will lead, sooner or later, to a point (E in Fig. 1) where the constraint of the constant factor will operate in the opposite manner. From this point on, further units of labor lead to a less "favorable" proportion between l and K_0, so that each additional unit of labor will add less output than its predecessors.

Another widely used assumption about MPL is the so-called *law of diminishing product,* which states that as l increases, output will always increase less than proportionately, implying a concave production function (the explanation is the same as for the one given above from point E on). Although this second law avoids the indivisibility

assumption (which is not necessary in the neoclassical productivity theory, and may lead to some theoretical contradictions), it rests on an idea that is sometimes difficult to justify: that MPL will always decrease whatever the given amount of K may be.

Both laws admit the possibility that a level of l may be reached at which MPL = 0, after which further increments of l will cause the MPL to become negative. One could say that at this point the given capital stock will treat further additions of labor as a "disservice."

HISTORICAL DEVELOPMENT OF THE CONCEPT

The first formulation of the law of variable proportions can be found in a work by the French economist Anne-Robert-Jacques Turgot (1727–1781), who showed that when advances (seeds) on a given piece of land are increased, the product will first rise more than proportionately, but that after a certain point the diminishing product will prevail, until "the fertility of the soil being exhausted … an addition to the advances will add nothing whatever to the produce" (quoted in Sraffa 1925, pp. 327–328). The role of MPL in the explanation of labor's reward may be found in various forerunners of marginal revolution, and in the works of the earlier neoclassical economists—particularly William Stanly Jevons (1835–1882) and Carl Menger (1840–1921). Only in the 1890s, however, with the contributions of John Bates Clark, Alfred Marshall, Knut Wicksell, and Philip H. Wicksteed, was a coherent theory of distribution fully established. Marshall, also through numerical examples, proved that profit maximization requires that real wages equal MLP. Clark claimed that, according to the marginal theory, production and distribution become faces of the same process of determination of value (undoubtedly one of the main goals of neoclassical theory), and that each "social class gets what it contributes, under natural law, to the general output of industry" (Clark 1891, p. 313; see also Clark 1899, p. v).

A few years later, however, Wicksteed showed that the marginal theory of distribution, in order to be consistent, must assume a homogeneous production function of degree 1 (i.e., constant returns to scale). Only under this assumption, in fact, would the sum of factors' rewards, determined on the basis of their marginal products, be equal to the total output produced (this is the *product exhaustion theorem*). The assumptions about production processes and the "laws" governing income distribution thus became strictly interconnected, requiring the marginal theory of distribution, if it is to be consistent, to postulate a particular configuration of productive processes. Wicksell thus suggested using the following production function (later called Cobb-Douglas): $y = l^\alpha K^\beta$, with $\alpha > 0$, $\beta > 0$, $\alpha + \beta = 1$. This function, and the law of diminishing product of labor (and

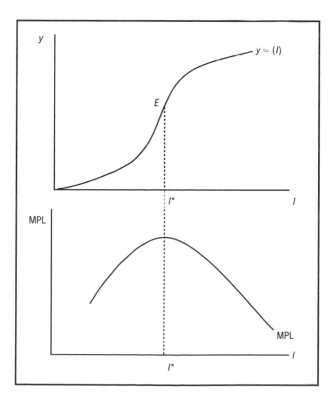

Figure 1: The Law of Variable Proportions

of capital) it incorporates, is still the most commonly used in neoclassical micro- and macroeconomic theory. It should be noted that the assumption of constant returns to scale represents a serious limitation, since it rules out the important phenomenon of increasing returns to scale—that is, it rules out the case for: $\alpha + \beta > 1$ (see Debreu 1959, p. 41, for a similar statement with regard to general economic equilibrium analysis).

SOME CRITICISMS

Soon after its formulation, the neoclassical theory of wages raised many "grumbles," as Dennis Robertson put it. One criticism concerned the distributive justice implied by what Clark defined as "natural law." It was pointed out that only the last—or better, the "marginal"—worker would be paid according to his or her contribution to production (equal to the marginal product), while all the other workers would be paid less than that, because under the assumption of diminishing product of labor, their marginal product is higher than that of the last worker employed. The marginal theory of distribution would therefore imply labor "exploitation."

Two points should be noted here. First, it makes sense to talk of a "first worker," a "second worker," and so on, only in a logical sense, since labor l is a homogeneous factor of production, and all that can really be discussed is the marginal product of the homogeneous factor l (Clark 1891, p. 308). Second, the "exploitation" (of both labor and other inputs) is denied by the assumption (fully compatible with other hypothesis about MPL) of constant returns to scale, which guarantees product exhaustion.

Contrary to Clark's claim, however, even if labor is considered a homogeneous factor, empirical evidence suggests that discrimination on labor markets may lead to wage differentials for equally productive worker groups. Beginning with the seminal work of Gary Becker in 1957, neoclassical theory has explained *discrimination* mainly as the outcome of personal prejudices of some groups (particularly employers) against others (women, racial minorities, etc.). Suppose that an employer (in a competitive product market) has a prejudice against a group, say women (although females and males have, by assumption, the same marginal productivity). On the basis of this prejudice, the employer will undervalue women's contribution to production, with the consequence that different equilibrium wages for the two groups will be fixed. The monetary wages of females and males are represented by w_f and w_m, respectively, so that labor market equilibrium conditions are given by   for males, and by

for females, where $d > 0$ is the "discrimination coefficient" that measures the employer's prejudice. Since MPL is the same for both men and women, it is easy

to realize that women will be paid *less* than their VMPL (i.e., $w_f = w_m - d$). According to this model, discrimination is possible only in the short run, however, since competition among employers and workers will eventually equalize the wages of the two groups.

Alternative non-neoclassical models explain the persistence of discrimination by focusing on the "segmented labor market approach," in a general noncompetitive theoretical framework. According to this approach, if the labor market is split into submarkets (think of the "dual" labor-market case, with a "primary" and a "secondary" segment), and if there are barriers to employee mobility, discrimination may take the form of occupational segregation, since workers who are discriminated against will be crowded into the only accessible labor market characterized by a lower equilibrium wage. In this case, however, unlike the neoclassical "taste model" presented above, all workers are paid according to their actual VMPL and wage differentials are the result of different labor supply conditions in the two submarkets, given the presence of barriers to employee mobility (see Smith 2003, ch. 6 and Ehrenberg-Smith 2003, ch. 12, for an exhaustive overview of discrimination theories).

Other criticisms concentrate on the "impossibility of disentangling the specific product of the various factors of production, even at the margin of their application" (Robertson 1931, p. 224). This argument rejects the very possibility of defining and measuring the marginal product of a factor (and particularly of labor). Among the various authors who have raised objections of this kind is J. A. Hobson, who did a good job synthesizing the various implications of the argument. In his view, if a productive process is characterized by cooperating factors employed in a well-defined proportion, an increase or a reduction of one of these factors (e.g., labor) will imply a reorganization of the entire process, thus modifying the average and marginal product of all the other fixed factors. If this is the case, it is not possible to attribute the corresponding change in output to one variable factor alone. Marshall, following Francis Y. Edgeworth, claimed that Hobson mistakenly assumed a discrete "violent check" in the supply of one input, rather than referring to continuous variations at the margin. In this case, the changes in the marginal product of the fixed factors would be negligible. In other words, Hobson's critics maintain that he was wrong because he was referring to a "broad" variation , while rigorously marginal productivity theory is concerned with the infinitesimal variation . Here, the relevance of the distinction between the marginal product and the marginal productivity of labor becomes apparent.

Hobson, however, was clearly discussing quite a different problem, which can be explained in the following way: If inputs used in a productive process must be employed in a well-defined fixed proportion, the principle of variation is not effective, and consequently the marginal product of labor (or of any other input) is a meaningless concept. An increase in one unit of labor will probably yield no additional output, while the withdrawal of one unit of labor will cause a notable diminution of both total product and the contribution of other inputs. In other words, if capital has to be considered as a specified physical endowment of goods, it could be combined only with a specified amount of labor (unless it is a sort of "butter capital" or "jelly capital," as John B. Clark put it, that can employ a widely variable quantity of labor). This position is still supported by many opponents to neoclassical theory, and it was partially supported by some of the older neoclassical economists, such as Léon Walras and Vilfredo Pareto.

There is a less radical way to consider Hobson's criticism. Although an extra unit of labor may cause an increase in total output, this can only occur if the productive process is reorganized by way of a change in technique of production, such as an increase in the division of labor. But this means that one is not working on the same production function, but rather "jumping" from one function to another one. In this case, there would be little sense in talking about the marginal product of labor in a static framework. The idea of a change in the technological configuration as the employment of labor is changed is a characteristic feature of modern theory of economic growth and particularly of the literature on increasing returns (a line of thought of this kind can be traced back to Adam Smith, passing through Allyn A. Young up to the contributions in the late 1990s of James Buchanan and Yong J. Yoon with their notion of "generalized increasing returns").

Hobson's criticism anticipated most of the elements later discussed in the famous "Cambridge Capital Controversies" that raged from the mid-1950s to the mid-1970s between neoclassical economists in Cambridge, Massachusetts, and post-Keynesian economists in Cambridge, United Kingdom. Although the controversy was mainly concerned with the nature and the unit of measure of capital, it nevertheless had serious implications for the consistency of the whole marginal theory of distribution. In fact, the main theoretical result of the debate was that if one considers a production process that employs (given the assumption of constant returns to scale) at least one other factor of production in addition to labor (i.e., "capital"), then, in general, it will be impossible to derive distributive shares from the specification of production function. Furthermore, the critics pointed out that, in general, other "strange" phenomena—such as "capital inversion" or the "re-switching of techniques"—may occur, which would undermine the principle of variation.

In conclusion, the only case consistent with the marginal productivity theory is that of a "one-commodity" economy, in which capital (in line with Clark's definition) is indistinguishable from consumption goods, and in which the only specific input is represented by labor. But in this case, as the critics have pointed out, both Ricardian and Marxian theories of value and distribution hold.

SEE ALSO *Becker, Gary; Cambridge Capital Controversy; Crowding Hypothesis; Economics, Labor; Economics, Marxian; Economics, Neoclassical; Economics, Neo-Ricardian; Economics, Post Keynesian; Employment; Exploitation; Income Distribution; Labor Demand; Labor Force Participation; Labor Market; Labor Market Segmentation; Labor Supply; Marginalism; Marshall, Alfred; Returns to Scale; Returns, Diminishing; Smith, Adam; Wages*

BIBLIOGRAPHY

Becker, Gary S. 1957. *The Economics of Discrimination.* Chicago: University of Chicago Press.

Buchanan, James, and Yong J. Yoon. 1999. Generalized Increasing Returns, Euler's Theorem, and Competitive Equilibrium. *History of Political Economy* 31 (3): 512–523.

Clark, John B. 1891. Distribution as Determined by a Law of Rent. *Quarterly Journal of Economics* 5 (3): 289–318.

Clark, John B. 1899. *The Distribution of Wealth: A Theory of Wages, Interest, and Profits.* London: Macmillan, 1927.

Colacchio, Giorgio, and Anna Soci. 2003. On the Aggregate Production Function and Its Presence in Modern Macroeconomics. *Structural Change and Economic Dynamics* 14 (1): 75–107.

Debreu, Gerard. 1959. *Theory of Value: An Axiomatic Analysis of Economic Equilibrium.* New York: Wiley.

Edgeworth, Francis Y. 1911. The Theory of Distribution. In *Papers Relating to Political Economy.* Vol. I, ed. Francis Y. Edgeworth, 13–60. New York: Burt Franklin, 1925.

Ehrenberg, Ronald G., and Robert S. Smith. 2003. *Modern Labor Economics.* 8th ed. Reading, MA: Addison-Wesley.

Georgescu-Roegen, Nicolaus. 1935. Fixed Coefficients of Production and the Marginal Productivity Theory. *Review of Economic Studies* 3 (1): 40–49.

Gravelle, Hugh, and Ray Rees. 2004. *Microeconomics.* 3rd ed. Edinburgh Gate, U.K.: Pearson Education.

Harcourt, Geoffrey C. 1972. *Some Cambridge Controversies in the Theory of Capital.* Cambridge, U.K.: Cambridge University Press.

Hicks, John R. 1932. Marginal Productivity and the Principle of Variation. *Economica* 35 (February): 79–88.

Hobson, John A., 1909. *The Industrial System: An Inquiry into Earned and Unearned Income.* Reprints of Economic Classics. New York: Augustus M. Kelley, 1969.

Marshall, Alfred. 1920. *Principles of Economics.* Vols. I and II. 9th (variorum) edition, with annotations by C. W. Guillebaud. Cambridge, U.K.: Cambridge University Press, 1961.

Robertson, Dennis. 1931. Wage Grumbles. In *Readings on the Theory of Income Distribution*, ed. American Economic Association, 221–236. Philadelphia: Blakiston, 1946.

Smith, Stephen. 2003. *Labour Economics*. 2nd ed. London and New York: Routledge.

Sraffa, Piero. 1925. On the Relation Between Cost and Quantity Produced. In *Italian Economic Papers*, vol. III, ed. Luigi L. Pasinetti, 323–363. Bologna, Italy: Il Mulino, 1998.

Varian, Hal R. 1999. *Intermediate Microeconomics: A Modern Approach*. 5th ed. New York: W. W. Norton.

Wicksell, Knut. 1901. *Lectures on Political Economy*. Vol. I. London: Routledge, 1934.

Wicksteed, Philip H. 1894. *The Co-ordination of the Laws of Distribution*. Classics in the History of Economics. Aldershot, UK: Edward Elgar, 1992.

Young, Allyn A. 1929. Increasing Returns and Economic Progress. *The Economic Journal* 38 (December): 527–542.

Giorgio Colacchio

LABOR, SURPLUS: CONVENTIONAL ECONOMICS

Surplus labor models are a class of models for analyzing developing countries as dual economies with a modern capitalist sector and a traditional precapitalist sector. The precapitalist sector is viewed as having a large pool ("unlimited supplies") of labor from which the capitalist sector may draw at constant cost. While these models are often described as finding their inspiration in the old classical economists and Karl Marx, the 1954 model of W. Arthur Lewis and its extensions are technically more neoclassical than truly classical. The Lewis model was elaborated and formalized by many others, most notably John C. H. Fei and Gustav Ranis (1964), with important theoretical contributions from Amartya Sen (1966) and Stephen Marglin (1976). Questions have been raised as to the historical relevance of the neoclassical labor surplus models (Schultz 1964; Myint 1971; Arrighi 1973; Williamson 1985).

In the Lewis model, the economy is divided into two sectors, a traditional precapitalist sector and a modern capitalist sector. Lewis emphasized that this sectoral distinction is not identical to that between manufacturing and agriculture, as there may be both traditional (craft) manufactures and capitalist agriculture. The traditional sector is characterized by a large pool of labor, available to the modern sector at a constant (subsistence) wage. The wage is exogenous and above the marginal product of labor in the traditional sector. Thus the labor supply in the modern sector is infinitely elastic. Lewis stated that the marginal product of labor in the traditional sector could be small, zero, or even negative, but whereas he also emphasized that this was not an assumption of fundamental importance, later developers and critics of the model devoted considerable attention to this assumption. For Lewis, the supply of labor is considered "unlimited" as long as the labor supply exceeds labor demand at the subsistence wage rate. The demand for labor in the modern sector is determined by the stock of capital. Under such conditions, labor shortage is never a constraint on the expansion of the modern sector. As demand is also not a constraint on expansion in the Lewis model, the modern sector hires labor out of the traditional sector, and output increases. Profits in the modern sector rise and are reinvested, fueling capital accumulation. This is how successful "development" is defined. Eventually, the marginal product of labor and the wage will become equal in both the traditional and modern sector, and dualism comes to an end. With the equalization of the wage in the two sectors, the presumption is that the wage will now be "neoclassically" (i.e., "market") determined.

A number of criticisms have been made of the Lewis model (see, for example, Leeson 1979; Bharadwaj 1979). First, it has been argued that the model assumes that employment transfer proceeds at the same rate as capital accumulation in the modern sector, and that this will not be the case if there is laborsaving technological change in that sector. Lewis did recognize that there are two forces working in opposite directions—capital accumulation increasing employment and technical advance which may reduce employment—though he rejected the argument that the latter would outweigh the former on empirical grounds in his original article. Second, a number of critics have asserted that the situation in many developing countries is precisely the opposite of what Lewis assumed: There is significant unemployment and underemployment in urban areas and full employment in rural areas. A defense of Lewis might point out that the traditional/modern distinction is not the same as the rural/urban distinction, and that what appears as full employment in some areas is disguised unemployment; people are working, but their transfer from the traditional to the modern sector will not reduce output in the traditional sector, or will only reduce output there by the amount that the individual was consuming. Third, it has been noted that Lewis assumes away the problem of the creation of a capitalist or entrepreneurial class in developing countries, whereas in fact this is one of the main obstacles to development. Fourth, critics have argued that real and nominal wages in the modern sector do not appear to behave in the way they are pictured in the Lewis model—they both are able to rise quite rapidly—and the relation of wages and employment also differs in that rates rise even in an atmosphere of significant unemployment. Fifth, Lewis's assumption that the sectors are homogeneous has been criticized with arguments developed that each sector can be quite heterogeneous, generating conflicts that affect the accumulation process. Finally, the assumption that "perfect competition" holds in the capitalist sector has been attacked both for ignoring the way in which monopoly characteristics had been inherited from the colonial era and for the neoclassical implications for the analysis of investment, allocation, and factor payments.

The Lewis model has also been criticized on historical grounds. Jeffrey Williamson (1985) argues that the early British experience does not confirm the model, while Giovanni Arrighi (1973) has attacked the argument that the model applies to southern Africa. One of the primary challenges of colonial capitalism was getting the indigenous populations to work as wage laborers or grow cash crops when they still had possession of means of production for producing the means of subsistence. In addition to forced labor and land alienation, the requirement that taxes be paid in colonial currency was one of the most important means of pressuring Africans to work on plantations and in mines or to grow cash crops.

Others challenging Lewis concerning surplus labor in developing nations included Theodore Schultz (1964) and Hla Myint (1971). Schultz studied the 1918–1919 influenza epidemic in India and the changes in output resulting from the reduction of the labor force, concluding that the surplus labor theory is false. Sen (1967) replied that the surplus labor doctrine refers to changes in the labor force resulting from the operation of economic incentives and principles, and that the influenza epidemic does not qualify. A single family member leaving the traditional sector is not the same as an entire family dying from influenza. Myint (1971) critiqued the idea that if a family member leaves a traditional farm, the other family members will increase their labor services to maintain a target level of output. Many of these critiques confuse modern/traditional with manufacturing/agriculture and, moreover, continue to ignore Lewis's claim that the assumption of zero marginal productivity is not crucial, that the marginal product of labor can be zero, positive, or negative, and that the supply of labor is considered "unlimited" as long as the labor supply exceeds labor demand at the subsistence wage rate.

SEE ALSO *Development Economics; Dual Economy; Economics, Neoclassical; Labor, Surplus: Marxist and Radical Economics; Lewis, W. Arthur*

BIBLIOGRAPHY

Arrighi, Giovanni. 1973. Labor Supplies in Historical Perspective. In *Essays on the Political Economy of Africa*, eds. Giovanni Arrighi and John S. Saul, 180–234. New York: Monthly Review Press.

Bharadwaj, Krishna. 1979. Towards a Macroeconomic Framework for a Developing Economy: The Indian Case. *Manchester School* 47 (3): 270–302.

Fei, John C. H., and Gustav Ranis. 1964. *Development of the Labor Surplus Economy: Theory and Policy.* Homewood, IL: Irwin.

Leeson, P. F. 1979. The Lewis Model and Development Theory. *Manchester School* 47 (3): 196–210.

Lewis, W. Arthur. 1954. Economic Development with Unlimited Supplies of Labour. *Manchester School* 22 (2): 139–191.

Marglin, Stephen A. 1976. *Value and Price in the Labour-Surplus Economy.* Oxford: Clarendon.

Myint, Hla. 1971. *Economic Theory and the Underdeveloped Countries.* New York: Oxford University Press.

Schultz, Theodore W. 1964. *Transforming Traditional Agriculture.* New Haven, CT: Yale University Press.

Sen, Amartya K. 1966. Peasants and Dualism With or Without Surplus Labor. *Journal of Political Economy* 74 (5): 425–450.

Sen, Amartya K. 1967. Surplus Labour in India: A Critique of Schultz's Statistical Test. *Economic Journal* 77 (305): 154–161.

Williamson, Jeffrey G. 1985. The Historical Content of the Classical Labor Surplus Model. *Population and Development Review* 11 (2): 171–191.

Mathew Forstater

LABOR, SURPLUS: MARXIST AND RADICAL ECONOMICS

The theory of capitalist accumulation devised by Karl Marx (1818–1883) rests upon the labor theory of value, according to which capitalists (i.e., owners of the means of production) appropriate the surplus value produced by the workers (i.e., owners of labor power or the capacity to labor) whose labor power they purchase. Capitalists then sell the products in which surplus value is embodied, and keep the profits for themselves. If, after commodities are sold, capitalists were to end up with an amount of capital equal to that spent purchasing the elements of the production process—that is, without profits—they would not invest. Investments are profitable, however, because the product can be sold for a sum greater than the original investment. In the production process, workers produce not only value but *surplus value*—that is, value greater than the value of their labor power; it is the sale of surplus value that is the source of profits. The value of the means of production is incorporated, unchanged, in the product, as machines and tools wear out and are eventually replaced by others. The difference between the value of labor power (i.e., the amount capitalists spend in wages) and the value labor power produces in the production process (i.e., the amount capitalists collect once the product is sold) is the profit capitalists appropriate. To understand why this is so, it is necessary to examine the main features of the capitalist production process.

Labor power, under capitalism, is a commodity that has the property of producing value. The value of labor power, like the value of any other commodity, is determined by the labor time necessary for its production and reproduction. As labor power is a capacity of living workers, its value is resolved in the labor time necessary for the production of the means of subsistence (i.e., a historically established bundle of commodities) necessary for the maintenance, and reproduction over time, of the individuals whose livelihood depends on their ability to sell their labor power in exchange for wages (Marx [1867] 1967, pp. 169–171). The use-value of labor power is its exercise in the production process where, combined with means of production and various materials, it produces specific useful goods, or use-values. Capitalists purchase the elements of the production process: means of production, raw materials or already processed materials, and labor power. They consume the use-value of labor power by setting the workers to work. Capitalists control the labor process and own its products, a quantity of use-values which, when sold, become commodities imbued with value and exchange-value (Marx [1867] 1967, pp. 174–175).

Workers sell their labor power for wages sufficient for the sustenance of themselves and, to a variable extent, their families. Once sold, the use-value of their labor power belongs to the capitalist who, being in control of the production process, can fix the length of the working day within limits set by the outcome of struggles between the capitalist class and the working class (Marx [1867] 1967, p. 235; Weeks 1981, p. 69). The working day can be divided in two parts of varying duration. During a number of hours that depends on the quantity of labor time necessary to produce the workers' means of subsistence, workers produce a value equivalent to their wages. In this portion of the working day, workers engage in *necessary labor*, which is spent in necessary labor time. It is necessary because workers need to replenish their energies and because capitalists need a productive labor force. The working day, however, lasts longer than the time necessary to produce the value of the wages. Workers are compelled to engage in surplus labor, creating value for the capitalist during surplus labor time. Capitalists seek to lengthen the quantity of surplus labor time by keeping wages low, thus decreasing the quantity of necessary labor time. The lower the value of the commodities necessary to maintain and reproduce labor power, the lower the wages and the higher the quantity of surplus labor time. The ratio of surplus labor to necessary labor, which can also be stated as the ratio of the surplus value to the value of the wages or vari-

able capital, is the rate of surplus value that "expresses the degree of exploitation of labor-power by capital, or of the laborer by the capitalist" (Marx [1867] 1967, pp. 216–218). The higher the rate of exploitation, the greater the profits and the power of the owners, who constantly strive to increase the rate of exploitation by lengthening the working day or by introducing technology intended to speed up the production process or replace workers with machines.

In the processes of capital accumulation, the proportion of capital invested in means of production (i.e., constant capital) and labor power (i.e., variable capital) can remain constant or it can change. If it remains constant, the more capital is invested, the greater the demand for laborers; as technology remains the same, the rate of exploitation remains unchanged. Growth in the demand for labor can lead to higher wages as long as profits are not diminished. When wages rise to the extent of undermining profits, capitalists may choose to slow down investments, thus producing a decline in employment and wages, or they may force workers to labor longer hours, thus lengthening the proportion of the working day spent in surplus labor. With the development of the forces of production (i.e., technological changes increasing the productivity of labor), it becomes possible for capitalists to augment their profits while reducing, at the same time, the demand for labor: more capital is invested in constant capital and less is spent in wages or variable capital. The greater the productivity of labor, the lower the quantity of labor time spent in necessary labor, the greater the proportion of the working day spent in surplus labor, and, therefore, the greater the profits.

Technological changes and growth in the productivity of labor result in changes in the division of labor and in the quantity and quality of the demand for labor. Changes in the division of labor increasing the demand for more skilled labor result in higher wages for those fortunate enough to have those skills, or access to the necessary training to acquire such skills. At the same time, these changes devalue formerly needed skills and push masses of workers into underemployment and unemployment. The relatively privileged position of skilled workers, however, is not permanent, as capitalists seek to lower wages through processes of de-skilling (i.e., breaking up skilled jobs into their constituent elements) even as they develop new technologies that eventually will render such jobs obsolete, in a never-ending cycle of skilling and deskilling that exploits and discards workers as mere things to be used as needed in the process of capital accumulation (Braverman 1974).

Quantitative changes in the demand for labor reflect changes in the composition of total capital invested; that is, in the proportion of capital invested in constant and variable capital. As capital investment and the productivity of labor increase, the demand for labor decreases relative to the quantity of capital invested (Marx [1867] 1967, p. 629). These changes in the composition of capital are reflected in fluctuations in the employment rate and growth in unemployment. It would seem that there are too many workers, that the labor force is increasing too fast, that workers are having too many children, and so on. But, as Marx observed, this apparent increase in the size of the laboring population is an illusion: "it is capitalistic accumulation itself that constantly produces ... a relatively redundant population of laborers ... a surplus population" (Marx [1867] 1967, p. 630). As capitalists use increasingly productive technology (e.g., assembly lines, automation), less and less labor time is needed to produce larger quantities of products and a growing proportion of workers become unemployed and even unemployable, thus constituting a "reserve army of labor" or *relative surplus population* (RSP), which has important economic and political effects: its presence limits the bargaining power of workers even at times of economic growth.

Within a national economy, the RSP can assume three forms: (1) the *floating RSP*, which is manifested when rapid and drastic technological changes substantially alter the location and kind of capital investments and the organization of production, thus producing rapid declines in employment; (2) the *latent RSP*, which emerges in rural areas as agribusiness replaces small, labor-intensive farming and farmworkers migrate to the urban and industrial areas; and (3) the *stagnant RSP*, which includes masses of workers permanently expelled from the labor force, able to obtain only irregular employment but remaining largely unemployed, constituting a large reserve of very low-paid, low-skilled, and unskilled labor power (e.g., today's poverty and near poverty population in the United States, largely dependent on welfare and irregular, minimum-wage employment). The stagnant RSP becomes "a self-reproducing and self-perpetuating element of the working class, taking a proportionally greater part in the general increase of that class than the other elements" (Marx, [1867] 1967, p. 640).

SURPLUS LABOR AND SOCIAL CLASS

Exploitation is "a social (society-wide) phenomenon under capitalism" (Weeks 1981, p. 64); it is at the core of the Marxist concept of social class, as an exploitative relation between capitalists and workers. While this seems a clear and useful definition, changes in the forces of production since the mid-nineteenth century have produced qualitative changes in the social and technical divisions of labor, thus altering the composition of the working population. In advanced capitalist social formations, like the United States, the proportion of workers exploited at the point of production, producing surplus labor for the owners of capital, has declined relative to the proportion of workers employed in services, white-collar, technical, professional, and managerial jobs. Automation and information technologies have contributed to the decline in the proportion of well-paid blue-collar workers that, in the United States, were considered "the backbone of the middle class."

Were Marxist social scientists to define the working class using as the sole criteria the production of surplus labor by manual workers, they would have to conclude that the size of this class is dwindling. The Marxist theorist Nicos Poulantzas (1936–1979), for example, argued that only productive workers (i.e., workers who produce surplus value) are part of the working class, unlike unproductive workers, whose work is located in the other spheres of the mode of production (e.g., circulation). Not all productive workers, however, are members of the working class; technicians and engineers, for example, occupy a contradictory class position, for they contribute to the production of surplus value while placed in positions of authority over the labor process, thus representing the power of capital. Classes cannot be identified solely on economic criteria; ideological and political criteria—namely, location in the relations of production and the social division of labor—matter as well (Poulantzas 1973, pp. 31–35).

GLOBALIZATION, SURPLUS LABOR, AND CLASS

When examining classes empirically, at the level of social formations, the capitalist/working class dichotomy is submerged under the heterogeneity of the technical and social division of labor, and the existence of noncapitalist classes, such as the petty bourgeoisie (independent producers) and the peasantry. Social scientists are compelled to introduce additional criteria for defining classes, such as, for example, *contradictory* class locations based on property relations, levels of skills and knowledge, and location in authority relations (e.g., Wright 1997). The heterogeneity of the working population does not obliterate, however, the importance of the underlying division between capitalists and workers and the significance of surplus labor in the process of capital accumulation. As capitalists seek to increase profits and lower labor costs, they continuously revolutionize the organization of production and change the kind and location of investments. Capitalist accumulation strategies result in changes in the quantity and quality of the demand for labor, changes in the social and technical division of labor, and, consequently, changes in the social stratification profile that can be documented in a given society at a given time. These changes reflect not only technological imperatives and competition among capitalists, but the extent of capitalist power over the working classes.

In the United States, where labor is relatively powerless if compared with its counterpart in Western Europe, globalization has resulted in declining benefits and real wages for the working classes; a decline in job security, benefits, and employment opportunities for the middle classes; and deepening wealth and income inequality. Downsizing, outsourcing, deindustrialization, growth in poorly paid service jobs, temporary and contingent employment, and, consequently, growth in the size of all the forms of the RSPs, especially the stagnant RSP, are some of the effects of capitalist efforts to lower labor costs.

The value of labor power in poorer countries is very low, thus resulting in a higher rate of exploitation; capitalists seeking higher profits flock to those countries, intensifying inequality and the growth of their RSPs, thus triggering massive migration flows toward the wealthy countries. The working classes in the wealthy capitalist countries, therefore, face national and global RSPs that have effectively contributed to the undermining of workers' bargaining power. Contributing to the lowering of the value of labor power in the rich countries is the export of cheap commodities from China and other exceedingly low-wage countries, which thus lowers the overall cost of the bundle of commodities necessary for the maintenance and reproduction of the working population.

To conclude, at the level of analysis of social formations, surplus labor plays a lesser role in the identification of social classes. However, at the level of analysis of the capitalist mode of production, globally considered or within a country, it is not possible to understand changes in the empirically observable stratification system without taking into account the dynamics of class exploitation and capital accumulation, which, as capitalists pursue the appropriation of as much surplus labor as feasible, constantly alter the structure of opportunities of all working people.

SEE ALSO *Accumulation of Capital; Class; Labor, Surplus: Conventional Economics; Marx, Karl; Profits; Surplus Value; Unemployment*

BIBLIOGRAPHY

Braverman, Harry. 1974. *Labor and Monopoly Capital: The Degradation of Work in the Twentieth Century.* New York: Monthly Review Press.

Marx, Karl. [1867] 1967. *Capital.* Vol. 1. New York: International Publishers.

Poulantzas, Nicos. 1973. On Social Classes. *New Left Review* 78: 27–54.

Weeks, John. 1981. *Capital and Exploitation.* Princeton, NJ: Princeton University Press.

Wright, Erik O. 1997. *Class Counts: Comparative Studies in Class Analysis.* Cambridge, U.K.: Cambridge University Press.

Martha E. Gimenez

LABOR CAMPS

SEE *Concentration Camps.*

LABOR DEMAND

The "demand for labor" is usually understood by economists to mean the demand for labor services by a firm, an industry, or the economy at a given real wage. In a capitalist economy, labor becomes a commodity that is bought and sold on the market just like any other commodity, such as bread or butter. Labor is a unique commodity, however, and when an employer buys labor, he or she obtains a worker's "labor power" which is the amount of services that the employer gets from the worker. These services depend on the power the employer has over the worker. If there is high unemployment, for example, the worker is in a weak position and greater labor services can be extracted from him or her. The amount of labor services that the employer obtains (not only in terms of hours of work, but in terms of the efficiency of those services) also depends on the nature of the employment contract, the real wage paid to the worker, the conditions of employment, and the attitude of the employer to the worker (and vice versa).

Labor services consist of three components: the number of workers (employees), the average hours worked per worker, and the efficiency per hour of the worker. There are several institutional and legal constraints on employers in most developed countries. For example, there may be laws against discrimination, equal pay legislation, minimum wages (henceforth, the term *wages* refer to real wages), occupational health and safety requirements, hiring and firing restrictions, and penalty rates for overtime.

The demand for labor is a derived demand: Firms wish to hire workers to produce goods and services that they sell in order to earn profits. Alfred Marshall, in his *Principles of Economics* (1930) suggested that labor demand becomes more responsive to wage changes if the substitution possibilities between labor and capital increase. In other words, the easier it is to substitute capital for labor, the greater the share of wages in total costs, and the more responsive the other factors of production are to their prices.

Much of the formal economics literature is based on simple models of firm behavior in a perfectly competitive economy (for a closed economy, that is, without any international trade), assuming that labor is a homogeneous commodity. In a prototype model, a firm is assumed to maximize profits (or minimize costs) subject to a so-called "well-behaved" production function that depends on homogeneous labor and capital. By simple mathematical manipulation, it is easy to show that the firm's demand for labor is a negatively sloped marginal revenue product (MRP) curve, and that employment is determined by equating the marginal revenue product of labor with the wage rate. In such models, it is usually assumed that labor and capital are substitutable (usually in a Cobb-Douglas production function). There are some difficulties, however, in moving from a firm labor-demand function to an industry or aggregate labor-demand function because of the possible interactions between firms, the heterogeneity of labor, and other factors.

In most of these models, it is assumed that the technology of production is given and unchanging. Alternatively, technological change is simply an exogenous variable that falls like manna from heaven on all existing inputs. Labor services are often assumed to be such that hours of work and employees are perfectly substitutable.

The impact of technological change on the labor market and on labor mobility is very significant, but it often has contradictory effects. Technological change is usually defined as being either a change in the product or a change in the process of production. Technological change that leads to the introduction of new products will lead to either new firms being set up or old firms expanding into a new product line, which would lead to increased employment through job creation and job destruction. Job destruction leads to the closing down of firms producing some products that are replaced by new firms producing new products. However, demand for a new product may lessen demand for competing products, leading to a reduction in labor demand elsewhere in the economy. Similarly, a technological change in the production process may lead to the substitution of capital for unskilled labor, and hence to a decrease in labor demand. It may also lead to an increase in the demand for skilled labor, however, due to a complementarity of capital with skilled labor.

In more advanced models, labor is treated as a "quasi-fixed" input, like a capital good (see Oi 1962; Nickell 1986). In other words, there are significant fixed costs associated with changing employment, due to hiring and firing costs. Usually, it is assumed that these costs of adjustment are quadratic (implying increasing marginal costs of adjustment), so that if there is an increase in the demand for goods the impact on the demand for labor is spread out over a few periods. In the short run, the demand for labor adjusts slowly in response to any external shock. Given that there are costs of adjustment, the firm would find it easier to either adjust the hours of work of existing workers or hire casual part-time workers. It is cheaper, however, to hire and fire casual part-time workers. European countries that have a more regulated labor market, with larger hiring and firing costs, have been found to have a slower adjustment process to shocks. However, the evidence on this is very controversial and needs further research (see Blanchard 2006).

There has been a large amount of econometric work to estimate the impact of a change in real wage rates (corrected for inflation) on labor demand holding the level of production constant using large datasets. Most of these studies have found that elasticity (the percentage change in labor demand in response to a 1 percent change in the real wage rate) lies between −0.15 and −0.75, with "a best guess" of −0.30. However, studies of the impact of minimum wages on employment suggest that there is no significant impact (see Card and Krueger 1995). David Neumark and William Wascher have found otherwise, however, perhaps because it is mainly unskilled labor, while usual studies of labor demand are for skilled and unskilled labor taken as a whole. The scale elasticity (i.e., the impact of increased output) is almost unity: a 1 percent increase in the level of production (output) leads to a 1 percent increase in labor demand.

Firms demand labor services from employees who provide honest, committed, and productive work at wage rates that the employer determines (either unilaterally or as a bargain between the employer and employee). Ideally, employers would like to employ workers who take a positive long-term interest in their work and make useful suggestions to improve the production process. In general, firms have flexibility in the wage (and other conditions of work, including perquisites) they offer to their employees. There are also theories of deferred payment, tournaments to provide a stimulus to get wage increases, and "efficiency wages." It has been shown that employers can get higher productivity from their workers, and hence make higher profits, if they pay a higher real wage. This idea was first put forward in a classic paper by Harvey Leibenstein (1957), who argued that in a developing country, paying higher wages led to workers getting better nutrition and providing better productivity.

This essential link between wages and productivity, or "efficiency wages," was extended in a series of papers: In 1984, Carl Shapiro and Joseph Stiglitz put forward the view that higher wages decreased shirking by employees; Steven Salop argued in 1979 that higher wages lowered worker turnover, increased productivity, and increased profits; and Andrew Weiss (in 1980) and George Akerlof (in 1982) both showed that if employers paid higher wages as a partial gift, workers would reciprocate by providing greater effort. Thus, there is no unique negative relationship between the real wage and employment, because an employer who pays a wage in excess of the "market wage" gets greater productivity. Lowering the wage does not increase employment. Experimental economics, particularly the work of Ernst Fehr and Simon Gächter, has shown the importance of considerations of "reciprocity" (e.g., fairness, equity, and other issues) in the employment relationship.

In a globalized world, the demand for labor becomes more confused as various activities are "outsourced." In other words, the firm can produce a larger quantity of output by either hiring more labor, buying more capital goods, improving its technology, or simply by outsourcing a particular activity. Call centers in less developed countries are good examples of this. Hence, the link between the output of a firm and its demand for labor is no longer constrained by a given production function.

There has been a large amount of econometric analyses of the demand for labor, suggesting, in general, a negative link between wages and employment. There are important policy implications that can flow from the research about minimum wages, but the results are contradictory and controversial (see Card and Krueger 1995; Neumark and Wascher 1992). Similarly, the efficiency wage literature also throws some doubt on a simple negative relation between wages and employment. The literature on hiring and firing costs has been used to suggest that a deregulated labor market would lead to higher employment, but this is still being debated.

SEE ALSO *Economics, Labor; Employment; Labor; Labor Force Participation; Labor, Marginal Product of; Labor Market; Labor Market Segmentation; Labor Supply; Wages*

BIBLIOGRAPHY

Akerlof, George A. 1982. Labor Contracts as Partial Gift Exchange. *Quarterly Journal of Economics* 97 (4): 543–569.

Akerlof, George A., and Janet L. Yellen, eds. 1986. *Efficiency Wage Models of the Labor Market*. Cambridge, U.K.: Cambridge University Press.

Blanchard, Olivier. 2006. European Unemployment: The Evolution of Facts and Ideas. *Economic Policy* 21 (45): 5–59.

Card, David, and Alan B. Krueger. 1995. *Myth and Measurement: The New Economics of the Minimum Wage*. Princeton, NJ: Princeton University Press.

Fehr, Ernst, and Simon Gächter. 2000. Fairness and Retaliation: The Economics of Reciprocity. *Journal of Economic Perspectives* 14 (3): 159–181.

Griliches, Zvi 1969. Capital-Skill Complementarity. *Review of Economics and Statistics* 51 (4): 465–468.

Hamermesh, Daniel S. 1993. *Labor Demand*. Princeton, NJ: Princeton University Press.

Junankar, P. N. 1982. *Marx's Economics*. Oxford: Philip Allan.

Lazear, Edward P. 1995. *Personnel Economics*. Cambridge, MA: MIT Press.

Leibenstein, Harvey. 1957. The Theory of Underemployment in Backward Economies. *Journal of Political Economy* 65 (2): 91–103.

Marshall, Alfred. 1930. *Principles of Economics*. 8th ed. London: Macmillan.

Marx, Karl 1867. *Capital*. Vol. 1. London: Lawrence and Wishart, 1977.

Neumark, David, and William Wascher. 1992. Employment Effects of Minimum and Subminimum Wages. *Industrial and Labor Relations Review* 46 (1): 55–81.

Nickell, Stephen. 1986. Dynamic Models of Labor Demand. In *Handbook of Labor Economics*, Vol.1, ed. Orley C. Ashenfelter, and Richard Layard. Amsterdam: North Holland.

Oi, Walter J. 1962. Labor as a Quasi-Fixed Factor. *Journal of Political Economy* 70 (6): 538–555.

Salop, Steven. 1979. A Model of the Natural Rate of Unemployment. *American Economic Review* 69 (1): 117–125.

Shapiro, Carl, and Joseph Stiglitz. 1984. Equilibrium Unemployment as a Worker Discipline Device. *American Economic Review* 74 (3): 433–444.

Solow, Robert. 1990. *The Labor Market as a Social Institution*. Oxford, U.K.: Blackwell.

Weiss, Andrew. 1980. Job Queues and Layoffs in Labor Markets with Flexible Wages. *Journal of Political Economy* 88 (3): 526–538.

P. N. Junankar

LABOR FORCE PARTICIPATION

The labor force participation rate is defined as the proportion of a population that is either employed for pay or profit (for one hour or more in the reference week or fortnight) or looking for paid work over some period of time. By definition, people who are carrying out unpaid work in the home or voluntary work are not counted as employed.

The concepts of employment and unemployment are more easily defined for a developed capitalist economy that has a market for wage labor. In less developed countries (LDCs), where wage labor is not a predominant form of employment, the concept of unemployment becomes "fuzzy": The line between employment in the informal sector (e.g., selling cigarettes on street corners) and unemployment is not clearly defined (see Turnham 1993). Similarly, the concept of "looking for work" becomes vague when social security benefits are not available and when labor markets are not developed. Often, when the unemployed are unable to find work for any length of time they give up looking for work and hence are not in the labor force (they are the so-called "discouraged workers"). In societies that provide welfare benefits to people with disabilities, people often move between the unemployed and disabled categories, and hence the participation rate as measured is unclear. Because the concept of unemployment is problematic in some countries, economists often compare employment-population ratios instead of participation rates.

Social customs, culture, and institutions (including the legal framework) play a large part in the participation of women and younger people in the labor market. In LDCs where there is no compulsory schooling, children are part of the labor force. In certain cultures where religion plays an important role, females do not engage in paid work and hence are not part of the labor force.

It is common to distinguish between the participation rate of males and females, and more detailed studies look at differences in the participation rates of several subgroups, such as married females and single females, whites and blacks, young and old, migrants and natives. In general, female labor force participation rates have been rising and male participation rates have been falling in most countries of the Organization for Economic Cooperation and Development (OECD), except for Japan, where male participation rates have risen. Male participation rates for older workers have been rising since the mid-1990s, possibly because of better employment conditions and better superannuation provisions for retirement after sixty-five years of age, or due to (in the United States) provision of health care for employed workers. Note, however, that the participation rate of both males and females has fallen in the United States since 2000, and whether this is a trend fall or a cyclical fall is a contentious issue (see Aaronson et al. 2006 and Juhn and Potter 2006). Participation rates tend to first rise with age and then fall as people get older. Participation rates of more educated people are usually higher than those of less educated people.

During World War II many women from the combatant countries worked in the war industries, and after the end of the war continued in the labor force. The increase in female participation rate is sometimes explained by the change in the structure of the economy from a dominant manufacturing sector to a dominant services sector that demands (allegedly) "feminine" skills such as computer keyboard skills. The increased level of education of females has also led to increased female participation, especially in white-collar jobs, often in part-time employment. The changing social mores that came with the women's liberation movement and the increased access to and ease of contraception via the Pill, which pro-

vided greater control over and timing of childbearing, lowered fertility rates and increased female participation rates. Increased real wages of women, as well as the introduction of equal pay legislation in many OECD countries, increased female participation rates. The development of household appliances (e.g., washing machines, microwave ovens, and so on) that lower time spent in household work for females have also had a positive impact on female participation rates (see Blau and Ferber 1992).

Male participation rates have declined with a fall in employment in the manufacturing sector, especially for older males who were made redundant and were unable to find work in the newer industries. However, in most OECD countries expanding economies (and perhaps the tightening of access to welfare benefits) appear to have increased participation rates for all males (including older males) since about 2000.

It is important to note that the labor force participation rate depends on both demand and supply factors: For example, a higher proportion of women are working if the demand for the skills that women offer is high. Generally, participation rates are procyclical: They rise during booms and fall in recessions. If for some reason employers discriminate against women in one country, their participation rate is lower than in a society where such discrimination does not exist. Similarly, women's participation rate is higher when they place a lower value on their time spent at home, and so are willing to supply more labor.

Economic analysis of labor force participation begins with neoclassical models of utility maximization subject to a budget constraint: Individuals are assumed to be maximizing their individual welfare (dependent on consumption and leisure or nonmarket time) subject to a given wage rate and some nonlabor income (either from social security or from family sources). (Usually the models are based on individual maximization, rather than family decision-making.) This typically provides an individual with a "reservation wage" that depends on the value of leisure (or nonmarket time). A "reservation wage" is defined as that wage below which the individual prefers not to work. Individuals have different reservation wages depending on their preferences for leisure, their access to nonlabor incomes, and their educational background. Female labor force participation is more difficult to analyze due to their roles as household managers, childbearers and caretakers, and paid market work. Even though social mores have changed over the past few decades, women continue to do the same amount of unpaid household work.

Models that allow for family decision-making (where the husband and wife choose whether to work or not, and decide who produces "household goods," e.g., child care at home, meals at home, etc.) are more complex and difficult to estimate econometrically. Some models treat these as "bargaining models" in a game theoretic context. In general, the probability of a wife working is positively related to her husband working (Pencavel 1998). This may, of course, also be explained in terms of "assortative mating,"—that is, highly educated and well paid males tend to marry highly educated and well paid females.

In a life-cycle context, males invest in education in their youth, then work and acquire pension or superannuation benefits, and retire in older age. Females invest in education (more so since World War II), work for some time, have children and leave the labor force, return to the labor force when the children are of school-leaving age, and then work until retirement. This stylized life-cycle behavior is easily explained by simple models of utility maximization. Participation rates of young people decreased with the increased participation in education in the postwar period. Retirement decisions were based on availability of pension or social security funds, accumulation of wealth over the life cycle, and health and family considerations.

There is an important interaction between the tax and welfare systems and participation rates, which makes the budget constraint nonlinear and sometimes nonconvex: Simple models of maximization of utility become complex and difficult to estimate. It is often argued that welfare benefits tend to lower participation rates, especially of women, as their nonlabor income is higher and hence their valuation of nonmarket time is higher. Child care support for families generally increases participation rates for married females.

To summarize, the research on labor force participation has expanded dramatically over the last decade, especially studies of the impact of tax and welfare policy changes. There is little hard evidence to support the popular view that welfare and social security provide disincentives to work. Most of the empirical evidence is based on simple static (one-period) individualistic models that do not allow for family decision-making. Work on household decision-making is still in its early stages, and further research is needed that allows for life-cycle decisions that include household saving jointly with labor-supply decisions and family formation and dissolution. Most empirical studies of labor-force participation find that noneconomic considerations play an important role in explaining behavior.

SEE ALSO *Business Cycles, Real; Education, Unequal; Employment; Game Theory; Gender Gap; Inequality, Gender; Inequality, Racial; Labor; Labor Demand; Labor Market; Labor Supply; Utility Function; Wages; Work; Work and Women*

BIBLIOGRAPHY

Aaronson, Stephanie, Bruce Fallick, Andrew Figura, et al. 2006. The Recent Decline in the Labor Force Participation Rate and Its Implications for Potential Labor Supply. *Brookings Papers on Economic Activity* 1: 69–134.

Blau, Francine, and Marianne A. Ferber. 1992. *The Economics of Women, Men, and Work.* 2nd ed. Englewood Cliffs, NJ: Prentice Hall.

Blundell, Richard, and Thomas Macurdy. 1999. Labor Supply: A Review of Alternative Approaches. In *Handbook of Labor Economics,* vol. 3A, ed. Orley C. Ashenfelter and David Card, 1559–1695. Amsterdam: North-Holland.

Card, David. 1994. Intertemporal Labor Supply: An Assessment. In *Advances in Econometrics,* ed. Christopher Sims, 49–78. Cambridge, U.K.: Cambridge University Press.

Hotchkiss, Julie L. 2006. Changes in Behavioral and Characteristic Determination of Female Labor Force Participation, 1975–2005. *Economic Review* 91 (2): 1–20.

Juhn, Chinhui, and Simon Potter. 2006. Changes in Labor Force Participation in the United States. *Journal of Economic Perspectives* 20 (3): 27–46.

Killingsworth, Mark R. 1983. *Labor Supply.* Cambridge, U.K.: Cambridge University Press.

Killingsworth, Mark R., and James J. Heckman. 1986. Female Labor Supply: A Survey. In *Handbook of Labor Economics,* vol. 1, ed. Orley C. Ashenfelter and Richard Layard, 105–204. Amsterdam: North-Holland.

Pencavel, John. 1986. Labor Supply of Men. In *Handbook of Labor Economics,* vol. 1, ed. Orley C. Ashenfelter and Richard Layard, 3–102. Amsterdam: North-Holland.

Pencavel, John. 1998. The Market Work Behavior and Wages of Women. *Journal of Human Resources* 33: 771–804.

Senesky, Sarah. 2005. Testing the Intertemporal Labor Supply Model: Are Jobs Important? *Labour Economics* 12: 749–772.

Turnham, David. 1993. *Employment and Development: A New Review of Evidence.* Paris: Organization for Economic Cooperation and Development.

P. N. Junankar

LABOR LAW

The purpose of labor law is to protect the interests of employers and employees in the workplace. Labor laws grant employers and employees the right to engage in certain conduct such as collective bargaining, strikes, and lockouts, in pursuit of their demands.

In the United States the area of labor law is governed by federal and state statutory law, judicial decisions and regulations, and decisions of administrative agencies. The National Labor Relations Act (NLRA), also known as the Wagner Act, enacted by Congress on July 5, 1935, marks the foundation of modern U.S. labor law. The NLRA covers all employers and employees involved in businesses that affect interstate commerce. The NLRA protects workers' rights to strike, associate freely with one another, join labor organizations, and bargain collectively without interference. The NLRA also prohibits employers and unions from engaging in "unfair labor practices" and requires both parties to engage in good-faith negotiations to resolve their disputes.

The NLRA was amended in 1947 by the Taft-Hartley Act (29 U.S.C. § 141 et seq.), which was aimed at reducing the number of industrial disputes and strengthening the power of employers in their dealings with unions. The Taft-Hartley Act was a response to problems that emerged during World War II (1939–1945), such as closed-shop and union-shop agreements, secondary boycotts, and strikes that often resulted in violence. Under a closed-shop agreement, employees are required to join the union as a precondition of employment. Closed shops are the opposite of open shops, which are characterized by the unlawful refusal to hire persons or give them preference in hiring based on their membership in a union. Union-shop agreements do not require employees to be union members as a precondition of employment, but do require employees to join the union or pay union dues within a set period of time after being hired.

The Taft-Hartley Act outlawed the closed shop in the United States, but permits the union shop in states that have not enacted "right-to-work" laws. Right-to-work laws are statutes that discourage collective bargaining and prohibit unions from making union membership a condition of employment. Currently, there are twenty-two states that have right-to-work laws, including Florida, Texas, Virginia, North Carolina, Arizona, Georgia, and Nevada. According to the Bureau of Labor Statistics and the U.S. Census Bureau, the share of jobs in the manufacturing sector rose from 25.4 in 1970 to 34.3 in 2000 in right-to-work states, and all right-to-work states registered a net gain in manufacturing payrolls despite the loss of nearly 875,000 manufacturing jobs nationwide during this period. Moreover, from 1978 to 2000, right-to-work states had lower average annual unemployment rates for all but five years. However, in 2000, per capita disposable income was approximately 10 percent higher in union-shop states than in right-to-work states, and both the poverty rate and income inequality remained higher in right-to-work states than in union-shop states.

The National Labor Relations Board (NLRB) was established under the NLRA to hear disputes between employers and employees. The NLRB's purpose is (1) to prevent and remedy unfair labor practices, whether committed by labor organizations or employers, and (2) to establish whether or not certain groups of employees

desire labor organization representation for collective-bargaining purposes, and if so, which union. The NLRB is composed of five members whose five-year terms are staggered. There is a long-standing tradition that the board consist of a split in political party affiliation, usually a 3 to 2 split in favor of the president's party. The president designates the chairman of the NLRB. The NLRB's membership as of 2007 included Robert J. Battista (chairman), Wilma B. Liebman, Peter Carey Schaumber, Dennis P. Walsh, and Peter N. Kirsanow.

Usually, both labor and management are represented by attorneys who file grievances in writing with the NLRB, prepare and submit evidence, and argue their positions in the grievances. In cases where the employer-employee relationship is not governed by the NLRA, that relationship may be governed by other federal statutes such as the Federal Service Labor-Management Relations Act (5 U.S.C. § 7101 et seq.) or the Railway Labor Act (29 U.S.C. § 101). State law may also govern the employer-employee relationship where federal statutes do not apply.

Since 2005, new labor legislation has been enacted in several states seeking to improve standards associated with child labor, drug and alcohol testing, equal employment opportunity, human trafficking, the minimum wage, the prevailing wage, time off, wages paid, and worker privacy, among other areas. Currently, seventeen states and the District of Columbia have a higher minimum-wage rate than the federal minimum-wage rate of $5.15 per hour. Kansas and Ohio are the only two states with a minimum-wage rate lower than the federal rate.

The labor movement has been instrumental in the establishment of laws protecting workers' rights around the globe. For example, over 90 percent of all nations have some kind of minimum wage law. Eighteen out of twenty-seven members of the European Union have national minimum wages, and the People's Republic of China, too, has established a monthly minimum wage for full-time workers and an hourly minimum wage for part-time workers. Moreover, labor-rights advocates in Europe have had success pushing through legislation that strengthens maternity and paternity rights and protects individuals from discrimination on the basis of age, religion, and sexual orientation, as well as gender, race and disability. The 35-hour maximum work week in France and the Working Time Directive in the United Kingdom, which covers working time, rest breaks, and the right to paid annual leave, are two of the most progressive pieces of labor legislation.

With the growth of democracy and capitalism worldwide, labor law will become more important in balancing the interests of employers and employees in the twenty-first century.

SEE ALSO *Employment; Labor; Law; Occupational Safety; Regulation; Unions; Wages; Work; Work Week*

BIBLIOGRAPHY

Gould, William B. 1994. *A Primer on American Labor Law.* 4th ed. Cambridge, MA: MIT Press.

Labor and Labor Relations. 1994. *American Jurisprudence* 48 (2nd. ed.) §§ 1–7. Rochester, NY: Lawyers Cooperative Publishing.

Rifkin, Bernard, and Susan Rifkin. 1979. *American Labor Sourcebook.* New York: McGraw-Hill.

Wilson, William T. 2002. *The Effect of Right-to-Work Laws on Economic Development.* A Mackinac Center for Public Policy Report. Midland, MI: Mackinac Center for Public Policy.

Klint W. Alexander

LABOR MARKET

According to textbooks such as Ronald G. Ehrenberg and Robert S. Smith's *Modern Labor Economics* (2005), a "labor market" is the place where labor services are bought and sold. The term *labor* is equated to the term *work*, not only manual work but also knowledge work. Sometimes, the place where labor services are bought and sold is a clearly identifiable one such as a construction site or a lawyer's office. Other times, the place is ill-defined, as for the work of most readers of this article, who are hired in one location and who perform labor services in a number of others, such as offices, libraries, home offices, airplane lounges, and hotel rooms.

Labor markets are defined in overlapping ways—by geography (the New York City labor market), occupation (the labor market for economists), or skill level (the labor market for college graduates).

Whatever the defining criterion may be, labor markets always have two sides: labor demand and labor supply. On the labor demand side are firms (including companies, not-for-profit organizations, and government agencies), which hire labor in order to produce goods and services. On the labor supply side are workers, who sell their time in exchange for compensation which, in standard terminology, is called the wage.

On both sides of the labor market, the relevant parties engage in purposeful behavior. In the core model of economics, companies seek to maximize the net present value of profit, which is the difference between the revenues they take in from the goods and services they sell and the costs they incur in producing those goods and services. Individuals, for their part, are assumed to seek to maximize utility, which depends positively on the goods they are able to buy with their income and negatively on the amount of leisure foregone while working.

The amount of labor demanded and supplied are both functions of the wage. The amount of labor demanded in a labor market decreases with the wage, all other things being equal. This negative relationship arises for two reasons: a higher wage induces existing employers to hire fewer workers than they would have if the wage had been lower, and it may induce some of these employers to go out of business entirely and hire nobody. On the other hand, the amount of labor supplied to a labor market increases with the wage, all other things being equal. Here too, there are two basic reasons: a higher wage in one labor market induces some workers to enter that labor market from other labor markets and also induces some individuals who are outside the labor market (the old, the young, full-time students) to seek work in this labor market.

Of course, other things are frequently not equal; labor demand and labor supply are functions of these other things as well. For instance, an improvement in product market conditions will cause more labor to be demanded at any given wage than before, and heightened prestige for a given occupation will cause more labor to be supplied at any given wage than before.

As with other markets, a labor market is said to clear when the amount of labor demanded equals the amount of labor supplied. It is said to be in equilibrium when the economy tends toward a particular set of conditions and, once there, tends to stay there.

Whether an equilibrium is characterized by market clearing or not depends on which equilibrating forces are free to operate in the labor market in question. In the standard labor market models, three fundamental equilibrating forces are postulated. First, firms are free to hire as many or as few workers as they want depending on wages and other conditions of employment. Second, workers are free within limits to move from one labor market to another or into and out of the labor force depending on wages and other conditions of employment. And third, the wage paid is free to rise or fall depending on supply and demand conditions.

When all three of these equilibrating forces are free to operate, the labor market is expected to clear in equilibrium. Wages and employment will therefore reflect supply and demand conditions.

The market-clearing model provides enormous insight. It explains, for example, why workers in the United States are paid so much, why workers in Mexico are paid so little, and why professional athletes are paid so much more than farm laborers.

These examples also highlight two important types of restrictions on equilibration in labor markets. First, every country imposes restrictions on international migration.

Because of the large differences in labor market earnings, a great many workers in Mexico and other countries would like to become American workers, but U.S. immigration law prohibits them from doing so. An estimated 6 million Mexican workers have taken matters into their own hands and have entered the United States illegally. Second, workers differ in terms of their productivity and skills. It is effectively impossible for farm laborers to acquire the skills needed to become professional athletes.

Beyond these barriers to equilibration, which are ubiquitous, there are also settings in which one of the equilibrating forces, the wage rate, is not free to adjust. Wages may be set above the market-clearing level by a variety of institutional forces including minimum wages, trade unions, multinational corporations, public-sector pay policies, and national labor codes. When this happens, the predictable consequence is unemployment. The high rate of unemployment in Europe compared to North America is usually explained in such terms. Infrequently, the wage in a labor market is set not above the market-clearing level but below it. The government of Singapore did this to try to hold down labor costs and maintain international competitiveness. That nation's wage-restraint policy was halted only when employers persuaded the government to allow them to raise wages so that they could attract more workers and increase production.

Moving beyond this basic labor market model, a number of other features are at the forefront of labor economics modeling today. Efficiency wage models recognize that a higher wage may increase worker productivity, because existing workers have greater incentives to work more efficiently and/or because firms that pay higher wages attract a larger pool of applicants, from whom they can hire more selectively. Human capital models recognize that workers' skills and productivity can be augmented through education and training. Imperfect information and matching models recognize that it takes time and resources for workers to find appropriate jobs and for firms to find appropriate workers. Models of labor market segmentation and dualism recognize that "good jobs" and "bad jobs" may coexist for workers of a given skill level. Labor market discrimination models recognize that employers, coworkers, and customers may have prejudicial tastes that they exercise in the labor market. In all of these areas, the consequences for employment and wage levels have been carefully worked out.

Finally, a fundamental aspect of labor market economics is that labor markets do not operate in isolation. Wages and employment levels in one geographic area, occupation, or skill group are determined not just by conditions in that labor market but by conditions in other labor markets as well. Multi-sector labor market models, though more complicated than models of individual labor markets, offer insights that models of single labor markets cannot—for example, the understanding that the solution to urban unemployment may be rural development.

SEE ALSO *Employment; Labor Demand; Labor Force Participation; Labor Supply; Wages*

BIBLIOGRAPHY

Ehrenberg, Ronald G., and Robert S. Smith. 2005. *Modern Labor Economics*. 9th ed. Boston: Pearson Addison Wesley.

Gary S. Fields

LABOR MARKET SEGMENTATION

Labor market segmentation theory (LMS) has two principle elements: (1) the labor market can be modeled as consisting of a small number of distinct markets offering different wages, and (2) workers, particularly those from racial and ethnic minorities, women, and new entrants, cannot necessarily find employment in the segment that offers them the highest compensation.

The most common version of LMS is the dual labor market model. This divides the labor market into a primary labor market with well-developed internal labor markets, offering secure long-term employment and higher wages for well-educated, experienced, and senior workers, and a secondary labor market with little job security, short-lived jobs, and wages independent of education and experience. For men, a statistical model of wages with two sectors predicts individual wages much better than does a model with the same number of parameters but only one sector. Moreover, in one sector education and experience have a positive effect on wages, whereas in the other they do not. For women, the dual labor market model does not fit the data well.

Mainstream labor economists have also sometimes modeled the labor market as consisting of two sectors: government and private, manufacturing and nonmanufacturing, skilled and unskilled, and so on. But LMS differs from mainstream models of the labor market in two important ways. First, it implies that low wages are associated with undesirable job characteristics, whereas conventional models imply that workers in jobs with otherwise undesirable characteristics receive a compensating (higher) wage differential. Second, in LMS, wages do not adjust to clear the market. There are workers who are qualified for desirable jobs but are unable to find employment in those jobs.

In fact, high wages are often associated with good job characteristics. There is relatively little evidence that workers are compensated for bad job characteristics. This is not decisive evidence in favor of LMS. Advocates of the standard view argue that we have relatively poor data on workers' earnings potential. Workers with high earnings potential take their compensation partly in the form of high wages and partly in the form of better working conditions, which explains the positive relation between wages and working conditions.

LMS is sometimes interpreted incorrectly as meaning that there is little mobility among sectors. Low mobility might mean most workers are happy where they work. In contrast, workers initially trapped in the secondary sector would change sectors upon obtaining primary-sector employment. The existence of queues for good jobs is the most significant departure of LMS from the conventional view, but it is difficult to test. Although compared with secondary-sector jobs, primary-sector jobs pay more and have characteristics that most people prefer; some secondary workers may not be excluded from primary jobs, but instead prefer secondary jobs and willingly accept the lower pay. However, the overrepresentation of some groups in the secondary sector is only consistent with free choice if their members are more likely than others to like secondary jobs. For some groups, such as African Americans, this is implausible and suggests that some workers in the secondary sector would prefer primary-sector employment.

SEE ALSO *Dual Economy; Harris-Todaro Model*

BIBLIOGRAPHY

Dickens, William T., and Kevin Lang. 1985. A Test of Dual Labor Market Theory. *American Economic Review* 75 (September): 792–805.

Doeringer, Peter, and Michael A. Piore. 1971. *Internal Labor Markets and Manpower Analysis.* Lexington, MA: D.C. Heath.

Kevin Lang

LABOR SUPPLY

For economists, "labor supply" usually means the hours of work, usually per week, offered for pay or profit. This definition therefore excludes unpaid household work and voluntary work. Usually, the question of labor-force participation (the question of whether a person is working or looking for work) is treated separately. Research on both the theoretical and applied labor supply exploded in the 1980s and 1990s, with the work ranging from models of individual behavior in a static one-period model to dynamic multi-period models for a household. Simple theoretical models that gave a backward-bending supply curve (where labor supply first increased and then decreased with wage rates, for which little evidence exists) have given way to empirical labor-supply curves that are usually (but not always) positively sloped with respect to the wage rate. Beginning in the late twentieth century, much of the focus of research has been on labor supply as a whole, not on particular firms, industries, or occupations.

The concept of "labor supply" is defined for economies with a well-developed labor market; that is, a market where wage labor is employed. The concept of labor supply in less developed countries (LDCs) is less clearly defined, because culture, history, and institutions affect labor supply. In some LDCs, women are not involved in the formal labor market, and the labor activities that women perform may be limited by tradition, either for religious or cultural reasons. Because precapitalist conditions exist in LDCs, labor in these nations is often tied to a particular feudal lord, and the worker does not have the freedom to move from one employer to another, or from one location to another.

In LDCs, as the economy develops, labor moves from the agricultural sector to the industrial sector. W. Arthur Lewis, in his seminal 1954 paper "Economic Development with Unlimited Supplies of Labour," put forward a dual-economy model in which the surplus agricultural labor (defined as labor with a zero marginal product) moved to the industrial (modern) sector, providing a nearly infinite supply of labor at a constant wage. This provided a boost to economic development because the industrial sector could expand with a "surplus" (i.e., a profit) being created with cheap labor. The rapid growth of the Chinese economy in the first decade of the twenty-first century provides an example of how surplus labor from agriculture can provide a boost to economic growth.

In general, there are important differences in labor supply for males and females. Biology, history, and society have led to women spending more time in housework, child rearing, and various other domestic duties. For various reasons, including discrimination, society appears to have accepted a gender segregation of roles in the labor market. For example, women work in the textile industry while men work in mining, and women work as primary school teachers while men work as lawyers. Fortunately, many of these stereotypes are breaking down slowly, at least in most Western countries.

The labor supply in a particular economy can increase through population growth (natural increase), immigration, an increase in people employed or looking for work, and through workers offering longer hours of work in each period. Although the labor supply of different educational or skill levels is considered in many models, the issue of the efficiency of labor services (i.e., how hard and diligently a person works) is usually ignored.

In most models of labor supply, the determination of the hours of work is derived from an assumption of utility-maximizing individuals who face given wage rates and prices and a time constraint. In all these models, it is assumed that there is a disutility from work—that is, it is assumed that people do not like working. There is a good deal of evidence, however, from psychologists, sociologists, and industrial relations experts that work provides an individual with a set of contacts, imposes a time structure on the waking day, provides social status and identity, and enforces activity (see Jahoda 1982). Further, an unemployed person often suffers from a level of despair that may lead to mental illness.

Standard neoclassical models are set up to analyze competitive capitalist economies with a well-developed wage-labor market. The utility function, which is unchanging over the life cycle, depends on leisure and consumption goods. An increase in the wage rate leads to a substitution effect (leisure becomes expensive) and an income effect (a person can purchase more leisure and goods). If leisure is a normal good, then these two effects work in opposite directions. The net effect of a wage rate change is therefore ambiguous. The introduction of income taxes and social security payments make the analysis more complex, since the budget constraint becomes nonlinear.

In a novel extension to the concept of labor supply, George Becker argued in a 1965 paper that individuals choose "commodities" that are produced by combining consumer goods with the individual's time. Hence, a consumer good that is purchased, such as meat, also needs time (e.g., cooking time, washing-up time) to form the "commodity" called dinner. The time used in cooking thus has an "opportunity cost." Alternatively, the "dinner" can be purchased in a restaurant with less time spent in obtaining it. The choice of cooking at home or eating out depends on the opportunity costs of time. For a professional person, the opportunity costs of cooking a meal are generally too high. This approach is especially useful in analyzing nonmarket work done (mainly) by women.

In an early model, labor supply was dependent on current wages and (expected) future wages, such that people would offer to work less in the current period if future wages were expected to be higher. Robert Lucas and Leonard Rapping deal with the intertemporal substitution of labor in "Real Wages, Employment, and Inflation" (1969). In advanced models, labor supply is dependent on the planned time path of consumption goods and leisure, along with a choice of saving and wealth accumulation

over an entire lifetime. A critical assumption in these dynamic models is of a utility function that is not affected by habits or learning (intertemporal separability over time), as this could make the wage rates depend on individual's behavior (see Card 1994). There are significant differences in the labor supply of males and females due to cultural and institutional factors. Typically, the female labor supply is significantly affected by the number of preschool children in the family.

Expanded models of labor supply allow for joint household decision making, with bargaining between husband and wife (see Vermeulen 2002). The aggregate supply of hours depends on the number of people who are willing to work (given wage offers and their reservation wage) and the hours offered per person. Individuals are assumed to work out a "reservation wage," meaning a wage below which they are not willing to work because the opportunity cost of leisure is too high. This reservation wage is obviously influenced by an individual's age, education, experience, family commitments, social security benefits, and wealth status. Changes in the minimum wage are likely to lead to a change in the distribution of reservation wages, because the idea of "fair wages" will also change (see Falk, Fehr, and Zehnder 2005). Changes in reservation wages can also affect the aggregate supply of labor.

It is generally assumed that the individual can work as many hours at a given wage as she or he desires (either within a firm, choosing different offers from different firms, or with multiple jobs). It is also usually assumed that there are no institutional constraints (e.g., a specified work week for a full-time person), and that the nonavailability of work (i.e., involuntary unemployment) is not a factor. Most estimates of labor supply are based on people who are working. This creates a selection bias, because it excludes those who want to work but cannot find work or have refused the wage offered to them. However, an individual can influence his or her wage through an appropriate investment in human capital, such as acquiring new skills or additional education. In some labor markets (especially for highly skilled labor) an individual may be able to bargain for a package of wages, hours, and other perquisites.

Some empirical regularities have been seen in OECD (Organisation for Economic Co-operation and Development) countries in the post-war period. These include an increase in the number of women working, a decrease in the number of older males working, a fall in the average number of hours worked, and educated people working longer hours. Most of the research on this subject has focused on an econometric estimation of labor supply for males, females, and households. Econometric estimation has moved progressively from time-series data to cross-section data to panel data. Most estimates of labor supply find a small positive link between wages and hours worked—known as "elasticity," the percentage increase in labor supply as a result of a one percent change in the wage rate—although there is a large element of "unexplained" variance. A major interest has been the extent to which welfare benefits and changes in tax rates affect the labor supply. Policy changes in these and other areas could affect people's decision whether or not to seek work. Again, because most labor-supply models are based on data on working people, the possibility of selection bias must be considered.

Labor supply is also important from a policy perspective. How people respond to changes in tax rates, social security payments, and other institutional features like minimum wages are all relevant. Much of the evidence is based on simple models of single-person (or "unitary") households, and is thus subject to debate. The evidence on many of these issues is very controversial, especially the impact of minimum wage on employment. And as Richard Blundell and Thomas Macurdy point out, there is little evidence to support the view that welfare programs have a disincentive effect on the labor supply.

Even though there have been significant advances in the theoretical modeling of labor supply, and in econometric estimation techniques, there are still large gaps in our understanding of the impact of policy changes on labor supply. Models need to be extended to households in which people decide simultaneously whether to work and how many hours to work over a longer period, including their saving behavior, and with some allowance made for the existence of demand-constrained choices. The existence of persistent unemployment in most OECD economies suggests that a basic underlying assumption of labor supply models is unrealistic, namely that workers can choose whether to work and how many hours to work.

SEE ALSO *Economics, Labor; Employment; Human Capital; Labor; Labor Demand; Labor Force Participation; Labor Market; Selection Bias; Wages*

BIBLIOGRAPHY

Becker, George. 1965. A Theory of the Allocation of Time. *Economic Journal* 75 (299): 493–517.

Blau, Francine D., and Marianne A. Ferber. 1992. *The Economics of Women, Men, and Work*. 2nd ed. Englewood Cliffs, NJ: Prentice-Hall.

Blundell, Richard, and Thomas Macurdy. 1999. Labor Supply: A Review of Alternative Approaches. In *Handbook of Labor Economics*, Vol. 3A, eds. Orley C. Ashenfelter and David Card. Amsterdam: North Holland.

Card, David. 1994. Intertemporal Labor Supply: An Assessment. In *Advances in Econometrics*, ed. Christopher Sims. Cambridge, U.K.: Cambridge University Press.

Card, David, and Alan B. Krueger. 1995. *Myth and Measurement: The New Economics of the Minimum Wage*. Princeton, NJ: Princeton University Press.

Chang, Yongsung, and Sun-Bin Kim. 2006. From Individual to Aggregate Labor Supply: A Quantitative Analysis Based on a Heterogeneous Agent Macroeconomy. *International Economic Review* 47 (1): 1–27.

Falk, Armin, Ernst Fehr, and Christian Zehnder. 2005. The Behavioral Effects of Minimum Wages. IZA Discussion Paper No. 1625. Bonn, Germany: Institute for the Study of Labor.

Jahoda, Marie. 1982. *Employment and Unemployment: A Social-Psychological Analysis*. Cambridge, U.K.: Cambridge University Press.

Killingsworth, Mark R. 1983. *Labor Supply*. Cambridge, UK: Cambridge University Press.

Killingsworth, Mark R., and James J. Heckman. 1986. Female Labor Supply: A Survey. In *Handbook of Labor Economics*, Vol. 1, eds. Orley C. Ashenfelter and Richard Layard. Amsterdam: North Holland.

Lazear, Edward P. 1995. *Personnel Economics*. Cambridge, MA: MIT Press.

Lewis, W. Arthur 1954. Economic Development with Unlimited Supplies of Labour. *Manchester School of Economic and Social Studies* 22: 139–192.

Lucas, Robert E., Jr., and Leonard A. Rapping. 1969. Real Wages, Employment, and Inflation. *Journal of Political Economy* 77 (5): 721–754.

Mortensen, Dale T., and Christopher A. Pissarides. 1999. New Developments in Models of Search in the Labor Market. In *Handbook of Labor Economics*, Vol. 3, eds. Orley C. Ashenfelter and David Card. Amsterdam: North Holland.

Neumark, David, and William Wascher. 1992. Employment Effects of Minimum and Subminimum Wages. *Industrial and Labor Relations Review* 46 (1): 55–81.

Pencavel, John 1986. Labor Supply of Men. In *Handbook of Labor Economics*, Vol. 1, eds. Orley C. Ashenfelter and Richard Layard. 1986. Amsterdam: North Holland.

Senesky, Sarah. 2005. Testing the Intertemporal Labor Supply Model: Are Jobs Important? *Labour Economics* 12 (6): 749–772.

Vermeulen, Frederic. 2002. Collective Household Models: Principles and Main Results. *Journal of Economic Surveys*. 16 (4): 533–564.

P. N. Junankar

LABOR THEORY OF VALUE

Fundamentally, the labor theory of value is a prohibition: it asserts that produced means of production cannot be sources of surplus value, and hence of profit. Once seen as an essential component of Marxian economics, it is now a divisive issue even amongst economists who describe themselves as Marxist. It is rejected by many non-neoclassical economists, and of course by the neoclassical school in general. However, it is still championed by several subschools of Marxian economics, and will no doubt always be part of the ideological appeal of anti-capitalist political parties.

The concept that work, or relative effort, was the just determinant of the ratio in which two commodities were freely exchanged was first aired by Aristotle (c. 450–388 BCE) in his *Nicomachean Ethics*. Starting from the premise that "the good has rightly been declared to be that at which all things aim" (Bk. 1, chap. 1), Aristotle deduced that, for justice to prevail, commodities should exchange in relation to the amount of work embodied in them: "Let A be a builder, B a shoemaker, C a house, D a shoe. The builder, then, must get from the shoemaker the latter's work" (Bk. 5, chap. 5). However, Aristotle subsequently added demand, or utility, as the basis of exchange, thus conflating the two great traditions in the determination of value and exchange: that relative prices are set either by the objective effort expended in production, or by the subjective utility enjoyed in consumption.

By the time of Adam Smith (1723–1790) and David Ricardo (1772–1823), these two perspectives were regarded as essentially contradictory. The then-dominant classical school subscribed to the former, while the then-nascent neoclassical tendency asserted the latter. However, though Smith identified work as the basis of exchange, and labor as its measure, he also argued that nonhuman inputs could be productive, and hence sources of profit: "labouring cattle, therefore, … not only occasion … the reproduction of a value equal to their own consumption, … but of a much greater value" (Smith [1776] 1904, Bk. 2, chap. 5). He also argued that only "in that early and rude state of society which precedes both the accumulation of stock and the appropriation of land" (Bk. 1, chap. 6) could commodities actually exchange in proportion to the labor embodied in them.

Ricardo also treated labor as a measure of value, rather than its sole source. The assertion that labor was not only the measure but also the source of value, and hence profit, was first made by Karl Marx (1818–1883).

Marx argued that profit could originate even when commodities exchanged at their costs of production. He assumed that commodities exchanged at their value, where value was "socially necessary labor-time," so that capitalists purchased labor at its value, which was a subsistence wage (the value of *labor-power*, signified by v). These commodities might take, say, six hours of direct and indirect labor to produce (where indirect labor included the depreciation of machinery and consumption of raw materials).

Marx then drew a crucial distinction between labor (actual work activity) and labor-power (working ability). Workers receive a wage that is equal to the value of their labor power; however, the value created by workers will normally be greater than this. Surplus value (signified by s) arises from the fact that the working day is longer (typically twelve hours in Marx's day) than the time required for laborers to create value equal to the value of labor-power (say, six hours). Surplus value arises from the unpaid labor time that accrues to capitalists as a legal right, and not because of capitalists' contribution to production. The capitalist gains this unpaid labor time "for free" from the labor contract. Expansions in the length of the workday, increases in the speed of work, or productive changes in the organization of work will all extend this gap between the value of labor-power (v) and the value of labor activity ($v + s$), giving rise to a surplus (s).

So, in Marx's analysis, surplus value does not arise because commodities exchange above their value: the commodity that is produced is exchanged according to its value, and laborers are paid a wage that is equal to the value of labor-power. Exploitation, which for Marx means the creation of surplus value, occurs because workers create value that is greater than the value of their labor power. Marx argued that labor-power is the only commodity with the capacity for value greater than its own value, and he regarded the distinction between labor and labor-power as his important contribution to political economy.

Marx assumed that s/v, the "rate of surplus value," was constant across industries, though it could of course vary over time. He was emphatic that all other inputs to production (signified by c and measured by their depreciation) made no net contribution to surplus: "However useful a given kind of raw material, or a machine … may be, though it may cost £150 … it cannot, under any circumstances, add to the value of the product more than £150" (Marx [1867] 1887, chap. 8). Surplus, and therefore profit, thus emanated solely from labor.

The rate of profit, which Marx defined as $s/(c + v)$, was positively related to the rate of surplus value and negatively related to the ratio of c to v (c/v, the ratio of capital to labor, which Marx termed the *organic composition of capital*). Allied with an alleged tendency for the organic composition of capital to rise over time, this led to Marx's prediction of a falling rate of profit that would ultimately lead to the demise of capitalism via a socialist revolution.

Critics of Marx's economics have long argued that the dilemma for the labor theory of value was that it could not be made consistent with the competitive equalization of the rate of profit across different industries, when the organic composition of capital differed from one industry to another. Marx's solution of what became known as the *transformation problem* was strongly challenged by Ladislaus von Bortkiewicz (1868–1931) and remains a contentious issue within Marxian economics.

By the end of the twentieth century, economists inspired by Marx had broken into two broad camps: those who accept the labor theory of value and those who do not (most of whom would describe themselves as belonging to other schools of non-neoclassical thought). Indeed, one of the most influential present-day economists inspired by Marx, Ian Steedman, believes that "the project of providing a materialist account of capitalist societies is dependent on Marx's value magnitude analysis only in the negative sense that continued adherence to the latter is a major fetter on the development of the former" (Steedman 1977, p. 207).

Anwar Shaikh (1984) presents an orthodox defense of Marx's value theory. Two other important attempts to sustain the labor theory of value are the *temporal single system* interpretation that the determination of price from value is a dynamic process in which the labor theory of value can be sustained (Foley 2000), and the empirical argument that, while subject to theoretical criticism, the proposition that prices are proportional to labor values is empirically valid (Cockshott and Cottrell 1998, 2005). Both the theoretical and empirical defenses are subject to criticism from other non-neoclassical economists (Mongiovi 2002; Podkaminer 2005).

Most critiques of the labor theory of value, as with Steedman's pivotal contribution, effectively discourage consideration of other aspects of Marx's thought, such as his philosophy of dialectical materialism. An exception here is Steve Keen's argument that Marx's philosophy itself contradicts the labor theory of value. Keen argues that, after 1857, the concept of a dialectic between the objective use-value of a commodity and its exchange-value became Marx's fundamental axiomatic base, rather than the labor theory of value itself.

Marx mocked Ricardo for not having an explanation of the gap between the value of labor and labor-power: "Value of labour is not identical with wages of labour. *Because* they are different. *Therefore* they are not identical. This is a strange logic. There is basically no reason for this other than that it is *not* so in practice." In contrast, Marx argued that "what the capitalist acquires through exchange is labour capacity: this is the exchange value which he pays for. Living labour is the use value which this exchange value has for him, and out of this use value springs the surplus value and the suspension of exchange as such" (Marx [1857] 1973, pp. 561–562).

The distinction between use-value and exchange-value was also central to Marx's explanation of surplus value in *Capital*: "The past labor that is embodied in the labor-power, and the living labor that it can call into action ... are two totally different things. The former determines the exchange-value of the labor power, the latter is its use-value" (Marx [1867] 1887, chap. 7, sec. 2). Keen (1993) asserts that Marx misapplied this dialectic to machinery to sustain the labor theory of value, and that when properly applied, Marx's dialectic concludes that the means of production are also sources of surplus value. This critique thus maintains Marx's philosophy, while also rejecting the labor theory of value.

SEE ALSO *Exchange Value; Immiserizing Growth; Marx, Karl: Impact on Economics; Primitive Accumulation; Relative Surplus Value; Surplus Value; Transformation Problem; Value*

BIBLIOGRAPHY

Aristotle. [c. 350 BCE] 1980. *Nicomachean Ethics.* Trans. W. D. Ross. Oxford: Oxford University Press. http://classics.mit.edu/Aristotle/nicomachaen.html.

Cockshott, W. Paul, and Allin F. Cottrell. 1998. Does Marx Need to Transform? In *Marxian Economics: A Reappraisal,* ed. Riccardo Bellofiore, Vol. 2, 70–85. New York: St. Martin's Press.

Cockshott, W. Paul, and Allin F. Cottrell. 2005. Robust Correlations between Prices and Labour Values: A Comment. *Cambridge Journal of Economics* 29: 309–316.

Foley, Duncan K. 2000. Recent Developments in the Labor Theory of Value. *Review of Radical Political Economics* 32: 1–39.

Keen, Steve. 1993. Use-value, Exchange-value, and the Demise of Marx's Labor Theory of Value. *Journal of the History of Economic Thought* 15: 107–121.

Marx, Karl. [1857] 1973. *Grundrisse.* Trans. Martin Nicolaus. London: Penguin. http://www.marx.org/archive/marx/works/1857/grundrisse/.

Marx, Karl. [1867] 1887. *Capital.* Vol. 1. Trans. Samuel Moore and Edward Aveling. Moscow: Progress Publishers. http://www.marx.org/archive/marx/works/1867-c1/index.htm.

Mongiovi, Gary. 2002. Vulgar Economy in Marxian Garb: A Critique of Temporal Single System Marxism. *Review of Radical Political Economics* 34: 393–416.

Podkaminer, Leon. 2005. A Note on the Statistical Verification of Marx: Comment on Cockshott and Cottrell. *Cambridge Journal of Economics* 29: 657–658.

Shaikh, Anwar. 1984. The Transformation from Marx to Sraffa. In *Ricardo, Marx, Sraffa: The Langston Memorial Volume,* eds. Alan Freeman and Ernest Mandel, 43–84. London: Verso.

Smith, Adam. [1776] 1904. *An Inquiry into the Nature and Causes of the Wealth of Nations.* Ed. Edwin Cannan. London: Methuen. http://www.econlib.org/library/Smith/smWN1.html.

Steedman, Ian. 1977. *Marx After Sraffa.* London: NLB.

Steve Keen

LABOR UNION

A labor union is typically an association of wage and salary earners aimed at improving the welfare of its associates through raising the bargained wage above the competitive level, improving working conditions, and preserving occupational levels. These aims can be achieved by unions using a number of strategies, according to the institutional framework under which unions and employers operate, general economic conditions, and political economy considerations.

In most industrialized economies, wages are largely determined through collective agreements between unions and employer confederations. Total output is shared between the two parts according to the relative bargaining power. These agreements are usually binding for a proportion of total employees that does not include union members only. The proportion of contracts usually covered by collective agreements is known in the literature as *union coverage*. The membership rate among wage and salary earners is referred to as *union density*.

The bargaining process may take place at the firm, industry, regional, or national level and may involve other issues, such as the work schedule, working conditions, holidays, and training. The attitude of unions during the bargaining process may differ, according to how much they internalize the consequences of the bargaining decisions on the economy as a whole. This amounts to unions being more or less coordinated with employer confederations in defining bargaining outcomes that can be beneficial or detrimental for economy-wide growth and welfare. Alternatively unions may adopt bargaining strategies aimed at improving the welfare of their associates only, regardless of the consequences on the economic system. For example, unions mainly representing insiders—that is, employed workers—may bargain for a higher wage, therefore improving the welfare of associated employees, despite the adverse effect on outsiders, including the unemployed and new entrants in the labor market.

Sometimes unions' actions and organization may be defined and managed under specific regulations. For example, in the United States public sector workers do not have the right to strike, while in other countries certain limitations apply in order to guarantee a minimum amount of public services during collective actions. Other regulations apply to the collection and management of union dues. For example, all employees may be required to pay union dues within a fixed period of time after hiring, although unions may be limited in their ways of spending financial resources collected from nonmembers.

One possible representation of union preferences is based on the assumption that union members are identical. The union objective function consists then of the expected utility of the representative member. This amounts to the utility associated, respectively, to the state of employment and unemployment, that is, by the real wage W and the reservation wage $\overline{W}$, weighted by the probability of being in each of the two states. With N and L being, respectively, the labor force and the employment level, and $v(\cdot)$ an indirect utility function, this can be written as $E(U) = \dfrac{L}{N} v(W) + \left(1 - \dfrac{L}{N}\right) v(\overline{W})$ with $v'(W) > 0;\ v''(W) \leq 0$.

Union members are, however, typically heterogeneous. In this case, the union objective function will depend on the mechanisms regulating the functioning of the union. If unions are perfectly democratic organizations, then their objectives will typically depend on the preferences of the median member. However, because they are collective organizations, unions respond to political economy incentive structures, like firms and political parties, and their leaders may be assigned discretionary power. In this case, union leaders may operate for objectives that are different from their organization's statutory objectives.

Wage-bargaining models can be classified into two main theoretical frameworks, known in the literature as *right to manage* and *efficient bargaining*. Under the right-to-manage approach, unions and firms bargain over the wage, with firms setting labor demand given the bargained wage. As a result, the bargaining outcome will always be on the labor-demand curve. This approach can be rationalized under a simple Nash framework, with the bargained wage W^* being the result of the following maximization problem: $\max_{W} B = V(W)^{\gamma} \Pi(W)^{1-\gamma}$, where $V(W)$ and $\Pi(W)$ are, respectively, the bargaining outcome gains for unions and firms, and γ (with $0 < \gamma < 1$) is the bargaining power of unions. A higher wage will increase the employed workers' utility, but at the same time it will lower the firms' profits per worker as well as the aggregate employment level.

Under the efficient bargaining approach, it is shown that unions and firms can reach bargaining outcomes that are Pareto-improving with respect to the right-to-manage hypothesis. The bargaining equilibrium is then located on the contract curve, that is, on the locus of the tangency points between firms' isoprofit curves and unions' indifference curves. The exact location of the equilibrium on the contract curve will depend on the relative bargaining power γ. The empirical evidence is mainly consistent with the first setting.

Historically, in many industrialized countries, union density rates have increased especially during the expansion of the industrial sector. Recent decades, characterized by a declining industrial sector and the development of a service-oriented economy in many advanced economies, have witnessed heterogeneous patterns in union density rates, with a decline in some countries and an increase in others. These patterns seem to have followed the general institutional settings prevailing in each country as well as the ability of unions to adapt their objectives and strategies to new economic environments. As a result union density rates across Organization for Economic Cooperation and Development (OECD) countries display a significant amount of variation, from a minimum of around 10 percent in France, the United States, and Spain in 2001 to a maximum of around 80 percent in Finland and Sweden. The same is true for union coverage that ranges from a minimum of 14 percent in the United States to above 90 percent in Austria, Belgium, Finland, France, and Sweden. Even within the same country, unions are characterized by different membership rates across sectors. For example, in the United States private sector unions represent around 8.5 percent of workers, whereas public sector unions represent around 30 percent of workers in their sector.

SEE ALSO *Game Theory; Labor; Negotiation; Unions; Wages*

BIBLIOGRAPHY

Booth, Alison. 1995. *The Economics of the Trade Union.* Cambridge, U.K.: Cambridge University Press.

Cahuc, Pierre, and André Zylberberg. 2004. *Labor Economics.* Cambridge, MA: MIT Press.

Pencavel, John. 1991. *Labor Market Under Trade Unionism: Employment, Wages and Hours.* Cambridge, MA: Blackwell.

Luca Nunziata

LABOUR PARTY (BRITAIN)

The Labour Party currently led by Tony Blair (b. 1953) has formed the governments of Britain since 1997 through its successes at three consecutive general elections in 1997, 2001, and 2005. It is now a party committed to the "New Labour" ideas of its leader, who maintains a "third-way approach" that accepts that both the state and public enterprise should jointly contribute to Britain's economic recovery. Peter Mandelson and Roger Liddle in their book *The Blair Revolution* (1996) state that "New Labour believes that it is possible to combine a free-market economy with social justice: liberty of the individual with wider opportunities for all; One Nation security with efficiency and competitiveness" (p. 1).

As part of this strategy Blair forced the party to drop its traditional Clause 4 when he became leader in 1994, replacing it with an amorphous alternative and thus abandoning a commitment to public ownership, playing down the importance of traditional trade-union and working-class demands, and opening up the possibility of the party capturing more white-collar and middle-class support, the middle ground in British politics. He was able to do so largely because of the way in which both Neil Kinnock (b. 1942), leader between 1983 and 1992, and John Smith, leader from 1992 to 1994, had transformed the party after Labour's disastrous general election of 1983. Gerald Kaufmann, a Labour MP, had described Labour's manifesto of 1983 "as the longest suicide note in history," tied as it was to nationalization in the hands of an increasingly left-wing party that was becoming unpopular in the country and that was ultimately out of power from 1979 until 1997.

In the early 1980s the Labour Party was organized into local constituency Labour parties, which were usually dominated by the bloc-vote influence of the trade unions and often could be operated by a small minority of activist members. The trade unions and left-wing activists usually dominated the local parties, and therefore their representatives often held sway in the annual national conference of the party, which often elected a predominantly left-wing National Executive Committee. Fearful that a small extreme minority could easily dominate the party, Kinnock pressed for a number of reforms, including instigating four policy reviews between 1988 and 1991, one of which, *Meet the Challenge and Make the Change* (1989), challenged Labour's shibboleth of nationalization. His policy reviews also ended Labour's commitment to full employment and universal provision within Britain's welfare state. Kinnock set up committees to be responsible for Labour's manifesto commitments and policies, the centralizing authority around the Labour leader. Trade union power at the annual party conference was also reduced to 40 percent of the vote, considerably less than the 1987 bloc vote, and the rest of the vote was based upon an individual ballot of rank-and-file members. The method of electing the party leader was changed, and by the late 1980s the voting in leadership and deputy-leadership elections was established on the basis of One Member One Vote (OMOV). Effectively, then, Kinnock centralized power around the Labour Party leader, neutralized left-wing policies, and reduced the power of the trade unions within their local constituencies and at party conference. It was out of these changes that Blair was able to press forward with his more moderate to right-wing agenda of "New Labour."

The present Labour Party is thus a far cry from the organization formed as the Labour Representation Committee in 1900, which became the Labour Party in 1906. This had been an alliance of trade unions and socialist groups committed to operating as an independent working-class organization within a parliamentary system. Led at various times by James Keir Hardie (1856–1915), Ramsay MacDonald (1866–1937), and Arthur Henderson (1863–1935), it had emerged quickly, was drawn into the wartime coalition of World War I (then referred to as the "Great War,") and was able to form its first, albeit minority, Labour government in 1924. By that time the party had become officially socialist as a result of accepting Clause 4 (clause 3d) in its 1918 constitution, which committed it to the public ownership of the means of production. MacDonald's first government was short-lived, but its essential moderation helped to allay the fears of newspapers that announced the first Labour government's formation in January 1924 with the headlines "Lenin dead, MacDonald in power." This government was defeated in the 1924 general election, which was dominated by the Zinoviev, or "Red Letter," scare, in which what was almost certainly a forged letter was published as evidence that the Soviet Union wished to use the Labour Party to extend the influence of communism in Britain.

MacDonald formed another, minority, Labour government in 1929, but it too was defeated after a brief existence as a result of the mounting economic crisis of 1931, when the Labour cabinet was divided on cutting unemployment benefits by 10 percent. The government resigned but MacDonald continued as prime minister of a national government, and Labour was decimated, cut down from 289 to 52 seats, in the general election of October 1931.

Labour remained in the political wilderness until May 1940, when Clement Attlee (1883–1967), elected leader in 1935, became a member of Winston Churchill's wartime cabinet. Out of office, the party rethought its policies, and partly because of this, and partly because of the leftward shift during World War II, it won the general election of July 1945 with 393 seats and a thumping majority of 146 seats in the House of Commons. As a result, Attlee led his first administration from 1945 to 1950, and narrowly won a second term from 1950 to 1951. These two Attlee governments were immensely talented, with members such as Ernest Bevin (1881–1951), a foreign secretary who pushed for the North Atlantic Treaty Organization in 1949, and Aneurin (Nye) Bevan (1897–1960), who inspired the introduction of the National Health Service in 1948.

Nevertheless, in the early 1950s the Labour government was divided, and it collapsed after Bevan left in 1951 over his opposition to the threatened prescription charges on medicines. The Labour Party was defeated at the 1951 general election and remained out of office for thirteen years, during which it was divided between its left-wing public-ownership groups and its right wing, led

by Labour Leader Hugh Gaitskell, who wanted to drop public ownership from his policies. Gaitskell died in 1963, but Labour returned to power under the then moderate, but once left-wing, Harold Wilson (1916–1995) in 1964, and won again in the 1966 general election. However, the Wilson administrations faced serious economic problems, had to devalue the pound, and fell out with the trade unions over how to deal with strikes. Defeated in the 1970 general election, the party brokered a deal with the trade unions in the early 1970s that saw it win two general elections in 1974. Nevertheless, the Wilson and James Callaghan governments of 1976 to 1979 were unable to introduce policies of redistributing income in return for the small wage increases that trade unions were going to accept under the so-called "social contract," and as a result the Labour Party lost the general election of 1979 following the strike-prone "winter of discontent."

The Labour Party came under the influence of left-wing trade unionists in the early 1980s when led by Michael Foot (b. 1913). However, the disastrous general election of 1983 augured the change of leadership and a move to the right that occurred under Neil Kinnock, John Smith (1938–1994), and Tony Blair. It is now epitomized by the "New Labour" party of Tony Blair.

SEE ALSO *Multiparty Systems*

BIBLIOGRAPHY

Laybourn, Keith. 1988. *The Rise of the Labour Party, 1890–1979*. London: Edward Arnold.

Laybourn, Keith. 2000. *A Century of Labour*. London: Sutton.

Mandelson, Peter, and Roger Liddle. 1996. *The Blair Revolution: Can New Labour Deliver?* London: Faber and Faber.

McKibbin, Ross. 1974. *The Evolution of the Labour Party*. Oxford: Oxford University Press.

Morgan, Kenneth O. 1987. *Labour People: Leaders and Lieutenants*. Oxford: Oxford University Press.

Keith Laybourn

LADEJINSKY, WOLF
1899–1975

Wolf Isaac Ladejinsky significantly influenced global debates and policy surrounding rural development and cold war strategy. He was perhaps the most influential advocate of using agrarian reforms to win the support of the peasantry in order to preempt communist appeals— "stealing communist thunder," in one of his memorable formulations. The most significant effect of his policies was, perhaps, the decade of social conservatism resulting from post–World War II land reforms in Taiwan and, especially, Japan.

Ladejinsky fled Soviet power in the Ukraine in 1922, after expropriation of his father's business. His life was subsequently dedicated to the defeat of communism. In his view—much influenced by Bolshevik successes—communist mobilization fed on unattended peasant grievances; the remedy was preemptive policy against rural injustice.

Four years after landing in New York City, Ladejinsky entered Columbia University; he graduated in 1928. Though he made extensive studies of Soviet state farms as a graduate student, he did not finish his PhD Ladejinsky began working for the U.S. Department of Agriculture in 1935; by the end of the World War II, he was head of the Department's Far East division. In 1945 he joined General Douglas McArthur's staff overseeing American occupation forces in Japan, where he forcefully advocated land reform to promote social peace and centrist politics during reconstruction. Ladejinsky's "root-and-branch" land reform in Japan under occupation authority broke the power of large landlords and established the landless as small farmers. Farmers became the backbone of conservative governance that served many American foreign-policy objectives. Contemporary consensus is that land reforms contributed significantly to postwar Japan's political stability and economic growth. Ladejinsky's model of "stealing communist thunder" by redistributing land was also successful in Taiwan, in ways parallel to developments in Japan, but proved impossible to implement in China, where Mao Zedong's revolution promoted agrarian reform.

Time magazine observed in 1955 that the "Americanization of Wolf Ladejinsky was a copybook success story. An immigrant, he won an education and renown as a U.S. agricultural expert who helped to stymie the Communists in the Far East." Ironically, this successful anticommunist was accused of having communist sympathies by Eisenhower's secretary of agriculture; Ladejinsky lost his job in 1955 as one of many victims of anticommunist hysteria organized by Senator Joseph McCarthy.

After having had both success and failure in Asia, and losing his government job, Ladejinsky served as adviser to the U.S.-backed Diem regime in South Vietnam from 1956 to 1961. Vietnam proved more like China than Japan; Ladejinsky's attempt to use land reform as the antidote to communism foundered on the inability of Diem's regime to confront landlords. Ladejinsky subsequently served as adviser to the Ford Foundation and World Bank, concerned with Indonesia, Nepal, and the Philippines. He ended his career in India, keenly observing rural dynamics and promoting agrarian reform until his death in 1975.

SEE ALSO *Land Reform; Landlords*

BIBLIOGRAPHY

Rorty, James. 1955. "The Dossier of Wolf Ladejinsky." *Commentary* 19 (4): 326–334.

Rosen, George. 1977. "Wolf Ladejinsky: 1899–1975." *Journal of Asian Studies* 36 (2): 327–328.

Stavis, Ben. 2004. "Tireless (and Frustrated) Advocate of Land Reform." http://astro.temple.edu/~bstavis/courses/215-ladejinsky.htm.

Walinsky, Louis J., ed. 1977. *Agrarian Reform as Unfinished Business: The Selected Papers of Wolf Ladejinsky.* New York and London: Published for the World Bank by Oxford University Press.

Ronald J. Herring

LAFARGUE, PAUL
1842–1911

Paul Lafargue was a Haitian-Cuban-French Marxist economist, activist, politician, and writer, who considered himself black and referred to himself as African in letters to the German socialist Friedrich Engels. One might say with much justification that Lafargue was Cuba's first socialist.

FAMILY BACKGROUND AND EDUCATION

Lafargue was born on January 15, 1842, in Santiago, Cuba, the most popular and culturally Africanized part of the country to this day. His father, Francisco/François Lafargue (b. c. 1791–1803, d. 1870), was a wine seller, landowner (with New Orleans, Cuban, and Bordeaux properties), and tobacco or coffee planter. His mother was Ana Virginia Armaignac/Armagnac (1803 or 1810–1899). His paternal grandparents were Jean Lafargue (d. c. 1791–1803), a French colonist in St. Domingue from the Bordeaux area, and Catalina Piron (d. after 1891), a "mulatto" woman from St. Domingue. His maternal grandparents were Abraham Armagnac, the scion of a French Jewish colonialist family in St. Domingue, and Margarita Fripie/Frijie, a Carib woman residing in Kingston, Jamaica. François's mother, Caralina, fled from St. Domingue to Santiago, Cuba, probably in 1803, after the death of her French husband, Jean Lafargue, François's father, during the Haitian Revolution (1791–1803). She evidently was pregnant with François at the time of the flight, for he was born in Santiago.

In 1891, when Paul was running for the Chamber of Deputies from Bordeaux, his grandmother Catalina provided proof of her husband's French nationality. This implies that by this time Catalina also had marriage documents, or some other written token of her son's legal relationship to Jean Lafargue. Francisco was registered with the French consul in Santiago as a Frenchman, as evidently was his mother, Catalina. Actually, however, Francisco was a French citizen by virtue of article 59 of the 1685 Code Noir, which provided that any slave freed from French captivity became a French citizen. This implies that Catalina or her ancestors were freed slaves, and suggests that her descendants had documents in 1891 to prove her French slave and freedman origins.

In any case, Catalina Lafargue was among the approximately twenty thousand civilian refugees who fled from the island of Hispaniola to Cuba during the Haitian Revolution. In 1809 the Spanish government of Cuba forced Catalina and her son Francisco to flee once more. She went to New Orleans because Louisiana was the nearest location with a large French population and culture. They remained in the French Quarter and neighboring areas from about 1809 until 1814. In New Orleans the Lafargues were well-established Creoles as well. Catalina apparently never remarried, and little more is known about her.

Paul Lafargue's parents married in 1834, evidently in Santiago, Cuba. During the next seventeen years, they had one child, Paul (or Pablo, his name at baptism), and acquired property in Cuba, New Orleans, and perhaps in other places as well. The Lafargue's Cuban property included slaves, which they held at least until 1866. Paul attended the Colegio de Santiago, a Jesuit primary and middle school. Between 1814 and 1851, his parents acquired the property that made Francisco a landowner, wine seller, and slave-managed coffee plantation owner.

In 1851, three years after the Revolution of 1848 had eliminated slavery in France and its colonies, Paul's parents leased their Cuban property, La Maison de Saint Julian, with its slaves, and moved to Bordeaux, France. Paul was nine years old at the time. His parents retained possession as well of a house in Santiago. Apparently, relatives of theirs who remained in Cuba managed the leased property and the house. Paul's parents left at this time to avoid the increasingly burdensome laws directed against free blacks and mulattoes.

In Bordeaux, which at that time had a population of around 180,000, Paul studied for eight years under a private teacher, a Messieur Roger-Mice, and then in the lycées of Bordeaux and Toulouse. In the lycées, he received a good education in classical languages, literature, philosophy, and science.

Under Napoléon, a boarding school system existed in which boys spent ten months a year at gender-segregated school for eight or nine years, seeing little of their families. They wore military uniforms. Lycées for boys in Bordeaux at that time included the Lycée Michel Montaigne and Lycée Bertrand de Born. Lafargue evidently lived at home while attending one of these lycées. Lycées for boys in Toulouse included the Academie Royale de Toulouse (established 1345). Lafargue graduated from the Toulouse lycée in 1861 with a baccalaureate degree.

After completing lycée, Lafargue moved to Paris to study pharmacy, hoping to become an apothecary. He changed his mind, however, and enrolled at the Faculté de Medecin in Paris, studying medicine there from 1861 to 1865. His professors included his mentor, Jules-Antoine Moilin, and Carriere, his advisor. Moilin, a psychologist, also wrote on social economics, and was a left-wing radical who was ultimately executed by the government. Carriere, whose first name is not known, was himself driven into exile and began teaching physics and chemistry in London at St. Bartholomew's Hospital Medical School (now part of the University of London). Having been expelled from the University of Paris in 1863 for insulting church and state, Lafargue elected to continue his medical studies in London, gaining entrance to St. Bartholomew's in 1865 with Carriere's help. Lafargue graduated in July 1868 as a physician, qualified for the Royal College of Surgeons as an assistant surgeon, and practiced at the hospital.

MARRIAGE AND CHILDREN

Lafargue had joined the social democratic labor movement in France. Because of his residence in England for medical school, he was accredited as a representative of the Prudhonist French labor party and the French section of the First International in London in 1865. At that time, he was converted to Marxism by debates with Karl Marx at the meetings and at Marx's home. He met Marx's daughter Laura (1845–1911), and they were married in 1868. They had three sons, all of whom died in infancy or early childhood—Charles Étienne (1868–1872), François (1870–1870), and Marc-Laurent (1871–1872).

For their honeymoon, Paul and Laura were supposed to come to the United States, where his parents owned property in New Orleans, but Paul's commitments to the international socialist movement preempted this trip. Quite possibly, the Lafargues, or the Armagnacs, had and still have relatives and descendents in New Orleans and/or the United States, because this was fifty-four years after they had left New Orleans, and seventeen years after they had left the Caribbean for Europe. If they owned property in New Orleans, presumably someone had been in charge of managing their property during that period, and that someone was likely to have been a relative. The Lafargue family was well established in both Bordeaux and Louisiana in the nineteenth century.

REVOLUTIONARY ACTIVIST AND POLITICIAN

After completing his medical residency in London in 1870, Lafargue moved back to Bordeaux with his wife. That year, he participated in the Paris Commune. As a result, he was arrested, and his papers were burned by police in Paris and Bordeaux. Lafargue founded the Marxist labor party in France, as well as the French, Spanish, and Portuguese sections of the First International. From 1872 to 1882, he and Laura lived in London, and then returned again to France. From 1891 to 1893 Lafargue represented a district in Lille in the Chamber of Deputies. In 1898 he also completed a thesis in law.

WRITING CAREER

Lafargue was a prolific writer, but his lasting legacy is to have introduced Marx's magnum opus, *Das Kapital*, to France and Italy. In 1890 Lafargue began work on a French translation of excerpts from *Kapital* that encompassed only the first nine chapters. The selected excerpts presented Marx's theory of historical materialism and class struggle, his distinction between use value and exchange value, his labor theory of value, and the beginning of his scheme of simple reproduction. Published in 1893, this translation featured an introduction by Vilfredo Pareto, which was intended as a refutation. This version of *Kapital* was also published in Italian in 1894 with a translation by Pasquale Martignetti, an Italian socialist and the translator into Italian of two of Engels's works.

The inclusion of Pareto's introduction in this version of *Kapital* was particularly significant. Pareto approved the theory of historical materialism and class struggle, but opposed the labor theory of value. He did not address the theory of simple reproduction. At this time, he was a supporter of socialism, and in this book, he began the research that led in 1897 to the construction of his renowned general equilibrium model of socialist economic planning. This collaboration between a Marxist theorist and a quasi-socialist economist (Pareto) is unique at this high level of rigor, and has had immense consequences for the theory of macroeconomic modeling for more than a century, despite the later waning of Pareto's sympathy for socialism. All national economic planning owes its origin to *Kapital*.

Although Marxist theoreticians had been writing and talking about trusts for decades, none had published a book on the subject until Lafargue published *Les trusts américains* in 1903. Using *Moody's Manual*, he identified 793 trusts, capitalized at $69.781 million, out of a total

U.S. "fortune" of $485 million. Five railroad groups held additional capital. He focused his analysis on the petroleum, tobacco, and steel trusts, in which most of this capital was concentrated, and discussed their leading firms: Standard Oil, American Tobacco, United States Steel, and the Morgan, Gould-Rockefeller, Harriman-Kuhn-Loeb, Vanderbilt, and Pennsylvania railroad groups. Lafargue offered a straightforward empirical analysis, with no novel argumentation or conclusions.

The Right to Be Lazy was first published in French as a series of articles in *L'Egalite* in 1880, then appeared as a pamphlet the following year, and was first translated into English in 1898. It was a sardonic attack on the Protestant ethic that Lafargue argued underlay capitalism. Rather than a right to work, workers had a right not to work, or to work as little as possible. Lafargue took this idea from Aristotle's dictum that merchants and other workers had no time to develop the mind, and so were inferior to pure intellectuals or philosopher kings. Practically, implementing this idea would have the effect under capitalism of reducing unemployment by sharing the available paid work. Lafargue, however, argued not only for abolishing work, but that people engage in hedonism with their newly found free time. This pamphlet became the most translated socialist work after the *Communist Manifesto*, and was translated into Russian before the latter had been.

The modern Zerowork tradition may be said to have begun with Harry Cleaver (b. 1944) of the University of Texas and the two issues of the New York journal *Zerowork* published in 1975 and 1977. The journal engaged in polemics leading back to the materialist class struggle theory of classical Marxism of the 1848–1917 period, and against the idealist tendency promoting Marx's philosophical ideas of the early 1840s. These polemics even represented the Russian Communist leader Leon Trotsky (1879–1940) as an idealist. A liberal strand of this movement, led by Jeremy Rifkin, argues that it is now technologically possible to abolish work. Another strand followed the economic anthropologist Marshall Sahlins (b. 1930) and others in showing that primitive hunter-gatherers worked less than the proletariat in capitalist societies, because they are not forced by capitalists to produce economic surplus value to be extracted; thus, they limit their desires, producing only what is necessary for subsistence. This tradition may be viewed as a Lafarguean movement, in inspiration, one attempting to show that work is neither desirable nor necessary, or even possible.

SEE ALSO *Haitian Revolution; Labor; Marx, Karl; Marxism; Monopoly; Pareto, Vilfredo; Slavery; Socialism; Syndicalism; Unions; Work*

BIBLIOGRAPHY

PRIMARY WORKS

Engels, Frederick, Paul Lafargue, and Laura Lafargue. 1959–1963. *Correspondence*. Trans. Yvonne Kapp. 3 vols. Moscow: Foreign Languages Publishing House.

Lafargue, Paul. 1903. *Les trusts américains* [The American trusts]. Paris: V. Giard and E. Brière.

Lafargue, Paul. 1972. *The Right to Be Lazy, and Other Studies*. Trans. Charles H. Kerr. New York: Gordon Press. (Orig. pub. 1907.)

Lafargue, Paul. 2002. *Essays zur Geschichte, Kultur, und Politik* [Essays on history, culture, and politics], ed. Fritz Keller. Berlin: Karl Dietz.

SECONDARY WORKS

Boa, Paul. 1962. Evocación de Pablo Lafargue. *Cuba Socialista*, no. 6.

Derfler, Leslie. 1991. *Paul Lafargue and the Founding of French Marxism, 1842–1882*. Cambridge, MA: Harvard University Press.

Derfler, Leslie. 1998. *Paul Lafargue and the Flowering of French Marxism, 1882–1911*. Cambridge, MA: Harvard University Press.

Hartel, W. C. 1962. The French Colonial Party, 1895–1905. PhD diss., Ohio State University.

Keller, Fritz. Paul Lafargue (1842–1911). Marxists' Internet Archive. http://www.marxists.org/deutsch/archiv/lafargue/biog/index.htm.

Tremblay, Jean-Marie, ed. Paul Lafargue, 1842–1911. Les classiques des sciences sociales. http://classiques.uqac.ca/classiques/lafargue_paul/lafargue_paul.html.

Julian Ellison

LAGGING, LEADING, AND COINCIDENT INDICATORS

The *index of leading indicators* comprises economic indicators that generally turn down and up prior to the business cycle peaks and troughs designated by the Business Cycle Dating Committee of the National Bureau of Economic Research. The *index of coincident indicators* consists of data series whose turning points tend to coincide with peaks and troughs in overall economic activity, and the *index of lagging indicators* comprises indicators whose turning points generally occur after recessions and recoveries begin.

The three indexes are published by the Conference Board, a not-for-profit business-membership organization. Prior to 1996, they were published by the Bureau of Economic Analysis (BEA) of the U.S. Department of Commerce.

The ten components of the leading index are:

1. The length of the workweek for production workers in manufacturing.
2. Initial weekly claims for unemployment insurance.
3. Manufacturers' new orders for consumer goods and materials.
4. A measure of slower deliveries by vendors.
5. Manufacturers' new orders for nondefense capital goods.
6. Permits issued for the construction of new housing units.
7. Stock prices.
8. The inflation-adjusted money supply.
9. Consumer expectations.
10. The difference between the interest rate on ten-year Treasury securities and the federal funds rate, which banks charge one another on short-term loans.

Various explanations have been offered for why these indicators turn up and down before the economy does. Stock prices, for example, are regarded as a reflection of people's confidence in the economy, and such confidence (or the lack thereof) is self-fulfilling. If people think the economy will do well, they will behave in ways (e.g., spending more freely) that will cause the economy to do well. Also, changes in stock prices create changes in wealth that—with a lag—lead to changes in consumer spending.

While the leading index is intended to predict cyclical turning points in the economy, it has major weaknesses as a forecasting tool. One weakness is that the time period between the turn in the index and the turning point for the economy varies greatly, before both recessions and recoveries. In 1993, when the BEA revised the index, it reported that the lead time provided by its new index had varied in the post–World War II (1939–1945) period from five months before the July 1953 peak to twenty months before the August 1957 peak, and that the lead time provided by the index that was being replaced had varied even more—from two months before the recessions that began in 1981 and 1990 to twenty months before the August 1957 peak. Under a widely accepted rule of thumb that a decline in the index is not meaningful until it has lasted at least three months, the leading indicators failed to signal the recessions that began in 1981 and 1990. Also, the index sometimes gives a false signal of a recession, as in 1984, when a large drop in the index was not followed by a downturn in the economy.

The BEA has pointed out, too, that the size of a drop in the leading index is not a sign of the severity of an ensuing recession; a mild recession may be preceded by a sharp drop in the index, and a severe recession may be preceded by a moderate decline in the index.

The coincident index includes:

1. The number of employees on nonagricultural payrolls.

2. Inflation-adjusted personal income less transfer payments (such as unemployment insurance benefits).

3. Industrial production (a measure of the output of the manufacturing, mining, and utility industries).

4. Inflation-adjusted manufacturing and trade sales.

The index is regarded as a gauge of the current health of the economy, although in the "jobless" recovery from the recession that ended in November 2001, payroll employment did not hit its low until August 2003.

The index of lagging indicators comprises:

1. The average duration of unemployment (inverted).

2. The ratio of inventories to sales in manufacturing and trade.

3. The change in labor cost per unit of output in manufacturing.

4. The average prime rate of interest charged by banks.

5. Commercial and industrial loans outstanding (adjusted for inflation).

6. The ratio of consumer credit outstanding to personal income.

7. The change in the consumer price index for services.

These series measure the types of forces (debt burdens, for example, and price and credit pressures) that build up during expansions and that can bring an expansion to a close if they build up excessively. Thus, the ratio of the coincident index (which measures economic activity) to the lagging index serves as a leading indicator of recessions. A decline in the ratio during an expansion, suggesting that expansion-threatening forces are building up faster than economic activity is increasing, is a leading indicator of a possible recession.

The Conference Board publishes cyclical indexes for a number of countries other than the United States, and the makeup of those indexes differs somewhat from that of the U.S. indexes. For example, the coincident index for Mexico includes retail sales and the (inverted) unemployment rate, and the leading index for Australia includes the sales to inventories ratio.

SEE ALSO *Business Cycles, Real; Equity Markets; Industry; Inflation; Inventories; Leisure; Maximization; Misery Index; Money, Supply of; Stock Exchanges; Unemployment; Unemployment Rate; Utility Function*

BIBLIOGRAPHY

Frumkin, Norman. 2004. *Tracking America's Economy.* 4th ed. Armonk, NY: Sharpe.

Green, George R., and Barry A. Beckman. 1993. Business Cycle Indicators: Upcoming Revision of the Composite Indexes. *Survey of Current Business* 73 (10): 44–51.

Stekler, H. O. 2003. Interpreting Movements in the Composite Index of Leading Indicators: Use Them with Caution. *Business Economics* 38 (3): 58–61.

Edward I. Steinberg

LAGRANGE MULTIPLIERS

Lagrange Multipliers is a mathematical device introduced to find local extrema of a function subject to constraints. Problems of this general type are ubiquitous in the social sciences. For instance, they arise as optimization problems for quantities that depend on variables that satisfy some additional relations. An example in neoclassical economics is the optimization problem of the utility function with restrictions imposed by a fixed budget.

A typical problem of this type involves a function $f(x_1, \dots x_n)$, say, dependent on n variables. One seeks values for the variables x_i so that f has a local extremum; that is, f has a local maximum or minimum. This requirement is equivalent to the statement that all partial derivatives of f vanish:

$\partial f / \partial x_i = 0$ for all $i = 1, \dots, n$.

Quite often the variables x_i are not independent of each other but must satisfy some additional conditions. In such cases one cannot simply solve the above condition on the partial derivatives of f since the variables x_i are not independent of each other. The Lagrange multiplier technique can be employed in cases where the constraints on the variables can be expressed as equations:

$g_\alpha(x_1, \dots, x_n) = 0$, for $\alpha = 1, \dots, k$.

In such cases the above extremization problem can be expressed in a different form. Consider a new function F defined through the relation:

$$F(x_1, \dots, x_n, \lambda_1, \dots, \lambda_k) = f(x_1, \dots, x_n) + \Sigma \ \lambda_\alpha g_\alpha(x_1, \dots, x_n).$$

This definition introduces k new variables λ_α—one for each constraint g_α. The sum in the above expression is over α. The new variables λ_α are called Lagrange multipliers.

In terms of F it is possible to express the previous problem of constrained extremization as a simple extremization problem. Since F depends on $n + k$ variables, finding local extrema for F can be split up into two sets of equations:

$\partial F/\partial x_i = \partial f/\partial x_i + \partial g/\partial x_i = 0$ for all $i = 1, \ldots, n$.

as well as:

$\partial F/\partial \lambda_\alpha = g_\alpha = 0$ for all $\alpha = 1, \ldots, k$.

The second set of equations imposes the constraints ($g_\alpha = 0$), while the first set imposes a new condition. This apparently new condition actually reduces to the condition that the partial derivatives of f vanish once the constraints $g_\alpha = 0$ are taken into account.

As an example from neoclassical economics, consider the problem of optimizing utility for a consumer who can buy two commodities, a and b, with price per unit p_a and p_b, respectively. The consumer is constrained to spend within his or her budget w. Let the number of commodities of each kind, a and b, purchased by the consumer be given by x_a and x_b, respectively. The budget of the consumer imposes the constraint:

$p_a x_a + p_b x_b \leq w$.

This states simply that the total price paid for the two commodities should be less than the available budget. In many neoclassical models the inequality is transformed into an equality. This is justified by hypothesizing one of a number of characteristics of consumer behavior. One hypothesis that justifies this modification is that the consumer is "insatiable" that is, the consumer will buy to the maximum of his or her buying ability. In any case, these hypotheses lead to the modified constraint:

$p_a x_a + p_b x_b = w$.

The utility function u is a measure of the happiness of the consumer. The utility is a function of x_a and x_b: $u = u(x_a, x_b)$. Consumers in neoclassical economics base their behavior on maximizing their utility function while satisfying the budgetary constraint. This problem is of the general type discussed above with $f = u(x_a, x_b)$, and $g(x_a, x_b) = p_a x_a + p_b x_b - w$. To illustrate the method, consider a utility function given by $u(x_a, x_b) = x_a x_b$.

To apply the Lagrange multiplier method one constructs a new function:

$F(x_a, x_b, \lambda) = u(x_a, x_b) + \lambda g(x_a, x_b) = x_a x_b + \lambda(p_a x_a + p_b x_b - w)$.

Setting the partial derivatives of F to zero, one finds:

$0 = \partial F/\partial x_a = x_b + \lambda p_a$

$0 = \partial F/\partial x_b = x_a + \lambda p_b$

$0 = \partial F/\partial \lambda = p_a x_a + p_b x_b - w$

These equations can be solved to yield:

$x_a = w/2p_a$

$x_b = w/2p_b$.

These give the proportions of each of the commodities that optimize the utility function. The Lagrange multiplier

$\lambda = -w/2p_a p_b$

has an economic interpretation. The Lagrange multiplier can be expressed as a derivative of F:

$\lambda = \partial F/\partial w$.

It tells one how F changes when w is varied. Since on the extremum of F, the constraint is satisfied F coincides with u, the utility. The Lagrange multiplier is thus a measure of how the utility u changes when the budget w is varied, with this interpretation the Lagrange multiplier λ is called the shadow price.

SEE ALSO *Constrained Choice; Maximization; Minimization; Shadow Prices; Utility Function*

BIBLIOGRAPHY

Courant, R. 1988. *Differential and Integral Calculus,* Vol. II. Trans. E. J. McShane. New York: Wiley.

Varian, Hal R. 1996. *Intermediate Microeconomics.* New York: W. W. Norton.

Ansar Fayyazuddin

LAGRANGE MULTIPLIER TEST

SEE *Specification Tests.*

LAGS, DISTRIBUTED

Often when we try to model statistical relationships, we tend to use contemporaneous values. For example, if we want to model changes in consumption because of a change in disposable income, we may try to run the regression $\Delta y_t = \alpha + \beta \Delta x_t + \varepsilon_t$, where Δy_t is the percentage change in consumption and Δx_t is the percentage change in the disposable income, α and β are the regression parameters, and ε_t is the random error. The relationship works very well, but it has been documented that people demonstrate "consumption inertia"—that is, the consumption habits of consumers do not change right away in response to an increase in the disposable income. Because consumption expectations are formed by past changes in income, this class of models is called backward-looking expectations models. The best way to capture consumption inertia is to include in the regression model not only the current change in disposable income but also previous changes. If an independent variable (Δx_t) appears more than once, with different time lags, then the model is called a distributed lag model. Generally, with only one dependent variable and one explanatory variable, the distributed lag model is represented as $y_t = \beta_0 x_1 + \beta_1 x_{t-1} + \beta_2 x_{t-2} + \ldots + \beta_n x_{t-n} = \sum_{i=0}^{n} \beta_i x_{t-i} + \varepsilon_t$. The β_i are coefficients, x_{t-i} are the lagged values of the explanatory variable and ε_t is the independent white noise random error.

To demonstrate the distributed lag model empirically, with personal consumption data let y_t, be the change in U.S. personal consumption expenditure in quarter t, and x_t be a change in U.S. personal disposable income in quarter t. The results of a regression of one lag of personal disposable income are:

$y_t = .005 + .124\ x_t + .142\ x_{t-1}$ (3.52) (1.89) (2.17) (t-stats).

This illustrates that a 1 percent change in disposable income induces 0.124 percent of the change in the current consumption. However, last quarter's change in disposable income has statistically significant (t-statistics in the parenthesis) influence on the change in the consumption. A 1 percent increase in disposable income would cause about 0.142 percent increase in current consumption. The implication of this finding is that changes in personal disposable income have lasting influence on the changes in consumption.

The obvious statistical question then is why estimate the model with only one lag. How many lags are appropriate? This has long been one of the problems with the distributed lag models, even in the early work of Irving Fisher (1937) in the 1930s. Researchers such as Jan Tinbergen (1949) suggest including lags until the coefficients of the lagged variables become insignificant or the signs of the coefficient become erratic. There are several problems with this kind of ad hoc specification. First, there is no guidance in terms of lag length. Second, if the sample size is small, then as the lag length increases statistical inference may be somewhat shaky, with fewer degrees of freedom. Finally, successive lags tend to have high correlations (multicollinearity), leading to smaller t-ratios and incorrect inferences.

One way to reduce the number of lags and the extent of multicollinearity is to use L. M. Koyck's (1954) adap-

tive expectations model. In this type of model, in addition to the explanatory variable a lagged dependent variable is included and is represented as $y_t = \alpha + \beta_1 x_t + \beta_2 y_{t-1} + \upsilon_t$, where υ is the error term. The adaptive expectation model can be illustrated by using the data on personal consumption expenditures and disposable income. The results of the model are:

$y_t = .007 + .067\ x_t + .107\ y_{t-1}$

The coefficients of the above model have some interesting interpretations. The coefficient of disposable income (x_t) shows short-run impact of a change in disposable income on consumption. A 1 percent change in disposable income would cause a 0.67 percent increase in consumption in the short run. The estimate 1.15 percent $(0.107/(1 - 0.067))$ provides the long-run impact of a change in disposable income on consumption. The results reveal that a 1 percent increase in disposable income would cause consumption to go up by 1.15 percent in the long run.

If the dependent variable is random, the lagged dependent variable may also be random, and including a random explanatory variable in the model may produce biased and inconsistent estimates. Thus, in order to use this model it is essential to verify that the lagged dependent variable is not correlated with the random errors. In addition, in the above models serial correlation in the errors cannot be tested using normal autocorrelation statistics. One of the assumptions of infinite distributed lag models such as Koyck's is that the coefficient on the lag variables declines geometrically as the lag length increases. If the coefficients do not behave in this manner, then the above lag structure may not be suitable. In these circumstances, you need a more flexible model that would incorporate a variety of lag structures, such as Shirley Almon's (1965) distributed lag models.

To estimate a flexible model such as Almon, we must a priori specify the lag length to verify the changes in the size of the coefficients. If βs decrease at first and then increase with higher lags, β_is can then be approximated by a second-degree polynomial because we have one size change. The more the turning points, the higher the degree of polynomials. We can illustrate the Almon distributed lag model by using the data on personal consumption and disposable income. First, we assume that change in consumption depends on the current change and preceding two-quarter change in disposable income. Second, we also assume that β_i can be approximated by a second-degree polynomial. The results of this estimation of are $y_t = 0.006 + 0.121 z_0 - 0.047 z_1 - 0.064 z_2$, where zs are constructed as a linear combination of x (change in disposable income) series. For this example of two lags and second-degree polynomial, the zs are:

$$z_0 = \sum_{i=0}^{3} x_{t-i} = (x_t + x_{t-1} + x_{t-2})$$

$$z_1 = \sum_{i=0}^{3} i x_{t-i} = (x_{t-1} + 2x_{t-2})$$

$$z_2 = \sum_{i=0}^{3} i^2 x_{t-i} = (x_{t-1} + 4x_{t-2}).$$

From the above estimates, original βs can be obtained and are presented as $y_t = 0.006 + 0.103x_t + 0.121x_{t-1} + .001x_{t-2}$.

The above values are provided in standard econometric software programs. Although this model offers more flexibility than Koyck's model, there are still problems with this technique. First, there is no real guidance as to the selection of lag length or the degree of polynomial. Second, the constructed *z*s are likely to exhibit multicollinearity, which may lead to statistically insignificant coefficients due to large standard errors. Nevertheless, the distributed lag models in general are very useful in modeling issues when the dependent variable exhibits delayed reaction to changes in the independent variable.

SEE ALSO *Error-correction Mechanisms; Vector Autoregression*

BIBLIOGRAPHY

Almon, Shirley. 1965. The Distributed Lag between Capital Appropriations and Expenditures. *Econometrica* 33: 178–196.

Fisher, Irving. 1937. Note on a Short-Cut Method for Calculating Distributed Lags. *International Statistical Bulletin* 29: 323–327.

Koyck, L. M. 1954. *Distributed Lags and Investment Analysis.* Amsterdam: North-Holland.

Tinbergen, Jan. 1949. Long-Term Foreign Trade Elasticities. *Metroeconomica* 1: 174–185.

Bala G. Arshanapalli

LAISSEZ-FAIRE

The doctrine of laissez-faire was first systematically developed by the physiocrats in France. It was at first primarily considered a moral doctrine that sanctified the freedom of the individual and had implications for economic life, not just an economic policy doctrine. Later laissez-faire came to be understood mainly as an economic policy doctrine.

Folklore has it that during the reign of Louis XIV (1638–1715), the finance minister, Jean-Baptiste Colbert (1619–1683), asked a group of French businessmen what the government could do to aid the cause of commerce, and the response was *laissez-faire*, or let the people do as they freely choose. The social-philosophic doctrine that emerged opposed government interference in economic affairs beyond providing the minimum functions of ensuring peace, administering justice, and providing basic public goods. In the English-speaking world, the laissez-faire doctrine came to be identified with Adam Smith (1723–1790) and in particular the argument for free trade associated with *An Inquiry into the Nature and Causes of the Wealth of Nations* (1776).

The moral theory aspects of the doctrine of laissez-faire remained in classical political economy, but the economic policy implications came to dominate the debates around the doctrine. The idea of economic freedom and limited government would be developed in the century after Adam Smith by Jeremy Bentham (1748–1832), J. B. Say (1767–1832), Frédéric Bastiat (1801–1850), and John Stuart Mill (1806–1873). Even as Mill made an explicit case for exceptions to the laissez-faire principle in economic life, he argued that "laisser-faire, in short, should be the general practice: every departure from it, unless required by some great good, is a certain evil" (Mill [1848] 1976, p. 950).

From the beginning, however, critics of laissez-faire attempted to paint a picture of extremism and lack of concern for the least advantaged in society. This characterization of the position was immortalized by Charles Dickens's (1812–1870) portrayal of Scrooge (a thinly veiled depiction of Herbert Spencer [1820–1903]) and the claim that rather than give aid to the poor we should allow the surplus population to decline naturally. But as Jacob Viner (1892–1970) pointed out in his "The Intellectual History of Laissez Faire," only "unscrupulous or ignorant opponents of it and never its exponents" used the term *laissez-faire* to mean a position of "philosophical anarchism, or opposition to any governmental power or activity whatsoever" ([1960] 1991, p. 200). Instead, the term *laissez-faire* as used by its systematic exponents meant freedom of choice and trade and a limitation on the scope of governmental activities to defense against foreign powers, establishment of a system of justice to prevent members of the society from oppressing others in that society, and the maintenance of essential public works and institutions. Laissez-faire, Frank Knight (1885–1972) declared, "simply means freedom, in the particular case of economic policy: freedom of economic conduct from dictation by government" ([1967] 1999, p. 435).

The nonsubtle reading of laissez-faire argues that the position is claiming that the individual pursuit of self-interest is enough to realize a benevolent social order irrespective of the social rules of interaction that are in place. In fact, the critics read the doctrine as insisting that there is an absence of governance, rather than just limits on the scope of government. In this regard, advocates of the doctrine of laissez-faire are accused of being unreasonable and doctrinaire. F. A. Hayek (1899–1992), in fact, argues that nothing has done more harm to the cause of economic liberalism than a "wooden insistence" on the principle of laissez-faire (1945, p. 17). A more nuanced and appropriate reading of laissez-faire would emphasize the essential role of institutions of governance (though not necessarily provided only by government) in explaining how a benevolent social order can result from individuals freely choosing.

Critical to understanding the defense of the doctrine of laissez-faire are two subsidiary arguments. First, the defender of laissez-faire must present a demonstration through the logic of economic analysis of the "invisible hand" proposition (see, e.g., Nozick 1974, pp. 18–22). Second, the defender of laissez-faire will proceed to conduct a comparative analysis (both theoretical and empirical) of market versus governmental decision-making within the sphere of economic affairs (see, e.g., Buchanan and Tullock 1962). The combination of these two subsidiary arguments, often alongside a moral stance derived from natural law theory, can be found in almost any presentation of the laissez-faire position from Smith to Hayek, from Bastiat to Milton Friedman (1912–2006).

As Viner pointed out in his essay "Adam Smith and Laissez Faire," even when Smith "was prepared to admit the system of natural liberty would not serve the public welfare with optimum effectiveness, he did not feel driven necessarily to the conclusion that government intervention was preferable to laissez faire. The evils of unrestrained selfishness might be better than the evils of incompetent and corrupt government" (Viner [1927] 1991, p. 104). In order to justify intervention, Smith argued, one would have to demonstrate not only that individuals freely choosing would not advance the public welfare, but also that government officials would be in a position to know better what was in a man's interest than he would be himself. This was a position that Smith vehemently refused to concede in the realm of economic affairs. As Smith put it:

> The statesman, who should attempt to direct private people in what manner they ought to employ their capitals, would not only load himself with a most unnecessary attention, but assume an authority which could safely be trusted, not only to no single person, but to no council or senate whatever, and which would no-where be so dangerous as in the hands of a man who had folly and presumption enough to fancy himself fit to exercise it. (Smith [1776] 1976, bk. IV, chap. 2, p. 478)

On the other hand, the individual from the vantage point of his local situation is in a better position to judge what is the best course of action for himself. Smith, it is important to stress, did not presume that acting self-interestedly was enough to ensure a benevolent social order. Self-interest is what guides the statesman to overburden himself; it is also what leads to Oxford dons not satisfying the educational demands of their students (Smith [1776] 1976, bk. V, chap. 1, p. 284) and to teachers of religious doctrine being less zealous and hardworking in the state-supported religious sects as compared to those sects that rely solely on voluntary contributions (bk. V, chap. 1, p. 309). Self-interest also leads the businessman to conspire with his competitors to set prices (bk. I, chap. 10, p. 144) and to seek out protection from foreign competitors (e.g., bk. IV, chap. 2, pp. 489–490). It is self-interest that is behind the sophistry of the merchants and the manufacturers in the quest for monopolistic status, just as it is self-interest among professors and preachers when they seek secure incomes and protection from competitors in the instruction of philosophy and religious doctrine.

Self-interest is also what drives the refinements in the division of labor, the coordinative activities of an economy guided by relative price movements, and the innovations of the entrepreneur. Self-interest is not unique to laissez-faire, but a regime of laissez-faire (within the specified institutions of natural liberty) will channel self-interest in a direction that will maximize the likelihood of a social order of peace and prosperity. When the institutions of natural liberty are absent, or government attempts to thwart their development, Smith's claim was that tyranny and poverty would result. As he put it in the notebooks that preceded the *Wealth of Nations*:

> Little else is requisite to carry a state to the highest degree of opulence from the lowest barbarism, but peace, easy taxes, and a tolerable administration of justice; all the rest being brought about by the natural course of things. All governments which thwart this natural course, which force things into another channel or which endeavor to arrest the progress of society at a particular point, are unnatural, and to support themselves are obliged to be oppressive and tyrannical. (Smith [1776] 1976, p. xl)

The laissez-faire doctrine would latter become identified with the *harmony of interest* doctrine, a doctrine that claimed that the competing interests of individuals could be reconciled through the market mechanism. The proposition is actually older than Smith, and can be traced back to Voltaire (1694–1778). In the sixth of his *Letters Concerning the English Nation*, Voltaire discusses how even passionate warring factions can be reconciled through commerce:

> Take a view of the Royal Exchange in London, a place more venerable than many courts of justice,

where the representatives of all nations meet for the benefit of mankind. There the Jew, the Mahometan, and the Christian transact together, as though they all professed the same religion, and give the name of infidel to none but bankrupts. There the Presbyterian confides in the Anabaptist, and the Churchman depends on the Quaker's word. At the breaking up of this pacific and free assembly, some withdraw to the synagogue, and others to take a glass. This man goes and is baptized in a great tub, in the name of the Father, Son, and Holy Ghost: that man has his son's foreskin cut off, whilst a set of Hebrew words (quite unintelligible to him) are mumbled over his child. Others retire to their churches, and there wait for the inspiration of heaven with their hats on, and all are satisfied. (Voltaire [1733] 1994, pp. 29–30)

This *doux-commerce* thesis, which argued that commerce was a civilizing influence on humanity, has been identified with Montesquieu (1689–1755) and Voltaire, and then received its systematization in the works of David Hume (1711–1776) and Smith. It is very much a part of the underlying argument for the laissez-faire doctrine. Understanding the logic of this argument and its implications came to be synonymous with becoming an economist or a classical political economist.

Critics of the laissez-faire doctrine emerged from the beginning and tended to focus on variants of the following arguments through the years:

1. Poverty traps that cannot be escaped through free choice.

2. General glut that results from overproduction or underconsumption.

3. Monopoly power that emerges naturally in the market and allows businesses to exploit consumers.

4. Exploitation of the working class that pushes wages down to subsistence and compels laborers to work in harsh and unsafe conditions.

5. External economies that generate situations where desirable goods are underproduced on the market, and undesirable goods are overproduced on the market.

6. Public goods that are not supplied by the market due to free-rider problems.

Beginning in the late nineteenth and continuing throughout the twentieth century, a stream of economic schools of thought rose to challenge the presumption for laissez-faire. In fact, the American Economic Association was formed by economists who were decidedly non-laissez-faire thinkers, but instead were government reformers and activists. Laissez-faire was identified in their minds

with an economic policy of noninterventionism, which meant that the social ills of monopoly, unemployment, inequality, and exploitation would go unchecked. The institutional school of Thorstein Veblen (1857–1929), John Commons (1862–1945), and Clarence E. Ayres (1891–1972) was critical of the laissez-faire doctrine. John Maynard Keynes (1883–1946) declared "The End of Laissez Faire" in the 1920s, and the development of Keynesian economics in the 1930s and 1940s transformed the discipline of economics from one that sought philosophic understanding to one that provided tools for social control. Mid-century arguments for market socialism and market failure theory added to the dismissal of the presumption for laissez-faire that was in the classics from Smith to Mill. And the arguments against laissez-faire from Karl Marx (1818–1883) to Paul Samuelson relied on some version of the six critiques listed above. Even the most sophisticated modern criticisms of laissez-faire (e.g., asymmetric information, network externalities, or behavioral irrationalities) rely on a variant of these basic criticisms that have been leveled since the beginning of the history of the idea.

The argumentative strategy of the opponents of laissez-faire usually took the form of: (1) characterization of the laissez-faire position as based on unrealistic assumptions concerning man (e.g., atomistic and hyperrationality); (2) depiction of reality that highlighted deviations from what would be theoretically optimal (e.g., deviations from marginal cost pricing); and (3) a willful ignoring of the costs of decision-making when government is called upon to serve as a corrective to social ills.

During the twentieth century, three figures emerged as the heirs to Adam Smith and the defenders of the laissez-faire doctrine—F. A. Hayek (1974 Nobel Prize in Economics), Milton Friedman (1976 Nobel Prize in Economics), and James Buchanan (1986 Nobel Prize in Economics). Keep in mind what was argued in the beginning of this entry concerning Smith's argument—that there were two intellectual moves in the laissez-faire argument: first, the invisible hand; second, the comparative analysis on nonmarket decision-making. Hayek, Friedman, and Buchanan argued that more often than not the breakdown of the invisible hand was a consequence of governmental policy that had previously not been considered by the critics of laissez-faire. Adam Smith, they reminded everyone, did not argue that self-interest under any conceivable set of circumstances would produce a beneficial social order. Self-interest within a system of clearly defined and strictly enforced property rights could be relied upon to channel self-interest to serve the public welfare, but if property rights are unclear or weakly enforced, self-interest may very well produce undesirable outcomes. The tragedy of the commons, in other words, is not a challenge to Smith (or Hayek, Friedman, and

Buchanan) but a confirmation of their basic insight into how the "invisible hand" works. Second, even if the market order failed to produce the best of all possible outcomes (as it inevitably always did at any point in time), the critic must not leave the costs of governmental decision-making unexamined (including unintended and undesirable consequences). The standard twentieth-century argument for interventionism presumed both that the government possessed the knowledge to solve the problem, and that the decision process was relatively cost-less because the government actors were acting as economic eunuchs. Works such as Hayek's *The Road to Serfdom* (1945) and *The Constitution of Liberty* (1960), Friedman's *Capitalism and Freedom* (1962) and *Free to Choose* (1980, with Rose Freidman), and Buchanan's *The Limits of Liberty* (1975) and *Democracy in Deficit* (1977, with Richard Wagner) challenged the government as corrective presumption, and helped forge a revitalized case for laissez-faire in the late twentieth century.

In the narrative on laissez-faire just constructed, little reference was made to the actual historical record for the simple reason that such a discussion would require multiple entries. The critics of laissez-faire attribute the late nineteenth-century robber barons, the miserable working conditions of the poor in early twentieth century, the Great Depression, and the bigotry of racial segregation to laissez-faire capitalism. The defenders of laissez-faire, on the other hand, reject each of these interpretations and attempt to show either that the root cause of the problem was government interference with the competitive process or that the competitive forces of the economy were in fact alleviating the problem at the time that government stepped in to claim credit for easing social tension. One side sees market forces as ameliorating social ills and reconciling conflicts, while the other side sees the market as augmenting social ills and aggravating conflicts. This has been an ongoing argument for three centuries, and it does not appear to be resolvable in a clear-cut empirical manner. Instead, the debate turns on analytical arguments, empirical evidence and counterevidence, and explicit or implicit moral judgments.

SEE ALSO *Austrian Economics; Bentham, Jeremy; Capitalism; Competition; Economics, Classical; Free Trade; Government; Hayek, Friedrich August von; Liberty; Market Fundamentals; Markets; Mill, John Stuart; Natural Rights; Naturalism; Physiocracy; Smith, Adam; Social Statics*

BIBLIOGRAPHY

Buchanan, James M. 1975. *The Limits of Liberty: Between Anarchy and Leviathan.* Chicago: University of Chicago Press.

Buchanan, James M., and Gordon Tullock. 1962. *The Calculus of Consent: Logical Foundations of Constitutional Democracy.* Ann Arbor: University of Michigan Press.

Buchanan, James M., and Richard E. Wagner. 1977. *Democracy in Deficit: The Political Legacy of Lord Keynes.* New York: Academic Press.

Friedman, Milton. 1962. *Capitalism and Freedom.* Chicago: University of Chicago Press.

Friedman, Milton, and Rose Friedman. 1980. *Free to Choose: A Personal Statement.* New York: Harcourt.

Hayek, Friedrich A. 1945. *The Road to Serfdom.* Chicago: University of Chicago Press.

Hayek, Friedrich A. 1960. *The Constitution of Liberty.* Chicago: University of Chicago Press.

Keynes, John Maynard. 1926. *The End of Laissez Faire.* London: Hogarth.

Knight, Frank H. [1967] 1999. Laissez-Faire: Pro and Con. In *Selected Essays by Frank H. Knight*, ed. Ross Emmett, vol. 2. 435–453. Chicago: University of Chicago Press.

Mill, John Stuart. [1848] 1976. *Principles of Political Economy.* New York: Kelley.

Nozick, Robert. 1974. *Anarchy, State, and Utopia.* New York: Basic Books.

Smith, Adam. [1776] 1976. *An Inquiry into the Nature and Causes of the Wealth of Nations.* Chicago: University of Chicago Press.

Viner, Jacob. [1927] 1991. Adam Smith and Laissez Faire. In *Essays on the Intellectual History of Economics*, ed. Douglas Irwin, 85–113. Princeton, NJ: Princeton University Press.

Viner, Jacob. [1960] 1991. The Intellectual History of Laissez Faire. In *Essays on the Intellectual History of Economics*, ed. Douglas Irwin, 200–225. Princeton, NJ: Princeton University Press.

Voltaire. [1733] 1994. *Letters Concerning the English Nation.* Ed. Nicholas Cronk. Oxford: Oxford University Press.

Peter J. Boettke

LAKATOS, IMRE
1922–1974

The pivotal philosophical debate of twentieth-century Anglo-American philosophy originated with Thomas Kuhn's 1962 *The Structure of Scientific Revolutions.* Kuhn (1922–1996), along with Imre Lakatos and Paul Feyerabend (1924–1994), made the history and sociology of science central to conceptions of scientific progress and rationality. Lakatos, a Hungarian émigré who escaped the failed 1956 revolution, became Karl Popper's (1902–1994) best and favored student, but he joined forces with Kuhn and Feyerabend against Popper's refusal to see scientific method as having historical roots and hence being subject to change. Lakatos maintained Popper's anti-positivist view that scientific knowledge has no epistemological foundation, but that progress occurred through continual criticism and revision. Lakatos made the historicism in that view explicit by critically elaborating Popper's approach into an interpretative method for the history of science and mathematics. Instead of Popper's ahistorical "logic of scientific discovery" Lakatos saw an historically *changing* logic of criticism and the growth of scientific knowledge. But like Popper and Feyerabend, and unlike Kuhn, Lakatos recommended a normative conception of scientific method, analogous to normative philosophical models of political or civic processes. Lakatos created his critical theory of science using a sui generis historiographical approach for reconstructing the scientific present as a value-laden history of progress and decline.

The historiographical toolkit is Lakatos's methodology of scientific research programs. In contrast to Popper's confrontations of falsifiable theories, with their risky predictions and hence potential refutations, Lakatos argued that individual theories are poorly chosen "units" for scientific change. In practice, as Kuhn and Feyerabend dramatically demonstrated, the best theories can be formally inconsistent; they may contradict stable observations or received theories, or they may violate traditional canons of scientific method—not all at once, but individually or opportunistically, as needed for theory improvement. Lakatos also assumed no theory-neutral observational basis to conclusively refute a single theory. Hence there was no guarantee that confirmatory or refuting data might not itself be reinterpreted and overturned, thus making conclusive refutation of single theories either impossible or subject to unrealistic and overcomplex methodological criteria.

This messy and chaotic milieu of chronic uncertainty requires the intelligence and flexibility of working scientists, whose theories Lakatos organized in terms of long-term research programs. These need not coincide with projects of individual researchers. Instead, they are a post festum historical reconstruction used to characterize scientifically recognized progress or failure. Lakatos proposes a philosophical model to characterize just what, in long-term patterns of theory choice, empirical discovery, and interpretation, led to a recognition, perhaps erroneous, by scientific communities as achievement or decline. A research program, then, was defined as a series of theories that were loosely united by a shared hard core of key principles, ranging from inchoate metaphysical ideas to favored modeling approaches; a positive heuristic of plans for generating theoretical improvements, and turning theories into operational models for addressing open problems, hopefully creating novel confirmations or predictions; ancillary touchstone and observational theories, used to interpret and organize a changing basis of

theory-laden "facts" relevant to the program; a protective belt of theories or models insulating the program from critical attack; perhaps ad hoc theories or models needed as temporary fixes; an inventory of Kuhnian puzzles, contradictions, and anomalies awaiting resolution; and an environment of competing research programs against which relative progress is gauged.

Thus "scientific" describes not individual theories, but sequences of theories in time, not necessarily coordinated by any single individual or group. Such science, then, is either progressive or degenerating, the outcome measured by the presence or absence of novel confirmations, persistent puzzles and contradictions, powerful model development, and more or less ad hoc fixes—all of these judged relative to competing programs with a shared domain of problems, relevant phenomena, and research objectives. Lakatos's historiography of research programs is a theory of modern scientific progress in which a role for scientific truth is reduced in proportion to the Faustian ambitions of theoreticians and experimenters.

Lakatos and others rewrote episodes from the histories of various sciences, using research program categories: the phlogiston and oxygen programs of Joseph Priestley (1733–1804) and Antoine-Laurent Lavoisier (1743–1794); the wave and corpuscular programs for light; nineteenth-century atomic-versus-phenomenological theories of heat; modern plate tectonics; classical political economy from Adam Smith (1723–1790) to David Ricardo (1772–1823) and Karl Marx (1818–1883); and several segments of twentieth-century physics. These projects led to successes and failures, the latter occurring when a major change, like the replacement of classical physics with relativity theory, or the emergence of modern science altogether, is forced into Lakatos's research program categories, which can be thought of as a nuanced conception of Kuhn's "normal science," and absent Kuhn's confusing normative views. Lakatos saw this historical work as "scientific," meaning that methodological reflection itself was an ongoing, theory-laden activity of understanding the "phenomena" of the scientific past. As in science proper, no perfect match is expected between historical theory and historical data, implying, as Lakatos points out, no "true" scientific consciousness: our knowledge of science is imperfect and uncertain, just as in science proper. Lakatos's dialectical histories demonstrated that understanding past knowledge is possible only through some contemporary normative criteria for what counts as scientific, whether clearly articulated or not. His project was to make that condition of historical knowledge his primary lesson for the new philosophy of science. Lakatos and others carried out this project by using the methodology of scientific research programs as a historiographical guide and toolkit. Feyerabend identified the characteristic feature of modern scientific knowledge as a constantly expanding horizon of facts. Lakatos thought it best to comprehend that post-Renaissance process using normative and philosophical concepts that make historical knowledge an object of rational, even scientific, self-understanding.

SEE ALSO *Kuhn, Thomas; Philosophy of Science; Popper, Karl; Science; Scientific Method*

BIBLIOGRAPHY

Kuhn, Thomas S. 1962. *The Structure of Scientific Revolutions.* Chicago: University of Chicago Press.

Lakatos, Imre. 1976. *Proofs and Refutations: The Logic of Mathematical Discovery.* Eds. John Worrall and Elie Zahar. New York: Cambridge University Press.

Lakatos, Imre. 1978. *Mathematics, Science, and Epistemology.* Eds. John Worrall and Gregory Currie. New York: Cambridge University Press.

Lakatos, Imre. 1978. *The Methodology of Scientific Research Programmes.* Eds. John Worrall and Gregory Currie. New York: Cambridge University Press.

Lakatos, Imre, and Alan Musgrave, eds. 1970. *Criticism and the Growth of Knowledge.* New York: Cambridge University Press.

Popper, Karl Raimund. 1959. *Logic of Scientific Discovery.* New York: Basic Books.

John Kadvany

LAND CLAIMS

A *land claim* is the pursuit of recognized territorial ownership by a group or individual. In modern nation-states, the vast majority of such claims have been advanced by indigenous peoples who have been dispossessed of land and resources in the course of imperial expansion and nation building. In the context of a worldwide rise in aboriginal political power since the 1970s, aboriginal leaders have initiated land claims in an effort to reverse the marginalization of Native societies in countries dominated by non-Native peoples and to provide a means of wealth and security. While indigenous peoples have pursued land claims across much of the globe since at least the early 1980s (see Fondahl et al. for Russian examples), they have become particularly well developed in the countries that have emerged out of the former British settler colonies: Canada, the United States, Australia, and New Zealand. As with so many other struggles for the acknowledgement of minority rights, land claims are often marked by protest and conflict between, on one side, sets of property owners, corporations, and governments that stand to benefit from the maintenance of the status quo and, on the other side, aboriginal peoples who hope to regain control of territory and resources. In the context of social science research and study, understanding land claims requires consideration of the intersection of geography, politics, economics, and social pluralism.

At the root of the pursuit of modern land claims is the assertion of *title* by aboriginal peoples. Claimants argue that they hold ownership of land and resources based upon long-term occupation and use of particular territories. Thus, for a land claim to proceed, title must be ascertained and recognized by a country's legal institutions. In different jurisdictions, recognition of Native title has varied greatly. In Canada, for example, aboriginal claims of ownership are backed by the Royal Proclamation of 1763, in which the British Crown affirmed Native ownership of land and resources in Britain's North American colonies where obvious occupation and use was in evidence. Under this law, British settlers were obliged to negotiate in good faith with Native peoples for the transfer of land and resources (Usher 2003, p. 377). Since the early 1990s, land and resource claims advanced by a number of Native groups in British Columbia have been based on the historical fact that the requirements of the Proclamation have not been met in the province (Rossiter and Wood 2005, pp. 358–359). The United States, another outgrowth of British colonization, also recognized the existence of aboriginal title through the negotiation of historic treaties between the federal government and individual Native groups (Hendrix 2005, p. 765). Modern land claims in the United States, such as those advanced in the 1980s and 1990s by the Western Shoshone Nation in Nevada (see Luebben and Nelson 2002) have resulted from failures of governments to live up to the terms of these treaties. By contrast, in Australia the recognition of the existence of aboriginal title prior to settlement by British colonists only emerged in 1992 with a High Court ruling that entrenched the principle in the country's body of common law (Davies 2003, p. 28). Whatever the case, however, once the general principle of prior indigenous title has been accepted by a state, land claims by Native groups may then be pursued in order to regain or affirm clear ownership in cases where such ownership has not been superseded through recognized legal means, yet practical control of territory has been lost to either government or private interests.

When countries' legal institutions recognize the existence of Native title in relation to territory where aboriginal control has been superseded, they place demands on governments and other property holders to either extinguish Native title through accepted channels or return control over land and resources to claimants. As with the acknowledgement of Native title, the means of extinguishment has varied greatly between countries. In Canada (Usher 2003, p. 366) and the United States (Hendrix 2005, p. 764), negotiated agreements (treaties) between governments and aboriginal groups have been the typical means of title extinguishment. However, in Australia the existence of freehold property resulting from government land alienation schemes developed in the late nineteenth and early twentieth centuries is recognized in that country's body of law as an adequate means of extinguishment (Davies 2003, p. 28). As uneven as the approaches are, once title is said to be extinguished, governments consider claims to be settled and no further action can be pursued by claimants in relation to questions of ownership.

The principal means of modern title extinguishment, and thus the main outcome of modern land claims negotiations, has been the negotiation of durable and comprehensive treaties. While often focused on the return of land and resources to aboriginal control, treaties are not marked by this feature alone. As land claims launched by aboriginal peoples against modern nation-states often involve territory that is occupied by cities or other intensive and permanent land use, the return of land can be extremely problematic. In such cases, or in cases where two or more groups launch overlapping claims, negotiated settlements between Native groups and governments often include monetary compensation in lieu of returned territory. Further, issues of tax status, education and health provision, and linkage (social, political, economic) with non-Native territories are also frequently addressed in the negotiation of treaties. As Usher notes (2003, p. 379), in Canada treaty negotiations are increasingly marked by a concern with providing claimants with the opportunity to build governance and management capacity through education and partnership. Thus, far from simply serving to settle land and resource disputes between indigenous and settler populations, the treaties that result from land claim negotiations are often required to address the social, political, and economic marginalization of Native populations that has arisen out of colonial situations.

While land claims hold out the possibility of transforming the material (and therefore social) conditions of life for aboriginal peoples in the former settler colonies of the world, they also, as Hendrix argues, provide a possible means through which the historical and geographical memories of settler populations might be reworked. The dominant narratives of American and Australian settlement treat the period prior to European contact as prehistoric; the lands were empty and awaiting improvement by industrious hands, so goes the story. By successfully reclaiming land and resources through resort to the institutions put in place by colonial societies, however, Native peoples across the world are taking back ownership of more than territory. Insisting upon official recognition of precontact occupancy and title, marginalized cultures are writing themselves back into history and, therefore, into the fabric of modern nation-states.

SEE ALSO *Annexation; Colonialism; Decolonization; Indigenismo; Indigenous Rights; Native Americans; Natives*

BIBLIOGRAPHY

Davies, Jocelyn. 2003. Contemporary Geographies of Indigenous Rights and Interests in Rural Australia. *Australian Geographer* 34(1): 19–45.

Fondahl, Gail, Olga Lazebnik, Greg Poelzer, and Vasily Robbek. 2001. Native "Land Claims," Russian Style. *The Canadian Geographer / Le Géographe Canadien* 45 (4): 545–561.

Hendrix, Burke A. 2005. Memory in Native American Land Claims. *Political Theory* 33 (6): 763–785.

Luebben, Thomas E., and Cathy Nelson. 2002. The Indian Wars: Efforts to Resolve Western Shoshone Land and Treaty Issues and to Distribute the Indian Claims Commission Judgment Fund. *Natural Resources Journal* 42 (4): 801–833.

Rossiter, David, and Patricia K. Wood. 2005. Fantastic Topographies: Neo-Liberal Responses to Aboriginal Land Claims in British Columbia. *The Canadian Geographer / Le Géographe Canadien* 49 (4): 352–366.

Usher, Peter J. 2003. Environment, Race, and Nation Reconsidered: Reflections on Aboriginal Land Claims in Canada. *The Canadian Geographer / Le Géographe Canadien* 47 (4): 365–382.

David A. Rossiter

LAND GRANTS
SEE *Development, Rural.*

LAND REFORM

The term *land reform* refers principally to the redistribution of agricultural land from existing private or public landowners to tenant farmers, agricultural laborers, or collective farmers who work on such land without owning it. The absence of ownership or equivalent secure rights to land carries numerous negative consequences. These include lack of ability, or motivation, to invest in the land; stagnant agricultural productivity; rural poverty and malnutrition; lack of status and power for the landless; pressures to flee rural poverty for ill-equipped cities; land degradation; and a dearth of rural families with assets or savings.

By contrast, successful redistributive land reform can confer broad benefits, including increased crop production and improved nutrition, reduction of rural poverty, greater grassroots empowerment and a lessening of social unrest, reduced pressure for urban migration, better environmental stewardship, and the creation of wealth in the beneficiaries' hands.

Widespread positive results from redistributive land reforms have been experienced by well over a billion people since World War II ended in 1945. While land reform is not a panacea against rural poverty, it has been a foundational element for effective economic and social development in many settings. Fully a billion others are potential future beneficiaries.

This entry begins with a brief historical perspective, then looks at major post–World War II land reforms, followed by some key program-design considerations, a review of where land reform remains relevant today, and the broader economic, social, and political issues likely to influence decisions about undertaking future land-reform programs.

HISTORY

Documented land reforms occurred in ancient Greece in the sixth century BCE and Republican Rome in the second century BCE. Perhaps reminding us how controversial land reform can be if not adequately designed or explained, the brothers Gracchi successive tribunes or leaders of the Republic, were assassinated, largely because of their support for redistributive land reform. There is also an Old Testament reference to the requirement of land redistribution every fiftieth year, in the "year of the jubilee" (Leviticus 25:23), although scholars are unsure of the extent of actual implementation.

A major land reform was carried out around the beginning of the French Revolution (1789), after which the reasonably satisfied French peasantry largely sat out the (mostly urban) violence and upheaval. About the same time, a democratic and nonviolent land reform began in Denmark.

A variety of land-reform undertakings are found in nineteenth-century Europe. Notable among them was the emancipation of the Russian serfs by Czar Alexander II (1818–1881) in 1861, accompanied by a major distribution of land (however, heavy repayment obligations were imposed on the land recipients). While President Abraham Lincoln (1809–1865) emancipated the slaves in 1863 in the midst of the Civil War in the United States, this was unfortunately not followed by redistribution to the freed slaves of the southern plantation lands on which they had worked: Most were left socially and economically disempowered, many working as sharecroppers with insecure tenure and paying high rents on the same lands on which they had worked as slaves.

The twentieth century before World War II saw a number of democratic and nonviolent land reforms, including many in European countries, as well as several violent civil upheavals that were significantly fueled by the grievances of landless or near-landless peasants. The Mexican peasantry supported a revolution (1910) and fought a subsequent civil war, eventually receiving perpetual land rights beginning in the 1930s. The Russian peasantry, still land-hungry, supported the 1917 revolution and received land, but later were forced to turn that land over to collective farms (1930s). A weak republican government in Spain made indecisive efforts to redistribute land in the 1930s, ultimately collapsing before the catalyzing acts of peasants who wanted land and seized it, and large landowners and their allies who feared communism or anarchy, and helped foment a successful military rebellion (the 1936–1939 Spanish Civil War).

POST–WORLD WAR II

There have been three principal waves of land reform since 1945. The first, during the decade following World War II, occurred largely where the war had catalyzed or helped speed regime change.

Leading examples were land-to-the-tiller programs in Japan, Taiwan, and South Korea—with tenant farmers receiving ownership of the same land on which they had been tenants—carried out under U.S.-supported noncommunist regimes. In mainland China, the Communists conducted a similar reform (but accompanied by antilandlord violence) when they took power in 1949, but this was followed by forced collectivization of all farmland in the mid-1950s. This period also included involuntary collectivizations carried out by Eastern European communist regimes that were within the Soviet sphere—even though the great majority of affected farmers had already been individual owners. Poland was a notable holdout, maintaining its system of small owner-operated farms.

A second wave of land-reform efforts occurred as many countries gained independence from colonial powers from the late 1940s onward. But most of these reforms were poorly designed and had little impact. The handful of successes—mainly land-to-the-tiller programs—included a few Indian states (each state legislates its own land-reform rules), notably West Bengal and Kerala in the 1970s and 1980s, and also included South Vietnam, under the threat of a communist insurgency, during the 1970–1973 period.

Also of importance during this time were programs taking large estates for redistribution to farm laborers, continuing in postwar Mexico, going forward in 1950s Bolivia, and undertaken in 1980s El Salvador, the latter again under the threat of a communist insurgency. The El Salvador reform also included a land-to-the-tiller program for tenant farmers.

There were also many failures during this period. These included other Latin American attempts, chiefly involving large estates, such as occurred in Brazil,

Colombia, and (reversed through the 1954 U.S.-sponsored overthrow of the regime) Guatemala. Failures in Asia, mostly attempts to redistribute tenanted land or above-"ceiling" land, included most Indian states, Pakistan, Bangladesh, Indonesia, and the Philippines, among others. In Africa, where land-redistribution efforts have centered on regions of white-owned estate land, many programs have shown slow progress (South Africa) or gone far astray (Zimbabwe, apparently benefiting largely the president's cronies and militia, while evicting most farm laborers).

One impetus to land reforms that has largely disappeared with the demise of militant Marxist ideology was the threat of communist insurgency built upon the promise of land, which led both to revolutionary land reforms (Russia, China, Cuba, Nicaragua, Vietnam) and to protective, anticommunist land reforms (South Vietnam, El Salvador). But some such insurgent movements persist (the Naxalites in eastern India, the New People's Army in the Philippines), and extralegal efforts to occupy large estates, though well short of armed insurgency, are still found in countries like Brazil.

The latest wave of postwar land reform has involved efforts to break up the large collective farms that existed under many communist regimes (*decollectivization*) and to give ownership or equivalent secure individual land rights to the former collective-farm workers (*privatization*). Progress has varied on these two aspects: China was the first to decollectivize (1979–1983) but has only partially privatized the resulting individual farms; Vietnam has now done both, as have most (but not all) Eastern European countries; Russia and Ukraine have formally privatized, but the former collectives remain the major operating units, usually renting in from their workers the individual land rights those workers have received. Finally, some countries, such as North Korea and Cuba, have neither broken up the collectives nor given individual land rights. Where physical breakup has occurred, it has generally affected cropland, but left grazing land as commons lands available for joint use.

PROGRAM DESIGN

Accumulated land-reform experience indicates numerous features of program design, subject to deliberate change, which can play an important role in determining success or failure. Three features of continuing importance are discussed below.

First, will "full-size" farms, or something much smaller, be the goal? If a full-size farm by local standards, say two to three acres, is to be allocated, then multiplying this size farm by the number of households needing land often indicates that 20 to 40 percent of the country's cropland will have to be taken and redistributed. In most con-

temporary settings, such a program is politically and financially impractical.

Thus, it is important that recent research in many countries, such as India, now indicates that the "benefits curve" rises extremely rapidly with the first few thousand square feet of land distributed. In particular, distributing a homestead plot of one-tenth acre or even less, to supplement the family's existing livelihood, not only affords room to erect a small house, but beyond that allows an area for intense cultivation and for keeping one or two animals. This results in substantial increments to that family's nutrition, income, and status. Yet distribution of such homestead plots to nearly all the landless may require only 1 percent or less of the country's cropland, changing judgments as to political and financial feasibility—as currently in India—in a dramatically favorable way. The disproportionately large contribution of small plots to agricultural production has also been seen in many collective-farming systems where the workers were permitted to have "private plots" near their homes for personal cultivation, as well as in the "garden plots" that many of these countries have allowed urban households to maintain on the peri-urban fringe.

Second, will the land reform be heavily publicized? China's program to give former collective (now individual) farmers secure, long-term rights exemplifies the impact of publicity. An earlier, 1998 law was widely publicized, and achieved over 40 percent effective implementation by mid-2001. A later, 2002 law, although providing even stronger rights to the farmers, received little publicity, and by mid-2005 achieved only minimal additional implementation among farmers unaware of their rights.

Finally, will beneficiaries receive support, such as technical advice and farm credit? While wide agreement exists that this is desirable, there remains disagreement as to how vital it may be in particular settings. It would be rare, however, that an otherwise-feasible land redistribution should be delayed because such complementary programs were not yet available.

Still another measure might be noted, one that has stirred considerable recent debate. That is the impact of giving confirmatory land-rights documents (titles) to those already in reasonably uncontested possession of land (by contrast, there is little question that beneficiaries of redistribution of land that had been privately owned by someone else, such as tenants receiving the land of former landlords, or agricultural laborers receiving the land of former plantation owners, should receive confirmatory documentation). The issue as to titling those in already-existing uncontested, but undocumented, possession is more complex than may be immediately evident. Some customary or traditional land rights may exist as distinct elements or layers that may be difficult to separately describe and document; some may be held by groups rather than individuals; and in some settings those who actually hold the rights may be preempted (through corruption or chicanery) by false claimants when a documentation process occurs. The benefits of giving documentation to uncontested existing possessors appear to be situational, emerging most clearly in urban settings.

CURRENT NEEDS

The two most populous developing countries at the beginning of the twenty-first century, China and India, are also the two most critical arenas for further land reform measures. Both countries have already adopted the essential laws, but both need to move to much wider implementation. In China's case, such efforts would involve renewed publicity and expanded formal documentation for farmers' long-term land rights. In India, the central government needs to help finance, and the individual states need both to finance and implement, a widespread homestead-plot program.

There are many additional settings where land reform efforts could have a major impact. Homestead-plot programs, for example, hold important potential in Indonesia, Pakistan, and Bangladesh, and in a number of other Asian, African, and Latin American countries with significant numbers of landless poor. And, in some settings, unused or underutilized land in large estates may still be sufficient in quantity and cheap enough in price to provide full-size farms to many of the rural poor: for example, in Brazil and further significant parts of Latin America, as well as in some parts of Africa with large-farm colonial legacies.

Also, communist or formerly communist countries that have not yet done so must eventually confront the twin tasks of decollectivizing and privatizing their inefficient and low-productivity collective-farm sectors, among them North Korea and Cuba. Others, like Russia and Ukraine, which have formally privatized, will have to facilitate the actual breakup of the large farms.

Altogether, the remaining potential for land reform is at least as great as what was carried out globally during the six decades after World War II.

BROADER ECONOMIC, SOCIAL, AND POLITICAL ISSUES

Every land reform, no matter how well designed, has to take account of broader economic, social, and political challenges and issues in the particular country.

Economic Issues Land reform neither creates nor destroys land: It simply puts an existing population into a relationship with an existing agricultural land base that is likely to be fairer and more productive than the present one. One consideration is that the accumulated evidence now indicates that small farms are, in terms of total factor productivity (that is, with regard to the value of land, capital, and labor inputs), generally more productive than larger farms in less-developed-country settings. Such countries are typically short on land, short on capital, and long on labor. Hence it makes good economic sense to have many motivated families—and ownership provides crucial motivation—applying family labor intensively on small farms while using as little capital (machinery, pesticides, etc.) as possible to achieve a given production result.

A related economic point on which there is general agreement is that large farms with a large number of laborers working together—such as most plantations or collective farms—are generally inefficient, because of the great difficulty of supervising labor on these far-flung operations with their complex and variable sequences of tasks.

A further economic point: Viable land reform in the transitional (communist or formerly communist) societies entails no land costs, since the land to be redistributed is presently publicly owned. And improved design will greatly reduce total land costs in traditional developing-country settings, wherever policymakers opt for a program based on homestead plots rather than full-size farms.

A final economic point, applicable in both traditional land-reform settings and those of the transitional societies, is whether recipients of individual land rights should be restricted in selling or leasing those rights, and if there are such restrictions, how broad should they be and how long should they last? There is disagreement on these issues: Such restrictions may improvidently prevent the creation of wealth in the hands of land-reform beneficiaries, but they may also forestall hasty sales at a low price or leases having adverse terms. Restrictions that are temporary and narrower (e.g., no land sales to foreigners or no large accumulations of land) may be easier to justify than long-term and broad restrictions, which may also be widely ignored and eventually abandoned (as in Mexico).

Social Issues This entry noted above some of the likely consequences of successful redistributive land reform. There are also broader social consequences that are likely for the newly landowning families, such as reduced infant and child mortality resulting from better nutrition; the affordability of increased school-going, including for girls; and increased participation in community affairs for those with the status of "landowner."

Political Issues To communicate the economic and social case for land reform is, in many settings, to move considerably toward achieving the necessary political support.

Three additional factors, important to what is sometimes called "democratic land reform," are likely to bolster such political support: (1) acquiring any privately held land needed for the land reform on the land market through voluntary sales, or (if the acquisition is involuntary) paying a fair and reasonable price; (2) coupled with this, treating any acquisition of privately held land simply as something needed for a higher social purpose (like land needed for a highway or hospital), not as a judgment that landlords are bad; and (3) giving the beneficiaries a free choice as to how they wish to organize their farming.

SEE ALSO *Chiapas; Ladejinsky, Wolf*

BIBLIOGRAPHY

Deininger, Klaus. 2003. *Land Policies for Growth and Poverty Reduction*. Washington, DC: World Bank; New York: Oxford University Press.

Field, Erica. 2005. Property Rights and Investment in Urban Slums. *Journal of the European Economic Association* 3(2–3): 279–290.

Ghimire, Krishna B., ed. 2001. *Whose Land? Civil Society Perspectives on Land Reform and Rural Poverty Reduction*. Rome: Popular Coalition to Eradicate Hunger and Poverty; Geneva: UN Research Institute for Social Development.

Lerman, Zvi, Csaba Csaki, and Gershon Feder. 2004. *Agriculture in Transition: Land Policies and Evolving Farm Structures in Post Soviet Countries*. Lanham, MD: Lexington.

Mitchell, Robert, and Tim Hanstad. 2004. Small Homegarden Plots and Sustainable Livelihoods for the Poor. LSP Working Paper 11. Rome: UN Food and Agriculture Organization.

Prosterman, Roy, and Jeffrey Riedinger. 1987. *Land Reform and Democratic Development*. Baltimore, MD: Johns Hopkins University Press.

Thiesenhusen, William C. 1995. *Broken Promises: Agrarian Reform and the Latin American Campesino*. Boulder, CO: Worldview.

Toulmin, Camilla, and Julian Quan, eds. 2000. *Evolving Land Rights Policy and Tenure in Africa*. London: Department for International Development.

Zhu, Keliang, Roy Prosterman, Ye Jianping, et al. 2006. The Rural Land Question in China: Analysis and Recommendations Based on a Seventeen-Province Survey. *New York University Journal of International Law and Politics* 38(4): 761–839.

Roy L. Prosterman

LANDLORDS

A landlord is a person or organization that rents out real estate, holding the rights to receive the rentals paid by tenants. Usually a landlord has a freehold estate, a legal right to the possession of, and income from, real estate. A land-lord can also be a tenant who subleases the premises to another tenant. A lease divides the estate into a leased fee estate for the owner and a leasehold estate for the renter, the latter providing rights of possession, as laid out in the lease, for a specified duration. If the lease expires and the tenant continues to have possession, he has a tenancy at sufferance.

"Land" in this context includes all space that can be controlled, including territory with water and in the atmosphere, and "real estate" consists of the land and the objects attached to the land, the rest being movable property. Land that is common property, such as the oceans beyond the jurisdiction of governments, are rent free, although international organizations and international law can be considered landlords if they can enforce their authority.

HISTORY OF LAND TENURE

"Land tenure" is the pattern of land ownership. In some small-group societies, the community as a whole often owns territory. The land can either have open access by anyone, or be allocated to families for use, but without inheritance. In some cases, an individual or family has periodic access to lands forming the commons of a village, and families have access to the commons for hunting, fishing, and gathering. Some societies provide priority rights to land when a member makes improvements on the site.

Social scientists such as Franz Oppenheimer have theorized that such land tenure changed mostly because of conquest, as the conquerors became the landlords and the original inhabitants became tenant farmers. In Europe after the collapse of the Roman Empire, the feudal system took hold, where serfs became attached to the land held by the aristocracy.

As trade became more widespread, land became more of a commodity that could be exchanged and operated by landlords for profit rather than for governing power. This change was facilitated in the United Kingdom by the "enclosure" movement, in which the aristocracy took over land that had been held collectively by village residents. The landlords switched much of the enclosed land from farming to raising sheep, and the expelled villagers had to move to cities where they became vagabonds and beggars, some of whom suffered from hunger and illness. Eventually, many became "proletarians" who had little choice but to work for the emerging Industrial Revolution for low wages.

Modern markets for the sale and rental of real estate and of mortgages on real estate are based on having secure and transferable titles to real estate, including the ability to verify a deed to real property. A governmental cadastre or registry of deeds and titles of ownership of estates in land facilitates the real estate market. During the Middle Ages in Europe, manorial court rolls recorded the titleholders and descriptions of the landholdings. As land become more marketable, the registration of deeds by governments developed to facilitate loans and transactions. In the United States, the recording of titles is the responsibility of the states, usually implemented at the county level. In the United Kingdom, governmental registration of land titles was not fully developed until the twentieth century with the Land Registration Acts of 1925 and 2002.

In his book *The Mystery of Capital*, Peruvian economist Hernando de Soto has emphasized that the absence of land titles has hampered economic development, as squatters avoid building improvements when they fear that their investment may be confiscated. Societies with communal or governmental land can obtain similar security with long-term (e.g., ninety-nine-year) transferable leaseholds.

In Latin America, the Spanish and Portuguese seized land from the Indians and turned the native population into tenants working on large estates, the "latifundia," as well as working small plots of land for their subsistence. In the southern states of the United States, the Indians were mostly expelled, and plantations utilized slaves imported from Africa.

Although Americans commonly think of the frontier as having been settled by homesteading, most of the western lands were not settled that way but were granted to various special interests such as the railroads, veterans, land-grant colleges, and speculators. As Henry George (1871) described, much land was obtained through dishonest means, such as by fraudulent titles. In California, the Southern Pacific Railroad became the largest landlord, giving the company great political clout.

In continental Europe, the aristocracy continued to own much of the land after the end of feudalism. In Germany, the Prussian aristocrats, called Junkers, owned half the land. In Russia, where the aristocracy remained landlords after the serfs were legally freed, revolution gained popular support with the slogan, "land and liberty," as popular movements for liberation have recognized a close relationship between liberty and landownership.

In the United States, some two-thirds of the people live in owner-occupied homes, but commercial and industrial land value remains highly concentrated. Landowners and real estate interests have great political clout, which they maintain with significant contributions to political campaigns. As a result, landowners obtain great tax benefits relative to those from other property and sources of income.

The tax benefits of real estate owners include being able to deduct mortgage interest and property taxes from taxable income and to exchange rental properties while deferring payment of capital gains taxes. Further, owner-occupants have a large capital-gains exemption, and in most places, they enjoy a rather light property tax on their land value relative to the civic benefits that raise their land values and rentals.

LANDLORDISM

The term *landlordism* is used in sociology and anthropology to refer to land tenure and status relationships with three characteristics: The land tenure is extremely unequal, the landlords tend to be rentiers who receive rent but do not actively manage their lands, and the landowning class controls and benefits most from the government.

The most stark examples of landlordism are the landed aristocracy and the large landed estates, as in Latin America, but most economies today have significant landlordism. Landlords of dilapidated buildings in blighted areas are disparagingly called "slumlords."

Since the supply of land is fixed, as the population and wealth grow, a rising demand for land increases rentals and land prices. Much of the gains from increased productivity flow to the landowners as rent and site values. Land value is enhanced even more by public works. The political clout of landowners induces government to place much of the tax burden on labor and enterprise, thus implicitly subsidizing landownership. Landlordism is thus endemic in most economies today, even if it is not as obvious as in the more visible form of a landed agricultural aristocracy.

Some governments have enacted rent control in order to set a maximum rental paid by tenants. Such price controls create shortages of rental units and can discourage maintenance.

In developing countries, prevailing landlordism has induced movements for land reform, a change in land tenure to a more widespread ownership of land. Land reformers have usually advocated a redivision of the land by splitting up large estates. In some cases, the "reform" has granted land to the politically well connected and to inefficient farmers. An effective way to accomplish land reform is by taxing the land value, which then induces the large holders who are not using their land efficiently to sell their land, thus accomplishing redistribution with greater productivity. This policy was implemented to some degree by Japan in the latter 1800s and Taiwan after 1950.

LANDLORD–TENANT LAW AND RELATIONSHIPS

The landlord–tenant relationship is governed by private law as set by the lease and by governmental law regarding landlording. A lease is a contract of tenancy, which transfers some of the rights of possession from the landlord as lessor to the tenant as lessee. A tenant has the right of quiet enjoyment, meaning an unmolested, tranquil use, free from interference or disturbance. However, the landlord retains the right of entry either with advance notice or in an emergency. Upon the expiration of the lease, the landlord is entitled to reversion, that is, to retake possession.

The lease provides an implied if not explicit warranty of habitability that requires the landlord to maintain the premises in a reasonably safe condition, but tenants can be held liable for the damage they cause. Usually the landlord pays the property taxes, but in a gross lease, usually for commercial real estate, the tenant pays the gross costs of occupancy, including real property taxes, utilities, insurance, and operating expenses. For residential leases, the landlord usually does the maintenance and pays the taxes and insurance, although tenants pay for any renters' insurance on their personal property.

The lease can specify a fixed time interval of tenancy, or go from month to month. If there is no written lease or no specified time, the relationship is a tenancy at will, subject to termination by the landlord or the tenant at any time. If the tenant remains after the expiration of a lease, the tenant remains liable for the rent. Governmental law limits the power of a landlord to choose a tenant. In the United States, the Civil Rights Act of 1968 prohibits discrimination in housing based on national origin, race, religion, or color. In 1974, sex or gender discrimination was added. The 1988 Fair Housing Act extended antidiscrimination protection to familial status. The Americans with Disabilities Act prohibits discrimination that denies the equal use of property due to physical or mental disabilities. State laws can duplicate or extend the application of antidiscrimination law; for example, the California Fair Housing Laws prohibit discrimination based on sex, color, race, religion, marital status, ancestry, or national origin.

Tenants can exploit landlords as well by causing damage and taking advantage of laws that delay eviction. Landlords can protect themselves by screening tenants in legal ways, by visiting where they live, observing the condition of their car, asking parents of young tenants to cosign leases, making tenants responsible for minor repairs, and providing a discount for prompt payments of rental (which is better psychologically than fines for late payment).

Landlords in the United States are also vulnerable to civil asset forfeiture, that is, the confiscation of their property if the police suspect that there is illegal drug activity on the premises, even if the landlord is not aware of it. While large-scale landowners and developers typically have political clout, they sometimes use their political power at the expense of other real estate owners, such as

when a government uses eminent domain to forcibly take real estate from some owners and transfer it to private developers, a practice that was widely reported in *Kelo v. City of New London* (2005). The Supreme Court's decision alarmed many property owners, who feared the case would facilitate more real estate "takings" by governments, and some states have enacted laws limiting such wide powers of eminent domain.

SEE ALSO *Aristocracy; Class, Rentier; Common Land; Land Claims; Land Reform; Latifundia; Rent*

BIBLIOGRAPHY

De Soto, Hernando. 2000. *The Mystery of Capital: Why Capitalism Triumphs in the West and Fails Everywhere Else.* New York: Basic Books.

George, Henry. 1871. *Our Land and Land Policy, National and State.* San Francisco: White and Bauer.

Oppenheimer, Franz. 1908. *The State: Its History and Development Viewed Sociologically.* Trans. John M. Gitterman. New York: Huebsch, 1922.

Rhodes, David, and Mark Bevan. 2003. *Private Landlords and Buy to Let.* Heslington, U.K.: Centre for Housing Policy, University of York.

Fred Foldvary

LANDLORDS, ABSENTEE

The term "absentee landlord" describes the situation where a person with the ultimate ownership of land—and this may be an actual person, a corporate entity, or even the state itself—does not personally use the land but instead extracts payment for its use by another. In one sense most landlords are "absent" in that the land is let for a rent to another person who enjoys physical possession and use of it, but an "absentee landlord" is a more pejorative description. It is meant to signify a landowner whose only interest in the land is to extract its economic value and who pays little or no regard to the state of the land or the welfare—economic, social, or political—of the person who is paying the rent. Such landlords are "absent" both in the sense that they have little or no social, emotional, or physical attachment to the land, and also because in many cases they are physically distant from the land, preferring either to regard the land as if it were merely an entry on a profit and loss account or, in some cases, to appoint a more local agent who will manage the land for the landlord on a purely commercial basis.

Historically absentee landlords have generated both social and economic problems on a grand scale, especially when the absenteeism is allied with external domination of the local territory. The Protestant owners of lands in Catholic Ireland in the seventeenth century and the mainly English absentee landowners of Prince Edward Island, Canada, in the eighteenth century are well-known examples of how absentee ownership can go hand in hand with "colonial" dominance, but this is not merely an historical problem. Absentee owners of Scottish Highland sporting estates; anonymous state control of land in less developed countries; corporate investors (e.g., pension funds) in city center business districts; absentee owners of Midwestern agribusinesses in the United States; and absent landlords of low-quality, deteriorating residential properties in most of our major cities are just a few examples from the twenty-first century.

Absentee landlords are perceived to be a threat to the economic and social viability of communities. By extracting value from the land (rent) but not spending or reinvesting in the local community, absentee landlords produce an outward flow of economic capital. They drain the local community. When accompanied by a constant turnover of short-term tenants, the social capital of a community is diminished and all of those community activities that depend on the interest and commitment of stable residents are lost. Given that absentee landlords may regard the land as merely another form of economic asset, rather than as a social and economic resource for the community in which the land is situated, many absentee landlords observe only the bare minimum of standards in relation to the land and the buildings on it. Properties owned by absentee landlords often are in a poor state of repair and building and zoning controls are either ignored or observed to the minimum standard permitted. An effective local management team can prevent some of the worse excesses, but the geographically absent landlord may be slow to respond to requests from the tenants or the local authorities. In many cases such landlords will simply sidestep calls for repairs or renovations and attempt to avoid local taxation.

Absentee landlords also generate numerous legal problems. Enforcing obligations in letting arrangments, serving of notices for the enforcement of tenants' rights, and ensuring observance of public rights affecting the property (for example public access routes and rights of way) are common problems. In extreme cases in countries without a systematic register or record of land ownership, it may be difficult to identify who actually is the ultimate owner and this can lead to problems of squatting as well as making the land economically stagnant.

The economic and social cost of absentee landlords can be considerable and many countries or localities have attempted to impose regulatory or legal requirements either in order to curb absenteeism or to remove its harmful effects. These have included public access to land reg-

isters in order to identify absent owners, tax incentives for owners who maintain an economic presence in the local community and penal local taxes for those draining the local economy, enhanced procedures for the recovery of land for local landlords when faced with defaulting tenants, compulsory enfranchisement (sale of the land to the tenant) on long leases, and the enhancement of enforcement powers for violators of building codes.

Martin J. Dixon

LANGUAGE

SEE *Psycholinguistics.*

LARGE SAMPLE PROPERTIES

In empirical work, researchers typically use estimators of parameters, test statistics, or predictors to learn about a given feature of an underlying model; these estimators are functions of random variables, and as such are themselves random variables. Data are used to obtain estimates, which are realizations of the corresponding estimators—that is, random variables. Ordinarily, the researcher has available only a single sample of n observations and obtains a single estimate based on this sample; the researcher then wishes to make inferences about the underlying feature of interest. Inference involves the estimation of a confidence interval, a p-value, or a prediction interval, and it requires knowledge about the sampling distribution of the estimator that has been used.

In a small number of cases, exact distributions of estimators can be derived for a given sample size n. For example, in the classical linear regression model, if errors are assumed to be identically, independently, and normally distributed, ordinary least squares estimators of the intercept and slope parameters can be shown to be normally distributed with variance that depends on the variance of the error terms, which can be estimated by the sample variance of the estimated residuals. In most cases, however, exact results for the sampling distributions of estimators with a finite sample are unavailable; examples include maximum likelihood estimators and most nonparametric estimators.

Large sample, or asymptotic, properties of estimators often provide useful approximations of sampling distributions of estimators that can be reliably used for inference-making purposes. Consider an estimator

$$\hat{\theta}_n = g(Y_1, \ldots, Y_n)$$

of some quantity θ. The subscript n denotes the fact that $\hat{\theta}_n$ is a function of the n random variables $Y_1, ..., Y_n$; this suggests an infinite sequence of estimators for $n = 1, 2, ...$, each based on a different sample size. The large sample properties of an estimator $\hat{\theta}_n$ determine the limiting behavior of the sequence $\{\hat{\theta}_n \mid n = 1, 2, ...\}$ as n goes to infinity, denoted $n \rightarrow \infty$. Although the distribution of $\hat{\theta}_n$ may be unknown for finite n, it is often possible to derive the limiting distribution of $\hat{\theta}_n$ as $n \rightarrow \infty$. The limiting distribution can then be used as an approximation to the distribution of $\hat{\theta}_n$ when n is finite in order to estimate, for example, confidence intervals. The practical usefulness of this approach depends on how closely the limiting, asymptotic distribution of $\hat{\theta}_n$ approximates the finite-sample distribution of the estimator for a given, finite sample size n. This depends, in part, on the rate at which the distribution of $\hat{\theta}_n$ converges to the limiting distribution, which is related to the rate at which $\hat{\theta}_n$ converges to θ.

CONSISTENCY

The most fundamental property that an estimator might possess is that of consistency. If an estimator is consistent, then more data will be informative; but if an estimator is inconsistent, then in general even an arbitrarily large amount of data will offer no guarantee of obtaining an estimate "close" to the unknown θ. Lacking consistency, there is little reason to consider what other properties the estimator might have, nor is there typically any reason to use such an estimator.

An estimator $\hat{\theta}_n$ of θ is said to be weakly consistent if the estimator converges in probability, denoted

$$\hat{\theta}_n \xrightarrow{P} \theta$$

This occurs whenever

$$\lim_{n \rightarrow \infty} P(|\hat{\theta}_n - \theta| < \varepsilon) = 1$$

for any $\varepsilon > 0$. Other, stronger types of consistency have also been defined, as outlined by Robert J. Serfling in *Approximation Theorems of Mathematical Statistics* (1980). Convergence in probability means that, for any arbitrarily small (but strictly positive) ε, the probability of obtaining an estimate different from θ by more than ε in either direction tends to 0 as $n \rightarrow \infty$.

Note that weak consistency does not mean that it is impossible to obtain an estimate very different from θ using a consistent estimator with a very large sample size. Rather, consistency is an asymptotic, large sample property; it only describes what happens in the limit. Although consistency is a fundamental property, it is also a minimal property in this sense. Depending on the rate, or speed, with which $\hat{\theta}_n$ converges to θ, a particular sample size may or may not offer much hope of obtaining an accurate, useful estimate.

A sequence of random variables $\{\hat{\theta}_n \mid n = 1, 2, ...\}$ with distribution functions F_n is said to converge in distribution to a random variable $\hat{\theta}$ with distribution function F if, for any $\varepsilon > 0$, there exists an integer $n_0 = n_0(\varepsilon)$ such that at every point of continuity t of F, $|F_n(t) - F(t)| < \varepsilon$ for all $n \geq n_0$. Convergence in probability implies convergence in distribution, which is denoted by $\hat{\theta}_n \xrightarrow{d} \hat{\theta}$.

Often, weakly consistent estimators that can be written as scaled sums of random variables have distributions that converge to a normal distribution. The Lindeberg-Levy Central Limit Theorem establishes such a result for the sample mean: If $Y_1, Y_2, ..., Y_n$ are independent draws from a population with mean μ and finite variance σ^2, then the sample mean

$$\bar{Y}_n = n^{-1} \sum_{i=1}^{n} Y_i$$

may be used to estimate μ, and

$$\frac{1}{\sigma} n^{1/2} (\bar{Y}_n - \mu) \xrightarrow{d} N(0,1)$$

The factor $n^{1/2}$ is the rate of convergence of the sample mean, and it serves to scale the left-hand side of the above expression so that its limiting distribution, as $n \rightarrow \infty$, is stable—in this instance, a standard normal distribution. This result allows one to make inference about the population mean μ—even when the distribution from which the data are drawn is unknown—by taking critical values from the standard normal distribution rather than the often unknown, finite-sample distribution F_n.

Standard, parametric estimation problems typically yield estimators that converge in probability at the rate $n^{1/2}$. This provides a familiar benchmark for gauging convergence rates of other estimators. The fact that the sample mean converges at rate $n^{1/2}$ means that fewer observations will typically be needed to obtain statistically meaningful results than would be the case if the convergence rate were slower. However, the quality of the approximation of the finite-sample distribution of a sample mean by the standard normal is determined by features such as skewness or kurtosis of the distribution from which the data are drawn. In fact, the finite sample distribution function F_n (or the density or the characteristic functions) of the sample mean can be written as an asymptotic expansion, revealing how features of the data distribution affect the quality of the normal approximation suggested by the central limit theorem. The best-known of these expansions is the Edgeworth expansion, which yields an expansion of F_n in terms of powers of n and higher moments of the distribution of the data. Among those who explain these principles in detail are Harald Cramér in *Biometrika* (1972), Ole E. Barndorff-Nielsen and David Roxbee Cox in *Inference and*

Asymptotics (1994), and Pranab K. Sen and Julio M. Singer in *Large Sample Methods in Statistics: An Introduction with Applications* (1993).

Many nonparametric estimators converge at rates slower than $n^{1/2}$. For example, the Nadarya-Watson kernel estimator (Nadarya 1964; Watson 1964) and the local linear estimator (Fan and Gijbels 1996) of the conditional mean function converge at rate $n^{1/(4 + d)}$, where d is the number of unique explanatory variables (not including interaction terms); hence, even with only one right-hand side variable, these estimators converge at a much slower rate, $n^{1/5}$, than typical parametric estimators. Moreover, the rate of convergence becomes slower with increasing dimensionality, a phenomenon often called the curse of dimensionality. Another example is provided by data envelopment analysis (DEA) estimators of technical efficiency; under certain assumptions, including variable returns to scale, these estimators converge at rate $n^{2/(1 + d)}$, where d is the number of inputs plus the number of outputs. Léopold Simar and Paul W. Wilson discuss this principle in the *Journal of Productivity Analysis* (2000).

The practical implications of the rate of convergence of an estimator with a convergence rate slower than $n^{1/2}$ can be seen by considering how much data would be needed to achieve the same stochastic order of estimation error that one would achieve with a parametric estimator converging at rate $n^{1/2}$ while using a given amount of data. For example, consider a bivariate regression problem with $n = 20$ observations. Using a nonparametric kernel estimator or a local linear estimator, one would need m observations to attain the same stochastic order of estimation error that would be achieved with parametric, ordinary least-squares regression; setting $m^{1/5} = 20^{1/2}$ yields $m \approx 1,789$.

The large sample properties of parametric and nonparametric estimators offer an interesting trade-off. Parametric estimators offer fast convergence, therefore it is possible to obtain meaningful estimates with smaller amounts of data than would be required by nonparametric estimators with slower convergence rates. But this is valid only if the parametric model that is estimated is correctly specified; if not, there is specification error, raising the question of whether the parametric estimator is consistent. On the other hand, nonparametric estimators largely avoid the risk of specification error, but often at the cost of slower convergence rates and hence larger data requirements. The convergence rate achieved by a particular estimator determines what might reasonably be considered a "large sample" and whether meaningful estimates might be obtained from a given amount of data.

CENTRAL LIMIT THEOREM

Aris Spanos, in his book *Probability Theory and Statistical Inference: Econometric Modeling with Observational Data*

(1999, pp. 464–465), lists several popular misconceptions concerning the large sample properties of estimators. It is sometimes claimed that the central limit theorem ensures that various distributions converge to a normal distribution in cases where they do not. The Lindeberg-Levy central limit theorem concerns a particular scaled sum of random variables, but only under certain restrictions (e.g., finite variance). Other scaled summations may have different limiting distributions. Spanos notes that there is a central limit theorem for every member of the Levy-Khintchine family of distributions that includes not only the normal Poisson, and Cauchy distributions, but also a set of infinitely divisible distributions. In addition, continuous functions of scaled summations of random variables converge to several well-known distributions, including the chi-square distribution in the case of quadratic functions.

SEE ALSO *Central Limit Theorem; Demography; Maximum Likelihood Regression; Nonparametric Estimation; Sampling*

BIBLIOGRAPHY

Barndorff-Nielsen, Ole E., and David Roxbee Cox. 1989. *Asymptotic Techniques for Use in Statistics*. London: Chapman and Hall.

Barndorff-Nielsen, Ole E., and David Roxbee Cox. 1994. *Inference and Asymptotics*. London: Chapman and Hall.

Cramér, Harald. 1972. On the History of Certain Expansions Used in Mathematical Statistics. *Biometrika* 59 (1): 205–207.

Fan, Jianqing, and Irène Gijbels. 1996. *Local Polynomial Modelling and Its Applications*. London: Chapman and Hall.

Nadarya, E. A. 1964. On Estimating Regression. *Theory of Probability and Its Applications* 10: 186–190.

Sen, Pranab K., and Julio M. Singer. 1993. *Large Sample Methods in Statistics: An Introduction with Applications*. New York: Chapman and Hall.

Serfling, Robert J. 1980. *Approximation Theorems of Mathematical Statistics*. New York: Wiley.

Simar, Léopold, and Paul W. Wilson. 2000. Statistical Inference in Nonparametric Frontier Models: The State of the Art. *Journal of Productivity Analysis* 13 (1): 49–78.

Spanos, Aris. 1999. *Probability Theory and Statistical Inference: Econometric Modeling with Observational Data*. Cambridge, U.K.: Cambridge University Press.

Watson, G. S. 1964. Smooth Regression Analysis. *Sankhya*, series A, 26: 359–372.

Paul W. Wilson

LASPEYRE'S INDEX

SEE *Price Indices; Quantity Index.*

LASSWELL, HAROLD
1902–1978

Harold Lasswell was an influential social scientist who contributed to the field of political science through research on political psychology, quantitative methods, and public policy. Lasswell was born in Donnellson, Illinois, to a schoolteacher and Presbyterian minister. At the age of sixteen, Lasswell received a scholarship to study at the University of Chicago, and he later completed graduate studies at the London School of Economics. Lasswell was a faculty member at the University of Chicago from 1922 to 1938 and at Yale University from 1946 to 1970. Lasswell died in 1978 in New York City.

Laswell's approach to political science was behavioral, and he was a part of the "Chicago school" of sociology. The Chicago school was a group of academicians in the 1920s and 1930s who focused on the urban environment, specifically through ethnographic fieldwork and an emphasis on social issues. Lasswell believed that propaganda was a key tool in public policy making, arguing that the citizenry was largely uninformed and often did not understand what was in its best interest. Lasswell was one of the first scholars to define and systematically explore the concept of propaganda, through his book *Propaganda Technique in World War I* (1927).

Lasswell's work on propaganda later expanded into a more general research agenda on communication. Lasswell contributed to the field by suggesting that more than one "channel" of media can carry a message. His model of communication is shown through a basic question: "Who says what, in which channel, to whom, and with what effect?" This model identified the several different components of communication in a political sphere: "Who" involved the political body or agency communicating, "what" is the gist of the message or idea, "channel" is the venue of communication, "whom" is the target audience, and "effect" is the policy outcome. His model encouraged systematic thinking about political communication and the psychological and policy implications of different forms of communication. Perhaps Lasswell's most famous and widely read work is his general treatise on politics, *Politics: Who Gets What, When, and How* (1936), which is an abridged but more general commentary on his model of communication.

Lasswell's work shifted in the later stages of his career to more of an emphasis on the policy sciences. Many see him as the father of policy sciences, and his work in that area is certainly among the first and most influential. Lasswell's research became larger in scope and resulted in policy-making frameworks that were more comprehensive and less concerned with narrow theorizing. Lasswell's ideas were rooted in his early work on propaganda—actors in the policy process were seen as sometimes irra-tional and pursuing goals that would ultimately harm them, and this led to a need for policies that went beyond those based in simple rational choice. Lasswell argued that misguided political behavior could easily undermine democracy, and called attention to the need for policy-makers to consider both expressed and unexpressed constituent needs.

Lasswell argued that the role of the policy sciences was to produce knowledge for democracy. His emphasis on contextualism influenced quantitative research in important ways, guiding analysts to consider as many external influences as possible in their research. Lasswell believed that the role of the analyst was both scientist and activist—the policy analyst cannot be completely objective in selection of goals, but should work toward objectivity in analysis of results. Although some have cast Lasswell as a positivist, his approach had both positivist and postpositivist themes.

Lasswell's approach to political science and public policy was met with some criticism. Many disagree with Lasswell's assertion that citizens often do not understand what they need, finding his approach to be at once paternalistic and naïve. Some also believe that Lasswell's view of the policy analyst is a romanticized one, exaggerating the impact that the analyst can have on policy making and ignoring issues with using objective data for political decision-making.

SEE ALSO *Media; Political Psychology; Political Science; Propaganda; Public Opinion; Sociology, Political*

BIBLIOGRAPHY

PRIMARY WORKS

Lasswell, Harold. [1927] 1971. *Propaganda Technique in World War I.* Cambridge, MA: MIT Press.

Lasswell, Harold. [1936] 1966. *Politics: Who Gets What, When, and How.* New Haven, CT: Meridian Books.

Lasswell, Harold. [1948] 1976. *Power and Personality.* Westport, CT: Greenwood Press.

SECONDARY WORKS

Ascher, William, Barbara Hirschfelder-Ascher. 2004. Linking Lasswell's Political Psychology and the Policy Sciences. *Policy Sciences* 37 (1), 23–36.

Bell, Wendell. 1993. H. D. Lasswell and the Futures Field: Facts, Predictions, Values, and the Policy Sciences. *Futures* 25 (8): 806.

Farr, James, Jacob S. Hacker, Nicole Kazee. 2006. The Policy Scientist of Democracy: The Discipline of Harold D. Lasswell. *American Political Science Review* 100 (4), 579–587.

David W. Pitts

LATIFUNDIA

A *latifundium* is a large piece of contiguous land that belongs to a single individual or family. It is a form of property as well as a mode of production that for centuries has determined the socioeconomic structures in many parts of the world, even through to the present day. Historically, latifundia were owned by members of the aristocracy, conferring upon them considerable social and political power and providing them with the income needed to support a lavish lifestyle.

To become the owner of a latifundium did not require much capital. Through ways more or less legal, latifundisti appropriated lands from the public domain and took over the holdings of poor peasants. The size of latifundia varied: from 600 acres in ancient Rome, which guaranteed the owner a senatorial seat, to the estates of Polish magnates extending over 250,000 acres, to those of *hacendados* in Mexico of over half a million. From the beginning, latifundia were commercial enterprises dedicated primarily to growing produce and livestock for profit, both for distant and nearby urban markets. In *On Agriculture*, Cato the Elder (234–149 BCE) emphasized the importance of latifundia being located near good roads and waterways so as to get the crops to their markets. All later forms of latifundia—haciendas, plantations, and Balkan *chifliks*—followed the same model and reproduced the same form of class domination: a paternalistic landlord ruling over a mass of laborers—slaves, landless peasants, manorial serfs, or peons. Latifundisti maintained political control in the provinces as well, despite being absentee landlords who resided in urban centers and left management of their estates to *villici*, or hired administrators.

The term *latifundium* is synonymous with other terms commonly used for large estate systems: Russia's *pomiestny*, Prussia's *Junkerdom*, Poland's magnate estate, and Latin America's hacienda (*fazenda* in Brazil, *estancia* in Argentina, *fundo* in Chile, *finca* in Bolivia and Peru). The term itself carries with it a wide range of negative connotations that comprise what may be called a "black legend." Ancestors of slave plantations, the ancient Roman latifundia have been described as the model for imperialism, colonialism, and modern slavery. A latifundista was a landlord who monopolized huge tracts of land, much of which he left fallow "by virtue of indolence." The system has been blamed for hindering modernization, preventing social mobility and the rise of the middle classes, making a few people very rich and bringing dire misery to the many, and finally for destroying the peasantry and unraveling rural society. The black legend was famously summed up by Pliny the Elder (23–79 CE) as *latifundia perdidere Italiam*, causing the ruin of Rome, together with its provinces—Egypt, North Africa, Gaul, Spain, and Sicily.

Latifundia were originally a Roman phenomenon. There were no large landholding fortunes before then, neither in ancient Greece nor in the early Roman republic, where laws systematically restricted the size of a family's property (the average farm was four acres). Extensive holdings first appeared in the fourth century BCE when Rome converted part of its newly conquered territory in Italy into state domain and then rented it out to wealthy people. These first latifundia, some 1,000 acres in size, became common in Etruria and southern Italy. Wars with Carthage further enriched a Roman patriciate who—excluded from trade and commerce—invested their war booty into large latifundia so as to make profits along capitalistic lines.

Prolonged warfare and centuries of conquest eventually concentrated the land in the hands of a few and pushed small peasants off the land. Before long, the city of Rome was overrun with dispossessed paupers.

By 23 BCE the newly formed Roman Empire was one hundred times larger than the republic had been at the time of the Punic Wars, and latifundisti were cultivating the soil of their immense estates with armies of slaves. In Nero's time (37–68 CE), Pliny tells us, half the land of the North African province was divided up among six patricians and organized in huge latifundia farmed by slaves and native peasants. "Life on the great estate," splendidly illustrated in mid-second-century mosaics in Tunisia, became a popular art genre. But it was an ultimately oppressive system that gave rise to slave revolts, like the one famously led by Spartacus in 73 to 71 BCE.

In the final years of the Roman Empire, these slave workers were replaced by *coloni*, small tenant farmers who became permanently attached to the estates (*glebae adscripti*) and evolved eventually into feudal serfs. Latifundia persisted in Italy, Gaul, Spain, southern Britain, along the Rhine, and in the eastern Byzantine Empire for centuries after the fall of Rome; in Sicily they survived until the 1950s. Even if, after the German invasions, a new class of landowners began to emerge as different groups adapted the Roman agrarian system to their particular needs, there still existed considerable continuity over the centuries, from the Roman latifundium and its slaves to the manor and its serfs.

The conquest of the Americas and the expansion of the world economy in the sixteenth century created ideal conditions for exporting the European manorial system. While vast commercial estates emerged in the New World, agrarian capitalism also began to flourish throughout much of Europe.

Beyond the Elbe River, for example, and in the eastern part of the Austrian Empire, feudal lords transformed their large properties into *Gutsherrschaften*. In Poland, especially in the Ukraine and Lithuania, immense lands and power became increasingly concentrated in the hands of the magnates. In Spain, the south was turned into large latifundia, established on formerly Moorish land (they had virtually abolished the manor system). All these market- and profit-oriented latifundia were farmed by peasant-serfs through a system of compulsory labor.

There were no market economies or commercial estates in the New World before the Europeans arrived and only the merest hint of a landed aristocracy in the Aztec and Incan empires. The profit-oriented latifundia system came with the colonists, and it carefully reproduced the European model. With few exceptions, the haciendas traced their origins to the sixteenth century, when viceroys divided up the Indians and the land (*encomiendas*) among the conquerors. In time, with a minimum outlay of capital, *encomenderos* became latifundisti (*hacendados*), the Indians became their peons, and the latifundium (hacienda) the most highly visible social and economic institution of the countryside.

The traditional monolithic model of the Latin American *latifundium* emphasized its continuity with late-medieval Spain. The landowner had aristocratic pretensions and displayed ostentatious patterns of consumption. He tied the laborers to the estate through debt peonage, built his great house to resemble a fortress, made the estate self-sufficient, and paid lip service to a kind of unproductive mentality. This "feudal" representation of the latifundium was challenged by dependency theorist André Gunder Frank (1929–2005), among others, who saw the latifundia as actively engaged in capitalist modes of production and the world market. Similarly, the North American plantation system, based on African slave labor, must be seen as a capitalist enterprise.

Similar patterns existed in Asia as well. In the Philippines, for example, Spanish latifundia were established on the land of Dominican friars and were farmed by Tagalog and Chinese laborers who were relieved of their "public corvées" to sustain the priests' cash-crop-export enterprise. In Vietnam, latifundia arrived with the French, who wanted to turn the colony into a major exporter of agricultural products. In India, it was the British who established an abusive and irresponsible absentee landowner system. Only in China had the system existed independently for centuries, until the 1600s, when it gave way to tenancy.

By the eighteenth century, latifundia dominated the life of the world's rural peripheries. Associated with serfdom and debt-peonage, the institution came under harsh criticism from scholars and bureaucrats who espoused physiocratic doctrines, while estates were the target of violent peasant attacks.

Despite calls for change, nearly all agricultural production for the world market was still controlled by latifundia in the nineteenth century, and the concentration of land had significantly increased. In Bohemia, Hungary, the Balkans, Poland, Germany, Ireland, Chile, and Mexico, more than half of the land belonged to large estates, some of which achieved truly princely dimensions. The secularization and subsequent sale of ecclesiastic property gave rise to new latifundia in southern Italy and Spain, as well as in Latin America. Many economists saw small-scale farming as economically wasteful, and even some social democrats like Karl Kautsky (1854–1938) argued in favor of the modern latifundium.

The nineteenth-century latifundia system survived the abolition of slavery and serfdom, replacing them with various contractual arrangements and modes of labor control. Junker land was now being cultivated by day laborers and seasonal Slavic workers. While the Balkan *chifliks* were regulated by the bailiff system, the system of rent-racking (landlords raising rents exorbitantly upon expiration of leases) in Ireland did not change at all.

The development of industrial capitalism in Europe created new market conditions and new possibilities for agrarian systems in Latin America—a development that political independence from the Old World only served to promote. Coffee, cereal, and sugar plantations expanded, these often owned by Creoles and mestizos. Latifundia also expanded exponentially following the confiscation and sale of the vast holdings of the Catholic Church. And finally, as the nonrural sectors declined during the Latin American wars of independence, latifundisti gained an unprecedented degree of political power, often running their own private regional states. Not only did they control the conservative parties and the military, but they often had the support of the liberals as well.

As new market opportunities opened up in the nineteenth century, latifundisti moved effortlessly with the times, acquiring credit from banks to purchase more land and expand the number of laborers. Their ways of operating were neither "traditional" nor "modern," neither feudal nor capitalist, as can be seen by the example of the Barracco latifundium system in southern Italy.

This new commercial growth was accompanied by the emergence of an impoverished and embattled landless proletariat. Their plight placed latifundia, once again, at the center of the so-called agrarian question. Circa 1900, latifundisti still owned and cultivated one-fourth of the total agricultural land of Germany and half of the arable land of Romania and Hungary, employing a full one-third of the population (six million workers) in this latter country. It was then that peasant movements and progressive parties joined forces to declare war on the latifundia, calling for the expropriation of vast tracts of land. Following

World War I (1914–1918), the old order seemed doomed (at least in Europe and Mexico), and national agrarian reforms began expropriating land belonging to absentee owners and corporations.

The last vestiges of latifundism definitively vanished from Europe in the second half of the twentieth century, while still maintaining a toehold as late as the 1950s in Italy and the 1970s in Spain. In Latin America, however, the latifundium remains a dominant and even expanding form of productive organization that has profitably adjusted itself to the modern, dynamic, and export-oriented economy of late capitalism. With the exception of Mexico, Latin American agriculture is twice as large a sector as manufacturing, and three times as large as commerce. The greater part of the national wealth of many of these countries depends upon the production of coffee, sugar, bananas, cotton, and beef. The beef-producing latifundia, in particular, are expanding, benefiting from the international "hamburger connection."

As Stanley Stein cautioned in 1961, we should not underestimate the political resilience of Latin America's socioeconomic elites and their ability to adapt the latifundia system to late capitalism, using their influence to persuade sympathetic governments to provide infrastructure and protection. Although profitable, this system exacerbates the old latifundia/minifundia dichotomy, for Latin America's agrarian structure is the most unequal in the world: ten of the fourteen countries with the highest concentration of land in the hands of single individuals are to be found there. This inequitable distribution lies at the root of the region's persistent poverty. It was also the fundamental cause of civil wars and social uprisings in Guatemala, El Salvador, and Nicaragua during the 1980s and 1990s and more recently in Brazil and in the Mexican state of Chiapas.

SEE ALSO *Landlords; Plantation*

BIBLIOGRAPHY

Chevalier, François. 1952. *La formation des grands domains au Mexique: Terre et société aux XVIe–XVIIe siècles.* Paris: Institut d'Ethnologie. Trans. Alvin Eustis. 1963. *Land and Society in Colonial Mexico: The Great Hacienda.* Berkeley: University of California Press.

Edelman, Marc. 1992. *The Logic of the Latifundio: The Large Estates of Northwestern Costa Rica since the Late Nineteenth Century.* Stanford, CA: Stanford University Press.

Florescano, Enrique, ed. 1975. *Haciendas, latifundios, y plantaciones en América Latina.* Mexico City: Siglo Veintiuno Editores.

Petrusewicz, Marta. 1996. *Latifundium: Moral Economy and Material Life in a European Periphery.* Trans. Judith C. Green. Ann Arbor: University of Michigan Press.

Stein, Stanley J. 1961. Tasks Ahead for Latin American Historians. *Hispanic American Historical Review* 41 (3): 424–433.

Table Ronde International du CNRS. 1995. *Du latifundium au latifondo: Un héritage de Rome, une création médiévale ou moderne?* Actes de la Table Ronde International du CNRS (1992). Paris: Diffusion de Boccard.

Wolf, Eric, and Sidney Mintz. 1957. Haciendas and Plantations in Middle America and the Antilles. *Social and Economic Studies* 6: 380–412.

Marta Petrusewicz

LATINO NATIONAL POLITICAL SURVEY

The Latino National Political Survey (LNPS) of 1989–1990 is a nationally representative dataset designed to measure the political attitudes and behaviors of the three major Latino subgroups in the United States: Mexicans, Puerto Ricans, and Cubans. The principal investigators of the LNPS consisted of four political scientists—Rodolfo de la Garza, Angelo Falcon, F. Chris Garcia, and John A. Garcia. Temple University's Institute for Survey Research conducted the survey.

DESCRIPTION OF THE LNPS

Data collection for the survey began in July 1989 and continued through March 1990. Latinos in the survey consist of individuals who reported having at least one parent or two grandparents (in any combination) of Mexican, Puerto Rican, or Cuban ancestry. The LNPS dataset includes 2,817 Latino respondents (1,546 Mexicans, 589 Puerto Ricans, and 682 Cubans).

The LNPS is the primary dataset examining the political attitudes and behaviors of Latinos on a national basis. According to the LNPS codebook, the survey contains a variety of variables, including the following broad categories: family history, organizational membership, political participation, voting behavior, attitudes toward a wide variety of political issues, attitudes toward a variety of racial/ethnic/national origin groups, and typical demographic characteristics (e.g., age, sex, and generational status). The dataset also includes information on the phenotype of respondents.

THE USES OF THE LNPS

The LNPS dataset has been disseminated widely. Indeed, it is available to researchers at the Inter-University Consortium for Political and Social Research (ICPSR).

Social science researchers, public policy practitioners, and the mass media have used the dataset.

The LNPS has been used widely by social scientists. Thirty-one articles based on the LNPS are abstracted in *ISI Web of Science* and/or *Sociological Abstracts*. These were published in eighteen journals, including *American Journal of Political Science, Applied Economics Letters, Armed Forces & Society, British Journal of Political Science, Cambridge Journal of Economics, Centro Journal, Demography, Hispanic Journal of Behavioral Sciences, International Migration Review, Journal of Family and Economic Issues, Journal of Health Care for the Poor and Underserved, Political Behavior, Population Research & Policy Review, PS: Political Science & Politics, Social Forces, Social Science Quarterly, The Sociological Quarterly,* and *Transforming Anthropology,* and one forthcoming article in the *Ethnic and Racial Studies* journal. Two journals—*Hispanic Journal of Behavioral Sciences* and *Social Science Quarterly*—stand out in terms of publishing the most articles using the LNPS. Indeed, *Hispanic Journal of Behavioral Sciences* devoted an entire issue (volume 18, issue 2) to work on the LNPS in 1996 (Garcia et al. 1996).

The LNPS has been applied to a broad range of social science topics, including the political attitudes of Latinos, the correlation between discrimination and phenotypes, residential patterns among Latino groups, and migration/immigration issues facing Latino groups. For example, in 2002 the *Social Science Quarterly* published an article titled "Latino Phenotypic Discrimination Revisited: The Impact of Skin Color on Occupational Status" (Espino and Franz 2002) based on the LNPS. This work showed that dark-skinned Mexicans and Cubans—but not Puerto Ricans—held less prestigious occupations than their lighter-skinned counterparts. In addition, *Social Science Quarterly* published another article in 2003 titled "The Corrosive Effect of Acculturation: How Mexican Americans Lose Political Trust" (Michelson 2003) using the LNPS. This particular article showed how political trust among Mexican Americans decreases with greater acculturation and exposure to mainstream society.

Social sciences such as economics and anthropology have also utilized the LNPS. For example, the journal *Applied Economics Letters* published an article in 2002 entitled "Passing on Blackness: Latinos, Race, and Earnings in the USA" (Darity, Hamilton, and Dietrich 2002). The article used previous findings from the LNPS to examine labor-market outcomes of people with Latino ancestry who also self-identify as black. Similarly, the anthropological journal *Transforming Anthropology* published an article in 2005 titled "Bleach in the Rainbow: Latin Ethnicity and Preference for Whiteness" (Darity, Dietrich, and Hamilton 2005). Like the economics-based

study, this article examines Latinos, particularly Puerto Ricans, who self-identify as black. The article cited a previous study that examined racial self-characterization categories ranging between black and white.

The LNPS has also been used in recent years by public policy agencies to better understand the political attitudes and voting behaviors of Latinos. Groups such as the Pew Hispanic Center, a Washington, D.C., think tank, and the Center for Information and Research on Civic Learning and Encouragement have utilized the LNPS to better comprehend the political behaviors of this increasingly influential population group.

Furthermore, the national media have also used the LNPS. In the early 1990s the Associated Press (AP)—specifically *USA Today* (Benedetto 1991)—and *El Sol del Valle* (Contreras 1995) referenced the LNPS. Each of these news pieces discussed political and related attitudes and behaviors of Latinos. The AP's usage of the LNPS demonstrates the wide application of this dataset.

LIMITATIONS OF THE LNPS

Despite the major contributions and the wide use of the LNPS, the dataset has some limitations. First, it focuses on only three Latino subgroups (Mexicans, Puerto Ricans, and Cubans). This creates a problem in generalizing the observed trends to other Latino groups such as Dominicans, Central Americans, and South Americans.

Second, as is typical of cross-sectional surveys, the information collected provides only a "snapshot" of individuals' attitudes and behaviors at a single point in time (1989–1990). Thus, researchers using the LNPS cannot analyze temporal changes related to political attitudes and behaviors. Moreover, the data are now quite dated. Many important changes have taken place since 1990, especially with respect to the politics of immigration. Longitudinal datasets need to be developed in order to capture the major demographic, social, economic, and political changes taking place within the Latino population.

Third, while the LNPS has a major focus on the political attitudes and behaviors of Latinos, other important dimensions (immigration, education, health, work, and gender relations) of the Latino experience are neglected or receive little attention. A new dataset, funded by private and public agencies and research centers, will be available in the fall of 2007 through the University of Washington's "WISER" Web site and the ICPSR. The new dataset, titled the Latino National Survey (LNS), focuses on the same ethnic groups as the LNPS (Mexicans, Cubans, and Puerto Ricans). This new survey is based on a random sample of 8,634 respondents interviewed by telephone. The sample is drawn from fifteen states and the District of Columbia. Selection of the states was based on Latino population estimates using U.S.

Census data. The LNS covers broader issues compared to the LNPS, including, but not limited to, inter- and intra-group relations, transnationalism, education, and gender.

SEE ALSO *Ethnicity; Latino/a Studies; Latinos; Race; Racial Classification; Survey; Surveys, Sample*

BIBLIOGRAPHY

Benedetto, Wendy. 1991. Three Largest Hispanic Groups Vary on Political Attitudes. *USA Today*, September 30.

Contreras, Raoul. 1995. Surprises in Survey of "Latinos." *El Sol del Valle*, December 28.

Darity, William, Jr., Darrick Hamilton, and Jason Dietrich. 2002. Passing on Blackness: Latinos, Race, and Earnings in the USA. *Applied Economics Letters* 9 (13): 847–853.

Darity, William, Jr., Darrick Hamilton, and Jason Dietrich. 2005. Bleach in the Rainbow: Latin Ethnicity and Preference for Whiteness. *Transforming Anthropology* 13 (2): 103–109.

De la Garza, Rodolfo, Angelo Falcon, F. Chris Garcia, and John A. Garcia. 1998. *Latino National Political Survey, 1989–1990* [Computer file]. 3rd ICPSR Version. Ann Arbor, MI: Inter-University Consortium for Political and Social Research.

Espino, Rodolfo, and Michael M. Franz. 2002. Latino Phenotypic Discrimination Revisited: The Impact of Skin Color on Occupational Status. *Social Science Quarterly* 83 (2): 612–623.

Garcia, F. Chris, Angelo Falcon, and Rodolfo de la Garza. 1996. Ethnicity and Politics: Evidence from the Latino National Political Survey—Introduction. *Hispanic Journal of Behavioral Sciences* 18 (2): 91–103.

Michelson, Melissa R. 2003. The Corrosive Effect of Acculturation: How Mexican Americans Lose Political Trust. *Social Science Quarterly* 84 (4): 918–933.

Rogelio Saenz
Misael Obregón
Beverly Pratt

LATINO/A STUDIES

The academic discipline of Latino/a studies examines the experience of the Latino/a population of the United States and is rooted in the inception of Chicano/a and Puerto Rican/Boricua studies in the late 1960s and early 1970s. The adoption of the panethnic term *Latino/a* recognizes the origins of Mexican Americans, Puerto Ricans, Cuban Americans, and members of other Latin American and Caribbean societies, thereby enveloping the heterogeneity of this diverse population. Latino/a studies programs in institutions of higher education have provided not only needed attention to the struggle of Latinos/as in the United States but also academic legitimacy for Latino/a students and faculty and recognition of the interdisciplinary interests of Latinos/as.

The civil rights movements of the 1950s and 1960s facilitated the implementation of Latino/a studies scholarship in U.S. colleges and universities. Activists fighting against systemic racism and discrimination provided an impetus for Latino/a students and faculty seeking scholarship that met the needs of Latinos/as in the United States. At the time Latinos/as were essentially invisible in mainstream white America. For instance, although both Chicanos/as and Puerto Ricans represented the two largest Latino/a subgroups in the United States, their incorporation by conquest resulted in their limited participation and integration into political, social, and economic institutions.

The systemic exclusion and historical underrepresentation of people of color was reproduced in academic institutions of higher education. Scholars studying U.S. race relations regularly failed to take a critical view of the social, economic, and political disparities and realities of the Latino/a population. For example, scholars with research interests in the Mexican-origin population of the United States were "primarily concerned with understanding the reasons for the perceived inability of Mexicans to assimilate into American society in the manner of other ethnic groups, from Europe" (García, Lomelí, and Ortiz 1984, p. 1). Therefore Latino/a students and faculty sought to establish academic programs that rejected the colonizing ideology of white America, advocating instead the development of scholarship that provided students with critical knowledge and training of Latino/a culture and history (Rodriguez 1990; Muñoz 1984). The implementation of Latino/a studies programs concentrating on the issues affecting Latino/a communities and the development of resolutions that dealt with these were the goals of Latinos/as who were privileged to be affiliated with colleges and universities (Rodriguez 1990; Muñoz 1984).

With these issues in mind, Chicanos/as and Puerto Ricans paved the way for the development of Latino/a studies. Latino/a students and faculty pioneered changes at historically white colleges and universities, beginning with the creation of the first Chicano/a studies program at California State University, Los Angeles, in 1968 and following with Chicano/a studies programs at universities in the Southwest and Puerto Rican/Boricua studies programs in the Northeast. Despite these accomplishments, Latino/a studies programs have experienced a number of challenges. Marginalized within their respective institutions, programs have been underfunded, denied autonomy, and at times, subsumed within other programs in their respective colleges and universities (Cabán 2003).

Influential in the creation of Latino/a studies scholarship were Latino/a student activists who protested and participated in strikes that confronted racial and class oppression (Muñoz 1984); Latino/a faculty also played pivotal roles in the creation of Latino/a studies programs. Julian Samora (1920–1996), the first Chicano to receive a doctorate degree in sociology and anthropology—in 1953 from Washington University in Saint Louis—was particularly important in establishing the field of Chicano/a studies. In addition to cofounding the National Council of La Raza and creating the Mexican American Legal Defense and Educational Fund, Samora mentored hundreds of undergraduate students and supervised the completion of more than fifty doctoral degrees at the Notre Dame University. His accomplishments influenced studies in the areas of bilingual education and immigration. In 1989 Michigan State University established a Latino/a research organization in his name, the Julian Samora Research Institute.

Likewise Frank Bonilla influenced the development of Puerto Rican/Boricua studies. Anne Quach chronicled Bonilla's U.S. military experience, describing how it motivated his pursuit of an academic career (Quach 2004). His own interests, along with those of other young social activists, spurred the formation of the Puerto Rican Hispanic Leadership Forum, thus paving the way for the establishment of Aspira (Quach 2004). Aspira is the first national nonprofit organization to empower Latino/a youth through the development of leadership skills that motivate Latino/a community advancement. These organizations, which seek to meet the needs of Puerto Ricans and other Latinos/as, originated from a response to the racism and discrimination that Puerto Ricans faced in the United States. Bonilla's interests also focused on issues of globalization and immigration (Quach 2004). Both Samora and Bonilla, along with many others, were pivotal forces in addressing the needs of Latinos/as in the United States, and they mentored many others toward initiating change.

In spite of their turbulent beginnings, Latino/a studies programs have gained academic legitimacy and produced scholarship directed toward multidisciplinary interests (Cabán 2003). Traditionally social science scholars in the disciplines of sociology and political science, for instance, focused Latino/a research in the areas of politics, sociology, political science, and economics. However, the emergence of interdisciplinary research within the field has sprung from the very nature of the heterogeneity of the Latino/a origin population and resulted in a hybrid that acknowledges the diverse cultures and disciplinary interests of Latinos/as (Masud-Piloto 2003). By the 1990s Latino/a studies scholarship encompassed nontraditional areas of study, such as border studies, women's studies, and performance and film studies (Masud-Piloto 2003). Further developments included the incarnation of "a multidisciplinary academic field that explores the diversity of localized and transnational experiences of Latin American

and Caribbean national origin populations in the United States" (Cabán 2003, p. 6).

The origin of Latino/a studies scholarship was a response to the racial and class oppression faced by Chicanos/as and Puerto Ricans. Although programs face internal divisions and marginalization within their respective academic institutions, Latino/a studies programs continue to meet the needs of Latinos/as and to inspire students and faculty to examine various areas of research, thereby acknowledging the diversity of the Latino/a population.

SEE ALSO *Boricua; Ethnicity; Immigrants to North America; Immigrants, Latin American; Immigrants, New York City; Latino National Political Survey; Mexican Americans; Nuyoricans; Politics, Latino; Race; Whiteness*

BIBLIOGRAPHY

Aspira Association. http://www.aspira.org/.

Cabán, Pedro A. 2003. Moving from the Margins to Where? Three Decades of Latino/a Studies. *Latino Studies* 1 (1): 5–35.

García, Eugene E., Francisco A. Lomelí, and Isidro D. Ortiz. 1984. *Chicano Studies: A Multidisciplinary Approach*. New York and London: Teachers College Press.

Julian Samora Research Institute. 2006. The Julian Samora Virtual Collection.

Masud-Piloto, Felix. 2003. Response to Pedro Cabán Latino Studies: Moving Forward while Looking Back. *Latino Studies* 1 (1): 43–46.

Muñoz, Carlos, Jr. 1984. The Development of Chicano Studies, 1968–1981. In *Chicano Studies: A Multidisciplinary Approach*, ed. Eugene E. García, Francisco A. Lomelí, and Isidro D. Ortiz, 5–18. New York and London: Teachers College Press.

Rodriguez, Clara. 1990. Puerto Rican Studies. *American Quarterly* 42 (3): 437–455.

Quach, Anne. 2004. From the "Bulge" to the Halls of Academia: Frank Bonilla's Hunger for Education Opened His Eyes to the World. *Narratives* 4 (2): 88. http://utopia.utexas.edu/explore/latino/narratives/08_PDFs/bonilla_frank.pdf.

Aurelia Lorena Murga

LATINOS

The Latino population represents the largest minority group and most rapidly growing ethnic group in the United States. This population is composed of a variety of subgroups tracing their origins to Mexico, the Caribbean, Central America, South America, and Spain. While Latinos represented one-sixteenth of the U.S. population in 1980, they were one-seventh of the U.S. population in 2005, when they numbered 42.7 million. They accounted for two-fifths of the nearly 70 million people added to the national population between 1980 and 2005. Population projections indicate that Latinos will continue to drive the demographic changes in this country throughout the twenty-first century. Indeed, they are expected to make up 46 percent of all people projected to be added to the U.S. population between 2000 and 2030. Thus, by 2030 Latinos are predicted to number 73.1 million, accounting for one-fifth of all people in the nation.

This entry provides an overview of the emergence of the terminology to describe this population, the mode of incorporation of the major Latino populations into the United States, and the contemporary social and economic standing of the Latino population in the country.

THE IDENTIFICATION OF LATINOS

In the United States, race and ethnicity have been central to public discourse, government, and economics. Throughout U.S. history racial and ethnic categories functioned as a basis for inequality and discrimination. Governmental changes to identifiers during the twentieth century came as a result of the pursuit of civil and equal rights by minorities in areas regarding education, housing, employment, and public services. For instance, mid-twentieth-century civil unrest and subsequent legal challenges compelled the Federal Office of Management and Budget to develop the term *Hispanic* in 1970 to mean "a person of Mexican, Puerto Rican, Cuban, Central or South American or other Spanish culture or origin, regardless of race" (Hayes-Bautista and Chapa 1987, p. 64). While many adopted the Hispanic ethnic identity, many others eschewed the term as it failed to take into account the unique origins and historical experiences of distinct subgroups. Therefore, the term *Latinos* has been widely adopted as a more acceptable term of self-identification by people of Latin American ancestry.

Despite pan-ethnic identifiers, the groups that make up the Latino population have diverse histories, cultures, and modes of incorporation into the United States. For instance, the initial incorporation of some groups occurred through warfare, while that of others was the result of civil unrest. For all groups, economics—the search for favorable employment—has been an attraction to the United States.

HISTORICAL OVERVIEW AND MODES OF INCORPORATION OF LATINO GROUPS

Over the course of 185 years, nearly 15 million people from Latin America migrated on a legal basis to the United States, according to the U.S. Department of

Homeland Security in 2006. The majority of this movement took place during the late twentieth and early twenty-first centuries (77% of the 15 million immigrated after 1970). About 45 percent of all immigrants who entered the United States legally between 1970 and 2005 originated from Latin America. Mexico alone accounted for one-fifth of all legal immigrants entering the country during this period. The ten countries with the most Latinos immigrating to the United States from 2000 to 2005 were Mexico (867,417), El Salvador (139,390), Dominican Republic (127,066), Cuba (97,988), Colombia (91,808), Guatemala (78,594), Peru (58,318), Ecuador (47,094), Nicaragua (36,620), and Venezuela (32,500).

Latino groups have entered the United States at different periods under varying conditions. The two groups that have been in the United States the longest, Mexicans and Puerto Ricans, were initially incorporated into the United States through warfare. Numerous other groups—including Cubans, Guatemalans, Nicaraguans, and Salvadorans—have sought asylum in the United States due to warfare in their home countries. Still, the majority of Latin American immigrants came to the United States for economic reasons, drawn by labor opportunities and propelled by poor employment prospects in their home countries.

Mexicans Mexicans, approximately three-fifths of all Latinos living in the United States, have been in the country the longest. Mexicans were incorporated through the Mexican-American War that Mexico lost, along with approximately half of its land, to the United States under the Treaty of Guadalupe Hidalgo of 1848. Mexicans who were living on what was now U.S. land were given the choice to remain and become U.S. citizens or return to Mexico. They overwhelmingly elected to remain on their land. Although Mexican Americans were guaranteed all rights as U.S. citizens, including respect for their property, culture, and language, as former Mexicans they became, at best, second-class citizens.

In actuality, Mexican Americans experienced colonization and exploitation as whites from other parts of the United States entered the acquired territories. Colonization included the loss of land due to legal and extralegal means, according to Rodolfo Acuña (2000) and David Montejano (1987). Mexican Americans became a landless proletariat and provided inexpensive labor for Anglo settlers. Similar to the situation that African Americans experienced in the South, Mexicans and Mexican Americans in the Southwest experienced great legal and illegal violence, discrimination, oppression, and disenfranchisement.

During the opening decades of the twentieth century, Mexicans fled political and civil unrest to the United States. Ironically, during a period when the United States was creating policies to keep southern and eastern Europeans and Asians from entering the country, many industrialists and growers welcomed Mexican immigrants as cheap labor for a growing economy. By the mid-1920s their growing presence, the country's economic instability, and the xenophobic attitudes of whites compelled the U.S. government to evict Mexicans from the country. For example, approximately 500,000 Mexicans—roughly one-third of the Mexicans enumerated in the 1930 U.S. census—were repatriated to Mexico during the Great Depression. Within ten years the United States and the Mexican government colluded to establish the Bracero Program to deal with U.S. labor shortages associated with World War II; because of its wide popularity among U.S. employers, the Bracero Program was extended nearly two decades beyond the conclusion of the war. The program allowed United States employers to actively recruit and import Mexican contract labor to meet their needs. In all, approximately 4.7 million Mexicans came to the United States under this program. Since the 1970s, there has been a significant increase in Mexican immigrants and settlers. The entrance of U.S. capital into Mexico—in the form of the Border Industrialization Program and the North American Free Trade Agreement—have altered social and economic structures in Mexico that have helped to create the movement of workers (some of these displaced) to the United States. The combination of "old-timers" (those whose roots extend back multiple generations) and "newcomers" (those who have come to the United States in the recent past) has created a diverse Mexican-origin population, as described by Rogelio Saenz in his census report *Latinos and the Changing Face of America* (2004).

Puerto Ricans Puerto Ricans share a colonized past with Mexico. Indeed, the island of Puerto Rico has been marked by colonial exploitation beginning with its colonization by Spain and continuing into the present as a Commonwealth of the United States. The history of Puerto Rico is similar to that of other Latin American countries that have been under the sovereignty of colonial nation-states. The native people of the island were first colonized in 1493 by the Spanish. When this population declined as a result of forced labor and disease, according to the writers Joe R. Feagin and Clairece Booher Feagin in their book *Racial and Ethnic Relations* (1999), slaves were brought in to fill the labor gap until 1873, when slavery was abolished. Rule over Puerto Rico was ceded to the United States as result of the Spanish-American War and the subsequent signing of the Treaty of Paris in 1898. Puerto Ricans received U.S. citizenship with the passage of the Jones Act of 1917 and gained self-governance in 1952. However, although Puerto Ricans are U.S. citizens, island residents are not allowed to vote in U.S. presidential elections, but they are required to enlist in military service to the United States.

Puerto Rico functioned economically in an agricultural system until the late 1940s when a rapid program of industrialization, known as Operation Bootstrap, was introduced by then Governor Luis Munoz Marin. Operation Bootstrap allowed locally tax-exempt U.S. corporations to develop industries on the island, which placed an economic burden on the Puerto Ricans who were required to finance the necessary infrastructure through high personal taxes. Although Puerto Rican migration to the U.S. mainland existed prior to the rapid-industrialization projects, massive unemployment in the 1970s resulted in the migration of approximately one-third of the island's population to the United States (Feagin and Feagin 1999).

Due to their U.S. citizenship status, Puerto Ricans tend to migrate in a circular pattern. Over the years many have settled in the United States. Puerto Ricans have subsequently had a major impact on mainstream American culture, especially in cities such as New York, where ethnic enclaves have existed since the 1920s.

Cubans The island of Cuba became a U.S. protectorate in early 1900, and in the middle of the twentieth century, through revolution, it became a socialist state. U.S. interest in Cuba arose out of economic investments by U.S. businesses. The United States became the major market for Cuban goods and a provider of essential supplies needed to sustain the island's economic system. The political instability on the island began in the 1930s and lasted through the 1950s; student-led protests, along with instability within the Cuban polity, threatened the economic, social, and political interests of capitalist Cuban elites, U.S. investors, and as a result the governments of both countries. Socioeconomic disparities led to the establishment of a socialist state with Fidel Castro in power beginning in 1959. Castro's rise to power resulted in large-scale emigration of the middle and upper classes, who sought asylum in the United States. As advantaged political refugees fleeing what was labeled as a communist state by those who were adversely affected by Castro's rise to power, Cuban refugees were offered numerous resettlement benefits by the United States.

Other refugees accepted into the United States in 1980, however, were not provided resettlement programs. This group, referred to as *Marielitos* (after the Cuban port from which they left, Mariel Bay), were drawn from the lower classes and were largely black. While the group included some criminals, the media exaggeratedly portrayed *Marielitos* as "undesirables," write Alejandro Portes and Robert L. Bach in their book *Latin Journey: Cuban and Mexican Immigrants in the United States* (1985, p. 87). The group was confronted with a negative reaction from the American mainstream and their own communities, notes Juan González in his book *Harvest of Empire: A History of Latinos in America* (2000).

Still, the favorable economic and human-resource assistance that the early waves of Cubans received helped some to achieve upward mobility in the United States. Cuban enclave enterprises have been highly successful in Miami and have helped integrate Cuban immigrants, according to Portes and Bach (1985).

Nicaraguans Significant immigration to the United States by Nicaraguans is often recognized as beginning in the late 1970s at the end of the regime of Anastasio Somoza Debayle. Immigrants were escaping a repressive government whose actions had impoverished the majority of the population, destabilized the economy, and started a U.S.-supported revolution. Nicaraguan immigration was characterized by three subsequent waves.

The initial arrivals were limited in number and composed of upper-class or elite families—industrialists, large landowners, and top businessmen—escaping the Sandinista takeover of the country. Many had the financial means and education required to establish themselves in the United States. Their arrival and presence was therefore much less noticeable than subsequent arrivals.

The second phase of Nicaraguan migration occurred in the early 1980s and consisted of political asylum–seeking urban, middle-class professionals and business personnel escaping a dysfunctional economy destabilized by political turmoil. Some used prior degrees and skills to find jobs, but the majority of immigrants were reduced to labor occupations until they could better accommodate themselves. State assistance was provided for them as long they had legal documentation. Improper documentation resulted in deportation procedures.

The third wave of immigrants began in the mid-1980s and consisted of laborers and peasants escaping the Contra war and a disrupted economy. Many resorted to the informal economy in order to earn subsistence wages. These arrivals initiated a recognizable flow that alarmed many Americans, who urged the U.S. government to respond.

Unlike the Cuban experience, but much like that of other Central and South Americans, Nicaraguans were hardly welcomed to the United States or given much opportunity for permanent settlement. By the late 1980s the Reagan administration's support for the Contra military was overtly stopped, and the flood of refugees to the United States seeking asylum increased exponentially. In an effort to stop the flow of refugees, the United States detained and incarcerated all new arrivals while their cases for asylum were processed. The U.S. Immigration and Naturalization Services classified most as illegal aliens and initiated deportation. Established Nicaraguans attempted to intercede, but U.S.-supported political changes in Nicaragua compelled democratic changes and prompted refugees to return. In contrast to other refugee groups, Nicaraguans were offered no resettlement programs, note Portes and Alex Stepick in *City on the Edge: The Transformation of Miami* (1993).

CONTEMPORARY AMERICA

Latinos have comparable, yet distinct immigration experiences. Foreign policies and territorial ambitions coupled with the United States' need for cheap labor established the initial ties between Latin America and the United States, paving the way for immigration and setting the stage for Latino identity in the United States, as described by José Calderón in his contribution to *Latin American Perspectives* (1992). Latino Americans who settled in the United States are represented in all socioeconomic classes and at various stages of assimilation or acculturation. Latino subgroups have established distinct communities around the country. Ethnic enclaves attract newcomers that reinvigorate immigrant culture, and each successive generation blends with mainstream American culture, shaping a new identity for Latinos.

There is a significant amount of stratification within the Latino population, notes Saenz (2004). Cubans and South Americans tend to have the highest levels of socioeconomic achievement in the United States, while Mexicans, Puerto Ricans, Dominicans, and, to some extent, Central Americans are positioned at the bottom of the socioeconomic ladder.

Nonetheless, due to their increasing numbers, Latinos have begun to achieve some degree of political success. Furthermore, because they are situated in urban areas and in the most populous states, they are a group that politicians must acknowledge. However, other forces tend to limit the political power of Latinos: They are a young population (with many not old enough to vote), many Latinos cannot vote because they are not U.S. citizens, and they are noticeably divided across national origin and class lines.

The presence of a diverse and growing Latino population may diminish Anglo cultural dominance and introduce a sense of multiculturalism to U.S. society. As Latinos retain and assert their own ethnic identities, they add cultural distinction to their respective geographical centers across the United States.

As a consumer group, Latinos have been recognized by marketing agencies and corporations who previously had failed to target this large group and their buying potential, observes Arlene Dávila in *Latinos, Inc.: The Marketing and Making of a People* (2001). In this regard, the influence of Latinos in the labor market and their presence as a consumer force impact economics in the United States and abroad.

SEE ALSO *Boricua; Bracero Program; Citizenship; Cuban Revolution; Ethnicity; Identity; Immigrants to North America; Immigrants, Latin American; Immigrants, New York City; Latino/a Studies; Mexican Americans; Naturalization; Nuyoricans; Politics, Identity; Politics, Latino; Race*

BIBLIOGRAPHY

Acuña, Rodolfo. 2000. *Occupied America: A History of Chicanos.* 4th ed. New York: Pearson Longman.

Alba, Richard. 1999. Immigration and the American Realities of Assimilation and Multiculturalism. *Sociological Forum* 14 (1): 3–25.

Bean, Frank D., and Marta Tienda. 1999. The Structuring of Hispanic Ethnicity: Theoretical and Historical Considerations. In *Majority and Minority: The Dynamics of Race and Ethnicity in American Life*, 6th ed., ed. Norman R. Yetman, 202–217. Boston: Allyn and Bacon.

Calderón, José. 1992. "Hispanic" and "Latino": The Viability of Categories for Panethnic Unity. *Latin American Perspectives* 19 (4): 37–44.

Carrigan, William D., and Clive Webb. 2003. The Lynching of Persons of Mexican Origin or Descent in the United States, 1848 to 1928. *Journal of Social History* 37 (2): 411–438.

Dávila, Arlene. 2001. *Latinos, Inc.: The Marketing and Making of a People.* Berkeley: University of California Press.

Feagin, Joe R., and Clairece Booher Feagin. 1999. *Racial and Ethnic Relations.* 6th ed. Upper Saddle River, NJ: Prentice Hall.

González, Juan. 2000. *Harvest of Empire: A History of Latinos in America.* New York: Viking.

Hayes-Bautista, David E., and Jorge Chapa. 1987. Latino Terminology: Conceptual Bases for Standardized Terminology. *American Journal of Public Health* 77 (1): 61–68.

Hirschman, Charles, Richard Alba, and Reynolds Farley. 2000. The Meaning and Measurement of Race in the U.S. Census: Glimpses into the Future. *Demography* 37 (3): 381–393.

Leogrande, William M. 1985. The United States and Nicaragua. In *Nicaragua: The First Five Years*, ed. Thomas W. Walker, 425–446. New York: Praeger.

Leonard, Thomas M. 2003. The Cuban Revolution, 1959–1961. In *Revolutions: Theoretical, Comparative, and Historical Studies*, 3rd ed., ed. Jack A. Goldstone, 201–211. Belmont, CA: Wadsworth/Thomson Learning.

Montejano, David. 1987. *Anglos and Mexicans in the Making of Texas, 1836–1986.* Austin: University of Texas Press.

Portes, Alejandro, and Robert L. Bach. 1985. *Latin Journey: Cuban and Mexican Immigrants in the United States.* Berkeley: University of California Press.

Portes, Alejandro, and Rubén G. Rumbaut. 1996. *Immigrant America: A Portrait.* 2nd ed. Berkeley: University of California Press.

Portes, Alejandro, and Alex Stepick. 1993. *City on the Edge: The Transformation of Miami.* Berkeley: University of California Press.

Reimers, David M. 1985. *Still the Golden Door: The Third World Comes to America.* New York: Columbia University Press.

Saenz, Rogelio. 2004. *Latinos and the Changing Face of America.* New York: Russell Sage Foundation and Population Reference Bureau.

Snipp, C. Matthew. 2003. Racial Measurement in the American Census: Past Practices and Implications for the Future. *Annual Review of Sociology* 29 (August): 563–588.

U.S. Department of Homeland Security. 2006. *2005 Yearbook of Immigration Statistics.* Washington, DC: U.S. Department of Homeland Security, Office of Immigration Statistics.

Jesus A. Garcia
Aurelia Lorena Murga
Rogelio Saenz

LATITUDES

SEE *Social Judgment Theory.*

LAUSANNE, SCHOOL OF

The expression "School of Lausanne" indicates the body of ideas and analytical techniques associated with the early mathematical formulations of general economic equilibrium, due to Léon Walras (1834–1910) and Vilfredo Pareto (1848–1923); later writers working in that field are occasionally classified as belonging to the School of Lausanne as well.

In 1870, the Frenchman Léon Walras was appointed to the newly created chair of political economy at the University of Lausanne, Switzerland. Walras aimed at attacking *La Question Sociale* (the problem of the distribution of social wealth) by means of a new approach to economics and social economics revolutionizing its philosophical foundations. He aimed at discovering the scientific laws of the most equitable distribution of the most abundant production. Walras pursued this project during his entire life, but he only managed to achieve a systematic presentation of his *Pure economics* (*Éléments d'économie politique pure*, 1874–1877, 1889, 1896, 1900). As Walras surrendered to age and fragile health, in the end his theory of distribution of social wealth (*social economics*) and his theory of production of social wealth (*applied economics*) had to appear as collections of articles under the titles *Études d'économie sociale* (1896) and *Études d'économie politique appliquée* (1898).

In 1893 the Italian Vilfredo Pareto succeeded Walras, taking over the chair officially on October 23, 1894. While retaining Walras's general equilibrium approach, Pareto severed it from social economics and renounced its use as a conceptual tool to deal with *La Question Sociale*, thereby denying that it can serve any purpose as an instrument for social reform. In fact, Pareto came from a quite different ideological tradition and was much more concerned with the demonstration of the advantages of free trade than with *La Question Sociale*. Their philosophical backgrounds are not quite the same either. Walras was an heir to the tradition of French rationalism whereas Pareto was influenced by the English empiricists. In fact, notwithstanding the rather similar mathematical models, Walras and Pareto strongly disagreed regarding to what general equilibrium is supposed to refer. The relationship of individual choices and the market was also interpreted in radically different ways. Whereas for Walras free and absolute competition is a pure, idealized mechanism that logically comes before the actual individual actions, Pareto takes the individual actions as his starting point and sets them in the context of perfect competition as a market form. There are hints of this change of approach beginning with Pareto's *Cours d'Économie politique professé à l'Université de Lausanne* (1896–1897). However, it was in the *Manuale di Economia politica con una introduzione alla scienza sociale* (*Manual of political economy, with an introduction to social science*, 1906) that Pareto set out the foundation of the modern theory of rational choice, characterized by an ordinal ordering of preferences.

This was perhaps the last important contribution of the Lausanne School to economic theory. Later, in fact, Pareto turned away from the study of individual logical action (pertaining to economics) and dedicated himself to the study of non-logical actions (the domain of sociology). The few articles written by Pasquale Boninsegni (1869–1939), who succeeded Pareto at Lausanne and taught at the University until 1939, did not supply theoretical advances comparable to his predecessors' achievements.

The School of Lausanne is important not only for its theoretical contributions, but also for its attempt to couch them in mathematical form, or at any rate for having interpreted economic mechanisms by means of mathematical procedures. Walras and Pareto paved the way for the mathematization of economics, and accordingly the School is often referred to as the Mathematical school.

This feature attracted the attention of some renowned mathematicians, beginning with those participating in Karl Menger's Vienna seminar in the 1930s and later with some at the Cowles Commission for Research in Economics in Chicago.

These new contributors shifted the focus of research toward the formal aspects of the general equilibrium approach, in particular the issues of existence, uniqueness, and stability of equilibrium, leaving the heuristic aspects aside. The existence and uniqueness of a general equilibrium solution were established in the 1950s. The issue of its stability, however, has not yet been solved, and there are indications that it will remain unsettled. In other words, one can prove that under some carefully chosen assumptions in a perfectly competitive world individual choices are mutually compatible; but it is highly unlikely that such coordination actually takes place.

SEE ALSO *Competition; Economics; Equilibrium in Economics; General Equilibrium; Marginalism; Mathematical Economics; Neocolonialism; Ordinality; Pareto, Vilfredo; Rational Choice Theory; Utility Function; Walras, Léon*

BIBLIOGRAPHY

Busino, Giovanni, and Pascal Bridel. 1987. *L'école de Lausanne de Léon Walras à Pasquale Boninsegni.* Lausanne, Switzerland: Université de Lausanne.

Ingrao, Bruna, and Giorgio Israel. 1990. *La mano invisibile. L'equilibrio economico nella storia della scienza* [The Invisible Hand: Economic Equilibrium in the History of Science]. Trans. Ian McGilvray. Cambridge, MA: MIT Press.

Roberto Baranzini

LAW

The importance of law is much more easily determined than its definition. Law is perhaps the most conspicuous arena wherein theory and practice meet. Law often acts as a catalyst in society, introducing ideas and solutions that might not otherwise take hold. Law can also act as a barrier to social progress and justice. The civil rights legislation of the 1960s, constructed in part to end desegregation in the U.S. South, is an example of law as a catalyst. The very laws overturned by the civil rights legislation illustrate how law can impede social change. Law also reacts to cultural and moral developments and can be understood as responding to a new social consensus or understanding. In this sense the same civil rights legislation that acted as a catalyst in one region of the United States can be said to have simultaneously reflected a growing national consensus; in this case, a national judgment that racial segregation in public schools was a gross violation of American ideals.

But if law, and the study of law, is important because of its obvious connection to social problems and social change, what exactly is it? For a straightforward definition one need only consult *Black's Law Dictionary,* which describes law as "a rule of civil conduct prescribed by the supreme power in a state," or more fully, a law is a "general rule of human action, taking cognizance only of external acts, enforced by a determinate authority, which authority is human, and among human authorities is that which is paramount in a political society."

These definitions are helpful in identifying some important features of the law and legal systems. Not surprisingly, however, such definitions cannot entirely capture other salient features of what is meant by the term *law.* A more comprehensive approach to the question of what law is involves taking a closer look at some of the most important components of law. Finally, some of the different types of law must be examined, as well as methods of approaching the study of law.

ELEMENTS OF THE LAW

In what remains one of the most elegant and insightful investigations into the nature of law, the English scholar H. L. A. Hart opens his 1961 book *The Concept of Law* by noting that law is a unique discipline. Chemists, professors of French literature, and medical doctors do not expend a great deal of intellectual energy on the question of what comprises chemistry, French literature, or medicine. Yet scholars who study law, also known in this context as *jurisprudence* or *philosophy of law*, have created a voluminous literature dedicated to the question of the essence of law.

This seems rather odd, given that most of us would have no problem identifying examples of "the law." Hart describes five features that we would expect to find in a legal system ([1961] 1994, p. 3). First, there are laws mandating some actions (e.g., wearing a seatbelt in a car) while prohibiting others (e.g., driving the car above a certain speed limit). If citizens run afoul of such laws, and are convicted as such, there are prescribed punishments. Second, there are rules that require citizens to repay those whom they have injured in some way. Third, there are laws that allow citizens to create legally recognized relationships that did not exist before; for example, marriage and contract laws. Fourth, there are courts created by law for the express purpose of determining when and how laws have been broken and what recompense is warranted. Finally, there is a special category of law that concerns how new laws are created. Article 1 of the U.S. Constitution is an example of this sort of law, as it specifies how Congress as the legislative branch can create new law.

But note that these bare minimum characteristics describe a *legal system*, not necessarily the *law* itself. How might one understand the difference? Although there is some conceptual overlap between the two terms and they are often used interchangeably, generally, legal systems are concrete attempts to instantiate laws within a given political community. Some examples include the U.S. legal system, the British legal system, and the Chinese legal system. Social scientists can describe various legal systems with more precision than they can the more ambiguous concept of law itself. A legal system can be explained by reference to its constitution, legal traditions, and the actual practices of a government; a flow chart can show the defining governing bodies, powers, checks, and legal rights and responsibilities. However, defining and understanding various legal systems does not do away with the need to understand law as conceptually distinct from the various legal systems that attempt to instantiate and embody different understandings of law. One need only consider, as Hart notes, that the very constitutional conventions that establish modern legal systems have something to do with law, yet cannot themselves be understood as identical with the legal systems they create. Legal systems, however they may differ from nation to nation, are attempts to instantiate law.

What, then, is the purpose of law? Law exists to secure social and public goods, which include such important political priorities as order, justice, equality, and liberty. In short, and paraphrasing legal scholar Ronald Dworkin's introduction to his influential 1986 tome *Law's Empire*, we "live in and by the law," pursuing our goals and relationships, our identities and our livelihoods, within the framework created and maintained by a system of laws.

But this does not capture all the essential elements of what law is or how law works in society. A system of law has by definition at least an element of coercion. Laws that proscribe or enjoin behaviors have attached to them penalties that must be enforced by some level of government. As Hart's example of a marriage law illustrates, not every law has a punitive or coercive element to it, but given the impossibility of voluntary and unanimous adherence to laws, coercion and punishment are necessary components of a legal system.

This notion of coercion leads naturally to the questions of authority and legitimacy and their relation to a society's laws. By what authority are laws made, and who has the right to enforce them? One answer to this question is based purely on power: Whoever can impose laws and enforce them has authority. But this answer collapses any understanding of what is lawful into a mere description of who holds power. It undercuts a basic intuition that law serves a normative purpose and can be imposed by a legitimate governing body. Most liberal constitutional democracies, at a procedural minimum, understand a legitimate governing body to be one that enjoys the consent of those governed by its laws and is ultimately accountable for its representation of its citizens through fair and regular elections.

Legitimacy itself is best understood as a normative or moral concept, and it highlights the link between law and morality. Scholars differ as to exactly how morality and law are related, and as to how morality should inform descriptions and theorizing about law, but there is some general agreement that describing law accurately entails some measure of understanding of what actors in the legal arena aim to do. Thus one is brought back to the social goals mentioned previously: justice, order, freedom, and the like. These are inherently normative concepts, the realization of which can be understood as making society somehow better. Traffic laws, for example, aim at providing an orderly and safe means of transportation. This in turn protects the value one's society places on life, commerce, free movement, and so on. To be sure, there are often tensions between social goods, such as liberty and security, and laws are often inefficient means of promoting or securing such goods (indeed, laws themselves can be instruments of injustice). Moreover, the content of morality and law are not identical. Many citizens might consider a given behavior, for example gossiping, to be immoral without thinking that it should also be illegal. Nevertheless, there does seem to be a connection between law, its social function, and morality. It is difficult to persuasively describe what law is without making at least some reference to a society's understanding of what law ought to be.

TYPES OF LAW

Legal emphases and specialties have proliferated to the point where categorizing all the different types of law is a Herculean task. In addition to traditional subject areas such as contract law, torts, criminal law, and constitutional law, prospective lawyers, social scientists, and interested laypersons can expect to find new avenues of research and study in environmental law, election law, intellectual property law, Internet law, and law pertaining to the rights of indigenous peoples, to name just a few. With that in mind, a few words are in order about some of the central areas of law: constitutional law, criminal law, and torts.

Constitutional Law A constitution acts as the framing document of a given political entity. Often, constitutions will include an aspirational preamble, a declaration or bill of rights, explicit means whereby the constitution may be amended, and the basic framework of the government's bodies in their executive, legislative, or judicial functions. Constitutions vary a great deal, not only in their allotment of political responsibility but also in their means of interpretation. In the British parliamentary system the executive and legislative functions are both found in Parliament, whereas the U.S. Constitution places legisla-

tive duties with Congress and executive duties with the president. In some European nations a court must review the constitutionality of every piece of legislation; in the United States the Supreme Court does not review the constitutionality of a law unless a citizen or state pursues the issue through the lower courts.

Constitutional law, then, is the practice of law that concerns itself both with applying constitutional norms to contemporary issues and with arguments about the constitution itself. An example of the former is found in deciding how to apply constitutional provisions to new technologies or developments. For example, the framers of the U.S. Constitution forbade "unreasonable search and seizure" but could not have anticipated how to apply this norm to telephone technology and wiretapping. Constitutional law is also the purview of those who might want to change the constitution itself.

Criminal Law One of the major areas addressed by constitutional law is criminal law. Criminal law addresses wrongs that are public in nature. District attorneys prosecute crimes in the name of the people of their particular state, province, or city. This is because some wrongs are seen as injuring not only the individual victim, but also the wider public. Criminal law includes prohibited and required actions as well as the safeguards in place to ensure fair trials and sentencing. Obviously this area is most closely identified with the coercive element of law.

Torts Not all wrongs committed between citizens are considered public wrongs that would be tried in a criminal court. These other wrongs are called *torts*, or civil wrongs, and these sorts of cases are what is commonly meant when lawsuits are filed between citizens. One of the chief differences between civil and criminal trials is that in a civil trial the state acts as a facilitator in the attempt to resolve the conflict, whereas in a criminal trial the state, in its executive function, is itself a party in the dispute. Another key difference is that damages in a civil trial are usually monetary; in a criminal trial prison time in addition to monetary fines is a frequent punishment. Occasionally the same event can result in both a criminal and civil trial. One famous example of this is the 1994 murder of Ron Goldman and Nicole Brown Simpson. O. J. Simpson was found not guilty in the criminal case brought against him by the state of California in 1995, but the parents of Ron Goldman sued successfully for damages in civil court in 1997.

TWO METHODOLOGICAL AIDS

The topic of law can certainly seem overwhelming given the innumerable manifestations of law, debates over its essence and application, and differing social science approaches in how to describe law and its relation to politics and society. There are two methodological aids that may be helpful for anyone interested in pursuing the study of law regardless of discipline (i.e., law school, sociology of law, philosophy of law).

The Central Case The "central case" method is useful for trying to determine what counts as law or a legal system, given that such descriptions are not always a clear matter of either-or categorization. For example, international law courts have many of the salient features of a legal system save one, coercion. There is as yet no authority superior to a nation-state to enforce international law. If coercion is a necessary feature of a legal system, should international law be categorized as law, or something else? The legal philosopher John Finnis in his 1981 book *Natural Law and Natural Rights* builds on insights from the ancient Greek philosopher Aristotle and contemporary legal philosopher Joseph Raz in presenting the central case as a useful tool (pp. 9–16).

What the central case method allows one to do is articulate several key elements of a legal system and thus identify an authoritative definition of law without having to then dismiss every example that does not exhibit every single key element, or does not exhibit them to the same degree. For example, one might describe the central case of constitutional government as being one that includes the rule of law, regular and fair elections, separation of powers, and an independent judiciary. A political scientist working on comparative legal systems can identify nations whose legal systems fulfill these criteria, as well as nations that are missing one of these elements (e.g., an independent judiciary). We might describe such a nation's legal system as being a somewhat watered-down version of the central case. The central case method is a useful tool that allows observers to describe legal and social phenomena with enough flexibility to allow for real-world conditions that are not always amenable to orderly categorizations.

The Internal Point of View Another of H. L. A. Hart's contributions to the study of law is the internal point of view (Hart [1961] 1994, pp. 89–91). The social scientist or observer who utilizes the internal point of view counts as worthwhile knowledge the self-understanding of the actors in any given system or social group. Consider for example U.S. Supreme Court Justice Oliver Wendell Holmes's famous definition of law in his 1897 "The Path of the Law" address, that law is the "prophecies of what the courts will do in fact" (1920, p. 173). Whatever merit this view of law might have, it does not take into account what judges and lawmakers understand themselves to be doing. Legislators who pass laws, and judges who interpret them, understand themselves to be doing more than merely guessing how judges will rule on various situations

in the future. Hart's point is not that one need adopt the viewpoint of the judge, or anyone else, as one's own. Rather, his argument is that one cannot accurately describe social phenomena without taking the internal view into account, precisely because those internal views are themselves part of the social phenomena and they help explain actions taken by legal actors in the system.

When faced with any study or explanation of legal behavior or phenomena, the notion of the internal point of view is helpful. Does a particular study of why judges decide cases the way they do take into account how judges understand their own role? If not, do the authors offer a persuasive explanation for their methodological choices? If nothing else, understanding Hart's endorsement of taking into account the internal point of view encourages the student of law and legal phenomena to be aware of important questions regarding the objectivity and accuracy of legal theorists and social scientists.

SEE ALSO *Authority; Crime and Criminology; Government; Judiciary; Jurisprudence; Justice; Legal Systems; Litigation, Social Science Role in; Regulation; State, The*

BIBLIOGRAPHY

Barber, Soterios A., Walter F. Murphy, James E. Fleming, and Stephen Macedo, eds. 2003. *American Constitutional Interpretation.* 3rd ed. New York: Foundation Press.

Dworkin, Ronald. 1986. *Law's Empire.* Cambridge, MA: Harvard University Press.

Finnis, John. 1981. *Natural Law and Natural Rights.* Oxford: Oxford University Press.

Fuller, Lon. 1969. *The Morality of Law.* 2nd ed. New Haven, CT: Yale University Press.

Gardner, Brian A., ed. 2004. *Black's Law Dictionary.* 8th ed. St. Paul, MN: Thomson West.

Hamilton, Alexander, James Madison, John Jay, et al. 2003. *The Essential Federalist and Anti-Federalist Papers*, ed. David Wootten. Indianapolis, IN: Hackett.

Hart, H. L. A. [1961] 1994. *The Concept of Law.* 2nd ed. Oxford: Oxford University Press.

Holmes, Oliver Wendell. 1920. *Collected Legal Papers.* New York: Harcourt, Brace, and Howe.

Raz, Joseph. 1979. *The Authority of Law: Essays on Law and Morality.* Oxford: Oxford University Press.

Unger, Roberto Mangabeira. 1983. *The Critical Legal Studies Movement.* Cambridge, MA: Harvard University Press.

Micah J. Watson

LAW, ADMINISTRATIVE
SEE *Administrative Law.*

LAW, JOHN
1671–1729

John Law was an outstanding monetary theorist who, unusually for a theorist, was given the opportunity to implement his monetary theory as policy. This he did during the 1716–1720 period through the Indies Company (Compagnie des Indes), which was popularly known as the Mississippi Company. The shares of this company rose from a low of 150 livres in 1717 to a high of over 10,000 in early January 1720, producing in the process Europe's first major stock-market boom. Such was the success of Law's policy in its initial phases that he was made controller-general of finances, a position akin to prime minister of France, at the start of 1720. Fearing that Law's success with the Mississippi Company was regenerating the French economy, the British government authorized the South Sea Company to carry out similar debt-management style operations in 1720, resulting in a considerable boom in share prices in London up to August 1720. The subsequent collapses of both the Mississippi and the South Sea companies in the autumn of 1720 had considerable repercussions in delaying the development of the financial systems of France and, to a lesser extent, Great Britain until well into the nineteenth century. As a result of the failure of his company, Law was excoriated by contemporaries and later by a long line of distinguished economists including Richard Cantillon (1680–1734), Adam Smith (1723–1790), Karl Marx (1818–1883), and Alfred Marshall (1842–1924).

These criticisms were unfair to Law in that he was a man with thoroughly modern conceptions of money and banking. Law had the advantage that he was born the son of an Edinburgh goldsmith in 1671 at a time when goldsmiths were becoming embryonic bankers. His early career did not result in him following this banking gene. Instead, Law became a rake, a gambler, and a philanderer in London in the early 1690s. He killed a rival, Edmund Wilson, in a duel in Bloomsbury in 1694. Arrested for killing Wilson, Law was sentenced to death. However, he escaped from the gallows, most probably assisted by high-ranking members of the government. Law was forced to travel to the Continent. There, using his mathematical knowledge, he made a fortune at the gambling tables. He also became highly interested in the banking systems that he observed in Italy and Holland. Law's new interest in banking encouraged him to send proposals to the English and Scottish authorities in 1704 and 1705.

Law outlined his monetary theory in two major works: *John Law's Essay on a Land Bank*, written around 1704 but not published until 1994, and *Money and Trade Considered* (1705). In the former work, Law became the first economist to introduce the term *demand* in its proper economic sense into English. He then introduced the concept of the demand for money, and showed how inflation could arise when the demand for money was out of line with the supply of money. These were extraordinary achievements for someone writing in the first decade of the eighteenth century. In *Money and Trade*, he attempted to show the real role of money in the economy, contending that an increase in the money supply would generate increases in economic activity when there were unutilized resources in the economy, as was the case in Scotland in 1705. Law presented a rudimentary, circular flow-of-income model of the economy, the money-in-advance requirement, and the law of one price.

Law was provided with the opportunity to implement his monetary theories in France after the death of Louis XIV in 1715. In 1716 Law created the General Bank, and followed this a year later with the establishment of the Company of the West, which became the Mississippi Company. The General Bank, later transformed into the Royal Bank, attempted to solve France's monetary crisis through the issue of banknotes, while the Mississippi Company addressed the problems of debt management and the development of colonial trade, particularly that of North America, where the Mississippi Company claimed ownership of all the lands between the British holdings in the Carolinas and those of the Spanish in Texas. In theory, this meant that the company had claims to half of the current contiguous United States. Law hoped that by swapping the equity of the Mississippi Company for government debt, he could greatly reduce France's debt problem. Initially, the system worked, and people flocked to Paris to invest in the company. However, Law had created a financial circuit that was out of line with the real economy. When he attempted to address this problem in May 1720 by reducing the value of shares and paper money, confidence in the system was lost, and by December 1720 he was forced to flee from France. He was nearly brought back to France in 1723, at the invitation of the regent, Philippe (1674–1723), duke of Orléans. However, the latter's sudden death stopped that possibility. Law died in Venice in 1729.

Law believed that money was the value *by which* goods are exchanged and not the value *for which* goods are exchanged. This placed him on the outside of most economic theory of his time, because he was asserting that money did not need to be intrinsically valuable. He wanted to rid the monetary system of the use of gold and silver, and replace these metals with paper money and bank credit. For a short period in France, he showed that this was possible, but it would take another 250 years before the final link with the gold standard was broken by the decision of the United States to refuse to guarantee the price of the dollar in terms of gold.

SEE ALSO *Bubbles; Demand; Economic Crises; Gold Standard; Mercantilism; Monetary Theory; Money, Demand for; Quantity Theory of Money*

BIBLIOGRAPHY

PRIMARY WORKS

Law, John. 1705. *Money and Trade Consider'd, with a Proposal for Supplying the Nation with Money.* Edinburgh: Andrew Anderson.

Law, John. [1934] 1980. *John Law: Oeuvres complètes.* Ed. Paul Harsin. Paris: Vaduz.

Law, John. 1994. *John Law's "Essay on a Land Bank."* Ed. Antoin E. Murphy. Dublin: Aeon.

SECONDARY WORKS

Du Tot, Nicolas. 2000. *Histoire du système de John Law (1716–1720).* Ed. Antoin E. Murphy. Paris: INED.

Faure, Edgar. 1977. *La banqueroute de law.* Paris: Gallimard.

Hamilton, Earl J. 1967. John Law of Lauriston: Banker, Gamester, Merchant, Chief? *American Economic Review* 37: 273–282.

Hamilton, Earl J. 1968. John Law. In *International Encyclopedia of the Social Sciences.* Vol. 9. New York: Macmillan.

Murphy, Antoin E. 1986. *Richard Cantillon: Entrepreneur and Economist.* Oxford: Clarendon.

Murphy, Antoin E. 1997. *John Law: Economic Theorist and Policy-Maker.* Oxford: Clarendon.

Antoin E. Murphy

LAW AND ECONOMICS

Since the 1970s, a new approach to the analysis of law has developed. Known as *law and economics*, its focus is on identifying the effects of legal rules. Law and economics addresses questions like these: What is the effect on the number of automobile accidents of legal rules that hold negligent drivers responsible for harms that they cause? What is the influence on the amount of pollution of laws that penalize firms for releasing harmful wastes into the environment? Does the death penalty reduce the number of murders, and if so, by how much? In seeking to answer such questions, economic analysts generally assume that individuals and firms want to avoid legal sanctions, and the analysts often use data and statistics to verify their theoretical predictions.

Despite its name, the law and economics approach is not necessarily concerned with matters of money or markets. Determining the effects of the death penalty, for example, involves, among other things, consideration of whether an incensed individual would be deterred from shooting someone by fear of the punishment of execution.

The *economic* aspect of law and economics lies in its emphasis on incentives in predicting behavior. In the field of economics proper, the incentives are to make profits or to find a good price; here the incentives are to avoid legal sanctions.

Because economic analysis of law allows the effects of legal rules to be ascertained, the approach is useful for evaluating and comparing rules with regard to their social desirability. If, for example, it is found that the death penalty fails to deter murders carried out by incensed individuals, then it might be concluded that the death penalty is undesirable as a punishment for such murders.

Economic analysis of law has been controversial, mainly because it is centered on identifying the effects of legal rules rather than on the fairness of the rules, the focal issue of traditional analysis. The economic approach to law can be traced in significant respects to the English philosopher Jeremy Bentham (1789), and its modern pioneers include Ronald Coase (1960), Guido Calabresi (1970), and Richard Posner (1972). Posner is also an exponent of the hypothesis that the legal rules that exist are approximately rational in the sense that the consequences of their use are socially desirable.

This entry will provide two illustrations of the economic approach to the analysis of law and will make comparisons with traditional analysis of law. The first illustration concerns legal liability for harm caused in accidents, such as automobile accidents, oil spills, and construction mishaps like the collapse of a crane. A major effect of legal liability is that it fosters the taking of precautions. For instance, in order to avoid being held liable for harm due to an oil spill, the owner of a supertanker might install better navigation devices or hire more experienced crews. Or consider a numerical example: Suppose that if a person does not take a precaution, it is certain that his activity will cause harm of $100,000, for which he would be held liable. If he takes the precaution, however, he would definitely prevent the harm. The precaution would cost $30,000. Then the person would be induced to spend the $30,000 because it would save him a liability expense of $100,000. Such logic underlies the conclusion that, under many forms of liability, parties will be led to take socially desirable risk-reducing steps, and empirical evidence suggests that the liability system has often substantially reduced harm from accidents.

A number of complications arise in assessing how the threat of liability for accidents affects behavior. One issue involves liability insurance, which covers insured parties if they are held liable for harm. If the owner of a supertanker has liability insurance protecting it against having to pay for harm caused by an oil spill, the owner's reason to invest in navigation devices to prevent spills might be dulled. However, the liability insurer might insist that the owner install such devices. Another complication is that parties who cause harm might themselves suffer harm in accidents, as is true in automobile accidents. In this situation, parties have a strong reason to avoid causing accidents, regardless of the threat of being held liable. Taking such factors into account is necessary to obtain good estimates of the influence of liability on accidents.

Given analysis of the effects of liability in reducing accidents, questions about legal policy can be addressed. For example, would raising the amount that has to be paid for oil spills significantly reduce the number of oil spills? A radical question is whether, in some areas of activity, it is worthwhile using the liability system at all. This question is an important one in view of the high costs of the liability system. It is estimated that for every dollar that an accident victim receives through the liability system, approximately one additional dollar is spent on lawyers, making the liability system extremely expensive for society to employ. For that reason, economic analysis suggests that, unless the liability system substantially reduces the number of some type of accident, the system may not be worthwhile for that type of accident. Consider automobile accidents. Liability may not much reduce the number of automobile accidents, since the fear of being injured in an accident (or of being arrested for drunk driving) may already provide most drivers with a sufficient motive to drive with reasonable care. Hence, it might be advantageous for society to do away with the liability system for automobile accidents (something that has largely been done in a number of American states).

The foregoing economic analysis of legal liability for accidents may be contrasted with traditional legal analysis of the topic. Traditional analysis stresses the perceived fairness of liability, and notably, the view that an individual who wrongly injures another ought to compensate the victim for his losses. Under traditional analysis, liability is often seen as desirable *without* real regard to the degree to which it reduces the number of accidents or the costs of its use (or to the ability of accident victims to obtain compensation through their insurance policies). At the same time, economic analysts have generally not considered notions of the fairness of liability, although this issue is now beginning to receive some attention from them.

The second illustration of the economic approach to the analysis of law relates to a specific legal doctrine. When a person is making a contract, the law may impose on the person an obligation to disclose material information to the other party to the contract. For example, if a person is selling a home with a leaky basement, the person might be required to disclose this fact to the buyer. Or if an oil company is purchasing land and believes oil is likely to be found there, the company might have a duty to disclose this information to the seller.

Under the economic approach to law, emphasis is given to ascertaining the effects of a disclosure obligation. In the case of leaky basements, a principal effect of a disclosure obligation is that buyers will know about problems and will be able to take appropriate remedial steps, such as not storing valuables in the basement. Hence, a disclosure obligation for such problems as leaky basements may be socially desirable. However, the case of oil and land is different. If oil companies must reveal their knowledge about the high oil-bearing potential of land, they will have to pay significantly higher amounts to purchase land with promising potential. This will tend to reduce the willingness of oil companies to make investments, such as in geological surveys, to locate land with good oil-bearing potential. (Note that this issue of acquisition of information is not relevant in the case of leaky basements—homeowners will automatically learn about leaks, just because they live in their homes.) Therefore, it might not be desirable to obligate buyers to disclose what they know in situations like that of an oil company purchasing land (and, in fact, the law sometimes does not impose an obligation to disclose in these situations).

Under traditional analysis of law, the consideration of a disclosure obligation has mainly to do with whether it would be seen as unfair or immoral not to disclose information at the time of contracting. From this perspective, it might be thought that both a homeowner with knowledge of a leaky basement and an oil company with knowledge that there is probably valuable oil under a person's land ought to reveal their information, for it would be underhanded, and perhaps akin to a lie, not to do so. Under traditional analysis, there would be no obvious reason to draw a distinction between the two types of cases, and the effects of the disclosure obligation on behavior and outcomes would not be the focus of attention.

These two illustrations show the importance of economic analysis of law, that is, of identifying the effects of legal rules, and the contrast between economic analysis and traditional analysis of law. Over time, economic analysis of law is likely to have a major, if not a revolutionary, influence on the understanding of law and on lawmaking activity.

SEE ALSO *Information, Asymmetric; Insurance; Mechanism Design*

BIBLIOGRAPHY

Bentham, Jeremy. [1789] 1973. An Introduction to the Principles of Morals and Legislation. In *The Utilitarians*, 5–398. Garden City, NY: Anchor.

Calabresi, Guido. 1970. *The Costs of Accidents: A Legal and Economic Analysis.* New Haven, CT: Yale University Press.

Coase, Ronald. 1960. The Problem of Social Cost. *Journal of Law and Economics* 3: 1–44.

Posner, Richard A. [1972] 2003. *Economic Analysis of Law.* Boston: Little, Brown. 6th ed. New York: Aspen.

Shavell, Steven. 2004. *Foundations of Economic Analysis of Law.* Cambridge, MA: Harvard University Press.

Steven Shavell

LAW AND ORDER

The term *law and order* refers to a prominent theme of Richard Nixon's (1913–1994) successful 1968 campaign for the American presidency. Law and order became a potent campaign symbol for Nixon, and related themes have sometimes surfaced in later Republican presidential campaigns—especially in 1972 and 1988. The term *law and order* is a political symbol capturing public anxieties about civil unrest, urban riots, black militant groups (which, some charged, fomented violence), and rising crime rates. Later events, such as the violence in the Boston area in response to court-ordered busing, widely publicized crime sprees like the Son of Sam murders in New York City, and continued rising crime rates, stoked fears of societal breakdown during the 1970s and gave law-and-order appeals additional resonance. These developments, sometimes connected with subtle racial appeals, contributed to the erosion of the Democratic Party's dominant position in American politics after 1968.

1962 TO 1965: VIOLENT RESISTANCE TO CIVIL RIGHTS

After a period of relative domestic tranquility in the 1950s, the 1960s came as a rude shock to many Americans. Between 1961 and 1964, violent actions by southern whites bent on defending racial segregation became commonplace. Demonstrators at sit-ins and freedom riders, black and white, faced actual or threatened violence and mass arrests on fabricated charges. More violence erupted as federal officials attempted to carry out court-ordered desegregation. When black student James Meredith sought to enroll at (and integrate) the University of Mississippi, thousands of segregationists rioted, resulting in two deaths and forcing President John F. Kennedy (1917–1963) to mobilize thousands of troops to restore order.

As the civil rights movement continued, it was met with more violence. Police in Birmingham, Alabama, deployed dogs and high-pressure water cannons against unarmed civil rights demonstrators in 1963. The murders of National Association for the Advancement of Colored People (NAACP) leader Medgar Evers in Jackson, Mississippi, in 1963 and of three civil rights workers near Philadelphia, Mississippi, in 1964 fed fears of mounting social unrest. A 1963 bombing of a Birmingham black church killed four little girls, and Alabama state troopers attacked unarmed voting-rights marchers with dogs and electric cattle prods in March 1965. These cumulative shocks to the national consciousness were amplified by the 1963 assassination of President Kennedy in Dallas, Texas.

1965 TO 1970: BLACK MILITANT GROUPS AND URBAN UNREST

In response to white violence against civil rights activists, some black leaders adopted increasingly belligerent rhetoric. The rise of black radicalism was personified in militants like Stokely Carmichael (1941–1998) and H. Rap Brown. As political scientists Donald Kinder and Lynn Sanders noted, the new rhetoric frightened many whites. There was "less talk of nonviolence and more of self-defense; less yearning for integration and more for solidarity and black nationalism; 'We Shall Overcome' was replaced by Black Power and 'burn, baby, burn'" (1996, p. 103). The image of neatly-dressed blacks pummeled by vicious white violence faded, replaced by images of blacks rampaging through city streets, torching cars and buildings and looting stores. The initial trigger for the changing imagery was the August 1965 Watts riot in Los Angeles. As Kinder and Sanders described the Watts riot:

> The violence raged unchecked for three days, and three days longer in sporadic eruptions. Blacks looted stores, set fires, burned cars, and shot at policemen and firemen. Before the violence was halted, 14,000 National Guard troops, 1,000 police officers and 700 sheriff's deputies were pressed into service.... In the end, 1,000 buildings were damaged, burned, looted or completely destroyed; almost 4,000 people were arrested; more than 1,000 were injured seriously enough to require medical treatment; and 34 were dead, all but three of them black. (Kinder and Sanders 1996, p. 103)

Watts was only the beginning, as 1966, 1967, and 1968 each brought more unrest. In 1967, 250 serious uprisings occurred, including the Detroit riots, which killed forty-three people. More disturbances erupted in multiple cities after the assassination of Martin Luther King Jr. in April 1968. As Kinder and Sanders observe:

> For one long, hot summer after another, Americans watched what appeared to be the coming apart of their own country. On the front page of their morning newspapers and on their television screens in the evening appeared dramatic and frightening pictures of devastation and ruin: cities on fire, mobs of blacks looting stores and hurling rocks at police, tanks rumbling down the avenues of American cities.... Discussion of the "race

problem" in America ... centered on the threat that inner-city blacks posed to social order and public safety. (Kinder and Sanders 1996, p. 103)

In 1968 the Kerner Commission released a report on the civil disturbances, warning that the United States was "moving toward two societies, one black, one white—separate and unequal." The urban violence and Kerner Commission report created an opening for Republicans to pounce on the law-and-order theme. Republican presidential candidate Richard Nixon blasted the report for "blaming everybody for the riots except the perpetrators of violence," promising "retaliation against the perpetrators" that would be "swift and sure." As noted by journalists Thomas Edsall and Mary Edsall, Nixon's running mate, hard-line Maryland governor Spiro Agnew (1918–1996), summoned black leaders in Baltimore to a stormy meeting where he accused them of cowardice for refusing to renounce black militant leaders like Stokely Carmichael and H. Rap Brown. Speaking of the violence in Baltimore after the King assassination, Agnew charged: "The looting and rioting which has engulfed our city during the past several days did not occur by chance. It is no mere coincidence that a national disciple of violence, Mr. Stokely Carmichael, was observed meeting with local black power advocates and known criminals in Baltimore three days before the riots began" (quoted in Edsall and Edsall 1991, p. 85).

The 1968 Democratic national convention met in Chicago following the June 1968 assassination of Democratic presidential candidate Robert Kennedy. Chaotic scenes of police beating demonstrators in Chicago's streets and parks echoed the tumult within the convention hall, as party delegates splintered over the Vietnam War (1957–1975). By 1965 almost all American homes had televisions, bringing searing images of one dramatic (and sometimes horrifying) event after another into the public consciousness. The racial subtext to much of the unrest of the 1960s is unmistakable. As Kinder and Sanders note:

> The riots opened up a huge racial rift. Fear and revulsion against the violence were widespread among both white and black Americans, but whites were much more likely to condemn those who participated in the riots and more eager for the police and National Guard to retaliate against them. Where blacks saw the riots as expressions of legitimate grievances, whites were inclined to explain them as eruptions of black hatred and senseless criminality.... To many white Americans, then, the civil disorders of the 1960s amounted to an appalling collective mugging. (Kinder and Sanders 1996, p. 104).

Liberals, then, faced the unenviable task of explaining why, after leading the fight to pass major civil rights laws, blacks appeared to be responding not with gratitude, but with annual explosions of violence, looting, and destruction.

As political analyst James Sundquist observes, the potency of law-and-order themes was evident as early as 1966, when Ronald Reagan (1911–2004) easily won the governorship of California after promising to "get tough" on welfare, crime, riots, and student unrest. In October 1966, the Republican Coordinating Committee charged that officials in the Lyndon B. Johnson (1908–1973) administration had "condoned and encouraged disregard for law and order." In an August 29, 1967, press conference, House Republican leader Gerald R. Ford (1913–2006) proclaimed:

> The war at home—the war against crime—is being lost. The Administration appears to be in full retreat. The homes and the streets of America are no longer safe for our people. This is a frightful situation.... The Republicans in Congress *demand* that the Administration take the action required to protect our people in their homes, on the streets, at their jobs.... There can be no further Administration excuse for indecision, delay or evasion. When a Rap Brown and a Stokely Carmichael are allowed to run loose, to threaten law-abiding Americans with injury and death, it's time to slam the door on them and any like them—and slam it hard! (quoted in Sundquist 1983, p. 385)

As Sundquist notes, Ford's statement illustrates that "by 1967, the Republicans were pulling out all the stops" (on the law and order issue). In 1968 "the issue was propelled by so many events that it hardly needed partisan exploitation" (1983, p. 385).

The cumulative effect of civil-rights violence, assassinations, urban rioting and unrest, the tumult at the 1968 Democratic convention, and the comparatively peaceful 1968 Republican convention in Miami was to create a climate unmistakably ripe for Republican law-and-order appeals. Many Americans were shell-shocked by the rising crime rates and domestic violence of the 1960s, amplified by the increasingly controversial Vietnam War, with antiwar demonstrators burning their draft cards and soldiers coming home, some in body bags, others maimed. In May 1970, Ohio National Guardsmen opened fire on antiwar protesters at Kent State University, killing four students and injuring nine. Many Americans sympathized more with the shooting guardsmen than with the dead students—a sentiment captured in Neil Young's protest song "Ohio" (written immediately after the Kent State shootings and performed by Crosby, Stills, Nash, and Young).

The song characterized conservative sentiment as celebrating the shootings: "should've been done long ago."

LAW AND ORDER IN THE 1968 CAMPAIGN

The political context in 1968 was clearly ripe for a campaign centering on law and order. The Nixon campaign eagerly seized the opening. Nixon's selection of Agnew as his running mate sent an unmistakable signal that if elected president he would "crack down" hard on rioters, draft protesters, and others perceived as contributing to or fomenting social and urban unrest. At the 1968 Republican convention, Nixon began his acceptance speech: "As we look at America, we see cities enveloped in smoke and flame. We hear sirens in the night." Nixon's speech continued by attacking Democratic-sponsored government programs for the unemployed, the poor, and cities as "reaping an ugly harvest of frustration, violence, and failure across the land." Nixon's campaign advertisements, too, reinforced the law-and-order theme. As Kinder and Sanders note:

> Nixon's television advertisements played upon Americans' fear of crime. While voiceovers pointed to sharp increases in violent crime and blamed the Democrats, the television viewer witnessed scenes of riots and buildings in flames, montages of urban decay, a lonely policeman on the beat, a mugging, crowds taunting the police, faces of anxious and perplexed Americans, and a woman walking alone on a deserted city street as darkness fell. (Kinder and Sanders 1996, p. 226)

After Nixon's election victory in 1968, Agnew, as vice president, demonstrated a slashing, attack-dog speaking style that further expanded on law-and-order themes. As noted by Sundquist, Agnew toured the country to support Republican candidates, attacking and denouncing "permissivists," "avowed anarchists and communists," "misfits," the "garbage" of society, "thieves, traitors and perverts," and "radical liberals" (1983, p. 387). This rhetoric is anything but subtle in positioning the Republican Party as representing the masses of "middle America" that abide by society's rules, are horrified by social violence, and support harsh crackdowns against it—a group that later would be targeted by the appeal of the 1972 Nixon campaign to the "silent majority." By implication, Agnew sought to position Democrats as representing less savory elements: antiwar radicals, draft-card burners, urban rioters, black militants, hippies, and practitioners of recreational drug use and sexual activity. Agnew's language, then, expanded the law-and-order theme to imply that Democrats sympathized not only with those who encouraged and practiced crime and violence (i.e., black militants, urban rioters, and draft-card burners), but also with

groups that encouraged a more general social permissiveness and breakdown of traditional moral values—that is, permissivists, radical liberals, and perverts. These themes foreshadowed Nixon's 1972 reelection campaign, which would successfully brand Democratic presidential candidate George McGovern as the candidate of "acid, amnesty, and abortion."

1972 TO 2007: LAW-AND-ORDER THEMES RECYCLED

Since 1972, explicit law-and-order themes have become less central issues in most campaigns. However, a major exception was the 1988 presidential campaign, when George H. W. Bush portrayed Democratic candidate Michael Dukakis as "soft" on violent crime in a campaign that critics charged appealed to racial prejudices. The campaign featured the story of William "Willie" Horton, a black convict who, released from prison on a weekend furlough (a controversial program supported by Massachusetts governor Dukakis), escaped to Maryland, where he attacked a couple in their home. Republican strategists openly exploited the Horton case. One television advertisement, sponsored by an independent pro-Bush group, showed a sinister and unruly-looking Horton in a mug shot, while an announcer recounted Horton's crimes, emphasized by the words *kidnapping, raping,* and *stabbing* appearing in large print on the screen. Republican strategist Lee Atwater (1951–1991) promised that "by the time this election is over, Willie Horton will be a household name." Later, he said "the Horton case is one of those gut issues that are value issues, particularly in the South, and if we hammer at these over and over, we are going to win." As Kinder and Sanders note, Atwater joked to a Republican gathering, "There is a story about Willie Horton, who, for all I know may end up being Dukakis' running mate.... Maybe [Dukakis] will put this Willie Horton on the ticket when all is said and done" (1996, p. 255).

The 1988 campaign illustrates the political dangers for Democrats of not responding adequately to Republican efforts to brand them as "soft on crime." Especially in the more conservative South, Democrats have responded by emphasizing crime-fighting credentials and support for the death penalty. Bill Clinton used this formula successfully in his 1992 and 1996 presidential campaigns, and in 2005 Democrat Timothy Kaine won the governorship of Virginia, a conservative state. Kaine successfully fended off Republican attacks on his personal opposition to the death penalty by promising to uphold death sentences handed down by Virginia juries. The law-and-order campaign theme most clearly applies to the 1968 presidential campaign. However, it has spawned similar campaign themes, usually pursued by Republicans eager to portray Democrats as "soft on crime," with varying degrees of success.

LAW AND ORDER AND VIGILANTISM IN AMERICAN LIFE AND FILM

Paradoxically, the appeal of law-and-order themes has potentially contributed to citizen vigilantism at times. American history offers numerous examples of citizens "taking the law into their own hands." White southerners' lynchings of blacks are but one example of vigilante actions defending a social order that is anything but admirable. In 1898, for instance, the majority-black port city of Wilmington, North Carolina, was consumed by a race riot in which an unknown number of blacks (probably dozens) were murdered and hundreds more banished by an armed white mob bent on establishing white supremacy in local and statewide politics. Historian Timothy Tyson described the actions and motives of riot instigators as follows:

> On Nov. 10, 1898, heavily armed columns of white men marched into the black neighborhoods of Wilmington. In the name of white supremacy, this well-ordered mob burned the offices of the local black newspaper, murdered perhaps dozens of black residents—the precise number isn't known—and banished many successful black citizens and their so-called "white nigger" allies. A new social order was born in the blood and the flames, rooted in what *News and Observer* publisher Josephus Daniels, heralded as "permanent good government by the party of the White Man." (Tyson 2006)

Tyson added that the riot "marked the embrace of virulent Jim Crow racism" nationwide. The Red Shirts, a paramilitary arm of the then-white-supremacist Democratic Party, had rampaged across North Carolina before the 1898 election, disrupting black church services and Republican meetings, and attacking blacks, who leaned Republican. These violent, vigilante actions were justified as necessary to preserve a cherished social order, white supremacy, by any means necessary. That their actions were neither lawful nor orderly probably never crossed the minds of either the Red Shirts or the white participants in the Wilmington riot.

Similarly, some anti-immigration activists along the U.S.-Mexican border have launched vigilante efforts to deter would-be undocumented immigrants from crossing from Mexico into the United States. Ranch Rescue is one such group, which styles itself as a defender of U.S. borders and private property rights against what it calls "criminal aliens" and "terrorists" out of a belief that law enforcement is unable or unwilling to act appropriately toward these ends. In 2005 Ranch Rescue founder Casey Nethercutt lost his southern Arizona ranch to satisfy a court judgment levied against him and other Ranch Rescue members for seizing and traumatizing two Mexican immigrants (Pollack 2005). The Wilmington riots and the Ranch Rescue case illustrate behaviors that are probably driven by the conviction that to restore law and order—or a cherished social goal—requires violating law and order at least temporarily.

The vigilantism inherent in the actions of the Wilmington riot instigators and Ranch Rescue members is also reflected in some American films. In movies like the *Death Wish* series starring Charles Bronson (1921–2003) and *The Punisher* (1989 and 2004), vigilantism is celebrated, with a curious and unmistakable implicit message: exacting revenge sometimes requires violating law and order—even abandoning the rule of law altogether. Law and order, then, has morphed from an often-potent political symbol from the 1960s through the 1980s to a notion that some action films celebrate violating—but whose impact in real-world politics is largely blunted.

SEE ALSO *Law; Rule of Law*

BIBLIOGRAPHY

Edsall, Thomas Byrne, and Mary D. Edsall. 1991. *Chain Reaction: The Impact of Race, Rights, and Taxes on American Politics.* New York: Norton.

Kinder, Donald R., and Lynn M. Sanders. 1996. *Divided by Color: Racial Politics and Democratic Ideals.* Chicago: University of Chicago Press.

National Advisory Commission on Civil Disorders. [1968] 1988. *The Kerner Report: The 1968 Report of the National Advisory Commission on Civil Disorders.* New York: Pantheon.

Pollack, Andrew. 2005. Two Illegal Immigrants Win Arizona Ranch in Court. *New York Times,* August 19. http://www.nytimes.com/2005/08/19/national/19ranch.htm.

Sundquist, James L. 1983. *Dynamics of the Party System: Alignment and Realignment of Political Parties in the United States.* Rev. ed. Washington, DC: Brookings Institution.

Tyson, Timothy B. 2006. The Ghosts of 1898: Wilmington's Race Riot and the Rise of White Supremacy. *Raleigh News & Observer,* November 17. http://www.newsobserver.com/1370/story/511596.html.

Fred Slocum

LAW OF LARGE NUMBERS

Classical statistics assumes simple random sampling in which each sample of size *n* yields different values. Thus, the value of any statistic calculated with sample data (for example, the sample mean) varies from sample to sample.

A histogram (graph) of these values provides the sampling distribution of the statistic.

The law of large numbers holds that as n increases, a statistic such as the sample mean ($\bar{X}$) converges to its true mean (μ)—that is, the sampling distribution of the mean collapses on the *population mean*. The *central limit theorem,* on the other hand, states that for many samples of like and sufficiently large n, the histogram of sample means will appear to have a normal bell-shaped distribution. As the sample size n is increased, the distribution of the sample mean becomes normal (central limit theorem), but then degenerates to the population mean (law of large numbers). This process is shown in Figure 1. For an infinite number of samples, each of size $n = 5$, drawn from an exponential distribution with a mean of one, the probability density function (pdf) of $\bar{X}$ is right skewed, but for $n = 30$ the pdf appears more bell-shaped, and for $n = 90$ it is approximately normal. As n gets larger and larger (approaching infinity) the pdf of $\bar{X}$ appears to be a thick line at a mean of one, which illustrates the law of large numbers. Remember, however, that even as n goes to infinity, within two standard deviations of the mean there will continue to be approximately 95 percent of the distribution. It is the standard error of the mean ($\sigma / \sqrt{n}$) that keeps shrinking.

More technically, a distinction is made between the weak law of large numbers and the strong law of large numbers. The *weak law of large numbers* states that if X_1, X_2, X_3, ... is an infinite independent and identically distributed sequence of random variables, then the sample mean

$$\bar{X} = (X_1 + X_2 + X_3 + \ldots + X_{n-1} + X_n) \,/\, n$$

converges in probability to the population mean μ. That is, for any positive small number ε,

$$\lim_{n \to \infty} P(|\bar{X}_n - \mu| < \varepsilon) = 1.$$

The *strong law of large numbers* states that if X_1, X_2, X_3, ... is an infinite sequence of random variables that are independent and identically distributed with $E(|X_i|) = \mu < \infty$, for all i, then

$$P(\lim_{n \to \infty} \bar{X}_n = \mu) = 1.$$

That is, the sample average converges almost surely to the population mean μ.

Students, scientists, and social commentators have been and continue to be befuddled by the law of large numbers versus the central limit theorem. Although the law of large numbers was articulated by Jacob Bernoulli (1654–1705) in the seventeenth century, in the nineteenth century *curve fitting* and the finding of *normality in nature* were popular. It was believed that if the sample was big enough then it would be normal (not understanding that the central limit theorem applies to $\bar{X}$ and not to a single sample of size n). For instance, Adolphe Quetelet (1797–1874), originator of the "average man," made his early reputation by arguing that bigger and bigger samples would yield a bell-shaped curve for the attribute being sampled. He did not make the connection between the mean of one random sample and the distribution of means from all such samples (see Stigler [1986] for this history). By the law of large numbers, the larger the sample size the more the sample will look like the population (the sampling distribution of $\bar{X}$ appears to collapse on μ).

To this day, confusion exists among those who should know the difference between the law of large numbers and the central limit theorem. For example, in his otherwise excellent book, *Against the Gods,* Peter Bernstein wrote:

> Do 70 observations provide enough evidence for us to reach a judgement on whether the behavior of the stock market is a random walk? Probably not. We know that tosses of a die are independent of one another, but our trials of only six throws typically produced results that bore little resemblance to a normal distribution. Only after we increased the number of throws and trials substantially did theory and practice begin to come together. The 280 quarterly observations resemble a normal curve much more closely than do the (70) year-to-year observations. (Bernstein 1996, p. 148)

SEE ALSO *Central Limit Theorem; Classical Statistical Analysis; Random Walk; Risk; Sampling; Statistics*

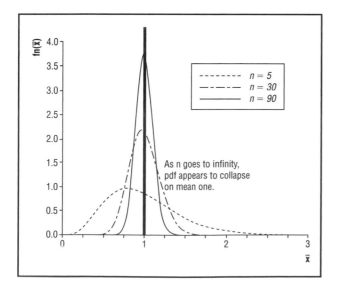

Figure 1: Sample mean pdf. expotential (1) population.

BIBLIOGRAPHY

Bernstein, Peter. 1996. *Against the Gods: The Remarkable Story of Risk.* New York: Wiley.

Stigler, Stephen. 1986. *The History of Statistics: The Measurement of Uncertainty before 1900*. Cambridge, MA: Belknap.

William E. Becker

LAW OF MORTALITY

SEE *Morbidity and Mortality.*

LAW OF ONE PRICE

SEE *Purchasing Power Parity.*

LAY THEORIES

Laypeople, like scientists, develop and use theories to help them understand and respond to their social world. *Lay theories*, then, are the theories people use in their everyday lives. Lay theories are often captured by proverbs such as "the early bird gets the worm" (Protestant work ethic), "you can't teach an old dog new tricks" (entity theory), and "it's never too late to turn over a new leaf" (incremental theory). Such lay theories often reflect the core beliefs of people living in a given culture or environment. Since the 1990s there has been greater recognition that people's perceptions are filtered through and guided by their lay theories and thus there is not one universal way for people to perceive and respond to the same social information.

Researchers—namely cognitive, social, personality, and developmental psychologists—have identified different kinds of lay theories and their far-reaching impact on judgments and behaviors toward the self, individual others, and groups. Lay perceivers can rather easily report their lay theories, agreeing or disagreeing with simple, straightforward sentences reflecting those ideas (e.g., "people who work hard succeed"). Yet people are generally unaware of the tremendous impact that their lay theories have on them and on others, such as guiding decisions on whom to ask out on a date, what career path to choose, whom to vote for for president, and whether to befriend or avoid members of certain groups. As one example, individuals who hold the lay theory that people cannot change their personality, morality, or intelligence (e.g., entity theory) tend to give up in the face of an academic or social failure; often judge a defendant as guilty based on minimal negative information about his or her character; and frequently endorse stereotypes of socially stigmatized groups.

Lay theories are readily used in everyday life in part because they are socially transmitted and shared but also because they are functional. Like scientific theories, lay theories provide understanding, prediction, and a sense of control over one's social world. However, unlike scientific theories, lay theories need not be objective, testable, or true. Lay theories serve people's needs to label their observations as reflecting a correct social reality. Lay theories such as the Protestant work ethic can fulfill important values (e.g., value of hard work). People may use lay theories as well to justify their attitudes and prevailing social norms. For example, the Protestant work ethic is an ingredient in racism toward African Americans at the hands of European Americans in the United States; African Americans are sometimes seen as not conforming to the work ethic (not working hard enough) and thus deserving disadvantage. Some lay theories may serve many cognitive, social, and psychological functions, and other lay theories may serve only one. What is more, some lay theories are more or less useful to certain members of a culture (e.g., relatively advantaged or disadvantaged group members) or more or less useful in certain contexts (e.g., at home or at work).

In summary, lay theories have far-reaching implications for understanding how people work. Lay theories can both drive and justify thought and behavior that impact the self and others.

SEE ALSO *Attitudes; Attribution; Norms; Social Cognition; Social Judgment Theory; Stereotypes*

BIBLIOGRAPHY

Furnham, Adrian. 1988. *Lay Theories: Everyday Understandings of Problems in the Social Sciences*. New York: Pergamon.

Levy, Sheri R., Chi-yue Chiu, and Ying-yi Hong. 2006. Lay Theories and Intergroup Relations. *Group Processes and Intergroup Relations* 9 (1): 5–24.

Sheri R. Levy

LAZARSFELD, PAUL FELIX
1901–1976

The Austrian sociologist Paul Lazarsfeld studied law, social psychology, and mathematics at the University of Vienna under the direction of Ernst Mach, physicist and founding figure in the field of philosophy of science. Lazarsfeld received his PhD in applied mathematics in 1925. In 1929 he founded a research institute for applied social psychology connected with Karl Buhler's research center in Vienna, then moved to the United States on a Rockefeller Foundation grant in 1933. While at Princeton

University directing the Office of Radio Research, Lazarsfeld studied the listening habits of radio audiences, the first of many studies on the media and public opinion. In 1940 he moved to Columbia University in New York to direct the Bureau of Applied Social Research, where he conducted extensive empirical social research and later joined the sociology department. At Columbia University Lazarsfeld collaborated with prominent sociologists such as Robert Staughton Lynd (1892–1970) and Robert K. Merton (1910–2003). Lazarsfeld continued to work at Columbia University until 1970, when he moved to the University of Pittsburgh, where he taught until his death in 1976.

Along with Albert Einstein (1879–1955), Enrico Fermi (1901–1954), Max Horkheimer (1895–1973), Theodor Adorno (1903–1969), and Niels Bohr (1885–1962), Lazarsfeld was part of an intellectual migration of academics from Europe during the early stages of Nazism. Many moved to the United States where they conducted research free from government interference and created a wealth of intellectual activity in U.S. universities.

Lazarsfeld's research in the field of sociology, particularly in the areas of social and applied psychology, used statistics to determine the influence of radio and print media on Americans' voting habits and personal preferences. Concerning himself with the development of empirical social science methods, Lazarsfeld applied his background in mathematics in the field of sociology, conducting independent and corporate-funded research on public opinion, voting, and popular culture. Written contributions to the field of empirical social science and survey research include *The People's Choice* (1944), with Bernard Berelson and Hazel Gaudet, a study of how public opinion was formed prior to elections; *Radio Listening in America* (1948), an analysis of radio listening habits; and *Voting* (1954), with Berelson and William N. McPhee, an inquiry into the determining factors of candidate selection. These publications placed Lazarsfeld's Bureau for Applied Social Research at the forefront of postwar American sociology.

Lazarsfeld is considered a pioneer in the field of media research. His research, both quantitative and qualitative, provided a scientific framework to study media influence on political attitudes. Lazarsfeld's research on radio listeners and the effect of radio listening on public preferences was used by market researchers, pollsters, and political campaigns to better understand the relationship between popular culture and public tastes. One of the first to systematically study the media, Lazarsfeld's research influenced mass communications theory, survey research, public opinion, and polling. In his theory of the two-step flow, Lazarsfeld explained how media information flows from opinion leaders to the larger public. He is also cred-

ited with introducing the concept of agenda setting, which was further developed by a later generation of social theorists. His empirical social analysis was later criticized by C. Wright Mills in *The Sociological Imagination* (1959). Lazarsfeld is credited with educating a generation of sociologists and bringing the academic discipline of sociology into the modern era, incorporating social and applied psychology and mathematics into the field to solve substantive sociological problems.

SEE ALSO *Communication; Lynd, Robert and Helen; Media; Merton, Robert K.; Political Psychology; Political Science; Public Opinion; Radio Talk Shows*

BIBLIOGRAPHY

Berelson, Bernard, Paul F. Lazarsfeld, and William N. McPhee. 1954. *Voting: A Study of Opinion Formation in a Presidential Campaign.* Chicago: University of Chicago Press.

Converse, Jean. 1987. *Survey Research in the U.S.: Roots and Emergence, 1890–1960.* Berkeley: University of California Press.

Katz, Elihu, and Lazarsfeld, Paul F. 1955. *Personal Influence.* New York: Free Press.

Lazarsfeld, Paul F. 1948. *Radio Listening in America.* New York: Prentice-Hall.

Lazarsfeld, Paul F., Bernard Berelson, and Hazel Gaudet. 1944. *The People's Choice.* New York: Duell, Sloan, and Pearce.

Mills, C. Wright. 1959. *The Sociological Imagination.* London: Oxford University Press.

Weimann, Gabriel. 1994. Is There a Two Step Flow of Agenda Setting? *International Journal of Public Opinion* 6 (4): 323–340.

James Freeman

LAZARUS, RICHARD S.
SEE *Coping.*

LEADERS

Leadership is influencing the performance of group members toward the achievement of organizational goals through persuasion, example, direction, control, or oversight. There are two inherent conflicts in the very idea of leadership in a democratic society. The first is embodied in the British statesman and orator Edmund Burke's (1729–1797) distinction between employing one's own best judgment in service of constituents (a trustee), and trying as assiduously as possible to implement the will of the majority, regardless of whether it seems right to the "leader" (a delegate):

> Your representative owes you, not his industry only, but his judgment; and he betrays, instead of serving you, if he sacrifices it to your opinion ("Speech to the Electors of Bristol," November 3, 1774, reprinted in Laski, 1998).

This point is deeper than the indeterminacy of the social choice problem, raising instead a paradox in the nature of leadership itself. There is a distinction, dating back at least to Plato, between *rulers* (members of an elite, born and socialized to rule by virtue of merit), and *leaders* (people chosen by the people from among themselves). If decisions are truly democratic, why does a society need leaders in the first place?

An interesting example of the tension between leading the people and simply implementing their will can be found in the October 1944 diary of British member of Parliament Sir Cuthburt Headlam (1999, entry for 10/12/44): "Never was a party so leaderless as the Conservative party is today." What leader was it that Sir Headlam held in such low esteem? Winston Churchill, perceived by history as one of the great wartime leaders of all time. But in terms of advancing the fortunes of his party, Churchill either did not care or could not be bothered. Who was right: Headlam or history? In voters' minds, Headlam's view was correct. Churchill was unceremoniously dumped from office, with his Conservatives so resoundingly defeated in July 1945 that the opposition Labour Party gained a majority of more than 180 seats.

The second inherent conflict divides transactional leadership and transformational leadership. Transactional leadership is close to Taylorist principles of management and control, focusing on mechanism design and incentive compatibility, assuming that rewards and punishment motivate workers. The successful transactional leader compensates workers in a strict hierarchy in exchange for their service to the collective goal.

Transformational leaders begin with a vision, and persuade subordinates to share that vision. Inspiration, rather than either direction or control, is the objective. Transformational leaders believe that success comes first and last through deep and sustained individual commitment among followers.

These two distinctions suggest the following schematic representation of leadership.

It is useful to consider in more detail two accounts of charismatic leadership that have had a large impact both in the training of leaders and in the academy. The first of these is by the German social theorist Max Weber; the second is the work of contemporary management theorist Bernard Bass.

THEORIES OF CHARISMATIC LEADERSHIP

Weber believed that there are three types of systems in which leadership matters. The first is traditional/feudal; the second is charismatic leadership; and the final type, the highest achievement of leadership in an evolutionary sense, is the legal/rational leader, whose authority is based on expertise, experience, and technical training.

Traditional leadership authority is based on tradition and patriarchy, suppressing conflict but substituting an irrational and capricious order. Government actions arbitrate competition among those seeking favors, income, and other advantages, with leaders personally collecting fees. This system allows for some mobility among the classes, but the actual functions of government are based on loyalty, not merit.

Charismatic authority derives from the exceptional sacrifice, heroism, or exemplary character of the leader. Claims to charismatic authority are bolstered by assertions of destiny, being "chosen" or selected, or other supernatural signs. But pure charismatic leadership does not rely, or even allow, any other administrative or governmental organizations. If an organization relies on charismatic leadership, it may collapse into chaos if the leader dies or leaves, because subordinates act out of personal regard for that individual leader rather than the organization as an abstraction.

Source of authority		
Style of leadership	Delegation	Trusteeship
Transactional	*The committee chair.* Ad hoc style of leadership. Short-term, few resources, limited and group-determined goals. Everybody gets something for participating	*The general.* Military command; extreme hierarchy, harsh punishment, complete authority over subordinates
Transformational	*The quarterback.* Charismatic and inspirational, but focused on needs and wants of subordinates. Teamwork, shared responsibility, focus is as much on transformation of team members themselves as on ultimate goals	*The savior.* Classic true charismatic leader, narcissistic focus on internal vision, willing to sacrifice underlings to achieve that vision

The highest expression of the potential for leadership authority, for Weber, was rational/technical/legal authority. Weber argued that bureaucracy is "the exercise of control on the basis of knowledge" (1947, p. 339). The leader is controlled and disciplined by rules and procedures, and open commitment to these procedures is the entire basis for the leader's authority. The office holder is constrained to impersonal, official obligations and commands, and cannot benefit either directly or indirectly from decisions. In the hierarchy of offices, it is office holders, not persons, who exercise authority. Real leadership requires extensive training and demonstrated expertise and experience. Deference and obedience are owed not to individuals, but to the impersonal order.

Bass accepted many of Weber's claims, but adapted for his own purposes the idea of charismatic rather than legal/rational relations among leaders and subordinates. In his *Leadership and Performance Beyond Expectations* (1985) Bass began with what seems like a paradox, from the perspective of Weberian or Taylorist perspectives on leadership. Why is it that most leaders are able to elicit only competent performance from employees? Why are some leaders able to elicit much more, and to make the workers happier and more fulfilled at the same time?

The explanation Bass offered is that the transactional, contractual approach described by Weber, and the charismatic leader Weber admired but considered anachronistic, could be combined into a new synthesis. Truly successful leadership depends on charisma, and successful organizations must nurture and promote charismatic individuals to leadership positions.

Bass created a taxonomy of personalities in an organization. The mix of personalities on teams, and the profile of the leader, might have as much to do with the success of the team as the abilities of the team and the technical nature of the task. He calls the three personality types self-oriented, task-oriented, and interaction-oriented. Task-oriented personalities are self-sufficient, resourceful, competitive, and motivated by intellectual challenges if they are not distracted. Self-oriented personalities are disagreeable, introverted, and often jealous, but they can be motivated by their desire for personal success and rewards. Interaction-oriented personalities are motivated by contact and interaction with others, and have much lower needs for autonomy or personal rewards.

Bass claimed that charismatic, transformational leaders could have an unexpectedly large impact on nearly any organization, so long as they consciously focused on three things. First, subordinates must be made to feel aware of the importance of their tasks and the importance of performing well. Part of this "importance" rests in expectation of reward, but much of it could simply be expectation of recognition and respect.

Second, Bass argued it was important to make subordinates aware of their needs for personal growth, development, and accomplishment. That is, the specific tasks being worked on today might be less important, both to the individual and the organization, than the impact that task might have on the employee's career. Finally, Bass claimed that transformational leaders must motivate their subordinates to work for the good of the organization rather than exclusively for their own personal gain or benefit. This might be achieved by making subordinates feel they belong, or can depend on each other, in a variety of ways, but the important thing is reconciling collective goals and individual fulfillment.

SEE ALSO *Authority; Leadership*

BIBLIOGRAPHY

Bass, Bernard M. 1985. *Leadership and Performance Beyond Expectations.* New York: Free Press.

Weber, Max. 1947. *The Theory of Social and Economic Organization.* Trans. A. M. Henderson and Talcott Parsons. New York: Free Press.

Michael Munger

LEADERSHIP

The study of leadership is not only a search for understanding the thoughts and actions of leaders, but also an investigation into how to improve the performance and motivation of both individuals and groups. Given the importance of leadership to the success of groups, organizations, or even entire civilizations, there are few more pressing questions than, "What is leadership?" Attempts to answer this question are evident in early discussions of the notion of leaders. Governments, businesses, industries, and private organizations have all turned to behavioral scientists to better understand how organizations work efficiently, how managers can improve workers' performance, how teamwork and commitment can be instilled, and how an environment conducive to change can be structured.

DEFINING LEADERSHIP

The notion of leadership "connotes images of powerful, dynamic individuals who command victorious armies, direct corporate empires from atop gleaming skyscrapers, or shape the course of nations" (Yukl 2002, p. 1). Yet, considerable debate exists among researchers regarding an understanding of who exerts influence, what kind of power or influence is exerted, when and where leadership takes place, and why and how this phenomenon occurs.

As many definitions of leadership exist as do authors who have studied the concept. Conceptions and definitions of *leader* and *leadership* have been reviewed by Carroll Shartle (1956), Bernard Bass (1960), and James Hunt and colleagues (1982), among others. Some of the more recent definitions focus on influence, collective understanding, effectiveness, and facilitation:

- "Leadership appears to be a working relationship among members in a group, in which the leader acquires status through active participation and demonstration of his or her capacity to carry cooperative tasks to completion" (Bass and Stogdill 1990, p. 77).

- "Leadership is a process of giving purpose [meaningful direction] to collective effort, and causing willing effort to be expended to achieve purpose" (Jacobs and Jaques 1990, p. 281).

- "A definition of leadership that would be widely accepted by the majority of theorists and researchers might say that 'leadership is a process of social influence in which one person is able to enlist the aid and support of others in the accomplishment of a common task'" (Chemers 1997, p. 1).

- "Leadership is influencing people—by providing purpose, direction and motivation—while operating to accomplish the mission and improving the organization" (Department of the Army 1999, pp. 1–2).

The common thread in the majority of definitions is that leadership is an active process of one person exerting influence over one or more other persons toward a common goal or objective. However, the similarities end there, and leadership definitions do not always fit into the applications for which they are used. For example, Bernard Bass and Ralph Stogdill's definition of leadership does not fully account for hierarchical structures, and T. Owens Jacobs and Elliot Jaques's definition does not address the interactive nature of leadership between a superior and a subordinate. A more adequate definition of leadership needs to account for both the individual person and the situational context. The definition provided by the U.S. Army is comprehensive and useful. Therefore, this entry also defines leadership as "influencing people—by providing purpose, direction and motivation—while operating to accomplish the mission and improving the organization" (U.S. Army 1999, pp. 1–2).

Having defined leadership, it is necessary to examine assumptions about the topic. Some commentators assume that certain individuals are predisposed to be leaders, while others are not. If the person is the most important predictor of leadership success, then personnel selection matters most. However, other scholars assume that context is most important in developing leaders. If the situational variables are the most influential aspects of leadership success, then the training models employed would seem most important. A review of the historical approaches to leadership will highlight these two divergent approaches.

A REVIEW OF THE HISTORICAL STUDY OF LEADERSHIP

An understanding of the historical literature and the changing philosophies behind leadership studies add meaning and depth to current integrated theories. The concepts examined provide a framework for understanding current models and examining future directions.

Traits and Attributes Theories Few areas of research have had a more controversial history than that on leadership traits and attributes. One question that researchers have tried to answer is "who is exerting the influence?" During the nineteenth and early twentieth centuries, "great man" theories dominated leadership discussions. The great man concept suggested that leaders possessed special traits or characteristics that allowed them to ascend above others and enhanced their ability to be leaders (Hollander and Offermann 1990b). This view is often linked to the nineteenth-century philosopher Thomas Carlyle, who wrote "the history of the world is but the biography of great men" (1841). In short, the attributes of effective leaders were seen as inborn and permanent, and they applied to various circumstances. Later, Francis Galton expounded on this concept in *Hereditary Genius* (1869), where he argued that reputation flows from heredity.

The great man theory led to hundreds of research studies that looked at personality traits, physical characteristics, intelligences, and values to differentiate leaders from followers. In the early 1900s, psychologists developed intelligence testing to measure individual differences in analytic ability. Initial findings that intelligences correlated with leadership led researchers toward searching for additional nonintellective traits that might be predictors of behavioral tendencies (Chemers 1997).

Ralph Stogdill was the first researcher to summarize the results of these studies. He examined 124 studies to determine the characteristic differences between leaders and followers. He came to two major conclusions. First, Stogdill found slightly higher intelligence measures for leaders, as well as positive relationships between leadership and adjustment, extroversion, and dominance. However, Stogdill failed to find traits that were universally associated with leadership and could be reliably used to predict who might be an emerging leader. Stogdill concluded that "a person does not become a leader by virtue of the possession of some combination of traits" (1948, p. 63). Later, Richard Mann (1959) came to the same conclusions that although individuals with certain characteristics were more likely to be successful leaders, leaders were not altogether different from followers. As a result, later researchers erroneously concluded that personal traits and attributes alone could not be used to predict future leadership success.

It was not until the publication of a meta-analysis by Robert Lord, Christy de Vader, and George Alliger (1986) that such traits as intelligence and personality regained favor with leadership researchers. Their article reexamined the relationship between personality traits and leadership perceptions and emergence. In contrast with the conclusions of earlier nonquantitative literature reviews on traits and leadership, Lord and his colleagues utilized the literature investigated by Mann in his 1959 review and subsequent relevant studies and found that prior research on trait theories was misinterpreted as applying to leader effectiveness when it actually applied to the relationship between leader traits and leader emergence. Using meta-analytic techniques, their results supported social perception theories where several traits were expected to be related to leadership perception. Specifically, they found that intelligence, masculinity-femininity, and dominance were significantly related to followers' perceptions of their leader's effectiveness. Shelley Kirkpatrick and Edwin Locke (1991) found that successful leaders' traits include drive, the desire to lead, honesty and integrity, self-confidence, cognitive ability, and competence. Overall, as the study of traits and attributes in relation to leadership continued, the beginnings of the study of leadership as a behavioral phenomenon began.

Behavioral Theories After World War II (1939–1945), researchers emphasized the observable aspects of leadership in order to differentiate not only the nature of leadership and leader activity but also the behavioral patterns of effective leaders (Chemers 1997). A research program at Ohio State in the 1940s attempted to measure leadership behavior as group members described the behavior of the leader. From this data, John Hemphill (1950) quantified 150 behavior descriptors that were incorporated into the Leader Behavior Description Questionnaire (LBDQ), which is still used as a measure in leadership research. Andrew Halpin and Ben Winer (1957), while adapting the LBDQ for use in the U.S. Air Force, identified *initiating structure* and *consideration* as two fundamental dimensions of leader behavior. Earlier, Daniel Katz and Robert Kahn (1966) had attempted to identify general styles of leadership. From interviews with subordinate employees or "followers," they recognized two general styles: *production-oriented* and *employee-oriented*. The former is focused on planning, preparation, direction, and end-state productivity. In contrast, employee-oriented leaders identified with followers, exemplified openness, and showed concern for the well-being of subordinates.

With the limitations of behavioral approaches for explaining why some leaders are more effective than others, leadership researchers shifted their focus away from what leaders *are* toward developing a better understanding of what leaders actually *do*, and how such behaviors relate to leader effectiveness (i.e., how often a leader communicates with followers, what types of reward and discipline methods he or she uses, and the decisions leaders make).

Although behavioral approaches to leadership generated great interest, they also generated a number of controversies, including accusations of inconsistencies in findings (Bass and Stogdill 1990). For example, there are significant variations in most relationships between leadership styles and behaviors and the various indicators of leadership effectiveness, such as morale and satisfaction (Bryman 1992). These inconsistencies in the literature instigated the emergence of contingency approaches to leadership to account for differences found across situations.

Contingency and Situational Theories Contingency and situational theories examine both the tasks and the follower characteristics to specify what behavior is required of effective leaders. The circumstance in which leader-follower interaction takes place plays a major role in the process of leadership. Captured in the situational leadership approach are the quality of relationships, tasks, and activities to be performed, perceptions of the leader based on history, the motivation of both the leader and the follower, and personal characteristics influencing the situation. There exist several contingency and situational theories, but perhaps the most commonly researched were F. E. Fiedler's (1967) *contingency theory* of leadership, Paul Hersey and Kenneth Blanchard (1969) *situational leadership model*, Robert House's (1971) *path-goal theory* of leadership, and Victor Vroom and Philip Yetton's (1973) *normative decision model*.

Fiedler's contingency model proposes that leader effectiveness is a function of the match between the leader and specific situational factors, including position power, task structure, and leader-member relations. Fiedler's model differentiates between *task-oriented* and *relationship-oriented* leadership styles, but also measures ratings of the person with whom employees are least able to work. Fiedler found that the effectiveness of the leader-follower interaction was contingent upon the factors of leader-follower relationship, task structure, and leader position. If these factors were all high or all low, it was determined that a task-centered leader would be most effective. However, if the factors were mixed, an employee-centered leader was found to be most effective (Fiedler 1967).

Further, Fiedler argued that leaders cannot adjust their behavior to changing circumstances. If a leader's style is not appropriate for the specific situation, the leader will not be successful and an organization must change the leader. However, most contemporary theorists believe that leaders can adjust their style. If that is so, what should leaders consider in making adjustments?

Hersey and Blanchard's situational leadership model sought to answer this question. There was little evidence to support a relationship between leader behavior and leader effectiveness. Instead, the relative effectiveness of these two elements often depended on the context of the task. Hersey and Blanchard used the terms *task behaviors* and *relationship behaviors* and sought to explain why leadership effectiveness varies across these two dimensions. In their model, they depicted task behavior and relationship behavior as orthogonal dimensions. They argued that this approach is useful because certain combinations of task and relationship behaviors may be more effective in certain situations than in others.

Another contingency model deals with different aspects of leader-follower relationships. Path-goal theory is based on the idea that it is the leader's responsibility to clarify the path, remove obstacles, motivate his or her followers, and provide feedback to achieve organizational goals while setting guidelines on how to accomplish those goals. Path-goal theory examines the contingency of the leader's effectiveness at increasing a subordinate's motivation along a pathway leading to a certain goal. House proposed three areas that would affect the path-goals relationship: the task, the characteristics of the followers, and the nature of the group to which the followers belong. The theory hypothesizes that certain subordinates will respond better to directions when a task is unstructured (e.g., developing building plans) than when a task is structured (e.g., air traffic controlling) (House and Dessler 1974). The response is contingent upon differences in both the individual and the task. More importantly, understanding the effects of the nature of the task should influence how leaders behave.

Another influential model within the contingency approach is the normative decision model from Vroom and Yetton. In this model, emphasis is placed on increasing followers' involvement. The leader's method of including followers is contingent upon such constraints as time, talents, and resources. Another important aspect of the model is to what extent the support of followers is critical to successful outcomes. The implications of this model are that leaders who possess an awareness of their subordinates' involvement can improve the decision-making process.

All of these models have helped to develop an understanding of leadership complexities. Although contingency theories dominated leadership research for decades, a number of writers have questioned the methods used to tests these theories (Yukl 2002). For example, J. C. Wofford and Laurie Liska (1993) quantitatively reviewed 120 path-goal studies and found that only seven of the moderators used were significant. Katherine Miller and Peter Monge (1986) meta-analyzed research on the effects of participation in decision making on satisfaction and productivity. Results failed to support the contingency model predictions.

Transactional Theories Transactional models describe a process-oriented exchange between leaders and followers. As Edwin Hollander and Lynn Offermann (1990a) explained, transactional models focus on the follower's perceptions of the leader's actions. The concern for process stems from the social exchange between leaders and followers as a function of effectiveness (Shaw and Costanzo 1982). These models emphasize persuasive influence instead of compelled compliance. Hollander developed a transactional leadership model, and in its context coined the term *idiosyncratic credit*. Idiosyncratic credits are often defined as a tit-for-tat exchange. Hollander (1958) explained that leadership was a social exchange transaction between leaders and followers where "legitimacy" was the currency of the exchange. To have a successful transaction, the leader must provide direction, guidance, and technical knowledge, as well as recognition of followers' inputs. In turn, followers increase their receptiveness and add legitimacy to the leader's influence (Hollander 1993).

By demonstrating competency, assisting the achievement of group goals, and conforming to group norms, leaders demonstrate commitment to the group and in turn earn credits (Chemers 1997). By obtaining credits, the leader gains latitude to explore new and perhaps nonnormative ideas, methods, and courses of action, all of which can potentially lead to innovations. Overall, the successful employment of the idiosyncrasy credit exchange leads to legitimacy in shaping the perceptions of subordinates. In a cyclical nature, from the leader-follower exchange, group performance is increased (Green and Mitchell 1979).

Other relationship- and influence-oriented theories include *implicit leadership* theory, *leader-member exchange* theory, and *Pygmalion* theory. According to implicit leadership theory, a leader's behavior will not be effective unless the person is perceived as a leader (Calder 1977). Leader-member exchange theory (Graen and Ginsburgh 1977) proposes that leaders have *in-groups* of trusted individuals within their organization. Subordinates in the *out-group* are supervised through a more formal authority process. Another approach is referred to as Pygmalion theory. A critical component of this theory is the self-fulfilling prophecy, which suggests that raising leader expectations regarding follower achievement produces an improvement in the followers' performance (Eden 1990). Over nearly three decades, researchers have found that if leaders have confidence in followers and set high goals and expectations for them, then the followers' likelihood of success is higher due to a self-fulfilling prophecy effect (see Eden et al. [2000] for a review of this literature).

From a theoretical perspective, a common complaint against these theories is their lack of generalizability to women and to established work groups (White and Locke 2000). For example, several Pygmalion studies, with the exception of D. Brian McNatt's (2000) meta-analysis, have reported weak effect sizes when controlling for gender (Eden et al. 2000). Indeed, McNatt reported significant differences in the effect sizes across different leadership contexts, with the results stronger in the military, with men, and for followers for whom low expectations were initially held.

R. E. Kelly (1988) brought attention to the active role of followers in achieving group success. He argues that a prerequisite to effective leadership is followership. Effective followers are "intent on high performance and recognize that they share the responsibility for the quality of the relationship they have with their leaders" (Potter et al. 2000, p. 130). The study of followership includes an understanding of two separate dimensions of follower initiative: performance and relationships. Successful organizations that have the ability to change in positive directions have leaders who value and encourage partners, and followers who seek to become partners (Potter et al. 2000).

The relationship and influence theories have furthered scientific understanding of the leadership phenomena. They have also assisted in answering the question, "Can we develop leaders?" However, these theories do not address the most pressing questions. For example, how do leaders build more enlightened and transformational forms that create referent effects beyond mere legitimacy? Modern theories have sought to explain these challenges. These more recent ideas are examined under the umbrella of *new-genre* theories.

New-genre Theories *New genre* refers to theories that have dominated leadership research since the 1980s, including charismatic, inspirational, transformational, and visionary leadership (Bass 1998; Bryman 1992). New leadership approaches emphasize symbolic leader behavior, visionary and inspirational messages, emotional feelings, ideological and moral values, individualized attention, and intellectual stimulation. Charismatic and transformational leadership theories have turned out to be the most frequently

researched theories since the early 1990s (Judge and Piccolo 2004), with the accumulated research showing that charismatic and transformational leadership is positively associated with leadership effectiveness and a number of important organizational outcomes across many different types of organizations, situations, levels of analyses, and cultures (see Avolio, Bass, Walumbwa, and Zhu [2004] for a summary of this literature).

Hollander and Offermann described transformational leadership "as an extension of transactional leadership, but with greater leader intensity or follower arousal" (1990a, p. 88). The study of transformational leadership is rooted in Max Weber's (1946) notion of a leader. In this theory, leaders are seen as active transforming agents, changing the outlook and behavior of their followers (Burns 1978). Transformational leaders may employ one or more of the core competencies of transactional leadership to obtain greater outcomes.

Factor analytic studies have recognized four key components of transformational leadership (Bass 1985; Avolio and Howell 1992): (1) charismatic leadership or idealized influence; (2) inspirational motivation; (3) intellectual stimulation; and (4) individualized consideration. Transformational leaders act as role models to their subordinates. The use of power is a last resort for a transformational leader. Transformational leaders motivate and inspire subordinates by providing meaning and challenge through emphasis on teamwork. Inspirational motivation leads to internalization. Leaders ensure an open exchange of ideas by allowing mistakes, soliciting new methods for problem solving, and evaluating followers' processes rather than just situational outcomes. The leader acts as a coach, teacher, and mentor for each subordinate, providing individual attention and feedback, both positive and negative (Bass 1996).

Components of transformational and transactional leadership principles are incorporated into training strategies used by governments, corporations, and sports teams. As a result of training and education, transformational leaders motivate and enable followers to accomplish more than what is expected, set increasingly higher goals, and achieve higher standards. Transformational leadership is particularly evident in successful teams when coaches increase performance by providing motivation and inspiration. In contrast, current research on *in extremis* leadership, or leadership of teams facing death (e.g., fire departments, SWAT teams, and the military) shows that the environment itself provides the inherent motivation. Therefore, leaders in these extreme environments focus on continual learning and shared risk to build competency, loyalty, and trust (Kolditz 2007).

Like transformational leadership, the concept of charismatic leadership is an outgrowth of Max Weber's description of a form of influence based on follower perceptions that the leader possesses certain enviable characteristics. Weber proposed that charisma can occur when a leader with certain qualities emerges during a crisis to propose a new vision (Weber 1946). Charismatic leaders exert enormous power and influence over followers, especially followers searching for direction or for guidance during times of crisis. Leadership is considered charismatic when it "inspires the follower with challenge and persuasion, providing a meaning and understanding" (Bass 1996, p. 5). Robert House (1977) developed a theory of charismatic leadership based on the premise that charisma has a distinct effect on followers. Charismatic leaders tend to be self-confident and achievement-motivated; they also desire to assert influence, and they possess strong convictions. These types of leaders advocate change and are able to mass followers in support of their own vision. Other theories centering on charisma focus on attributes (Conger and Kanungo 1987), self-concept (Shamir et al. 1993), and social contagion (Meindl 1990).

One of the latest new-genre approaches to leadership is the framework proposed in *authentic leadership* theory (Gardner et al. 2005; Avolio and Gardner 2005; Avolio, Gardner, Walumbwa, et al. 2004). This theory holds that high levels of leader self-awareness, self-regulation, and transparency, among other things, will increase the leader's positive effects on their followers. Another current approach to understanding leadership evaluates the unique characteristics of leaders in life and death situations or *in extremis* leaders. These leaders demonstrate inherent motivation, continuous learning, shared risk, common lifestyle with their followers, competency, trust, and loyalty (Kolditz 2007).

A 2004 meta-analysis by Avolio and colleagues compared studies in which the researcher manipulated new-genre leadership with studies that manipulated traditional theories (e.g. behavioral, trait, or contingency theories) (Avolio, Reichard, Hannah, et al. 2004). Results showed that new-genre approaches to leadership had appreciably larger effects than those based on traditional leadership theories for both affective and cognitive dependent variables, while traditional theories had a slightly larger effect on more proximal behavioral outcomes. These findings appear consistent with the core focus of these theories. New-genre theories, such as transformational leadership, are believed to have strong affective and cognitive components, and they are thus positively linked to such dependent variables as liking, trust, or intellectual engagement. Conversely, research on contingency and other more transactional leadership approaches has focused more on short-term behavioral change.

Studies suggest that researchers will continue to examine leadership in search of both an understanding of the thoughts and actions of leaders and improvements to organizational performance and motivation.

SEE ALSO *Behaviorism; Conformity; Hierarchy; Organizations; Personality, Cult of; Political Science; Pygmalion Effects; Self-Fulfilling Prophecies*

BIBLIOGRAPHY

Avolio, Bruce J., Bernard M. Bass, Fred O. Walumbwa, and W. Zhu. 2004. *Multifactor Leadership Questionnaire: Manual and Sampler Test.* 3rd ed. Redwood City, CA: Mind Garden.

Avolio, Bruce J., and William L. Gardner. 2005. Authentic Leadership Development: Getting to the Root of Positive Forms of Leadership. *Leadership Quarterly* 16 (3): 315–338.

Avolio, Bruce J., William L. Gardner, Fred O. Walumbwa, et al. 2004. Unlocking the Mask: A Look at the Process by which Authentic Leaders Impact Follower Attitudes and Behaviors. *Leadership Quarterly* 15 (6): 801–823.

Avolio, Bruce J., and Jane M. Howell. 1992. The Impact of Leader Behavior and Leader-follower Personality Match on Satisfaction and Unit Performance. In *Impact of Leadership*, eds. Kenneth E. Clark, Miriam B. Clark, and David P. Campbell, 225–236. Greensboro, NC: Center for Creative Leadership.

Avolio, Bruce J., Rebecca J. Reichard, Sean T. Hannah, et al. 2004. 100 Years of Leadership Intervention Studies: A Meta-Analysis. Peer reviewed paper presented at the Gallop Leadership Institute Summit, Omaha, NE.

Bass, Bernard M. 1960. *Leadership, Psychology, and Organizational Behavior.* New York: Harper.

Bass, Bernard M. 1985. *Leadership and Performance Beyond Expectations.* New York: Free Press.

Bass, Bernard M. 1996. *A New Paradigm of Leadership: An Inquiry into Transformational Leadership.* Alexandria, VA: U.S. Army Research Institute.

Bass, Bernard M. 1998. *Transformational Leadership: Industrial, Military, and Educational Impact.* Mahwah, NJ: Erlbaum.

Bass, Bernard M., and Ralph M. Stogdill. 1990. *Bass and Stogdill's Handbook of Leadership: Theory, Research, and Managerial Applications.* 3rd ed. New York: Free Press.

Bryman, Alan. 1992. *Charisma and Leadership in Organizations.* London: Sage.

Burns, James M. 1978. *Leadership.* New York: Harper and Row.

Calder, Bobby J. 1977. An Attribution Theory of Leadership. In *New Directions in Organizational Behavior*, eds. Barry M. Staw and Gerald R. Salancik, 179–204. Chicago: St. Clair.

Carlyle, Thomas. 1841. Lecture I: The Hero as Divinity. In *On Heroes, Hero-Worship, and the Heroic in History.* London: Fraser. http://www.gutenberg.org/dirs/etext97/heros10.txt.

Chemers, Martin M. 1997. *An Integrative Theory of Leadership.* Mahwah, NJ: Erlbaum.

Conger, Jay A., and Rabindra N. Kanungo. 1987. Behavioral Theory of Charismatic Leadership in Organizational Settings. *Academy of Management Review* 12: 637–647.

Department of the Army. 1999. *Army Leadership: Be, Know, Do.* FM 22–100. Washington, DC: Author.

Eden, Dov. 1990. *Pygmalion in Management: Productivity as a Self-fulfilling Prophecy.* Lexington, MA: Lexington Books.

Eden, Dov, Dvorah Geller, Abigail Gewirtz, et al. 2000. Implanting Pygmalion Leadership Style through Workshop Training: Seven Field Experiments. *Leadership Quarterly* 11 (2): 170–210.

Fiedler, F. E. 1967. *A Theory of Leadership Effectiveness.* New York: McGraw-Hill.

Galton, Francis. 1869. *Hereditary Genius: An Inquiry into its Laws and Consequences.* London: Macmillan.

Gardner, William L., Bruce J. Avolio, Fred Luthans, et al. 2005. "Can You See the Real Me?" A Self-based Model of Authentic Leader and Follower Development. *Leadership Quarterly* 16 (3): 343–372.

Graen, G. B., and S. Ginsburgh. 1977. Job Resignation as a Function of Role Orientation and Leader Acceptance: A Longitudinal Investigation of Organizational Assimilation. *Organizational Behavior and Human Performance* 19: 1–17.

Green, S. G., and T. R. Mitchell. 1979. Attributional Process of Leaders in Leader-member Interactions. *Organizational Behavior and Human Performance* 23: 429–458.

Halpin, Andrew W., and Ben J. Winer. 1957. A Factorial Study of the Leader Behavior Descriptions. In *Leader Behavior: Its Descriptions and Measurements*, eds. Ralph M. Stogdill and Alvin E. Coons, 39–51. Columbus: Ohio State University, Bureau of Business Research.

Hemphill, John K. 1950. Relations Between the Size of the Group and the Behavior of "Superior" Leaders. *Journal of Social Psychology* 32: 11–22.

Hersey, Paul, and Kenneth H. Blanchard. 1969. Life Cycle Theory of Leadership. *Training and Development Journal* 23 (2): 26–34.

Hollander, Edwin P. 1958. Conformity, Status, and Idiosyncrasy Credit. *Psychological Review* 65: 117–127.

Hollander, Edwin P. 1993. Legitimacy, Power, and Influence: A Perspective on Relational Features of Leadership. In *Leadership Theory and Research: Perspectives and Directions*, eds. Martin M. Chemers and Roya Ayman, 29–48. San Diego: Academic Press.

Hollander, Edwin P., and Lynn R. Offermann. 1990a. Relational Features of Organizational Leadership and Followership. In *Measures of Leadership*, eds. Kenneth E. Clark and Miriam B. Clark, 83–98. West Orange, NJ: Leadership Library of America.

Hollander, Edwin P., and Lynn R. Offermann. 1990b. Power and Leadership in Organizations: Relationships in Transition. *American Psychologist* 45: 179–189.

House, Robert J. 1971. A Path-Goal Theory of Leader Effectiveness. *Administrative Science Quarterly* 16: 321–352.

House, Robert J. 1977. A 1976 Theory of Charismatic Leadership. In *Leadership: The Cutting Edge*, eds. James G. Hunt and Lars L. Larson, 189–207. Carbondale: Southern Illinois University Press

House, Robert J., and G. Dessler. 1974. A Path-goal Theory of Leadership: Some Post Hoc and a Priori Tests. In *Contingency Approaches to Leadership*, eds. James G. Hunt and Lars L. Larson, 29–55. Carbondale: Southern Illinois University.

Hunt, James G., Uma Sekaran, and Chester A. Schriesheim. 1982. *Leadership: Beyond Establishment Views.* Carbondale: Southern Illinois University Press.

Jacobs, T. Owens, and Elliot Jaques. 1990. Military Executive Leadership. In *Measures of Leadership*, eds. Kenneth E. Clark and Miriam B. Clark, 281–295. West Orange, NJ: Leadership Library of America.

Judge, Timothy A., and Ronald F. Piccolo. 2004. Transformational and Transactional Leadership: A Meta-Analytic Test of their Relative Validity. *Journal of Applied Psychology* 89: 755–768.

Katz, Daniel, and Robert L. Kahn. 1966. *The Social Psychology of Organizations.* New York: Wiley.

Kelly, R. E. 1988. In Praise of Followers. *Harvard Business Review* 66 (6): 142–148.

Kirkpatrick, Shelley A., and Edwin A. Locke. 1991. Leadership: Do Traits Matter? *Academy of Management Executive* 5: 48–60.

Kolditz, Thomas A. 2007. *In Extremis Leadership: Leading as if Your Life Depended on It.* Hoboken, NJ: Wiley.

Lord, Robert G., Christy L. de Vader, and George M. Alliger. 1986. A Meta-analysis of the Relation Between Personality Traits and Leadership Perceptions: An Application of Validity Generalization Procedures. *Journal of Applied Psychology* 71 (3): 402–410.

Mann, Richard D. 1959. A Review of the Relationships between Personality and Performance in Small Groups. *Psychological Bulletin* 56 (4): 241–270.

McNatt, D. Brian. 2000. Ancient Pygmalion Joins Contemporary Management: A Meta-analysis of the Result. *Journal of Applied Psychology* 85 (2): 314–322.

Meindl, J. R. 1990. On Leadership: An Alternative to the Conventional Wisdom. In *Research in Organizational Behavior*, eds. B. M. Staw and L. L. Cumming, 159–203. Greenwich, CT: JAI Press.

Miller, Katherine I., and Peter R. Monge. 1986. Participation, Satisfaction, and Productivity: A Meta-analytic Review. *Academy of Management Journal* 29: 727–753.

Potter, Earl H., William E. Rosenbach, and Thane S. Pittman. 2000. Followers as Partners: The Best Evidence of Good Leadership. In *Military Leadership: In Pursuit of Excellence*, eds. Robert L. Taylor and William E. Rosenbach, 128–137. 4th ed. Boulder, CO: Westview.

Shamir, Boas, Robert J. House, and Michael B. Arthur. 1993. Motivational Effects of Charismatic Leadership: A Self-Concept Based Theory. *Organization Science* 4: 577–594.

Shartle, Carroll L. 1956. *Executive Performance and Leadership.* Englewood Cliffs, NJ: Prentice-Hall.

Shaw, Marvin E., and Philip R. Costanzo. 1982. *Theories of Social Psychology.* 2nd ed. New York: McGraw-Hill.

Stogdill, Ralph M. 1948. Personal Factors Associated with Leadership: A Survey of the Literature. *Journal of Psychology* 25: 35–71.

Vroom, Victor H., and Philip W. Yetton. 1973. *Leadership and Decision-making.* Pittsburgh, PA: University of Pittsburgh Press.

Weber, Max. 1946. The Sociology of Charismatic Authority. In *From Max Weber: Essays in Sociology*, eds. and trans. H. H. Gerth and C. Wright Mills, 245–252. New York: Oxford.

White, Susan S., and Edwin A. Locke. 2000. Problems with the Pygmalion Effect and Some Proposed Solutions. *Leadership Quarterly* 11 (3): 389–415.

Wofford, J. C., and Laurie Z. Liska. 1993. Path-goal Theories of Leadership: A Meta-Analysis. *Journal of Management* 19: 857–876.

Yukl, Gary A. 2002. *Leadership in Organizations*. 5th ed. Upper Saddle River, NJ: Prentice Hall.

Dennis P. O'Neil

LEADERSHIP, CONTINGENCY MODELS OF

One of the earliest theories of leadership that deliberately included features of the situation was proposed by the Austrian-born American psychologist Fred E. Fiedler (1967). According to Fiedler's *contingency model of leader effectiveness*, the performance of a group is a joint function of the style of the leader and key attributes of the context. Broadly stated, the model identifies appropriate "matches" of different leadership styles for particular types of situations.

Fiedler characterized leader style as varying across a single dimension of socioemotional orientation versus task orientation. Socioemotional orientation denotes a leader who is primarily concerned with maintaining positive social relations, whereas task orientation denotes a leader who is primarily concerned with task structure and accomplishment. This stylistic orientation is assessed by having a leader complete a "least preferred coworker" (LPC) attitude scale. Comparatively high (or lenient) LPC scores are interpreted as an indication of a socioemotional orientation, while low (or harsh) LPC scores are interpreted as an indication of a task orientation. The assumption that a social-relations orientation and a task orientation are opposite ends of a single continuum differs from other popular approaches to conceptualizing leader style (e.g., the Ohio State University–based conceptualization of consideration and structuring proposes two independent dimensions of leadership style).

Situations are judged in terms of how much control they afford the leader. High-control situations are those that provide a leader with strong subordinate support, clear task structure, and substantial power that is tied to the leader's formal position. The model posits that in extremely high-control situations and extremely low-control situations, leaders who are low LPC (i.e., task oriented) will be more effective than high LPC (i.e., socioemotional oriented) leaders. For more intermediate-control situations, the ordering of leader effectiveness is reversed, and high LPC leaders are predicted to be comparatively more effective. The precise underlying social process that might explain this pattern of association has been a major topic of study throughout the model's history.

Fiedler developed his model from data collected over a large number of work groups in a great variety of settings. As the results of these studies were used to induce the model's principles, subsequent research efforts have attempted to verify the proposed interaction of leader style and leader circumstance. By and large, these later attempts at verification have met with mixed success. Meta-analytic efforts (designed to summarize results across many studies) do suggest the model may be valid in certain extreme combinations of subordinate support, task structure, and leader position–based power (Peters et al. 1985). However, the magnitude of these effects for the observed associations of LPC with group performance in specific situations is not great. Moreover, there is some evidence that performance may actually decrease as situational control decreases (Schriesheim et al. 1994; Vecchio 1977). This suggests that performance may be maximal (and, therefore, situations should be created) where high LPC leaders are located within settings of extremely high situational control (i.e., positive leader-subordinate social relations, maximum task structure, and strong leader position power). Because much prior research has focused on within-setting comparisons of leaders, this across-setting comparison deserves further study.

Despite these concerns, Fiedler's contingency model of leadership is important for its emphasis on the interplay of leader style and the situation, and its suggestion that, in some settings, it may be more reasonable to modify or engineer the situation to fit the leader's personality, rather than attempt to modify the leader's style.

SEE ALSO *Leadership; Meta-Analysis*

BIBLIOGRAPHY

Fiedler, Fred E. 1967. *A Theory of Leadership Effectiveness*. New York: McGraw-Hill.

Fiedler, Fred E., and Martin M. Chemers. 1984. *Improving Leadership Effectiveness: The Leader Match Concept*. 2nd ed. New York: Wiley.

Peters, Lawrence H., Darrell Hartke, and John T. Pohlmann. 1985. Fiedler's Contingency Theory of Leadership: An Application of the Meta-analysis Procedures of Schmidt and Hunter. *Psychological Bulletin* 97: 274–285.

Schriesheim, Chester A., Bennett J. Tepper, and Linda A. Tetrault. 1994. Least Preferred Co-worker Score, Situational Control, and Leadership Effectiveness: A Meta-analysis of Contingency Model Performance Predictions. *Journal of Applied Psychology* 79: 561–573.

Vecchio, Robert P. 1977. An Empirical Investigation of the Validity of Fiedler's Model of Leadership Effectiveness. *Organizational Behavior and Human Performance* 19: 180–206.

Robert P. Vecchio

LEADING INDICATORS

SEE *Lagging, Leading, and Coincident Indicators.*

LEAGUE OF NATIONS

The League of Nations, inaugurated in 1920, was the first major international organization to attempt to tie individual nation-state security to international security. Envisioned as a collective security—rather than a collective defense—organization, the League of Nations attempted to replace individual nation-state self-interest with an altruistic vision of international justice and cooperation. In a first for international law, the Covenant of the League committed every signatory to settle disputes through arbitration before going to war. The centerpiece of the League Covenant was Article 10, which bound the League to collectively preserve "the territorial integrity and existing political independence of all Members."

Despite its all-encompassing mandate to preserve peace and security of the international community though mutual action, the League was not the first international organization to espouse such goals. The Concert of Europe (1815–1900) and the two Hague Conferences (1899 and 1907) had each in their way advanced the issue of international cooperation on the world stage, but both had serious limitations. The Concert of Europe was limited by the fact that only the Great Powers of Europe took part, and its means of conflict resolution (arbitration) only worked as long as each power agreed to submit. For their part, the two Hague Conferences were more inclusive (twenty-six and forty-four states, respectively) and accomplished more with respect to codifying into international law the peaceful settlement of disputes. The three Hague Conventions that arose from these conferences, along with the Permanent Count of Arbitration, presaged the Covenant of the League of Nations.

The League was born out of the experience of World War I. Many politicians believed the war had occurred in large part due to the brutal nature of *realpolitik* and the secretive diplomacy and shifting alliances between the Great Powers. For Woodrow Wilson, president of the United States from 1912 to 1920, the League of Nations represented a capstone of a morally based foreign policy; one designed to replace the dangerous balance of power politics with a more transparent and cooperative system between sovereign, democratic states governed by the principle of national self-determination. Wilson articulated his vision several times during his presidency, but his most famous statement on the League concluded his famous Fourteen Points speech presented before the U.S. Congress on January 8, 1918: "A general association of nations must be formed under specific covenants for the purpose of affording mutual guarantees of political independence and territorial integrity to great and small states alike."

The League was an integral part of the Treaty of Versailles, negotiated in early 1919 and enacted on January 10, 1920. The League began operations in Geneva, Switzerland, with Sir Eric Drummond its first secretary general. Structurally, the League consisted of a council, an assembly, and a secretariat—a structure that would subsequently serve as the model for the United Nations. The Council was originally designed to have nine members: the five great powers (Britain, France, Italy, Japan, and the United States with permanent seats, as well as four temporary rotating members (the first four were Belgium, Brazil, Greece, and Spain). However, despite an ardent cross-country campaign by Wilson, which eventually contributed to his debilitating stroke, the isolationist Senate failed to ratify the treaty and the United States never officially joined the League. Thus, the Council consisted of eight members until 1922, when two additional small states were added. In 1926 the Council was further increased to fifteen members, including Germany.

The foremost goal of the League was the prevention of another world war, and the League Covenant included calls for disarmament and dispute resolution through arbitration in the International Court or inquiry before the League Council. The central focus of the Covenant was the set of articles outlining the principles and responsibilities of collective security. Article 16 declared that any state that went to war without first vetting disputes through the League processes would be deemed to have committed an act of war against all other member states of the League. Building upon the idea of deterrence through the threat of "all against one," the collective members were then expected to sever all trade and financial relations with the aggressor state. Notably member states were not legally obliged to apply military sanctions, although Article 16 claims that military sanction may be "a political and moral duty incumbent to states." The League's architects, including Wilson, believed that this collective security system would ultimately preempt the precarious alliance behavior and arms races that had caused war repeatedly in the past.

The League did enjoy numerous successes, particularly in settling territorial disputes such as those between Albania and Yugoslavia (1921), Germany and Poland over Upper Silesia (1922), and Greece and Bulgaria (1925). Yet it is largely the League's spectacular failures that stand out when accounting for its fate. Conventional wisdom holds that the refusal of the U.S. Senate to ratify the Treaty of Versailles crippled the League from the outset. Other reasons for failure are both structural and operational. Reflecting its origins as an international organization with members of varying power and interests, the League Covenant contained structural compromises needed to ensure member state ratification and participation. The biggest of these concessions was the discrepancy between Articles 5 and 10. Article 10 promised collective preservation of territorial integrity and political independence of all member states, whereas Article 5 required all decisions taken by the League Council be made on the basis of unanimity of the members in attendance. Article 5 thus ensured a veto for any member of the Council who undertook aggressive action against another member.

Operationally the League was hampered throughout its existence by the reluctance of its member states to intervene in international disputes and apply collective security mechanisms. One of the most egregious cases was the League's weak response to Japan's invasion of Manchuria in 1931. Instead of sanctioning Japan, the League failed to take decisive action for more than seven months—partly due to the structural flaw of the League Council, which enabled Japan (as a permanent member) to delay League action. The League finally sent observers, but only after Japan formally withdrew from the League. By 1934 the League's lack of teeth would become readily evident again in the case of Italy's invasion of Ethiopia (which solicited only a weak set of economic sanctions on the part of the League) and Adolf Hitler's obvious rearming of Germany. Ultimately, the declaration of World War II—which the League was designed to prevent—spelled the demise of the institution. Although the League lingered on through the war, it finally faded into irrelevance and it functions were formally turned over to the newly created United Nations in 1945.

SEE ALSO *Alliances; Confederations*

BIBLIOGRAPHY

Knock, Thomas J. 1992. *To End All Wars: Woodrow Wilson and the Quest for a New World Order.* New York: Oxford University Press.

Link, Arthur S., ed. 1966–1994. *The Papers of Woodrow Wilson.* 69 vols. Princeton, NJ: Princeton University Press.

Northedge, F. S. 1986. *The League of Nations: Its Life and Times, 1920–1946.* New York: Holmes & Meier Publishers.

Scott, George. 1973. *The Rise and Fall of the League of Nations.* London: Hutchison & Co.

Catherine Weaver

LEAKEY, RICHARD
1944–

Born into a family with a legacy of seeking out the origins of humankind, Richard Erskine Leakey was the second of the three sons of Louis Leakey (1903–1972) and Mary Leakey (1913–1996). Both of Leakey's parents were renowned for their archaeological finds and influenced future generations of Leakeys toward the study of human origin. Louis Leakey had been born in Nairobi, Kenya, to missionary parents. Young Louis learned the culture, language, and traditions of the Kikuyu people and was even initiated as a member of the Kikuyu tribe at the age of thirteen. Louis later completed studies at Cambridge University in the fields of anthropology and archaeology. Louis and his wife Mary were both instrumental in shaping the fields of archaeology, paleoanthropology, and primatology due to their many discoveries.

Young Richard was often in the field with his parents on digs, and found his first fossil, of an ancient pig, at the age of six. During his youth, he had a horrible time with bullying in school and eventually left school to pursue his interest in observing and tracking animals. He initially resisted the idea of following the career path of his parents and decided to start a safari business. His business was fairly successful until his curiosity about paleontology led him in a different direction. Leakey began to go on fossil hunting expeditions in East Africa with colleagues of his parents. In 1967 he became part of an expedition funded through one of his father's research projects: Richard served as the field leader for a trip to the Lower Omo Valley in Ethiopia. In this area, the team found many early hominid fossils that were at least 130,000 years old.

Around this time, Leakey married Margaret Cropper, who traveled with him on the Omo Valley expedition. He faced difficulty early in his career because he lacked the credentials that many anthropologists and archaeologists possessed. Thus, he returned to school and completed the requirements to gain entry into a university. After he completed his entrance exam, he aimed to pursue higher education, but was soon distracted by his curiosity about a particular archaeological site and his desire to obtain a position with the National Museums of Kenya. He chose not to attend college.

Leakey's interest in further excavating Kenya was inspired by a flight from Omo to Nairobi. The aerial view

INTERNATIONAL ENCYCLOPEDIA OF THE SOCIAL SCIENCES, 2ND EDITION

provided him with a glimpse of what appeared to be fossil-bearing sedimentary rock. He determined that he would obtain funding to go back to that area and find fossils on Kenyan land. His excavations in the area around Kenya's Lake Turkana would yield many significant finds and result in his distinguished career in the field of paleoanthropology. In 1968 he began the first of many excavations at this site. He also began to lobby for a position with the National Museums of Kenya. He was named administrative director of the museums in May of 1968 and remained in this position until 1989.

Leakey and his wife Margaret had one daughter named Anna, who was born in 1969, but they were divorced soon after this time. Richard then met and fell in love with Meave Epps, a zoologist who had recently completed her PhD at the University of North Wales. They married and had two children: Louise born in 1972, and Samira born in 1974. Leakey established a camp in Koobi, which became the site of one of his best-known discoveries, called *skull 1470*. This discovery helped him mend a long-standing rift with his father that was instigated by conflicts between Richard's role as the director of the National Museum and his father's center, which had been in existence for many years. Richard was able to show skull 1470 to his father just before Louis died on a trip to London in October 1972.

The discoveries by Leakey's team of the *Homo habilis* skull in 1972 and the *Homo erectus* skull in 1975 were significant findings. Leakey's health began to suffer thereafter due to kidney disease, and he had to receive a kidney from his brother Phillip in 1979. Leakey is most well-known for the discovery in 1984 of what would become known as Turkana Boy, a *Homo erectus* skeleton roughly 1.6 million years old. Two members of his team have been credited with working with him on this find: Alan Walker and Kamoya Kimeu. It is one of the most complete *Homo erectus* skeletons ever found, and it has brought Leakey and Kenya worldwide acclaim in the field of paleoanthropology.

Leakey resigned his post as director of the National Museums of Kenya amidst a wave of controversy in 1989. Leakey had been appointed director of the Kenya Wildlife Service by President Daniel Arap Moi. In this capacity, he spoke out against the rampant practice of elephant poaching and created many enemies because of the confrontational methods of his antipoaching campaign. In 1993 Leakey lost both of his legs in a suspicious plane crash, although within a few months he was walking again on artificial limbs.

Accusations of corruption and fraud led to his resignation from his post with the Kenya Wildlife Service in 1994. In 1995 Leakey created a political party, called Safina, which stood in opposition to the Kenyan African National Union. Leakey was subjected to a public beating and humiliation in the streets by opponents. His tense relationship with political leaders and poachers in the country was a primary cause of this attack. Leakey was reappointed to a position with the Kenya Wildlife Service in 1999, but resigned again in 2001. His daughter Louise completed a PhD in paleontology at the University of London and has followed in the footsteps of her parents. She and her mother, Meave, continue to lead annual expeditions to the Turkana Basin. Leakey remains active, lecturing and writing books on the preservation of wildlife and the environment. He has authored seven books related to his life and work, including *Origins Reconsidered* (1992) and *The Origin of Humankind* (1994).

SEE ALSO *Anthropology; Anthropology, Biological; Archaeology; Primates*

BIBLIOGRAPHY

Harris, Scott. 1996. Richard Leakey: Africa's Passionate Voice for Nature. *E: The Environmental Magazine* 7 (4): 10.

Johanson, Donald. 1999. The Leakey Family. *TIME* (March 29). http://www.time.com/time/time100/scientist/profile/leakey.html.

Leakey, Richard. 1984. *One Life: An Autobiography*. Salem, NH: Salem House.

Leakey Foundation. http://www.leakeyfoundation.org.

Lewin, Roger. 1989. Leakey Leaves Kenya Museums. *Science* (New Series) 243 (4890): 473.

Kijua Sanders-McMurtry

LEARNED HELPLESSNESS

The term *learned helplessness* was coined by psychologists Martin Seligman and Steven Maier in 1967 to describe the behavior of dogs who, after experiencing inescapable electric shocks behaved as if they were helpless. As with many terms in psychology, *learned helplessness* is both descriptive and explanatory. Learned helplessness describes a constellation of maladaptive passive behaviors that animals (dogs, rats, cats, fish, mice, and humans) frequently exhibit following exposure to uncontrollable events. Learned helplessness is also a cognitive, expectancy-based explanation; after repeated, inescapable, aversive helplessness, animals *expect* to be helpless and do not attempt to change the situation—they have *learned* that their actions are ineffective.

Research on learned helplessness began in the 1960s at Richard L. Solomon's (1918–1995) psychology lab at the University of Pennsylvania. Graduate students Russell

Leaf and J. Bruce Overmier had discovered that after Pavlovian conditioning with unavoidable mild shocks, the lab dogs were useless for any subsequent experiments that required learning how to avoid or escape shock. The majority of the dogs would sit and passively endure the aversive but otherwise physically harmless shock. This phenomenon piqued the interest of graduate students Maier and Seligman, who set out to show that the dogs had learned more than just Pavlovian conditioning. Maier and Seligman suggested that the dogs had learned that when shocked, nothing they did mattered—they had learned that they had no control over their environment. This explanation was unusually "cognitive" given the behaviorist climate of that era.

Most early research on learned helplessness used a three-group, two-phase, experimental design to make sure that uncontrollability was the cause of the helplessness. In the first phase, one group experienced controllable aversive stimuli; for example, they could learn to avoid a shock by jumping across a barrier into a safe area. A second, "no control" group also experienced the aversive stimuli, but had no means by which to escape it. To make sure that subsequent differences in helplessness were not due to differences in the rate or length of exposure to the uncontrollable stimuli, experimenters pair, or yoke, each "no control" animal with a "has control" animal. The "no control" animal only experiences the aversive stimuli when the "has control" animal does. Researchers call this a "yoked control group." Animals in a third naive control group experience no aversive stimuli at all. In the second phase, the experimenters subject all three groups to aversive stimuli in a new controllable context; in other words, all have equal opportunity to escape.

In Seligman's studies, usually about two-thirds of the "no-control" dogs display helpless behavior in the new situation. Six percent of the naive control group dogs also displayed helplessness, which Seligman suggests may have been due to prior traumatic experiences. Typically helpless animals show signs of stress, such as lethargy, dejection, and reduced appetite, dominance aggression, sexual appetite, and serotonin levels.

These studies demonstrated that for most animals, uncontrollable aversive experiences have devastating effects on subsequent learning, motivation, and emotion. Seligman reports that therapy for dogs with learned helplessness required dragging them into the safe area a number of times before they began to respond on their own. On a positive note, Seligman and colleagues also found that they could "immunize" dogs against learned helplessness by giving them several trials of escapable shock before exposing them to inescapable shock.

Donald Hiroto and Seligman (1974) subsequently extended this research paradigm to humans, using insolu-

ble discrimination problems rather than shocks. It is important to note that in this transition from animals to humans, stimuli aversiveness was not the only parameter to change; the transition also included a shift from simple taskless stimuli to tasks such as unsolvable discrimination problems or puzzles. This shift has complicated the explanation of learning deficits following failure. Additionally, human susceptibility to learned helplessness varies considerably across individuals and situations. These differences correlate with a variety of characteristics: low mastery behavior, anxiety, depression, need for structure, and ego value of academic performance, to name a few. Nonetheless, the core features of the learned helplessness phenomenon remain: (1) following an uncontrollable situation, people exhibit a variety of learning, motivational, and emotional deficits, including increased vulnerability to depression and anxiety; (2) previous exposure to controllable aversive events immunizes people against learned helplessness; and (3) forced exposure to controllable contingencies reverses learned helplessness.

A significant portion of research on learned helplessness in humans has focused on its relationship with reactive depression. One of the earliest, and perhaps most fertile, explanations of learned helplessness as a cause of depression was Lyn Abramson, Seligman, and John Teasdale's 1978 reformulation of learned helplessness theory using concepts from Bernard Weiner's attribution theory. This reformulation recognizes that much of life is uncontrollable, yet not everyone is depressed by it. According to the reformulation of learned helplessness theory, whether depression results from helplessness situations depends on the attributions people make about the causes of the negative event. Depression is more likely if persons attribute negative events to internal causes ("it's me"), stable causes ("it's going to last forever"), or global causes ("it's going to mess up everything I do"). This pessimistic style is evident in a student who attributes her poor math performance to "being a girl" (internal and stable) and assumes that failure in a specific math class will mean the end of her medical school dream (a global attribution). In contrast, a student who attributes failure on an exam to not studying is protected from depression because he or she has attributed it to an internal ("I didn't study"), unstable ("I can study next time"), and specific ("failing on this test isn't going to mess up my whole life") cause. Each of these causal attributions has a different effect on subsequent behavior. Global attributions generalize helplessness across tasks and time, internal attributions imply a sense of failed responsibility, and stable attributions imply that it is not possible to change the parameters of the current situation.

A large body of research has found long-term individual differences in explanatory style and vulnerability to helplessness. Persons who have experienced a significant childhood loss (e.g., the death of a parent) or trauma (e.g., sexual or physical abuse) are more likely to develop pessimistic explanatory styles. Research has also found that parents and children have correlated explanatory styles, and messages from peers, teachers, media, and other community members have an impact on children's explanatory style. The repercussions of explanatory style is still being studied, for example, the effects of pessimistic explanatory style on negative health outcomes, occupational success, and the quality of social relationships.

The concept of learned helplessness has also been used extensively in educational and social psychology; for example, there is now an impressive body of research on individual differences in persistence following failure on evaluative and learning tasks. Some people's motivation is unaffected by experiencing failure; rather, they use failure as an additional source of information. Consequently, their performance quickly rebounds when given solvable problems. In contrast, "helpless" people appear to crumble under the experience of failure, or even just difficulty. They may regress to a lower skill level, exhibit negative affect, and conclude that they lack ability. Learned helplessness theory argues that helplessness following failure-feedback is the result of learning that responses and outcomes are noncontingent, which interferes with subsequent learning. Research in achievement motivation has found, however, that helplessness following failure can also be a strategic way to protect self-worth (e.g., "If I don't try, failing won't make me look bad"). Achievement motivation researchers call this an ego or performance goal.

A large and productive body of research has explored individual differences in resiliency and helplessness through the lens of achievement goals. Researchers have identified two major goal orientations: *mastery* or *task* goals and *performance* or *ego* goals. Mastery goals focus on intrinsic reasons for learning, which protects against learned helplessness. Performance goals focus on extrinsic reasons for learning—demonstrating one's ability and competing with others—which reduces vulnerability to learned helplessness. Recent research has extended these concepts by distinguishing between ego goals that focus on the display of skill (performance approach) and ego goals that focus on avoiding displays of incompetence (performance avoidance).

Finally, from an information-processing perspective, Grzegorz Sedek (1990) has described the phenomenon of learned helplessness as a state of cognitive exhaustion produced by nonproductive problem solving. This perspective reminds us that giving up is also an adaptive response because animal brains have finite energy resources. Helplessness behavior may be an adaptive avoidance of indiscriminant persistence. From this perspective, helplessness is not so much "learned" as it is "triggered."

There is little disagreement among researchers that helplessness as described by Seligman is a real and fascinating phenomenon; however, there is less consensus about its cause. Presently, separate bodies of research (learning theory, cognitive theory, cognitive behavioral therapy, achievement motivation, and information processing) support the existence of the helplessness phenomenon, but each gives a somewhat different explanation of its cause (i.e., helplessness as learned, helplessness as a cognitive interpretation of events, helplessness as a form of ego protection, and helplessness as an adaptive conservation of resources). Future research should intentionally compare these causes and the perhaps differential conditions under which they occur.

SEE ALSO *Attribution; Classical Conditioning; Depression, Psychological; Locus of Control; Motivation; Operant Conditioning; Pavlov, Ivan; Positive Psychology; Psychotherapy; Resiliency; Self-Efficacy; Seligman, Martin; Vulnerability*

BIBLIOGRAPHY

Abramson, Lyn Y., Martin E. P. Seligman, and John D. Teasdale. 1978. Learned Helplessness in Humans: Critique and Reformulation. *Journal of Abnormal Psychology* 87: 49–74.

Alloy, Lauren B., and Lyn Y. Abramson. 1982. Learned Helplessness, Depression, and the Illusion of Control. *Journal of Personality and Social Psychology* 42: 1114–1126.

Buchannan, Gregory McClellan, and Martin E. P. Seligman, eds. 1995. *Explanatory Style*. Hillsdale, NJ: Erlbaum.

Hiroto, Donald S., and Martin E. Seligman. 1975. Generality of Learned Helplessness in Man. *Journal of Personality and Social Psychology* 31 (2): 311–327.

Maier, Steven F., and Martin E. P. Seligman. 1976. Learned Helplessness: Theory and Evidence. *Journal of Experimental Psychology: General* 105: 3–46.

Sedek, Grzegorz, and Miroslav Kofta. 1990. When Cognitive Exertion Does Not Yield Cognitive Gain: Toward an Informational Explanation of Learned Helplessness. *Journal of Personality and Social Psychology* 58 (4): 729–743.

Seligman, Martin E. P. 1972. Learned Helplessness. *Annual Reviews* 23: 407–412.

Seligman, Martin E., and Steven F. Maier. 1967. Failure to Escape Traumatic Shock. *Journal of Experimental Psychology* 74 (1): 1–9.

Joan M. Martin
Jennie K. Gill

LEARNED OPTIMISM

SEE *Learned Helplessness; Seligman, Martin.*

LEARNING

SEE *Developmental Psychology; Education, Remedial; Education, Unequal; Education, USA; Intelligence; Learned Helplessness; Reinforcement Theories.*

LEARY, TIMOTHY
1920–1996

Timothy Francis Leary was a psychologist, scientist, and philosopher who made substantive contributions to interpersonal theory and methodology and also gained notoriety for his endorsement of and research on hallucinogens. Born in Springfield, Massachusetts, on October 22, 1920, Leary was an only child raised by his mother's family in a devout Irish Catholic household. His father, a successful dentist and prominent member of the community, left the family when Leary was thirteen years old. Initially expelled from the University of Alabama for spending a night in the women's dormitory, he appealed the dismissal in 1945 and was awarded his bachelor's degree in psychology while serving in the army during World War II (1939–1945).

Leary met his first wife, Marianne, in 1944 while serving as a psychometrician at Deshon General Hospital in Butler, Pennsylvania. A year later they were married in the same hospital before departing for the state of Washington, where Leary began work on his master's degree. In 1946 Leary received his master of science degree under the supervision of renowned psychologist Lee Cronbach (1916–2001) at Washington State University. The title of his master's thesis was "The Clinical Use of the Wechsler/Mental Ability Scale: Form B," which he later retitled "The Dimensions of Intelligence." Following the completion of his master's degree, Leary entered the doctoral program in clinical psychology at the University of California, Berkeley. In 1950 he received his PhD in clinical psychology with the dissertation "The Social Dimensions of Personality: Group Process and Structure."

Leary's seminal monograph, *The Interpersonal Diagnosis of Personality: A Functional Theory and Methodology for Personality Evaluation*, was a direct product of his doctoral thesis. First published in 1957, Leary considered his monograph to be a methodological extension of the interpersonal theory of Harry Stack Sullivan (1892–1949). According to Leary, the emotional, interpersonal, and social life of individuals could be best understood as attempts to avoid anxiety. Leary's monograph focuses on five levels of personality that include: (1) public communication, (2) conscious communication, (3) private communication or preconscious symbolization, (4) unexpressed or unconscious communication, and (5) the value or ego-ideal.

The majority of Leary's monograph is devoted to the development of a two-dimensional circumplex model of personality, his most lasting contribution to clinical psychology. Developed by Leary in collaboration with several of his mentors at Berkeley, the circumplex model presents a methodology for measuring interpersonal behavior using a collection of simple and specific behavioral descriptors. Each behavior is situated along a continuum defined by two dimensions: dominance-submission and hostility-affiliation. Sixteen generic interpersonal themes are identified along the circumference of a circle where the two dimensions comprise the circle's axes. The circumplex model can be utilized for a variety of purposes, including the assessment of the structure of personality, temporal variation in personality, and variability in personality due to situational context. Extensions and revisions of the Leary circumplex continue to be developed with the primary goal of better measuring and understanding the multifaceted and complex nature of interpersonal relationships.

After a brief tenure as assistant professor at Berkeley (1950–1955), Leary worked as director of the prestigious Kaiser Foundation in Oakland, California (1955–1958), where he applied his circumplex model to understand the process of group psychotherapy. During the time of his greatest academic achievements, Leary experienced a personal tragedy when his wife committed suicide in 1955, leaving him to raise their eight-year-old daughter and six-year-old son.

In 1958 Leary left Berkeley with his two children and moved to Harvard, where he accepted a position as lecturer at Harvard's Center for Personality Research and began the most controversial period of his academic career. In collaboration with his Harvard colleagues, most notably Richard Alpert and Ralph Metzner, Leary started an experimental research program examining the effects of psychedelic/hallucinogenic drugs on behavioral change. In a series of studies with Metzner, Leary explored the rehabilitative effects of psilocybin on young criminal offenders at the Massachusetts Correctional Facility in Concord. Leary believed that psilocybin, under guided professional supervision, could act as a conduit for internal reflection and behavioral change. In a second series of studies, Leary's doctoral student, Walter Pahnke (1931–1971), examined the effects of psilocybin on the mystical and religious experiences of volunteer seminary students, hypothesizing that psychedelic drugs would facilitate such experiences.

Leary's research, and his expulsion from Harvard in 1963, would catapult him into the public spotlight, where he became a counterculture icon. Popularizing the catch phrase "Turn on, Tune in, Drop Out" in the 1960s, Leary was an open advocate of the use of psychedelic drugs as a method of exploring and expanding consciousness. He

INTERNATIONAL ENCYCLOPEDIA OF THE SOCIAL SCIENCES, 2ND EDITION

published several books on the subject, including *The Psychedelic Experience* (1964), coauthored with his former Harvard colleagues Metzner and Alpert. A controversial and outspoken figure throughout his life, Leary died of prostate cancer in 1996.

SEE ALSO *Castaneda, Carlos; Consciousness; Drugs of Abuse; Hallucinogens; Personality*

BIBLIOGRAPHY

Greenfield, Robert. 2006. *Timothy Leary: A Biography*. New York: Harcourt.

Leary, Timothy. 1957. *Interpersonal Diagnosis of Personality: A Functional Theory and Methodology for Personality Evaluation*. New York: Ronald Press.

Leary, Timothy. 1983. *Flashbacks: An Autobiography*. New York: Tarcher/Putnam.

Metzner, Ralph, Ralph Alpert, and Timothy J. Leary. 1964. *The Psychedelic Experience: Manual Based on the Tibetan Book of the Dead*. Berkeley, CA: University Books.

Jamie D. Bedics
David C. Atkins

LEAST SQUARES, ORDINARY

Ordinary least squares (OLS) is a method for fitting lines or curves to observed data in situations where one variable (the response variable) is believed to be explained or caused by one or more other explanatory variables. OLS is most commonly used to estimate the parameters of linear regression models of the form

$$Y_i = \beta_1 + \beta_2 g_2(Z_{i2}) + \cdots + \beta_K g_K(Z_{iK}) + \varepsilon_i. \quad (1)$$

The subscripts i index observations; ε_i is a random variable with zero expected value (i.e., $E(\varepsilon_i) = 0$, for all observations $i = 1, \ldots, n$); and the functions $g_1(), \ldots, g_k()$ are known. The right-hand side explanatory variables $Z_{i2}, \ldots, Z_{iK}$ are assumed to be exogenous and to cause the dependent, endogenous left-hand side response variable Y_i. The $\beta_1, \ldots, \beta_K$ are unknown parameters, and hence must be estimated. Setting $X_{ij} = g_j(Z_{ij})$ for all $j = 1, \ldots, K$ and $i = 1, \ldots, n$, the model in (1) can be written as

$$Y_i = \beta_1 + \beta_2 X_{i2} + \cdots + \beta_K X_{iK} + \varepsilon_i. \quad (2)$$

The random error term ε_i represents statistical noise due to measurement error in the dependent variable, unexplained variation due to random variation, or perhaps the omission of some explanatory variables from the model.

In the context of OLS estimation, an important feature of the models in (1) and (2) is that they are linear in parameters. Since the functions $g_j()$ are known, it does not matter whether these functions are linear or nonlinear. Given n observations on the variables Y_i and X_{ij}, the OLS method involves fitting a line (in the case where $K = 2$), a plane (for $K = 3$), or a hyperplane (when $K > 3$) to the data that describes the average, expected value of the response variable for given values of the explanatory variables. With OLS, this is done using a particular criterion as shown below, although other methods use different criteria.

An estimator is a random variable whose realizations are regarded as estimates of some parameter of interest. Replacing the unknown parameters $\beta_1, \ldots, \beta_K$ and errors ε_i in (2) with estimators $\hat{\beta}_1, \ldots, \hat{\beta}_K$ and $\hat{\varepsilon}$ yields

$$Y_i = \hat{\beta}_1 + \hat{\beta}_2 X_{i2} + \cdots + \hat{\beta}_K X_{ik} + \hat{\varepsilon}_i. \quad (3)$$

The relation in (2) is called the population regression function, whereas the relation in (3) is called the sample regression function. The population regression function describes the unobserved, true relationship between the explanatory variables and the response variable that is to be estimated. The sample regression function is an estimator of the population regression function.

Rearranging terms in (3), the residual $\hat{\varepsilon}_i$ can be expressed as

$$\hat{\varepsilon}_i = Y_i - \hat{\beta}_1 - \hat{\beta}_2 X_{i2} - \cdots - \hat{\beta}_K X_{ik}. \quad (4)$$

The OLS estimators $\hat{\beta}_1, \ldots, \hat{\beta}_K$ of the parameters $\beta_1, \ldots, \beta_K$ in (2) are obtained by minimizing the error sum-of-squares

$$ESS = \sum_{i=1}^{n}$$
$$\hat{\varepsilon}_i^2 = [Y_i - \hat{\beta}_1 - \hat{\beta}_2 X_{i2} - \cdots - \hat{\beta}_K X_{ik}]^2 \quad (5)$$

with respect to $\hat{\beta}_1, \ldots, \hat{\beta}_K$. Hence the OLS estimator of the population regression function (2) minimizes the sum of squared residuals, which are the squared distances (in the direction of the Y-axis) between each observed value Y_i and the sample regression function given by (3).

By minimizing the sum of squared residuals, disproportionate weight may be given to observations that are outliers—that is, those that are atypical and that lie apart from the majority of observations. An alternative approach is to minimize the sum

$$\sum_{i=1}^{n} |\ddot{\varepsilon}_i|$$

of absolute deviations; the resulting estimator is called the least absolute deviations (LAD) estimator. Although this estimator has some attractive properties, it requires linear programming methods for computation, and the estimator is biased in small samples.

To illustrate, first consider the simple case where $K = 1$. Then equation (2) becomes

$$Y_i = \hat{\beta}_1 + \varepsilon_i \qquad (6)$$

In this simple model, random variables Y_i are random deviations (to the left or to the right) away from the constant β_1. The error-sum-of-squares in (5) becomes

$$\text{ESS} = \sum_{i=1}^{n} \hat{\varepsilon}_i^2 = [Y_i - \hat{\beta}_1]^2. \qquad (7)$$

This can be minimized by differentiating with respect to $\hat{\beta}_1$ and setting the derivative equal to 0; that is,

$$\partial \text{ESS}/\partial \beta_1 = -2 \sum_{i=1}^{n} (Y_i - \hat{\beta}_1) = 0$$

and then solving for $\hat{\beta}_1$ to obtain

$$\hat{\beta}_1 = n^{-1} \sum_{i=1}^{n} Y_i.$$

In this simple model, therefore, the OLS estimator of β_1 is merely the sample mean of the Y_i. Given a set of n observations on Y_i, these values can be used to compute an OLS estimate of β_1 by simply adding them and then dividing the sum by n.

In the slightly more complicated case where $K = 2$, the population regression function (2) becomes

$$Y_i = \beta_1 + \beta_2 X_{i2} + \varepsilon_i. \qquad (8)$$

Minimizing the error sum of squares in this model yields OLS estimators

$$\hat{\beta}_2 = \sum_{i=1}^{n} (X_{i2} - \bar{X}_2)(\bar{Y}_i - Y) / \sum_{i=1}^{n} (X_{i2} - \bar{X}_2)^2 \qquad (9)$$

and

$$\hat{\beta}_1 = \bar{Y} - \hat{\beta}_2 \bar{X}_2$$

where $\bar{X}_2$ and $\bar{Y}$ are the sample means of X_{i2} and Y_i, respectively.

In the more general case where $K > 2$, it is useful to think of the model in (2) as a system of equations, such as:

$$Y_1 = \beta_1 + \beta_2 X_{12} + \dots + \beta_K X_{1K} + \varepsilon_1$$
$$Y_2 = \beta_1 + \beta_2 X_{22} + \dots + \beta_K X_{2K} + \varepsilon_2$$
$$\vdots$$
$$Y_n = \beta_1 + \beta_2 X_{n2} + \dots + \beta_K X_{nK} + \varepsilon_n.$$

This can be written in matrix form as

$$Y = X\beta + \varepsilon \qquad (10)$$

where Y is an $(n \times 1)$ matrix containing elements $Y_i, \dots, Y_n$; X is an $(n \, Y \, K)$ matrix with element X_{ij} in the i-th row, j-th column (elements in the first column of X are equal to 1); β is a $(K \times 1)$ matrix containing the unknown parameters $\beta_1, \dots, \beta_K$; and ε is an $(n \times 1)$ matrix containing the random variables $\varepsilon_1, \dots, \varepsilon_n$. Minimizing the error-sum-of-squares yields the OLS estimator

$$\hat{\beta} = (X'X)^{-1} X'Y. \qquad (11)$$

This is a $(K \times 1)$ matrix containing elements $\hat{\beta}_1, \dots, \hat{\beta}_K$. In modern software, $\hat{\beta}$ is computed by inverting the $(K \times K)$ matrix $X'X$ using the Q-R decomposition. The OLS estimator can always be computed, unless $X'X$ is singular, which happens when there is an exact linear relationship among any of the columns of the matrix X.

The Gauss-Markov theorem establishes that provided

i. the relationship between Y and X is linear as described by (10);

ii. the elements of X are fixed, nonstochastic, and there exists no exact linear relationship among the columns of X; and

iii. $E(\varepsilon) = 0$ and $E(\varepsilon\varepsilon') = \sigma^2 I$,

the OLS estimator $\hat{\beta}$ is the best (in the sense of minimum variance) linear, unbiased estimator of β. Modified versions of the OLS estimator (e.g., weighted least squares, feasible generalized least squares) can be used when data do not conform to the assumptions given above.

The variance-covariance matrix of the OLS estimator given in (11) is $\sigma^2(X'X)^{-1}$, a $(K \times K)$ matrix whose diagonal elements give the variances of the K elements of the vector $\hat{\beta}$, and whose off-diagonal elements give the corresponding covariances among the elements of $\hat{\beta}$. This matrix can be estimated by replacing the unknown variance of ε, namely σ^2, with the estimator $\hat{\sigma}^2 = \hat{\varepsilon}'\hat{\varepsilon}/(n - K)$. The estimated variances and covariances can then be used for hypothesis testing.

DISCOVERY OF THE METHOD

Robin L. Plackett (1972) and Stephen M. Stigler (1981) describe the debate that exists over who discovered the OLS method. The first publication to describe the method was Adriene Marie Legendre's *Nouvelles méthodes pour la détermination des orbites des comètes* in 1806 (the term *least squares* comes from the French words *moindres quarrés* in the title of an appendix to Legendre's book), followed by publications by Robert Adrain (1808) and Carl Friedrich Gauss ([1809] 2004). However, Gauss made several claims that he developed the method as early as 1794 or 1795; Stigler discusses evidence that supports these claims in his article "Gauss and the Invention of Least Squares" (1981).

Both Legendre and Gauss considered bivariate models such as the one given in (8), and they used OLS to predict the position of comets in their orbits about the sun using data from astronomical observations. Legendre's approach was purely mathematical in the sense that he viewed the problem as one of solving for two unknowns in an overdetermined system of n equations. Gauss ([1809] 2004) was the first to give a probabilistic interpretation to the least squares method. Gauss reasoned that for a sequence $Y_1, \ldots, Y_n$ of n independent random variables whose density functions satisfy certain conditions, if the sample mean

$$\bar{Y}_n = n^{-1} \sum_{i=1}^{n} Y_i$$

is the most probable combination for all values of the random variables and each $n \geq 1$, then for some $\sigma^2 > 0$, the density function of the random variables is given by the normal, or Gaussian, density function

$$f(Y_i) = \frac{1}{\sigma\sqrt{2\pi}} \exp[\frac{1}{2}\sigma^{-2} Y_i^2].$$

In the nineteenth century, this was known as the law of errors. This argument led Gauss to consider the regression equation as containing independent, normally distributed error terms.

The least squares method quickly gained widespread acceptance. At the beginning of the twentieth century, Karl Pearson remarked in his article in *Biometrika* (1902, p. 266) that "it is usually taken for granted that the right method for determining the constants is the method of least squares." Beginning in the 1870s, the method was used in biological, genetic applications by Pearson, Francis Galton, George Udny Yule, and others. In his article "Regression towards Mediocrity in Hereditary Stature" (1886), Galton used the term *regression* to describe the tendency of the progeny of exceptional parents to be, on average, less exceptional than their parents, but today the term *regression analysis* has a rather different meaning.

Pearson provided substantial empirical support for Galton's notion of biological regression by looking at hereditary data on the color of horses and dogs and their offspring and the heights of fathers and their sons. Pearson worked in terms of correlation coefficients, implicitly assuming that the response and explanatory variables were jointly normally distributed. In a series of papers (1896, 1900, 1902, 1903a, 1903b), Pearson formalized and extended notions of correlation and regression from the bivariate model to multivariate models. Pearson began by

considering, for the bivariate model, bivariate distributions for the explanatory and response variables. In the case of the bivariate normal distribution, the conditional expectation of Y can be derived in terms of a linear expression involving X, suggesting the model in (8). Similarly, by assuming that the response variable and several explanatory variables have a multivariate normal joint distribution, one can derive the expectation of the response variable, conditional on the explanatory variables, as a linear equation in the explanatory variables, suggesting the multivariate regression model in (2).

Pearson's approach, involving joint distributions for the response and explanatory variables, led him to argue in later papers that researchers should in some situations consider nonsymmetric joint distributions for response and explanatory variables, which could lead to nonlinear expressions for the conditional expectation of the response variable. These arguments had little influence; Pearson could not offer tangible examples because the joint normal distribution was the only joint distribution to have been characterized at that time. Today, however, there are several examples of bivariate joint distributions that lead to nonlinear regression curves, including the bivariate exponential and bivariate logistic distributions. Aris Spanos describes such examples in his book *Probability Theory and Statistical Inference: Econometric Modeling with Observational Data* (1999, chapter 7). Ronald A. Fisher (1922, 1925) later formulated the regression problem closer to Gauss's characterization by assuming that only the conditional distribution of the response variable is normal, without requiring that the joint distribution be normal.

CURRENT USES

Today, OLS and its variants are probably the most widely used statistical techniques. OLS is frequently used in the behavioral and social sciences as well as in biological and physical sciences. Even in situations where the relationship between dependent and explanatory variables is nonlinear, it is often possible to transform variables to arrive at a linear relationship. In other situations, assuming linearity may provide a reasonable approximation to nonlinear relationships over certain ranges of the data. The numerical difficulties faced by Gauss and Pearson in their day are now viewed as trivial given the increasing speed of modern computers. Computational problems are encountered, however, in problems with very large numbers of dimensions. Most of the problems that are encountered involve obtaining accurate solutions for the inverse matrix $(X'X)^{-1}$ using computers with finite precision; care must be taken to ensure that solutions are not contaminated by round-off error. Åke Björck, in *Numerical Methods for*

Least Squares Problems (1996), gives an extensive treatment of numerical issues involved with OLS.

SEE ALSO *Classical Statistical Analysis; Cliometrics; Econometric Decomposition; Galton, Francis; Ordinary Least Squares Regression; Pearson, Karl; Regression Analysis; Regression Towards the Mean; Statistics*

BIBLIOGRAPHY

Adrain, Robert. 1808. Research Concerning the Probabilities of the Errors Which Happen in Making Observations, &c. *The Analyst, or Mathematical Museum* 1: 93–109.

Björck, Åke. 1996. *Numerical Methods for Least Squares Problems.* Philadelphia: SIAM.

Fisher, Ronald Aylmer. 1922. The Goodness of Fit of Regression Formulae and the Distribution of Regression Coefficients. *Journal of the Royal Statistical Society* 85 (4): 597–612.

Fisher, Ronald Aylmer. 1925. *Statistical Methods for Research Workers.* Edinburgh: Oliver and Boyd.

Galton, Francis. 1886. Regression towards Mediocrity in Hereditary Stature. *Journal of the Anthropological Institute* 15: 246–263.

Gauss, Carl Friedrich. [1809] 2004. *Theory of the Motion of the Heavenly Bodies Moving about the Sun in Conic Sections.* Trans. Charles Henry Davis. Mineola, NY: Dover.

Gauss, Carl Friedrich. 1866–1933. *Werke.* 12 vols. Göttingen, Germany: Gedruckt in der Dieterichschen Universitätsdruckerei.

Legendre, Adriene Marie. 1806. *Nouvelles méthodes pour la détermination des orbites des comètes.* Paris: Courcier.

Pearson, Karl. 1896. Contributions to the Mathematical Theory of Evolution III: Regression, Heredity, and Panmixia. *Proceedings of the Royal Society of London* 59: 69–71.

Pearson, Karl. 1900. Contributions to the Mathematical Theory of Evolution VIII: On the Correlation of Characters Not Quantitatively Measurable. *Proceedings of the Royal Society of London* 66: 241–244.

Pearson, Karl. 1902. On the Systematic Fitting of Curves to Observations and Measurements. *Biometrika* 1 (3): 265–303.

Pearson, Karl. 1903a. Contributions to the Mathematical Theory of Evolution: On Homotyposis in Homologous but Differentiated Organs. *Proceedings of the Royal Society of London* 71: 288–313.

Pearson, Karl. 1903b. The Law of Ancestral Heredity. *Biometrika* 2 (2): 211–228.

Plackett, Robin L. 1972. The Discovery of the Method of Least Squares. *Biometrika* 59 (2): 239–251.

Spanos, Aris. 1999. *Probability Theory and Statistical Inference: Econometric Modeling with Observational Data.* Cambridge, U.K.: Cambridge University Press.

Stigler, Stephen M. 1981. Gauss and the Invention of Least Squares. *Annals of Statistics* 9 (3): 465–474.

Paul W. Wilson

LEAST SQUARES, THREE-STAGE

The term *three-stage least squares* (3SLS) refers to a method of estimation that combines system equation, sometimes known as *seemingly unrelated regression* (SUR), with two-stage least squares estimation. It is a form of instrumental variables estimation that permits correlations of the unobserved disturbances across several equations, as well as restrictions among coefficients of different equations, and improves upon the efficiency of equation-by-equation estimation by taking into account such correlations across equations. Unlike the two-stage least squares (2SLS) approach for a system of equations, which would estimate the coefficients of each structural equation separately, the three-stage least squares estimates all coefficients simultaneously. It is assumed that each equation of the system is at least just-identified. Equations that are underidentified are disregarded in the 3SLS estimation.

Three-stage least squares originated in a paper by Arnold Zellner and Henri Theil (1962). In the classical specification, although the structural disturbances may be correlated across equations (*contemporaneous correlation*), it is assumed that within each structural equation the disturbances are both homoskedastic and serially uncorrelated. The classical specification thus implies that the disturbance covariance matrix within each equation is diagonal, whereas the entire system's covariance matrix is nondiagonal.

The Zellner-Theil proposal for efficient estimation of this system is in three stages, wherein the first stage involves obtaining estimates of the residuals of the structural equations by two-stage least squares of all identified equations; the second stage involves computation of the optimal instrument, or weighting matrix, using the estimated residuals to construct the disturbance variance-covariance matrix; and the third stage is joint estimation of the system of equations using the optimal instrument. Although 3SLS is generally asymptotically more efficient than 2SLS, if even a single equation of the system is misspecified, 3SLS estimates of coefficients of all equations are generally inconsistent.

The Zellner-Theil 3SLS estimator for the coefficient of each equation is shown to be asymptotically at least as efficient as the corresponding 2SLS estimator of that equation. However, Zellner and Theil also discuss a number of interesting conditions under which 3SLS and 2SLS estimators are equivalent. First, if the structural disturbances have no mutual correlations across equations (the variance-covariance matrix of the system disturbances is diagonal), then 3SLS estimates are identical to the 2SLS estimates equation by equation. Second, if all equations in the system are just-identified, then 3SLS is also equivalent to 2SLS equation by equation. Third, if a subset of m

equations is overidentified while the remaining equations are just-identified, then 3SLS estimation of the *m* over-identified equations is equivalent to 2SLS of these *m* equations.

The 3SLS estimator has been extended to estimation of a nonlinear system of simultaneous equations by Takeshi Amemiya (1977) and Dale Jorgenson and Jean-Jacques Laffont (1975). An excellent discussion of 3SLS estimation, including a formal derivation of its analytical and asymptotic properties, and its comparison with full-information maximum likelihood (FIML), is given in Jerry Hausman (1983).

SEE ALSO *Instrumental Variables Regression; Least Squares, Two-Stage; Regression; Seemingly Unrelated Regressions*

BIBLIOGRAPHY

Amemiya, Takeshi. 1977. The Maximum Likelihood and the Nonlinear Three-stage Least Squares Estimator in the General Nonlinear Simultaneous Equation Model. *Econometrica* 45 (4): 955–968.

Dhrymes, Phoebus J. 1973. Small Sample and Asymptotic Relations Between Maximum Likelihood and Three Stage Least Squares Estimators. *Econometrica* 41 (2): 357–364.

Gallant, A. Ronald, and Dale W. Jorgenson. 1979. Statistical Inference for a System of Simultaneous, Non-linear, Implicit Equations in the Context of Instrumental Variable Estimation. *Journal of Econometrics* 11: 275–302.

Robinson, Peter M. 1991. Best Nonlinear Three-stage Least Squares Estimation of Certain Econometric Models. *Econometrica* 59 (3): 755–786.

Sargan, J. D. 1964. Three-stage Least-Squares and Full Maximum Likelihood Estimates. *Econometrica* 32: 77–81.

Zellner, Arnold, and Henri Theil. 1962. Three-stage Least Squares: Simultaneous Estimation of Simultaneous Equations. *Econometrica* 30 (1): 54–78.

Mitali Das

LEAST SQUARES, TWO-STAGE

Two-stage least squares (2SLS or TSLS) is an alternative to the usual linear regression technique (ordinary least squares, or OLS), used when the right-hand side variables in the regression are correlated with the error term. 2SLS uses additional information to compute asymptotically unbiased coefficients (i.e., approximately unbiased in large samples), in contrast to the OLS coefficients, which are biased even in large samples.

In the regression model with *k* explanatory variables and *n* observations

$$y_i = b_1 x_{i1} + b_2 x_{i2} + \cdots + b_k x_{ik} + e_i$$

OLS will produce biased coefficients if any of the *x* variables is correlated with the error *e*. Such correlation may occur if any of the *x* variables is measured with error, if relevant variables are left out of the specification, or if any *x* variables are endogenous (determined in part by *y*.)

Suppose the investigator has a list of q ($q \geq k$) instrumental variables, $z_1, \ldots, z_q$, where to qualify as an instrument each *z* must be correlated with one or more *x* variables and must be uncorrelated with the error term. In the *first-stage* regressions, each *x* is regressed on the instruments and the fitted value $\hat{x}$ is computed. By construction, $\hat{x}$ will be a proxy for *x* that is uncorrelated with the error term *e*. In this way, $\hat{x}$ is purged of the correlation that made *x* unsuitable for use in the regression. In the *second stage* regression, *y* is regressed on the set of fitted $\hat{x}$'s. The estimated coefficients from this second stage are the two-stage least squares estimates of *b*. Appropriate adjustments are made to compute standard errors and other statistics associated with the regression, as the statistics reported directly in the second-stage regression are not valid.

In the simple case of one explanatory variable and one instrument, the formulas for the OLS and 2SLS coefficients are given by, respectively

$$\hat{b}_{OLS} = \frac{\sum_{i=1}^{n} y_i x_i}{\sum_{i=1}^{n} x_i^2} \qquad \hat{b}_{2SLS} = \frac{\sum_{i=1}^{n} y_i z_i}{\sum_{i=1}^{n} x_i z_i}$$

Note that modern software computes 2SLS coefficients directly, rather than actually computing two stages of regression.

The difficult task in using 2SLS is to specify a list of instruments known a priori to be uncorrelated with the error term. In a linear simultaneous equation model, all exogenous variables (those variables not determined in the model) are candidates to serve as instruments. In particular, a variable may serve both as an explanatory variable and as an instrument (*x* and *z*) if it is uncorrelated with the error. *Identification* requires that the number of instruments, *q*, be equal to or greater than the number of right-hand side variables, *k*.

2SLS is an *instrumental variable* (IV) estimator and the terms 2SLS and IV are often used interchangeably. Estimators closely related to 2SLS include the generalized method of moments (GMM) for nonlinear estimation, three-stage least squares (3SLS) for estimation of systems of equations, and limited-information maximum likelihood (LIML).

2SLS is a well-established technique, particularly in economics. Difficulties due to *weak instruments*, where the correlation between *x* and *z* is very low, constitute an ongoing area of investigation.

SEE ALSO *Error-correction Mechanisms; Least Squares, Ordinary; Least Squares, Three-Stage; Properties of Estimators (Asymptotic and Exact); Regression*

BIBLIOGRAPHY

Wooldridge, Jeffrey M. 2005. *Introductory Econometrics: A Modern Approach*, 3rd ed. Mason, OH: Thomson/South-Western.

Richard Startz

LEBANESE CIVIL WAR

The Lebanese civil war erupted in April 1975 and ended in October 1990. Since its independence in 1943, Lebanon has been governed by a confessional political system in which parliamentary seats and governmental and civil service positions are distributed among religious sects in accordance with their population ratio. The 1926 constitution, which officially recognizes the distribution of cabinet positions and governmental jobs on a sectarian basis, was supplemented at the time of independence in 1943 by an informal "gentlemen's agreement," the National Pact, at the time of independence. According to this agreement, the president has to be a Maronite Christian, the prime minister a Sunni Muslim, the speaker of the Parliament a Shia Muslim, and the deputy speaker a Greek Orthodox. The Muslims shunned pan-Arabism and recognized Lebanon's independence; Christians agreed to the Arab character of the country and eschewed western protection. This consociational democracy was based on cooperation and moderation among mainly Maronite and Sunni elites, perpetuated a weak state, and institutionalized the sectarian differences. Despite its defects, though, the Lebanese political system established order and stability from 1943 until 1975, weathering the crises of 1952 and 1958.

CAUSES OF THE WAR

Several developments in the 1960s undermined the precarious Lebanese republic. First, socioeconomic developments exacerbated economic inequalities. The Lebanese economy was characterized by free trade, low industrialization, low taxation, and minimal state intervention. Hence, the state was in position to effectively address the needs of the poorer segments of the population. Also, economic differences overlapped with sectarian differences:

Whereas Christians in general disproportionately benefited from the economic growth, the Shia remained at the bottom of the socioeconomic ladder. Second, demographic trends changed the population ratio between sects. The Shia had the highest fertility rate, followed by the Sunnis. The distribution of political power, which was based on the 1932 census, ceased to reflect demographic realities, and these developments augmented the Muslim demand for institutional reform. The rise of radical and populist forces undermined the power of the traditional Sunni and Shia elites. Third, and most importantly, regional events put immense burdens on the Lebanese political system. The rise of Arab nationalism in the 1950s exacerbated the sectarian tensions in Lebanon. Although Sunni Muslims were supportive of the anti-western policies of Egyptian president Gamal Abdel Nasser (1918–1970), the Maronites adamantly refused to allow Lebanon to join the pro-Nasser camp. Lebanon was on the brink of civil war in 1958 when the Maronite president asked for help from the United States. The landing of the U.S. marines in Beirut quelled the violence, and a compromise candidate, Fuad Chehab, was elected president. After the 1967 Six Days War and their expulsion from Jordan in 1970, Palestinian guerillas chose Lebanon as the main base of their operations against Israel. The November 1969 Cairo agreement between Lebanon and the Palestinian Liberation Organization (PLO) gave the PLO extraterritorial rights. The entrenchment of the PLO in Lebanon provoked Christian resentment because it further changed the demographic ratio to the disadvantage of Christians, and it brought fierce reprisals from the Israelis, who held the Lebanese government responsible for the actions of the Palestinians. The Lebanese army was unable to control the PLO or to defend the country against Israeli incursions. The insecurity in southern Lebanon led to the dislocation of Shia villagers to urban peripheries. Furthermore, after Hafez al-Assad (1930–2000) assumed the presidency of Syria in 1970, Syria pursued a more assertive and ambitious foreign policy in Lebanon. The ruling Alawite minority perceived the Shia of Lebanon as a counterweight against the Sunni majority of Syria and the Palestinians.

By 1975 two main coalitions were confronting each other. On the one hand, Maronite Christians came together under the rubric of the Lebanese Forces (LF), which was dominated by the Phalange Party led by Bashir Gemayel (1947–1982). The LF was in favor of the continuation of the existing confessional system of government in Lebanon and opposed any institutional reform benefiting the Muslims. Moreover, it espoused the end of Palestinian extraterritorial rights. During the conflict, the LF toyed with the idea of creating a small Christian state in Mount Lebanon, an idea that was rejected by several more moderate Maronite leaders. On the other hand was an amalgam of groups that demanded the end of the confessional system and sympathized with the Palestinian goals. The Lebanese National Movement (LNM) included the Progressive Socialist Party (PSP) led by the Druze leader Kamal Jumblatt (1917–1977), the Amal militia headed by the Shia leader Musa al-Sadr (1928–1978?), the Syrian Social Nationalist Party (SSNP), the Communists, the Arab nationalist Ba'th Party, and the Sunni al-Murabitun militia, and it had the support of the PLO.

FIGHTING FROM 1975 TO 1985

Fighting broke out between Palestinian guerrillas and the Phalange in April 1975, and several months later Lebanon was engulfed in full-scale civil war. The first phase of the civil war continued for eighteen months. By December 1975 the LNM was on the verge of defeating the LF, but Syria intervened to prevent that outcome because the ruling Alawite regime in Syria feared that the dissolution of Lebanon or the leftist and PLO domination of Lebanon would jeopardize its rule over the Sunni majority in Syria. Both the United States and Israel gave tacit agreement to Syria's intervention, which resulted in de facto partition of Lebanon. With the Syrian army in control of most of the country, the LF, the PLO, the Druze, and the pro-Israeli Free Lebanon Army established themselves in different parts of the country. The United Nations Interim Force in Lebanon (UNIFIL) became a buffer between the pro-Israeli militia and the PLO.

From 1976 to 1982 the conflict between the PLO and Israel continued unabated. In March 1977 Jumblatt was assassinated, and the LNM was beset by factionalism. In August 1978 al-Sadr disappeared while on a trip to Libya. Meanwhile, the relations between the LF and Syria deteriorated, and the Syrian regime suppressed the Muslim Brotherhood after much bloodshed. In 1981 Syrian-Israel relations deteriorated further, and Israel initiated a large-scale invasion of Lebanon in 1982. The Israeli goals were the destruction of PLO autonomy, the weakening of the Syrian influence in Lebanon, and most ambitiously, the reconstruction of the Lebanese state under the control of Gemayel, who allied himself with the Israelis. The invasion achieved its first goal, as the PLO was obliged to leave West Beirut in 1982 and later, Tripoli in 1983 after the Syrian attacks. However, the Israeli army's defeat of the Syrian forces did not end Syrian influence, which was rapidly restored with Soviet support. Gemayel was assassinated in September 1982, shortly after he was elected president. A security pact signed between Israel and Lebanon in May 1983 was later abrogated. Moreover, the LF massacres of Palestinian refugees in the Sabra and Shatila camps surrounded by the Israeli army in September 1982 left the Israeli goal of establish-

ing order in Lebanon in tatters. A multinational force composed of U.S., French, and Italian forces landed in West Beirut in October 1982, but its mission became a disaster when the U.S. and French barracks were devastated by suicide bombing attacks in October 1983. The Israelis withdrew from most of Lebanon in 1985, but remained in control of the southern border zone by sponsoring a Christian-dominated militia, the South Lebanon Army. The Israeli occupation eventually ended in May 2000, but it had contributed to the Islamic mobilization of the Shia and the rise of Hezbollah as the most powerful local organization in Lebanon. Support from the Islamic republic of Iran and the cooperation of Syria contributed to the emergence of Hezbollah as an effective guerrilla organization with extensive social services.

END OF THE CIVIL WAR

The later 1980s saw intra-sectarian conflict among the Muslims and Christians and the complete fragmentation of the state authority in Lebanon. The Shia militia Amal took over West Beirut in February 1984, and tensions between Amal and the Palestinians erupted into open conflict—the "war of the camps"—in 1985, prompting the Syrian occupation of West Beirut in 1987. Armed rivalry between Hezbollah and Amal from 1988 to 1990 resulted in the establishment of the former as a major force in Beirut. Among Christians, General Michel Aoun (b. 1935), the commander of the Lebanese army, emerged as a strong contender for leadership; President Amine Gemayel appointed him prime minister in 1988 in defiance of the National Pact. Aoun vehemently opposed Syrian interference and portrayed himself as a secular nationalist leader. He clashed with the LF for control of the Christian enclave and declared a "war of liberation" against Syria in March 1989. He was ultimately unsuccessful, and was forced into exile in 1991. With his defeat, the Lebanese Civil War came to an end.

A principal reason for the end of active hostilities was the exhaustion brought on by the fifteen years of warfare. None of the groups was able to establish dominance over others, and sectarian divisions continued as before. Syria emerged as the hegemonic power in Lebanon, with U.S. endorsement, and achieved veto power over all important political decisions. The Ta'if Agreement (1989), which was signed by the surviving Lebanese parliamentarians and crystallized the ethos of "no victor and no vanquished," amended the constitution but did not dismantle confessionalism. By its terms, the power of the president was reduced in favor of the prime minister and the speaker of the Parliament, and the parliamentary seats were equally distributed between Christians and Muslims. All the militias were disarmed in March 1991 with the exception of Hezbollah, which continued its "resistance" against Israel in the border zone. Syria did not completely withdraw from Lebanon until 2005.

SEE ALSO *Arab-Israeli War of 1967; Civil Wars; Communalism; Conflict; Democracy, Consociational; Ethnic Conflict; Ethnic Fractionalization; Muslims; Palestine Liberation Organization (PLO); Palestinians; Phalangists; Suez Crisis*

BIBLIOGRAPHY

Dekmejian, Richard Hrair. 1978. Consociational Democracy in Crisis: The Case of Lebanon. *Comparative Politics* 10 (2): 251–256.

El-Khazen, Farid. 2000. *The Breakdown of the State in Lebanon, 1967–1976.* Cambridge, MA: Harvard University Press.

Fisk, Robert. 2002. *Pity the Nation: The Abduction of Lebanon.* 4th ed. New York: Nation Books.

Khalaf, Samir. 2002. *Civil and Uncivil Violence in Lebanon.* New York: Columbia University Press.

Picard, Elizabeth. 1996. *Lebanon: A Shattered Country: Myths and Realities of the Wars in Lebanon.* Revised ed. New York: Holmes and Meier.

Rabinovich, Itamar. 1986. *The War for Lebanon, 1970–1985.* Revised ed. Ithaca, NY: Cornell University Press.

Gunes Murat Tezcur

LE BON, GUSTAVE
SEE *Race and Psychology.*

LE DUC THO
1911–1990

Phan Dinh Khai was born the son of a midlevel Vietnamese civil servant in Nam Ha Province of French Indochina on October 14, 1911. He changed his name to Le Duc Tho when he became a committed revolutionary during his teenage years. In 1929 Tho joined with Ho Chi Minh (1890–1969) and other Vietnamese radicals in founding the Indochinese (later Vietnamese) Communist Party. For agitating against French rule, Tho and his comrades spent much of the 1930s in French colonial prisons. During World War II (1939–1945), Tho helped to organize the Viet Minh, the Communist-led resistance movement against the Japanese occupiers of Indochina. By the end of the war, Tho was a member of the Central Committee of the Communist Party and a leader of the Viet Minh. When France tried to retake Indochina in 1945, Tho led southern Viet Minh resistance during the Indochina War (1946–1954). With the defeat of the

French, North Vietnam gained independence. Tho became a member of the Politburo in 1955 and secretary of the Central Committee in 1960.

During the Vietnam War (1956–1975), Tho returned south to organize Viet Cong guerrilla resistance against U.S. forces and the South Vietnamese government. In 1968, when peace talks began in Paris between the United States and North Vietnam, Tho participated as a lead negotiator for the Communist side. For years, Tho stonewalled the talks with nonnegotiable demands for U.S. withdrawal and the dismantling of South Vietnam's government. In 1970 Tho agreed to meet in private with U.S. national security adviser Henry Kissinger. Over the next two years, these secret back-channel discussions gradually resolved the many difficult issues involved in disengaging the United States from the Vietnam War. Finally, in October of 1972, Kissinger revealed to the world that "peace is at hand," just in time to help President Richard Nixon (1913–1994) obtain reelection by a landslide. After one last round of U.S. bombing killed thousands of Vietnamese civilians, Tho and Kissinger signed the Paris Peace Accords on January 25, 1973.

For their role in ending the American phase of the Vietnam War, Tho and Kissinger were jointly awarded the 1973 Nobel Peace Prize. Tho was the first Asian ever to win this honor—but he declined the award, saying that peace had not yet come to his country. Instead, Tho returned to South Vietnam to supervise the North Vietnamese offensive that delivered a Communist victory in 1975. A decade later, Tho told U.S. television viewers: "We hope American wives and mothers will never again allow their husbands and sons to go to die in another Vietnam War anywhere in the world" (quoted in Dowd 1985, p. A4). Tho remained active in party leadership after the war and oversaw the Vietnamese invasion of Cambodia in 1978, but he opposed economic reforms introduced by his government in the 1980s. Out of step with changes in Vietnamese Communism, Tho resigned his official posts in 1986 and retired. He died of cancer on October 13, 1990.

SEE ALSO *Anticolonial Movements; Communism; Guerrilla Warfare; Kissinger, Henry; Liberation Movements; Nixon, Richard M.; Nobel Peace Prize; Vietnam War*

BIBLIOGRAPHY

Current Biography 1975. 1975. Le Duc Tho. 235–238. New York: Wilson.

Dowd, Maureen. 1985. Kissinger and Le Duc Tho Meet Again. *New York Times* May 1: A4.

Lewis, Flora. 1973. Le Duc Tho. *New York Times.* January 24: 18.

Pace, Eric. 1990. Le Duc Tho, Top Hanoi Aide, Dies at 79. *New York Times.* October 14: 32.

Pearson, Richard. 1990. Le Duc Tho Dies at 78. *Washington Post*. October 14: B1.

Glen Gendzel

LEE, ROBERT E.
1807–1870

Robert Edward Lee was the most famous general of the Confederate forces during the American Civil War (1861–1865). Lee served as commander of the Army of Northern Virginia and eventually general-in-chief of the entire Confederate Army until the war's completion in 1865.

Lee was born January 19, 1807, in Westmoreland County, Virginia. His father, whom he barely knew, was the famous Revolutionary War hero, Henry "Light Horse Harry" Lee (1756–1818). In 1829 Robert E. Lee graduated second in his class without a single demerit at the United States Military Academy in West Point, New York. In 1831 Lee married Mary Custis (1808–1873), a great-granddaughter of Martha Washington (1731–1802). Together they had seven children.

During the Mexican War (1846–1848), Lee served on the staff of General Winfield Scott (1786–1866). As an engineer, Lee directed the placement and transport of heavy artillery in the Veracruz landing and subsequent march to Mexico City in 1847. In 1852 he became superintendent of West Point. In 1859 he commanded a force of marines that together with local militia put down John Brown's (1800–1859) raid of the Harpers Ferry armory.

Lee headed the Department of Texas from 1860 until March 1861. In April, in Washington, D.C., he was offered and then declined the command of the Union (North) Army. Within the month, he had joined the Confederate Army. In 1862 he assumed command of the Army of Northern Virginia, leading Confederate forces to decisive victories at such battles as Second Bull Run (August 1862), Fredericksburg (December 1862), and Chancellorsville (May 1863). He and his army suffered a crushing defeat at the Battle of Gettysburg in July 1863, arguably the turning point of the American Civil War. Shortly after the defeat at Petersburg, Lee surrendered the Confederate forces to Union general Ulysses S. Grant (1822–1885) on April 9, 1865, at Appomattox Courthouse in rural Virginia.

Following the war, Lee served as president of Washington College (later renamed Washington and Lee College) in Lexington, Virginia. He died of pneumonia on October 12, 1870, and was buried underneath the chapel at Washington College.

TRADITIONALIST AND REVISIONIST HISTORY ON LEE

Much of the literature on Robert E. Lee can be categorized by two historical perspectives. The *traditionalist* perspective interprets Lee as noble and full of virtue, fighting for the South out of a sense of duty to protect his Virginia homeland and confronted by forces beyond his control that compelled him to serve and fight against the Union. This perspective originated in the 1870s, was reinforced and consolidated over the following decades, and culminated with the publication of Douglas Freeman's four-volume biography, *Lee* (1934). In contrast, Thomas Connelly's *Marble Man* (1977) exemplifies the *revisionist* perspective, which took a more critical view of Lee as a southerner and as a soldier.

Proponents of these perspectives contest much about Lee's life, but three debates remain especially salient. The first surrounds Lee's views on slavery (Fellman 2000, esp. chap. 4). Traditionalists resurrected a Lee that was anti-slavery, and fought for the Confederacy despite this. They cite as evidence Lee's letters where he referred to slavery as a "moral and political evil" and that Lee manumitted slaves held by his father-in-law, George Washington Parke Custis (1781–1857), after the latter's death. Nevertheless, this did not mean Lee supported abolition; although Lee spoke of slavery as a moral and political evil, in the same correspondence he also claimed that slavery was God's will, that "blacks are immeasurably better off here [enslaved] than in Africa … the painful discipline they are undergoing, is necessary for their instruction as a race…. Their emancipation will sooner result from the mild and melting influence of Christianity, than the storms and tempest of fiery Controversy" (Freeman 1934, p. 372).

The second debate focuses on Lee's responsibility for the Confederate defeat at the crucial Battle of Gettysburg in 1863. Many traditionalists, such as Confederate general Jubal Early (1816–1894), generally blamed General James Longstreet (1821–1904) for his slow execution of Lee's plan to attack Union forces at Cemetery Ridge on July 2, 1863. Revisionist critics, including historical novelist Michael Shaara, author of *The Killer Angels* (1974), attribute the Confederate loss to Lee's poor judgment in attacking a Union force that possessed superior ground and material and a greater quantity of troops.

A third debate centers on Lee's involvement with the secessionist movement and his subsequent decision to serve in the Confederate forces in 1861. Proponents of both perspectives agree on two facts regarding this issue: (1) that Lee viewed secession as illegal, and (2) that he was offered, and declined, the position of commander of Union forces by the U.S. government. Traditionalists argue that Lee tortured over the decision to fight for the Confederacy, ultimately deciding to fight out of a sense of "duty" to Virginia: "If secession destroyed the Union, Lee intended to resign from the army and to fight neither for the South nor for the North, unless he had to act one way or the other in defense of Virginia" (Freeman 1934, p. 423). Revisionist Connelly, while conceding that Lee equated secession as "nothing but revolution," questions the traditionalist interpretation, asking: "One wonders why Lee did not endeavor to use his influence within Virginia to squelch the secession movement? He certainly might have been able to do it" (1977 p. 198). In addition, "almost instantaneously the secession movement which he supposedly abhorred was a holy cause, and the Union he loved had become a deadly enemy" (p. 201). In contrast with the "tragic hero" of Freeman's Lee, Connelly's is "a child of the seventeenth-century New England mind, and not of the later Enlightenment," one whose "belief implied an unquestioning spirit which submitted to unseen forces … and a denial of the reasoning process" (p. 199). Yet no evidence exists that Lee was active in the secessionist movement. His service in Texas immediately prior to Virginia's secession makes it difficult to suggest that Lee was a secessionist conspirator.

Scholars and students of history and the social sciences should take special note of Robert E. Lee as a model of historiography—an example of how interpretations of the past may serve the interests of those living in the present.

SEE ALSO *Confederate States of America; Davis, Jefferson; Mexican-American War; Secession; U.S. Civil War*

BIBLIOGRAPHY

Connelly, Thomas. 1977. *The Marble Man: Robert E. Lee and His Image in American Society.* New York: Knopf.

Fellman, Michael. 2000. *The Making of Robert E. Lee.* New York: Random House.

Freeman, Douglas. 1934. *R. E. Lee: A Biography.* New York: Scribner's.

Shaara, Michael. 1974. *The Killer Angels: A Novel.* New York: Ballantine.

Brent J. Steele

LEE, SPIKE
SEE *Bamboozled.*

LEFEBVRE, HENRI
1901–1991

Known as the "father of the dialectic," Henri Lefebvre was a key figure in the dissemination of the theory and method of dialectical materialism outside of Communist countries in the twentieth century, thanks to his widely translated *Le matérialisme dialectique* (Dialectical Materialism, 1939) and other works that emphasized a philosophically rigorous approach to the work of Karl Marx (1818–1883), G. W. F. Hegel (1770–1831), and Friedrich Nietzsche (1844–1900). One of the first serious French commentators on these scholars, Lefebvre pioneered their translation and popularization. He advocated the application of dialectical materialism as a methodology, even when it challenged Marxist orthodoxy. Lefebvre encouraged the elaboration of social critique by later generations, including the Situationniste Internationale group, 1960s student activists, 1970s Marxist critics of urban governance, and the 1980s critical postmodernists in the United States. Lefebvre was a witness to both world wars and to the modernization of everyday life in France, including the industrialization of the rural economy and the suburbanization of its cities.

In the early 1950s, Lefebvre was the measure of orthodoxy for pre-Stalinist French Marxism, until his humanism and interest in the alienated quality of everyday life led to expulsion from the Parti Communiste Français. These themes can be found in his series of works on the banality (*quotidiennté*) of everyday life under capitalism, *Critique de la view quotidienne* (Critique of Everyday Life, 4 vols., 1958–1981), in which he examines such topics as the requirement to commute long distances and work long hours. Reacting against his youthful romanticism and Martin Heidegger's (1889–1976) metaphysical critique of *Alltäglichkeit* (everydayness, banality), rather than seek an aesthetic or poetic solution to the problem of alienation, Lefebvre argued for concrete changes in collective practice. Contemporary social life is not just banal, it is the deliberate outcome of a bureaucratized, consumption-oriented society, suggesting that changes in its organization are required, not more refined individual sensibilities.

The commercialized and inauthentic ambient environment in cities, suburban developments, and housing design inspired his critiques of contemporary planning practice and the development of a critical theory of the production of these environments as social spaces. In collaboration with members of the Situationniste Internationale, whom he met in Strasbourg while establishing one of the first sociology departments in France, he championed the revolutionary potential of the ludic and the carnivalesque. This perspective informed the strategy of Lefebvre's later students in May 1968 at the University of Nanterre when they initiated student unrest in Paris. The inconclusive outcome was seen at the time as a failure of Lefebvre's Marxist humanism. However, interest in his pioneering appreciations of the spatial matrix and rhythms of urban life resumed in the 1990s.

Lefebvre was widely influential as a critic of structuralism, a founder of rural sociology, and an analyst of the role of the state in the creation of favorable conditions for capitalists and for the organization of production. He stressed that this took material and performative, rather than ideological forms. Capitalism is embodied, it is a built environment and landscape, and it is lived in the rhythms and divisions of our days.

SEE ALSO *Capitalism; Cultural Landscape; Hegel, Georg Wilhelm Friedrich; Humanism; Marx, Karl; Marxism; Materialism, Dialectical; Methodology; Nietzsche, Friedrich; Praxis; Protest; Resistance; Structuralism*

BIBLIOGRAPHY

Lefebvre, Henri. [1974] 1991. *The Production of Space.* Trans. Donald Nicholson-Smith. Oxford: Blackwell.

Shields, Rob. 1999. *Lefebvre: Love and Struggle—Spatial Dialectics.* London: Routledge.

Rob Shields

LEFT AND RIGHT

Left and *Right* are benchmarks of spatial understandings of politics. Such descriptions are widely used as shorthand for communicating information about relative policy positions. The origin of the terms, designating positions of factions in the French revolutionary assembly, reflects a transformation from a vertical, or hierarchical, understanding of politics to a horizontal, or democratic, arrangement of conflict. Thus, the spatial metaphor is not just useful; it is fundamental to the way that people decipher democracy.

The terms should be used with care, however. There is some consistency in the meaning of *left* and *right* for political position across time and space. But the particular associations between left and right and definite policy positions are inexact and changeable. And many issues and perspectives correspond only loosely, at best, to a position on a stylized left-right dimension.

ORIGINS

The first use of the left-right spatial metaphor was in France, in the period following the Revolution of 1789. Before the revolution, the polity had been divided into caste-like "estates." The first estate was the clergy; the second was the hereditary nobility. The third estate (artisans and professionals) was more numerous but politically weaker.

French society was explicitly hierarchical, with the monarch being superior to all estates. "Position" was defined by class and station, which were in turn decided at birth. The idea of political positions as ideative views of the good, rather than simply shared interests of the estate or class one belonged to, had little place in such a system.

But the French Revolution, literally and figuratively, leveled many of the institutions of France. Historians Alexis de Tocqueville and Francois Guizot, separately looking back decades later at the impact of the French Revolution, both used the word "leveling" to describe its primary political impact. But this meant that two traditional links had been broken. First, the inherent connection between a fixed caste and its place in society was uprooted. Second, all citizens took an equal place in the society, each equally worthy of respect and equally politically powerful.

With the passing of the static caste-based conception of French society, citizens sought some effective way of mentally organizing the new, often chaotic, situation. What was required was a mental construction based on politics (the contest among equals, on a level playing field), not class or estate (immutable vertical distinctions of social privilege and political advantage). The replacing of the vertical understanding of hierarchy with the spatial metaphor of political disputes among equals may have been inevitable. Spatial imagery was the result of the new vision citizens in a democracy had of the alternatives open to them.

The French National Convention, meeting in September 1792 in the aftermath of the dissolution of the Legislative Assembly, was chaotic and unruly. A significant plurality of the deputies elected to the convention was independent. They were too poorly organized to raise issues on their own, but at more than 500 they were numerous enough to determine the outcome on most votes. They were seated in the middle section of the huge hall, an area referred to as "the Plain."

The Gironde, the party physically located on the right of the hall (in the convention as had been true in the two previous assemblies), controlled the government in this period. They were pro-business, and advocated only mild and marginal reform of institutions. Their power base lay in the relatively conservative provinces.

The denizens of "the mountain," the high benches on the far left of the assembly hall, were the most organized opposition to the Girondins. These overtly populist Jacobins agitated for change, for radical reform, and for anything else that made it more difficult for the Gironde to control the country. Their focus was on centralization of power in Paris, reform of banks and the monetary system, and widespread nationalization of the assets and wealth of the first two estates.

The Gironde, the party on the right, proved unable to pursue its mix of military defense, free trade economics, and fiscal restraint. By the spring of 1793, the government collapsed. The Jacobins, the party seated on the left of the hall, seized its opportunity to implement a variety of collectivist reforms and political purges. These general associations, with the party of the right defending the status quo and the party of the left attempting to implement reforms and significant changes, persists in our political language still.

GENERAL CATEGORIES OF MEANINGS OF LEFT AND RIGHT

Spatial descriptions of positions have become nearly generic, like using "Coke" as a name for any carbonated cola drink. But it is a mistake to think that such generic designations have more than colloquial meaning in any specific political situation. Further, the generic meanings themselves are contradictory, or at least fundamentally different.

Keeping this caveat in mind, there are at least three broad categories of meaning for the labels Left and Right.

1. *Divisions with respect to perspective on property.* Left: Public ownership of the means of the production, government uses its power to redistribute wealth and power to achieve near-equality. Right: Private ownership, capitalist economy, government uses its power to preserve deep disparities in wealth and social status.

2. *Divisions with respect to status quo policy of current government.* Left: Radical reformers, seek to change status quo policies and break free from outmoded or repressive rules of the past. Right: Conservative defenders of the status quo, tradition, and customary relations.

3. *Fairness-based divisions.* Left: Emphasize fairness in terms of outcomes. In different ways, this perspective is embodied in such thinkers as Jean-Jacques Rousseau, Karl Marx, or John Rawls. Right: Emphasize fairness in terms of process, and stability of use of traditional processes. Examples include Robert Nozick's focus on historical principles, or Edmund Burke's defense of tradition and custom.

PROBLEMS: TIME, CULTURAL UNDERSTANDING, AND STRATEGIC ACTION

The use of the left-right spatial metaphor makes several hidden assumptions that are arguable, at best. First, there is a single primary dimension of political and social conflict in the society. Second, this dimension and its connection to specific issues and beliefs are constant over time. Third, this dimension of conflict is transcultural, imply-

ing that the same understanding of left-right imagery and its connection to everyday politics is broadly shared.

It is more likely that, though the use of left-right as a means of organizing discourse about politics is generally useful, the actual meaning of the end points, or extremes, of Left and Right are both time-bound and culturally specific.

SEE ALSO *Cleavages; Jacobinism; Political Parties*

BIBLIOGRAPHY

Downs, Anthony. 1957. *An Economic Theory of Democracy.* New York: Harper and Row.

Hinich, Melvin, and Michael Munger. 1994. *Ideology and the Theory of Political Choice.* Cambridge, U.K.: Cambridge University Press.

Kitschelt, Herbert, with Anthony McGann. 1996. *The Radical Right in Western Europe: A Comparative Analysis.* Ann Arbor: University of Michigan Press.

Michael Munger

LEFT WING

The term *left wing* originated with the seating arrangement of the French National Assembly of 1791. The deputies representing the Third Estate, the ordinary people, were seated to the left of the president's chair on an elevated section called the Mountain, while the nobility, the Second Estate, sat on the right side of the chamber. Between them sat a mass of deputies, known as the Plain, who did not belong to any particular faction.

CHANGING MEANINGS

Originally most members of the French National Assembly seated on the left were moderate reformers who called for a constitutional monarchy and a unicameral legislature for France. On the right sat the delegates who supported the more conservative royalist, aristocratic, and clerical interests. But the Left/Right labels took on new meanings during the course of the French Revolution, which began in 1789. The Left became increasingly radicalized as Maximilien Robespierre (1758–1794), Louis Saint-Just (1764–1794), Jean-Paul Marat (1743–1793), and the powerful Jacobin clubs (the most famous political group of the French Revolution) gained influence. Under their sway, King Louis XVI (1754–1793) was executed, a republic was declared, and the Reign of Terror (the period of the French Revolution when thousands of people were executed) commenced. Anyone who opposed the monarchy, or *ancien régime* (old order), was regarded as a member of the Left. Although differing on the political objectives, the Left and the Right shared similar economic views. Both factions supported laissez-faire capitalism and free markets, ideas later espoused solely by the right wing. Some radicals on the far Left, though, held that the revolution's promise of equality could only be achieved by redistributing wealth and land. Recognizing that genuine equality could not be fully realized without government intervention on behalf of the poor, the Left in European politics generally came to embrace socialism.

LEFT-RIGHT POLITICAL SPECTRUM

Political scientists and historians typically use the Left-Right political spectrum to classify modern political ideologies. At the extreme left end of the Left-Right divide are the communists and revolutionary socialist groups, such as the syndicalists, who historically endorsed the use of armed rebellion for achieving power and totalitarian means for imposing their socialist schemes. Moving toward the left-center of the spectrum are the social democrats, Christian socialists, Fabian socialists, Proudhonists, evolutionary socialists, and various groups associated with trade union movements. These groups believe that socialism can be established through democratic and incremental methods. At the opposite side of the political spectrum are such groups as the fascists, who believe in a centralized autocratic government often headed by a dictatorial leader. The far Right typically favors a corporatist economy and the mobilization of the nation against Marxist internationalism. Often these ideologies were espoused by military dictatorships, such as that of Juan Perón (1895–1974) of Argentina. On the right-center are the royalists or monarchists, followed by other traditional conservatives, such as British politician and orator Edmund Burke (1729–1797). Anarchists and libertarians were and are difficult to position on the Right-Left political continuum, since there are left-wing and right-wing variants of each.

What it means to be a left-winger varies depending on the country, culture, and particular issue. Since the eighteenth century until the latter part of the twentieth century, right- and left-wing ideologies battled mostly over questions of economics and class. The Left sought to equalize wealth and property while the Right defended the propertied interests of the privileged classes. Left-wingers always saw themselves as defenders of the disadvantaged and oppressed against the privileged elite. For them the equality of humankind was both a biological given and a political goal. The afflictions from which people have historically suffered, such as poverty, war, strife, crime, and so on, would be eradicated, they held, as advances toward greater economic, social, racial, and gender equality were made. The Left generally opposed at least in principle the institutionalization of sexual distinc-

tions. Since the natural equality of people is assumed, they blamed the persistence of social and economic inequalities on the maldistribution of wealth and property which fosters in turn the social prejudices that perpetuate and entrench the class system. Left-wingers tended to be social and economic levelers who believed that human nature itself can be transformed and improved through governmental action. People are born good, they held, but their natural goodness is corrupted by the environment. Hence leftists had an enormous faith in the efficacy of their political schemes to perfect human nature. Most social problems, it followed, could be remedied by economic fixes or social engineering. To achieve these ends, left-wing movements advocated central economic planning and nationalization of the economy. They were and are generally hostile to intermediary groups and associations such as local governing authorities, religious institutions, civic organizations, privately owned businesses, and traditional family structures that impede the power of the central government to reconstruct society in a more egalitarian direction.

During the French Revolution the Jacobins violently attacked the Roman Catholic Church and attempted to replace Christianity with the worship of "Reason." Left-wing ideologies continue today to be generally secular. The separation of church and state is a basic principle to the Left. Some believe that all religious expression should either be strictly limited or suppressed, while more religiously tolerant leftists would argue only that religion should play no part in political discourse.

THE LEFT WING IN THE TWENTY-FIRST CENTURY

Beginning in the latter part of twentieth century, moral, cultural, and social issues, such as abortion, gay rights, secularism, feminism, and multiculturalism, rather than economic or class questions, have come to characterize Left-Right political struggles. The Left typically today supports the legalization of gay marriage, extending abortion rights, and opening the national borders to unrestricted immigration. Opponents of these policies are sometimes accused of being hatemongers, homophobes, male chauvinists, and racists. These cultural wars have almost totally replaced the economic class warfare that once dominated Western politics. The central creed of the post-Marxist Left, as historian Paul Gottfried (1943–) argued in his *The Strange Death of Marxism: The European Left in the New Millennium* (2005), is no longer the elimination of economic classes but the establishment of the therapeutic-managerial state in which all gender, ethnic, racial, and cultural distinctions have been abolished.

The Left in the early twenty-first century would include the European Social Democrat and Green parties, the Labour Party of Great Britain, the much weakened European Communist parties, and the liberal wing of the United States Democratic Party. Left-wing political movements are still strong and active on the South American and African continents. As self-proclaimed Marxist Peoples' Democracies, the governments of Cuba and North Korea are leftist as well. American neoconservatism, some critics argue, should be considered a movement of the Left rather than the Right since it, like the French Jacobins, gives primacy to the principle of equality and supports global crusades to spread human rights and democracy.

The term *left wing* is rarely embraced by those who profess beliefs that would place them on the left end of the political spectrum. Rather the preferred label is *progressive,* which implies a commitment to egalitarianism and a willingness to promote governmental programs to help the poor, disadvantaged, and minorities. In the early 2000s the term was usually employed as a pejorative label by such right-wing political commentators as Rush Limbaugh, Bill O'Reilly, Ann Coulter, and Michelle Malkin, who applied it to their ideological adversaries.

SEE ALSO *Communalism; Egalitarianism; Fabianism; French Revolution; Jacobinism; Labor Union; Left and Right; Monarchy; Neoconservatism; Progressives; Republicanism; Right Wing; Socialism; Socialism, Christian; Syndicalism; Unions*

BIBLIOGRAPHY

Gottfried, Paul Edward. 2005. *The Strange Death of Marxism: The European Left in the New Millennium.* Columbia: University of Missouri Press.

Kuehnelt-Leddihn, Erik von. 1990. *Leftism Revisited: From de Sade and Marx to Hitler and Pol Pot.* Washington, DC: Regnery Gateway.

W. Wesley McDonald

LEGACY EFFECTS

Legacy effects are the impacts that one generation leave on the environment for future generations to inherit. There are very few parts of the globe where human beings have not left their imprint or legacy. Archeological evidence suggests that from the earliest times the human, the hunter, was responsible for the extermination of numerous other forms of life—flora and fauna—a pattern that persists today. The early civilizations changed watercourses, initiated farming, and denuded landscapes of many species of trees and shrubs; the barren lands of the eastern Mediterranean, for example, are largely a legacy of the classical period of ancient Greece. The advent of industrialization and mass production has resulted not only in further damage to the natural landscape as massive resource depletions take place, but also legacies of unsightly built environments.

Legacy effects are not all negative, at least in terms of public perception. Although the classical period saw the destruction of woodlands, it did leave a legacy of fine buildings that are seen by most as environmental attributes. The dividing line between what is a negative legacy effect on the environment and what is not is sometimes a fine one to draw and depends on who is being consulted.

Legacy effects occur because of the lack of a full allocation of long-term property rights to resources, which leads to excessive myopia in decision making. The 1987 report of the World Commission on Environment and Development, *Our Common Future* (the Brundtland Report), emphasizes that sustainable development requires current generations to leave an adequate legacy of resources for future generations. To achieve this goal, individuals have to take responsibility for resources. Without a complete legal definition of who owns these resources, however, it is difficult to ensure that adequate conservation is achieved. If this is not accomplished, then what is known as the "tragedy of the commons" becomes apparent as individuals in each generation excessively exploit resources with no regard to future needs or the implications for future generations.

Dealing with legacy effects poses a variety of public policy challenges. Ideally, property rights should be allocated across generations so that decisions regarding current consumption are made with due cognizance of their implications for future generations. Because the lack of adequate property-rights allocations in the past has burdened current generations with environmental costs, an inevitable degree of remedial action may be justified. In many countries, for example, large sums are being spent on cleaning watercourses where runoff from mining activities prevents plants or fish from living, on removing dams to allow salmon to move upstream, and on reforestation. The general approach to these legacy situations is to apply some form of informal benefit-cost analysis that seeks to weigh the immediate costs of remediation against the social benefits for future generations. In many cases, the financial burden for such measures is spread across communities as the state directly shoulders the burden, but in other cases there may be requirements for particular groups to pay. It may, for example, be necessary for a land developer to clean contaminated soil associated with a previous land use before new construction is allowed. In some cases, this latter approach can actually pass part of the cost back to those who caused the problem; in the land use example, the seller of the contaminated site will get a lower price for it.

The embrace of legacy effects in the public policy process often encounters an informational problem. Technology changes over time, and the long-term environmental implications of any action are difficult to fully assess, particularly when there are major technological or social changes taking place. In general, the world's current generations are materially better off than previous generations; its members live longer and there is also evidence that in many respects the environment is locally less polluted than it was forty or fifty years ago. Consequently, simply thinking in terms of the costs of future remedial actions to counter ongoing environmental intrusions may produce overestimates. Additionally, there are some current actions now that we do not understand well enough to be able to assess their legacy effects, either negative or positive. The lack of any real indication of the risks involved makes "insurance" policies difficult to formulate in these circumstances, and hence many advocate abstinence from any actions without knowing their full implications.

To combat current environmental effects that we know will be passed on to future generations, a number of micro- and macrostrategies have been adopted. At the micro level, many countries seek to economize on excessive resource depletion by stimulating recycling—for example, by requiring payment of a deposit at the time of purchase of an item, which is refunded when the item is returned for recycling. These initiatives encompass such items as bottles and cans, and even motor vehicles in some Scandinavian countries. There are also various standards that effectively "sunset" any adverse environmental effects—for example, the compulsory use of biodegradable materials for some products, or term limits on fisheries.

Macro legacy effects include global warming and the handling of nuclear products. Both of these are long-term matters affecting generations extending far into the future. They also have international ramifications; the effects represent a legacy with implications for citizens of other countries. Efforts to deal with this type of intergenerational externality have involved the United Nations (e.g., the International Atomic Energy Agency) and a series of global summits (resulting in, for example, the Kyoto Protocol).

SEE ALSO *Natural Resources, Nonrenewable; Pollution; Tragedy of the Commons*

BIBLIOGRAPHY

Button, Kenneth J., Roger Stough, Peter Arena, et al. 1999. Dealing with Environmental Legacy Effects: The Economic and Social Benefits of Acid Mine Drainage Remediation. *International Journal of Environment and Pollution* 12 (4) 459–475.

World Commission on Environment and Development. 1987. *Our Common Future*. Oxford: Oxford University Press.

Kenneth Button

LEGAL SYSTEMS

A legal system is a mechanism for creating, interpreting, and enforcing laws in a given jurisdiction. The major legal systems in the world include civil law, common law, socialist law, religious law, and customary law. Most nations have incorporated aspects of some or all of these systems, or developed variations on each system, into their own legal system.

CIVIL LAW

The civil law system is the predominant legal system in the world. It developed out of Romano-Germanic law—the law of continental Europe—based on a mixture of Roman, Germanic, ecclesiastical, feudal, commercial, and customary law. The beginnings of the civil law tradition can be traced to the Twelve Tables, written in 449 BCE, which laid the foundation for Roman law and would eventually become one of the most advanced systems of law in history.

Following the rise of the nation-state system in Europe, natural or civil codes were established in several countries, including France, Spain, Germany, and several Latin American and East Asian countries. The purpose behind the civil codes was to create a unified system of laws or statutes derived from basic principles and upon which judicial decisions are based. Perhaps the most widely known civil code is the Napoleonic Code established in France in 1804, which is the foundation for the civil law systems of Quebec and Louisiana. The German Civil Code, too, provides the legal foundation for the civil law systems of the former Soviet bloc countries, Japan, South Korea, China, and Taiwan. Most of Latin America also uses the civil law system as a result of the influence of its former colonial masters in Europe.

A distinguishing feature of the civil law system is that it is based on the idea of flexibility and judicial discretion in interpreting the law. Different schools of judicial interpretation exist in most civil law countries, and the law tends to be a product of these competing schools. Judicial disregard of precedent is considered to be a strength of the civil law system because it allows for alternative interpretations of the law that may be more compatible with the facts and circumstances of a particular case. One of the results of this more flexible approach in applying the law is that judicial opinions tend to be more concise, as courts discuss only the relevant legislation that applies rather than detailing how a decision was reached. However, the civil law system is still subject to the vagaries and uncertainties of judge-made law where the role of precedent has little influence.

COMMON LAW

Common law systems can be found in many nations that were former colonies or territories of England. The common law originated with the unification of England and the institutional stability provided by William the Conqueror (c. 1027–1087) after 1066. In 1215 King John (1167–1216) elevated the importance of the common law at Runnymede when he signed the Magna Carta. The Magna Carta freed the church, localized the court system, and codified the basic principles of the common law. By the sixteenth century, the common law system had supplanted the civil law system in England, and over time it would become more reliable as a consistent record of case law for judges and lawyers developed.

An important aspect of the common law is the role of precedent or the principle of *stare decisis* ("let that stand which has been stated"). The common law represents the law as expressed by judges in the form of judicial decisions based on precedent rather than statutes. These judicial decisions, if issued by the highest court in a jurisdiction, are binding on all other lower courts within that same jurisdiction. To ensure predictability in the law, high courts are expected not to overturn their own precedents in the absence of strong justification. Though new rules are adopted from time to time and judicial decisions can be overturned, these new rules or decisions also become binding precedents, thus restoring certainty to the law.

In the early twenty-first century, every state in the United States, except Louisiana, utilizes the common law system. Most state statutes provide that the common law, equity, and statutes in effect in England in 1603 be deemed part of the law of the jurisdiction. The common law system also constitutes the basis of the legal systems of Canada (except for Quebec), Australia, Hong Kong, India, Malaysia, New Zealand, and South Africa, among other nations. Each of these common law jurisdictions recognizes the importance of the adversarial system and the fundamental principles of law that have been adopted over the centuries by way of custom and precedent.

SOCIALIST LAW

Socialist law is the legal system used in most Communist states. It is based on the civil law system and Marxist-Leninist ideology. During the cold war period, it was incorporated into the legal systems of the Soviet Union and its former satellite states in Central and Eastern Europe. These systems were built on the notion that the state, rather than private individuals, should own most of the property within its jurisdiction.

When the cold war ended and the Soviet Union collapsed in 1989, support for the socialist legal model waned considerably. Some states, such as China, Cuba, Vietnam, and North Korea, continue to practice their own version of socialist law; however, most of these states have modified their legal systems in response to the growing popularity of market-oriented reforms and the inevitable forces of globalization.

RELIGIOUS LAW

Religious law is based on the sacred texts of religious traditions, which advocate norms, principles, or rules as revealed by God that are intended to govern human behavior. Most of the major religions of the world, including Islam, Christianity, and Hinduism, espouse a particular code of ethics or morality that is believed to be required by God and necessary to promote justice within a state. Many nations incorporate religious law into their national legal systems and, in some cases, there is no separation between religion and the state in administering these systems.

Islamic law, or *sharia*, is based on the Qu'ran, the primary source of Islamic jurisprudence, and the *sunna*, which purportedly incorporates the practices of the Prophet Muhammad (c. 570–632). Muslims believe that there is no distinction between religious and secular life and, therefore, national laws should reflect Islamic principles. Nations practicing some version of Islamic law in 2007 include Afghanistan, Saudi Arabia, Iran, Iraq, Pakistan, Indonesia, Libya, Morocco, Algeria, Turkey, Egypt, Kuwait, Tunisia, Syria, Sudan, Mauritania, and Lebanon, to name a few.

Canon law is a legal system developed by the Catholic Church and based on the Bible, the foremost source of Christian law. The Code of Canon Law has been compiled, organized, and revised over the centuries to reflect changes in the Catholic Church's hierarchical, administrative, and judicial practices. Today, the canon law system, which consists of its own courts, judges, lawyers, and legal code of ethics, makes up the legal system of the Vatican in Rome.

Hindu law is a body of rules and principles set forth in the *Manu Smriti* and practiced by the Hindus. It is one of the oldest religious systems in the world and is characterized by beliefs and practices rooted in ancient Vedic culture. Hinduism is the third-largest religion in the world, and its followers are concentrated mainly in India. During the occupation of India by the British, Hindu law was recognized by the British government, but it has been corrupted by the imposition of British common law and secularization.

Other major religious legal systems include the Baha'i faith (Iran), halacha (Jewish law), Buddhist law (Tibet and Southeast Asia), and Confucian law (China).

CUSTOMARY LAW

Customary law is law developed from the bottom up. It consists of established patterns of behavior that are capable of being observed, and it gives rise to expectations that guide people's actions. An important feature of customary law is that it is not imposed, or handed down, by some coercive institution or individual, but is instead created through mutual recognition and acceptance. Customary law consists of two elements: (1) an observable practice; and (2) a conception that the practice is required by or consistent with a prevailing norm (*opinio juris*). Customary international law is a type of customary law that refers to the "law of nations" and the rules developed over time as a result of state practice and *opinio juris*.

SEE ALSO *Administrative Law; Judiciary; Law; Law and Economics; Law and Order; Rule of Law*

BIBLIOGRAPHY

Benson, Bruce. 1990. *The Enterprise of Law: Justice without the State.* San Francisco: Pacific Research Institute for Public Policy.

Glendon, Mary Ann, Michael Wallace Gordon, and Christopher Osakwe. 1985. *Comparative Legal Traditions: Texts, Materials, and Cases on the Civil Law, Common Law, and Socialist Law Traditions with Special Reference to French, West German, English, and Soviet Law.* St. Paul, MN: West.

Hogue, Arthur. [1966] 1985. *Origins of the Common Law.* Indianapolis, IN: Liberty Fund.

Merryman, John. 1985. *The Civil Law Tradition: An Introduction to the Legal Systems of Western Europe and Latin America.* 2nd ed. Stanford, CA: Stanford University Press.

Plucknett, Theodore. 1956. *Concise History of the Common Law.* 5th ed. Boston: Little, Brown.

Souaiaia, Ahmed. 2002. *Islamic Law and Government.* Lincoln, NE.: Writers Club Press.

Zubaida, Sami. 2003. *Law and Power in the Islamic World.* London: Tauris.

Klinton W. Alexander

LEGENDS

SEE *Storytelling.*

LE GUIN, URSULA K.
1929–

Ursula K. Le Guin is a prolific writer of science fiction, children's literature, poetry, and a great many essays and nonfiction works. She was born Ursula Kroeber in Berkeley, California, the daughter of anthropologist Alfred Louis Kroeber (1876–1960), known for his work among Native American tribes, and Theodora Kracaw Kroeber (1897–1979), a psychologist and the author of the best-selling *Ishi in Two Worlds: A Biography of the Last Wild Indian in North America* (1961). Raised by parents whose professional interests centered on observation and analysis, words, myth, and storytelling, Le Guin developed a fascination with strange worlds and places early on in her life. She submitted her first science fiction piece to *Astounding Science Fiction Magazine* at age eleven (it was rejected). In 1947 she left California to attend Radcliffe College in Cambridge, Massachusetts, where she received a B.A. in Romance literature in 1951. She continued her education at Columbia University, where she earned an M.A. and a Fulbright Scholarship in 1952. Sailing to France in 1953, she met the historian Charles Le Guin, whom she married in Paris several months later. The couple have lived for more than fifty years in Portland, Oregon, where they raised their three children.

The ostensible uneventfulness of Le Guin's life stands in stark contrast to her extraordinary career and the range and variety of her work. With seventeen novels, eleven children's books, more than a hundred short stories, two collections of essays, five volumes of poetry, and two volumes of translations and screenplays to her name, and having been lavished with numerous literary prizes, including the National Book Award, five Hugos, five Nebulas, the Kafka Prize, and several lifetime achievement awards, she figures as one of the most distinguished writers of her generation. Fighting at the forefront of the civil rights, feminist, and antiwar movements of the 1960s, Le Guin first gained fame with her 1969 novel *The Left Hand of Darkness*, an exploration of the effects of sexual identity and (non)gender on an androgynous race in an imaginary country set in the distant future. Both here and in her other science fiction works, such as the award-winning *The Dispossessed: An Ambiguous Utopia* (1974), *Worlds of Exile and Illusion* (1996), and *The Telling* (2000), Le Guin puts a strong emphasis on the social sciences, especially on sociology and anthropology, using strange, alien cultures to explore and assess aspects of her own culture.

Praised for her ability to invent credible imaginary worlds populated with highly likeable human and nonhuman characters, Le Guin's work is different from that of other fantasy writers because she is primarily concerned with the human condition. She often uses the alien, nonearthly settings of her stories to present a critical perspective on sociocultural and political issues in our own world, imaginatively exploring new possibilities of living and being in alternative cultures. Politically progressive, witty, and a brilliant stylist, Le Guin has not only gained her reputation as a writer of "speculative fiction": With her nonfiction works, such as *Dancing at the Edge of the World: Thoughts on Words, Women, Places* (1989) and

Steering the Craft (1998), she has also established her name as an incisive social and cultural critic.

SEE ALSO *Science Fiction*

BIBLIOGRAPHY

Cadden, Michael. 2005. *Ursula K. Le Guin Beyond Genre: Fiction for Children and Adults.* New York: Routledge.

Cummins, Elizabeth. 1993. *Understanding Ursula K. Le Guin.* Rev. ed. Columbia: South Carolina University Press.

Rochelle, Warren C. 2001. *Communities of the Heart: The Rhetoric of Myth in the Fiction of Ursula K. Le Guin.* Liverpool, U.K.: Liverpool University Press.

renée c. hoogland

LEIJONHUFVUD, AXEL
SEE *Price vs. Quantity Adjustment.*

LEISURE

Leisure is not an essential human characteristic or pursuit. Yet it has a history and a variety of cultural manifestations (in language, rituals, and recurring occasions and events) determined by a variety of historical settings. Through its bewildering array of forms, leisure's only constant is its relation to work. Work and leisure are a mutually defining pair in their origin and through their historical development. Indeed, as work changed, so did leisure.

Originally, and still today among hunters and gatherers, humans had no abstract, general word for subsistence-related activities. The concept of work emerged with humans' ability to control other humans—primarily with slavery. As humans recognized work as a distinctive cultural reality, so too did they begin to recognize freedom from work and control as leisure.

The combined human concept of work and leisure as "figure and ground" (as a mutually defining, historical pair) is demonstrated by some of the first words for the pair: The Greek word for work (*a-scholia*, meaning "not leisure") was defined by its negative relation to leisure (*scholê*), just as the Latin *neg-otium* (not leisure) was defined in relation to *otium* (leisure).

In the classical age and the medieval world, leisure was the basis of culture—it represented the privilege of the few founded on the slavery of the many. As Aristotle famously noted, for the rich and powerful, the purpose of work and economic concerns was the freedom to become more fully human by doing those activities that were more complete in themselves, such as the liberal (free) arts, philosophy, politics (including all forms of free civic engagement), contemplation, and celebration. Over the centuries, leisure became so identified with learning and culture that the Greek word for leisure (*scholê*) developed as the etymological root of words for "school" and "scholarship" in many modern languages.

The positive view of leisure as work's purpose and fulfillment persisted in the West until the Reformation, when, as a variety of scholars beginning with Max Weber recognized, the cultural valuations of leisure and work became reversed. Weber understood that the modern view of work—summed up as "one does not work to live; one lives to work"—represented an historical revolution (Pieper 1952, p. 40).

After the sixteenth century, what Hannah Arendt called the modern "glorification of work," and Joseph Pieper described as "the rise of the world of total work" progressively eclipsed leisure as the basis of culture. The spread of capitalism and the marketplace commodified and rationalized leisure as well as work. More and more kinds of previously free activities were drawn into the marketplace, and various products were being produced to be bought and sold.

In the modern age, leisure is no longer widely valued among the newly emerging business classes or their socialist critics as the freedom to realize human potential. Writers such as Thorstein Veblen and Friedrich Engels, defining humanity as "Homo Faber" (man-the-worker/tool maker) insisted that work was the essential human characteristic. Veblen saw leisure as an example of the conspicuous consumption of the rich, a dangerous example for society that tempted its productive members to forget that work was the foundation of human morality and solidarity.

Increasingly, residents of the West have tended to turn from leisure to work as the time to realize their humanity, as the glue that holds humans in society, and as the fundamental moral imperative. However, all have not been true believers in the Protestant work ethic; its later secularized version, the "spirit of capitalism"; or socialist work-utopias. Early in the nineteenth century, as labor was increasingly rationalized and brought into the marketplace, working classes in Europe and America began a struggle for shorter working hours that lasted over a century and cut work time nearly in half.

The primary motive driving this process, one of the longest and most broadly based social movements in the history of the Western world, was workers' desire to have more leisure to spend with family, friends, and neighbors—and, according to a popular nineteenth-century doggerel, "to do with as we will." At the beginning of the labor movement in the United States, Philadelphia jour-

INTERNATIONAL ENCYCLOPEDIA OF THE SOCIAL SCIENCES, 2ND EDITION

neymen carpenters, after striking for a ten-hour work day in 1827, resolved that "all men have a just right, derived from their Creator, to have sufficient time each day for the cultivation of their mind and for self-improvement." Union leaders regularly repeated these sentiments for over a century, fully expecting that the "progressive shortening of the hours of labor" would eventually elevate leisure to life's center, reducing "human labor to its lowest terms" (Hunnicutt 1988, p. 322).

Ever since the founding of the United States, myriad believers in progress agreed that industry and the free market must eventually provide all people with enough "necessaries," as well as the steadily increasing leisure to enjoy them. As early as 1794, the U.S. inventor Samuel Hopkins foresaw a two- or three-hour work day, an expectation repeated regularly until the 1920s and 1930s, when influential scientists and economists such Julian Huxley and John Maynard Keynes confidently predicted, on the basis of a century-long economic trend, that the marketplace would soon provide everyone with all that they might rationally need in exchange for two or three hours of work a day. Before the twentieth century ended, it was believed, leisure would replace the economy as mankind's primary concern.

Clearly, such predictions were wrong. Instead of the "progressive shortening of the hours of labor," there has been little or no increase in leisure since the years of the Great Depression. In the early 1990s, the sociologist Juliet Schor presented a persuasive case that leisure had been declining over the previous three decades in the United States. These changes have coincided with the commodification and trivialization of leisure. More importantly, the nineteenth-century and early twentieth-century vision of the expansion of life beyond the pecuniary realm as a logical part of industrial progress has been forgotten.

Instead of following the lead of sociologists, educators, and economists of the early part of the twentieth century, who were trying to prepare the nation for "the worthy use of leisure," social scientists now assume that leisure is valuable mainly because it contributes to recreational spending, and because it allows people to recuperate for more work and to "adjust" to the pressure of modern life. The millennia-long belief that as humans get enough of the things that money can buy they might then live a fuller and happier life by moving up to freer and better things has been obscured by the modern credo that eternal economic growth and perpetual work expansion and job creation are humanities' *summa bona*. The concept of "work without end" has replaced the old dream of expanding leisure as humanities' final challenge.

SEE ALSO *Sports; Veblen, Thorstein; Weber, Max; Work; Work Day; Working Day, Length of*

BIBLIOGRAPHY

Arendt, Hannah. 1958. *The Human Condition.* Chicago: University of Chicago Press.

Aristotle. 1981. *The Politics.* Trans. Benjamin Jowett and Jonathan Barns. London: Penguin.

Hunnicutt, Benjamin. 1988. *Work Without End: Abandoning Shorter Hours for the Right to Work.* Philadelphia: Temple University Press.

Pieper, Joseph. 1952. *Leisure, the Basis of Culture.* Trans. Alexander Dru. New York: Pantheon Books.

Schor, Juliet. 1991. *The Overworked American: The Unexpected Decline of Leisure.* New York: Basic Books.

Veblen, Thorstein. [1899] 1994. *The Theory of the Leisure Class.* New York: Dover.

Weber, Max. 1930. *The Protestant Ethic and the Spirit of Capitalism.* Trans. Talcott Parsons. London: Allen and Unwin.

Benjamin Hunnicutt

LEMONS

SEE *Akerlof, George A.*

LENDER OF LAST RESORT

All advanced economies have relatively sophisticated banking systems. The commercial banks that make up the system operate on the basis of the *law of large numbers.* They accept deposits in the form of government-issued currency or transfers of cash reserves from other banks. The commercial banks then lend a large fraction of these reserves to businesses and individuals. This means that the claims of depositors against the banks exceed the banks' holdings in cash reserves by a wide margin. Banks are able to operate in this manner because the law of large numbers is at work. A single bank has a large number of depositors, whose deposit and withdrawal patterns vary widely. On any given day, deposits and withdrawals largely cancel out, permitting banks to meet their necessary net payments with relatively small cash reserves. Banks are able to operate in this manner because depositors are confident that their banks will always honor their requests to transfer funds or make withdrawals.

A system that is based on confidence can collapse if confidence fails. If depositors fear that their bank might be unable to honor all their requests for funds, they may "run on" the bank: The law of large numbers breaks down as depositors attempt to withdraw their funds from the bank. Since most of the bank's assets are tied up in loans that cannot be sold quickly to other financial institutions, the bank may have to stop payment.

In general, bank runs stem from one of two sources. Runs on individual banks may occur when depositors suspect that a bank is insolvent, that is, its net worth is negative. If the bank is in fact solvent (it has positive net worth), it should be able to borrow cash from other banks, enabling it to weather the run. General bank runs, affecting all banks in an area or throughout the economy, occur when depositors fear that the failure of other banks will trigger the failure of their own banks. Thus, depositors have the incentive to run on solvent banks. Because the bank run is general, individual banks cannot borrow from other banks, which are also under pressure. In the absence of a bank able to inject large quantities of legal currency into the banking system, the entire system is liable to collapse. A bank able to provide currency to the banking system in such situations is called a *lender of last resort*.

The importance of a lender of last resort to the banking system was recognized in 1797 by Sir Francis Baring (1740–1810), a London financier, and Henry Thornton (1760–1815), a London banker. Both argued that the Bank of England should respond to a large increase in the demand for currency by the English public by increasing the amount of currency issued by the Bank. Failure to meet the increased demand for currency would drain liquidity from the financial system, causing many solvent financial firms to fail. Widespread financial failure would be followed by an economic downturn.

Although the Bank of England did, on occasion, play the role of a lender of last resort (O'Brien 2003), the bank's directors rejected calls to formally accept the role of lender of last resort, even after Walter Bagehot (1826–1877) made the classic case for it in 1873 (Bagehot [1873] 1999), further developing Thornton's ([1802] 1939) analysis. The bank's directors argued that promising to act as the lender of last resort would prompt banks to take on more risk, a behavior known as *moral hazard*. The result would be perverse: a lender of last resort might lead to more bank failures. In subsequent decades, the Bank of England held no larger gold reserves than it had before, refusing to commit to serve as Great Britain's lender of last resort.

One of the purposes in establishing the Federal Reserve System in the United States was to improve the ability of the U.S. monetary system to meet increases in the demand for currency. Before 1914, the United States did not have a central bank, and increased demand for currency by rural banks during the harvest season resulted in several banking crises. The creation of the Federal Reserve System made it possible for commercial banks to obtain reserves by using short-term commercial loans as collateral for loans from the Federal Reserve banks. The

United States experienced no liquidity crises from 1914, when the Federal Reserve System began operations, until the early 1930s, when the Federal Reserve's failure to respond to large increases in the demand for currency contributed to the failure of more than ten thousand banks and to the severity of the Great Depression. Following the lead of Irving Fisher (1867–1947) and Henry C. Simons (1899–1946), Hyman Minsky (1919–1996) developed an argument in favor of a lender of last resort based on a *financial fragility hypothesis*. Minsky argued that overextension of credit by the banking system could lead to a general collapse of credit in the absence of a lender of last resort. In the post–World War II period, the Federal Reserve has acted on several occasions to prevent liquidity crises from developing.

SEE ALSO *Banking; Banking Industry; Casino Capitalism; Central Banks; Federal Reserve System, U.S.; Financial Instability Hypothesis; Insurance; Law of Large Numbers; Lombard Street (Bagehot); Minsky, Hyman; Moral Hazard*

BIBLIOGRAPHY

Bagehot, Walter. [1873] 1999. *Lombard Street: A Description of the Money Market*. New York: Wiley.

Minsky, Hyman P. 1975. *John Maynard Keynes*. New York: Columbia University Press.

O'Brien, Denis. 2003. The Lender-of-Last-Resort Concept in Britain. *History of Political Economy* 35 (1): 1–19.

Thornton, Henry. [1802] 1939. *An Enquiry into the Nature and Effects of the Paper Credit of Great Britain*. Ed. F. A. von Hayek. London: Allen and Unwin.

Neil T. Skaggs

LENIN, VLADIMIR ILITCH
1870–1924

Vladimir Ulianov was born in 1870, and in the 1890s he chose *Lenin* as his revolutionary pseudonym. Lenin formed the Bolshevik Party in 1903 and used it to conduct a Communist revolution in November 1917. As the first leader of the Soviet Union, he consolidated power and introduced a socialist system.

At a time when Western Marxists rapidly were deciding that socialist goals could be achieved through parliamentary action, Lenin firmly rejected Western democracy as a way of improving the lot of the workers. Conceding that workers were attracted to short-term economic gains, Lenin insisted in *What Is to Be Done?* (1901–1902) that a revolution was still possible by use of a tightly organized, centralized party that adhered strictly to orthodox Marxist ideas. Lenin's party proved very popular among the ethnic Russian workers and peasants in central Russia who worked part-time in the cities. After the overthrow of the tsar in March 1917, he won majority support in the elections of the soviets of central Russian cities. In an election in late November 1917 he won only 25 percent of the vote in the nation. He lost the truly peasant areas (both Russian and non-Russian), but won a strong plurality in the major cities and the peasant population surrounding the cities in the northwest region of the country.

When a military coup failed in September 1917, Lenin drove his reluctant lieutenants to seize power on November 7, and he became head of government (chairman of the Council of People's Commissars). Yet, he had established the party as the major political instrument, and really ruled as chairman of the Central Committee and Politburo of the Communist Party.

Lenin had only five years to rule the Soviet Union before he was disabled by a stroke. The first three of these years were marked by civil war, and the next two by a desperate effort to restore the economy. These five years made it clear that Lenin was determined to establish a quite centralized political system. He banned other parties, strengthened central control over the Communist Party, and even created a Communist International (Comintern) to subordinate foreign Communist parties to Moscow.

The great mystery about Lenin concerns the type of socialist economic system he would have left in place if he had lived longer. He died at the age of 54, and he had only five years in power, three of them during a fierce civil war. His *State and Revolution* ([1918] 1993) combined an anarchic vision of the long-term future that embraced Marx's "withering away of the state with a medium-range centralized view of an economy run by the state with the precision of a post office."

But when the civil war ended, Lenin introduced a New Economic Policy (NEP) that legalized private agriculture and trade in an effort to restore the economy. The question is whether he eventually would have established a state-directed economy, as Josef Stalin did in 1929, or whether he would have accepted a more mixed economy. No one knows, of course, but he did leave in place a highly centralized political system that Stalin could use to consolidate power and do with as he wished.

The major theoretical—and practical—contribution of Lenin to Marxism was his insistence that a country could jump easily from feudalism to socialism where the bourgeoisie was weak and avoid the long capitalist stage of the West. In practice, this meant that such a revolution was possible in Russia. But in his *Imperialism: The Highest*

Stage of Capitalism, Lenin laid a broader theoretical base behind this theory. He argued that Western capitalism had postponed revolution by exploiting colonies and semi-colonies, and that this was so necessary to the survival of Western economies that the struggle for colonies led them to war. In this terrible war, the whole capitalist system would collapse around the world. This doctrine was called Marxism-Leninism, and Lenin's anticolonial addition was a crucial element in making communism attractive in the Third World.

SEE ALSO *Bolshevism; Bureaucracy; Capitalism; Communism; Imperialism; Leninism; Marxism; Oligarchy; Peasantry; Russian Revolution; Socialism; Stalin, Joseph; Trotsky, Leon; Union of Soviet Socialist Republics*

BIBLIOGRAPHY

Lenin, V. I. [1901–1902] 1993. *What Is to Be Done?: Burning Questions of Our Movement.* New York: International Publishers.

Lenin, V. I. [1918] 1993. *State and Revolution.* London: Penguin.

Jerry Hough

LENINISM

The term *Leninism* refers to the political and economic ideas associated with Vladimir Ilyich Lenin (1870–1924), leader of the Russian Bolshevik Party and of the Soviet Union following the revolution of October 1917. Lenin saw himself as a follower of Karl Marx (1818–1883) and sought to give Marx's ideas practical expression.

In *What Is to be Done?* (1902), Lenin advocated the formation of a disciplined and centralized organization of professional revolutionaries in Russia to agitate for socialism, rather than the looser grouping favored by other Russian Marxists. Initially, he viewed this as necessary only because of the need to organize clandestinely in czarist Russia, where revolutionary groups were illegal, but later he generalized this model. Lenin argued that it was necessary in all advanced countries to build parties consisting of the most militant and class-conscious members of the working class in order to combat ruling-class ideology and overcome divisions between workers. This revolutionary vanguard would have the clarity of purpose and independence of action necessary to win a majority to its program during a period of major political and economic crisis, and to lead a successful socialist revolution.

Lenin's Bolsheviks put his theory into practice in Russia during the course of 1917, but within a few years the revolution that they led had degenerated into a one-party regime that bore little resemblance to the ideal of workers' democracy defended in his *State and Revolution* (1918). Lenin's critics see this as proof of an undemocratic impulse in his basic outlook, while his defenders argue that the revolution's degeneration was a consequence of adverse circumstances, including a brutal civil war, economic collapse, external threats, and the failure of revolution to spread successfully to more economically advanced countries, such as Germany. Certainly before the early 1920s there was always much disagreement, discussion, and debate in Lenin's party, in sharp contrast to the monolithic dictatorship that developed under his successor, Joseph Stalin (1878–1953), and to the practice of most Communist parties around the world that claimed, following Stalin, to be committed to the tenets of *Marxism-Leninism.*

Among Lenin's most influential theoretical contributions is his analysis of imperialism and war. Drawing on the work of the British economist J. A. Hobson (1858–1940), Lenin argued in *Imperialism: The Latest Stage of Capitalism* (1917) that the imperialist expansion by the world's major powers in the late nineteenth century was an outgrowth of the development of monopoly capitalism, in which economic power in the advanced countries is increasingly concentrated in a relatively small number of large firms, industrial capital merges with big banks, and there is growing integration of private companies and the state. Competition between capitals for markets thus gives rise, on Lenin's account, to military and territorial competition between nation states, which he viewed as the underlying explanation of the world war that broke out in 1914. On this analysis, rivalries and wars between major powers are rooted in the dynamic of capitalist development itself, and can only be eliminated by radically restructuring the economic system and replacing capitalism with socialism.

SEE ALSO *Bolshevism; Communism; Imperialism; Lenin, Vladimir Ilitch; Maoism; Marxism; One-Party States; Revolution; Russian Revolution; Socialism; Stalin, Joseph; Union of Soviet Socialist Republics*

BIBLIOGRAPHY

Harding, Neil. 1983. *Lenin's Political Thought: Theory and Practice in the Democratic and Socialist Revolutions.* Atlantic Highlands, NJ: Humanities Press.

Le Blanc, Paul. 1990. *Lenin and the Revolutionary Party.* Atlantic Highlands, NJ: Humanities Press.

Lenin, V. I. 1970. *Selected Works.* Moscow: Progress Publishers.

Liebman, Marcel. 1975. *Leninism under Lenin.* Trans. Brian Pearce. London: Merlin Press.

Philip Gasper

LEONTIEF, WASSILY
1905–1999

Wassily Leontief was born into an academic family on August 5, 1905, in Saint Petersburg, Russia. He earned his undergraduate degree from the University of Saint Petersburg. Upon completing his doctoral dissertation at the University of Berlin in 1928, Leontief started his professional life at the Institute of World Economics at the University of Kiel. He moved to the United States to work for the National Bureau of Economic Research in 1931 and then Harvard University in 1932. He served as the director of the Harvard University Research Project until 1973. Leontief left Harvard for New York University in 1975 to found the Institute for Economic Analysis. He was awarded the Nobel Prize in economic sciences in 1973.

Leontief's greatest achievement was the creation of a new area of economics, namely *input-output analysis.* In 1941 he published the classic *Structure of American Economy,* which laid the foundation for what is now known as a *social accounting matrix.* Such a matrix gives a snapshot of all transactions in an economy between and within producing sectors, households, factors of productions, institutions, and consumers at a level of disaggregation permissible by the availability of data.

Leontief was one of the first to discuss the issue of simultaneous estimation of demand and supply curves and the problems of identification. His work on aggregation and index numbers (1936) has also had a lasting impact. Leontief was one of the early contributors to the theory of aggregation in production relations (1947). He derived conditions under which one can identify structural mathematical relationships from reduced-form equations. His empirical research on the pattern of trade in the United States (1953) led to the well-known Leontief paradox. Later in life, he wrote on a number of diverse subjects, including the environment, population growth, automation, and defense.

The common thread in all his works was his love of general equilibrium analysis and his attempt to provide an empirical foundation to the theoretical work of the French economist Léon Walras (1834–1910). Leontief went well beyond that and brought the role of intermediate inputs to the forefront.

Input-output analysis was developed on the premise that different sectors of production in an economy are interconnected via production relations. One of the fundamental concepts in input-output analysis is the distinction between *direct* and *indirect* input requirements. This distinction led to the *Leontief multiplier,* which gives the total inputs required to produce a given level of final use as the sum of direct requirements and an infinite series (first round, second round, etc.) of indirect requirements. A sector can be more labor intensive (or, more polluting) than another in terms of the direct coefficient, but less so in terms of the total coefficient.

The Heckscher-Ohlin theorem on international trade suggests that a country should export goods that use more intensely the factor of production in which the country is relatively abundant; a country should import goods that use more intensely the factor of production in which the country is relatively less abundant. For example, China, which is relatively more abundant in labor, should export labor-intensive goods, whereas the United States, which has relatively more capital, should export capital-intensive goods. Using a 1947 input-output table for the United States, Leontief (1953) found an apparent contradiction between reality and the predictions of the Heckscher-Ohlin theorem. Leontief showed that the United States was apparently exporting labor-intensive goods. The Leontief paradox arises if one uses total coefficients (rather than the direct coefficients) in deriving labor and capital requirements. Direct coefficients are defined per unit of output, but the total coefficients are defined per unit of final use. Leontief made this distinction very clear. He lists the two as "requirements per million dollars of output" and "requirements per million dollars of final output." He defined capital and labor requirements for competitive imports as those that would be required if the imports were replaced by domestic production. Leontief found that capital and labor ("man" years) per million dollars of U.S. exports in 1947 were 2,550,780 and 182,313 respectively (in U.S. dollars and 1947 prices). The corresponding figures for competitive imports were 3,091,339 and 170,004 respectively. Thus the capital-labor ratio for a million dollars worth of exports is smaller than the capital-labor ratio for a million dollars worth of competitive imports.

The similarity between the Marxian labor theory of value and input-output analysis has led some to speculate that Leontief was influenced by Karl Marx (Bailey 1994). Perhaps Leontief was influenced indirectly by Marx, but it is more likely that both Marx and Leontief had a common source of inspiration in the French physiocrat François Quesnay (1694–1774), who considered a three-way classification of the French economy—farmers, manufacturers, and landowners.

SEE ALSO *Input-Output Matrix; Social Accounting Matrix*

BIBLIOGRAPHY

Bailey, R. E. 1994. A Voyage Round Economics: The New Palgrave Dictionaries of Economics, and Money, and Finance. *Economic Journal* 104: 660–675.

Leontief, Wassily. 1936. Composite Commodities and the Problem of Index Numbers. *Econometrica* 4 (1): 39–59.

Leontief, Wassily. 1941. *The Structure of American Economy, 1919–1929: An Empirical Application of Equilibrium Analysis.* Cambridge, MA: Harvard University Press.

Leontief, Wassily. 1947. Introduction to a Theory of the Internal Structure of Functional Relationships. *Econometrica* 15 (4): 361–373.

Leontief, Wassily. 1953. Domestic Production and Foreign Trade: The American Capital Position Reexamined. *Proceedings of the American Philosophical Society* 97: 332–349.

Sajal Lahiri

LEONTIEF MATRIX

SEE *Input-Output Matrix.*

LEONTIEF-SONO SEPARABILITY CONDITION

SEE *Separability.*

LERNER, ABBA

SEE *Economics of Control.*

LERNER INDEX

SEE *Competition, Imperfect.*

LESBIANISM

SEE *Sexual Orientation, Determinants of.*

LEVELLERS

The term *leveller* has a long history. It seems to have emerged in its modern understanding during the early years of the English Revolution (1640–1660), when it was used to designate the perceived political aims of the Long Parliament (so called because the Parliament sat from 1640–1653, long after it would ordinarily have been disbanded). Later, it referred to a group of agitators both within and outside of the New Model Army (NMA), which had been formed in 1645 by Parliament in the course of the Civil War/Revolution against Charles I. Yet the Levellers are notoriously difficult to pin down, due in part to the heterogeneity of their composition, the shifting nature of their demands, and the fact that the group of radicals the term is understood to designate rejected the appellation.

The Levellers arose out of agitation for the release of John Lilburne (1615–1657). Lilburne had been a radical cause célebre under King Charles I (r. 1620–1649), who had him publicly whipped, pilloried, and imprisoned in 1638 for publishing Puritan tracts. Lilburne was released from prison in 1641 and became a soldier in the Parliamentary army. He was imprisoned again in 1644 for advocating liberty of conscience and the interests of common soldiers, both of which would be successful planks in later Leveller agitation.

In what is generally understood to be the founding document of the Leveller movement, Richard Overton and William Walwyn published *A Remonstrance of Many Thousand Citizens* in 1646. They demanded the release of Lilburne and listed a number of political and social demands that would become the backbone of Leveller ideology. Most significantly, the *Remonstrance* demanded annual parliaments, an expansion of the voting franchise, a form of progressive taxation, the abolition of the House of Lords, liberty of religious conscience, and a written constitution.

Though the Levellers propagandized with success among civilians, their greatest inroads were made in the New Model Army, which at this time had become the de facto government of England. They combined the political concerns of the *Remonstrance* with the concerns of the army, including inaction on back pay and the failure of Parliament to produce amnesty for acts committed during the Civil War. Plans to disband the NMA and raise a new army for the invasion of Ireland made these concerns more acute, as they threatened to eliminate the political clout of the army.

The NMA Levellers elected Agitators, or New Agents, from each regiment to press these concerns, and with Overton, Lilburne, and Walwyn they produced *The Case of the Armie Truly Stated* and the *Agreement of the People* (1647), vowing that the army would not disband or be deployed until their demands were met.

The tracts were debated at Putney in October and November of 1647, with much of the debates centered around the franchise. Oliver Cromwell, Henry Ireton, and a handful of officers represented the Grandees (the officers of the NMA) against the Agitators, with Ireton taking the lead. Ireton began the attack by cynically arguing that the Agitators had presented a "levelling" scheme (hence the

term) that would result in "communism" and ultimately "anarchy." He claimed that the *Agreement*, if adopted, would extend the franchise to persons (including "foreigners") "with no interest" (as manifested in land) in England, and that it would therefore threaten the country's stability. The Agitators responded that they had risked their lives in war, and thus had more "interest" in England than those who had merely risked land. Though arguments for universal manhood suffrage were made, this does not seem to have been the general aim of the Agitators, and such arguments appear for the most part specifically related to suffrage among soldiers.

The general mood of the Agitators tended toward suffrage of persons considered "independent" (i.e., holders of small property) and did not include such persons as "servants and beggars." This position met with surprising success among NMA officers, including Colonel Thomas Rainborough, who became an eloquent spokesman for their cause. On the whole, the Agitators' aims may be summed up in their oft-repeated self-designation—they were for "liberty and propriety," as opposed to "community and levelling."

Though the *Agreement* enjoyed the support of a wide swath of officers and rank-and-file soldiers, it was scuttled by a familiar Cromwellian combination of force, fraud, and circumstance. The Levellers ceased to be a political force after 1648. The terms *leveller* and *levelling*, however, almost immediately entered the political lexicon, mostly on Ireton's terms. As early as 1649, the term *leveller* was in use by Gerrard Winstanley and William Everard, the founders of the Digger colony at St. George's Hill in Surrey, which sought to lay the foundations of a communist society. The group alternately referred to themselves as "True Levellers." A popular Ranter named Abiezer Coppe decried the murder of the "Levellers (so called)" and (in a typically apocalyptic flourish) promised that, as a result, the risen Lord was now going to "levell … in good earnest."

Though Leveller arguments could, in part, be seen at the root of John Locke's *Two Treatises* and other Whig thinking, the terms *leveller* and *levelling* came to represent a sort of radical redistribution of political and economic power, usually synonymous with anarchy. As such it was something of a "hot potato" for those so accused, with the notable exception of the eighteenth-century revolutionary Irish underground organization called the White Boys, who also referred to themselves as Levellers.

The term enjoyed a renaissance of sorts in England around the time of the French Revolution. Elites bankrolled societies for "the Preservation of Liberty and Property against Republicans and Levellers," with "republican" replacing "community." Edmund Burke categorized republican agitation as "mad" levelling schemes that sought to "pervert the natural [i.e., hierarchical, hereditary] order." Levelling thus retained a strong association with "anarchy," "chaos," and rule by the "rabble." The radical pamphleteer Thomas Paine, whose writings owe a deep (if unwitting) debt to the seventeenth-century Levellers, sought to distance himself from such accusations and turn them on his critics, arguing that a hereditary aristocracy was itself a levelling scheme that ignored merit and elevated the bad, corrupt, and incompetent to positions of power by virtue of birth.

If Paine sought to distance democratic reform from accusations of levelling, plebeian revolutionaries who followed in his wake were less skittish regarding the term, which was used interchangeably in such circles with *radical reformer*. The radical writer Thomas Spence (1750–1814) derived some of his ideas regarding land redistribution from the Diggers, or True Levellers, and he was publishing excerpts from seventeenth-century Leveller writings in his *Pig's Meat, or Lessons for the Swinish Multitude* in the late eighteenth century. In Spence's example, British ultra-radicals reveled in accusations of levelling (and in being part of the "swinish multitude"). The publisher Samuel Waddington's *Medusa*, an ultra-radical publication, spoke approvingly of "levelling," as did the poet Richard "Citizen" Lee, who, perhaps confirming reactionary fears, combined the term with an affection for the guillotine. The wildly popular ultra-radical preacher (and son of a slave) Robert Wedderburn was enormously fond of metaphors of levelling, and he was tried for seditious blasphemy in 1819 partly for linking Jesus Christ with such concerns.

Levelling tended to fall from use in the nineteenth century, when it was replaced by *radical, socialist, communist*, and other terms that reflected the political landscape of the time. The seventeenth-century Levellers became a subject of great interest both for socialist and Whig historians in the early twentieth century after the discovery of Clarke's minutes of the Putney Debates. These permitted a serious appraisal of just what the Levellers had stood for, and the term has lost its pejorative sense as many of their demands have been achieved and even superseded.

BIBLIOGRAPHY

Gentiles, Ian. 1992. *The New Model Army in England, Ireland and Scotland 1645–1653*. London: Blackwell.

Herzog, Don. 2000. *Poisoning the Minds of the Lower Orders*. Princeton, NJ: Princeton University Press.

Hill, Christopher. 1961. *The Century of Revolution 1603–1714*. Edinburgh: T. Nelson.

Hill, Christopher. 1972. *The World Turned Upside Down: Radical Ideas in the English Revolution*. London: Temple Smith.

MacPherson, C. B. 1962. *The Political Theory of Possessive Individualism: From Hobbes to Locke*. Oxford: Clarendon.

Morton, A. L. 1970. *The World of the Ranters: Religious Radicalism in the English Revolution*. London: Lawrence and Wishart.

Morton, A. L., ed. 1975. *Freedom in Arms: A Collection of Leveller Writings*. New York: International Publishers.

Underdown, David. 1971. *Pride's Purge: Politics in the Puritan Revolution*. Oxford: Clarendon.

Wolfe, Don, ed. 1944. *Leveller Manifestoes of the Puritan Revolution*. New York: Thomas Nelson.

Christopher J. Lamping

LEVERAGE

Leverage is the indebtedness of a company, or the process of increasing the indebtedness of a company (as in the phrases "highly leveraged company" or "acquiring leverage"). It is usually measured by one of two *gearing* ratios. *Capital* or *financial gearing* is the amount of debt that a company has relative to its total capital. Alternatively, *income gearing* is the ratio of a company's debt to its total income.

Until the twentieth century, income gearing was the common measure of leverage. This reflected a corporate practice in which the only possible gainful use of debt—that is, aside from its traditional unproductive use in financing consumption or government—was to finance commerce or industry. It followed that the key indicator in determining the amount of borrowing was the possible income that it might generate in trade or production.

With the emergence of active markets in corporate finance toward the end of the nineteenth century in Britain and the United States, the scope for the gainful employment of leverage extended beyond commerce and industry, and into the capital market itself. Once that market became sufficiently large, the return from profitable trade in it was determined by the total amount of capital that could be turned over in that market. In these circumstances, the major consideration was no longer possible future income in trade or production, because these are irrelevant in determining income from arbitraging in the capital market, but the amount of capital that could be applied to a profitable arbitrage. That amount of capital, and hence the income from it, was maximized by adding borrowing to equity. From this emerged the measure of leverage common today, namely the ratio of debt to total capital.

The roots of this change in definition, in the changing business of finance, was obscured in the 1950s by the famous Modigliani-Miller theorem, which claimed to prove that the value of a corporation is not affected by the division of its capital into equity and debt. But this is under the assumption of a perfect capital market, with no arbitrage possibilities, so that the return on debt was ultimately provided by income from commerce or industry, rather than further financial transactions. The "theorem" set off a number of hares in the academic finance literature to determine whether variations in leverage were caused by capital market imperfections or differences in the tax treatment of interest on debt, as opposed to the tax liability on the return to equity.

By the mid-2000s it was increasingly recognized that the business opportunities available to a company and its liquidity are clearly affected by its leverage. A company with $1 million of equity, tied up in productive equipment and work in progress, is a relatively illiquid company that may experience financial difficulties if a larger than expected bill needs to be paid. That same company with an additional $10 million of debt invested in the money market is a highly liquid company that can cope with larger-than-expected payments. Such a company can undertake new projects without having to waste management time in finding financial backers. Most importantly, it can itself engage in speculative buying and selling of companies in the capital market without reducing its liquidity, as long as that market stays liquid. With the expansion of capital market financing beyond the United States and United Kingdom into Europe and emerging markets elsewhere, leverage is becoming an increasingly widely used way of making medium-sized businesses into large corporations without the tedium of expanding productive or commercial capacity.

SEE ALSO *Capital; Capitalism, Managerial; Corporations; Equity Markets; Finance; Financial Instability Hypothesis; Financial Markets; Liquidity; Loans; Modigliani-Miller Theorems; Overlending; Wealth*

BIBLIOGRAPHY

Auerbach, Alan J. 1992. Leverage. In *The New Palgrave Dictionary of Money and Finance*, eds. Peter Newman, Murray Milgate, and John Eatwell, pp. 574–577. London: Macmillan.

Barclay, Michael J., Leslie M. Marx, and Clifford W. Smith Jr. 2003. The Joint Determination of Leverage and Maturity. *Journal of Corporate Finance* 9 (2): 149–167.

Myers, Stewart C. 1977. Determinants of Corporate Borrowing. *Journal of Financial Economics* 5 (2): 147–175.

Jan Toporowski

LEVIATHAN
SEE *Hobbes, Thomas; Social Theory.*

LÉVI-STRAUSS, CLAUDE
1908–

Anthropologist and philosopher Claude Lévi-Strauss, one of the leading figures in structuralism, was born in France in 1908. He studied philosophy in Paris and taught sociology at the University of São Paolo, Brazil, from 1934 to 1938. During these years, Lévi-Strauss traveled in Brazil and lived intermittently with the Amazonian tribes, especially the Nambikwara. The result of this early contact of Lévi-Strauss with precapitalist societies formed the basis of his first book, *The Elementary Structures of Kinship* (1949). He returned to Paris in 1939 to fulfill his military service requirement but had to flee France and the advancing Nazi threat, a flight that brought him to New York. In New York, he lectured at the New School for Social Research and came into contact with the linguist Roman Jakobson (1896–1982), with the Department of Anthropology at Columbia University and the anthropologist Franz Boas (1858–1942), and with the fieldwork- and practice-oriented American anthropology.

The encounter with Jakobson proved decisive for the development of Lévi-Strauss's structuralism. Taking from Émile Durkheim (1858–1917) the notion that religion is part of a symbolic system of human understanding of humanity, Lévi-Strauss developed the theory of human culture as a logical, coherent, but unconscious system of interlocking symbolic subsystems (such as religion, kinship, mythology, and economics). Elaborating further on Marcel Mauss's (1872–1950) theory of gift exchange as a local theory of reciprocity, Lévi-Strauss was able to expand his analysis of symbolic exchange to include marriage and kinship patterns. Jakobson's theory of structural linguistics brought all these theorizations of Lévi-Strauss into a neat package that claims to explain human behavior and culture as an intricate system of analogies between the tactile and the symbolic universe of humanity. His whole scheme of explanation rests on the fundamental notion of Jean-Jacques Rousseau (1712–1778) of savage nobility, where the true nature of the human is only to be found in the state of nature, prior to the corruption of the human by civilization and the development of private property. Lévi-Strauss's indebtedness to Rousseau is evident both in his autobiographical work *Tristes tropiques* (1955), one of the most eloquent and beautifully written books in anthropology, and in *The Savage Mind* (1962, the English title an inadequate translation of the original French *La Pensée sauvage*, with its double meaning of "thinking savage" or "wild pansy").

Lévi-Strauss's structuralism owes its foundational premise to Jakobson and Russian linguist Nikolai Trubetzkoy's (1890–1938) elaboration on the significance of *phonemes* for linguistic structure. Jakobson and Trubetzkoy had shown that phonemes provided linguistic structures with a specific economy of terms of meaning, and that the relationship between those terms is more significant than the terms themselves. Therefore the relationship between the terms that signify death, for instance, is a universal constant, despite the fact that the specific terms are universally different. One way of detecting the significance of the relationship of terms, Lévi-Strauss claims, originally in his three-volume *Mythologiques* (1964–1968) and later in *The View from Afar* (1983), is by looking at myths that are universally constituted by *mythemes* (analogous to the linguistic phonemes). These mythemes, despite the fact that they appear in different terms in the myths encountered throughout in the world, underline the fact that all societies have engaged in the deciphering of the foundational question, which for Lévi-Strauss is always the same, namely, the riddle of the transition from nature to culture, from animality to humanity. Thus myths are the results of unconscious explanations about the origins of humans. The insularity of structuralism as a theory of explanation prompted anthropologist Clifford Geertz in his *The Interpretation of Cultures* to proclaim that Lévi-Strauss has "made for himself an infernal culture machine" (1973, p. 355).

Lévi-Strauss lives in Paris. He has taught for many years at the Collège de France and in 1973 was elected to the Académie française.

SEE ALSO *Anthropology, U.S.; Boas, Franz; Structuralism*

BIBLIOGRAPHY

PRIMARY WORKS

Lévi-Strauss, Claude. 1962. *La Pensée sauvage.* Paris: Plon.

Lévi-Strauss, Claude. 1969. *The Elementary Structures of Kinship.* Rev. ed. Trans. James Harle Bell, John Richard Stermer, and Rodney Needham. London: Eyere & Spottiswoode.

Lévi-Strauss, Claude. 1970. *The Raw and the Cooked.* Vol. 1 of *Mythologiques.* Trans. John and Doreen Weightman. London: Jonathan Cape.

Lévi-Strauss, Claude. 1973. *From Honey to Ashes.* Vol. 2 of *Mythologiques.* Trans. John and Doreen Weightman. London: Jonathan Cape.

Lévi-Strauss, Claude. 1973. *Tristes tropiques.* Trans. John and Doreen Weightman. London: Jonathan Cape (Orig. Pub. 1955).

Lévi-Strauss, Claude. 1978. *The Origin of Table Manners.* Vol. 3 of *Mythologiques.* Trans. John and Doreen Weightman. London: Jonathan Cape.

Lévi-Strauss, Claude. 1985. *The View from Afar.* Trans. Joachim Neugroschel and Phoebe Hoss. New York: Basic Books.

SECONDARY WORKS

Boon, James A. 1972. *From Symbolism to Structuralism: Lévi-Strauss in a Literary Tradition.* New York: Harper.

Geertz, Clifford. 1973. *The Interpretation of Cultures: Selected Essays.* New York: Basic Books.

Neni Panourgiá

LEWIN, KURT
1890–1947

Kurt Lewin was a psychologist with wide-ranging interests in psychological theory, child development, personality, social psychology, and social issues. He was born on September 9, 1890, to a Jewish family in Prussia. His family moved to Berlin in 1905 to provide access to better educational institutions for their children. Lewin entered the University of Berlin in 1910 and completed requirements for the PhD in 1914, under the direction of Carl Stumpf (1848–1936), director of the psychology laboratory since 1894. Lewin then enlisted in the kaiser's army as a private, rose to the rank of lieutenant, was wounded in combat and awarded the Iron Cross. After discharge from the military, he returned to the university and began lecturing and conducting research, receiving an appointment as privatdozent in 1921. He was promoted to *Aussenordenlicher Professor* in 1927. In 1932 Lewin accepted an appointment as visiting professor at Stanford University. His sojourn allowed him to form friendships with a number of American psychologists who assisted him in immigrating to the United States after Adolf Hitler (1889–1945) and the Nazis took control of Germany in 1933. Lewin held a two-year appointment at Cornell University, moved to the University of Iowa from 1935 to 1944, and then to the Massachusetts Institute of Technology from 1944 until his death, from a heart attack, on February 12, 1947.

While in Berlin, Lewin began to study psychological issues considered too complex by the experimental psychologists of the time. He was interested in child development, human motivation and emotion, and personality. He considered the development of theories about these processes to be critical, and the use of experiments to test theory-based hypotheses as essential to progress in psychology. Lewin's overarching theoretical approach was *field theory*, which asserted that human behavior was a function both of the person and the environmental forces acting on the person at the time, giving rise to his famous equation $B(behavior) = f(function)[P(person), E(environment)]$. He and his students designed experiments in which theoretically defined variables were manipulated by complex changes in the social and physical environment. Theories focusing on complex intrapsychic processes and equally complex experimental manipulations were Lewin's unique contributions to the psychology of his time, as well as his legacy in the psychology that would develop after his death. Two books, *A Dynamic Theory of Personality* (1935) and *Principles of Topological Psychology* (1936), provide systematic treatments of his approach. His many experimental reports display his innovations in research methods. Early criticisms of Lewin's work focused on the difficulty and unfamiliarity of the concepts he employed, as well as the complexity of the experimental protocols he used. Over time, these criticisms faded as the psychological issues he explored became important research topics, while the details of his theoretical work received less and less attention. His style of experimentation was adopted by his students and colleagues, notably Leon Festinger (1919–1989), and became a robust tradition in social psychology.

Lewin had a lifelong dream of establishing a research institute that would conduct applied research focused on social issues such as prejudice, intergroup conflict, and social change. He succeeded in establishing the Research Center for Group Dynamics at MIT in 1944, and the Commission on Community Interrelations for the American Jewish Congress in 1945 in New York. An outgrowth of this work was the development of the National Training Laboratories, within which the T-group, or sensitivity training, was created.

Lewin is regarded by many social psychologists as the father of their discipline. He is certainly one of the field's towering ancestral figures, for two reasons. His unique combination of theory with bold experimentation provided the conceptual and methodological tools to study complex human social interaction. And, from his days in Berlin until his death in Massachusetts, he attracted and inspired dozens of students who used those tools to develop many of the central theories and findings in social psychology, including group dynamics, level of aspiration, social comparison processes, and action research.

SEE ALSO *Social Psychology*

BIBLIOGRAPHY

Lewin, Kurt. 1935. *A Dynamic Theory of Personality.* Trans. Donald Adams and Karl Zener. New York: McGraw-Hill.

Lewin, Kurt. 1936. *Principles of Topological Psychology.* Trans. Fritz Heider and Grace M. Heider. New York: McGraw-Hill.

Marrow, Alfred J. 1969. *The Practical Theorist: The Life and Work of Kurt Lewin.* New York: Basic Books.

Darwyn E. Linder

LEWIS, OSCAR
1914–1970

The anthropologist Oscar Lewis is best known for devising the "culture of poverty" theory and applying the life history and family studies approach to studies of urban poverty. The concept of the culture of poverty is cited often, especially in the popular press, and at times it is misapplied as an argument that supports the idea of "blaming the victim." Not surprisingly, given the continuing salience of debates about the causes of poverty, Oscar Lewis's legacy within anthropology and the social sciences is still very much debated. Indeed, the notion of a "culture of poverty" has since reemerged in discussions of the "urban underclass." While most researchers view the causes of poverty in terms of economic and political factors, there is still a strain of thinking that blames poverty on the behavior of the poor.

Oscar Lewis was born on December 25, 1914, in New York City, and he was raised in upstate New York. He received a BA in history from the City College of New York While in college he met his future wife, the former Ruth Maslow, who would also become his co-collaborator in many of his research projects. He enrolled in graduate school in history at Columbia University, but under Ruth Benedict's guidance he switched to anthropology. Partially due to a lack of funding, his PhD dissertation on the impact of white contact on Blackfoot culture was library based. After graduating he took on several jobs, including United States representative to the Inter-American Indian Institute in Mexico, which led him to begin conducting research on the peasant community of Tepoztlán. Lewis's critique of Robert Redfield's 1930 study of the same village is considered a classic in Mexican anthropology. Lewis's research shows, in contrast to Redfield's, that peasant culture in Tepoztlán is not based on "folk" solidarity but is rather highly conflictual, driven by struggles over land and power. In 1948 Lewis joined the faculty at the University of Illinois at Urbana-Champaign, where he was one of the founders of the anthropology department.

During his tenure at Illinois, Lewis produced his best-known works including *Five Families* (1959), *The Children of Sánchez* (1961), and *Anthropological Essays* (1970). In both *Five Families* and *The Children of Sánchez*, Lewis describes the culture of poverty theory and provides rich insights on urban poverty in Mexico through the narratives of his informants. In *Anthropological Essays*, Lewis reiterates the culture of poverty theory, which at its most basic level is an adaptation to economic circumstances: "The culture of poverty is … a reaction of the poor to their marginal position in a class-stratified, highly individuated, capitalistic society" (Lewis 1970, p. 69). Included in Lewis's trait list of the culture of poverty are feelings of inferiority and aggressiveness, fatalism, sexism, and a low

INTERNATIONAL ENCYCLOPEDIA OF THE SOCIAL SCIENCES, 2ND EDITION

level of aspiration. Lewis saw the culture of poverty as resulting from class divisions, and therefore present not only in Mexico but throughout the world.

Because Lewis's description of the poor went against the clean-cut image presented by the Mexican media, there was, within Mexico, harsh criticism of the notion of a culture of poverty. This response, as Miguel Díaz-Barriga (1997) points out, obfuscates the overlap between Lewis's representations of the urban poor and Mexican social thinkers such as Samuel Ramos and Octavio Paz. Díaz-Barriga shows that in their interviews, many of Lewis's informants ironically played off of well-known stereotypes of the urban poor, and that Lewis took their statements literally.

In the United States, the culture of poverty theory became well known through its application in Daniel Moynihan's 1965 report for the Department of Labor, *The Negro Family: The Case for National Action*, which informed national policymaking, including Lyndon B. Johnson's War on Poverty. By focusing on the "pathologies" that emerged from slavery, discrimination, and the breakdown of the nuclear family, Moynihan saw the emergence of a culture of poverty among the African American poor. This emphasis on the pathologies of poverty has since been reframed in terms of theories of the urban underclass that seek to understand the urban poor as being both economically and culturally isolated from the middle-class. While sociologists such as William Julius Wilson (1980) have devised sophisticated understandings of the urban underclass, this concept, especially in the popular press, has become a stand-in for arguments that see the causes of poverty in terms of cultural pathologies.

In their well-known 1973 refutation of the application of the culture of poverty theory, Edwin Eames and Judith Goode argued that many of the characteristics associated with poverty, including matrifocal families and mutual aid, are rational adaptations. The continuing prevalence of poverty, they stated, must be understood in terms of restricted access to and attainment of job skills. Studies that pathologize the poor have received justified criticism for privileging middle-class values, being vague about the overall characteristics of poverty and their interrelations, and viewing matrifocal households as being a cause rather than a result of poverty. The historian Michael Katz argues that, when given educational and employment opportunities (instead of dead-end service sector jobs), the urban poor aspire to succeed as much as their middle-class counterparts. Katz convincingly calls for a historical understanding of the educational, housing, and economic policies that have generated urban poverty.

As evidenced by essays marking the fortieth anniversary of the Moynihan Report in the popular press, many continue to believe that the culture of the poor must be understood as a cycle of broken households and disruptive behavior. This renewed cycle of applying the culture of poverty theory represents the pathological ways that American society has sought to overcome class-based and racial inequalities. Indeed, it is easier to blame the poor for their poverty than to do the hard work of understanding the historical and economic factors that have generated poverty and the policy options that can transform cities.

When Oscar Lewis died, on December 16, 1970, social scientists were beginning to forcefully criticize his work for blaming the victim. Lewis's death at fifty-five years old was particularly untimely because he was not able to respond to these critiques. Indeed, the social sciences lost an opportunity to engage Lewis's responses and, perhaps, reach agreement on more fruitful ways to explore urban poverty.

SEE ALSO *Culture of Poverty; Moynihan Report; Moynihan, Daniel Patrick; Poor, The; Poverty*

BIBLIOGRAPHY

PRIMARY WORKS

Lewis, Oscar. 1951. *Life in a Mexican Village: Tepoztlán Restudied.* Urbana: University of Illinois Press.

Lewis, Oscar. 1959. *Five Families, Mexican Case Studies in the Culture of Poverty.* New York: Basic Books.

Lewis, Oscar. 1961. *The Children of Sanchez: Autobiography of a Mexican Family.* New York: Random House.

Lewis, Oscar. 1970. *Anthropological Essays.* New York: Random House.

SECONDARY WORKS

Díaz-Barriga, Miguel. 1997. The Culture of Poverty as *Relajo. Aztlan, A Journal of Chicano Studies* 22 (2): 43–65.

Eames, Edwin, and Judith Granich Goode. 1973. *Urban Poverty in a Cross-Cultural Context.* New York: Free Press.

Katz, Michael. 1986. *In the Shadow of the Poorhouse: A Social History of Welfare in America.* New York: Basic Books.

Katz, Michael. 1989. *The Undeserving Poor: From the War on Poverty to the War on Welfare.* New York: Pantheon.

Leacock, Eleanor Burke, ed. 1971. *The Culture of Poverty: A Critique.* New York: Simon and Schuster.

Moynihan, Daniel P. 1965. *The Negro Family: The Case for National Action.* U.S. Department of Labor. http://www.dol.gov/oasam/programs/history/webid-meynihan.htm.

Redfield, Robert. 1930. *Tepoztlán, a Mexican Village: A Study of Folk Life.* Chicago: University of Chicago Press.

Rigdon, Susan M. 1988. *The Culture Facade, Art, Science, and Politics in the Work of Oscar Lewis.* Urbana: University of Illinois Press.

Wilson, William Julius. 1980. *The Declining Significance of Race: Blacks and Changing American Institutions.* Chicago: University of Chicago Press.

Miguel Díaz-Barriga

LEWIS, W. ARTHUR
1915–1991

William Arthur Lewis was quintessentially Caribbean. Born on January 23, 1915, in colonial St. Lucia of immigrant Antiguan parents who were both schoolteachers, he spent much of his life living in Britain or the United States but working on the problems of the Caribbean, Africa, Latin America, and Asia. In 1933, on a government scholarship, Lewis went to the London School of Economics (LSE) to do the Bachelor of Commerce degree. He graduated with first-class honors in 1937 and received a scholarship to do the PhD in economics, which he completed in 1940. In 1979, Lewis shared the Nobel Prize in economics with Theodore Schultz for pioneering research into economic development, in particular the problems of developing countries.

Lewis's great achievements were in economics, but he also had a distinguished career as an administrator. He was UN Economic Adviser to Kwame Nkrumah, the prime minister of Ghana, deputy managing director of the UN Special Fund, vice-chancellor of the University of the West Indies (1960–1963), and founder of the Caribbean Development Bank (1970–1974). By his account, this experience taught him more about policy than economics and motivated his publications on development planning. Scholarly enrichment came from his travels (Lewis 1994, p. xlviii).

Lewis published extensively on industrial economics after 1937, then published *Overhead Costs* in 1948 and dropped the subject. In 1948, at age thirty-three, Lewis became a full professor at the University of Manchester. There, he tackled development economics, addressing: (1) the fundamental forces determining the rates of growth of agricultural and industrial countries or sectors; (2) the relative price of agricultural and industrial products; and (3) distribution—the adjustment of the real wage rate and wage share of output as capital accumulates. As Lewis tells it, one day in August 1952, on the road in Bangkok, he saw the common solution to these problems: Use the classical assumption of "an unlimited supply of labor" available to a capitalist sector from an indigenous noncapitalist sector "at subsistence wages" (Lewis 1992). Unlimited supplies keep the wage low and fairly constant and generate a high rate of profit and a low relative price of agricul-

tural output. They also allow creation of new capital with technological progress, a rising rate of profit and savings, and expanded employment and output in the capitalist sector without raising consumption per worker. This initially causes faster growth in industrial countries because they reap all the benefits of technological progress. However, as industrial countries face rising wages, they export capital and encourage immigration, thereby allowing the growth rate of surplus labor countries to catch up. How much growth these capital exports generate for surplus labor countries depends partly on their natural resources, capital stock, demand in industrial countries, and the terms of trade. Lewis published this solution in his classic 1954 article, "Economic Development with Unlimited Supplies of Labour."

In 1963, Lewis took up a new professorship of political economy at Princeton University, a position he held until his death on June 15, 1991. At Princeton, Lewis used the growth channel of his "unlimited supplies" model to clarify the evolution of the international economic order since 1870. Trade is the principal link through which growth of industrial countries causes growth of the labor-surplus countries. Moderated growth in industrial countries causes slower growth of surplus-labor countries, unless an alternative growth engine is found. One option is a greater share of the markets of industrial countries, but this is unreliable. Preferable is growing trade among surplus-labor countries. This alternative trade engine could arise if a sufficient number of the large surplus-labor countries, such as India and Brazil, can end trade dependence on industrial countries, achieve self-sustaining growth, and provide alternative markets to the others. Lewis published these findings in his book *The Evolution of the International Economic Order* (1978) and his 1980 Nobel Lecture, "The Slowing Down of the Engine of Growth." By his logic, the current explosion of growth in excess of 7 percent per annum in Brazil, China, and India should provide much stimulus for the development of other surplus labor economies.

Lewis's Bangkok inspiration was rooted more firmly in influences of economic historians of the British nonrevolutionary socialist Fabian Society. Leading earlier members Barbara and J. L. Hammond (1917) had argued that the English industrial revolution was possible mainly because the emerging bourgeoisie could attract a large redundant rural labor force into urban industrial activity at low and constant wage rates. Lewis's firsthand knowledge of the Caribbean and observations of Egypt and Asia convinced him that a similar exodus could also underwrite an industrial revolution in those and similar countries where many nonindustrial subsistence workers contribute a zero or negative marginal product. However, an attendant condition was active trade unions and an emerging class of entrepreneurs or an active government operating democratically and dedicated to making and accumulating capital. Lewis (1949) summarized the main arguments in a Fabian pamphlet, foreshadowing the arguments of the 1954 paper.

From the start, economists questioned the updated classical assumption, the assumption that surplus labor only creates new capacity within the capitalist sector, along with Lewis's pessimism about the ability of surplus-labor countries to win a greater share of developed-country markets. Schultz (1964) used neoclassical data, competitive conditions, the assumption of rationality, and evidence from Egypt and Asia to argue that the marginal product of labor is neither zero nor negative. With transformation of traditional agriculture, rural wages could fall low enough relative to the marginal product in agriculture to enable full employment. Lewis's views amounted to assuming either an uncompetitive market or a distorted preference for leisure among agricultural workers.

Lewis himself viewed peasants as hardworking and thrifty and held that the main problem was a capitalist sector that is too small or disinclined to transform agriculture by accumulating capital (Lewis 1936, 1949, 1954, 1955, 1968, 1979). Amartya K. Sen (1966) also objected to Schultz, citing contrary evidence for India and observing that Lewis's assumption really means that the marginal product in the capitalist sector is greater than the average product of the subsistence sector. Nevertheless, Lewis's essential difference with Schultz on the capitalist wage is that its floor is set by the average productivity of the self-employed. As William Darity (1984) observed, Lewis employed an economic anthropology of traditional agricultural systems. Subsistence workers were household and community members who could not be easily dismissed without damaging established family and social norms. They could opt for the average benefits of the family operation rather than a lower capitalist real wage and thereby cause a breakdown of Adam Smith's law of demand.

Perceptive critiques of Lewis also came from the Caribbean. In three major proposals on Caribbean industrialization, Lewis proposed attracting multinational corporations to lead the process (Lewis 1950, 1951; UN 1951). Lloyd Best lampooned the strategy, naming it "industrialisation by invitation" and calling Lewis an "Afro-Saxon" (Best 1999). Multinational corporations would continue to import labor-displacing capital, re-create surplus labor, repatriate high rents, avoid the push for good governance, and promote repression of radical labor and neglect of the peasantry, as Lewis himself had complained (Lewis 1936). More important, the subsistence sector included viable entrepreneurs and collaborators producing and accumulating capacity and trading with the capitalist sector, not as pain and trouble but for the pleasure of building an alternative to the legacies of slav-

ery and strict indenture. The market for labor was tighter than Lewis implied and rising real wages were inevitable (Best 1975). Once import substitution started in the Caribbean, this became evident, but Lewis found it perplexing (Lewis 1958, 1968).

Yet Lewis's formulations can accommodate the Caribbean critique. His geometry of the marginal product of labor features diminishing returns to capital scarcity and an implicit production function that may not be algebraic and is dynamic, taking into account net capital accumulation, technical progress, increasing returns, and an underlying multiplier linked to the capitalist employment rate and the ratio of the marginal product of labor to its maximum. It allows residual profit at a rate different from the marginal product of capital and an independent distribution identity, and can be updated to account for rents on imported capital and production and accumulation of domestic capacity. With deliberate domestic capacity creation and supporting policy for their indigenous sectors, abundant externalities and stabilized rentals on imported capacity can replace Lewis's cheap constant wage as the driver of the savings mechanism, and surplus-labor countries need not be pessimistic about winning higher market share in industrial countries over time in the context of rising real wages. These adjustments would still be consistent with Lewis's view of how to achieve balanced growth, clarified in his 1949 note on "Colonial Development" in United Nations (1951) and in Lewis (1954, 1964). So, Lewis's independent marginal product function and his associated price, distribution, and growth theories represented major steps in clarifying how surplus-labor countries grow and the wider world economy evolves. They hold as limiting cases, providing an updated classical alternative to the increasingly dominant neoclassical theory of growth and trade, and they still apply to many countries of the world today. Viewed in this light and his time, Arthur Lewis was among the best of his generation and one of the greatest economists of all time.

SEE ALSO *Development; Development Economics; Dual Economy; Economics, Nobel Prize in; Fabianism; Industrialization; Labor, Surplus: Conventional Economics; Nkrumah, Kwame; Noncompeting Groups; Peasantry; Sen, Amartya Kumar; Subsistence Agriculture; Wages*

BIBLIOGRAPHY

PRIMARY WORKS

Lewis, W. A. 1936. The Evolution of the Peasantry in the British West Indies. Typescript of document available in the West Indian Collection, University of the West Indies Library.

Lewis, W. A. 1949. Colonial Development. *Transactions of the Manchester Statistical Society*, Section 1948-49, 1–30. January 12.

Lewis, W. A. 1950. The Industrialization of the British West Indies. *Caribbean Economic Review* 11 (1): 1–61.

Lewis, W. A. 1951. Industrial Development in the Caribbean. Port of Spain, Trinidad and Tobago: Caribbean Commission.

Lewis, W. A. 1954. Economic Development with Unlimited Supplies of Labour. *The Manchester School of Economic and Social Studies* 22 (2): 139–191.

Lewis, W. A. 1955. *The Theory of Economic Growth*. London: Allen and Unwin.

Lewis, W. A. 1958. Employment Policy in an Underdeveloped Area. *Social and Economic Studies* 7 (3): 42–54.

Lewis, W. A. 1964. Jamaica's Economic Problems. *The Gleaner*. Kingston, Jamaica: The Gleaner Company.

Lewis, W. A. 1968. Reflections on Unlimited Labour. Discussion Paper No. 5. Research Project. Princeton, NJ: Princeton University, Woodrow Wilson School.

Lewis, W. A. 1977. *Labour in the West Indies: The Birth of Workers' Movement*. London: New Beacon Books (first published by Fabian Society, as Research Series No. 44, 1939).

Lewis, W. A. 1978. *The Evolution of the International Economic Order*. Princeton, NJ: Princeton University Press.

Lewis, W. A. 1979. The Dual Economy Revisited. *Manchester School of Economic and Social Studies* 47 (3): 211–229.

Lewis, W. A. 1979. Sir Arthur Lewis, Autobiography. In *Nobel Lectures, Economics 1969–1980*, ed. Assar Lindbeck. Singapore: World Scientific Publishing Company, 1992. http://nobelprize.org/nobel_prizes/economics/laureates/1979/lewis-autobio.html.

Lewis, W. A. 1980. The Slowing Down of the Engine of Growth. *American Economic Review*, 70 (4): 555–564.

Lewis, W. A. 1994. Autobiographical Account. In *Sir William Arthur Lewis Collected Papers 1941–1988*. Vol. 1, ed. P. A. M. Emmanuel. Bridgetown, Barbados: Institute of Social and Economic Research.

SECONDARY WORKS

Best, Lloyd. 1968. Outline of a Model of Pure Plantation Economy. *Social and Economic Studies* 17(3): 283–326.

Best, Lloyd. 1975. A Biography of Labour. In *Caribbean Economy: Dependence and Backwardness*, ed. G. Beckford, 147–158. Kingston, Jamaica: University of the West Indies, Institute of Social and Economic Research.

Best, Lloyd. 1999. Economic Theory and Economic Policy in 20th Century West Indies: "The Lewis Tradition of Town and Gown." The Fourth Annual Sir Arthur Lewis Memorial Lecture. Basseterre, St. Kitts. http://www.eccb-centralbank.org.

Darity, William. 1984. Review of *Selected Economic Writings of W. Arthur Lewis*, ed. Mark Gersovitz. *Journal of Development Economics* 14: 266–273.

Hammond, J. L., and Barbara Hammond. 1917. *The Town Labourer 1760–1832: The New Civilisation*. London: Longmans, Green.

Schultz, Theodore. 1964. *Transforming Traditional Agriculture*. New Haven, CT: Yale University Press.

Sen, Amartya K. 1966. Peasants and Dualism With or Without Surplus Labour. *Journal of Political Economy* 74 (5): 425–450.

United Nations, 1951. Measures for the Economic Development of Under-Developed Countries: Report by a Group of Experts Appointed by the Secretary-General of the United Nations. New York: Author.

Vanus James

LEXICOGRAPHIC PREFERENCES

Once behavioral economists took seriously the limited information-processing capacity of the human brain (bounded rationality), they had to replace the neoclassical economic theory of consumer choice. The previous theory assumed additivity—the capacity to weight and add up all of the various features of all goods and thus rank and compare them to maximize utility within one's budget. Lexicographic preferences are consistent with bounded rationality. Economists conceive of a consumer having a manageable list of product characteristics organized ordinally, like an alphabetized dictionary. Consumers compare products with respect to the highest-ranked characteristic, and if one product is imagined better in that characteristic, the search stops and purchase ensues. If not, the consumer goes on to the next characteristic and repeats the procedure. This requires much less information processing than the additive model. It implies that other product features cannot compensate for failure to qualify on the first priority features. Price can be considered as just another product characteristic, and it may not be at the top of the list.

Theorists such as Peter Earl (1983) added uncertainty considerations to the basic conception without the computational requirements of attaching numerical probabilities to the satisfaction expected from consuming a product. A consumer may conceive of an acceptable gamble beyond which possible gains are not attractive.

Lexicographic preferences have implications for producers. Earl suggests that advertising should be aimed at changing consumers' priority rankings rather than emphasizing their product's strong points. If products are comparable with respect to high priority features, it may pay to introduce new product dimensions to meet emerging and created demands ahead of competitors. The theory lends itself to market surveys of yes-no questions rather than complicated sets of numerical tradeoffs.

In modern marketing, firms invest heavily in brand preeminence, perhaps hoping to displace any kind of characteristic comparison, simple or weighted. Further, firms search for how to create an image with which the

422 INTERNATIONAL ENCYCLOPEDIA OF THE SOCIAL SCIENCES, 2ND EDITION

consumer personally identifies. An emotional trigger that forestalls comparison is the ultimate lexicographic process. People do not necessarily have either probable values attached to products or priority lists for all categories of purchases. Decisions to buy may be formed in the particular case and are description, context, and procedure dependent. Daniel Kahneman (1999) suggests that people imagine an answer to the subjective happiness question on the fly, instead of retrieving preferences from memory. Stores aim to create impulse purchases.

A complementary conception of choice conserving of mental energy involves allocating one's budget to broad categories of spending all within a total budget constraint. Once the categories are set, there may be little substitution of items from one budget to another. Further, there seems to be a class of products that are pursued initially regardless of cost.

Some economists consider the inability of lexicographic preferences to provide deterministic formal support for the theory of market equilibrium as a drawback, while others were never fascinated with theoretical equilibrium in the first place.

SEE ALSO *Choice in Economics; Choice in Psychology; Cognition; Economic Psychology; Economics, Behavioral; Endogenous Preferences; Equilibrium in Economics; Gambling; Happiness; Information, Economics of; Preferences; Preferences, Interdependent; Rationality; Risk; Uncertainty; Utility, Subjective*

BIBLIOGRAPHY

Earl, Peter E. 1983. *The Economic Imagination: Towards a Behavioural Analysis of Choice.* Brighton, U.K.: Wheatsheaf.

Kahneman, Daniel. 1999. Objective Happiness. In *Well-Being: The Foundations of Hedonic Psychology*, eds. Daniel Kahneman, Ed Diener, and Norbert Schwarz, 3–25. New York: Russell Sage Foundation.

Thaler, Richard H. 1985. Mental Accounting and Consumer Choice. *Marketing Science* 4 (3): 199–214.

A. Allan Schmid

LIABILITIES

SEE *Wealth.*

LIBERAL PARTY (BRITAIN)

The Liberal Party in Britain was formed in March 1988 as the Social and Liberal Democratic Party (SDP) when the Liberal Party merged with the Social Democratic Party. A vote in July 1989 finalized its new name as the Liberal Democrats. The two merging parties had merely strengthened the alliance between the two parties that had existed from 1981 and that had operated since that year under the dual leadership of David Steel (Liberal) and David Owen (SDP). In 1988 Owen refused to agree to the merger and Steel, although he led the Liberals into the merger, declined to lead the new party. The leadership of the new party fell to Paddy Ashdown who won a contest against Alan Beith, in July 1988. Ashdown now led a small struggling party whose position was thwarted by the fact that Owen continued to operate outside the merger with his short-lived continuing SDP, and Michael Meadowcroft, Liberal member of Parliament (MP) for Leeds West, refounded the by now miniscule Liberal Party. Nevertheless, since that period the Liberal Democrat leaders Ashdown, Charles Kennedy, and Ming Campbell have successfully revived the status of the Liberal Democrats, and indeed the old Liberal Party, to a level of political success not seen since the 1929 general election.

The revival of the Liberal Democrats began with a by-election victory at Eastbourne in October 1990, an event that contributed to the fall from office of Prime Minister Margaret Thatcher. It continued to secure victories in parliamentary by-elections and in municipal contests, although it won only twenty seats in the House of Commons in the 1992 general election, securing only 18 percent of the vote, an insufficient number to project it to major success under the first-past-the-post (winner takes all) British system of electing the House of Commons. Nevertheless, the Liberal Democrats have continued to grow in number and influence, largely on a mixture of Liberal policies, and have risen to approximately 60 members of Parliament (MPs).

Traditionally the Liberal Party has been committed to free trade but by the 1980s it was drifting toward the view that government might, under some circumstances, be justified in intervening in economic growth. It also supported the Conservative Party in Europe in 1993 by endorsing the Conservative government and the Maastricht Treaty in 1993. The Party supported the Labour Party under Prime Minister Tony Blair, following the general election of 1997, and particularly supported the Labour government's moves toward devolution for both Scotland and Wales, the Celtic areas that the Liberal Democrats and the old Liberal Party had traditionally considered to be their strongholds. However, its distinctive demand for proportional representation in elections marks it off from the Conservative and Labour parties, who prefer to maintain the existing winner-takes-all strategy of British parliamentary politics. Although Blair set up a commission on changes in the voting system under Lord Roy Jenkins of Hillhead, LDP leader in the House of Lords, to examine alternative political systems and to make recommendations, the Labour government has shown scant interest in any system that would undermine its massive parliamentary majorities secured under the winner-takes-all system. Nevertheless, the Liberal Democrats had an indication of what might be elected when the European elections of June 1999 were conducted on a basis of proportional representation. Under the winner-takes-all system used in 1994 they secured only two members of the European Parliament (MEPs) with 17 percent of the vote. In 1999 they secured ten MEPs with only 13 percent of the vote.

Although it attracts support from across the social divide, the Liberal Democrat Party tends to attract middle-class and professional people committed to the ongoing protection of individual rights but who are prepared to accept that the state has an important social role to fulfill. It is now no longer the party of big business as it was in the nineteenth century but more that of the small shopkeeper and the small businessperson. It also represents the interests of some of the old right-wing Labour voters who left the Labour Party in 1981 to form the SDP, and which finally flowed into the Liberal Democrats.

Despite its growth, the Liberal Democratic Party of today is a far less successful party than the old Liberal Party that emerged in the mid-nineteenth century, even though its policies are still largely in tune with the old Liberal Party. The Liberal Party is considered to have emerged at a meeting at Willis's Rooms in 1859 when the Whigs, Peelite Tories who opposed protectionism, and radicals met to serve under Lord Palmerston. The group was subsequently led by Lord John Russell and W. E. Gladstone, who firmly established Gladstonian Liberalism in his 1868–1874 and 1880–1885 ministries and drew considerable support from the nonconformist religions at this time. From the start the Liberal Party was committed to free trade, religious toleration, efficiency, and an international policy of promoting peace. Although the Nonconformist association has long gone, most of the other policies are reflected in the modern Liberal Democrats. The Liberal Party operated throughout the country in Liberal clubs organized into constituencies through local bodies that denoted their number: the Liberal Two Hundred or the Liberal Four Hundred. These groups were brought together and given a sense of unity by the formation of the National Liberal Federation in 1877.

Under Gladstone the Liberals split in 1886 on the issue of Home Rule for Ireland, the Home Rule supporters siding with Gladstone and the Unionists, who favored the continuation of the union with Ireland, moving with Joseph Chamberlain into the Conservative Party. Lord Rosebery, who succeeded Gladstone in 1894, pressed for

issues such as temperance, strongly supported by the Nonconformists and the disestablishment of the Welsh Church. However, the divided party struggled until 1905 when it replaced the Conservatives and won a general election in 1906. This brought about a landslide Liberal victory, which sustained the Liberal Party in office until 1915 with the help of two further general elections in 1910. During these years the Liberals, greatly influenced by their parliamentary leader Henry Campbell-Bannerman, Prime Minister Herbert Asquith, and their Chancellor of the Exchequer, David Lloyd George, introduced the Liberal social reform of old-age pensions and national insurance, which were designed to alleviate poverty and avoid the need for a costly break-up of the New Poor Law. However, though these were remarkable developments, the Liberal Party found difficulty in prosecuting effectively Word War I, which started in 1914, and Asquith formed a wartime coalition government in 1915. As a result when Asquith resigned as prime minister in 1916, perhaps with the expectation of being brought back, Lloyd George stepped into the breach. The result was a split within the Liberal Party, which was not officially healed until 1923. Even then the Liberal Party remained divided, and by the 1930s there was the Lloyd George group, the Samuel group, which was the old Liberal Party, and the Sir John Simon Liberals, who joined the Conservative Party. Long before this final split the Labour Party had replaced the Liberal Party as the progressive party of government in British politics. Over the next fifty years the Liberals declined as a party, with occasional revivals under Jo Grimond and Edward Thorpe as well as a brief period of a Lib-Lab Pact in 1977–1978. However, none of this brought the revival of the Liberal Party back to the position of being a party of government, and even under the modern Liberal Democratic Party the prospects of forming a government remain extremely remote.

SEE ALSO *Multiparty Systems*

BIBLIOGRAPHY

Cook, Chris. 1998. *A Short History of the Liberal Party 1900–1997*. London: Macmillan.

Dangerfield, George. 1936. *The Strange Death of Liberal England*. Stanford, CA: Stanford University Press, 1997.

Grigg, John. 1978. *Lloyd George: The People's Champion, 1902–1911*. London: Eyre Methuen.

Searle, George R. 1992. *The Liberal Party: Triumph and Disintegration, 1886–1929*. London: Macmillan.

Stevenson, John. 1992. *Third Party Politics in Britain since 1945*. Oxford: Blackwell.

Keith Laybourn

LIBERALISM

Liberalism has been conceived of as at once a political philosophy, as an allied political movement, and as a way of thinking about the foundations and practices of government. Liberalism has historically been defined by a great diversity of ideas, largely due to the changing contexts within which and against which liberal thought has taken shape. Despite this diversity, there are a number of basic premises common to all liberal traditions. The most central of these is a valorization of the individual and of individual liberty, and much liberal debate has concerned the conceptions of human nature that undergird these terms. Linked to this, liberal thought has been preoccupied with how individuals should govern and be governed with the least possible intervention or coercion. While liberalism arose simultaneously with the Enlightenment as an often revolutionary response to religious and absolutist forms of government, liberal democracy has, in the aftermath of the Cold War, become the dominant form of government.

HISTORY

While the term *liberal* was not commonly used until the mid-nineteenth century, much liberal thought traces its origins to early modern writing, and in particular to John Locke's (1632–1704) writings on natural law in the context of the Glorious Revolution of 1688. Against the doctrine of the divine right of kings, Locke ([1690] 1988) argued that individuals are God's property and as such have a natural right to the means of survival—life, health, liberty, and property. The social contract is not, as it was in Thomas Hobbes (1588–1679), necessitated by fear, but rather secures the protection of the natural rights that individuals enjoyed in the state of nature. Locke's most lasting contributions to liberal theorizing were his conception of civil society as a society of free men, equal under the rule of law, and the link he drew between liberty and property. Locke's thought and in particular the emphasis he placed on consensual government would become central in the formulation of the American Declaration of Independence and the U.S. Constitution.

With the eighteenth-century Scottish Enlightenment and the rise of free market capitalism, liberal thought came to entail a more encompassing framework, including most importantly an economic theory. Against mercantilism, Adam Smith (1723–1790) argued in *The Wealth of Nations* ([1776] 2000) that a free market economy, if left to its own devices, would automatically regulate itself through an "invisible hand." Smith viewed human nature as inherently propelled by self-interest that is, however, softened by the capacity for "sympathy." Through the process of competition, individuals would fulfill their self-interest and, in the process, produce a balanced society. On the European continent, the Enlightenment tradition was defined by a much more rationalist conception of human nature that centered on the individual ability to reason and to direct change. The conceptions of individual reason and limited government in the work of Immanuel Kant (1724–1804) and Wilhelm von Humboldt (1767–1835) in Germany and Voltaire (1694–1778) and the Marquis de Condorcet (1743–1794) in the context of the French Revolution (1789–1799) had a lasting influence on liberal thought.

In the nineteenth century, English liberal thought developed an increasingly rationalistic turn. Starting with the utilitarianism of Jeremy Bentham (1748–1832) and James Mill (1773–1836), increasing trust is placed in the human capacity for reason and for the rational design of social institutions. The principle of utility, which in Adam Smith was reduced to individual calculations unknowable to the sovereign, now becomes the basis of governing society as a whole. Human action, argue the utilitarians, needs to be judged according to whether it promotes the greatest happiness for the greatest number of people. John Stuart Mill (1806–1873), while placing himself within the utilitarian tradition, argued that representative democracy was the best system to ensure that everyone had the freedom to pursue his own conception of happiness. In his most seminal contribution to liberal thought, *On Liberty* ([1859] 1989), Mill sought to fuse his father's utilitarianism with a strong defense of individuality and personal autonomy. His argument hinged on the idea of character and "self-development" based on a notion of human nature as perfectible. By extension, however, Mill's argument allowed for gradations of democracy based on the principles of civilization and progress that, especially in the colonies, entailed the justification of despotism (Mehta 1999).

In the early twentieth century, in the context of the crisis of the free market regime and the rise of socialism, a more state-centered strand of liberalism developed in Britain that sought to balance individual freedoms with equality in the form of welfare provisions. Elaborated in the work of sociologist Leonard Hobhouse (1864–1929) and later supported by the economic theories of John Maynard Keynes (1883–1946), the "new liberalism" was central to the development of the welfare state. In the aftermath of World War II (1939–1945) and in the context of the Cold War, a liberal conception and critique of totalitarianism arose in the work of Karl Popper (1902–1994) and in Isaiah Berlin's (1909–1997) conception and valuation of negative liberty (freedom from) over positive liberty (freedom to). For much of the century, however, welfare-state liberalism remained hegemonic in liberal thought and politics.

However, in the context of the crisis of the 1970s and rising critiques of the welfare state, liberal debate on the role of the state was reinvigorated. Arguing against the aggregating postulates of utilitarianism, John Rawls's (1921–2002) *A Theory of Justice* (1971) proposes a neo-Kantian, rights-based conception of "justice as fairness." Against a teleological conception of the good, this contractarian approach is premised on a heuristic device Rawls terms the "original position" in which individuals are imagined to be behind a "veil of ignorance" about their potential standing and attachments within society. From this position of distance and ignorance, individuals will rationally decide on a generalizable principle of justice. Importantly, this conception enables Rawls to move away from making any substantive claims about the public good or liberal society, to instead propose a proceduralist conception of justice based on rights rather than any particular version of the good. Partly as a response to his critics, Rawls (1993) later proposed the concept of political liberalism. Here, the question of pluralism is addressed by reducing the conception of justice to the idea of public reason defined by an "overlapping consensus." According to Rawls, this revised conception is necessitated in order to guarantee the stability of society in the context of diverging conceptions of the good.

In a 1974 critique of *A Theory of Justice*, Robert Nozick (1938–2002) proposes a minimal state, responsible primarily for the protection of private property. Friedrich von Hayek (1899–1992), who had throughout the period of welfare-state liberalism argued against state intervention into the economy, became one of the most influential proponents of a return to classical liberalism. Drawing on the Scottish Enlightenment tradition, Hayek proposed that society and in particular the economic sphere were unknowable to policymakers and would be governed by a "spontaneous order" as long as state intervention would be reduced to sustaining a peaceful order. Hayek's theorization of the limits of state reason became one of the most influential tracts in the rise to hegemony of neoliberalism in the last decades of the twentieth century.

LIBERALISM AND ITS CRITICS

Critiques of liberalism have usually converged on liberalism's disembodied conception of the individual. Edmund Burke's (1729–1797) writing on the French Revolution ([1790] 2001) lay the groundwork for the conservative critique of liberalism. Burke posited the organic nature of traditions evolved over time against what he perceived to be the ephemeral and dangerous rationalism of the Enlightenment. More recently and in explicit response to John Rawls, what has come to be known as the *communitarian critique* faults liberalism on both an ontological and a normative basis. The individual, communitarians like Michael Sandel (1984) argue, is not presocial; rather, the

individual only emerges through and within social and communal relations. Secondly, a society of atomized individuals is undesirable, since it removes the individual from the relations through which life becomes intelligible (MacIntyre 1981) and morally meaningful (Taylor 1979).

In his critique of liberal conceptions of freedom, Karl Marx (1818–1883) argued that the political emancipation of the individual is enabled by removing all difference from the political to the private realm. The liberal conception of autonomy is thus fictitious in that an individual's socioeconomic and religious particularities continue to exist outside liberalism's purview. Later, and here more explicitly linking liberalism to the rise of capitalism, Marx showed the ambiguities of liberal emancipation, famously suggesting that capitalism freed workers to sell their labor-power in the market place and simultaneously "freed" them from the means of production.

Similarly concerned with the constitution of the individual, Michel Foucault (1926–1984) viewed liberalism as a political rationality, as a practical way of thinking about the modalities and targets of government. Liberalism entails both the critique of previous ways of governing and the rise of new modalities of power that seek to produce a citizenry capable of self-government. Processes of responsibilization, disciplining, and normalization are thus not antithetical to liberalism, but rather the condition for liberal forms of rule. Liberal freedom is here not conceived of as the gradual removal of state intervention, but as entailing a new regime of power and a new approach to how one should govern oneself and others.

SEE ALSO *Cold War; Colonialism; Foucault, Michel; French Revolution; Globalization, Social and Economic Aspects of; Hobbes, Thomas; Identity; Locke, John; Marx, Karl; Marxism; Neoliberalism; Pluralism; Rawls, John*

BIBLIOGRAPHY

Berlin, Isaiah. 1969. Two Concepts of Liberty (1958). In *Four Essays on Liberty.* Oxford: Oxford University Press.

Burke, Edmund. [1790] 2001. *Reflections on the Revolution in France.* Ed. J. C. D. Clark. Stanford, CA: Stanford University Press.

Foucault, Michel. 2004. *Naissance de la biopolitique: Cours au collège de France, 1978–1979* [The birth of biopolitics]. Eds. François Ewald, Alessandro Fontana, and Michel Senellart. Paris: Éditions Gallimard.

Hayek, Friedrich A. von. 1978. *The Constitution of Liberty.* Chicago: University of Chicago Press.

Hobhouse, Leonard T. 1911. *Liberalism.* New York: Holt.

Locke, John. [1690] 1988. *Two Treatises of Government.* 3rd ed. Cambridge, U.K.: Cambridge University Press.

MacIntyre, Alisdair. 1981. *After Virtue: A Study in Moral Theory.* Notre Dame, IN: University of Notre Dame Press.

Marx, Karl. 1977. On the Jewish Question (1844). In *Karl Marx: Selected Writings*, ed. David McLellan, 39–57. Oxford: Oxford University Press.

Mehta, Uday Sing. 1999. *Liberalism and Empire: A Study in Nineteenth-Century British Liberal Thought.* Chicago: University of Chicago Press.

Mill, John Stuart. 1989. *On Liberty* (1859). In *J. S. Mill: "On Liberty" and Other Writings*, ed. Stefan Collini, 1–116. Cambridge, U.K.: Cambridge University Press.

Nozick, Robert. 1974. *Anarchy, State, and Utopia.* New York: Basic Books.

Popper, Karl. 1945. *The Open Society and Its Enemies.* London: Routledge.

Rawls, John. 1971. *A Theory of Justice.* Cambridge, MA: Belknap.

Rawls, John. 1993. *Political Liberalism.* New York: Columbia University Press.

Sandel, Michael. 1984. The Procedural Republic and the Unencumbered Self. In *Political Theory* 12 (1): 81–96.

Smith, Adam. [1776] 2000. *An Inquiry into the Nature and Causes of the Wealth of Nations.* New York: Modern Library.

Taylor, Charles. 1979. Atomism. In *Powers, Possessions, and Freedom: Essays in Honour of C. B. Macpherson*, ed. Alkis Kontos, 39–61. Toronto, ON: Toronto University Press.

Antina von Schnitzler

LIBERALISM, BLACK

SEE *Black Liberalism.*

LIBERALIZATION, ORDER OF

SEE *Liberalization, Trade.*

LIBERALIZATION, TRADE

In 1960 less than one-sixth of the countries in the world had open trade policies. Most countries had various types of trade restrictions such as high tariff rates (taxes on imports) and extensive nontariff barriers (such as quotas that restricted the physical quantity of specific imports allowed into a country). In addition, the official exchange rate often exceeded the black-market exchange rate, and governments exercised monopoly controls on exports and other trade-related matters. Yet by 2000 three-quarters of the countries in the world had removed many of these impediments and were now open to international trade. This is a remarkable transformation and highlights the importance of trade liberalization in the global economy.

What precipitated the extensive trade liberalization that occurred? Much of the credit is usually given to the sixty years of multilateral trade negotiations that has resulted in ever-lower trade barriers under the auspices of the General Agreement on Tariffs and Trade (GATT). Since GATT's inception in 1947, manufacturing tariffs in industrialized countries have fallen from 40 percent to 4 percent, and world trade has increased eighteenfold. Initial GATT membership of 23 countries expanded to 148 countries and the trade rounds became the international forum in which member governments agreed on rules for the conduct of international trade. The multilateral trade agreements involved nondiscriminatory tariff reductions so that all countries benefited—the "most favored nation" clause—and the tariff cuts were "binding" and could not be restored at a later date.

Countries would not have agreed to lower levels of import protection unless there were good arguments in their favor. Trade liberalization allows countries to specialize production and export in their areas of relative strength and to import products that other countries can make at lower cost. It enables access to a wider range of products, and access to foreign products helps diffuse innovations and new technologies. Openness to trade provides additional competition that can spur local firms to greater efficiency and keeps domestic prices low.

In the context of developing countries, a series of country studies sponsored by the World Bank, the Organization for Economic Cooperation and Development (OECD), and the National Bureau of Economic Research demonstrated that trade barriers imposed significant costs, whereas trade openness appeared to be associated with improved economic performance, although the underlying empirical research has not gone unquestioned (Rodrik 1999). For these countries, import substitution using high effective rates of protection had been the dominant vehicle by which industrialization has proceeded. Initially, local suppliers would have to be nurtured and protected from the competitive pressures applied by long established foreign producers. Over time, domestic inefficiencies would decline as these "infants" learned from experience and were able to reduce costs of production. The end result would be a far more diversified and self-reliant industrial structure less dependent on the vagaries of international commodity prices. In the 1970s increasing disenchantment with this strategy emerged, and an alternative approach, identified as outward- (or export-) oriented and associated with East

Asian development, became more popular and trade barriers fell (Edwards 1993).

While trade barriers in manufacturing have fallen extensively, the trade liberalization agenda has expanded its scope and consequently run into considerable difficulties. In 1995 GATT's successor, the World Trade Organization (WTO), became operational. Whereas GATT focused on trade in goods, the WTO concentrates on trade in services, intellectual property, and agricultural subsidies. According to the OECD, rich countries spend $280 billion a year on agricultural producer support; agricultural price support amounts to 20 percent in the United States, 50 percent in Europe, and 80 percent in Japan. These agricultural subsidies are trade-distorting, encouraging supported farmers to produce more, and this in turn lowers world prices and hurts farmers in poor countries that have a comparative advantage in the production of these subsidized commodities. Poor countries want agricultural liberalization in rich countries, yet there has been little progress in persuading richer countries to dispense with these subsidies. This leads credence to the claims about unfairness in trade negotiations made by Kevin Watkins and Penny Fowler in *Rigged Rules and Double Standards* (2003).

Trade in services, especially related to issues of labor mobility across national boundaries, and TRIPs (trade-related aspects of intellectual property rights), which are of special interest to the pharmaceutical and software industries, are equally contentious issues. The latter is related to the manufacture of generic drugs and their sales to poor countries. Claims for "fair trade" rather than "free trade" cloud trade negotiations even further, because nongovernment organizations have been advocating "social clauses" in trade liberalization agreements relating to child labor, human rights, the environment, wages, and conditions. Their position is that trade sanctions should be imposed against countries that do not meet international standards in these areas.

Given these stumbling blocks and complications, it is not surprising that there has been a move away from multilateral forums to negotiated bilateral or regional trade agreements outside the WTO framework. More than 300 such preferential trade agreements exist as of 2007. Whether these agreements assist global trade liberalization or hinder the process is not clear (Bhagwati 2002).

Trade liberalization is only part of a broader globalization movement and it needs to be carefully sequenced with other policy reforms. In general, trade liberalization should precede financial liberalization, domestic financial liberalization should precede external financial liberalization, and direct investment liberalization should precede portfolio and bank loan liberalization (capital account liberalization). Free inflows of foreign financial capital should only be allowed at the tail end of a liberalization program, and controls on suddenly increased inflows of short-term capital may be warranted. The purpose of these controls is to quarantine economies from excessive "hot" money inflows and outflows that disrupt economic stability and lead to exchange rate misalignments.

Overall, the welfare effects of trade liberalizations fall within the realm of second-best economics. There is still dispute about the direction of causation in the association between openness to trade and East Asia's rapid growth. What role have trade liberalization packages played in the performance of outward-oriented economies? A number of these countries, such as Japan, Korea, Singapore, and Taiwan, have promoted exports, but in an environment where imports had not been fully liberalized. The success of the East Asian countries with export-led growth suggests that some selectively determined degree of government intervention played a key role. Imports and lower tariffs may stimulate productivity, but import competition may have little impact on productivity growth if the domestic producers are technologically backward: Benefits accrue only to domestic producers that are roughly comparable to their foreign counterparts. This, then, suggests a role for trade-adjustment packages and safety nets for those disadvantaged by trade liberalization.

SEE ALSO *Barriers to Trade; Quotas, Trade; Tariffs*

BIBLIOGRAPHY

Bhagwati, Jagdish. 2002. *The Wind of the Hundred Days.* Cambridge, MA: MIT Press.

Edwards, Sebastian. 1993. Openness, Trade Liberalization, and Growth in Developing Countries. *Journal of Economic Literature* 31 (September): 1358–1393.

Rodrik, Dani. 1999. *The New Global Economy and Developing Countries: Making Openness Work.* Baltimore, MD: Johns Hopkins University Press.

Watkins, Kevin, and Penny Fowler. 2003. *Rigged Rules and Double Standards: Trade, Globalization, and the Fight Against Poverty.* Oxford: Oxfam.

John Lodewijks

LIBERATION

Liberation entered the English language during the fifteenth century. In modern terms liberation has taken on a political meaning to describe a condition of being free from impediments and more particularly activities leading toward the removal of restrictions to free action by a group or a person defined by nationality, race, gender, sexual orientation, or class. *Free action* is used here in relation to other key concepts that are part of the modern discourse of political life: autonomy, self-determination, and sovereignty. The development of a modern sense of individual rights, or the rights of a group of people to make decisions over their lives without external interference, is central to the way people understand sovereignty in the early twenty-first century. Liberation is therefore associated with particular historical movements toward the realization of sovereignty over one's self, among a "people," or over a country. In the twentieth century liberation emerged as an important desire expressed through a number of movements—examples of which will be discussed below—that have defined the character of social and political struggles in the contemporary world.

LIBERATION FROM SLAVERY

The abolitionist movement sought to end the practice of slavery on a global scale by ending the slave trade and emancipating slaves held in bondage. The Emancipation Proclamation (1863) issued by Abraham Lincoln (1809–1865), for example, declares that all slaves in Confederate territory were to be "freed." The act of manumission also allowed slave owners to set their slaves free. The Haitian slave revolt (1791) against French slavery, led by Toussaint Louverture (1743–1803) on the island of Saint Domingue, heralded briefly the first free black republic. The slaves in Saint Domingue drew on the Declaration of the Rights of Man, adopted by the leaders of the French Revolution in 1789, to demand liberation from the bondage of slavery, allowing them to be considered free and equal human beings, a right denied to subjects in French colonies. Initially the demand of the slaves in Saint Domingue was to be freed from slavery in order to be part of the French Empire as free people. Later in the revolt, as pointed out by C. L. R. James (1901–1989) in *The Black Jacobins* (1938), this changed to a demand for independence after the refusal of France under the rule of Napoléon Bonaparte (1769–1821) to grant the slaves "the rights of man."

COLONIALISM AND NATIONAL LIBERATION

While the expansive empires of the Romans, the Ottomans, and the Greeks possessed what might be considered colonies, it was after the sixteenth century that colonialism took on its modern meaning and eventually led to national liberation struggles. Developments in navigation and the technologies of war along with the changing patterns of trade facilitated the expansion and intensification of colonial rule and settlement by European powers over the rest of the world. Colonialism therefore meant ruling over another territory and its peo-ples either indirectly, through local elites like chiefs, or directly where there was a settler population, as in Australia and large parts of Africa and Asia.

The existence of empires that controlled large swaths of territory from a remote center of political power was challenged by the emergence of self-determination and nationalism. These principles held that states and groups of people who shared an affinity had the right to rule over themselves. The right to self-determination came into conflict with the maintenance and possession of colonies. This dilemma led to a protracted debate among prominent European philosophers of liberal thought, including John Stuart Mill (1806–1873) and Alexis de Tocqueville (1805–1859). Some argued that "states," following the Treaty of Westphalia (1648), should observe the principle of self-determination and, where states existed, this principle should be upheld to preserve territorial integrity. However, this principle did not necessarily apply to "peoples."

Benedict Anderson has argued that as a sensibility, nationalism emerged first in the Latin American colonies among the Creole elites. While "nations" may define themselves based on the subjective sense of a shared language, culture, or history, Anderson argued that nations are "imagined political communities" (Anderson 1991, p. 6). As a political idea, it holds that a "people," however defined, have the right to self-government, self-rule, or self-determination, and this principle was formally adopted by the United Nations in 1960 with the Declaration on the Granting of Independence to Colonial Countries and Peoples. A "people," defined as such, could legitimately claim the right to independence, but this idea was not universally accepted, and the struggle to realize independence was taken up by a range of national liberation movements in Africa, Asia, and the Americas. In these movements *liberation* was used to refer to the right of peoples to rule themselves, free from foreign domination by an external occupying power, and to live under an independent political authority. The methods used to achieve the aims of liberation by these movements took various forms, from nonviolent political agitation, as exemplified by Mahatma Gandhi's (1869–1948) idea of satyagraha to end British control over India, to the use of force and guerrilla warfare, as in the cases of Cuba from Spain, Algeria from France, Angola from Portugal, Zimbabwe from Britain, East Timor from Indonesia, Tamil nationalists in Sri Lanka, and Palestine from Israeli occupation.

RACIAL OPPRESSION, DISCRIMINATION, AND LIBERATION

The expansion of imperial rule, from which modern colonial rule emerged, was also facilitated by the notion of "race" as understood by Count de Gobineau (1816–1882), a French diplomat and writer who categorized humans as belonging to and originating from different "racial stocks." It was believed that races had different strengths, capabilities, and weaknesses and that some races should be socially nurtured while others could be destroyed. Europeans of an Aryan stock were placed at the acme of the pyramid in Gobineau's typology. This "scientific racism" contributed to the practice of colonialism and also fostered forms of social discrimination against particular groups of people within states, such as Jews in Germany and Poland, the descendents of free slaves in the United States, and black South Africans. On this basis therefore various forms of racism took root and fostered relations of hierarchy and domination between states and within states.

Racial discrimination led to another sense in which *liberation* came to refer to the struggle to free societies and individuals from racist institutional practices and racist thinking. The civil rights movement in the United States, led by African Americans such as Dr. Martin Luther King Jr. (1929–1968), demanded an end to the practice of segregation of Americans of African descent in southern states. The American civil rights movement also demanded representation in the democratic political system through the vote. Racism, in the institutionalized form that was practiced in South Africa, led to the demand for liberation from the severe effects of social, economic, and spatial separation of people on the basis of race, a situation formalized as apartheid after 1948 with the coming to power of the Afrikaner Nationalist Party.

While institutionalized racism has been successfully challenged by liberation movements, with African Americans now having the vote and South Africa inaugurating a nonracial democracy in 1994 under the presidency of Nelson Mandela, some argue that the more enduring psychological aspects of racism's legacy continue to require a form of liberation. The Martinican-born psychiatrist Frantz Fanon (1925–1961) wrote in *Black Skin, White Masks* (1967) of the mental effects of racism on human beings, who need "mental liberation" to free the mind from racist ways of thinking about the self and others. Applying Fanon's insights to academic knowledge, Edward Said (1935–2003), an American literary theorist of Palestinian descent, showed how racist assumptions underpinned many European understandings of the "Orient" and continue to operate in the academy with negative political effects. Also influenced by Fanon, the South African political leader Steve Biko (1946–1977), who was killed in police custody, emphasized the need for black South Africans to liberate their minds from the acceptance of racism by developing a "black consciousness."

CLASS STRUGGLE AND THE LIBERATION OF THE WORKING CLASS

Liberation from racism and slavery has largely been based on the liberal premise that people are entitled to individual rights. Marxists, however, have argued that capitalist societies are also based on relations of exploitation defined by economic class distinctions between groups. For Karl Marx (1818–1883), liberation entailed freeing the working class from wage labor or "wage slavery," which kept workers dependent on their bosses for their material reproduction. Liberation, Marx and Friederich Engels (1820–1895) noted in *The German Ideology* (1846), was therefore a process that required the material reorganization of society through the rearranging of the economic relations of production, thereby creating a classless society: "People cannot be liberated as long as they are unable to obtain food and drink, housing and clothing in adequate quality and quantity" (Marx and Engels [1846] 1967, p. 437). Marxism has inspired significant political liberation movements, notably the Russian Revolution of 1917, which provided the most influential alternative model of liberation to the liberalism of the West after World War II (1939–1945) until the collapse of the Soviet Union in 1990.

GENDER, SEXUALITY, AND THE FREEDOM TO CHOOSE

Since the nineteenth century the term *liberation* has also been used in defining movements that advocate changes in attitudes toward gender and sexuality (Wollstonecraft [1792] 1993). The American journalist Gloria Steinem declared 1970 "the year of women's liberation." "Women's lib," or feminism, as this movement has come to be known, refers to a diverse range of movements and philosophies that share the idea that gender should not be the primary determinant of an individual's economic or sociopolitical rights, obligations, or opportunities. Women's liberation has involved demanding for women the rights to vote in a democracy, to receive the same pay as men, and to exercise choices over their own bodies. Women, proponents argue, need to be liberated from the strictures of a male-dominated or patriarchal society. This liberation applies not only to women but to the gendered roles that men and women are socialized into performing, which reinforce patterns of inequality and discrimination. This notion is distinct from the use of *liberation* to redefine sexual relations in society. Such movements advocate an end to discrimination based on sexual orientation. The gay and lesbian movements, for example, advocate a redefinition of marriage to include same-sex couples. Such marriages are now recognized as legal in some countries, but it remains an ongoing liberation struggle.

SEE ALSO *Anticolonial Movements; Apartheid; Aryans; Autonomy; Capitalism; Civil Rights Movement, U.S.; Colonialism; Empire; Feminism; French Revolution; Gandhi, Mohandas K.; Gender Gap; Gobineau, Comte de; Haitian Revolution; Human Rights; Imperialism; Jews; Liberation Movements; Liberation Theology; Marx, Karl; Marxism; Mill, John Stuart; Neocolonialism; Race; Racism; Revolution; Russian Revolution; Said, Edward; Self-Determination; Sexual Orientation, Social and Economic Consequences; Sexuality; Slave Resistance; Slavery; Social Movements; Sovereignty; Tocqueville, Alexis de*

BIBLIOGRAPHY

Amílcar, Cabral. 1975. National Liberation and Culture. *Transition* 45: 12–17.

Anderson, Benedict. 1991. *Imagined Communities: Reflections on the Origin and Spread of Nationalism.* Rev. ed. London and New York: Verso.

Biko, Steve. 1987. *I Write What I Like: A Selection of His Writings.* London: Heineman.

Césaire, Aimé. [1955] 1972. *Discourse on Colonialism.* Trans. Joan Pinkham. New York: Monthly Review.

Chatterjee, Partha. 1990. The Nationalist Resolution of the Women's Question. In *Recasting Women: Essays in Indian Colonial History*, eds. Kumkum Sangari and Sudesh Vaid. New Brunswick, NJ: Rutgers University Press.

Fanon, Frantz. 1967. *Black Skin, White Masks.* Trans. Charles Lam Markham. New York: Grove.

Garvey, Marcus. [1924] 1992. Aims and Objects of Movement for Solution of Negro Problem. In *Philosophy and Opinions of Marcus Garvey*, ed. Amy Jacques-Garvey. New York: Athencum.

Gobineau, Joseph-Arthur de. [1853] 1983. *The Inequality of Human Races.* Trans. Adrian Collins. Torrance, CA: Noontide.

James, C. L. R. [1938] 1989. *The Black Jacobins: Toussaint L'Ouverture and the San Domingo Revolution.* New York: Vintage.

Lenin, Vladimir Ilyich. [1914] 1968. The Right of Nations to Self-Determination. In *National Liberation, Socialism, and Imperialism: Selected Writings.* New York: International Publishers.

Locke, John. [1690] 1963. *Two Treatises of Government.* New York: Mentor.

Maistre, Joseph de. [1884] 1965. *Study on Sovereignty.* Trans. Jack Lively. New York: Macmillan.

Marx, Karl, and Friedrich Engels. [1846] 1967. *The German Ideology.* In *Writings of the Young Marx on Philosophy and Society*, eds. and trans. Loyd D. Easton and Kurt H. Guddat. New York: Double Day.

Mill, John Stuart. [1861] 1958. *Considerations on Representative Government.* Indianapolis, IN: Bobbs-Merrill.

Mohanty, Chandra Talpade, Anne Russo, and Lourdes Torres, eds. 1991. *Third World Women and the Politics of Feminism.* Bloomington: Indiana University Press.

Rousseau, Jean-Jacques. [1762] 1993. *The Social Contract and Discourses.* Trans. G. D. H. Cole. London: Dent.

Said, Edward W. 1978. *Orientalism.* London: Penguin.

Skinner, Quentin. 1998. *Liberty before Liberalism.* Cambridge, U.K.: Cambridge University Press.

Steinem, Gloria. 1970. Women's Liberation Aims to Free Men Too. *Washington Post*, June 7.

Tocqueville, Alexis de. [1835–1840] 2000. *Democracy in America.* Trans. and eds. Harvey C. Mansfield and Delba Winthrop. Chicago: University of Chicago Press.

Wollstonecraft, Mary. [1792] 1993. *A Vindication of the Rights of Woman.* London: Penguin.

Suren Pillay

LIBERATION, WOMEN'S
SEE *Women's Liberation.*

LIBERATION MOVEMENTS

A liberation movement is a type of social movement that seeks territorial independence or enhanced political or cultural autonomy (or rights of various types) within an existing nation-state for a particular national, ethnic, or racial group. The term has also been extended to or adopted by other types of groups (e.g., women and gays and lesbians) that seek to free themselves from various forms of domination and discrimination. National liberation movements have been an especially important force in the modern world, and scholars have been interested in explaining their origins, strategies, and impacts. The division of the globe into nation-states, many of the wars among these states, and the hundreds of historical and contemporary conflicts among states and ethnic groups—in short, fundamental aspects of the modern world—cannot be understood without also understanding liberation movements.

TWO TYPES OF LIBERATION MOVEMENTS

Some national liberation movements are based on identification with and loyalty to a population and "its" state (or prospective state), regardless of the ethnic or racial composition of this population. The national feeling and identity underlying such movements is sometimes called "civic nationalism." For example, the leading liberation organization in South Africa, the African National Congress (ANC), has long advocated a policy of "nonracialism" (in effect, multiracialism), maintaining that South Africa belongs to all people who live there, whatever their race or tribe. Nationalism in the United States is also generally understood as civic in nature, although ethnic and especially racial nationalism (white and black) has often competed with this understanding.

In fact many liberation movements are based on identification with and loyalty to a specific ethnic or racial group that may or may not live within the jurisdiction of a single state. In fact bringing all co-ethnics within a single nation-state, through territorial expansion if need be, has been the aim of a number of nationalist movements. This type of national identity is often called "ethnic nationalism." For example, the Zionist movement that founded the state of Israel may be understood as a type of ethnic (specifically, Jewish) nationalism. Similarly the Palestinian liberation movement, which has long been at odds with Zionism, is also mainly an ethnonationalist liberation movement—although a very small number of Israelis and Palestinians support the creation of a single "binational" state for both Jews and Palestinians that would incorporate Israel, the West Bank, and Gaza (i.e., historical Palestine).

The word *liberation*, originally meaning "setting free or releasing from," first entered the English language in the fifteenth century. The term was not widely used in a political sense until the mid-nineteenth century and especially the mid-twentieth century. National liberation movements can, however, be traced back to the late eighteenth century. The temporal and geographic span of such movements—ranging from the North and South American wars of independence in the late eighteenth and early nineteenth centuries to the related (but distinct) European nation-building processes of the mid- and late nineteenth century and continuing through the decolonization struggles in Asia and Africa in the mid-twentieth century and beyond—raises the question of just how similar these movements actually are. Yet despite the wide variation among national liberation movements in terms of historical context, social base, strategies, and specific aims, a common thread uniting them all has been the need to contend, whether as friend or foe, with the nation-building projects that have been so central to the modern world.

The modern nation-state, along with the movements seeking to bring this form of political and social life into existence—whether through intellectual argument, cultural imagining, or force of arms—has been a contradictory social phenomenon. Objectively the political form of the nation-state is thoroughly modern, having come into wide existence only within the last 200 years or so, as well as highly contingent, with the ability of any given national liberation movement to achieve its objective of nation-

hood dependent upon a host of historical variables. Yet subjectively the nation or "the people," despite (or perhaps because of) its existence as what Benedict Anderson (1991) calls an "imagined community," is necessarily understood as natural, eternal, and as unchanging as the sun. The two core elements of national liberation movements—the political task of obtaining state power (whether through seizure or creation) and the cultural process of constructing a "nation"—have therefore frequently coexisted uneasily. The efforts of artists, intellectuals, and political leaders in the vanguard of national liberation struggles—along with the mass movements they have sought (with varying success) to inspire—have been aimed at the creation of a nation-state that, by definition, did not yet exist; yet this struggle has been represented as the natural unfolding of an inevitable, historically preordained process.

The concept of democracy, the idea (and ideal) that the state should represent the interests of the nation or the people, has provided an important ideological justification for attempts to bring together the cultural and political dimensions of the nation-state form. Yet the inclusive, revolutionary-democratic equation of state, nation, and people, ushered into the modern era most powerfully by the French Revolution, has existed alongside the exclusionary practices of modern bureaucratic states, including the "purification" and standardization of a single national language, mass education aimed at spreading this language and an attendant national feeling, and even occasionally the mass expulsion or genocidal elimination of those unfortunates who do not belong to the "right" national or ethnic (including religious or linguistic) group—all in the quest to create an ethnically homogenous nation. Many national liberation movements, moreover, have ignored or even actively suppressed social antagonisms based on class and gender, for example, that would allegedly weaken national identity. Thus the "liberation" these movements have sought has typically been partial at best.

The nation-state has existed throughout its relatively brief history in a complex relationship with another great force that has shaped the modern world—capitalism. Although nineteenth-century liberal economic doctrine extolled the benefits of free trade, the rise of industrial capitalism in Europe was closely linked to mercantilism and state-led "national economies," a fact that "no economist of even the most extreme liberal persuasion could overlook," as E. J. Hobsbawm (1992, p. 28) notes. Anderson's (1991) argument that "print-capitalism" fueled the rise of the mass-circulating newspapers and books upon which the "imagined community" of the nation arose shows that the relationship between capitalism and the nation-state was cultural as well as economic. Furthermore the decolonization struggles of the post–World War II (1939–1945) era must of course be understood in relation to the dynamics of capitalist imperialism. Hobsbawm (1992) points out the close links forged in at least some anti-imperialist national liberation movements between the goals of political independence and social revolution. At the dawn of the twenty-first century—amid neoliberal celebrations of the weakening of state regulation of the economy (seen as the final unfettering of the free market), unprecedented worldwide flows of capital, people, and goods, *and* a resurgence of nationalist feeling—debate rages as to whether the nation-state form can survive capitalism's global expansion. Many analysts, especially Marxists, have long predicted that global capitalism would undermine "parochial" nationalist sentiments—though this seems no closer to realization than it was at the beginning of the twentieth century.

THE ORIGINS OF LIBERATION MOVEMENTS

What causes liberation movements? Why do they arise when and where they do? Clearly national or ethnic identity and solidarity alone do not automatically produce social movements, and to some extent national identity is itself a product of nationalist mobilization. Furthermore, while nationalism may help to facilitate capitalist economic activities—by encouraging a common language, for example, or by weakening potentially disruptive class identities—its functionality for capitalism does not explain the origins of national identity or nationalist movements in the first place.

Many scholars would argue that liberation movements arise for the same reasons any social movement emerges: widespread grievances, plus a preexisting collective identity (in this case, a widespread national or ethnic identity), plus some significant formal or informal organization or social ties among this self-identified population, plus a sense of political empowerment or efficacy, plus a political context that facilitates (or at least is not inimical to) collective action. As noted, however, national or ethnic identities may be more of an outcome than the initial cause of liberation movements. That is, liberation movements may initially focus on very specific grievances and only gradually address more general grievances and evolve into movements claiming to represent the aspirations of a national or ethnic group as such. During and after the transformation of such movements into national or ethnic movements, they typically help spread a sense of national or ethnic identity to growing numbers of people. Nationalist identities and movements, in short, typically evolve contemporaneously.

Some scholars have also proposed specific theories of nationalist or ethnic mobilization. These theories tend to focus on the political and social conditions that encourage specifically ethnic or national identities—as opposed especially to class identities—and that generate widespread grievances among ethnic and national groups. In one view, those socially and territorially segregated ethnic groups that come into economic or military competition with one another are especially likely to develop strong ethnic identities and to mobilize in collective self-defense. The wealthier and more powerful group may mobilize in reaction to a perceived threat, and the poorer and less powerful group may mobilize so as to improve its own collective interests. Paradoxically, competition may be especially fierce if the two communities are or become more nearly equal. This competition (and concomitant nationalist mobilization) may gradually erode to the extent that the two populations become socially integrated (through voluntary association, for example, or intermarriage), but it is likely to persist if the two groups remain "socially distant" from one another.

The political exclusion and domination of particular ethnic groups, on an explicitly ethnic basis, is also likely to encourage ethnonationalist identities and movements for political rights. Overseas imperialism in its colonial form strongly encouraged the formation of national identities and liberation movements even among groups that did not previously consider themselves members of the same group (the boundaries of colonies were typically established with little regard for the ethnic composition of the local populations). Identities such as "Indonesian" and "Mozambican"—let alone liberation movements based on these identities—did not exist prior to the creation of colonial states.

The strategies of liberation movements have generally been shaped by their organizational strength as well as by the responses of authorities (Irvin 1999). Some authorities have seen political advantages to extending rights to liberation movements or even granting territorial independence in colonial situations. Not surprisingly, authorities have been more accommodating to narrowly political movements, dominated by economic elites, that do not challenge the economic well-being of these authorities and their constituents. By contrast, authorities have strongly and usually violently resisted liberation movements that represent a threat to their economic interests, and such resistance has generally induced liberation movements to adopt more coercive strategies of their own, including forms of armed struggle such as guerrilla warfare and terrorism—the latter strategy especially common in colonies with large settler populations.

THE FUTURE OF LIBERATION MOVEMENTS

In an age of increasing globalization, some have suggested that the relative importance of nation-states is declining, as states find it increasingly difficult to control the movements of labor, commodities, and especially capital. In this view, the advantages of creating or controlling states (or subnational political units) are rapidly decreasing. And yet there are numerous instances of ongoing national liberation and ethnonational movements around the world. These movements have a range of goals—from national independence to regional autonomy—as well as varied social bases—from immiserated Palestinians in the West Bank and Gaza to wealthy elites in the Santa Cruz region of Bolivia. A short list of early twenty-first-century liberation struggles includes Irish nationalists in North Ireland, Tamils in Sri Lanka, Tibetans in China, Palestinians in the West Bank and Gaza, Kurds in Iraq and Turkey, Kashmiris in India, Muslims in southern Thailand, Chechens in Russia, Quebecois in Canada, Basques in Spain, Zapatistas and other indigenous groups in Mexico, Albanians in Yugoslavia (Kosovo), Acehnese in Indonesia, several ethnic groups in the northeastern states of India (including Nagaland and Tripura), and many others. Despite the enormous variety and complexity of such conflicts, their sheer number indicates that ethnonational and national liberation movements will remain extremely important for the foreseeable future.

SEE ALSO *African National Congress; Anticolonial Movements; Capitalism; Ethnicity; Ethnocentrism; French Revolution; Globalization, Anthropological Aspects of; Globalization, Social and Economic Aspects of; Liberation; Nationalism and Nationality; Nation-State; Revolution; Social Movements; Zionism*

BIBLIOGRAPHY

Anderson, Benedict. 1991. *Imagined Communities: Reflections on the Origin and Spread of Nationalism.* 2nd ed. New York: Verso.

Hobsbawm, E. J. 1992. *Nations and Nationalism since 1780: Programme, Myth, Reality.* 2nd ed. New York: Cambridge University Press.

Irvin, Cynthia L. 1999. *Militant Nationalism: Between Movement and Party in Ireland and the Basque Country.* Minneapolis: University of Minnesota Press.

Miller, Norman, and Roderick Aya, eds. 1971. *National Liberation: Revolution in the Third World.* New York: Free Press.

Olzak, Susan. 2004. Ethnic and Nationalist Social Movements. In *The Blackwell Companion to Social Movements*, eds. David A. Snow, Sarah A. Soule, and Hanspeter Kriesi, 666–693. Malden, MA: Blackwell.

Smith, Anthony D. 1991. *National Identity.* Reno: University of Nevada Press.

Smith, Tony. 1981. *The Pattern of Imperialism: The United States, Great Britain, and the Late-Industrializing World since 1815.* New York: Cambridge University Press.

Younis, Mona N. 2000. *Liberation and Democratization: The South African and Palestinian National Movements.* Minneapolis: University of Minnesota Press.

Jeff Goodwin
Gabriel Hetland

LIBERATION THEOLOGY

Liberation theology, or theology of liberation, is among the movements for social change that emerged in the Americas in the 1960s. Born within Christian churches, it upholds an understanding of the Christian faith as demanding an "option for the poor," that is, a continuous commitment to the self-liberation of the oppressed. From its inception, it has had important ties with grassroots organizations and actions for social change—siding with the victims of socioeconomic oppression and of political and military repression.

Since early on liberation theology attracted the attention of social scientists and policymakers, as its effects both belied scholarly assumptions—for example, religion having a decreasing influence and a predominantly conservative function in the larger society—and raised fears of grassroots opposition to capitalism among the economic, political, and military elites north and south of the Rio Grande.

ROOTS AND DEVELOPMENT

Several factors influenced the emergence of liberation theology. The growing resistance throughout the Americas in the 1960s to economic exploitation, political repression, and official complicity with both is indeed among these. This resistance, partially inspired by the Cuban Revolution (1959), found mounting echoes among urban youth, the poor, students, and intellectuals—including a rising number of church activists and thinkers. These stimulated attempts (including a "theology of revolution," "Christian left," and Christian "communitarianism") to ground the struggle against exploitation and repression in the biblical tradition, especially in Jesus's actions, words, death, and resurrection—and thus to disprove the claim (shared both by Christian capitalists and Marxist atheists) that the churches' social role could only be a conservative one. Following suit, churches started not only initiatives for economic development and respect of human rights, but also theological foundations for such initiatives. The Second Vatican Council (1962–1965), the social encyclicals of Popes John XXIII (1963) and Paul VI (1967), as well as the 1968 Second General Conference of Latin

American Roman Catholic Bishops, were all particularly influential in that change of direction—particularly through their explicit Christian affirmation of the divine right of all peoples to govern themselves democratically, and to have access to the material goods necessary to satisfy their basic material needs, even through revolutionary social, economic, and political change, if necessary. On the Protestant side, the World Conference on Church and Society in Geneva, sponsored by the World Council of Churches (1966), a follow-up Consultation on Church and Society in São Paulo, Brazil, sponsored by a provisional commission for the Unity of Latin American Evangelicals (1967), and the Third Latin American Evangelical Conference (Buenos Aires, 1969), all contributed to Protestant Christians' embracing movements for social justice. In both Protestant and Catholic quarters, a growing chorus of voices, official and otherwise, affirmed much more clearly from the 1960s on than in earlier times the Christian obligation to fight for socioeconomic justice, political democracy, human rights, and world peace, especially in defense of the poorer populations. Entwined with these, in the United States, the civil rights movement, the Black Power movement, the antiwar movement, the United Farm Workers movement, the women's movement, and the American Indian liberation movement, all contributed to the emergence of a rich diversity of theological reflections from the late 1960s on.

A first digest of some key ideas of a liberation theology, as well as a first Spanish use of the idiom itself, *theology of liberation*, appeared in the lecture "Hacia una teología de la liberación" (Toward a theology of liberation), delivered in 1968 to a clergy meeting in his native Peru by Roman Catholic priest Gustavo Gutierrez (b. 1923), dubbed "the father of liberation theology" since. About the same time, the former Brazilian Presbyterian pastor Rubem Alves (b. 1933), exiled in Princeton Theological Seminary, used the expression in his dissertation *Towards a Theology of Liberation*, with ideas converging with Gutierrez's. In 1969 the African Methodist Episcopal minister/theologian James H. Cone independently finished his book *A Black Theology of Liberation*, the cornerstone of black liberation theology—deeply inspired by the revolutionary call of the Black Power movement for the black population in the United States to take in its own hands the task of achieving equality, autonomy, and respect "by any means necessary," as well as by its criticism of the complicity of churches and theologians with white supremacy.

Throughout the 1970s and 1980s, the movement grew in numbers, visibility, and influence across the churches in the Americas. In response, military dictatorships—in at least ten countries of the Caribbean, Central America, and South America—unleashed violent repression against those linked to liberation theology. Among the hundreds of thousands of lives thus lost, Msgr. Oscar Arnulfo Romero, archbishop of San Salvador, murdered while celebrating mass in a hospital chapel in 1980, was the most remarkable victim of that backlash, becoming a popular saint-martyr symbolizing the Christian commitment to the liberation of the poor. That year, a document outlining the inter-American strategy of the Reagan administration stated: "U.S. foreign policy must begin to counter (not react against) liberation theology as it is utilized in Latin America by the 'liberation theology' clergy" (Committee of Santa Fe 1980).

The military repression; the stifling of dissent in Roman Catholicism under Pope John Paul II (1978–2005), with parallel processes in many Protestant churches; the accelerating impoverishment of Latin American peoples under the new global economy; the emergence of fragile democracies in the wake of most military dictatorships; and the growing appeal of Pentecostalism among the Latin American poor stunned and beset liberation theology through the last two decades of the twentieth century.

KEY IDEAS, DEBATES, AND REPERCUSSIONS

For liberation theology God is the God of the poor. God's self-revelation is first and foremost in, to, and through the poor—not least in the incarnation, birth, words, deeds, persecution, torture, execution, and resurrection of Jesus, as expressed, among others, in Matthew 25: 31–46. Modern poverty is not a result of accidental scarcity (as it might have been in other times and places), but of systemic exploitation by the few at the expense of the many. Poverty is the result of the sin of the powerful, not of the poor: the product of a free human rejection of God's call for caring for the poor and oppressed. Salvation is, therefore, inseparable from the radical embracing of God's option for the poor, and thus entailing, among others, a call against capitalist exploitation.

The theology of liberation has often been charged with reducing Jesus to a social revolutionary. Albeit the charge could be deemed unfair, the fact is that such an iconic image was quite pervasive during the first two decades of the history of the movement—more among some "followers" than amid the theologians in the movement proper. As the years went by, such images became less recurrent. As in any emerging movement fighting for deep structural change, liberation theology developed much more what distinguished it from conservative, dominant theologies, than what both might hold in common. Thus, an emphasis on the historical Jesus, on the human facet of the divine incarnation, and on the social dimensions of the life, message, passion, death, and resurrection of the Christ, have been critical in liberation theology. The image of Jesus in this theology is and has been that of someone essentially identified with "the least among us," whose entire life was (is, and will continue to be) radically revolutionary—and not just marginally or accidentally—and thoroughly world-shattering in terms economical, social, political, ethnic, linguistic, and gender-based.

For liberation theology, theology is only a second moment—a moment of reflection on the actual praxis of faith—and dominant theologies are, all too often, unconscious sacralizations of the self-interested faith praxis of the elites. Theological work requires, therefore, an effort of critical social analysis of the social conditions and interests shaping its course, so that all theology moves toward bearing the good news of God's liberation for the poor and oppressed. But, as Gutierrez would put it, what matters is not the fate of theology (not even of liberation theology), but the fate of the poor and oppressed.

Possibly, however, the most significant and enduring impact of liberation theology—including in places as distant as Chile, the Philippines, Korea, South Africa, and Los Angeles—has to do with its emphasis on the obligation of theology and theologians to involve themselves in the actual struggles for liberation of the oppressed themselves. One major facet of this emphasis on praxis are the so-called "basic ecclesial communities" (BECs): small gatherings of lay Christian neighbors—with or without a pastor present—to read the Bible in community, reflect on its practical demands for the larger life in community, and organize and mobilize to enact those demands in the real existence of the area. Such BECs sprouted in many places in South America and beyond (notably in Brazil, with estimates of more than 100,000 BECs in the 1980s touching the lives of several million people), turning the message of liberation theology into the actual development of neighborhood clinics, literacy campaigns, independent schools, labor unions, strikes, mass protests, housing projects, and neighborhood cleanups.

The social and political movements leading to the victories of more socially concerned leaders in Latin America from 1979 on (Nicaragua's Sandinistas, Haiti's Lavalas, Brazil's Workers Party, Venezuela's Chavez, Chile's Bachelet, and Bolivia's Evo Morales), are probably inexplicable without factoring in the influence, large or small, of liberation theology and BECs.

These initiatives have placed liberation theology, on the one hand, in dialogue and cooperation with other movements (Christian or not) fighting for social justice, democracy, equality, and peace, and therefore, on the other hand, also in conflict with both the elites—social, economic, political, military, and, often too, religious—of many nations, as well as with those Christians who view their faith from vantage points outside of the liberation of the poor and oppressed.

Liberation theology has been variously critiqued for being more Marxist than Christian; reducing the Christian faith, evangelization, and salvation to this—a worldly, socioeconomic agenda; promoting hatred of the rich, class warfare, and armed revolution; erasing the spiritual dimensions of the Christian faith; turning the church into a political party; and sacralizing the poor while demonizing the wealthy. Liberation theologians, responding more indirectly than directly to such accusations, have nuanced and deepened their reflections, especially from the 1980s on, while inspiring further critical analyses of the complex social and religious dynamics beneath the charges laid against them.

NORTH AMERICAN LINKAGES

The reach, yield, sway, and publicized persecution of Latin American Roman Catholic liberation theology have often created the impression that it is only, or at least mainly, a Latin American and/or Roman Catholic phenomenon. Liberation theology, however, developed simultaneously in North America, too, and, not much later, in Asia, Africa, and the Middle East.

Black liberation theology was the first North American liberation theology. U.S. Hispanic/Latino theologies followed not long after both Black and Latin American liberation theologies. Feminist, pacifist, Native American, Asian American, and Jewish liberation theologies came immediately thereafter, followed by lesbian and gay liberation theologies. Each one has both advanced the critique of the ways in which their own religious tradition has been an unwitting accomplice of oppression, and contributed to reinterpreting such tradition in further solidarity with the victims of oppression and with their struggles for liberation. In the process, several forums have contributed to the dialogue, reciprocal critique, and cross-pollination between these liberation theologies—the most significant being the EATWOT (Ecumenical Association of Third-World Theologians).

At the onset of the twenty-first century, the multiplicity of liberation theologies, as well as the diversity of situations in which they exist, does not allow for any sweeping diagnosis or prognosis. It can be said, however, that it is not possible any longer to preach Christian theology without facing, sooner or later, knowingly or not, the key question raised by liberation theology: What have we done for the poor and oppressed in our midst? Simultaneously, at least in Latin America, it is hardly possible any longer to administer politics (leftist, centrist, or right-wing; civilian or military; governmental or oppositional; democratic or otherwise), without facing the demands of a significant sum of Christians for respect, justice, and peace for all—beginning with the most vulnerable.

BIBLIOGRAPHY

The Committee of Santa Fe. 1980. *A New Inter-American Policy for the Eighties.* Washington, DC: Council for Inter-American Security.

Cone, James H. 1990. *A Black Theology of Liberation.* 20th Anniversary ed. Maryknoll, NY: Orbis Books.

Gutierrez, Gustavo. 1988. *A Theology of Liberation: History, Politics, and Salvation.* Trans. and ed. Sister Caridad Inda and John Eagleson. Maryknoll, NY: Orbis Books.

Levine, Daniel H. 1992. *Popular Voices in Latin American Catholicism.* Princeton, NJ: Princeton University Press.

Smith, Christian. 1991. *The Emergence of Liberation Theology: Radical Religion and Social Movement Theory.* Chicago: University of Chicago Press.

Otto Maduro

LIBERTARIANISM

From the customs of liberal society and the writings of John Locke (1632–1704), David Hume (1711–1776), Adam Smith (1723–1790), and myriad others, there emerged an ideological sensibility dubious of government activism, leery of collectivist urges, and resistant of nationalistic sentiments. It learned to accept commercial society and cosmopolitanism, and even celebrate them. It maintains a presumption of individual liberty. The name of this sensibility has varied in time and place, but in the United States since the 1970s the name has been *libertarianism.*

The signal feature of libertarianism is the distinction between voluntary and coercive action. Coercion is the aggressive invasion (including the threat of invasion) of one's property or freedom of consent (or contract). Libertarians maintain a logic of ownership whereby owners have a claim to the control and use of their property, a claim good against the world. The logic is exhibited throughout centuries of liberal society in the normal, legitimate goings-on of private parties. It emerges as intuitive and natural. Adam Smith wrote in *The Wealth of Nations* (1776) that "the obvious and simple system of natural liberty establishes itself of its own accord" (bk. 4, chap. 9). As for the determination of who owns what, there are universal norms, beginning with ownership in one's own person, and extending to property acquired within the family and in voluntary interaction with others (such as trade, production, and gift relations). Libertarians admit the holes and gray areas, but argue that the distinctions nonetheless hold much water, and that rival ideologies are also plagued by holes and gray areas, even more so.

Libertarians reject any "social contract" device as a way to bring political relations into "consent." They reject the idea that, whether by virtue of democracy or simply by maintaining residence within the polity, one voluntarily agrees to the government laws one lives under. Government is recognized as a special kind of organization, and might be said to enjoy a special kind of legitimacy, but it does not get a special dispensation on coercion. In the eyes of the libertarian, everything the government does that would be deemed coercive and criminal if done by any other party in society is still coercive. For example, imagine that a neighbor decided to impose a minimum-wage law on you. Since most government action, including taxation, is of that nature, libertarians see government as a unique kind of organization engaged in wholesale coercion, and coercion is the treading on liberty. This semantic, libertarians say, was central in eighteenth- and nineteenth-century custom and social thought, for example in Adam Smith's treatment of "natural liberty" and through the American founders, the abolitionists, John Stuart Mill (1806–1873), Herbert Spencer (1820–1903), and William Graham Sumner (1840–1910). (Indeed, libertarians will argue that the vocabulary of modern liberalism is in many respects a systematic undermining of the older vocabulary.)

To just about anyone, *coercion* has a negative connotation. And, indeed, libertarians generally oppose government action. That disposition holds not only against economic intervention, but extends to coercive egalitarianism (the welfare state), restrictions on personal lifestyle (such as drug prohibition), and extensive government ownership of resources. Libertarians also tend to oppose military action abroad, though some libertarians may favor it when they believe that it bids fair to reduce coercion on the whole (that is, across the globe).

Within libertarian thought, there has been much debate over whether the principle of liberty is absolute (that is, 100 percent), or, as Adam Smith held, simply a presumption (say, 90 percent). Most classical liberals regarded it as a presumption, as have the transitional figures Ludwig von Mises (1881–1973) and Friedrich Hayek (1899–1992), both originally from Austria, and the famous American economist Milton Friedman. In judging where coercive government policy should be accepted or even deemed desirable, the "maxim" libertarians appeal to broad sensibilities about consequences, including moral and cultural consequences, of alternative policy arrangements. They do not attempt to set out any complete or definitive characterization of such sensibilities, any algorithm of desirability, and they declare that it is unreasonable to demand that they do so, especially since the same demand is not made of rival ideologies.

In justifying the presumption of liberty, most libertarians, especially economists, emphasize the practical arguments—liberty works better than government intervention—but others have maintained that liberty has an ethical authority established quite separately from any consideration of practical results.

The emergence of libertarianism, as such, comes about from the retreat of classical liberalism (particularly after 1900) and, particularly in the United Kingdom and the United States, the concurrent change of the popular meaning of *liberalism*, such that those who kept up cosmopolitan, laissez-faire, antistatist views no longer had a name.

Mises, Hayek, and Friedman clung to the old term *liberalism*. The term *libertarian* was used occasionally, but was really seized by the critical figure of modern libertarianism, Murray N. Rothbard (1926–1995). Beginning in the 1960s, Rothbard reasserted the old definition of *liberty* and infused *libertarianism* with a paradigmatic content holding that institutionalized coercion is always wrong and government action always damaging to social utility. Libertarianism implied anarchism. A prodigious polymath and challenging, charismatic personality, Rothbard erected an integrated doctrine for ethics, politics, and economics.

Anarcho hyphenates (such as *anarcho-capitalism*) were discussed also by other libertarian theoreticians, notably favorably by David Friedman and critically by Robert Nozick (1938–2002). Rothbard, David Friedman, and others built on the notion that private ownership and voluntary exchange are intuitive and focal, and hence lend themselves to a kind of spontaneous adoption by decentralized social institutions. They speculated on how there could be a free market in the enforcement of property rights, like private security companies today. Later research on voluntary reputational practices and institutions, exemplified, for example, by credit reporting agencies, would lend support to the view that, in a world where practically all property is privately owned, government police would not be necessary to resolving disputes and maintaining internal order. As for defense from external aggression, Rothbard tended to argue that no foreign government would have plausible cause or the practical means to conquer an anarcho-libertarian society, while David Friedman admitted uncertainties. The anarcho speculations, as well as Rothbard's extreme claims for liberty, arguably diverted libertarians from the task of developing a persuasive, relevant ideology, and hindered the penetration of libertarian thinking into mainstream discourse.

Many of the same people in the United States who were fashioning modern libertarianism were also busy fashioning the so-called Austrian school of economics, named for the influence of the Austrians Mises and Hayek (who in 1974 was awarded a Nobel Prize in economics). Austrian economics is solidly pro-laissez-faire, but there has always been a tension between two types of thought.

One, exemplified by Mises and Rothbard, champions human reason as an engine of discovery of scientific truth and purports to deduce a priori the superiority of voluntary arrangements. The other, inspired by Smith and exemplified by Hayek, criticizes the pretense of knowledge. It views economic processes as a skein of local practices and peculiarities, with their own dialectics of change and correction, and hence largely unknowable to regulators or even the most assiduous intellectuals. Followers of Mises and Rothbard claim a scientific foundation for laissez-faire economics; followers of Smith and Hayek criticize the scientific claims of interventionist economics. All "Austrian" economists are at least broadly libertarian in their policy views, but many libertarians are mainstream in economic method; Milton Friedman and David Friedman, for example, though admiring of Hayek, would be sharply critical of Austrian economics, particularly the Mises-Rothbard version. In fact, Hayek surely had grave misgivings about that as well, and never favored the fashioning of a separate "Austrian" school of economics.

Another important figure in the resurgence of antistatist ideas was the novelist and pop-philosopher Ayn Rand (1905–1982). Like Rothbard a messianic personality, though with much less learning and scholarship, Rand too set forth a highly integrated belief system, "objectivism." However, Rand strongly favored government's function as the keeper of the peace, and, in sharp contrast to Rothbard, an anticommunist foreign policy. She detested libertarianism, and Rothbard attacked her movement as a cult.

Rothbard's paradigm was so clear and consistent that even the libertarians who soundly rejected his extreme claims for liberty nonetheless found themselves working out their ideas in relation to principles like those he propounded. Nowadays, there remain loyal Rothbardians, but most libertarians think more in the fashion of Smith, Hayek, and Friedman. They insist that government intervention, including taxation, is coercive, but they take the anticoercion principle to be, not a natural axiom, but a natural maxim. They see government as having at least one important and necessary function—the undoing of other governmental functions. (In contrast, Rothbard's vision of libertarian social transformation held that after long years of ideological stirrings, there would come the inevitable internal political crisis, yielding to a widespread awakening and some kind of spontaneous, bottom-up institutional house-cleaning.)

Libertarianism joins the mainstream conversation as a political persuasion anchored in the status quo, not some ideal libertarian society, and yet opposed to the status quo, favoring freer arrangements pretty much across the board. It is perhaps best represented by public-policy institutes, such as the Cato Institute and the Independent

Institute, that develop policy argumentation on an issue-by-issue basis. As for the academic world, the most notable libertarian strongholds are the economics department and law school at George Mason University.

Libertarianism is now a broad tent, rooted in policy issues and insistent on the Locke-Smith-Spencer-Rothbard definition of liberty. Within the tent, only a small portion would defend "anarchism," but all remain radical in the sense that they insist that government intervention is coercive, and on most issues they entertain and quite likely favor abolishing the government agency or interventions in question.

There has also existed since the 1970s in the United States a Libertarian Party. However, libertarians are usually not much interested in it, chiefly because they feel that within the American system third parties are impossible or even damaging to their own cause.

SEE ALSO *Freedom; Friedman, Milton; Hayek, Friedrich August; Mises, Ludwig Edler von; Philosophy, Political*

BIBLIOGRAPHY

Boaz, David. 1997. *Libertarianism: A Primer.* New York: Free Press.

Hayek, Friedrich. 1960. *The Constitution of Liberty.* Chicago: University of Chicago Press.

Klein, Daniel B. 2004. Mere Libertarianism: Blending Hayek and Rothbard. *Reason Papers: A Journal of Interdisciplinary Normative Studies* 27: 7–43. http://www.reasonpapers.com/pdf/27/rp_27_1.pdf.

Rothbard, Murray. 1978. *For a New Liberty: The Libertarian Manifesto.* Rev. ed. Lanham, MD: University Press of America.

Smith, Adam. [1776] 1904. *An Inquiry into the Nature and Causes of the Wealth of Nations.* 5th ed. Ed. Edwin Cannan. London: Methuen. http://www.econlib.org/library/Smith/smWN.html.

Daniel B. Klein

LIBERTY

The etymological origin of *liberty* is the Latin word *libertas*, from *liber*, which means "free." In the social sciences, *liberty* and *freedom* are often used interchangeably. However, in common parlance, a distinction can be made. *Freedom* is the more general term referring to a lack of restraint in all its manifestations. *Liberty*, in contrast, is typically used when discussing the political and legal aspects of the human condition, particularly those involving choice.

Liberty, as a political ideal, has had a profound influence over the course of human events going back to the eighteenth century. It was a central theme for both the American Revolution (1775–1783) and the French Revolution (1789–1799). Liberty was a fundamental motivation for the rise of the modern democratic state, capitalist economies, and the concern for human rights. In contemporary practice, a number of freedoms are commonly protected by the state, including assembly, association, press, religion, speech, thought, and trade. The importance and significance of liberty is widely acknowledged. Still, there are fundamentally different understandings about what it means and why it is valuable.

Benjamin Constant (1767–1830), for example, distinguishes between what he calls "liberty of the ancients" and "liberty of the moderns." *Ancient liberty* refers to the direct sharing of political power. It is the "active and constant" participation of citizens in the collective governing of their communities. Consequently, it can only be realized in smaller political units such as the city-state. Ancient liberty involves citizens being able to make truly meaningful contributions to political decisions on a continual basis, thus allowing them to play an intimate role in determining the course of their collective lives. This identification of liberty with ongoing collective political decision-making, however, entails the "complete subjection of the citizen to the authority of the community" (Constant [1820] 1988, p. 311). Still, authentic self-government brought such a "vivid and repeated pleasure" (p. 316) that citizens were willing to make great sacrifices to preserve this form of liberty. The problem is that too little value was attached to the rights of individual citizens.

With the emergence of larger political units like the nation-state, ancient liberty was no longer possible. "Lost in the multitude, the individual can almost never perceive the influence he exercises" (Constant [1820] 1988, p. 316). Liberty, therefore, became associated with individual rights and freedoms. This *modern liberty* consists in "peaceful enjoyment and private independence" (p. 316) for each citizen. It is made possible by legal guarantees such as the rule of law, freedom of expression, property rights, freedom of association, elected political representation, and the right to petition the government. The purpose of modern liberty is to give citizens the opportunity to choose and enjoy their own "private pleasures." The danger of this type of liberty is that people will get so absorbed in pursuing their personal happiness and interests that they neglect their political responsibilities, thereby allowing the government to overstep its limits.

Another well-known distinction is Isaiah Berlin's (1909–1997) understandings of negative and positive conceptions of liberty. On the one hand, *negative liberty* simply refers to the absence of external constraints and obstacles. It is freedom "from." Liberty, in this sense, is the ability to act without human or institutional hindrances. It is concerned with the boundaries of individual autonomy. Negative liberty deals with the question, "What is the area within which the subject—a person or group of persons—is or should be left to do or be what he is able to do or be, without interference by other persons?" (Berlin [1958] 1990, p. 121–122). *Positive liberty*, on the other hand, refers to being able to live an authentic or self-directed life. It is the freedom "to." This type of liberty is associated with concepts like self-mastery and self-realization. It is interested in the question, "What, or who, is the source of control or interference that can determine someone to do, or be, this rather than that" (p. 122).

Berlin notes that negative and positive liberty might be thought of as two sides of the same coin. The former focuses on the freedom that exists when there are no constraints on the individual, and the latter concentrates on the freedom that comes from personal self-determination. Berlin claims, however, that the theoretical development of these two types of liberty has led to divergent understandings. While the meaning of negative liberty remained the same, positive liberty took on a more psychological orientation. Positive liberty became associated with overcoming internal obstacles that thwarted self-mastery. Berlin contends that this understanding of liberty is dangerous because state coercion can be justified as a benevolent action. By coercing people into living according to their supposed authentic desires, the state is simply advancing positive liberty. Overlooked is the fact that individuals are still being constrained against their will and the state is assuming to know better the true interests of its citizens. Appeals to positive liberty, therefore, divert attention from the disquieting contradiction that the state is forcing its citizens to be free. Berlin sardonically observes that, in this case, "true" freedom is obtained "even while my poor earthly body and foolish mind bitterly reject it, and struggle against those who seek however benevolently to impose it" (Berlin [1958] 1990, p. 134).

Even though positive liberty can be used to justify political tyranny, the association of self-mastery with liberty may nonetheless reflect how humans tend to think about what it means to be free, at least in part. Charles Taylor argues that humans do have higher order, life-orienting aims that can be undermined by impulses and desires. Unhealthy indulgences, for example, may harm an individual's physical well-being. Irrational fears may prevent people from taking advantage of opportunities that are in their best interests. In these types of situations, "is freedom not at stake when we find ourselves carried away by a less significant goal to override a highly significant one?" (Taylor 1979, p. 185)

Positive liberty is also associated with having requisite resources and opportunities to act. T. H. Green (1836–1882), for example, contends that freedom is commonly recognized as involving the "positive power or capacity" to maximize human potential. Liberty involves not simply the lack of constraint; it also includes the ability to successfully pursue personal goals and ambitions. Green contends that this success depends on people having basic protections and services. Moreover, it is society's responsibility to provide this assistance. Positive liberty, consequently, requires the provision of educational opportunities, safety regulations for the workplace, and adequate housing. Without health and knowledge, people are not able to develop their faculties and make the most out of themselves.

Liberty, variously understood, has been a central concern for liberalism, the dominant political ideology of the modern age. John Locke (1632–1704), for example, considered individual liberty a natural right along with life, health, and property. The state, therefore, had a responsibility to protect the freedoms of its citizens. Thomas Jefferson (1743–1826) adopted Locke's theme for the Declaration of Independence, asserting that humans "are endowed by their Creator with certain unalienable rights," including "life, liberty, and the pursuit of happiness." This concern for individual freedom was further formalized in the first ten amendments to the Constitution, which provide citizens with rights that limit the power of the state.

John Stuart Mill (1806–1873) was also interested in protecting the liberty of citizens to think and act without interference by the state. He provides a seminal defense of civil liberties in his classic work, *On Liberty* (1859). His justification, however, was not based on natural or inalienable rights; it was based on utility. Mill claims that maximizing individual liberty creates the greatest utility for society. There are three fundamental types of civil liberties that need to be protected: (1) thought and opinion, (2) tastes and pursuits, and (3) association. The limits of these liberties should be based on what has come to be called the *harm principle*. "The only purpose for which power can be rightfully exercised over any member of a civilized community, against his will, is to prevent harm to others" (Mill [1859] 1978, p. 9).

Jean-Jacques Rousseau (1712–1778) provided a markedly different approach to protecting individual liberty. Instead of trying to limit the power of the state, he sought to align the individual will with the general will, which is the sovereign will of the people. To accomplish this task, there must be the "total alienation of each associate, together with all his rights, to the entire community" (Rousseau [1762] 1987, p. 24). In so doing, each citizen, "while uniting with all, obeys only himself and remains as free as before" (p. 24). The identification of the individual will with the general will means the state's decisions are simply reflections of each citizen's preferences. Consequently, people are not under the subjection of any other person. If citizens have preferences contrary to the general will, then it merely proves that they were "in error" about the good of the community and their true interests.

Liberal political philosophers may justify liberty in terms of natural rights or utilitarianism. They may advocate negative or positive understandings of liberty. Regardless, all liberal political theories share two basic assumptions: Freedom is a key human value and all individuals are equal in some primary sense. Equality is a necessary complement for liberty. At the same time, however, it can provide a significant challenge. The grant of liberty inevitably undermines equality. The imposition of equality inevitably requires restrictions on liberty. The proper balance of liberty and equality, therefore, is an issue that will always have to be addressed by liberal political theories.

SEE ALSO *American Revolution; Choice in Psychology; Citizenship; Civil Rights; Constitutions; Democracy; Freedom; French Revolution; Government; Human Rights; Individualism; Liberalism; Liberation; Mill, John Stuart; Natural Rights; Philosophy, Political; Political Theory; Privacy; Utilitarianism*

BIBLIOGRAPHY

Berlin, Isaiah. [1958] 1990. *Four Essays on Liberty.* New York: Oxford University Press.

Constant, Benjamin. [1820] 1988. *Constant: Political Writings.* New York: Cambridge University Press.

Green, T. H. [1880] 1986. *Lectures on the Principles of Political Obligation and Other Writings.* New York: Cambridge University Press.

Locke, John. [1690] 1988. *Two Treatise of Government.* New York: Cambridge University Press.

Mill, John Stuart. [1859] 1978. *On Liberty.* Indianapolis, IN: Hackett.

Rousseau, Jean-Jacques. [1762] 1987. *On the Social Contract.* Indianapolis, IN: Hackett.

Taylor, Charles. 1979. What's Wrong with Negative Liberty? In the *Idea of Freedom: Essays in Honour of Isaiah Berlin*, ed. Alan Ryan. 175–193. New York: Oxford University Press.

Johnny Goldfinger

LIBIDO

SEE *Psychoanalytic Theory.*

LIFE COURSE PERSPECTIVE

SEE *Developmental Psychology.*

LIFE-CYCLE HYPOTHESIS

The life-cycle hypothesis (LCH) is the theory of private consumption and saving developed by the Italian-born American economist Franco Modigliani (1918–2003) and his collaborators in the 1950s and 1960s. The LCH posits that individuals, trying to maintain a stable level of consumption over time, save in their working years for retirement. Consequently, lifetime resources, rather than current income, are what determine the level of consumption. On an aggregate level, growth in aggregate lifetime resources, often as a result of growth in productivity and a shift in demographics, ultimately determines the saving-income ratio in an economy. The macroeconomic implications of the LCH set it apart from the prevailing Keynesian theory at the time, which assumed that the saving-income ratio was determined by level of income.

Modigliani was awarded the Nobel Prize in economics in 1985, thanks in part to his construction and development of the life-cycle hypothesis. According to the Royal Swedish Academy of Sciences, the LCH represents "a new paradigm in studies of consumption and saving."

FROM THE GENERAL THEORY TO LCH

The standard consumption theory prior to LCH was established by John Maynard Keynes (1883–1946) in his groundbreaking *General Theory*, published in 1936. Keynes observed that aggregate consumption was determined by (current) income and would increase as income increased, but not as much. A theory of saving was not formally developed in Keynes's *General Theory*; however, it could be derived from the consumption function that the saving-income ratio was determined by the level of income and would increase as income increased. This implication was later found to contradict empirical evidence. U.S. national income accounts data did not show a rising saving rate over time. Nor did cross-country studies reveal that rich countries necessarily saved more.

In 1954 Modigliani first articulated the life-cycle hypothesis in a paper coauthored with Richard Brumberg (d. 1955). The LCH starts out from the framework that a household makes its consumption and saving decisions at any given time based on the household's lifetime resources. In other words, consumers choose their level of consumption in each period to maximize their utility subject to the constraint of their lifetime resources. With the added assumption that consumers prefer a stable pattern of consumption over time, it can be readily shown that households must save in their productive years for consumption after retirement.

The seemingly simple formulation of the LCH differed fundamentally with the accepted theory of the time. In the LCH setting, consumption in any period does not depend on current income but rather on lifetime resources; savings in any period, therefore, depend on the difference between lifetime resources and current income. In contrast to the traditional theory, which predicts that the rich save and the poor dissave, the LCH predicts that the rich and the poor save a similar share of their lifetime resources.

Milton Friedman independently reached the same conclusion at about the same time. In the setting of Friedman's permanent income hypothesis (PIH), lifetime resources are referred to as *permanent income*, and the difference between permanent income and current income as *transitory income*. A change in the level of permanent income affects the level of consumption much more than a change in transitory income. However, thanks to Friedman's assumption of an infinite life span for individuals, the PIH does not share the most important implication of the LCH presented below—that is, the aggregate saving-income ratio is first and foremost determined by the growth in an economy.

It is important to note that the LCH defines savings, S, as the change in aggregate private wealth, W, that is, $S = \Delta W$. Therefore, the saving rate, s, is simply

$$s \equiv S/Y = (\Delta W/W) \bullet (W/Y) = \rho w \qquad (1)$$

where ρ is the growth rate of the economy and w is the wealth-income ratio.

The two common sources of growth in an economy are population growth and productivity growth. In the case of population growth, the intuition is that as more young laborers enter the workforce, they would save more than what the retirees dissave and drive up the saving rate in the economy. Similarly, in the case of productivity growth, the younger population will have higher levels of consumption in their productive years and will save more as well, such that they can maintain their higher level of consumption after retirement. In aggregate, they will save more than the retirees dissave, and the saving rate will go up.

Some of the implications of the LCH are counterintuitive. As one can see from equation (1), the saving rate in an economy is not affected by per capita income in any way. When the wealth-income ratio is constant, the saving rate depends entirely on the growth rate. If there is zero

growth in the economy, the saving rate will be zero. A country with a higher long-run growth rate will save more proportionately than a country with lower growth, irrespective of the per capita income level.

The LCH also predicts that the wealth-income ratio is a decreasing function of growth and is largely determined by the typical length of retirement in the economy.

THE EXTENDED LCH

Although the LCH emphasizes the role of growth in savings determination, alternative saving motives and macroeconomic variables can also be analyzed in its framework. These extensions enhance the explanatory power of the pure LCH model.

Bequest had long been considered to be the primary motive for saving before the LCH. It is now generally considered part of the supporting cast. In the extended LCH setup with bequest, receiving an inheritance increases permanent income, and a bequest to the next generation can be considered a choice for the household in addition to consumption in any period. Bequest raises the wealth-income ratio and hence the saving rate. The net effect on consumption depends on whether households pass on more than they inherit.

Literature on the precautionary motive also dates back to well before the LCH. In the extended LCH formulation with uncertainty in future income, households save more so that they can maintain a smooth consumption pattern in case of an unanticipated drop in income. This effect should be more profound for young and old households because they have fewer assets to tap into for this purpose.

Another area of research is forced savings programs, such as Social Security in the United States and pensions. It is intuitive to see the substitute effect of these programs in that they replace private saving. In reality, however, these programs often have the unintended effect of inducing participants to retire early as benefits decline for people working beyond retirement age. The net result is unclear from a theoretical perspective. Ignoring these programs, however, will bias the savings and income measures downward.

Liquidity constraint prevents households from borrowing to maintain their preferred level of consumption when current income falls below permanent income. In the extended LCH with liquidity constraint, households cannot consume more than their current income, which typically results in higher levels of consumption in later years than in earlier years.

Periods of high inflation often cause consumers to overestimate their real income, which leads to undersaving. In addition, when the return on assets does not fully adjust to the increase in the price level, inflation will reduce the real value of such nominal assets as bank deposits and bonds, and will consequently lower permanent income.

EMPIRICAL EVIDENCE FROM THE UNITED STATES AND CROSS-COUNTRY STUDIES

The LCH variables are not directly observable, making the hypothesis difficult to test. In addition to equation (1), the most commonly tested LCH equation is the consumption function in the form of

$$C = \alpha YL + rW \qquad (2)$$

where C is consumption, YP is labor income, W is wealth, and r is asset return. Note that, under the LCH, YL is not consistent with current income in the national accounts; consumption does not include the portion of housing and durables purchased in a period but consumed later; and saving is not the residual of current income and current consumption but a comprehensive measure of change in nominal and real assets.

Despite these challenges, the LCH has been successful in explaining the saving behavior in many cross-section and time-series studies. Research in the 1960s, when data regarding private wealth in the United States and national income accounts for many Organization for Economic Cooperation and Development (OECD) countries first became available, accounted for the low saving-income ratio in the United States versus "poorer" countries under the LCH framework. Growth has also been proved to be the driving force behind the high saving-income ratio in Japan in the 1960s to 1970s and in China from the 1980s to 1990s.

Many studies have also documented evidence supporting the various extended versions of the LCH discussed above. Bequest and precautionary motives help explain why the wealth-income ratio does not decline as fast as the pure LCH predicts. Renewed interest in liquidity constraint has found the concept helpful in explaining the lower level of consumption in households' early years.

The LCH lends itself well to studying implications of policies designed to influence private consumption and saving, such as the Social Security program discussed above. Interest rate policy affects permanent income through the asset return variable directly and through its impact on housing and stock prices indirectly. In contrast to bequest, deficit financing increases current generations' permanent income at the cost of future generations.

SEE ALSO *Absolute Income Hypothesis; Consumption; Expectations; Modigliani, Franco; Permanent Income Hypothesis; Relative Income Hypothesis*

BIBLIOGRAPHY

Ando, Albert, and Franco Modigliani. 1963. The "Life-Cycle" Hypothesis of Saving: Aggregate Implications and Tests. *American Economic Review* 53 (1): 55–84.

Friedman, Milton. 1957. *A Theory of the Consumption Function.* Princeton, NJ: Princeton University Press.

Modigliani, Franco, and Richard Brumberg. 1954. Utility Analysis and the Consumption Function: An Interpretation of Cross-Section Data. In *Post-Keynesian Economics*, ed. Kenneth K. Kurihara, 388–436. New Brunswick, NJ: Rutgers University Press.

Modigliani, Franco, and Shi Larry Cao. 2004. The Chinese Saving Puzzle and the Life-Cycle Hypothesis. *Journal of Economic Literature* 42: 145–170.

Royal Swedish Academy of Sciences. 1985. Press Release: This Year's Economics Prize Awarded for Pioneering Studies of Saving and of Financial Markets. http://nobelprize.org/nobel_prizes/economics/laureates/1985/press.html.

Shi Larry Cao

LIFE EVENT MODEL
SEE *Life Events, Stress.*

LIFE EVENTS, STRESS

Interest in the relationship between life events and stress has sparked thousands of studies over the past several decades. The thrust of this research was that any event that required a person to change aspects of his or her life would have negative consequences for psychological and physical health. According to this perspective, whether the event was positive or negative did not matter. Rather, the most important variable in linking stress and illness was whether the event changed the status quo in one's life and required change. Therefore getting married (presumably a happy event for most) is considered more stressful than getting fired at work or the death of a close friend.

The stress associated with life events can be measured in a variety of ways. The Social Readjustment Rating Scale (SSRS) (Holmes and Rahe 1967) is the most widely used of such measures. It consists of a list of forty-three events in nine categories: personal, family, community, social, religious, economic, occupational, residential, and vocational life. The events are intended to represent significant changes in life that require adaptive or coping behavior. Each event is given a score: for example, death of a spouse is given a 100, marriage a 50, and troubles with boss a 23. Individuals are asked to indicate which of the events listed have occurred over a designated period (from six months to two years). The sum of the weights for the checked items is then summed as the life-change score for a given individual.

Although the SRRS has been widely used, it has also been widely criticized. The relationship between life events and illness is thought to be small, and problems such as validity of the weights applied, biases in how people remember personal life events, overlap between life events and illness (e.g., change in sleeping habits) that might be related to illness all point to limitations in measuring a relationship between life events and stress (Smith 1993). Importantly, however, the use of this measure has led to an understanding of the type of life events that seem to have the greatest impact on stress levels; those include events that are unwanted, random, uncontrollable, and close together in time.

More recent perspectives on stress and illness appreciate that stress is a complex process involving different types of appraisals and coping as well as short- and long-term consequences. Perhaps the most applied theory of stress—the transactional model (Lazarus and Folkman 1984)—defines stress as a relationship between the person and the environment that is appraised by the person as taxing or exceeding his or her resources and endangering his or her well-being. According to this view, stress is conceptualized in terms of cognitive appraisal and coping, and stress is considered a continuous process. Furthermore patterns of coping are thought to change from one stage of a stressful encounter to another. For example, in the early stages of coping with the breakup of a relationship, one may seek social support from friends in order to get sympathy, understanding, or another perspective. In time one may find it more effective to cope by reinterpreting the breakup in a positive light, such as how it contributed to personal growth or opened up new and better possibilities.

Research has concluded that an important resource for dealing with stress is social support. People who have strong ties with other people are generally healthier and better able to cope with stressful life events. Other people can help reduce stress in a variety of ways by providing different forms of emotional support (e.g., intimacy and a sense of value), informational support (e.g., advice and guidance), and instrumental support (e.g., physical and material assistance). All these sources of support relate to a range of better health outcomes.

Applications of the stress and coping model to a specific stressor, discrimination, illustrates that exposure to potentially stressful events does not necessarily lead to reduced well-being. A stress and coping approach to understanding the experience of discrimination highlights the importance of examining how stressors are cognitively appraised; the coping strategies targets use to deal with stressful events; and the personal, situational, and structural factors that affect cognitive appraisals and coping processes (Major, Quinton, and McCoy 2002). Members of stigmatized groups confront discriminatory events by engaging in a variety of coping responses that can protect them from or make them more vulnerable to the adverse effects of stress (e.g., James, Hartnett, and Kalsbeek 1983; Krieger and Sidney 1996). The ways one responds to stress in general and discrimination in particular are important in understanding outcomes associated with stress.

SEE ALSO *Coping; Diathesis-Stress Model; Hypertension; John Henryism; Racism; Resiliency; Stress; Stress-Buffering Model; Vulnerability*

BIBLIOGRAPHY

Holmes, T. H., and R. H. Rahe. 1967. The Social Readjustment Rating Scale. *Journal of Psychosomatic Research* 11: 213–218.

James, S. A., S. A. Hartnett, and W. D. Kalsbeek. 1983. John Henryism and Blood Pressure Differences among Black Men. *Journal of Behavioral Medicine* 6: 259–278.

Krieger, N., and S. Sidney. 1996. Racial Discrimination and Blood Pressure: The CARDIA Study of Young Black and White Adults. *American Journal of Public Health* 86: 1370–1378.

Lazarus, R. S., and S. Folkman. 1984. *Stress, Appraisal, and Coping*. New York: Springer.

Major, B., W. J. Quinton, and S. J. McCoy. 2002. Antecedents and Consequences of Attributions to Discrimination: Theoretical and Empirical Advances. In *Advances in Experimental Social Psychology*, vol. 34, ed. M. P. Zanna, 251–330. San Diego, CA: Academic.

Smith, J. C. 1993. *Understanding Stress and Coping*. New York: Macmillan.

Laura S. Richman

LIFE EXPECTANCY

SEE *Morbidity and Mortality.*

LIFE SPAN, HUMAN

SEE *Morbidity and Mortality.*

LIFESPAN DEVELOPMENT

SEE *Developmental Psychology.*

LIFESTYLES

Lifestyles is a term found in both popular and scholarly literatures, most often referring to health-related behaviors such as drug use and "unsafe" sex, various forms of deviance, and consumption choices. Two of the earliest uses of *lifestyles* are in the work of psychologist Alfred Adler and sociologist Max Weber. Unlike Freud, Adler viewed human behavior as oriented toward future goals rather than driven mechanistically by the past. In *The Science of Living* (1929), he employed the concept of "style of life" to describe the individual's way of striving toward a goal of perfection within his or her particular social context. In contrast to Adler's focus on the individual, Weber viewed lifestyles as socially structured, introducing *lifestyle* to differentiate between class and status. Weber argued that classes are defined by their relation to the production of goods, while status groups are differentiated according to their consumption of goods; the various ways in which groups consume goods cluster into distinctive lifestyles.

The common use of *lifestyles* in popular culture as well as in studies of health and deviance shares Adler's focus on the individual to explain behavior, often connecting deviant behaviors such as drug use or unsafe sex to individual life decisions. In the scholarly and policy literatures, variables such as nutrition, housing, risk-taking behavior, health attitudes and beliefs, and preventative health behavior are used as primary indicators of lifestyles. In particular, tobacco use, alcohol consumption, diet, and sexual and intravenous drug practices (e.g., prostitution, needle sharing) are used to predict negative health outcomes. Experts in this field agree that individuals who abstain from smoking and drug use, consume alcohol in moderation, eat a healthy diet, refrain from violence, and practice safer sex have better survival rates than those who do not.

While the use of *lifestyles* in the health and behavioral sciences centers largely on individual practices, a vibrant social science discourse, in the tradition of Weber, points out that risk factors such as those listed above are only proximate causes of disease. A more sociological approach thus examines these lifestyles in terms of the social factors that put certain groups at greater risk for these behaviors in the first place. For example, in *A Plague on Your Houses* (1998), Deborah Wallace and Rodrick Wallace argue that living conditions in low-income areas—such as overcrowding and persistent displacement due to urban renewal—result in outbreaks of substance abuse, violence, and contagious disease. Similarly, Carol Cunradi et al. (2000) demonstrate a causal link between neighborhood poverty and intimate partner violence. Other sociologists argue that deviant behavior does not inhere in particular individuals but is learned through social interaction. Contrary to the conventional wisdom of the time,

Howard Becker, for example, in *Outsiders: Studies in the Sociology of Deviance* (1963), finds that marijuana smokers do not naturally adopt deviant behavior because of flawed personalities or psychological problems but instead have to learn from others how to smoke marijuana. Later work in the sociology of deviance led to the concept of *subcultures*, which are characterized by the social organization of deviance as distinctive lifestyles.

The concept of *lifestyles* also appears prominently in the "culture of poverty" debate (see Lewis 1966). The culture of poverty thesis, widely disseminated in the Moynihan Report (1965), holds that the qualitatively different values held by the poor result in deviant lifestyles, which in turn lead to continued poverty. This argument has been criticized by sociologists such as Herbert Gans (1972, 1995), Ann Swidler (1986), and Elijah Anderson (1999), among many others, for its lack of attention to structural factors such as unemployment, inequality, and discrimination.

The socially structured nature of lifestyles is also emphasized in the sociology of consumption. In his famous study, *The Theory of the Leisure Class* (1899), Thorstein Veblen argued that the wealthy translate their money into symbols of prestige through "conspicuous consumption" and leisure. Veblen connects lifestyles to social hierarchy and explains that the lower classes emulate the "scheme of life" of the upper class. For Veblen, lifestyles are always observable, external, and conscious—in other words, conspicuous—that is, primarily enacted as vehicles for status and power.

Along these lines, economists, psychologists, and demographers explain lifestyles as sets of shared preferences. Tracing the development of American consumer culture, Lizabeth Cohen in *A Consumer's Republic* (2003) reveals that after World War II, merchants and advertisers moved away from treating consumers as a homogeneous group. Instead, marketers sought to "identify clusters of customers with distinctive ways of life and then set out to sell them idealized lifestyles constructed around commodities" (p. 299).

Target marketing both reflected and indeed created particular consumption patterns, defined not only by material goods but also by cultural frameworks for how to live, particularly through techniques such as "slice of life" advertising.

Another seminal work in the consumption literature is Pierre Bourdieu's *Distinction* (1984), which argues that the tensions of late capitalism are played out through consumption as social practice. In contrast to Veblen, Bourdieu emphasizes the habitual, internalized, and largely unconscious cultural practices implicated in lifestyles by explaining that people's class positions predispose them to certain lifestyles, which they experience as personal and freely chosen. Thus, Bourdieu creates a map of ostensibly natural and individual lifestyles—centered on taste—and reveals their socially patterned, cultural logic. His use of lifestyles is radically anti-individualist: Even seemingly idiosyncratic qualities such as ways of walking and talking are rooted in socially structured material inequality. Bourdieu's approach thus marks a significant advance over sociologists whose use of *lifestyle* as a secondary marker of class position draws superficial correlations between lifestyles and other variables such as race, ethnicity, political orientation, education, and urban/suburban/rural residence.

More generally, social theorists of contemporary culture, such as Lears (1983), Campbell (1987), and Bauman (1998), do not see a tight connection between class and consumption, instead linking lifestyles to the growing identity crisis of modernity, thus marking a shift from Bourdieu's structural analysis of the role of lifestyles in class reproduction. For instance, Don Slater contends in *Consumer Culture and Modernity* (1997), that "In theorizing pluralization and identity crisis, two terms keep appearing: 'expertise' and 'lifestyle.' Both denote features of modern life which manage, assuage, and organize anxieties about modern identity and at the same time can be used to exploit and intensify them" (p. 86). Lifestyles, which center on consumer goods, services, and experiences, thus become a vehicle for the modernist project of realizing the self. This centrality of lifestyles indicates, for some theorists, the instability of modern forms of social membership. Anthony Giddens, for example, argues in *Modernity and Self-Identity: Self and Society in the Late Modern Age* (1991) that the consumption of goods replaces the genuine development of the self. Since the 1980s, *lifestyle* has become increasingly detached from traditional demographic variables—class, race, or gender, for example—and has come to represent personal, voluntary choices about how to consume.

SEE ALSO *Anthropology; Bourdieu, Pierre; Class, Leisure; Conspicuous Consumption; Culture, Low and High; Distinctions, Social and Cultural; Ethnography; Gans, Herbert J.; Giddens, Anthony; Habitus; Lewis, Oscar; Moynihan Report; Neighborhoods; Popular Culture; Poverty; Relative Income Hypothesis; Suburbs; Veblen, Thorstein; Weber, Max*

BIBLIOGRAPHY

Adler, Alfred. 1956. *The Individual Psychology of Alfred Adler*, ed. Heinz Ansbacher and Rowena Ansbacher. New York: Basic Books.

Anderson, Elijah. 1999. *The Code of the Street: Decency, Violence, and the Moral Life of the Inner City*. New York: Norton.

Bauman, Zygmunt. 1998. *Consumerism, and the New Poor*. Philadelphia: Open University Press.

Becker, Howard. 1963. *Outsiders: Studies in the Sociology of Deviance*. London: Free Press of Glencoe.

Bourdieu, Pierre. 1984. *Distinction: A Social Critique of the Judgment of Taste*. Trans. Richard Nice. Cambridge, MA: Harvard University Press.

Campbell, Colin. 1987. *The Romantic Ethic and the Spirit of Modern Consumerism*. New York: Blackwell.

Cohen, Lizabeth. 2003. *A Consumers' Republic: The Politics of Mass Consumption in Postwar America*. New York: Knopf.

Cunradi, Carol, et al. 2000. Neighborhood Poverty as a Predictor of Intimate Partner Violence among White, Black, and Hispanic Couples in the United States: A Multilevel Analysis. *AEP*. 10 (5): 297–308.

Gans, Herbert. 1972. The Positive Functions of Poverty. *American Journal of Sociology* 78 (2): 275–289.

Gans, Herbert. 1995. *The War against the Poor: The Underclass and Antipoverty Policy*. New York: Basic Books.

Giddens, Anthony. 1991. *Modernity and Self-Identity: Self and Society in the Late Modern Age*. Stanford, CA: Stanford University Press.

Lears, T. J. Jackson. 1983. From Salvation to Self-Realization: Advertising and the Therapeutic Roots of the Consumer Culture, 1880–1930. In *The Culture of Consumption: Critical Essays in American History, 1880–1980,* ed. R. Fox and T. J. Lears, 1–38. New York: Pantheon.

Lewis, Oscar. 1966. The Culture of Poverty. *Scientific American* 215 (October): 19–25. Reprinted in *Urban Life: Readings in Urban Anthropology,* 3rd ed., ed. G. Gmelch and W. Zenner. pp. 393–404. Prospect Heights, IL: Waveland Press, 1996.

Slater, Don. 1997. *Consumer Culture and Modernity*. Cambridge, U.K.: Polity Press.

Swidler, Ann. 1986. Culture in Action. *American Sociological Review* 51: 273–86.

Veblen, Thorstein. 1899. *The Theory of the Leisure Class*. Mineola, NY: Dover, 1994.

Wallace, Deborah and Rodrick Wallace. 1998. *A Plague on Your Houses: How New York Was Burned Down and National Public Health Crumbled*. New York: New Left Books.

Weber, Max. 1966. Class, Status, and Party. In *Class, Status, and Power,* ed. R. Bendix and S. Lipset, 21–28. New York: Free Press.

Bethany E. Blalock
Jennifer M. Silva

LIKELIHOOD RATIO TEST

SEE *Specification Tests.*

LIKERT, RENSIS

SEE *Likert Scale.*

LIKERT SCALE

The Likert scale is arguably the most widely used type of attitude scale in the social sciences. The typical Likert scale appears as a collection of statements about an attitude object (person, group, institution, idea, etc.) reflecting favorable or unfavorable attitudes toward the object. Each statement is accompanied by a graded-response rating scale, typically with five response choices, the most commonly used being: "Strongly Agree," "Agree," "Undecided," "Disagree," and "Strongly Disagree." The respondent is instructed to select one of the response choices for each statement. To score the scale, the response choices are given weights to reflect the attitude continuum, typically weights of 1 to 5, 1 for the most unfavorable (or least favorable) attitude and 5 for the most favorable. The weights for the respondent's choices are then summed across all statements. The resulting total score may be interpreted normatively, with reference to some comparison group, or absolutely, with reference to theoretically or empirically chosen cut-off scores.

As examples, here are two contrasting items from a Likert scale on attitudes toward work:

1. Work is an activity to be avoided.

__Strongly Agree __Agree __Undecided __Disagree __Strongly Disagree

2. Work brings out the best of my abilities.

__Strongly Agree __Agree __Undecided __Disagree __Strongly Disagree

The first item reflects an unfavorable attitude toward work and therefore "Strongly Agree" is scored 1, "Agree" is scored 2, and so on, up to 5 for "Strongly Disagree." The second item, reflecting a favorable attitude, is scored 5 for "Strongly Agree," 4 for "Agree," and so on, up to 1 for "Strongly Disagree."

The format of five response choices per statement is so widely used that some have mistakenly called any instrument using this format a Likert scale. But it is not the five-choice format that characterizes a Likert scale. Rather, it is the method used in developing the scale—Rensis Likert's method—that makes an instrument a Likert scale, regardless of the number of response choices used.

Likert's method is essentially the construction of an internally consistent scale. Likert's idea, innovative for its time in the 1930s, was to use total score as the criterion for item selection, on the assumption that total score was a "best estimate" of a respondent's attitude. Likert proposed two different methods of item selection: (1) *item analysis*, in which selection is based on the correlation of item score with total score; and (2) the employment of a *criterion of internal consistency*, which is used to examine, for each statement, the difference in average item score between high-scoring and low-scoring groups defined on the basis of total score. Both methods turned out to be variants of the same general method for constructing internally consistent scales.

Likert's insight was that psychometric methods (at that time used only in ability and achievement test construction) could be applied to attitude measurement, just as Louis Thurstone's insight was that psychophysical methods, such as the method of equal-appearing intervals, could be used in attitude measurement. Louis Guttman, the third pioneering great of attitude measurement, invented a unique scaling method based on a rigorous definition of unidimensionality and its implications for the rank-ordering of attitude statements and respondents. Whereas Thurstone's method scaled stimuli (attitude statements) and Likert's method scaled responses and respondents, Guttman's method scaled both stimuli and respondents simultaneously. However, Guttman's method was rather difficult to apply, and Thurstone's method was quite labor-intensive. Consequently, Likert's method became the method of choice for constructing attitude measures and other self-report instruments, especially with the advent of computers and statistical computer programs. Nowadays, the application of Likert's method often begins with a factor analysis of a large pool of statements, followed by the (Likert) scaling of high-loading statements for each factor. The usual criterion for item retention is contribution to internal consistency reliability. All the techniques of psychometrics, including—more recently—item response theory, can be applied to the construction of Likert scales.

Likert scales are essentially rating scales, hence they are susceptible to the problems of rating scales. Many of these problems involve *response sets*, which comprise response tendencies that are independent of the semantic content of the attitude statements. Response sets may result in errors of three kinds: (1) *mean error*, the tendency to center responses around some preferred mean value (*leniency error*, when the preferred mean is high, and *strictness error*, when the preferred mean is low); (2) *variance error*, the tendency to restrict or to expand the rating range regardless of correspondence to reality; and (3) *covariance error*, the tendency to rate all statements similarly (also called the *halo effect*). These errors may be avoided or minimized by various procedures described in psychometric texts.

Likert scales are also self-report scales, hence they are susceptible to the biases implicit in self-disclosure. Clerical errors aside, responses to a Likert scale reflect the extent to which a respondent decides to "self-disclose," which, in turn, depends on the ability and the motivation of the respondent to self-disclose. Ability to self-disclose is affected by such factors as reading comprehension (of the scale's statements, instructions, etc.), experience, and familiarity with the subject matter of the scale. Motivation to self-disclose is more difficult to parse; respondents may be motivated by any number of reasons to understate or to overstate their attitudes. Such distortion may be avoided or minimized if the scale administrator has credibility and rapport with the respondents.

Likert scales can be measures of either stable or changeable attitudes. It behooves scale constructors to determine which kind of attitude they are measuring by conducting test-retest and longitudinal studies. These studies are especially important when the scale constructor intends (for theoretical or other purposes) to measure one kind of attitude rather than the other.

Finally, unless it is actual self-report that is of interest (as, for example, in opinion surveys), Likert scales should be validated against other independent indicators of the attitude(s) being measured. As psychometric instruments, Likert scales have to meet the basic psychometric requirements of reliability and validity.

SEE ALSO *Guttman Scale; Reliability, Statistical; Scales; Surveys, Sample; Validity, Statistical*

BIBLIOGRAPHY

Likert, Rensis. 1932. A Technique for the Measurement of Attitudes. *Archives of Psychology* 22 (140): 5–54.

Rene V. Dawis

LIMINALITY

SEE *Turner, Victor.*

LIMITS IN PROBABILITY

SEE *Probability, Limits in.*

LIMITS OF GROWTH

The proposition that economic growth could not continue indefinitely was first put in a formal quasi-mathematical manner by Thomas Malthus's (1766–1834) pamphlet *An Essay on the Principle of Population* (1798). Malthus's essential propositions were that "population, when unchecked, increases in a geometrical ratio. Subsistence increases only in an arithmetical ratio. A slight

acquaintance with numbers will shew the immensity of the first power in comparison of the second" (Malthus 1798, chap. I.18).

Malthus's analytic concept, of a clash between variables growing at fundamentally different rates, failed to take root in economic methodology, which instead came to be dominated by concepts of stability and equilibrium. Also, contrary to Malthus's assumptions, both food and income per capita grew in Europe over the next two centuries.

However, world population also continued to grow, and at an accelerating exponential rate, rising from about one billion in Malthus's time to four billion by the early 1970s. The specter of population outrunning food production was once again raised by the biologist Paul R. Ehrlich in *The Population Bomb* (1968). The oil engineer M. King Hubbert (1956) hypothesized that economic growth would exhaust oil supplies during the twenty-first century. And, in *The Limits to Growth* (1972), Donella Meadows and colleagues argued that complex interactions between population, resources, and pollution would limit economic growth.

Ehrlich's analysis, like Malthus's, focused predominantly on the relationship between population and food output. On the basis of verbal hypotheses, Ehrlich presented a number of future scenarios with short-term quantitative predictions that were soon falsified. The key weaknesses in Ehrlich's analysis were the extrapolation of short-term trends, and the expectation that these trends would manifest in near-immediate problems. However, these short-term trends were not maintained. For example, Ehrlich's book coincided with the "green revolution" in agriculture and extensive birth control programs, which undermined his predictions of imminent widespread famines.

Hubbert's argument differs from those of Malthus and Ehrlich by considering a nonrenewable resource as the limit, rather than food. Hubbert proposed a logistic depletion of total reserves, so that actual oil output would follow a bell-like curve, peaking in the early twenty-first century when approximately half the planet's finite stock of oil had been mined. Though the model works well for given deposits, its aggregate outcome is disputed. Critics argue that technological change and price incentives will increase the amount of recoverable reserves indefinitely. Adherents assert that the physical limit will ultimately assert itself, thus limiting economic growth because alternative energy sources to oil have lower net energy gains than oil.

Meadows and colleagues present a sophisticated case for limits to growth using a systems dynamics computer model known as World3. The key features of a systems dynamics model are: (1) the model consists of a set of coupled difference or differential equations (that are represented as flowcharts rather than symbolic equations); (2) the model specifies both positive and negative feedbacks between variables; and (3) time relationships between variables are depicted (there is, for example, a fifteen-year lag between the emission of a chlorofluorocarbon molecule at sea level and its entry into the stratosphere, where it will destroy about 100,000 ozone molecules for about one century before decaying).

Whereas Malthus and Ehrlich presumed the rates of population change remained constant, World3 made this and other rates of change depend on feedbacks from other variables. For example, the fertility rate is affected by negative feedbacks from per capita gross domestic product (GDP), social services, and per capita expenditure on birth control—so that increasing incomes reduce the rate of population growth. Overcrowding and pollution are positively linked to the death rate—so that increasing pollution also reduces the rate of population growth.

World3 allows for technological change that enables increased output per unit of input—an effect that reduces the severity of physical constraints on growth over time. The model is also designed to accept different specifications of ultimate physical constraints, while specifying base-level estimates related to known levels in 1970. Physical constraints included both *sources*, or fixed nonrenewable resources such as land and oil, and *sinks*, or the capacity of the ecosystem to absorb pollutants.

As an aggregative numerical model, World3 has to reduce some multifaceted phenomena—such as population, food, pollution, and technology—to index numbers that represent each variable's current level and a set of influences on other variables over time. The model's numerical outcomes are thus not predictions but broad scenarios, where increases in some index numbers—for example, pollution—cause severe dampening effects upon others, such as population or average human welfare. The model also operates at a global level, and thus omits the possibility that some interrelations, and therefore crises, may be localized (for example, land degradation problems are more likely to be severe in Africa and Australia than in Europe and Japan).

In *The Limits to Growth*, World3's index values were calibrated to ensure rough compliance of the model with data from 1900 till 1970. The model was then run forward to the year 2100 under a range of different scenarios—starting from "business as usual"—and then adding a layered range of alternative futures, with changes to population growth norms, accepted levels of pollution, rates of technical change, and desired levels of consumption. Differing levels of physical constraints were also considered.

In contrast to Malthus and Ehrlich, the Meadows group concluded that it was feasible that the world could provide a high-quality life for the entire human population for the indefinite future. However, they also concluded that current growth patterns were likely to overshoot this ideal, leading to some form of severe crisis that would cause world population to fall precipitously in the middle of the twenty-first century.

The Meadows study was a popular success, selling millions of copies, but it was also highly controversial. Critics attacked it on four main grounds, asserting that it:

- Applied unrealistically low-capacity constraints
- Underestimated the market's response to price signals and the adaptability of technology
- Based crucial causal relations on inadequate data
- Used an inappropriate modeling technique

The Meadows group rejects these criticisms on the general ground that they result from applying a mistakenly reductionist approach to their holistic study. For example, they allege that the criticism about capacity constraints being set too low ignores the corollary that, with higher capacity constraints, there is an increased likelihood of pollution levels overwhelming the planet's sinks. In their *30-Year Update*, published in 2004, they argue that to really disprove their conclusions, one or more of the following assumptions has to be disproved (Meadows et al. 2004, pp. 175–176):

- "Growth is considered desirable."
- "There are physical limits to the sources of materials … and there are limits to the sinks that absorb waste products."
- "The growing population and economy receive signals … that are distorted, noisy, delayed…. Responses to those signals are delayed."
- "The system's limits are not only finite, but erodable when they are overstressed … there are strong nonlinearities—thresholds beyond which damage rises quickly and can become irreversible."

They also argue that the systems dynamics approach to modeling is superior to the general equilibrium approach favored by economists. One of the disappointments for the Meadows group has been the lack of adoption of systems dynamics methods by other social sciences—and in particular, by economics.

The 1972 report predicted that environmental issues would dominate early twenty-first century politics. That expectation is confirmed by the widespread political acceptance that global warming is occurring—the underlying cause of which is the emission of far more carbon dioxide than the planet's carbon-absorbing sinks can process, and the degradation of those sinks in a feedback process. CO_2 levels have risen from 325 parts per million at the time of *The Limits to Growth* report to 380 parts per million in 2006, consistent with the report's predictions.

Nicholas Stern (2006), using accepted economic computable general equilibrium methods, has amplified the political acceptability of the proposition that global warming will limit growth potential. However, Stern makes much milder predictions of a 5 to 10 percent fall in mid-twenty-first century global GDP because of climate change, and he asserts that addressing global warming will cost only 1 percent of annual GDP. *The Limits to Growth*'s standard run, on the other hand, contemplates a fall in human welfare of more than two-thirds from its peak level. Its sustainable society achieves high human welfare, but requires population stabilization policies, limits on material production, and innovation in food technology, in addition to the power generation, transport efficiency, and pollution abatement contemplated by Stern.

The Meadows group is broadly pessimistic about whether these policies will be implemented in time. In the *30-Year Update*, they argue that humanity's "ecological footprint" (Meadows et al. 2004, p. xv, following Wackernagel and Rees 1996) exceeded its carrying capacity by more than 20 percent in 2000. They therefore predict that, given the lags in systemic adjustments and the erosion of physical limits, the twenty-first century will experience an "overshoot." Their policy recommendations, which were intended to avoid overshoot in 1970, are now designed to limit the impact of overshoot to oscillations and a diminished carrying capacity, rather than a serious collapse.

SEE ALSO *Change, Technological; Club of Rome; Economic Growth; Green Revolution; Malthus, Thomas Robert; Malthusian Trap; Natural Resources, Nonrenewable; Overpopulation; Ricardo, David*

BIBLIOGRAPHY

Campbell, Colin J., and Jean H. Laherrère. 1998. The End of Cheap Oil. *Scientific American*. March: 78–83.

Cole, H. S. D., Christopher Freeman, Marie Jahoda, and K. L. R. Pavitt, eds. 1973. *Models of Doom: A Critique of The Limits to Growth*. New York: Universe.

Ehrlich, Paul R. 1968. *The Population Bomb*. London: Pan.

Greene, David L., Janet L. Hopson, and Jia Li. 2006. Have We Run Out of Oil Yet? Oil Peaking Analysis from an Optimist's Perspective. *Energy Policy* 34: 515–531.

Hubbert, M. King. [1956] 2006. Nuclear Energy and the Fossil Fuels. *Energy Bulletin*. http://www.energybulletin.net/13630.html.

Malthus, Thomas Robert. 1798. *An Essay on the Principle of Population*. London: J. Johnson. http://www.econlib.org/library/Malthus/malPop.html.

Meadows, Donella, Dennis Meadows, Jørgen Randers, and William W. Behrens III. 1972. *The Limits to Growth: A Report for the Club of Rome's Project on the Predicament of Mankind*. London: Pan.

Meadows, Donella, Jørgen Randers, and Dennis Meadows. 2004. *The Limits to Growth: The 30-Year Update*. White River Junction, VT: Chelsea Green.

Stern, Nicholas. 2006. *Stern Review: The Economics of Climate Change*. Cambridge, U.K.: Cambridge University Press.

Trainer, F. E. 1985. *Abandon Affluence!* London: Zed.

Wackernagel, Mathis, and William E. Rees. 1996. *Our Ecological Footprint: Reducing Human Impact on the Earth*. Philadelphia: New Society.

Watkins, G. C. 2006. Oil Scarcity: What Have the Past Three Decades Revealed? *Energy Policy* 34: 508–514.

Steve Keen

LINCOLN, ABRAHAM
1809–1865

Abraham Lincoln, the sixteenth president of the United States, was born February 12, 1809, in a log cabin in Kentucky. His opinions against slavery seem to have been shaped while he was a boy, partly by his father's antislavery opinions, partly by the fact that his father took everything Lincoln earned until he was of majority, and partly by a trip to New Orleans where he witnessed the institution in operation.

Lincoln's political career began in 1832, when he ran as a Whig for the Illinois state legislature from the town of New Salem and lost. He won two years later, though, and began studying law. New Salem was not a promising town, and Lincoln moved to Springfield in 1837. There he honed his legal skills, ultimately becoming one of Illinois's most prominent attorneys and, in the 1850s, a successful corporate lawyer. It was also in Springfield that he met Mary Todd (1818–1882), whom he married in 1842. They had four sons together, only one of whom lived past eighteen.

After four terms in the legislature, Lincoln was elected to Congress in 1846. To the extent that he made a name for himself in Washington, it was by challenging the grounds on which the Mexican War began. Lincoln was not reelected. Discouraged about politics, he focused on his practice instead. The Kansas-Nebraska Act (1854), which allowed Kansas to decide whether it would have slavery and sparked a virtual civil war within the territory, reengaged Lincoln. He won his fifth legislative term but resigned to run for the U.S. Senate, a campaign he lost in 1855.

The following year, he joined the Republican Party, which positioned him for his most dramatic campaign to date: his 1858 race for the Senate against one of the country's best-known Democrats, Stephen A. Douglas (1813–1861). Lincoln's acceptance of the nomination has come to be known as his "House Divided" speech. Equally famous is the series of debates he had with Douglas in seven different towns across the state. The Lincoln-Douglas debates drew thousands of observers and national press attention as the two men argued about whether or under what circumstances slavery should be allowed to spread into the territories. Douglas tried to undermine Lincoln by painting him as an abolitionist (Lincoln actually did not target slavery in the states where it already existed; his goal was to keep it from moving into the territories), and Lincoln pressed on the moral aspect of slavery and Douglas's position. Lincoln lost the contest, but gained nationwide recognition, which he leveraged in a prominent 1859 speech at New York's Cooper Union.

Despite Lincoln's rising prominence, he remained a man with little political baggage. That made him an appealing compromise candidate for the Republicans at their 1860 convention. In November Lincoln ran against three other candidates, including his old nemesis, Douglas. Lincoln won with just 39.8 percent of the popular vote, but a clear majority of electoral votes.

Despite Lincoln's repeated assertions that he was interested only in keeping slavery out of the territories, southerners were convinced that he wanted to abolish it completely and immediately. South Carolina was the first state to secede from the Union, on December 20, 1860. Six states followed shortly thereafter, and four more joined after the rebels opened fire on Fort Sumter on April 12, 1861.

Lincoln initially believed that a number of Unionists in the South would rise up against the Confederate government, so for the first year of the war he favored a strategy that avoided targeting slavery. As late as the spring of 1862, Lincoln believed in trying to compensate slaveowners in places such as the border state of Kentucky for their property, and he thought freed blacks should be sent to colonies elsewhere, on the grounds that blacks and whites could not live together. By July 1862, Lincoln realized that the Confederacy did not have a critical mass of Union supporters, and he decided to hit at the rebels' point of vulnerability. In issuing the Emancipation Proclamation on January 1, 1863 (he had issued a preliminary version the previous September), he believed he was striking at the Confederates in two ways: First, the proclamation would deny southerners their slaves, and second, it would also deny them the workforce that kept the Confederate army going. The proclamation was limited, however, affecting only those parts of the South that were in rebellion and out of the Federals' reach.

Lincoln was fundamentally moderate. He was also a man of his times. Both these points account for his approach to the slavery question as president. Critics have assailed Lincoln's slowness on emancipation, but he believed the Constitution limited his powers in this regard. Because of these constitutional concerns, he issued the proclamation as a military measure. One thing is clear from the historical record, however, and that is that Lincoln was always personally opposed to slavery. He was also willing to change, and he did. In fact, it is difficult to generalize about most of Lincoln's policies because he underwent such transformation in office. For instance, Lincoln abandoned his positions on compensation and colonization and, in the summer of 1864, when he was under great pressure to abandon emancipation as a condition for peace, he staked his career on protecting freedmen, saying he would be "damned" if he abandoned them. He also approved of Sherman's March through Georgia and later into the Carolinas, a maneuver that amounted to hard, if not total, war—a far cry from his gentler approach at the war's outset.

Even as he moved toward harder war, Lincoln wanted a soft peace. His early efforts at reconstruction called for Louisiana to establish a new state government when just 10 percent of the voters in the 1860 election took a loyalty oath and accepted emancipation. Many in Congress deemed this to be too lenient, but Lincoln at the end of his life appeared to be determined to return the rebel states to the fold with as little rancor as possible, while simultaneously protecting and advancing the rights of blacks. This included extending the vote to at least some African Americans. Lincoln was preparing a new reconstruction plan when he was assassinated April 14, 1865—Good Friday—while watching a play. He died the next morning.

While we will never know Lincoln's precise plans for Reconstruction or how they would have changed in response to the contingencies of the day, it seems fair to say that Reconstruction would have been markedly different under Lincoln. Instead, his successor, Andrew Johnson (1808–1875), proved to be a white supremacist who easily bent to the wishes of southern elites. This led to such tragic consequences as the Black Codes, laws that all but reinstated slavery in many parts of the South. Johnson's ready acquiescence to southern demands prompted Congress to wrest control of Reconstruction from the president and impose its own plan on the South, which proved to be to the short-term benefit of black southerners but provoked a bitter and violent response from whites in the region.

SEE ALSO *Slavery; U.S. Civil War*

BIBLIOGRAPHY

Carwardine, Richard. 2006. *Lincoln.* New York: Knopf.

Donald, David Herbert. 1995. *Lincoln.* New York: Simon and Schuster.

Gienapp, William E. 2002. *Abraham Lincoln and Civil War America: A Biography.* New York: Oxford University Press.

McPherson, James M. 1990. *Abraham Lincoln and the Second American Revolution.* New York: Oxford University Press.

Thomas, Benjamin P. 1952. *Abraham Lincoln: A Biography.* New York: Knopf.

Jennifer L. Weber

LINDBLOM, CHARLES EDWARD
1917–

Raised in Turlock, California, Charles Edward Lindblom attended Stanford University and then went to graduate school at the University of Chicago. Shortly after he began teaching economics at the University of Minnesota in 1939, the department chair rebuked Lindblom "for giving a talk to an undergraduate club on … Lange's concept of market socialism." He subsequently "met with many other sharp intolerances" from faculty and did not receive tenure. After moving to Yale, he found greater diversity of thought but nevertheless "was heavily influenced by the intolerances of the discipline of economics" (*Democracy and Market System*, 1988, p. 17).

Although the tensions were framed in terms of "good economics," not ideological disagreement, the response to his dissertation (*Unions and Capitalism*, 1949) was telling: Whereas the text offered a symmetrical analysis depicting corporate and union power relations on a collision course likely to lead to serious problems including inflation, reviewers were sure the author was calling for limits on collective bargaining. Lindblom's subsequent work reveals that he already was contemplating restraints on corporate executive discretion.

Lindblom's research questions and methodology were so out of favor that the Yale economics chair urged him to resign, predicting he would "die on the vine" and never be promoted to full professor. However, coteaching and scholarly collaboration with Robert Dahl led to a joint appointment in political science and a gradual shift of attention toward a discipline that recognized the landmark nature of his work. Lindblom chaired the political science department from 1972 to 1974 and later was named to Yale's most prestigious chair as Sterling Professor of Economics and Political Science. He served as president of the Association for Comparative Economic Studies and of the American Political Science Association.

Lindblom helped found the Institution for Social and Policy Studies, intended to move the university's social sciences into interdisciplinary conversation while enhancing their relevance to public issues. As director from 1974 to 1980, Lindblom led mapping projects designed to frame research questions with the professional care normally reserved for the conduct of research. Present-day research on the not-for-profit sector traces partly to an exploratory ISPS project, as do Richard Nelson and Sidney Winter's evolutionary economics and Robert Lane's studies of market and personality.

In a presidential address to political scientists titled "Another State of Mind" (1982), Lindblom argued that "conventional theory is embarrassingly defective. It greatly needs to call more heavily on radical thought" (p. 20). At four regional political science meetings, he asked audiences: "Suppose—just to limber up our minds—that we faced the fanciful task of designing … a political/economic system that would be highly resistant to change. How to do it?" A "simple and fiendishly clever" approach would be "to design institutions so that any attempt to alter them automatically triggers punishment" ("The Market as Prison," 1982, p. 324). Far from fanciful, something approaching that arrangement occurs as market systems imprison policy, sometimes via tangible constraints, as when officials fear businesses will move if "excessively" regulated. More insidious and fundamental are imprisonments of mind, a wide range of helpful policy options becoming unthinkable because their adoption would require deviating from tightly held and carelessly examined beliefs about corporation and market.

Politics, Economics, and Welfare (1953, with Robert Dahl) remains the most systematic comparison yet attempted of the price system, hierarchy, polyarchy, and bargaining as political-economic processes of rational calculation and social decision-making. It closes with an insight still fresh generations later: "Through what social processes should action take place? Clearly the answer … (depends on another) question: What kind of human being is wanted?" (p. 523).

The idea of incrementalism introduced therein was refined in "The Science of 'Muddling Through'" (1959), which still garners hundreds of citations annually. The core idea, derived in part from Lindblom's training in marginalist economic analysis, was a challenge to the Western political tradition's extreme faith in reason: Analysis is inevitably incomplete, excessively costly, and a poor guide to big changes; political interactions negotiating smaller changes often are both more feasible and more reliable. *A Strategy of Decision* (1963, with David Braybrooke) and *The Intelligence of Democracy* (1965) offered detailed treatments of mutually adjusting interaction as a method of analyzing and determining policy moves, the latter still unparalleled regarding forms of mutual adjustment other than bargaining.

Neither critics nor followers did especially well by disjointed incrementalism. Many readers reduced the concept's nuances to the oversimplified notion of small steps, degenerating into arguments that Aaron Wildavsky subsequently pilloried as the search for the "magic size" of an increment. Some perceived incrementalism as overly conservative (Dror 1964, Etzioni 1966), seemingly blaming the decision strategy for conservative tendencies in U.S. politics, or perhaps failing to recognize that, in principle, "A fast-moving sequence of small changes can more speedily accomplish a drastic alteration of the status quo than can an only infrequent major policy change" ("Still Muddling, Not Yet Through," 1979, p. 520).

Goodin and Waldner (1979) argued that actually practicing incrementalism would be more difficult than it sounds. Some theoretical understanding is needed to decide where and how to intervene, and to determine how long to monitor a policy trial before deciding whether to change it. They pointed as well to difficulties posed by threshold and sleeper effects and questioned the idea that small changes are always less dangerous and more reversible. To the claim that reforms can be thought of as experiments, they found nontrivial difficulties in actually learning from early trials. A number of analysts pointed to circumstances where the value of incrementalism would be reduced, including Schulman's (1975) recognition that large-scale policy choices such as the lunar program sometimes have to be undertaken completely if they are to work at all.

Lindblom acknowledged the validity of some of these insights but found that the critics had not really proposed an alternative way of grappling with the basic predicament: "Incremental policy making is weak, often inefficacious, inadequate to the problem at hand; and the control over it often falls into the wrong hands. It is also usually the best that can be done," given the imprisoning effects of corporation and market, gross political inequalities, and elite-catalyzed impairments in political thinking by citizens, government functionaries, and social scientists (*Democracy and Market System*, 1988, p. 11). Neo-incrementalists recently have begun to take up the challenge, responding to the critics' concerns and extending incrementalist thought to deal better with inequality and with institutional malfunctioning (Collingridge 1992; Hayes 2001).

Lindblom returned to studying the economic side of political life in *Politics and Markets* (1977), winner of the APSA Woodrow Wilson Award, which concluded, "The large private corporation fits oddly into democratic theory and vision. Indeed, it does not fit" (p. 356). The work garnered sufficient public notice to evoke an attacking ad by Mobil in *The New York Times*. The "privileged position of business" and political-economic inequalities were central in *The Policy-Making Process* (1993, originally written in 1973), a soon-classic text for policy-oriented courses. *The Market System* (2001) summarized the great merits of market systems as social coordinating mechanisms, simultaneously offering an elegant overview of systemic defects not encompassed in conventional analyses of market failure.

Usable Knowledge (1979, with David Cohen) argued that professional social inquiry is "incapacitated in contributing to social problem solving because of its own metaphysics, fashions, traditions, and taboos" (p. 95). *Inquiry and Change* (1990), another APSA best book award winner, analyzed inequality as a barrier to rationality while contrasting the analysis-heavy ideal of scientifically guided society with a more egalitarian and cognitively realistic self-guiding society. Among many barriers to self-guiding society, foremost is impairment, Lindblom argued: Not only corporation and government, but family, school, church, and media hamper development of capacities for probing problems and possibilities. Social scientists can assist people in understanding and shaping their societies by conducting partisan analysis challenging the status quo better than by aiming for avowedly neutral, supposedly authoritative knowledge that actually is forever unattainable.

Although following in the tradition of the Enlightenment, then, Lindblom's "aspiration to improve social problem solving ... pursues inquiry and the resourceful utilization of its results more than it pursues firm knowledge. Thus, it rewrites Kant's 'Dare to know!' as 'Dare to inquire!' "(*Inquiry and Change*, p. 301).

SEE ALSO *American Political Science Association; Corporations; Corporatism; Economics; Incrementalism; Marginalism; Norms; Pluralism; Political Science; Public Policy*

BIBLIOGRAPHY

PRIMARY WORKS

Lindblom, Charles E. 1949. *Unions and Capitalism*. New Haven, CT: Yale University Press.

Lindblom, Charles E. 1959. The Science of "Muddling Through." *Public Administration Review* 19:79–88.

Lindblom, Charles E. 1965. *The Intelligence of Democracy: Decision Making Through Mutual Adjustment*. New York: The Free Press.

Lindblom, Charles E. 1977. *Politics and Markets: The World's Political-Economic Systems*. New York: Basic Books.

Lindblom, Charles E. 1979. Still Muddling, Not Yet Through. *Public Administration Review* 39 (6): 517–526.

Lindblom, Charles E. 1982. Another State of Mind. *American Political Science Review* 76 (1): 9–21.

Lindblom, Charles E. 1982. The Market as Prison. *Journal of Politics* 44 (2): 324–336.

Lindblom, Charles. 1988. *Democracy and Market System*. Oslo: Norwegian University Press.

Lindblom, Charles E. 1990. *Inquiry and Change: The Troubled Attempt to Understand and Shape Society*. New Haven, CT: Yale University Press.

Lindblom, Charles E. 1993. Concluding Comment: A Case Study of the Practice of Social Science. In *An Heretical Heir of the Enlightenment: Politics, Policy, and Science in the Work of Charles E. Lindblom*, ed. Harry Redner, 343–373. Boulder, CO: Westview Press.

Lindblom, Charles E. 2001. *The Market System: What It Is, How It Works, and What to Make of It*. New Haven, CT: Yale University Press.

Lindblom, Charles E., and David Braybrooke. 1963. *A Strategy of Decision: Policy Evaluation as a Social Process*. New York: Free Press of Glencoe.

Lindblom, Charles E., and David K. Cohen. 1979. *Usable Knowledge: Social Science and Social Problem Solving*. New Haven, CT: Yale University Press.

Lindblom, Charles E., and Robert A. Dahl. 1953. *Politics, Economics, and Welfare: Planning and Politico-Economic Systems Resolved into Basic Social Processes*. New York: Harper.

Lindblom, Charles E., and Edward J. Woodhouse. 1993. *The Policy-Making Process*, 3rd ed. Englewood Cliff, NJ: Prentice Hall.

SECONDARY WORKS

Collingridge, David. 1992. *The Management of Scale: Big Organizations, Big Technologies, Big Mistakes*. New York: Routledge.

Dror, Yehezkel. 1964. Muddling Through—"Science" or Inertia? *Public Administration Review* 24 (3): 153–157.

Etzioni, Amitai. 1967. Mixed-Scanning: A "Third" Approach to Decision-Making. *Public Administration Review* 27 (5): 385–392.

Goodin, Robert, and Ilmar Waldner. 1979. Thinking Big, Thinking Small, and Not Thinking at All. *Public Policy* 27: 1–24.

Hayes, Michael T. 2001. *The Limits of Policy Change: Incrementalism, Worldview, and the Rule of Law*. Washington, DC: Georgetown University Press.

Schulman, Paul R. 1975. Nonincremental Policy Making: Notes Toward an Alternative Paradigm. *American Political Science Review* 69 (4): 1354–1370.

Edward J. Woodhouse

LINEAR REGRESSION

Linear regression refers to a linear estimation of the relationship between a dependent variable and one or more independent variables.

Social researchers typically assume that two variables are linearly related unless they have strong reasons to believe the relationship is nonlinear. In general, a linear relationship between a dependent variable (Y) and an independent variable (X) can be expressed by the equation $Y = a + bX$, where a is a fixed constant. The value of the dependent variable (Y) equals the sum of a constant (a) plus the value of the slope (b) times the value of the independent variable (X). The slope (b) shows the amount of change in Y variable for every one-unit change in X. The constant (a) is also called the *Y-intercept*, which determines the value of Y when $X = 0$.

Theoretically, if the dependent variable Y can be perfectly estimated by the independent variable X, then the y should be precisely located on the predicted line. The equation of the predicted line can be expressed as $\hat{Y} = a + bX$. The $\hat{Y}$ ("Y hat") represents the predicted value Y. However, actual social data never follow a perfect linear relationship. In fact, the actual observed value of Y is rarely on the predicted line. Therefore, it is necessary to take the deviations between the predicted value and actual value into account through the linear regression model. In the linear regression model, for every X value in the data, the linear equation will predict a Y value on the "best-fitting" line. This "best-fitting" line is called a *regression line*. The linear regression model should then be expressed as $Y = a + bX + e$. The e is the error term, or a residual, which represents the distance between predicted value ($\hat{Y}$) and the actual Y value in the data.

The goal of linear regression estimation is to develop a procedure that identifies and defines the straight line that provides the best fit for any specific set of data. A basic approach of linear regression is to estimate, by minimizing the residuals, the values for the two regression coefficients (a and b) based on the observed data. In other words, the predicted errors estimated by regression equation must be smaller than the errors made with any other linear relationship. To determine how close the predicted scores are to the observed scores, the method of Ordinary Least Squares (OLS) is the most popular approach used in the linear regression.

OLS estimates regression equation coefficients (a and b) that minimize the error sum of squares. That is, the OLS approach sums the squared differences between each observed score (Y) and its score predicted by the regression equation $\hat{Y}$, and produces a quantity smaller than that obtained by using any other straight linear equation. The result is a measure of overall squared error between the line and the data: Total squared error = $\Sigma(Y - \hat{Y})^2$.

In Figure 1 the distance between the actual data point (Y) and the predicted point on the line ($\hat{Y}$) is defined as $Y - \hat{Y}$. The best-fitting line to the data should thus show a sum of absolute values of $Y - \hat{Y}$ to be the minimum, or the

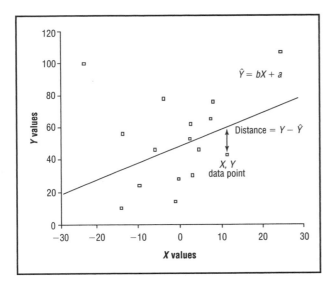

$\hat{Y} = bX + a$

Distance $= Y - \hat{Y}$

X, Y
data point

Figure 1

sum of distances between $Y-\hat{Y}$ to be the shortest if there are only two sets of X and Y. Because some of these distances will be positive and some will be negative, the sum of the residuals, $\Sigma(Y-\hat{Y}) = \Sigma e$, is always zero. The process of squaring removes the negative signs so that the sum of these squared errors is greater than zero. Also, it minimizes the sum of all the squared prediction errors.

Under certain ideal conditions, OLS is in fact superior to other estimators. If these necessary assumptions are true, OLS is the best linear unbiased estimator of corresponding population parameters. The OLS assumptions include:

1. Linearity. The relationship between the dependent variable (Y) and independent variable(s) (Xs) has to be linear. But sometimes the true relationship is better described by a curve.

2. Normality. It is assumed that y has a normal distribution for every possible value of X. This assumption is especially important in small samples for the marked skewness or severe outliers of residuals.

3. Homoscedasticity. It is assumed that the population variance of Y is the same at all levels of X. This assumption of homoscedasticity is required for regression t and F tests, as well as difference-of-means tests and analysis of variance.

4. No autocorrelation. The sample observations are assumed to be independent of each other if they were individually and randomly selected from a large population. That is, there should be no correlation between errors and X variables (Hamilton 1992, pp. 110–111).

However, perfect data fitted with all OLS assumptions are rather rare in practice. For example, the OLS assumptions may be violated by problems of a nonlinear relationship, omitting relevant independent variables (Xs) including irrelevant independent variables (Xs), correlation between X and errors, X measured with errors, heteroscedasticity, non-normal distribution, and multicollinearity, and so on. To deal with these problems, certain nonlinear robust estimators are better and more efficient than the OLS estimation, which will yield unbiased estimations of the correlation between X and Y variables. Therefore, the selection of regression techniques is highly dependent on the characteristics of the selected data.

SEE ALSO *Logistic Regression; Ordinary Least Squares Regression*

BIBLIOGRAPHY

Hamilton, Lawrence C. 1992. *Regression with Graphics: A Second Course in Applied Statistics.* Belmont, CA: Duxbury Press.

Chiung-Fang Chang

LINEAR SYSTEMS

Linear systems are systems of equations in which the variables are never multiplied with each other but only with constants and then summed up. Linear systems are used to describe both static and dynamic relations between variables.

In the case of the description of static relations, systems of linear algebraic equations describe invariants between variables such as:

$$a_{11}x + a_{12}x_1 = c_1$$
$$a_{21}x + a_{22}x_2 = c_2$$

Here, one would be interested in the values of x_1 and x_2 for which both equations hold. This system of equations can easily be written in matrix form:

$$\begin{pmatrix} a_{11} & a_{12} \\ a_{21} & a_{22} \end{pmatrix} \begin{pmatrix} x_1 \\ x_2 \end{pmatrix} = \begin{pmatrix} c_1 \\ c_2 \end{pmatrix}$$

or, more concisely:

$$Ax = c$$

The solution can be written as $x = A^{-1}c$ if the matrix A is invertible. Another frequent application of systems of linear algebraic equations is the following:

$$y_i = b_0 + b_1 x_{i1} + b_2 x_{i2} + b_3 x_{i3} + \ldots + b_m x_{im} + e_i$$

The above is a regression equation stating that for every object i, its attribute Y has a value that can be expressed as the weighted sum of its attributes X_1 through X_m, with a measurement error of E (whose variance should be a minimum in the classical regression analysis). The term linear is derived from the fact that the graphical representation of the above equation for $m = 1$ is a straight line (with intercept b_0 and slope b_1). The above equation holds for all i, thus the system of equations:

$$y_1 = b_0 + b_1 x_{11} + b_2 x_{12} + b_3 x_{13} + \ldots + b_m x_{1m} + e_1$$
$$y_2 = b_0 + b_1 x_{21} + b_2 x_{22} + b_3 x_{23} + \ldots + b_m x_{2m} + e_2$$
$$\ldots$$
$$y_n = b_0 + b_1 x_{n1} + b_2 x_{n2} + b_3 x_{n3} + \ldots + b_m x_{nm} + e_n$$

for all n objects is often written in the abbreviated form, using matrices and vectors,

$$y = Xb + e$$

where y and e are column vectors containing all y_i and e_i, respectively ($i = 1 \ldots n$), b is a row vector containing all b_j ($j = 0 \ldots m$), and X is a $n \times (m + 1)$ matrix (with n rows and $m + 1$ columns) containing x_{ij} in the cells in row i and column j (where $x_{i0} = 1$ for all i). Here one is interested in the values of the regression coefficients b_j ($j = 0 \ldots m$) which minimize the variance of the regression residual E. This is solved by calculating $e^T e$ which is the sum of the squares of the still unknown e_i and calculating the derivatives of $e^T e$ with respect to all (also unknown) b_j. These derivatives will be 0 for $e^T e = min$, and the solution of this minimization problem is expressed as follows:

$$\frac{\partial b^T X^T X b}{\partial b} = 0 \quad \text{for} \quad b = (X^T X)^{-1} y$$

Linear systems are also used to describe dynamic relationships between variables. An early standard example from political science is English physicist Lewis Fry Richardson's (1881–1953) model of arms races, which consists of the following simplifying hypotheses:

- The higher the armament expenses of one military block, the faster the increase of the other block's armament expenses (as the latter wants to adapt to the threat as quickly as it can).

- The higher the armament expenses of a military block, the slower those expenses will increase (as it becomes more difficult to increase the proportion of military expenses with respect to the gross national product).

Calling the armament expenses of the two blocks x_1 and x_2, respectively, and their increase rates $x\dot{x}_1$ and $x\dot{x}_2$, respectively, one can model the increase rates as proportional both to the military expenses of the other block and the nonmilitary expenses of the own block (the total expenses x_1^{max} and x_2^{max} being constant), with some proportionality constants a, b, m, and n:

$$x\dot{x}_1 = m(x_1^{max} - x_1) + ax_2 = g - mx_1 + ax_2 \quad g = mx_1^{max}$$
$$x\dot{x}_2 = bx_1 + n(x_2^{max} - x_2) + h + bx_1 - nx_2 \quad h = nx_2^{max}$$

or, in shorter form:

$$\begin{pmatrix} \dot{x}_1 \\ \dot{x}_2 \end{pmatrix} = \begin{pmatrix} g \\ h \end{pmatrix} + \begin{pmatrix} -m & b \\ a & -n \end{pmatrix} \begin{pmatrix} x_1 \\ x_2 \end{pmatrix}$$
$$\dot{q} = c + Aq$$

Such linear systems of differential equations usually have a closed solution, that is, there is a vector-valued function $q(t)$ that fulfills this vector-valued differential equation. Usually, the precise form of $q(t)$ is not very interesting, but generally speaking it has the form:

$$q(t) = \theta_1 q_1 e^{\lambda_1 t} + \theta_2 q_2 e^{\lambda_2 t} + q_s$$

where q_1, q_2 and q_s are constant vectors and θ_1, θ_2, λ_1 and λ_2 are constant numbers of which mainly q_s, λ_1 and λ_2 are of special interest. q_s is the stationary state of the system of differential equations, that is, once the system has acquired this state, it will never leave that state, as the derivatives with respect to time vanish. λ_1 and λ_2 are the so-called eigenvalues of the matrix A, which, as the exponents of the two exponential functions in the above equation, determine whether the function $q(t)$ will grow beyond all limits over time or whether the two first terms in the right-hand side of the above equation will vanish as time approaches infinity. For negative values of both λ_1 and λ_2 the latter will happen, and the overall function will approach its stationary state (in which case the stationary state is called *stable* or an *attractor* or *sink*). If both eigenvalues are positive, then the function will grow beyond all limits (in which case the stationary state is called *unstable* or a *repellor* or *source*). If one of the λs is positive while the other is negative, the stationary is also unstable, but is called a *saddle point* because the function will first approach the stationary state and then move away. There is a special case when λ_1 and λ_2 are pure imaginary numbers—which happens if $4ab < 0$ and $m = n = 0$, as $\lambda_{1,2} = -\frac{m+n}{2} \pm \sqrt{4ab + (m-n)^2}$. In the arms race model this is not a reasonable assumption, as one block would increase its arms expenses faster, the smaller the arms expenses of the other block are (exactly one of a and b would be negative and the respective block would behave strangely, the other constant would be positive, so the other block would behave normally) and both would increase or decrease its arms expenses regardless of what their current values are ($m = n = 0$ means that there is no influence of the current value of arms expenses upon its change for both blocks). In this case both variables x_1 and x_2 oscillate around the stationary state.

The example demonstrates that systems of linear differential equations always have a closed solution, which can be expressed in several different forms. There is always exactly one stationary state (except in the case that the matrix *A* is not invertible) that can either be a sink or a source or a saddle or a center. Nonlinear systems often have more than one stationary state, but their behavior can be analyzed in a similar way, taking into account that a linear approximation of a nonlinear system behaves approximately the same in a small neighborhood of each of its stationary states.

SEE ALSO *Input-Output Matrix; Matrix Algebra; Nonlinear Systems; Simultaneous Equation Bias; Vectors*

BIBLIOGRAPHY

Arnold, Vladimir I. 1973. *Ordinary Differential Equations.* Cambridge, MA: MIT Press.

Richardson, Lewis Fry. 2003. *Mathematics of War and Foreign Politics.* In *The World of Mathematics*, vol. 2, ed. James R. Newman. Mineola, NY: Dover Publications.

Robinson, Derek J. S. 1991. *A Course in Linear Algebra with Applications.* River Edge, NJ: World Scientific.

Klaus G. Troitzsch

LINGUISTIC TURN

"Where word breaks off no thing may be": This line from a poem by Stefan George was repeatedly cited by the German philosopher Martin Heidegger (1889–1976) to indicate his version of the linguistic turn, which affected many philosophers in the early twentieth century—literary scholars already having made the turn, whether consciously or not (Heidegger [1959] 1982, p. 63). The phrase *linguistic turn* actually was coined by the philosopher Gustav Bergman, a former member of the Vienna circle, who made an effort to reformulate philosophy with regard to syntax and interpretation and was given new currency by the American philosopher Richard Rorty (b. 1931). Currently it is extremely popular, but the phenomenon is far from unprecedented (Rorty 1992; and see Jay 1982). Friedrich Nietzsche's idea of "the infinite interpretability of all things" (Nietzsche [1901] 1967, p. 327) is an analogy drawn from language, and a century later Hans-Georg Gadamer (1900–2002) carried on the criticism of Kant's transcendental turn (1975, p. 176)—that is, his "metacriticism" of Kant, which Jacques Derrida likewise recalled (Michelfelder and Palmer 1989, p. 102; cf. Derrida 1978). Renaissance humanism, too, was in part a linguistic—a philological, a rhetorical, and a literary—protest against the excessive abstraction of scholasticism, following the lead of the ancient Sophists and orators (Kelley 1991).

The linguistic turn was apparent also in the "new rhetoric" of the mid-twentieth century, which drew attention to the habits and conventions of language, as when Michel Foucault (1926–1984) denied the control of speakers and writers over their own discourse (e.g., Foucault 1970). The arts of speaking and writing are based on conscious imitation, but every literate person moves in linguistic channels carved by predecessors, deposited in the memory, and repeated in different contexts. Particular languages produce semantic fields that make possible communication and dialogue; and linguistic usage—for example, *topoi*, copulas, and word combinations—has its own inertial force that acquires meaning apart from the intentions of users. This is one reason for distrusting the "intentional fallacy" in interpreting texts.

One of the most impressive vistas opened up by the linguistic turn is the modern philosophy of hermeneutics in the form given by Gadamer, who, following Heidegger, extended the line of thought in the direction suggested not by Nietzsche (as did Heidegger and Derrida) but rather by the German philosopher and historian Wilhelm Dilthey (1833–1911). Rejecting revolutionary ruptures as a condition of understanding, Gadamer preserved belief in a kind of continuity that made communication and "dialogue" possible not only between speakers but also over time (Gadamer 1975). There are no absolute beginnings, no understanding without prejudice, and the "fore-structures of understanding" provided by language and the "life-world." Pursuing the old quest for "the I in the Thou," Gadamer accepts the horizon-structure of experience but doubles it to accommodate the contexts of past as well as the inquiring present. Language is a continuum making interpretation possible, but it does not permit the sort of retrospective mind reading assumed by the "empathy" of Romantic hermeneutics. That meaning is always constructed in the present is the hermeneutical condition of Gadamer's historicism. To understand, in short, is always to understand *differently*.

An important offshoot of hermeneutics is reception theory, or reception history (*Rezeptionsgeschichte*), which follows Gadamer in shifting attention from writing to reading. In fact, intellectual history is more concerned with the intention of authors and meaning of their texts than with their "fortune" in later contexts. Paul Ricoeur's "semantic autonomy" of texts is the condition of interpretations and misinterpretations accompanying the reception of writings (Ricoeur 1981, 63ff). For him, the poles of interpretation are hermeneutics of tradition and hermeneutics of suspicion, the first locating the position of Gadamer, who seeks an experience of tradition, the second that of Foucault, who is devoted to the critique of ideology. For Gadamer, "tradition" and continuity produce the common ground of understanding and communication which, via ideas, connects present and past; for Foucault, they mean entrapment in or complicity with ideology and a denial of the ruptures between the successive *epistemes* that represent decipherable codes (critically fabricated *Weltanschauungen*) of culture and patterns of underlying power relations.

This is also to some extent the noble dream of the German approach to intellectual history that is the "history of concepts" (*Begriffsgeschichte*), an effort to reconstruct an intellectual field through the history of terms and families of terms such as the English study of "keywords" (Williams 1983, and see Richter 1995). Under the influence of J. G. A. Pocock, Quentin Skinner, and others, political thought has turned its attention to questions of terminology and vocabulary rather than abstract systems (Pocock 1971; Tully 1988). Likewise, *Begriffsgeschichte* is a species of cultural history focusing on semantic change and the historical context of ideas, and it depends on metahistorical considerations to determine the meanings behind the keywords being analyzed. Such enterprises began thirty years ago, before databases such as Proteus and ARTFL made possible a much more extensive searching of semantic fields, but nonetheless they have greatly enriched the practices of intellectual and social history after the linguistic turn.

The linguistic turn has had an impact across the whole range of disciplines, whether through the idea of social construction or through the extension of the interpretive method into the human and even the natural sciences (Bernstein 1980; Nelson, Megill, and McCloskey 1987). The result was to place the observer in the field of observation, that is, the discipline, in the search for meaning. In anthropology this meant not the establishment of general "scientific" knowledge, but rather the hermeneutical "interpretation of cultures," in Clifford Geertz's phrase (Geertz 1973); and so it was in the other social and human sciences, which after the linguistic turn took language rather than mathematics as the model of understanding. For some scholars this represented the threat of relativism or the basis for a claim to postmodernism, but in any case it permitted a more critical approach to the social sciences.

The "new cultural history" proclaimed in the 1980s also included a linguistic turn, drawing extensively on post-Marxist literary theory and the idea of history as a text to be read. Some social scientists have resisted this move toward the social construction of knowledge, and a decade later a number of scholars affected to take their disciplines "beyond the cultural turn" (Hunt 1987; Bonnell and Hunt 1999). In any case, there is no turning back.

SEE ALSO *Meaning*

BIBLIOGRAPHY

Bernstein, Richard J. 1980. *The Restructuring of Social and Political Theory*. Philadelphia: University of Pennsylvania Press.

Bonnell, Victoria E., and Lynn Hunt. 1999. *Beyond the Cultural Turn*. Berkeley: University of California Press.

Derrida, Jacques. 1978. *Edmund Husserl's "Origins of Geometry": An Introduction*. Trans. John P. Leavey. Pittsburgh, PA: Duquesne University Press.

Gadamer, Hans-Georg. 1975. *Truth and Method*, eds. Garrett Barden and John Cumming. New York: Continuum.

Foucault, Michel. [1966] 1970. *The Order of Things: An Archaeology of the Human Sciences*. New York: Pantheon Books.

Geertz, Clifford. 1973. *The Interpretation of Cultures*. New York: Basic Books.

Heidegger, Martin. [1959] 1982. *On the Way to Language*. Trans. Peter D. Hertz. New York: Harper and Row.

Hunt, Lynn. 1987. *The New Cultural History*. Berkeley: University of California Press.

Jay, Martin. 1982. Should History Take a Linguistic Turn? In *Modern Intellectual History*, eds. Dominick LaCapra and Steven Kaplan, 86–110. Ithaca, NY: Cornell University Press.

Kelley, Donald R. 1991. *Renaissance Humanism*. Boston: Twayne.

Michelfelder, Diana P., and Richard Palmer, eds. 1989. *Dialogue and Deconstruction: The Gadamer-Derrida Encounter*. Albany: State University of New York Press.

Mueller-Vollmer, Kurt. 1986. *The Hermeneutics Reader*. Oxford: Oxford University Press.

Nelson, John S., Allan Megill, and Donald N. McCloskey. 1987. *The Rhetoric of the Human Sciences*. Madison: University of Wisconsin Press.

Nietzsche, Friedrich. [1901] 1967. *The Will to Power*, ed. Walter Kaufman. New York: Random House.

Pocock, J. G. A. 1971. *Politics, Language, and Time*. Chicago: University of Chicago Press.

Richter, Melvin. 1995. *The History of Political and Social Concepts*. New York: Oxford University Press.

Ricoeur, Paul. 1981. *Hermeneutics and the Human Sciences*. Trans. John B. Thompson. Cambridge, U.K.: Cambridge University Press.

Rorty, Richard, ed. 1992. *The Linguistic Turn*. Chicago: University of Chicago Press.

Tully, James, ed. 1988. *Meaning and Context: Quentin Skinner and His Critics*. Princeton, NJ: Princeton University Press.

Williams, Raymond. 1983. *Keywords: A Vocabulary of Culture and Society*. London: Fontana.

Donald R. Kelley

LINGUISTICS

SEE *Psycholinguistics; Anthropology, Linguistic.*

LIQUIDITY

An asset is considered to be liquid if it can be: (1) easily exchanged; (2) quickly exchanged; and (3) exchanged at little or no cost. For example, currency (coins and paper money) is an extremely liquid asset, whereas consumer durables and housing are very illiquid assets. Other assets, such as money in the bank, stocks, and bonds, fall between these two extremes, depending on the nature of their market. Hence, if someone needed to sell illiquid assets to raise money, say, as a result of a bad income shock, he should expect a loss, because he will not get the full value of his illiquid assets in a distress sale.

Even though the goal of holding assets is to obtain a return, firms and consumers regularly hold currency, which offers no return. The reason for this, first put forth by John Maynard Keynes (1883–1946), is that "bills and call loans are more 'liquid' than investments, i.e., more certainly realizable at short notice without loss" ([1930] 1971, p. 59). According to John R. Hicks (1904–1989), this is the first time the term *liquid* was used to describe the ability of an asset to be converted to cash without suffering a loss, and sets the foundation for Hicks's subsequent *liquidity preference framework* (a theory of nominal interest rate determination) and the *IS-LM framework* (a theory of determination of aggregate output and the interest rate) (see, for example, Mishkin and Serletis 2007).

These Keynesian models lead to the conclusion that an increase in the money supply (everything else remaining equal) lowers interest rates. This is known as the *liquidity effect*. However, Milton Friedman (1912–2006), the 1976 Nobel laureate in economics, argued that an increase in the money supply might not leave everything else equal, and that there are other possible effects of an increase in the money supply on interest rates, such as the *income effect*, the *price-level effect*, and the *expected-inflation effect*. In fact, the empirical evidence, mainly based on vector autoregressions (VARs), seems to indicate that money and interest rates are positively rather than negatively related, thereby producing a *liquidity puzzle*. There have been many attempts to unravel this puzzle (e.g., Eichenbaum 1992; Strongin 1995; Christiano et al. 1996). In general, as more variables are introduced and as the VAR specification is refined, it produces results consistent with traditional Keynesian and monetarist analysis (see, for example, Cochrane 1998).

A purely theoretical concept that is also due to Keynes is the idea of a *liquidity trap*—an extreme case of ultrasensitivity of the demand for money to interest rates. In this case, the money demand curve is completely flat in the liquidity preference framework and the LM curve is horizontal in the IS-LM framework, meaning that increases in the money supply are absorbed without any decline in interest rates. Thus monetary policy is without

effect and fiscal policy is the only means of economic control. The empirical evidence, however, indicates that although the demand for money is sensitive to interest rates, a liquidity trap has never existed.

Over the years, several measures of liquidity have been employed. For example, for individual assets, liquidity can be measured by a *liquidity premium*—the lower the liquidity premium, the more liquid (and the more like money) the asset is. If one wanted to obtain an aggregate measure of liquidity, one would add the assets together, giving higher weights to those assets with lower liquidity premiums. In this regard, the money measures currently in use by central banks around the world (known as *monetary aggregates*) are simple-sum indices in which all financial assets are assigned a constant and equal (unitary) weight. This index is M_t in $M_t = \sum_{j=1}^{n} x_{jt}$ where x_{jt} is one of the n components of the monetary aggregate M_t. This summation index implies that all financial assets contribute equally to the money total, and it views all components as dollar-for-dollar perfect substitutes. Such an index, there is no question, represents an index of the stock of nominal financial wealth, but cannot, in general, represent a valid structural economic variable for the liquidity services of financial assets in the economy.

In light of the foregoing arguments, there have been many attempts at properly weighting financial assets within a simple-sum aggregate. With no theory, however, any weighting scheme is questionable. William A. Barnett (1980) applied economic aggregation and index number theory and constructed monetary aggregates based upon W. Erwin Diewert's (1976) class of superlative quantity index numbers. The new aggregates are Divisia quantity indices, named after François Divisia (1889–1964), who first proposed the index in 1925. The Divisia index (in discrete time) is defined as

$$\log M_t^D - \log M_{t-1}^D = \sum_{j=1}^{n} w_{jt}^*(\log x_{jt} - \log x_{j,t-1}),$$

according to which the growth rate of the aggregate is a weighted average of the growth rates of the component quantities, with the Divisia weights being defined as the expenditure share averaged over the two periods of the change, $w_{jt}^* = \frac{1}{2}(w_{jt} + w_{j,t-1})$, for $j = 1, \ldots, n$, where

$$w_{jt} = \frac{\pi_{jt} x_{jt}}{\sum_{k=1}^{n} \pi_{kt} x_{kt}},$$

is the expenditure share of asset j during period t, and π_{jt} is the user cost of asset j, derived in Barnett (1978), $\pi_{jt} = \frac{R_t - r_{jt}}{1 + R_t}$, which is the opportunity cost of holding a dollar's worth of the jth liquid asset.

Above r_{jt} is the market yield on the jth asset, and R_t is the yield available on a benchmark asset that is held only to carry wealth between multiperiods. At the margin, the greater the difference between R_t and r_{jt}, the greater is the liquidity services that asset j yields.

SEE ALSO *Capital; Financial Instability Hypothesis; Financial Markets; Friedman, Milton; Interest Rates; IS-LM Model; Keynes, John Maynard; Leverage; Liquidity Premium; Liquidity Trap; Loans; Monetary Theory; Money; Money, Demand for; Neutrality of Money; Overlending*

BIBLIOGRAPHY

Barnett, William A. 1978. The User Cost of Money. *Economics Letters* 1: 145–149.

Barnett, William A. 1980. Economic Monetary Aggregates: An Application of Aggregation and Index Number Theory. *Journal of Econometrics* 14: 11–48.

Christiano, Lawrence J., Martin Eichenbaum, and Charles Evans. 1996. The Effects of Monetary Policy Shocks: Evidence from the Flow of Funds. *Review of Economics and Statistics* 78: 16–34.

Cochrane, John. 1998. What Do the VARs Mean? Measuring the Output Effects of Monetary Policy. *Journal of Monetary Economics* 41: 277–300.

Diewert, W. Erwin. 1976. Exact and Superlative Index Numbers. *Journal of Econometrics* 4: 115–145.

Eichenbaum, Martin. 1992. Comments on "Interpreting the Macroeconomic Time Series Facts: The Effects of Monetary Policy" by C. Sims. *European Economic Review* 36: 1001–1011.

Hicks, John R. Liquidity. 1962. *The Economic Journal* 72: 787–802.

Keynes, John Maynard. [1930] 1971. *A Treatise on Money*. 8th ed. Vol. 2. London: Macmillan.

Mishkin, Frederic S., and Apostolos Serletis. 2007. *The Economics of Money, Banking, and Financial Markets*. 3rd Canadian ed. Toronto: Pearson.

Strongin, Stephen. 1995. The Identification of Monetary Policy Disturbances: Explaining the Liquidity Puzzle. *Journal of Monetary Economics* 35: 463–497.

Apostolos Serletis

LIQUIDITY PREMIUM

Liquidity premium is the amount of monetary return that one would be willing to forgo for the convenience or security of disposing of an asset quickly and with minimal or no cost. The power of disposal of an asset is measured in terms of how easily it can be sold as well as in terms of the

degree of expected capital risk if the asset is liquidated (Keynes [1936] 1964, p. 226).

Each asset has an expected total return (an "own rate of return") composed of q—the expected income from employing the asset in production; c—the carrying cost; a—the expected capital gains (appreciation or depreciation); and l—liquidity premium. An own rate of return for an asset is calculated in the following way: $q - c + a + l$. Thus liquidity premium is one of the elements that constitute the value of an asset. Assets are differentiated according to combinations of expected monetary returns and liquidity premiums they are anticipated to offer (Carvalho 1999, p. 126).

The state of expectations refers not merely to subjective assessments of what events might or might not occur but also to the anticipated costs of undertaking alternative courses of action (Kregel 1998). So long as there are alternative ways to store value and money is one of them, the option of not "using" money—that is, not purchasing capital assets—and hedging against uncertainty affects investment in less liquid capital assets (Davidson 1978). Thus liquidity premium is an expression of the "return" from holding money as an asset (Keynes [1936] 1964, p. 227). This return establishes the standard that expected yields of capital assets must achieve. In order for capital assets to be purchased, their prices must be at a level at which the expected yield ($q - c$) equals the liquidity premium l. Consequently the expected return of a capital asset has to be such as to compensate for its degree of illiquidity given the degree of uncertainty felt by asset holders. The degree of uncertainty determines the liquidity premium (Carvalho 1999, p. 127).

Liquidity reduces the uncertainty about fulfilling future commitments and, implicitly, about future income and capital returns. The willingness to borrow and purchase capital assets depends on business enterprises' perception of borrower's risk, whereas the willingness of banks to make the requested loans depends on their perception of lender's risk (Minsky 1975). The assessment of these types of risks depends on the state of expectations and on the margins of safety or the amount of monetary returns that borrowers and lenders are willing to forgo to be liquid—in other words, on liquidity premium.

These margins of safety vary across time and geopolitical space with the tendency for perception of higher risks and thus with higher liquidity preference in developing countries (Dow 1995, p. 8). At the international level, this can result in a tendency for liquid portfolio investment rather than greenfield foreign direct investment in "emerging markets." Because liquidity premium is a manifestation of the margin of safety thought necessary to deal with uncertainty and perceived capital risk, it enters the determination of domestic and global level composition of investment, output, and employment.

SEE ALSO *Carrying Cost; Equilibrium in Economics; Equity Markets; Expectations; Financial Instability Hypothesis; Keynes, John Maynard; Liquidity; Minsky, Hyman; Money, Demand for; Risk; Uncertainty; Yield*

BIBLIOGRAPHY

Carvalho, Fernando. 1999. On Banks' Liquidity Preference. In *Full Employment and Price Stability in a Global Economy*, eds. Paul Davidson and Jan Kregel, 123–138. Cheltenham, U.K., and Northampton, MA: Edward Elgar.

Davidson, Paul. 1978. *Money and the Real World*. London: Macmillan.

Dow, Sheila. 1995. Liquidity Preference in International Finance: The Case of Developing Countries. In *Post-Keynesian Economic Theory*, ed. Paul Wells, 1–14. Boston, Dordrecht, Netherlands, and London: Kluwer Academic.

Keynes, John M. [1936] 1964. *The General Theory of Employment, Interest, and Money*. New York: Harcourt Brace.

Kregel, Jan. 1998. Aspects of a Post Keynesian Theory of Finance. *Journal of Post Keynesian Economics* 21 (1): 111–124.

Minsky, Hyman. 1975. *John Maynard Keynes*. London: Macmillan.

Wray, Randall. 1990. *Money and Credit in Capitalist Economies: The Endogenous Money Approach*. Aldershot, U.K.: Edward Elgar.

Zdravka Todorova

LIQUIDITY TRAP

The inability of a nation's central bank to decrease the interest rate when it is already very close to zero is known as the "liquidity trap." It was first referred to by John Maynard Keynes in his 1936 "General Theory." It was John Hicks, however, who—by laying the foundations of the IS-LM model in the 1930s in an attempt to present and popularize Keynes's main propositions—put forward the concept of the liquidity trap and its policy implications.

The IS-LM presentation of an economy became a very popular tool for macroeconomic analysis and for policy propositions after World War II (1939–1945). In an IS-LM model, the IS curve is a negatively sloped curve that presents the locus of points in which investment (I) equals savings (S) for all possible combinations of interest rates and levels of output (Y). The LM curve is a positively sloped curve that presents the locus of points in which the demand for money or liquidity preference (L) is equal to money supply (M) for all possible combinations of interest rates and level of income (Y). The intersection point of the two curves represents the equilibrium interest rate and output of an economy. The IS curve represents the real sector of the economy and it shifts outward to the right when aggregate demand increases (and inward to the left when demand decreases). The LM curve represents the monetary sector of the economy and it shifts outward to the right with an expansionary money policy (and inward to the left with a contractionary policy). Hence, economic analysis based on IS-LM analysis suggests that an appropriate mix of fiscal and monetary policies can bring the economy to equilibrium with full employment.

It is argued that the lower left segment of the LM curve is very flat, and that for very low (close to zero) interest rates it becomes horizontal. The reason is that at very low interest rates, economic agents prefer to keep cash for liquidity purposes. Financial assets are not as desirable in this situation because their liquidity is lower and their yield is close to zero. Hence, the liquidity preference schedule becomes infinitely elastic due to investors' expectation that the rate of interest cannot fall any further, and because bond prices are so high that no one expects them to rise still higher. In this flat state, the economy is in "liquidity trap," meaning that interest rates are so low that people are indifferent between holding money or other assets. The demand for money is therefore infinitely elastic.

The liquidity trap hypothesis has led to a theoretical dispute over the extent to which the demand for money depends on interest rates. Neoclassical and monetarist economists argue that the interest rate is determined in the real sector, and that money, by being neutral, makes monetary policy an ineffective tool. Keynesians, on the other hand, argue that interest rates are defined in the money market, and that money is not neutral. In fact, the liquidity trap hypothesis rests on the neutrality of money, whereas Keynes's analysis of conditions of less than full employment is predicated on the nonneutrality of money. Another implication of a liquidity-trap situation is that neoclassical analysis becomes inconsistent at such low interest rates, since the system can be in equilibrium at less than full employment. In fact, the liquidity trap argument suggests that the neoclassical case has no equilibrium solution; that is, it does not include a positive interest rate that will equate investment and demand.

According to neoclassical analysis, interest rates are the equilibrators of both capital and goods markets. Interest rates keep investment equal to saving at full employment levels, and as a result the real full equilibrium of the economy is independent of nominal prices. The neoclassical proposition, often associated with the quantity theory of money, states that the interest elasticity of money demand is zero, and that with perfect flexibility of all wages and prices (present and future), full employment will be maintained. On the other hand, Keynes's suggestion is that a perfectly competitive economy does not, in fact, tend automatically toward full employment. The inflexibility of wages and prices, the low interest-elasticity of investment demand, and the liquidity trap might all suffice to prevent attainment of full employment equilibrium.

According to Keynesians, if the economy is stuck in a liquidity trap, a shift of the IS curve to the left (lower aggregate demand) does not allow for the intersection of aggregate demand and supply curves, suggesting that wages and prices will fall continuously and there will be no equilibrium. In other words, the problem with the neoclassical analysis is that equilibrium output, either on the supply side or on the demand side, does not respond to the price drop in the liquidity-trap case. In fact, as Keynes argued, it is possible for interest rates to fall so low in the neoclassical model that neither an expansionary monetary policy nor falling prices could ever increase the level of demand-side equilibrium output. Thus, with employment determined in the labor market and demand caught in the liquidity trap, the neoclassical model offers no solution.

The British economist Arthur Pigou attempted to remove this inconsistency in the neoclassical model by suggesting that falling prices would increase consumers' real wealth, leading to increased spending and reduced saving (the "real balance effect"). The rise in real consumption that occurs with falling prices would shift the IS curve out and raise the level of demand-side equilibrium output. This solution to the inconsistency in the neoclassical model generally implies that, after a long period of falling wages and prices, equilibrium will be reestablished. However, in the 1930s, the U.S. economy seemed to reach a different result: a fairly stable low level of employment with wages and prices dropping to a fixed level. Another solution to inconsistencies arising from the neoclassical analysis in liquidity trap conditions is the rigid-wage hypothesis, which allows for the equilibrium intersection between demand and supply.

Keynes mentioned that he was not aware of there ever having been a liquidity trap. Yet in 1998, Japan's interest rate was almost zero and output had barely changed, even in the face of expansionary monetary policy by the Bank of Japan, the nation's central bank. Thus, the Japanese government pursued an expansionary fiscal policy in its effort to increase output. The liquidity trap analysis should therefore clearly be part of the argument, which reveals that Keynesian economics teaches us that the automatic adjustment mechanism of competition cannot be relied upon for purposes of achieving certain policy objectives, such as full employment and price stability.

SEE ALSO *Economics, Keynesian; Interest Rates; Keynes, John Maynard; Liquidity; Money; Money, Demand for; Policy, Monetary; Unemployment*

BIBLIOGRAPHY

Blaug, Mark. 1997. *Economic Theory in Retrospect*. 5th ed. Cambridge, U.K.: Cambridge University Press.

Branson, William H. 1989. *Macroeconomic: Theory and Policy*. 3rd ed. New York: Harper & Row.

Tobin, James. 1993. Price Flexibility and Output Stability: An Old Keynesian View. *Journal of Economic Perspectives* 7 (1): 45–65.

Persefoni V. Tsaliki

LITERATURE

The word *literature* can simply mean a body of published texts, as in, "Are you familiar with the literature on global warming?" In a more restrictive sense, it alludes to creative works of the imagination. Conventionally these are divided into poetry, drama, and fiction. This concept of literature is a relatively recent one, first used in the late eighteenth century.

BEGINNINGS

The English word *literature* derives from the Latin *litteratura*, from *littera* (a letter of the alphabet). Most European languages—Romance, Germanic, and Slavic—have direct Latin cognates of similar meaning. Originally, *literature* in English signified knowledge of books, book learning, and familiarity with *letters*, that is, written works. Creative writing was termed *poesy* or *poetry* in English, irrespective of its form, from the Greek word for "to create." The earliest forms of poesy or what we would now call *literature* were the oral narratives of preliterate cultures—myths and folktales—handed down in written form. These include the oldest known literary text, the Sumerian *Epic of Gilgamesh* (3000 BCE), ancient Egyptian tales from 2000 BCE, Indian poems in Sanskrit (such as the Hindu epics *Ramayana* and *Mahabharata*), and ancient Chinese poetry. Homer's epics, *The Iliad* and *The Odyssey* (eighth century BCE), and the tragedies of Sophocles, Aeschylus, and Euripides (fifth century BCE) stand at the beginnings of the Western canon, or the body of literature generally accepted as worthy of study. Indeed, ideas of literary excellence were already present in the Dionysia festivals in Athens, when Greek playwrights competed for prizes. In a comedy that won first prize in 405 BCE, *The Frogs*, Aristophanes (c. 450–388 BCE) contrasted two preeminent tragedians—Aeschylus (525–456

BCE) and Euripides (c. 484–406 BCE)—clearly revealing the Athenians' general familiarity with their dramas. Through attending epic or dramatic performances, a largely unschooled populace could be exposed to *poesy* or *literature*.

Some of the first Greek libraries were established to gather together accurate copies of the prize-winning dramas. The earliest known library—a collection of Babylonian clay tablets—dates from the twenty-first century BCE. Other ancient examples are the libraries at Nineveh (in modern Iraq), at Egyptian temples, and at the temple at Jerusalem, as well as the Hellenistic libraries of Alexandria and Pergamum, established under royal patronage, and Roman libraries, both private and public. The famous Library of Alexandria, estimated at 500,000 scrolls, was joined to a research center (the Museion or Museum), encouraging the systematic study of philology, that is, language and letters. Literary commentary was already practiced in classical Greece; the best-known examples are those of Plato and Aristotle (fourth century BCE), followed in Roman times with Horace (65–8 BCE), Plutarch (c. 46–120 CE), and Pseudo-Longinus (first century CE), as well as the third-century Neoplatonist Plotinus, whose ideas would resound in the romantic era. The work of these ancient Greco-Roman libraries and commentators established crucial ideas of literary evaluation and the literary canon that would influence Renaissance and later scholarship.

"Poetic" works in verse and prose were produced from antiquity through the Middle Ages and the Renaissance without being considered *literature*. In Europe these included imaginative works in Greek and Latin, as well as later texts in the vernacular languages, such as the Norse, Irish, and Germanic epics (including the Old English poem *Beowulf*), courtly love poems of medieval France, the *Divine Comedy* of Dante Alighieri (1265–1321), the tales of Giovanni Boccaccio (c. 1313–1375), the poetry of Geoffrey Chaucer (c. 1342–1400), and the plays of William Shakespeare (1564–1616). The term *literature* first enters English in the late fourteenth century (according to the authoritative *Oxford English Dictionary*) in the original sense of literacy or acquaintance with books.

MODERN DEFINITION

It is not until the late eighteenth century, with such developments as the growth of the modern nation-state; the rise of printing, publishing, and literacy; and the move from aristocratic patronage to commercial support of writing, that *literature* came to signify a body of literary texts. In this general sense, literature includes creative writing (poetry, fiction, drama, and essays), popular narratives, and works produced by philosophers, historians,

religious and social thinkers, travelers, and nature writers, as exemplified in standard literary histories or reference volumes like the *Oxford Companion to American Literature*. In the more restricted sense of imaginative literature, the definition alludes to what in French is called *belles letters* or "fine writing" (a term also sometimes used in English but now tinged with the dismissive meaning of light or artificial dabbling). Imaginative literature can be defined by its fictional and autotelic nature, the dominance of the aesthetic function within it, and its special use of language, which René Wellek (1903–1995) and Austin Warren (1899–1986) in *Theory of Literature* characterized as follows: "Poetic language organizes, tightens, the resources of everyday language, and sometimes does even violence to them, in an effort to force us into awareness and attention" ([1949] 1978, p. 24). Complexity and appeal to generations of readers are also viable characteristics.

AESTHETICS AND NATIONALISM

The nineteenth century brought about an increasing emphasis on the aesthetic properties of literature and the rise of the field of literary criticism, independent of philosophy or rhetoric. The romantic poets fostered a sense of literature as the field of unique genius and stressed the aesthetic experience of reading. Literature was also increasingly seen as an important element in constructing a unified national consciousness and providing citizens with a sense of their cultural heritage, both through the training of students and through the accumulation of literary works in research libraries and their interpretation by specialists. Famously defining the critic's object of study as "the best which has been thought and said in the world" in his *Culture and Anarchy* ([1869] 1993, p. 190), Matthew Arnold (1822–1888) played an important role in making literature and literary criticism prominent in Anglo-American culture, vying with philosophy and religion as a way to reflect on the world.

In British and American colleges, the core curriculum was already heavily concentrated on the classics, the study of the languages and literatures of ancient Greece and Rome. English literature was introduced in the 1820s at London and other universities, followed much later in the century by Oxford, Cambridge, and American universities, aided by an influx of women entering college. The national literature was seen as offering a valuable unifying cultural tradition, both in Britain after the shock and disruptions of World War I (1914–1918), and in the United States after the Civil War (1861–1865) and massive waves of immigration in the second half of the nineteenth century. The Victorians produced a staggering array of novels, short stories, and poetry to feed a rapidly growing, increasingly literate and middle-class reading public. The realistic novel became the dominant literary mode in Western literature, with a growing tendency toward a split between lowbrow or popular fiction—due to a proliferation of new subgenres, such as the romance, the mystery, and science fiction—and highbrow literature, made up of critically approved fiction, poetry, and drama.

Modernist literature of the beginning decades of the twentieth century moved away from the realism and naturalism of the nineteenth century, toward experimentation, disruption of chronology and causality, and increasing complexity, a style more suited to developments in the twentieth century. Here T. S. Eliot (1888–1965) played a crucial role in elevating literature to a high art through his poetry and literary criticism, which helped develop the American formalist New Criticism and *The Great Tradition* (1948) school of F. R. Leavis (1895–1978) in Britain. This led to the mid-twentieth-century view, aptly summarized by Peter Widdowson, of high literature as "a select(ive) and valuable aesthetic and moral resource to replenish those living in the spiritual desert of a mass civilization" (1999, p. 59).

THE CANON AND BEYOND

What is deemed of literary significance or high literature is to a large extent the purview of the national educational system, where academic critics establish the canon of works considered worthy of reading and study at the school and college level. The canon in its original meaning refers to the authoritative set of orthodox, established texts of the Christian church. The biblical canon excludes a number of texts deemed heretical, such as gnostic writings. Similar exclusionary policies have been seen in literary canonization, leading to postmodernist disruptions of the canon under the pressures of new authors and literary theories, including feminism, queer theory, poststructuralism, deconstruction, and postcolonial studies. From the 1960s onward, the canon, long seemingly the domain of dead white males, was opened up to women, people of color, and other minorities. It was again in flux, with the emergence of these new writings and new genres, such as New Journalism or the nonfiction novel, as well as the self-reflective playfulness of postmodern fiction.

Literature is now increasingly in competition with film, television, and other mass media. Nevertheless, it is sustained by a huge publishing industry, bookselling businesses, the school and university systems, academic and public libraries, and the seemingly infinite resources of the Internet. In his study *On Literature*, J. Hillis Miller notes the crucial feature of creative writing: "A literary work is not, as many people assume, an imitation in words of some pre-existing reality, but on the contrary, it is the creation or discovery of a new, supplementary world, a meta-world, a hyper-reality. This new world is an irreplaceable

addition to the already existing one. A book is a pocket or portable dreamweaver" (2002, p. 18). Although threatened by the visual culture of the twenty-first century, literature still retains its unique quality of being able to generate alternative realities through the use of words as signs without visible referents.

BIBLIOGRAPHY

Arnold, Matthew. [1868] 1993. *Culture and Anarchy: An Essay in Political and Social Criticism.* Ed. Stefan Collini. New York: Cambridge University Press.

Baldick, Chris. 2004. *The Concise Oxford Dictionary of Literary Terms.* 2nd ed. Oxford, U.K.: Oxford University Press.

Guillory, John. 1990. Canon. In *Critical Terms for Literary Study,* ed. Frank Lentricchia and Thomas McLaughlin, 233–249. Chicago: University of Chicago Press.

Hart, James D., and Phillip W. Leininger, eds. 1995. *The Oxford Companion to American Literature.* 6th ed. New York: Oxford University Press.

Miller, J. Hillis. 2002. *On Literature.* London: Routledge.

Wellek, René, and Austin Warren. [1949] 1978. *Theory of Literature.* Harmondsworth, U.K.: Penguin.

Widdowson, Peter. 1999. *Literature.* London: Routledge.

Williams, Raymond. 1976. *Keywords: A Vocabulary of Culture and Society.* New York: Oxford University Press.

Elżbieta Foeller-Pituch

LITIGATION, SOCIAL SCIENCE ROLE IN

Judicial opinions have four elements: (1) jurisdiction (the court's authority to adjudicate this dispute); (2) findings of fact (what happened); (3) conclusions of law (what laws apply to these facts); and (4) order (what the court directs to be done). Social science is utilized in all four parts. For example, social scientists debate the merits of existing and proposed law, and their writings may be brought to the attention of judges, legislators, and government administrators (Meier et al. 1986, and Dixon and Gill 2002). They are most directly active, as participants, in finding fact, usually as expert witnesses. John L. Solow and Daniel Fletcher describe the role of the antitrust economist as "reaching conclusions about factual issues like the existence of market power or barriers to entry, and drawing causal links between firms' actions, market outcomes, and claimed damages" (2006, p. 31).

The law categorizes two kinds of fact: legislative and adjudicative. Legislative fact is about generalizations. For example, courts often want to know if a screening device (for school admission, or for employment or termination, for example) is "valid." But the effectiveness of a device used to screen plaintiffs cannot be tested on them, because validation requires observations on success or failure of persons who achieved the positions the plaintiffs have been denied. As a Fifth Circuit panel observed, "We fail to understand how passing scores conclusively establish the demographics of the qualified applicant pool if passing scores mean nothing with respect to predicting the quality of future firefighters" (*Dean v. City of Shreveport* 2006, p. 457). A validity study therefore is always legislative fact. The most famous legislative fact argument in litigation, appearing in an appeals brief by Louis Brandeis, was put together by his social scientist sister-in-law, Josephine Goldmark. Brandeis argued that as women are physically and socially different from men, it is appropriate that they have special protective legislation (*Muller v. Oregon* 1908). In *United States v. Virginia* (1996), in contrast, plaintiffs' experts argued convincingly that academically qualified women who could pass the same physical test as men needed only equal assessment.

To accept legislative fact requires that the court extrapolate from one population to another. When faced with an explicit recognition that such extrapolation is required, some judges have been reluctant to do it, despite precedential acceptance by the Supreme Court of Kenneth Clark's "doll studies," which showed that both white and black children prefer to play with white dolls. Clark had tested some children at issue in the U.S. Supreme Court's decision in *Brown v. Board of Education* (1954), which held that race is an unconstitutional basis for school assignment, but the Court referred only to his larger studies of children not connected with this case (Beggs 1995). In contrast, a massive study that contended that harsher sentences (particularly for execution) are handed down more often in black-on-white murder cases (i.e., black murderer of a white victim) than in cases involving any other race combination was rejected because it was legislative fact, where what the Court required was evidence that the particular sentence being challenged was tainted with racial bias (*McCleskey v. Kemp*, 1987). In another example, the First Circuit Court of Appeals rejected a sociologist's argument that "relies on evidence from one locality to establish the lingering effects of discrimination in another" (*Wessman v. Gittens* 1998, p. 804).

Adjudicative fact is particular. Much of what the social scientist expert does is devise ways to measure the concepts that seem relevant to the law. Redistricting, jury representation, antitrust, and equal employment opportunity issues inherently call for such social science fact. To show that juries are unrepresentative of "the community," for example, one needs a measure of that community, as well as of the jurors. Even if population demographics are stable, individuals may come and go, and not be available

for jury duty. The Hispanic population may be younger and more likely to be single and renting—and therefore implicitly more mobile—than the non-Hispanic population. As Hispanics tend to live in identifiable areas, one can describe their mobility directly from address-based data sources. Inferring characteristics of a set of people from data describing their tract or block or zip code is called *geocoding*.

In another example, invalid implicit screening devices may be used to make employment decisions. An implicit device might be a prejudice held, perhaps unknowingly, by the decision-maker, for example, thinking that fat people are lazy. According to R. Matthew Wise, "social framework evidence is the product of social science research that an expert compiles and uses to construct a frame of reference for specific issues central to the resolution of a case" (2005, p. 548). That is, particular evidence offered by such an expert may be an amalgam, applying legislative fact to case-specific attributes. Whether that type of study will be admitted is always in question.

Three other distinctions loom large in explaining the role of the social scientist as expert witness. First, laws are about events, whereas data are almost always about situations. Changing one's residence is an event, but most data describe the population in an area at one time, and then at another. Hiring and firing are events, but the majority of employment-discrimination analyses have compared situations, such as the racial composition of a firm's employees with the racial composition of a subset of a proximate area's workforce. In another example, one seldom observes the collusion implied in some antitrust charges; that event is inferred from situations, such as where stores are located and the prices of their goods.

The complaining party's expert tries to explain the relationship between the outcome and the alleged events, excluding other, benign events that could have led to the same outcome. The defending party's expert tries to show that it likely was benign events that led to the same outcome, and also argues that plaintiffs' descriptions of the situations are themselves incorrect or misleading. An example in which how one defines a variable determines the statistical result is *McReynolds v. Sodexho Marriott Services, Inc.* (2004), where the plaintiffs' expert does not measure "promotions" as defendant firm defines them. Courts generally dislike plaintiffs' analyses that have not considered alternative explanations for the events complained about. The defendant may prevail merely by criticizing the plaintiffs' "proof." For example, "A statistical analysis which fails to control for equally plausible non-discriminatory factors overstates the comparison group and, under the facts of this case, cannot raise a question of fact for trial regarding discriminatory impact" (*Carpenter et al. v. The Boeing Company*, 2004, *affirmed* 2006).

Second, the social scientist's evidence is subject to legal distinctions, such as the difference between *disparate treatment* (in which actions are at issue) and *disparate impact* (in which the action's effect is at issue). Measuring the "cost" of gasoline at its market price (opportunity cost), evaluating damages to resorts from oil spills by lost consumer surplus, failing to distinguish allowable from nonallowable behavior as causes for an outcome in antitrust litigation, and using the wrong basis for a survey are examples of legal mistakes made in social science evidence. See, for example, *Rebel Oil Company, Inc. v. Atlantic Richfield Company* (1996), *In the Matter of Oil Spill by the Amoco-Cadiz off the Coast of France on March 16, 1978* (1992), *Williamson Oil Co. v. Philip Morris* (2003), *Citizens Financial Group, Inc. v. Citizens National Bank of Evans City* (2004), and *Autozone v. Tandy Corp.* (2001).

Third, although both an eyewitness and a social science witness may present adjudicative fact as they see it, the social scientist provides *circumstantial* evidence. (Social scientists would call it *inferential* evidence.) Therefore, social science results must be reported probabilistically. The social scientist cannot be "certain" in the way an eyewitness can.

However, no matter how firmly held, eyewitness testimony is often wrong—it, too, is probabilistic. See *United States v. Veysey* (2003), referring to Judge Frank Easterbrook's discussion of probabilistic evidence in *Branion v. Gramley*, 1988: "Much of the evidence we think of as most reliable is just a compendium of statistical inferences."

Estimates of the fallibility of eyewitness identification (legislative fact) sometimes are allowed into evidence, sometimes not. Thus, although a social scientist cannot testify that "X did not do Y," he may be called upon to testify that although Z says that X did Y, Z may be mistaken; or that such mistakes happen in such and such circumstances, more or less to such an extent. On the fallibility of eyewitness identification, see Munsterburg (1909), Loftus and Monahan (1980), and Bradfield and Wells (2000). Similarly, "forensic" experts often allude to a certainty in their identification (e.g., by handwriting, fingerprints) that social scientists find offensive. Social science research about the fallibility of forensic evidence is sometimes admitted in rebuttal, sometimes excluded.

Geocoding is a powerful method of examining voting patterns, even though individual ballots remain secret. Social scientists have debated whether gerrymandering had been directed by race (impermissible) or party (permissible) in situations when the outcome of the vote is known and the race of the voters is inferred. J. Morgan Kousser attributes the setting of district boundaries to the majority's attempt to prevent minority successes (1999).

In *Thornburg v. Gingles* (1986) the Supreme Court found race to be too important a factor to let the redistricting stand; and in *Hunt v. Cromartie* (2001) it found that race was not important enough to disallow the redistricting. (See Grofman 1998 for social science studies concerning judicial redistricting decisions.)

The federal judicial system had no formal rules of evidence until 1975, prior to which judges usually accepted a witness as an "expert" if he was regarded to be one by others in the same "field" (*Frye v. United States* 1923). Although the institution of rules of evidence gave judges the authority to determine the expertise of proffered experts, decisions at first were little affected. "Junk science" was sometimes determinative (Huber 1991). In *Daubert v. Merrill Dow Pharmaceuticals, Inc.* (1993) the Supreme Court held that the Federal Rules of Evidence superseded *Frye*. Trial judges were instructed to exclude expert testimony they found insufficiently reliable or unhelpful to a fact finder.

The decisions of the "Science Evidence Trilogy"—*Daubert, Joiner v. General Electric Company* (1997), and *Kumho Tire Co. v. Carmichael* (1999)—now govern the use of scientific and technical testimony. Joëlle Anne Moreno describes the slowness with which *Daubert* principles have been applied to criminal cases, and the resulting bias against rebuttal experts offered by defendants (2004). John V. Jansonius and Andrew M. Gould (1998) and Mark S. Brodin (2004) discuss the problem of applying the Science Evidence Trilogy to social science. Credentials remain important. Practice has not evolved to focus solely on the proposed testimony. For example, in *Gary Price Studios, Inc. v. Randolph Rose Collection, Inc.* (2006), a proffered expert's method for evaluating damages was internally contradictory. The judge took pains to show that the witness was not otherwise qualified, when the rules would have allowed him to dismiss the testimony as clearly incorrect and therefore unhelpful.

Subjects amenable to expert study are fast expanding as imaginative attorneys find new ways to argue for their clients. Courts are increasingly willing to hear evidence from statistical models. For example, adjudicative studies based on samples at one time were not acceptable; see *United States v. United Shoe Machinery Corp.* (1953), in which Judge Wyzanski drew his own sample, breaking that tradition. "The Court arbitrarily selected from a standard directory of shoe manufacturers, the first 15 names that began with the first letter of the alphabet, the first 15 names that began with the eleventh letter of the alphabet, all 8 of the names that began with the twenty-first letter of the alphabet, and the first seven of the names that began with the twenty-second letter of the alphabet" (p. 305). Now, over fifty years later, the parties' experts would do the sampling, presumably more skillfully. Opposing experts may come from different fields. Some judges complain that they do not have the skills to resolve technical disputes, and sometimes they engage their own experts, as the Rules of Evidence permit.

BIBLIOGRAPHY

Beggs, Gordon J. 1995. Novel Expert Evidence in Federal Civil Rights Litigation. *American University Law Review* 45 (5) 1–75.

Bradfield, Amy L., and Gary L. Wells. 2000. The Perceived Validity of Eyewitness Identification Testimony: A Test of the Five *Biggers* Criteria. *Law and Human Behavior* 24 (5): 581–594.

Brodin, Mark S. 2004. Behavioral Science Evidence in the Age of *Daubert*: Reflections of a Skeptic. Boston College Law School Research Paper 24. http://lsr.nellco.org/bc/bclsfp/papers/24.

Brown v. Board of Education, 347 U.S. 483, 495 (1954).

Carpenter et al. v. The Boeing Company, 2004 WL 2661691 (2004).

Dean v. City of Shreveport, No. 04–31163 (5th Cir. 2006).

Dixon, Lloyd, and Brian Gill. 2002. Changes in the Standards for Admitting Expert Evidence in Federal Civil Cases since the *Daubert* Decision. *Psychology, Public Policy, and Law* 8: 251–308.

Grofman, Bernard, ed. 1998. *Race and Redistricting in the 1990s*. New York: Agathon Press.

Huber, Peter W. 1991. *Galileo's Revenge: Junk Science in the Courtroom*. New York: Basic Books.

Hunt v. Cromartie, 526 U.S. 541 (1999); on remand, 133 F.Supp.2d 407 (E.D. N.C. 2000); reversed, 532 U.S. 234 (2001).

Jansonius, John V., and Andrew M. Gould. 1998. Expert Witnesses in Employment Litigation: The Role of Reliability in Assessing Admissibility. *Baylor Law Review* 50 (267): 282–286.

Kousser, J. Morgan. 1999. *Colorblind Injustice: Minority Voting Rights and the Undoing of the Second Reconstruction*. Chapel Hill: University of North Carolina Press.

Loftus, Elizabeth, and John Monahan. 1980. Trial by Data: Psychological Research as Legal Evidence. *American Psychologist* 35 (3): 270.

Meier, Paul, Jerome Sacks, and Sandy L. Zabell. 1986. What Happened in Hazelwood: Statistics, Employment Discrimination, and the 80% Rule. In *Statistics and the Law*, ed. Morris H. DeGroot, Stephen E. Fienberg, and Joseph B. Kadane, 1–48. New York: John Wiley.

Michelson, Stephan. 2006. *The Expert: The Statistical Analyst in Litigation*. Hendersonville, NC: LRA Press.

Moreno, Joëlle Anne. 2004. What Happens When Dirty Harry Becomes an (Expert) Witness for the Prosecution? *Tulane Law Review* 79 (1): 1–54.

Munsterberg, Hugo. 1909. *On the Witness Stand*. New York: Doubleday and Page.

Solow, John L., and Daniel Fletcher. 2006. Doing Good Economics in the Courtroom: Thoughts on *Daubert* and

Expert Testimony in Antitrust. *Journal of Corporation Law* 31:489–502.

United States v. United Shoe Machinery Corp., 110 F.Supp. 295 (D.Mass. 1953).

United States v. Veysey, 334 F.3d 600 (2003).

Wessman v. Gittens, 160 F.3d 790 (1998).

Wise, R. Matthew. 2005. From Price Waterhouse to Dukes and Beyond: Bridging the Gap between Law and Social Science by Improving the Admissibility Standard for Expert Testimony. *Berkeley Journal of Employment and Labor Law* 26: 545–581.

Stephan Michelson

LITTLE RED BOOK

The "little red book" was a Western nickname for the *Quotations from Chairman Mao Tse-tung*, a collection of Mao Zedong's (1893–1976) quotations published in 1964 under the auspices of the People's Liberation Army (PLA). It is most commonly referred to in China as a "little treasure book." This pocket-sized quotation book contained more than four hundred select quotations from Mao's speeches and writings. It was widely circulated in China and around the world during the infamous Cultural Revolution (1966–1976). By the time the Chinese Communist Party finally ordered a halt to the printing of the book in February 1979, at least one billion official copies had already been printed. Some estimates put the total as high as five billion copies worldwide. This impressive number made the little red book one of the most popular publications in the world in the twentieth century.

The little red book was born during a campaign to study Mao's political thought that was initiated in 1959 by General Lin Biao (1907–1971). Hoping to further his own political ambitions, Lin Biao asked the staff of the *People's Liberation Army Daily* to compile a small collection of Mao's quotations in 1964. Its original compiler was Xian Xiaoguang, an editor who worked for the newspaper. Once the book was approved, it immediately became popular among PLA soldiers, since most of them had little education and found it difficult to read Mao's original writings. Lin ordered that a free copy be issued to every soldier.

When the Cultural Revolution began in 1966, Mao's personality cult had reached its peak and demand for the quotation book hit an all-time high. After several revisions, the 88,000-word book was finally made available to the public. It soon became a political bible and a source of spiritual inspiration. Every person in China had at least one copy, and its reading and recital became a daily ritual.

People would carry the little red book everywhere and studied it religiously; they could get into trouble for showing disrespect for the book or for misquoting it. The little red book was carried by millions of Red Guards during the Cultural Revolution, and it became a symbol of China's rebellious and revolutionary youth.

The influence of this publication was tremendous. Mao's formal writing was too difficult for ordinary peasants and workers to read, and this quotation book quickly became a useful literacy reader. It also provided a simplified version of Mao's basic ideas and served as a central tool for the widespread political indoctrination of Communist ideology. The little red book socialized an entire generation of Chinese, and some of its passages remain in use today. Nevertheless, the Chinese Communist Party later denounced the book, and blamed it for its harmful effect on the holistic understanding of Mao's thought.

The downfall of Lin Biao and the end of the Cultural Revolution brought an abrupt end to the worship of Mao and his quotation book. In recent years, the little red book has become a popular collectable item. But as a political reader, it has lost its old status.

SEE ALSO *Communism; Mao Zedong; Maoism*

BIBLIOGRAPHY

Fang, Houshu. 1966. Dangdai zhongguo chubanshi shang teshu de yiye (A Special Page in the History of Chinese Printing). http://news.xinhuanet.com/book/2004-07/13/content_1595006.htm.

MacFarquhar, Roderick, ed. 1993. *The Politics of China: 1949–1989.* New York: Cambridge University Press.

Baogang Guo

LITTLE ROCK NINE

SEE *Civil Rights, Cold War.*

LIVERPOOL SLAVE TRADE

In 1740 Thomas Augustine Arne set the words of James Thompson's poem "Rule Britannia" to music. This poem emphasized how Britain was a "Blest Isle" of liberty and that "Britons never will be slaves." Yet at the same time Britain was one of the major suppliers of Africans to the Americas as a slave labor force. In the course of the eighteenth century British ships forcibly transported an esti-

mated 2.5 million individuals from Africa. This accounted for 40 percent of an estimated six million Africans carried by ships of all nations.

LIVERPOOL'S ROLE IN THE TRADE

By the 1740s Liverpool had emerged as Britain's leading slave port, eclipsing London and Bristol, its nearest rivals. Rawley and Behrendt point out in *The Transatlantic Slave Trade* (2005) that the "adroitness of the Liverpool merchant community" was one of a number of factors accounting for Liverpool's rise to prominence (p. 167). The sailing of the *Blessing* and the *Liverpool Merchant* in 1700 marked Liverpool's entry into the trade. Over the next century approximately 5,300 slave ships sailed from Liverpool, accounting for almost one-half of 11,000 British slave ship clearances. By the end of the century Liverpool's dominance was still more pronounced, as three-quarters of all British slaving ventures cleared from Liverpool. Behrendt (1991) points out that approximately 779 slave ship captains were active in Liverpool between 1785 and the abolition of the trade in 1807. Many were migrants from Scotland and the Isle of Man, attracted by career opportunities in the trade.

Liverpool vessels traded for slaves at a wide variety of locations on the West African coast, although the Bight of Biafra developed as a particularly important source of supply from the second quarter of the eighteenth century. John Dawson and William Boats, two of Liverpool's leading slave merchants, controlled a significant share of the market at Bonny in the Bight of Biafra in the late eighteenth century. Captains trading at Bonny had to be skilled in negotiating with African merchants for the supply of slaves. They were often assisted in this trade by surgeons who carefully inspected the men, women, and children brought from the interior by African merchants.

CONTEMPORARY ATTITUDES AND ASSUMPTIONS

Copious business records were generated by British merchants who regarded the shipping of enslaved Africans as "morally indistinguishable from shipping textiles, wheat, or even sugar" (Eltis et al. 1999, p. 1). In contrast, few detailed personal accounts of captains engaged in the British slave trade have survived. Three examples are available for eighteenth-century Liverpool: Hugh Crow, James Irving, and John Newton. The best known is undoubtedly Newton, an evangelical clergyman who composed the hymn "Amazing Grace" in 1772. In his *Thoughts upon the African Slave Trade*, published in 1788, Newton bitterly regretted his former career as a slave captain. He explained that when he commanded the *Duke of Argyle* and the *African* between 1750 and 1752 he had no idea that the trade was wrong. He stated that "I never had a scruple upon this head at the time. ... What I did I did ignorantly; considering it as the line of life which Divine Providence had allotted me" (Martin and Spurrell 1962, pp. 98–99).

His profound guilt and contrition are unlikely to be typical of other men engaged in the trade. Crow probably provides a more typical example of how slave traders reacted to abolitionist debate. Reflecting on his slave trading career in Liverpool between 1790 and 1807, Crow asserted that "it has always been my decided opinion that the traffic in negroes is permitted by that Providence that rules over all, as a necessary evil" (Crow 1830, pp. 132–133).

As the letters and journals of James Irving, a Scottish surgeon and captain, were not intended for publication, they provide a more accurate insight into the cultural assumptions and mind-set of a practitioner in the trade. On his third slaving venture, Irving wrote to his wife from New Calabar (Bight of Biafra) in August 1786 and informed her that trade was slow. He estimated that the process of bartering for slaves would take nine or ten weeks. After completing the Middle Passage from Africa to the West Indies, Irving wrote to his wife in December 1786 and informed her that they were awaiting the sale of their "very disagreeable cargo." He ended this long conversational letter abruptly, and pointed out that "I think I'll desist [writing] as our black cattle are intolerably noisy and I'm almost melted in the midst of five or six hundred of them" (Schwarz 1995, pp. 112–113). Irving's description of the 526 Africans confined in the stifling heat of the ship's hold as "black cattle" sheds light on the brutal inhumanity of the slave trade. Irving failed to recognize the humanity of the Africans and viewed them as inferior and eligible for enslavement.

After five voyages as a surgeon, Irving was promoted to his first command. Three weeks after sailing from Liverpool on May 3, 1789, the *Anna* was shipwrecked on the Atlantic coast of Morocco. Irving and his crew were captured and enslaved and spent fourteen months in captivity. Redeemed through the efforts of British consular officials, Irving remained completely blind to the irony of his situation and within a month of returning to Liverpool had agreed to command another slave ship. Irving had no compunction about returning to his former occupation of enslaving Africans, and his captivity prompted no reflection on the morality of the trade. Despite his personal experience as a chattel slave, he recognized no similarities with the transatlantic slave trade principally because he did not accept that Africans were fellow humans. Irving died during this second captaincy of the *Ellen* on December 24, 1791. His correspondence indicates how older attitudes sustaining the trade were deeply entrenched, and that a slave trader who valued his own freedom had no qualms about depriving Africans of their liberty.

Historical controversy continues to center on the extent to which Liverpool's rapid growth in the eighteenth century was linked primarily to the wealth generated by the slave trade. The complex and enduring legacies of the transatlantic slave trade were explored in an exhibition opened at the Merseyside Maritime Museum in Liverpool in 1994. This gallery, entitled "Transatlantic Slavery: Against Human Dignity," was groundbreaking as it was the first permanent exhibition of its kind in the world. The new International Slavery Museum opening in Liverpool in August 2007 will considerably extend the scope of the original exhibition.

SEE ALSO *Freedom; Insurance Industry; Liberty; Shipping Industry; Slave Trade; Slave-Gun Cycle; Slavery; Slavery Industry*

BIBLIOGRAPHY

Behrendt, Stephen D. 1991. The Captains in the British Slave Trade from 1785 to 1807. *Transactions of the Historic Society of Lancashire and Cheshire* 140: 79–140.

Crow, Hugh, 1830. *Memoirs of the Late Captain Hugh Crow of Liverpool.* London: Frank Cass, 1970.

Eltis, David, Stephen D. Behrendt, David Richardson, and Herbert S. Klein, 1999. *The Trans-Atlantic Slave Trade: A Database on CD-Rom.* Cambridge, U.K.: Cambridge University Press.

Martin, Bernard, and Mark Spurrell, eds. 1962. *The Journal of a Slave Trader (John Newton) 1750–1754.* London: The Epworth Press.

Rawley, James A., with Stephen D. Behrendt, 2005. *The Transatlantic Slave Trade: A History.* Rev. ed. Lincoln and London: University of Nebraska Press.

Schwarz, Suzanne, ed. 1995. *Slave Captain: The Career of James Irving in the Liverpool Slave Trade.* Wrexham, U.K.: Bridge Books.

Tibbles, Anthony J., ed. 2005. *Transatlantic Slavery: Against Human Dignity.* Liverpool, U.K.: Liverpool University Press.

Suzanne Schwarz

LOAN PULLING

SEE *Loan Pushing.*

LOAN PUSHING

One of the international social interactions that occurs between countries is lending by banks of one country (the *creditor*) to individuals or the government of a different country (*the debtor*). *Loan pushing* refers to the attempt of a creditor with market power to sell a higher volume of credit at a higher rate of interest to a debtor than the creditor would if it lacked market power. The creditor's market power may stem from a low number of credit suppliers or from the formation of a consortium or syndicate of creditors, such as a consortium of four hundred international banks negotiating with a single country. *Loan pulling*, in contrast, is the effort of a debtor to gain more credit if it is not faced with loan pushing but rather with *credit rationing*, which means that the debtor does not get as much credit as it would like at a given interest rate. If the debtor has no market power, it will not get more credit than the rationing creditor wants to give it.

Jonathan Eaton and Mark Gersovitz (1981) show that many countries, but by far not all countries, are credit rationed. William Darity (1986), Barry Eichengreen (1989), and Kaushik Basu (1991) have collected anecdotal evidence for loan pushing. Articles by Thomas Ziesemer (1997) and Ashwini Deshpande (1999) describe loan pushing and related forms of excessive lending.

THEORY

A theoretical model for loan pushing is presented in Figure 1. Imagine that a bank consortium uniting all banks and thereby constituting a monopoly is the supplier of credit and a country is the debtor. The debtor would like to incur debt L for any given interest rate i as indicated by the curve DD'. All combinations of interest, i, and credit volume, L, along the line DU_0 are considered to be as good as getting no credit. The monopolist creditor gets the amount of

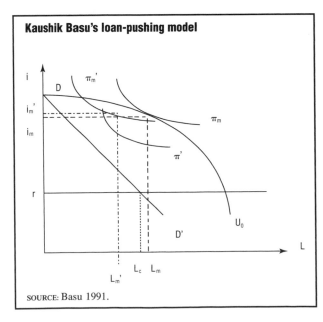

Kaushik Basu's loan-pushing model

Figure 1

money to be lent, L, from the world market at interest cost rL. The monopolist obtains interest revenue iL and assumes it will get the money back.

The monopolist now can choose between two types of behavior. It can either be customer friendly, offering a contract on the curve DD', or it can look at its profits and try to maximize them. In the latter case, the monopolist creditor will recognize that curves such as π' (or π_m) represent combinations of interest rates and credit volumes that have equally large profits and therefore are called *isoprofit lines*. But a curve with higher interest and credit volume represents higher profits. The monopolist knows that the debtor will not accept a contract with interest and credit volume making the debtor worse off than getting no credit; the debtor therefore will reject offers represented by points to the upper right of DU_0. The highest profit the creditor can get is therefore a combination such as (L_m, i_m). The monopolist can achieve this by telling the customer "either you take this or you get no credit at all." This is called a *take-it-or-leave-it offer*. The debtor accepts because it is slightly better off with the contract than without it.

Of course, this scenario works only if there is no competitor offering a better contract to the debtor and only if the monopolist creditor really is a monopolist. Compared to a situation without monopoly power, where the debtor can get L_c at interest rate r, the interest rate is higher and the credit volume is larger, as stated in the definition of *loan pushing* above. Therefore, (L_m, i_m) is also called the *loan-pushing equilibrium*, and (L_c, r) is called the *competitive equilibrium*.

Now, eliminate the assumption that the creditor is sure to receive its money back with interest. Instead, the creditor may expect *sovereign risk*—a political problem caused by governments that wish to protect debtors who refuse to pay (repudiation)—and expect to get only some payment, which increases with the money lent, say $b(L)$. This scenario is illustrated in Figure 2. The creditor would want to make sure that it does not lend more than it can get back. If the creditor can impose a punishment $b(L)$ on the repudiating debtor, the creditor would prefer to limit the credit such that the punishment is as large as the money to be paid, $b(L) = (1 + i)L$, or, $i = b(L)/L - 1$. The profit $(i - r)L$, after insertion of this constraint with equality is, $b(L) - (1 + r)L$. Its maximum now is where the $b(L)$ curve in Figure 2 has the maximum distance from the $(1 + r)L$ curve, at L_r. If the debtor wants less credit, there is no problem; but if the debtor wants more credit, it will not be offered and the debtor is called to be rationed at L_r.

UNDERSTANDING THE 1982 DEBT CRISIS

An essential feature of the debt crisis in the beginning of the 1980s was the sharp rise in the world market interest

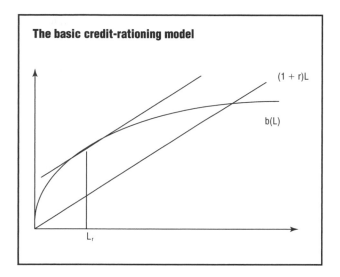

The basic credit-rationing model

Figure 2.

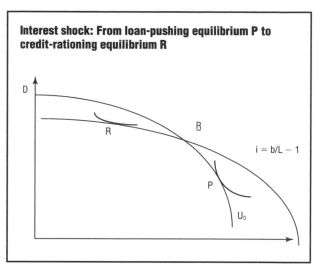

Interest shock: From loan-pushing equilibrium P to credit-rationing equilibrium R

Figure 3.

rate *r*. If credit markets were competitive, as at the equilibrium (r, L_c) in Figure 1, the horizontal line would shift up and L_c would fall. Similarly, if the economy is and remains in a loan-pushing equilibrium, it moves along the reservation-utility line DU_0 to the upper left, resulting in (L_m', i_m') with higher interest rates i_m and a lower credit volume, as isoprofit lines can be shown to flatten for a higher world interest rate *r* and moving from π^* to $\pi^{*'}$.

If the country is and remains in the credit-rationing regime shown in Figure 2, the line $(1 + r)L$ becomes steeper when *r* rises, and therefore the profit maximizing point moves to lower credit volumes. However, whereas the evidence described above indicated that there was loan pushing before the 1982 crisis, the evidence after the crisis was that the balance of trade in goods and services had shifted to positive values and credit was limited to ensure that interest could be paid. Basu (1991) suggested that this would indicate that there was a shift from loan pushing to credit rationing. Ziesemer (1997) showed that this is possible if, in terms of Figure 3: (1) the credit-rationing function, $i = b(L)/L - 1$, intersects with the DU_0-line; (2) the former is flatter than the latter; (3) the initial equilibrium is the loan-pushing equilibrium *P*; and (4) the increase in the world market interest rate is large enough to come to a credit-rationing equilibrium *R* rather than to an equilibrium between *P* and the intersection point *R̄*. A flat function $b(L)/L$ means that the punishment function must have a slope that is not decreasing too strongly with the credit volume *L*. The crucial point then is that, for some countries, credit rationing does not prevent crises but occurs upon an interest shock in order to avoid high losses from sovereign risk after the crisis, which was preceded by loan pushing.

BEYOND THE MODEL

Why is it profit-maximizing to push rather than to ration? There are several answers to this question. First, banks make the salaries of sales agents dependent on profits, $(i - r)L$. Selling more and at higher interest rates maximizes agents' salaries (Darity 1986).

Second, third parties, such as a firm selling machines to a debtor country paid by the credit money, *L*, and being a client of the bank(s), may play a role. For example, the client may be a current bad risk that the bank can get rid of by giving the credit, which is used to increase the revenue when the machines are sold. The bank may now substitute a current risk of the firm by a future risk from the debtor country. Or, more generally, the firm has higher revenue and deposits more money in the bank, thus enhancing expected bank profit. Deshpande (1999) extends the loan-pushing part of Basu's (1991) model to include a third party and a more general cost function. Deshpande also provides anecdotal evidence and discusses the role of large and small banks in a syndicate.

Third, illegal activity may occur. For example, a bank manager may own shares of the firm, which increase in value if the firm can sell machines to the debtor country. A gain for the manager is exchanged for a risk for the bank. Fourth, economies of scale and scope of the bank may be valued higher than the new risk from the debtor country, especially if the latter is perceived to be low.

BIBLIOGRAPHY

Basu, Kaushik. 1991. *The International Debt Problem, Credit Rationing, and Loan Pushing: Theory and Evidence.* Princeton, NJ: Princeton University Press.

Darity, William, Jr. 1986. Did the Commercial Banks Push Loans on the LDCs? In *World Debt Crisis: International Lending on Trial*, ed. Michael P. Claudon, 199–225. Cambridge, MA: Ballinger.

Deshpande, Ashwini. 1999. Loan Pushing and Triadic Relations. *Southern Economic Journal* 65 (4): 914–926.

Eaton, Jonathan, and Mark Gersovitz. 1981. Debt With Potential Repudiation: Theoretical and Empirical Analysis. *Review of Economic Studies* 48 (2): 289–309.

Eichengreen, Barry. 1989. The U.S. Capital Market and Foreign Lending, 1920–1955. In *Developing Country Debt and Economic Performance*. Vol. 1: *The International Financial System*, ed. Jeffrey Sachs, 107–155. Chicago: University of Chicago Press.

Ziesemer, Thomas. 1997. From Loan Pushing to Credit Rationing: A Brief Note on Interest Shocks in a Model by Basu. *Journal of Institutional and Theoretical Economics* 153 (3): 569–578.

Thomas Ziesemer

LOANS

A loan is a type of debt. In general, a loan refers to anything given on the condition of its return or the repayment of its equivalent. All material things can be lent, but the most common type of loan is the monetary loan. Like all debt instruments, a loan implies the redistribution of financial assets over time between the lender and the borrower.

In a monetary loan, the borrower initially receives an amount of money from the lender, which he pays back, usually in regular installments. This service is generally provided at a cost, referred to as interest on the debt. The provision of loans is one of the principal tasks of financial institutions. A loan also may be acknowledged by a bond, a promissory note, or a mere oral promise to repay.

The concept of loans dates back to the very old ages of the agricultural era, when people had started living in organized societies. However, it developed and became widespread with the use of money. Because of biblical injunctions against usury, the early Christian church forbade the taking of interest. In feudal European society, loans were little needed by the great mass of relatively self-sufficient and noncommercial farmers and serfs, but kings, nobles, and members of the church community borrowed heavily for personal expenditures. The role of the moneylender was undertaken back then by merchants and other townsmen, especially the Jews, while various devices were found for circumventing the prohibition of usury.

The development of money lending among the Jews as their almost exclusive occupation began in the twelfth century, and it was probably the consequence of the persecutions during the First Crusade; Jews at this time could not own land or vineyards, so money lending was one of the few occupations open to the Jews as a means of livelihood. In addition, the Catholic Church's prohibition against money lending for Christians provided Jews with a unique opportunity to step into this void in establishing themselves as bankers. The laws regarding pawn-broking also became increasingly more detailed. During the Middle Ages, local rulers prohibited Jews from occupying most professions, so they were pushed into marginal occupations that were considered socially inferior, such as money lending.

Historically, attacks on usury have often been connected with anti-Semitism. Moreover, Judaism has been a more lenient religion with respect to lending than other religions. The Torah and later sections of the Hebrew Bible criticize the taking of interest, but interpretations of the biblical prohibition vary. One common interpretation is that Jews are forbidden to charge interest upon loans made to other Jews but allowed to charge interest on transactions with non-Jews. However, the Hebrew Bible itself gives numerous examples where this prohibition was evaded. Moreover, legislation concerning the Jews recognized the rabbinical law. According to the latter, for instance, a Jew who had advanced money on a stolen article was entitled to recover the amount he had loaned for it, including interest, if he could swear that he did not know it had been stolen.

By contrast, many religions prohibit the charge of interest. The most prominent example is that of Islam. Sharia, the Islamic law, does not allow the collection and payment of interest (*riba*). However, as Maxime Robinson demonstrates in his book *Islam and Capitalism* (1974), even the Islamic prohibition of usury and other kinds of transactions was no barrier to the continuation and elaboration of pre-Islamic capitalistic practices. The Koranic revelation, therefore, did not bring into being an exemplary moral economic system that was fundamentally different from any other existing economic system. Thus, Islamic prohibitions on usury were circumvented with the establishment of Islamic banks. Islamic banks have the same purpose as conventional banks but are believed to obey the rules of Sharia. Islamic banking is based on the sharing of profit and loss and the prohibition of interest. According to a common practice used to lend money for a purchase, a bank might buy the item itself from the seller and resell it to the buyer at a profit while allowing the buyer to pay for it in installments. To protect themselves against default, Islamic banks retain ownership of the item until the loan is paid.

The United States has an old tradition of lending. Americans have long relied on credit, which, for day-today matters, typically took the form of charge accounts with local retailers. In the early years of the United States, when it was primarily an agrarian society, income for many people rested upon when the crops were harvested and sold. Credit and charge accounts, rather than the more structured repayment of an installment purchase, were more individual in nature, relying heavily on the personal relationship between the consumer and the retailer. Credit cards and other more modern and impersonal means of credit and charge-account purchasing became a fixture in the consumer-retailer relationship in the 1950s. However, even today the traditional, more personal and informal types of charge accounts do exist. Without extending some sort of credit to customers, many businesses in the past simply would not have been able to operate. Today's modern means, the credit card, has greatly reduced the degree to which individual retailers personally extend credit to consumers. However, credit itself remains as essential to the retail economy as it has ever been.

The history of formal lending in the United States is also deeply related to the rise of homeownership in the lower socioeconomic classes. Formal lending, in terms of institutional lending, has long been the means by which many have been able to buy their own home. Before institutionalized lending that was accessible to those who were not wealthy, people relied on private loans or small, regional networks serving a particular ethnic or professional group. These types of lending situations, however, did not nurture and support homeownership in the same ways, or for as great a percentage of people, as does formal or institutional lending today.

The early types of formal mortgages were extended by insurance companies. The terms of these mortgages, however, were often quite risky for the borrower, with the balance of power distinctly tipped toward the lender in ways that would be deemed unfair and even predatory by today's standards. Savings and loan associations also evolved, although they remained separate from traditional banks, which could offer checking accounts and other services, until the 1970s, when banking regulations changed. Once those regulations changed, savings and loan associations became almost indistinguishable from the typical bank of today, but their loan practices became the universal standard among many of today's financial institutions. The practices have been revised continuously through the years by regulations meant to ensure that minorities and women were able to have equal access to fair lending.

Today, banks and finance companies usually extend loans against collateral, such as stocks, personal effects, and mortgages on land and other property. Credit activity is considered to be strongly correlated with consumption, and it is expanding due to the gradually decreasing savings rates of typical households. Financial institutions are the ones responsible for extending loans, and they make a large share of their profits out of this activity. The low penetration of loans to an economy, as is the case in the developing countries of central and southeastern Europe, attracts many foreign direct investments in those countries.

Bank loans and credit are considered to be one way to increase the money supply. Policymakers, such as many central bankers, take into account credit growth developments in their decisions about interest-rate movements. Another aspect of the internationalization of loans is the ability of the participants of economic activity—governments, companies, and households—to borrow from abroad under better terms and conditions.

Apart from those who have access to financial markets, the establishment of organizations such as the International Monetary Fund and the World Bank allow the provision of loans to countries experiencing economic problems. This financial assistance enables countries to encounter economic difficulties, reconstruct, and restore conditions for economic growth. Moreover, Muhammad Yunus of Bangladesh, who was awarded the Nobel Peace Prize for providing, through his Grameen Bank, small loans known as micro-credit to poor people without any collateral showed that loans can be accessible and provide support even to those who have no financial security.

SEE ALSO *Banking; Banking Industry; Discounted Present Value; Equity Markets; Financial Instability Hypothesis; Financial Markets; Hedging; Leverage; Liquidity Premium; Microfinance; National Debt; ROSCAs*

BIBLIOGRAPHY

International Monetary Fund. 2006. IMF Lending. International Monetary Fund, September. http://www.imf.org/external/np/exr/facts/howlend.htm.

Robinson, Maxime. 1974. *Islam and Capitalism.* Trans. Brian Pearce. New York: Pantheon Books.

Secor, Sharon. 2004–2006a. A Brief History of Formal Lending in the United States. Direct Lending Solutions. http://www.directlendingsolutions.com/history_of_lending .htm.

Secor, Sharon. 2004–2006b. *Credit History: Before There Was Plastic … The Earliest Charge Accounts.* Direct Lending Solutions. http://www.directlendingsolutions.com/history_of_credit .htm.

Tran, Mark. 2006. Pioneering Economist Wins Nobel Prize. *Guardian Unlimited,* October 13. http://business.guardian.co.uk/story/0,,1921726,00.html.

Eleni Simintzi

LOBBYING

Lobbying is the process by which an organized interest communicates its concerns and preferences to governmental policy makers in order to influence a policy decision. Lobbyists are the individuals who directly attempt to persuade policy makers to take a particular action. They may be full-time employees of a corporation or an interest group, but are often contract lobbyists hired by an interest group. Additionally, governmental employees act as legislative liaisons for their agencies and at the state level a small percentage of lobbyists are volunteers. Regardless of the extent to which lobbying persuades policy makers, a topic debated by scholars, lobbying serves instrumentally at several stages of policy making. Therefore, understanding the process of lobbying complements knowledge of how policy is made.

HISTORY

The first use of the term *lobby* seems to have been in the mid-seventeenth century when the large anteroom near the English House of Commons floor became known as the lobby. It was a public room in which members of Parliament could be easily approached by individuals seeking favors, called lobby agents. In the early 1800s in the United States those who petitioned government officials in lobbies or common areas were called lobbiers and later lobbyists. This label transferred to their petitioning activity, termed lobbying. Members of Congress did not have private offices until after 1900 so influence seekers commonly buttonholed them in the rotunda of the U.S. Capitol. Similarly, state legislators could be easily waylaid in the halls and anterooms of their capitol buildings as private offices did not appear in some states until the mid-1970s.

FORMS OF LOBBYING AND THEIR ROLES

In the United States, lobbying plays a role in all three branches of government, though legislative lobbying gains the most attention in scholarship and in the media. In Congressional and state legislatures, lobbyists provide drafts of bills to sympathetic members who introduce them, given the need to show policy entrepreneurship and in order to lower the cost of bill preparation by staff. Later, in the committee stage, lobbyists focus mostly on rallying their base rather than persuasion. They typically contact two kinds of legislators: those who are sympathetic ideologically to their client and those who represent a constituency in which their company or group has a strong presence. Similarly, on a floor vote, lobbyists again focus mostly on their base, but if necessary they try to persuade fence-sitting legislators to gain sufficient support for the bill's passage.

Lobbyists provide technical expertise about the issue and expected effects of the policy as well as political intelligence about the electoral consequences of a member's vote. The most important means of presenting information are testimony at committee hearings and contacting legislators directly, tactics used by 95 percent of Washington lobbyists. Lobbyists can more easily contact legislators if they represent an organized interest whose members constitute a significant portion of the legislator's constituency. Mobilizing a group's members to contact a legislator, known as grassroots lobbying, has become an important tool in politics. Lobbyists often control another resource—money—in the form of Political Action Committee (PAC) campaign contributions, which may help secure access to legislators and, some allege, influence floor votes. Political scientists caution that many forces besides money influence a congressperson's vote, and detecting money's direct impact on voting has been limited.

Lobbying also extends to the federal executive branch and the U.S. court system. Starting with the presidency, since 1974 the Office of Public Liaison has served as the White House's primary means of interaction with organized interests. Interests gain access to prominent officials, and the White House receives information and lobbying support from organized interests. It is not always clear what the interests gain from this approach. More transparently, interests lobby bureaucrats in the regulatory process. Whenever Congress enacts legislation, an agency must write rules for implementation, a process open to public comments and hearings, in which lobbyists regularly participate. Agencies pay attention to comments because regulations can be legally challenged for a variety of reasons.

Indeed, legal challenges and influencing the courts are also part of the domain of lobbying; however, lobbyists cannot directly contact judges about rulings, so in this approach organized interests use indirect lobbying techniques. The first technique is lobbying during judicial selection. At the federal level lobbyists simply encourage senators to vote for the confirmation of judicial nominees favorable to their group's concerns, while in the thirty-eight states where judges stand for election, interest groups get more directly involved in campaigning. A second means is actual litigation either through an organization's defending itself or sponsoring a test case. A final means of influencing courts is by submitting *amicus curiae* briefs on cases with which the organized interest is not involved as a litigant, yet has a policy interest. These briefs advance legal and social arguments that may not be raised by the litigants. When seemingly technical rule-making by bureaucrats or rulings by courts affect policies of interest to their clients, lobbyists attempt to influence these decisions.

REGULATION

In regulating lobbying by organized interests, the primary focus at both the federal and state levels has been on registration and public visibility, rather than restricting activity. Lobbying is protected by the First Amendment, which guarantees the right "to petition the Government for a redress of grievances." The Federal Regulation of Lobbying Act of 1946 was the first law to require lobbyists at the national level to register, but court rulings substantially narrowed the range of groups that had to register. The Lobby Disclosure Act of 1995 established a meaningful registration requirement for nearly all organizations engaged in direct lobbying. In 2005 36,689 individuals lobbied Congress, according to PoliticalMoneyLine, an independent campaign finance Web site. States began oversight of lobbying in the 1960s, primarily by requiring lobbyist registration and disclosure of expenditures. In the 1990s many states tightened their rules, often imposing gift bans, so that in the early 2000s state laws are substantially more stringent than federal law. The Center for Public Integrity reported that 47,000 organized interests were registered to lobby in state capitals in 2004, employing more than 38,000 individual lobbyists.

SEE ALSO *Interest Groups and Interests; Pressure Groups*

BIBLIOGRAPHY

Federal Lobby Directory. PoliticalMoneyLine. http://www. fecinfo.com.

Gordon, Neil. 2005. State Lobbyists near the $1 Billion Mark. Center for Public Integrity. http://www.publicintegrity.org.

Lowery, David, and Holly Brasher. 2004. *Organized Interests and American Government.* New York: McGraw-Hill.

Safire, William. 1993. *Safire's New Political Dictionary.* New York: Random House.

Virginia Gray

LOBOTOMY

Lobotomy describes a class of psychosurgical techniques that involve the cutting of nerve fibers in the prefrontal area of the brain with the intent to calm severely disturbed psychiatric patients. These procedures are designed to disrupt the limbic system, the area of the brain most closely associated with regulating emotion.

António Egas Moniz (1874–1955), a Portuguese neurologist, is credited as initiating the widespread use of psychosurgery. In 1935 Moniz attended a presentation by psychologist Carlyle Jacobsen at the Second International Neurological conference in London. Jacobsen noted that destruction of the prefrontal area in monkeys eliminated "experimental neurosis," a pattern of frustrated behavior in response to errors when monkeys were given problem-solving tasks. Moniz questioned Jacobsen as to whether similar procedures could be used in humans to eliminate anxiety. Moniz and his colleague Almeida Lima initially treated psychiatric patients by using alcohol injections to destroy parts of the frontal lobes. By the end of 1935 Moniz and Lima were performing prefrontal leucotomy, a technique that involved cutting open the skull and severing nerve connections using a surgical instrument with a wire loop on the end called a leucotome.

In 1936 Moniz published encouraging results from twenty patients. Of these Moniz reported fourteen were either cured or showed improvement. Interest in lobotomy and for other dramatic procedures like insulin-induced coma and electroconvulsive therapy grew rapidly in response to the social pressures of a growing number of psychiatric patients in state hospitals during the 1930s and 1940s. Available treatments prior to the rise of psychosurgical techniques consisted primarily of the use of heavy sedatives, such as opiates or barbiturates. Psychoanalysis was growing in popularity but was impractical for widespread use in hospital settings especially among patients with severe disorders, such as those with schizophrenia. In recognition of his contribution to medicine, Moniz was awarded the Nobel Prize in 1949.

Lobotomy's greatest promoter was Walter Freeman, a U.S. neuropsychiatrist. Freeman corresponded with Moniz and closely followed the reports of his work. Freeman and neurologist James Watts established a practice and began performing their first lobotomies in 1936. Although Watts was trained as a surgeon while Freeman was not, the two often performed the operation together. After performing several surgeries using Moniz's technique, Freeman and Watts developed a technique that involved drilling burr holes in both sides of the skull to be used as landmarks for making more precise cuts. Their procedure became known as the standard Freeman-Watts lobotomy. Freeman and Watts published *Psychosurgery* in 1942, which included reports about their patients, descriptions of the procedure, and theoretical explanations.

Freeman became discontent with inconsistent results of standard prefrontal lobotomy—particularly among schizophrenic patients who he felt were less benefited the longer their disorder progressed without psychosurgery. In 1946 Freeman performed the first transorbital lobotomy. Nonsurgical professionals could perform this procedure within a few minutes without anesthesia often during an office visit. The transorbital lobotomy involved inserting a sharp instrument resembling an ice pick through connective tissue between the eye and the orbital bones, and then thrusting the instrument upward to sever neural connections. After years together Watts split with Freeman over Freeman's characterization of transorbital lobotomy as a minor operation and eager use of the procedure. Freeman went on to perform or supervise approximately 3,500 transorbital lobotomies and train many others to perform them in a tour of state hospitals to popularize the procedure.

The use of lobotomy declined rapidly with the advent of drug treatments in the mid-1950s such as chlorpromazine to treat schizophrenia. Introduction of viable alternatives strengthened support for lobotomy's critics. Critics included Nolan Lewis, director of New York State Psychiatric Institute, who spoke at a psychiatric symposium in 1949 that included Freeman and Watts and challenged the validity of evidence in favor of lobotomy. Lewis claimed widespread underreporting of unsuccessful surgeries. He also questioned whether quieting the patient was really a cure or more a convenience to psychiatric caregivers. Patients were often described after surgery as emotionless zombies, impulsive, or lacking initiative. In a published critique in 1949, Jay Hoffman, chief of the Veteran's Administration's Neuropsychiatric Service, noted that results were typically deemed successful as long as patients showed improvement over their condition during hospitalization, but that family members were often unhappy with the results, as patients did not return to their prediagnosis, normal selves (Hoffman 1949).

Although technical improvements in psychosurgery allow more precise destruction of specific cells or neural circuits, ethical questions surrounding the irreversibility of these procedures have led to legal restrictions limiting psychosurgery to a treatment of last resort.

SEE ALSO *Ethics in Experimentation; Medicine; Neuroscience*

BIBLIOGRAPHY

Hoffman, Jay L. 1949. Clinical Observations Concerning Schizophrenic Patients Treated by Prefrontal Leukotomy. *New England Journal of Medicine* 241: 233–236.

Valenstein, Elliot S. 1973. *Brain Control: A Critical Examination of Brain Stimulation and Psychosurgery.* New York: Wiley.

Valenstein, Elliot S. 1980. *The Psychosurgery Debate: Scientific, Legal, and Ethical Perspectives.* San Francisco: W. H. Freeman.

Valenstein, Elliot S. 1986. *Great and Desperate Cures: The Rise and Decline of Psychosurgery and Other Radical Treatments for Mental Illness.* New York: Basic Books.

Craig C. Jackson

LOCATION THEORY

SEE *Spatial Theory.*

LOCKE, JOHN
1632–1704

John Locke was an English philosopher who is often seen as the founder of liberalism and a major source of inspiration for the American founding. Born into a Parliamentarian family near Bristol, Locke attended the prestigious Westminster school in London and then Christ Church College at Oxford. In 1666 he became a friend and secretary of Anthony Ashley Cooper (1621–1683), later the first earl of Shaftesbury, a prominent Whig politician. After the arrest of Shaftesbury and a number of other Whigs for their opposition to royalism and Catholicism, Locke fled to Holland in 1683, returning to England only after the Glorious Revolution of 1688 expelled James II (1633–1701) and installed William of Orange (1650–1702) on the throne. While he had been working on what were to become his major writings for several decades, it was not until this time that they were published: *A Letter Concerning Toleration*, which advocated religious toleration and a separation of church and state, the *Two Treatises of Government*, which argued for limited government and private property, and *An Essay Concerning Human Understanding*, which advanced an empiricist view of human knowledge, were all published in 1689. While the former two works appeared anonymously, the latter was published under Locke's name and quickly made him famous. Other important works of his later life included *Some Thoughts Concerning Education* (1693) and *The Reasonableness of Christianity* (1695). By the time he died in 1704, Locke had become one of the most prominent and influential philosophers of his time.

The second of Locke's *Two Treatises of Government* is often regarded as the founding text of liberalism. In this work, he posits that there is no natural or divine source of legitimate political power and thus that government must be based on consent. In the "state of nature" that exists when there is no political authority, he claims, the law of nature (which obliges people not to harm others) tends to be inadequately obeyed and enforced, and so people agree to create a government through a social contract. The purpose of the contract and hence of government is to protect people's lives, liberties, and property, and to achieve this end Locke advocates a limited government with institutional safeguards such as separate legislative and executive branches, common judges, and standing laws that apply equally to everyone. Locke puts a special emphasis on the protection of property rights, as he claims this will encourage people to be industrious and thus to increase productivity and raise the society's standard of living. While people are understood to have tacitly consented to the government under which they live even if they were not a part of the original social contract, the people always remain supreme, and thus when the government violates its trust the people can and should exercise their right to revolution. With his arguments for natural rights, government by consent, constitutionalism, private property, and religious toleration, Locke is one of the major sources of the ideology of the American founding and indeed of the modern world.

SEE ALSO *Enlightenment; Hobbes, Thomas; Labor Theory of Value; Natural Rights; Property; Rousseau, Jean-Jacques; Social Contract; State of Nature*

BIBLIOGRAPHY

Dunn, John. 1969. *The Political Thought of John Locke: An Historical Account of the Argument of the "Two Treatises of Government."* Cambridge, U.K.: Cambridge University Press.

Grant, Ruth. 1987. *John Locke's Liberalism.* Chicago: University of Chicago Press.

Locke, John. [1689] 1988. *Two Treatises of Government.* Ed Peter Laslett. Cambridge, U.K.: Cambridge University Press.

Zuckert, Michael P. 2002. *Launching Liberalism: On Lockean Political Philosophy.* Lawrence: University Press of Kansas.

Dennis C. Rasmussen

LOCUS OF CONTROL

Locus of control was the brainchild of psychologist Julian Rotter, who based his concept on the social learning theory idea that the generalized expectancies of people govern their actions. Rotter assumed that people vary in the degree to which they perceive the things that are happening to them as being under their own internal control or under the control of outside forces. Using this latter locus of control dimension, at one end of the continuum are the internal individuals who see themselves as being "captains of their own ships," whereas at the other end of the continuum are the external persons who see themselves as being ruled by powerful people or outside forces. In more technical psychological terms, the internal loci of control people believe that through their own behaviors, they have command over the reinforcements in their lives; conversely the external loci of control people see the reinforcements in their lives as being driven by causal sources that are independent of their own actions.

HISTORY OF CONCEPT

Since the publication of the 1962 article "Internal Versus External Control of Reinforcement: A Major Variable in Behavior Therapy" by Julian Rotter, Melvin Seeman, and Shephard Liverant, there have been more published papers on this construct than perhaps any other new idea in all of psychology. At the start of the twenty-first century there were literally thousands of studies that focused on locus of control. This surge of interest regarding locus of control probably stemmed from the fact that it represented a logical step as the field of psychology moved beyond the previous strict tenets of stimulus-response behaviorism. On this point Rotter believed that to understand the actions of higher order organisms such as human beings, people's expectancies about their behaviors being reinforced needed to be taken into account. Thus he reasoned that people use their personal experiences to develop expectations as to whether they can or will be rewarded for their actions. Beyond the inherent appeal of these underlying social learning and generalized expectancies ideas, another reason for the explosion of interest probably was the fact that Rotter produced a short and valid self-report instrument for measuring locus of control. That is to say part of this tremendous growth reflected the availability of a valid instrument for use by researchers.

RESEARCH EVIDENCE

In 1966 Rotter published what has come to be called the Rotter IE Control Scale. It contained twenty-three items (plus six fillers), each with a paired option. For each item the respondent is asked to select which of two options is most true of him or her. Thus consider item #2 on the Rotter IE Control Scale, where the respondent is asked to select from the following two choices: option A, "Many of the unhappy things in people's lives are partly due to bad luck," or option B, "People's misfortunes result from the mistakes that they make." In this item #2 option A represents a response indicating an external locus of control, whereas option B represents an internal locus of control. The more of the external items that the person selects as being most applicable to him or her, the more external is that person's overall score.

The IE scale has been shown to be reliable and valid. Likewise factor analyses have revealed that the items fall into two clusters, with one factor pertaining to a sense of mastery and a second factor tapping the degree to which citizens perceive that they can play significant roles in political institutions.

Along with Rotter's IE scale, the following other adult indices related to locus of control have been introduced and validated: (1) the Nowicki-Duke Locus of Control Scale; (2) the Crandall, Katkovsky, and Crandall Intellectual Achievement Responsibility Questionnaire; and (3) the Wallston and Wallston Health Locus of Control Scale. Additionally indices such as the Nowicki-Strickland Locus of Control Scale for Children have been developed for use with children of various ages.

From the outset Rotter suggested that an external locus of control was implicated in neurotic maladjustment. In support of this general proposition persons with external as compared to internal loci of control have been shown to be more unhappy, depressed, and suicidal. Likewise those clients who do not improve over the temporal course of psychotherapy have loci of control scores that remain external, whereas those psychotherapy clients who improve over treatment have scores that have become more internal. Turning to achievement-related performances in school, external loci of control people repeatedly have done more poorly than internal loci learners. Furthermore studies consistently have shown that external more than internal loci of control people have disadvantages in physical health-related matters. Specifically compared to internals, the external loci of control persons have worse sleeping, exercise, and eating patterns, and they also are more prone to hypertension.

The counterproductive outcomes produced by external as compared to internal loci of control persons may relate to many externals' lack of belief in hard work, along with their unwillingness to expend high efforts. Also because externals believe that their lives are ruled by chance factors and/or powerful forces residing outside of themselves, they are quite passive and do not take protective measures when it comes to health matters (e.g., wearing seatbelts or sunscreen). They also tend not to be planful and future oriented because they do not see themselves as being capable of effective proactive behaviors. As such instead of taking a task-oriented "I can do something" approach to anticipate any stressors that they may encounter, external loci of control people are rather fatalistic about their coping skills in particular and their lives more generally. Moreover the externals relative to internals are not attentive to their surrounding environments, and they are not very knowledgeable about health-related matters. Accordingly the externals probably could not act in healthy ways even if they wanted to do so. Not surprisingly, therefore, externals greatly prefer avoidance behaviors rather than the problem-solving tactics used by internal loci of control people.

CRITIQUE OF LOCUS OF CONTROL THEORY

In spite of its huge influence in the field of psychology, the locus of control concept has been criticized. In one noteworthy critique, the 1995 publication *Judgments of Responsibility: A Foundation for a Theory of Social Conduct* by Bernard Weiner, the author reasoned that the concept of "locus of control" was misleading and, in fact, that locus and control should be considered as two distinct dimensions involving causality—locus (internal versus external) and control (controllable versus uncontrollable). On this point Weiner held that a person could have an internal locus, and yet believe that she or he either was or

was not in control; similarly people could hold external loci, and yet believe that they either were or were not in control. Thus, for example, efforts and ability are both internal in their loci, but effort is controllable and ability is uncontrollable. Weiner's important point, therefore, is that there actually are two independent dimensions of causality, and that the Rotter theory may be incorrect in assuming that an internal locus always means that the person also is in control, and that an external locus always means that the person is not in control.

IMPLICATIONS

Locus of control may have been the most prominent new construct to appear in the interface of social, clinical, personality, and health psychology in the last three decades of the twentieth century. Loci of control scale scores have produced many robust correlations with outcome markers pertaining to psychological disorders, psychotherapy, school achievements, and physical health. Perhaps most importantly the locus of control concept solidified the importance of human expectancies in governing how people cope. As such locus of control facilitated the transition of psychology from an earlier emphasis on stimulus-response behaviorism to the twenty-first-century emphasis on cognitive and mental factors. Moreover locus of control has contributed to other theories such as learned helplessness, attributional biases, self-efficacy, hope, and optimism.

SEE ALSO *Attribution; Hope; Learned Helplessness; Optimism/Pessimism; Psychotherapy; Rotter's Internal-External Locus of Control Scale; Validity, Statistical*

BIBLIOGRAPHY

Lefcourt, Herbert M., and Karina Davidson-Katz. 1991. Locus of Control and Health. In *Handbook of Social and Clinical Psychology: The Health Perspective*, eds. C. R. Snyder and Donelson R. Forsyth, 246–266. New York: Pergamon Press.

Rotter, Julian B. 1954. *Social Learning and Clinical Psychology*. New York: Prentice-Hall.

Rotter, Julian B. 1966. Generalized Expectancies for Internal Versus External Control of Reinforcement. *Psychological Monographs* 80 (Whole No. 609).

Rotter, Julian B., June E. Chance, and E. Jerry Phares. 1972. *Applications of a Social Learning Theory of Personality*. New York: Holt, Rinehart and Winston.

Rotter, Julian. B., Melvin Seeman, and Shephard Liverant. 1962. Internal Versus External Control of Reinforcement: A Major Variable in Behavior Therapy. In *Decisions, Values and Groups*, Vol. 2, ed. Norman F. Washburne, 473–516. New York: Pergamon Press.

Weiner, Bernard. 1995. *Judgments of Responsibility: A Foundation for a Theory of Social Conduct*. New York: Guilford Press.

C. R. Snyder

LOGIC

Logic is the study of persuasive reasoning. As such, it concerns arguments that successfully convey credibility from a set of premises to a conclusion. Given this broad definition, there are many possible avenues of discourse and logicians have studied everything from formal inference patterns, to the logic of causation, possibility and necessity, obligation, and inference to the best explanation. Nonetheless, formal deductive and inductive logic are the most historically significant branches of logic, even for the social sciences.

The discipline of logic evolved as a prominent branch of philosophy from the time of Aristotle and marks the first time in history that anyone began to systematize the forms of good reasoning. This systematization was of great benefit to philosophers as they attempted to know the universe of knowledge—covering both nature and human relations—on the basis of intuitive thought, rather than empirical analysis. As the sciences eventually pulled away from philosophy (first "natural philosophy" as it evolved into physics in about the seventeenth century, and then the social sciences arguably following in the eighteenth century, as they too learned that knowledge could be formulated on an empirical basis), it is only natural that they would develop their own methods of inquiry, separate from those of philosophers. Nonetheless, the special relationship of logic to the earliest forms of scientific analysis has survived to the twenty-first century, and has had great influence over the modes of inquiry in economics, history, sociology, anthropology, political science, and psychology, that make up the social sciences.

Logic is logic, whether it is applied to the social sciences, or any other field of inquiry. There is no special type of logic that is particularly suitable to the social sciences, just as there is not one for the natural sciences. The principles of valid reasoning are the same no matter what the subject, and are expressible in symbolic notation that is concerned only with the form, rather than the content, of what is uttered. To say "if I have a dollar then I have some money" is no different, logically, than to say, "If one is president of the United States then one is an American citizen." The form of this type of "if, then" statement ($P \Rightarrow Q$) is known as a "conditional," and, along with "not," "or," "and," and "if and only if" ($-, \vee, \&, \Leftrightarrow$), it forms the backbone of logical syntax. The idea that it is then possible to devise more complex statements using these connectives, to formulate premises and then to draw a conclusion, is to present the form of a "valid" argument in deductive logic, which is one where the conclusion follows *necessarily* from the premises. As long as the relationship between the premises and conclusion is a deductive one—which is to say that if the premises are true then the conclusion cannot help but be true—then the conclusion

follows inevitably from the premises, and does not require any sort of empirical data to support it.

> If it is raining then the streets will be wet.
> It is raining.
> _____
> Therefore, the streets will be wet.

This is, however, a long way from saying that such an argument is "sound" (that is, both valid and true) and it is here that the first limit of logic is reached in the social sciences, for as practitioners of an empirical discipline, social scientists are concerned to know whether an argument is sound (for instance whether its premises are true), and not just whether its form is valid. Therefore, we need to gather data in the world to assess this. No matter how powerful the principles of logic, in modern social scientific inquiry logic cannot provide the sole means for testing a theory, since logic is concerned not with truth, but with validity, yet the truth of a theory depends crucially on its conformity with actual experience. Pure logic can be done in an armchair, but science needs to go out into the world (if not for experiment, at least for observation).

In his or her search for causes, it is therefore incumbent upon social scientists to dig deeper into the subject, and find some way to assess whether a statement like "if one uses the death penalty then crime will drop" is true, and this is a tricky business, which deductive logic, at least, cannot adjudicate. However, there is another branch of logic that deals with "inductive" inferences that is much more conducive to empirical inquiry, and which some have felt represents the very type of reasoning that is used in science. In contrast to deduction—which deals with moving from general statements to the particular conclusions that follow from them—with induction one moves from particular statements to a general conclusion, somewhat as if one is gathering data points to see if they form a pattern. This resembles, at least ideally, the form of reasoning that a social scientist uses when he or she is searching for a general regularity. For example, if one were to argue that:

> Kennedy's tax cut in 1961 stimulated the economy
> Reagan's tax cut in 1981 stimulated the economy
> Bush's tax cut in 2003 stimulated the economy
> _____
> Therefore, tax cuts always (usually, generally) stimulate the economy

one is engaging in a form of reasoning that is familiar to social scientists, who seek to make causal explanations and to formulate general theories based on historical evidence. The problem, however, is that this form of reasoning is not valid, as has famously been shown by the Scottish philosopher David Hume. Specifically, the above argument has a hidden assumption (common to all inductive arguments), which is to think that there is a relevant similarity between the future and the past. But this assumption does not always hold. Moreover, even if this assumption is borne out in some cases, it is important to recognize that there is a distinction to be made between "causation" and "correlation" in the social sciences, such that, no matter how solid one's evidence may be, it is always possible that even the strongest correlation may represent only an accidental connection. Try as one might to obtain the sort of certainty that the "necessary connection" of deductive logic has provided, the social sciences have found this an elusive goal. This represents no particular flaw in the social sciences, for the natural sciences—or indeed any fact-based discipline—would also seem to suffer from this same difficulty.

Nonetheless, the social sciences have embraced the power of logic and have used it in various ways throughout their history to bolster their conclusions and to capitalize on the strengths of clear reasoning. The development of modern probability theory, and especially the invention of regression analysis in statistics, has been a very useful tool for social scientists to identify patterns in their data and to make sure that their hypotheses do not outrun them. The models of rationality that have been used throughout economics and political science—in particular those of rational choice and game theory—reflect another important way that the power of logic has had an impact on research design and model building in modern social science. In psychology, too, where experiments are designed to assess rational cognitive function by using thinly disguised logic games, one sees the influence of logic in social inquiry. Such reliance on logical modes of behavioral analysis, however, has come at a cost, for the new trend of "behavioral economics," and the more general movement toward more realistic and experimental models in the social sciences, have revealed limitations in some of the classic theories in social science. Assumptions about "rational economic man," for instance, may work ideally in our theoretical models, but break down when faced with the irrationality and fractured logic of everyday human experience that constitutes the subject matter of the social sciences.

In another avenue, however, the principles of logic have been unquestionably useful in the social sciences, and that is in research design, the formulation of hypotheses, and the analysis and synthesis of data and theory in social inquiry. Taking a page from the "scientific method" that is allegedly used in the natural sciences, some methodologists have argued that, as empirical disciplines, the social sciences should follow the "five-step method" of observation, hypothesis formulation, prediction, experiment (or learning from experience), and assessment. Despite the storied literature in the philosophy of science, provided by philosophers of science Karl Popper and Thomas Kuhn, that has rightly caused philosophers and others to rethink this simplistic model of scientific method, there is a nugget of truth in it for any discipline that cares to be empirical, which is to be ruthless about the comparison of one's theory to the data. If a theory tells an individual to expect something, and one does not find it, then there is an inescapable problem for the theory. In a statement attributed to American physicist Richard Feynman, "It doesn't matter how beautiful your theory is. If it doesn't agree with experiment, it's wrong." This form of reasoning is directly related to the "conditional" in our earlier consideration of valid arguments, for it is trivially true that every conditional statement (if P, then Q) implies (indeed, is equivalent to) its "contrapositive" (if not Q, then not P). Thus, if one's social scientific theory states, "If one is a thirteen-year-old boy then one has had an Oedipus Complex" and one finds a thirteen-year-old boy who has *not* had an Oedipus Complex, then the original theory is wrong. If a theory has even one exception, then it is not universally true and must either be discarded, or modified in some way to deal with this anomaly. As Popper demonstrated, here the power of logical certainty may be appreciated, since the contrapositive relationship is one of deductive, not inductive, reasoning and therefore may be relied upon as rock solid in its epistemological status.

The role of logic in the social sciences is a mixed one. As in the natural sciences one realizes that, if it is to explain the world, any empirical theory must go beyond the homilies of deductive reasoning and venture forth into the world of experience, with the chance of being wrong as the price of expressing a truth that is not trivial. Still, as we have seen, the power and benefits of logic have not been without value to the social sciences.

SEE ALSO *Game Theory; Hypothesis and Hypothesis Testing; Rational Choice Theory; Scientific Method; Theory*

BIBLIOGRAPHY

Haack, Susan. 1978. *Philosophy of Logics.* Cambridge, U.K.: Cambridge University Press.

Kneale, William, and Martha Kneale. 1962. *The Development of Logic.* New York: Oxford University Press.

Kuhn, Thomas. 1962. *The Structure of Scientific Revolutions.* Chicago: University of Chicago Press.

Little, Daniel. 1990. *Varieties of Social Explanation.* Boulder, CO: Westview Press.

Martin, Michael, and Lee McIntyre, eds. 1994. *Readings in the Philosophy of Social Science.* Cambridge, MA: MIT Press.

Popper, Karl. 1965. *Conjectures and Refutations: The Growth of Scientific Knowledge.* New York: Harper Torchbooks.

Rosenberg, Alexander. 1988. *The Philosophy of Social Science.* Boulder, CO: Westview Press.

Lee C. McIntyre

LOGIC, SYMBOLIC

Symbolic logic is sited at the intersection of philosophy, mathematics, linguistics, and computer science. It deals with the structure of *reasoning* and the formal features of information. Work in symbolic logic has almost exclusively treated the deductive validity of arguments: those arguments for which it is *impossible* for the premises to be true and the conclusion false. However, techniques from twentieth-century logic have found a place in the study of inductive or probabilistic reasoning, in which premises need not render their conclusions certain.

The historical roots of logic go back to the work of Aristotle (384–322 BCE), whose *syllogistic reasoning* was the standard account of the validity of arguments. Syllogistic reasoning treats arguments of a limited form: They have two premises and a single conclusion, and each judgment has a form like "all people are mortal," "some Australian is poor," or "no politician is popular."

The discipline of symbolic logic exploded in complexity as techniques of algebra were applied to issues of logic in the work of George Boole (1815–1864), Augustus de Morgan (1806–1871), Charles Sanders Peirce (1839–1914), and Ernst Schröder (1841–1902) in the nineteenth century (see Ewald 1996). They applied the techniques of mathematics to represent propositions in arguments *algebraically*, treating the validity of arguments like equations in applied mathematics. This tradition survives in the work of contemporary algebraic logicians.

Connections between mathematics and logic developed into the twentieth century with the work of Gottlob Frege (1848–1925) and Bertrand Russell (1872–1970), who used techniques in logic to study mathematics. Their goals were to use the newfound precision in logical vocabulary to give detailed accounts of the structure of mathematical reasoning, in such a way as to clarify the definitions that are used, and to make fully explicit the commitments of mathematical reasoning. Russell and Alfred North Whitehead's (1861–1947) *Principia Mathematica* (1912) is the apogee of this project of *logicism*.

With the development of these logical tools came the desire to use them in different fields. In the early part of the twentieth century, the *logical positivists* attempted to put all of science on a firm foundation by formalizing it: by showing how rich theoretical claims bear on the simple observations of experience. The best example of this is the project of Rudolf Carnap (1891–1970), who attempted to show how the logical structure of experience and physical, psychological, and social theory could be built up out of an elementary field of perception (Carnap 1967). This revival of empiricism was made possible by developments in logic, which allowed a richer repertoire of modes of construction or composition of conceptual content. On an Aristotelian picture, all judgments have a particularly simple form. The new logic of Frege and Russell was able to encompass much more complex kinds of logical structure, and so with it, theorists were able to attempt much more (Coffa 1991).

However, the work of the logical positivists is not the enduring success of the work in logic in the twentieth century. The radical empiricism of the logical positivists failed, not because of external criticism, but because logic itself is more subtle than the positivists had expected. We see this in the work of the two great logicians of the mid-twentieth century. Alfred Tarski (1902–1983) clarified our view of logic by showing that we can understand logic by means of describing the *language* of logic and the valid arguments by giving an account of *proofs*. However, we view logic by viewing the *models* of a logical language, and taking a valid argument as one for which there is no model in which the premises are true and the conclusion false. Tarski clarified the notion of a model and he showed how one could rigorously define the notion of *truth* in a language, relative to these models (Tarski 1956). The other great logician of the twentieth century, Kurt Gödel (1906–1978), showed that these two views of logic (proof theory and model theory) can agree. He showed that in the standard picture of logic, validity defined with proofs and validity defined by models agree (see von Heijenhoort 1967).

Gödel's most famous and most misunderstood result is his *incompleteness* theorem: This result showed that any account of proof for mathematical theories, such as arithmetic, must either be completely intractable (we can never list all of the rules of proof) or incomplete (it does not provide an answer for every mathematical proposition in the domain of a theory), or the theory is inconsistent. This result brought an end of the logicist program as applied to mathematics and the other sciences. We cannot view the truths of mathematics as the consequences of a particular theory, and the same holds for the other sciences (see von Heijenhoort 1967).

Regardless, logic thrives. Proof theory and model theory are rich mathematical traditions, their techniques have been applied to many different domains of reasoning, and connections with linguistics and computer science have strengthened the discipline and brought it new applications.

Logical techniques are tools that may be used whenever it is important to understand the structure of the claims we make and the ways they bear upon each other. These tools have been applied in clarifying arguments and analyzing reasoning, and they feature centrally in the development of allied tools, such as statistical reasoning.

One contemporary debate over our understanding of logic also bears on the social sciences. We grant that using languages is a social phenomenon. How does the socially mediated fact of language-use relate to the structure of the information we are able to present with that use of language? Should we understand language as primarily *representational*, with inference valid when what is represented by the premises includes the representation of the conclusion, or should we see the social role of assertion in terms of its *inferential* relations? We may think of assertion as a social practice in which the logical relations of *compatibility* and *reason-giving* are fundamental. Once we can speak with each other, my assertions have a bearing on yours, and so logic finds its home in the social practice of expressing thought in word (Brandom 2000).

SEE ALSO *Aristotle; Empiricism; Logic; Models and Modeling; Philosophy; Social Science; Statistics in the Social Sciences*

BIBLIOGRAPHY

Brandom, Robert. 2000. *Articulating Reasons: An Introduction to Inferentialism.* Cambridge, MA: Harvard University Press.

Carnap, Rudolf. 1967. *The Logical Structure of the World, and Pseudoproblems in Philosophy.* Trans. Rolf A. George. New York: Routledge and Kegan Paul.

Coffa, J. Alberto. 1991. *The Semantic Tradition from Kant to Carnap: To the Vienna Station,* ed. Linda Wessels. Cambridge, U.K.: Cambridge University Press.

Ewald, William, ed. 1996. *From Kant to Hilbert: A Source Book in the Foundations of Mathematics.* Oxford: Oxford University Press.

Russell, Bertrand, and Alfred North Whitehead. 1912. *Principia Mathematica.* Cambridge, U.K.: Cambridge University Press.

Tarski, Alfred. 1956. *Logic, Semantics, Metamathematics: Papers from 1923 to 1938.* Trans. J. H. Woodger. Oxford: Clarendon.

von Heijenhoort, Jan. 1967. *From Frege to Gödel: A Source Book in Mathematical Logic, 1879–1931.* Cambridge, MA: Harvard University Press.

Greg Restall

LOGISTIC REGRESSION

The logistic regression model is used when the dependent variable is categorical. A categorical variable is one whose numerical values serve only as labels distinguishing different categories. When a categorical variable has only two mutually exclusive outcomes, the *binary* logistic regression model is used. The logistic regression model had its origins in the biological sciences of the early twentieth century (Berkson 1944) but has subsequently found wide applicability in many areas of social science. The logistic regression model can be used for all data types but is most commonly used for cross-sectional data.

There are three different ways to derive or view the logistic regression model. In the first approach, one assumes that there is an unobserved or latent variable related to the observed outcome. For example, an individual's decision to enter the labor force is made by comparing his or her unobserved reservation wage to the market wage. Only if the market wage exceeds the reservation wage does the individual enter the labor force. Secondly, the model can be viewed as a probability model for the dependent variable. Thirdly, the model can be derived from random utility theory or discrete choice model formulation (see McFadden 1974).

BINARY CASE

In the binary case, some event Y either occurs ($Y = 1$) or not ($Y = 0$). The linear probability regression model (LPM) is given by:

$$(1) \qquad Y = X\beta + \epsilon$$

where $\beta X = \beta_0 + \beta_1 {}^* X_1 + \beta_2 {}^* X_2 + \ldots + \beta_k {}^* X_k$, and ε is the random error term.

The set of independent variables X affecting the event Y can be either continuous or categorical. The LPM model is problematic. First, the dependent variable Y is not constrained to lie between 0 and 1, and thus may produce nonsense probabilities. Also, the linear assumption holds that for every unit increase in X, the probability of Y occurring increases by the same amount. In many applications this assumption is not tenable. For example, the effect of an additional child on the probability of a female entering the labor force is assumed to be constant. It makes more sense to assume decreasing marginal effects of the number of children on the probability of a female entering the labor force. Also, the effect of changes in a specific X on the probability of Y does not depend on the other independent variables. In most applications this is also an unrealistic assumption. In the example above, the effect of an additional child on the probability of a female entering the labor force is assumed to be independent of, say, her husband's income.

The logistic regression model was formulated to address these issues and can be written as:

(2) $\quad \text{Ln}\,(P/1 - P) = X\beta + \epsilon$

where P = Probability (Y = 1).

The dependent variable is the log of the odds ratio of the event Y occurring or the logit of Y. Since the probability is between 0 and 1, the odds ratio goes from 0 to ∞ and the logit (an increasing function of P) goes from $-\infty$ to $+\infty$. Thus, the dependent variable in the logistic model is not constrained. The logistic model uses the cumulative logistic probability function to constrain the probability P to be between 0 and 1. In theory, any probability distribution can be used, however the most popular choices include the normal, uniform, and the logistic distributions. The uniform distribution gives rise to the linear probability model, while the normal distribution gives rise to the probit model. In most binary applications, the logit and the probit models are very similar. Historically, for ease of computation, mathematical tractability, and ease of interpretability, the logistic model was the preferred choice. Solving for P in the logistic model, one obtains:

(3) $\quad P = 1/(1 + \exp\{-X\beta\}).$

The probability P is now nonlinear in X. The effect of changes in X on the probability P are the smallest at the extreme points of the variable X or when P is close to 0 or 1, which makes sense in most applications. In addition, the effect of a unit change in a specific X on P now depends on all of the independent variables X. The appropriate estimation method for the logistic model is the maximum likelihood estimation (MLE) method, since only Y and not P is observed. The MLE estimates are consistent and asymptotically normal and efficient. In addition, the standard likelihood ratio and Wald tests on the coefficients can be used. Since this is a nonlinear model, the marginal effect of X on Y can be estimated using either the point of means of the variables or by averaging the marginal effect over all of the sample observations. The standard measures of goodness of fit are overly pessimistic in this model, and other measures that are used include the *count R-squared statistic*, which gives the average correct predictions of the model over the two outcomes of Y, or the *pseudo R-squared statistic*, which is the likelihood ratio statistic comparing the general model with the restricted model where all of the slope parameters ($\beta_1 = \beta_2 = \ldots \beta_k = 0$) are zero.

EXTENSIONS TO POLYCHOTOMOUS AND MULTIVARIABLE SITUATIONS

There are several approaches to modeling the polychotomous (more than two categories) case, including the *multinomial logistic model*. Similarly, the *multivariate logistic model* may be used in the modeling of two or more choice variables. Other relevant distinctions are made among ordered, unordered, and sequential choice variables. An individual choosing among no work, part-time work, or full-time work is facing an *ordered variable*. The choice of mode of daily transportation by car, bus, train, or bicycle is an example of an *unordered variable*. The decision of a high school graduate to attend college or not and then, if college is chosen, to decide on a major program is an example of a *sequential choice variable*.

A problematic feature of the multinomial logistic model is the property of independence from *irrelevant alternatives* (IIA). The IIA property states that the choice between any two alternatives is made independent of the remaining alternatives. In situations where there are close substitutes in the set of alternatives, this property is unlikely to hold true. In the mode of transportation example, adding a blue bus to the choice set affects all of the probabilities assigned to each category. Thus, by adding enough buses of different colors, one can make the probability of driving a car arbitrarily small. One can formally test for IIA in the multinomial logistic model or use other models, such as the *multinomial probit model*, which does not have this property. Unlike the dichotomous single variable situation, there are now major differences between the logistic and probit models and many more types of models to choose from.

SEE ALSO *Maximum Likelihood Regression; Probabilistic Regression; Probability Distributions; Regression; Specification Tests*

BIBLIOGRAPHY

Amemiya Takeshi. 1981. Qualitative Response Models: A Survey. *Journal of Economic Literature* 19 (4): 1483–1536.

Berkson, Joseph. 1944. Application to the Logistic Function to Bio-Assay. *Journal of the American Statistical Association* 39: 357–365.

Hosmer, David W., and Stanley Lemeshow. 2000. *Applied Logistic Regression*. 2nd ed. New York: Wiley.

Long, J. Scott. 1997. *Regression Models for Categorical and Limited Dependent Variables*. Thousand Oaks, CA: Sage.

McFadden, Daniel. 1974. Conditional Logit Analysis of Qualitative Choice Behaviour. In *Frontiers in Econometrics*, ed. Paul Zarembka, 105–142. New York: Academic Press.

Menard, Scott. 2002. *Applied Logistic Regression Analysis*. 2nd ed. Thousand Oaks, CA: Sage.

William Veloce

LOGIT REGRESSION

SEE *Logistic Regression.*

LOG-LINEAR MODELS

Within the realm of regression modeling, the term *log-linear* is used in two distinct ways. In the first case, it refers to nonlinear model specifications that—following a logarithmic transformation—become linear and can be estimated using tools available for the classical linear regression model. Most importantly, they can be estimated using ordinary least squares when assuming that the error terms are independent and normally distributed with mean 0 and equal variance σ^2. The multiplicative or double-log model and the exponential or semi-log model are two such nonlinear specifications. The multiplicative model takes on the form

$$y_i = \beta_0 \prod_{j=1}^{m} x_{ij}^{\beta_j} \exp(\varepsilon_i), \qquad (1)$$

or, in its log-transformed equivalent,

$$\ln y_i = \ln \beta_0 + \sum_{j=1}^{m} \beta_j \ln x_{ij} + \varepsilon_i, \text{ with } \varepsilon_i \text{ i.i.d. } N(0,\sigma^2),$$

where $\ln y_i$ is the dependent variable for observation i, $\ln x_{ij}$ is the j-th covariate or predictor variable, $\beta_0,\ldots,\beta_m$ are parameters to be estimated and ε_i are the error terms. The multiplicative model implies that a 1 percent change in x (not $\ln x$) yields a β percent change in y. It is frequently used to model large-scale traffic flows and migration flows. A well-known application in economics is the Cobb-Douglas production function that links output to capital and labor in a double-log specification, and where the parameters are the associated elasticities. The exponential or semi-log model takes on the form

$$y_i = \beta_0 \exp\left(\sum_{j=1}^{m} \beta_j x_{ij} + \varepsilon_i\right),$$

or, equivalently,

$$\ln y_i = \ln \beta_0 + \sum_{j=1}^{m} \beta_j x_{ij} + \varepsilon_i, \text{ with } \varepsilon_i \text{ i.i.d. } N(0, \sigma^2).$$

The exponential specification is most well-known for modeling unlimited and rapid population growth over time, where the dependent variable y represents the population, and time is the only covariate. The parameter β associated with time is the population growth rate, and a one-unit increase in time is expected to change the population by 100β percent.

In the second case, the term *log-linear model* is used to refer to a particular class of generalized linear models (GLM), the so-called "Poisson models." GLMs share a common mathematical structure in which the expected value of the dependent variable is functionally linked to a linear predictor. Unlike the multiplicative and exponential model, the Poisson regression model cannot be trans-formed into a classical linear regression model for which the link function is the identity function. Instead, the dependent variable is a count variable with Poisson-distributed non-negative integers as possible outcomes, and the link function connecting the expected value of Y with the linear predictor is the natural logarithm. For a Poisson-distributed random variable, the probability of observing k occurrences is

$$P(Y = k) = (\lambda^k e^{-k})/k!$$

where $\lambda = E(Y)$ is the expected number of occurrences. A Poisson model stipulates a systematic relationship between the expected value and the predictor variables such that

$$\lambda = E(Y_i) = \exp\left(\beta_0 + \sum_{j=1}^{m} \beta_j x_{ij}\right)$$

or, equivalently,

$$\ln \lambda_i = \ln E(Y_i) = \beta_0 + \sum_{j=1}^{m} \beta_j x_{ij}$$

for observations $i = 1, 2, \ldots, n$.

The parameters β_j are estimated iteratively from the maximum-likelihood expression, typically using the Newton-Raphson estimation procedure. Today, most statistical software programs include estimation routines for Poisson regression models. Several measures, including the most frequently used χ^2-distributed log-likelihood ratio, provide an assessment of the goodness-of-fit of the estimated model to the observed data. The estimates of the parameters can be tested for significance using a t-distribution. A broad range of phenomena are suitable to be modeled in a Poisson regression setting. Characteristic of such phenomena is the comparatively low chance of occurrence per fixed unit of time (or space). This applies to, for example, counts of the number of automobile fatalities per month, the number of disease incidents per week, the number of species found in an ecosystem, and the frequency of severe weather events per year. The oldest and probably most cited application is the study by Ladislaus Josephovich von Bortkiewicz (1868–1931) in which he analyzed the probability of a soldier being killed through the kick of a horse. In his now-famous book on the laws of small numbers, von Bortkiewicz showed that rare events follow a Poisson distribution. The book appeared sixty-one years after the French mathematician Siméon Denis Poisson (1781–1840) had published his famous treaty on the limiting distribution—which is now rightfully named the "Poisson distribution"—of the binomial distribution when the probability of occurrence is small and the number of trials is large.

Whereas the origins of regression models go back to the German mathematician and physicist Johann Carl Friedrich Gauss (1777–1855) and the French mathematician Adrien-Marie Legendre (1752–1833), extensions from the classical model to GLMs were made primarily over the last forty years. Credit goes to the seminal 1972 article by the statisticians John Ashworth Nelder and Robert William MacLagan Wedderburn. Nelder's 1983 book—coauthored with Peter McCullagh—still serves as the authoritative reference on GLMs. Recent refinements of Poisson models allow for relaxing the equidispersion assumption (i.e., for a Poisson-distributed random variable the expected value equals the variance). Advances also include mixed Poisson models in which, for instance, normally distributed random effects are added, or an abundance of zero-outcomes is accounted for in a so-called zero-inflated Poisson model. Although these advances make the log-linear regression model more flexible and suitable for a wider range of phenomena, their applicability needs to be thoroughly scrutinized, especially in situations where the linearity may be inappropriate, where the dispersion changes over time (or space), or where the observations are not independent.

SEE ALSO *Linear Regression; Regression*

BIBLIOGRAPHY

Bortkiewicz, Ladislaus Josephovich von. 1898. *Das Gesetz der kleinen Zahlen* [The Law of Small Numbers]. Leipzig, Germany: Teubner.

McCullagh, Peter, and John A. Nelder. 1983. *Generalized Linear Models*. London: Chapman and Hall.

Nelder, John A., and Robert William MacLagan Wedderburn. 1972. Generalized Linear Models. *Journal of the Royal Statistical Society* Series A 135 (3): 370–384.

Poisson, Siméon Denis. 1837. *Recherches sur la probabilité des jugements en matière criminelle et matière civile*. Paris: Bachelier, Imprimeur Libraire.

Brigitte Waldorf

LOMBARD STREET (BAGEHOT)

In the second half of the nineteenth century, world financial activity was centered in London. Within the city, the core of the financial district was Lombard Street, named after the bankers and financiers from northern Italy who centuries before had established their businesses there. In 1873, Walter Bagehot, editor of *The Economist* magazine, published a book that explained the workings of the London financial market. He titled it *Lombard Street: A Description of the Money Market*.

Lombard Street quickly became the main resource for understanding the workings of the London financial industry, replacing Henry Thornton's *Enquiry into the Nature and Effects of the Paper Credit of Great Britain*, published seven decades earlier in 1802. In *Lombard Street*, Bagehot briefly surveyed the origins of the London market and the reasons for its existence before undertaking a detailed description of the functions of a host of financial market participants, both public and private.

Lombard Street examines both the technical workings of the market and the government's policy actions within the market, as determined by the chancellor of the Exchequer and the directors of the Bank of England. It describes the activities of joint-stock banks, private banks, and bill brokers, all of which was of great interest to large numbers of contemporary readers. But the signal contribution of *Lombard Street* is Bagehot's discussion of how the Bank of England should behave toward other banks, especially when the money market was under stress.

The Bank Charter Act of 1844 had separated the Bank of England into an Issue Department, which issued bank notes backed by gold reserves, and a Banking Department, which was free to behave like an ordinary commercial bank. Critics of the Bank Act, including Bagehot's father-in-law James Wilson, founder of *The Economist*, argued throughout the 1850s and 1860s that the Bank's support of the money market during commercial crises was crucial and that the Bank of England should hold larger reserves of gold to meet the increased demand for gold during such periods. However, none of the critics developed a well-rounded case for the Bank to act as a central bank before Bagehot wrote.

Bagehot recognized that, though the Bank of England had no legal obligation to act as the nation's central bank, it in fact had done so since before 1800. Because the Bank kept the gold reserve for the entire economy, it had no choice but to act as a central bank. This meant that the Bank of England had to meet the banking system's liquidity needs during crises and that the Bank should act as lender of last resort when the increased demand to hold gold by individuals threatened the ability of solvent banks to meet their commitments.

Although the principle that the Bank of England would act as the banking system's lender of last resort was widely accepted after 1873, the British government implemented no legislation requiring the Bank to do so. Rather, the government assumed that the Bank would conduct its business appropriately. The Bank in fact did not hold larger gold reserves after 1873; in relation to the size of the banking system, the Bank's reserve shrank. The absence of any major crises over the next four decades prevents historians from knowing how the Bank of England would have behaved during a crisis.

SEE ALSO *Economic Crises; Finance; Financial Instability Hypothesis; Financial Markets; Fleet Street; Lender of Last Resort; Wall Street*

BIBLIOGRAPHY

Bagehot, Walter. [1873] 1999. *Lombard Street: A Description of the Money Market.* New York: John Wiley & Sons.

Thornton, Henry. [1802] 1978. *An Enquiry into the Nature and Effects of the Paper Credit of Great Britain*, ed. F. A. von Hayek. Fairfield, NJ: A. M. Kelley.

Wood, John H. 2003. Bagehot's Lender of Last Resort: A Hollow Hallowed Tradition. *The Independent Review* 7 (3): 343–351.

Neil T. Skaggs

LONELINESS

Social scientists agree that loneliness stems from the subjective experience of deficiencies in social relationships and that these deficiencies are unpleasant, aversive, and exceptionally common. Objectively deficient social relationships (i.e., social isolation) do not necessarily correspond with feeling lonely. Thus, it is common to appear alone but not feel lonely, and to feel lonely within a seemingly rich social relationship network. This potential paradox highlights an important distinction between quantitative and qualitative aspects of social relationships.

MODELS AND MEASUREMENT OF LONELINESS

Theoretical perspectives on loneliness differ concerning the nature of loneliness, whether loneliness stems from internal or situational causes, and where such causes occur developmentally. Psychoanalysts view loneliness as a pathological result of internal factors rooted in childhood. Sociologists view loneliness as a normative event stemming from societal influences that occur throughout development. From cognitive perspectives, loneliness occurs when people perceive discrepancies between their desired and actual patterns of relationships, with desired patterns stemming from previous relationships and comparisons of one's own relationships to those of similar others (i.e., social comparison). Although different perspectives contribute uniquely to our understanding, the cognitive perspective serves as the dominant model for studying loneliness.

The measurement of loneliness depends inherently on theoretical conceptualizations of the construct. Unidimensional views of loneliness posit a common core of experience that varies in intensity regardless of the antecedents or causes of feeling lonely. Many unidimensional scales exist, but the UCLA Loneliness Scale is the most commonly used. This measure assesses loneliness via self-report without using the terms *lonely* or *loneliness*, thereby reducing social desirability influences. Extensive psychometric work indicates that it is a reliable and valid measure of loneliness.

Multidimensional measures involve assessments of perceived quality and quantity of social interaction across multiple domains such as romantic, friendship, family, and community relationships. Multidimensional views of loneliness have become more common in the research literature, spurring intensive psychometric work on these types of scales. Two multidimensional views of loneliness have received considerable research attention. The first breaks down loneliness into distinct components that reflect stable enduring traits or transitory states tied strongly to situation/context. Studies examining these components using specialized scales typically yield test-retest correlations that are higher (indicating greater stability) for measures assessing trait loneliness than for measures assessing state loneliness, suggesting that this distinction is valid. A second multidimensional view involves a distinction between social loneliness that results from a lack of relationships that provide a sense of belonging (e.g., friendships) and emotional loneliness that occurs when people lack relationships that foster deep connection or feelings of attachment (e.g., romantic relationships). Many scales designed to measure social and emotional loneliness exist, and research findings suggest that this distinction is also a valid one.

PERSONALITY, DEVELOPMENT, AND CONTEXT

Studies examining associations between personality characteristics and loneliness consistently show that extroverted people report less loneliness, whereas highly neurotic people often feel lonely. Low self-esteem, shyness, and pessimism also correspond to higher levels of loneliness. It remains unclear whether these personality traits lead to loneliness by limiting social contact and preventing the formation and maintenance of quality relationships, whether feeling lonely biases self-assessment of personality, or whether personality predisposes one to develop few relationships, and the subsequent lack of relationships reciprocally influences one's personality. There remains a need for continued research that delineates causal paths among personality characteristics and loneliness.

Most children understand that being alone does not necessarily mean one is lonely, and that people can feel lonely when they do not appear to be alone. Adolescents experience more loneliness than do other individuals due to necessary restructuring of social groups to include friendships and other social relationships outside of the family during transitions to elementary, junior high, and high school. Family environments also influence the development of relationships in that children surrounded by parental conflict exhibit social anxiety and avoidance that contribute to loneliness.

Young adults face many contextual events, such as moving out of the home or going away to college, that require the development of new social ties. During these transitions, interpersonal difficulties may hinder the development of new social relationships, leaving one feeling lonely. Shy people who maintained a few high-quality relationships during high school may suddenly feel very lonely away at college when their shyness interferes with opportunities to make new friends. Although these types of life transitions often foster feelings of temporary loneliness that subside over time for most people, some individuals remain chronically lonely, suggesting that interpersonal difficulties or personality characteristics contribute to feelings of loneliness across the life span.

During adulthood, contextual transitions including college graduations and the establishment of careers present challenges to existing social networks and the need to form new relationships. New obstacles include individualistic or competitive work environments that make the formation and maintenance of satisfying relationships difficult. As adults, people place less emphasis on friendships than on intimate or romantic relationships. Although intimate relationships provide protection from loneliness, relationship quality is vital as adults in strained or unsatisfying relationships often report feeling lonely.

Elderly individuals face a number of challenges to maintaining their social networks, including the loss of relationships with coworkers through retirement, reduced contact with adult children, and the deaths of spouses or friends. Decreased functional mobility, cognitive impairment, and physical illness strain existing relationships and impede the establishment of new relationships. Despite these challenges, the elderly are less lonely on average than are college students, and increases in loneliness occur only among individuals eighty years and older. Married men and women report less loneliness than do elderly widows and widowers and men and women who are divorced or never married. Spouses in elderly couples provide functional support in addition to companionship and emotional connection, suggesting multiple ways in which marriage serves to protect against feelings of loneliness. For those without spouses, friendships with similar others provide more protection against loneliness than do relationships with adult children and neighbors.

LONELINESS, HEALTH, AND COPING

Consistent links between loneliness, life satisfaction, and anxiety exist, and loneliness is associated with depression independently of age, gender, physical health, cognitive impairment, network size, and social activity involvement.

In addition, loneliness influences well-being and feelings of hopelessness independently of associations with social isolation and perceived social support. Loneliness also relates to physical health, as evidenced by its consistent associations with alcohol abuse, admission of the elderly to nursing homes, suicide, and mortality.

Although loneliness uniquely influences physical health, potential causes for these connections have received varying degrees of support. One view posits that loneliness affects health through maladaptive behaviors including smoking, drinking, poor exercise habits, and substandard dietary practices; however, lonely and nonlonely people rarely differ in the frequency of such behaviors. Alternative models argue that loneliness influences physical reactions to stress including cardiovascular activation, cortisol production, immunocompetence deficiencies, and sleep disruptions that link directly to development of cardiovascular disease, susceptibility to disease and infection, and diminished restorative processes that maintain overall resilience. Emerging findings provide initial support for these links, suggesting promising avenues for future research.

Strategies for coping with loneliness include changing actual relationships, expectations about relationships, or reducing the importance of relationships. Attempts to change one's social relationships are active coping strategies wherein feelings of loneliness motivate people to form new relationship ties. Changing expectations about social relationships involves cognitive restructuring of how people view the social relationships of others. Attempts to reduce the importance of social relationships or engage in diversionary activities are passive coping strategies that often do little to alleviate loneliness.

Researchers have begun to explore the success of intervention programs in reducing feelings of loneliness, and promising findings have emerged. Social skills training for children and young adults provide the tools needed to effectively initiate, develop, and maintain satisfying social relationships. College orientation, mentoring, and buddy-pairing programs provide social contact with similar others in hopes of fostering relationship development during a transitional period when loneliness is quite common. Finally, interventions that effectively reduce loneliness among older adults target specific groups (e.g., divorcées or widows) and provide social contact opportunities with similar others as well as information that is useful for maintaining established social relationships.

BIBLIOGRAPHY

Brashears, Matthew E., Miller McPherson, and Lynn Smith-Lovin. 2006. Social Isolation in America: Changes in Core Discussion Networks over Two Decades. *American Sociological Review* 71 (June): 353–375.

Peplau, Leticia A., and Daniel Perlman, eds. 1982. *Loneliness: A Sourcebook of Current Theory, Research, and Therapy.* New York: Wiley-Interscience.

Russell, Daniel W. 1996. The UCLA Loneliness Scale (Version 3): Reliability, Validity, and Factor Structure. *Journal of Personality Assessment* 66 (1): 20–40.

Russell, Daniel W., Carolyn E. Cutrona, Arlene de la Mora, and Robert B. Wallace. 1997. Loneliness and Nursing Home Admission among Rural Older Adults. *Psychology and Aging* 12 (4): 574–589.

Steptoe, Andrew, Natalie Owen, Sabine R. Kunz-Ebrecht, and Lena Brydon. 2004. Loneliness and Neuroendocrine, Cardiovascular, and Inflammatory Stress Responses in Middle-Aged Men and Women. *Psychoneuroendocrinology* 29: 593–611.

Weiss, Robert S. 1973. *Loneliness: The Experience of Emotional and Social Isolation.* Cambridge, MA: MIT Press.

W. Todd Abraham
Daniel W. Russell

LONELY CROWD, THE

The Lonely Crowd, published in 1950, was written by sociologist David Riesman (1909–2002) in collaboration with Reuel Denney (1913–1995) and Nathan Glazer (b. 1923). Initially expected to sell only several thousand copies, this study of the links between social structure and national character has sold over 1.4 million copies from its initial publication, making it the best-selling sociology book in the United States.

Writing in the post–World War II (1939–1945) period, Riesman sought to understand what kinds of character structures were being encouraged by the social institutions of modern society, including capitalist corporations, political institutions, and the mass media. He proposed three different character types. The *tradition-directed type* was the product of unchanging societies in which social patterns were rooted in the past. The traditional character was rigid, insular, and not open to innovation. The development of industrial society, however, required a new character type. The nineteenth century saw the rise of what Riesman called the *inner-directed type*. This character received its essential structure in its youth, through strong family and community socialization. Unlike the traditional type, the inner-directed person could change and develop, but only following the direction of his or her *inner gyroscope*, whose essential pattern had been determined in youth.

Riesman argued that in the mid-twentieth century the *inner-directed type* was being replaced by a new character type. Modern organizations demanded people who took their cues from what other people expected of them.

These *other-directed* individuals used their *social radar*, rather than an inner gyroscope, to guide their values and actions. They preferred to be loved rather than esteemed. Their character was not shaped primarily by family or religion, but rather was strongly influenced by peer culture and the mass media.

When it was first published, *The Lonely Crowd* received many critical reviews, but nonetheless resonated widely in American society. Readers could appreciate the social changes within twentieth-century American society; they experienced firsthand the growing power of corporations and the greater presence of the media, including television, which was then in its infancy. They could—or thought they could—identify inner- and other-directed people among their relatives and friends, and detect differences between generations. Riesman himself, of course, proposed these terms as *ideal types*, with most people in modern society combining elements of the different character types.

The popularity of the book was also due to the clear, declarative writing style that artfully mixed interview data with evidence culled from magazines, movies, and even children's books. *The Lonely Crowd* was a jargon-free, wide-ranging analysis of the sort that sociology has largely since abandoned. To some extent, it is a period piece. Many of its assertions have since proved wrong, most notably a demographic hypothesis that tied the rate of population growth to national character type, a hypothesis that Riesman himself abandoned in the 1969 edition. But other hypotheses about the tenuous balance between the social conformity demanded by society and desires for autonomy among individuals continue to demand attention, even as the paradoxical phrase, "the lonely crowd," has entered into public discourse as an image of anomie within affluent society.

SEE ALSO *Alienation; Conformity; Glazer, Nathan; Intersubjectivity; Organization Man*

BIBLIOGRAPHY

Lipset, Seymour Martin, and Leo Lowenthal, eds. 1961. *Culture and Social Character: The Work of David Riesman Reviewed.* New York: Free Press of Glencoe.

Riesman, David, with Reuel Denney and Nathan Glazer. 1950. *The Lonely Crowd: A Study of the Changing American Character.* New Haven, CT: Yale University Press.

Diane Barthel-Bouchier

LONGEVITY

SEE *Morbidity and Mortality.*

LONGITUDINAL DATA

SEE *Data, Longitudinal.*

LONGITUDINAL
RESEARCH

SEE *Research, Longitudinal.*

LONGITUDINAL
SURVEYS

SEE *Panel Studies.*

LONG MARCH, THE

SEE *Chinese Revolution.*

LONG PERIOD
ANALYSIS

The forces that operate on economic processes are manifold and complex. In the eighteenth century philosophers of the Scottish and French Enlightenments, influenced in part by developments in the natural sciences (notably Newtonian mechanics) sought to identify the mechanisms that regulate social life. With the displacement of feudalism by a nascent market system as the dominant mode of material provisioning, an obvious question arose concerning whether the interactions of countless self-interested economic actors could generate benign social outcomes. Thomas Hobbes, in *Leviathan* (1651), had argued that a powerful state was necessary to contain the destructive potential of human nature. Mercantilist policies were partly grounded in the view that the market is an unreliable guarantor of the commonwealth's prosperity. In *The Fable of the Bees* (1724) Bernard Mandeville suggested that sentiments and behaviors commonly regarded as vices—envy, cupidity, gluttony, lust, pride—underpinned national economic well-being by stimulating demand for services and for the products of industry. Mandeville, who delighted in poking respectable opinion in the eye, had put his finger on a distinctive feature of capitalism: that markets to a significant degree generate order out of the self-interested behavior of atomistic agents. But he provided no scientific account of how markets coordinate the decisions of individual economic actors.

Market outcomes are not always benign. But capitalism is not chaotic. Somehow commodities get produced using sophisticated technologies that require the cooperation of many workers performing specialized tasks at different locations. The commodities are produced not in random quantities but in amounts that roughly match the demand for them. Resources get channeled from declining industries into expanding sectors. The process can be messy, and occasionally it falters. Yet the system manages to reproduce itself, to grow and to undergo structural and technological transformation. It is able to do all this without the intervention of a conscious coordinating hand.

ADAM SMITH'S FOUNDATION

Adam Smith is credited with providing the first systematic account of how markets generate order. His argument owes a good deal to Richard Cantillon's *Essai sur la nature du commerce en général* (1755) and to Anne Robert Jacques Turgot's *Réflexions sur la formation et la distribution des richesses* (1769–1770). Smith's argument is set out in book 1, chap. 7 ("Of the Natural and Market Price of Commodities") of the *Wealth of Nations* (1776). The chapter outlines a method of analysis that grounded theoretical economics until the middle of the twentieth century. That method, long period analysis, starts from the premise that in a market economy competition manifests itself as a tendency for profit rates to equalize across all lines of production. Smith drew a distinction between the natural price of a good and the market price. The natural price, which later generations of economists called the long period equilibrium price, is the price that would, if it obtained, be just sufficient to cover the commodity's cost of production, where cost is understood to include a normal rate of return for the owners of the capital invested in the enterprise. The market price of a good is the price that is actually observed. Smith argued that the natural price is a center of gravitation toward which market prices are pushed by the dominant and persistent forces operating in a market economy. Accidental and temporary circumstances may cause market prices to rise above or fall below the natural price, but "they are constantly tending towards it" (Smith 1776, book 1, chap. 7, p. 65).

The mechanism that pushes market prices toward their long period equilibrium levels is what coordinates the self-interested activity of the economy's participants. We may reasonably suppose that the owners of capital will prefer to invest it in enterprises that earn high rates of return rather than in enterprises that earn low rates of return. That is why, from the economist's point of view, a normal return on investment is an element of cost: The market prices of a good must, on average, be sufficient not only to cover labor costs, the costs of raw materials, and the cost of depreciation of physical equipment; if the price is not high enough to give the owners of capital the same rate of return they could obtain in other lines of production, the owners will eventually transfer their capital to those other sectors. As capital flows into the high return sectors, the output of those sectors increases, and as the supply of those commodities becomes more abundant, their *market* prices fall, lowering the rate of profit in those sectors. In the sectors that are experiencing an outflow of capital, outputs decline, causing market prices and hence rates of return to rise. The overall tendency is for rates of return to converge, provided there are no impediments to the movement of capital, and for prices to move toward their natural levels, which are consistent with equalization of profit rates. (If there are barriers to the movement of capital, such as patents or monopolistic control of particular necessary resources, the mechanism nevertheless operates, but the long period position will then be characterized by profit rate differentials.) The flow of capital in pursuit of its highest return brings the structural composition of production capacity into line with the composition of demand. It is also the principal mechanism by which economic systems absorb new technologies and adjust to major changes in the regulatory or institutional framework or in the availability of natural resources. It is what Smith meant by the "invisible hand" (1776, book 4, chap. 2, p. 477).

CLASSICAL ECONOMICS AND NEOCLASSICAL THEORY

The adjustments just described take place over long stretches of time, as capital goods wear out and are replaced by new and usually different ones; hence the label "long period method." This method proved immensely useful for analyzing the determination of relative prices and the closely connected question of what determines the distribution of income among social classes. But the method makes no presumption about how the variables of the economy are determined. Historically two broad approaches to the explanation of prices and distribution may be identified—the surplus approach of Karl Marx and the classical political economists, in particular Smith and David Ricardo, and neoclassical supply and demand theory. The theories differ with respect to the data they treat as parametric in explaining prices. The classical economists and Marx took the social product, the real wage, and the technology of production as givens in their attempts to explain relative prices and the rate of profit. Perhaps the feature that distinguishes the approach most starkly from modern economics is its conception of the real wage as a socially and institutionally conditioned variable. (A later variation of the theory, associated with Piero Sraffa, treats the profit rate as the parametric distribution variable.) The marginalist or neoclassical theory

that emerged in the last decades of the nineteenth century explains prices and incomes in terms of the interaction of price-elastic demand and supply functions derived from a somewhat different set of data: the preferences of economic agents, the economy's endowment of productive resources and the distribution of that endowment among the members of society, and the technology of production. The two frameworks arrive at different explanations of prices and distribution, but until the middle of the twentieth century they utilized the same long period method, in which market forces are understood to move the economy toward a fully adjusted position characterized by a uniform rate or profit across sectors.

In the twentieth century, however, mainstream neoclassical economics underwent a shift in method, in which long period analysis gradually gave way to models of temporary or intertemporal general equilibrium. These models drop the requirement that equilibrium be characterized by a uniform profit rate and instead define equilibrium entirely in terms of market clearing—the absence of excess demand. (Intertemporal equilibrium models assume the existence of complete futures markets—markets existing in the present, which reflect agents' beliefs about the probability distributions of all future contingent states of nature; in temporary equilibrium models, equilibrium occurs when agents' short-term expectations about prices and quantities are fulfilled.) The emergence and then ascendance of these approaches appear to be related to two considerations. First, they may reflect an attempt to avoid capital theoretic problems that are evident in long period versions of the neoclassical theory (the same problems may well be present in intertemporal and temporary equilibrium models, but in such models they are less transparent). Second, these models were in part motivated by a desire to move beyond the static analysis of the long period approach and to depict the patterns of change that every actual economy undergoes over time. But the models are themselves limited in their ability to depict actual economic processes: Complete futures markets do not exist, and short-period equilibria can explain the temporal sequence of prices and outputs only if the equilibria are *actually established* by market forces. A distinct advantage of the long period method is that the equilibrium values established by the theory need not be achieved in reality: The explanatory value of long period models lies in the supposition that the equilibrium positions established by such models are centers of gravitation for the actually observed values of the variable, which may deviate from the values predicted by the theory for any number of accidental or random causes.

The long period method has been the target of criticism as well. Among institutionalist economists there is a long tradition of skepticism toward equilibrium analysis. More troublesome perhaps is the fact that the stability of long period positions is notoriously difficult to establish in both the surplus approach and neoclassical applications of the method. The stability of an equilibrium position refers to the position's status as a center of gravitation: Under what is it reasonable to suppose that an accidental disturbance of the system will set in motion a set of adjustments that move the economy back to toward the long period position? If the conditions necessary to ensure a return to the equilibrium are excessively strict, we cannot take it for granted that the long period position is a center of gravitation, and in that case the method's claims to capture real-world processes are weakened.

SEE ALSO *Cantillon, Richard; Capitalism; Economics, Classical; Economics, Neo-Ricardian; Economics, Post Keynesian; Equilibrium in Economics; Keynes, John Maynard; Long Run; Markets; Marx, Karl; Prices; Ricardo, David; Smith, Adam; Surplus; Turgot, Jacques*

BIBLIOGRAPHY

Eatwell, John. 1982. Competition. In *Classical and Marxian Political Economy*, ed. Ian Bradley and Michael Howard. London: Macmillan.

Garegnani, Pierangelo. 1976. On a Change in the Notion of Equilibrium in Recent Work on Value and Distribution. In *Keynes' Economics and the Theory of Value and Distribution*, ed. John Eatwell and Murray Milgate. London: Duckworth, 1983.

Milgate, Murray. 1979. On the Origin of the Notion of "Intertemporal Equilibrium." *Economica* 46: 1–10.

Smith, Adam. 1776. *An Inquiry into the Nature and Causes of the Wealth of Nations*, ed. E. Cannan. Chicago: University of Chicago Press, 1976.

Gary Mongiovi

LONG PERIOD PRICES

SEE *Long Period Analysis.*

LONG RUN

The term *long run* entered economic analysis as economists started considering different time horizons in their analyses. All the consequences of economic events may not occur immediately, nor may they all happen at the same time. The concepts of long and short run were thus introduced in order to cope with these problems. In a long-run context, all consequences are assumed to be finished, whereas in the short run only some effects are taken into account.

CLASSICAL AND NEOCLASSICAL PERSPECTIVES

The term was explicitly used for the first time in the works of the Cambridge economist Alfred Marshall (1842–1924), who detailed a concept of long-run equilibrium that became broadly accepted and used in the scientific community. Implicitly, the classical economists of the eighteenth century, Adam Smith (1723–1790) and David Ricardo (1772–1823), already used the concept of a long-run equilibrium, as did Karl Marx (1818–1883) after them. The former focused attention on so-called "normal" or long-period positions of the economy in conditions of free competition and the corresponding system of "natural values" and a uniform rate of profits. These natural values guarantee the payment of wages, profits, and rents so that no extra profits occur. In contrast, "market values" are the observed prices that are influenced by all sorts of factors, both systematic and accidental, persistent and temporary. Market values do not necessarily converge to their natural values but are considered to gravitate around their natural levels. Marx had a similar view on the long-run position of the economy. The classical economists determined the rate of profits and relative prices in terms of given levels of output, given technical alternatives, and a given wage rate (or share of wages).

The neoclassical economists of the nineteenth century and early twentieth century used a related methodology. Their theories attempted to determine prices, income distribution, and quantities simultaneously in terms of given endowments, technical alternatives, and preferences. Their works led to the elaboration of general equilibrium analysis, which, in contrast to partial equilibrium analysis, focuses on the economic system as a whole. Among the neoclassical economists, Marshall in *Principles of Economics* (1890) made a distinction between four different types of equilibria: temporary, short run, long run, and secular equilibrium. In temporary or very short run equilibrium, supply is fixed, and the price is solely determined by demand. In the short run, supply itself is not fixed, but the production is constrained by a given plant and equipment. As a consequence, productive capacity is given in a short run. In the long run, supply can adjust perfectly to demand via an adjustment of productive capacity within the prevailing production technology. Finally, in the secular or very long run, technical knowledge may change. Although neoclassical authors developed the tools for handling short-run problems, the long-run analysis remained dominant.

EXTENSIONS AND CRITICISM

John Maynard Keynes (1883–1946) called for focused attention on short-run problems with his witticism in *A Tract on Monetary Reform*: "*In the long run we are all dead*"

491

(Keynes 1923, p. 65). An investigation of the impact of effective demand on output, given productive capacities, is at the center of Keynes's magnum opus *The General Theory of Employment, Interest, and Money* (1936). His conclusion is that the demand side of the economy is of crucial importance not only in the short run but in the long run as well. This argument is studied in terms of income and employment multipliers, which originally were suggested by the British economist Richard Kahn (1905–1989), who augmented Marshall's distinction of long and short run with a classification as regards cost. In the short period, firms face fixed costs, and windfall profits or losses might occur. By contrast, costs are entirely variable in the long run because all factors of production become flexible, at least in principle. Companies can freely enter and exit industries, which leads to a uniform profit rate throughout the economy. Contrary to previous authors, the U.S. economist Milton Friedman (1912–2006) defined the long period with regard to adaptive expectations. In numerous works he investigated the effects of monetary policies and discovered that they were moderate in the short run and practically nil in the long. He maintained that there is no long-term trade-off between inflation and unemployment because of the influence of expectations regarding inflation on the behavior of forward-looking agents. Exogenous shocks can only affect the economy in the short run, whereas they have no influence in the long run. In contrast to Keynes, Friedman stated that the long run is determined entirely by supply-side conditions and effective demand does not matter. An even more radical point of view, based on the theory of rational expectations, was established by the U.S. economist Robert Lucas (b. 1937). In his contributions to the theory of endogenous growth, he argued that the economy would converge to a balanced path, irrespective of short-run perturbations. This balanced path is considered to be a close approximation to any actual development, and thus the attention should focus on it.

The different types of long-run equilibria mentioned are also known as "stationary equilibria," "steady states," and "intertemporal equilibria." The relative importance of either long-run or short-run analysis has varied considerably over time. Whereas classical and neoclassical economists predominantly treated long-run problems, Keynes drew attention to the short run. In correspondence to the different problems at hand, the methods applied varied vastly, from micro to macro and from static to dynamic. A convincing unification of the long- and short-run points of view is not yet in sight. The time horizon and therefore the distinction between short and long run seem to remain crucial in economics.

SEE ALSO *Exchange Value; Expectations; Friedman, Milton; Kahn, Richard F.; Keynes, John Maynard;* *Long Period Analysis; Lucas, Robert E., Jr.; Marshall, Alfred; Marx, Karl; Ricardo, David; Short Period; Short Run; Smith, Adam*

BIBLIOGRAPHY

Garegnani, Pierangelo. 1976. On a Change in the Notion of Equilibrium in Recent Works on Value and Distribution. In *Essays in Modern Capital Theory*, ed. Murray Brown, Kazuo Sato, and Paul Zarembka, 25–45. Amsterdam: North-Holland.

Keynes, John M. 1923. *A Tract on Monetary Reform.* London: Macmillan.

Keynes, John M. 1936. *The General Theory of Employment, Interest, and Money.* New York: Harcourt, Brace.

Kurz, Heinz D., and Neri Salvadori. 1998. *Understanding "Classical" Economics: Studies in Long-period Theory.* London: Routledge.

Marshall, Alfred. [1890] 1920. *Principles of Economics.* 8th ed. London: Macmillan.

Wolfgang Eichert
Rita Strohmaier

LONG RUN PRICES
SEE *Long Period Analysis.*

LONG-TERM MEMORY
SEE *Mood Congruent Recall.*

LONG WAVES

Since the beginning of the twentieth century, observers of the world economy have been analyzing long-term regularities associated with the behavior of the leading economies. Statistical analysis of more than a century of price behaviors and output series in the United States and Britain led Nikolai Kondratieff (1892–1938), a Russian Marxist economist, to conclude in the 1920s that boom-and-bust long-wave cycles exist and that their duration is between fifty and sixty years. The study of key growth indicators of industrial and world output between 1826 and 1968 by Ernest Mandel (1995) found that the periods 1826 to 1847, 1848 to 1873, 1874 to 1893, 1894 to 1913, 1914 to 1939, and 1940 to 1967 were marked with striking fluctuation in the average rates of growth, with ups and downs between successive long waves ranging from 50 to 100 percent. His analysis provided strong evidence of long waves in capitalist development.

In the 1930s the economist Joseph Schumpeter (1883–1950) endorsed the long-wave concept as a reasonable explanation of macroeconomic activity, and he named the pattern, after Kondratieff, *K-waves*. Schumpeter's own work focused on the clustering of innovations during the phase of economic depression (the *Winter phase*). He used the terms "swarms of technological progress" and "gales of creative destruction" to describe this phase. Innovations are hypothesized to cluster during the Winter phase because only then do firms resort to the highly risky strategy of introducing basic, new-to-the-world innovations. This phase is thought to be a key driver of new techno-economic paradigms or structural shifts in the economy. Societies' adjustments to the basic innovations take the form of S-shaped growth or learning life cycles and are accomplished in the latter three phases (Spring, Summer, and Autumn) of the long waves. Here, firms extract profit from the dominant technologies, rather than seeking new innovations.

Long waves are most often written about during periods of economic downturns and are viewed as a way out of an impending crisis. They receive considerably less press during times of prosperity because the long-wave theory would suggest the less popular hypothesis, namely, that the good times will not last.

ORIGIN

Long waves are not thought to be unique to the nineteenth and twentieth centuries. Some authors have traced them back in Europe over five hundred years, others have identified nineteen such waves dating back to printing and paper in 930, and others assert that they go back at least five thousand years. This entry, however, discusses only the last five such waves (between 1800 and 2025), which represent the industrialization of modern economies. Each appears to have a dominant technology driver, but technology is only one part of a much broader innovation system that is responsible for the long-wave phases. The transportation systems, communication modes, primary energy sources, manufacturing processes, corporate organizational structures, and public administration approaches appear to be unique to particular waves and provide the all-important context for the full depth and breadth of the technology to flourish for each long wave. Thus, long waves arise from the clustering of fundamental innovations that initiate technological revolution and that in turn create leading commercial and industrial sectors. (See Table 1.)

THEORY

According to Schumpeter, long waves are caused by the demand for solutions to new problems, and innovative firms supply these solutions. Each new wave has its own unique innovative character, its own identity, but it is composed of four common phases. The four phases, often described as seasons, are thought of as dramatic mood changes of the economy that can be anticipated by individuals and can influence their actions. As discussed previously, the Winter (depression) phase is characterized by a collapse of the price system, which forces the economy into a sharp period of retrenchment. A three-year collapse is followed by a fifteen-year deflationary work out period where risky innovation takes place.

The Spring phase (the inflationary growth phase) requires approximately twenty-five years to complete and is characterized by wealth accumulation, new innovation, great upheaval and displacement, and significant social unrest. The exponential growth reaches its limit, inefficiencies build up in the system, and a Summer (stagflation, recession) phase is entered and lasts for twenty to

Long waves and critical drivers				
Innovation domain	**1st to 2nd wave 1800–1856**	**2nd to 3rd wave 1856–1916**	**3rd to 4th wave 1916–1970**	**4th to 5th wave 1970–2025**
Key technology	Steam power	Steel, electricity	Oil	Information technology, microelectronics, biotechnology
Transportation modality	Railroads, steam engines	Automobiles	Aircraft	Spacecraft
Communication technology	Periodicals	Telegraph, telephone	Radio, television	Internet, World Wide Web
Global energy source	Wood	Coal	Oil	Natural gas
Process innovation	Factory	Scientific management, assembly line	Mass production, in-house research and development	Minimal inventory, flexible man
Corporate organization	Hierarchy	Division	Matrix	Network, virtual company
U.S. Public Administration	Jacksonian Populism	Merit-based Civil Service	New Deal	Deregulation
Wars	War of 1812	American Civil War	World War I, World War II	Vietnam War, Iraq War

SOURCE: Adapted from Devezas, Linstone, and Santos 2005.

Table 1

twenty-five years. The Autumn (deflationary growth, plateau) phase of seven to ten years follows with rapid rises in prices, selective industry growth, a strong feeling of affluence, and a general isolationist mood in the citizenry. Interest in long-wave theory waned in the 1940s, 1950s, and 1960s (and again in the 1990s) because predicting a downturn during boom times was not fashionable, but the theory resurged when a new group, known as neo-Shumpeterians, sought to explain the economic downturns of the 1960s, 1970s, and 1980s.

EMPIRICAL SUPPORT

Kondratieff was the first to use regression procedures to reveal long waves in economic time series data, and Jay Forrester's computer simulation of the macroeconomic process also reproduced long-wave patterns of roughly fifty years. While subsequent econometric research using time series data and equilibrium assumptions do not find unambiguous support for them, long-wave supporters argue that methodologies based on equilibrium assumptions are flawed because today's economy is structurally unstable and evolutionary in nature. They suggest long waves need to be measured by observations of physical events associated with the economy, like innovations, rather than traditional economic measures.

Robert Metz's study (2005) of over fifteen thousand innovations during the 1750–1991 period found innovation clusters peaking in 1840, 1890, 1935, and 1986, followed by an upswing in economic growth eighteen years later, thereby confirming the depression-trigger innovation hypothesis. At the beginning of a long-wave cycle, innovations usually center around one country and a few breakthrough technologies; however, the creation of a new techno-economic system, as shown in Table 1, requires sustained innovations in the related, complementary areas.

POLICY SIGNIFICANCE

If, as asserted above, long waves are a consequence of the inner dynamics of economic growth, then policy makers can put forth prescriptions during different phases of the economic cycle. For example, a government's policy would have its greatest impact on innovation during the Winter phase, for entrepreneurs need to be encouraged most then. During the Spring phase, governments have to keep a check on inflation to ensure that the economy does not overheat. During the Summer phase of stagflation or recession, the government can offer policies to stimulate the economy. The last prescriptive area is during the Autumn phase, when government policies should be most concerned about controlling inflation. Another interesting finding is that international political economists have studied the relationship between long waves and war and find that wars and revolutions are much more likely to occur during the economic-upswing phase.

LEGITIMATE CONCERNS

Some economists argue that long waves have less validity in a post–World War II (1939–1945) economy given the monetary and fiscal tools available to governments. They cite Federal Reserve Chairman Alan Greenspan's providing of massive liquidity after the dot-com bust of 2000 to prevent a Kondratieff Winter. Wave supporters counterargue that the resulting debt from this policy has become unsustainable and only temporarily postponed the pending Winter phase for a few years. As evidenced by the above arguments, the timing of each phase is critical to policymakers and economists. Unfortunately, long-wave theory lacks precision in this domain, particularly in the area of explaining the downswing at the end of the prosperity phase.

SEE ALSO *Business Cycles, Political; Business Cycles, Real; Business Cycles, Theories; Depression, Economic; Financial Instability Hypothesis; Lucas Critique; Panics; Recession; Say's Law; Shocks*

BIBLIOGRAPHY

Ayres, Robert. 1990. Technological Transformations and Long Waves. *Technological Forecasting & Social Change* 37 (1): 1–37.

Devezas, Tessaleno, Harold Linstone, and Humberto Santos. 2005. The Growth Dynamics of the Internet and Long Wave Theory. *Technological Forecasting & Social Change* 72 (8): 913–935.

Linstone, Harold. 2002. Corporate Planning, Forecasting, and the Long Wave. *Futures* 34 (3–4): 317–336.

Mandel, Ernest. 1995. *Long Waves of Capitalist Development: A Marxist Interpretation, Based on the Marshall Lectures Given at the University of Cambridge.* 2nd rev. ed. London and New York: Verso.

Metz, Robert. 2005. Empirical Evidence and Causation of Kondratieff Cycles. Presented at the NATO Advanced Research Workshop on Kondratieff Waves, Warfare, and World Security, February 14–18, 2005. Covilhã, Portugal.

Wymbs, Cliff. 2004. Telecommunications: An Instrument of Radical Change for Both the 20th and 21st Centuries. *Technological Forecasting & Social Change* 71 (7): 685–703.

Clifford Wymbs

LOOKING-GLASS EFFECT

The *looking-glass effect*, or the *looking-glass self*, may be defined as people's conceptualization of their own views of self, based on how they perceive that others view them. The concept has provided a captivating theoretical springboard for social scientists from a broad variety of disciplines. Sociologists and psychologists have historically focused on this effect more than researchers in other fields, however, because of the effect's inherent focus on both society and the individual as critical shaping forces in the development of human identity.

The term *looking-glass effect* was coined by Charles Horton Cooley, a social psychologist, in his 1902 treatise entitled *Human Nature and the Social Order*. Cooley's assertion that people derive their attitudes about themselves based on how others perceive them drew on earlier works by William James and inspired the work of George Herbert Mead, founder of the school of thought known as *symbolic interactionism*.

Central to the existence of the looking-glass self is the presence of a social audience; to learn about themselves, people require others to provide self-relevant information. Gordon Gallup's work with chimpanzees highlighted the necessity of a history of social interaction to the existence of self-knowledge (Gallup 1977). In a series of investigations, Gallup and his colleagues demonstrated that chimpanzees that were reared in isolation from other chimpanzees responded to their reflections in a mirror in a very different fashion from their socially informed, non-isolated counterparts. Whereas nonisolates recognized themselves in a mirror and evidenced recognition of a researcher-induced change in their physical appearance, isolates never demonstrated knowledge that they were viewing a reflection of themselves in the mirror. Without a prior history of information about themselves gleaned from interactions with other chimpanzees, isolates were seemingly devoid of a concept of self.

Though Cooley's original notion of the looking-glass self implied that people imagine how others must view them and, as a result, develop self-attitudes based on these imagined evaluations by others, it did not detail whether or not these imagined evaluations were accurate. It assumed, rather, that people should be able effectively to learn about themselves from social feedback from others. Later work revealed, however, that people's self-evaluations may not be rooted in others' *actual* evaluations but in people's *beliefs* about how others evaluate them (Shrauger and Schoeneman 1979). So, in effect, people could misperceive others' attitudes about themselves and, correspondingly, report self-attitudes that did not align with others' real evaluations.

Findings that the looking-glass effect may not provide people with accurate self-evaluations challenged the informative utility of the effect but paved the way for future investigations concerning it. Much of this work has revealed that people's own feelings of self-worth, or self-

esteem, play a role in how they think that others view them. People who have more positive self-evaluations tend to believe that others view them positively as well. Likewise, people who view themselves negatively are more likely to believe that others view them in the same negative light. As a result, a more nuanced definition of the looking-glass effect is people's evaluations of themselves based on their own self-attitudes and their perceptions, which are influenced by these self-attitudes, of how others view them (Tice and Wallace 2003).

SEE ALSO *James, William; Mead, George Herbert; Primates; Self-Concept; Social Influence; Social Isolation; Social Psychology*

BIBLIOGRAPHY

Cooley, Charles H. 1902. *Human Nature and the Social Order.* New York: Scribner's.

Gallup, Gordon G. 1977. Self-recognition in Primates: A Comparative Approach to the Bidirectional Properties of Consciousness. *American Psychologist* 32: 329–338.

Shrauger, J. Sidney, and Thomas J. Schoeneman. 1979. Symbolic Interactionist View of Self-Concept: Through the Looking Glass Darkly. *Psychological Bulletin* 86: 549–573.

Tice, Dianne M., and Harry M. Wallace. 2003. The Reflected Self: Creating Yourself As (You Think) Others See You. In *Handbook of Self and Identity*, eds. Mark Leary and June Tangney, 91–105. New York: Guilford.

Jorgianne Civey Robinson

LORDE, AUDRE

SEE *Womanism.*

LOSS FUNCTIONS

The *loss function* (or *cost function*) is a crucial ingredient in all optimizing problems, such as statistical decision theory, policymaking, estimation, forecasting, learning, classification, financial investment, and so on. The discussion here will be limited to the use of loss functions in econometrics, particularly in time series forecasting.

When a forecast $f_{t,h}$ of a variable Y_{t+h} is made at time t for h periods ahead, the loss (or cost) will arise if a forecast turns out to be different from the actual value. The loss function of the forecast error $e_{t+h} = Y_{t+h} - f_{t,h}$ is denoted as $c(Y_{t+h}, f_{t,h})$. The loss function can depend on the time of prediction, and so it can be $c_{t+h}(Y_{t+h}, f_{t,h})$. If the loss function does not change with time and does not depend on the value of the variable Y_{t+h}, the loss can be written simply as a function of the error only, $c_{t+h}(Y_{t+h}, f_{t,h}) = c(e_{t+h})$.

Clive Granger (1999) discusses the following required properties for a loss function: (1) $c(0) = 0$ (no error and no loss); (2) $\min_e c(e) = 0$, so that $c(e) \geq 0$; and (3) $c(e)$ is monotonically nondecreasing as e moves away from zero so that $c(e_1) \geq c(e_2)$ if $e_1 > e_2 > 0$ and if $e_1 < e_2 < 0$.

When $c_1(e)$, $c_2(e)$ are both loss functions, Granger (1999) shows that further examples of loss functions can be generated: $c(e) = ac_1(e) + bc_2(e)$, $a \geq 0$, $b \geq 0$ will be a loss function; $c(e) = c_1(e)^a c_2(e)^b$, $a > 0$, $b > 0$ will be a loss function; and $c(e) = 1(e > 0)c_1(e) + 1(e < 0)c_2(e)$ will be a loss function. If $h(\cdot)$ is a positive monotonic nondecreasing function with $h(0)$ finite, then $c(e) = h(c_1(e)) - h(0)$ is a loss function.

LOSS FUNCTIONS AND RISK

Granger (2002) notes that an expected loss (a risk measure) of financial return Y_{t+1} that has a conditional predictive distribution $F_t(y) \equiv Pr(Y_{t+1} \leq y|I_t)$ with $X_t \in I_t$ may be written as

$$\mathbb{E}c(e) = A_1\int_0^{\infty} |y - f|^{\theta} dF_t(y) + A_2\int_{-\infty}^0 |y - f|^{\theta} dF_t(y),$$

with A_1, A_2 both > 0 and some $\theta > 0$. Considering the symmetric case $A_1 = A_2$, one has a class of volatility measures $V_{\theta} = \mathbb{E}[|y - f|^{\theta}]$, which includes the variance with $\theta = 2$, and mean absolute deviation with $\theta = 1$.

Zhuanxin Ding, Clive Granger, and Robert Engle (1993) study the time series and distributional properties of these measures empirically and show that the absolute deviations are found to have some particular properties, such as the longest memory. Granger remarks that given that the financial returns are known to come from a long-tail distribution, $\theta = 1$ may be more preferable.

Another problem raised by Granger is how to choose optimal L_p-norm in empirical works, to minimize $\mathbb{E}[|\varepsilon_t|^p]$ for some p to estimate the regression model $Y_t = X_t\beta + \varepsilon_t$. As the asymptotic covariance matrix of $\hat{\beta}$ depends on p, the most appropriate value of p can be chosen to minimize the covariance matrix. In particular, Granger (2002) refers to a trio of papers (Nyquist 1983; Money et al. 1982; and Harter 1977) that find that the optimal $p = 1$ from Laplace and Cauchy distribution, $p = 2$ for Gaussian, and $p = \infty$ (min/max estimator) for a rectangular distribution. Granger (2002) also notes that in terms of the kurtosis κ, H. L. Harter (1977) suggests using $p = 1$ for $\kappa > 3.8$; $p = 2$ for $2.2 \leq \kappa \leq 3.8$; and $p = 3$ for $\kappa < 2.2$. In finance, the kurtosis of returns can be thought of as being well over 4, so $p = 1$ is preferred.

We consider some variant loss functions with $\theta = 1, 2$ below.

LOSS FUNCTIONS AND REGRESSION FUNCTIONS

Optimal forecasting of a time series model depends extensively on the specification of the loss function. *Symmetric quadratic loss function* is the most prevalent in applications due to its simplicity. The optimal forecast under quadratic loss is simply the conditional mean, but an *asymmetric loss function* implies a more complicated forecast that depends on the distribution of the forecast error as well as the loss function itself (Granger 1999), as the expected loss function is formulated with the expectation taken with respect to the conditional distribution. Specification of the loss function defines the model under consideration.

Consider a stochastic process $Z_t \equiv (Y_t, X_t')'$, where Y_t is the variable of interest and X_t is a vector of other variables. Suppose there are $T + 1 (\equiv R + P)$ observations. We use the observations available at time t, $R \leq t < T + 1$, to generate P forecasts using each model. For each time t in the prediction period, we use either a rolling sample $\{Z_{t-R+1}, \ldots, Z_t\}$ of size R or the whole past sample $\{Z_1, \ldots, Z_t\}$ to estimate model parameters $\hat{\beta}_t$. We can then generate a sequence of one-step-ahead forecasts $\{f(Z_t, \hat{\beta}_t)\}_{t=R}^T$.

Suppose that there is a decision maker who takes a one-step point forecast $f_{t,1} \equiv f(Z_t, \hat{\beta}_t)$ of Y_{t+1} and uses it in some relevant decision. The one-step forecast error $e_{t+1} \equiv Y_{t+1} - f_{t,1}$ will result in a cost of $c(e_{t+1})$, where the function $c(e)$ will increase as e increases in size, but not necessarily symmetrically or continuously. The optimal forecast $f_{t,1}^*$ will be chosen to produce the forecast errors that minimize the expected loss

$$\min_{f_{t,1}} \int_{-\infty}^{\infty} c(y - f_{t,1}) dF_t(y),$$

where $F_t(y) \equiv Pr(Y_{t+1} \leq y|I_t)$ is the conditional distribution function, with I_t being some proper information set at time t that includes $Z_{t-j}, j \geq 0$. The corresponding optimal forecast error will be

$$e_{t+1}^* = Y_{t+1} - f_{t,1}^*.$$

Then the optimal forecast would satisfy

$$\frac{\partial}{\partial f_{t,1}} \int_{-\infty}^{\infty} c(y - f_{t,1}^*) dF_t(y) = 0.$$

When we interchange the operations of differentiation and integration,

$$\int_{-\infty}^{\infty} \frac{\partial}{\partial f_{t,1}} c(y - f_{t,1}^*) dF_t(y) \qquad \mathbb{E}\left(\frac{\partial}{\partial f_{t,1}} c(Y_{t+1} - f_{t,1}^*)|I_t\right)$$

the *generalized forecast error*, $g_{t+1} \equiv \frac{\partial}{\partial f_{t,1}} c(Y_{t+1} - f_{t,1}^*)$,

forms the condition of forecast optimality:

$$H_0: \mathbb{E}(g_{t+1}|I_t) = 0 \ a.s.,$$

that is, a martingale difference (MD) property of the generalized forecast error. This forms the optimality condition of the forecasts and gives an appropriate regression function corresponding to the specified loss function $c(\cdot)$.

To see this, consider the following two examples. First, when the loss function is the squared error loss

$$c(Y_{t+1} - f_{t,1}) = (Y_{t+1} - f_{t,1})^2,$$

the generalized forecast error will be $g_{t+1} \equiv \frac{\partial}{\partial f_t} c(Y_{t+1} - f_{t,1}^*) = -2e_{t+1}^*$ and thus $\mathbb{E}(e_{t+1}^*|I_t)$

$= 0 \ a.s.$, which implies that the optimal forecast

$$f_{t,1}^* = \mathbb{E}(Y_{t+1}|I_t)$$

is the conditional mean. Next, when the loss is the check function, $c(e) = [\alpha - 1(e < 0)] \cdot e \equiv \rho_\alpha(e_{t+1})$, the optimal forecast $f_{t,1}$, for given $\alpha \in (0, 1)$, minimizing

$$\min_{f_{t,1}} \mathbb{E}\left[c(Y_{t+1} - f_{t,1})|I_t\right]$$

can be shown to satisfy

$$\mathbb{E}[\alpha - 1(Y_{t+1} < f_{t,1}^*)|I_t] = 0 \ a.s.$$

Hence, $g_{t+1} \equiv \alpha - 1(Y_{t+1} < f_{t,1}^*)$ is the generalized forecast error. Therefore,

$$\alpha = \mathbb{E}[1(Y_{t+1} < f_{t,1}^*)|I_t] = Pr(Y_{t+1} \leq f_{t,1}^*|I_t),$$

and the optimal forecast $f_{t,1}^* = q_\alpha(Y_{t+1}|I_t)$ is the conditional α-quantile.

LOSS FUNCTIONS FOR TRANSFORMATIONS

Granger (1999) notes that it is implausible to use the same loss function for forecasting Y_{t+h} and for forecasting h_{t+1} $= h(Y_{t+h})$ where $h(\cdot)$ is some function, such as the log or the square, if one is interested in forecasting volatility. Suppose the loss functions $c_1(\cdot)$, $c_2(\cdot)$ are used for forecasting Y_{t+h} and for forecasting $h(Y_{t+h})$, respectively. Let e_{t+1} $\equiv Y_{t+1} - f_{t,1}$ will result in a cost of $c_1(e_{t+1})$, for which the optimal forecast $f_{t,1}^*$ will be chosen from $\min_{f_{t,1}} \int_{-\infty}^{\infty} c_1(y - f_{t,1}) dF_t(y)$, where $F_t(y) \equiv Pr(Y_{t+1} \leq y|I_t)$. Let $\varepsilon_{t+1} \equiv h_{t+1}$ $- h_{t,1}$ will result in a cost of $c_2(\varepsilon_{t+1})$, for which the optimal forecast $h_{t,1}^*$ will be chosen from $\min_{h_{t,1}} \int_{-\infty}^{\infty} c_2(h - h_{t,1})$ $dH_t(h)$, where $H_t(h) \equiv Pr(h_{t+1} \leq h|I_t)$. Then the optimal forecasts for Y and h would respectively satisfy

$$\int_{-\infty}^{\infty} \frac{\partial}{\partial f_{t,1}} c_1(y - f_{t,1}^*) dF_t(y) = 0,$$

$$\int_{-\infty}^{\infty} \frac{\partial}{\partial h_{t,1}} c_2(h - h_{t,1}^*) dH_t(h) = 0.$$

It is easy to see that the optimality condition for $f_{t,1}^*$ does not imply the optimality condition for $h_{t,1}^*$ in general. Under some strong conditions on the functional forms of the transformation $h(\cdot)$ and of the two loss functions $c_1(\cdot)$, $c_2(\cdot)$, the above two conditions may coincide. Granger (1999) remarks that it would be strange behavior to use the same loss function for Y and $h(Y)$. This awaits further analysis in future research.

LOSS FUNCTIONS FOR ASYMMETRY

The most prevalent loss function for the evaluation of a forecast is the symmetric quadratic function. Negative and positive forecast errors of the same magnitude have the same loss. This functional form is assumed because mathematically it is very tractable, but from an economic point of view, it is not very realistic. For a given information set and under a quadratic loss, the optimal forecast is the conditional mean of the variable under study. The choice of the loss function is fundamental to the construction of an optimal forecast. For asymmetric loss functions, the optimal forecast can be more complicated as it will depend not only on the choice of the loss function but also on the characteristics of the probability density function of the forecast error (Granger 1999).

As Granger (1999) notes, the overwhelming majority of forecast work uses the cost function $c(e) = ae^2$, $a > 0$, largely for mathematical convenience. Asymmetric loss function is often relevant. A few examples from Granger (1999) follow. The cost of arriving ten minutes early at the airport is quite different from arriving ten minutes late. The cost of having a computer that is 10 percent too small for a task is different from the computer being 10 percent too big. The loss of booking a lecture room that has ten seats too many for your class is different from that of a room that has ten seats too few. In dam construction, an underestimate of the peak water level is usually much more serious than an overestimate (Zellner 1986).

There are some commonly used asymmetric loss functions. The check loss function $c(y, f) \equiv [\alpha - 1 (y < f)] \cdot (y - f)$, or $c(e) \equiv [\alpha - 1(e < 0)] \cdot e$, makes the optimal predictor f the conditional quantile. The check loss function is also known as the *tick function* or *lil-lin loss*. The asymmetric quadratic loss $c(e) \equiv [\alpha - 1(e < 0)] \cdot e^2$ can also be considered. A value of $\alpha = 0.5$ gives the symmetric squared error loss.

A particularly interesting asymmetric loss is the *linex function* of Hal Varian (1975), which takes the form

$$c_1(e, \alpha) = \exp(\alpha e_{t+1}) - \alpha e_{t+1} - 1,$$

where α is a scalar that controls the aversion toward either positive ($\alpha > 0$) or negative ($\alpha < 0$) forecast errors. The linex function is differentiable. If $\alpha > 0$, the linex is exponential for $e > 0$ and linear for $e < 0$. If $\alpha < 0$, the linex is exponential for $e < 0$ and linear for $e > 0$. To make the linex more flexible, it can be modified to the double linex loss function by

$$c(e) = c_1(e, \alpha) + c_1(e, -\beta), \qquad \alpha > 0, \beta > 0,$$

$$= \exp(\alpha e) + \exp(-\beta e) - (\alpha - \beta)e - 2$$

which is exponential for all values of e (Granger 1999). When $\alpha = \beta$, it becomes the symmetric double linex loss function.

LOSS FUNCTIONS FOR FORECASTING FINANCIAL RETURNS

Some simple examples of the loss function for evaluating the point forecasts of financial returns are the out-of-sample mean of the following loss functions studied in Yongmiao Hong and Tae-Hwy Lee (2003): the squared error loss $c(y, f) = (y - f)^2$; absolute error loss $c(y, f) = |y - f|$; trading return $c(y, f) = -\text{sign}(f) \cdot y$ (when y is a financial asset return); and the correct direction $c(y, \hat{y}) = -\text{sign}(f) \cdot \text{sign}(y)$, where $\text{sign}(x) = 1(x > 0) - 1(x < 0)$ and $1(\cdot)$ takes the value of 1 if the statement in the parentheses is true and 0 otherwise. The negative signs in the latter two are to make them the loss to minimize (rather than to maximize). The out-of-sample mean of these loss functions are the mean squared forecast errors (MSFE), mean absolute forecast errors (MAFE), mean forecast trading returns (MFTR), and mean correct forecast directions (MCFD):

$$MSFE = P^{-1} \sum_{t=R}^{T} (Y_{t+1} - f_{t,1})^2,$$

$$MAFE = P^{-1} \sum_{t=R}^{T} |Y_{t+1} - f_{t,1}|,$$

$$MFTR = -P^{-1} \sum_{t=R}^{T} \text{sign}(f_{t,1}) \cdot Y_{t+1},$$

$$MCFD = -P^{-1} \sum_{t=R}^{T} 1(\text{sign}(f_{t,1}) \cdot \text{sign}(Y_{t+1}) > 0).$$

These loss functions may further incorporate issues such as interest differentials, transaction costs, and market depth. Because the investors are ultimately trying to maximize profits rather than minimize forecast errors, MSFE and MAFE may not be the most appropriate evaluation criteria. Granger (1999) emphasizes the importance of model evaluation using economic measures such as MFTR rather than statistical criteria such as MSFE and MAFE. Note that MFTR for the buy-and-hold trading strategy with sign $(f_{t,1}) = 1$ is the unconditional mean return of an asset because $MFTR^{\text{Buy\&Hold}} = -P^{-1} \sum_{t=R}^{T} Y_{t+1} \rightarrow -\mu$ in probability as $P \rightarrow \infty$, where $\mu \equiv \mathbb{E}(Y_t)$. MCFD is closely associated with an economic measure as it relates to market timing. Mutual fund managers, for example, can adjust investment portfolios in a timely manner if they can predict the directions of changes, thus earning a return higher than the market average.

LOSS FUNCTIONS FOR ESTIMATION AND EVALUATION

When the forecast is based on an econometric model, to the construction of the forecast, a model needs to be estimated. Inconsistent choices of loss functions in estimation and forecasting are often observed. We may choose a symmetric quadratic objective function to estimate the parameters of the model, but the evaluation of the model-based forecast may be based on an asymmetric loss function. This logical inconsistency is not inconsequential for tests assessing the predictive ability of the forecasts. The error introduced by parameter estimation affects the uncertainty of the forecast and, consequently, any test based on it.

However, in applications, it is often the case that the loss function used for estimation of a model is different from the one(s) used in the evaluation of the model. This logical inconsistency can have significant consequences with regard to comparison of predictive ability of competing models. The uncertainty associated with parameter estimation may result in invalid inference of predictive ability (West 1996). When the objective function in estimation is the same as the loss function in forecasting, the effect of parameter estimation vanishes. If one believes that a particular criteria should be used to evaluate forecasts, then it may also be used at the estimation stage of the modeling process. Gloria González-Rivera, Tae-Hwy Lee, and Emre Yoldas (2007) show this in the context of the VaR model of RiskMetrics, which provides a set of tools to measure market risk and eventually forecast the value-at-risk (VaR) of a portfolio of financial assets. A VaR is a quantile return. RiskMetrics offers a prime example in which the loss function of the forecaster is very well defined. They point out that a VaR is a quantile, and thus the check loss function can be the objective function to estimate the parameters of the RiskMetrics model.

LOSS FUNCTION FOR BINARY FORECAST AND MAXIMUM SCORE

Given a series $\{Y_t\}$, consider the binary variable $G_{t+1} \equiv 1(Y_{t+1} > 0)$. We consider the asymmetric risk function to discuss a binary prediction. To define the asymmetric risk with $A_1 \neq A_2$ and $p = 1$, we consider the binary decision problem of Clive Granger and Hashem Pesaran (2000b), and Tae-Hwy Lee and Yang Yang (2006) with the following 2×2 payoff or utility matrix:

Utility	$G_{t+1} = 1$	$G_{t+1} = 0$
$G_{t,1}(X_t) = 1$	u_{11}	u_{01}
$G_{t,1}(X_t) = 0$	u_{10}	u_{00}

where u_{ij} is the utility when $G_{t,1}(X_t) = j$ is predicted and $G_{t+1} = I$ is realized ($i, j = 1, 2$). Assume $u_{11} > u_{10}$ and $u_{00} > u_{01}$, and u_{ij} are constant over time; $(u_{11} - u_{10}) > 0$ is the utility gain from taking correct forecast when $G_{t,1}(X_t) = 1$; and $(u_{00} - u_{01}) > 0$ is the utility gain from taking correct forecast when $G_{t,1}(X_t) = 0$. Denote

$$\pi(X_t) \equiv \mathbb{E}_{Y_{t+1}}(G_{t+1}|X_t) = Pr(G_{t+1} = 1|X_t).$$

The expected utility of $G_{t,1}(X_t) = 1$ is $u_{11}\pi(X_t) + u_{01}(1 - \pi(X_t))$, and the expected utility of $G_{t,1}(X_t) = 0$ is $u_{10}\pi(X_t) + u_{00}(1 - \pi(X_t))$. Hence, to maximize utility, conditional on the values of X_t, the prediction $G_{t,1}(X_t) = 1$ will be made if

$$u_{11}\pi(X_t) + u_{01}(1 - \pi(X_t)) > u_{10}\pi(X_t) + u_{00}(1 - \pi(X_t)),$$

or

$$\pi(X_t) > \frac{(u_{00} - u_{01})}{(u_{11} - u_{10}) + (u_{00} - u_{01})} \equiv 1 - \alpha.$$

By making a correct prediction, our net utility gain is $(u_{00} - u_{01})$ when $G_{t+1} = 0$, and $(u_{11} - u_{10})$ when $G_{t+1} = 1$. Put another way, our opportunity cost (in the sense that you lose the gain) of a wrong prediction is $(u_{00} - u_{01})$ when $G_{t+1} = 0$ and $(u_{11} - u_{10})$ when $G_{t+1} = 1$. Since a multiple of a utility function represents the same preference, $(1 - \alpha)$ can be viewed as the utility gain from correct prediction when $G_{t+1} = 0$, or the opportunity cost of a false alert. Similarly,

$$\alpha \equiv \frac{(u_{11} - u_{10})}{(u_{11} - u_{10}) + (u_{00} - u_{01})}$$

can be treated as the utility gain from correct prediction when $G_{t+1} = 1$ is realized, or the opportunity cost of a failure-to-alert. We thus can define a cost function $c(e_{t+1})$ with $e_{t+1} = G_{t+1} - G_{t,1}(X_t)$:

Cost	$G_{t+1} = 1$	$G_{t+1} = 0$
$G_{t,1}(X_t) = 1$	0	$1 - \alpha$
$G_{t,1}(X_t) = 0$	α	0

That is,

$$c(e_{t+1}) = \begin{cases} \alpha & \text{if } e_{t+1} = 1 \\ 1 - \alpha & \text{if } e_{t+1} = -1 \\ 0 & \text{if } e_{t+1} = 0 \end{cases},$$

which can be equivalently written as $c(e_{t+1}) = \rho_\alpha(e_{t+1})$, where $\rho_\alpha(e) \equiv [\alpha - 1(e < 0)e]$ is the check function. Hence, the optimal binary predictor $G_{t,1}^\dagger(X_t) = 1(\pi(X_t) > 1 - \alpha)$ maximizing the expected utility minimizes the expected cost $E(\rho_\alpha(e_{t+1})|X_t)$.

The optimal binary prediction that minimizes $\mathbb{E}_{Y_{t+1}}(\rho_\alpha(e_{t+1})|X_t)$ is the conditional α-quantile of G_{t+1}, denoted as

$$\begin{aligned} G_{t,1}^\dagger(X_t) &= Q_\alpha^\dagger(G_{t+1}|X_t) \\ &= \arg\min_{G_{t,1}(X_t)} \mathbb{E}_{Y_{t+1}}(\rho_\alpha(G_{t+1} - G_{t,1}(X_t))|X_t). \end{aligned}$$

This is a maximum score problem of Charles Manski (1975).

Also, as noted by James Powell (1986), using the fact that for any monotonic function $h(\cdot)$, $Q_\alpha(h(Y_{t+1})|X_t) = h(Q_\alpha(Y_{t+1}|X_t))$, which follows immediately from observing that $Pr(Y_{t+1} < y|X_t) = Pr[h(Y_{t+1}) < h(y)|X_t]$, and noting that the indicator function is monotonic, $Q_\alpha(G_{t+1}|X_t) - Q_\alpha(1(Y_{t+1} > 0)|X_t) = 1(Q_\alpha(Y_{t+1}|X_t) > 0)$. Hence,

$$G_{t,1}^\dagger(X_t) = 1(Q_\alpha^\dagger(Y_{t+1}|X_t) > 0).$$

where $Q_\alpha(Y_{t+1}|X_t)$ is the α-quantile function of Y_{t+1} conditional on X_t. Note that $Q_\alpha^\dagger(G_{t+1}|X_t) = \text{argmin} \; \mathbb{E}_{Y_{t+1}}(\rho_\alpha(e_{t+1})|X_t)$ with $e_{t+1} \equiv G_{t+1} - Q_\alpha(G_{t+1}|X_t)$, and $Q_\alpha^\dagger(Y_{t+1}|X_t) = \arg\min \mathbb{E}_{Y_{t+1}}(\rho_\alpha(u_{t+1})|X_t)$ with $u_{t+1} \equiv Y_{t+1} - Q_\alpha(Y_{t+1}|X_t)$. Therefore, the optimal binary prediction can be made from binary quantile regression for G_{t+1}. Binary prediction can also be made from a binary function of the α-quantile for Y_{t+1}.

LOSS FUNCTIONS FOR PROBABILITY FORECASTS

Francis Diebold and Glenn Rudebusch (1989) consider the probability forecasts for business-cycle turning points. To measure the accuracy of predicted probabilities, that is, the average distance between the predicted probabilities and observed realization (as measured by a zero-one dummy variable). Suppose we have time series of P probability forecast $\{p_t\}_{t=R+1}^T$, where p_t is the probability of the occurrence of a turning point at date t. Let $\{d_t\}_{t=R+1}^T$ be the corresponding realization with $d_t = 1$ if a business-cycle turning point (or any defined event) occurs in period t and $d_t = 0$ otherwise. The loss function analogous to the squared error is Brier's score based on the quadratic probability score (QPS):

$$QPS = P^{-1} \sum_{t=R}^{T} 2(p_t - d_t)^2.$$

The QPS ranges from 0 to 2, with 0 for perfect accuracy. As noted by Diebold and Rudebusch (1989), the use of the symmetric loss function may not be appropriate, as a forecaster may be penalized more heavily for missing a call (making a Type II error) than for signaling a false alarm (making a Type I error). Another loss function is given by the log probability score (LPS)

$$LPS = -P^{-1} \sum_{t=R}^{T} \ln\left(p_t^{d_t}(1-p_t)^{(1-d_t)}\right),$$

which is similar to the loss for the interval forecast. Major mistakes are penalized more heavily under LPS than under QPS. Further loss functions are discussed in Diebold and Rudebusch (1989).

Another loss function useful in this context is the Kuipers score (KS), which is defined by

KS = Hit Rate − False Alarm Rate,

where the hit rate is the fraction of the bad events that were correctly predicted as good events (power, or 1— probability of Type II error), and the false alarm rate is the fraction of good events that have been incorrectly predicted as bad events (probability of Type I error).

LOSS FUNCTION FOR INTERVAL FORECASTS

Suppose Y_t is a stationary series. Let the one-period-ahead conditional interval forecast made at time t from a model be denoted as

$$J_{t,1}(\alpha) = (L_{t,1}(\alpha),\ U_{t,1}(\alpha)),\ t = R, \ldots, T,$$

where $L_{t,1}(\alpha)$ and $U_{t,1}(\alpha)$ are the lower and upper limits of the ex ante interval forecast for time $t + 1$ made at time t with the coverage probability α. Define the indicator variable $X_{t+1}(\alpha) = 1[Y_{t+1} \in J_{t,1}(\alpha)]$. The sequence $\{X_{t+1}(\alpha)\}_{t=R}^{T}$ is IID Bernoulli (α). The optimal interval forecast would satisfy $\mathbb{E}(X_{t+1}(\alpha)|I_t) = \alpha$, so that $\{X_{t+1}(\alpha) - \alpha\}$ will be an MD. A better model has a larger expected Bernoulli log-likelihood

$$\mathbb{E}\alpha^{X_{t+1}(\alpha)}(1-\alpha)^{[1-X_{t+1}(\alpha)]}.$$

Hence, we can choose a model for interval forecasts with the smallest out-of-sample mean of the negative predictive log-likelihood defined by

$$-P^{-1} \sum_{t=R}^{T} \ln\left(\alpha^{x_{t+1}(\alpha)}(1-\alpha)^{[1-x_{t+1}(\alpha)]}\right).$$

LOSS FUNCTION FOR DENSITY FORECASTS

Consider a financial return series $\{y_t\}_{t=1}^{T}$. This observed data on a univariate series is a realization of a stochastic process $Y^T \equiv \{Y_\tau : \Omega \to \mathbb{R},\ \tau = 1, 2, \ldots, T\}$ on a complete probability space $(\Omega, \mathfrak{F}_T, P^T_0)$, where $\Omega = \mathbb{R}^T \equiv x^T_{\tau=1}\mathbb{R}$ and $\mathfrak{F}_T = B(\mathbb{R}^T)$ is the Borel σ-field generated by the open sets of $\mathbb{R}^T$, and the joint probability measure $P^T_0(B) \equiv P_0[Y^T \in B]$, $B \in B(\mathbb{R}^T)$ completely describes the stochastic process. A sample of size T is denoted as $y^T \equiv (y_1, \ldots, y_T)'$.

Let σ-finite measure ν^T on $B(\mathbb{R}^T)$ be given. Assume $P^T_0(B)$ is absolutely continuous with respect to ν^T for all $T = 1, 2, \ldots$, so that there exists a measurable Radon-Nikodým density $g^T(y^T) = dP^T_0/d\nu^T$, unique up to a set of zero measure-ν^T.

Following Halbert White (1994), we define a probability model P as a collection of distinct probability measures on the measurable space $(\Omega, \mathfrak{F}_T)$. A probability model P is said to be correctly specified for Y^T if P contains P^T_0. Our goal is to evaluate and compare a set of parametric probability models $\{P^T_\theta\}$, where $P^T_\theta(B) \equiv P_\theta[Y^T \in B]$. Suppose there exists a measurable Radon-Nikodým density $f^T(y^T) = dP^T_\theta/d\nu^T$ for each $\theta \in \Theta$, where θ is a finite-dimensional vector of parameters and is assumed to be identified on Θ, a compact subset of $\mathbb{R}^k$ (see White 1994, Theorem 2.6).

In the context of forecasting, instead of the joint density $g^T(y^T)$, we consider forecasting the conditional density of Y^t, given the information $\mathfrak{F}_{t-1}$ generated by Y_{t-1}. Let $\varphi_t(y_t) \equiv \varphi_t(y_t|\mathfrak{F}_{t-1}) \equiv g^t(y_t)/g^{t-1}(y^{t-1})$ for $t = 2, 3, \ldots$ and $\varphi_1(y_1) \equiv \varphi_1(y_1|\mathfrak{F}_0) \equiv g^1(y^1) = g^1(y_1)$. Thus the goal is to forecast the (true, unknown) conditional density $\varphi_t(y_t)$.

For this, we use a one-step-ahead conditional density forecast model $\psi_t(y_t; \theta) \equiv \psi_t(y_t|\mathfrak{F}_{t-1}; \theta) \equiv f^t(y_t)/f^{t-1}(y^{t-1})$ for $t = 2, 3, \ldots$ and $\psi_1(y_1) \equiv \psi_1(y_1|\mathfrak{F}_0) \equiv f^1(y^1) = f^1(y_1)$. If $\psi_t(y_t; \theta_0) = \varphi_t(y_t)$ almost surely for some $\theta_0 \in \Theta$, then the one-step-ahead density forecast is correctly specified, and it is said to be optimal because it dominates all other density forecasts for any loss functions as discussed in the previous section (see Granger and Pesaran 2000a, 2000b; Diebold et al. 1998; Granger 1999).

In practice, it is rarely the case that we can find an optimal model. As it is very likely that "the true distribution is in fact too complicated to be represented by a simple mathematical function" (Sawa 1978), all the models proposed by different researchers can be possibly misspecified and thereby we regard each model as an approximation of the truth. Our task is then to investigate which density forecast model can approximate the true conditional density most closely. We have to first define a metric to measure the distance of a given model to the truth, and then compare different models in terms of this distance.

The adequacy of a density forecast model can be measured by the conditional Kullback-Leibler information criterion (KLIC) (1951) divergence measure between two conditional densities,

$$I_t(\varphi: \psi, \theta) = \mathbb{E}_{\varphi_t}[\ln \psi_t(y_t) - \ln \psi_t(y_t; \theta)],$$

where the expectation is with respect to the true conditional density $\varphi_t(\cdot | \mathfrak{F}_{t-1})$, $\mathbb{E}_{\varphi_t} \ln \psi_t(y_t | \mathfrak{F}_{t-1}) < \infty$, and $\mathbb{E}_{\varphi_t} \ln \psi_t y_t | \mathfrak{F}_{t-1}; \theta) < \infty$. Following White (1994), we define the distance between a density model and the true density as the minimum of the KLIC

$$I_t(\varphi: \psi, \theta_{t-1}^*) = \mathbb{E}_{\varphi_t}[\ln \psi_t(y_t) - \ln \psi_t(y_t; \theta_{t-1}^*)],$$

where $\theta_{t-1}^* = \arg \min I_t(\varphi: \psi, \theta)$ is the pseudotrue value of θ (Sawa 1978). We assume that θ_{t-1}^* is an interior point of Θ. The smaller this distance is, the closer the density forecast $\psi_t(\cdot | \mathfrak{F}_{t-1}; \theta_{t-1}^*)$ is to the true density $\varphi_t(\cdot | \mathfrak{F}_{t-1})$.

However, $I_t(\varphi: \psi, \theta_{t-1}^*)$ is unknown since θ_{t-1}^* is not observable. We need to estimate θ_{t-1}^*. If our purpose is to compare the out-of-sample predictive abilities among competing density forecast models, we split the data into two parts, one for estimation and the other for out-of-sample validation. At each period t in the out-of-sample period ($t = R + 1, \ldots, T$), we estimate the unknown parameter vector θ_{t-1}^* and denote the estimate as $\hat{\theta}_{t-1}$. Using $\{\hat{\theta}_{t-1}\}_{t=R+1}^T$, we can obtain the out-of-sample estimate of $I_t(\varphi: \psi, \theta_{t-1}^*)$ by

$$I_P(\varphi: \psi) \equiv \frac{1}{P} \sum_{t=R+1}^T \ln\left[\varphi_t(y_t)/\psi_t(y_t; \hat{\theta}_{t-1})\right]$$

where $P = T - R$ is the size of the out-of-sample period. Note that

$$I_P(\varphi: \psi) = \frac{1}{P} \sum_{t=R+1}^T \ln\left[\varphi_t(y_t)/\psi_t(y_t; \theta_{t-1}^*)\right]$$
$$+ \frac{1}{P} \sum_{t=R+1}^T \ln\left[\psi_t(y_t; \theta_{t-1}^*)/\psi_t(y_t; \hat{\theta}_{t-1})\right],$$

where the first term in $I_P(\varphi: \psi)$ measures model uncertainty (the distance between the optimal density $\varphi_t(y_t)$ and the model $\psi_t(y_t; \theta_{t-1}^*)$), and the second term measures parameter estimation uncertainty due to the distance between θ_{t-1}^* and $\hat{\theta}_{t-1}$.

Since the KLIC measure takes on a smaller value when a model is closer to the truth, we can regard it as a loss function and use $I_P(\varphi: \psi)$ to formulate the loss-differential. The out-of-sample average of the loss-differential between model 1 and model 2 is

$$I_P(\varphi: \psi^1) - I_P(\varphi: \psi^2) =$$
$$\frac{1}{P} \sum_{t=R+1}^T \ln\left[\psi_t^2(y_t; \hat{\theta}_{t-1}^2)/\psi_t(y_t; \hat{\theta}_{t-1}^1)\right],$$

which is the ratio of the two predictive log-likelihood functions. With treating model 1 as a benchmark model (for model selection) or as the model under the null hypothesis (for hypothesis testing), $I_P(\varphi: \psi^1) - I_P(\varphi: \psi^2)$ can be considered as a loss function to minimize. To sum up, the KLIC differential can serve as a loss function for density forecast evaluation as discussed in Yong Bao, Tae-Hwy Lee, and Burak Saltoglu (2007).

LOSS FUNCTIONS FOR VOLATILITY FORECASTS

Gloria González-Rivera, Tae-Hwy Lee, and Santosh Mishra (2004) analyze the predictive performance of various volatility models for stock returns. To compare the performance, they choose loss functions for which volatility estimation is of paramount importance. They deal with two economic loss functions (an option pricing function and a utility function) and two statistical loss functions (the check loss for a value-at-risk calculation and a predictive likelihood function of the conditional variance).

LOSS FUNCTIONS FOR TESTING GRANGER-CAUSALITY

In time series forecasting, a concept of causality is due to Granger (1969), who defined it in terms of conditional distribution. Tae-Hwy Lee and Weiping Yang (2007) use loss functions to test for Granger-causality in conditional mean, in conditional distribution, and in conditional quantiles. The causal relationship between money and income (output) has been an important topic that has been extensively studied. However, those empirical studies are almost entirely on Granger-causality in the conditional mean. Compared to conditional mean, conditional quantiles give a broader picture of a variable in various scenarios. Lee and Yang (2007) explore whether forecasting the conditional quantile of output growth may be improved using money. They compare the check (tick) loss functions of the quantile forecasts of output growth with and without using the past information on money growth, and assess the statistical significance of the loss-differential of the unconditional and conditional predictive abilities. As conditional quantiles can be inverted to the conditional distribution, they also test for Granger-causality in the conditional distribution (using a nonparametric copula function). Using U.S. monthly series of real personal income and industrial production for income, and M1 and M2 for money, for 1959 to 2001, they find that out-of-sample quantile forecasting for output growth, particularly in tails, is significantly improved by accounting for money. On the other hand, money-income Granger-causality in the conditional mean is quite weak and unstable. Their results have important implications for monetary policy, showing that the effectiveness of monetary policy has been underestimated by merely testing Granger-causality in mean. Money-income Granger-causality is stronger than it has been known, and therefore the information on money growth can (and should) be more widely utilized in implementing monetary policy.

SEE ALSO *Autoregressive Models; Generalized Least Squares; Least Squares, Ordinary; Logistic Regression; Maximum Likelihood Regression; Optimizing Behavior; Regression; Regression Analysis; Time Series Regression*

BIBLIOGRAPHY

Bao, Yong, Tae-Hwy Lee, and Burak Saltoglu. 2007. Comparing Density Forecast Models. *Journal of Forecasting* 26: 203–225.

Diebold, Francis X., and Glenn D. Rudebusch. 1989. Scoring the Leading Indicators. *Journal of Business* 62 (3): 369–391.

Diebold, Francis X., Todd A. Gunther, and Anthony S. Tay. 1998. Evaluating Density Forecasts with Applications to Financial Risk Management. *International Economic Review* 39: 863–883.

Ding, Zhuanxin, Clive W. J. Granger, and Robert F. Engle. 1993. A Long Memory Property of Stock Market Returns and a New Model. *Journal of Empirical Finance* 1: 83–106.

González-Rivera, Gloria, Tae-Hwy Lee, and Santosh Mishra. 2004. Forecasting Volatility: A Reality Check Based on Option Pricing, Utility Function, Value-at-Risk, and Predictive Likelihood. *International Journal of Forecasting* 20 (4): 629–645.

González-Rivera, Gloria, Tae-Hwy Lee, and Emre Yoldas. 2007. Optimality of the RiskMetrics VaR Model. Unpublished manuscript, University of California, Riverside.

Granger, Clive W. J. 1969. Investigating Causal Relations by Econometric Models and Cross-Spectral Methods. *Econometrica* 37: 424–438.

Granger, Clive W. J. 1999. Outline of Forecast Theory Using Generalized Cost Functions. *Spanish Economic Review* 1: 161–173.

Granger, Clive W. J. 2002. Some Comments on Risk. *Journal of Applied Econometrics* 17: 447–456.

Granger, Clive W. J., and M. Hashem Pesaran. 2000a. A Decision Theoretic Approach to Forecasting Evaluation. In *Statistics and Finance: An Interface*, eds. Wai-Sum Chan, Wai Keung Li, and Howell Tong. London: Imperial College Press.

Granger, Clive W. J., and M. Hashem Pesaran. 2000b. Economic and Statistical Measures of Forecast Accuracy. *Journal of Forecasting* 19: 537–560.

Harter, H. L. 1977. Nonuniqueness of Least Absolute Values Regression. *Communications in Statistics—Theory and Methods* A6: 829–838.

Hong, Yongmiao, and Tae-Hwy Lee. 2003. Inference on Predictability of Foreign Exchange Rates via Generalized Spectrum and Nonlinear Time Series Models. *Review of Economics and Statistics* 85 (4): 1048–1062.

Koenker, Roger, and Gilbert Bassett Jr. 1978. Regression Quantiles. *Econometrica* 46 (1): 33–50.

Kullback, L., and R. A. Leibler. 1951. On Information and Sufficiency. *Annals of Mathematical Statistics* 22: 79–86.

Lee, Tae-Hwy, and Weiping Yang. 2007. Money-Income Granger-Causality in Quantiles. Unpublished manuscript, University of California, Riverside.

Lee, Tae-Hwy, and Yang Yang. 2006. Bagging Binary and Quantile Predictors for Time Series. *Journal of Econometrics* 135: 465–497.

Manski, Charles F. 1975. Maximum Score Estimation of the Stochastic Utility Model of Choice. *Journal of Econometrics* 3 (3): 205–228.

Money, A. H., J. F. Affleck-Graves, M. L. Hart, and G. D. I. Barr. 1982. The Linear Regression Model and the Choice of p. *Communications in Statistics—Simulations and Computations* 11 (1): 89–109.

Nyquist, Hans. 1983. The Optimal Lp-norm Estimation in Linear Regression Models. *Communications in Statistics—Theory and Methods* 12: 2511–2524.

Powell, James L. 1986. Censored Regression Quantiles. *Journal of Econometrics* 32: 143–155.

Sawa, Takamitsu. 1978. Information Criteria for Discriminating among Alternative Regression Models. *Econometrica* 46: 1273–1291.

Varian, Hal R. 1975. A Bayesian Approach to Real Estate Assessment. In *Studies in Bayesian Econometrics and Statistics: In Honor of Leonard J. Savage*, eds. Stephen E. Fienberg and Arnold Zellner, 195–208. Amsterdam: North Holland.

West, Kenneth D. 1996. Asymptotic Inference about Prediction Ability. *Econometrica* 64: 1067–1084.

White, Halbert. 1994. *Estimation, Inference, and Specification Analysis*. Cambridge, U.K.: Cambridge University Press.

Zellner, Arnold. 1986. Bayesian Estimation and Prediction Using Asymmetric Loss Functions. *Journal of the American Statistical Association* 81: 446–451.

Tae-Hwy Lee

LOST CAUSE

SEE *Vindication.*

LOTTERIES

Lotteries are most frequently government-sponsored alternatives to primarily illegal numbers games whereby the participants win cash prizes if they match a series of numbers or symbols. It can be argued that lotteries date back to biblical times (the process of "casting lots") and there is considerable historical evidence of lotteries from the sixteenth century forward as a means by which municipalities raised funds for government finance. In the eighteenth and nineteenth centuries numerous lotteries raised very significant revenues to build roads, canals, courthouses, and so on, and in particular, to finance wars (Gribbin and Bean 2006). In the modern era of lotteries (presumed to have begun in 1964 with the initiation of the New Hampshire lottery in the United States), lotteries have generally not generated commensurately large revenues, but have served as an alternative revenue source that is politically expedient due to both participant and nonparticipant perceptions.

Lottery players generally cite the expected utility of a potential win as justification for playing, or at the least, the utility derived from thinking about what they would do with the money if they win. There is limited entertainment value in lottery instruments beyond these measures of expected utility, and no skill. Lottery players also recognize that even if they do not win, their money is designated for a generally desirable beneficiary group such as public schools, the elderly, or specific public works projects. Lottery commissions recognize the lack of entertainment value in their games and thus must constantly innovate to maintain player interest in participation.

Nonplayers appreciate that lotteries allow them to shift a portion of the municipal tax burden to those who do not understand or care about the long odds of winning. Their perception is the opposite of the advertising slogan, that is, "you cannot lose if you do not play." Legislative leaders understand lotteries for what they have become: tax revenue sources that are not perceived as such, that allow the government representatives to take advantage of fungibility to shift funds to whichever projects or groups they choose, while maintaining the perception of effective earmarking for a desirable recipient group (Borg and Mason 1988).

From a procedural standpoint, lottery games fall into two basic categories: instant games and lotto games. Instant games are mostly scratch-off instruments whereby the player uses a coin or some other means to remove a coating from areas on a card, attempting to match a particular series of like symbols to win a predetermined amount. These games represent a relatively minor portion of the revenue raised by lotteries, but the area in lottery administration that requires the most innovation to maintain player interest. Lotto games are closer to the illegal numbers games mentioned above, requiring the winning player to match from three to six numbers, most frequently printed on ping-pong balls drawn from a container. The payouts in these games are substantial, ranging from hundreds to hundreds of millions of dollars. Most of

these lotto games reflect odds that follow simple mathematical combinations, for example $_xC_6$ is a standard for many U.S. state games, where x is 49 numbers, 53 numbers, or some other magnitude. The $_{53}C_6$ game implies that odds of winning are 1 in approximately 22 million. Longer odds are encountered in multistate games that also imply that the last ball drawn reflects a specific number (e.g., the "powerball").

Lottery games are generally available in a large number of retail locations including grocery stores, convenience stores, and other establishments that are licensed by the municipality to distribute the tickets. Ticket sellers receive a commission for selling the tickets (frequently around 5% of sales) and many also share in the good fortune of winners with extra compensation. Evidence suggests that play increases when ticket availability is found close to either one's home or workplace. Consequently, lottery ticket sales are frequently higher per capita in large cities as opposed to small towns and rural areas (Clotfelter and Cook 1989).

There are other significant demographic characteristics of lottery players that identify the implications of the tax inherent in lottery games. Consistently, researchers have discovered that lottery players tend to be older, and frequently members of racial and ethnic minority groups. Far more players come from large municipalities. There is significant crossover between states and countries whenever jackpots of the lotto games become large, and women tend to play lottery games slightly more than men. From an economic standpoint, the most significant demographic reality of lotteries is that while lottery play increases with income, it does so at a declining rate, suggesting that the routinely 50 percent tax rate inherent in lottery games is regressive (Clotfelter and Cook 1989, among many).

Among the other economic implications of lotteries, lotteries are inefficient from a tax standpoint. The responsiveness of demand for lotto games to price changes is often greater than one in absolute value, implying that taxes inherent in lottery games do not raise the same levels of revenue for the same cost as other tax sources. This reflects the luxury nature of lotto tickets in the player's market basket. The magnitude of this effect is mitigated whenever a municipality increases the frequency of lotto games during the week, so current trends have reduced this effect somewhat (Mason, Steagall, and Fabritius 1997). Lottery tax revenues are generally relatively small compared to other tax sources, and are not as stable given that their magnitudes frequently depend on rollovers, and the impact that they have on player frenzy. Earmarking of lottery revenues to specific recipients is a bait-and-switch process that motivates players to justify their involvement while legislative bodies shift funds away from the designated recipient simultaneously. Numerous studies have shown that designated recipients of lottery revenues, for example, public education, are often worse off after the creation of a lottery (see, for example, Gribbin and Bean 2006). As more states adopt lotteries, the competition for lottery player dollars becomes more intense while the attractiveness of playing lottery games wane. This makes it likely that future lottery revenues generated by all states will diminish.

In summary, lotteries are a means by which legislative groups motivate individuals to provide tax revenue that they do not perceive as such in exchange for minute chances of winning cash awards. The economic consequences of these lotteries are just as condemning. Perhaps the best perspective on lotteries is that "your odds of winning are almost as good if you do not play." The forty-one states in the United States and many municipalities around the world should learn this lesson to generate more stable and more conscientious government revenue generation.

SEE ALSO *Expected Utility Theory*

BIBLIOGRAPHY

Borg, Mary O., and Paul M. Mason. 1988. The Budgetary Incidence of a Lottery to Support Education. *National Tax Journal* 41: 75–85.

Clotfelter, Charles T., and Philip J. Cook. 1989. *State Lotteries in America.* Cambridge, MA: Harvard University Press.

Gribbins, Donald W., and Jonathan J. Bean. 2006. Adoption of State Lotteries in the United States, with a Closer Look at Illinois. *Independent Review* 10 (3): 351–365.

Mason, Paul M., Jeffrey W. Steagall, and Michael M. Fabritius. 1997. The Elasticity of Demand for Lotto Tickets and the Corresponding Welfare Effects. *Public Finance Quarterly* 25 (5): 474–490.

Paul M. Mason

LOUIS XVI

SEE *French Revolution; Left Wing.*

LOVE CANAL

In 1894 entrepreneur William T. Love began building a canal to connect the Niagara River to Lake Ontario. The canal was to provide water and hydroelectric power for the city of Niagara Falls, New York. Some eighty-four years later, however, the canal became a symbol of the threat of toxic chemical wastes to human communities and the environment, and Love Canal became a moniker for a social movement whose advocates believe that all people are entitled to protection from such hazards.

Love sold his partially completed sixteen-acre canal at public auction in 1947. There was a nationwide depression that had left him short of funds, and the invention of alternating electrical current had rendered his hydroelectric project obsolete. Hooker Chemicals and Plastic Corporation (later known as Hooker Chemical Corporation, and more recently as Occidental Chemical Corporation or OxyChem) bought the site after determining it was isolated and sparsely populated at the time and had an impermeable clay substrate, which made it a good location for a chemical waste landfill. According to New York state officials, the city of Niagara Falls and some federal agencies (including the military) regularly dumped chemical and other wastes at the site, in addition to the approximately 21,800 tons of chemical wastes dumped by Hooker until 1952. The company sold the site for one dollar in 1953 to the Niagara Falls Board of Education, which intended to eventually construct a grade school and playground on it.

Subsequent events ignited controversy over who—Hooker or the Niagara Falls Board of Education—was legally responsible for the exposure of the public to the chemical wastes and the resulting illnesses experienced by families who resided in the area. Despite the restrictions and risk stipulations in the deed conveyed to the Board of Education by Hooker, the Board decided to develop the land above the fill site and its surrounding area. The Board authorized construction of an elementary school on the site in 1955, the city constructed a sewer line through the canal in 1960, and developers constructed homes and streets next to the site. The toxic chemicals stored there eventually seeped from their ruptured and deteriorated containers into the soil, basements, and storm sewers. In April 1978, Michael Brown, a reporter for the *Niagara Gazette*, wrote a series of articles on hazardous wastes in the Niagara Falls area. By August 1978, the New York health commissioner declared a state of emergency in the area, and 239 families were evacuated. Five days later President Jimmy Carter approved emergency financial aid to permanently relocate these families. In March 1980 the president declared a state of emergency at Love Canal and funded the permanent evacuation and relocation of an additional 780 families. Brown drew national attention to the disaster in his 1980 book *Laying Waste: The Poisoning of America by Toxic Chemicals.*

State and federal investigations into the conditions at the landfill identified 248 different chemicals and 82 chemical compounds, 11 of which were known carcinogens. These toxins included benzene, toluene, chloroform, carbon tetrachloride, lindane, and trichlorophenol that was contaminated with the carcinogen dioxin. Residents exposed to these and other chemicals reported miscarriages, birth defects, cancer, and asthmatic, urinary, and convulsive disorders. Beginning in 1979, residents initiated a series of lawsuits against Hooker, the city, the Board of Education, and several public agencies. In April 1980 the State of New York filed a $635 million lawsuit against Occidental Petroleum (OxyChem's parent company) and its two subsidiaries, charging that the companies were responsible for the Love Canal disaster. The New York Supreme Court announced three years later a $20 million settlement of the 1,337 claims filed. Occidental Petroleum agreed in 1989 and later paid the Environmental Protection Agency $129 million for cleanup costs.

Epidemiological evidence of chemical exposure causing abnormal rates of acute and chronic illness has been controversial. Studies conducted by scientists and by the New York State Department of Health as recently as 1997 found that the residents who lived closest to the canal experienced rates of certain diseases (for example, liver disorders and lymphomas, leukemia, and several other cancers) that were no different from those of control groups who lived elsewhere in the county and in upstate New York. Other findings showed, however, that Love Canal residents had higher rates of spontaneous abortions, childhood disorders, lung and respiratory disorders, and female genitourinary cancers.

In 1988, based on its own five-year study and further investigation by the Environmental Protection Agency, the New York State Department of Health concluded that a segment of the canal area was again habitable and proposed to resettle the area. Lois Gibbs, who had organized the Love Canal Homeowners Association in 1978 and whose son had attended the contaminated elementary school, energized the public to fight against the state's effort to move families back to the canal area. In 1981 Gibbs founded the Citizens' Clearinghouse for Hazardous Wastes (later renamed as the Center for Health, Environment, and Justice).

The Citizens' Clearinghouse became a national resource that provided guidance and education to many of the grassroots groups and people of color who opposed chemical wastes and emissions in their communities and neighborhoods. These groups and their supporters helped define the early agenda of the American environmental justice movement, and they drew media and political attention to socioeconomic inequities (e.g., environmental racism) associated with waste facility siting, industrial emissions, and regulatory enforcement. Their collective efforts galvanized public awareness of these issues during the 1980s and 1990s and bridged other major social movements involving civil rights, feminism, and worker safety.

SEE ALSO *Disaster Management; Environmental Impact Assessment; Justice; Pollution; Racism; Toxic Waste*

BIBLIOGRAPHY

Axelrod, David. 1981. *Love Canal: A Special Report to the Governor and Legislature: April 1981.* Albany, NY: New York State Department of Public Health. http://www.health.state.ny.us/nysdoh/lcanal/lcreport.htm.

Brown, Michael Harold. 1980. *Laying Waste: The Poisoning of America by Toxic Chemicals.* New York: Pantheon.

Bullard, Robert D. 1993. Anatomy of Environmental Racism and the Environmental Justice Movement. In *Confronting Environmental Racism: Voices from the Grassroots,* ed. Robert D. Bullard, 15–39. Boston: South End Press.

Center for Health, Environment, and Justice. http://www.chej.org/.

Domokos-Bays, Becky L. 1997. The Role of the Citizen's Clearinghouse for Hazardous Wastes as an Agent of Adult Education in the Environmental Justice Movement from 1981–1995. PhD diss., Virginia Polytechnic Institute and State University, Blacksburg.

Fletcher, Thomas H. 2003. *From Love Canal to Environmental Justice: The Politics of Hazardous Waste on the Canada–U.S. Border.* Peterborough, Ontario: Broadview.

Gibbs, Lois Marie. 1998. *Love Canal: The Story Continues.* Rev. ed. Gabriola Island, British Columbia: New Society.

Grossman, Karl. 1994. The People of Color Environmental Summit. In *Unequal Protection: Environmental Justice and Communities of Color,* ed. Robert D. Bullard, 272–297. San Francisco: Sierra Club.

Mazur, Allan. 1998. *A Hazardous Inquiry: The Rashomon Effect at Love Canal.* Cambridge, MA: Harvard University Press.

New York State Department of Health. September 2002. *Love Canal Follow-up Health Study—September 2002.* Albany, NY: Author. http://www.health.state.ny.us/nysdoh/lcanal/902news.htm.

Niagara Gazette. 1980. Love Canal Chronology. May 23. http://ublib.buffalo.edu/libraries/projects/lovecanal/chronology_menu.html.

Online Ethics Center for Engineering and Science. 2004. *Love Canal—An Introduction.* Cleveland, OH: Case Western Reserve University. http://onlineethics.org/environment/lcanal/index.html.

Taylor, Dorceta. 2000. The Rise of the Environmental Justice Paradigm. *American Behavioral Scientist* 43 (4): 508–580.

University Archives. 1998. *Love Canal Collection.* Buffalo: University of New York at Buffalo, University Libraries.

Whalen, Robert P. 1978. *Love Canal: Public Health Time Bomb, A Special Report to the Governor and Legislature: September 1978.* Albany, NY: New York State Department of Health. http://www.health.state.ny.us/nysdoh/lcanal/lctimbmb.htm.

John K. Thomas

LOWE, ADOLPH

SEE *Economics of Control.*

LOWI, THEODORE J.
1931–

Theodore J. Lowi is known within the fields of political science, sociology, and law for his statement of interest-group liberalism, a theory of political power in the United States widely accepted (particularly in the 1970s and 1980s) as an alternative to the pluralist theory of political power advocated by Robert A. Dahl (b. 1915). In *The End of Liberalism* (1979) Lowi presumed that single-power-elite theories of U.S. politics are generally incorrect, in that Lowi described political power as wielded by different elites in different policy areas. But his interpretation of this research finding was very different from the pluralist interpretation. Lowi argued that such fragmented power leads to the control of most domestic policy areas by special-interest coalitions of interest groups, administrators, and legislative committee members, who are unresponsive to control by legislative and executive leaders, or by the judiciary. Lowi's use of the term *liberalism* in this theory does not refer to the political opinions of some Americans, but to the term's use in political philosophy, referring to those defining democracy according to some process of decision making, rather than to those referring to standards of justice in the substance of government action. Lowi argued that liberalism in the process sense had come to permeate the values of legislative, executive, and judicial decision makers in the United States, so that laws were written and interpreted without useful reference to clear standards of justice and administration. He argued that as a consequence, lower-level executive decision makers interpreted the practical meaning of legislation after a process of bargaining with organized interest groups, thereby forming a special-interest policymaking coalition specific to a particular area of public policy. To reform interest-group liberalism, Lowi advocated institutional changes to promote the statement of clear standards in legislation and administration of public policy, such as judicial prohibition of legislation lacking such clear standards.

In 1976 a survey of political scientists ranked Lowi as having "made the most significant contribution to the discipline" from 1970 to 1976 (Roettger 1978). During the 1970s Lowi's interpretation of power and policymaking was not effectively challenged by other scholars. The power-elite theory of C. Wright Mills had been discredited within political science by the criticisms of the pluralists, led by Robert A. Dahl (Mills 1956; Dahl 1961), although political scientists often apply a version of elite theory to foreign policy decisions. The more complex elitist theory of Thomas R. Dye (ranked third in the above survey) and L. Harmon Zeigler simply included Lowi's policy-area elites as a part of their description of a national policymaking elite numbering in the thousands (1975,

pp. 274–276, 394). Faced with about twenty case studies of particular national policy areas tending to support Lowi's theory, the pluralists did not attempt a general criticism of Lowi's views. Instead, they directed their research at dealing with the question of control of the political agenda (Polsby 1980). Lacking much in the way of opposing argument, Lowi's views about power and policymaking were preeminent for about a decade. However, research by a later generation of pluralists found that many areas of domestic policymaking actually show numerous interest groups in contention with one another, thereby precluding domination of a policy area by a single coalition (Walker 1991). These neopluralist critics agreed that the pattern described by Lowi can be found in some areas, known as "policy niches."

The End of Liberalism is based on Lowi's previous delineation of three types of public policies: distributive, regulatory, and redistributive. (Lowi added a fourth, government reform, somewhat later.) Distributive policies encompass the distribution of particular benefits, usually material ones such as government contracts, grants, and construction projects. As interest groups cooperate to divide up such goods, distributive policies tend to exhibit little conflict and are characterized by interest-group liberalism. Regulatory policies regard the passage and enforcement of legal regulations such as labor law, civil rights law, environmental rules, and so forth. Such policy areas often show the politics of pluralist conflict among interest groups, unless the regulations set unenforceable standards, in which case interest-group liberalism prevails. Redistributive policies take wealth from the rich and give to the poor, and are characterized by class politics, uncommon in the United States. Lowi's contrasts among these three types of policies are now widely accepted by political scientists.

SEE ALSO *Elite Theory; Lynd, Robert and Helen; Networks; Social Movements*

BIBLIOGRAPHY

Dahl, Robert A. 1961. *Who Governs?* New Haven, CT: Yale University Press.

Dye, Thomas R., and L. Harmon Zeigler. 1975. *The Irony of Democracy.* 3rd ed. North Scituate, MA: Duxbury.

Lowi, Theodore J. 1964. American Business, Public Policy, Case Studies and Political Theory. *World Politics* 16 (July): 677–715.

Lowi, Theodore J. 1979. *The End of Liberalism.* Rev. ed. New York: Norton.

Mills, C. Wright. 1956. *The Power Elite.* New York: Oxford University Press.

Polsby, Nelson W. 1980. *Community Power and Political Theory.* 2nd ed. New Haven, CT: Yale University Press.

Roettger, Walter B. 1978. Strata and Stability: Reputations of American Political Scientists. *PS* 11: 6–12.

Walker, Jack L., Jr. 1991. *Mobilizing Interest Groups in America.* Ann Arbor: University of Michigan Press.

Andrew McFarland

LOWIE, ROBERT
1883–1957

Robert Harry Lowie, an Austrian-American anthropologist, was one of the leaders of Franz Boas's (1858–1942) first generation of students. Lowie was noted for his contributions to American Indian ethnography, social structure, and ethnological theory.

Born to a middle-class Jewish family in Vienna, Austria, Robert Lowie was the son of Samuel Lowie, a Hungarian-born businessman, and Ernestine Kuhn Lowie, the daughter of a Viennese physician. Immigrating with his family at the age of ten, he attended public school in New York City. In 1901 Lowie graduated with a BA in classics from the City College of New York. After teaching briefly in the New York school system, he enrolled in Columbia University, where he was soon attracted to anthropologist Franz Boas and his embodiment of German scientific ideals. Entering the doctoral program in anthropology in 1904, Lowie earned his PhD in 1908 with a dissertation on "The Test-Theme in North American Mythology."

Robert Lowie joined curator Clark Wissler (1870–1947) at the American Museum of Natural History, which sponsored Lowie's first field work in 1906 among the Lemhi (Northern Shoshone) of Idaho. The following year, Lowie officially joined the staff of the museum as an assistant, becoming assistant curator in 1909 and associate curator in 1913. During his tenure at the museum, Lowie carried out most of his ethnographic fieldwork, studying the Assiniboine, Northern Blackfoot, Chipewyan, Hidatsa, Southern Ute, Southern Paiute, Northern Paiute (Paviotso), Washo, and Hopi. Despite this wide range, Lowie's specialty was the Native peoples of the Great Plains, particularly the Crow of Montana. He first worked among them in 1907, returning every summer from 1910 to 1916, and again in 1931.

In most respects, Lowie's ethnography was thoroughly Boasian. Motivated by the "salvage paradigm," predicated on the disappearance of Native cultures, in his ethnography he focused on a general cultural survey that called for the mapping of cultures and languages. His fieldwork was also holistic and comprehensive, studying every aspect of a group's culture from artifacts to social organization to religion and mythology.

After spending a year teaching anthropology at the University of California, Berkeley (1917–1918), Lowie joined the faculty as an associate professor in 1921, becoming a full professor in 1925 and retiring in 1950. During the 1930s, Lowie developed a new areal interest: South America. He edited and translated the writings of Curt Nimuendajú (1883–1945), a German-Brazilian ethnographer of the Ge-speaking peoples of Brazil. These interests led to his planning and support for the *Handbook of South American Indians* (1946–1959), edited by his student Julian Steward (1902–1972).

Many of Lowie's books stemmed from his interest in summarizing the state of anthropological knowledge and communicating it to a broadly educated general audience; these included *Culture and Ethnology* (1917), *Primitive Society* (1920), *Primitive Religion* (1924), and *Social Organization* (1948). His interest in cultural critique, expressed in *Are We Civilized?* (1929) and other essays of the 1920s, led to his *Toward Understanding Germany* (1954), a detailed anthropological analysis of a European society.

In anthropological theory, Robert Lowie was known for his empiricism, inspired by youthful influences of Ernst Mach (1838–1916) and Ernst Haeckel (1834–1919). Lowie thought it important to emphasize facts and distinguish them from interpretation, amassing full and accurate evidence with an aversion to premature generalization. At the center of his interests was social organization, both in kinship and in voluntary associations such as Plains Indian military societies. *Primitive Society*, his major work on the subject, embodied the Boasian critique of Lewis Henry Morgan's (1818–1881) unilinear evolution. Lowie's famed characterization of culture as "a thing of shreds and patches" expressed the Boasian belief that while the sources of any given culture might be diverse, they were integrated in a unique pattern. Lowie extended this approach in his formulation of the method of controlled comparison. His interest in the philosophy of science revealed itself in his *History of Ethnological Theory* (1937), one of the first summaries of its kind. Like all his work, it was distinguished for its grasp of international scholarship.

In 1933, at the age of fifty, Lowie married Luella Cole (1893–1970), a psychologist; they had no children. In the course of his long career, Lowie received many professional honors, including service as the editor of *American Anthropologist* (1924–1933) and president of the American Folklore Society (1916–1917), American Ethnological Society (1920–1921), and American Anthropological Association (1935–1936). A socialist in his youth, he was a pacifist during World War I (1914–1918) and a passionate opponent of Nazism. Robert Lowie died of cancer in Berkeley; his papers are preserved at the Department of Anthropology of the American Museum of Natural History and the Bancroft Library at the University of California, Berkeley.

SEE ALSO *Anthropology; Boas, Franz; Ethnography; Jews; Native Americans; Nazism; Observation, Participant; Pacifism; Socialism*

BIBLIOGRAPHY

PRIMARY WORKS

Lowie, Robert H. 1908. The Test-Theme in North American Mythology. *Journal of American Folklore* 21: 97–148.

Lowie, Robert H. 1916. Plains Indians Age-Societies: Historical and Comparative Summaries. *American Museum of Natural History, Anthropological Papers* 11: 877–992.

Lowie, Robert H. 1917. *Culture and Ethnology.* New York: McMurtrie.

Lowie, Robert H. 1920. *Primitive Society.* New York: Boni and Liveright.

Lowie, Robert H. 1924. *Primitive Religion.* New York: Boni and Liveright.

Lowie, Robert H. 1929. *Are We Civilized? Human Cultures in Perspective.* New York: Harcourt, Brace.

Lowie, Robert H. 1935. *The Crow Indians.* New York: Farrar and Rinehart.

Lowie, Robert H. 1937. *The History of Ethnological Theory.* New York: Farrar and Rinehart.

Lowie, Robert H. 1948. *Social Organization.* New York: Rinehart.

Lowie, Robert H. 1954. *Toward Understanding Germany.* Chicago: University of Chicago Press.

Lowie, Robert H. 1959. *Robert H. Lowie, Ethnologist: A Personal Record.* Berkeley: University of California Press.

Lowie, Robert H. 1960. *Selected Papers in Anthropology.* Ed. Cora Du Bois. Berkeley: University of California Press.

SECONDARY WORKS

Murphy, Robert F. 1972. *Robert H. Lowie.* New York: Columbia University Press.

Radin, Paul. 1958. Robert H. Lowie. *American Anthropologist* 60: 358–361.

Steward, Julian H. 1946–1959. *Handbook of South American Indians. Bureau of American Ethnology Bulletin* 143, Vols. 1–7. Washington, DC: Smithsonian Institution.

Steward, Julian H. 1974. Robert Harry Lowie: June 12, 1883–September 21, 1957. *Biographical Memoirs* 44 (6): 175–212. Washington, DC: National Academy of Sciences.

Ira Jacknis

LOW-INCOME LIFESTYLES

SEE *Lifestyles.*

LOYALISTS

Loyalism is a form of group identity based on the idea of fealty to the political status quo. The status quo is typically an imperial order like the Spanish or British empires or the French *ancien régime.* Sometimes, as in the Spanish case, the term *royalist* is used, while at other times *counterrevolutionary* may be applied. What is significant from the point of view of nationalism and ethnic studies is that in some cases entire ethnic groups may define themselves through their loyalty to a monarch. In colonial situations, numerous ethnic groups like the Ambonese in Indonesia or Karen of Burma favored retention of the colonial tie and were "loyal" in this way. However, these groups did not rely on loyalty to the empire as a prop of identity. In historical terms, use of the word *loyalist* has therefore principally focused on those "British" peoples who defined themselves through their loyalty to the British Empire in North America and Ireland.

In the American colonies in the mid-eighteenth century, there was no movement for independence. The settlers, 98 percent of them Protestant and 80 percent deriving from the British Isles, were content to remain in the empire. They defined themselves as English-speaking Protestants who had won a victory for Britain in the Seven Years' War (1756–1763) against the Catholic French and their Indian allies in North America. The sphere of battle covered present-day Canada (Quebec, Ontario, Nova Scotia) as well as the United States (New York, Pennsylvania) in one undifferentiated whole. George Washington (1732–1799) played an important role on the British side.

Prior to about 1774, the identity of the American loyalists could well be described as dualistic. On the one hand, they saw themselves as "Americans" with a distinct geographical and cultural particularity. On the other hand, they identified with the British flag, language, and (Protestant) religion against the Spanish and French, as well as the British Empire and its mission (Colley 1992). Independence altered this calculus for roughly two-thirds of the colonists, but one-third remained loyal to the British Crown. Persecution—extending to tarring and feathering and land seizures—led most to downplay their allegiance or flee. Approximately 19,000 loyalists fled to present-day Canada, forming the United Empire Loyalists. These loyalists were the first major British Protestant settlers in Canada and largely laid down the dialect, ideology, and institutions of English-speaking Canada. In 1812 key loyalists like Sir Isaac Brock (1769–1812) and the Mohawk leader Joseph Brant's son John Brant played a role in rebuffing the American invasion of Canada. This became part of the mythology of the United Empire Loyalists, which was celebrated a century later by British Canadians, most of whom were not descendants of the American loyalists, but of subsequent waves of American economic migrants and British immigrants (Kaufmann 1997).

At the time of Canadian confederation in 1867, roughly half the English-speaking population of Canada was of Scottish or Irish-Protestant extraction. The large-scale movement of Irish-Protestant settlers to Canada brought the other major "loyalist" ethnic group together with its Canadian soul mate. Protestants in Ireland were mainly the descendants of English and Scottish settlers from the early 1600s. The Anglo-Irish elite derived from a longstanding high-church Anglican population whose cultural life was centered upon Dublin. However, the bulk of the Protestant population was "planted" by the British Crown from Elizabethan times (post–1600), mainly in the nine northern counties comprising Ulster.

Irish loyalism was initially divided because Presbyterians and other dissenting sects experienced discrimination (such as the nonrecognition of marriages) from the Anglican authorities. Fired by Whig ideas, Presbyterians were in the forefront of both the American Revolution (1775–1783) and the uprising of the United Irishmen in Ireland in 1798. Both movements sought independence from Britain and were inspired by liberalism rather than anti-Catholicism. However, popular conflict at the everyday level between Protestants and Catholics was a reality upon which political entrepreneurs could draw. After all, there was a history of sectarian strife and bloodshed, especially around the English Civil War in the 1640s. As the United Irishmen began to seek support from the Catholic Defender movement, with its Catholic-rights agenda, a countermovement sprang up among the Protestants. This movement coalesced into the Loyal Orange Order, formed in 1795 near Portadown in County Armagh after a series of local sectarian skirmishes. Based on the structures of freemasonry, Orangeism rapidly spread throughout Ireland, where it espoused an ideology of loyalty to Protestantism and to the Crown, which served as the political defender of Protestantism in the British Empire (Haddick-Flynn 1999).

Orangeism was soon exported to Scotland and England (by 1810) and Canada (by 1820) with returning British soldiers and through Irish-Protestant emigration. In Canada, it was so successful that it surpassed the Irish organization in numbers soon after 1900. The late nineteenth century saw the emergence of a full-blown Britannic nationalism, an expression of pride in British ethnic origins and political achievements that spanned Britain, Ireland, Canada, Australasia, and South Africa (Cole 1970). This imperial sentiment colored loyalism in Canada and Ireland. But it never displaced the metropole-settler dualism that is the hallmark of loyalist identity.

The decline of the British Empire drove home the local (or settler) side of loyalist identity for Canadians (as well as Australians, Scots, and Newfoundlanders), leading to new expressions of local nationalism in these places. In Canada, loyalism died hard, as witnessed in the 1965 debate over whether to retain the Union Jack or adopt a new maple leaf flag (Buckner 2004). In Ireland, the home rule crisis of 1884 to 1886 proved the last time that the Irish Protestants could count on Unionist support from mainland Britain. After the second home rule crisis of 1912 to 1914, Irish Protestants began to militarily organize and mentally prepare themselves to go it alone in the six Protestant-majority counties in the northeast of Ulster. The Northern Ireland Act of 1922 recognized the Protestant-dominated Northern Ireland state, restoring the British loyalty of the Ulster-Protestants. However, this loyalism was tested again in the 1960s when agitation by the 35 percent Catholic minority led the British government to press loyalists to reform their system of local government and housing, and share power with Catholics. When such reforms were not forthcoming, the British stepped in to directly rule the province, but by then the Irish Republican Army (IRA) military and terror campaign was in full swing. Twenty-five years of bombing and violence ensued, as the British army and its loyalist auxiliaries (local police and defense regiments) tried to subdue the IRA.

With the IRA ceasefires in 1995 and 1997, and the Good Friday Agreement of 1998, some saw a new dawn for Northern Ireland. Catholics made gains toward economic and political parity with Protestants, but power sharing, premised on the inclusion of Sinn Fein/IRA in government, proved a nonstarter for most Protestants. By 2007, decommissioning of IRA weapons remained the main obstacle to peace, but changes within loyalism were also important. Loyalists have increasingly turned inward, shifting from being "loyal" to "rebel" Unionists (Kaufmann 2007). Skeptical of Britain for "selling us out," they have begun to celebrate their Scottish roots, their Ulster-Scots dialect, and their role in anti-British episodes like the American Revolution and even the United Irish uprising. Though most identify as "British," this label does not connote civic attachments to the British state, but rather an ethnic attachment to the Ulster-Protestants and their six-county homeland of "Ulster."

SEE ALSO *American Revolution; Colonialism*

BIBLIOGRAPHY

Buckner, Phillip, ed. 2004. *Canada and the End of Empire.* Vancouver: University of British Columbia Press.

Cole, Douglas. 1970. Canada's "Nationalistic" Imperialists. *Journal of Canadian Studies* 5 (3): 43–70.

Colley, Linda. 1992. *Britons: Forging the Nation, 1707–1837.* New Haven, CT: Yale University Press.

Haddick-Flynn, Kevin. 1999. *Orangeism: The Making of a Tradition.* Dublin: Wolfhound.

Kaufmann, Eric. 1997. Condemned to Rootlessness: The Loyalist Origins of Canada's Identity Crisis. *Nationalism and Ethnic Politics* 3 (1): 110–135.

Kaufmann, Eric P. 2007. *The Orange Order: A Contemporary Northern Irish History.* Oxford: Oxford University Press.

Eric P. Kaufmann

LSD

SEE *Drugs of Abuse; Hallucinogens.*

LUCAS, ROBERT E., JR.
1937–

Born September 15, 1937, in Yakima, Washington, Robert E. Lucas Jr. was the first child of the owners of the Lucas Ice Creamery, which did not survive the 1937–1938 downturn. After completing his BA in history at the University of Chicago in 1959, he enrolled in graduate school at the University of California at Berkeley, where he became interested in economic history and decided he needed more background in economics. This brought him back to the University of Chicago, where he became so interested in economics that he obtained his PhD in this field in 1964. Lucas worked at Carnegie Mellon University, originally known as the Carnegie Institute of Technology, until 1974, when he returned once again to the University of Chicago. In 1995 Lucas received the Nobel Memorial Prize in Economics "for having developed and applied the hypothesis of rational expectations, and thereby having transformed macroeconomic analysis and deepened our understanding of economic policy." Indeed he is often considered the preeminent macroeconomist of the last quarter of the twentieth century.

Lucas is one of the founding fathers of new classical macroeconomics, which contrasts sharply with the Keynesian insights that dominated macroeconomics through the 1960s. The new classical paradigm starts from the premise that economics has to account for the decisions made by firms and people in ways that are consistent with the idea of optimizing behavior, because ad hoc assumptions about their behavior are not compatible with the microfoundations of economic theory. At the same time Lucas criticized the typical Keynesian assumptions that markets do not clear and that economic agents do not always pursue optimizing strategies. In addition he challenged adaptive expectations economists for working with models that forecast better than agents, thereby leaving space for the non-neutrality of money in the short run. These insights are associated with, among others, Milton Friedman and Anna Schwartz. Instead, Lucas obliterated the distinction between the short run and the long run. Overall then Lucas may be viewed as replacing earlier ad hoc treatments with an approach squarely based on the microfoundations of incentives, information, and optimization.

Lucas has made contributions to a wide variety of fields, including financial economics, monetary theory, public finance, international economics, and economic growth. In the last he contributed the insights that human capital accumulation has significant external effects and that learning by doing plays an important role in the process of human capital accumulation. He is known especially for the so-called Lucas critique, according to which parameters of economic relationships are likely to change due to policy changes, rendering them unreliable for making policy recommendations. By overturning the basis for governmental fine-tuning, this transformed thinking on economic policy and inspired Lucas to develop powerful and operational methods for drawing conclusions from models that avoid this pitfall. In particular he is known for his efforts to embed theories in general equilibrium dynamics.

The attempts of Lucas and his colleagues to create microfoundations for macroeconomics ran into a major stumbling block in the shape of the Sonnenschein-Debreu-Mantel results, which established that the standard microeconomic model has almost no implications for macrobehavior. In response macroeconomists have turned to representative agent analysis (Kirman 1992) and endeavored to incorporate some kind of bounded rationality (Sargent 1993; Sent 1997). In some sense, this is moving them away from Lucas's original insights.

BIBLIOGRAPHY

PRIMARY WORKS

Lucas, Robert E. 1972. Expectations and the Neutrality of Money. *Journal of Economic Theory* 4 (2): 103–124.

Lucas, Robert E. 1976. Econometric Policy Evaluation: A Critique. *Carnegie-Rochester Conference Series on Public Policy* 1: 19–46.

Lucas, Robert E. 1981. *Studies in Business-Cycle Theory.* Cambridge, MA: MIT Press.

Lucas, Robert E. 1987. *Models of Business Cycles.* Oxford: Basil Blackwell.

SECONDARY WORKS

Chari, Varadarajan. 1998. Nobel Laureate Robert E. Lucas Jr.: Architect of Modern Macroeconomics. *Journal of Economic Perspectives* 12 (1): 171–186.

Kirman, Alan P. 1992. Whom or What Does the Representative Individual Represent? *Journal of Economic Perspectives* 6 (2): 117–136.

Sargent, Thomas J. 1993. *Bounded Rationality in Macroeconomics: The Arne Ryde Memorial Lectures.* Oxford: Clarendon.

Sent, Esther-Mirjam. 1997. Sargent versus Simon: Bounded Rationality Unbound. *Cambridge Journal of Economics* 21 (3): 323–338.

Esther-Mirjam Sent

LUCAS CRITIQUE

In an extremely influential 1976 article, American economist Robert E. Lucas Jr. questioned the ability of econometric models to predict the effect of policy experiments. According to Lucas, reduced-form econometric models are not able to provide useful information about the outcomes of alternative policies because the structure of the economy changes when policy changes.

Lucas describes the economy in time, t, by a vector y_t of state variables, a vector x_t of exogenous forcing variables, and a vector ε_t of independent and identically distributed random shocks. One estimates the values of a fixed parameter vector θ, with the F function of behavioral relationships suggested by economic theory:

$$y_{t+1} = F(y, x, \theta, \varepsilon) \qquad (1)$$

With knowledge of F and θ, policy evaluation becomes straightforward. However, F and θ derive from (optimal) decision rules of the economy. It is the central assumption that once F and θ are approximately known, they will remain stable under arbitrary changes in the behavior of x_t. To assume stability of (F, θ) under alternative policy rules is to assume that agents' views about the behavior of shocks to the system are invariant under changes in the true behavior of these shocks. The empirical implication is that the estimated vector θ is not invariant but will change with policy interventions, which invalidates forecasts and policy predictions. Under (1), Lucas (1976) discusses in turn the aggregate consumption function, the investment function (reconsidered in Oliner et al. 1996), and the popular Phillips curves of the 1970s.

The reaction to the Lucas critique has been to formulate dynamic macromodels with rational expectations and optimizing foundations. Empirical evidence has suggested that price and real variables exhibit gradual responses to shocks. Given that forward-looking specifications with those desirable foundations do not replicate features from the data, reconsiderations have followed, such as Arturo Estrella and Jeffrey Fuhrer (2002) in macromodels and George Evans and Garey Ramey (2006) under adaptive expectations.

Other studies have delved into the framework in (1). Jesper Lindé (2001) examines money demand (MD) and consumption functions (CF) to see whether the θ-parameters are dependent on the monetary policy Taylor-rule (TR). There are two sets of observations [1, 2,..., T/2; and (T/2) + 1,..., T] under the assumption that TR changes unexpectedly after T/2 periods from one monetary policy regime to another. See also Richard Clarida et al. (2000) on shifting monetary policies at the U.S. Federal Reserve.

Estimating parameter vectors for all functions in both subperiods (θ^1 and θ^2), Lindé employs breakpoint tests to see whether the null hypothesis of equal parameters is rejected and concludes that the Lucas critique is quantitatively important in a statistical sense. It remains to be seen whether changes in the θ-parameters are sufficiently large to cast doubt on forecasting exercises. The methodology then tests, according to the Lucas critique, whether the null (H_0: $\theta^1_{MD} = \theta^2_{MD} | \theta^1_{TR} \neq \theta^2_{TR}$) is false. If the computed probabilities of rejecting parameter stability in MD and TR at the same time are low, the power of the test (defined as $1 - \beta$, where β is the type-II error or the probability of not rejecting H_0 given that H_0 is false) is low in small samples. Simulations in Lindé suggest this is indeed the case, although the tests are given the best possible environment for detecting regime shifts. This implies that the methodology used is not capable of detecting the relevance of the Lucas critique in small samples. This negative finding suggests further work along these lines seems warranted.

SEE ALSO *Economics, New Classical; Expectations; Expectations, Rational; Lucas, Robert E., Jr.; Policy, Fiscal; Policy, Monetary*

BIBLIOGRAPHY

Clarida, Richard, Jordi Gali, and Mark Gertler. 2000. Monetary Policy Rules and Macroeconomic Stability: Evidence and Some Theory. *Quarterly Journal of Economics* 115: 147–180.

Estrella, Arturo, and Jeffrey Fuhrer. 2002. Dynamic Inconsistencies: Counterfactual Implications of a Class of Rational Expectations Models. *American Economic Review* 92 (4): 1013–1028.

Evans, George, and Garey Ramey. 2006. Adaptive Expectations, Underparametrization, and the Lucas Critique. *Journal of Monetary Economics* 53 (2): 249–264.

Lindé, Jesper. 2001. Testing for the Lucas Critique: A Quantitative Investigation. *American Economic Review* 91: 986–1005.

Lucas, Robert E., Jr. 1976. Econometric Policy Evaluation: A Critique. *Carnegie-Rochester Conferences in Public Policy* 1: 19–46. Supplemental Series to the *Journal of Monetary Economics*.

Oliner, Stephen, Glenn Rudebusch, and Daniel Sichel. 1996. The Lucas Critique Revisited: Assessing the Stability of Empirical Euler Equations for Investment. *Journal of Econometrics* 70: 291–316.

Andre V. Mollick

LUCK

Luck exerts a dramatic influence over people's lives. It has the power to transform the improbable into the possible; to make the difference between life and death, reward and ruin, happiness and despair. But how do psychologists examine this elusive concept, and what has this work revealed?

Some researchers have examined why some people are consistently lucky while others encounter little but ill fortune. This work has employed a variety of methods, including interviews, diary studies, personality questionnaires, and laboratory-based research. The findings suggest that luck is not a magical ability or the result of random chance. Instead, although lucky and unlucky people have almost no insight into the real causes of their good and bad luck, their thoughts and behavior are responsible for much of their fortune. Lucky people tend to be skilled at creating and noticing chance opportunities, create self-fulfilling prophesies via positive expectations, and adopt a resilient attitude that transforms bad luck into good.

Take, for example, the notion of "lucky breaks." Lucky people consistently report encountering such opportunities whereas unlucky people do not. Researchers have conducted several experiments to discover whether this is due to differences in their ability to spot such opportunities. One such experiment involved giving both lucky and unlucky people a newspaper, asking them to look through it, and asking them to state how many photographs were inside. Participants were unaware that a large opportunity had been placed in the newspaper, in the form of an advertisement announcing: "Tell the Experimenter You Have Seen This and Win $250." The message took up half of the page and was written in type that was over 2 inches high. However, the unlucky people tended to miss the ad and the lucky people tended to spot it. Why was this the case?

Personality tests suggest that unlucky people are generally much more tense and anxious than lucky people, and research has shown that anxiety disrupts people's ability to notice the unexpected. In one experiment, people were asked to watch a moving dot in the center of a computer screen. Without warning, large dots would occasionally be flashed at the edges of the screen. Nearly all participants noticed these large dots. The experiment was then repeated with a second group of people, who were offered a large financial reward for accurately watching the center dot. This time, people were far more anxious during the experiment. They became very focused on the center dot and over one-third of them missed the large dots when they appeared on the screen. The harder they looked, the less they saw. And so it is with luck: unlucky people miss chance opportunities because they are too focused on looking for something else; lucky people are more relaxed and open, and therefore see what is there rather than just what they are looking for.

Another important aspect of the psychology of luck revolves around the way in which lucky and unlucky people deal with the ill fortune in their lives. Imagine an individual is chosen to represent his or her country in the Olympic Games. The participant competes in the games, does very well, and wins a bronze medal. How happy would the person feel? Most people would probably be overjoyed and proud of their achievement. Now imagine instead that the individual competes at the same Olympic Games a second time. This time he or she does even better, and wins a silver medal. How happy would the person feel now? Most people think that one would feel happier after winning the silver medal. This is not surprising. After all, the medals are a reflection of one's performance, and the silver medal indicates a better performance than a bronze medal. But research suggests that athletes who win bronze models are actually happier than those who win silver medals. And the reason for this has to do with the way in which the athletes think about their performance. The silver medalists focus on the notion that if they had performed slightly better, then they would have perhaps won a gold medal. In contrast, the bronze medalists focus on the thought that if they had performed slightly worse, then they would not have won anything at all. Psychologists refer to one's ability to imagine what might have happened, rather than what actually did happen, as counterfactual thinking.

Lucky people use a certain type of counterfactual thinking to soften the emotional impact of the ill fortune that they experience in their lives. In one study, lucky and unlucky people were presented with some imaginary scenarios and asked how they would react. For example, one such scenario involved the following:

> Imagine that you are waiting to be served in a bank. Suddenly, an armed robber enters the bank, fires a shot and the bullet hits you in the arm. Would this event be lucky or unlucky?

Unlucky people tended to say that this would be enormously unlucky and it would be just their bad luck to be in the bank during the robbery. In contrast, lucky people viewed the scenario as being far luckier, and often spontaneously commented on how the situation could have been much worse. Lucky people tend to imagine spontaneously how the bad luck they encounter could have been worse and, in doing so, they feel much better about themselves and their lives. This, in turn, helps keep their expectations about the future high, and, increases the likelihood of them continuing to live a lucky life.

People have searched for an effective way of improving the good fortune in their lives for many centuries. Lucky charms, amulets, and talismans have been found in virtually all civilizations throughout recorded history. Such beliefs represent people's attempts to control and enhance their luck. Research suggests the time has come for them to put their lucky charms away, and start to change the way they think and behave.

SEE ALSO *Magic; Miracles; Mysticism; Risk; Social Psychology*

BIBLIOGRAPHY

Bandura, A. 1982. The Psychology of Chance Encounters and Life Paths. *American Psychologist* 37 (7): 747–755.

Medvec, V. H., S. F. Madey, and T. Gilovich. 1995. When Less is More: Counterfactual Thinking and Satisfaction among Olympic Medalists. *Journal of Personality and Social Psychology* 69 (4): 603–610.

Vyse, S. 1997. *Believing In Magic: The Psychology of Superstition.* Oxford: Oxford University Press.

Wiseman, R. 2003. *The Luck Factor.* London: Random House.

Richard Wiseman

LUCY

SEE *Johanson, Donald.*

LUDDITES

Few groups have been more misunderstood and have had their image and name more frequently misappropriated and distorted than the Luddites. The term *Luddite* has typically referred to an individual who is opposed to technological change, and is derived from various tales in the Midlands stocking trade about an apprentice named Ned or Edward Ludd who broke his frame or needles in response to his master's strict discipline. (No actual person named Ned Ludd has been identified.) The Luddites were not, as popularizers of theories of technology and capitalist apologists for unregulated innovation claim, universally technophobes. They were artisans—primarily skilled workers in the early-nineteenth-century English textile industry. When faced with attempts to drive down their wages through the use of machines (operated at lower wages by less-skilled labor) the Luddites turned to wrecking the offensive machines and terrorizing the offending owners in order to preserve their wages, their jobs, and their trades. These men objected not only to the threat to their wages, but also to the production of cheap, inferior goods, which they feared would damage the reputation of their trades. Machines were not the only, or even the major, threat to the textile workers of the Midlands and North, however. The Prince Regent's Orders in Council, barring trade with Napoleonic France and nations friendly to France, cut off foreign markets for the British textile industry. Even more importantly, high food prices required more of each laborer's shrinking wages. Machines and those masters who used them to drive down wages were simply the most accessible targets for expressions of anger and direct action.

LUDDITE DEMOGRAPHICS

The Luddites varied by region and profession. In the Midlands counties of Nottinghamshire, Leicestershire, and Derbyshire, the Luddites comprised (almost exclusively) workers in the framework-knitting and lace trades. Midlands Luddism began in 1811 and ended in 1817 with the executions of men convicted for their roles in the 1816 attack on John Heathcoat's Loughborough mill. Yorkshire Luddism centered on the woolen trade. Most Yorkshire Luddites were croppers (highly skilled artisans who cropped the nap off of woven woolen cloth to smooth it), but the croppers found support among other skilled workers, such as saddle-makers. Yorkshire Luddism began in early 1812 and ended with the executions of several convicted Luddites in York in 1813. Luddism in the Cotton Districts surrounding Manchester encompassed not only trade-based protest but also political agitation. Luddites there were made up largely of cotton weavers, supported at times by colliers and by women in no trade at all, but spinners also played an important role in Luddite riots in Manchester and Flintshire. In Manchester, north Cheshire, and north Derbyshire, Luddism was frequently joined to food rioting and agitation for political reform.

PRIOR HISTORY OF MACHINE-BREAKING

The Luddites were neither the first nor only machine wreckers. Because organized, large-scale strikes were impractical due to the scattering of factories throughout different regions, machine-wrecking, which E. J. Hobsbawm calls "collective bargaining by riot," had occurred in Britain since the Restoration. For example, in 1675 narrow weavers in the area of Spitalfields destroyed "engines," power machines that could each do the work of several people, and in 1710 a London hosier employing too many apprentices in violation of the Framework Knitters Charter had his machines broken by angry framework knitters, also called stockingers. Even parliamentary action in 1727, making the destruction of machines a capital felony, did little to stop the activity. In 1768 London sawyers attacked a mechanized sawmill. Following the failure in 1778 of the stockingers' petitions to Parliament to enact a law regulating "the Art and Mystery of Framework Knitting," Nottingham workers rioted, flinging machines into the streets. In 1792 Manchester weavers destroyed two-dozen Cartwright steam looms owned by George Grimshaw. Sporadic attacks on machines (wide knitting frames, gig mills, shearing frames, and steam-powered looms and spinning jennies) continued, especially from 1799 to 1802 and through the period of economic distress after 1808.

THE COURSE OF LUDDISM

The first incident during the years of the most intense Luddite activity, 1811 to 1813, was the March 11, 1811, attack upon wide knitting frames in a shop in the Nottinghamshire village of Arnold, following a peaceful gathering of framework knitters near the Exchange Hall in Nottingham. In the preceding month, framework knitters had broken into shops and removed jack wires from wide knitting frames, rendering them useless without inflicting great violence upon the owners or incurring risk to the stockingers themselves; the March 11 attack was the first in which frames were actually smashed and the name "Ludd" was used. The grievances consisted, first, of the use of wide stocking frames to produce large amounts of cheap, shoddy stocking material, and, second, of the employment of "colts," workers who had not completed the seven-year apprenticeship required by law. Employers' violations not only of the law against hiring "colts," but of a number of other laws as well—such as the prohibition against the use of the gig mill and the limitation on the number of looms any weaver could possess—provided Luddites with justification for direct action against the employers. In probably the best example of such validation, the framework knitters, who launched the Luddite protests in Nottingham in 1811, justified their actions by referring to their own originary or constitutive charter, the 1663 Charter of the Company of Framework Knitters.

Frames continued to be broken in many of the villages surrounding Nottingham. The March 23, 1811, and April 20, 1811, *Nottingham Journal* reported several weeks of almost nightly attacks in the villages, all successful and carried out with no arrests. The summer of 1811 was quiet, but a bad harvest helped to renew disturbances in November, when, as the story goes, stockingers assembled in the wooded lands near Bulwell and were led in attacks on a number of shops by a commander calling himself Ned Ludd.

Midlands authorities' letters dated November 13 and 14, 1811, request that the government dispatch military aid because "2,000 men, many of them armed, were riotously traversing the County of Nottingham." In December 1811 public negotiations between the framework knitters and their employers, the hosiers, failed to result in the return of wages, piece rates, and frame rents to earlier levels or in any satisfactory improvement of the framework knitters' economic circumstances. Frame-breaking continued in Nottinghamshire, Derbyshire, and Leicestershire through the winter and early spring of 1812. It resurfaced in 1814 and again in Leicestershire in the autumn of 1816.

The first signs of the spread of Luddism to the cotton-manufacturing center of Manchester and its environs in Lancashire, Cheshire, and Flintshire materialized in December 1811 and January 1812. Manchester Luddism centered on the cotton-weaving trade, which was suffering from the use of steam-powered looms, but Luddites there were active in defense of the spinning trade as well. In Manchester, unlike Nottingham, large factories housed the offensive machinery. Large numbers of attackers tended to carry out the Luddite raids in and around Manchester; these also often coincided with food riots, which provided crowds that were large enough to carry out the factory attacks. Luddite activity continued in Lancashire and Cheshire into the summer of 1812 and blended into efforts to establish larger trade combinations and into political reform, but the force of Luddism dissipated following the acquittal of dozens of accused Luddites in Lancaster later that year.

The factory owners and cloth merchants of the woolen industry in the West Riding of Yorkshire were the targets of Luddism in that county. Although West Riding Luddites represented a variety of skilled trades, the most active and numerous by far were the cloth dressers, called croppers, whose work was threatened by the introduction of the shearing frame. The croppers' work consisted of using forty- or fifty-pound handheld shears to cut, or crop, the nap from woven woolen cloth in order to make a smooth and salable article. They were threatened by two types of machines. The gig mill, which had been prohibited by law since the rule of Edward VI, was a machine that raised the nap on woolen cloth so that it might be sheared more easily. The shearing frames actually mechanized the process of shearing and reduced the level of skill and experience necessary to finish an article of woolen cloth, even though the machines could not attain the quality of hand-cropped cloth. From January 1812 through midspring, Luddite attacks in Yorkshire concentrated on small cropping shops as well as large mills where frames were used. In April, Luddites began to attack mill owners and raided houses and buildings for arms and lead. Luddism began to lose steam after the failed attack upon Rawfolds Mill and the murder of mill owner William Horsfall by George Mellor and other Luddites. By the next winter, West Riding Luddism had run its course, even though after the January 1813 executions of Mellor and other Luddites a few more threatening letters were sent to public officials.

In all three regions, Luddites responded to the distressing concurrence of high food prices, depressed trade caused by the wars and by the trade prohibitions imposed under the Orders in Council, and changes in the use of machinery so as to reduce wages for the amount of work done. That machinery alone was not the primary cause of Luddite anger is evident in the cessation of Luddism. Luddite activities ended following the rescinding of the Orders in Council, some wage and usage concessions, and some reduction in food prices. While Malcolm Thomis (1970) has argued that Luddism was not a concerted agitation for political reform, but simply a common label applied to a range of unconnected protestors in different trades in different regions, it is perhaps more accurate that there were several Luddisms (see Randall 1991; Binfield 2004). Despite its brief run, Luddism ought to be understood, as J. L. Hammond and Barbara Hammond (1919) and E. P. Thompson (1963) have argued, as an important step in the formation of a class-consciousness and in the development of labor unions in Britain.

SEE ALSO *Machinery; Machinery Question, The; Technology; Technophobia*

BIBLIOGRAPHY

Bailey, Brian. 1998. *The Luddite Rebellion.* Stroud, U.K.: Sutton.

Binfield, Kevin, ed. 2004. *Writings of the Luddites.* Baltimore, MD: Johns Hopkins University Press.

Hammond, J. L., and Barbara Hammond. 1919. *The Skilled Labourer, 1760–1832.* London and New York: Longmans, Green.

Hobsbawm, E. J. 1964. *Labouring Men: Studies in the History of Labour.* London: Weidenfeld and Nicolson.

Jones, Steven E. 2006. *Against Technology: From the Luddites to Neo-Luddism.* New York: Routledge.

Navickas, Katrina. 2005. The Search for 'General Ludd': The Mythology of Luddism. *Social History* 30 (3): 281–295.

Randall, Adrian. 1991. *Before the Luddites: Custom, Community, and Machinery in the English Woollen Industry, 1776–1809.* Cambridge, U.K., and New York: Cambridge University Press.

Rule, John. 1986. *The Labouring Classes in Early Industrial England, 1750–1850.* London and New York: Longman.

Sale, Kirkpatrick. 1995. *Rebels against the Future: The Luddites and Their War on the Industrial Revolution: Lessons for the Computer Age.* Reading, MA: Addison-Wesley.

Thomis, Malcolm I. 1970. *The Luddites: Machine-Breaking in Regency England.* Newton Abbot, U.K.: David and Charles; Hamden, CT: Archon Books.

Thompson, E. P. 1963. *The Making of the English Working Class.* London: Gollancz.

Kevin Binfield

LUDIC DIMENSION

SEE *Rituals.*

LUKACS, GEORG
1885–1971

Georg Lukacs was a Hungarian Marxist philosopher who was profoundly influential on leftist social thought and whose reputation has fluctuated in light of a long life of controversy and productivity. Like his early friend and contemporary, Karl Mannheim, Lukacs was originally trained in Neo-Kantian philosophy, especially Georg Simmel's formalist aesthetics. The theme of form overcoming matter through collective action, prominent in this period as an account of artistic schools, became a hallmark of Lukacs's generally realist aesthetic sensibility as well as his approach to revolutionary politics.

The turning point in Lukacs's life came in 1917 with the onset of the Bolshevik Revolution. As Lukacs himself put it, he became eager to play St. Augustine to Lenin's Jesus. He thus spent the rest of his life systematizing and justifying Communist ideology, including service as a high-ranking party official in both Moscow and Budapest. While often the dutiful apparatchik, Lukacs sometimes dissented and distanced himself from Leninist and Stalinist policies, more so after Stalin's death, albeit through the communist practice of "self-criticism." Here Lukacs may be compared with Martin Heidegger, who originally saw Hitler as his standard-bearer but then withdrew from Nazi politics once his own ambitions were thwarted—though never with a formal renunciation.

To his defenders, Lukacs's most enduring legacy is a scholarly recovery of the Hegelian roots of Marxism, otherwise known as "Marxist humanism." Instead of reading

Marx as a strict economic determinist or scientific materialist, as a focus on *Capital* might suggest, Lukacs stressed Marx's original training in dialectics as applied to the law. On this basis, Lukacs popularized the term "alienation" to express what he called the "reification" of social relations, whereby people come to be defined in terms of properties that are subject to exchange relations. Following Marx, the key human property for Lukacs is labor, which he understood more as an open-ended and dynamic "praxis" than a mathematical constant in a production function.

This rather existentialist conception of the Marxist project influenced the Frankfurt School's emphasis on culture in the 1920s and was revived as a distinctly post-Stalinist "Western Marxism" in the 1960s, which continues to underwrite most academic Marxist theory, especially in the humanities. However, Lukacs used his revisionist reading of Marx to idealize Lenin's practice of organizing a vanguard of intellectuals to consolidate class consciousness in the workers, rendering them a "proletariat" possessed of what Lukacs called the "objective possibility" of revolutionizing society.

The continuing allure of Lukacs's version of Marxism lies in its thoroughly formal characterization of the conditions for revolutionary politics, one that does not presuppose the success of any historic revolutions. That the first Marxist revolution occurred in Russia, not Germany as Marx had predicted, and that it lost many of its admirers after Lenin's death, did not deter Lukacs from developing the basis for what feminists nowadays call a "standpoint" theory oriented toward groups that combine centrality to and alienation from the means of production of society. Whichever group occupies such a position is potentially the party of revolution.

SEE ALSO *Alienation; Collective Action; Communism; Existentialism; Frankfurt School; Hegel, Georg Wilhelm Friedrich; Kant, Immanuel; Lenin, Vladimir Ilitch; Mannheim, Karl; Marx, Karl; Revolution; Russian Revolution; Stalin, Joseph; Stalinism*

BIBLIOGRAPHY

Lichtheim, George. *Georg Lukacs.* 1970. New York: Viking Press.

Lukacs, Georg. [1923] 1967. *History and Class Consciousness: Studies in Marxist Dialectics.* Trans. Rodney Livingstone. London: Merlin Press.

Steve Fuller

LULA

SEE *Integration.*

LUMPENPROLETARIAT

The word *lumpenproletariat* means literally "ragged proletariat." In the view of Karl Marx (1818–1883) and Friedrich Engels (1820–1895), the lumpenproletariat consists of people who subsist on the margins of society and scavenge a living from illegal or semi-legal activities, such as prostitution and petty thieving, and the underworld involved therein. The attitude of Marx and Engels to this group is extremely negative. In the locus classicus of the *Communist Manifesto* (1848), they are described as "the dangerous class, the social scum, that passively rotting mass thrown off by the lowest layers of old society" (McLellan 1977, p. 229). While such a group might be swept into joining the proletarian cause in a revolution, "its conditions of life," continued Marx and Engels, "prepare it far more for the part of a bribed tool of reactionary intrigue." And this description found empirical confirmation in the role that Marx conceived the lumpenproletariat to have played in the 1851 coup d'état of Louis Bonaparte (1808–1873) in France.

The reason for this negative assessment of the lumpenproletariat by Marx and Engels can be found in their conception of the role of classes in historical development. A class was defined by its relationship to, and potential control of, the means of production. In ancient society, the ruling class owned the slaves; in feudal society, the king and the barons owned the land; in contemporary society, the capitalists owned the factories and the proletariat owned (and was compelled to sell) its labor. According to Marx and Engels, as history unfolded, each new class was swept to power by its ability to gain control over the ever-changing forces of production. In their own society, they foresaw the decline of the bourgeoisie due to inherent crises in capitalism and the coming to power of the increasingly class-conscious proletariat who, as the majority of society, would be able to organize the productive forces with which they worked for the benefit of all rather than the few.

In this optimistic scenario, the lumpenproletariat had no positive role to play. This was because they had only a negative role vis-à-vis the forces of production. Whereas the proletariat was intimately involved in the forces of production in that industrialization made them more numerous, more cohesive, and more antipathetic to their exploitation therein, the lumpenproletariat, being essentially rootless and venal, could have no clear historical destiny.

This view found some confirmation in the 1851 coup d'état of Louis Bonaparte. It is in his analysis of the class context of this coup, titled the *Eighteenth Brumaire of Louis Bonaparte* (1852), that Marx most fully described his view of the lumpenproletariat. In a period of French history where neither the rising proletariat nor the declining bourgeoisie could attain political power, the lumpenproletariat could come to dominate by selling itself to

Louis Bonaparte, who was "an adventurer blown in from abroad, raised on the shield by a drunken soldiery, which he has bought with liquor and sausages and which he must continually ply with sausage anew" (McLellan 1977, p. 317). Louis Bonaparte could achieve this by relying on the army, which was itself "the swamp-flower" of the peasant lumpenproletariat.

Thus Marx's view of the "ragged" section of the proletariat is very different from *The Ragged Trousered Philanthropists* (1914) of Robert Tressell's (1870–1911) famous social realist novel. Being outside the process of production, the lumpenproletariat were not a class in the sense in which Marx and Engels usually used the term. Unlike the proletariat itself, the evolving industrial process subjected them to no revolutionary imperatives. They were either outside the process altogether or effectively counterrevolutionary in that they depended on the aristocracy or the bourgeoisie for their day-to-day existence.

The views of Marx and Engels are in sharp contrast with the anarchist tradition exemplified by, for example, their rival Mikhail Bakunin (1814–1876). For him, destruction was a precondition for building a new society and it was only those outside normal society who could be expected to have the necessary destructive urge that could go as far as terrorism and assassination. A more modern version of the view that salvation can only be found in the excluded was explored in the work of Herbert Marcuse (1898–1979), for whom the all-pervasive conformity of present society could only be disrupted by "the substratum of outcasts and outsiders, the exploited and persecuted of other races and other colours, the unemployed and the unemployable" (Marcuse 1968, p. 201). An advocacy of the revolutionary potential of the lumpenproletariat in the developing world can be found in Franz Fahon's *Wretched of the Earth*. From a more negative point of view there are obviously echoes of the views of Marx and Engels in contemporary discussions of the emergence of an "underclass."

SEE ALSO *Anarchism; Class; Class Consciousness; Communism; Marx, Karl; Marxism; Napoléon Bonaparte; Poverty; Proletariat; Working Class*

BIBLIOGRAPHY

Draper, Hal. 1972. The Concept of the "Lumpenproletariat" in Marx and Engels. *Economies et Sociétés* 6 (12): 2285–2312.

Fanon, Frantz. [1961] 1965. *The Wretched of the Earth*. New York: Grove.

Marcuse, Herbert. 1968. *One Dimensional Man*. London: Penguin.

McLellan, David, ed. 1977. *Karl Marx: Selected Writings*. Oxford: Oxford University Press.

David McLellan

LUMPY GOODS
SEE *McFadden, Daniel L.*

LUMUMBA, PATRICE
1925–1961

Patrice Lumumba was an outspoken African nationalist politician and first prime minister of the Democratic Republic of the Congo. He played a central role in the chaotic and hastily executed decolonization in the Belgian Congo in 1960. His assassination in 1961 by Belgian and American security services, who conspired with his Congolese political enemies, earned him a lasting place as an eloquent and courageous African champion against the excesses of Western governments and corporations.

Lumumba was born in 1925 in Kasai Province, in what was then the Belgian Congo. He completed primary school at a Catholic mission in 1943. He then worked as a clerk for a mining company before joining the Belgian Congo junior civil service as a postal clerk in Stanleyville. His life was typical of the *evolue* underclass of Western-educated and urbanized Africans, who kept the colonial system functioning. Despite his limited education, he was a good writer and brilliant orator.

The recession of the mid-1950s, which occurred as postwar Belgium sought to extract the maximum return from its investments in the Congo, led to high African urban unemployment and mounting discontent. In 1956 an *evolue* group in Léopoldville issued a manifesto calling for independence within thirty years. But both Lumumba, who led the *Mouvement National Congolais* (MNC), and Joseph Kasavuba, the leader of the rival *Alliance des Ba-Kongo* (ABAKO), called for immediate independence.

In response to urban riots in 1959, the Belgian government convened a conference in Brussels to determine the future of the Congo. Lumumba was placed under arrest and charged with inciting anticolonial riots, but when the MNC won a convincing majority at local elections, Lumumba was freed to attend the conference. Under pressure from the MNC, the Belgian government announced that general elections would be held in May 1960 for the newly created national and provincial assemblies, and for a national senate nominated by the provincial assemblies, with independence for the Congo on June 30, 1960. This would be the first experiment with democracy in the colony's history.

Lumumba and the MNC advocated a unitary state with a strong central government. However, parochial interests, with the support of Belgian colonial interests, led to a profusion of ethnic and regional parties. The

MNC emerged as the largest party in the national assembly, but it was unable to govern without a coalition. Parochial tribal-based parties dominated the provincial assemblies.

Following the election, Lumumba became the independent nation's prime minister, with Kasavubu serving as president. At the independence ceremony, Baudouin I, the king of the Belgians, praised Belgian colonialism, provoking Lumumba to a stinging impromptu critique of Belgian colonial rule and the exploitation of Western mining companies. In 1960, many in the West were shocked at an African publicly criticizing a European head of state. Coming in the midst of the cold war, it led the Eisenhower administration in America to view him as "pro-Communist."

Within days, the Congolese army, drawn from the poorest and most marginalized segment of the population, mutinied. With the support of Belgian mining companies, Katanga Province declared its independence under Governor Moise Tshombe. Lumumba appealed to the United Nations for support, but the Security Council divided along cold war lines.

In September 1960, President Kasavubu dismissed Lumumba's government, and Joseph Mobutu, the army chief-of-staff, arrested Lumumba. With the connivance of the U.S. Central Intelligence Agency and Belgian Security Lumumba was handed over to his enemies in Katanga, who murdered him on January 17, 1961.

The Lumumba legacy, like that of John F. Kennedy, has been shrouded by his untimely assassination in a mantle of unrealized promise. On one level, as the hapless victim of Belgian pride and American cold war paranoia, he was to be buried in the past and forgotten. Yet to many non-Europeans in America, the Caribbean, and Africa, the outspoken and charismatic African nationalist became a hero in the struggle against white racism and oppression, one of the martyrs of African liberation. His assassination and the widespread accusations (later confirmed) of American CIA involvement may have served as a warning to others in the anticolonial struggle, but to many ordinary black people, his murder was a confirmation of Western excess, duplicity, and racism. While Lumumba is a forgotten figure in the mainstream Western consciousness, to many black intellectuals his fate remains an indelible stain, a lasting reminder of Western neocolonialism.

SEE ALSO *Anticolonial Movements; Central Intelligence Agency, U.S.; Colonialism; Liberation Movements; Nationalism and Nationality; Neocolonialism*

BIBLIOGRAPHY

De Witte, Ludo. 2001. *The Assassination of Lumumba.* Trans. Ann Wright and Renée Fenby. New York: Verso.

Gibbs, David N. 1991. *The Political Economy of Third World Intervention: Mines, Money, and U.S. Policy in the Congo Crisis.* Chicago: University of Chicago Press.

Kanza, Thomas. 1979. *The Rise and Fall of Patrice Lumumba: Conflict in the Congo.* Boston: G. K. Hall.

David Dorward

LUNDBERG, ERIK
1907–1987

The Swedish economist Erik Filip Lundberg was born in Stockholm into an academic family. His father, Filip Lundberg, was a famous insurance mathematician. After studying economics and mathematics at Stockholm University, Erik Lundberg spent 1931 to 1933 in the United States, where he came under the influence of Wesley C. Mitchell (1874–1948), founder of the National Bureau of Economic Research. Mitchell inspired in Lundberg an interest in empirical research and a certain skepticism toward theory.

Despite this influence, Lundberg wrote a theoretical PhD thesis titled *Studies in the Theory of Economic Expansion*. This thesis earned him an international reputation among economists, but it was his only theoretical work. Lundberg's thesis was completed in December 1936, a few months after the publication of John Maynard Keynes's (1883–1946) *General Theory of Employment, Interest, and Money*. The disposition of Lundberg's work was to some extent adapted to the then-current climate of discussion generated by the *General Theory*, but Lundberg was little influenced by Keynes's book in any other sense. Lundberg, unlike Keynes, discussed both the production side and demand side of the economy, though Lundberg's demand-side theory is similar to Keynes's.

The starting point for Lundberg and for the Stockholm school was to a great extent the Swedish economist Knut Wicksell (1851–1926), though Lundberg was also influenced by Eugen Böhm-Bawerk (1851–1914) and Friedrich August von Hayek (1899–1992), according to whom capital was perceived as time consumption. Prior to Keynes, capital in this sense—that is, the length of the production cycle from raw materials through semi-manufactured products, investment products, and final products—played a role in explaining the business cycle.

Lundberg developed these lines of reasoning, in the spirit of the Stockholm school, into a sequence analysis. The combination of the accelerator principle, which determined investment and the multiplier via consumption, analyzed in a sequence of periods, was shown to cause instability in free market economies. This theory was dynamic in contrast with Keynes's *General Theory*. Keynes analyzed the equilibrium situations in the economy and compared them with one another, while Lundberg analyzed processes in disequilibrium, namely, the development of the economic system over time. Paul Samuelson (1939) later simplified Lundberg's theory in an elegant mathematical formulation.

After completing his doctoral thesis, Lundberg was drawn into analysis work and economic advisor tasks. He became head of the Swedish National Institute of Economic Research in 1946 and there developed inflation-gap analysis, based on his thesis. The inflation-gap hypothesis was measured, in a closed economy, as the difference between the aggregated effective demand and the production capacity at full employment. Lundberg's years of empirical work resulted in 1953 in his great *Konjunkturer och ekonomisk politik* (Business Cycles and Economic Policy). This is a rich book with retrospective references to economic developments and discussions during the period between the world wars. The book also deals with the conditions for stabilization policy and the efficiency of regulated and planned economies compared to free markets. The significance of free market prices for efficient allocation of resources is also an important theme, one that aroused considerable interest in Swedish economic policy debates.

Lundberg's *Produktivitet och räntabilitet* (Productivity and Rate of Return; 1961) studies the significance of capital formation for economic growth. Lundberg observed, for instance, that the small ironworks of Horndal in central Sweden had not made any net investment during a period of fifteen years, only investing in some maintenance work. Despite this, labor productivity increased by 2 percent a year. This is usually termed the *Horndal effect* and has since been studied under the label *learning by doing*.

Lundberg's final major work was *Instability and Economic Growth* (1968). One of the issues in this book concerns the relationship, if there is one, between instability and growth. Lundberg found no such relationship.

Lundberg ranks as Sweden's leading economist during the postwar period. He was chairman of the International Economic Association (1968–1971) and of the Nobel committee for economics (1974–1979). Because Lundberg was skeptical toward theory and worked eclectically, it is impossible to definitively establish his attitudes toward many social problems, apart from a deeply rooted economic liberalism. Lundberg had a pronounced sense of humor that could occasionally wound colleagues and students, but he was a good person and as a debater and advisor he epitomized integrity and honesty. He was not as successful as a teacher. His excess of

approaches and ideas could easily confuse an inexperienced doctoral student, and few of his students continued on an academic path.

SEE ALSO *Stockholm School*

BIBLIOGRAPHY

Lundberg, Erik. 1937. *Studies in the Theory of Economic Expansion*. Trans. Nils G. Sahlin and Florianne Dalberg. London: King and Son.

Lundberg, Erik. 1953. *Konjunkturer och ekonomisk politik*. Stockholm: Swedish National Institute of Economic Research and Studieförbundet Näringsliv och Samhälle.

Lundberg, Erik. 1957. *Business Cycles and Economic Policy*. Trans. J. Potter. Cambridge, MA: Harvard University Press.

Lundberg, Erik. 1961. *Produktivitet och räntabilitet*. Stockholm: Studieförbundet Näringsliv och Samhälle.

Lundberg, Erik. 1968. *Instability and Economic Growth*. New Haven, CT: Yale University Press.

Lundberg, Erik. 1995. *Studies in Economic Instability and Change: Selected Writings Through Five Decades, Together with an Obituary by William J. Baumol*, ed. Rolf G. H. Henriksson. Stockholm: SNS Förlag.

Samuelson, Paul A. 1939. Interactions Between the Multiplier Analysis and the Principle of Acceleration. *The Review of Economics and Statistics* 21 (2): 75–78.

Villy Bergström

LUXEMBOURG INCOME STUDY

The Luxembourg Income Study (LIS), a research center and microdata archive, was founded in 1983 by Timothy Smeeding, Lee Rainwater, Gaston Schaber, and a team of multidisciplinary researchers in Europe. With support from the government of Luxembourg, LIS and its staff became an independent nonprofit institution in 2002. LIS is organized as a consortium of countries with financing from the national science foundations and other funders in the participating countries, as well as from the Luxembourgian government. LIS operations are governed by a board whose members represent the countries that provide data and financing. Janet Gornick, a political economist and sociologist based in the United States, became overall director of LIS in September 2006. Markus Jäntti, an economist in Finland, took up the post of LIS Research Director in 2005.

LIS has four goals:

1. To harmonize cross-national data, thus relieving researchers of this task, relying on an expert staff

that carries out the harmonization work and provides support services for users.

2. To provide a method allowing researchers to access these data under privacy restrictions required by the countries providing the data.

3. To create a system that allows research requests to be received and results returned quickly to users at remote locations.

4. To promote comparative research on the economic and social well-being of populations across countries.

In 2006, LIS included data from thirty countries, mostly in Europe and North America, but also including Australia, Israel, and Taiwan. The database contained over 150 datasets, organized into five time periods (known as *waves*) spanning the years 1968 to 2002. Wave six is due to come online in 2007. The data can be accessed in multiple ways. Researchers can write programs (in SPSS, SAS, or STATA) and send them via electronic mail directly to the LIS server; results are returned to the researcher, with average processing time under two minutes. There is also a web-based tabulator that allows users to construct tables using keywords. The LIS website provides a set of country-level indicators (known as *Key Figures*), including measures of inequality and poverty for each LIS dataset.

Extensive documentation for each dataset details technical aspects of the original survey, a record of the harmonization process, and institutional information on tax and transfer programs corresponding to the microdata variables. The LIS website also houses a comparative welfare states database and a family policy database; both contain an array of country-level policy indicators. These policy databases are widely used by LIS microdata researchers, who often seek to link policy variables to microlevel outcomes.

Reports based on LIS data have appeared in books, journal articles, and dissertations, and are often featured in the popular media. Each completed study is made available in the LIS Working Paper series, which numbered more than 450 papers by Fall 2006. The LIS website offers a Working Papers search engine, a complete set of abstracts, and most of the papers in full text.

Beginning in 2005, LIS expanded by adding a wealth data project. The Luxembourg Wealth Study (LWS) established a network of producers of microdata on household wealth and has, like LIS, harmonized the country-specific data into a common template, including comparable measures of net worth and its components. The LWS project will help to set guidelines for wealth data producers, as the LIS project has with income data.

LIS conducts annual training workshops that introduce researchers to the database and to cross-national research on wages, income, employment, and social policy. Between 1988 and 2006, more than five hundred scholars attended the workshops. LIS publishes a newsletter twice yearly, which is mailed to over 1,400 scholars in thirty-five countries.

The LIS microdatasets include income, employment, and demographic variables at the person and household level. Since LIS's inception, these microdatasets have been used by more than a thousand researchers in many countries to analyze economic and social policies and their effects on outcomes including poverty, income inequality, employment status, wage patterns, gender inequality, family formation, child well-being, health status, immigration, political behavior, and public opinion.

One of the most fruitful uses of LIS is for the study of income distributions across the richest countries of the world. Figure 1, derived from LIS's Key Figures, summarizes income distributions in the LIS countries, using four measures of inequality (ratios of tenth and ninetieth centiles to the median; the 90–10 "decile ratio," and the Gini coefficient). This figure shows clearly that income distributions vary dramatically across countries, with variation seen at both the bottom and the top of the distributions. The figure also reveals loose clusters of countries, with lower levels of inequality in the Nordic countries, moderate levels in most of the continental European countries, and higher levels in southern Europe and in the English-speaking countries of Australia, Canada, Ireland, the United Kingdom, and, most especially, the United States. Notably, the former communist countries of eastern Europe report remarkably varied levels of income inequality.

LIS-based research has catalyzed changes in national policies—for example, British policy toward children, based on the work of Jonathan Bradshaw (Bradshaw and Chen 1997)—and has informed the United Nations, the Organization for Economic Cooperation and Development (OECD), and other major bodies about poverty, inequality, and employment outcomes across countries. Results based on LIS have been published in and lauded by *Science* (Butz and Torrey 2006), *The Lancet* (Lynch et al. 2001), and major academic journals in the fields of economics, political science, sociology, comparative public policy, and social measurement. A twenty-year anniversary volume, published by *The Socio-Economic Review* in 2004, further summarizes and explains the accomplishments of LIS (Smeeding 2004).

In 2006 LIS completed a comprehensive internal review of its data template and harmonization rules in order to improve the quality of the LIS data and to identify ways to increase cross-country comparability in response to changes in the previous two decades in the participating countries' social policies and survey content. This review also led to a restructuring of the pen-

Social distance and social exclusion

(numbers given are percent of median in each nation and Gini coefficient)

	P10 (Low income)	Length of bars represents the gap between high and low income individuals	P90 (High income)	P90/P10 (Decile ratio)	Gini coefficient[1]
Czech Republic 1996	59		179	3.01	0.259
Luxembourg 2000	57		184	3.24	0.260
Norway 2000	57		159	2.80	0.251
Sweden 2000	57		168	2.96	0.252
Finland 2000	57		164	2.9	0.247
Slovak Republic 1996	56		162	2.88	0.241
Netherlands 1999	56		167	2.98	0.248
Austria 2000	55		173	3.17	0.260
Denmark 1992	54		155	2.85	0.236
Hungary 1999	54		194	3.57	0.295
France 1994	54		191	3.54	0.288
Switzerland 2002	54		182	3.38	0.274
Germany 2000	54		177	3.29	0.264
Romania 1997	53		180	3.38	0.277
Slovenia 1999	53		167	3.15	0.249
Belgium 2000	53		174	3.31	0.277
Poland 1999	52		188	3.59	0.293
Taiwan 2000	51		196	3.81	0.296
Canada 2000	48		188	3.95	0.302
United Kingdom 1999	47		215	4.59	0.345
Estonia 2000	46		234	5.08	0.361
Japan 1992[2]	46		192	4.17	0.315
Australia 1994	45		195	4.33	0.311
Italy 2000	44		199	4.48	0.333
Spain 2000	44		209	4.78	0.340
Greece 2000	43		207	4.77	0.338
Israel 2001	43		216	5.01	0.346
Ireland 2000	41		189	4.56	0.323
United States 2000	39		210	5.45	0.368
Mexico 2002	33		309	9.36	0.471
Russia 2000	33		276	8.37	0.434
		0 50 100 150 200 250 300 350			
Average[3]	50		194	4.09	0.302

(1) Gini coefficients are based on incomes which are bottom coded at one percent of disposable income and top coded at ten times the median disposable income.
(2) Japanese gini coefficent as calculated in Gottschalk and Smeeding (2000) from 1993 Japanese Survey of Income Redistribution.
(3) Simple average.

SOURCE: Authors' calculations from the Luxembourg Income Study (http://www.lisproject.org/keyfigures.htm).

Figure 1

sion and family benefits data, an expansion of the person-level data, and a substantial increase in the number of labor market variables included in LIS. These revisions enabled the many researchers who use LIS primarily for employment research to go further in their comparative analyses.

Thereafter LIS anticipated adding new datasets for all of the participating LIS countries; the newest wave of data (LIS's sixth wave) was to include datasets from approximately 2004. In addition, LIS anticipated adding two new countries in 2007: South Korea and Japan. LIS also continued to work to bring in datasets from Portugal, New Zealand, and Turkey.

LIS's income surveys have mostly come from high-income countries, as classified by the World Bank. Of the thirty countries participating as of 2006, twenty-one are high-income and nine are upper-middle-income (Czech Republic, Estonia, Hungary, Mexico, Poland, Romania, Russia, Slovak Republic, and Taiwan). One of LIS's main priorities is to substantially increase the inclusion of middle-income countries. LIS intends to add microdata, at multiple points in time, from ten middle-income countries, including, for example, Brazil, Bulgaria, Chile, China, Indonesia, and South Africa.

SEE ALSO *Discrimination; Gini Coefficient; Inequality, Income; Poverty; Social Exclusion*

BIBLIOGRAPHY

Bradshaw, Jonathan R., and Jun-Rong Chen. 1997. Poverty in the UK: A Comparison with Nineteen Other Countries. *Benefits* 18: 13–17.

Butz, William P., and Barbara Boyle Torrey. 2006. Some Frontiers in Social Science. *Science* 312 (5782): 1898–1900.

Gottschalk, Peter, and Timothy M. Smeeding. 2000. Empirical Evidence on Income Inequality in Industrialized Countries. In *Handbook of Income Distribution*, Vol. 1, eds. Anthony B. Atkinson and François Bourguignon, 261–307. New York: Elsevier.

Luxembourg Income Study. http://www.lisproject.org.

Lynch, John, George Davey Smith, Marianne Hillemeier, et al. 2001. Income Inequality, the Psychosocial Environment, and Health: Comparisons of Wealthy Nations. *The Lancet* 358 (9277): 194–200.

Smeeding, Timothy M., guest ed. 2004. *Socio-Economic Review* 2 (2): 149–339.

Janet C. Gornick
Timothy M. Smeeding

LUXEMBURG, ROSA
1870 or 1871–1919

Rosa Luxemburg was a Polish Marxist revolutionary as well as the most relevant figure of the left wing of the German Social Democratic Party (SPD). Together with Leo Jogiches (1867–1919), she was the leader of the Social Democratic Party of the Kingdom of Poland. Breaking with SPD for its support of World War I (1914–1918), with Karl Liebknecht (1871–1919) she founded the Spartacist League (*Spartakusbund*), which became in 1918 the German Communist Party (KPD). Luxemburg was killed during the German Revolution of January 1919 by the paramilitary *Freikorps*, and by the order of the SPD chancellor Friedrich Ebert.

At Zurich University Luxemburg trained in law and economics. Indeed, many of her writings can be seen as an original and undogmatic reprise, critique, and development of Marxist critical political economy. By 1898 she was widely known for her trenchant and astute criticism of the mounting revisionism. In *Social Reform or Revolution?* (1899), the pamphlet she wrote against fellow SPD member Eduard Bernstein, Luxemburg strongly objected to the idea that capitalism was entering a phase of social and economic stabilization, with the end of class polarization and the attenuation of economic crises. Skeptical about the law of a tendential fall in the profit rate, she nevertheless defended "collapse theory," but with too generic a reference to the lack of demand for commodities. She also stressed the essential link between money and value, justifying Marx's notion of abstract labor as a real abstraction that actually comes into being with the unity of production and circulation.

She refined her argument after 1907 when she started teaching economics at the SPD party training center in Berlin. While preparing her lectures (which were posthumously collected in *Introduction to Political Economy*, 1921) she stumbled upon a difficulty in Marx. Luxemburg stressed what she called the "law of the tendential fall" of the "relative" wage—that is, of the share in the new value added that goes to workers—as the other side of relative surplus value extraction. In her view, though, the real wage may grow when the productive power of labor rises, the former always lagging behind the latter. Workers' consumption is thus decreasing. Hence the question: Can capitalist investments fill the gap, and guarantee the smooth development of capitalist extended reproduction? In the *Accumulation of Capital* (1913) Luxemburg attacked Marx's schemes of reproduction for promoting the illusion that in a "closed" setting capitalism can go on as "production for the sake of production," and only disproportional crises can occur. Imperialism is seen as the consequence of the need to find new markets in non-capitalist areas. In the end, collapse due to lack of effective demand was certain: To avoid slipping into "barbarism," socialist revolution was historically necessary.

She was fiercely attacked by critics who hit some blind spots in her formulation (which was written in haste in a few months) but missed the core of her position, stated most clearly in the *Anti-Critique* (written in jail in 1916–1917). Capital must be analyzed first of all as a macro-monetary circuit. Therefore, the issue at stake is that capitalists cannot recover from monetary circulation more than they injected into it, advancing either constant or variable capital. From this theoretical stance, the realization problem opens to the problem of finance as fundamental in a monetary production economy. This does not mean that Luxemburg's view was correct: She discarded the distinction between "financial" and "industrial" capital, so her question could not have an answer. But her approach was more farsighted than her critics understood because she opened a new problematic (Bellofiore 2004).

Two interpreters who clearly perceived this were Joan Robinson (1951) and Michal Kalecki (1967). Robinson saw that the key issue in Luxemburg was that accumulation depends on the incentive to invest. Kalecki extended her position, showing that capitalism can find effective demand not only through net exports, but also through state deficit spending financed by the central. However, it must not be forgotten that in the last instance, crises erupt because of relative surplus value extraction: Although it induces a fall in the wage share, it also systematically upsets the conditions of equilibrium for capitalist reproduction, and then provokes disproportions and leads to a general "glut." Realization crises are failures to sell products at prices that recoup expected profitability due to inadequate aggregate demand. They are rooted in the dynamics of exploitation within the capitalist labor processes where valorization—that is, the production of surplus value starting from a given value—immediately occurs.

Customarily, Luxemburg's position is labeled as determinist and under-consumptionist (which is clearly wrong), and her political perspective is condemned as spontaneist. A convincing rebuttal of this reading was put forward by Norman Geras (1976). What is relevant is Luxemburg's opposition to Lenin. As Rossana Rossanda succinctly states, Luxemburg "never maintained that the masses could do without an organized vanguard which, for her, was identified with the party. However, the need for the latter was not derived from the absence of a *political* dimension of working class struggles as such, but from the objective fragmentation of these struggles, which a unifying strategy could alone overcome" (1970, p. 224).

In recent decades, interest in Luxemburg has shifted from discussion about her political, social, and economic thought to her pacifism, her love for nature, and her anticipation of some traits of contemporary feminism (Nye 1994).

SEE ALSO *Accumulation of Capital; Economic Crises; Feminism; Imperialism; Kalecki, Michal; Robinson, Joan; Socialism*

BIBLIOGRAPHY

Bellofiore, Riccardo. 2004. "Like a Candle Burning at Both Ends": Rosa Luxemburg and the Critique of Political Economy. *Research in Political Economy* 21: 279–297.

Geras, Norman. 1976. *The Legacy of Rosa Luxemburg.* London: New Left Books.

Hudis, Peter, and Kevin B. Anderson. 2004. *The Rosa Luxemburg Reader.* New York: Monthly Review Press.

Luxemburg, Rosa. [1913] 2003. *The Accumulation of Capital.* London: Routledge.

Luxemburg, Rosa. [1921] 1972. *The Accumulation of Capital: An Anti-Critique.* New York: Monthly Review Press.

Nye, Andrea. 1994. *The Thought of Rosa Luxemburg, Simone Weil, and Hannah Arendt.* London: Routledge.

Robinson, Joan. 1951. Introduction. In *The Accumulation of Capital.* London: Routledge and Kegan Paul.

Rossanda, Rossana. 1970. Class and Party. *Socialist Register.* 217–231.

Riccardo Bellofiore

LYING

People who are lying are trying to mislead others. If an attempt to mislead is conscious, entails misstatement of fact, and promises a payoff, it is usually considered a lie. Alongside its denotative meaning, *lying* is a pejorative term. In one investigation, college students rated the social desirability of 555 one-word descriptions of a person. According to these ratings, the most negative thing one can say about a person is not that the person is greedy, incompetent, prejudiced, or cruel. The most negative thing one can say is that the person is a liar.

Lying is related to other phenomena. Like deception, lying involves false communication. However, deception is a broader concept. Biologists have discussed deception by fireflies, possums, and plants, but few would claim that plants can lie. As lying is one type of deception, so are there many types of lies: lies of omission and commission, white lies, and high-stakes lies.

Lying has intrigued scholars for thousands of years. Theologians have debated the morality of deceit, and epistemologists have puzzled over apposite logical problems like the liar's paradox. Lying has been a recurrent literary theme. Novelists have dazzled their readers with fictional deception and counterdeception; playwrights have captivated audiences with both dramatic and comic lies.

Social scientists' interest in lying grew from a practical concern, the need to detect lies. In a 1917 *Journal of Experimental Psychology* article, Harvard doctoral student John Marston described his efforts to construct a lie detection technology, based on the premise that lying is accompanied by changes in blood pressure. Marston's work gave rise to the polygraph, an apparatus that monitors several indices of autonomic functioning. Once polygraphs came to be used in examinations for truthfulness, the accuracy of this lie detector became a matter of scientific debate. Reviewing evidence on both sides of this controversy, the U.S. National Academy of Sciences concluded in 2003 that the polygraph detects lies at rates that are better than chance but imperfect. In the National Academy's view, polygraph examinations are poorly suited for screening large populations of people that include only a small percentage of liars.

Soon after Marston's psychophysiological venture, Hugh Hartshorne and Mark May developed methods for measuring character. In their 1928 book *Studies in Deceit*, Hartshorne and May reported many character tests, including a test for lying in children. This written self-report instrument asked children about conduct that is socially approved but rare. Thus, the child was asked, "Do you always obey your parents cheerfully and promptly?" Across thirty-six such items, some children claimed that they were always good and never bad. The authors maintained that these children were lying, while acknowledging that some might get high "lie scores" because they were exceedingly conventional. Hartshorne and May's clever test inspired the inclusion of "Lie scales" on subsequent self-report instruments. These seek to identify individuals who are falsifying their self reports.

Inspired by these pioneering efforts, social scientists have illuminated several aspects of lying: the demography of deceit, deceptive behavior, and veracity judgments.

DEMOGRAPHY OF DECEIT

Lying is most likely universal. It has been found in all cultures ever studied. In a 2003 investigation, Lawrence Sugiyama and associates reported some relevant cross-cultural evidence: that farmers in a preliterate culture perform as well as Harvard students on difficult reasoning problems, so long as the reasoning would prevent them from being duped in a social exchange. These results suggest that cheating is a pan-cultural component of social life. Indeed, evolutionists have attributed the large size of the human brain to selection pressures imposed by the ever-escalating Machiavellian intelligence of our ancestors' scheming peers.

Psychologists have ventured estimates of the frequency of lying in everyday life. In one investigation, college students logged all the lies they told over a period of several weeks. Their records imply that the average student lies once or twice per day, once in every three to five social interactions. In another study, thousands of people from around the world were asked how many lies the typical person tells in a week. Their estimates varied widely, but the median estimate was that typical person lies seven times a week, or once a day.

Social scientists have analyzed deception at the institutional level. Historians have revisited large-scale military deceptions, like the Allies' duping of Nazi Germany before the Normandy landing in 1944. Political scientists have described constraints on the use of duplicity by the intelligence services of democracies. Financial analysts have noted international differences in institutional corruption. According to Transparency International, an anticorruption organization based in Berlin, the most corrupt countries in the world in 2005 were Bangladesh and Chad. The least corrupt were Iceland, Finland, and New Zealand. Economic factors help explain international differences in corruption. Highly corrupt countries are poor and pay their civil servants poorly by local standards. Psychological factors may also play a role. Controlling for differences in income, countries are more corrupt if they feature a collective culture, rather than an individualistic culture.

Researchers have documented socioeconomic, racial, and family differences in lying. Armed with the character tests they developed, Hartshorne and May reported in 1928 that students from a low socioeconomic background are more likely to cheat than those from a higher background. In 2002 sociologists Judith Blau and Elizabeth

Stearns reported a discrepant finding: that white students of high socioeconomic status are most likely and black students are least likely to condone cheating. Perhaps socioeconomic differences in cheating have changed over the years. In any case, there are family influences on deception. In 1982, a team of investigators measured 54 different personality traits on each member of 415 families in Hawaii. The researchers found that family members resemble one another in personality. This was expected. However, the researchers also found that family members resemble one another in the tendency to lie. Indeed, family similarities proved to be stronger on Lie Scales embedded within the investigators' personality tests than on any of the other traits measured.

Social scientists have explored sex differences in lying. Although some have maintained that the sexes differ in the propensity to lie, it appears that a larger difference is in motives for deception. Women are more likely to lie to spare others' feelings, while men more often lie out of self-interest. Relative to women, men are more suspicious of what they hear. Although there is little evidence that the sexes differ in the ability to discriminate lies from truths, women are more willing than men to accept politely what others say. Perhaps these sex differences reflect differential socialization experiences.

DECEPTIVE BEHAVIORS

Do people act in distinctive ways when they are lying? Are there behavioral signatures from which lying can be inferred?

Certain behaviors appear to accompany deceit on certain occasions. Medical researchers Alan Hirsch and Charles Wolf analyzed a videotape of Bill Clinton during Clinton's August 17, 1998, appearance before a federal grand jury. While giving testimony that a judge later found to be false, Clinton displayed 20 of 23 putative signs of deception. Clinton, for example, made more speech errors when denying a sexual relationship with Monica Lewinsky than when answering perfunctory questions. While testifying about Lewinsky, Clinton showed a tendency to touch his nose—which the authors dubbed a "Pinocchio phenomenon."

Although Hirsch and Wolf's videotape analysis is certainly provocative, it reflects a single case. One wonders if the 20 behaviors that accompanied Clinton's suspect testimony accompany most lies. To address this issue, psychologist Bella DePaulo and colleagues analyzed research data on 158 potential deception cues from 120 independent samples of lie- and truth-tellers. They considered facial cues, bodily cues, vocal cues, and verbal cues, organizing the evidence around a series of questions.

None of the 158 behaviors these reviewers examined is a perfect indicator of deception, always displayed when a person is lying and never otherwise displayed. Even so, some cues bear a statistical relationship to deception. Compared to truth-tellers, liars are less forthcoming. They sound distant, appear tense, and convey a negative impression. Invariably actuarial, cues to deception vary to a considerable extent across situations, across liars, and across lies. Attempts to conceal fear may, for instance, be exposed by inadvertent signs of fear.

For lie detection, it is best to assemble evidence from multiple cues. German psychologist Gunter Kohnken has advocated a multi-cue approach for assessing the truthfulness of statements. This so-called Statement Validity Analysis has been used in Europe to evaluate legal testimony, particularly the testimony of children who allege sexual abuse. As a component of Statement Validity Analysis, the witness's account of an event is checked against nineteen criteria presumed to be indicative of truthfulness. Criterion-Based Content Analysis (CBCA) deems as truthful, for example, witnesses who spontaneously correct themselves, admit a lack of memory, and recount events in a nonchronological order. Research studies corroborate the value of this content-based system, suggesting that CBCA can discriminate lies from truths with an accuracy of about 70 percent.

VERACITY JUDGMENTS

Alongside these research efforts are lay attempts to uncover deceit. Nonscientists make judgments of deception every day, and these judgments have consequences. Some business negotiations succeed and others fail because of the negotiators' judgments of one another's truthfulness. Some marriages end in a month and others last fifty years because of the partners' beliefs about one another's veracity. Lay judgments of deception have special significance in U.S. courtrooms, where jurors are the only lie detectors. Whenever witnesses give conflicting testimony, jurors must decide who is telling the truth. Thus under American law a defendant's fate can hinge on her (or his) demeanor, and those who appear guilty are often found guilty.

Social scientists have investigated lay theories of lying. As they have discovered, people share beliefs about behaviors that accompany deceit. In a 2006 investigation a global deception research team found that the most common stereotype in the world about deception is that liars avoid eye contact. Residents of 75 countries said that liars avoid eye contact, expressing this belief in 42 different languages. In response to the open-ended question "How can you tell that others are lying?" two thirds of the respondents worldwide mentioned that liars avert gaze, and when they mentioned more than one way to tell when others are lying, they mentioned gaze aversion first.

Do people in fact avoid eye contact when lying? There is not much evidence to support this belief. In the findings reviewed by DePaulo and colleagues, people who are telling small lies show no tendency to avert gaze, and those who are telling bigger lies show only a weak gaze aversion. Even if there is a kernel of truth to the stereotype of the gaze-aversive liar, this belief is overdrawn. In a study by communications scholar Timothy Levine, college students were asked to rate the eye contact of peers they saw on videotape. When informed that the peers were lying, students perceived them to be averting gaze.

Apologists for the American legal system contend that jurors are good at spotting deception. Unfortunately, research suggests that they are not. In 2006 psychologists Charles Bond and Bella DePaulo reviewed results from hundreds of experiments on people's attempts to detect lies in real time with no special aids. Under these circumstances, people average 54 percent correct lie-or-truth judgments when 50 percent would be expected by chance. Although lie detection rates vary from study to study, much of the variation appears to be artifactual, and the highest accuracy achieved by any group to date barely exceeds 70 percent. People usually presume that their acquaintances are telling the truth. Most people appear honest even when they are lying, and a few appear dishonest even when they are telling the truth. Individual differences in social competence may underlie differences in apparent honesty, psychologist Robert Feldman has found. Although skills at feigning honesty continue to develop through middle childhood, even three-year-olds can dupe adults, researcher Michael Lewis reports.

BIBLIOGRAPHY

Bond, Charles F., Jr., and Bella M. DePaulo. 2006. Accuracy of Deception Judgments. *Personality and Social Psychology Review* 10 (3): 214–234.

DePaulo, Bella, et al. 2003. Cues to Deception. *Psychological Bulletin* 129: 74–118.

Godson, Roy, and James J. Wirtz, eds. 2002. *Strategic Denial and Deception: The Twenty-First Century Challenge.* New Brunswick, NJ: Transaction.

Lewis, Michael, and Carolyn Saarni, eds. 1993. *Lying and Deception in Everyday Life.* New York: Guilford.

Rogers, Richard. 1997. *Clinical Assessment of Malingering and Deception.* 2nd ed. New York: Guilford.

Vrij, Aldert. 2000. *Detecting Lies and Deceit: The Psychology of Lying and the Implications for Professional Practice.* Chichester, U.K.: Wiley.

Charles F. Bond Jr.

LYNCHINGS

Lynchings, illegal killings performed by groups of people under service to justice, race, or tradition, are a phenomenon seen across human history, from ancient cultures through contemporary ones, in pre-modern and modern Europe, Asia, Africa, and the Americas. Across cultures and eras, mobs have perpetrated lynchings in order to punish what they have perceived as behavior that violates societal norms. The definition of deviant behavior varies widely across cultural contexts, but most commonly lynch mobs have collectively murdered those they have accused of transgressions such as murder, rape, theft, the crossing of racial boundaries, or witchcraft. Roberta Senechal de la Roche argues in "The Sociogenesis of Lynching" (1997) that lynchings are more likely to occur in times and places where great social distance exists between deviants and those offended by their behavior. Lynchings have meaning as performances of collective violence, with mobs resorting to varying degrees of ritual, such as selecting a site of symbolic significance for a mob execution, the desecration of a victim's body, or taking trophies or affixing signs to a victim's corpse. With such ritualistic punishment, mobs have sought to emphasize particular values and the cleansing of a community of a victim's alleged offense.

In the last several centuries, lynchings have arisen amid cultural conflict over changing legal systems, particularly when certain social groups have perceived themselves as alienated from or unprotected by the formal legal system. This was the case in the United States in the early to mid-nineteenth century, when lynching arose south and west of the Allegheny Mountains amid profound shifts in understandings of law and the criminal justice system. On the southern, midwestern, and far western frontiers of the United States in the 1830s, 1840s, and 1850s, white Americans seized upon lethal group violence unsanctioned by law—particularly hangings—to enforce mandates of racial and class hierarchy and to pull into definition tenuous and ill-defined understandings of social order and community. Collectively murdering Native Americans, Mexicans, African American slaves and free blacks, and working-class, nonlanded whites, white Americans rejected growing due-process legal reforms that offered the promise of fairness to the unpopular and powerless by protecting the rights of those accused of crimes. Invoking popular sovereignty, a notion stemming from the American Revolution that government was rooted in the people and could be reclaimed by them if their life, liberty, and property were threatened, lynchers imitated customary public punishments, the pillory and the gallows, even as reformers sought to abolish those institutions on grounds of humanitarianism and the maintenance of public order.

In the late nineteenth and early twentieth centuries, the ranks of lynchers included rural landholding elites and members of the rural and urban working classes. Significant numbers of lynchings occurred in the American West and Midwest. On the southwest borderlands of Texas, New Mexico, Arizona, and California, lynchers killed hundreds of Mexicans following the American conquest of those territories in the mid-nineteenth century and during the era of the Mexican Revolution in the 1910s. Beyond racial animosities, lynchings in the West and Midwest in the nineteenth and early to mid-twentieth centuries were motivated by criminal justice concerns and class prejudices revolving around the landed elite's protection of property on the range. For instance, in California between 1875 and 1947, lynch mobs killed thirty-five whites, fifteen Mexicans, nine Native Americans, three Chinese, and two African Americans. In Iowa during the same era, by contrast, lynchers murdered twenty-three white men and one Native American.

However, the vast majority of lynchings in the United States occurred in the South, where mobs killed at least 2,805 persons, 2,462 of them African American, between 1882 and 1930. Stewart E. Tolnay and E. M. Beck (1995) document the leading states for lynching as Mississippi (452 victims), Georgia (381), and Louisiana (274). In the South in the late nineteenth and early twentieth centuries, lynching became a dramatic and frequent means for whites to seek to assert racial hierarchy over African Americans. Lynchings were concentrated in Cotton Belt and Gulf Plain counties that had seen significant recent black in-migration and where African Americans composed from half to three-fourths of the population. Lynchings often stemmed from violent disputes in which African American laborers had resisted the authority of planter-class whites or the indignities of the emerging Jim Crow system that segregated blacks from whites in public spaces. In some Cotton Belt jurisdictions, such as Caddo, Bossier, and Ouachita parishes in Louisiana, whites completely abandoned formal criminal justice institutions in favor of rampant lynching violence that reaffirmed white supremacy. In another social setting that became conducive to lynching, the growth of towns and cities mixed whites and blacks from different parts of the South. In these novel urban locales, thousands of whites sometimes participated in highly ritualistic lynchings of African Americans, as for example in the mob execution of Jesse Washington in Waco, Texas, on May 15, 1916.

Lynchings waned in the early to middle decades of the twentieth century, as antilynching advocates such as Ida B. Wells-Barnett (1862–1931), the NAACP (National Association for the Advancement of Colored People), and Jessie Daniel Ames (1883–1972) protested the injustices of mob violence. During the same decades, a significant southern, white middle class developed that opposed lynching and placed its faith instead in formal law, especially the death penalty. The U.S. House of Representatives passed several antilynching laws, but these were defeated in the U.S. Senate (on June 13, 2005, the Senate approved a resolution apologizing to the descendants of lynching victims for its historical failure to enact antilynching legislation). Brief surges in lynchings in and outside of the South during World War I (1914–1918), the Great Depression, and World War II (1939–1945) raised fears that the practice could be reviving. However, lynching lost its public face in succeeding decades and went underground. In the latter decades of the twentieth century, small groups of whites murdered African Americans such as Emmett Till in northern Mississippi in August 1955; Michael Donald in Mobile, Alabama, in March 1981; and James Byrd Jr., in Jasper, Texas, in June 1998; as well as civil rights workers Andrew Goodman, Michael Schwerner, and James Chaney in Neshoba County, Mississippi, in June 1964.

In the late twentieth and early twenty-first centuries, lynchings occurred in such places as Latin America, sub-Saharan Africa, the Middle East, and the urban United States. In these locales, crowds of people have lethally punished alleged perpetrators of crime and have sought to explain their actions by citing ineffectual, distant, or corrupt criminal justice institutions.

SEE ALSO *Jim Crow; Race Relations; Wells-Barnett, Ida B.*

BIBLIOGRAPHY

Brundage, W. Fitzhugh. 1993. *Lynching in the New South: Georgia and Virginia, 1880–1930.* Urbana: University of Illinois Press.

Brundage, W. Fitzhugh, ed. 1997. *Under Sentence of Death: Lynching in the South.* Chapel Hill: University of North Carolina Press.

Pfeifer, Michael J. 2004. *Rough Justice: Lynching and American Society, 1874–1947.* Urbana: University of Illinois Press.

Senechal de la Roche, Roberta. 1997. The Sociogenesis of Lynching. In *Under Sentence of Death: Lynching in the South,* ed. W. Fitzhugh Brundage, 48–76. Chapel Hill: University of North Carolina Press.

Tolnay, Stewart E., and E. M. Beck. 1995. *A Festival of Violence: An Analysis of Southern Lynchings, 1882–1930.* Urbana: University of Illinois Press.

Michael J. Pfeifer

LYND, ROBERT AND HELEN

Robert Stoughton Lynd was born on September 26, 1892, in New Albany, Indiana, and died on November 1, 1970,

in Warren, Connecticut. In 1921 he married Helen Merrell, who was born on March 17, 1896, in LaGrange, Illinois, and died on January 30, 1982, in New York City. The two social scientists were best known for their community studies *Middletown* (1929) and *Middletown in Transition* (1937). During World War I, Robert, a Princeton graduate, turned to the ministry as the only institution working for spiritual values. After doing missionary work at a Standard Oil camp, he launched a muckraking attack on Standard Oil and John D. Rockefeller Jr. Both infuriated and impressed by Lynd, Rockefeller's chief aide for the social sciences, Raymond Fosdick, hired him to undertake a study on the church in a small city for the Rockefeller-funded Institute of Social and Religious Research. That work became the basis for *Middletown.*

THE *MIDDLETOWN* STUDIES

The Lynds began their study in Muncie, Indiana, in 1923 after choosing it as a representative American city. They quickly convinced the institute that one could not study the church in a vacuum but had to study it in an integrated fashion. They argued that one should study modern society as one would examine a primitive culture. Adopting the British school of functional anthropology, they concentrated on how the culture as a whole worked.

The Lynds split Middletown culture into six activities: getting a living, making a home, training the young, using leisure, engaging in religious activities, and engaging in community activities. Indebted most of all to Thorstein Veblen and his concept of pecuniary culture, the Lynds demonstrated how that culture dominated Middletown society. Everything followed from occupations and the consequent split into business and working classes. The way one earned a living dominated the culture from one's leisure time to one's church denomination.

Despite a lack of methodological training, the Lynds produced a sophisticated work of sociological research. They used well-conceived questionnaires for all organizations, interviewed representative samples of the population, and innovatively included the questionnaires in an appendix. Despite its methodological rigor, the institute refused the work because of its admitted biases and use of class perspective and for being, as William F. Ogburn noted, "too interesting to be science" (quoted in Lynd 1929).

As the Lynds attempted to gain control of the manuscript, Robert wrote the section on consumerism for inclusion in a book for the President's Committee on Social Trends, "Recent Social Trends." That piece followed the emphasis in *Middletown* on spending as dominating American life and used empirical techniques to argue for a change in society. The Lynds' works were among the first not only to identify a consumer society but also to criticize it. After the release of the Middletown manuscript in 1928, it quickly became a best seller, winning praise from social scientists and the general public.

In 1935 the Lynds decided to restudy Muncie. They recognized that American sociologists had not conducted follow-up studies of communities and had paid insufficient attention to social change. Furthermore, they felt that the Great Depression would provide an excellent case study in how outside forces compel local areas to alter the status quo. They also realized that like most American social scientists of their time, they had overlooked the issue of social and political power.

In *Middletown in Transition* (1937) the coauthors discovered that Middletown in fact was not in transition. The most noticeable change, apart from the infusion of federal funds, was the total resistance of the community to change and the solidification of existing attitudes and institutions. In regard to power, the dominant Ball family had come to control even more of the economic and political structure. Producers of canning jars, one of the few products more in demand during the Depression, the Balls used their profits to buy up local bankrupt industries, contributed heavily to local charities, and controlled both political parties.

INFLUENCE AND CRITICISMS

Although the first Middletown book has had greater influence as a pioneering community study and historical source, the second volume also influenced later social scientists in the study of power. Although the concentration of power in one family in Muncie was not characteristic of larger communities, both Floyd Hunter's study of Atlanta, *Community Power Structure* (1953), and C. Wright Mills's *The Power Elite* (1956) saw power as being concentrated in small groups. Later pluralistic views such as Robert Dahl's 1961 examination of New Haven, *Who Governs?*, questioned the Lynds' results and biases.

The Middletown works represented the apex of the Lynds' influence, although both of them continued to produce important theoretical works independently. During the 1950s both Lynds were accused of being Communists, and the Middletown books were removed from United States Information Agency libraries around the world. Both Robert and Helen were committed social activists and students of Marxism. They were also extremely popular teachers, Robert at Columbia and Helen at Sarah Lawrence. As fear of communism increased in the United States, several congressional committees subpoenaed the left-wing faculty to testify before them. While Helen testified before the Jenner Committee and kept her job, Robert suffered a nervous breakdown from which he never recovered. Their son Staughton

would go on to become one of the leaders of the new left academia during the 1960s and 1970s.

SEE ALSO *Case Method; Case Method, Extended; Community Power Studies; Dahl, Robert Alan; Hunter, Floyd; McCarthyism; Occupational Status; Political Science; Power; Sociology; Survey; Veblen, Thorstein; Working Class*

BIBLIOGRAPHY

Etkowitz, Henry. 1979–1980. The Americanization of Marx: *Middletown* and *Middletown in Transition*. *Journal of the History of Sociology* 2: 41–57.

Fox, Richard Wightman. 1983. Epitaph for Middletown: Robert S. Lynd and the Analysis of Consumer Culture. In *Culture of Consumption: Critical Essays in American History 1880–1980*, ed. Richard Wrightman Fox and T. J. Jackson Lears, 101–142. New York: Pantheon.

Igo, Sarah E. 2005. From Main Street to Mainstream: Middletown, Muncie and "Typical America." *Indiana Magazine of History* 101: 239–266.

Lynd, Robert S. 1929. Problems of Being Objective. Social Science Research Council. Charles E. Merriam Collection, University of Chicago: August.

Smith, Mark C. 1994. Robert Lynd and Knowledge for What. In *Social Science in the Crucible: The American Debate over Objectivity and Purpose, 1918–1941*, 120–158. Durham, NC: Duke University Press.

Mark C. Smith

LYND, STAUGHTON
1929–

Staughton Lynd, historian, radical political activist, and labor lawyer, was born on November 22, 1929, to the sociologists Robert and Helen Lynd, best known for their path-breaking Middletown studies. Like his parents, whose socialist views strongly influenced their son, Lynd pursued an academic career, graduating from Harvard in 1951 and obtaining a PhD in history from Columbia in 1962. Staughton Lynd, however, acquired notoriety not as a scholar but as a civil rights and antiwar activist.

Lynd came from a Quaker background. He was inducted into the U.S. army during the Korean War as a noncombatant conscientious objector, but discharged for his leftist sympathies. After leaving the army, Lynd and his wife, Alice Niles, joined the Macedonia cooperative community in Georgia. While teaching at Spelman College in Atlanta, Lynd became involved in the civil rights movement and in 1964 he organized Freedom Schools for the Student Nonviolent Coordinating Committee (SNCC) during the legendary Mississippi Freedom Summer of

1964. In the fall of that year, Lynd moved on to become an assistant professor of history at Yale University, but his focus was on the fledgling movement against the war in Vietnam. He traveled to Hanoi in December 1965, along with fellow peace activist Tom Hayden and Marxist historian Herbert Aptheker. Lynd saw the trip as a mission to prevent the escalation of the war; it resulted in his passport being temporarily revoked by the State Department, though the federal government did not initiate criminal prosecution. The trip did, however, probably cost him tenure at Yale.

As an antiwar activist with the Students for a Democratic Society (SDS), he was involved in organizing mass demonstrations and providing support for income tax and draft resistance. When parts of the New Left embraced violence in the late sixties and early seventies, Lynd remained firmly committed to the ideals of nonviolent grassroots mobilization. In 1973 he enrolled in the University of Chicago law school, obtained a law degree, and in 1976 became a labor lawyer in Youngstown, Ohio, where he represented and helped organize steelworkers, sometimes in conflict with their unions. Legal strategies, in Lynd's view, needed to be devised in close contact with working people and bolstered by radical direct action. His fields of activity have included the rights of retired and disabled workers, the struggle against plant closings, and efforts to create interracial labor alliances.

Lynd's scholarly publications have always closely mirrored his interests and commitment as an activist, beginning with his 1962 dissertation on class conflict in the Revolutionary era. In addition, he has published books on slavery, oral histories of working-class activism, and, in 2004, an account of the 1993 prison revolt in Lucasville, Ohio. In 1998 Kent State University established the Staughton Lynd Collection, which includes materials from the 1930s to the year 2000.

Staughton Lynd has often been referred to as a Quaker influenced by Marxism. His socialism has always remained skeptical of dogma and tied to his strong belief in communitarian democracy, pacifism, and social justice. Not content to criticize American capitalism from the position of a middle-class intellectual, his life has been dedicated to helping empower poor people and minorities.

SEE ALSO *Activism; Civil Rights Movement, U.S.; Left Wing; Lynd, Robert and Helen; Marxism; Prisons; Protest; Slavery; Vietnam War; Working Class*

BIBLIOGRAPHY

Lynd, Staughton. 2004. *Lucasville: The Untold Story of a Prison Uprising.* Philadelphia: Temple University Press.

Lynd, Staughton, and Alice Lynd, eds. 2000. *The New Rank and File.* Ithaca, NY: ILR Press.

Polsgrove, Carol. 2001. *Divided Minds: Intellectuals and the Civil Rights Movement.* New York: Norton.

Manfred Berg

M

MAALOUF, AMIN

SEE *Identities, Deadly.*

MACCOBY, ELEANOR
1917–

Eleanor Emmons Maccoby is a leader and innovator in theory and research on the social development of the child. The Barbara Kimball Browning Professor of Psychology Emerita at Stanford University, she received her BA from the University of Washington and her MA and PhD from the University of Michigan. After working at Harvard University for several years, she joined the Stanford faculty in 1958.

Maccoby's wide-ranging interests include theories of socialization, gender differences, and the effects of divorce on the child. She has examined the socialization process from early childhood through adolescence. With John Martin (Maccoby and Martin 1983) she has provided a virtually book-length review of the history of theories of child development within the family, relating these theories to current issues in socialization. In a highly influential early work, Maccoby and Carol Nagy Jacklin (1974) concluded that, contrary to popular conceptions, the evidence does not support the notions that girls, relative to boys, are more social, have lower self-esteem, are better at rote learning and repetitive tasks, are less analytic, are more affected by heredity, lack achievement motivation, and are more auditory. They did find preliminary evidence that girls have a greater verbal ability than boys, that

boys excel in visual-spatial and mathematical ability, and that boys are more aggressive.

Basic to Maccoby's approach to socialization is the notion of interaction, taken in two senses: (1) face-to-face interaction in the process of socialization and (2) systemic interaction between biological factors and socialization. With respect to face-to-face interaction, Maccoby rejects the notion that socialization is a top-down process in which adults mold the essentially passive child. Rather, from the beginning there is true interaction between child and caregiver in the sense that each participant's actions are contingent, at least in part, on the actions of the partner. She expands significantly on the notion of bidirectionality most frequently attributed to Richard Bell (1968). The implication of bidirectionality is that the child is an active participant in his or her own socialization.

A second basic influence on socialization is the biological endowment of the child. In this context, Maccoby cites potential constitutional differences between boys and girls. These differences, in turn, influence the interaction of the child with others. An example would be the play separation of boys and girls in relatively unsupervised settings. Maccoby (1990) provides evidence that boys have a more rough-and-tumble style of play, termed a restrictive or constricting interaction style. This is aversive to girls, who have a more enabling or facilitating style (Leaper 1991). The result is play separation and contrasting socialization within these separated peer groups.

Maccoby and Robert Mnookin (1992) surveyed the effect of the current process of divorce on the child. They regard the institution of no-fault divorce as introducing a new social regime, the social and legal implications of which continue to emerge. They conclude that, under the proper circumstances, the experience of divorce is not necessarily damaging to the child and that it is possible for life to proceed in a relatively normal fashion in these families.

SEE ALSO *Divorce and Separation; Gender; Gender Gap; Socialization*

BIBLIOGRAPHY

Bell, Richard Q. 1968. A Reinterpretation of the Direction of Effects in Studies of Socialization. *Psychological Review* 75 (2): 81–95.

Leaper, Campbell. 1991. Influence and Involvement in Children's Discourse: Age, Gender, and Partner Effects. *Child Development* 62: 797–811.

Maccoby, Eleanor E. 1990. Gender and Relationships: A Developmental Account. *American Psychologist* 45: 513–520.

Maccoby, Eleanor E., and Carol Nagy Jacklin. 1974. *The Psychology of Sex Differences*. Stanford, CA: Stanford University Press.

Maccoby, Eleanor E., and John A. Martin. 1983. Socialization in the Context of the Family: Parent-Child Interaction. In *Handbook of Child Psychology*, ed. Paul H. Mussen. Vol. 4: *Socialization, Personality, and Social Development*, ed. E. Mavis Hetherington, 1–101. 4th ed. New York: Wiley.

Maccoby, Eleanor E., and Robert H. Mnookin. 1992. *Dividing the Child: Social and Legal Dilemmas of Custody*. Cambridge, MA: Harvard University Press.

Starkey Duncan

MACHEL, SAMORA
1933–1986

Samora Machel was the first president of Mozambique following independence in 1975. He came to prominence in the 1960s during the struggle to end Portuguese colonial rule over Mozambique and was influential as a leader of the Mozambique Liberation Front, known as Frelimo for the Portuguese name, Frente de Libertação de Moçambique. Machel was born on September 29, 1933, to a rural family in southern Mozambique, and as a child he attended a Catholic mission school. He worked briefly as an orderly, trained as a nurse from 1952 to 1954, and was then employed as a nurse in the capital city, where he continued his nursing education. He and Sorita Tchaiakomo had a common-law relationship, and they had four children together. Machel married Josina Machel in 1969 during the armed struggle, and they had one child before Josina died in 1971. He married Graça Machel in 1975, and they had two children.

European nations began the process of granting independence to their African colonies in the 1950s and 1960s, but Portugal refused to end its colonial ties. As a result, the anticolonial movements in the Portuguese colonies, including Mozambique, were forced to operate clandestinely. Machel was greatly influenced by his experiences in the colonial medical services, where he witnessed racial divisions among workers and in the treatment of patients. He began attending secret nationalist meetings, and in 1961 he met and was deeply inspired by Eduardo Mondlane (1920–1969), who emerged as the leader of the Mozambican liberation movement. Within a year Machel had attracted the attention of the Portuguese secret police and had to leave Mozambique in 1963 when he joined Frelimo in exile in Tanzania. Machel joined the military sector of Frelimo and trained in Algeria. The first shots of the armed struggle were fired in 1964, and by 1966 Machel was the commander of the Frelimo army. His contribution to the development of Frelimo's politics included his perspective that the independence struggle was not a racial issue of black against white, but was a struggle for freedom from the colonial system, an issue that continued to be contentious for many years. He was also a strong voice for socialism within Frelimo. After Mondlane's assassination in 1969, Machel emerged as the leader of Frelimo and as president of Mozambique after the Portuguese fascist government was overthrown in 1974.

As president, Machel focused on unifying Mozambique and implementing an ambitious socialist program of reforms. Many enterprises were nationalized, education and health were dramatically expanded to serve ordinary Mozambicans, and new laws were introduced to support women, peasants, and others who had been marginalized under colonialism. But Mozambique was one of the poorest nations in the world, and it was difficult to sustain the planned changes. South Africa and Zimbabwe, both ruled by white-minority regimes in the 1970s, helped form and support an anti-Frelimo organization known as Renamo (for Resistência Nacional de Moçambique, Mozambique National Resistance). Machel found himself mired in an intractable guerrilla war as Renamo wrought extensive damage and destruction in Mozambique throughout the 1980s, ending with a peace accord in 1992.

Machel himself was a casualty of that war. In October 1986 he traveled to Zambia to participate in talks designed to bring an end to Renamo's attacks. As his plane returned to Mozambique on October 19, it crashed under suspicious conditions. The plane, a Tupelov 134, apparently followed a beacon that the Soviet pilots believed would bring them to their airfield in Mozambique. Instead they crashed into a low hill inside South Africa at Mbuzini. Samora Machel and twenty-four other passengers, including other members of the government, were killed. South African officials claimed that the accident was a result of pilot error. Most Mozambicans and many others believe that the crash was orchestrated by the South African apartheid regime. Despite several investigations, including testimony as part of South Africa's postapartheid Truth and Reconciliation Commission, the exact circumstances of the crash have not been determined. More than twenty years later, President Armando Guebuza of Mozambique promised to further investigate Machel's death, saying the government "would not rest" until the events that led to the death of his predecessor were clarified.

SEE ALSO *Anticolonial Movements; Apartheid; Colonialism; Decolonization; Inequality, Racial; Liberation Movements; Pan-Africanism; Racism; Resistance; Socialism; Truth and Reconciliation Commissions*

BIBLIOGRAPHY

Christie, Iain. 1989. *Samora Machel: A Biography.* London: Panaf.

Munslow, Barry, ed. 1985. *Samora Machel, An African Revolutionary: Selected Speeches and Writings.* Trans. Michael Wolfers. London: Zed.

Público. 2006. Guebuza promete investigar morte de Samora Machel. September 27.

Souto, Amélia, and António Sopa. 1996. *Samora Machel: Bibliografia (1970–1986).* Maputo, Mozambique: UEM Centro de Estudos Africanos.

Kathleen Sheldon

MACHIAVELLI, NICCOLÒ
1469–1527

The Renaissance political thinker Niccolò Machiavelli shocked Christian Europe by declaring that success in politics both necessitates and excuses any means used to achieve it. Born in 1469 in Florence to a family of some prominence but modest means, Machiavelli probably received a humanistic education in his youth, enabling him to become head of the Second Chancery of the Florentine Republic in 1498. This office brought him into close contact with a number of Renaissance potentates, inciting his penetrating mind to form a stern, indeed, cynical view of politics. After the republic's fall in 1512, Machiavelli retired to his small landed property to study ancient writers and reflect on political affairs.

In 1513 Machiavelli wrote *The Prince,* a slender book in the traditional mirror-of-princes genre. His advice to princes, however, was far from traditional. Rather than exhorting them to practice the virtues, he encouraged them to "know how to enter into evil, when forced by necessity" (Chap. XVIII), on the grounds that "a man who wants to make a profession of good in all regards must come to ruin among so many who are not good" (Chap. XV). In particular, he argued that princes should not hesitate to use deceit and violence to maintain their state and secure their subjects. This advice transformed the European tradition of "reason of state" (Lat. *ratio status,* Fr. *raison d'état*). Whereas the medieval proponents of this tradition had considered the necessity to break moral rules for the common good to be exceptional, and thus reconcilable with a community of virtue, Machiavelli assumed necessary evil to be a regular aspect of politics, thus separating it from ethics. Machiavelli's pithy maxims to this effect inspired generations of writers who called for strong measures to build the modern state, such as Gabriel Naudé in France and Johann Gottlieb Fichte in Germany. His approach also legitimized the ruthlessness of many statesmen who constructed it, including Thomas Cromwell, Cardinal Richelieu, Napoleon, and Mussolini.

From roughly 1515 to 1520, Machiavelli belonged to a circle of educated Florentines who met in the Oricellari Gardens and whose political views reflected the civic strand of Renaissance humanism. Drawing on the Aristotelian and Ciceronian notion of citizenship, civic humanism advocated *vivere civile,* a life of intense involvement with public affairs, based on a humanistic education and framed by the institutions of a republic. Accordingly, they believed that men ought to deliberate wisely and serve capably in the offices of their city, while also practicing the virtues, fostering concord, upholding liberty, and attaining greatness. Machiavelli's exposure to this ideal prompted his major republican writings, the *Discourses on Livy* (c. 1518), the *Art of War* (1521) and the *Florentine Histories* (1525). In these works Machiavelli followed Renaissance fashion by taking the Roman republic as a model. According to Machiavelli, Rome maintained its liberty because it provided the commoners with a representative, the Tribune of the Plebs, who checked the tyrannical ambitions of the nobles with his power to veto any law and intercede with any action of the magistrate. Having this share in authority also made the commoners loyal enough to be armed for war in large numbers, enabling Rome to conquer a vast empire and attain unprecedented greatness. Moreover, Rome's superior institutions were brought to life by the "good customs" of its citizens, allowing nobles and commoners to conduct their struggles over wealth and power without bloodshed and settle them by compromise.

The fact that civic humanism formed Machiavelli's historical context has led a number of historians, most prominently J. G. A. Pocock (1975) and Quentin Skinner (1978), to conclude that Machiavelli was a civic humanist himself. More penetrating analysis, however, reveals that Machiavelli's republican writings rest on the same premises on human nature and ethics as *The Prince*, and they consequently propose corresponding maxims of action: "As all those demonstrate who reason on a *vivere civile*, and as every history is full of examples, it is necessary to whoever disposes a republic and orders laws in it to presuppose that all men are bad" (*Discourses on Livy* I.3.1). To found, as well as to reform a republic, an autocrat must therefore kill all those opposed to equality before the law. The good customs of the citizens are not only acquired by habituation under threat of punishment, they also are continuously degraded by their natural ambition and thus must be constantly renewed by exemplary and excessive punishments. Republics can execute policies more effectively than principalities because the majority can easily crush the minority, regardless of the harm done to individuals. Republics wage aggressive wars because the citizens need to satisfy their ambition abroad in order to mitigate conflict at home, and because security rests on striking first and acquiring empire. In other words, the "reason of state" forms the core of Machiavelli's republican thought as well. He made this fact most explicit when he claimed that "where one deliberates entirely on the safety of his fatherland [i.e., republic], there ought not to enter any consideration of either just or unjust, merciful or cruel … one ought to follow entirely the policy that saves its life and maintains its liberty" (*Discourses on Livy* III.41).

Preference must therefore be given to the older view of Machiavelli as a bold, if not reckless, thinker who broke with civic humanism and the entire classical tradition by limiting political thought to what men do rather than what they ought to do. According to the German historian Friedrich Meinecke (1924), this impulse led Machiavelli to probe and reveal the full extent of the reason of state, while the philosopher Ernst Cassirer (1946) believed that it prepared the ground for the empirical approach of modern political science by making no distinction between legitimate and illegitimate states. According to the British philosopher Isaiah Berlin (1953), it led Machiavelli to undermine the Western belief in a cosmos unified by reason. The political scientist Sheldon Wolin (1960) noted that it made Machiavelli conceive of politics as a struggle between conflicting interests. The philosopher Leo Strauss (1963) observed that this impulse prepared Machiavelli to lower the ethical standards that human beings ought to follow. It was in these ways that Machiavelli lit the flame of modernity.

BIBLIOGRAPHY

PRIMARY WORKS

Machiavelli, Niccolò. 1513. *The Prince*. Trans. Harvey C. Mansfield. Chicago: University of Chicago Press, 1998.

Machiavelli, Niccolò. c. 1518. *Discourses on Livy*. Trans. Harvey C. Mansfield and Nathan Tarcov. Chicago: University of Chicago Press, 1996.

Machiavelli, Niccolò. 1521. *Art of War*. Trans. Christopher Lynch. Chicago: University of Chicago Press, 2003.

Machiavelli, Niccolò. 1525. *Florentine Histories*. Trans. Laura F. Banfield and Harvey C. Mansfield, Jr. Princeton, NJ: Princeton University Press, 1988.

SECONDARY WORKS

Berlin, Isaiah. 1953. The Originality of Machiavelli. In *Studies on Machiavelli*, ed. Myron P. Gilmore, 147–206. Florence: Sansoni, 1972.

Cassirer, Ernst. 1946. *The Myth of the State*. New Haven, CT: Yale University Press.

Meinecke, Friedrich. [1924] 1984. *Machiavellism: The Doctrine of Raison d'Etat and Its Place in Modern History*. Trans. Douglas Scott. Boulder, CO: Westview.

Pocock, J. G. A. 1975. *The Machiavellian Moment: Florentine Political Thought and the Atlantic Republican Tradition*. Princeton, NJ: Princeton University Press.

Skinner, Quentin. 1978. *The Foundations of Modern Political Thought*. Vol. 1, *The Renaissance*. Cambridge, U.K.: Cambridge University Press.

Strauss, Leo. 1987. Niccolò Machiavelli: 1469–1527. In *History of Political Philosophy*, 3rd ed., ed. Leo Strauss and Joseph Cropsey, 296–317. Chicago: University of Chicago Press.

Wolin, Sheldon S. 1960. *Politics and Vision: Continuity and Innovation in Western Political Thought*. Boston: Little, Brown.

Markus Fischer

MACHIAVELLIANISM

SEE *Machiavelli, Niccolò; Realism, Political.*

MACHINE FUNCTIONALISM

SEE *Functionalism.*

MACHINERY

The adoption of new machinery, as part of technological progress, is a very controversial issue in economic analysis. Many analysts consider technology, the diffusion of technology, and technological advancements, to be very effective in promoting and attaining economic progress. Others consider machinery and new technologies to be major factors in reducing employment and the de-skilling of labor. These controversial views on machinery reflect the dual character of technology, which simultaneously creates and destroys labor positions.

Historically, the massive introduction of machinery in the production process took place with the advent of the capitalist economic system, and it was made possible by the subdivision and specialization of the labor process in the early stages of the capitalist mode of production. Adam Smith, in his famous example of the pin factory, showed very eloquently that the subdivision of the labor process into small consecutive tasks dramatically increases labor productivity and, more importantly, allows for the introduction of machines in the production process.

David Ricardo (1772–1823) was the first economist who discussed in detail the issue and consequences of technological progress in society. At first, he agreed with Smith that the mechanization of the production process is good for all social groups within an economy. The introduction of machinery increases productivity, lowers costs and, in competitive environments, lowers the prices of commodities. Eventually, all members of society benefit from the lowering of prices. Both the unemployment that is induced by technological change and the consequent substitution of capital for labor is only temporary, according to Say's Law, which guarantees full employment in the economy.

Ricardo later revised his position, however, arguing that the introduction of machinery in the production process may not benefit the working class, since it may create conditions for permanent unemployment. This could occur if the expenditures on machines are not financed out of savings (new investments) but through the transformation of circulating to fixed capital (simple replacement of labor with capital). If the latter takes place, unemployment will rise and be permanent, and society will suffer. In both cases, however, Ricardo was supportive of a public policy favoring the introduction of machines into the production process. He argued that entrepreneurs will either search for higher profits by increasing productivity through technological progress, or they will invest in profitable projects abroad, rendering the domestic working class doomed to unemployment. Thus, the mechanization of the production process in an economy increases productivity and lowers per unit costs rendering the economy competitive in the international environment.

In Ricardo's presentation of the question of machinery (as in James Mill's), a certain confusion exists. At one point he argues that the substitution of capital for labor generates unemployment, but at the same time he stresses the benefits of genuine cost-reducing improvements in techniques. The theory that technological unemployment automatically generates compensatory adjustments was introduced by John Ramsay McCulloch in the 1820s. According to this approach, all technically displaced labor

will necessarily be absorbed in the making of the machines themselves. This approach rests on the idea that, under perfect competition, innovations result in price reductions and an expansion of output. If demand is elastic, total receipts rise and the employer will increase his expenditures on either consumption or investment. If, however, demand is unresponsive to lower prices, the purchasing power in the economy still rises and consumers can acquire goods from other sectors, alleviating the increase in their sectoral demand. Either way, directly or indirectly, labor-saving machinery entails the expansion of output in an economy, which eventually causes the reabsorption of those displaced by machines.

Knut Wicksell (1851–1926), drawing upon compensation theory, argued that in analyzing the effect of labor displacement due to the introduction of machinery in the production process, the fact that unemployment creates feedback and domino effects in an economy should be considered. For instance, an increase in unemployment due to the displacement of labor will decrease wages and increase in profits. This rise in profits then brings about more investment and, by extension, more employment opportunities. In addition, the technological process introduced by machines increases productivity, lowers costs and prices, and eventually increases an economy's demand and, most likely, employment.

An increase in labor productivity is important in the capitalist mode of production because the motive force of capitalism is the drive for profits. Quite simply, more profits can be attained if labor productivity rises. According to Marx, the inner nature of capital is its self-expansion (accumulation), which imposes on individual capitals a fierce competition for higher profits and survival. An increase in labor productivity leads to per-unit cost reductions. This allows the entrepreneur to act in the competitive arena according to the following two pricing options: (1) if the price remains the same, the capitalist can attain a higher profit margin and, eventually, more profits; (2) if the price declines, the entrepreneur can drive his competitors out of the market, thus enjoying the benefits of a higher market share. Hence, rising labor productivity becomes an essential condition for capital's survival. Labor productivity rises if the amount of value that a worker produces in a given time rises. In today's economies, with the existing physical and legislative barriers (labor laws) to workers employment, an increase in surplus value (which translates into potential profits for the capitalist) can take place primarily through the introduction of new machinery.

The introduction of machinery into the labor process has changed the nature of the labor process itself. These changes include the intensification of work, the introduction of methods that further promote the division of labor, and the specialization and work rationalization that serve to simplify and standardize work so that it can be done in the least amount of time at the lowest cost to business. Technology is a particularly effective mode of getting workers to expend a greater amount of labor power while they are on the job. As a result, more output can be obtained by employing more capital and less labor. Prior to the 1960s, technology was applied primarily to industrial production and to manual work processes. These forms of mechanization reached their height in the automation of assembly lines and in "continuous-flow" processes, which raised industrial productivity enormously. The dominant form of new technology applied to work processes today is electronic technology, which allows a worker to operate several testing machines at the same time, thus serving exactly the same purpose as increasing labor productivity.

The introduction of machines in the production process has also changed the character of the labor process. Since the equipment makes all essential decisions, many skills are removed from the worker's task, making the worker perform more repetitive functions at a more productive rate. Labor is in this way intensely divided and de-skilled. With the division of work and the mechanization of the production process, the real subsumption of labor to capital takes place. Once a new technology is finally rationalized and prepared for mass production, in the long run it will de-skill most workers. Hence, mechanization and de-skilling are the logical outcome of capital's need to exploit living labor. However, there is no perfectly linear descent of skill levels of the labor force, because new technologies may also raise the skill level of certain groups of specialized laborers.

In the face of rapid technological change, workers have great difficulty in recognizing that changes in their jobs are caused by management's desire for greater profits, and not by the machinery itself. The famous movement of Luddites at the beginning of the nineteenth century shows the impotence of the working class to realize the real cause of jobless economic progress. At that time, British workers were against the introduction of labor-saving machines, and in many cases they destroyed factories and machines. The fact is, however, that the historical tendency of capitalism is the growth of surplus labor (as a reserve army of unemployed). Moreover, the more skillful the labor, the more they will be unemployed, since the way capitalism introduces machinery in the production process encourages unskilled labor.

SEE ALSO *Division of Labor; Labor, Surplus: Conventional Economics; Luddites; Machinery Question, The; Marx, Karl; Productivity; Relative Surplus Value; Ricardo, David; Say's Law; Surplus Population; Unemployment*

BIBLIOGRAPHY

Baumol, William J., Sue Anne Batey Blackman, and Edward N. Wolff. 1989. *Productivity and American Leadership.* Cambridge, MA: MIT Press.

Blaug, Mark. 1985. *Economic Theory in Retrospect.* 4th ed. New York: Cambridge University Press.

Botwinick, Howard. 1993. *Persistent Inequalities: Wage Disparity Under Capitalist Competition.* Princeton, NJ: Princeton University Press.

Braverman, Harry. 1998. *Labor and Monopoly Capital: The Degradation of Work in the 20th Century.* 25th Anniversary ed. New York: Monthly Review Press.

Carson, R. B. 1991. *Economic Issues Today: Alternative Approaches.* 5th ed. New York: St. Martin's Press.

Ricardo, David. 1817. *The Principles of Political Economy and Taxation.* Amherst, NY: Prometheus Books, 1996.

Persefoni V. Tsaliki

MACHINERY QUESTION, THE

The "machinery question" was developed by the economist David Ricardo (1772–1823) in the chapter "On Machinery," he added to the third edition of *On the Principles of Political Economy and Taxation* in 1821. This question related, in his words, to the "influence of machinery on the interests of the different classes of society" and particularly to the "opinion entertained by the labouring class, that the employment of machinery is frequently detrimental to their interests" ([1821] 1951). Ricardo's argument was presented as a recantation of his "previous opinion" on this question and marks the beginning of a debate that is still going on. This argument is based on the example of "a capitalist" with a £20,000 investment and particularly on how that capital is used over three succeeding years.

During the first year, a fraction (£7,000) of this sum is "invested in fixed capital," the remaining part (£13,000) is "employed as circulating capital in the maintenance of labour." Under conditions of simple reproduction, the gross revenue emerging at the end of the year must be £15,000, of which a part (£2,000, if the profit rate is 10%) is the net revenue (profit) of the year. The remaining sum (£13,000) is put back into the operation as the circulating capital of the next year.

In the second year, a process of mechanization begins, and half of the laborers previously employed in producing the gross revenue (wage goods plus profit goods) are transferred to the production of new machinery. Thus, the gross revenue emerging at the end of the year is £7.500, of which £2,000 is retained as the capitalist's profit.

INTERNATIONAL ENCYCLOPEDIA OF THE SOCIAL SCIENCES, 2ND EDITION

In the third year, the new machinery appears and is worth £7.500, or half of the gross revenue previously produced by the given number of laborers. Thus, the circulating (wage) capital of this year cannot be greater than £7.500 (half of the gross revenue produced in the previous year) minus the £2,000 profit, so that it actually falls to £5.500 from the £13,000 of previous years. Hence, the real wage rate (the wage goods given in exchange for one labor-year) falls to less than half of what it was initially.

Ricardo's argument cannot be understood without a number of qualifications. First, his "capitalist" is understood to be the only capitalist within a closed economy (a self-sufficient farmer or an industrial dictator) who cannot buy, but must produce, the new machinery. Ricardo's special assumption is that this production is realized without increasing the total capital employed—that is, without extra saving out of the capitalist's profit (which is unproductively consumed).

In addition, the "introduction of machinery" has two meanings. One refers to machinery *still to be built*, the other to machinery *already built*. While the former is the meaning adopted in the example above, the latter is adopted in other chapters of the *Principles* as well as in Ricardo's "previous opinion" which held that the introduction of machinery is beneficial to all classes of society. Since the two meanings reflect two equally legitimate assumptions, Ricardo's diverging conclusions in different phases of his life (as well as in different chapters of his principles) are not contradictory, so that his latest argument is an unnecessary recantation.

Ricardo's argument also requires that a distinction be made between national revenue (consumption goods) and national product (consumption goods plus instrumental goods), as well as between the consumption goods exchanged for productive labor (circulating capital in Ricardo's sense, or free capital in Jevons's sense) and the instrumental goods that assist labor in production (fixed capital in Ricardo's sense, or invested capital in Jevons's sense).

Ricardo's special assumption on savings as an unchanging magnitude is reflected in his idea that machinery be "suddenly discovered and extensively used." This assumption was designed to elucidate "a principle," not to explain current reality. This principle relates to the different role that capital plays in the demand for labor, depending on whether it is circulating (free) or fixed (invested). It also relates to the possibility that the gross revenue of a society (wages plus profits) may not increase—and may even fall—when its net revenue (profit) increases.

One interpretation of Ricardo's argument claims that what this is about, and what it warns against, is technological unemployment. This interpretation misses the change in the composition of national product (and of total capital) resulting from the (sudden) introduction of new machines and is focused instead on the impact on employment of a change in their technical coefficients. Ricardo's argument holds even if the new machines were identical to those already in use, provided they be produced without additional savings.

Another interpretation regards the "Ricardo effect"—by which "machinery and labor are in constant competition, and the former can frequently not be employed until labor rises"—as the core of Ricardo's argument. But the "Ricardo effect" deals with the causes, not the effects, of the introduction of machinery, and it is put forward, along with other qualifications, at the close of the machinery chapter in order to deny the "inference that machinery should not be encouraged."

Searching for episodes in economic history to confirm Ricardo's argument, the Nobel laureate John R. Hicks has alluded to the declining conditions of the working classes during the early phase of Britain's industrialization (1969). More properly, perhaps, Ricardo's argument could be used to explain the dramatic conditions of the working classes in the early phase of the Soviet Union's industrialization.

SEE ALSO *Change, Technological; Marx, Karl; Ricardo, David*

BIBLIOGRAPHY

Barkai, Haim. 1986. Ricardo's Volte-Face on Machinery. *Journal of Political Economy* 94 (June): 595–613.

Berg, Maxine. 1980. *The Machinery Question and the Making of Political Economy, 1815–1848*. Cambridge, U.K.: Cambridge University Press.

Hayek, Friedrich A. 1969. Three Elucidations of the Ricardo Effect. *Journal of Political Economy* 77 (2): 274–285.

Hicks, John R. 1969. *A Theory of Economic History*. Oxford: Clarendon.

Hollander, Samuel. 1971. The Development of Ricardo's Position on Machinery. *History of Political Economy* 3 (1): 105–135.

Maital, Shlomo, and Patricia Haswell. 1977. Why Did Ricardo (Not) Change His Mind! On Money and Machinery. *Economica* 44 (176): 359–368.

Meacci, Ferdinando. 1998. Further Reflections on the Machinery Question. *Contributions to Political Economy* 17 (1): 21–37.

Ricardo, David. 1821. *On the Principles of Political Economy and Taxation*. Cambridge, U.K.: Cambridge University Press, 1951.

Samuelson, Paul A. 1988. Mathematical Vindication of Ricardo on Machinery. *Journal of Political Economy* 96 (2): 274–282.

Samuelson, Paul A. 1989. Ricardo Was Right! *Scandinavian Journal of Economics* 91 (1): 47–62.

Samuelson, Paul A. 1994. The Classical Classical Fallacy. *Journal of Economic Literature* 32 (2): 620–639.

Schumpeter, J. A. [1954] 1994. *History of Economic Analysis.* London: Routledge.

Ferdinando Meacci

MACMILLAN, HAROLD
1894–1986

Maurice Harold Macmillan was the prime minister of Great Britain from 1957 to 1963. A member of a famous publishing family, Macmillan was born in Brixton, England, on February 10, 1894. He was educated at Eton and Oxford University, and served in the British army during World War I (1914–1918). Macmillan was elected as a Conservative to the House of Commons in 1924. During the Conservative governments of Stanley Baldwin (1867–1947) and Neville Chamberlain (1869–1940), he criticized their appeasement policies toward Nazi Germany. During World War II (1939–1945), Macmillan served as a civilian official in the Ministry of Supply and later as a British liaison to American forces in North Africa and the Mediterranean. In this position, Macmillan developed a friendship with American general and future president Dwight D. Eisenhower (1890–1969).

From 1951 until 1957, Macmillan served in various cabinet positions under prime ministers Winston Churchill (1874–1965) and Anthony Eden (1897–1977). Appointed chancellor of the Exchequer in 1955, Macmillan succeeded Eden as prime minister in 1957. Eden resigned in part because his foreign policy strained British relations with the United States through his controversial military intervention in the Suez Canal and his effort to develop an independent nuclear deterrent.

Consequently, Macmillan was determined to develop a more cooperative, harmonious relationship with the United States in cold war foreign and defense policies. Both Republican president Eisenhower and Democratic president John F. Kennedy (1917–1963) valued Macmillan's advice and diplomatic support. Macmillan persuaded Kennedy to deliver Polaris nuclear missiles to Britain in 1962, advised Kennedy during the 1962 Cuban missile crisis, and helped to negotiate the 1963 Partial Nuclear Test Ban Treaty with the Soviet Union. Macmillan also oversaw the continuing dismemberment of the British Empire as such former colonies as Malaya, Kenya, and Nigeria became independent nations. He tried but failed to overcome French opposition to Britain's application for membership in the European Economic Community.

In domestic and economic policies, Macmillan pursued a moderate course. He assured working-class Britons that his Conservative government would not dismantle the Labour-initiated welfare state and would manage it more efficiently. He also promised to promote economic growth through tax cuts and fewer regulations on business. Macmillan's centrist yet reformist rhetoric and policies contributed to a sharp increase in the Conservative majority of seats in the 1959 parliamentary elections.

Disagreements among cabinet officials about how to solve Britain's problems with its balance of payments and Macmillan's unpopular wage freezes to control inflation contributed to the loss of Conservative seats in the by-elections of 1961 and Macmillan's decision to make major changes in his cabinet in 1962. The growing disunity of the Conservative Party and declining support for Macmillan's government were intensified by the Profumo affair of 1963. John Profumo (1915–2006), secretary of state for war, misled Macmillan and the House of Commons in March 1963 about his adulterous relationship with Christine Keeler, a showgirl who also had a relationship with the Soviet embassy's naval attaché. Labour members of the House of Commons asserted that such a relationship by the secretary of state for war endangered national security in the cold war.

In June 1963, Profumo publicly admitted his deceit and resigned from the cabinet, House of Commons, and Privy Council. Suffering from declining health and less credibility with the public and Parliament, Macmillan resigned as prime minister on October 18, 1963. He retained enough influence within the Conservative Party, however, to ensure that Sir Alec Douglas-Home (1903–1995), instead of Rab Butler (1902–1982), succeeded him as prime minister. Still tainted by the Profumo scandal, the Conservative Party lost its majority in the House of Commons in the 1964 parliamentary elections, and Labour Party leader Harold Wilson (1916–1995) became prime minister.

Macmillan retired from politics in 1964 and rarely commented on British politics publicly. During the 1980s, however, Macmillan was rumored to be displeased with some of Prime Minister Margaret Thatcher's more aggressive privatizing and monetarist economic policies. Busy with the chairmanship of the Macmillan publishing firm, Macmillan became a peer in 1984 as the earl of Stockton and died in Sussex on December 29, 1986.

SEE ALSO *Balance of Payments; Chamberlain, Neville; Churchill, Winston; Cold War; Colonialism; Conservative Party (Britain); Decolonization; Eisenhower, Dwight D.; Empire; Imperialism; Kennedy, John F.; National Security; Parliament, United Kingdom; Suez Crisis; Thatcher, Margaret*

BIBLIOGRAPHY

Denning, Lord Alfred. 1999. *John Profumo and Christine Keeler: 1963*. London: Stationery Office.

Hennessy, Peter. 2001. *The Prime Minister: The Office and Its Holders since 1945*. New York: St. Martin's.

Horne, Alistair. 1989. *Harold Macmillan*, Vol. 1: *Politician: 1894–1956*. New York: Penguin.

Lee, Sabine, and Richard Aldous, eds. 1999. *Harold Macmillan: Aspects of a Political Life*. New York: Palgrave Macmillan.

Sean J. Savage

MACROECONOMICS

The field of economics is divided into two subfields: macroeconomics and microeconomics. Macroeconomics is the study of the economy as a whole. It examines the cyclical movements and trends in economy-wide phenomena, such as unemployment, inflation, economic growth, money supply, budget deficits, and exchange rates. By contrast, microeconomics focuses on the individual parts of the economy. It studies decision making by households and firms and the interaction among households and firms in the marketplace. It considers households both as suppliers of factors of production (labor, land, capital, entrepreneurship) and as ultimate consumers of final goods and services. It also analyzes firms both as suppliers of goods and services and as demanders of factors of production.

Because the economy-wide events studied in macroeconomics arise from the interaction of many households and firms, macroeconomics is inevitably rooted in microeconomics. When economists study the economy as a whole, they must consider the decisions of individual economic actors. For example, to understand what determines gross savings (a macroeconomic issue), they must think about the intertemporal choices facing an individual—in response to a certain change in interest rates on deposits, whether to increase or decrease saving by decreasing or increasing consumption (a microeconomic issue).

Macroeconomic events and the state of the economy affect all members of society. Businesspeople forecasting the demand for their products and services should anticipate how consumers' incomes will grow. Pensioners and people living on fixed incomes have concerns about potential price increases that could affect the cost of living. Unemployed persons looking for jobs always hope that the economy will grow fast so that firms will increase their labor force. Even politicians are affected by the state of the economy, which could influence the outcome of presidential or congressional elections. For instance, in purely democratic societies, the popularity of political leaders currently in office could fade in the event of adverse macroeconomic conditions (e.g., high inflation and/or unemployment) because voters are keenly aware of such conditions and their potential impact. It is, therefore, no surprise that economic policy is always a primary issue of debate for candidates during campaigns.

MACROECONOMIC VARIABLES

Economists assess the success of an economy's overall performance by studying how it could achieve high rates of output and consumption growth. For the purpose of such an assessment, three macroeconomic variables are particularly important: gross domestic product (GDP), the unemployment rate, and the inflation rate.

Gross Domestic Product The GDP equals the total value of goods and services produced in a country during a year. Economic growth is, therefore, a sustainable increase in the amount of goods and services produced in an economy over time. However, *economic growth* is different from *economic development*. Noneconomists usually make little or no distinction between the two terms, using them interchangeably. Going further than GDP growth, economic development can be defined as "a multi-dimensional process of change focused on the betterment of the community, state, and/or country … and aimed at producing more 'life sustaining' necessities such as food, shelter, and health care and broadening their distribution, raising standards of living and individual self esteem, and expanding economic and social choice" (Todaro 2005, p. 4).

Development theories have started to look beyond GDP per capita as a sole measure of development and to consider other measures, such as health-care availability, educational attainment, equality of income distribution, and political freedom. GDP growth, though necessary, is not a sufficient condition for economic development. Modern theories try to explore other requirements for *sustainable* economic development, including the availability of sound government policies and institutions, infrastructure, lack of trade barriers, and fair judicial systems.

Capital accumulation is an essential factor for economic growth and development, which typically involve large-scale investments in infrastructure, industry, education, health, and financial sectors. Simon Kuznets (1901–1985) argued that levels of economic inequality can change as countries develop and, hence, accumulate more capital. Presumably, countries at early stages of development have relatively equal distributions of income because levels of per capita income and capital are low. As a country develops, more capital is accumulated and income distribution becomes unequal in favor of the owners of capital. Eventually, more-developed countries move back to lower levels of inequality either directly, through social welfare programs and other redistribution mechanisms, or indirectly, through "trickle down" effects.

Macroeconomists usually try to evaluate the economy's growth and development performance either in comparison to other economies (cross-sectional analysis) or over time (time-series analysis). In other words, macroeconomists investigate why the economies of many developing countries in Asia, Africa, Latin America, and eastern Europe tend to grow at a slower rate than those of developed countries, and how the rate of economic growth for a certain country can be improved over time.

Although sustainable growth is always desired by economic policymakers, economies do not always grow steadily and sometimes undergo periods of slowdown or expansion. Slowdowns in economic growth are called *recessions*. Severe economic slowdowns are called *depressions* (e.g., the Great Depression). During recessions, aggregate incomes decrease, as does the demand for goods and services. As a result, firms realize less profit, more firms go out of business, and, therefore, job opportunities become scarce.

On the other hand, economies can sometimes grow unusually fast. These periods of rapid economic growth are called *expansions*, and particularly strong expansions are called *booms*. During an expansion, businesses witness increasing growth and, hence, profits; incomes are higher because more people get raises and promotions; and, as a result, the demand for goods and services increases, which causes firms to realize even more profits, and more job opportunities become available. Given their importance, macroeconomists have a keen interest in analyzing economic fluctuations and whether policymakers can (or should) do anything about them.

Unemployment Rate The second most important macroeconomic concept is the unemployment rate, which is a key indicator of the condition of the labor market. The unemployment rate is defined as the percentage of people willing to be employed at the prevailing wage rate, yet unable to find job opportunities. When the unemployment rate is high, work is not only hard to find, but also less rewarding as people already holding jobs might find it difficult to get wage increases or promotions. A low unemployment rate is an indication of good economic performance. Thus, keeping workers employed is always a chief concern of economic policymakers.

Inflation The third most important macroeconomic concept is inflation, which is an increase in the overall level of prices measured by the consumer price index. This index shows how the value of money changes over time. Inflation is one of the primary concerns of economists and

policymakers because it imposes a variety of costs on the economy. When the inflation rate is high, the real value of money erodes. People on fixed incomes, such as pensioners who receive a fixed dollar payment each month, cannot keep up with the rising cost of living. Inflation also redistributes wealth among the population in a way that has nothing to do with merit. When there is a sustained period of inflationary pressure, lenders and workers lose while borrowers and employers benefit because many work and loan contracts in the economy are specified in terms of money. Another cost of inflation is that it discourages saving. The income tax treats the nominal interest earned on savings as income, even though part of the nominal interest rate merely compensates for inflation. This reduces the after-tax real interest rate, and hence makes saving less attractive.

International Trade Another major macroeconomic topic is international trade, which is the exchange of goods and services across international borders. Because modern economies are highly interdependent, macroeconomists often study the impact and desirability of free trade agreements. They also study the causes and effects of trade imbalances, which occur when the quantity of goods and services that a country sells abroad (its exports) differs significantly from the quantity of goods and services its citizens buy from abroad (its imports).

ORIGIN AND EVOLUTION

Until the 1930s, most economic analysis did not separate microeconomic behavior from macroeconomic behavior. The 1776 publication of *The Wealth of Nations* by the Scottish economist Adam Smith (1723–1790) marked the birth of classical economics. Along with Smith, the major representatives of this school of economic thought include David Ricardo (1772–1823), Thomas Robert Malthus (1766–1834), and John Stuart Mill (1806–1873).

Classical economists emphasized the optimization of private economic agents, the adjustment of relative prices to equate supply and demand, and the efficiency of free markets. The classical theory dominated economic analysis till the late 1920s. Its main presumption is that the economy works better when government intervention is kept at a minimum because the behavior of different economic agents tends to achieve self-interests that are consistent with the overall well-being of the economy. Classical economists believed that the market itself would correct for any economic imbalance or turbulence without the need for government intervention. Any disequilibrium in a single market would eventually result in an automatic correction via the interaction between the two sides of the market, supply and demand, with the help of price flexibility. This flexibility would always ensure that macroeconomic equilibria in the national economy are a result of automatic equilibria (clearance) in single markets. Classical economists also believed that the utilization of more inputs of production can be translated into higher levels of national output and income.

The Great Depression that began in 1929 in the United States was the worst economic catastrophe in the country's history. During the depression, the United States experienced massive unemployment and greatly reduced incomes. This devastating period caused many economists to question the validity of classical economic theory, which seemed incapable of explaining the Great Depression. Classical economists believed that factor supplies and available technology determined the level of national income. However, real income in the United States decreased by 30 percent between 1929 and 1933 even though factors of production and technology remained unchanged. Therefore, many economists believed that a new theory was needed to explain such a large and sudden economic downturn and to identify government policies that might reduce the economic hardship so many people faced.

The British economist John Maynard Keynes (1883–1946) revolutionized the way economists think with his book, *The General Theory of Employment, Interest, and Money* (1936). It was pathbreaking in several ways. The two most important are, first, that it introduced the notion of aggregate demand as the sum of consumption, investment, and government spending. Second, it showed that full employment could be maintained only with the help of government spending.

Keynes proposed that low aggregate demand is responsible for the low income and high unemployment that characterize economic downturns. He criticized the classical theory for assuming that factor supply alone determines national income and that prices are flexible. In contrast to the classical theory, Keynes asserted that, in the short run, changes in aggregate demand rather than aggregate supply influence national income. Moreover, automatic economic equilibria are not necessarily ensured in the Keynesian world. In fact, economic balance can only occur by chance. Consequently, government intervention is sometimes sought in order to correct for economic instability.

The work of Keynes remains a central point of reference even today because all economic schools of thought label themselves in relation to the ideas initially developed by Keynes in his *General Theory*. Since the breakdown of the Keynesian consensus in the early 1970s, macroeconomics witnessed the emergence of a number of competing schools of thought consisting of economists who share a broad vision of how the economy as a whole works. Two "new" schools in particular have been highly influential:

the new classical and the new Keynesian. These new schools share the view that macroeconomic theories should be based on solid microeconomic foundations.

Most economists use the term *new classical* broadly to describe the many challenges to Keynesian orthodoxy that prevailed in the 1960s. New classical economists advocate models in which wages and prices adjust quickly to clear markets. More recently, many new classical economists have turned their attention to *real business cycle theory*, which uses the assumptions of the classical theory—especially flexible prices—to explain short-run economic fluctuations.

New Keynesian economists, on the other hand, believe that market-clearing models cannot explain short-run economic fluctuations, and so they advocate models with sticky wages and prices. New Keynesian research is aimed at explaining how wages and prices behave in the short run by identifying more precisely the market imperfections that make wages and prices sticky.

Even though they sometimes reach differing conclusions, the various schools of thought are not always in direct competition with one another. It is unlikely that one of the current schools of economic thought perfectly captures the workings of the economy. Rather, each theory contributes a small piece of the overall puzzle.

THEORETICAL, EMPIRICAL, AND POLICY SIGNIFICANCE

Like all scientists, economists rely on both theory and observation. Macroeconomists usually try to explain the economic world as it is and consider what it could be. For this purpose, they use many types of data to measure the performance of an economy. They collect data on incomes, prices, unemployment, and many other economic variables from different periods and different countries. They then attempt to formulate theories that could help explain these data. They try to answer such questions as: Why do incomes increase over time? Why do some countries have high rates of inflation while others maintain stable prices? What causes recessions and how can economic policy be used to reduce their incidence and scale?

The goal of studying macroeconomics, however, is not just to explain economic events but also to improve economic policy. Macroeconomic policies are government actions designed to influence the performance of the economy as a whole. By understanding how government policies affect the economy, economists can help policymakers do a better job and avoid serious mistakes.

The policy goals that macroeconomists typically associate with the discipline include economic growth, price stability, and full employment. Policymakers always face three fundamental macroeconomic questions: (1) How can the rate of economic growth be increased and sustained? (2) How can unemployment be reduced? (3) How can inflation be kept under control? To find answers to these questions, policymakers can implement the tools of three major types of macroeconomic policy: monetary policy, fiscal policy, and structural policy.

The term *monetary policy* refers to the management of the nation's money supply (cash and coins, although modern economies have other forms of money such as savings and time deposits and money market mutual funds). Most economists agree that changes in the money supply affect important macroeconomic variables, including national output, employment, interest rates, inflation, stock prices, and the exchange rate. In almost all countries, monetary policy is implemented by a government institution called the *central bank*.

Fiscal policy refers to decisions that determine the government's budget, including the amount and composition of government expenditures and government revenues. The balance between government spending and taxes is a particularly important aspect of fiscal policy. When the government spends more than it collects in taxes, it runs a *deficit*, and when it spends less, the government's budget is in *surplus*. There is a consensus among economists that fiscal policy can have an important impact on the overall performance of the economy.

Finally, the term *structural policy* includes government policies aimed at changing the underlying structure, or institutions, of the economy. The move away from government control of the economy and toward a more market-oriented approach in many formerly communist countries, such as Poland, the Czech Republic, and Hungary, is a large-scale example of structural policy. Many developing countries have tried similar structural reforms. Supporters of structural policy hope that by changing the basic characteristics of the economy or by restructuring its institutions they can stimulate economic growth and improve living standards.

POLICY DEBATE

Different analytical approaches lead to different policy conclusions. For example, a Keynesian approach would have governments run a surplus during the boom period of business cycles and a deficit during a recession. On the other hand, classical economists would prefer that the government not intervene to correct for short-term economic fluctuations; they believe this will distort the way free markets function. Others argue that using taxation as a macroeconomic policy tool has no effect on the economy; rational individuals tend to save when they receive tax cuts because they expect the government to raise taxes in the future to pay off its deficit.

As articulated in Mankiw (2004), there are three unresolved questions pertaining to monetary and fiscal policies, each of which is central to political debates: First, should policymakers try to stabilize the economy? Second, should monetary policy be made by rule rather than by discretion? Third, should the government balance its budget?

With regard to the first debate on whether monetary and fiscal policymakers should try to stabilize the economy, proponents argue that policymakers should take an active role in leading the economy to stability. When aggregate demand is inadequate to ensure full employment, policymakers should act to boost spending in the economy. When aggregate demand is excessive and there is a risk of inflation, policymakers should act to lower spending. Such policy actions put macroeconomic theory to its best use by leading to a more stable economy. Opponents argue that there are substantial difficulties associated with running fiscal and monetary policies. One of the most important problems is the time lag that often occurs with policy. Economic conditions change over time. Thus, policy effects that occur with a lag may hit the economy at the wrong time, leading to a more unstable economy. Therefore, policymakers should refrain from intervening in order to avoid doing any harm to the economy.

As for the controversy on whether monetary policy should be made by *rule* rather than by *discretion*, advocates assert that discretionary monetary policy does not limit incompetence and abuse of power. For example, a central banker may choose to create a *political business cycle* to help a particular candidate. One way to avoid such a problem is to force the central bank to follow a monetary rule that is flexible enough to allow for some unforeseen circumstances that could affect the economy. Critics of this view argue that discretionary monetary policy allows flexibility, which gives the central bank the ability to react to unforeseen situations quickly.

Finally, macroeconomists have long debated whether the government should balance its budget or run a deficit. Advocates of a balanced budget argue that future generations of taxpayers will be burdened by public debt if the government accumulates annual deficits in the present. Opponents of the balanced budget approach argue that the problems caused by government debt are overstated and that the future generation's burden of debt is relatively small when compared with their lifetime incomes. If public spending on education and health is reduced, for example, this could lead to lower economic growth in the future, which would certainly not make future generations better off.

SEE ALSO *Inflation; Involuntary Unemployment; Microeconomics; Natural Rate of Unemployment*

BIBLIOGRAPHY

Baumol, William J., and Alan S. Blinder. 2006. *Macroeconomics: Principles and Policy*. 10th ed. Mason, OH: Thomson South-Western.

Colander, David C. 2006. *Macroeconomics*. 6th ed. Boston: McGraw-Hill/Irwin.

DeLong, J. Bradford, and Martha L. Olney. 2006. *Macroeconomics*. 2nd ed. New York: McGraw-Hill/Irwin.

Dornbusch, Rudiger, Stanley Fischer, and Richard Startz. 2004. *Macroeconomics*. 9th ed. New York: McGraw-Hill/Irwin.

Frank, Robert H., and Ben S. Bernanke. 2004. *Principles of Macroeconomics*. 2nd ed. New York: McGraw Hill/Irwin.

Hall, Robert E., and Marc Lieberman. 2006. *Macroeconomics: Principles and Applications*. 3rd ed. Mason, OH: Thomson South-Western.

Keynes, John M. 1936. *The General Theory of Employment, Interest, and Money*. Cambridge, U.K.: Cambridge University Press.

Mankiw, N. Gregory. 2003. *Macroeconomics*. 5th ed. New York: Worth.

Mankiw, N. Gregory. 2004. *Principles of Macroeconomics*. 3rd ed. Mason, OH: Thomson South-Western.

McEachern, William A. 2006. *Macroeconomics: A Contemporary Introduction*. 7th ed. Mason, OH: Thomson South-Western.

Miller, Roger LeRoy, and David D. VanHoose. 2004. *Macroeconomics: Theories, Policies, and International Applications*. 3rd ed. Mason, OH: Thomson South-Western.

Samuelson, Paul A., and William D. Nordhaus. 2005. *Macroeconomics*. 18th ed. Boston: McGraw-Hill/Irwin.

Schiller, Bradley R. 2006. *The Macro Economy Today*. 10th ed. Boston: McGraw-Hill/Irwin.

Snowdon, Brian, and Howard R. Vane, eds. 1997. *A Macroeconomics Reader*. London: Routledge.

Todaro, Michael P., and Stephen C. Smith. 2005. *Economic Development*. 9th ed. Boston: Addison-Wesley.

Tucker, Irvin B. 2006. *Macroeconomics for Today*. 5th ed. Mason, OH: Thomson South-Western.

Khaled I. Abdel-Kader

MACROECONOMICS, STRUCTURALIST

Macroeconomics as taught in North American and European universities does not reflect the particular set of problems faced by most developing countries. Indeed, more than simply reflecting different stages of industrialization, underdeveloped—or developing—countries followed very different development paths altogether, characterized by foreign technology, independently of their production factors (excess workforce), structural heterogonous domestic production, and structural inflation. Structuralist macroeconomics in contrast addresses specif-

ically the economic development of Latin America. Incidentally, "underdeveloped economies" is a term coined by *dependendist* theorists such as Mauro Marini (1975) and Dos Santos (1978), who were largely influenced by the work of Andre Gunder Frank. This theory states that backward countries could never fully develop since they lack a national bourgeoisie class that could lead the industrialization process. The Economic Commission for Latin America and the Caribbean (ECLAC), however, took a softer view, coining the term "developing countries," which eventually could "catch up" with industrial countries (Amsden 1989).

Structuralism finds its roots in ECLAC, a United Nations institution created soon after World War II to compensate Latin American countries for being left out of the Marshall Plan. One of the founding fathers of structuralism is Raúl Prebisch, an Argentinean who was executive director of ECLAC from 1950 to 1963. Prebisch was critical of various economic doctrines, including the critical views advocated by Keynes and Kalecki, that failed to consider the particularities of developing countries.

Prebisch was a university professor in Buenos Aires and a founding member and first governor of the Central Bank of Argentina, a post he held until 1943. Perhaps his most famous book, *The Economic Development of Latin American and Its Principal Problems* (1949), often referred to as the "manifesto" of Latin American development, propelled him into the position of ECLAC executive secretary. Prebisch held considerable influence over economists and policy makers. After leaving ECLAC, Prebisch became the first director of the United Nations Conference on Trade and Development (UNCTAD).

STRUCTURALISM IN THEORY

After the demise of the Bretton Woods system, there was an ideological movement in academic circles toward neoliberal ideology. This intellectual shift can be characterized by three principal ideas. (1) Public deficits were seen as the main cause of inflation because they increase demand over supply. As such, there was a movement against state intervention in the product and financial markets (Bielschowsky 1998). (2) Expansionary credit policies were seen as the main cause of interest rate increases. (3) Structural trade imbalances were considered to be the result of limited savings. Therefore, the principal way to eliminate the discrepancy is by opening up the financial markets to external finance.

This ideology, advocated in particular by the International Monetary Fund and the World Bank, spread through academic and policy circles in Latin America. These policies, known today as the Washington Consensus, were adopted by most governments with disastrous consequences, since they did not take into consideration the specific set of economic problems facing Latin American countries.

Latin American economies are characterized by two overall macroeconomic problems: dependence on the external sector and technological backwardness. In turn, these can be expanded into the following six stylized facts (Pinto 1973):

1. Having been colonies, Latin American countries were open economies: They were subjected to certain external markets for which they produced specialized goods and services based on their comparative (absolute or relative) advantage: They supplied raw materials to capitalist economies and imported manufactured goods. They were prices takers, with terms favorable to industrialized countries, for which overvalued exchange rates are an important instrument (Kregel 2004).

2. Exports are not linked to the structure of domestic production. As a result, developing countries are highly dependent on imports according to the dominant mode of production (the primary export model before World War II; the import substitution model from the 1950s to the 1970s; the secondary export mode from 1980 until now).

3. There exists an imbalance in the structure of production: Industrial participation increased rapidly without a corresponding change in the agricultural sector or in the production of know-how and technology suitable for their factors of production.

4. There exists an imbalance between the productive sector and other substructures of the economy. The infrastructure was inadequate for industrialization, and the process of finance switched from the external to the internal markets, without developing a deep financial system.

5. The external dependence on imports induced higher income elasticities of imports and exports, and a highly price-inelastic demand for imports and exports, requiring overvalued exchange rates to reduce costs.

6. Exchange rate devaluations are an important transmission mechanism that induces inflationary pressures via magnified exchange-rate pass-through effects to prices, along with unequal income distribution that undermines the purchasing power of workers. Devaluations come with reductions in nominal wages (Noyola 1957).

Another important structuralist is Lance Taylor (1979, 1983, 1991), who believed that institutions and their behavior were the main determinants of resource allocation. Influenced largely by ECLAC, he approached development by first identifying stylized facts. First, "sectoral distinctions" are required in any analysis of development. In particular, Taylor argues that we must distinguish on the one hand between traded and home-goods production sectors, both highly dependent on imports, and between the agricultural (or traditional) and industrial sectors on the other. Second, financial markets tend to be underdeveloped. Third, distribution and class struggles are key components of the story of underdevelopment. In turn, these "centers of power" (Taylor 1991, p. 5) influence pricing and production decisions. Fourth, "unresolved distributional conflicts" are the source of inflationary pressures. Fifth, dependency on imports makes the economy dependent on foreign exchange.

MAIN ISSUES OF STRUCTURALISM

Given these facts, macroeconomic structuralists developed two important concepts. The first is "structural inflation" caused by factors unrelated to demand. In particular, given the openness of Latin American countries, there is a magnified pass-through effect from variations in the exchange rate to domestic prices. Latin American countries historically have had external current account deficits requiring external finance to cover the balance-of-payments deficit. External public borrowing, however, shifted toward external private borrowing (debt) and bond and shares issuance in the 1980s and 1990s.

The second concept concerned the unequal terms of trade, based on the price inelasticity of demand for imports and exports, and income inelasticity of demand. As a result, exchange rate movements do not induce equilibrium in the current account, which can be attained only through economic stagnation.

With respect to external financing, Prebisch and other structuralists were against relying on foreign direct investment (FDI) as well as foreign private credits, for two important reasons. First, while it is true that initially FDI was an important source of external capital (1940–1960), capital outflows soon were much higher than capital inflows, thereby exacerbating the existing fragile balance of payments. Second, while foreign investment increased, the imported technology was largely unsuitable for Latin America. Fajnzylber (1990) argued that FDI was less of a black box than an "empty hole."

As for external debt, there was not much concern in the 1970s when interest rates were kept low. However, once interest rates were pushed up in 1979, it had dramatic implications for Latin American countries. Initially, capital movements reversed (1980s) and exchange rates devalued, preventing Latin American countries from financing their balance-of-payments account. In the late 1980s, financial markets were liberalized, a process that continued through the early 1990s. External financing shifted to the bond market, which induced the 1994 crisis and the Tequila effect, which increased foreign direct investment importance, although these were of a different nature. Now, foreign direct investments are principally in the form of cross-border acquisitions and mergers, proving equally as unstable as movements in the bond market.

STRUCTURALIST POLICIES

Given the above discussion, what are the principal structuralist policy proposals? While we can identify several, the more relevant and important ones include the following.

1. Following Keynesians, structuralists believe that the emphasis of policy should be output, growth, and employment. To achieve growth, however, structuralists believe that the state should play a vital role.

2. Growth can result only from placing the emphasis on the domestic, internal industrial economy rather than relying on the export sector. As such, policies aim at eliminating the countries' reliance on foreign demand for their primary exports (especially raw materials). As a result, import-substitution policies, such as government-imposed tariffs on imports, are seen as important policy elements.

3. Because of the technological backwardness of many sectors, an industrial policy of improving production technologies in lagging sectors is crucial.

4. End the perception of "old colonies" and reevaluate the role of developing countries and their relationship with other countries.

SEE ALSO *Balance of Payments; Development Economics; Economic Commission for Latin America and the Caribbean (ECLAC); Exchange Rates; Income Distribution; Interest Rates; Macroeconomics; Markup Pricing; North-South Models; Prebisch, Raúl; Prebisch-Singer Hypothesis; Singer, Hans; Taylor, Lance*

BIBLIOGRAPHY

Amsden, A. 1989. *Asia's Next Giant*. New York and Oxford: Oxford University Press.

Amsden, A. 2004. La Sustitución de Importaciones en las Industrias de Alta Tecnología. Prebisch Renace en Asia. *Revista de la CEPAL* 84.

Bielschowsky, R. 1998. Cincuenta Años del Pensamiento de la CEPAL. Una Reseña. In *Cincuenta Años de Pensamiento de la CEPAL*, vol. 1, ed. R. Bielschowsky, 9–91. Mexico City: Fondo de Cultura Económica.

Dos Santos, T. 1978. *Imperialismo y Dependencia*. Mexico City: Ediciones Era.

Fajnzylber, F. 1990. Industrialización en América Latina: De la Caja Negra Al Casillero Vacío. In *Cincuenta Años de Pensamiento de la CEPAL*, vol. 2, ed. R. Bielschowsky, 817–851. Mexico City: Fondo de Cultura Económica.

Kalecki, M. 1954. The Problem of Financing Economic Development. Reprinted in *Collected Works of Michał Kalecki*, vol. 5. Oxford: Clarendon Press, 1993.

Kregel, J. 2004. Do We Need Alternative Financial Strategies for Development in Latin America? Paper presented at the Cuarto Seminario de Economía Financiera, IIE, UNAM, México.

Marini, Mauro. 1975. *Dialéctica de la Dependencia*. Mexico City: Ediciones Era.

Noyola, J. 1957. Inflación y Desarrollo Económicoen Chile y México. In *Cincuenta Años de Pensamiento de la CEPAL*, vol. 2, ed. R. Bielschowsky, 273–286. Mexico City: Fondo de Cultura Económica.

Pinto, A. 1975. Raices Estructurales de la Inflación en América Latina. In *Lecturas Del Fondo de Cultura Económica Nº 3*, Mexico.

Pinto, Anibal. 1973. *Inflación: raíces estructurales*. Ensayos de Anibal Pinto, Lecturas 3, El trimestre Económico. Mexico City: Fondo de Cultura Económica. 2nd ed., 1985.

Taylor, Lance. 1979. *Macro Models for Developing Countries*. New York: McGraw-Hill.

Taylor, Lance. 1983. *Structuralist Macroeconomics: Applicable Models for the Third World*. New York: Basic Books.

Taylor, Lance. 1991. *Income Distribution, Inflation and Growth: Lectures on Structuralist Macroeconomic Theory*. Cambridge, MA: MIT Press.

Noemi Levy-Orlik
Louis-Philippe Rochon

MACROFOUNDATIONS

The macrofoundations of economic activity consist of institutions (rules, norms, laws, and conventions) that define the social context within which economic processes take place. These economic processes include individual decision-making, production, exchange, and the determination of aggregate output and employment. Note that macrofoundations as defined here are understood strictly as social structures that shape the processes responsible for generating both microeconomic and macroeconomic outcomes. This is not to overlook the fact that the latter, themselves, frequently provide a type of "macrofoundation" for the former. For example, the existence of involuntary unemployment creates a social context that can be expected to impact significantly on the behavior of individual workers.

Macrofoundations can differ between regions and over time. They play an important role in supplementing the price mechanism as a means of coordinating economic activity.

FROM MICROFOUNDATIONS TO THE MACROFOUNDATIONS OF ECONOMIC ACTIVITY

Economists have long been interested in the microeconomic underpinnings of economic decisions and outcomes. This "microfoundations" project deems individual decision making to be the root source of all economic phenomena, and hence the basic "building block" of all economic theory. But an important oversight of this project is that, as much as individuals create the societies in which they live, so, too, does society shape and mold individuals—their preferences, habits, beliefs, aspirations, and so forth. For example, exposure to the customs and laws of North America causes individuals to habitually keep to the right when driving on the road, and to regard such behavior as normal. But exposure to the customs and laws of the United Kingdom would result in the same individuals habitually keeping to the left, and coming to regard this different behavior as normal. The macrofoundations project calls attention to the importance of the social context in which economic activity takes place, and the role of this social context as a determinant of economic decisions and outcomes.

In particular, the macrofoundations of an economy are understood to supplement the workings of the price mechanism as a means of coordinating economic activity. Keynesian macroeconomists have long doubted the capacity of the price mechanism to coordinate economic activity so as to automatically create full employment. The macrofoundations project goes further, pointing out that the price mechanism does not even suffice to ensure the orderly reproduction of the economy from one period to the next, at any level of economic activity. Hence the price mechanism alone cannot coordinate expectations if there is fundamental uncertainty about the future (including the future states of markets and the prices determined therein). Nor can it coordinate actions pursuant to conflicts of interest that occur outside the sphere of market exchange—for example, at the point of production. But the economy's macrofoundations can assist in the coordination of both expectations formation and conflict resolution. By specifying behavioral procedures of the form "in event of *x*, do *y*," they provide a source of information about likely future actions and outcomes, and hence a basis for forming expectations in what would otherwise be a world of behavioral flux. For example, it is easier for workers to predict their future income if their employer is committed to a convention of retaining employees on current terms regardless of trade fluctuations, than it would

be if wages and employment were made contingent on the future state of the labor market.

Furthermore, macrofoundations can ameliorate conflict, by regularizing relations between parties with mutually exclusive interests. For example, the conventional authority that is vested in a production supervisor can be used to settle disputes amongst subordinate operatives that might otherwise create prolonged disruptions to a production process. (Note that this last example draws attention to the fact that institutions sometimes codify power relations. Some economists regard the latter—together with related concepts such as the class structure of capitalism and the associated unequal ownership of wealth—as also being part of the economy's macrofoundations.) In this way, the macrofoundations of economic activity have been likened to a computer's operating system, providing a stable macroscopic environment within which particular actions (in the case of a computer, tasks using specialized software; in the case of an economy, specific economic activities) take place.

THEORETICAL, EMPIRICAL, AND POLICY SIGNIFICANCE OF MACROFOUNDATIONS

The existence of macrofoundations poses several challenges for economic theory. First and most obviously, it raises questions about the level of aggregation at which economic inquiry should begin. Rather than starting with an isolated individual conceived *sui generis*, the existence of macrofoundations necessitates that consideration be given to the societal norms, conventions, laws, and so forth to which the individual is exposed if his or her decision making and behavior are to be understood. This, in turn, requires a search for the macrofoundations pertinent to different particular facets of economic activity (such as corporate behavior, the workings of the labor market, or the determination of macroeconomic outcomes). Some economists believe that what is necessary in this regard is appeal to stylized facts about the operation of actually existing economies. This means that the macrofoundations project can be associated with economic theory that is spatially and temporally contingent rather than universal.

The macrofoundations project has already had an impact on empirical inquiry, with studies suggesting that economic outcomes such as unemployment can be explained by means of exclusive reference to macroinstitutional variables. Finally, the concept of macrofoundations has important policy implications. It suggests that, rather than treating the economy as a given "state of nature," policymakers can (and do) contribute to the constitution of the economy by creating institutions that add to its macrofoundations. These include laws governing the limits to and operation of markets, and conventions (such as the Taylor rule in monetary economics) that determine the objectives and pursuit of policy interventions.

SEE ALSO *Economics, Keynesian; Macroeconomics; Microeconomics; Microfoundations; Policy, Monetary; Taylor Rule*

BIBLIOGRAPHY

Colander, David C. 1993. The Macrofoundations of Micro. *Eastern Economic Journal* 19 (4): 447–457.

Colander, David C., ed. 1996. *Beyond Microfoundations: Post Walrasian Macroeconomics.* Cambridge, U.K.: Cambridge University Press.

Cornwall, Wendy. 1999. The Institutional Determinants of Unemployment. In *Growth, Employment, and Inflation: Essays in Honour of John Cornwall*, ed. Mark Setterfield. 254–269. London: Macmillan.

Hodgson, Geoffrey M. 1994. The Return of Institutional Economics. In *The Handbook of Economic Sociology*, eds. Neil J. Smelser and Richard Swedburg. 58–76. Princeton, NJ: Princeton University Press.

Kotz, David M., Terrence McDonough, and Michael Reich. 1994. *Social Structures of Accumulation: The Political Economy of Growth and Crisis.* Cambridge, U.K.: Cambridge University Press.

Mark Setterfield

MADISON, JAMES
1751–1836

James Madison was born in King George County, Virginia, in March 1751 and died at "Montpelier," his country estate, in June 1836. The fourth president of the United States, Madison was one of early America's most significant contributors to the developing social sciences, especially through his political and constitutional thought and writings.

Madison was born into a prominent Virginia family, the first son of James Madison Sr. and Nelly Conway. Madison's education began in King and Queen County, Virginia, where he was taught by Donald Robertson, a Scottish teacher who ran a school there. His education continued under the Reverend Thomas Martin, a private tutor who was a graduate of the College of New Jersey (now Princeton University), which Madison himself later attended, graduating in 1771. At Princeton, Madison was influenced in lasting ways by the college president, John Witherspoon (1723–1794), who had come to America in 1768 partly through the efforts of Benjamin Rush (1746–1813), who at the time was a young American medical student studying in Edinburgh. Madison stayed on at Princeton after the completion of his undergraduate degree to study with Witherspoon more closely. As his correspondence shows, by the time he left college Madison was clearly well acquainted with the major thinkers of Western political thought, including Plato (c. 428–347 BCE), Aristotle (384–322 BCE), Huigh de Groot (1583–1645), Thomas Hobbes (1588–1679), and John Locke (1632–1704), as well as the works of the Scottish Enlightenment, including David Hume's multivolume *History of England* (1754–1762). Madison also came away from Princeton—as did many of his classmates—a fiery supporter of the building Revolutionary cause and with a desire to promote religious freedom.

CHAMPION OF RELIGIOUS FREEDOM

From at least the early 1770s Madison was known to have championed religious freedom in his home colony of Virginia, a subject to which in 1785 he contributed "A Memorial and Remonstrance against Religious Assessments." There, Madison wrote:

> Torrents of blood have been spilt in the old world, by the vain attempts of the secular arm, to extinguish Religious discord, by proscribing all difference in Religious opinion. Time has at length revealed the true remedy. Every relaxation of narrow and rigorous policy, wherever it has been tried, has been found to assuage the disease. The American Theatre has exhibited proofs that equal and compleat liberty, if it does not wholly eradicate it, sufficiently destroys its malignant influence on the health and prosperity of the State. (Hutchinson 1956, pp. 302–303)

FATHER OF THE CONSTITUTION

While Madison is remembered in the early twenty-first century as a champion of religious freedom and for his support of the separation of church and state, he is even better remembered for his instrumental part in the deliberations at the Constitutional Convention held at the statehouse in Philadelphia in the summer of 1787. That convention resulted in the drafting of the U.S. Constitution, a document that showed Madison's imprint at many key points. It is for this that he is remembered as the "Father of the Constitution." Part of that legacy was the "three-fifths" compromise, whereby, for the purposes of taxation and representation, five blacks were considered equivalent to three whites. Like Thomas Jefferson and others of their generation, the slaveholding Madison was not able to reconcile—even in his own mind—the political realities of slavery in eighteenth-century America with the Enlightenment principles of freedom and liberty.

It is also on related constitutional issues that Madison is best known as a social science writer. Madison (with Alexander Hamilton and John Jay) was one of the three authors who under the pen name of *Publius* composed the *Federalist*, a collection of eighty-five essays first published in 1787 in New York newspapers. It was written with an eye to assuring ratification of the Constitution, and Madison is thought to have written twenty-nine of the *Federalist* essays. His most famous papers were *Federalist* No. 51, No. 39, and No. 10, an essay on the causes, nature, and remedies for the problem of factions. In that paper Madison merged his intimate knowledge of Scottish Enlightenment texts, including Hume's *History of England*, with his personal experiences of American social and political developments. Madison countered Charles-Louis de Secondat (Montesquiéu, 1689–1755) and other European and American political theorists, who argued in a civic republican vein that republican government could not long exist in a large country such as the United States. Madison wrote:

> Extend the sphere, and you take in a greater variety of parties and interests; you make it less probable that a majority of the whole will have a common motive to invade the rights of other citizens; or if such a common motive exists, it will be more difficult for all who feel it to discover their own strength, and to act in unison with each other. (Carey and McClellan 2001, p. 48)

Madison was also one of the principal framers of the Bill of Rights, the first ten amendments to the U.S. Constitution, which went into effect in 1791.

SEE ALSO *American Revolution; Aristotle; Bill of Rights, U.S.; Church and State; Constitution, U.S.; Federalism; Freedom; Hobbes, Thomas; Hume, David; Locke, John; Plato; Presidency, The; Slavery; Smith, Adam*

BIBLIOGRAPHY

Banning, Lance. 1995. *The Sacred Fire of Liberty: James Madison and the Founding of the Federal Republic.* Ithaca, NY: Cornell.

Carey, George W., and James McClellan, eds. 2001. *The Federalist, by Alexander Hamilton, John Jay, and James Madison.* Gideon ed. Indianapolis, IN: Liberty Fund.

Hutchinson, William T., et al., eds. 1962. *The Papers of James Madison.* Vol. 8. Chicago: University of Chicago Press.

Ketcham, Ralph Louis. 1971. *James Madison: A Biography.* New York: Macmillan.

Rakove, Jack N. 2002. *James Madison and the Creation of the American Republic.* Ed. Oscar Handlin, 2nd ed. New York: Longman.

Mark G. Spencer

MADNESS

Every society considers some of its members to be "mad," "crazy," "insane," or "mentally ill." Regardless of the particular term that is used, the core aspect of madness lies in its *incomprehensibility*. Universally, when social action seems to lack purpose, intent, or reason, observers are likely to apply labels of *madness* to it. To say that incomprehensibility is the major criterion observers use to classify madness is not just to say that they fail to understand or empathize with a person's motives. Rather, it implies that the behaviors of the mad seem beyond the realm of understanding. This lack of comprehensibility distinguishes madness from other types of behaviors that violate social norms. For example, murders that stem from recognizable motives such as jealousy, quarrels, or vengeance are not viewed as signs of mental illness. Someone who randomly kills a stranger without any possible motive usually cannot be placed in any socially recognizable category of murderer, and is likely to be viewed as mad.

Historically, labels of madness were reserved for people whose behaviors fell well outside the boundaries of normal social interaction. Beginning with the earliest written records, madness encompassed behaviors that appear to be "without reason." The ancient Greek philosopher Socrates (c. 470–399 BCE), for example, noted that the Greeks of his time "do not call those mad who err in matters that lie outside the knowledge of ordinary people: madness is the name they give to errors in matters of common knowledge" (Rosen 1968, p. 94). Since ancient times, societies have also recognized a second type of madness that features profound sadness and withdrawal that is not proportionate to the social circumstances of the sufferer. The eminent German psychiatrist Emil Kraepelin (1856–1926), writing at the turn of the nineteenth century, codified these two categories of disorder as *dementia praecox* or schizophrenia and manic-depressive or affective conditions, which remain as major types of disorders.

SOCIAL RESPONSES TO MADNESS

While the core meaning of madness as incomprehensibility is universal, the boundaries of this label, as well as the specific behaviors that fall within it, are culturally specific and highly variable. The social responses to people who are considered mad have diverged considerably across cultures and throughout time. The simplest social groups, where individuals are bound to a small number of kin and group members throughout their lives, typically respond to those they consider mad with sympathy and tolerance, and attempt to maintain them in the group with little stigma. The Yoruba of Ghana provide a typical example. "The majority of chronic schizophrenics in rural districts," according to M. J. Field in *Search for Security*

(1960), "are treated with such patient and sustained kindness by their relatives and tolerance by their neighbors that the prognosis for their recovery is probably better than it would be were they herded with other patients in understaffed mental hospitals" (p. 453).

With growing social complexity comes a lower tolerance for the aberrant behavior of the mad. Most Western societies have associated madness with unpredictability and violence and have shunned and excluded the mentally ill from social life. In ancient Israel, Greece, and Rome, for example, the mad often roamed through the countryside and were commonly mocked, ridiculed, and abused. Likewise, in medieval Europe, the mentally disordered did not participate in community life, were stigmatized, and often treated harshly. The French philosopher Michel Foucault (1926–1984), however, asserts in *Madness and Civilization* (1961) that before the seventeenth century madness was linked to wisdom and insight and "man's dispute with madness was a dramatic debate in which he confronted the secret powers of the world" (1965, p. xii). While Foucault probably exaggerates the respect shown to the mad during this period, it is true that no formal institutions existed to confine the mad and they were left to roam the countryside at liberty, provided that they did not create disturbances.

The breakdown of social cohesiveness in Western societies resulted in a more dramatic exclusion of those who were viewed as mad. Confinement in mental institutions arose between the sixteenth and nineteenth centuries in western Europe and at the beginning of the nineteenth century in the United States. This growing segregation reflected growing urbanization, geographic mobility, and immigration that contributed to the breakdown of cohesive communities.

In the United States, the initial mental hospitals of the early nineteenth century emphasized what was called moral treatment that provided individualized and sympathetic care within small residential facilities. By the middle of the nineteenth century, however, mental institutions had become much larger and more bureaucratic. Under such circumstances, moral treatment became more problematic. The new profession of psychiatry developed around these formal institutions, and nearly all early psychiatrists had positions in mental hospitals. These facilities served as the central institution devoted to the care of the mentally ill until well into the next century. By the beginning of the twentieth century, their residents were often elderly, from impoverished backgrounds, and members of disadvantaged ethnic groups. Many stays were long term, and often persons who entered these institutions ultimately died within them. But some individuals passed through them for short stays and may have benefited from their experience. To be sure, mental institutions had serious flaws, including their huge size, overcrowding, geographic isolation, involuntary confinement, depersonalization, and coercive and custodial treatment. Nevertheless, they provided the most seriously ill persons an integrated range of services—housing, food, symptom management, medical treatment, a place for social interaction, and respite from stressful community conditions—in one centralized location.

Beginning in 1955, the use of mental hospitals to confine the mad began to break down in the United States as the average number of residents in state and county mental hospitals started to decline from a peak of 550,000 to 370,000 in 1969 to about 60,000 in 1998. Taking growing population size into account, the number of residents in state and county mental hospitals fell from 339 per 100,000 persons in 1955 to 91.5 in 1975 and to only 21 in 1998. A variety of factors led to the steep decline in the use of traditional mental institutions. The introduction of psychotropic drugs in the mid-1950s, political and legal movements devoted to stiffening requirements for institutional commitment, the expansion of the civil rights of mental patients, and the growth of community treatment all played a role. But the development of government entitlement programs, notably Medicare, Medicaid, Social Security Disability Insurance, and housing supplements, were the most significant facilitators of community treatment.

EXPANDING DEFINITIONS OF MADNESS

Until the end of the nineteenth century, the category of madness was largely reserved for people who behaved in bizarre and incomprehensible manners. At that time, the boundaries of this category began to undergo a dramatic expansion. Stimulated by the rise of psychoanalysis, outpatient treatment developed as a parallel system to inpatient mental hospitals. In contrast to the generally impoverished, poorly educated, and socially marginal persons who resided in mental hospitals, outpatient clients were often financially well-off, highly educated, and intellectually sophisticated. Over the course of the century, the type of problems associated with outpatient psychiatric care expanded from severe and disabling disorders to encompass people with problems of living, such as troubled marriages, wayward children, and lack of purpose in life. In contrast to the declining population of public mental hospitals, treatment in outpatient mental health settings in the United States increased by over twentyfold between 1955 and 2000.

A major change in the response to the mentally ill occurred in 1980 when the psychiatric profession codified hundreds of different mental illnesses in the *Diagnostic and Statistical Manual* (*DSM*-III). This manual includes not only the sorts of incomprehensible behaviors that have always been viewed as forms of madness, but also numerous forms of emotional, behavioral, psychophysiological, and many other disorders that extend well beyond the traditional boundaries of madness. It reflected the idea that mental illnesses, like physical illnesses, were specific disease entities that were likely to have biologically based causes. The *DSM*'s categories of mental illness have expanded to the extent that population surveys estimate that half of all Americans will experience some mental illness during their lifetimes, and over a quarter have some disorder at any given time. At the same time, there has been an explosive growth in the use of psychotropic medications. These medications, first introduced in the 1950s, have exponentially expanded to the point that 10 percent of women and 4 percent of men consume them in any given month. Indeed, three of the seven largest selling prescription drugs of any sort are now antidepressant medications.

MADNESS IN THE TWENTY-FIRST CENTURY

The concept of madness has simultaneously shrunk and expanded over the course of recent history. As *mental illness* has replaced *madness* as the term most likely to be applied to incomprehensible behaviors, fewer people experience exclusion, confinement, and stigma. The social distance between the mad and the normal has decreased with the growing emphasis on the similarities between mental and physical illnesses and on the perceived biological origins of mental illness. At the same time, this concept has expanded as more behaviors are regarded as signs of mental illness, more people are seen as suffering from this condition, and more individuals seek help from medical and mental health professionals.

The evolution of madness into mental illness has brought both benefits and costs. On the one hand, it has led to efforts to destigmatize the mentally ill and treat them less coercively, as well as to a growing understanding of the causes of and effective responses to these conditions. On the other hand, no adequate program has replaced the many services mental hospitals used to provide, and the most seriously ill do not receive adequate care in the community. In addition, the expansion of the boundaries of mental illness have medicalized many normal behaviors and led to an overconsumption of psychotropic medications. The responses to madness at the beginning of the twenty-first century are far better than for most of Western history, but still have much room for improvement.

SEE ALSO *Foucault, Michel; Mental Health; Mental Illness; Psychotherapy; Psychotropic Drugs; Schizophrenia; Stigma*

BIBLIOGRAPHY

Field, M. J. 1960. *Search for Security: An Ethno-Psychiatric Study of Rural Ghana.* Evanston, IL: Northwestern University Press.

Foucault, Michel. 1965. *Madness and Civilization: A History of Insanity in the Age of Reason.* Trans. Richard Howard. New York: Pantheon.

Grob, Gerald N. 1994. *The Mad among Us: A History of the Care of America's Mentally Ill.* New York: Free Press.

Horwitz, Allan V. 1982. *The Social Control of Mental Illness.* New York: Academic Press.

Horwitz, Allan V. 2002. *Creating Mental Illness.* Chicago: University of Chicago Press.

Lunbeck, Elizabeth. 1994. *The Psychiatric Persuasion: Knowledge, Gender, and Power in Modern America.* Princeton, NJ: Princeton University Press.

Rosen, George. 1968. *Madness in Society: Chapters in the Historical Sociology of Mental Illness.* New York: Harper.

Allan V. Horwitz

MAFIA, THE

The Mafia is an organized crime formation with Sicilian roots; branches in France, Tunisia, and the Americas; and a recent presence in Russia and Eastern Europe. Its historical successes vis-à-vis other criminal groups, particularly in the United States, have made the word *mafia* (whose origin has never been convincingly traced) a brand name for organized crime. Recently repressed on both sides of the Atlantic, the Mafia, as such, may be on the wane, although reduced vigilance could allow a resurgence.

Intrinsically secretive and violent, organized crime is best known through criminal investigations, yet police models, influenced by concerns of state, pose analytical problems for social science research. Early interpretations of the Sicilian Mafia—for example, Gaetano Mosca's article in the 1933 *Encyclopedia of the Social Sciences*—emphasized two aspects associated with Sicily's western provinces, historically dominated by quasi-feudal latifundia: a "mafiist" attitude valorizing self-help justice, as expressed through the concept *omertà* (silence before the law); and localized bands known as *cosche* (singular *cosca*) dedicated to animal rustling, extortion, and occasionally kidnapping for ransom. Although the menace of violence accompanied these activities, most murders resulted from inter- and intra-cosca rivalry for "turf." The surrounding "mafiist" attitude impeded investigations, as did the political connections of mafiosi who "made elections" as the suffrage expanded.

In the 1960s foreign scholars of Sicily, swayed by that decade's profound distrust of policing institutions, wrote about mafia with a small *m* and without the definite article. Rather than an *associazione a delinquere* (criminal association) with boundaries, rules and goals, mafia was the sum of individual mafiosi wielding power through private violence. In the 1980s and 1990s, however, innovative Sicilian prosecutors, responding to the Mafia's assumption of a commanding role in trafficking heroin to the United States, "turned" several mafiosi into justice collaborators, eliciting ethnographically rich personal narratives. (Palermo-based Tommaso Buscetta was the first of these, offering testimony to the prosecutor Giovanni Falcone, who was assassinated in 1992.) This and a corresponding citizens' antimafia movement encouraged new research, much of it by Sicilian scholars, which revealed the Mafia to have a greater institutional capacity than had been imagined before.

Antecedents of the Mafia date to the late 1800s in Sicily, when a newly unified Italian state sought to transform feudal and ecclesiastical holdings into private property, impose taxes, and draft soldiers, but without building institutions that could govern the resulting banditry and chaos. Self-anointed "mafias" filled the breach, claiming to restore order while earning revenue from manipulating disorder. Enterprises of many kinds were extorted for a *pizzo* (a "beak full") as the price for protection, and pressed to distribute employment opportunities in ways that leveraged the racketeers' local influence. Using their electoral clout, mafiosi also insinuated themselves with local, regional, and national governments, receiving licenses to carry weapons and "fix" inconvenient trials. Older, established *capi* (bosses) rarely went to jail, whereas younger *picciotti* (henchmen and enforcers) experienced incarceration as no more than a perfunctory interruption of their affairs. When criminal convictions occurred, the cosca functioned as a mutual-aid society, taking care of imprisoned members' families. Prisons, in turn, were nerve centers of inter-cosca communication. (In contemporary accounts, generalized "mafiism," earlier defined as the integument of the Mafia, is downplayed as part of a racialized "myth of Sicily" and an obstacle to serious inquiry.)

The state's tolerant stance toward the Mafia was reversed by Benito Mussolini, but after World War II mafiosi reemerged to protect influential landowners from restive peasants, intimidating and even murdering their left-wing leaders. In addition, they offered electoral support to politicians of the newly constituted Christian Democratic Party—a cold war accommodation that enabled the penetration of modern domains such as urban real estate and construction, public works, and the administration of the land reform enacted in 1950. In the 1970s mafiosi with strong transatlantic connections—among them Gaetano Badalamenti, a resident of a town near the Palermo airport, and the above mentioned Buscetta—

oversaw the shift from Marseille to Palermo of labs for refining heroin.

The audacity of the early narcotics traffickers was a provocation to the *Corleonesi*, an aggressive Mafia faction named for the fact that its leaders—Luciano Liggio, his protégé Salvatore (Totò) Riina, and Bernardo Provenzano (famously fugitive for forty years)—hailed from the interior town of Corleone. Allying with powerful capi in the Palermo region, this coalition raised capital for drug deals through kidnapping, which was normally disapproved of by the Mafia, and waged a murderous "war" whose victims—the *perdenti*, or losers—included many relatives and associates of Buscetta. The Corleonesi also advocated and carried out assassinations of public figures, among them Falcone.

The depositions of justice collaborators in the antimafia trials of the 1980s and 1990s, amplified by recent research, shed new light on the Mafia's social organization and culture. Territorially grounded, the cosca, or "family," is to some extent kin-oriented, with membership extending from father to sons, uncles to nephews, and through the fictive-kin tie of godparenthood. Yet, becoming a mafioso is also a matter of talent. Sons of cosca members believed to lack "criminal reliability" are passed over in favor of promising delinquents from unrelated backgrounds, and members seeking to induct large numbers of their own kin are viewed with suspicion. In effect, the word *family* is metaphorical—an evocation of the presumed solidarity of kinship. Mutual good will is further induced by idiosyncratic terms of address and linguistically playful nicknames. In a rite of entry inspired by Freemasons in nineteenth-century prisons, the Mafia novice holds the burning image of a saint while his sponsor pricks his finger and, mixing the blood and ashes, has him swear an oath of life-long loyalty and omertà, against the penalty of death. (1960s researchers doubted the existence of such a rite; Mosca's essay makes no mention of it.)

Within the cosca, senior bosses hold the elected leadership positions, distribute moneys accumulated through extortion, and are responsible for the behavior of those novices whom they have personally sponsored. The *picciotti* are expected to show deference, take greater risks, and funnel their earnings upward. Ambitious upstarts occasionally murder their patrons, however, and seize power. The gossip and treachery intrinsic to cosca politics are considered affairs of men; women are excluded not only from meetings, but also from banquets and hunting parties, where masculine identity is asserted and novices socialized into the practice of violence. Nevertheless, the Mafia wife is usually from a Mafia family, enjoys the refinements provided by her husband's money and status, assists in hiding fugitives, and willingly shelters his assets from the confiscatory power of the state. Most Mafia women know far more than they are free to discuss, even with family and friends.

Breaking with the past, contemporary scholars dispute the cosca's autonomy. Similar to other fraternal organizations, multiple local chapters are shown to foster mutual recognition across a broad terrain—an asset for long-distance trafficking in cigarettes, narcotics, and, of late, clandestine sex workers and migrants. In the 1890s in the bandit corridor that straddled interior Sicily, mafiosi organized the theft and hidden slaughter of livestock for sale in urban markets (at one point, including Tunisia); in the orchards near Palermo, they controlled not only the protection of crops and water for irrigation, but also the movement of citrus fruit to the Brooklyn docks. Recent research further suggests a relationship between far-flung trafficking, generally more lucrative than neighborhood rackets, and the Mafia's felt need to create structures and lay down rules at a translocal level. One example is the *Cupola*, or "Commission," set up to coordinate groups in the province of Palermo, and then throughout western Sicily, in the 1960s through 1980s, to which intermediate districts sent representatives. At first considered derivative of a U.S. Mafia Commission dating to the 1930s, it is now believed to have had a forerunner in a similar Sicilian structure, the *Conferenza*, at the turn of the twentieth century.

Knowledge of the U.S. Mafia initially expanded with Estes Kefauver's Senate hearings in 1950 and 1951; the FBI's 1958 analysis following the spectacular if accidental 1957 raid of a secret meeting in Apalachin, New York; the McClellan Committee hearings on labor racketeering, prompted by the same event; and the probes of Robert Kennedy, chief counsel to John McClellan and then attorney general (until 1964). Under Kennedy, the Justice Department negotiated the terms by which a low-level mafioso, Joe Valachi, would testify about his experiences in the Mafia—testimony that exposed, among other things, the illusive term *cosa nostra*.

More or less sidestepping these state-centered sources, social scientists of the time analyzed organized crime in relation to the difficulties faced by early twentieth-century immigrants—Irish and Jewish as well as Italian—as they tried to earn a livelihood, benefit from corrupt political machines, and resist being criminalized by racism. (In the case of Italians, racial stereotyping included accusations of membership in a mysterious "black hand" organization, and numerous lynchings; eleven Sicilians were victims of the largest mass lynching in U.S. history in New Orleans, in 1891.) Images in print media, film, and television further complicate social analysis. The novel *The Godfather* (1969) and its film versions (1970s), produced by Italian Americans upset with racial stereotypes, romanticize their subject for outsiders. Other films such as Martin Scorsese's

Goodfellas (1990), based on the 1985 book *Wiseguy* by journalist Nicolas Pileggi, and the television serial *The Sopranos* (in which Italian Americans have also been involved) dramatize a model of masculinity that combines a haughty attractiveness with a dangerous readiness to retaliate against any perceived offense with gratuitous violence.

In light of several new sources—autobiographies (albeit self-serving) like Joseph Bonanno's (1983); complex investigations pursued under the Racketeer Influenced Corrupt Organizations (RICO) statute of 1970; collaborative investigations with Italian authorities, unraveling, for example, the "pizza connection" network of heroin delivery to the East Coast and Midwest; telephone intercepts; and the impressive reporting of dedicated journalists—organized crime is now analyzed less in relation to impoverished immigrant communities and more in relation to New World opportunities attracting already experienced racketeers from abroad (who, in the case of Sicilians and southern Italians, made voyages back and forth, tending to affairs and, especially during the fascist period, evading surveillance). Underlying the opportunities was an American dynamic of race and class: As WASP elites enacted rigid laws to interdict "vices" associated with newcomers, vast black markets took shape—for drugs, prostitution, gambling, and most spectacularly, alcohol, prohibited from 1919 to 1933 by constitutional amendment.

Immigrant Italian communities were assets to the racketeers who came—a source of recruits for smuggling operations and easily conditioned to respect omertà. New York, with a million Sicilians and southern Italians by 1920 (not to mention the large number who worked on the Brooklyn waterfront), became the center of gravity for the U.S. Mafia. Yet the immigrant communities also suffered from having to harbor predatory entrepreneurs. Nor did they circumscribe figures such as Nick Gentile, who migrated from Sicily in 1905, joined a "family" in Philadelphia, sold fraudulent goods in Pittsburgh and Kansas City, trafficked heroin in New Orleans and Texas, and bootlegged liquor from Canada to Milwaukee and San Francisco. His close associates—Alfonse "Scarface" Capone in Chicago and, in New York, Joe "the Boss" Masseria and Charles "Lucky" Luciano—were also well-connected. A competing New York faction led by Salvatore Maranzano, the youthful Bonanno's patron, had especially strong links to Castellammare del Golfo, a Sicilian town with a history of Mafia involvement in citrus exports.

Following prohibition, the most telling instance of New World opportunities attracting Old World mafiosi developed out of the 1956 Narcotics Control Act. Concerned about mounting drug arrests—aware, too, of the pending loss of Havana, Cuba, (playground of Jewish mobster Meyer Lansky and the Tampa mafiosi Santo Trafficante, senior and junior), as a point of entry—Bonanno led a delegation of American capi to Palermo where, at a strategic meeting at the Grand Hotel of the Palms in 1957, they franchised out to a select group of Sicilians the business of distributing heroin throughout the United States—a harbinger of Badalamenti's and Buscetta's audacity, and of the pizza connection.

Money earned from protecting and trafficking in illegal "vices" has helped American mafiosi colonize many fields: loansharking, especially to addicted gamblers; Las Vegas casinos and tourism; trash-hauling and construction companies; coin-operated slot machines and laundromats; and schemes for kickbacks, extortion, truck jackings, and cargo theft and no-show jobs at ports, airports, wholesale markets, convention centers, hotels, and restaurants. Quickly accumulated capital has also been important in bribing police and prosecutors; insinuating the Mafia into municipal politics; penetrating labor unions; and paying for first-class trial lawyers. However, with its heady possibilities for risk, vice-related crime takes a large toll in violence. During the Prohibition Era, Sicilian bootleggers and smugglers both allied with and warred against "outside" Irish and Jewish gangsters, near-outside Neapolitan gangsters, and their own compatriots. Al Capone's Valentine's Day massacre of a rival gang in 1929 in Chicago, and the bloody "Castellammarese war" between the Massaria and Mazarano factions in New York in 1930, are landmarks of American Mafia lore.

Significantly for social theory, such crises, and the unwanted attention they draw, prompt peacemakers to push for higher-level organizational innovations. Thus in 1931, Luciano negotiated the systematization of five Mafia "families" in New York, each with an elected capo, an appointed *consigliere*, several subgroups or "crews," and a ceiling on new initiates. (More could join only upon the death of existing members, which greatly enlarged the category of Mafia "wannabes.") The five heads, together with Capone of Chicago (the next-largest hub of Mafia activity, after New York) and Stefano Magaddino, a Bonanno relative in Buffalo, agreed to form an overarching Commission to rule on pending murders. Articulating territorial power with the far-flung entrepreneurial activities of individual mafiosi, this body pledged to meet with bosses from across the country every five years. (The Apalachin meeting took place during an off year, in part to assess the 1956 Narcotics Act.) This was the Commission that many believed inspired the Sicilian *Cupola*—perhaps via the 1957 meeting at the Palms—until the discovery of the much earlier *Conferenza*.

By the 1930s the U.S. Mafia had surpassed other, mainly Jewish and Irish, organized crime formations in

both firepower and discipline, yet its very organizational coherence was a source of destabilizing leadership struggles, as illustrated by New York's Gambino family. Police investigators concluded, although without bringing charges, that in 1957 the family's namesake (not its founder) Carlo Gambino, together with Vito Genovese, arranged for the then-boss, Albert Anastasia, to be murdered while receiving a shave at his favorite barbershop. Anastasia is believed to have leveled his predecessor in 1951. Gambino died a natural death, but his anointed successor (and brother-in-law), Paul Castellano, was gunned down in 1985 on orders of the up-and-coming John Gotti—who, in turn, was "ratted out" by a coconspirator, Sammy "the Bull" Gravano, who turned state's witness in the context of intensified antimafia pressure in 1988. Similarly, in their brutal assault on the *perdenti*, the Corleonesi either ignored or manipulated the *Cupola*, carrying out numerous murders without its permission and with impunity, then took it over as an instrument of repression.

SEE ALSO *Cold War; Crime and Criminology; Drug Traffic; Ethnicity; Gambling; Immigrants to North America; Immigrants, New York City; Latifundia; Mussolini, Benito; Organizations; Prisons; Prostitution; Violence*

BIBLIOGRAPHY

Block, Alan, A. 1980. *East Side, West Side: Organizing Crime in New York, 1930–1950.* Cardiff, U.K.: University College, Cardiff Press.

Blok, Anton. 1974. *The Mafia of a Sicilian Village, 1860–1860: A Study of Violent Peasant Entrepreneurs.* New York: Harper and Row.

Bonanno, Joseph, with Sergio Lalli. 1983. *A Man of Honor: The Autobiography of Joseph Bonanno.* New York: Simon and Schuster.

Chubb, Judith. 1982. *Patronage, Power, and Poverty in Southern Italy: A Tale of Two Cities.* Cambridge: MIT Press.

Gambetta, Diego. 1993. *The Sicilian Mafia: The Business of Protection.* Cambridge, MA: Harvard University Press.

Gardaphé, Fred L. 2006. *From Wiseguys to Wise Men: The Gangster and Italian American Masculinities.* New York: Routledge.

Gentile, Nick. 1963. *Vita di Capomafia.* Rome: Editori Riuniti.

Landesco, John. [1929] 1968. *Organized Crime in Chicago.* Intro. Mark H. Haller. Chicago: University of Chicago Press.

Lupo, Salvatore. 1993. *Storia della mafia: dalle origini ai giorni nostri.* Rome: Donzelli Editore.

Maas, Peter. 1968. *The Valachi Papers.* New York: Bantam.

Messinger, Chris. 2002. *The Godfather: How the Corleones Became "Our Gang."* Albany: State University of New York Press.

Nelli, Humberto S. [1976] 1981. *The Business of Crime: Italians and Syndicate Crime in the United States.* Chicago: University of Chicago Press.

Paoli, Letizia. 2003. *Mafia Brotherhoods: Organized Crime Italian Style.* Oxford: Oxford University Press.

Pezzino, Paolo. 1995. *Mafia: industria della violenza. Scritti e documenti inediti sulla mafia dalle origini ai giorni nostri.* Florence: La Nuova Italia.

Raab, Selwyn. 2005. *Five Families: The Rise, Decline, and Resurgence of America's Most Powerful Mafia Empires.* New York: St. Martin's.

Riall, Lucy. 1998. *Sicily and the Unification of Italy: Liberal Policy and Local Power, 1859–1866.* Oxford: Clarendon.

Santino, Umberto, and Giovanni La Fiura. 1990. *L'impresa mafiosa: dall'Italia agli Stati Uniti.* Palermo: Franco Angeli, Centro Siciliano di Documentazione Giuseppe Impastato.

Schneider, Jane, and Peter Schneider. 2003. *Reversible Destiny: Mafia, Antimafia and the Struggle for Palermo.* Los Angeles and San Francisco: University of California Press.

Siebert, Renate. 1996. *Secrets of Life and Death: Women and the Mafia.* London and New York: Verso.

Stille, Alexander. 1995. *Excellent Cadavers: The Mafia and the Death of the First Italian Republic.* New York: Vintage.

Jane Schneider

MAGIC

In ancient times, the term *magic* referred to the doctrines and practices of the "magi," a Zoroastrian caste of priests centered in Persia. The term meant "gift of God" in its original language, but as individuals claiming to be magi contacted Mediterranean cultures, it came to mean any itinerant specialist in fortune-telling or other forms of the occult. Europeans looked positively upon the magi because in the New Testament the magi were celebrated in Matthew's account of the nativity of Jesus. But by 500 BCE the term magi also had a pejorative sense as many impostors made a living by pretending to possess supernatural powers gained in the mysterious East. The *ars magica*, or "the practices of would-be magi," usually meant the tricks of showmen, a sense that followed the word "magic" when it entered English. For this reason, in the most popular usage, a "magic" trick performed by a "magician" typically means an illusion performed on stage as contrived entertainment.

In a more objective ethnographic sense, however, the concept of magic is useful in describing a common form of vernacular belief, as well as an important emphasis in a variety of new religions. The twentieth century occult revivalist Aleister Crowley (1874–1947) defined magic in a quasi-objective sense as "the science and art of causing change to occur in conformity with will" (Adler 1986,

p. 8). His practice, however, involved the use of rituals intended to "cause change" through the use of occult forces. Folklorists and anthropologists have likewise seen similar tendencies in a variety of cultures, and so magic could be defined more precisely as any traditional ritual that seeks to protect or benefit an individual through the private appropriation of supernatural forces.

During his research among Micronesian fishers (1914–1920), British anthropologist Bronislaw Malinowski found that magical practices were based on practical, utilitarian needs of those engaging in professions with high degrees of personal risk, particularly open-sea fishing. Malinowski argued that "where man can rely completely upon his knowledge and skill, magic does not exist," while in activities "full of danger and uncertainty, there is extensive magical ritual to secure safety and good results" (Malinowski 1954, pp. 30–31). Subsequently, ethnographers found similar practices among other cultures with a high degree of personal risk (such as fishing, mining, or lumbering) or where success is largely due to unpredictable factors (gambling, sports competitions, or the law).

Most common forms of magic are simple, including watching for omens of a lucky or unlucky venture, preparing and carrying amulets intended to bring fortune, or engaging in simple rituals at the start of an activity. Folklorist Don Yoder saw many of these as forms of "folk religion" and argued that they included any religious or quasi-religious practice observed but not positively prescribed by the institutionalized sect to which one belonged. However, more elaborate, privately maintained magic-religious traditions have also survived in ethnic communities alongside these common omens and rituals. These traditions are often termed "ceremonial magic," and involve complicated rituals and magical paraphernalia. The rituals are similar in structure to blessings and prayers carried out in religion, but as Malinowski noted, they are often pragmatic in intent, serving to ensure success in an individual's economic or private matters.

Practitioners of such rituals normally define their art as "natural" or "white" magic because the forces that they use are the same as those honored in their dominant religion and their functions are supportive of their communities' core ethics. In addition, as sociologist Hans Sebald found in a 1978 study of witchcraft traditions in Franconia (a region in southern Germany), magic often served as a convenient alternative in complex family disputes where calling in legal or religious officials would have caused a scandal. Nevertheless, such traditions are viewed with considerable suspicion by mainstream religious authorities.

The conventional distinction between "black" and "white" magic derives from this longstanding tension between vernacular practitioners and the law. In fact, scholars agree that few explicitly "satanic" or explicitly evil magicians ever existed. Prosecutors of the early modern (1500–1700) witch trials obtained confessions describing explicit devil worship and evil magic, but these descriptions were certainly obtained by coercion and torture. Sound ethnographic studies show that virtually all practicing "magicians" claimed to be "white" witches whose rituals supported the religious and ethical values of their communities.

Jealous religious authorities considered all private magic rituals, however, to be unnecessary (the literal meaning of "superstitious"), foolish, and at worst, a potentially dangerous form of "black" magic. "There is Mention of Creatures that they call *White Witches*, which do only *Good-Turns* for their Neighbours," the Massachusetts Puritan minister Cotton Mather said shortly before the outbreak of the Salem Witch Trials (1692), adding, "I suspect that there are none of that sort; but … If they *do good*, it is only that they *may* do *hurt*" (Mather 1689, p. 4). To be truly divine, that is, the exercise of supernatural powers needed to be limited strictly to institutionally approved specialists. Any use of allegedly "good" magic outside of orthodox religion was often defined as "black" magic for that reason alone. In addition, magical rituals that cast misfortune on an individual, or which explicitly call on demonic powers are the most strongly proscribed as "dark arts" by mainstream religions and, at times, by civil authorities as well.

The more elaborate traditions involve a belief that an unexplained illness or misfortune could be explained in terms of a curse cast by another person, deliberately or inadvertently. Hence the magic user's first task was to diagnose the source of the inquirer's problem, then to conduct a ritual intended to remove its influence and frequently, turn the curse back against the one who cast it. Such magical specialists also fabricate and sell fetishes intended to protect its purchaser. Often these traditions are complex enough that they need to be preserved in writing, either privately maintained manuscripts passed down in a family or circle of practitioners, or in print editions available from specialists. Among these "magic books," the most notorious include the Germanic *Sixth and Seventh Books of Moses* and the Jewish qabbalist *Key of Solomon*.

A further development in magic occurred in England during the 1890s when a group of academics revived the medieval European traditions of ceremonial magic as a new religious movement. The Order of the Golden Dawn attracted many followers, chief among them the Irish poet William Butler Yeats (1865–1939), whose writings include frequent references to magical rituals that he performed. Crowley's Ordo Templi Orientis (O.T.O.) was another influential faction in this movement. Predictably, Crowley was repeatedly denounced by religious authorities as a "black" magician who dabbled in Satanism. Although Crowley, a vocal critic of orthodox Christianity, at times encouraged this image, the rituals he practiced were in fact not diabolical in nature or intent. Nevertheless, the popular image of an evil "black" magician whose powers are countered by a benevolent "white" magician has become a cliché in popular fantasy and children's literature.

More influentially, in 1954 Briton Gerald Gardner published a manuscript titled "Ye Bok of ye Art Magical," supposedly the record of rituals preserved by a secret coven of English witches. In fact, the manuscript was based on publications of the Golden Dawn circles, but Gardner's writings inspired the growth of a vigorous "Neo-Pagan" religious movement that has developed into a strong alternative religion in both Great Britain and North America. A number of ethnographic studies of contemporary witchcraft revival (particularly anthropologist Sabina Magliocco's 2004 study) show that the use of magic has had profound impact on its followers. Magic, Magliocco argues, is not simple make-believe but a powerful means of inducing spiritually transformative experiences.

The common perception of "magic" in terms of illusion or ignorance is therefore simplistic. Magical beliefs need to be seen in the larger context of their practitioners' social and religious worldviews. Only by seeing a magical tradition as an integral part of a culture's definition of reality can we understand why it attracts and maintains followers

SEE ALSO *Anthropology; Ethnography; Ethnology and Folklore; Luck; Malinowski, Bronislaw; Religion; Risk; Rituals; Taboos*

BIBLIOGRAPHY

Adler, Margot. 1986. *Drawing Down the Moon: Witches, Druids, Goddess-Worshippers and Other Pagans in America Today.* 2nd ed. Boston: Beacon.

Davies, Owen. 2003. *Cunning-Folk: Popular Magic in English History.* London: Hambledon and London

Ellis, Bill. 2003. *Lucifer Ascending: The Occult in Folklore and Popular Culture.* Lexington: University of Kentucky Press.

King, Francis. 1989. *Modern Ritual Magic: The Rise of Western Occultism.* Rev. ed. New York: Avery.

Magliocco, Sabina. 2004. *Witching Culture: Folklore and Neo-Paganism in America.* Philadelphia: University of Pennsylvania Press.

Malinowski, Bronislaw. [1925] 1954. *Magic, Science and Religion.* Garden City, New York: Doubleday.

Mather, Cotton. [1689] 2002. *Memorable Providences Relating to Witchcrafts and Possessions. The Internet Sacred Text Archive.* http://www.sacred-texts.com/pag/twp/twp03.htm.

Sebald, Hans. 1978. *Witchcraft: The Heritage of a Heresy.* New York: Elsevier.

Yoder, Don. 1974. Toward a Definition of Folk Religion. *Western Folklore* 33: 2–15.

Bill Ellis

MAGNA CARTA

Emerging as a thirteenth-century agreement between crown and aristocracy, the language of Magna Carta (literally, "great charter") proved pregnant with meaning for later generations. The charter came to be seen as representing wider legal and political principles, especially those of lawful and limited government.

The charter was drafted against a backdrop of complex political and military disputes. At the center of each was King John (c. 1167–1216), the Plantagenet ruler of England, Wales, Ireland, and much of northern France. A descendant of the Normans who had conquered England a century earlier, John would become the first to reside permanently in England. He was crowned king in 1199 and immediately faced competing claims on his French territories, not least those of King Philip II (1165–1223) of France. In a series of wars with Philip and his allies, John lost much of his continental holdings by 1204. The following years saw him invade successively—and more successfully—Scotland, Ireland, and Wales. To exacerbate these military demands, John fell foul of Pope Innocent II (d. 1143). In 1207 the king contested the pope's nominee for archbishop of Canterbury, Stephen Langton (c. 1150–1228). As a result, the pope placed England under an interdict on religious worship, excommunicated the king, and sided with Philip.

In attempting to pay for his military activities, John imposed increasing financial demands on the Anglo-Norman aristocracy. Combined with complaints about royal interference with the administration of justice, the result was rebellion against the king. In 1212 John acquiesced to the pope, agreeing to surrender his kingdoms to the papacy as feudal overlord and repurchasing them from him. An invasion of England was narrowly avoided the following year when the French fleet was destroyed. John then invaded France in 1214 in the hope of reclaiming his territories there. He suffered a major defeat at Bouvines, resulting in the loss of most of his remaining continental possessions.

John soon faced additional problems within England. Encouraged by Archbishop Langton, the Anglo-Norman barons there remonstrated against the king's financial demands and judicial interference. In May 1215 they took London by military force. A truce was sought and representatives met at Runnymede, a meadow west of London on the river Thames, in June 1215. After much discussion, they agreed to a document of compromises called the Articles of the Barons. This was superseded by the charter subsequently known as Magna Carta. Formally, Magna Carta was a royal letter written in Latin dealing with a wide variety of issues: the freedom of the church, feudal customs, taxation, trade, and the law. This was not the first attempt to limit political power by a written charter. In England, for example, the Charter of Liberties issued by Henry I (c. 1068–1135) predated Magna Carta by over a century. Magna Carta was also similar to contemporaneous continental charters and legislation. Many of its rules came from a common pool of European political and legal thought, not least the canon law of the church. In the short term, the most potentially radical element of Magna Carta was probably the provision for a commission of barons to ensure royal compliance. But this came to nothing. Contrary to subsequent interpretation, it had little to do with the lesser landholders or the vast peasantry of England.

John renounced Magna Carta almost immediately. The pope, too, issued a papal bull against the agreement because it had been imposed by force. Civil war returned. Numerous barons now aligned themselves with Louis (1187–1226), Philip's son and later Louis VIII of France, who invaded England in May 1216 with a significant army. Louis subsequently occupied London, where he was received enthusiastically by the barons and was proclaimed king of England. John made some military gains, but died of dysentery in October 1216. With his death, the barons' complaints were less pressing. John's nine-year-old son, Henry III (1207–1272), was seen as more politically malleable and was crowned English king. His regent, William Marshall (c. 1146–1219), one of the signatories of Magna Carta, revised and reissued the document in November 1216. Marshall was also able to convince most of the rebellious barons to renew their loyalty to the crown, ending the war. In 1217 a treaty was signed, and Louis left England. Another revision of Magna Carta that year separated the document into two sections: a brief Charter of the Forest concerning the royal forests, and the remaining text, the larger Magna Carta. Henry III reissued a still shorter version of Magna Carta in 1225. This version was confirmed by Edward I (1239–1307) in 1297.

The vague wording of Magna Carta, combined with changing social structures, meant that its text was continually reinterpreted. This is already evident in the fourteenth century. In general, the charter was largely ignored for centuries. By the seventeenth century, however, it took on greater significance in conflicts between king and Parliament. Lord Chief Justice Edward Coke (1552–1634) was especially important in popularizing the belief in Magna Carta's wider constitutional principles. With parliamentary ascendancy in the late seventeenth century, it continued to play an important role in debates both in and out of Parliament. In the eighteenth century, Magna Carta served as a touchstone for American independence and constitutional government. In England, the nineteenth century brought a more balanced assessment of its historical meaning and the removal of most of its antiquated provisions from English law.

The document retains a deeply symbolic importance throughout the English-speaking world. The American Bar Association erected a monument at Runnymede in 1957. In May 2003 the Australian Parliament opened Magna Carta Place in Canberra. In the early twenty-first century, four copies of the original charter remain: two in the British Library and one each in the cathedral archives at Lincoln and Salisbury.

SEE ALSO *Democracy; Feudalism; Monarchy; Monarchy, Constitutional; Sovereignty*

BIBLIOGRAPHY

Breay, Claire. 2002. *Magna Carta: Manuscripts and Myths.* London: British Library.

Hindley, Geoffrey. 1990. *The Book of Magna Carta.* London: Bury St. Edwards.

Holt, J. C. 1985. *Magna Carta and Medieval Government.* London: Hambleton.

Holt, J. C. 1992. *Magna Carta.* 2nd ed. Cambridge, U.K.: Cambridge University Press.

Seán Patrick Donlan

MAHATHIR MOHAMAD
1925–

Tun Dr. Mahathir bin Mohamad, to give him his formal Malaysian designation, was the fourth prime minister of Malaysia. He was in power from 1981 to 2003, more than twenty-two years. Mahathir, an ethnic Malay and a Muslim, was born in 1925 in Alor Setar in northwestern Malaysia. He was trained during colonial times as a medical doctor at the University of Malaya in Singapore, graduating in 1947. As prime minister, he was widely credited with the transformation of Malaysia into a prosperous, fully employed, newly industrialized country that became a magnet for illegal immigrants from Indonesia, Burma (Myanmar), and Bangladesh. He is best known in the West as an outspoken advocate of "Asian values" and a critic of Zionism and Western hypocrisy. Mahathir is also widely seen as an authoritarian leader who was prone to cronyism and not adequately respectful of human rights.

Mahathir is a member of the United Malays National Organization (UMNO), the party that with its ethnic Chinese and Indian allies has ruled Malaysia since independence from the British in 1957. Mahathir was elected to parliament in 1964, but lost his seat in 1969 and was expelled from the party after criticizing the prime minister, Tunku Abdul Rahman (1903–1990). After readmission to the UMNO, Mahathir was again elected to parliament in 1974. He then became minister of education and from 1976 served as deputy prime minister. Throughout his career, Mahathir was both a strong advocate for the advancement of the indigenous Malay majority and one of the most vocal critics of Malay stereotyping. He held a strong conviction that racial harmony in Malaysia (and elsewhere) requires all communities to stand at approximately equal levels of prosperity, and he became frustrated when some sections of the Malay community encountered difficulties in their attempts to advance economically, despite the strong preferences afforded to them by Mahathir's government.

During his twenty-two years in power, Mahathir was successful in creating a prosperous and sizable *Bumiputra* (literally, "sons of the soil," that is, indigenous) middle class. During the colonial period, commerce and industry had been dominated by the Chinese and the professions by ethnic Indians. With Mahathir in power, the Bumiputra came to dominate Malaysia's civil service, police, and military; they also gained a foothold in commerce, industry, and the professions. However, this progress was achieved at a substantial price. Quotas on non-Malay students in the universities, for example, prompted many non-Malay Malaysians to seek higher education in the United Kingdom, Australia, the United States, and elsewhere, and many never returned to Malaysia. In addition, emphasis on the national language in education led to a noticeable decline in the country's standard of English, which eventually resulted in the partial reversal of language policies in education.

During Mahathir's tenure, Malaysia evolved from a predominantly rural, low-income economy in the 1970s to a middle-income economy with full employment and social indicators similar to high-income economies. This was achieved through state-dominated capitalism, openness to foreign investment, and authoritarian political policies. Mahathir's economic policies were always nationalistic, although based on exports and guided capitalism. Following the 1997 Asian financial crisis, Mahathir rejected the advice of the International Monetary Fund (IMF) and imposed a fixed exchange rate and capital controls. He was widely criticized for this move, but the results were much better in Malaysia than in neighboring countries that had followed IMF advice, and Malaysia weathered the crisis with relatively little damage to either growth or investment. However, the crisis did produce difficulties with respect to undocumented immigrants, who flocked to Malaysia because of its relative prosperity and high demand for labor. Officials have attempted to repatriate migrants, amid the complaints of private-sector firms, particularly in construction, plantation agriculture, and low-skill manufacturing, about the impact of this policy on their labor forces. Mahathir also promoted a number of large-scale pet projects aimed at modernizing the economy and turning it into a high-tech center for the region. Some of these projects were eventually cancelled, with others looking more and more like white elephants.

Mahathir is perhaps best known in the West for his strong views on Asian values and his rejection of Western moral leadership. He argues that Asian societies place more value on the community than on the individual, and he considers the guidance of an authoritarian government as necessary to ensure stability and rapid economic development in Asian societies. Mahathir has also been a fierce critic of Israel. His relationships with the United States and other Western governments, most notably the United Kingdom and Australia, have often been tense, with much criticism flowing in both directions. American vice president Al Gore, for example, endorsed reform in Malaysia in a speech delivered in Kuala Lumpur in 1998, a speech that Mahathir described as "rude." The Western critique centered on the authoritarian nature of Mahathir's rule, particularly the curtailment of the press and other freedoms, draconian internal security laws, political repression, and harassment of rivals, notably Anwar Ibrahim, the former finance minister and deputy prime minister who was jailed on corruption and sodomy charges. Anwar had led a reform movement emphasizing the dangers of corruption and nepotism under Mahathir. Mahathir has been highly critical of the 2003 invasion of Iraq by U.S.-led forces and of the U.S. policy of detention without trial for prisoners held at Guantánamo Bay and elsewhere.

Mahathir has remained outspoken and influential in Malaysia since his retirement from active politics in 2003. In May 2006 he described his handpicked successor, Prime Minister Abdullah Ahmad Badawi, as "gutless" and "kowtowing" after Abdullah abandoned a project to build a bridge to replace the causeway joining Malaysia to Singapore. Many Malays and moderate Muslims elsewhere regard Mahathir with great respect for the economic achievements of his administration and his willingness to state independent views with eloquence and force.

BIBLIOGRAPHY

Khoo Boo Teik. 1996. *Paradoxes of Mahathirism: An Intellectual Biography of Mahathir Mohamad.* New York: Oxford University Press.

Mahathir bin Mohamad. 1970. *The Malay Dilemma.* Singapore: Times Books International.

Milne, R. S., and Diane K. Mauzy. 1999. *Malaysian Politics under Mahathir.* London: Routledge.

James Cobbe

MAJORITARIANISM

Majoritarianism is a stark philosophical position defended explicitly by nearly no one but which many debates invoke rhetorically. Majoritarianism is more fundamental than majority rule, which is simply one of many possible political decision rules. Any democratic system obliges the government to respond to the desires of citizens. Any republican system requires that the people understand their obligations to each other and to the larger nation. Majority rule bridges the gap between the two systems of obligation in a particular way. Leaders and policies are selected by majority rule, and citizens have a duty of participation to ensure that choices are not made by minority factions of the population.

Majoritarianism, by contrast, if it were to be implemented fully, would require something closer to what Plato has Thracymachus tell us in *The Republic*: "Justice is the interest of the strongest." Any policy that thwarts or frustrates "the majority," by this notion, is inherently and intrinsically undemocratic and destroys the moral fiber of the nation.

In policy debates majoritarianism is most commonly invoked as a counterclaim to arguments for increased diversity or multicultural policies. The claims take the form of an identification of what "we," the majority, stand for: "we are a Christian nation" or "we are an English-speaking nation" are common majoritarian appeals. Other examples of asserted majoritarianism include Richard Nixon's "Silent Majority," for whom he claimed to speak, or Wilmot Robertson's book *The Dispossessed Majority* (1972). Robertson's is perhaps the most extreme and tendentious version of majoritarianism in the U.S. context, with its concern for the separation of ethnic groups because of the impossibility of true assimilation.

Though majority rule is not the same as majoritarianism, they are closely related. There are a variety of formal results regarding the potential for purely majoritarian institutions to produce just outcomes. On the negative side, Kenneth Arrow (1963) generalized the Marquis de Condorcet's finding, rediscovered by Duncan Black

(1958), that purely majoritarian choice will generally produce results that are either arbitrary (indeterminate) or imposed (dictatorial, so control of the agenda is tantamount to choosing the outcome). On the positive side, May's Theorem demonstrates that even simple majority rule has several desirable properties and can avoid the chaos of Arrow's result when there are only two alternatives.

Many political theorists point to John Rawls's *Political Liberalism* as the most important counterpoint to a philosophical majoritarian perspective. Rawls argues that no one conception of identity should dominate and so no one majority can be said have primacy. Instead, Rawls advances a conception of "overlapping consensus," with each individual committed to fair and respectful treatment of citizens who hold different conceptions of the good, whether it be political or religious.

SEE ALSO *Arrow, Kenneth J.; Condorcet, Marquis de; Democracy; Dictatorship; Majority Rule; Majority Voting; Nixon, Richard M.; Plato; Rawls, John; Separatism; Tyranny of the Majority*

BIBLIOGRAPHY

Arrow, Kenneth. [1951] 1963. *Social Choice and Individual Values*. 2nd ed. New York: Wiley.

Black, Duncan. 1958 *The Theory of Campaigns and Elections*. New York: Cambridge University Press.

May, Kenneth O. 1952. A Set of Independent Necessary and Sufficient Conditions for Simple Majority Decisions. *Econometrica* 20: 680–684.

Rawls, John. 1993. *Political Liberalism*. Cambridge, MA: Harvard University Press.

Robertson, Wilmot. 1972. *The Dispossessed Majority*. Cape Canaveral, FL: H. Allen.

Michael Munger

MAJORITIES

Majorities are defined as proportions larger than 50 percent of the total. This concept is fundamental to the theory and practice of democracy because of the democratic principle of equal human worth. The moral equality of people suggests that deference often should be given to the opinions of the majority when political conflicts require a collective resolution.

BENEFITS AND ATTRACTIVENESS OF MAJORITIES

Several rationales can be used to justify this partiality toward majorities (Dahl 1989). First, it maximizes self-determination by allowing more people to live under conditions they prefer. Second, it maximizes average utility by benefiting the largest number of individuals. Third, it is likely to produce beneficial decisions because people are well informed.

Majorities commonly are treated with special consideration in many areas of the democratic political process. They exert their strongest influence on decision-making activities. Majorities usually have primary control over decision-making institutions and are generally in a position to dictate outcomes. Consequently, forming and maintaining majorities is an important feature of democratic politics.

The attractiveness of majorities for democratic decision making was demonstrated formally in 1952 by Kenneth May, who showed that in choosing between two alternatives, only majority rule satisfies four reasonable conditions for a democratic process: It produces outcomes that are decisive, anonymous, neutral, and positively responsive.

MULTIPLE ALTERNATIVES AND MINORITY INFLUENCE

When the choice set includes more than two alternatives, there may not be a naturally occurring majority winner. In these situations voting procedures can be used that still reflect the basic principles of majority rule. A runoff system, for example, involves a two-stage election. It begins with a preliminary election. If there is no majority winner, the two candidates with the highest vote totals advance to a head-to-head runoff in which majority rule can be used. An amendment procedure, which often is used in legislatures, also uses majority rule to choose among more than two alternatives. A winner is chosen through a series of pairwise votes decided by majority rule. At each stage the winning alternative advances to face a different competing option.

Variations of majority rule such as unanimity and supermajorities empower minorities in certain situations. The unanimity rule, which requires unanimous consent, effectively gives veto power to any individual voter. A supermajority rule, which requires a proportion greater than a simple majority, also leaves open the possibility of minority control over the outcome of a decision. Similarly, with the plurality rule a winner is chosen on the basis of receiving the largest proportion of votes. In this case an alternative can win with less than a majority.

TWO-PARTY AND MULTIPARTY SYSTEMS

The importance of the use of majorities for exerting political power in a democracy makes it a significant concern for political actors. Political institutions and conditions, however, can affect the way political power is pursued. Two-party political systems, for example, provide unique strategic environments for parties, candidates, and voters. Competing parties and candidates have an incentive to make their platforms more appealing to centrist voters to maximize their vote totals (Downs 1957). Consequently, voters typically are presented with two relatively moderate alternatives. People who support third-party or independent candidates have an incentive to cast ballots strategically for one of the two major parties to avoid "wasting" their votes.

In contrast, multiparty systems often require the formation of coalitions among competing political parties to establish ruling majorities. Consequently, parties and candidates can achieve political power without having broad-based support. They can concentrate their platforms to appeal to more narrow constituencies that are large enough to secure political representation. Once seated, they can negotiate with others to create a majority coalition. Therefore, voters in a multiparty system often have a wider range of alternatives from which to choose and less motivation to vote strategically.

TYRANNY OF THE MAJORITY

Although majorities have certain normative advantages related to the principle of equal moral worth, they also present dangers in the form of majority tyranny. Political power in the hands of the majority leaves minorities susceptible to harm or exploitation. The criticism of democracy as a form of mob rule reflects the suspicion that an unconstrained majority will misuse its power.

The problem of majority tyranny often is addressed through political institutions in which majority rule is balanced with the protection of minorities. In the *Federalist Papers* the abuse perpetrated by majority factions is identified as a primary obstacle to political justice and the well-being of the American state. Consequently, certain institutional structures and principles were included in the American Constitution and the Bill of Rights, including federalism, the division of powers, checks and balances, and the freedoms enumerated in the First Amendment.

Majorities in a democracy can have an oppressive effect on private individuals in civil society. Alexis de Tocqueville observed that the thoughts and opinions of individuals in a democracy are susceptible to majority tyranny: "[A majority] uses no persuasion to forward its beliefs, but by some mighty pressure of the mind of all upon the intelligence of each it imposes its ideas and makes them penetrate men's very souls" (Tocqueville 2000, p. 435). This power over public opinion is due in part to the influence of the principle of equality. When individuals are considered equal, there is an inclination to view the greater number in a majority as providing evidence of superior thought. There is also a propensity for individuals to be ostracized socially when they publicly disagree with the majority opinion. These tendencies make a democratic society vulnerable to uniformity of thought and a dearth of new ideas.

The concept of majorities plays a critical role in democratic thought and practice similar to that of freedom and equality. It provides a general standard for structuring democratic decision making. It also influences the behavior of political actors, who must keep in mind the political advantages of being in the majority. The power that democracies give majorities may be justified normatively. However, it should be viewed with caution. The power majorities have to exert control over the political process allows them to sacrifice the interests of minorities.

SEE ALSO *Dahl, Robert Alan; Democracy; Majoritarianism; Majority Rule; Majority Voting; Minorities; Political Science; Politics; Tocqueville, Alexis de; Tyranny of the Majority*

BIBLIOGRAPHY

Dahl, Robert Alan. 1989. *Democracy and Its Critics*. New Haven, CT: Yale University Press.

Downs, Anthony. 1957. *An Economic Theory of Democracy*. New York: Harper.

May, Kenneth. 1952. A Set of Independent Necessary and Sufficient Conditions for Simple Majority Decision. *Econometrica* 10: 680–684.

Tocqueville, Alexis de. 2000. *Democracy in America*. 1st ed. Trans. George Lawrence, ed. J. P. Mayer. New York: Perennial Classics. (Orig. pub. 1835–1840.)

Johnny Goldfinger

MAJORITY RULE

The principle of majority rule in elections and decision-making was introduced in medieval Germanic law and canon law as a consequence of failures to make decisions by unanimity. In fact, in any community, the formation of two or more factions or parties may lead to procedures requiring the counting of votes and the achievement of a majority threshold.

The majority principle has been praised for being the only system that satisfies the following criteria: (1) decisiveness, but only when there are no more than two alternatives (e.g., candidates, parties, or policy proposals) to choose from; (2) anonymity or voter equality; (3) neutrality with respect to issues, so the status quo or the largest group does not have an advantage; and (4) monotonicity, or a positive response to changes in voter preference.

If there are only two alternatives along a single issue or ideological dimension, such as the left-right axis, majority rule tends to give the victory to the alternative closer to the median voter's preference. By definition, the median voter—that is, the voter whose preference is located in an intermediate position with less than half of voters on each of the two sides—is always necessary to form a consistent majority in a single dimension. Since the median voter's preference minimizes the sum of the distances from all other individual preferences, the winner by majority rule in a two-alternative contest minimizes aggregate distance and thus maximizes social utility.

However, this model relies on two strong assumptions: a single-dimensional issue space and only two alternatives. If the set of issues submitted to a majority decision is not bound, the introduction of new issues creating a multidimensional space can change the winner. In a multidimensional space, an alternative—such as a party or candidate's platform that includes a "package" of proposals on several issues—can make the majority winner unpredictable, depending on which issue takes higher salience in voter choice. In the long term, there can be a series of successive winners relying on different salient issues, with no foreseeable "trajectory."

When there are more than two alternatives, even in a single-dimensional space, majority rule can be indecisive and unable to produce a winner. Several procedures loosely related to the majority principle can then be adopted. With plurality or relative majority rule, the winner is the alternative that obtains a higher number of votes than any other alternative while not requiring a particular proportion of votes, a result that may imply minority support. Plurality rule has traditionally been used for political elections in the United Kingdom and in former British colonies, including the United States, Canada, and India. Majority runoff requires an absolute majority of votes in the first round of voting, while in a second round the choice can be reduced to the two candidates receiving the highest number of votes in the first round, so as to secure majority support for the winner. Such a system is used for presidential elections in France and in some other countries, including many in Latin America. A majority-preferential vote also requires an absolute majority of voters' first preferences, while successive counts of further preferences are made to find a candidate with majority support. This system is used in Australia.

With both plurality and majority-runoff or majority-preferential voting, the median voter's preference can be defeated or eliminated in the first or successive rounds. This implies that the nonmedian winner by any of these procedures might be defeated by another candidate by

absolute majority if the choice between the two were available. Extreme minority candidates who are broadly rejected by citizens can paradoxically win by these procedures, based on the majority principle. Majority rule is, thus, dependent on irrelevant alternatives; it encourages strategies aimed at altering the number of alternatives, such as divide and win and merge and win, as well as nonsincere or strategic votes in favor of a less-preferred but more-likely-to-win alternative.

Even when majority rule is decisive and maximizes social utility, as in a single-dimensional space with only two alternatives, it can produce a tyranny of the majority, where one group always wins and there is a permanent losing minority. There has been a long history of concern with the perils of the tyranny of the majority for good democratic governance. Remedies include constitutional guarantees on individual and minority rights, judicial review of decisions made by a majority, mechanisms requiring supermajorities and consensual decisions, and separate elections for different issues, as can be provided by institutional frames of division of powers and decentralization. With separate elections, different majorities and minorities may emerge on different issues, thus creating a broad distribution of political satisfaction or social utility.

If a permanent minority subsists, it may try to secede and establish its own independent democratic system. A previous minority within a large country would then become a local majority and increase the total number of citizens identified with collective decisions and social utility. However, a consistently outvoted minority may not be able to secede because it lacks the military capability to do so or would have to accept resource-poor land or territory.

The major alternative to the principle of majority rule is proportional representation. This system implies representative government, that is, decision-making in two stages: election by voters and decisions made by elected representatives. If the two stages are decided by majority rule, the winner is "a majority of the majority, who may be, and often are, but a minority of the whole" (Mill 1861, chap. 7). In contrast, if the voters' election is held with proportional representation and the elected representatives make decisions by majority rule, typically by forming multiparty legislative and cabinet coalitions, the system will generally produce a close fit between electoral and legislative majorities. Nonmajority principles are, thus, necessary to guarantee majority government.

SEE ALSO *Democracy; Majoritarianism; Majority Voting; Plurality; Tyranny of the Majority; Utilitarianism*

BIBLIOGRAPHY

Arrow, Kenneth. 1963. *Social Choice and Individual Values*. 2nd ed. New York: Wiley.

Dahl, Robert A. 1989. *Democracy and Its Critics.* New Haven, CT: Yale University Press.

Downs, Anthony. 1957. *An Economic Theory of Democracy.* New York: Harper.

May, Kenneth O. 1952. A Set of Independent, Necessary, and Sufficient Conditions for Simple Majority Decision. *Econometrica* 20: 680–684.

Mill, John Stuart. 1861. *Considerations on Representative Government.* London: Parker, Son, and Bourn.

Riker, William H. 1982. *Liberalism against Populism: A Confrontation between the Theory of Democracy and the Theory of Social Choice.* San Francisco, CA: Freeman.

Josep M. Colomer

MAJORITY VOTING

In the majority voting system, voters cast their ballots for their preferred candidate and the winner of the election is the candidate who receives a majority of the votes, which is 50 percent plus one vote. When there are only two candidates in an election, majority voting is an attractive voting scheme. With more than two candidates, complications may arise.

Social choice theorist Kenneth Arrow, writing in 1951, lists some simple features of a fair and just voting system, and majority voting meets most of his criteria. Majority voting is what Arrow calls monotonic, or responsive. This means, simply, that one voter cannot cause candidate A to win by changing her vote from supporting candidate A to supporting candidate B. This may seem obvious: if candidate A loses support, that candidate ought to be less, not more, likely to win. Yet in many voting schemes this is not the case. Majority voting with runoff elections, a very popular voting scheme, violates monotonicity. This would occur in a three-candidate election, when candidate A could win a runoff election against candidate B alone, but not candidate C alone. Suppose A and C get the most votes, so move on to the runoff, where A loses. But now suppose a set of voters changes their votes from A to B in the first round of the runoff election, and that this means A and B now face off in the runoff. Despite having lost votes, A now wins the election. Arrow further specified that a fair and just voting system must count all votes equally, which majority voting does. No one voter is a dictator, and no group of voters gets more power than any other group. Similarly, majority voting is not biased toward any of the possible outcomes. For example, some systems name the status quo the winner in the event of a tie, thus introducing a bias for the status quo.

Majority voting has attractions beyond the properties Arrow points out. It is simple for voters. All they must do is select one preferred candidate, and they need do so only once. Provided there are only two candidates and an odd-numbered electorate, majority voting always results in elections with clear winners. By definition, one of the two candidates must get a majority of the votes cast. In elections with more than two candidates, majority vote winners accurately reflect the aggregate preferences of the group. If most voters prefer one candidate over all other candidates, that candidate wins. More technically, this means that majority voting always results in the selection of what social choice theorists call a Condorcet winner. This means that the candidate who wins is the candidate who would receive a majority of votes over any other candidate if the election were between only those two candidates. In other words, in an election among candidates A, B, and C, candidate A is a Condorcet winner if A could win an election against candidate B alone and also win an election against candidate C alone.

There is, however, one serious downfall to majority voting: Often where there are more than two candidates, no candidate will receive a majority of the vote. In this sense, majority voting is not decisive. If no candidate receives 50 percent plus one vote, there is no winner of the election. This means that in most cases, pure majority voting is not practicable. In response to this problem, electoral systems must provide a means of deciding elections when majority voting does not offer a winner. Two of the most popular variants are plurality voting and majority voting with runoff elections. In plurality voting, the winner is declared to be whichever candidate receives the most votes, regardless of whether or not that candidate receives a majority of the vote. In majority voting with runoff, the two candidates with the most votes run again in a second election. The candidate who receives a majority of the votes in the second election is then declared the winner.

These two variants on majority rule, unfortunately, often produce very different outcomes, a troubling contradiction to the concept of democracy: The voting mechanism used in the election, not the attitudes and beliefs of the electorate, may well be the deciding factor in determining who wins. Philosopher Jean-Jacques Rousseau believed that allowing the body politic to select its own government would supply a government that provides for the common good of all the voters, a concept he described in his 1762 work *On the Social Contract* as the general will. But if electoral outcomes rely at least as much on voting schemes as they do on the will of the body politic, the notion of democratic elections providing an infallible general will becomes suspect. In response to this problem, social choice theorist William H. Riker argues in his 1982 *Liberalism against Populism* that the outcome of all elections is thus dubious and that government ought, therefore, to be as limited as possible.

SEE ALSO *Democracy; Elections; Electoral Systems; Majoritarianism; Tyranny of the Majority; Voting; Voting Patterns; Voting Schemes*

BIBLIOGRAPHY

Arrow, Kenneth J. 1963. *Social Choice and Individual Values.* 2nd ed. New Haven, CT: Yale University Press. (Orig. pub. 1951.)

Riker, William H. 1982. *Liberalism against Populism: A Confrontation between the Theory of Democracy and the Theory of Social Choice.* San Francisco: W. H. Freeman.

Rousseau, Jean-Jacques. 1987. On the Social Contract. In *The Basic Political Writings.* Trans. and ed. Donald A. Cress. Indianapolis, IN: Hackett. (Orig. pub. 1762.)

Saari, Donald G. 2001. *Decisions and Elections: Explaining the Unexpected.* Cambridge, U.K.: Cambridge University Press.

Kristin Kanthak

MALCOLM X
1925–1965

Malcolm X, a Muslim minister and Black Nationalist leader, was the most formidable race critic in American history. More effectively than anyone before or since, he exposed the moral and legal hypocrisy of American democracy and the ethical contradictions of white Christianity.

Malcolm Little was born in Omaha, Nebraska, to a Baptist preacher and a West Indian immigrant, both of whom were followers of Marcus Garvey (1887–1940), an early proponent of Black Nationalism. Malcolm's first introduction to white supremacy came in infancy, when the Ku Klux Klan drove his family out of town. The harassment continued in Lansing, Michigan, where the Little home was destroyed by arson, and where Malcolm's father was allegedly murdered by another white hate group. His mother had a nervous breakdown and had to be institutionalized, and her six children became wards of the state. After stints in various foster homes, Malcolm dropped out of school and landed in a juvenile detention facility. In his teens, he made his way first to Boston and then to New York, where as "Detroit Red" he became a fixture of the underworld. He dabbled in drugs, prostitution, numbers running, and armed robbery, and was arrested and convicted of the latter a few months shy of his twenty-first birthday.

While incarcerated, he experienced two major conversions. The first was intellectual: realizing that lack of education was a major contributing factor to black oppression, he set himself to read everything he could get his hands on. The second was religious: he became a follower of Elijah Muhammad's (1897–1975) Nation of Islam, a sui generis American religious sect that embraces the trappings of orthodox Islam while propagating a mythology and inverting white supremacist ideology to proclaim black supremacy instead. The Nation of Islam flourishes in prisons in particular, where its strict code of personal discipline helps many former substance abusers to become clean. It was at this time that Malcolm, in keeping with the Nation's custom, dropped his last name, bequeathed him by slave owners, and took an *X* in its place, to mark his lost African ancestry. Upon Malcolm's release in 1952, his brilliance, dedication, and charisma, along with the debating skills he had honed in prison, brought him to the highest ranks of the Nation's leadership. He became its national spokesperson, second only to Elijah Muhammad himself, and was appointed minister-in-charge of the prestigious Temple Number Seven in Harlem.

Malcolm X quickly distinguished himself as the most feared, controversial, and articulate race critic in the United States. Since the overt racist violence of southern conservatives was obvious, and was effectively exposed in the media by the Reverend Martin Luther King Jr. (1929–1968) and the civil rights movement, Malcolm focused his critique on the covert racist violence of northern liberals. His attack on these liberals was brutal and persistent. He exposed the responsibility they bore for the creation of the black ghetto, with its poverty, drugs, crime, unemployment, bad schools, and bad housing. While King praised white liberals for their support of the civil rights movement, Malcolm castigated them for their hypocrisy in opposing legal segregation in the South while maintaining de facto segregation in the North.

Although he was often accused of preaching hate and violence, Malcolm simply exposed what was already there. White America had always been hateful and violent toward blacks: 244 years of slavery had been followed by 100 years of segregation. Black America had tried and failed to "overcome" using the principles of love and nonviolence. Now it was time for righteous anger and "non-nonviolence." In other words, blacks needed to start defending themselves and their freedom, just as whites had always done. Only in this way could they affirm their humanity. Malcolm is often contrasted with King, and the latter, a frequent target of Malcolm's sharp tongue, kept a wary distance from him, but by the end of their lives each was moving closer to the other's position. King had become much more radical, and Malcolm much more universal in outlook.

In 1964 Malcolm X broke with Elijah Muhammad and converted to Sunni Islam, taking many of his followers with him. The year that followed marked the first time in Malcolm's career that he was free to think and speak for himself. It was a period of intense change and creativity, during which he abandoned the racist ideology of the Nation of Islam and tentatively began to reach out to whites and to the mainstream civil rights movement. After a pilgrimage to Mecca, Saudi Arabia, he took the name El-Hajj Malik El-Shabazz, and founded the Muslim Mosque Inc. and the Organization of Afro-American Unity—a religious and a political organization, respectively. He traveled widely, visiting countries in the Middle East, Africa, and Europe, explaining the black struggle for justice in the United States and linking it with other liberation struggles throughout the world. He also collaborated with the writer Alex Haley (1921–1992) on an autobiography. On February 21, 1965, Malcolm X was assassinated at the Audubon Ballroom in New York City, in front of a large crowd that included his wife and children. Three men connected with the Nation of Islam were convicted of the crime; it was widely suspected, though never proven, that Elijah Muhammad himself ordered the assassination.

There are many questions that arise out of Malcolm X's account of his life as told to Haley, especially the circumstances of his father's death, the timing of his conversion to Sunni Islam, who set fire to Malcolm's home, and Malcolm's sexual orientation. No one has raised these questions as sharply and as controversially as Bruce Perry in *Malcolm: The Life of a Man Who Changed Black America* (1991). Though his biography received much attention when published, it had little impact on the thinking about Malcolm X among most scholars, largely because Perry's sources have proven difficult to check.

In 1992 the Spike Lee film *Malcolm X* made *The Autobiography of Malcolm X* (1965) a best seller, and sparked a renewal of interest in Malcolm. In the early twenty-first century, he was more popular than ever in the African American community, especially among the young. His name, words, and face adorn T-shirts, buttons, and the covers of rap albums. His writings, books about him, and tapes of his speeches are sold by street vendors, at cultural festivals, and in bookstores. His two most significant speeches, "Message to the Grass Roots" and "The Ballot or the Bullet," were delivered in the last year of his life—one immediately before his break with the Nation of Islam, and the other soon after. In both of these speeches, he pushed the basic theme that he had sounded from the beginning of his career: black pride. It was by far his most influential notion, yielding Black Power, Black Theology, African American studies, and much else. This cultural philosophy was his lasting bequest to his people, whom he loved so deeply and for whom he died.

SEE ALSO Black Power; Civil Rights; King, Martin Luther, Jr.; Nation of Islam

BIBLIOGRAPHY

Breitman, George, ed. 1970. *By Any Means Necessary: Speeches, Interviews, and a Letter.* New York: Pathfinder Press.

Cone, James H. 1991. *Martin & Malcolm & America: A Dream or a Nightmare?* Maryknoll, NY: Orbis.

Goldman, Peter. 1979. *The Death and Life of Malcolm X.* 2nd ed. Urbana: University of Illinois Press.

Malcolm X. [1965] 1990. *Malcolm X Speaks: Selected Speeches and Statements.* Ed. George Breitman. New York: Grove.

Malcolm X, with Alex Haley. [1965] 1973. *The Autobiography of Malcolm X.* New York: Ballantine.

Perry, Bruce. 1991. *Malcolm: The Life of a Man Who Changed Black America.* New York: Talman.

James H. Cone

MALINCHISTAS

The term *malinchistas* is used by Mexicans and Mexican-origin populations in the United States to refer to community members who "sell out," adopt the value system of the dominant culture, and implicitly accept the terms of their own subordination. These persons seek to prove themselves as exceptions and embody traits associated with the dominant culture, while they shun those associated with their own. *Malinchismo* may be defined broadly as the pursuit of the novel and foreign, coupled with rejection and betrayal of one's own culture.

This term is linked to the history and myth of a sixteenth-century indigenous woman named Malinalli Tenepali (Malintzin), popularly known as La Malinche or Doña Marina (c. 1502–1527). One of the most legendary figures involved in the conquest of Mexico, La Malinche was of Nahua origin and served as interpreter, guide, and concubine to Hernán Cortés (c. 1484–1547). Knowledge about La Malinche's life before meeting Cortés is derived from the biography that the Spanish soldier Bernal Díaz del Castillo (c. 1495–1584) provides when he recounts La Malinche's reunion in 1524 with her mother and half brother in his *La historia verdadera de la conquista de la Nueva España* (The True History of the Conquest of New Spain, written in 1568, published in 1632). Díaz del Castillo states that La Malinche was a born a Nahua to royal indigenous parents in Tenochtitlán, experienced the death of her father and the remarriage of her mother, and was banished by her mother and enslaved to the Chontal Maya from the coastal area of Tabasco, whose cacique, in turn, gave her to Cortés, along with other virgins for sexual and domestic services, as a welcoming gift. She became Cortés's lover, gave birth to two mestizo sons, and served as an intermediary and translator between Cortés and Moctezuma (c. 1466–1520). She later married a Spanish soldier named Juan Jaramillo, and gave birth to a forgotten mestiza daughter. She died in 1527 at the age of twenty-five.

Many historians consider La Malinche's participation as crucial in enabling Cortés to defeat Moctezuma and topple the Aztec Empire in 1521. La Malinche's abilities in her native Nahuatl and her proficiency in Yucatán dialects proved indispensable to Cortés. La Malinche spoke both Nahuatl (her mother tongue) and other dialects of the Yucatán Peninsula, and, most importantly, she knew the conventions of a register of Nahuatl *tecpilla-tolli* (lordly speech), a difficult and indirect rhetorical style used among the Nahuatl-speaking elite. With these special skills, she was able to negotiate successfully for Cortés and counsel him about the intentions of the people with whom he was dealing.

The concept of *malinchismo* emerged in post-independence nineteenth-century Mexican nationalist historiography and literature. After her representations in Spanish and indigenous sources as a powerful woman commanding respect (for example, Spanish Christian interpretations tend to redeem Doña Marina through accounts of her heroism, religious conversion, and cultural assimilation), Mexicans began to condemn her treacherous role in the conquest of Mexico and focused on her sexuality. The depiction of La Malinche's "willful betrayal" centers on the events leading to the Spanish massacre of the people of Cholula prior to the Spanish occupation of Tenochtitlán in 1519. According to Francisco López de Gómara (c. 1511–1566) in his *La conquista de México* (1552) and Bernal Díaz del Castillo in the *Historia verdadera*, La Malinche was given the opportunity to leave the Spaniards for the protection of the Cholulans, even to the point of entering into marriage with a Cholulan nobleman, but she chose instead to inform Cortés of the Cholulans' plans to ambush the Spaniards. Her role in interrogating Cuauhtémoc (c. 1496–1525), the last ruler of the Aztecs, during his imprisonment and in interpreting his confession prior to execution during Cortés's expedition to Honduras is considered confirmation of her treachery. The acts have been considered acts of free and reprehensible choice. An analogue of La Malinche in African American culture is Uncle Tom from Harriet Beecher Stowe's 1852 antislavery novel, *Uncle Tom's Cabin*. Just as La Malinche has been stereotyped as an indigenous woman that sells out her people to the Spanish conquistadors, Uncle Tom has become the stereotype for an African American who is too eager to please whites. Both La Malinche and Uncle Tom "betray" their respective community of origin.

Numerous nineteenth-century Mexican novels depict La Malinche as Eve, the woman to blame for the fall of the Aztec Empire; the child doomed by birth prophecy; the indigenous woman desiring the white man; the ambitious schemer using men for her own egotistical ends; the whore; and the scapegoat for centuries of Spanish colonization. In the twentieth century, Octavio Paz's (1914–1998) essay "Los hijos de la chingada" (Sons of the Violated One) from his collection *El laberinto de la soledad* (The Labyrinth of Solitude, 1950) depicts La Malinche as *"la chingada"* (the violated one), lover, and mistress. La Malinche's redemption lies in her role as the mother of the first mestizos, though Mexicans remain alienated from their past and suffer as *hijos de la chingada*. In short, *malinchismo* portrays indigenous Mexicans as victims of Spanish aggression facilitated by Malinche's lasciviousness and treachery.

The notion of *malinchismo* is profoundly misogynistic. The elements of *malinchismo* were set in the twentieth century: La Malinche is perceived as cursed at birth, driven by an unbridled sexual appetite, unprincipled in pursuit of her own ends regardless of the incalculable price that others must pay for her actions, and culpable for bloody deeds carried out by Cortés and his soldiers.

La Malinche entered into the United States cultural lexicon under the influence of the Chicano movement of the 1960s and 1970s. During this period, Chicano (male) nationalists labeled Chicana feminists and Chicana lesbians as *malinchistas*. Chicana feminist and lesbian writer Cherríe Moraga engages these negative depictions in her essay "A Long Line of Vendidas" in the collection *Loving in the War Years: Lo que nunca pasó por sus labios* (What Never Passed Her Lips, 1983). Chicano playwright and screenwriter Luis Valdés in his play *Los vendidos* (1967) labeled *vendidos* (sellouts) or *malinchistas* those working-class Chicanos and Chicanas who become middle-class Mexican Americans closely aligned with mainstream, middle-class U.S. Anglo cultural values, while they deny their own Mexican working-class heritage. In the late 1970s and early 1980s, Moraga and other Chicana cultural critics and literary writers, however, began to recast the icon of La Malinche as a positive role model for women. They have sought to convert La Malinche into a woman of empowerment and to provide new liberatory potential for the myth. While La Malinche appears frequently as a traitor and scapegoat from the male point of view, feminists in the late twentieth century reclaimed her tale as that of a woman who played a central role in the Western Hemisphere's formation.

SEE ALSO *Latinos; Uncle Tom*

BIBLIOGRAPHY

Alarcón, Norma. 1989. Traddutora, Traditora: A Paradigmatic Figure of Chicana Feminism. *Cultural Critique* 13: 57–87.

Alcalá, Rita Cano. 2001. From Chingada to Chingona: La Malinche Redefined, or, a Long Line of Hermanas. *Aztlán* 26 (2): 33–61.

Candelaria, Cordelia. 2005. Malinche, La. In *The Oxford Encyclopedia of Latinos and Latinas in the United States*, Vol. 3, eds. Suzanne Oboler and Deena J. González, 48–50. Oxford: Oxford University Press.

Cypess, Sandra Messinger. 1991. *La Malinche in Mexican Literature from History to Myth*. Austin: University of Texas Press.

Day, Stuart A. 2005. La Malinche in the Neoliberal '90s. In *Staging Politics in Mexico: The Road to Neoliberalism*, 122–139. Lewisburg, PA: Bucknell University Press.

Díaz del Castillo, Bernal. [1632] 1963. *The Conquest of New Spain*. Trans. John M. Cohen. New York: Penguin.

Díaz del Castillo, Bernal. [1632] 1974. *Historia verdadera de la conquista de la Nueva España*. Mexico City: Editorial Porrúa.

Gladstein, Mimi R. 2005. Malinche, La. In *Encyclopedia Latina: History, Culture, and Society in the United States*, Vol. 3, eds. Ilán Stavans and Harold Augenbraum, 60–62. Danbury, CT: Grolier Academic Reference.

Glantz, Margo, ed. 1994. *La Malinche, sus padres y sus hijos*. Mexico City: UNAM.

Hassig, Ross. 1998. The Maid of the Myth: La Malinche and the History of Mexico. *Indiana Journal of Hispanic Literature* 12: 101–134.

Karttunen, Frances. 1997. La Malinche and Malinchismo. In *Encyclopedia of Mexico: History, Society, & Culture*, Vol. 2, ed. Michael S. Werner, 775–778. Chicago and London: Fitzroy Dearborn.

López de Gómara, Francisco. [1552] 1987. *La conquista de México*. Madrid: Historia 16.

Moraga, Cherríe. 1983. A Long Line of Vendidas. In *Loving in the War Years: Lo que nunca pasó por sus labios*, 90–144. Boston: South End.

Paz, Octavio. 1961. The Children of La Malinche. In *The Labyrinth of Solitude*. Trans. Lysander Kemp. New York: Grove.

Paz, Octavio. [1950] 1983. Los hijos de la Malinche. In *El laberinto de la soledad*, 59–80. Mexico City: Fondo de Cultura Económica.

Pérez, Emma. 1999. *The Decolonial Imaginary: Writing Chicanas into History*. Bloomington: Indiana University Press.

Pratt, Mary Louise. 1993. "Yo soy la Malinche": Chicana Writers and the Poetics of Ethnonationalism. *Callaloo* 16 (4): 859–873.

Rebolledo, Tey Diana. 1995. *Women Singing in the Snow: A Cultural Analysis of Chicana Literature*. Tucson: University of Arizona Press.

Rebolledo, Tey Diana, and Eliana S. Rivero, eds. 1993. *Infinite Divisions: An Anthology of Chicana Literature*. Tucson: University of Arizona Press.

Mark A. Hernández

MALINOWSKI, BRONISLAW
1884–1942

Bronislaw Kaspar Malinowski is one of the most charismatic personalities in the history of anthropology. Malinowski defined long-term ethnographic fieldwork as the hallmark of social anthropology. His functionalist approach dominated British social anthropology well into the 1950s. He was a powerful promoter of social anthropology as an academic discipline, both by teaching a whole generation of students and by securing research grants through appeal to the usefulness of ethnographic knowledge to projects of development. A European intellectual with wide-ranging interests, Malinowski was gifted at learning languages and was a brilliant writer. Much of today's fascination with Malinowski revolves around the circumstances of his pioneering fieldwork in Melanesia from 1914 to 1918: how he happened to choose his field sites; how he positioned himself toward the "natives," colonial administrators, and academic colleagues; how important the method of participant observation was in relation to other data collection techniques; and how different ethnographic experiences were expressed in different forms of writing.

Born in Krakow, Malinowski first studied physics and philosophy, receiving a doctorate from Jagiellonian University in 1908. His readings during this time were broad, with Friedrich Nietzsche (1844–1900) and the physicist-philosopher Ernst Mach (1838–1916) among his intellectual influences (*Early Writings* [1993]). He spent a further year at Leipzig University studying *Völkerpsychologie* (cultural psychology) with Wilhelm Wundt (1832–1920). In 1910 Malinowski traveled to Britain and started to study ethnology with Edward Westermarck (1862–1939) and Charles Gabriel Seligman (1873–1940) at the London School of Economics. He was to remain attached to the London School of Economics for most of his academic career, becoming a reader in 1923 and a professor in 1927. Just before the outbreak of World War II (1939–1945), Malinowski was on sabbatical in the United States and decided not to return to Europe. He became a professor of anthropology at Yale University in 1942, but died the same year.

Malinowski's writings cover a range of different regions (Australia, Melanesia, Mexico), but his most famous works are ethnographic studies of the Trobriand Islands in the southwest Pacific. In *Argonauts of the Western Pacific* (1922), Malinowski describes the *kula*, a system of ceremonial exchanges between a group of islands. In Malinowski's view, the *kula* is primarily about establishing reciprocal ties, whereas economic gain is only of secondary importance. Magic, religion, and myth are central themes in many of his works. For example, in *Coral Gardens*

(1935), Malinowski analyzes the function of magic spells in Trobriand horticulture. This work also presents most clearly the powers of Malinowski's linguistic approach. *Crime and Custom* (1926) is a pioneering work in legal anthropology. Showing that a society's ideals about proper conduct must be clearly distinguished from everyday reality, Malinowski carves out a distinctly anthropological perspective on law and society. A number of his works are concerned with Trobriand sexuality and family relations (e.g., *Sex and Repression* [1927]) and reflect Malinowski's enduring interest in Sigmund Freud's (1856–1939) psychoanalytic theories. His more theoretical works, such as *A Scientific Theory of Culture* (1944), have not preserved the same appeal as his ethnographies. Some of his wartime writings are devoted to a passionate defense of liberalism (*Freedom and Civilization* [1944]). His posthumously published fieldwork diary (1967) remains controversial because of racist remarks, but has also significantly deepened the understanding of his ethnographic oeuvre.

SEE ALSO *Anthropology, British*

BIBLIOGRAPHY

Malinowski, Bronislaw. 1922. *Argonauts of the Western Pacific: An Account of Native Enterprise and Adventure in the Archipelagoes of Melanesian New Guinea.* London: Routledge.

Malinowski, Bronislaw. 1926. *Crime and Custom in Savage Society.* New York: Harcourt.

Malinowski, Bronislaw. 1927. *Sex and Repression in Savage Society.* New York: Harcourt.

Malinowski, Bronislaw. 1935. *Coral Gardens and Their Magic: A Study of the Methods of Tilling the Soil and of Agricultural Rites in the Trobriand Islands.* 2 vols. London: Allen and Unwin.

Malinowski, Bronislaw. 1944. *A Scientific Theory of Culture and Other Essays.* Chapel Hill: University of North Carolina Press.

Malinowski, Bronislaw. 1944. *Freedom and Civilization.* Ed. A. V. Malinowska. New York: Roy.

Malinowski, Bronislaw. 1967. *A Diary in the Strict Sense of the Term.* Trans. Norbert Guterman. London: Routledge and Kegan Paul.

Malinowski, Bronislaw. 1993. *The Early Writings of Bronislaw Malinowski.* Eds. Robert J. Thornton and Peter Skalnik. Trans. Ludwik Krzyzanowski. Cambridge, U.K.: Cambridge University Press.

Young, Michael. 2004. *Malinowski: Odyssey of an Anthropologist, 1884–1920.* London and New Haven, CT: Yale University Press.

Stefan Ecks

MALNUTRITION

Malnutrition describes the measurable impairment to individual health and well-being resulting from insuffi-cient or unbalanced food intake relative to physiological needs. The term is often compared and contrasted with *hunger*, which refers to the subjective feeling of discomfort caused by lack of food, and *food insecurity*, which describes lack of access to nutritionally adequate food in a socially acceptable manner. Malnutrition usually arises in situations of national or regional *food shortage* (its acute form is *famine*), where geographic regions or nations lack adequate food supply, and *food poverty*, where households lack resources (*entitlements*) to produce or acquire adequate nourishment. But individual *food deprivation* also occurs when national and household availabilities are adequate but distribution is inequitable; in famine situations, some always eat well. *World hunger* is a composite term covering insufficient availability, access, and utilization of food at global, national, household, and individual levels.

The United Nations Food and Agricultural Organization (FAO) and the World Bank, working from national food production and trade statistics along with household income figures relative to the price of a minimum food basket, estimate that some 800 million people in developing countries are food insecure. This is despite aggregate increases in agricultural production and improvements in market infrastructure that, since the 1970s, have made it technically possible to feed everyone a nutritionally adequate basic diet. The largest proportions of food-insecure households and undernourished children exist in South Asia, where endemic poverty is high; numbers are growing also in sub-Saharan Africa, where political instability and HIV-AIDS interfere with food production, marketing, income generation, and intergenerational care.

Within households, pregnant and lactating women, adolescent girls, infants and young (especially weaning-aged) children, and elders are particularly vulnerable to malnutrition where they suffer intrahousehold discrimination in access to food and care relative to their nutritional needs. This vulnerability is further elevated by excessive workloads, infections, malabsorption syndromes, environmental contamination, and insufficient health services. Public health nutritionists study *nutrition over the life cycle*, beginning with gestational nutrition and breast-feeding, to identify these culturally specific age- and gender-related patterns of malnourishment and to institute more effective food and nutrition policies and practices.

Undernutrition includes both protein-energy (protein-calorie) malnutrition and specific micronutrient deficiencies. Manifestations include growth failure in children, underweight and weight loss in adults, extra burdens of disease, and functional impairments to physical activity, work performance, cognitive abilities, reproductive outcomes, and social life. From the 1930s through the late 1960s, nutritionists working with the FAO, the World Health Organization (WHO), and the United Nations University (UNU) made prevention of protein deficiency (the "protein gap") the priority for interventions. In the 1970s emphasis shifted to energy (calories) on the reasoning that if nutritionally deprived children (or adults) could get sufficient quantities of their traditional balanced diet, protein would take care of itself. Increasing food energy also fit the agricultural-intensification agenda of the green revolution that was producing piles of rice, wheat, and to a lesser extent maize in Asia and Latin America but reducing protein-balanced cereal-legume crop mixes. Malnutrition, conceptualized as a factor in longer-term national economic growth and development, also became part of integrated national nutrition and rural development strategies. These strategies were promoted by the World Bank and other foreign-assistance agencies, which launched national maternal-child health and school feeding programs, targeted food subsidies, agricultural diversification and marketing programs as well as income generation and nutrition and health education efforts. *Basic needs* investments in education, health, clean water, and sanitation tried to address poverty alleviation and malnutrition together while contributing to longer-term economic growth.

In the late 1980s and early 1990s priorities and framing shifted yet again, this time to ending "hidden hunger." With UNICEF taking the lead, the World Summit for Children (WSC) in 1990 set goals to reduce—by half—mild to moderate energy-protein malnutrition, which had been implicated in more than half of child deaths in the developing world, and virtual elimination of vitamin A, iodine, and iron deficiencies as public health problems. By this time dietary diversification had practically eliminated beriberi (thiamin deficiency, associated with polished rice diets), pellagra (niacin deficiency, associated with maize), kwashiorkor (protein deficiency, associated with dependence on a starchy tuber or sap), rickets (associated with too little vitamin D and exposure to sunlight), and scurvy (vitamin C deficiency). The WSC initiatives combined nutrient supplementation, food fortification, and food-based strategies as strategies to end vitamin A deficiency blindness and impaired immune response, cretinism and goiter (associated with severe gestational and later deficiencies of iodine), and severe iron deficiency anemias. At the same time the WSC's goal was to correct more moderate deficiencies, which researchers showed could depress physical and intellectual development, work performance, and child survival.

Subsequently the World Food Summit (1996) and the Millennium Development Goals set additional targets and action plans for reducing world hunger numbers and proportions by half, along with their causes, by 2015. In follow-up, nongovernmental organizations (NGOs) and community-based organizations, collaborating with governments and international agencies, increasingly frame approaches in terms of *livelihood security* (income generation, microcredit, female education) and *rights-based development* or *the right to adequate food* (emphasizing government accountability and public-private-community partnerships and participation). NGOs also play a growing role in *humanitarian assistance*, including the SPHERE project, which disseminates principles, minimum technical standards, and best practices for responding to disasters. Although international *famine early warning systems*—and attendant obligations for food aid response—have eliminated most severe malnutrition apart from areas of political instability, active conflict, or oppression, seasonal and chronic malnutrition persist where people lack access to markets and government or international assistance and among those experiencing the immediate economic displacements of globalization. Local and global studies analyzing these contexts of malnutrition suggest that to reduce malnutrition and poverty everywhere, it is necessary to overcome the economic, political, and social exclusion of women by improving women's education, entitlements, livelihoods, and empowerment, especially across South Asia, and providing fairer access to land, water, infrastructure, and terms of trade.

Although conventionally through the 1980s *malnutrition* usually referred to *undernutrition*, caused primarily by poverty and improper diet, there has since been increased attention to overweight, obesity, and nutritional "diseases of civilization," including diabetes, coronary heart disease, and certain cancers associated with unhealthy diets and behaviors. These syndromes are on the rise also in developing countries, which are experiencing dietary transitions away from traditional, balanced local diets based on grains, legumes, oilseeds, and small amounts of animal protein plus fruits and vegetables toward modern, unbalanced, global diets characterized by more processed and "fast" foods that are higher in fats and simple sugars. Nutritionists studying the etiology of malnutrition now find overweight and underweight individuals residing in the same households, as both low- and higher-income people fill up on cheaper, calorie-dense snacks and sugary beverages. Genetically modified foods and corporate control over the global food system are additional contentious issues for the present and future.

SEE ALSO *Disease; Famine; Food; Green Revolution; Needs, Basic; Nutrition; Poverty; Public Health; Undereating; World Bank, The*

BIBLIOGRAPHY

DeRose, Laurie, Ellen Messer, and Sara Millman, eds. 1998. *Who's Hungry? And How Do We Know? Food Shortage, Poverty, and Deprivation.* Tokyo: United Nations University Press.

Food and Agricultural Organization. 2006. State of Food Insecurity in the World. http://www.fao.org/SOF/sofi/.

Runge, C. Ford, Benjamin Senauer, Philip G. Pardey, and Mark W. Rosegrant. 2003. *Ending Hunger in Our Lifetime: Food Security and Globalization*. Baltimore, MD: Johns Hopkins University Press.

World Health Organization. 2007. Global Database on Child Growth and Malnutrition. http://www.who.int/nutgrowthdb/.

Ellen Messer

MALTHUS, THOMAS ROBERT
1766–1834

Malthus is now a word, like *Luther* or *Marx* or *Darwin*, that connotes both much more and much less than the individual to whom it refers. The important social-scientific ideas associated with *Malthus* are:

1. the inevitability of population pressures in human societies,

2. scarcity as the central principle of economic analysis,

3. "spontaneous order" and the futility of political revolution,

4. Poor Laws and "welfare dependency,"

5. the theory of general unemployment, and

6. the struggle for existence.

Thomas Robert Malthus—always known as "Robert" or "Bob," never as "Thomas"—was born in Surrey, England, on February 13, 1766, the younger son of Daniel Malthus (1730–1800), a country gentleman. He died in Bath on December 29, 1834, and is buried in Bath Abbey. Educated first privately, then at Warrington Academy and at Jesus College, Cambridge, he graduated BA as Ninth Wrangler in 1788, residing at Cambridge for a further year to read divinity, then was ordained deacon in June 1789 and priest in 1791. Although elected a fellow of his college in 1793, he served a country curacy at Okewood in Surrey from 1789 until 1803, when he became rector of Walesby in Lincolnshire, relinquished his fellowship, and married. In 1805 Malthus was appointed first professor of history and political economy at the East India College, a position he held until his death. He also retained the benefice of Walesby as a nonresident, appointing a curate.

While still curate of Okewoood, Malthus wrote the book that made him famous: *An Essay on the Principle of Population* (1798). Though greatly enlarged in 1803 and appearing in four further editions during his lifetime, the first *Essay* contains the seeds of all "Malthusian" social-scientific ideas save possibly the theory of general unemployment.

HUMAN POPULATION: THE "RATIOS" AND THE "CHECKS"

The first *Essay* was written to show the unfeasibility of William Godwin's *Political Justice* (1796). Godwin (1756–1836) believed that humans are naturally "benevolent," and that the moral evil we perceive is caused by social institutions, which should therefore be dismantled. But if Godwin's "beautiful system of equality" is fully realized, all property equally divided, and marriage, wage labor, government, and law abolished, the economic and social constraints on procreation are removed and population can grow *geometrically* (exponentially) at first. As fertile land becomes scarce, food needed to support more people cannot be produced at the same rate. Malthus assumes "no limits … to the productions of the earth" (p. 26), but suggests that food can only be made to increase, at the utmost, *arithmetically* (linearly). Hence per capita income must fall. Long before it reaches the "subsistence" (zero population-growth) level, falling real income reawakens "the mighty law of self-preservation": Theft and falsehood undermine the mutual trust on which "benevolence" depends; "self-love resumes his wonted empire and lords it triumphant over the world" (p. 190); and the most able and powerful convene to institute "some immediate measures to be taken for general safety" (p. 195). Property rights reappear, together with sanctions for their violation, requiring the restoration of government. Wage labor is reintroduced to ration scarce food to the landless. Marriage comes back to assign responsibility for the feeding and care of children. Godwin's "beautiful fabric of the imagination vanishes at the severe touch of truth" (p. 189).

Malthus acknowledged that the "principle of population" was not new. That human populations multiply "like mice in a barn" (Cantillon [1755] 2001, p. 37) when unconstrained by resource scarcity was taken for granted by all eighteenth-century social theorists. Malthus's new wrinkle, occasionally hinted at by his predecessors and recognizably formulated by James Anderson in 1777, was an analysis of the effects of population growth with scarce land. When natural resources are limited, human fecundity makes population pressure inevitable. Rational individuals may and often do respond with some variety of the *preventive check*: measures to restrict procreation ranging from "moral restraint" (delay of marriage without "irregular gratification," Malthus's preferred solution) to contraception, as recommended by "neo-Malthusians" such as the young John Stuart Mill (1806–1873), but which

Malthus himself ruled out as un-Christian, and subversive of the work ethic. Failing any or enough of these, the real incomes of some must fall so low that the *positive check* will operate: Population will be arrested by famine, starvation and disease, high infant mortality, and shortened adult lifespan.

SCARCITY AND DIMINISHING RETURNS

Though the economists Richard Cantillon (1680–1734), François Quesnay (1694–1774), Adam Smith (1723–1790), and others were conscious of land scarcity, they did not integrate the concept into their economic analyses. For Smith, the brake upon economic growth was shortage of capital, not of land. Now a capital shortage can always be remedied by the "parsimony" of capitalists, and hence is not a necessary feature of economic analysis. But land scarcity is given by nature and is permanent.

Successive applications of labor and capital to a given supply of land result in ever-diminishing returns: at the extensive margin as lower-quality land is brought into cultivation; and at the intensive margin as each successive unit of the variable factor (labor-plus-capital) has less of the fixed factor (land) to work with. Between 1798 and 1815 the analytical implications of the first *Essay* gradually became clear to Malthus himself and to Robert Torrens (1814–1884), Sir Edward West (1782–1828), and David Ricardo (1772–1823). In the latter year each published papers expounding the so-called "classical" theory of rent: Land is cultivated up to the point at which the diminishing marginal product of labor-plus-capital is equal in value to the competitively determined factor cost; capitalist farmers divide the factor payment into profits and wages; and landlords get a surplus ("rent") equal to the excess value of intramarginal production over total cost of production.

Two years later Ricardo codified all this in his *Principles of Political Economy* (1817). Adam Smith's "chearful" study of the *Wealth of Nations* was replaced by a "dismal science" of scarcity, and "classical political economy" was born. Half a century later, economists in England, Austria, Switzerland, and the United States generalized diminishing returns to construct "neoclassical" production theory. All factors are substitutable, and the contribution of each and every factor is subject to diminishing returns when all other inputs are constant. When the production functions implied by this analysis are confronted with isomorphic utility functions, generalized resource scarcity implies the "budget constraints" of the latter, and economic theory becomes an investigation of constrained maximization by rational agents. The present-day view of economics as the study of the allocation of scarce resources between competing ends is a direct consequence of Malthus's *Essay on Population.*

"SPONTANEOUS ORDER" AND THE FUTILITY OF POLITICAL REVOLUTION

Edmund Burke's *Reflections on the French Revolution* (1790) rested on a view of civilized human societies as dynamically unstable systems. An exogenous dissolution of the social fabric producing anarchy causes society to collapse into a state of "tyranny," from which it can only be dislodged by successful counterrevolutionary action. Godwin's answer to Burke accepted the assumption of instability, but supposed that the effect of anarchy is to launch society upon a growth-path of never-ending progress toward the goal of human perfectibility. Malthus's decisive intervention in the debate undermined both Godwin's argument and Burke's. Anarchy may be morally superior to the status quo as Godwin believed. But the "laws of nature" then operate: first to produce a state of affairs *inferior* to the status quo; and because of this, eventually to restore the system to its original state. Political revolution is therefore costly, futile, and self-reversing.

Malthus's conception of human societies as dynamically *stable* systems is a corollary of the theory of "spontaneous order" attributed by F. A. Hayek to Scottish Enlightenment thinkers, in particular David Hume (1711–1776) and Adam Smith, each of whom Malthus had studied with great care. Things get to be the way they are not because anyone intended and planned the present state; rather, the status quo is the unintended consequence of countless private, self-regarding decisions in the past. It is stable in the sense that those now in a position to effect change prefer things as they are, and have strong incentives to restore equilibrium if it is exogenously disturbed.

This conception is of the highest scientific importance, for Burke's and Godwin's arguments are equally defective. By postulating instability of the status quo they leave unexplained and inexplicable the way society becomes what it is. Malthus's stable equilibrium model is not only central to all subsequent economic analysis: It is an essential feature of all present-day attempts to explain social phenomena as the outcome of rational choice by individuals.

THE POOR LAWS AND "WELFARE DEPENDENCY"

In 1798 and in all subsequent recensions of the *Essay on Population* (1803, 1806, 1807, 1817, 1826), Malthus criticized the Elizabethan Poor Laws then in force in England, first, because they tended to "increase population without increasing the food for its support" (1803, p.

358); and second, because any transfer to the indigent "diminishes the shares that would otherwise belong to the more industrious, and more worthy members" of the working class (1803, p. 358). The "more worthy" are those in whom "a spirit of independence still remains," and the "poor-laws are strongly calculated to eradicate this spirit" by lowering the cost to individuals of "carelessness, and want of frugality," and by weakening the incentive to postpone marriage and procreation (1803, p. 359). Because "dependent poverty ought to be held disgraceful," the poor laws, by removing that stigma, "create the poor which they maintain" (1803, pp. 359, 358). What is now called "welfare dependency" was clearly recognized by Malthus not as moral turpitude among the lower orders but as their rational response to a perverse set of incentives.

The incentives are perverse because it is through the preventive check alone that the working class can obtain higher wages and a larger share of national income. Malthus, following Smith, William Paley (1743–1805), and many others, saw that the "subsistence" wage is a cultural variable. If workers raise their sights and come to expect a higher real income before marrying, the aggregate labor supply will be reduced and the equilibrium real wage increased to match their expectations. In terms of the "classical" theory of rent, factor cost rises and the share of income going to both capitalists and laborers increases at the expense of rents. Welfare dependency, in contrast, reduces both the absolute and the relative income of workers.

THEORY OF GENERAL UNEMPLOYMENT

Like his eighteenth-century predecessors, Malthus saw economic activity as driven by "effectual demand." His *Principles of Political Economy* (1820), written partly to criticize Ricardo's value theory, attempted in chapter 7 to explain the post-1815 depression as a "general glut" in commodity markets. An increase in parsimony by capitalists diverts expenditure from "unproductive" to "productive" labor, thereby increasing the supply of goods while reducing the demand. Therefore, unless landlords and others of "the rich" can increase "unproductive expenditure" (personal services, luxuries, etc.) correspondingly, excess supply will drive down prices and profits, "check for a time further production," and throw labor out of employment (1820, p. 354).

Ricardo, James Mill (1773–1886), Jean-Baptiste Say (1767–1832), and most other contemporaries rejected the possibility of "general gluts" on the grounds that produced goods must count as expendable income for those who own them, therefore "supply creates its own demand." Malthus and Ricardo continued the debate in their celebrated correspondence, but Malthus's formulation was never sufficiently clear to convince the latter, and his theory—shared to some extent by Jean Charles Léonard de Sismondi (1773–1842) and Thomas Chalmers (1780–1847)—was treated by J. S. Mill and most later economists as a regrettable mistake.

John Maynard Keynes (1883–1946), however, was a lifelong admirer of Malthus, whom he called "the first of the Cambridge economists," and he abetted Piero Sraffa (1898–1983) in his recovery and edition of the Ricardo-Malthus correspondence. When in the early 1930s Keynes was beginning to construct his own quite different theory of demand-led aggregate production and employment he was inspired, if not exactly influenced, by Malthus's conscientious though flawed attempt to do justice to the whole of economic reality; and he averred that "the almost total obliteration of Malthus's line of approach and the complete domination of Ricardo's … has been a disaster to the progress of economics" (Keynes 1972, p. 98).

THE "STRUGGLE FOR EXISTENCE"

In October 1838, shortly after returning from the voyage of the *Beagle*, Charles Darwin "read for amusement Malthus's *Population*, and being well prepared to appreciate the struggle for existence … it struck me that under these circumstances favourable variations would tend to be preserved and unfavourable ones to be destroyed [implied in chapter 3 of the *Essay*, where the phrase "struggle for existence" occurs]. Here then I had at last got hold of a theory by which to work" (Darwin 1974, p. 71).

Modern biology is "Malthusian" in two analytically distinct ways. In the short run in which all genes may be taken as given, the science of ecology—a study of the general equilibrium of coexisting species in defined space—generalizes Malthus's partial equilibrium analysis of human populations to explain what J. S. Mill called "the spontaneous order of nature." In the long run in which there is genetic mutation and adaptation of species, the theory of organic evolution generalizes Scottish Enlightenment "conjectural history" central to Malthus's anti-Godwin polemic.

The dominance of scarcity in human affairs is never a welcome message. From the first, Malthus's work has provoked vigorous controversy, ranging from technical and sometimes cogent objections to details of his arguments by fellow economists to outraged vilification by Romantics, Marxists, Christian Socialists and advocates of the welfare state, few of whom seem to have read what Malthus actually wrote.

BIBLIOGRAPHY

PRIMARY WORKS

Malthus, Thomas Robert. [1798] 1966. *An Essay on the Principle of Population as It Affects the Future Improvement of Society, with Remarks on the Speculations of Mr Godwin, M.*

Condorcet, and Other Writers. Facsimile reprint Royal Economic Society. London: Macmillan.

Malthus, Thomas Robert. [1803, 1806, 1807, 1817, and 1826] 1989a. *An Essay on the Principle of Population; or A View of Its Past and Present Effects on Human Happiness; with an Inquiry into Our Prospects Respecting the Future Removal or Mitigation of the Evils Which It Occasions.* 2 vols. Ed. Patricia James. Cambridge, U.K.: Cambridge University Press for the Royal Economic Society.

Malthus, Thomas Robert. [1820, 1836] 1989b. *Principles of Political Economy, Considered with a View to Their Practical Application.* 2 vols. Ed. John Pullen. Cambridge, U.K.: Cambridge University Press for the Royal Economic Society.

Malthus, Thomas Robert. 1986. *The Works of Thomas Robert Malthus.* 8 vols. Ed. E. A. Wrigley and David Souden. London: Pickering and Chatto.

SECONDARY WORKS

Anderson, James. 1777. *An Inquiry into the Nature of the Corn Laws, with a View to the Corn Bill Proposed for Scotland.* Edinburgh, U.K.: Mundell.

Burke, Edmund. [1790] 2003. *Reflections on the Revolution in France and on the Proceedings in Certain Societies in London Relative to that Event.* Ed. Frank M. Turner. New Haven, CT: Yale University Press.

Cantillon, Richard. [1755] 2001. *Essay on the Nature of Commerce in General.* Trans. Henry Higgs, with a new introduction by Anthony Brewer. New Brunswick NJ: Transaction Publishers.

Darwin, Charles, and Thomas Henry Huxley. 1974. *Autobiographies.* Ed. Gavin de Beer. London: Oxford University Press.

Godwin, William. [1793, 1796, 1798] 1946. *Enquiry Concerning Political Justice and Its Influence on Morals and Happiness.* 3rd ed. 2 vols. Photographic facsimile, ed. F. E. L. Priestley. Toronto: University of Toronto Press.

Hollander, Samuel. 1997. *The Economics of Thomas Robert Malthus.* Toronto: University of Toronto Press.

James, Patricia. 1979. *Population Malthus: His Life and Times.* London: Routledge.

Keynes, John Maynard. [1933] 1972. Thomas Robert Malthus: The First of the Cambridge Economists. In *The Collected Writings of John Maynard Keynes*, vol. 10. London: Macmillan for the Royal Economic Society.

Ricardo, David. [1817] 1951. *On the Principles of Political Economy and Taxation.* Volume 1 of *The Works and Correspondence of David Ricardo.* Ed. Piero Sraffa. Cambridge, U.K.: Cambridge University Press.

Waterman, Anthony M. C. 1991. *Revolution, Economics, and Religion: Christian Political Economy, 1798–1833.* Cambridge, U.K.: Cambridge University Press.

Waterman, Anthony M. C. 1998. Reappraisal of "Malthus the Economist," 1933–1997. *History of Political Economy* 30 (2): 293–324.

Winch, Donald. 1987. *Malthus.* Oxford: Oxford University Press.

Winch, Donald. 1996. *Riches and Poverty: An Intellectual History of Political Economy in Britain, 1750–1834.* Cambridge, U.K.: Cambridge University Press.

Anthony M. C. Waterman

MALTHUSIAN TRAP

The Reverend Thomas Robert Malthus was born in Surrey in 1766 and died in 1834. He was the son of a clergyman and one of eight children. Malthus was educated at Jesus College, Cambridge, and later became a professor of history and political economy at the East India Company's College at Haileybury in Hertfordshire. His most famous work, the *Essay on the Principles of Population*, was published in 1798 when he was thirty-two. It has been interpreted partly as a reaction to the utopian thought of William Godwin (1756–1836) and others, as well as that of Malthus's own father. It is an extension and formalization of the work of the classical economist Adam Smith (1723–1790) and others who had laid down some of the basic ideas concerning the tendency of population to outstrip resources.

Malthus's theory, in brief, was that humankind is permanently trapped by the intersection of two "laws." The first law concerned the rate at which populations can grow. He took the "passion between the sexes" to be constant, and investigations showed that under conditions of "natural" fertility (with early marriage and no contraception, abortion, or infanticide), this would lead to an average of about fifteen live births per woman. This figure is confirmed by modern demography. Given normal mortality at the time, and taking a less than maximum fertility, this will lead to what Malthus called *geometrical growth* of one, two, four, eight, sixteen, and so on. Only thirty-two such doublings are needed to lead from one original couple to a world population of over six billion persons.

The second premise was that food and other resource production will grow much more slowly. It might double for a generation or two, but could not keep on doubling within an agrarian economy. Thus there could, in the long run, only be an arithmetical or linear growth of the order of one, two, three, four. Incorporated into this later theory was the law of diminishing marginal returns on the further input of resources, especially labor. Underpinning the scheme was the assumption that there was a finite amount of energy available for humans through the conversion of the sun's energy by living plants and animals. The conclusion was that humankind was *trapped*, a particular application in the field of demography of the more general pessimism of Adam Smith. Populations would grow rapidly for a few generations, and then be savagely cut back. A crisis would occur, manifesting itself in one (or a combination) of what Malthus called the three "positive" checks acting on the death rate: war, famine, and disease.

After the publication of this theoretical account of the "laws" of the trap, Malthus undertook a great deal of empirical research, traveling through Europe and reading widely in history and anthropology. On the basis of this research, he published what is termed the second edition of *The Principles* (1803) but which is, in effect, a very different book. Basically, Malthus turned his laws of population into tendencies, likelihoods, or probabilities, to which there were exceptions. The trap became avoidable, for he had discovered in England itself, as well as in Switzerland and Norway, that there were what he called "preventive checks" that could act to suppress fertility to a level that would be in line with resource growth. He divided these checks into "moral restraint" (celibacy and delayed marriage) and "vice" (contraception of all kinds, abortion, and infanticide), of which he disapproved.

Malthus believed that the only force strong enough to overcome the biological drive to mate was a set of desires created in societies and cultures where people were affluent, unequal, and ambitious for social status, and thus willing to forgo the delights of large families for other goals. A mixture of human avarice and human reason could lead people to avoid the Malthusian trap.

Malthus's work was hugely influential at the practical level. He contributed to the discussion of the reform of England's Poor Law and to the ideas of how to run the British Empire, many of whose administrators he taught at the East India Company's College. He is also the only social scientist who has had a revolutionary effect in the biological sciences. His idea that humans normally suffer from very high mortality rates, that war, famine, and disease periodically cut swathes through historical populations, was seminal. Entirely independently, both Charles Darwin (1809–1882) and Alfred Russel Wallace (1823–1913) described how reading Malthus's *Principles* provided them with the key to unlock the secret of human evolution, that is, the principle of the survival of the fittest, random variation, and selective retention.

There have been a number of criticisms of the Malthusian framework. His predictions were not fulfilled, at least in the middle term. Malthus wrote before the huge resources of energy locked up in coal and then oil became widely available for human use. For a while, from the middle of the nineteenth century, it looked as if the Malthusian trap was no longer operative. A combination of science (in particular chemistry) and new resources had made it possible to more than double production in each generation. First England, then parts of Europe, Japan, and elsewhere, escaped from the trap. It appeared that Malthus's laws could be inverted: population grew slowly, resources exponentially.

Ester Boserup (1981) and others have suggested that Malthus mistook cause for effect. It is argued that human ingenuity will find solutions to population pressure and indeed that growth of population is one of the necessary spurs to technical innovation and the development of civilizations. For example, the transformations from tribal to settled peasant civilizations, and then from peasantries to advanced industrial societies, were propelled and made possible by the growth of population.

At a more abstract level, thinkers on the Far Left, such as Chinese Communist leader Mao Zedong (1893–1976), argued that Malthusianism was merely a capitalist philosophy, and that under communism, populations would automatically stabilize at the right level. This view is inverted and reflected by a number of Catholic writers who argue that since God has planned our lives, and since all forms of contraception are immoral, there is no need to worry about the so-called laws of population. There is no trap.

Others point out that there is no simple correlation between rapid population growth and economic advance. For example, since the mid-twentieth century, India has become richer and less famine-prone as its population has grown, while a number of sparsely populated areas in the Horn of Africa have suffered from the Malthusian trap. So there are clearly many intermediary variables.

Yet it is too early to forget Malthus, as the Chinese decided after a generation of the Communist experiment. In the early twenty-first century, as resources reach their limits and the external costs of the massive use of carbon energy become apparent in pollution and global warming, it appears that the ghost of Malthus has arisen again. Likewise, as we realize the ability of microorganisms to outpace human medicine, our ability to overcome disease in an increasingly crowded world seems at risk. Finally, the tensions that lead to war are further aggravated by shortages and crowding.

Malthus's realistic message that we can postpone the crises of war, famine, and disease but that they will almost certainly strike again in a much more serious way within an increased total population, again makes sense. His advice, that only by stabilizing and probably reducing total population levels through the rational control of fertility, seems ever more salutary. Like all traps, the Malthusian trap can be avoided. Yet it can only be circumvented if people remain constantly aware of its nature as specified by the lucid first theoretical exponent of the biological limits imposed by human nature and the physical world.

SEE ALSO *Malthus, Thomas Robert; Population Growth; Population Studies*

BIBLIOGRAPHY

Boserup, Ester. 1981. *Population and Technology.* Oxford: Blackwell.

James, Patricia. 1979. *Population Malthus: His Life and Times.* London: Routledge and Kegan Paul.

Macfarlane, Alan. 1997. *The Savage Wars of Peace: England, Japan, and the Malthusian Trap.* Oxford: Blackwell.

Malthus, Thomas. [1798] 1982. *An Essay on the Principle of Population.* London: Penguin.

Petersen, William. 1979. *Malthus.* Cambridge, MA: Harvard University Press.

Alan Macfarlane

MANAGEMENT

Management is a set of functions and tasks performed by individuals and groups for the purpose of enabling an organization to achieve its objectives. From one perspective, management consists of planning, organizing, staffing, directing, and controlling (Koontz and O'Donnell 1982). From another perspective, management is distinguishable from, yet operates in tandem with, leadership, which consists of envisioning, enabling, and energizing functions and tasks (Nadler and Tushman 1990). In short, leaders formulate organizational strategy, set direction, mobilize resources, and motivate people to perform, whereas managers execute organizational strategy by clarifying expected behavior, instituting measurements, and administering rewards and punishments (Kotter 1990).

The distinction between management and leadership is relatively new, largely because for much of the twentieth century the majority of industries in the United States and other nations were characterized by oligopoly (a few firms possess concentrated market power) or monopoly (one firm possesses sole market power). When a firm—an organization—possesses market power, it does not need much in the way of leadership because customers have little or no choice in terms of alternative products or services and because there are few or no rival firms that pose competitive threats. In such circumstances a firm needs only management to ensure that organizational objectives will be met.

Irrespective of the competitive structure of particular industries, traditionally managers and leaders of business (and nonbusiness) enterprises have maximized the objectives of those enterprises. Such maximizing behavior is consistent with the utility maximization principle that underlies both classical and neoclassical microeconomics (Marshall 1923) and with the optimization principle that is at the core of management science (Starr and Miller

1960). But when it comes to management, there is a plethora of concepts, evidence, and experience that indicates that management settles for second- or even third-best when it comes to organizational performance (Simon 1947). An especially influential example in this regard is the work of Frederick W. Taylor (1911), the father of scientific management, who early in the twentieth century showed that management consistently and systematically underperformed. Applying the principles of industrial engineering to the design of work, Taylor demonstrated how most jobs could be reconstructed to enhance productivity with no change in the quantity or mix of factors of production—land, capital, and especially labor. Taylor's work ultimately led to the development and widespread adoption of motion time management (MTM), or time study, whereby jobs were reengineered to maximize efficiency and standard times were set for workers to perform those jobs, with consequent pay rewards if workers overperformed and pay penalties if workers underperformed.

Taylor's conception of management was a single-minded one in which supervisors (and, by inference, managers) did the thinking and issued orders with which workers would presumably comply. But workers proved to be far more independent-minded, even obstreperous, than Taylor envisioned, and they often banded together to attempt to influence and change their terms and conditions of employment. A prime example of this was the industrial union movement of the 1930s, during which workers from a wide variety of companies sought official recognition in order to negotiate collective bargaining agreements with the managements of those companies. That these efforts were strongly resisted by company management is readily evident from historical accounts of labor violence during this period (Rayback 1966).

Ironically, the scientific management movement was followed by, and in significant respects supplanted by, the "human relations" movement, which was founded on the principle that workers are social beings rather than only or even primarily economic beings. The well-known work of Elton Mayo (1933) and his colleagues, which was conducted at the Hawthorne Works of the Bell Telephone System, showed that workers' job performance could be greatly enhanced if management paid close attention to workers' social needs rather than merely to their economic needs (Roethlisberger and Dickson 1939). This research was instrumental to the adoption by many companies of employee counseling and industrial welfare programs aimed at addressing workers' noneconomic needs. Yet at the same time companies strongly and in some cases militantly opposed workers' efforts to form independent unions and bargain collectively with their employers. Responding to these developments during the Great Depression, the U.S. Congress in 1935 passed the landmark National Labor Relations Act (NLRA), establishing unionization and collective bargaining as labor policy for the private sector—a policy that was ultimately upheld by the U.S. Supreme Court.

As management thought and practice continued to evolve, more attention was paid to *external* and *internal alignment*. External alignment refers to the relationship of an enterprise to its external environment and involves the scanning of economic, political, legal, and social developments, the analysis of competitive opportunities and threats, the positioning of the enterprise in its particular sector or industry, and ultimately the formulation of a business strategy and specification of strategic objectives. Internal alignment refers to the linkages among and balancing of elements such as organization structure, reward systems, decision-making processes, human-capital skills and capabilities, and organization culture, all of which are key to the implementation of business strategy.

Each of these external and internal alignment dimensions is the province of specialized academic research; a leading example is Alfred Chandler's work on organizational structure. Chandler (1962) postulated that an organization's structure was fundamentally shaped by the organization's strategy, which meant (among other things) that there is no one ideal organization structure for all enterprises. Based on this reasoning, a classical functional structure aligned well with certain businesses' strategies, whereas product-based, geographical-based, and matrix structures aligned well with other businesses' strategies. From this work there developed a more robust contingency model of organizational structure, and similar contingency models were applied to other elements of internal organizational alignment. The main insight or message of such contingency models is that there is no one best way to operate a business in any of its key dimensions.

As the competitive advantage of business enterprises has come to lie more with human or intellectual assets (capital) than with physical assets (capital), much attention has been devoted to the management of human resources for competitive advantage. In this regard there is considerable empirical evidence that decentralized organizational structures and decision making together with team-based work lead to superior performance compared to hierarchical organization structures, centralized decision making, and individual-based work. In particular the notion that competitive advantage can be achieved through the "high-involvement" management of people has taken hold quite firmly in management circles (Pfeffer 1994); from this perspective, employees are managed as assets. But it is also the case that competitive advantage can be achieved through "low-involvement" management of people, most especially through outsourcing and short-term employment contracting, in which employees are managed as labor expense to be controlled (Lewin 2001).

Both types of human-resource management practices can lead to positive economic returns to a business enterprise.

Finally, much attention has been devoted to the types of incentives systems that best harmonize the interests of business owners and employees, including management employees. The underlying concern, captured by the notion of agency theory, is that management and employees are agents of the principals or owners of a business and as such seek to maximize their own interests rather than those of the principals or owners (Jensen and Meckling 1976). To combat this problem, incentive systems that tie at least some of the pay of managers and employees to the performance of the business have been widely advocated. Such incentives include profit-sharing, bonuses, gain-sharing, productivity-sharing, commissions, stock ownership, and stock-option plans (Lewin and Mitchell 1995). What these plans have in common is that they pay off when a business does well and do not pay off when a business does poorly, which is analogous to what happens to the owners of a business, including shareholders.

SEE ALSO *Business; Competition; Corporations; Labor; Leadership; Management Science; Marshall, Alfred; Maximization; Organization Theory; Organizations; Principal-Agent Models; Profits; Simon, Herbert A.; Taylorism*

BIBLIOGRAPHY

Chandler, Alfred D. 1962. *Strategy and Structure.* Cambridge, MA: MIT Press.

Jensen, Michael, and William Meckling. 1976. Theory of the Firm: Managerial Behavior, Agency Costs, and Ownership Structure. *Journal of Financial Economics* 3: 305–360.

Koontz, Harold, and Cyril O'Donnell. 1982. *Essentials of Management.* 3rd ed. New York: McGraw-Hill.

Kotter, John P. 1990. What Leaders Really Do. *Harvard Business Review* 68 (3): 103–111.

Lewin, David. 2001. Low Involvement Work Practices and Business Performance. Paper presented at the Fifty-third Annual Meeting, Industrial Relations Research Association. Champaign, IL.

Lewin, David, and Daniel J. B. Mitchell. 1995. *Human Resource Management: An Economic Perspective.* 2nd ed. Cincinnati, OH: South-Western.

Marshall, Alfred P. 1923. *Principles of Economics.* 8th ed. London: Macmillan.

Mayo, Elton. 1933. *The Human Problems of an Industrial Civilization.* New York: Macmillan.

Nadler, David A., and Michael L. Tushman. 1990. Beyond Charismatic Leaders: Leadership and Organization Change. *California Management Review* 32 (1): 77–90.

Pfeffer, Jeffrey. 1994. *Competitive Advantage through People.* Boston: Harvard Business School Press.

Rayback, Joseph G. 1960. *A History of American Labor.* New York: Free Press.

Roethlisberger, Fritz W., and W. J. Dickson. 1939. *Management and the Worker.* Cambridge, MA: Harvard University Press.

Simon, Herbert A. 1947. *Administrative Behavior.* New York: Free Press.

Starr, Martin K., and David W. Miller. 1960. *Executive Decisions and Operations Research.* New York: Prentice Hall.

Taylor, Frederick W. 1911. *The Principles of Scientific Management.* New York: Harper and Brothers.

David Lewin

MANAGEMENT SCIENCE

Management science is the experimental study and systematic application of a coordinated process for reaching individual and collective goals by working with and through human and nonhuman resources to continually improve value added to the world.

In historical non-Western civilizations, management topics were addressed by Egyptian pharaohs, Chinese mandarins, pre-Hispanic American chiefs, and Arabic scholars like Ibn Khaldun (1332–1406). However, in Western civilization after the Protestant Reformation, worldly prosperity achieved through hard work in this life became a sign of divine approval, and individuals became motivated to exercise self-discipline at work to earn eternal salvation. Adam Smith (1723–1790) provided the economic rationale for free trade and capitalism to increase individual, group, and national wealth—while critiquing the effects of the division of labor. During the Industrial Revolution, the technological development of steam power, railroad transportation, enormous factories, and production changes required new management skills to rapidly handle large flows of material, people, and information over great distances.

Frederick W. Taylor (1856–1915) was the first to develop a science of the management of others' work for controlled adaptation of labor to the needs of financial capital in his 1911 work, *The Principles of Scientific Management.* His model was the machine with its cheap, interchangeable parts, each of which does one specific function. Taylor attempted to do to complex organizations what engineers had done to machines, and this involved making individuals into the equivalent of machine parts. Just as machine parts were easily interchangeable, cheap, and passive, so too should the human parts be the same in the machine model of organizations.

This approach involved breaking down each task to its smallest unit to figure out the one best way to do each job. Then the engineer, after analyzing the job, would teach it to the worker and make sure the worker performed only those motions essential to the task. Taylor attempted to control each element of work and to limit human behavioral variability in order to increase productivity.

The results were profound. Productivity under *Taylorism* went up dramatically. New departments, such as industrial engineering, personnel, and quality control, arose. There was also growth in middle management as there evolved a separation of planning from operations. Rational rules replaced trial and error; management became formalized and effectiveness increased. Henry Ford (1863–1947) successfully applied scientific management processes in the mass production of inexpensive automobiles using the assembly line. He reduced car assembly time from 728 hours to 93 minutes and increased market share by 40 percent.

Of course, scientific management did not come about without criticism. First, the old-line managers resisted the notion that management was a science to be studied, not a status that was conferred at birth or by inheritance or acquired through an intimidating physical presence or force of personality. Second, many workers resisted the dehumanization of their work due to managerial overcontrol of the labor process in a way that ignored workers' conceptual and craft skills and deprived them of discretionary time-motion options and work design input. The industrial engineer with a clipboard and a stopwatch, standing over workers to control their task motions and work pace, became a hated figure and led to group resistance.

To counter and complement Taylor's emphasis on external control of labor, three major approaches have developed over the years, focusing on the following managerial emphases: internal flexibility, internal control, and external flexibility.

First, with respect to emphasizing the internal flexibility of managers, the human relations approach, based on the experiments of Fritz J. Roethlisberger (1898–1974) and William J. Dickson (1904–1989) described in *Management and the Worker* (1939), demonstrated that work is not merely a mechanical, physical act but an expression of multiple psychosocial needs requiring managerial flexibility. When managers give special attention to employees, productivity is likely to improve regardless of whether working conditions improve—the Hawthorne effect. In *The Functions of the Executive* (1938), Chester I. Barnard (1886–1961) reinforced this view of the organization as a social system requiring employee cooperation and acceptance of workplace authority. Kurt Lewin (1890–1947), in *Frontiers in Group Dynamics* (1946), further demonstrated that human work systems could not be understood—much less improved—without factoring in the social-psychological impact of group dynamics in decision making and work performance.

Second, with respect to emphasizing the internal control of managers, Max Weber (1864–1920) maintained that efficient, impersonal coordination of standardized procedures by means of a hierarchy of formal authorities to ensure bureaucratic internal control of labor was the prototypical new role for managers in any organization. Herbert A. Simon (1916–2001) further demonstrated, in *The New Science of Management Decision* (1960), that the internal organization of firms was the result of decisions made by managers facing uncertainty about the future and costs in acquiring information in the present. Under decision theory, Simon claimed that managers have only "bounded rationality" and are forced to make decisions not by "maximizing" but by "satisficing," that is, setting an aspiration level that, if achieved, they will be happy enough with. If the aspiration level is not achieved, managers will try to change either their aspiration level or their decision to internally control labor.

Third, with respect to emphasizing external flexibility, Paul Lawrence and Jay Lorsch, in *Organization and Environment* (1968), maintained that the context of fast-paced uncertainty and global risks required modern managers to creatively adapt and acquire external resources to thrive. They argued that a rapidly changing external environment demanded a dynamic, open-systems approach to management with an organizational feedback structure more like an "adhocracy" than a bureaucracy. One of the first contingency theorists, Fred E. Fiedler, in *Leader Attitudes and Group Effectiveness* (1958), argued that managerial performance depended (was contingent) upon the manager's match with three situational factors: leader-member relations, task structure, and position power.

In summary, the four major approaches to management compete and complement each other, requiring both control and flexibility to demonstrate managerial excellence.

SEE ALSO *Labor; Management; Taylorism*

BIBLIOGRAPHY

Barnard, Chester I. 1938. *The Functions of the Executive.* Cambridge, MA: Harvard University Press.

Fayol, Henri. [1916] 1949. *General and Industrial Management.* Trans. Constance Storrs. London: Pittman.

Fiedler, Fred E. 1958. *Leader Attitudes and Group Effectiveness.* Urbana: University of Illinois Press.

Lawrence, Paul, and Jay Lorsch. 1967. *Organization and Environment: Managing Differentiation and Integration.* Cambridge, MA: Harvard University Press.

Lewin, Kurt. 1947. Frontiers in Group Dynamics. *Human Relations* 1 (2): 143–153.

Mayo, Elton. 1933. *The Human Problems of an Industrial Civilization.* New York: Macmillan.

Roethlisberger, Fritz J., and William J. Dickson. 1939. *Management and the Worker: An Account of a Research Program Conducted by the Western Electric Company, Hawthorne Works, Chicago.* Cambridge, MA: Harvard University Press.

Simon, Herbert Alexander. 1960. *The New Science of Management Decision.* New York: Harper.

Taylor, Frederick. 1911. *The Principles of Scientific Management.* New York: Harper.

Weber, Max. 1946. *From Max Weber: Essays in Sociology.* Trans. and eds. H. H. Gerth and C. Wright Mills. New York: Oxford University Press.

Joseph A. Petrick

MANAGERIAL CLASS

The idea of a distinct managerial class with interests that diverge from those of both the capitalist class and the working class is associated with three broad theoretical agendas in the social sciences: (1) the explication of the historical and sociological significance of the rise to power of a layer of intellectuals and state bureaucrats in socialist (communist) countries ostensibly committed to achieving a "classless society"; (2) the analysis of a putative separation of ownership and control within the modern capitalist corporation; and (3) the attempt to delimit and more rigorously define a "middle class" occupying a mediating position between capital and wage labor in advanced capitalist societies. The concept is closely associated with the notion of a rising "new class" of technocrats and intellectuals whose class project is to subordinate modern society to the rules of bureaucratic rationality and the imperatives of science and technology. It is also linked to the idea of a "managerial revolution," which has rendered obsolete the Marxist theory of the centrality of the capital-labor struggle to the social dynamics of modern or postmodern societies.

Speculation regarding the global ascendancy of a "new" managerial class reached its high point during the early to middle phases of the cold war, finding expression in the thesis that modern, industrialized societies, whether nominally socialist or capitalist, were "converging" toward a unitary (technocratic) model of social and economic organization, one dominated by the requirements of efficiency, productivity, and social responsibility. According to this convergence thesis, the movement of Western capitalist societies toward greater government intervention in the economy and the expansion of the welfare state was no less inexorable than the economic and political liberalization and eventual democratization of the Soviet-bloc countries. In East and West alike, these processes would be guided by an increasingly self-conscious class of technocrats and intellectuals seeking a middle ground between the freewheeling, individualistic capitalism of a bygone era and the stultifying authoritarianism of "actually-existing socialism."

The demise of "real socialism" in Eastern Europe and the Soviet Union in the 1990s and the growing influence in the capitalist West of neoliberal policies and ideological nostrums following the profitability crises of the 1970s called into question the continuing theoretical salience of the idea that capitalists and wage workers alike were being eclipsed by a rising new class of "managerial experts." Indeed, it is arguable that these developments have combined to reduce significantly the influence and relative weight of managerial and technocratic strata in the post-Soviet era, encouraging the revival of a more traditional capitalism, one that "can—and must—manage with a substantially smaller buffer between capital and labour than it did during the more economically prosperous, but also more politically perilous, days of the Cold War" (Smith 1997).

THE MANAGERIAL REVOLUTION

In *The Modern Corporation and Private Property* (1932), Berle and Means sounded an early alarm concerning the centralization of economic power in the hands of large-scale corporations and the usurpation of power within them by a class of professional managers whom they saw as increasingly unaccountable to shareholders and the general public alike. The immediate impact of this thesis in the crisis-ridden 1930s was to encourage the notion of a "managerial revolution" among many socialist intellectuals disillusioned by the experience of Stalinism in the Soviet Union. This idea found inchoate expression in Lewis Corey's *The Crisis of the Middle Class* (1935) and a more fully blown elaboration in Bruno Rizzi's *The Bureaucratization of the World* (1939) and especially James Burnham's *The Managerial Revolution* (1941). Theorists of a managerial revolution argued that capitalism was in the process of being replaced, not by working-class socialism, as Marx had anticipated, but by a new "collectivist" social formation ruled by a new class of bureaucrats and technocrats.

The Berle-Means thesis of a "separation of ownership from control" was to be given a decidedly positive inflection by many institutional economists and sociologists in the postwar era (notably Talcott Parsons, Neil Smelser, Ralf Dahrendorf, Daniel Bell, and John Kenneth Galbraith) who saw this separation as conducive to an attenuation of conflict between socially irresponsible capitalists and socialist-minded workers, as well as to the tri-umph of meritocratic, democratic, and technocratic principles over the prerogatives of property ownership.

MARXISM, THE MIDDLE CLASS, AND THE IDEA OF A MANAGERIAL CLASS

The revival of interest in Marxist class theory and socialist politics in the 1960s and 1970s brought to the fore a new set of concerns pertaining to the character and role of the professional, managerial, and other "middle" strata of the advanced capitalist countries. In Europe, in particular, concrete questions of socialist political strategy compelled many left-wing intellectuals to confront the issue of the numerical decline of the industrial working class and the class position of new layers of waged and salaried employees in corporate bureaucracies, service industries, and state apparatuses.

The specifically professional or managerial elements of these new strata were often seen as belonging to a "new middle class." Reprising in some ways the earlier ideas of Corey and Burnham, Alvin Gouldner (1979) suggested that a "New Class" of technical intelligentsia was arising in the bureaucratic organizations of such societies; but unlike the earlier theorists of "managerial revolution," he saw this class as in conflict with other bureaucratic elements and as comprising nonmanagerial intellectuals as well. For Gouldner, New Class intellectuals had come to monopolize the "culture of critical discourse," emerging as a somewhat flawed "universal class" with its own specific project of social reconstruction and domination.

Most Marxists, however, denied that the new middle class of unproductive but "socially reproductive" salaried workers possessed a determinate set of homogeneous interests or was capable of articulating a coherent class project distinct from the bourgeoisie and the working class. In one influential and controversial formulation proposed by Barbara and John Ehrenreich (1978), such elements constituted a "Professional-Managerial Class … consisting of salaried mental workers who do not own the means of production and whose major function in the social division of labor may be described broadly as the reproduction of capitalist culture and capitalist social relations." But this class was seen as extremely diverse, and the Ehrenreichs did not regard it as a truly independent factor in the class dynamics of modern capitalist or post-capitalist societies. Other Marxists denied that the professional and managerial strata constituted a class at all, insisting instead that they occupied "contradictory locations" within class relations (as in the formulation by Erik Olin Wright). It was commonly assumed that in the course of class struggle between capital and labor, this new middle class would tend to polarize in terms of their allegiances to the more fundamental social classes defining capitalist society.

Marxist theorists of this persuasion also typically denied that the ruling bureaucratic oligarchies within the communist states constituted a new managerial ruling class, regarding them either as remnants of the old class society within social formations in transition to classless communism or as a "state capitalist" ruling class. Many reasserted the thesis of Russian revolutionary leader Leon Trotsky in *The Revolution Betrayed* (1936) that the Stalinist oligarchy was a brittle and dysfunctional stratum lacking the attributes of a fully formed social class and destined to fragmentation as the Soviet Union either moved forward to socialism (through an international extension of the socialist revolution) or backward to capitalism (the inevitable result of a too-prolonged isolation of the Soviet "workers state" from the international division of labor).

THE FUTURE OF THE CONCEPT

The idea of an ascendant managerial class capable of exercising a class hegemony over advanced, industrialized societies lost favor in the new era of corporate downsizing, neoliberalism and capitalist globalization that opened in the 1980s. Nevertheless, the role of intellectual, managerial, and technocratic elements in assuring the continuous reproduction of capitalist culture and social relations remains a vital one. In particular, since the advent of Frederick Taylor's project of "scientific management," capital has been reliant on a special stratum of salaried "hired guns" to safeguard its interests against the demands and struggles of the wage-earning class. However, with the shift of radical social analysis from capital-labor relations to "identity politics," increasing attention has been devoted to the persistent obstacles to entry into the intellectual elites and upper management experienced by women, racial minorities, and others designated as "undesirables" (see, for example, Darity 1996). The intersections of class, race, and gender provide a rich new field of inquiry for a concept that has proven to be both resilient and acutely susceptible to the vagaries of ideological fashion.

SEE ALSO *Bureaucracy; Capitalism; Class; Class Conflict; Class Consciousness; Culture; Hierarchy; Institutionalism; Knowledge Society; Managerial Society; Marxism; Middle Class; New Class, The; Oligarchy; Parsons, Talcott; Socialism; Stalinism; Stratification; Trotsky, Leon; Union of Soviet Socialist Republics*

BIBLIOGRAPHY

Darity, William, Jr. 1996. The Undesirables, America's Underclass in the Managerial Age: Beyond the Myrdal Theory of Racial Inequality. In *An American Dilemma Revisited: Race Relations in a Changing World*, ed. Obie Clayton Jr., 112–137. New York: Russell Sage Foundation.

Ehrenreich, Barbara, and John Ehrenreich. 1978. The Professional-Managerial Class. In *Between Labor and Capital*, ed. Pat Walker, 5–45. Montreal: Black Rose Books.

Gouldner, Alvin W. 1979. *The Future of Intellectuals and the Rise of the New Class*. New York: Seabury.

Smith, Murray E. G. 1997. Rethinking the "Middle Class": Ideological Constructions and Contradictory Structural Locations. *Brock Review* 6 (1/2): 56–73.

Zeitlin, Maurice. 1974. Corporate Ownership and Control: The Large Corporation and the Capitalist Class. *American Journal of Sociology* 79 (5): 1073–1119.

Murray Smith

MANAGERIAL SOCIETY

SEE *Managerial Class.*

MANDEL, ERNEST
1923–1995

Ernest Mandel, a professor at the Free University of Brussels, was a renowned Marxist scholar and one of the best-known Trotskyists of the second half of the twentieth century. In the 1960s he emerged as a leading figure of one of several organizational contenders to the mantle of the Fourth International, the "world party" founded by the exiled Russian communist leader Leon Trotsky in 1938 with the dual aim of overthrowing world capitalism and combating the Stalinist "bureaucratic degeneration" of Russia's socialist revolution of 1917.

Mandel's commitment to achieving a worldwide socialist democracy profoundly influenced all aspects of his scholarship. He wrote some thirty books and about two thousand articles, including such major works as *Marxist Economic Theory* (1968), *From Stalinism to Eurocommunism* (1978), *Late Capitalism* (1975), *Trotsky as Alternative* (1995), and *Power and Money: A Marxist Theory of Bureaucracy* (1992).

Mandel's economic works were centrally concerned with demonstrating the continuing relevance of Karl Marx's critical analysis of the capitalist mode of production to both the postwar boom of the 1950s and 1960s and to the subsequent period of stagflation and declining profitability that had begun in the early 1970s. In *Late Capitalism*, he sought to show how the inexorable laws of motion of advanced capitalism must eventually result in severe economic crises, which in turn would give a major impetus to the global class struggle between capital and labor. While advocating a multicausal explanation of capitalist economic crisis, he also defended Marx's view that the average rate of profit was the key variable determining the fortunes of capitalist societies and that its tendency to fall was largely due to technological innovations that displaced living wage labor (the sole source of surplus value) from the capitalist production process.

In his Marshall Lectures delivered at Cambridge University in 1978 (published in 1980 as *Long Waves of Capitalist Development*), Mandel expanded on an original argument, first advanced in *Late Capitalism*, that the history of the capitalist mode of production had been characterized not only by the short-term industrial cycles analyzed by Marx, but also by four successive "long periods" of development, each characterized by a particular form of productive technology. The duration of each period was approximately fifty years, and each could be subdivided into an initial long wave of accelerating economic growth, corresponding to generally high rates of profit, and a subsequent long wave of decelerating growth, marked by lower profit rates.

The argument owed something to the Russian economist Nikolai Kondratieff's theory of long cycles of economic development, but departed from it by insisting that an expansionist wave following a wave of stagnation is not due to a corrective mechanism inherent in the functioning of capitalism, but depends on strictly noneconomic factors such as wars of conquest and decisive victories by capital over labor in the class struggle. The issue of whether capitalism had passed from a wave of stagnation to one of expansion by the twenty-first century sparked controversy among those adhering to Mandel's theory of long waves.

Non-Marxists sometimes criticized Mandel for allowing his dedication to Marxist orthodoxy to constrain an otherwise creative and fertile intellect. Marxist critics complained about his theoretical eclecticism, historical objectivism, and political opportunism. Nevertheless, his writings and personal example left a deep impression on many scholars and activists shaped by the youth radicalization of the 1960s.

SEE ALSO *Capitalism; Economic Crises; Long Waves; Marx, Karl; Rate of Profit; Trotsky, Leon*

BIBLIOGRAPHY

Achcar, Gilbert, ed. 1999. *The Legacy of Ernest Mandel.* London: Verso.

Murray E. G. Smith

MANDELA, NELSON
1918–

Nelson Rolihlahla Mandela is South Africa's iconic elder statesman and winner of the 1993 Nobel Peace Prize.

After almost fifty years of antiapartheid activism as a leader in the African National Congress (ANC), including over twenty-seven years in prison (1962–1990), Mandela became South Africa's first democratically elected president in 1994. Since stepping down from the presidency in 1999, he has continued to play a visible role in South African and international affairs.

Born into the royal Tembu family near Umtata in the Transkei, Mandela attended missionary schools prior to entering Fort Hare University College in 1939. Suspended for participation in student protests in 1940, he moved to Johannesburg, completing a bachelor's degree through correspondence in 1942. Working and studying part time, he qualified as an attorney through apprenticeship and passage of the qualifying exam in 1952.

His political career began in 1944, when he became a founding member of the Youth League of the ANC. He was prominent in efforts to galvanize the senior ANC to greater militancy that culminated in passage of the Program of Action in 1949. Dropping his opposition to collaboration with communists and Indian nationalists in the wake of their determined opposition to the relentless post-1948 implementation of apartheid, Mandela was at the center of the ANC-led Defiance Campaign (1952–1953), uniting Africans and antiapartheid volunteers of all races and ideological persuasions in nonviolent protest actions. Elected provincial president of the Transvaal ANC and deputy national president of the ANC in 1953, he was banned from political activity by the government and forced to resign. For the remainder of the decade, he concentrated on organizational activities behind the scenes. Only during the long-running treason trial (1956–1961) of 156 ANC members and their non-African allies was Mandela highly visible as lawyer, witness, and spokesman from the dock.

After the defendants in the treason trial were acquitted, Mandela went underground to organize support for unsuccessful mass protests in May 1961. Popularly dubbed the "Black Pimpernel," surfacing sporadically in South Africa and during a seven-month overseas trip, he evaded arrest and prison for seventeen months. While underground, he participated in clandestine meetings of the ANC (banned in 1960 under the Unlawful Organizations Act in the wake of the Sharpeville massacre) at which the ANC decided to end its policy of nonviolence. Mandela and other leaders of the banned ANC and its also proscribed ally, the Communist Party, then formed a unit called Umkhonto we Sizwe (Spear of the Nation) in mid-1961 to conduct sabotage and prepare for eventual guerrilla warfare. In August 1962 Mandela was apprehended by the police in Howick, Natal, and in November 1962 he was sentenced to five years in prison for incitement to strike and leaving the country illegally.

Subsequent to the separate arrest of nine other leaders at the underground Rivonia headquarters of Umkhonto we Sizwe in Johannesburg in July 1963, Mandela was brought from Robben Island prison to face trial with them on charges of sabotage. In the glare of worldwide publicity at the end of the trial, he delivered a dramatic final statement from the dock, concluding that "the ideal of a democratic and free society ... is an ideal for which I am prepared to die."

Receiving a life sentence (instead of the death sentence that could have been passed), Mandela returned to Robben Island and became the world's most famous political prisoner. Despite South African efforts to black out news about him, the world increasingly became aware of his assertive demands that the government adhere to prison regulations and his leadership of fellow inmates across the political spectrum. Transferred to Pollsmoor prison on the mainland in 1982 and then to a cottage in Victor Verster prison in 1987, Mandela became the star of a deft and media-smart campaign for unconditional release from prison. Simultaneously, he conducted secret talks with government ministers to set the stage for negotiations to achieve majority rule.

Released unconditionally from prison on February 11, 1990, by the newly elected president F. W. de Klerk, Mandela immediately assumed the leadership of the ANC's negotiations with the Nationalist Party government. Against a backdrop of rising violence, he showed repeated willingness to compromise with former opponents without abandoning the goal of nonracial constitutional democracy based on one person, one vote. In November 1993 an agreement was reached on a constitution, and in December 1993 Mandela and de Klerk were jointly awarded the Nobel Peace Prize.

Victorious at the head of the ANC ticket in the country's first election open to all citizens, Mandela assumed the presidency of South Africa on May 10, 1994. During his five-year term, he won extraordinary respect at home and abroad for his advocacy and practice of national reconciliation. After completion of his presidency, he turned to international issues, successfully mediating ethnic strife in Burundi. He also spoke out strongly on HIV/AIDS, urging both the South African government and the international community to greater commitment. In June 2004, shortly before his eighty-sixth birthday, he announced his retirement from public life.

SEE ALSO *African National Congress; Apartheid; Colonialism; Mandela, Winnie*

BIBLIOGRAPHY

Johns, Sheridan, and R. Hunt Davis Jr., eds. 1991. *Mandela, Tambo, and the African National Congress: The Struggle against Apartheid, 1948–1990.* New York: Oxford University Press.

Mandela, Nelson. 1994. *Long Walk to Freedom: The Autobiography of Nelson Mandela.* Boston: Little Brown.

Sampson, Anthony. 1999. *Mandela: The Authorized Biography.* New York: Knopf.

Sheridan Johns

MANDELA, WINNIE
1936–

Nomzamo Winifred Zanyiwe Madikizela was Columbus and Gertrude Madikizela's fifth child, born on September 26, 1936, in Pondoland Hills in Bizana (near Transkei), South Africa. Winnie's father encouraged her to complete a diploma at the prestigious Jan Hofmeyr School of Social Work in Johannesburg. She became the first black female social worker at Baragwanath Hospital. She would later complete a bachelor's degree in International Relations from the University of Witwatersrand. Winnie married political activist and leader of the African National Congress (ANC) Nelson Rolihlahla Mandela on June 14, 1958. Winnie and Nelson moved to Soweto and immediately began a life together fighting the oppressive apartheid regime of South Africa. Winnie became actively involved in the ANC Women's League and participated in protests against various obstructions to black South Africans' freedom, including the requirement for blacks to carry "passes" in order to travel within the country. Blacks that were caught without passes could be subjected to abuse and jail time. Nelson and Winnie were under tremendous scrutiny by the South African government. Nelson left the country to avoid being arrested for treason. He was arrested upon his return for inciting black South African workers to strike and for leaving the country without proper traveling documents. In 1962, Nelson would begin a twenty-eight year incarceration.

Winnie worked for the Johannesburg Child Welfare Society and was continually placed under numerous bans for her suspected affiliation with ANC. She was fired from various jobs due to repeated harassment of her employers by South African police. She also faced consistent bans inhibiting her ability to raise her two children, Zeni and Zindzi. In 1970, Winnie was detained for 491 days in Pretoria Prison before being released on house arrest. Frequent threats against Winnie's life, including a bomb explosion outside of her home, led her twelve-year-old daughter Zindzi to write a letter of appeal to the United Nations for her mother's protection. Winnie would be arrested and jailed two additional times, in 1974 and in 1976, after the Soweto student uprising against Bantu education led to the police beating and killing of many children. Winnie was viewed as an instigator and was arrested under the Internal Security Act. Winnie became an executive member of the Federation of South African Women, the Black Parents Association, and continued supporting the efforts of the ANC. She inspired many black South Africans and was known as the "Mother of the Nation." After her release from jail in 1976, she was banished for nine years to a remote black township known as Brandfort. For a time, she lived with no heat, no toilet, and no running water in a three-room shack she shared with Zindzi. Her eldest daughter, Zeni, married Prince Thumbumuzi of Swaziland in 1978.

Winnie was linked with radical factions of ANC during the 1980s and her legacy became tarnished by several key incidents, which eventually led to her divorce in 1996 from then President Nelson Mandela. The incidents centered around a group of bodyguards she formed, known as the Mandela United Football Club. Winnie was implicated in the murder of fourteen-year-old ANC activist James "Stompie" Moeketsi and numerous other beatings and deaths associated with the Football Club. When she appeared before the Truth and Reconciliation Commission, Bishop Desmond Tutu (b. 1931) begged her to admit her mistakes and Winnie acquiesced with the words "things went horribly wrong." She was convicted on 43 counts of fraud in 2003 and is considered a leading anti-apartheid activist and controversial figure around the world.

SEE ALSO *African National Congress; Anticolonial Movements; Apartheid; Colonialism; Mandela, Nelson; Truth and Reconciliation Commissions*

BIBLIOGRAPHY

Appiah, Kwame Anthony, and Henry Louis Gates, eds. 2004. *Africana: Civil Rights; An A-to-Z Reference of the Movement that Changed America.* Philadelphia: Running Press.

Harrison, Nancy. 1985. *Winnie Mandela: Mother of a Nation.* London: Victor Gollancz.

Hunter-Gault, Charlayne. April 5, 2003. Winnie Mandela Resigns ANC Post. *Cable News Network.* http://edition.cnn.com/2003/WORLD/africa/04/25/mandela.sentencing.

Mandela, Nelson. 1994. *Long Walk to Freedom: The Autobiography of Nelson Mandela.* New York: Little, Brown and Company.

Wines, Michael. 2004. No Jail for Winnie Mandela. July 6. *The New York Times.* http://www.nytimes.com/.

Kijua Sanders-McMurtry

MANIAS

The American Psychiatric Association (APA) defines *mania* as a period of unusually elated or irritable mood that is accompanied by at least three other symptoms (APA 2000). The symptoms of mania can include physical restlessness or overly active behavior; rapid speech or unusual talkativeness; racing thoughts; markedly diminished need for sleep (e.g., feeling rested after only a couple hours of sleep); inflated self-esteem; difficulty focusing attention; and excessive involvement in pleasurable activities without regard to undesirable consequences, such as reckless spending, sexual behavior, or driving. A manic episode is diagnosed if symptoms last for at least one week or lead to hospitalization, and if the symptoms are extreme enough to cause either distress or interference with social or occupational functioning. A person in a manic episode may feel invincible and enthusiastic, but family and friends may perceive manic activity as alarming.

The APA defines several other types of related episodes as well. *Hypomania* is milder than mania; it is diagnosed if the above symptoms are present for at least four days and produce noticeable changes in functioning without significant distress or impairment. *Mixed* episodes meet criteria for a full manic episode, but include concurrent depressive symptoms.

Bipolar disorders are defined based on the types of episodes experienced. Bipolar I disorder includes the presence of at least one lifetime manic or mixed episode. Bipolar II disorder is characterized by at least one lifetime episode of hypomania, along with at least one episode of depressive symptoms. *Cyclothymia* is defined by milder fluctuations of manic and depressive symptoms, which never meet the severity of full-blown manic or depressive episodes, but which are present at least 50 percent of the time for two years. The term *bipolar* reflects the fact that most (but not all) people with an episode of mania or hypomania will experience depressive episodes during their lifetime. No biological tests are used to diagnose bipolar disorder. Findings of large studies indicate that approximately 3.9 percent of people will meet diagnostic criteria for bipolar I or II disorders (Kessler et al. 2005), and that approximately 4.2 percent will meet diagnostic criteria for cyclothymia during their lifetime (Regeer et al. 2004).

Researchers have documented above-average rates of bipolar disorder among the world's most famous artists, authors, and composers (Jamison 1993). Unaffected family members of people with the disorder appear to be more creative than those affected by the disorder (Richards et al. 1988). In addition, family members of those with the disorder appear to have elevated levels of accomplishment in their careers (Johnson 2005).

Despite these intriguing correlates, bipolar disorders remain among the most devastating of psychiatric conditions. Suicide rates among people hospitalized for bipolar I disorder are twelvefold higher than those in the general population (Harris and Barraclough 1997). Most people remain unemployed a year after hospitalization for mania (Keck et al. 1998). As a consequence, bipolar disorders have been projected to become a leading cause of medical disability worldwide (Murray and Lopez 1996).

What causes this disorder? Bipolar disorder is one of the most genetic of psychiatric illnesses. Twin studies comparing rates of disorder in identical and fraternal twins suggest that 60 to 85 percent of the variability in whether or not people will develop bipolar I disorder is explained by genes (McGuffin et al. 2003). About 10 percent of the children of a parent with bipolar I disorder will develop a bipolar disorder. It is likely that a set of genes, rather than a single gene, contributes to cause the disorder.

Although there is no cure for bipolar disorder, medications are considered the best form of treatment. Medications are typically recommended throughout the life course, as people with one episode of mania are at extremely high risk for further episodes. Treatment guidelines recommend lithium as the medication of choice. Lithium has been shown to help prevent relapses, to reduce severity of episodes when they do occur, and to decrease suicidality. Unfortunately, many people find the side effects of lithium difficult to tolerate. Other medications, such as antiseizure and antipsychotic medications, have been licensed by the U.S. Food and Drug Administration for the treatment of mania. These treatments are often supplemented with medications to treat depressive symptoms (although antidepressant medications are not recommended without a mood stabilizer because they can trigger manic symptoms).

Although medicine is the primary approach to treatment, stressors and sleep loss can trigger episodes of bipolar disorder. Given this, as well as the devastating consequences of the disorder, psychosocial treatments can be used to supplement medication. Psychoeducation and family therapy can help prevent hospitalization, and cognitive therapy, focused on changing self-critical thoughts, helps reduce the risk of depression (Miklowitz and Johnson 2006).

SEE ALSO *Madness; Psychotropic Drugs; Schizophrenia*

BIBLIOGRAPHY

American Psychiatric Association. 2000. *Diagnostic and Statistical Manual of Mental Disorders* (*DSM*-IV-TR). 4th ed., text rev. Washington, DC: APA.

Harris E. C., and B. Barraclough. 1997. Suicide as an Outcome for Mental Disorders: A Meta-Analysis. *British Journal of Psychiatry* 170 (3): 205–228.

Jamison, Kay Redfield. 1993. *Touched with Fire: Manic-Depressive Illness and the Artistic Temperament.* New York: Free Press.

Johnson, Sheri L. 2005. Mania and Dysregulation in Goal Pursuit: A Review. *Clinical Psychology Review* 25 (2): 241–262.

Keck, Paul E., Jr., et al. 1998. 12-Month Outcome of Patients with Bipolar Disorder Following Hospitalization for a Manic or Mixed Episode. *American Journal of Psychiatry* 155 (5): 646–652.

Kessler, Ronald C., et al. 2005. Lifetime Prevalence and Age-of-Onset Distributions of DSM-IV Disorders in the National Comorbidity Survey Replication. *Archives of General Psychiatry* 62 (6): 593–602.

McGuffin, Peter, et al. 2003. The Heritability of Bipolar Affective Disorder and the Genetic Relationship to Unipolar Depression. *Archives of General Psychiatry* 60 (5): 497–502.

Miklowitz, David J., and Sheri L. Johnson. 2006. The Psychopathology and Treatment of Bipolar Disorder. In *Annual Review Clinical Psychology.* Vol. 2, 1–37. Palo Alto, CA: Annual Reviews.

Murray, Christopher J. L., and Alan D. Lopez. 1996. *The Global Burden of Disease: A Comprehensive Assessment of Mortality and Disability from Diseases, Injuries, and Risk Factors in 1990 and Projected to 2020.* Cambridge, MA: Harvard University Press.

Regeer, E. J., et al. 2004. Prevalence of Bipolar Disorder in the General Population: A Reappraisal Study of the Netherlands Mental Health Survey and Incidence Study. *Acta Psychiatrica Scandinavica* 110 (5): 374–382.

Richards, Ruth, et al. 1988. Creativity in Manic-Depressives, Cyclothymes, Their Normal Relatives, and Control Subjects. *Journal of Abnormal Psychology* 97 (3): 281–288.

Sheri L. Johnson
Christopher Miller

MANIC DEPRESSION

Many lay people use the name *manic depression* to refer to a disorder that is more formally called *bipolar disorder* within the diagnostic system of the American Psychiatric Association. In this formal diagnostic system, there are three forms of bipolar disorder. *Bipolar I disorder*, the most severe form, is defined by a single episode of *mania*. Manic episodes are characterized by a period of expansive, elevated, or irritable moods, along with such symptoms as diminished need for sleep, rapid speech, grandiosity, agitation or increased activity, racing thoughts, and increased engagement in pleasurable activities that have potential to cause trouble. The symptoms must last for at least one week and create severe impairment. *Bipolar II disorder* is a milder form of the disorder, defined on the basis of *hypomania* and recurrent depression. Hypomania is characterized by the same set of symptoms as mania, but symptoms must only last for four days and do not create severe impairment. *Cyclothymia* is defined by frequent ups and downs that are not severe enough to meet the criteria for hypomania or mania.

Two measures commonly used to verify diagnoses within research studies include Michael B. First and M. Gibbons's 2004 Structured Clinical Interview for *DSM-IV* (*Diagnostic and Statistical Manual of Mental Disorders*, 4th ed.), and Jean Endicott and Robert L. Spitzer's 1978 Schedule for Affective Disorders and Schizophrenia. No biological markers are available to aid with diagnosis.

About 1 percent of the population experiences bipolar I disorder; it was estimated in 2005 by Ronald C. Kessler et al. that bipolar II disorder also affects approximately 1 percent of the population. Cyclothymia may affect 4 percent of the population, according to a 2004 study by E. J. Regeer et al. The vast majority of people with a single episode of mania will experience another episode during their lifetime, many within five years, reported Michael J. Gitlin et al. in 1995. A 2002 report by Lewis L. Judd et al. said that mild symptoms lingering between episodes are common. The median time of onset for this disorder has been estimated at twenty-five years of age, according to the report by Kessler et al., but at least 25 percent of affected people report that episodes began by age seventeen.

It is well established that bipolar disorder is biologically based: heritability accounts for as much as 85 percent of whether people develop mania, according to a 2003 report from Peter McGuffin et al. Neurobiological research in 2003 by Craig A. Stockmeier suggests that a set of brain regions, modulated by dopamine and serotonin, are involved in the disorder. Psychosocial variables, including negative life events, negative cognition, and family hostility and criticism can increase the risk of depressive episodes within this disorder, per several reports (Butzlaff and Hooley 1998; Monroe et al. 2001; Alloy et al. 2000). Sleep loss and events involving goal attainment can predict increases in mania over time (Johnson 2005a, 2005b; Malkoff-Schwartz et al. 1998, 2000).

Historically, treatments for this disorder, including psychotherapy alone or hospitalization, were not very effective. The discovery of lithium's mood-stabilizing effects led to dramatic gains in outcome. The dominant treatment approach is mood-stabilizing medication. The first-line treatment recommendation remains lithium, but if side effects are difficult to tolerate, anticonvulsant medications are also useful mood stabilizers. Antidepressants are often added to combat depression, but not without a mood stabilizer because antidepressants can provoke manic symptoms when administered alone (Altshuler et al. 1995; Goldberg and Whiteside 2002). Antipsychotic medications can address psychotic or agitation symptoms. Research in 2004 by Sheri L. Johnson and Robert L. Leahy indicates that family or individual talk therapy can be helpful supplements to medication.

SEE ALSO *Depression, Psychological; Manias*

BIBLIOGRAPHY

Alloy, Lauren B., Lyn Y. Abramson, Michael E. Hogan, et al. 2000. The Temple-Wisconsin Cognitive Vulnerability to Depression Project: Lifetime History of Axis I Psychopathology in Individuals at High and Low Cognitive Risk for Depression. *Journal of Abnormal Psychology* 109: 403–418.

Altshuler, Lori L., Robert M. Post, Gabriele S. Leverich, et al. 1995. Antidepressant-induced Mania and Cycle Acceleration: A Controversy Revisited. *American Journal of Psychiatry* 152: 1130–1138.

American Psychiatric Association. 2000. *Diagnostic and Statistical Manual of Mental Disorders* (*DSM*-IV-TR). 4th ed., text rev. Washington, DC: Author.

Butzlaff, Ronald L., and Jill M. Hooley. 1998. Expressed Emotion and Psychiatric Relapse: A Meta-analysis. *Archives of General Psychiatry* 55: 547–552.

Endicott, Jean, and Robert L. Spitzer. 1978. A Diagnostic Interview: The Schedule for Affective Disorders and Schizophrenia. *Archives of General Psychiatry* 35 (7): 837–844.

First, Michael B., and M. Gibbon. 2004. The Structured Clinical Interview for DSM-IV Axis I Disorders (SCID-I) and the Structured Clinical Interview for DSM-IV Axis II Disorders (SCID-II). In *Comprehensive Handbook of Psychological Assessment*. Vol. 2: *Personality Assessment*, eds. Mark J. Hilsenroth and Daniel L. Segal, 134–143. Hoboken, NJ: Wiley.

Gitlin, Michael J., Joel Swendsen, Tracy L. Heller, and Constance Hammen. 1995. Relapse and Impairment in Bipolar Disorder. *American Journal of Psychiatry* 152: 1635–1640.

Goldberg, Joseph F., and Joyce E. Whiteside. 2002. The Association between Substance Abuse and Antidepressant-induced Mania in Bipolar Disorder: A Preliminary Study. *Journal of Clinical Psychiatry* 63: 791–795.

Johnson, Sheri L. 2005a. Life Events in Bipolar Disorder: Towards More Specific Models. *Clinical Psychology Review* 25: 1008–1027.

Johnson, Sheri L. 2005b. Mania and Dysregulation in Goal Pursuit. *Clinical Psychology Review* 25: 241–262.

Johnson, Sheri L., and Robert L. Leahy, eds. 2004. *Psychological Treatment of Bipolar Disorder*. New York: Guilford.

Judd, Lewis L., Hagop S. Akiskal, Pamela J. Schettler, et al. 2002. The Long-Term Natural History of the Weekly Symptomatic Status of Bipolar I Disorder. *Archives of General Psychiatry* 59: 530–537.

Kessler, Ronald C., Wai Tat Chiu, Olga Demler, and Ellen E. Walters. 2005. Prevalence, Severity, and Comorbidity of 12-Month DSM-IV Disorders in the National Comorbidity Survey Replication. *Archives of General Psychiatry* 62 (6): 617–627.

Malkoff-Schwartz, Susan, Ellen Frank, Barbara Anderson, et al. 1998. Stressful Life Events and Social Rhythm Disruption in the Onset of Manic and Depressive Bipolar Episodes: A Preliminary Investigation. *Archives of General Psychiatry* 55: 702–707.

Malkoff-Schwartz, Susan, Ellen Frank, Barbara Anderson, et al. 2000. Social Rhythm Disruption and Stressful Life Events in the Onset of Bipolar and Unipolar Episodes. *Psychological Medicine* 30: 1005–1016.

McGuffin, Peter, Fruhling Rijsdijk, Martin Andrew, et al. 2003. The Heritability of Bipolar Affective Disorder and the Genetic Relationship to Unipolar Depression. *Archives of General Psychiatry* 60: 497–502.

Monroe, Scott M., Kate Harkness, Anne D. Simons, and Michael E. Thase. 2001. Life Stress and the Symptoms of Major Depression. *Journal of Nervous and Mental Disease* 189: 168–175.

Regeer, E. J., M. ten Have, M. L. Rosso, et al. 2004. Prevalence of Bipolar Disorder in the General Population: A Reappraisal Study of the Netherlands Mental Health Survey and Incidence Study. *Acta Psychiatrica Scandinavica* 110 (5): 374–382.

Stockmeier, Craig A. 2003. Involvement of Serotonin in Depression: Evidence from Postmortem and Imaging Studies of Serotonin Receptors and the Serotonin Transporter. *Journal of Psychiatric Research* 37: 357–373.

Sheri L. Johnson
Christopher Miller

MANIFEST DESTINY

SEE *Americanism; Annexation; Mexican-American War.*

MANIFOLDS

In mathematics, a manifold is a space that looks like a Euclidean space, locally around every point. Since a set is defined by its elements, two spaces can be seen as equivalent if there is a bijection (one-to-one correspondence) between them. There are different versions of this equivalence, depending on the structure of the bijection. When the two spaces are topological, the bijection is a homeomorphism if it is continuous and has a continuous inverse. If both spaces are Euclidean, the bijection is a C^K diffeormorphism if both it and its inverse are (or can be extended to be) of class C^K. A topological space is a J-dimensional topological manifold if for every point there exists a homeomorphism from some open subset of the J-dimensional Euclidean space to an open neighborhood of the point. If, in the Euclidean case, what one has is a C^K diffeormorphism, then the space is a C^K differentiable manifold.

A manifold has the property that, at every point, one can find a neighborhood that is just a transformation of a Euclidean space, preserving topological and/or differential properties. An example of this type of transformation is

from a circle to an ellipse, whereas going to a number eight would not be bijective, to a line would violate continuity, and to a triangle would violate differentiability.

Differentiable manifolds are the natural objects for the application of calculus, and the study of that application, differential topology, has proved useful in economic theory. These techniques were introduced to economics in 1970 by Gerard Debreu's proof that, generically in the space of exchange economies (that is, in almost all of them), competitive equilibria are isolated from one another. The argument is an application of the Transversal Density Theorem of differential topology.

Later, Darrel Duffie and Wayne Shafer used Grassmanian manifolds (the sets of linear subspaces of a given Euclidean space) to show that in exchange economies subject to uncertainty and endowed with real assets (those whose payoffs depend on the prices of commodities), a competitive equilibrium generically exists. This application was necessary because the dependence of payoffs on prices makes the space of revenue transfers across states of nature variable. The idea of Duffie and Shafer was to break that dependence, effectively weakening the concept of equilibrium but allowing the use of the manifold structure of the Grassmanian to guarantee its existence, and then to show that, generically, the weaker equilibrium is indeed equilibrium.

Another remarkable application of techniques of differential topology in economics is the proof by John Geanakoplos and Herakles Polemarchakis that in a generic economy with uninsurable risks, just by changing their trade in assets, and then competitively trading in commodity markets, all individuals could be better off than at the competitive equilibrium allocation. This result was also obtained from the Transversal Density Theorem.

But perhaps the most visible application of the concept is the result, claimed by Yves Balasko, that in economies described by the preferences of the individuals, the set of pairs of profiles of endowments and associated competitive equilibrium prices is a differentiable manifold. After this result, the equilibrium set of an economy is usually referred to as equilibrium manifold.

SEE ALSO *Topology*

BIBLIOGRAPHY

Balasko, Yves. 1975. The Graph of the Walras Correspondence. *Econometrica* 43 (5–6): 907–912.

Debreu, Gerard. 1970. Economies with a finite set of equilibria. *Econometrica* 38 (3): 387–392.

Duffie, Darrell and Wayne Shafer. 1985. Equilibrium in Incomplete Markets I: A Basic Model of Generic Existence. *Journal of Mathematical Economics* 14 (3): 285–300.

Geanakoplos, John D., and Herakles M. Polemarchakis. 1986. Existence, Regularity and Constrained Suboptimality of

Competitive Allocations when the Asset Market is Incomplete. In *Uncertainty, Information and Communication. Essays in Honor of Kenneth J. Arrow*, Vol. III, edited by Walter P. Heller, Ross M. Starr, and David A. Starret. New York: Cambridge University Press.

Andrés Carvajal

MANKILLER, WILMA
1945–

Wilma Pearl Mankiller struggled successfully against male dominance, white privilege, and significant health problems to become the first female principal chief of the Cherokee Nation. Her accomplishments occurred in a social context of poverty, failed federal government relocation programs, and social protest movements for American Indians. Her ability to secure government funding for her tribe reflected movement toward assimilation and societal integration for women and American Indians. Mankiller's support for Indian and female empowerment included social movements, politics, and protest. Thus, her legacy may also be viewed through the prism of resistance to oppression and oppositional culture.

Mankiller was born on November 18, 1945, in Tahlequah, Oklahoma, the sixth of eleven children of Charley Mankiller and Clara Irene Sitton. Her father's family had endured the Trail of Tears, the forced removal of Cherokees in 1839 from the Tennessee Valley to Oklahoma, where they lived in severe poverty and had to conduct tribal ceremonies in secret. Despite these hardships, her family remained a source of comfort for her and taught her to be proud of her heritage and her family name, Mankiller, which was a Cherokee title given to a person who safeguarded a Cherokee village.

In 1956, her family was relocated to San Francisco, California, as part of the Bureau of Indian Affairs' Indian Relocation Program, which attempted to sever Native Americans' ties with their land and culture, thus helping the U.S. government avoid responsibility for the institutionalized oppression of American Indians. Despite facing poverty, prejudice, and discrimination, Mankiller found inspiration and support at the American Indian Center in San Francisco. As a young adult, she took a job at a financial company, married, and had two daughters.

Her activism was sparked by the 1969 to 1971 seizure of Alcatraz Island by Native Americans. She and others in her family took part in the protest as a way to draw attention to the plight of Native Americans. Through this experience, Mankiller met and befriended many of the leaders of Native American empowerment movements. Soon afterward, Mankiller was diagnosed with polycystic kidney disease. Despite the diagnosis, Mankiller directed the Native American Youth Center in Oakland and continued her involvement in social protest movements on behalf of American Indians. She helped the Pit River tribe regain tribal land from the Pacific Gas and Electric Company, which tried to assert ownership over their land. Mankiller worked for the tribe for five years, organized a legal defense fund, and researched treaty rights and international law to aid their cause.

More interested in activism than in being a housewife, Mankiller divorced her husband and moved back to Oklahoma with her children in 1977. She used her skills acquired in San Francisco to work for the Cherokee Nation of Oklahoma as an economic stimulus coordinator. In 1981, Mankiller founded and directed the Cherokee Nation Community Development Department, which received acclaim for rehabilitating the small Cherokee community of Bell, Oklahoma. She accomplished this despite recovering from a serious car accident that killed a friend and receiving treatment for systemic myasthenia gravis, a form of muscular dystrophy.

In 1983, she ran for deputy chief of the Cherokee Nation. She won the election and became the Cherokee Nation's first female deputy chief despite death threats because of her sex. She was appointed the first female principal chief of the Cherokee Nation in 1985 after the presiding principal chief was nominated to lead the Bureau of Indian Affairs. In 1987, she won a tough election and, while actively leading the Cherokee Nation, underwent a kidney transplant in 1990. In 1991, Mankiller was reelected principal chief with 83 percent of the votes cast. In 1995, she chose not to run again and instead accepted a fellowship at Dartmouth College.

During her term as Cherokee chief, tribal revenue increased, $20 million was secured for construction projects, an $8 million Job Corps center was created, and funding was secured for programs aiding women and children and to reform the Cherokee judiciary. She also developed economic and educational empowerment programs in which women and men worked collectively for community improvement under the Cherokee tradition of *gadugi*, which emphasizes gender equity. In 1996, she was diagnosed with lymphoma and received treatment while continuing to write, edit, and participate in community organizations. In 1998, she was awarded the Presidential Medal of Freedom.

Wilma Mankiller nurtured economic development for American Indians and paved new paths to leadership for women of color. She exemplifies greater economic and political assimilation for women and American Indians. Mankiller's significance also rests in resistance to institutional and cultural racism and sexism through embracing social protest and oppositional culture.

SEE ALSO *American Indian Movement; Cherokees; Native Americans; Protest; Resistance; Trail of Tears; Women and Politics*

BIBLIOGRAPHY

Edmunds, R. David, ed. 2001. *The New Warriors: Native American Leaders since 1900.* Lincoln: University of Nebraska Press.

Mankiller, Wilma. 2000. *Mankiller: A Chief and Her People.* 2nd ed. New York: St. Martin's.

Mankiller, Wilma, Gwendolyn Mink, Marysa Navarro, Barbra Smith, and Gloria Steinem, eds. 1998. *The Reader's Companion to U.S. Women's History.* Boston: Houghton Mifflin.

Steven M. Frenk
Vasilios T. Bournas
Wayne Luther Thompson

MANNHEIM, KARL
1893–1947

Karl Mannheim was a Hungarian philosopher and sociologist who is usually credited with having established the sociology of knowledge as an autonomous field of inquiry—as opposed to, say, an application of Marxist or phenomenological sociology. Mannheim's intellectual trajectory resembled that of his contemporary, Georg Lukacs (1885–1971), with whom he remained friends until the rise of Nazism. Whereas Mannheim fled to London, Lukacs fled to Moscow, and their politics diverged accordingly from their original common Marxist roots. Both were grounded in the philosophy of culture and were early influenced by Georg Simmel's (1858–1918) conception of sociology as the science of forms of life. Each tried to ground a conception of objectivity from the "relationist" epistemology common to Karl Marx (1818–1883) and Simmel. This produced an interesting contrast in privileged standpoints and, implicitly, the vanguard of progressive politics. In response to Lukacs's "proletarian standpoint," where workers were understood as integral to, yet alienated from, the means of production, Mannheim proposed a "free-floating intelligentsia," an increasing segment of the middle class whose alienation reflects its detachment from the means of production.

Mannheim's sociology of knowledge was refined through a series of debates in both the German- and English-speaking worlds. Prior to the publication of his major work, *Ideology and Utopia* (1929), Mannheim corresponded with the art historian Erwin Panofsky (1892–1968) over the sense of "historicism" required of cultural interpretation. In contrast to Panofsky's view of art as the unique synthesis of various ongoing traditions, Mannheim stressed art's ability to capture the common experience of a generation. Indeed, "ideology and utopia" referred to contrasting attitudes toward history that might be shared by a generation: the backward-looking (conservative) ideology and the forward-looking (progressive) utopia.

Over his career, Mannheim cast this perspective in increasingly normative terms, culminating in the proposal of new modes of political education and broadcast media capable of instilling social democratic attitudes in the generation entrusted with reconstructing post–World War II Europe. Here he crossed swords with both liberals and elitists, including fellow émigrés Michael Polanyi (1891–1976) and Karl Popper (1902–1994), as well as T. S. Eliot (1888–1965), with whom Mannheim maintained a friendly rivalry until his death.

Two seminal theses in the sociology of knowledge are due to Mannheim: (1) a knowledge practice's validity is relative to its capacity to confer legitimacy on a particular social order; and (2) the social conditioning of a knowledge practice that is valid according to standard methodological criteria can be demonstrated by showing how the practice helps to reproduce—and sometimes even constitute—the criteria by which it is judged valid. Both theses remain controversial because they imply that the sociology of knowledge can challenge the philosophical theory of knowledge, epistemology, on its own grounds. Mannheim's challenge was later taken up by "social epistemology."

BIBLIOGRAPHY

Fuller, Steve. 2002. *Social Epistemology.* 2nd ed. Bloomington: Indiana University Press.

Mannheim, Karl. 1936. *Ideology and Utopia: An Introduction to the Sociology of Knowledge.* Trans. Louis Wirth and Edward Shils. New York: Harcourt.

Steve Fuller

MANSKI, CHARLES
SEE *Identification Problem; Reflection Problem.*

MANU, CODES OF
SEE *Brahmins.*

MAO ZEDONG
1893–1976

Mao Zedong (previously Mao Tse-tung) is undisputedly the preeminent figure in modern Chinese history, and also a commanding presence in the history of the twentieth century. The Mao-led Communist revolution in 1949 ended China's century of humiliation and laid the foundations of the rapidly developing nation of the early twenty-first century. But Mao also created much unnecessary social turmoil in the latter part of his political career; he did not know when to exit the historical stage gracefully. As a result, most Chinese today have a mixed view of Mao—a great leader who united and rejuvenated their massive country, but also one who left considerable human suffering in his wake. Mao is often compared to Qin Shihuangdi (259 BCE–210 BCE), the First Emperor of Qin, a brilliant but ruthless leader who created the first unified Chinese empire in 221 BCE.

Mao was a complex personality who was torn between admiration for China's past imperial glory and despair at its parlous condition in the closing decades of the nineteenth century, when he was born. As a young man, he struggled to reconcile the dichotomy in his mind (and in the minds of many others in his generation) between China's traditional civilization and the increasing demands of a modern world dominated by the advanced nations of Europe and North America. In Marxist-Leninist theory, Mao discovered a penetrating Western critique of the West, which enabled him to adopt many of its revolutionary premises (and promises) without abandoning China's own impressive cultural heritage. In direct intellectual descent from Mao, China's succeeding leaders continue to claim they are building socialism with Chinese characteristics, a somewhat ambiguous concept that has yet to be fully articulated, which (at least in the narrower area of economics) is often referred to as market socialism.

RISE TO POWER

Mao was born on December 26 into a moderately well-off peasant family in the village of Shaoshan in Xiangtan County, Hunan province, in south-central China, not far from the provincial capital of Changsha. He developed an early interest in political and international affairs, and his years at the First Provincial Normal School in Changsha, where he studied to be a teacher, brought him into contact with young men and women from all over the province. Seeking a wider stage after graduation, Mao set out for Beijing in 1918, where he studied and worked part-time in the library at Peking University, the nation's premier institution of higher education, and, at the time, a hotbed of radical political thinking among many of the faculty and students.

Mao took an active interest in the student-inspired May Fourth movement, which sparked off a country-wide nationalist upsurge directed against unwanted European and Japanese influence in China. Soon after, Mao

declared himself to be a Marxist-Leninist, without actually undertaking a thorough study of either the revolutionary doctrine or the Russian Revolution in 1917. After a short period as an elementary school principal and political activist back home in Hunan, he became a founding member of the Chinese Communist Party, which was formally established in Shanghai on July 23, 1921.

Consolidating Power Mao's rural background gave him a special interest in the peasantry, and he was often at odds with his more urban-oriented colleagues. In early 1927, after an intensive study of rural conditions in his native province, Mao wrote his seminal "Report on an Investigation of the Peasant Movement in Hunan," in which he predicted that the peasant masses would soon rise up and sweep away the old, feudal system of land ownership that exploited and oppressed them. The Communists, he argued, should lead the peasants or get out of the way. Chiang Kai-shek's (1887–1975) bloody coup in the spring of 1927 effectively destroyed the Communist organizations in Shanghai and other major cities, forcing them to find refuge in Jiangxi province, in the mountainous hinterland in south-central China, adjacent to Hunan where Mao had been born and raised. Mao was elected chairman of the new Jiangxi Soviet (local Communist government) in this isolated base area, but soon lost power to the Returned Student group (a reference to their study in Moscow), which took over party leadership and pushed him aside.

Mao finally came into his own during the famous Long March in 1934 to 1936, when the Communists had to flee from Nationalist leader Chiang Kai-shek's fifth and finally successful military encirclement campaign to surround their base area and destroy them. At the decisive Zunyi conference in January 1935, in the early part of this arduous 6,000-mile trek, Mao was recognized as the political and military leader of the Communist movement. At the Communists' new base area in Yan'an, a small county seat in China's arid northwest region, Mao built an elaborate system of ideology, organization, guerrilla warfare, and rural recruitment that led quickly to the emergence of a powerful political movement, backed up by its own military forces (the Red Army). Both the party and the army grew rapidly during the war against Japan, which had invaded China in July 1937, and the Communists emerged as a formidable competitor for state power with the Nationalists.

By the end of the war in 1945, Mao was hailed as the Party's leading political and military strategist, and, coincidentally, its preeminent ideological thinker. What was now called Mao Zedong thought was said to represent the Sinification of Marxism, that is to say, the adaptation of Marxist theory to China's actual historical conditions.

Mao's thought, reinforced through a powerful personality cult and an oppressive rectification campaign to tame his critics, was to become the ideological foundation of the Chinese Communist movement in subsequent years.

SUCCESS—AND FAILURE

Despite unfavorable odds, the Red Army (renamed the People's Liberation Army) employed superior strategic tactics to defeat the Nationalists in the civil war (1946–1949). Mao wasted no time in consolidating Communist rule; he proclaimed the founding of the People's Republic of China on October 1, 1949, and moved decisively to consolidate its borders and occupy and reintegrate Tibet. His intention was not merely to rebuild the shattered nation, but also transform it, which, with a staggering population of over 400 million, was the world's largest. In late 1949 to early 1950, Mao traveled to Moscow (his first trip abroad) and signed an alliance with the Soviets; but Mao and Soviet leader Joseph Stalin (1879–1953) neither liked nor trusted each other and their relationship was to prove unstable. The Korean War (1950–1953) could not have come at a worse time for the new regime, but at great cost Chinese troops succeeded in repulsing the U.S. advance into the north, near the Yalu River on the Chinese border.

Despite these international concerns, Mao launched a wide-ranging program of reconstruction and nationalization in major industrial and commercial cities such as Shanghai and Guangzhou (Canton). In the countryside, land was confiscated from the landlord class, many of whom were summarily executed by makeshift tribunals, and land passed (if only briefly) into the hands of the ordinary peasants. A comprehensive range of social reforms was also launched, including marriage reform favoring the female; a crackdown on crime, drugs, and prostitution; and clean-up campaigns targeted at government and business corruption. Although U.S. intervention had placed Taiwan beyond their grasp, by the mid to late-1950s things had gone very well for the Communists, and for this much credit must go to Mao and his fellow party leaders.

But Mao had ever more ambitious plans. He wanted to speed up the pace of economic growth, based on industrial development and the collectivization of agriculture; and he wanted to emancipate China from the bonds of the Soviet alliance, which he found increasingly restrictive. Unfortunately it was at this juncture, in the late 1950s, that Mao's hitherto deft political touch began to fail him and he launched two disastrous political campaigns that convulsed the country and ultimately damaged his reputation. The Great Leap Forward in 1958, calling for the establishment of small backyard factories in the towns and giant people's communes (consolidated co-operative enterprises) in the countryside, resulted in an economic lurch backward. The consequent three bitter years (1959–1961) saw rural peasants perish in the millions due to harsh conditions for the very young, the very old, and the disadvantaged. Chastened, and under criticism from his more moderate colleagues, Mao agreed to step back from the forefront of leadership; he turned his attention to the growing ideological polemic marking the growing Sino-Soviet split and left it to others to repair the untold damage at home.

In his heart, Mao believed that the Great Leap Forward had failed largely because too many party officials (cadres) did not boldly implement his policies; disparagingly, he compared them to old women tottering about in bound feet. He decided to purge these revisionist (pro-Soviet) officials and others said to be taking the capitalist road (more open to Europe and North America generally) from positions of authority. Mao and his militant party faction (the Gang of Four) called upon the nation's youth (primarily high school and university students) to rise up and call the errant officials to account. The result was the Great Proletarian Cultural Revolution, which witnessed the unusual spectacle of the top Communist leader declaring war on his own party organization. Millions of inflamed students and others donned Red Guard armbands, and, waving the *Little Red Book* (1966) of selected Mao quotations, they proceeded to carry out their assigned mission. The campaign tore the country apart from 1966 to 1969, forcing Mao to call for military intervention to restore order, and it dragged on destructively until his death in 1976. Still, from the perspective of foreign policy, the Cultural Revolution's sharp anti-Soviet orientation succeeded in liberating China from its underlying dependency on the Soviet Union, and prepared the nation for a more independent role in international affairs in the years ahead.

A BEGINNING, AND AN END

Despite his miscalculations with the Great Leap Forward and the Cultural Revolution, Mao wisely decided to play the American card in order to counterbalance growing Soviet military power on the conflict-prone Chinese border. With the surprise invitation to a U.S. table tennis team then in Japan to visit China, Mao set in motion the ping-pong diplomacy that led to U.S. president Richard Nixon's state visit to China in February 1972, which culminated in the landmark Shanghai communiqué calling for a more constructive relationship between the countries. Mao and Nixon toasted each other cordially in the Great Hall of the People in Beijing, laying to rest a generation of bitter enmity and setting the stage for the remarkable flowering of Sino-American relations that has continued into the early twenty-first century. It was to be

Mao's final hurrah; already in declining health (possibly suffering from Parkinson's disease), he gradually faded from the scene and passed away peacefully at age eighty-two on September 9, 1976.

In an official assessment of his lengthy career, the Communist Party hailed Mao as an illustrious national hero who laid the foundations of the new China, but at the same time a tragic figure with all too human frailties. Mao is buried in a grand mausoleum in Tiananmen Square in Beijing and he enjoys considerable popular approbation despite his rather clouded historical record. But while many people revere Mao, many others revile him, as they do the First Emperor of Qin, who lived some two thousand years earlier. For most Chinese though, many of whom were born well after Mao's death, he remains the human embodiment of China's national regeneration and its reemergence as a great world power.

English historian Lord Acton (1834–1902), in his famous observation on power, concluded that "great men are almost always bad men," and, in the case of Mao, there is considerable truth to this. Mao was a romantic visionary who set himself seemingly impossible goals, but he had the necessary qualities of leadership, persistence, and ruthlessness to reach them, at least to a degree. In addition to his political and military prowess, he is also considered a talented calligrapher and poet in the classical style, and he left behind a small corpus of work that is generally well regarded. But he was also something of an uncouth peasant who lacked personal polish, could be vulgar in his choice of words, and (even in his declining years) overly enjoyed the company of young women. As he aged, he became increasingly out of touch with political reality, vainly attempting to force the entire nation onto the Procrustean bed of his own ideological convictions (ideological fantasies, some would say).

Will history remember Mao Zedong? Undoubtedly, for Mao occupies a historical position comparable to individuals such as Alexander the Great, Julius Caesar, Genghis Khan, Napoleon Bonaparte, and Qin Shihuangdi—these individuals were a frustrating mix of good and bad, but they all left a distinctive imprint on their own historical ages. Like playwright William Shakespeare's Caesar, they "bestrode the narrow world like a Colossus," and to this day their achievements and failures are enshrined in countless volumes for future generations to read and ponder. The same will quite likely be true of Mao Zedong.

SEE ALSO *Chinese Revolution; Communism; Little Red Book; Maoism; Nixon, Richard M.*

BIBLIOGRAPHY

Li, Zhisui. 1994. *The Private Life of Chairman Mao: The Memoirs of Mao's Personal Physician.* Trans. Tai Hung-chao. New York: Random House.

Schram, Stuart R. 1969. *The Political Thought of Mao Tse-tung.* Harmondsworth, U.K.: Penguin.

Short, Phillip. 2001. *Mao: A Life.* New York: Holt.

Snow, Edgar P. 1968. *Red Star over China.* Rev. ed. New York: Grove. (Orig. pub. 1937.)

Spence, Jonathan D. 1999. *Mao Zedong.* New York: Viking.

Wylie, Raymond F. 1980. *The Emergence of Maoism: Mao Tse-tung, Ch'en Po-ta, and the Search for Chinese Theory, 1935–1945.* Stanford, CA: Stanford University Press.

Raymond F. Wylie

MAOISM

Maoism is an influential revolutionary ideology of the twentieth century. The term *Maoism*, despite its originating from the name of the People's Republic of China's former leader Mao Zedong, is used primarily outside of mainland China. The Communist Party of China (CPC) uses Mao Zedong Thought as its official ideology. Although Maoism is only a derivation of Marxism and Leninism, its impact has been worldwide. Maoism continues to inspire international Maoists everywhere—especially in Asia and Latin America—even as the Chinese have been moving increasingly away from it.

The crux of Maoism is a belief that Marxism and Leninism can be adapted to suit the conditions of developing countries in their struggle against capitalism and imperialism. According to Karl Marx, a Communist revolution will be organized by advanced productive forces, such as industrial workers, and is possible only in an advanced capitalist society. Chinese Communist leader Mao Zedong, however, believed that rural revolutions in a traditional society can become a stepping-stone for an advanced social revolution, and peasants can be allies of the industrial workers and thus should play a pivotal role in erecting socialism and communism. During the lengthy military struggle in the rural areas of China, Mao formulated his theory of New Democratic Revolution.

Mao's theory of revolution is based on the guerrilla war strategy, a disciplined Leninist party, and the united front. First of all, Mao believed that "political power comes from the barrel of a gun." He and his comrades developed the strategy of rural-based guerrilla warfare and fought the nationalist government in the countryside for two decades. This strategy provided a practical solution for a smaller and weaker revolutionary force to defeat a much stronger and powerful state power. During World War II (1939–1945), Mao further extended his theory into the strategy of the "protracted people's war," designed to mobilize a total, yet prolonged, war to figuratively bleed the Japanese invaders to death.

Second, Mao emphasized the importance of a disciplined, elitist political party with absolute control over a revolutionary army. He developed doctrines such as democratic centralism, mass line, and criticism and self-criticism. All of these doctrines have become operational principles of the CPC. Finally, while stressing the need for the leadership of the CPC, Mao embraced a corporatist strategy to extend the party control to other political parties and groups. His theory of united front appears to raise the status of many smaller parties from opposition to collaborative and participating parties, yet it denies these parties the right to become competitors with the CPC, and thus lays the groundwork for the corporatist party-state after 1949. For all these contributions, the CPC formally adopted Mao Zedong Thought as its official doctrine in the Seventh Party Congress of the CPC held in Yanan in 1945.

In his early revolutionary career, Mao was a populist practitioner of Marxism rather than a dogmatic follower. Mao's success in using his military strategy to seize political power in a big country such as China established Mao's charismatic legitimacy in China and throughout the developing world. In his later life, however, Mao became an ardent defender of Marxism after the death of Joseph Stalin. In his fight against the so-called revisionists, such as the Communist leader Nikita Khrushchev in the Soviet Union, Mao apparently became more dogmatic. He defended Stalin and was unremitting in his emphasis on the theory of "a continued revolution under proletarian dictatorship." Mao and his supporters believed that an important task of the revolution was to carry out the proletarian dictatorship and class struggle against old and new bourgeoisie.

Maoism also contains some utopian elements. Mao believed that industrialization and modernization could go hand in hand with socialist transformation. The ambitious Great Leap Forward program (launched in 1958) tried unrealistically to speed up the industrialization process, but suffered a major setback. Nevertheless, this did not stop Mao from launching another major political campaign, the Great Proletarian Cultural Revolution (1966–1976), to crush leaders "who are taking the capitalist road," and to transform political, social, and cultural superstructures that were considered to be unfitting with a socialist economy. Mao's quotation books (such as what became known in English as "The Little Red Book") became a spiritual guide for the millions of young students (Red Guards) who waged a war on the establishment. The subsequent chaos was eventually put to an end after Mao's death in 1976.

Although Mao Zedong Thought continues to be upheld as the CPC's official ideology, the radical and utopian elements have been discredited and revised. Worldwide, Maoism is still influential. The Maoist International Movement in the United States still supports a Maoist world revolution, and the Revolutionary Internationalism Movement continues to believe that the strategy of people's war is an effective means of Marxist revolution.

SEE ALSO *Chinese Revolution; Communism; Guerrilla Warfare; Imperialism; Khrushchev, Nikita; Leninism; Little Red Book; Mao Zedong; Marxism; Revolution; Socialism; Stalin, Joseph; Utopianism*

BIBLIOGRAPHY

Alexander, Robert J. 2001. *Maoism in the Developed World.* Westport, CT: Praeger.

Schram, Stuart R. 1969. *The Political Thought of Mao Tse-tung.* Rev. ed. New York: Praeger.

Spence, Jonathan D. 1999. *Mao Zedong.* New York: Viking.

Baogang Guo

MAQUILADORAS

Although the term *maquiladora* or *maquila* is often used interchangeably with *export assembly firm*, it refers to a company operating under a very specific tax regime initiated by the Mexican government in 1969, and it is applicable to only one type of export production first established in communities near the U.S.-Mexico border. The official definition of the maquiladora regime defines it as "temporary importation of goods necessary for the transformation, elaboration, or repair of products destined to be exported, without taxes [being levied] on these temporary imports" (de la O 2002, p. 200).

HISTORY OF THE MAQUILADORA

In September 1942, Mexico and the United States agreed to the Bracero Program in an attempt to alleviate wartime U.S. labor shortages in agriculture and other areas. Approximately 5 million Mexican men participated in this guest worker (bracero) program until it ended in 1964. With the mechanization of agriculture in the United States and the decrease in demand for Mexican labor, the Mexican government began planning alternate sources of employment. During a 1964 tour of the Far East, Minister of Industry and Commerce Campos Salas was introduced to the notion of export production zones. He envisioned this as an alternative for Mexico's economic development.

In December 1964, the United States unilaterally canceled the Bracero Program. As many as two hundred thousand braceros, comprising 40 to 50 percent of the border population, found themselves without jobs, leading to a buildup of social unrest. In response, the Mexican government inaugurated the Border Industrialization Program (BIP), later known as the Maquiladora Program. The purpose of the BIP was to promote export-led industrialization in northern Mexico, encouraging foreign investment in Mexican maquiladoras. Corollary objectives included the creation of employment and increasing the income of the border population to foment a stronger local economy. The pillars of the BIP were proximity to the United States; use of favorable articles of the U.S. Tariff Code, which permits firms to import goods manufactured abroad with U.S. components to reenter the United States, paying duty only on the value-added, cheap labor; and a Mexican government friendly to investors. Campos Salas was quoted in the *Wall Street Journal* (on May 25, 1976) as saying, "Our idea is to offer free enterprise an alternative to Hong Kong, Japan, and Puerto Rico" (Bustamante 1983, p. 233). This translated into tax incentives for foreign firms, lax enforcement of environmental laws, and a blind eye to the breaking of labor laws.

Initially, maquiladora enterprises were allowed to settle in a 20-kilometer strip along the Mexican border. After four years, however, Mexican government officials were disappointed with the results. Two important objectives of the program had been: (1) having foreign firms make use of Mexican products and firms (known as linkages with the local economy), and (2) the transfer of technology and know-how to Mexican managers and firms. Neither goal was being met. In addition, maquiladoras experienced high turnover rates, as workers frequently changed jobs, seeking incentives and bonuses to complement low wages. As a result, in 1972, the Mexican government expanded the zone to include all of Mexico. To encourage further growth, the Mexican government provided additional incentives to foreign firms, including lowering the minimum wage in the interior of the country, easing the ability of foreign firms to form joint ventures with Mexican corporations, and, after 1983, granting maquiladoras the opportunity to sell up to 40 percent of their products in Mexico.

At the beginning of the BIP, United States companies trickled across the border. By the late 1970s, however, transnational corporations had taken over the border economy. Since the 1980s, maquiladoras have been the engine driving the Mexican economy, providing more than 1,200,000 jobs.

EVOLUTION OF THE MAQUILADORA PROGRAM

Most scholars of Mexican development agree that the Maquiladora Program has progressed through four stages or generations. Jorge Carrillo, Alfredo Hualde, and Cirila Quintero Ramírez denote these as the stages of inception, growth, consolidation, and crisis. During the inception stage (1965–1982), the border region truly operated as an industrial enclave. Under the program's special directives, products were assembled solely for export. The rest of the country was ruled by import-substitution industrialization, which levied high tariffs to discourage imports and promoted production for the national market.

Most of the firms that participated in the program's first stage were labor-intensive operations seeking cheap labor. However, the jobs created did not go to the male agricultural workers laid off in 1964 by the termination of the Bracero Program. Managers preferred to hire young women, creating a labor force segregated by age and sex. In 1974, 80 percent of the maquiladora labor force was female. Younger women, between the ages of sixteen and twenty-four, were more likely to work in electronics assembly, while older women tended to work in the lower paying textile and garment industry (see Fernández-Kelly 1983).

Women were the cheapest source of labor available, and they were thus the preferred workers in Mexico (as they had been in the export processing zones of East Asia). Lower wages were justified through the "feminization" of assembly work. That is, assembly was designated as "unskilled" work, and women workers were held to have traditionally feminine skills (such as knowing how to sew and embroider), which were considered useful for such employment. Managers construed women as being "docile, undemanding, nimble-fingered, and uninterested in participating in unions" (Sklair 1993, pp. 171–172). Crucial in this framing was employers' desire that women not demand higher wages. Moreover, although high percentages of women were the primary or sole providers for their families, they were paid lower wages than their male counterparts. Maquiladora management treated women as secondary and supplemental earners deserving of lower wages.

The second stage of growth (1983–1994) was marked by changes in three main areas: (1) There was a shift to export-oriented industrialization, (2) there was an increased participation of men in the labor force, and (3) there was a movement of firms toward the interior of Mexico. Mexico's inability to pay its foreign debt in 1982 signaled the end of import-substitution industrialization and the opening of Mexican markets to foreign goods and production. Export production was promoted as a crucial means of earning needed foreign exchange to pay the debt and fulfilling International Monetary Fund (IMF) loan deferment agreements. The Maquiladora Program blossomed, assisted by changes in regulations—such as the ability to sell 40 percent of production within the newly opened Mexican markets and the devaluation of the peso. With the devaluation of the peso, foreign companies' dollars stretched further, while national firms, who earned pesos, struggled to compete as inputs, wages, and overhead costs increased overnight.

The ensuing economic crisis resulted in increased unemployment. Under these conditions, men's participation in the maquiladora labor force increased from 20 to 40 percent. This change did not signal an improvement in working conditions, but rather the precariousness of workers' situation. There was, however, a continued gender segregation of employment. A significant number of the new firms that settled in Mexico during this second stage were capital-intensive automobile and auto-parts maquiladoras. Because this was considered skilled work, men were preferred to women. These transplants, mostly from the United States, used a combination of old machinery, new computerized equipment, and selective implementation of flexible production techniques, such as teamwork, Just-in-Time (JIT) production, and Total Quality Management (TQM). However, they differed from the U.S. auto industry in a number of key ways. In particular, the selective adoption of work innovations was combined with low wages and heavy control of workers. Lastly, responding to high turnover rates and wages in the border region, there was a slight shift of firms to the interior of Mexico.

The third stage of consolidation (1995–2000) followed Mexico's signing of the North American Free Trade Agreement (NAFTA). Important changes in this stage included a strengthening of the Maquiladora Program, the rise of the "third generation maquila," and the geographical segmentation of firms. In effect, NAFTA regulations closely followed the Maquiladora Program tax regime, thus increasing the number of national and foreign firms taking advantage of these terms. Yet because of this similarity, the Maquiladora Program was slated to end in the year 2001. This would have ended the most important advantage of the maquiladoras, a 4 percent tax exemption on wages. In the end, however, the program was extended until 2007 due to the political clout of its lobby association. The future of the program continues to be debated at the highest levels of government.

NAFTA allowed U.S. and Canadian companies to move greater portions of their production processes (not only assembly, as previously allowed) to Mexico. In the garment industry, for example, this meant that design, cut, laundry, and trim operations could move south. New regulations also translated into a large number of Asian and some European firms moving to Mexico in order to take advantage of the all-important U.S. market. The number of firms joining the Maquiladora Program was also greatly enhanced by the devaluation of the peso that followed the signing of NAFTA, which cut wages again. However, wages in maquiladoras were now compared to those in East Asia, among the lowest in the world, and not those of the interior of the country.

The consolidation of maquiladoras was also related to geographical segmentation. Participation and competition in international markets drew more firms to Mexico based on low wages and geographical proximity to United States. Thus, the more labor-intensive firms seeking the lowest wages and costs of production (such as garments, footwear, and toy production) moved south, with the more capital-intensive sectors (electronic, automobile, and auto parts) remaining in the north of Mexico.

In the stage of consolidation, third-generation maquilas grew—those that moved beyond assembly to become highly productive, innovative, world-class firms. While most scholars agree these third-generation maquilas exist, there is great debate as to how widespread and complete the process of industrial upgrading has been. On the one hand, there has been enhanced participation of Mexican engineers and technicians, a crucial element of organizational learning. However, organizational innovations have occurred in only a few large automobile and auto-parts firms. Moreover, these innovations continue to be implemented selectively and in conjunction with low wages, worker control, and union marginalization, instead of the high wages and worker autonomy envisioned in the management philosophies. The result has been a hybrid system of greater productivity through the intensification of work. The majority of maquiladoras remain labor-intensive assemblers with a strong gender division of labor and little possibility for promotion.

The last stage in the development of the Maquiladora Program (2001–2006) was marked by the crisis brought about by the 2001 U.S. recession. Over 80 percent of Mexican production was destined for the U.S. market, so the U.S. recession sent shock waves throughout Mexico. All types of production facilities, including the important maquiladora industrial sector, saw a sharp decline in output and revenues. Many firms either shut down or moved to lower-wage countries, such those in East Asia and Central America, leaving the maquiladora sector in crisis.

GAUGING THE MAQUILADORA PROGRAM'S SUCCESS

In evaluating the performance of the Maquiladora Program, it is evident that the goal of development has not been completely fulfilled. The articulation of the local economy (through raw materials, components, and services) to maquiladora export production has been minimal with less than 3 percent of product components being from Mexico (see Carrillo, Hualde, and Quintero Ramírez 2005). Other than in the small number of third-generation maquilas, it is impossible to speak of technology transfer per se, but rather of technology relocation, since most of the technology used in maquiladoras is obsolete. However, in a smaller number of companies where advanced technology is used, the number of Mexican technicians and skilled workers has increased.

Not only has the Maquiladora Program not solved the problem of male unemployment caused by the termination of the Bracero Program, it has accentuated it. Women have been drawn to the border region by employment in the maquiladoras, while men have remained mostly unemployed. Border infrastructure has been pressed to the maximum, as cities and towns have spread into the countryside without public services. Moreover, maquiladoras have routinely disposed of toxic waste by either dumping it into public canals that pass through worker communities or by abandoning drums of waste in the desert. One study found that 60 percent of maquilas did not return toxic wastes to the United States, as required by maquiladora regulations (see León Islas 2004). While the program did create an economic boom, with the maquiladora industry bringing in the second-largest amount of revenue for Mexico after oil, it has also exacerbated social inequalities and created ecological disasters along much of the border.

SEE ALSO *Borders; Corporations; Gender; Labor; North American Free Trade Agreement; Technology, Transfer of*

BIBLIOGRAPHY

Bustamante, Jorge. 1983. Maquiladoras: A New Face of International Capitalism on Mexico's Northern Frontier. In *Women, Men and the International Division of Labor*, ed. June Nash and María Patricia Fernández-Kelly. Albany: State University of New York Press.

Carrillo, Jorge, Alfredo Hualde, and Cirila Quintero Ramírez. 2005. Recorrido por la historia de las maquiladoras en Mexico. *Comercio Exterior* 55 (1): 30–42.

De la O, María Eugenia. 2002. La flexibilidad inflexible: estudios de caso de plantas maquiladoras electrónicas en el norte de México. *Papeles de Población* July–September (33): 200–221.

Fernández-Kelly, María Patricia. 1983. *For We Are Sold, I and My People: Women and Industry in Mexico's Frontier*. Albany: State University of New York Press.

León Islas, Oscar. 2004. Apuntes de coyuntura: Nueva reglamentación para la industria maquiladora. *Comercio Exterior* 54 (1): 80–86.

Sklair, Leslie. 1993. *Assembling for Development: The Maquila Industry in Mexico and the United States*. Updated ed. San Diego: Center for U.S.-Mexican Studies, University of California-San Diego.

Nancy Plankey Videla

MARBURY V. MADISON

SEE *Supreme Court, U.S.*

MARCUSE, HERBERT
1898–1979

Herbert Marcuse was a German American social theorist and activist who gained prominence in the 1960s as "the father of the New Left." Born in Berlin to a prosperous Jewish family, Marcuse served in the German army during World War I and then studied in Berlin and Freiburg from 1919 to 1922. After working as a bookseller in Berlin, Marcuse returned to Freiburg in 1929 to study philosophy with Martin Heidegger. Although he was enthralled with Heidegger's thought, he was deeply dismayed by his teacher's political affiliation with the Nazis. Though his habilitation, *Hegel's Ontology and the Theory of Historicity* (1932), was not accepted because of the rising influence of nazism, Marcuse joined the Frankfurt Institute for Social Research in 1933 and became associated with the neo-Marxist Frankfurt school of critical social theory. In 1934 Marcuse fled Nazi Germany and relocated to Columbia University in New York, receiving U.S. citizenship in 1940. He published *Reason and Revolution* (1941), which established him as an insightful interpreter of the Hegelian-Marxian tradition of dialectical thinking.

Wanting to aid the war effort against the Nazis, Marcuse joined the Office of Strategic Services as an intelligence analyst in 1943. After the war he worked for the State Department until he returned to academia in 1952 and eventually landed a position at Brandeis, where he taught from 1954 to 1965. In 1955 he published *Eros and Civilization*, which argues, contrary to Freud, that civilization is not inevitably repressive, but that the unconscious harbors an instinctual drive toward happiness and freedom that is evident in works of art and other creative cultural products. While a "basic repression" of drives is necessary for civilization, Marcuse criticizes contemporary society's "surplus repression," especially its exploitive economic organization and unnecessary restriction of sexuality. He outlines an alternative form of social organization in which labor is non-alienated and sexuality is free and open.

In 1964 Marcuse published his most influential work, *One-Dimensional Man*, which argues that the technology and consumerism of advanced industrial society enables it to eliminate social critique and conflict by assimilating traditional voices of dissent, for example, the voice of the working class. The result is "one-dimensional man," who cannot think critically about society because it integrates him by continually creating and satisfying "false needs." Genuine social critique must therefore come from nonintegrated, socially marginalized voices. Marcuse's supplemental essay, "Repressive Tolerance" (1965), argues that the liberal conception of "tolerance" blunts social critique by demanding tolerance for oppressive speech. He insists upon a discriminating tolerance that prevents certain forms of intolerance from being voiced. Although criticized by Marxists, *One-Dimensional Man* was a seminal work of 1960s radical thought, and Marcuse began publishing articles, giving lectures, and advising student protest groups all over the world. He influenced such activists as Abbie Hoffman and Angela Davis, who was his student at Brandeis.

Marcuse died on a lecture tour in Starnberg, West Germany. Although his work has been criticized for its lack of empirical analysis, his provocative blend of Marxism and libertarian socialism has inspired much political activism and social critique.

SEE ALSO *Davis, Angela; Frankfurt School; Repressive Tolerance*

BIBLIOGRAPHY

Bokina, John, and Timothy J. Lukes, eds. 1994. *Marcuse: From the New Left to the Next Left.* Lawrence: University of Kansas Press.

Kellner, Douglas. 1984. *Herbert Marcuse and the Crisis of Marxism.* Berkeley: University of California Press.

Marcuse, Herbert. 1964. *One-Dimensional Man: Studies in the Ideology of Advanced Industrial Society.* Boston: Beacon, 1991.

Pippin, Robert, Andrew Feenberg, and Charles P. Webel, eds. 1988. *Marcuse: Critical Theory & the Promise of Utopia.* London: MacMillan Education.

William M. Curtis

MARGINAL COST

SEE *Average and Marginal Cost.*

MARGINAL PRINCIPLE

SEE *Marginalism.*

MARGINAL PRODUCTIVITY

A dominant theme in both the explication and legitimization of a market economy is that if individuals work hard and effectively, they will be appropriately rewarded. Typically understood as the Protestant ethic, the theme provides moral approval for hard work and asset accumulation, even though the terms *hard work, effectively,* and *appropriately* require technical specification and thereby a narrower meaning than the theme seems to offer at first glance. The moral injunction is transformed when translated into economic theory.

The foremost attempt to do so was by John Bates Clark (1847–1938) in the late nineteenth century. His ethical marginal productivity theory was an attempt to prove mathematically that people receive what they produce. Correctly formulated, the theory says something much less than that: namely, that the wage rate is only an element in an equilibrium equation and not a uniquely causal factor; indeed, that marginal productivity explains only the demand for labor and not the wage rate. The hold of the Protestant ethic is such that even though economists understand the more limited significance of marginal productivity, an inevitable tendency is for some economists to revert to Clark's ethical formulation.

That the marginal productivity theory is only a theory of the demand for labor is easily shown. Assuming (eventual) diminishing returns, the marginal product curve for a particular occupation slopes downward to the right. The wage rate is a function of the demand and supply of labor. The marginal product curve represents the demand for labor for the firm: As the wage rate falls, employers will hire more workers, and vice versa. The summation of the individual firms' marginal product curves yields the market-demand curve for labor. It, together with the labor-supply curve, determines the wage rate. In equilibrium, the intersection of the labor-demand and labor-supply curves will yield the amount of labor hired and the wage rate at which they are hired. The marginal productivity curve enters only into the determination of the labor-demand curve; to determine the wage rate (and employment) one must introduce the labor-supply curve. If, in a particular occupation, the supply of labor shifts to the right, there will be greater employment at a lower wage rate—even though workers are working as hard as before.

Another way of looking at the foregoing is to consider the downward-sloping curve as the value of the marginal product, constructed thusly: The marginal physical product, itself a result of technology, is the immediate cause of the downward slope; the marginal physical product must be multiplied by the price of the product, which is a function of the demand and supply of the product, all of which is separate from or external to the demand for labor. Workers may work as hard as they can, but at best this will only raise slightly the value of the marginal product curve; much more important is technology and the product price. The wage rate is governed largely by nonethical factors.

So, far from proving that people receive (the value of) what they produce, the theory, using the conventional assumptions, proves a tendency toward equal wages. Assume three occupations, each with its respective, negatively inclined marginal productivity curve. Let the three curves start at any three points on the vertical marginal product axis (employment is on the horizontal axis) and let them decline at different rates. The language, "one occupation is more productive than another," is predicated neither on one curve starting higher than another on the vertical axis, nor on one curve declining less rapidly than the other. It asserts something stronger, something that is analytically false. Assume further a labor-supply curve for each marginal productivity curve; their three respective intersections yield three wage rates, one for each occupation. The conventional assumptions are competition and labor mobility. Labor in the lowest-wage occupations will move to the higher-paying ones. The labor-supply curve shifts to the left in the formerly low-wage occupation, thereby raising the wage; and vice versa in the formerly high-wage occupations. The process, under the postulated static conditions, continues in principle until the same wage rate prevails in all three industries. The theory produces the result, not that one industry has higher wages because it is more productive than another(s), but that there is a tendency toward equal wages. That the tendency is not reached is due to immobility of labor, noncompetitive conditions, wages as not the only remuneration in a job, and evolutionary and dynamic changes in technology, tastes, and so on.

At any rate, marginal productivity theory is only a theory of the demand for labor and is itself dependent in part on technology and on the demand (relative to the supply) of the product of labor. Other marginalist formulations, with the exception of marginal utility as a theory of value, have not been given ethical status: marginal cost, marginal disutility, marginal efficiency of capital or of investment, marginal propensities to consume and to save, marginal rate of substitution, marginal tax rate, marginal revenue, marginal utility of money, and marginal rate of transformation are important and nonethical categories. So too is the marginal productivity theory as a theory of the demand for labor and employment of labor; it is, however, neither a theory of wages nor the Protestant ethic in economic garment.

SEE ALSO *Capital; Human Capital; Marginalism; Market Economy*

BIBLIOGRAPHY

Bronfenbrenner, Martin. 1971. *Income Distribution Theory.* Chicago: Aldine.

Clark, John Bates. 1899. *The Distribution of Wealth: A Theory of Wages, Interest, and Profits.* New York: Macmillan.

Hicks, John R. 1932. *The Theory of Wages.* New York: Macmillan.

Robinson, Joan. 1933. *The Economics of Imperfect Competition.* London: Macmillan.

Rothschild, Kurt W. 1993. *Employment, Wages, and Income Distribution: Critical Essays in Economics.* New York: Routledge.

Warren J. Samuels

MARGINALISM

Marginalism is one of two types of approaches to studying economic and political processes. Each is both a technique of analysis and a view of how both individual economic agents and the economy as a whole function in reacting to change and in causing change, and therefore policy. Marginalism, or incrementalism, gives effect to the methodological individualist perceptions that the meaning of human action is best comprehended at the level of individuals, that change takes place along various margins and not in totals, that decision making/policy is made in a composite manner, as the sum of the results of independent but interacting agents and institutions.

The system comprising all of such agents and institutions moves as a result of marginal adjustments to changes originating within and outside the domain of each. Government, for example, is no single decisional unit; decision making is incrementally developed by a multiplicity of agencies. Systems analysis, on the other hand, gives effect to the methodologic collectivist perception that the meaning of any marginal adjustment, agent or institution is a function of the total system of which it is a part. Systems analysis thus facilitates the study of the totality of interacting agents and institutions, therefore of group processes, and how agents and institutions generate and respond to large-scale social forces, problems, and so on. The systems approach to policymaking centers on the study of the economic and political structures and processes within which individual behavior takes place, just as the incrementalist or marginalist approach focuses on the individual behavior putatively independent of systemic structures, processes, and forces. Uniting the two types of approach enables the combined study of the impacts of system upon individuals and of individuals upon system. Moreover, no single mode exists for modeling either parts or wholes, incremental or systemic change. The variety of schools of thought operating in each approach is enormous; and the range of models runs from the single individual to the world system.

Marginalism gives effect to important aspects of change. One aspect is that a change in a variable is not likely to be a change in its totality; that is, in all of it, but a small increase or a small decrease here and /or there, along one margin but not another. For example, a typical change of tastes does not involve now buying fish and no longer buying pork, but a little more of one and a little less of the other. The change is said to take place at the margin. Another aspect is the impact of a change in one variable at its margin on another variable at its margin. The increase or decrease in purchases of fish may lead to a change in employment in the same direction, and vice versa for pork. The concept of elasticity, for example, relates proportionate changes in quantity to proportionate changes in price or income. A change in aggregate consumption spending will change income in the same direction and may also change investment in the same direction; but not every element comprising the total need change.

Another aspect of marginalism has to do with the tendency of an economy, or parts of it, to adjust so as to reach equilibrium. When consumption increases, leading to an increase in income, consumption further increases, though generally by an amount smaller than the initial increase, and investment also increases; eventually the increases in spending diminish to zero, which will be when spending equals income for one period and income equals spending for the next period; the economy is in equilibrium. As for that increase in investment, the increase in consumption and, with it, income tend to increase the expected rate of profit (marginal efficiency of capital, or MEC) not on all investment but on new investment; that is, investment at the margin; in the example, investment increases as the MEC increases relative to the interest rate, a proxy for alternative uses of money.

Still another aspect of marginalism is its use in optimization. If one defines optimization as when benefit equals cost, then an individual will optimize a line of expenditure at the point of purchase when the additional benefit of an increase in spending equals the cost so that there is no incentive to change spending. A firm will optimize its level of production when the marginal cost of a level of production equals the marginal revenue derived from its sale and when the marginal revenues of different periods and in different markets are equal. An agent is in both equimarginal equilibrium and optimization, when the last dollar spent on each line of spending equals the benefit derived from it, so there is no incentive to change the pattern of spending, given the pattern of tastes. In this simple model, equilibrium and optimization coincide. But, many production processes have increasing returns (marginal cost of another physical unit decreasing). If the good is priced equal to its marginal cost, the total production costs cannot be recovered. Pricing necessarily is an institutional matter of industry cost accounting and other conventions.

HISTORICAL PERSPECTIVE

Marginal analysis in economics originated in two initial forms. The English economist David Ricardo's theory of rent involved decreasing marginal returns in the form of food from additional increases in inputs so that rent was a differential. The returns are still positive, but decreasing, until they reach zero, eliciting no further increases in inputs. In the English jurist and philosopher Jeremy Bentham's utilitarianism, an activity is characterized by pain and pleasure, such that an activity will be conducted up so long as the pleasure exceeds the pain (perceived benefits are greater than perceived costs), to the point that the two are equal in magnitude. Whereas Ricardo's theory involves physical inputs and outputs, Bentham's theory involves subjective feelings of pain and pleasure.

In the late nineteenth century, albeit with many precursors, several economists used marginalism to construct a theory of value different from cost of production. In their view, the value of anything that is bought and sold is at the point where the marginal (last) buyer and seller agree as to the price of purchase and sale. The buyer derives marginal utility from additional acquisitions of the item. The level of marginal utility decreases as more is acquired. Tracking falling marginal utility is falling demand: Because marginal utility is decreasing, the individual buyer will purchase more only at lower prices. Sellers will sell more only if they receive more, due to increasing costs. This is the subjectivist, or Austrian, theory of value in which value is a function of scarcity, as opportunity cost meets subjective demands in the market.

All aspects of marginalist change have proven to be useful either as conjectural explanation, actual explanation, and/or a tool of analysis of how changes in variables occur and their consequences. In many interesting and important respects, the world changes at the margin.

LIMITATIONS

Marginalism, like all concepts and theories in economics, has its limits. One class of limits has to do with the identification of a margin. If one is going to make marginal comparisons, the arrays of margins must be specified. In some respects this is a matter of the physical monetary activity itself. But in other respects it depends on subjective identifications of the lines along which marginal change will be measured. This will depend in part on how firms and households are organized, on the cost accounting conventions adopted by firms and how they are applied, on legal requirements, and so on. The analysis of consumption usually centers on particular commodities or groups of commodities and may include attention to marginal adjustments between complementary goods and between substitutable goods. The analysis of production, undertaken by the typical multi-product firm, is more complicated. Here the assignment of costs between fixed and variable costs can take place along a variety of different identifications of margins and with numbers further influenced by the identification of products and product groups and of block levels of production, instead of single units, in the construction of cost accounting. For nonrival goods, marginal cost of another user is equal to zero. If users are to be charged the cost of the unit they use, some could pay nothing, while others pay some share of the fixed cost of production. Who is designated the marginal user is an institutional matter. Thus, if marginal productivity is the incremental increase (decrease) in total output associated with an increase (decrease) in input by one unit (which may be a block of units), the calculation is dependent on the definitions of product line, input, output, and margin.

Another class of limits involves what some economists perceive to be a superficial rendering of human activity. The question is whether people act as they are portrayed in theory, whether the maximizing or optimizing behavior is more complex than, perhaps even different from, that described in marginalist accounts, whether tastes are given or stable, and so on.

A different class of limits involves the larger system of things in which change—marginal change—takes place. If people make marginal adjustments in their buying and selling and other economic activity, the question involved is, in part, what is the market in which this takes place and how is it formed. Markets are created as firms and governments exercise strategic behavior and attempt to form and structure markets to accomplish their goals. Beyond markets alone, the larger system involves the overall structure of power, the legal-economic nexus, the set of macroeconomic policies pursued by governments, and so on, in which marginal adjustments take place and have effects.

Closely related limitations derive from the specification of the unit of analysis. The unit may be a representative firm, a particular industry, or an element of a particular country or of a particular region, as well as the world system. These and other limits apply to both marginal and systems analysis.

Also closely related is the evolutionary dynamics of the larger economic system, a process of change which manifests in changes at the margin but also, and more importantly, swamps marginal adjustments. Further limitations are imposed by theories centering on asymmetric information, expectations, uncertainty, strategic behavior, corporate goal formation, bounded information, and so on. In practice, the various strengths and limits are trumped by the research interests of particular economists and their respective schools of thought.

SEE ALSO *Economics, Neoclassical; General Equilibrium; Substitutability; Trade-offs*

BIBLIOGRAPHY

Easton, David. 1965. *A Systems Analysis of Political Life*. New York: Wiley.

Elster, Jon. 1989. *Nuts and Bolts for the Social Sciences*. Cambridge, U.K.: Cambridge University Press.

Lindblom, Charles E. 1958. Policy Analysis. *American Economic Review* 48 (June): 298–312.

Marshall, Alfred. 1890. *Principles of Economics*. London: Macmillan.

Robinson, Joan. 1933. *The Economics of Imperfect Competition*. London: Macmillan.

Samuels, Warren J. 1994. Part-Whole Relationships. In *The Elgar Companion to Institutional and Evolutionary Economics*, Vol. 2, ed. Geoffrey M. Hodgson, Warren J. Samuels, and Mark R. Tool, 142–146. Brookfield, VT: Edward Elgar.

Veblen, Thorstein. 1997. Why Is Economics Not an Evolutionary Science? In *Classics in Institutional Economics, The Founders, 1890–1945* Vol. 1, ed. Malcolm Rutherford and Warren J. Samuels, 2–27. London: Pickering and Chatto.

Warren J. Samuels

MARGINALIZATION

Marginalization comprises those processes by which individuals and groups are ignored or relegated to the sidelines of political debate, social negotiation, and economic bargaining—and kept there. Homelessness, age, language, employment status, skill, race, and religion are some criteria historically used to marginalize. Marginalized groups tend to overlap; groups excluded in one arena, say in political life, tend to be excluded in other arenas, say in economic status. Concern with marginalization is relatively recent. As the advance of democratization and citizenship swell the ranks of those "included" in the social order, the plight of those with limited access to the franchise and without rights or at least enforceable claims to rights becomes problematic.

Our discussion focuses on two main issues. First, what are marginalizing processes and how do they operate? Second, why are so many of the same groups—women, ethnic groups, religious minorities—marginalized in a variety of situations and institutions? Major approaches to marginalization are represented by neoclassical economics, Marxism, social exclusion theory, and recent research that develops social exclusion theory findings.

Neoclassical economists trace marginalization to individual character flaws or to cultural resistance to individualism. Their explanations of poverty stress the notion of the *residuum*, defined as those "limp in both body and mind." This residuum—the term was made famous by the

Cambridge economist, Alfred Marshall—will only work when forced to do so. Generous social policies encourage its members to stay out of the labor force. To explain why some groups are found disproportionately in the residuum, economists sometimes cite the presence of a "culture of poverty," which although adapted to alleviate the worst effects of poverty in fact reinforces it.

In contrast, Marxists see marginalization as a structural phenomenon endemic to capitalism. For Marx, the "reserve army of the proletariat," a pool of unemployed or partially unemployed laborers, is used by employers to lower wages. Together with déclassé elements, the most impoverished elements from the "reserve army" form the bases for the lumpenproletariat—in Marx's time, a motley conglomeration of beggars, discharged soldiers, prostitutes, and vagabonds. Marx also noted the presence of ethnic minorities, such as the Irish, in the "reserve army." He attributed the composition of the reserve army of labor and thus the lumpenproletariat to capitalist efforts to divide the working class along ethnic lines.

Although strongly influenced by Marxism, contemporary social exclusion theory stresses the importance of social networks and symbolic boundaries. Studying the economic recovery of the late 1970s, French sociologists noted that some groups—particularly migrants and youth—benefited relatively little from renewed growth. They concluded that sustained unemployment leads to poverty, which in turn leads to social isolation, including the breakup of families and the financial inability to fully participate in popular culture. Shorn of kin ties and cultural associations, the unemployed have difficulty finding a job and eventually become unemployable.

Current research has led to modifications of social exclusion theory. States and kin networks can play a significant role in moderating the effects of prolonged unemployment. Generous Dutch and Danish welfare states keep the unemployed out of poverty. In Italy and Spain the tendency of all unmarried adult children, including unemployed adult children, to remain in households with members who have ties to labor markets moderates social isolation. Less generous welfare states and the relatively early departure of adult children from households leaves the unemployed in France, Germany, and the United Kingdom especially susceptible to social isolation. Everywhere, immigrant workers, who do not receive the full benefits of the welfare state and whose families are often not integrated into job markets, remain marginalized.

Recent work by American sociologist Charles Tilly further stresses the importance of economic structures and social networks to marginalization. For Tilly, capitalist control of jobs combined with included groups' monopolization of job niches help explain why adult, native, white

men are privileged in many different hierarchies, whereas nonadult, migrant, nonwhite women are invariably among the excluded. He emphasizes that new job hierarchies within capitalist industry tend to be filled according to already existing social distinctions; employers use old distinctions to justify and buttress new workplace distinctions and maintain harmony by endorsing distinctions that already divide the labor force. In so doing, employers and included groups perpetuate existing social distinctions and reinforce them, creating durable inequality.

Increasingly, modern interpretations stress marginalization's collective character and the role of the state, elites, and entrenched groups in determining who is marginalized. But wherever it occurs, marginalization seldom begins afresh. Institutions typically fill new job hierarchies in line with existing social ranks. Groups marginalized in the past have the best chance of being marginalized in the future.

SEE ALSO *Education, Unequal; Inequality, Income; Inequality, Political; Lumpenproletariat; Marxism; Social Exclusion; Stratification*

BIBLIOGRAPHY

Gallie, Duncan, ed. 2004. *Resisting Marginalization: Unemployment Experience and Social Policy in the European Union.* Oxford: Oxford University Press.

Romero, Mary, and Eric Margolis, eds. 2005. *The Blackwell Companion to Social Inequalities.* Oxford: Blackwell.

Silver, Hilary. 1994. Social Exclusion and Social Solidarity: Three Paradigms. *International Labour Review* 133 (5–6): 531–578.

Tilly, Charles. 1999. *Durable Inequality.* Berkeley: University of California Press.

Michael Hanagan

MARIJUANA
SEE *Drugs of Abuse.*

MARITAL CONFLICT

In marriage, conflict occurs when the needs and desires of spouses diverge and are thus incompatible. Because spouses interact with each other regarding a number of issues important to their marriage over time, it is inevitable that conflict will occur to at least some degree in every marriage. It is not the existence of conflict in marriage per se that is detrimental to marital satisfaction or stability, but how spouses manage conflict when it occurs.

Conflicts can be settled positively through discussion, but in some cases may result in the escalation of arguing without resolution, or with each spouse ignoring the area of conflict in an attempt to prevent negative marital interactions. The quality of the marriage suffers when conflicts remain unresolved, and in some marriages the inability to successfully manage conflict can lead to physical abuse, sometimes with severe consequences. Understanding the causes and consequences of marital conflict has been the target of a growing body of empirical research, and the results of this research have been useful in developing therapeutic programs aimed at assisting spouses to manage conflict in a positive manner.

One influential model created by Caryl Rusbult and her colleagues to explain how spouses manage marital conflict is called the exit-voice-loyalty-neglect model (Rusbult and Zembrodt 1983). This model stipulates that spouses can respond to conflict in a positive or negative fashion, and in either an active or passive manner. Walking away from a partner during a conflict (exit), for example, reflects an active/negative way to deal with conflict, whereas ignoring the negative event (neglect) reflects a passive/negative way to deal with conflict. By contrast, openly discussing the conflict and attempting to resolve it (voice) reflects an active/positive way to deal with conflict, whereas hoping that the partner will work alone to solve the problem (loyalty) reflects a passive/positive manner of conflict resolution. In general, voice offers the best opportunity for resolving conflict, while the other options tend to prolong the conflict and erode marital quality.

A second influential model of understanding how spouses manage marital conflict has been developed by John Gottman (1994) over several years. In Gottman's original research, married couples that had reported being very happy or very unhappy with their marriage were asked to discuss areas of conflict in their marriage while being videotaped. Through careful observation of these interactions, it was found that unhappy spouses tended to frequently criticize each other, respond defensively to their partners' comments, treat their partners with contempt, and emotionally withdraw from the discussion. Gottman also found that the more spouses engaged in these four types of behaviors while managing conflicts, the more likely they were to experience declines in marital satisfaction and to eventually divorce.

When faced with marital conflict, certain people are more likely than others to engage in negative interpersonal behaviors. For instance, some people tend to be very anxious about how much their romantic partners love them, fearing that their partners may eventually abandon the relationship. When relationship conflicts occur, these anxious individuals are more likely to become very upset and to believe that their partners will leave them

(Campbell, Simpson, Boldry, and Kashy 2005). Also, people that chronically feel less loved by their partners behave more negatively toward their partners in the face of marital conflict (Murray, Bellavia, Rose, and Griffin 2003). Ironically, although these people fear the loss of their spouse and relationship, when conflicts arise, they tend to behave in ways that have been shown to destabilize marriages.

IMPACT ON HEALTH

The inability to successfully manage conflict in marriage is also linked with declines in physical well-being. Research in the late twentieth century revealed that marital disagreement is related to increased blood pressure and heart rate, as well as with alterations in immune functioning. For instance, in a 1998 study of 93 newlywed couples, Janice Kiecolt-Glaser and colleagues found that hostile interactions observed while couples attempted to resolve a relationship conflict were associated with increased levels of epinephrine (adrenaline), norepinephrine, and growth hormone, as well as greater immunological change over the subsequent twenty-four hours. This pattern of results was replicated in a sample of older couples who had been married an average of forty-two years. Therefore, because stressful interpersonal events can result in immunosuppression, which leaves people more vulnerable to a variety of illnesses, couples that are not effective at managing marital disagreement expose themselves to increased physiological stress over time, which leaves them vulnerable to health problems.

In a 1993 article, Craig Ewart finds that the presence or absence of negative behaviors directed toward spouses while discussing relationship conflicts is more responsible for physiological changes than are positive behaviors. For example, hostile marital interactions produced significant increases in blood pressure among patients with hypertension, whereas neither positive nor neutral behaviors were associated with change. Kiecolt-Glaser and colleagues also found that negative, but not positive, behaviors were related to decreases in immune functioning in both short- and long-term marriages. Therefore, responding to marital conflicts with negative interpersonal behaviors is particularly bad for the stability of the marriage and for one's physical health.

MARITAL THERAPY

Therapeutic approaches to marital therapy have been greatly influenced by research on conflict resolution in marriage. Overall, it is agreed that therapy is most effective when both spouses participate. Some therapeutic approaches focus directly on altering the behavior of spouses during conflicts. Spouses are taught to identify their negative interpersonal behaviors during conflict, to discontinue the use of these behaviors, and to engage in more positive forms of conflict resolution as suggested by the therapist. Alternatively, other therapeutic approaches assume that unhappiness with the marriage is directly related with negative conflict resolution behaviors, and thus focuses on the reasons why people are unhappy with their marriage.

Therapeutic approaches to marital conflicts operate on the premise that if spouses can understand the source of their marital unhappiness and work to make a better marriage, their behaviors in the face of marital conflicts will naturally improve. Both approaches are somewhat effective for improving conflict management in marriage.

SEE ALSO *Conflict; Disease; Divorce and Separation; Exit, Voice, and Loyalty; Hypertension; Infidelity; Marriage; Romance; Stress*

BIBLIOGRAPHY

Campbell, Lorne, Jeffry A. Simpson, Jennifer Boldry, and Deborah A. Kashy. 2005. Perceptions of Conflict and Support in Romantic Relationships: The Role of Attachment Anxiety. *Journal of Personality and Social Psychology* 88 (3): 510–531.

Ewart, Craig K. 1993. Marital Interaction—The Context for Psychosomatic Research. *Psychosomatic Medicine* 55 (5): 410–412.

Gottman, John Mordechai. 1994. *What Predicts Divorce? The Relationship between Marital Processes and Marital Outcomes.* Hillsdale, NJ: Erlbaum.

Kiecolt-Glaser, Janice K., Ronald Glaser, John T. Cacioppo, and William B. Malarkey. 1998. Marital Stress: Immunologic, Neuroendocrine, and Autonomic Correlates. *Annals of the New York Academy of Sciences* 840 (1): 656–663.

Murray, Sandra L., Gina M. Bellavia, Paul Rose, and Dale W. Griffin. 2003. Once Hurt, Twice Hurtful: How Perceived Regard Regulates Daily Marital Interactions. *Journal of Personality and Social Psychology* 84 (1): 126–147.

Rusbult, Caryl E., and Isabella M. Zembrodt. 1983. Responses to Dissatisfaction in Romantic Involvements: A Multidimensional Scaling Analysis. *Journal of Experimental Social Psychology* 19: 274–293.

Lorne Campbell

MARKET CLEARING

The concept of market clearing related initially to the capability of the aggregate economy to generate sufficient purchasing power to assure that the economy's aggregate output will find purchasers. When this is the case, the total value of the economy's output will be exactly equal to the total value of the economy's purchases. In short, the economy's aggregate demand will be the equivalent of aggregate supply so that a situation historically termed a *glut* of output will be nonexistent.

Concern about the possibility of a glut dates (at least) to late-eighteenth-century France, where production was directed by central authority toward luxury products intended for export (for example, tapestries, crystal, velvet) in order to increase the economy's ability to earn gold via trade. The fear that French purchasing power could become insufficient was quelled by the articulation of a generalization by Jean-Baptiste Say in 1803 that became known as "the Law of Markets." It maintained that, because the value generated by the process of production simultaneously generates an equivalent flow of factor payments, an insufficiency of purchasing power is impossible because "supply creates its own demand." The logic of Say's argument was introduced into England by John Stuart Mill in the mid-nineteenth century and continued to dominate academic thinking until the mid-1930s, as Ingrid Rima notes in her 2001 work. Traditional nineteenth-century thinkers concerned themselves primarily with the problems of value and distribution and the equilibration of competitive markets, although they also understood that monetary expansion could result in inflation. The argument that purchasing power in the aggregate economy might be deficient was largely the province of monetary reformers who were unaware that Say's Law was predicated on a barter interpretation of the aggregate economy so that money served simply as a convenience to facilitate exchange.

It was not until the depressed 1930s that attention was focused on the linkage between changes in monetary aggregates and changes in real economic activity. John Maynard Keynes wrote his *The General Theory of Employment, Interest, and Money* (1936) to challenge Say's Law on the ground that it is inapplicable to a monetary production economy: "Say's Law is not the true law relating the aggregate demand and supply functions" (p. 26), because in a monetary economy the aggregate demand function does *not* coincide with the aggregate supply function. In particular Keynes maintained that it is the part played by the aggregate demand function that has been overlooked (p. 89). Thus his theory focused on the components of aggregate expenditures, emphasizing the stable relationship between consumption and income and the great instability of investment expenditures in consequence of the inherent uncertainty of the marginal efficiency of capital (Davidson 1972) relative to the rate of interest paid for funds, whether these are borrowed or internally generated (Minsky 1982). The argument that followed was when aggregate effective demand falls short of the economy's resource capability (given the level of technical knowledge), the demand deficiency is evidenced principally in the involuntary unemployment of some part of its workforce (Keynes 1936;

Weintraub 1966). Thinkers who responded positively to Keynes's argument looked to fiscal policy, that is, reduced tax collections and increased government spending financed via bond sales to increase aggregate spending via the operation of the multiplier, which was expected to enable both commodity and labor markets to clear at a higher income level. The persuasiveness of the theory of aggregate demand culminated in the "Keynesian revolution," which shifted economists' perspectives to the behavior of the economy's macroeconomic magnitudes. The shift underscores the distinction between the market equilibrium of industry demand and supply curves and market clearing in the sense of equivalence of aggregate demand and aggregate supply, in which full employment was shown to be the economy's normal equilibrium state.

It is perhaps not surprising that the ink of *The General Theory* was hardly dry before John R. Hicks of Oxford University wrote "Mr. Keynes and the Classics: A Suggested Reinterpretation" (1937), in which he maintained that the criticism of indeterminacy that Keynes made against the classical theory of interest was equally the fault of his own liquidity preference theory. Hicks's reinterpretation suggested that by joining liquidity preference to abstinence theory, which he represented in terms of two new curves, the IS and the LM curves, it can be shown that savings are a function of both income and the interest rate. The intersection of the IS curve and the LM curve, which brings together the four variables of the interest rate problem, the savings function, the investment function, the system's monetary stock, and the liquidity preference function, will make the interest rate determinant. Thus Hicks and the Harvard professor Alvin Harvey Hansen (1953) integrated the general equilibrium approach introduced by Leon Walras in the 1870s to demonstrate mathematically that all markets are interdependent and simultaneously able to clear goods and factor markets via the guidance of an auctioneer through whom participants "re-contracted" until mutually satisfactory trades could be consummated. Thus began a counterrevolution against Keynes (sometimes called neo-Walrasianism) that reasserted the market clearing capability of an economy characterized by flexible wages and prices (Patinkin 1956). In a 1956 model that also incorporated the labor market, Don Patinkin maintained that Keynes did not adequately recognize the significance of price changes on the real value (that is, the purchasing power) of monetary balances and wealth as a mechanism for restoring commodity, bond, and labor market equilibriums with full employment. In effect the integration of Walrasian foundations onto Keynes's model, whose foundation is Marshallian, undermined the Keynesian revolution.

It was to address neo-Walrasianism challenges to Keynes's credibility that Robert Clower (1965) and Axel Leijonhufvud (1967) undertook reinterpretations of Keynes's *General Theory* as a disequilibrium problem attributable to information and coordination failures. They argued that markets clear when potential traders successfully make the adjustments needed for market clearing instead of lagging behind. The theoretical contributions of Clower and others underscored the inadequacy of the micro-foundations inherent in the so-called "Keynesian" framework. Their efforts encouraged an increasingly elaborate micro-approach to rationalize sticky wages and prices in efficiency terms (Barro and Grossman 1976). The essential research focus for many Keynesian economists thus became to identify the reasons for ongoing wage and price rigidities that impede market clearing and to explain the successes and failures of coordination or its absence (Weintraub 1979).

BIBLIOGRAPHY

Barro, Robert J., and Herschel I. Grossman. 1976. *Money, Employment, and Inflation.* New York: Cambridge University Press.

Clower, Robert. 1965. The Keynesian Counter-Revolution: A Theoretical Appraisal. In *The Theory of Interest Rates*, ed. Frank H. Hahn and Frank P. Brechling, 103–125. London: Macmillan.

Davidson, Paul. 1972. *Money and the Real World.* 2nd ed. London: Macmillan.

Hansen, Alvin Harvey. 1953. *A Guide to Keynes.* New York: McGraw-Hill.

Hicks, John R. 1937. Mr. Keynes and the Classics: A Suggested Reinterpretation. *Econometrica* 6: 147–159.

Keynes, John Maynard. 1936. *The General Theory of Employment, Interest, and Money.* New York: Harcourt, Brace.

Leijonhufvud, Axel. 1967. Keynes and the Keynesians: A Suggested Reinterpretation. *American Economic Review* 57 (2): 401–410.

Minsky, Hyman P. 1982. *Can "It" Happen Again?* Armonk, NY: Sharpe.

Patinkin, Don. 1965. *Money, Interest, and Prices.* 2nd ed. New York: Harper and Row.

Rima, Ingrid Hahne. 2001. *Development of Economic Analysis.* 6th ed. London and New York: Routledge.

Weintraub, E. Roy. 1979. *Microfoundations.* Cambridge, U.K.: Cambridge University Press.

Weintraub, Sidney. 1966. *A Keynesian Theory of Employment Growth and Income Distribution.* Philadelphia: Chilton.

Ingrid H. Rima

MARKET CLEARINGHOUSE

A clearinghouse is a third-party establishment that operates with stock exchanges to clear trades, collect and maintain margin monies, regulate delivery, and report trading data. All trades on an exchange go through the clearinghouse. Three million contracts trade each day on the Chicago Mercantile Exchange, and 1.5 billion shares change hands each day on the New York Stock Exchange (NYSE). If an exchange clearinghouse were to fail it would trigger a financial meltdown. When the stock market crashed in 1987 the Federal Reserve moved quickly to provide access to liquidity for exchange clearinghouses, and none failed.

The clearinghouse performs two principal functions: (1) accounting; and (2) contract guarantee. Accounting is a necessity, but it can be outsourced. The fundamental economic function of the clearinghouse is the contract guarantee, which makes large-scale anonymous trading feasible.

The accounting function is easy to understand and mechanically hard to complete. The clearinghouse keeps the books. At the end of the trading day (or on rare occasions during the trading day) the clearinghouse requires that traders balance their account. The guarantee function is harder to understand, but it is *the* reason for the clearinghouse. In any transaction a seller agrees to deliver at a price and a buyer agrees to take delivery at that price. But for transactions separated in time or space, payment and delivery are uncertain. The clearinghouse puts itself in the middle of each transaction. Technically, buyers buy from the clearinghouse and sellers sell to the clearinghouse. If the seller fails to deliver, he or she defaults to the clearinghouse. The clearinghouse delivers to the buyer. Traders on organized exchanges do not concern themselves with the creditworthiness of their trading partner because their trading partner is the clearinghouse.

In over-the-counter markets traders trade directly with other traders—there is no clearinghouse in the middle. In most over-the-counter markets trades take place only among principals (large financial institutions) that know each other very well.

The clearinghouse guarantee exposes the clearinghouse to default risk. Most traders operate on credit. The clearinghouse requires traders to post margins (collateral) on their accounts so that they have an incentive to perform, and if they do not perform the clearinghouse has immediate access to the collateral. Setting the correct margin involves walking a fine line: a margin too high pushes traders off organized exchanges, and a margin too low exposes the clearinghouse to excess risk.

eBay is an Internet auction site that bills itself as "The World's Online Marketplace." Traders meet virtually to agree on the terms of a trade for virtually any item. A big problem for eBay is that a few sellers do not deliver and a few buyers do not pay. If potential eBay traders do not have confidence in the performance of their trading partner, then they will not go to eBay for trades, and the exchange dies. eBay works hard to assure traders that their transactions will be consummated.

eBay bought PayPal, an electronic payments system, in 2002. Through PayPal, one can authorize credit card payments or electronic check transfers. PayPal provides eBay with an electronic accounting system, the first function of a clearinghouse. In addition, PayPal has begun to guarantee transactions. If one buys from a PayPal authorized seller using the electronic check payment method, then PayPal guarantees delivery of items that cost less than $1,000. PayPal also guarantees that the seller will receive payment.

In conclusion, exchanges provide an anonymous marketplace for traders in modern economies. Clearinghouses provide the assurance that delivery and payment occurs.

SEE ALSO *Financial Markets; Market Clearing*

BIBLIOGRAPHY

The Chicago Mercantile Exchange Education Center. http://www.cme.com/edu/course/intro/clrhouse9706.html.

Craine, Roger, and David Bates. 1999. Valuing the Futures Market Clearinghouse's Default Exposure During the 1987 Crash. *Journal of Money, Credit, and Banking* 31: 248–272.

Hull, John C. 2006. *Options, Futures, and Other Derivatives*. 6th ed. Upper Saddle River, NJ: Prentice Hall.

Roger Craine

MARKET CORRECTION

Market correction refers to a temporary reversal of an upward trend in security prices. Market corrections typically involve a drop of between 10 to 20 percent in security prices. Such declines are temporary secondary trends that are exhibited within a larger upward trend in security prices. Every asset class, including stocks, currencies, commodities, and real estate, has been subject to periodic episodes of corrections. History shows that a 20 percent correction occurs once every five years in the stock market.

The phenomenon of a correction can be understood better within a theoretical framework of an equilibrium asset pricing model. The prediction of a multifactor asset pricing model is:

$$\mu = \lambda_0 + B\lambda_K$$

where μ is a vector of expected returns to N securities, λ_0 is the risk-free parameter, B is a vector of factor sensitivities, and λ_K is a $(K \times 1)$ vector of factor risk premia. The equilibrium model predicts that changes in expected returns occur in response to changes in the risk-free rate, or in factor premia. An increase in expected return should lead to a drop in prices, which is, in turn, reflected as a market correction.

Some of these theoretical predictions are upheld by the data. It is now well accepted that most market corrections are preceded by a sharp jump in short-term interest rates. An increase in the risk-free rate of interest is predicted by theory to increase the expected return, and hence to lead to a drop in current prices. Market corrections have also been driven by a decline in earnings momentum. The decline in earnings momentum leads investors to revise downward their expectation of future profitability. This, in turn, leads to a drop in current stock prices.

Revised beliefs about economic conditions, however, only partially explain why corrections occur. In a challenge to rational asset pricing models, fear and greed have been advanced as explanations for market corrections. It is believed that market corrections curb excessive investor optimism, also labeled as greed. Fear of further market declines keeps markets down thereafter. The situation reverses when rational investors step in to exploit the buying opportunity created by price drops. Proponents of this irrational behavior offer the short-lived nature of a typical correction as evidence to bolster their view. The average length of a market correction over the period from 1872 to 2004 has been about twelve months. Security prices return to their precorrection levels after this period and, in fact, continue to trend upward thereafter. Such a reversal is inconsistent with a theoretical asset pricing model since the underlying economic conditions that may warrant a market correction do not experience a similar reversal.

Whatever processes underlie a market correction, investors can expect to experience steep drops in security prices periodically. They should also expect every asset category to experience such corrections. Globalization of financial markets has meant that international markets are also not immune to such corrections. Emerging markets experienced a steep market correction of greater than 20 percent during May to June of 2006. Higher volatility in emerging markets makes them more susceptible to frequent market corrections.

Experienced investors are able to weather market corrections with appropriate risk management strategies, the simplest of which is diversification. Diversification across different asset categories protects an investor from steep drops in any one market. Diversification also imposes the discipline of reallocating a portfolio to restore optimal allocations to beaten down sectors of the market. It is these buying activities that have enabled markets to recover soon after a sharp correction.

SEE ALSO *Bubbles; Financial Markets; Globalization, Social and Economic Aspects of; Interest Rates; Rationality; Stock Exchanges*

BIBLIOGRAPHY

Chordia, T., and L. Shivakumar. 2006. Earnings and Price Momentum. *Journal of Financial Economics* 80 (3): 627–656.

Cochrane, John H. 2005. *Asset Pricing.* 2nd ed. Princeton, NJ, and Oxford: Princeton University Press.

Fama, E., and K. French. 2002. The Equity Premium. *Journal of Finance* 57 (2): 637–659.

Selengut, S. 2005. Dealing with Market Corrections. *Risk Management.* 52 (12): 48.

Shefrin, Hersh. 2005. *A Behavioral Approach to Asset Pricing.* Amsterdam and Boston: Elsevier.

Padma Kadiyala

MARKET ECONOMY

A market economy is an economic system that allocates scarce resources based on the interaction of market forces of supply and demand. It is an economy that operates by voluntary exchange and is not planned or controlled by a central authority. A market economy, also called a free economy or free enterprise economy, is the conceptual opposite of a command economy, also known as a planned or government-controlled economy, where all goods and services are produced, priced, and distributed under government control. In the twenty-first century a market economy is most often associated with a capitalistic economy.

The market is a process in which individuals interact with one another in pursuit of their separate economic objectives. The basic principle under which the market functions is: If an individual has undisputed ownership of something and wishes to exchange it for another thing that is owned by someone else and the exchange is executed without violence, theft, or deception, then the individual becomes entitled to what the other person was previously entitled and vice-versa. Both parties to an economic transaction in the market benefit from it, provided the transaction is bilaterally voluntary and informed. In this way, through the market process everyone is able to escape coercion at the hands of any one buyer or seller by turning to another. The market prevents one person from interfering with another, allowing a high degree of autonomy. In addition, the society is able to reap the benefits from the division of labor and specialization and function.

The prices that emerge from voluntary transactions, which are motivated by separately self-interested individual behavior, generate a spontaneous order. Many economic theorists argue that these prices coordinate the activity of people in such a way as to make everyone better off. An individual who intends only his or her own gain (profit) by producing goods and services at the same time is satisfying the needs of other people for these goods and services. According to the Scottish economist Adam Smith, individuals pursuing their own self-interest are led as if by an "invisible hand" to behave in a socially desirable way by satisfying people's needs for goods and services (1976).

The result of the operation of a competitive market, efficient scarcity prices, in the absence of market failure is indispensable to the operation of the market system. Scarcity prices perform three functions in organizing economic activity: first, they transmit information about the divergent preferences of the economic actors; second, they provide an incentive to adopt least cost methods of production; finally, they determine who gets how much of the product. Prices can perform these functions only if the market is able to function freely; that is, able to function without any discretionary intervention, which results in distorting prices producing the undesirable results of shortages, queues, and low quality, as occurred in the Soviet Union. Before the collapse of the government-controlled economy of the Soviet Union, prices were set by the government, not by the market, below equilibrium. As a result, enterprises did not have an incentive to satisfy consumer demand.

Market-based economies require at least limited government intervention, because a market requires appropriate laws and institutions including defined property rights that are respected and enforced and procedures for guaranteeing the execution of contracts. Markets are also characterized by market failure; that is, an allocation of resources that is not efficient. The market is not able to produce public goods (defense, law and order), it is not able to include the social cost or benefits of externalities (environmental pollution, education), and it creates monopolies and oligopolies. The state takes on the responsibility of producing public goods and subsidizing positive externalities funded through taxation, while restricting negative externalities, monopolies, and oligopolies.

SEE ALSO *Market Clearinghouse; Markets*

BIBLIOGRAPHY

Friedman, Milton, and Rose Friedman. 1980. *Free to Choose: A Personal Statement*. New York: Harcourt Brace Jovanovich.

Smith, Adam. 1976. *An Inquiry into the Nature and Causes of the Wealth of Nations*. Oxford: Oxford University Press.

Aristidis Bitzenis
John Marangos

MARKET FUNDAMENTALS

The *market fundamental* (or fundamental value) of an asset is the discounted present value of the stream of future cash flows attached to the asset. When asset prices are determined by market fundamentals, the value of the asset depends positively on future expected cash flows and negatively on the discount rate used to obtain the present value. Although some estimates of market fundamentals move together with market values, they tend to exhibit lower volatility. This evidence, especially in the case of the stock market, suggests that asset prices deviate from their fundamental values.

The cash flows obtained by the owner of a stock are the dividends distributed by the firm. Since the source of dividends is the earnings generated by the firm, investors must take into account the factors behind earnings when forming expectations concerning future dividends. The most important factors that determine the evolution of expected earnings are the future profitability of current operations and future investment projects.

The second component of the market fundamental of stocks is the discount rate used to obtain the present value of dividends. Given a fixed stream of cash flows, an increase in expected future returns implies that the market fundamental decreases because the discount rate is higher. Expected returns for individual stocks and for the stock market as a whole are not constant, and different financial and macroeconomic variables contain significant information to forecast returns. This evidence implies that changes in expectations of future returns (i.e., changes in discount rates) can produce fluctuations in market fundamentals. In fact, John Campbell (1991) shows that movements in the aggregate stock market prices are mainly driven by news about future expected returns. However, Tuomo Vuolteenaho (2002) shows that stock returns for individual firms are mainly driven by cash-flow news, and that cash-flow news is largely idiosyncratic, while expected-returns news is common across firms. By a diversification argument, the results of both authors are compatible. Historically, the average real return on the stock market is higher than the real return on treasury bonds. The difference between both returns is denominated as *excess return*. It is a reward for holding a risky security. Hence, we can decompose the fluctuations in expected returns into changes in the expected return on a treasury bond and the expected excess return. John Campbell and John Ammer (1993) show that stock returns movement can be attributed to news about future excess returns, and that news about the return on a treasury bond has little impact. Therefore the most important component in the discount rate is the excess return. Since it is a reward for risk, the factors that determine its magnitude are investors' attitudes toward risk and the risk associated with the stock market. The variables that forecast excess returns are connected to macroeconomic activity. Returns forecasts are high at the bottom of business cycles and low at peaks.

Different valuation ratios have been proposed to anticipate the evolution of stock prices. The most common is the price-earnings ratio, which is computed as the quotient between the price of a stock and its earnings per share. Given the definition of market fundamental, the price-earnings ratio depends positively on future expected earnings growth and negatively on future expected returns. This ratio presents long cycles of approximately thirty years (for the U.S. aggregate stock market during the last century) together with shorter fluctuations. For the aggregate stock market, some authors argue that the price-earnings ratio incorporates significant information to predict future returns for long horizons (more than five years). This conclusion has been criticized mostly from a statistical point of view. John Cochrane (1992) argues in favor of the capacity of the price-dividend ratio to predict returns. The author shows that as the ratio is not constant, it must predict changes in dividend growth or changes in returns. He also provides evidence showing that almost all variation in the ratio is due to changes in returns forecasts.

The market fundamental of a house can be analyzed through similar arguments. It is the expected present value of future housing services. Because the value of housing services is not observable, some authors approximate this magnitude by the rental value of the house. This variable depends on a wide set of factors, such as the characteristics of the rental market or the evolution of the population. Different empirical studies emphasize the importance of the fluctuations in the discount rate in determining housing prices. Further, housing provides collateral services and allows for tax deductions. Intangible services and tax variables may also influence the value of the stock.

There are also other assets where the market fundamental may be hard to define. For instance, the exchange rate is the price of two currencies, and hence the relative price of two assets. Exchange rates may be influenced by the availability of international reserves, balance-of-payments deficits, and monetary and fiscal policies. These macroeconomic aggregates are usually referred to as market fundamentals. Economists build stylized models to evaluate the effects of these market fundamentals.

SEE ALSO *Bubbles; Business Cycles, Real; Discounted Present Value; Financial Markets; Market Correction; Ponzi Scheme; Rate of Profit; Risk-Return Tradeoff; Speculation; Stock Exchanges*

BIBLIOGRAPHY

Campbell, John Y. 1991. A Variance Decomposition for Stock Returns. *Economic Journal* 101: 157–179.

Campbell, John Y., and John Ammer. 1993. What Moves the Stock and Bond Markets? A Variance Decomposition for Long-Term Asset Returns. *Journal of Finance* 48 (1): 3–37.

Cochrane, John H. 1992. Explaining the Variance of Price-Dividend Ratios. *The Review of Financial Studies* 5 (2): 243–280.

Vuolteenaho, Tuomo. 2002. What Drives Firm-Level Stock Returns? *Journal of Finance* 57 (1): 233–264.

Manuel S. Santos
Miguel A. Iraola

MARKET POWER
SEE *Competition, Imperfect.*

MARKET PRICE
SEE *Exchange Value.*

MARKET PRICES
SEE *Spot Market.*

MARKET SOCIALISM
SEE *Socialism, Market.*

MARKETS

Several disciplines, among them economics, political economy, philosophy, ethics, and, as of the late twentieth century, sociology, anthropology, and geography, rely on the notion of a market to establish a nexus between those who wish to purchase a commodity and those seeking its sale at a mutually acceptable price or exchange value. While specialists in the latter three fields concern themselves with markets in the sense of trading places observable in the less developed economies of the world, modern economists are principally concerned with an explanation of pricing under different market conditions. For the philosophers of Greece, in particular Aristotle, exchanging an article for money was considered "unnatural." In *Politics* he observed that there is a double way of using every article. "There is its wear as a shoe and there is its use as an article of exchange" (I.9, 1977, pp. 39–41). The "natural" use of an article is for consumption, while its exchange for money is an improper or "unnatural" use. Clearly, the distinction the philosophers made between value in use and value in exchange in a market is a reflection of the contempt they had for mercantile activities.

EARLY RELIGIOUS AND POLITICAL VIEWS

The influence of the Greek philosophers on intellectual thought and human behavior was eclipsed by the fall of the Roman Empire in 476 CE. Their teachings were not rediscovered until translations were made from Aramaic sources by early Christian scholars in the twelfth and thirteenth centuries. Church scholars (the Scholastics) reinterpreted Greek ethics and philosophy to meld them with the Catholic Church's doctrines, including that of the "just price" as the market outcome that results from the moral behavior of both buyers and sellers, so that the resulting exchange value serves the common good. The central role of the "just price" derives from the papal bull *Unam Sanctum* (1302), enunciated by Pope Boniface VIII, which not only reflects the authority of Christian doctrine, but also implies the political priority of the state, vis-à-vis the family and the individual. Throughout the Middle Ages the dominant perspective about human behavior was that it should be guided by the goal of salvation.

By the mid-sixteenth century Church doctrines were challenged by the rise of nation-states and divine-right monarchies in England, France, Spain, and Holland. Their belief was that a nation's stock of gold was an index of its wealth and power, which led several of their thinkers to a theory of foreign trade that identified a favorable balance of trade (i.e., an export surplus) as the cause of national wealth. Merchant activity in foreign trade was thus accorded social status above artisans and manufacturers, while agricultural labor placed last. Interest in trade also promoted quantitative concepts and techniques, such as William Petty's *Political Arithmetic* (1690), to explain social phenomena. The logic of explaining prices in terms of the physical costs of producing goods thus replaced the subjective perspective inherent in the medieval notion of just price and its counterpart, the "just wage." The rise of the European nation state is thus intimately related to the development of political economy, and ultimately of capitalism.

OPTIMISTIC AND PESSIMISTIC APPROACHES

The view of the market that followed in the eighteenth century originated in the Scottish Enlightenment and was envisioned as the outcome of multiple individual choices adapting to evolutionary changes to promote maximum happiness for the greatest number of individuals. This optimistic vision underlies Francis Hutcheson's (1694–1746) *System of Moral Philosophy* (published posthumously in 1755), whose teachings influenced David Hume's natural order philosophy, which explored its beneficence to human freedom and happiness that is fully manifested in a market economy. Hume's work greatly influenced Adam Smith, whose *Theory of Moral Sentiments* (1759) explores the complementarity between sympathy and self interest that is central to the functioning of a market economy: In *The Wealth of Nations* Smith observes, "It is not from the benevolence of the butcher, the brewer, or the baker that we expect our dinner, but from their regard to their self interest" ([1776] 1977 Vol. 1, p. 10). Thus, Smith viewed the functioning of markets as the outcome, on the one hand, of the innate capability of humans to engage in moral behavior socially, while also serving their self interest.

Smith's starting point in *The Wealth of Nations* (1776) was to link the functioning of the economy to the division of productive labor as the basis for economic progress in raising the economy's standard of living. Increasing division of productive labor (by which Smith means labor that results in a vendible product), favors the expansion of markets, encouraging still further division of labor, while promoting a larger proportion of productive workers in the population. The market price of every commodity oscillates in accordance with the proportion actually brought to the market. Thus, the market price tends to converge to a price that pays the wages of labor (at their natural or subsistence level, the profits of capitalists (which competition pressures toward zero), and the rent of land (which tends to increase as population growth necessitates the use of inferior soils). The increasing division of labor enhances productivity and thereby ensures economic progress, broadens markets, and enhances the well being of each of the three great social classes: laborers, capitalists, and landlords.

Notwithstanding the optimism inherent in the invisible hand doctrine, the thesis that market wage rates tend toward the subsistence levels anticipated the pessimistic worldview of the nineteenth century that led Thomas Carlyle (1795–1881) to describe political economy as the "dismal science" (*Critical and Miscellaneous Essays* 1849, p. 84). While Smith attributed downward pressure on wages to the relatively greater bargaining power of employers, many who followed him, the English Economist Thomas Robert Malthus among them, attributed the tendency toward subsistence wages to the combined effect of population growth and rising food costs in consequence of diminishing returns. Classical thinkers were thus fully cognizant that the market allocates income shares among workers, capitalists and landowners, as well as goods among households. These forces led the English economist David Ricardo to offer the theory of comparative advantage to explain the gains inherent in international trade, which encourages improvements in productive technology and international division of labor, which will enhance worker productivity and the rate of profit, and help the working class to participate in the gains from trade.

The advent of the "marginal revolution" led by William Stanley Jevons in England, Carl Menger in Austria, and Leon Walras in Switzerland (who published almost simultaneously in the 1870s), introduced a subjective perspective as an alternate to the classical cost of production view of exchange value, which predicated values on the utilities that consumers placed on their purchase. Because it is their objective to maximize their total utilities, consumers reallocate their commodity holdings until they achieve a set of values that represents an equilibrium state from which no further improvement is possible. This is the vision that led subsequently, principally in the work of Leon Walras (1834–1910) and Vilfred Pareto (1848–1923), who jointly founded the Lausanne School in the twentieth century, that when viewing an economy in its entirety there is a tendency for all of its sectors to move toward simultaneous (i.e., general) supply and demand equilibriums in each of its commodity and factor markets. This is an outcome that lends itself toward representation in a group of simultaneous equations from which Walras demonstrated that it is possible to derive a mathematical solution for market outcomes, given the necessary data. In practice, of course, markets establish actual quantities and prices through the interaction of demand and supply.

PRINCIPLES OF ECONOMICS

An alternative to explaining market outcomes exclusively in terms of marginal utility, which built on the mature classical tradition of John Stuart Mill, and which is known as neoclassicism, emerged in England with the publication of Alfred Marshall's *Principles of Economics* (1890). Its distinguishing feature is its eclecticism, which joined marginal utility as underlying the demand side of market behavior (which he pioneered independently of the English economist and logician William Stanley Jevons [1835–1882]), with the classical cost of production explanation of the supply prices of output. By maintaining the interaction of demand (or utility) and supply (or cost or production) in determining prices, Marshall emphasized the central importance of the time periods during which competitive industries are able to make adjustments to consumer demands. In the short run, when inventory has already been produced, costs of production are relatively less important in setting prices than are consumer demands. The short run, during which investment in

fixed plant and resources are in place, outputs can be varied by changing inputs of labor and raw material so that costs of production become equally important as demand in establishing prices. In this period the number of firms in an industry becomes expanded or contracted in response to profits or losses, so that in the long run, when all inputs are variable, competitive prices will tend toward equality with the costs of production incurred in response to consumer demands. Thus, Marshall's focus (unlike the French economist Léon Walras's [1834–1910] general equilibrium) for explaining prices was on "short causal chains" of partial equilibrium to explain what happens in commodity and factor markets.

With the publication of Marshall's eighth edition of *Principles of Economics* in 1920, the basic supply and demand framework for conceptualizing market behavior and outcomes, along with the vision of economics as a moral science, was established in the United Kingdom and the United States. The only important addition was the subsequent recognition by scholars Edward Chamberlin and Joan Robinson that the commodities sold in most markets are fundamentally differentiated from competing products via advertising, packaging, design, and sales locales. The latter give individual firms a degree of control over selling prices that renders their markets monopolistically competitive. In other industries, the increasing returns that are inherent in large scale production cause firms to expand so that a few large firms (i.e., oligopolies, many of which are multinational firms) dominate markets in which prices deviate from competitive cost of production prices in consequence of both product differentiation and competition among few (rather than many) large firms. Globalization and electronic communication, along with the apparent widespread political preference for privatization and profit driven decision making, suggests an emerging overlap in the behaviors and outcomes in markets worldwide.

There is, however, an important difference between economies that have become privatized since the decline of communism in 1989 in the former Soviet bloc, and American and Western European capitalism. The transition from collectivism to market-oriented decision making has been accompanied by reductions in output, increased unemployment, and rising prices.

SEE ALSO *Economics, Classical; Economics, Neoclassical; Market Clearinghouse; Market Economy*

BIBLIOGRAPHY

Aristotle. 1977. *Politics.* Trans. H. Rackham. Loeb Classic Library, Vol. 21. Cambridge MA: Harvard University Press.

Bromley, R. J. 1974. *Periodic Markets, Daily Markets, and Fairs: A Bibliography.* Melbourne: Produced by the Dept. of Geography, Monash University, for the International

Geographical Union Working Group on Market Distribution Systems.

Carlyle, Thomas. 1849. *Critical and Miscellaneous Essays*. Philadelphia: Carey and Hart.

Marshall, Alfred. [1890] 1920. *Principles of Economics*. 8th ed. London: Macmillan.

Petty, William. 1899. *Political Arithmetic*. Vol. 11 of *The Economic Writings of Sir William Petty*, ed. Charles Hall. Fairfield, NJ: Augustus M. Kelley.

Rima, Ingrid H. 2000. *Development of Economic Analysis*. 6th ed. London and New York: Routledge.

Smith, Adam. [1759] 1982. *The Theory of Moral Sentiments*. 6th ed. Eds. D. D. Raphael and E. L. MacFre. Indianapolis, IN: Liberty Press.

Smith, Adam. [1776] 1977. *The Wealth of Nations*. New York: Everyman's Library.

Ingrid Rima

MARKOWITZ, HARRY M.
1927–

Harry Max Markowitz was born in Chicago, Illinois, on August 24, 1927, the only child of Morris and Mildred Markowitz. While he grew up during the Great Depression, his parents, who owned a small grocery store, were more than adequately able to provide for him during some difficult economic times in the United States. During his high school years, Markowitz developed an interest in philosophy that continued throughout his college years. After completion of his bachelor of philosophy degree in 1947, however, Markowitz decided to study economics.

Markowitz was particularly drawn to the "economics of uncertainty" through works by John von Neumann, Oskar Morgenstern, Jacob Marschak, and Leonard J. Savage. He received his MA in 1950 and his PhD in 1954. While at the University of Chicago, Markowitz was selected to join the prestigious Cowles Commission for Research in Economics. Markowitz developed the basic concepts of portfolio theory while working on his doctoral dissertation at the University of Chicago. In his brief autobiography published by the Nobel Foundation, he noted that his basic ideas for portfolio theory came to him while reading John Burr Williams's *Theory of Investment Value* (1938). Markowitz introduced modern portfolio theory to the world with his paper "Portfolio Selection," which appeared in the March 1952 issue of the *Journal of Finance*. He later published a more extensive explanation of portfolio theory in his book *Portfolio Selection: Efficient Diversification of Investments* (1959).

Before Markowitz's research, investors focused on evaluating the risks and rewards of individual securities when creating their portfolios. The goal of portfolio management was to identify individual securities that offered the highest expected return for a given level of risk and then build a portfolio from these securities. Correspondingly, if pharmaceutical company stocks had good risk–reward characteristics, then an investor could infer that creation of a portfolio entirely from these stocks was optimal. Markowitz formalized the intuition, however, that this logic was flawed. Formulating a mathematics of diversification, he asserted that investors should select portfolios based on their overall risk–reward characteristics. From the entire universe of possible portfolios, the ones that optimally balance risk and reward belong to what Markowitz called an efficient frontier of portfolios. Specifically, a portfolio on the efficient frontier is one in which: (1) no additional diversification can decrease the portfolio's risk for a given expected return, and (2) no additional expected return can be gained without increasing the portfolio's risk. Markowitz proposed that investors should select portfolios from those that lie on the efficient frontier. This work is considered by many to be the first pioneering contribution in the field of financial economics.

An indirect but significant additional contribution by Markowitz to the theory of financial economics occurred through the use of Markowitz's portfolio theory as a basis for developing the capital asset pricing model (CAPM). Thus, Markowitz's work on portfolio theory is regarded by many as establishing financial microanalysis as a prominent research area within economics and finance. Markowitz's work is also consistent with the Modigliani-Miller theorem, which implies that it is not in the interest of investors for firms to reduce risk through diversification, because investors can achieve diversification through their own portfolio choices.

Markowitz's work is not without criticism. Many challenge his assumption that rational investors are risk averters. In the world of speculation in financial markets, market bubbles and herd behavior do occur. In these situations, investors often demonstrate behavior of seeking risk or ignoring risk or both. Markowitz's work is also in conflict with the efficient market hypothesis, which implies that portfolio management is of limited value.

Upon leaving the University of Chicago in the early 1950s, Markowitz concentrated primarily on the application of mathematics and computer methods to problems of business decisions under uncertainty. Markowitz spent ten years on the research staff at the Rand Corporation. He then held various positions with Consolidated Analysis Centers, Inc. (1963–1968), the University of California at Los Angeles (1968–1969), Arbitrage Management Company (1969–1972), and International

Business Machines Corporation's T. J. Watson Research Center (1974–1983) before becoming a faculty member of Baruch College of the City University of New York in 1982. His most notable work falls in the areas of portfolio theory, sparse matrix techniques, and the SIMSCRIPT programming language. In 1989 he was awarded the von Neumann Prize in Operations Research Theory by the Operations Research Society of America and the Institute of Management Sciences. In 1990 Markowitz shared (with Merton H. Miller and William F. Sharpe) the Nobel Prize for Economics for theories on evaluating stock market risk and reward and on valuing corporate stocks and bonds.

SEE ALSO *Efficient Market Hypothesis; Modigliani-Miller Theorems; Von Neumann, John*

BIBLIOGRAPHY

Markowitz, Harry M. 1991. Harry M. Markowitz— Autobiography. In *Les Prix Nobel: The Nobel Prizes 1990*, ed. Tore Frängsmyr. Stockholm: Nobel Foundation. http://nobelprize.org/nobel_prizes/economics/laureates/1990/markowitz-autobio.html.

Vicki L. Bogan

MARKUP PRICING

The term *markup pricing* assumes that a hypothetical firm when setting a price makes it equal to average costs plus some reasonable profit margin that can be expressed as *cost times a markup*. There are different theoretical treatments of markup pricing, however. In the neoclassical theory of monopoly, the law of supply and demand is assumed and the markup is thought to be determined by the elasticity of demand. The post-Keynesian theory, on the other hand, assumes some monopolization of markets due to concentration, entry barriers, and collusion within or across industries and does not consider the law of supply and demand a relevant factor—that is, prices are not thought to respond to disequilibria in supply and demand. The markup is assumed to be determined by the degree of monopoly. Since the 1970s, theories of what is called *dynamic markup pricing* have also been developed.

NEOCLASSICAL THEORY OF MARKUP PRICING

The neoclassical theory assumes the existence of monopolies or monopolistic competition due to differentiated products. In a market for differentiated products, a large number of firms compete by selling similar products but they are not perfect substitutes for one another. A firm confronts certain limitations imposed by the nature of consumer demand—that is, the fact that consumers are more willing to buy products at lower prices than at higher ones. Thus, the firm's profit-maximization problem can be written as

$$\max_{y} p(y)y - c(y)$$

where $p(y)$ is the inverse demand function, and $c(y)$ the cost function.

The profit-maximizing condition is

$$p(y)\left[1 - \frac{1}{|\eta_D|}\right] = c'(y)$$

where $|\eta_D| \equiv |(p/y)(dy/dp)| > 1$ is the elasticity of demand in absolute value. Because consumer demand is inversely related to the price, η_D is never positive. The elasticity of demand must be greater than 1 in absolute value, or the condition is contradictory to nonnegative marginal cost, $c'(y) \equiv MC > 0$.

Rearranging the above, we obtain

$$p(y) = \frac{|\eta_D|}{|\eta_D| - 1} MC$$

or

$$\frac{p(y) - MC}{p(y)} = \frac{1}{|\eta_D|}.$$

The left side of the equation indicates the ratio of profit to price, while the right is the so-called Lerner index, which is inversely proportional to the elasticity of demand. The elasticity of demand $|\eta_D|$ is independently determined by consumer behavior. Hence, assuming that $|\eta_D| = 4$, we can see from the first formula that the price is equal to marginal costs times 4/3 times the marginal costs. In this theory, markup pricing is, therefore, an attempt by a firm to guess the market's elasticity of demand. Higher elasticity leads to a price closer to the competitive price.

POST-KEYNESIAN THEORIES OF OLIGOPOLISTIC PRICING

Theories of monopolistic and oligopolistic markets in post-Keynesian economics were developed based on the assumption that concentration, entry barriers, and collusion within or across industries prevent prices from responding to disequilibria in supply and demand. The markup is determined by the degree of the monopoly that gives the firm or entrepreneur the power to increase a markup on prime cost by raising price. This position is taken by post-Keynesian economists such as Michał Kalecki (1971), Maurice Dobb (1973), Joan Robinson (1965, 1971), Josef Steindl (1952), Paolo Sylos-Labini

(1969), Alfred S. Eichner (1973, 1976, 1980), Adrian Wood (1975), and Athanasios Asimakopulos (1975).

Kalecki (1971) holds the view that the different markups in different industries are determined by the degree of industrial concentration and that the different markups within one industry are determined by the distribution of power among the firms in the industry. This can be expressed as

$$p = mu + n\bar{p}$$

where u is the variable cost, $\bar{p}$ the weighted average price of all firms in the industry, and $m > 0$ and $0 < n < 1$ are coefficients that indicate the firm's position within the industry. The weighted averages, $\bar{m}$ and $\bar{n}$, which reflect the degree of industrial concentration, determine the average price in the industry and thus the average markup:

$$\bar{p} = \frac{\bar{m}}{1 - \bar{n}} \bar{u}$$
$$= (1 + \bar{\mu})\bar{u}.$$

whereby the factor before the $\bar{u}$ is the markup.

Target return pricing is a variant of markup pricing that is often found in post-Keynesian economics. Price is set to earn a profit margin that yields a target rate of return on capital at a standard volume of output:

$$p = ULC^N + UMC^N + \frac{\pi K}{x^N}$$
$$= (1 + \mu)(ULC^N + UMC^N)$$

where π is the target rate of return on capital, K the capital stock, x^N the normal output, ULC^N and UMC^N the unit labor and material costs respectively at a normal output, and μ the markup factor. The markup over variable cost $\mu VC = \pi K / x^N$ changes either because of changes in the target rate of return or in the capital-output ratio.

Studies by Robert F. Lanzilotti (1958), Wood (1975), and Eichner (1973, 1976, 1980) are concerned particularly with pricing decisions by large corporations. These economists maintain that prices are likely to be set so as to assure the internally generated funds necessary to finance a firm's desired rate of capital expansion:

$$p = VC + \frac{FC + CL}{CU^N}$$

where VC is variable cost, FC fixed cost, CL corporate levy (the desired internal funds to finance the investment expenditure), and CU^N normal capacity utilization. If variable and fixed costs are held constant, the markup is determined by corporate levy, though it may be limited by substitution, the entry of new firms, and government intervention.

Despite the fact that there are several accounts of the markup within post-Keynesian economics, post-Keynesian theories do nonetheless all share an assumption: that prices change primarily due to a change on the cost side (though this is less due to the law of supply and demand than would be the case for neoclassical theorists).

DYNAMIC MARKUP PRICING

According to dynamic markup pricing theorists, while firms can decide their own prices and markups, they are nonetheless guided by the need to build up customers in order to expand their future market shares. Firms also have to face competition with a few rivals in the oligopolistic market and threats from potential entrants into the market. Furthermore, customers may leave or switch to other firms. In this sense, the firms have restricted choice since their pricing decisions should be based on considerations of the current and future state of the market. In this dynamic framework, a firm's markup pricing is greatly dependent on other firms.

Economists such as Joe Staten Bain (1956), Sylos-Labini (1969), Franco Modigliani (1958), and David P. Baron (1973) have long argued that price and markup function as barriers to market entry set up by incumbents who wish to deter potential competition. This version of oligopolistic pricing is called *limit pricing* or *entry-preventing pricing*. Prices are set above the costs but below prices at which potential competitors could enter the market and earn positive profits. Pricing depends on many factors such as the degree of concentration, economies of scale, product differentiation, the absolute cost advantages of incumbents, and internal interdependence of oligopolistic firms.

Like other post-Keynesians, Nicholas Kaldor (1985) suggests that prices and markups are cost-determined, but he also takes the importance of customer relationships into account. In his view, a firm determines markup based on two opposing considerations: market-share expansion and capital expansion. On the one hand, each firm will choose a price and a markup as *low* as possible so that they can build up more customers to improve their market share. On the other hand, they also have an incentive to set their markup as *high* as possible to increase their own capital by means of *internal finance*. This is because firms want to prevent a situation in which they become financially constrained through excessive reliance on external finance. Note that the second point was usually neglected in the traditional neoclassical theories, in which internal and external finances are considered as near-perfect substitutes. Kaldor therefore views a markup merely as a residual between the cost and the price chosen after considering the market dynamics.

Edmund S. Phelps and Sidney Winter (1970) have provided the first rigorous theoretical analysis of this type of dynamic markup pricing theory. They point to customer-flow dynamics as a barrier to optimal markup pricing:

$$\frac{dn}{dt} = -\alpha(p - \bar{p}).$$

Here n is the number of a firm's own customers, p its own price, $\bar{p}$ the average price of all other firms in the industry, and α a positive constant. Therefore, if a firm charges a high price, it loses customers. They find that equality between marginal cost and price does not generally hold even in a stationary state. Thus an optimal markup is derived as the difference between those two.

IMPERFECT COMPETITION AND OLIGOPOLISTIC PRICING

More recent developments in oligopolistic pricing theory focus on *imperfect information* such as "judging quality by price" (Stiglitz 1984), "reputations" (Greenwald, Stiglitz, and Weiss 1984), and "search costs" (Stiglitz 1983) as the source of price rigidities and the markup.

SEE ALSO *Competition; Prices; Rate of Profit*

BIBLIOGRAPHY

Asimakopulos, Athanasios. 1975. A Kaleckian Theory of Income Distribution. *Canadian Journal of Economics* 8 (3): 313–333.

Bain, Joe Staten. 1956. *Barriers to New Competition: Their Character and Consequences in Manufacturing Industries.* Cambridge, MA: Harvard University Press.

Baron, David P. 1973. Limit Pricing, Potential Entry, and Barriers to Entry. *American Economic Review* 63 (4): 666–674.

Clarkson, Kenneth W., and Roger LeRoy Miller. 1982. *Industrial Organization: Theory, Evidence, and Public Policy.* New York: McGraw-Hill.

Dobb, Maurice. 1973. *Theories of Value and Distribution since Adam Smith.* Cambridge, U.K.: Cambridge University Press.

Eichner, Alfred S. 1973. A Theory of the Determination of the Mark-Up under Oligopoly. *Economic Journal* (Royal Economic Society) 83 (332): 1184–1200.

Eichner, Alfred S. 1976. *The Megacorp and Oligopoly: Micro Foundations of Macro Dynamics.* Cambridge, U.K.: Cambridge University Press.

Eichner, Alfred S. 1980. A General Model of Investment and Pricing. In *Growth, Profits, and Property: Essays in the Review of Political Economy,* ed. Edward J. Nell, 118–133. New York: Cambridge University Press.

Greenwald, Bruce, Joseph E. Stiglitz, and Andrew Weiss. 1984. Information Imperfections in the Capital Market and Macroeconomic Fluctuations. *American Economic Review* 74 (2): 194–199.

Kaldor, Nicholas. 1985. *Economics without Equilibrium.* Armonk, NY: Sharpe.

Kalecki, Michał. 1971. Costs and Prices. In his *Selected Essays on the Dynamics of the Capitalist Economy, 1933–1970.* Cambridge, U.K.: Cambridge University Press.

Lanzilotti, Robert F. 1958. Pricing Objectives in Large Companies. *American Economic Review* 48 (4): 921–940.

Modigliani, Franco. 1958. New Developments on the Oligopoly Front. *Journal of Political Economy* 64 (3): 215–232.

Phelps, Edmund S., and Sidney Winter. 1970. Optimal Price Policy under Atomistic Competition. In *Microeconomic Foundations of Employment and Inflation Theory,* ed. Edmund S. Phelps et al, 309–337. New York: Norton.

Robinson, Joan. 1965. *Collected Economic Papers.* Vol. 3. Oxford, U.K.: Blackwell.

Robinson, Joan. 1971. *Economic Heresies: Some Old-Fashioned Questions in Economic Theory.* London: Macmillan.

Semmler, Willi. 1984. *Competition, Monopoly, and Differential Profit Rates: On the Relevance of the Classical and Marxian Theories of Production Prices for Modern Industrial and Corporate Pricing.* New York: Columbia University Press.

Steindl, Josef. 1952. *Maturity and Stagnation in American Capitalism.* New York: Monthly Review Press.

Stiglitz, Joseph E. 1984. Price Rigidities and Market Structure. *American Economic Review* 74 (2): 350–355.

Stiglitz, Joseph E. 1987. Competition and the Number of Firms in a Market: Are Duopolies More Competitive Than Atomistic Markets? *Journal of Political Economy* 95 (5): 1041–1061.

Sylos-Labini, Paolo. 1969. *Oligopolio e progresso tecnico* [Oligopoly and Technical Progress]. Trans. Elizabeth Henderson. Cambridge, MA: Harvard University Press.

Tirole, Jean. 1988. *The Theory of Industrial Organization.* Cambridge, MA: MIT Press.

Varian, Hal R. 1992. *Microeconomic Analysis.* 3rd ed. New York: Norton.

Wood, Adrian. 1975. *A Theory of Profits.* Cambridge, U.K.: Cambridge University Press.

Willi Semmler
Mika Kato

MARRIAGE

Transformations in marriage during the twentieth century have inspired a large body of research. Marriage is both a social and legal institution. Although the criteria for who can be legally married vary cross-culturally, marriage is a conjugal state that generally has been reserved for two individuals of opposite sexes, of consenting age, and of no blood relation. Historically, the reasons for, function of, and frequency of marriage has varied by race or ethnicity, class, gender, and the social and economic structures of society. Regardless of such differences, the institution of marriage is viewed by social scientists as one of the most fundamental elements in the maintenance and reproduction of society itself.

Marriage differs in its relation to church and state, though both infer rights and obligations to members of the marital union. Religions often view marriage as a sacrament that reaffirms religious commitment, whereas wedlock is the legal state of matrimony. Even if a marriage is recognized by the state, it may not be recognized as valid by the church. In practice, church weddings often provide both a legal and religious contract between marriage partners.

Although marriage is defined most often as a union between two opposite-sex individuals, some societies and religious traditions allow for marriage between multiple partners: *polygamy*. Two forms of polygamy exist. Polygynous unions, in which a man is married to more than one wife, are the most common. Polygyny is currently practiced in some West African countries, particularly among more traditional members of society. When less formal arrangements are included in the definition—such as a man simultaneously being legally married to one woman while engaged in formal consort relationships with other women that are also expected to produce children—the prevalence of polygyny increases substantially. This latter type of polygyny, for instance, is found among wealthier Chinese in China, Taiwan, and the Chinese diaspora in Southeast Asia and North America. Polyandrous marriages, in which a woman is married to more than one husband, are relatively uncommon. Polyandry in the form of marriages to fraternal cohusbands has been reported in some areas of India.

Over time, there has been a shifting focus toward the emotional aspect of marriage in European and North American countries. In the United States prior to the twentieth century, marriage was viewed as a legal contract by which individuals joined in a marital union for social and economic reasons. During this time, marriages were more likely to be arranged by persons not party to the union itself. Following World War I, Americans began to place a greater emphasis on the emotional nature of marriage, and the notion of romantic love in marriage became more important. Furthermore, married persons were expected to invest their emotional energy into the spiritual growth of their marriage partners. The concept of marrying for love varies by cultures today. More industrialized societies are more likely to view love as the primary reason for forming a marital union, whereas less industrialized societies sometimes practice arranged marriage.

Marriage has long been associated with various benefits, including increased health and longevity. Married men in particular are less likely to engage in risky behaviors such as alcohol and drug use. Emotional satisfaction and increased economic well-being are also associated with marriage. Married people are less likely to experience anxiety and depression. Some theorists argue that there is something unique about the institution of marriage that bestows these benefits on the married couple. For instance, a spouse may serve as a monitor of their partner's health. This is supported by findings that married men are more likely than unmarried men to visit the doctor on a regular basis. Other theorists, however, argue that the benefits of marriage are more a factor of selection bias—that is, people with higher socioeconomic status and better health and emotional well-being are more likely to marry, whereas those lacking these characteristics are more likely to have short-lived marriages that end in divorce, or to forgo marriage altogether.

DEMOGRAPHIC TRENDS IN MARRIAGE

Over time, demographic trends in legal union formation have included changes in legal age restrictions, an overall retreat from marriage in western societies, and women's increased investment in their own human capital.

Legal age restrictions on who is eligible to marry have varied over time, cultures, and ethnicities. Historically, marriageable age has been closely tied to puberty, and it remains so in many less industrialized countries today. Currently, most North American and European countries have a minimum age of marital consent, usually age eighteen. The U.S. state or jurisdiction allowing for the youngest age at marriage without parental consent is Mississippi at age fifteen for women and age seventeen for men, whereas Puerto Rico requires both genders to be at least twenty-one. However, most states do allow for parental consent, and other statutory requirements may override these minimum age requirements for marriage. For instance, in Massachusetts if parents consent, women can marry as young as age twelve and men as young as age fourteen, whereas other states such as West Virginia, Kentucky, and Louisiana maintain the relatively advanced age of eighteen even with parental consent.

The marriage rate has been in decline in the United States and Europe since the end of World War II. Although the vast majority of people still report a desire to be married (80% of women and 78% of men), and most will eventually do so, there is a continuing trend to delay this step in the adult life course. The median age of first marriage in 1970 was twenty-three for men and twenty-one for women; by 2003 the median age of first marriage had risen to twenty-seven for men and twenty-five for women. (As these figures imply, the age difference between husbands and wives in most developed nations—including the United States—is small.)

A primary factor thought to at least partially account for the decreasing prevalence of marriage in the United States is the increase in women's human capital. Specifically, women have increased their investment in education, participation in the labor force, and relative annual earnings compared to men. Currently, more women (and men) go to college, thus delaying their economic stability and, subsequently, their transition to marriage. In 1970, 13 percent of American women aged twenty-five to twenty-nine had a bachelor's degree or higher, compared to 30 percent of women aged twenty-five to thirty-four in 2000.

The decline in marriage in more industrialized countries has accompanied an increase in female labor force participation. For instance, American women aged twenty-five to thirty-four increased their participation in the labor force from approximately 41 percent in 1970 to 70 percent in 2004. Marriage benefits also vary by gender. Despite their hours worked outside the home, women typically perform the majority of household chores—about 70 percent in the United States. Additionally, married men benefit in the job market more than married women do. Men (especially fathers) often have been afforded a "family wage"—that is, more money to support their families—because of their traditional role as family breadwinners. Women, too, have to deal with social norms, which often view the roles of wife and mother as incompatible with the role of worker. In many Western societies, women's increased participation in nonfamilial roles and investments in their own human capital has begun to close the gap in men's and women's contributions to family income. For instance, in 1987 only 24 percent of all married women earned more than their husbands, but by 2003 32 percent did.

THEORIES OF MARRIAGE

Different explanations exist as to how we select mates to form a unique marital bond. Social-exchange theories focus on the contextual characteristics of the larger marriage market, where individuals compare the assets and liabilities of prospective spouses. Mate selection criteria include income, wealth, home- versus labor-market production, and physical attractiveness. Once the benefits of marriage outweigh the benefits of remaining single for both partners, a legal union is formed. The specialization and trading model adopts a rational-choice perspective that views men and women as attempting to maximize personal gains through marriage. This model asserts that individuals exchange personal assets—be it income, wealth, home production, child rearing skills, or physical attractiveness—for a partner with the highest overall value on a related set of assets. Historically, men have specialized in and traded on their economic production, whereas women have specialized in and traded on their domestic production.

Career-entry theory is derived from job-search theory, which asserts that potential workers look for employment in the labor market until they find a job that satisfies the minimum qualifications necessary for acceptable employment. From the perspective of the worker, the sorting of individuals into jobs is maximized when the number of jobs available in the market increases. An analogous situation occurs during the process of spousal selection. A person wishing to form a marital union searches for a spouse in the marriage market. As with employment, individuals usually have a predetermined idea of the minimal characteristics necessary before a potential spouse is deemed acceptable. Once in the marriage market, individuals compete with others to find a spouse. High levels of human capital in women decrease the probability of marriage by extending women's marital search process and simultaneously raising their reservation wage for potential husbands. More importantly, from a career-entry perspective, men's economic volatility lowers the probability of marriage by creating long-term financial uncertainty for both men and the women who choose to marry them.

Psychodynamic theories often focus on how childhood experiences and family background influence partner selection. Individuals may model their potential spouses after their opposite-sex parents, or they may create images of the ideal spouse based on childhood experiences. Filter theory posits that we sift through potential mates based on predetermined criteria—often ascribed characteristics such as race and class. Homogamy filters include finding a potential mate that matches your characteristics such as propinquity, physical attractiveness, race, education, income, and religion. Propinquity is typically the strongest homogamy filter. Heterogamy filters include selecting a mate based on characteristics that are opposite such as gender.

Other researchers point to the historical roots of marriage in the system of patriarchy, which views wives as the property of their husbands. For instance, the tradition of wedding rings historically served to solidify a woman's status as the property of her husband. Until recently, legal views of rape and sexual assault within marriage supported the notion that wives were the property of their husbands. In 1736 the English chief justice Sir Matthew Hale stated that "the husband cannot be guilty of a rape committed by himself upon his lawful wife, for by their mutual matrimonial consent and contract the wife hath given up herself in this kind unto her husband, which she cannot retract" (cited in Russell 1990, p. 17). This statement, which came to be known as the "Hale Doctrine," was accepted by the U.S. legal system in 1857 under the *Commonwealth v. Fogarty* decision. Marital rape is now illegal in the United States and in all countries represented at the United Nations's women's conference of 1995. In the United States, however, current laws continue to treat marital rape as a crime less severe, with more lenient sentencing, than other forms of rape.

Nonwestern traditions also support the notion of women as property. The practice of paying a dowry is one example of how women have been seen as property to be transferred from their parents to their husbands. Under the dowry system, women are an economic liability. To increase a woman's attractiveness to a male suitor, the family of the bride produces various gifts of economic value to the potential groom and his family. Although this practice is becoming less common under the global capitalist system, various cultures around the world still adhere to the dowry system.

Anthropologists such as Levi-Strauss also note that marriage has been used as a structural tool to form political or commercial alliances across groups. Referred to as *alliance theory*, it maintains that the universal incest taboo motivates exogamy in marriage through a series of intimate kinship group exchanges of women as the wives of men who are members of a different group. Through this type of generalized exchange a marriage alliance between the two groups is formed and reciprocity is expected. Alliance theory argues that groups' circulation of women through the practice of trading wives links various social groups together to form complex structures of kinship, and ultimately, society itself.

MARRIAGE ALTERNATIVES

The drop in the marriage rate and the trend in delaying marriage have been accompanied by an increase in alternatives to traditional marriage. Marital dissolution (divorce), cohabitation, nonmarital childbearing, and gay marriage have become increasingly evident in European and North American countries. Marital dissolution in the United States, for instance, increased steadily during the decades following World War II, and began to level off during the 1990s with one in two U.S. marriages ending in divorce.

Cohabitation also has become an increasingly prevalent form of union formation in more-developed counties. Increases in cohabitation rates have spawned public debate regarding social policies that support the traditional marital union of a husband and wife, and have implications for the popularity of marriage as a larger social institution. Although modern forms of cohabitation were relatively unheard of before the 1960s, by 2003 4.6 million U.S. households were comprised of unrelated opposite-sex partners who were not married. Cohabitation types vary from short-term arrangements, to precursors to marriage, to replacements for legal union formation that is condoned by both church and state. In Sweden, for example, approximately 85 percent of partnered adults aged twenty-five to thirty-four were cohabiting as opposed to living as married couples. In other countries such as the United States, cohabitation is often a short-term arrangement followed by marriage or dissolution of the union. For instance, approximately 70 per-

cent of cohabiting American women marry their residential partner within five years of cohabitation. At the other extreme, 49 percent of cohabiting women dissolve their residential union during the first five years of cohabitation (this figure includes cohabiting women who both marry and divorce within the first five years of the original cohabitation).

As cohabitation has increased, some countries have begun to treat marital and cohabiting unions as legally equivalent. Legal rights inferred to cohabiting couples may include inheritance rights, alimony upon dissolution, retirement benefits for spouses, and streamlined adoption processes. Some other countries, including the United States, continue to distinguish marriage from cohabitation in social and legal policies. A bridge between cohabitation and marriage is available in some U.S. states: Certain states recognize common-law marriages. Under explicit (but varying) criteria—such as the length of time the couple has co-resided, whether they hold joint accounts, assets, and liabilities, and whether the partners refer to each other as "spouses"—cohabiting couples may be considered similar to legally married couples. However, allowances and the requirements needed to establish a common-law marriage vary from state to state.

Rates of childbearing outside of marriage also have been increasing, due in part to the more liberal acceptance of sex outside of marriage and increases in cohabitation and divorce. For instance, in Sweden most children are now born outside of marriage, mostly to cohabiting couples. In the United States, 5 percent of children were born to unmarried mothers in 1960 and this percentage increased to just fewer than 37 percent in 2005. Among non-Hispanic blacks nonmarital childbearing represents nearly 70 percent of all births. Social acceptance of premarital sex also has increased significantly since the 1960s. Despite these trends, people still report that marriage is the ideal situation in which to raise a child. In a survey of high school seniors in 1997 to 1998, only 8 percent of high school seniors stated that unmarried childbearing is a worthwhile alternative lifestyle.

Although marriage often is religiously and legally restricted to the union of two opposite-sex individuals, alternative expressions of intimate-adult commitment are increasingly common. One aspect of marriage that has been gaining public exposure during the twenty-first century is gay marriage. Although the United States generally restricts marriage to a union between opposite-sex adults, other countries allow for individuals of the same sex to marry. In 2001 the Netherlands became the first country to legalize same-sex marriage. Belgium and the Canadian provinces of Ontario and British Columbia followed suit in 2003. In 2004 Massachusetts became the first and only state in the United States to grant marriage licenses to two persons of the same sex.

Another legal option available to some same-sex couples is the civil union, which is a marriage-like union available in some European countries and in some U.S. states. One example is Germany's Registered Life Partnership, which grants to same-sex couples legal rights such as sharing a surname, the ability to enter together into contracts regarding property and finances, the right to refuse to testify against your partner, priority in immigration consideration, and health benefits. In 2000 Vermont was the first state in the United States to allow civil unions. Some states (such as California, Connecticut, Hawaii, Maine, New Jersey, and Vermont) allow for domestic partnerships or joint tax returns for same-sex couples. However, many U.S. states have reaffirmed the historical and religious sacrament of marriage between only a man and a woman. Currently, twenty-seven U.S. states have banned same-sex marriage. Eighteen of these have also banned civil unions.

SEE ALSO *Childlessness; Children; Cohabitation; Divorce and Separation; Dowry and Bride Price; Family; Feminism; Fertility, Human; Marriage, Interracial; Marriage, Same-Sex; Reproduction; Rituals; Romance*

BIBLIOGRAPHY

Bramlett, M. D., and W. D. Mosher. 2002. Cohabitation, Marriage, Divorce, and Remarriage in the United States. National Center for Health Statistics. *Vital Health Statistics* 23 (2).

Bumpass, Larry, and Hsien-Hen Lu. 2000. Trends in Cohabitation and Implications for Children's Family Contexts in the United States. *Population Studies* 54 (1): 29–41.

Fields, Jason. 2003. America's Families and Living Arrangements: 2003. Current Population Reports, P20-553. Washington, DC: U.S. Government Printing Office. http://www.census.gov/prod/2004pubs/p20-553.pdf.

Kiernan, Kathleen. 2004. Unmarried Cohabitation and Parenthood in Britain and Europe. *Law and Policy* 26: 33–55.

Lloyd, Kim M., Marta Tienda, and Anna Zajacova. 2001. Trends in Educational Achievement of Minority Students since Brown v. Board of Education. In *Achieving High Educational Standards for All: Conference Summary*. Division of Behavioral and Social Sciences and Education, National Research Council, eds. Timothy Ready, Christopher Edley Jr., and Catherine E. Snow, 149–182. Washington, DC: National Academy Press.

Russell, Diana E. H. 1990. *Rape in Marriage*. Bloomington: Indiana University Press.

Teachman, Jay D., Lucky M. Tedrow, and Kyle Crowder. 2000. The Changing Demography of America's Families. *Journal of Marriage and the Family* 62 (4): 1234–1246.

Thornton, Arland, and Linda Young-DeMarco. 2001. Four Decades of Trends in Attitudes toward Family Issues in the United States: The 1960s through the 1990s. *Journal of Marriage and Family* 63 (4): 1009–1037.

U.S. Bureau of the Census. 1970. Characteristics of the Population 1, pt. 1, U.S. Summary sec. 2. Washington, DC: Government Printing Office. http://www2.census.gov/prod2/decennial/documents/1970a_us2-01.pdf.

U.S. Bureau of the Census. 2000. A Half-Century of Learning: Historical Statistics on Educational Attainment in the United States, 1940 to 2000. Decennial Census PHC-T-41. Washington, DC: Government Printing Office. http://www.census.gov/population/www/socdemo/education/phct41.html.

U.S. Department of Labor Statistics. 2005. Women in the Labor Force: A Databook. Report 985. Washington, DC: Government Printing Office. http://www.bls.gov/cps/wlf-databook2005.htm.

Waite, Linda, and Maggie Gallagher. 2000. *The Case for Marriage: Why Married People Are Happier, Healthier, and Better Off Financially*. New York: Doubleday.

Kim M. Lloyd
Rosemary Yeilding

MARRIAGE, INTERRACIAL

Marriage is an important social institution. In every society, family values and social norms are in place to proscribe appropriate behavior regarding mate selection. Mate selection follows the pattern of like marries like—people aspire to marry those of the same age, race and ethnicity, educational attainment, religion, or social class. But then, finding an exact match in every characteristic is difficult. Matching based on certain characteristics may become more important than on some others. In most societies religion and race are often the two most important criteria. Religious and racial group boundaries are most likely the hardest to cross in marriage markets. In the United States, religious boundaries are breaking down and interfaith marriages have become more common over recent generations. Marriages crossing racial boundaries, on the other hand, still lag behind. This is not surprising because American society has a long history of racial inequality in socioeconomic status as a result of racial prejudice and discrimination. Race boundary is the most difficult barrier to cross.

Nevertheless, the racial marriage barrier in the United States appears to be weakening as well, at least for certain groups. Americans have had more contact opportunities with people of different racial groups in recent decades than in the past because increasingly, they work and go to school with colleagues from many groups. Because racial gaps in income have narrowed, more members of racial minorities can afford to live in neighborhoods that were previously monopolized by whites. Physical proximity creates opportunities to reduce stereotypes and to establish interracial connections and friendships. In addition, mixed-race individuals born to interracially married couples tend to help narrow social distance across racial groups because of their racially heterogeneous friend networks. The growth of the mixed-race population further blurs racial boundaries.

Attitudes toward interracial marriage have shifted over time as a result. In 1958, a national survey asked Americans for the first time for their opinions of interracial marriage. Only 4 percent of whites approved of intermarriage with blacks. Almost 40 years later, in 1997, 67 percent of whites approved of such intermarriages. Blacks were not asked this question until 1972; they have been much likelier to approve of intermarriage, reaching 83 percent in 1997. Social scientists take such expressions of attitudes with a grain of salt. Respondents who answer attitude questions in a survey may simply reflect their desire to fit in with the rest of society. Despite misgivings, people today may feel that it is inappropriate to express reservations about racial intermarriage. Many Americans, it appears, remain uneasy about interracial intimacy generally—and most disapprove of interracial relationships in their own families. Indeed, support for interracial marriage by white Americans lags far behind their support of interracial schools (96 percent), housing (86 percent), and jobs (97 percent). Still, such relationships are on the increase. Nationwide, interracial marriages have increased from only 310,000, accounting for .7 percent of all marriages in 1970, to about 1.5 million, 2.6 percent of all marriages in 2000. The actual number would be much greater if marriages between Hispanics and non-Hispanics were taken into account as well. The upward trend in intermarriage seemingly signals improved racial/ethnic relations, the incorporation of racial/ethnic minorities into American society, and the breakdown of racial/ethnic distinctions. Intermarriage, however, varies widely across racial groups.

RACIAL DIFFERENCES IN INTERRACIAL MARRIAGE

Who pairs up with whom partly depends on the population size of each racial group in the United States. The larger the group, the more likely group members are to find marriageable partners of their own race. The U.S. Census Bureau classifies race into four major categories: whites, African Americans, Asian Americans, and American Indians. Hispanics can belong to any of the four

racial groups but are considered as one separate minority group. Although whites form the largest group—about 70 percent of the population—just 4 percent of married whites aged 20 to 34 in 2000 had nonwhite spouses. The percent of interracial marriages is much higher for U.S.-born racial minorities: 9 percent for African Americans, 39 percent for Hispanics, 56 percent for American Indians, and 59 percent for Asian Americans (who account for less than 4 percent of the total population). To be sure, differences in population size for each group account for part of the variation in interracial marriage. For example, the Asian population is much smaller than the white population, which means that one Asian-white marriage affects the percentage of interracial marriage much more for Asians than for whites. Also because of their numbers, although just 4 percent of whites are involved in interracial marriages, 92 percent of all interracial marriages include a white partner. Clearly, racial minorities have greater opportunities to meet whites in schools, workplaces, and neighborhoods than to meet members of other minority groups.

Given population size differences, comparing rates of intermarriage among groups can be difficult. Statistical models used by social scientists nevertheless can account for group size, identify to the extent to which any group is marrying out more or less than one would expect given their population group size, and then reveal what else affects intermarriage. Results show that the lighter a group's skin color, the higher the rate of intermarriage with white Americans. Hispanics who label themselves as racially "white" are most likely to marry non-Hispanic

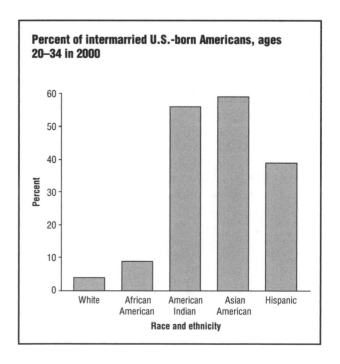

Percent of intermarried U.S.-born Americans, ages 20–34 in 2000

whites. Asian Americans and American Indians are next in their levels of marriage with whites. Hispanics who do not consider themselves racially white have low rates of intermarriage with whites. African Americans are least likely of all racial minorities to marry whites. Darker skin, in America, is associated with discrimination, lower educational attainment, lower income and residential segregation. Even among African Americans, those of lighter tone tend to do better both in the job market and in the marriage market.

EDUCATIONAL DIFFERENCES IN INTERRACIAL MARRIAGE

Highly educated minority members often attend integrated colleges, work in integrated surroundings, and live in neighborhoods that are integrated. Although they develop a strong sense of their group identity in such environments, they also find substantial opportunities for interracial contact, friendship, romance, and marriage. College-educated men and women are more likely to marry interracially than those with less education. The fact that Asian Americans attend college at relatively high rates helps to explain their high level of intermarriage with whites. The major exceptions to the strong effect of educational attainment on interracial marriage are African Americans.

Although middle-class African Americans increasingly live in integrated neighborhoods, African Americans still remain much more segregated than other minorities. College-bound African Americans often choose historically black colleges or colleges with a large and potentially supportive black student body. Their opportunities for contact with whites, therefore, are limited. After leaving school, well-educated African Americans are substantially less likely to live next to whites than are well-educated Hispanics and Asian Americans. One reason is that middle-class black Americans are so numerous that they can form their own middle-class black neighborhoods, while in most areas middle-class Hispanic and Asian American communities are smaller and often fractured by ethnic differences. In addition, racial discrimination against African Americans also plays a role. Studies demonstrate that whites resist having black neighbors much more than they resist having Hispanic or Asian American neighbors.

High levels of residential segregation accompanied by high levels of school segregation, on top of a pronounced history of racial discrimination and inequality, lower African Americans' opportunities for interracial contact and marriage. The geographic distance between blacks and whites is in many ways rooted in the historical separation between the two groups. In contrast, Hispanic and Asian Americans' distances from whites have more to do with their current economic circumstances. As those

improve, they come nearer to whites geographically, socially, and matrimonially.

SEX DIFFERENCES IN INTERRACIAL MARRIAGE

Black-white couples show a definite pattern: About two-thirds have a black husband and a white wife. Asian American–white couples lean the other way; three-fifths have an Asian American wife. Sex balances are roughly even for intermarried couples that include a white and a Hispanic or an American Indian. Clearly, white men have disproportionately more Asian American wives while white women have more black husbands.

In the mid-twentieth century, Robert Merton (1941) proposed a status exchange theory to explain the high proportion of black men–white women marriages. He suggested that men who have high economic or professional status but who carry the stigma of being black in a racial caste society trade their social position for whiteness by marriage. Meanwhile, some social scientists argue that racialized sexual images also encourage marriages between white women and black men. Throughout Europe and the West, fair skin tone has long been perceived as a desirable feminine characteristic; African Americans share that perception. For example, black interviewers participating in a national survey of African Americans rated black women interviewees with lighter skin as more attractive than those with darker skin. But they did not consider male interviewees with light skin any more attractive than darker-skinned men. Other social scientists argue that the sex imbalance is associated with the legacy of slavery. During the plantation era, the miscegenation was mostly marked by white males' exploitation of slave females. The lingering effect of this legacy discourages African American women from marrying whites despite their low rates of in-marriage due to the low availability of marriageable African American men.

Asian Americans have a different pattern; most marriages with whites have a white husband. Some speculate that Asian American women tend to marry white men because they perceive Asian American men to be rigidly traditional on sex roles and white men as more nurturing and expressive. Asian cultures' emphasis on the male line of descent may pressure Asian American men to carry on the lineage by marrying "one of their own." But what attracts white men to Asian American women? Some scholars suggest that it is the widespread image of Asian women as submissive and hyperfeminine. On TV and in cinema, relationships between whites and Asian Americans, though still rare, almost always involve white men and Asian American women. Yet, this image does not explain a smaller but significant proportion of marriages involving white women and Asian American men. Indeed,

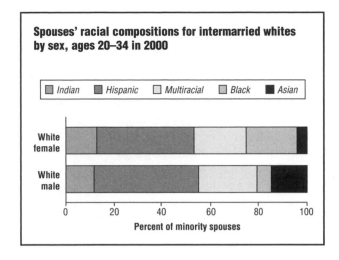

Spouses' racial compositions for intermarried whites by sex, ages 20–34 in 2000

Indian ▪ Hispanic □ Multiracial ▪ Black ■ Asian

White female

White male

0   20   40   60   80   100
Percent of minority spouses

education may be part of the reason, given that Asian American men and women have more years of schooling and highly educated minorities are much more likely to marry whites than their less educated counterparts. Yet perceptions of Asian Americans in American society are important as well. Asian Americans are generally believed to be smart, even though the spouses of some whites are not as educated. The stereotype is consistent with the social construction of Asian Americans as a model minority. This belief may well be another reason for a relatively high level of interracial marriages involving whites and Asian Americans.

SEE ALSO *Family; Marriage; Miscegenation; Race Relations*

BIBLIOGRAPHY

Alba, Richard D., and Victor Nee. 2003. *Remaking the American Mainstream: Assimilation and Contemporary Immigration.* Cambridge, MA: Harvard University Press.

Lichter, Daniel T., and Zhenchao Qian. 2004. *Marriage and Family in a Multiracial Society.* New York and Washington DC: Russell Sage Foundation and Population Reference Bureau.

Merton, Robert K. 1941. Intermarriage and the Social Structure: Fact and Theory. *Psychiatry* 4 (3): 361–374.

Qian, Zhenchao. 2005. Breaking the Racial Taboo: Interracial Marriage in America. *Contexts* 4 (4): 33–37.

Qian, Zhenchao, and Daniel T. Lichter. 2007. Social Boundaries and Marital Assimilation: Interpreting Trends in Racial and Ethnic Intermarriage. *American Sociological Review* 72 (1): 68–94.

Root, Maria P. P. 2001. *Love's Revolution: Interracial Marriage.* Philadelphia: Temple University Press.

Zhenchao Qian

MARRIAGE, SAME-SEX

Marriage is a vital social institution. The exclusive commitment of two individuals to each other nurtures love and mutual support; it brings stability to society. For those who choose to marry, and for their children, marriage also provides an abundance of legal, financial, and social benefits. In return it imposes weighty legal, financial, and social obligations (see *Goodridge v. Department of Public Health* 2003).

A growing number of jurisdictions around the world are according legal recognition to same-sex relationships. The types of recognition vary, some jurisdictions according all of the rights and obligations of marriage and others only according some. Similarly, some states within the United States have been expanding the rights and obligations accorded to same-sex couples, although others have acted to restrict or preclude the extension of rights and obligations to same-sex couples and their families.

BACKGROUND

Several countries have recognized that same-sex couples, like different-sex couples, both need and deserve to have their relationships accorded legal recognition. Some countries, such as Spain, the Netherlands, Belgium, and Canada, permit same-sex couples to marry. Other countries, such as France, Germany, Denmark, Norway, Iceland, Finland, Sweden, and Great Britain, offer many but not all of the rights and obligations of marriage.

Some of the differences among these countries include how they treat adoption (e.g., whether international adoptions are permitted), taxes, pension benefits, citizenship (whether at least one of the individuals entering into the relationship must be a citizen of the country recognizing the status), and the presumption of parenthood (whether a child born into the relationship will be presumed to be the child of both adults).

A separate issue is whether families involving same-sex couples will be recognized on a subnational level. Thus, relationships or incidents of relationships might be recognized in a particular city or region, even if they are not recognized nationally. For example, Buenos Aires recognizes civil unions, even though Argentina has not yet decided to do so, and New South Wales, Australia, has legislation regarding how property should be distributed upon the dissolution of a same-sex relationship, even though that is not true for all of Australia.

THE UNITED STATES

In the United States, the states differ greatly with respect to the ways that they treat same-sex relationships. Some states not only refuse to recognize same-sex relationships but also have passed state constitutional amendments precluding the legal recognition of same-sex marriage or same-sex unions more generally. These amendments have been open to a variety of interpretations. For example, the Ohio state constitutional amendment has been interpreted to preclude the extension of certain domestic violence protections to nonmarital couples, whether composed of individuals of the same sex or of different sexes.

Other states recognize same-sex unions but stop short of ascribing to those relationships all of the rights and obligations of marriage. For example, Hawaii recognizes reciprocal beneficiaries status, which permits both same-sex and different-sex couples to receive certain limited benefits specified by the legislature. California offers a much more robust array of benefits and responsibilities for domestic partners, although even this status is not the equivalent of marriage. Still other states, such as Vermont, accord to same-sex couples the rights and benefits of marriage, but call the relationship a civil union rather than a marriage. As of mid-2006, only Massachusetts recognized same-sex marriage.

Regardless of how the relationship is designated by the state, same-sex couples are not entitled to the numerous federal benefits that are accorded to different-sex married couples, because the U.S. Congress passed legislation in 1996 (the Defense of Marriage Act) specifying that only a marriage between a man and a woman will count as a marriage for federal purposes. The federal statute affects benefits in a broad range of areas, including social security, veteran's affairs, immigration, taxes, and bankruptcy, among others.

The Defense of Marriage Act was passed for a variety of reasons. Many of its supporters, whether or not they self-identify as part of the Religious Right, cite religious reasons as their justification—for example, by suggesting that God did not intend for same-sex couples to be able to marry. Other supporters worry that recognition of same-sex marriages would be too costly to the state or would somehow devalue different-sex marriage. Those asserting these arguments do not seem to appreciate that the same arguments have been or could be offered to justify preventing many types of marriages, including interreligious, interracial, or intergenerational marriage.

BENEFITS ON THE STATE LEVEL

While the Defense of Marriage Act precludes the extension of a substantial number of federal benefits, there are nonetheless a variety of matters of fundamental importance that are determined by state law. For example, there is no national law regarding adoption by same-sex couples—states determine that. There are at least two issues that should be discussed when adoption is being considered. Some states (e.g., Florida) prohibit those with a

same-sex orientation from adopting, even if the state permits unmarried individuals to adopt. An individual who had been raising a child for over ten years as a foster parent might be precluded from cementing that relationship through the vehicle of adoption if the would-be adoptive parent is in a relationship with someone of the same sex.

Other states permit gays and lesbians to adopt as individuals. However, they do not permit both members of a nonmarital couple to establish parental relations with the same child, which can result in great difficulties should the adults' relationship end because of death or estrangement. Suppose, for example, that a lesbian or gay man has custody of a child and is living with a partner. Further suppose that no other adult has parental rights to that child. In many states, the partner will not be allowed to adopt the child, which means that should something happen to the biological or adoptive parent, the child and the partner might be treated as legal strangers to each other.

Refusing to permit both members of a same-sex couple to establish legal relations with a child can have negative consequences, both materially and emotionally. If the partner is not legally recognized as a parent, then the partner's employer might not recognize the relationship between the partner and the child, which might mean that insurance or other employment benefits would not be extended to that child. The partner might also have more difficulty functioning as a parent, whether when meeting with teachers, visiting the child in the hospital, or authorizing medical treatment. In addition, if the partner will not be recognized by the state as a parent, that individual may have less incentive to form strong bonds with the child, to the detriment of both the partner and the child.

The difficulties that may arise because of a lack of a formally recognized relationship between the partner and the parent's child can occur analogously if the partners themselves cannot have their relationship formally recognized. If same-sex partners are not permitted to marry, an employer might not recognize the relationship between the two adults, which would mean that insurance benefits might not be extended to the partner. A partner who might otherwise stay home with a child or elderly parent might not be able to do so because of that lack of insurance coverage. Basically, there are a variety of benefits provided by third parties, such as an employer or the government, that will not be available unless same-sex partners can have their relationships legally recognized.

The benefits of legal recognition are nonfinancial as well. For example, hospital visitation and the ability to have a say in medical decision making may depend upon one's being able to establish a familial relationship with the patient. Were the states to permit same-sex couples to marry, many of these difficulties would be averted.

Marriage is also important because of the protections that will be provided should the relationship end because of death or dissolution. When married couples divorce or one of the parties dies, the state has a system in place specifying how property will be distributed or, perhaps, whether one member of the couple will be ordered to provide support for the other. When same-sex couples are precluded from marrying, they are unable to avail themselves of this system. Perhaps they will make private agreements or other arrangements that will avoid some of the difficulties that are caused by not having access to this system. However, for those who do not make the necessary arrangements beforehand, there is a definite risk that one of the parties may be treated unfairly.

Marriage also has symbolic importance to the parties themselves, as well as to society at large. By precluding same-sex partners from making a public commitment, the state is removing one of the ways that individuals act to strengthen their relationships, which means that the state is removing one of the supporting pillars of long-lasting relationships. Certainly, individuals can remain in committed relationships without marrying, and individuals who do marry may not remain in a committed relationship, so the claim is not that marriage is a necessary or sufficient condition for the maintenance of a healthy or long-lasting union. Further, it may well be that the couple can marry within their faith tradition. That said, however, the state's recognition of same-sex unions helps add stability to those relationships. Marriage gives individuals security so that they are more willing to invest in and make sacrifices for their relationships, which helps the individuals themselves, their families, and society as a whole.

The refusal to permit same-sex couples to marry has other negative effects as well. It sends a message to society that certain individuals either cannot commit to marriage or, perhaps, do not deserve the opportunity to marry. It also provides a rationale for the imposition of burdens on a particular group that might otherwise be difficult to justify. For example, limitations on adoption and markedly different criminal sentences for sexual relations between adults and minors have been rationalized by appealing to the mere possibility that different-sex couples might marry.

Jurisdictions vary with respect to whether they will recognize same-sex unions and, if they do, whether they will accord those unions the status or the rights and obligations of marriage. When states refuse to accord legal recognition to same-sex relationships, same-sex couples and their families are disadvantaged, so the growing number of jurisdictions recognizing such unions is a development that might be expected to diminish many of the difficulties that such families face.

SEE ALSO *Gender; Marriage; Politics, Gay and Lesbian*

BIBLIOGRAPHY

Goodridge v. Department of Public Health, 798 N.E.2d 941, 948 (Mass. 2003).

Lofton v. Secretary of Dept. of Children and Family Services, 358 F.3d 804 (11th Circuit 2004).

Merin, Yuval. 2002. *Equality for Same-Sex Couples: The Legal Recognition of Gay Partnerships in Europe and the United States*. Chicago: University of Chicago Press.

State v. Limon, 83 P.3d 229 (Kansas Appellate 2004), reversed, 122 P.3d 22 (2005).

Waaldijk, Kees. 2004. Others May Follow: The Introduction of Marriage, Quasi-Marriage, and Semi-Marriage for Same-Sex Couples in European Countries. *New England Law Review* 38 (3): 569–589.

Mark Strasser

MARRIAGE SQUEEZE HYPOTHESIS

SEE *Dowry and Bride Price.*

MARS

Since ancient times, the planet Mars has been seen as both a bright red light in the sky and an inspirer of aggressive behavior. Mars is the next planet out in the solar system from Earth, and its relative brightness in the night sky varies more than any other planet. Every two years and seven weeks, Mars changes its appearance from a dim spark to a bright red star. For this reason, Mars has represented a duality to humanity: It is both an inspiring astronomical object and the symbol of the God of War. It was Mars's variability and red hue which inspired, in the astronomers Nicolaus Copernicus and Johannes Kepler, an intense curiosity concerning its orbit, thus helping spawn the Scientific Revolution in the sixteenth century.

As the Scientific Revolution blossomed, this fascination with Mars continued and changed. Giovanni Schiaparelli's sighting of "canali," or canals, in the Martian landscape in 1877, followed by further reports of this phenomena by Percival Lowell, meant that Mars was the possible abode of extraterrestrial life and intelligence. The Lowellian concept of Mars as a dying planet was formed, and it came to be seen by some as a desert planet where a dead or dying civilization might be found. This spawned a host of fictional accounts of Martians, such as the *War of the Worlds* by H. G. Wells and the tales of John Carter of "Barsoom" (Mars) by Edgar Rice Burroughs.

Mars also inspired rocket developers such as Robert H. Goddard, and the planet was finally reached successfully by probes, beginning in 1964 with the American Mariner 4, which found a frozen desert covered with water channels, suggesting a previous Earthlike epoch.

In 1976, in a place on Mars called Cydonia, what appeared to be a massive archeological complex was discovered. On two separate orbits of the Viking A probe, images showed kilometer-sized objects resembling a pyramid near what looked like a carved humanoid face. NASA dismissed the images as illusions, but two engineers, Vincent DiPietro and Gregory Molenaar, investigated the images digitally. One person intrigued by these images was Richard Hoagland, a science reporter formerly with CBS News who organized a team of scientists and engineers called the Independent Mars Investigation Team, which validated the provocative nature of the images. However, Hoagland was criticized by other scientists for sensationalizing the results of the investigation. This effort was motivated by both the compelling nature of the images and the Lowellian folklore of Mars, but it was also a product of the tense cold war atmosphere of the early 1980s. This tension made researchers sensitive to any suggestion of a dead humanoid civilization, fearing the same fate might befall the inhabitants of Earth.

Another aspect of interest in the Cydonia objects was the very humanoid form suggested by the images, which recalled the fascination with the human form of previous epochs. For this reason, the Cydonia images were not only disturbing for their implications but also reassuring in their validation of the human experience, suggesting it is part of something cosmic. Since the cold war ended, Cydonia has become a favorite target of satellite images, which show that the objects are highly eroded, and thus very difficult to characterize. However, despite their eroded character—and continued efforts to dismiss them as merely geological formations—the objects still provoke mystery.

Mars as a whole continues to be an object of intense scientific investigation, with strong suggestions of primitive microbial biology, past and present, and past Earthlike conditions. Thus Mars may yet provide the answer to the age-old question of whether or not humanity is alone in the cosmos. Mars has also become the stated target of human exploration and settlement. Therefore, it can be said that Mars has provoked more human intellectual activity than any other planet and may be the setting for its greatest advances in the future.

SEE ALSO *Space Exploration*

BIBLIOGRAPHY

McDaniel, Stanley V., and Monical Rix Paxson, eds. 1998. *The Case for the Face: Scientists Examine the Evidence for Alien Artifacts on Mars.* Kempton, IL: Adventures Unlimited Press.

Wallbank, T. Walter, Alastair Taylor, and Nels Bailkey. 1967. *Civilization Past and Present.* 3rd ed. Glenview, IL: Scott, Foresman.

John Brandenburg

MARSHALL, ALFRED
1842–1924

The economist Alfred Marshall was born on July 26, 1842, in London, the second son of William Marshall, a clerk at the Bank of England, and Rebecca Marshall, née Oliver. He was educated at Merchant Taylors School (1852–1861) and took the mathematical tripos (1861–1865) at Saint John's College Cambridge as "second wrangler," that is, second in the first class honours list. This achievement gained him a fellowship at Saint John's, where his interests shifted to the moral sciences, initially philosophy and mental science. Marshall became a college lecturer (1868) and from the early 1870s began concentrating on economics. In 1877 he married Mary Paley, forcing his resignation from his college positions as college statutes then in force prohibited fellows to marry. From 1877 to 1881 Marshall served as principal and professor of political economy at Bristol University College. In 1883 he became a lecturer in economics at Oxford. In 1884 Marshall succeeded Henry Fawcett (1833–1884) as professor of political economy at Cambridge, a post he retained until 1908.

During his professorship at Cambridge, Marshall published his most significant book: *Principles of Economics* (1890). He had earlier published *The Economics of Industry* (1879) with his wife and *Pure Theory of Foreign Trade and of Domestic Value* (1879). Marshall gave most of his evidence to official government inquiries, on monetary and financial topics, on the poor laws, on national income accounting, and on local government finance during the 1880s and 1890s; and served as a member of the Labour Commission (1891–1894), set up by the government to inquire into labor unrest and recommend solutions thereto accordingly.

Marshall greatly expanded opportunities for the study of economics at Cambridge, an effort that culminated in the establishment of an economics and politics tripos in 1903. The Cambridge School of Economics he created was consolidated by his student A. C. Pigou (1877–1959), who became Marshall's successor as chair.

Other prominent students included John Neville Keynes (1852–1949) in the 1880s, and John Maynard Keynes (1883–1946) in 1905–06. In addition, Marshall was instrumental in the formation in 1890 of the British Economic Association, which became known as the Royal Economic Society in 1902.

Marshall published two further books, *Industry and Trade* (1919) and *Money, Credit, and Commerce* (1923), before he died on July 13, 1924. He left his books and papers to create the Marshall Library at the Cambridge Faculty of Economics and Politics, which honored him in 1932 by establishing the Marshall Lectures. An undergraduate Marshall Society for discussing social questions was formed in 1927.

Marshall's writings, especially *Principles of Economics*, made major contributions to economic theory. Marshall's ideas were often succinctly presented in diagrammatic form, a method he pioneered. Facilitating the understanding of real economic problems was a key element in Marshall's economics, reflecting his desire "to be read by businessmen" and explaining why the *Principles* remained in use as a text until the early 1950s. As a trained mathematician, Marshall also used algebra and the calculus in his economics, visible in the Mathematical Appendix included with all eight editions of the *Principles*. According to him, this was its proper place, since such reasoning could not add anything significant in formulating economic propositions. His frequent use of diagrams in the *Principles* invariably took place in the footnotes, and not in the text.

A major feature of Marshall's economics was its *partial equilibrium* method, which enabled him to concentrate on the key variable that explained a particular concept, while holding other less important variables constant. For example, his exposition of demand theory is presented primarily as a function of price, other things being equal, including the purchasing power of money, money income, prices of related commodities (substitutes or complementary goods), the time element in the analysis, and tastes, habits, and fashions. This approach simplified functional relationships considerably. However, the complexity of what was impounded in "the pound of *caeteris paribus*" made the method difficult to use in practice, contrary to Marshall's intentions. Furthermore, its use gave rise to potential logical conflicts; for example, when prices of all other commodities are held constant together with the purchasing power of money, the price of the commodity whose demand is being analyzed needs to vary.

Marshall's economic analysis in the *Principles* is organized in terms of supply and demand. After two preliminary sections, the *Principles* discusses demand (dependent on price and utility), supply (founded on his theory of production), and their combination to explain value (commodity prices) and distribution (factor prices and factor incomes). Much of Marshall's analysis is presented in diagrams featuring the *Marshallian cross* of a falling demand curve (reflecting generalized diminishing marginal utility) and a rising supply curve (reflecting generalized diminishing returns), with price the independent variable and quantity (supplied or demanded) the dependent variable, producing the stability, generally speaking, of the resulting equilibrium. Marshall departed from this simple presentation when circumstances demanded, as he did, for example, in his treatment of constant and increasing returns in terms of horizontal and falling supply curves (Marshall 1920, p. 464). However, since economic agents could also make decisions about quantities—for example, how much additional tea to consume, how much additional capacity to install in a factory, which invariably influenced prices—this technique was quite appropriate for Marshall, and following him, Keynes.

Marshall divided supply-and-demand analysis into specific time periods (market, short, and long) reflecting the degree of responsiveness of supply pertaining to them. During the market period, time is too short for supply to alter; supply is unresponsive to changes in price in the short period except from movements in stocks because the period is too short to increase stock by additional production. New output is confined to long-period situations when supply becomes fully flexible from changes in production induced by price changes. These time periods, although measured in clock time, do not reflect clock time per se. They depend on the technical production possibilities for the commodity being analyzed. Marshall also used time analysis for generalizing rent theory to incorporate quasi rent as the income of old capital investments. Like rent, quasi rent is price-determined, but only in the short run, defined as the time required before capital investments can be replaced.

The responsiveness in supply and demand of a commodity to changes in price was classified by Marshall in terms of their degrees of *elasticity*. Where responsiveness is proportionately equal to the price change, *unitary elasticity* applies. When responsiveness is less than the price change, the function exhibits *inelasticity*; if greater, it is described as *elastic*. Elasticity was an important, novel, and enduring feature of Marshall's price analysis.

Application of Marshall's theory of value to welfare economics by means of consumer surplus was another enduring contribution. Marshall defined *consumer surplus* as "the excess of the price which a consumer would be willing to pay rather than go without a certain commodity over that which he actually does pay" (1920, p. 124). Consumer surplus provided a measure of the benefit gained by consumers from their environment when individual consumer surpluses could be added. Marshall also noted that "a pound's worth of satisfaction" differed between people depending on their wealth and income levels, enhancing the difficulties in measuring consumers' welfare.

Marshall's theory of production carefully distinguished between the impact of scale and location on the cost of production. Size would generally elicit lower production costs over time. Marshall's discussion embodied static and dynamic elements, as well as factors incompatible with perfect competition, such as marketing and advertising expenses (Stigler 1941, pp. 77–83). Moreover, by dwelling on the locational advantages for firms as parts of industrial districts—the geographical concentration of industry—Marshall linked scale advantages to the size and concentration of an industry, as well as to the individual firm.

Marshall developed the *theory of the firm* as an important entity in economic decision making. This was implicit in his treatment of economies and diseconomies of scale, in his treatment of locational advantages, and in his analysis of monopoly and competition as specific market situations where competition meant monopolistic (imperfect) competition rather than an artificial construct of perfect competition. The pupils of Marshall's pupils, especially Dennis Robertson (1890–1963), Austin Robinson (1897–1993), and Joan Robinson (1903–1983), explicitly produced theories of the firm in their writings, including an innovative study of imperfect competition.

In *Money, Credit, and Commerce*, Marshall developed the *Cambridge cash balance equation* as his version of the quantity theory. This equation expressed the demand for money (the amount of income and wealth a person seeks to keep in the form of money) as follows: $D(M) = kPY + k'PW$, where k is the proportion of nominal income (PY) held in the form of money, and $k'k'$ the proportion of nominal wealth held in this way. These k's are the inverse of the respective velocities of circulation. Stating the quantity theory in this manner focused on individual demand for cash balances explicable in terms of transaction, precautionary, and speculative demands. Marshall's manner of looking at monetary relationships was also more amenable to statistical analysis.

Marshall's role in the history of economic thought is enormous. His *Principles* is the only nineteenth-century treatise still in wide use more than a hundred years later, even if, by modern standards, it is an unsatisfactory book (Blaug 1997, pp. 404–405). Marshall is the most important figure in economics from the formative decades of the 1890s to the 1920s, when marginalist economics became the dominant theory (Screpanti and Zamagni 1990, p. 177). Moreover, his theory accepts a general equilibrium framework but is presented in the more realistic and prac-

tical partial equilibrium form (Deane 1978, pp. 112–113). The centenary of Marshall's *Principles* in 1990 sparked many international celebrations, not only in England at Cambridge and the Royal Economic Society, but in Italy, Germany, France, North America, and even China. Close to 250 articles on Marshall's economics are collected in the eight volumes of John Wood's *Alfred Marshall: Critical Assessments* (1982, 1996). Marshall's writings clearly continue to be of use to students of economics.

SEE ALSO *Partial Equilibrium*

BIBLIOGRAPHY

Blaug, Mark. 1997. *Economic Theory in Retrospect.* 5th ed. Cambridge, U.K.: Cambridge University Press.

Deane, Phyllis. 1978. *The Evolution of Economic Ideas.* Cambridge, U.K.: Cambridge University Press.

Groenewegen, Peter. 1995. *A Soaring Eagle: Alfred Marshall, 1842–1924.* Cheltenham, U.K.: Edward Elgar.

Marshall, Alfred. [1890] 1920. *Principles of Economics.* 8th ed. London: Macmillan.

Marshall, Alfred. 1982. *Alfred Marshall: Critical Assessments.* 4 vols. Ed. John Cunningham Wood. London: Croom Helm.

Marshall, Alfred. 1996. *Alfred Marshall: Critical Assessments.* 2nd series. 4 vols. Ed. John Cunningham Wood. London: Routledge.

Screpanti, Ernesto, and Stefano Zamagni. 1990. *An Outline of the History of Economic Thought.* Trans. David Field. Oxford: Clarendon.

Stigler, George. 1941. *Production and Distribution Theories: The Formative Period.* New York: Macmillan.

Peter Groenewegen

MARSHALL, JOHN
SEE *Supreme Court, U.S..*

MARSHALL, THURGOOD
1908–1993

In 1967 Thurgood Marshall, who was born in Baltimore on July 2, 1908, became the first African American appointed to the United States Supreme Court. Marshall's twenty-four-year tenure as a justice was marked by a strong interest in protecting the rights of criminal defendants (e.g., protection against illegal search and seizure) and opposition to the death penalty (*Furman v. Georgia,*

1972). Marshall's appointment to the Court was part of a successful career as an advocate for the protection of civil rights. Marshall dedicated his career to enhancing access to every arena of public life, with a particular focus on education, housing, employment, and voting. He believed that promoting equal rights under the law was essential to the proper functioning of democracy. According to Marshall, "equal means getting the same thing, at the same time and in the same place" (*Brown v. Board of Education*, 1954). Marshall's dedication created a lasting legacy that encompasses numerous aspects of American jurisprudence. He died in Bethesda, Maryland, on January 24, 1993.

EDUCATION AND LAW PRACTICE

Thurgood (born Thoroughgood) Marshall developed an early interest in education. A cum laude graduate of Lincoln University, he believed that education is the only assured means of promoting both individual and communal success. To Marshall and his contemporaries, education was a necessary means of reshaping the status of American race relations.

After graduating from Lincoln, Marshall enrolled in Howard University Law School, where he met and worked with his mentor, Charles Hamilton Houston. As dean of Howard's law school Houston inculcated in his students a commitment to equal justice and a desire to challenge both legal and extralegal segregation. Paramount to that commitment was an emphasis on overturning the 1896 *Plessy v. Ferguson* Supreme Court decision. That decision was significant because it created a legal doctrine known as separate but equal and provided the legal justification for segregation in many areas, including education and public accommodations. Marshall was influenced deeply by Houston's belief that he and other Howard graduates could force the United States to live up to its promise of equality for all Americans. Marshall graduated from Howard in 1933 and opened up a practice in Baltimore that focused on civil rights cases involving issues such as police brutality, civil disobedience, and housing discrimination. Marshall later assisted the Baltimore branch of the National Association for the Advancement of Colored People (NAACP) in its civil rights efforts.

In 1935 Marshall won his first major desegregation case, *Murray v. Pearson*. Together with his cocounsel, Charles Hamilton Houston, Marshall represented the African American student Donald Gaines Murray, who had been denied admission to the University of Maryland Law School on the basis of its separate but equal admissions policy. Although Murray was a graduate of Amherst College with an impressive academic record, the state of Maryland defended his exclusion, arguing that black stu-

dents could attend other schools. Marshall had been denied admission to the University of Maryland Law School for the same reason five years earlier. In ruling against the state of Maryland the court of appeals argued that constitutional compliance could not be left to the will of the state. Marshall helped secure the first state-level victory toward overturning *Plessy*.

Murray became the first in a long line of successes for Marshall. As legal counsel for the NAACP he launched a comprehensive assault on the legally sanctioned practice of exclusion. In 1940 he won his first Supreme Court case, *Chambers v. Florida*. Over the course of his career Marshall argued thirty-two cases before the Supreme Court; winning twenty-nine, making him the most successful attorney to argue before the Court. As the U.S. solicitor general, appointed by President Lyndon Johnson, Marshall won fourteen of nineteen cases he argued before the Supreme Court.

Marshall successfully argued the 1944 case *Smith v. Allwright*. The case was significant because it overturned the "white primaries" that were prominent in the South. Marshall helped reduce the gap between the principle and practice of democracy by opening up the political process to all Americans. He continued to attack the separate but equal doctrine in cases such as *Shelley v. Kraemer* (1948) that struck down racially restrictive covenants. In two cases in particular, *McLaurin v. Oklahoma State Regents* (1950) and *Sweatt v. Painter* (1950), he fought against segregation in public education. *Sweatt* found that the state of Texas's creation of a separate law school for black students (now Texas Southern University) with inadequate facilities failed to meet the standard of substantive equality.

Although Marshall was successful in arguing the cases, he faced criticism from some black leaders who feared that his legal victories would jeopardize state funding for historically black colleges and universities. Marshall responded to the criticism by stating that "we are convinced that it is impossible to have equality in a segregated system, no matter how elaborate we build the Jim Crow citadel and no matter whether we label it the 'Black University of Texas,' 'The Negro University of Texas,' 'Prairie View Institute,' or a more fitting title, 'An Apology to Negroes for Denying them Their Constitutional Rights to Attend the University of Texas'" (*Sweatt v. Painter*, 1947).

BROWN V. BOARD OF EDUCATION

The 1954 case *Brown v. Board of Education of Topeka Kansas* was the culmination of Marshall's attack on the separate but equal doctrine. Unlike the prior cases *Brown* specifically outlawed racial segregation in American primary and secondary schools. Timing was critical for Marshall's agenda. Armed with his success in integrating institutions of higher education, Marshall and his NAACP colleagues sponsored five cases affirming their view that separate educational facilities were inherently inferior. Led by Chief Justice Earl Warren, the Court reached a 9–0 decision affirming that "separate educational facilities are inherently unequal" (*Brown v. Board of Education of Topeka*, 1954). Although *Brown* did not result in the immediate desegregation of American public schools (see *Brown II* [1955], *Swann v. Charlotte-Mecklenburg Board of Education* [1971], and *Milliken v. Bradley* [1974]), it created a firm foundation for judicial support of the civil rights movement and its efforts to integrate all areas of public and private life.

Marshall's commitment to protecting the rights and freedoms of individuals was not restricted to the United States. He investigated allegations of racism in the U.S. armed forces in Japan and South Korea and later assisted in drafting the constitution of Ghana. Thurgood Marshall fundamentally redefined the relationship between citizens and their government by promoting equal rights under the law.

SEE ALSO Brown v. Board of Education, *1954;* Brown v. Board of Education, *1955;* Civil Liberties; Civil Rights Movement, U.S.; Desegregation; Education, USA; Houston, Charles Hamilton; Schooling in the USA; Separate-but-Equal; Supreme Court, U.S.

BIBLIOGRAPHY

Brown v. Board of Education of Topeka, 347 U.S. 483, 495. 1954. http://caselaw.lp.findlaw.com/scripts/getcase.pl?court=US&vol=347&invol=483.

Brown v. Board of Education, 349 U.S. 294. 1955. http://caselaw.lp.findlaw.com/cgi-bin/getcase.pl?court=us&vol=349&invol=294.

Chambers v. Florida, 309 U.S. 227. 1940. http://supreme.justia.com/us/309/227/case.html.

Furman v. Georgia, 408 U.S. 238. 1972. http://supreme.justia.com/us/408/238/case.html.

McLaurin v. Oklahoma State Regents, 339 U.S. 637. 1950. http://supreme.justia.com/us/339/637/case.html.

Milliken v. Bradley, 418 U.S. 717. 1974. http://supreme.justia.com/us/418/717/case.html.

Plessy v. Ferguson, 163 U.S. 537. 1896. http://supreme.justia.com/us/163/537/case.html.

Shelley v. Kraemer, 334 U.S. 1. 1948. http://supreme.justia.com/us/334/1/case.html.

Smith v. Allwright, 321 U.S. 649. 1944. http://supreme.justia.com/us/321/649/case.html.

Swann v. Charlotte-Mecklenburg Board of Education, 402 U.S. 1. 1971. http://caselaw.lp.findlaw.com/cgi-bin/getcase.pl?court=us&vol=402&invol=1.

Sweatt v. Painter, 339 U.S. 629. 1950. http://caselaw.lp.findlaw.com/scripts/getcase.pl?court=US&vol=339&invol=629.

Warren, Earl. 1954. *Brown v. Board of Education of Topeka* 347 U.S. 483. 1954. http://www.nationalcenter.org/brown.html.

Williams, Juan. 2000. *Thurgood Marshall: American Revolutionary.* NY: Three Rivers Press.

Khalilah L. Brown-Dean

MARTYRDOM

Martyrdom is defined as voluntary death for a cause, often for a religious purpose or as the result of persecution. The terminology of martyrdom varies from region to region. The term *martyr* comes from the Greek *martur,* which means "witness," as does the Arabic *shahīd* (pl. *shudadā*). Martyrs thus bear witness to their cause by sacrificing their lives as proof of its validity. Eastern cultures tend to use words closer to "sacrifice," focusing on the valor of the agent; e.g., *sati,* "immolation" after the eponymous Hindu widow who sacrificed herself on her husband's pyre.

Although martyrdom is historically conditioned, these voluntary deaths have structural similarities, being rooted in traditions of the warrior-hero and religious sacrifice. The noble deaths of kamikaze pilots, Christian martyrs, Indian widows in *sati,* the Jews who committed mass suicide at Masada in 72 CE, or Moslems on *jihad* are all sacrifices that transform and sanctify (or divinize) the martyr. Martyrs put their lives on the line, choosing to sacrifice their lives for a cause rather than submit to an opponent and betray their principles. In dying on their own terms, martyrs die heroically, like archaic warriors in battle, sacrificing their lives for the tribe. To their communities, martyrs are god-like in their honor, nobility, and glory. Like King Oedipus or Christ, martyrs are scapegoats and saviors, dying that others may live. Martyrdom is the ultimate and apocalyptic vindication of the martyr's cause and proof of his or her righteousness. After death martyrs become saints in Christian tradition, divine in Japanese traditions, and hallowed in all traditions.

Martyrdom joins politics and metaphysics. The martyrs' moral authority becomes a means of confronting an enemy's superior political and military power, as it did when Antiochus IV persecuted the Maccabees, when Romans persecuted early Christians, when Japanese pilots faced the Allies in World War II, or presently, when Palestinians confront Israel and the United States. Martyrs are marginal agents—crossing the numinous boundary of death, they seek to harness a spiritual power to their own advantage. Being unnatural, voluntary or self-inflicted death is shocking, awesome in the fear and wonder it inspires. Why did the martyr die? If the martyr chose to die, what is worth dying for? At what point is life so unbearable that one is better off dead? What gave the martyr the strength to face death so bravely?

The power of martyrdom lies in its potential to change society: It forces an audience to think about ultimate questions (if only momentarily) and make moral judgments. These decisions can redress injustices and eventually change the world. Because the death of the martyr invests a cause with meaning, with numen or "weight," the cause is no longer ordinary. It has been sanctified with the offering of one life; perhaps it is worth the cost of many more. Martyrs draw public attention to the cause for which they died. Not only do they educate the audience, they strive to make their own views normative, converting (if not convincing) their critics. The propaganda value of martyrdom is so great that shrewd opponents avoid martyring their enemies, who are more dangerous dead than alive. In the Middle Ages, the cult of saints and the development of pilgrimage sites was of such political and economic importance that relics were stolen, traded, and even manufactured. Today, pilgrims still visit Karbala, Iraq, famous for its Shiite martyrs, and Rome for its early Christian martyrs. Historically, martyrs have meant economic prosperity, political authority, and social eminence.

The dynamics of martyrdom are unusually histrionic, as if the martyr's ordeal takes place in a transcendent, metaphysical arena or a universal courtroom of conscience that hears the martyr's case. As J. Huizinga's theory of play and his game theory suggest, opponents adopt strategies to win, but events unfold unpredictably and are subject to multiple interpretation. Martyrs feel deprived of what they deserve; they challenge existing authorities and offer their case to God and the world at large for judgment. Entrusted to Higher Powers, martyrs and their cause have moved into the realm of the sacred. But the ordeal is also public, a political spectacle in the here-and-now; at any one time, much is "in play," fluid, indeterminate, and ambiguous.

The martyr's power comes from holding the moral high ground of innocence and purity. Guilt and unworthiness must be pinned on the opponent. The spectacle of martyrdom is inherently biased in the martyr's favor insofar as endurance of suffering and death is taken as *prima facie* evidence that the martyr is in the right—that God is on the martyr's side. (Otherwise, how could the martyr face such terrible ordeals?) Even if death is clearly self-inflicted, the enemy is held responsible. He has forced the martyr to choose between life on the enemy's terms and death on the martyr's terms; he is the guilty persecutor. All martyrdom redounds ultimately to this choice between self-determination and submission to the will of another. Here, the warrior spirit affirms that death is preferable to subjection, dishonor, suffering, and the betrayal of beliefs;

whether in Imperial Japan, Christian antiquity, or contemporary Islamic circles, an honorable death is preferable to a life of degradation and misery.

Martyrs seek vindication and retribution for their innocent suffering, some definitive judgment denied them by existing society. Viewed strategically, martyrdom obliges the audience to avenge the innocent or share the guilt of the wrongdoers. If martyrs can turn public opinion against their opponents, they can undermine their enemies' power. The assassinations of Gandhi, Martin Luther King, and Stephen Biko not only stunned the world at large, they were of such great political consequence that they broke the resistance of the enemy camp. Shifting public opinion often takes the form of boycotts. During the civil rights era boycotts such as the Montgomery bus boycott in 1955 added momentum to the movement for racial equality. In the 1980s, divestment in South Africa hastened the end of apartheid. Individual protests can take the form of hunger strikes (a kind of slow martyrdom), such as that undertaken by suffragettes in their struggle for the franchise, or that of Gandhi, who undertook over a dozen long fasts against the British, or the seventy-five prisoners protesting their illegal detention in Guantánamo in 2005–2006. Such lesser martyrdoms can tweak the conscience of the world audience.

Although the ordeal or spectacle of martyrdom is biased in the martyr's favor, part of the audience may reject the martyr's voluntary death, viewing it as "a waste," "irrational," and "tragic," the "pathetic suicide" of a "brainwashed fanatic" or a "selfish act" that disregards family and community. The dead are called "victims," as if they had not acted willfully, but instead succumbed to circumstances beyond their control. The deaths of such fanatics do not lend credibility to the cause, but discredit it even further, even as the deaths of prominent leaders (or the moral support of living celebrities) lend credibility to a cause.

The intrinsic worthiness of a cause is critical, but not determinative in distinguishing martyrs from fools or criminals. The worthiness of a cause, the social status and deeds of the martyr, the martyr's behavior under stress, the strength of the enemy, the resources of both sides, and the sequence of actions are all variables "in play." While dying for freedom is clearly different from dying for the sake of a lost shoe, a range of causes exists whose importance might change in the public eye were a sufficient number of martyrs to bear witness: global warming, animal rights, or the malfeasance of corporations (e.g., Enron). The deaths of martyrs invest a cause with meaning, and this is cumulative. When a cause builds up sufficient "weight," it earns a public hearing and triggers change. In 1963, the self-immolation of the Buddhist monk Thich Quang Duc in Vietnam opened a flood of media coverage, facilitated by the letters of protest he left behind. Six other monks followed. The event is credited as the final turning point, the death knell of the Diem regime, which collapsed a few months later.

Martyrs lose their power when they lose their innocence, when the greater public rejects their cause and/or refuses to sanction their actions. Then martyrs become enemies (or persecutors themselves) engaged in open warfare with the rest of humanity. The cause must be worth the cost. Martyrs may gain attention and sympathy for their cause by offering their own lives, but they cross a line when others die. Martyrs have no right to deprive others of free choice, not to mention life itself. Belligerent nations in World War II (1939–1945) offer a clear example. Kamikaze pilots accepted that killing Americans was the price of vindicating the purity and divine purpose of their emperor and nation. Validating the cause, they also accepted the cost. But Americans and the Allies rejected the cause of Japan and called it "war." In the Middle East, the sides are of unequal power, but each has moral claims. To Israelis and their allies, Palestinian suicide bombers are terrorists who murder innocent bystanders, but Palestinians see themselves as victims of an occupation sanctioned by all Israelis and feel justified in fighting against that occupation. To them, Israeli bystanders are casualties in a war that has already cost the lives of many more innocent Palestinians.

Martyrdom operates within that indeterminate field where opinions change and variables are "in play." Affirmation and rejection are extremes of a continuum; advancement of the martyr's status depends on numerous contingencies. Sooner or later, the martyr's case gains public attention, but rational understanding of the martyr's grievances may not convert an audience driven by equally compelling drives. The audience's capacity for empathy is unpredictable. While historical conditions such as economic security or social similarity increase chances that the audience will identify with victims and feel compassion, studies of authoritarianism demonstrate that personality structure can diminish or even preclude empathy with others. No act of valor, no leader, no matter how august, can convert those who are deeply prejudiced.

What triggers empathy varies. The calculus of martyrdom favors elites, so that the death of one important leader outweighs the deaths of the innumerable nameless. Assassinated in 1980, only Archbishop Oscar Romero is honored as a martyr in the civil war in El Salvador, even though 30,000 others were exterminated by right-wing death squads between 1979 and 1981. The prestige of martyrs sacrificed lends authority to the cause, but the lack of martyrial "quality" can be addressed by an increase in "quantity" (the number of martyrs, the length and intensity of their suffering). All lives are not equal. Certain markers are more valuable than others. In 2003, a young American was killed by a bulldozer as she tried to prevent the Israeli army's destruction of homes in the Gaza Strip. A play based on her letters, "My Name Is Rachel Corrie," commemorates her life, as does a memorial Web site; she is the subject of various articles, media spots, etc. Corrie is not the first to die resisting the demolition of houses, but she is the first Westerner. Europeans and Americans can identify with such a young, attractive, and highly literate "peace activist," while Palestinians remain invisible. The less kinship the audience shares with martyrs, the more onerous the martyrs' suffering.

Examples of martyrdom or noble death are nearly universal. These include:

- *Judaism.* Kiddush Hashem (sanctification of the name) is found in Abraham's binding of Isaac; Rabbi Akiba, who was killed by the Romans in 135 CE; Hannah and her sons; and the killing of Jews in the Rhineland during the First Crusade. A dispute exists about the terminology used for those dying in the Holocaust. Traditionalists argue that Jews did not choose to die and therefore the term "martyr" is inappropriate. They are instead victims, murdered in war. But Yad Vashem (sponsor of the Holocaust Memorial in Jerusalem and the leader in Shoah research and education) calls itself "The Holocaust Martyrs and Heroes Authority." What matters to most people is that Jews were killed for no other reason than being Jewish.

- *Islam.* A spiritualized definition of martyrdom goes back to the Middle Ages and the distinction between the lesser *jihad*, the struggle against unbelievers, and the greater *jihad*, the struggle against evil. Martyrdom lies in intention; death on the battlefield is no guarantee of salvation. In present usage, any observant Muslim who dies gratuitously is a martyr. But martyrdom also has a militant side that goes back to Muhammad's grandson, Husayn ibn 'Ali, who was killed at Karbala in 680 in a battle against supporters of the caliphate for leadership of the community. Husayn's followers are Shiite and martyrdom is an honored goal; those of the caliphs, are Sunni. Also in this militant tradition are the Assassins (from *hashish*), a secret society of Nizari Isma'ilis (schismatic Muslims) who fought against European Crusaders in the Middle Ages. They called themselves *fedayeen*, meaning those "willing to sacrifice their lives," a term that survives in the second *intifada* (September 28, 2000, to the present).

- *Christianity.* Persecuted by Romans, early Christians, like Jews, saw themselves as "dying for God." Acts or passions record the martyrs' ordeals, many of which contain purported court records or eyewitness accounts. Protestants memorialized in *Foxe's Book of Martyrs* date from the sixteenth century, when Catholics persecuted Protestants in the Counter-Reformation. In Nagasaki, twenty-six Jesuit missionaries were martyred in 1597, and persecution continued under the Tokugawa shogunate costing several hundred lives. In 1981, members of the Irish Republican Army incarcerated at Maze prison went on a hunger strike in protest of the British government's refusal to grant them status as political prisoners (instead of ordinary criminals). Bobby Sands and nine others died and are widely commemorated in Ireland. In 1998, statues of ten twentieth-century Christian martyrs were unveiled at Westminster Abbey in London, among them, Martin Luther King Jr.

- *Hinduism.* The Hindu practice of *sati* was most frequent in western India from the tenth to nineteenth centuries. Outlawed by the British in 1829, it has survived sporadically up to the present. A new tradition borrowed from Christianity arose with the growth of nationalism in the nineteenth century and the struggle for an independent state in the twentieth century. While Gandhi is the most famous martyr, about a dozen others are deemed martyrs for the cause of Indian independence. While *satis* have altars and are treated as divine, of modern martyrs only Gandhi is occasionally commemorated at an altar.

- *Sikhism.* The Sikh theology of martyrdom (*śahīdī*) is first found in the Siri Guru Granth Sahib, scriptures compiled by the fifth master and first martyr, Guru Arjan Dev Ji (d. 1606), who called martyrdom "the game of love." Sikhs have suffered bitterly from persecutions by both Muslims and Hindus. Martyrdom is strongly associated with political resistance and the desire for political as well as religious autonomy, the Punjab being the possible Sikh homeland.

- *Buddhism.* The idea of dying for Buddha does not exist in Buddhism (which is atheistic); the notion of dying for something in the material world is similarly foreign, and Buddhism lacks a history of persecution. Nevertheless, the seven Buddhist monks who immolated themselves in Vietnam protesting the Diem regime's policies are deemed martyrs in both the East and the West. As with Hinduism, Sikhism, and Islam in modern times, in Buddhism the struggle for freedom and national identity can occasion martyrdom.

BIBLIOGRAPHY

Abeii, Mehdi, and Gary Legenhausen, ed. 1986. *Jihād and Shahādat: Struggle and Martyrdom in Islam.* Houston, TX: Institute for Research and Islamic Studies.

Cormack, Margaret, ed. 2002. *Sacrificing the Self: Perspectives on Martyrdom and Religion.* Oxford, U.K.: Oxford University Press.

Fields, Rona, ed. 2004. *Martyrdom: The Psychology, Theology, and Politics of Self-Sacrifice.* Westport, CT: Praeger.

Pettigrew, Joyce, ed. 1997. *Martyrdom and Political Resistance Movements: Essays on Asia and Europe.* Amsterdam: VU University Press.

Carole Straw

MARX, KARL
1818–1883

By identifying the rational core in the German philosopher Georg Hegel's writings, the German political philosopher Karl Marx not only clarified the essence of the human mind, but also conceptualized the relationship between Hegel's subjective and objective mind. Marx suggested that the objective mind had primacy over subjectivity. Identifying the sociohistorical essence of the mind (consciousness), Marx realized that the individual mind was a societal product and that the mind of a single individual was not just the mind of a single person, but that the individual mind was always and necessarily embedded in society and part of society. Marx and his colleague Friedrich Engels discussed the sociohistorical dimension of the mind extensively in their work *The German Ideology* (1932), in which they also suggested that language development paralleled the development of the mind, and that language developed historically from the need to interact with other humans.

Marx's sociohistorical conceptualization of the mind was part of his view on human nature, which states that the essence of human nature is its societal quality and thus humans should be understood in the context of the ensemble of societal relations. The idea that the mind is in its essence sociohistorical was not in contradiction to the notion of the era that the mind has a natural biological dimension. Marx in fact understood the English naturalist Charles Darwin's book on natural selection as the natural-historical foundation for his view. The difference between Marx, who regarded Darwin's theory highly, and Darwin was that for Marx it would be impossible to transfer rules that govern animal behavior to the history of human societies.

According to Marx, because of the sociohistorical quality of the mind, it is exposed to power in contexts and relations of production. This means that the ideas of the ruling class are also the ruling ideas and the ruling ideas are the cognitive expression of the ruling material relations. Thus, morality, religion, and metaphysics cannot be independent. Marx used the metaphor of a camera obscura to describe ideology or false consciousness. Marx knew about psychological phenomena such as optical illusions, the invertive function of the eye, and technological applications such as the camera obscura. He came to the conclusion that the mind has distorted views of the world (optical illusions) and that the mind works upside down (camera obscura). In ideological theories humans and their relations appear upside down but in reality these theories arise from the historical life processes of humans. This metaphor also appeared in Marx's first volume of the *Capital* (1867) on the fetish character of the commodity. Relationships among human beings appear as relationships among produced things (commodities), and these commodities seem to possess supernatural powers.

Marx connected the mind with power and with labor, the material activities and practices of humans. An analysis of the psychology and philosophy of his time, when cognitive processes were disconnected from real-life activities, demonstrates its significance. Ideas and conceptions of the mind are interwoven with the material activity of human beings. Thus, Marx believed that imagination, thinking, the mental interaction of humans should be understood as the direct outcome of material behavior. The same applies to mental productions as represented in the language of politics, laws, morality, religion, and metaphysics. For Marx real active human beings are the producers of their ideas and they are determined by a particular developmental stage of the productive forces. This conceptualization of the mind led to the famous idea that life is not determined by the mind, but the mind by life. It is not the mind of humans that determines their being, but to the contrary it is the societal being of humans that determines their mind. Although Marx had no doubts about the sociohistorical quality of the mind, he also believed that the mind could be developed further than the zeitgeist, or the existing societal realities of a particular time.

Marx moved according to his philosophy with its emphasis on productive activity (labor), from an objective mind understood by Hegel as law, morality, and ethics, to viewing the objective mind as industry. Accordingly, one should be able to understand the nature of humans in the objectified products of human labor. For Marx the history of industry and the developing objective existence of industry was the open book of human psychology. In the course of this argument, Marx expressed one of the first criticisms of the content of modern psychology: "A psychology, for which this book, the sensuously most tangible and accessible part of history, is closed, cannot become a real science with a genuine content" (1968, p. 543).

In terms of methodology, Marx urged philosophers to study concrete individuals who live in concrete historical societies and not to reflect upon the abstract individual beyond history and society. He suggested a methodology that begins with active humans in order to understand their ideas and imaginations. Human existence and history starts with the fact that humans must be able to live, which includes eating, drinking, clothing, shelter, and procreation. History in its course also leads to the development of new needs and at a certain point in history humans did not only find their means of living but they produced them. Thus, the history of humankind and the history of the mind should be studied in relation to the history of production.

Contemporary psychologists assume more or less implicitly that functions or domains such as consciousness, reasoning, language, memory, or perception belong to an individual mind, and often base their theories and research practices on an individualistic concept of the mind. However, a few psychologists based their theories on Marx's sociohistorical conceptualization of the mind. His ideas inspired the Soviet philosophical psychologist Sergej Rubinstein (1889–1960), the cultural-historical school with its most influential thinker Lev Vygotsky (1896–1934), the French psychologist Georges Politzer (1903–1942), the German thinker Klaus Holzkamp (1927–1995), and various forms of critical psychology. It also can be demonstrated that Marx inspired early American social psychology. In addition, followers of the Frankfurt school merged his theories, yet not his psychological writings, with psychoanalysis, and developed a Freudian-Marxist field of research.

BIBLIOGRAPHY

PRIMARY WORKS

Marx, Karl. [1859] 1961. Critique of Political Economy. In *Works: Volume 3*. Karl Marx and Friedrich Engels. Berlin: Dietz.

Marx, Karl. [1888] 1958. Theses on Feuerbach. In *Works: Volume 3*. Karl Marx and Friedrich Engels. Berlin: Dietz.

Marx, Karl. [1932] 1968. Economico-Philosophical Manuscripts of 1844. In *Supplementary Volume*. Karl Marx and Friedrich Engels. Berlin: Dietz.

Marx, Karl. 1964. Marx to Engels: December 19, 1860. In *Works: Volume 30 (Letters 1860–1864)*. Karl Marx and Friedrich Engels. Berlin: Dietz.

Marx, Karl, and Friedrich Engels. [1932] 1958. The German Ideology. In *Works: Volume 3*. Berlin: Dietz.

SECONDARY WORKS

Teo, Thomas. 2001. "Karl Marx and Wilhelm Dilthey on the Socio-Historical Conceptualization of the Mind." In *The Transformation of Psychology: Influences of 19th-Century Philosophy, Technology, and Natural Science,* edited by Christopher Green, Marlene Shore, and Thomas Teo, 195–218. Washington, DC: American Psychological Association.

Vygotsky, Lev S. 1978. *Mind in Society: The Development of Higher Psychological Processes.* Cambridge, MA: Harvard University.

Young, Robert M. 1996. "Evolution, Biology and Psychology from a Marxist Point of View." In *Psychology and Society: Radical Theory and Practice,* edited by I. Parker and R. Spears, 35–49. London: Pluto.

Thomas Teo

MARX, KARL: IMPACT ON ANTHROPOLOGY

Karl Marx was born in the Trier of the German Rhineland in 1818. He studied law and philosophy in Bonn and Berlin, completing a doctorate at the University of Jena in 1841. His thesis, "The Difference between the Democritean and Epicurean Philosophy of Nature," explored the earliest materialist philosophies of the two Greek atomists, and demonstrates the inception of a nascent scholarly interest in crafting a sophisticated materialist critique of German idealism. Not surprisingly, his earliest writings, *The Economic and Philosophical Manuscripts* (1844), as well as the unpublished "Theses on Feuerbach" (1845) and *The German Ideology* (1845), all represent attempts to conceptualize a practice-oriented methodology for analyzing history and society. This "historical materialist" approach evidences the first engagements between Marx and the work of nineteenth-century anthropology, particularly the writings of Lewis Henry Morgan (1818–1881), Sir Henry Maine (1822–1888), and Johann Jakob Bachofen (1815–1887). Within archaeology, Marx and his frequent coauthor Friedrich Engels (1820–1895) had a profound impact on the cultural historical approach of V. Gordon Childe (1892–1957) in the early twentieth century. And Marx continues to have an important influence on a range of archaeological approaches today, including new structuralist approaches to class analysis (e.g., Saitta 1994). But within sociocultural anthropology, overt reference to Marx did not reemerge until the 1960s. Although much of the reluctance to engage Marx through the first part of the twentieth century can be attributed to a disciplinary reaction against evolutionary theoretical models (especially in U.S. and Canadian anthropology), by the 1940s and 1950s the omission was clearly the product of outright political and scholarly censorship during the "red scares" and McCarthyism of that period. This had the effect of suppressing and ideologically orienting the contributions of U.S. anthropology, which were becoming increasingly dominant globally. As David Price (2004) has shown convincingly, the FBI's intrusions into anthropology during this period were extensive, frustrating and dismantling careers of anyone with activist interests, particularly anthropologists concerned with racial equity and desegregation. Anthropologists with obvious Marxist influence (e.g., Julian Steward and his students, Leslie White, and many others) were not able to claim that influence until the civil rights movement of the 1960s, when broad populist concern with social justice and widespread public disapproval over U.S. actions in Southeast Asia ushered in a new era of social activism.

When Marx did reemerge as a prominent influence in anthropology in the 1960s, he did so in three social theoretical manifestations: through a discussion of the relationship or "articulation" between capitalist and precapitalist social forms (particularly within the French Marxist tradition); through an investigation of the mechanics and practice of politics and ideological and class formation; and finally through an interrogation of capitalist influence on non-Western settings (laudably within the cultural ecological and political economic traditions, especially in the United States).

PRECAPITALIST SOCIAL FORMATIONS

A common rejection of Marx stems from the critique that his historical approach was evolutionary and ethnocentrically focused on the socioeconomic experiences of Europe. As a result, many believe his method to be inapplicable to contemporary non-Western societies. Indeed, this explains why in the early twentieth century Marx had a more relevant impact on archaeology than on sociocultural anthropology, which had become frustrated with the unilinear evolutionary claims of nineteenth-century anthropology. In answering this charge, the French Marxist tradition has been particularly interested in the relationship between global and local socioeconomic systems, questioning the relevance of Marx to the study of non-Western societies, particularly in Marx's later works such as the first French editions of *Capital,* volume 1 ([1867] 1990a) and *Grundrisse* ([1857] 1978), as well as a long list of unpublished papers and notes. The 1964 publication of *Pre-Capitalist Economic Formations,* with historian Eric Hobsbawm's insightful introduction, provided Marx's notes from 1857 to 1858, framing his conceptualization of the development of economic forms in human history. French Marxist anthropologists drew upon Marx's observations and their own studies of non-Western (principally African and Papuan) societies to query the analysis of societies without centralized political systems. In discussing such societies, where political relationships were based more on kinship or other traditional nonstate forms, they sought to develop a theory of materialism and structural analysis of modes of production that adequately explained transitions between various historical stages (instead of the transitions from feudalism to capitalism and capitalism to socialism and communism that Marx had primarily focused on). French Marxist anthropology is commonly seen as having followed two paths: one influenced by the philosopher Louis Althusser (1918–1990) and his reinterpretation of *Capital*, which attempted to apply Marxian analysis to all societies in an "overdetermined" fashion; and the other associated with Maurice Godelier (b. 1934), himself a student of the French structuralist Claude Lévi-Strauss (b. 1908), who advocated a more tempered incorporation of Marx's work that in fact rejected many of Marx's arguments about noncapitalist societies and economic determinism.

THE ANTHROPOLOGY OF POLITICS: CULTURE, IDEOLOGY, AND A THEORY OF PRAXIS

Marx's struggle to make sense of the mechanics of class and state formation through dialectics has been influential in the anthropology of politics. Marx's writing on the state were mostly confined to a series of case studies of France, including *The Eighteenth Brumaire of Louis Bonaparte* ([1852] 1964c) and *Class Struggles in France* ([1850] 1964b). Unlike his widely read but hastily composed populist pamphlet *The Communist Manifesto*, penned with Engels during the height of the European revolutionary events of 1848 (see Marx 1998), these political analyses were written retrospectively because he was forced from France, where he had been an active organizer and journalist, into exile in England. His other notable political analysis, *The Civil War in France* ([1871] 1933a), a rumination on the Paris Commune of 1871, was produced late in his life, along with his *Critique of the Gotha Programme* ([1875] 1933b), Marx's sole, if very vague, attempt to discuss the organization of communist society. Marx's "Theses on Feuerbach," in particular his famous eleventh thesis, "the philosophers have only explained the world, the point is to change it," is widely referenced for its emphasis on the importance of revolutionary practice. Beginning with the civil rights and other social movements in the 1960s, an increasing number of anthropologists became interested in social activism, prompting a thorough investigation of revolutionary politics and interrogation of the work of Marx and his intellectual progeny.

Marx's writings on politics and the state became influential in the early twentieth century among contemporaries concerned with developing strategies for revolutionary change, notably Antonio Gramsci (1891–1937) and Georg Lukács (1885–1971). Along with some members of the Frankfurt school, including Walter Benjamin (1892–1940), these scholars attempted to make sense of the role ideology and culture played in constraining or driving revolutionary change. Though decisively divergent from Marx's sociological emphasis on materialist philosophy and historical investigation of the category of labor, they do reflect Marx's lifelong preoccupation and frustration with the mechanics of socialist transition. The emphasis on culture and ideology has found currency, especially since the 1960s, with many anthropologists uncomfortable with the materialism of Marxian political economy, and often in reaction to the heavy-handed technological or environmental determinism of cultural materialists such as Marvin Harris. Michael Taussig and Jean and John Comaroff, with their concerns with investigating the symbolic organization of capitalist relations embedded in the politics of the state, fetishization, and cultural and religious institutions, are well-known for this kind of Marxian political tradition.

ANTHROPOLOGY, POLITICAL ECONOMY, AND GLOBALIZATION

Beginning in the 1940s and 1950s a group of scholars based in New York (including Elman Service, Stanley Diamond, and Julian Steward and his students, such as Eric Wolf and Sidney Mintz) spearheaded a new theoretical and methodological movement against a U.S. anthropology that for several decades had emphasized a more isolated approach to the study of individual cultures. Beginning with emphases on environment, ecology, and materiality, their approaches gradually evolved toward a sophisticated political economic analysis intent on assessing the impact of capitalism in non-Western societies, particularly in areas with a long history of entrenchment global processes, such as Latin America and the Caribbean. At the same time, anthropologists were influenced by numerous interdisciplinary studies of capitalism and development, including those by Andre Gunder Frank, Immanuel Wallerstein, Samir Amin, Walter Rodney, David Harvey, and others. There is a long list of anthropologists interested in the effects of capitalism on their subjects of study, some of whom have a more direct connection to materialist and cultural ecological approach than others. But regardless of their intellectual kinship, studies of political economy in anthropology from the early 1980s to the present can be divided, more or less, into two groups: one set of studies analyzing primarily the agency of subjects reacting to capitalist labor processes;

and the other focused on material objects (commodities) as entry points for understanding socioeconomic organization.

The first, subject-centered, track includes the many discussions of discipline, power, and alienation developed through the capitalist labor process, and typically they rely on Marx's more subject-oriented discussions of capitalism, such as his four-tiered typology of alienation in *Economic and Philosophical Manuscripts* ([1844] 1959). Since the 1980s anthropologists have produced a number of ethnographies analyzing capitalist power and discipline in global contexts, especially in the areas of industrial production and the exploitation of women and peasants, as well as rich analyses of flexibility in response to changing capitalist strategies of production. Aihwa Ong's 1987 discussion of Malaysian women factory workers and June Nash's 1979 study of Bolivian tin miners stand out as exceptional ethnographies that describe the structuring of and responses to labor transformation and alienation.

The second, object-oriented, variant of this political economic tradition relies more methodically on Marx's analysis of the commodity in *Capital* (1990a; 1990b). Sidney Mintz's groundbreaking study of the history of sugar production in Caribbean slave economies and its influence on the development of capitalism in Europe provides a model for this kind of political economic study (Mintz 1985). Focused on particular commodity objects and the global ordering of social relations that follows their cycles of production, exchange, distribution, and consumption, this "commodity biography" approach has proliferated not only in anthropology, but indeed across the social sciences (for summary, see Mantz and Smith 2006, pp. 78–80).

MARXIAN FUTURES?

Since the 1980s fewer anthropologists have been willing to claim identification with Marxism. The reasons are threefold. First, a disciplinary preoccupation with anthropology's colonial legacy has resulted in a reluctance to assert generalizable or lawlike claims about the cultural concept. Marxist approaches, as with other purportedly "grand narrative" approaches, have been decried in some circles as overly functionalist and even ethnocentric in their obsession with the global role of capital. Second, there was a general apathy toward the work of Marx following the end of the cold war. It is worth noting that the recent electoral victories by Marxist politicians throughout Latin America have no doubt contributed to a reenergizing of interest in Marxian scholarship in this area. Lastly, anthropologists appear to have embraced the more comfortable category of globalization as a way of understanding the wider net of capitalist influences around the world. Despite these ominous postscripts, this last point

should be taken to demonstrate the indelibility of Marxian influence in spirit, if not in practice, throughout a discipline that can no longer see its subjects as removed from an increasingly relevant and pervasive global capitalist organization.

SEE ALSO *Marxism; Mintz, Sidney W.; Wolf, Eric*

BIBLIOGRAPHY

Marx, Karl. [1844] 1959. *Economic and Philosophical Manuscripts of 1844.* Trans. Martin Milligan. Moscow: Foreign Languages Publishing.

Marx, Karl. [1848] 1998. *The Communist Manifesto: A Modern Edition.* New York: Verso.

Marx, Karl. [1850] 1964b. *Class Struggles in France.* New York: International Publishers.

Marx, Karl. [1852] 1964c. *Eighteenth Brumaire of Louis Bonaparte.* New York: International Publishers.

Marx, Karl. [1857] 1978. *Grundrisse.* Ed. and trans. David McClellan. New York: Harper and Row.

Marx, Karl. [1867] 1990a. *Capital: A Critique of Political Economy,* vol. 1, trans. Ben Fowkes. New York: Penguin Books in association with New Left Review.

Marx, Karl. [1871] 1933a. *The Civil War in France.* New York: International Publishers.

Marx, Karl. [1875] 1933b. *Critique of the Gotha Programme.* New York: International Publishers.

Marx, Karl. [1894] 1990b. *Capital: A Critique of Political Economy,* vol. 3, trans. Ben Fowkes. New York: Penguin.

Marx, Karl. 1964a. *Pre-Capitalist Economic Formations.* Ed. Eric Hobsbawm, trans. Jack Cohen. New York: International Publishers.

Marx, Karl, and Friedrich Engels. 1978. *The Marx-Engels Reader.* Ed. Robert C. Tucker. New York: Norton.

Mantz, Jeff W., and Jim H. Smith. 2006. Do Cellular Phones Dream of Civil War? The Mystification of Production and the Consequences of Technology Fetishism in the Eastern Congo. In *Inclusion and Exclusion in the Global Arena,* ed. Max Kirsch, 71–93. New York: Routledge.

Mintz, Sidney W. 1985. *Sweetness and Power: The Place of Sugar in Modern History.* New York: Penguin.

Nash, June. 1979. *We Eat the Mines and the Mines Eat Us: Dependency and Exploitation in Bolivian Tin Mines.* New York: Columbia University Press.

Ong, Aihwa. 1987. *Spirits of Resistance and Capitalist Discipline: Factory Women in Malaysia.* Albany: State University of New York Press.

Price, David H. 2004. *Threatening Anthropology: McCarthyism and the FBI's Surveillance of Activist Anthropologists.* Durham, NC: Duke University Press.

Saitta, Dean J. 1994. Agency, Class, and Archaeological Interpretation. *Journal of Anthropological Archaeology* 13: 201–227.

Jeffrey Mantz

MARX, KARL: IMPACT ON ECONOMICS

Karl Marx's economic analysis is mainly contained in three books: the three-volume *Capital*, the *Theories of Surplus Value*, also in three volumes, and the *Grundrisse*. In his economic works Marx tries "to lay bare the law of motion of modern society," that is to say, to discover social regularities described mainly as long-run tendencies. Marx's method of analysis begins with the observation of empirical reality in all its complexity and concreteness. From this reality he derives abstract concepts (determinative relations and interpretive categories), and then through these concepts he ends up once again with the concrete, whose reproduction now is structured according to the internal connections established by the theory. The adequacy of the theory and concepts that have been created is judged by the degree of correspondence between the most concrete categories and data derived from empirical reality. A characteristic example of this methodological approach is the determination of market prices (the most concrete category) by another set of more abstract prices known as prices of production, that is, prices that incorporate the economy's general rate of profit. Prices of production are in turn determined by an even more abstract type of prices called labor values. All these prices can be subjected to empirical testing.

Marx observes that capitalism is a historically specific system characterized by generalized commodity exchange and so, naturally, the starting point of his inquiry is the analysis of the commodity whose exchange value aspect (and not its use value aspect) is the dominant one. Exchange value is the external measure of the intrinsic property of commodities, which he calls *value*, defined as the total amount of socially necessary abstract (i.e., undifferentiated) labor time embodied in a commodity. In the process of exchange, one commodity, due to its possession of a set of useful properties, is chosen to function as the universal commodity against which all other commodities are compared and exchanged. The commodity that historically has performed the function of universal commodity more successfully than any other is gold. The ratio of the value of a commodity to the value of gold gives the direct price of the commodity. If the value of gold decreases (e.g., because of discoveries of new gold mines and technological change) the general price level, other things being constant, increases—and vice versa. This rudimentary theory of money, which is derived from a straightforward generalization of the theory of value, can be expanded to include both monetary systems that are convertible to gold and those that are not, and thus becomes relevant for new developments after 1970. At the same time, Marx's theory of value (together with the use of mathematical analysis and input-output data) has been shown to rather accurately predict market prices, and thus could become a viable alternative to neoclassical price theory (Shaikh 1984).

The analysis of the universal commodity and money leads to an investigation of the capitalist process of production. This process is described by the circuit $M - C (LP, MP) \ldots P \ldots C' - M'$, according to which capitalists invest an amount of money (M) in order to buy a set of commodities (C) consisting of commodity labor power (LP)—that is, the worker's capacity to work—and other means of production (MP), for the purpose of production (P) of a new set of commodities (C'), which when sold they expect to realize a sum of money greater than that of the initial investment, $M' > M$. This extra money is what really motivates the whole circuit of capitalist production as it is repeated on an expanded scale. The difference $M' - M > 0$, which Marx calls *surplus value*, stems from labor power, a special commodity characterized by its property of producing more value than the value of commodities that the worker buys with his money wage and consumes in order to reproduce his capacity to work. In contrast, the value of the means of production is either transferred to the final product all at once (as in the case of raw materials) or gradually through depreciation (as is the case with the plant and equipment) (*Capital I*). The distinction between *labor* and *labor power* is Marx's greatest discovery and contribution to political economy, because through this distinction the source of surplus value can be explained on the basis of equivalent exchanges. Marx argued that surplus value is created in the sphere of production by labor. The production sphere has primacy over the circulation sphere because the latter is supported by the surplus value produced in the former. Furthermore, the circulation sphere modifies and changes, within strictly specified limits, some of the results of the sphere of production. For example, surplus value in the sphere of circulation is redistributed to the various sectors of the economy in the form of profit according to its degree of capital intensity; however, the sum of the profits cannot exceed the amount of surplus value produced.

It is important to stress that there is no guarantee that the circuit of capital will necessarily be completed, as it can be interrupted at any stage by a number of unexpected factors. Thus, uncertainty and expectations are immanent in Marx's analysis of capitalism. Furthermore, the whole circuit begins and ends with money, a characteristic that allows the introduction of credit and also the hypothesis that savings may differ from investment, a difference that sets the stage for the development of an alternative to Keynes's theory of effective demand rooted in the process of capital accumulation.

According to Marx, the hallmark of the individual behavior of capitalists is the pursuit of profit as a purpose in itself, which forces them into two kinds of competition: the first with workers in the labor markets over wages and conditions of work, and the second with other capitalists in the commodity markets over the expansion of market share at the expense of their competitors. Capitalists cope with these two types of competition through the introduction of more fixed capital. As a consequence, mechanization of the labor process is used to raise the productivity of labor. The introduction of fixed capital both increases the scale of operation needed for minimum efficiency and reduces the unit cost of production. The latter implies that by reducing their prices innovating firms are able to expand their market share at the expense of less efficient firms. Thus, the process of capital accumulation leads to a small number of top firms controlling an increasing share of the total market. This is the reason why concentration of capital is the expected outcome implied by the nature of capital and by the operation of competition, which by no means diminishes over time. On the contrary, the very cause of mechanization—the pursuit of profit—continues to exist even with fewer firms, as competition among them intensifies. Meanwhile, the ever-increasing minimum-efficiency scale of operation requires higher investment that firms, especially the small ones, cannot undertake on their own, and thus there is pressure to merge, in order to avoid becoming the target of a hostile takeover. The resulting growth in the scale of production through the amalgamation of capitals is called *centralization of capital* and is another aspect of the operation of competition (*Capital I, III*). If there is a grand prediction that has been historically validated it is Marx's law of increasing concentration and centralization of capital.

Another grand prediction by Marx, which is also consistent with the available historical evidence, concerns the law of the falling rate of profit. This law is derived from the very purpose of capitalist production, which is the extraction of profits as an end in itself. As mentioned above, the realization of this goal entails mechanization of the production process through the introduction of fixed capital. On the one hand, this raises both the productivity of labor and profits for the firms that remain following concentration; on the other hand, however, the increase of fixed capital relative to labor leads to a falling profit rate. Marx noted that the fall in the rate of profit exerts a negative effect on the mass of real profits and, at the same time, a positive effect through the accumulation of capital. So long as the positive effect exceeds the negative, the mass of real profits expands at an increasing rate in a long wavelike pattern. Because new investment is a function of the rate of profit, it follows that a falling rate of profit at some point will necessarily slow down the rate of growth of new investment, thereby slowing down the rate of increase in the mass of real profits. As this tendency continues there will be a point at which the two (positive and negative) effects will cancel each other out and the change in the mass of profits will become zero. This means that the investment of the previous period will not contribute at all to an increase in profits and thus capitalists will have no interest in new investment. This is the point of "absolute overaccumulation of capital" that marks the onset of economic crisis. Its consequence is a slowdown in investment and rising unemployment. As more and more firms are led into bankruptcies and real wages fall, one can also observe the creation of new institutions, the emergence of new methods of management, and the diffusion of technological change. The combination of these processes results in a rising mass of profit (and a temporarily rising rate of profit) and sets the course for the reestablishment of the necessary conditions for another wave of expansion and contraction. Thus capitalism is both a growth- and crisis-prone system, as has also been documented in the literature on long economic cycles (see Shaikh 1992).

Marx's impact on economic thought has not received the recognition it deserves due to his view of the historical character of capitalist society and his vision of socialism. Thus, unfortunately, when orthodox economists discuss aspects of Marx's work, they generally do so to point out its alleged weaknesses rather than its strengths.

SEE ALSO *Communism; Competition, Marxist; Labor Theory of Value; Marxism*

BIBLIOGRAPHY

Marx, Karl. 1867–1894. *Capital.* 3 vols. Ed. Friedrich Engels. Moscow: International Publishers.

Shaikh, Anwar. 1984. The Transformation from Marx to Sraffa. In *Ricardo, Marx, Sraffa,* ed. Ernest Mandel and Alan Freeman, 43–84. London: Verso.

Shaikh, Anwar. 1992. The Falling Rate of Profit and Long Waves in Accumulation: Theory and Evidence. In *New Findings in Long-Wave Research,* ed. Alfred Kleinknecht, Ernest Mandel, and Immanuel Wallerstein, 175–202. London: Macmillan.

Lefteris Tsoulfidis

MARX, KARL: IMPACT ON SOCIOLOGY

The ideas of Karl Marx (1818–1883) on alienation, historical change, class relationships, the capitalist system, and social revolution have had a lasting impact on sociology, though interest in his work has fluctuated and sociologists have not always agreed about its relevance. In the classical period, for example, Émile Durkheim's 1897 "Review of Antonio Labriola, 'Essais sur la conception matérialiste de l'histoire'" (Essays on the Materialist Conception of History, 1896) argued that the materialist conception of history—which he believed Marx's *The Communist Manifesto* (1848) represented—was unproven and contrary to established facts. In "Bureaucracy," (1921) Max Weber offered a critical estimation of a socialist program's likelihood of success, while his *The Protestant Ethic and the Spirit of Capitalism* (1905) forwarded an idealist explanation of capitalism's rise to complement Marxist-materialist accounts.

Georg Simmel's *The Philosophy of Money* (1900) and Ferdinand Tönnies's *Gemeinschaft und Gesellschaft* (Community and Society, 1887) were also, in part, motivated by Marx's view of modernity as a unique historical experience. While these classical theorists approached Marx from a general sociological vantage point, later scholars adopted a Marxian perspective from which to consider sociological questions, including the influence of class structures on the state, the human sciences, and popular culture, as well as the dynamics of social stratification systems.

In early twentieth-century Europe, Italian Marxist Antonio Gramsci (*Selections from the Prison Notebooks*) inquired into how the ruling class's cultural "hegemony" can shape social institutions and thwart revolutionary spirit and action. In Germany, Georg Lukács similarly examined the relationship between *History and Class Consciousness* (1923). In his widely read and debated *Ideology and Utopia* (1929), Karl Mannheim (Hungarian born, schooled in Germany and France) tapped into Marxist ideas for research on the sociology of knowledge. Scholars at the Institute for Social Research—later known collectively as the Frankfurt school and including most notably Herbert Marcuse (*Reason and Revolution*, 1941; *One-Dimensional Man*, 1964), Max Horkheimer (*Critical Theory*, 1968), and Theodor Adorno (*Negative Dialectics*, 1966)—examined how commodity markets and bureaucratic planning shape science and popular culture (e.g., Horkheimer and Adorno 1972). Also in Germany, Jürgen Habermas adopted similar questions but further asked how ruling classes and their state representatives might suffer a *Legitimation Crisis* (1973), as well as how free communicative spaces can exist within the rubric of bureaucratic capitalism (*The Theory of Communicative Action*, vols. 1 and 2, 1981).

In France, Georges Canguilhem (*Ideology and Rationality in the History of the Life Sciences*, 1977) and Maurice Merleau-Ponty (*Adventures of the Dialectic*, 1955) appealed to Marx's ideas in their research on the human sciences. Their wider influence came through their students, most notably the structuralism of Louis Althusser (*For Marx*, 1965) and the poststructuralism of Michel Foucault (*The Archaeology of Knowledge*, 1969; *Discipline* *and Punish*, 1975). Later postmodern theorists such as Jacques Derrida (*Spectres of Marx*, 1993) and Ernesto Laclau and Chantal Mouffe (*Hegemony and Socialist Strategy*, 1985) were sympathetic to Marx's views for capturing the contemporary moment and animating political struggle, though they argued for incorporating nontraditional Marxist concerns such as racial, gender, national, and sexual identities into radical politics.

In England, historian E. P. Thompson's *The Making of the English Working Class* (1963) provided insight into class dynamics and historical social change, while Ralph Miliband (*The State in Capitalist Society*, 1969) debated Greek theorist Nicos Poulantzas (1969) on the relationship between social classes and the state—that is, "relative autonomy" versus "instrumentalist" theories. This dialogue inspired reexaminations of political power in Marxist terms, such as those found in Bob Jessop's *The Capitalist State: Marxist Theories and Methods* (1982). Also in England, Anthony Giddens adopted features of Marx's materialist approach in constructing *New Rules of Sociological Method* (1976) and his theory of "structuration" (Giddens 1984).

Outside the centers of European power, others picked up Marxian questions. African Marxist Frantz Fanon's *The Wretched of the Earth* (1961) offered a trenchant critique of French imperialism in Algeria. In Latin America, economist Raúl Prebisch's *The Economic Development of Latin America and Its Problems* (1950) examined relations of unequal exchange between "core" capitalist societies and those on their "periphery" in the world market. This perspective influenced dependency theory, whose main advocate was the German American scholar Andre Gunder Frank (*Capitalism and Underdevelopment in Latin America*, 1967). Frank argued that the "underdeveloped" conditions of many countries in the Americas resulted from economic and political exploitation visited upon them by capitalist powers. This perspective attracted the attention of Chilean president Salvador Allende and former Brazilian president Fernando Henrique Cardoso while in political exile.

In the United States, where Marx was generally eclipsed for the first half of the twentieth century, economist Paul Sweezy's works, *The Theory of Capitalist Development* (1942) and *Monopoly Capital* (1966), were influential in keeping a Marxist dialogue alive. The postwar period found sociologists such as C. Wright Mills using Marx's (and Weber's) work for a critical analysis of *The Power Elite* (1956), which was said to dominate political, economic, and military institutions. Adopting dialectics as his viewpoint, Bertell Ollman (1968) revealed the objective and subjective elements in Marx's approach to class and examined how the humanism in his early works shed light on the question of alienation (*Alienation: Marx's*

Conception of Man in Capitalist Society, 1971). Having previously fled Nazi Germany (Adorno and Horkheimer found a home at the New School for Social Research in New York City and Marcuse at the University of California, San Diego), Frankfurt school scholars and American Marxists, in combination with the U.S. political-cultural climate in the 1960s and 1970s, made conditions conducive for a new generation of scholars to rediscover Marx. Interest in Marx's humanism and alienation brought attention to the Frankfurt school's work on the culture industries and the mass media in the works of Douglas Kellner and Stuart Ewen. Other theorists of popular culture, such as Frederic Jameson, followed the postmodern lead to inquire about "the cultural logic of late capitalism."

Marx's impact on sociology advanced elsewhere on both theoretical and research fronts. Marx's political economy inspired Althusser's structural Marxism, which theorized the operation of social structures outside of human agency, and analytical Marxism, which placed the rational actor at the center of analysis (Elster 1985; Roemer 1986). One influential perspective sharing this latter approach was Erik Olin Wright's (1976) work on the "contradictory class locations" in advanced capitalism, as well as his studies of *Class, Crisis, and the State* (1978). Theda Skocpol's *States and Social Revolutions* (1979) advanced class analysis through a historical-comparative study of state formation, while Michael Burawoy (1990) examined how Marx's scientific commitments inform the history of political strategies of radical movements. Scholars outside of conventional Marxism, such as feminist theorists and researchers (Smith 1977) and criminologists (Richard Quinney), increasingly incorporated Marxist ideas in an intellectual climate that also brought renewed attention to the work on race relations previously done by W. E. B. Du Bois and Oliver Cox, each of whom Marx had influenced.

Perhaps the most influential strand of Marxist thought has been Immanuel Wallerstein's (1974–1989) *World Systems Analysis*. This perspective arose in dialogue with Russian theories about Asiatic modes of production, the French Annales school and its analyses of historical periods of the *longue durée* (Marc Bloch, Lucien Febvre, Fernand Braudel), and Latin American theorists of unequal exchange and other dependency theorists (*world-systems analysis*). After their introduction into the discipline, Wallerstein's models of core-periphery relations, the interstate system, long waves of capitalist development, the rise of antisystemic movements, and the transition out of the capitalist world economy have ever since shaped the work of world-systems analysts. Used in studies of development, social stratification (including race, class, and gender studies), and the sociology of knowledge, world-systems analysis arguably reached the status of a paradigm in itself by the late twentieth century.

Throughout the second half of the twentieth century, the number of journals devoted to Marxist studies proliferated, including the *New Left Review* (1960), *Capital & Class* (1977), *Thesis Eleven* (1980), *Praxis International* (1981), *Critical Sociology* (1987; formerly *The Insurgent Sociologist*, 1969–1987), *Rethinking Marxism* (1988), and *Historical Materialism* (1997). Not limited to sociologists, these journals provided a home for a wide variety of Marxist scholarship, something less in evidence in sociology prior to the 1960 to 1970 period. Marxist scholars also increasingly found professional institutionalization within reach both in the university system and in sociology's major organizations. For instance, in 1975 the American Sociological Association officially incorporated a Marxist section.

Marx's political-economic, materialist, and dialectical thought continues to inform research programs in sociology. Control of productive resources is a source of social power in capitalist society, shaping the conditions of work, discourse in the mass media, and state policies worldwide. These relationships have grown in scope since Marx's day, as have attempts by antisystemic movements to find local autonomy, cross-national cooperation, and solutions to ecological crises. With capitalist society and how to study it as its central subject matter, Marx's work remains a source of insight for all sociologists interested in studying the origins, the structure, and the nature of the change within the capitalist system.

SEE ALSO *Communism; Marxism*

BIBLIOGRAPHY

Burawoy, Michael. 1990. Marxism as Science: Historical Challenges and Theoretical Growth. *American Sociological Review* 55 (12): 775–793.

Elster, Jon. 1985. *Making Sense of Marx*. Cambridge, U.K.: Cambridge University Press.

Giddens, Anthony. 1984. *The Constitution of Society: Outline of the Theory of Structuration*. Cambridge, U.K.: Polity Press.

Horkheimer, Max, and Theodor Adorno. 1972. *The Dialectic of Enlightenment*. Trans. John Cumming. New York: Herder and Herder.

Ollman, Bertell. 1968. Marx's Use of Class. *American Journal of Sociology* 73 (5): 573–580.

Poulantzas, Nicos. 1969. The Problem of the Capitalist State. *New Left Review* 58: 67–78.

Roemer, John, ed. 1986. *Analytical Marxism*. Cambridge, U.K.: Cambridge University Press.

Smith, Dorothy E. 1977. *Feminism and Marxism: A Place to Begin, a Way to Go*. Vancouver, British Columbia: New Star.

Wallerstein, Immanuel. 1974–1989. *The Modern World-System*. Vols. 1–3. New York: Academic Press.

Weber, Max. 1921. *Wirtschaft und Gesellschaft* [Bureaucracy]. Tübingen, Germany: J. C. B. Mohr.

Wright, Erik Olin. 1976. Class Boundaries in Advanced Capitalist Societies. *New Left Review* 98: 3–41.

Paul Paolucci

MARXISM

Marxism is a family of critiques, theories, and political goals loosely organized around the theories and criticisms formulated by Karl Marx (1818–1883) in the middle of the nineteenth century. Central to this body of theory are several key ideas: the view that capitalism embodies a system of class exploitation; that socialism is a social order in which private property and exploitation are abolished; and that socialism can be achieved through revolution. Revolutionary leaders and theorists, and several generations of social scientists and historians, have attempted to develop these central ideas into programs of political action and historical research. The challenges for Marxist political parties fall in two general areas: how to achieve revolutionary political change (the problem of revolution); and what the ultimate socialist society ought to look like (the problem of the creation of socialism).

Marx was an advocate for socialism and for the ascendant political power of the working class (Newman 2005). His analysis of the need for political action by the proletariat was most fully expressed in *The Communist Manifesto*, jointly authored with Friedrich Engels. He was one of the early leaders of the International Workingmen's Association (the First International), founded in 1864. However, Marx's economic and political writings provide very little concrete guidance for the design of a socialist society. Socialism was to be an order in which exploitation and domination were abolished; it was to establish an end to the dominion of private property; it was to create an environment of democratic self-determination for the proletariat. Marx's own definition of socialism might have included these elements: collective ownership of the means of production, a centralized socialist party, political power in the hands of the proletariat, and the view that socialist reform will require the power of a socialist state. Marx also emphasized human freedom and "true democracy"—elements that could have been incorporated into nonauthoritarian forms of democratic socialism.

Much of the political platform of twentieth-century Marxism took shape following the death of Marx through a handful of more authoritarian theories, including especially those of Vladimir Lenin (1870–1924), Joseph Stalin (1878–1953), and Mao Zedong (1893–1976). The most catastrophic ideological results of twentieth-century communism bear only a tangential relationship to Marx's writings; instead, they bear the imprint of such revolutionary thinkers as Lenin, Stalin, Leon Trotsky (1879–1940), and Mao. Perhaps the most crucial flaw within twentieth-century communist thought was its authoritarianism: the idea that a revolutionary state and its vanguard party can take any means necessary in order to bring about communist outcomes. This assumption of unlimited political authority for party and state led to massive violations of human rights within Soviet and Communist regimes: Stalin's war on the *kulaks* (rich farmers), the Moscow show trials, the Gulag, Mao's Great Leap Forward and its resulting famine, and the Chinese Cultural Revolution. The dramatic economic failures of centralized Soviet-style economies derived from a similar impulse: the view that the state could and should manage the basic institutions and behaviors of a socialist society (Kornai 1992).

It is possible to formulate a nonauthoritarian conception of socialism based on a democratic socialist movement and a theory of a democratic socialist society. Indeed, it is possible to find support for such conceptions within the writings of Marx himself. The most influential Marxist parties of the twentieth century took another avenue, however. These parties emphasized the "dictatorship of the proletariat," the need for the working class to seize power by force, and the conviction that the "bourgeoisie" and its allies would not tolerate a peaceful transformation of the defining property relations of capitalism. The Bolshevik seizure of political power in the Russian Revolution (1917), the failed Spartacist uprising in Germany in 1918, and the Chinese Communist Revolution in 1949 all embodied the assumption that only a disciplined central party, supported by the masses, would be able to exercise the power necessary to overthrow the capitalist ruling class; and only a disciplined Communist government would be capable of enacting the massive social changes required for the establishment of communist society once in power. The dominant political ideology of communist parties and states in the twentieth century was antidemocratic and ruthless in its use of violence against its own citizens. (One of the few examples of a socialist regime that willingly submitted itself to popular referendum, and accepted defeat, was the government of Daniel Ortega in Nicaragua in 1990.)

Soviet Communism represented the earliest and most pervasive ascendancy by a communist party. After the seizure of power in the Russian Revolution, Lenin and Stalin exercised political power to force the rapid transformation of Soviet society and economy, and to preserve the power and privilege of the Communist Party. There was deep disagreement among the party's leadership about the right course for Soviet Communism. How should the development of agriculture and industry be balanced? How rapidly should socialist transition be performed?

How should the forces of the market and the state be involved in socialist transition? One school of thought advocated a gradual transformation of the Soviet economy and system of production, permitting the workings of market institutions and the emergence of an industrial bourgeoisie that would advance Soviet industrial capacity. The other school was ideologically opposed to permitting a propertied class to acquire power, and advocated a state-directed and more rapid transition to socialism. The New Economic Policy (NEP) of 1921 embodied the former strategy, and it was decisively rejected by 1928. From that point forward, Stalin demonstrated his intention of using the power of the state to force social changes that would propel the Soviet system into its communist future. Stalin's determination to defeat "counter-revolutionary *kulaks*" during the period of collectivization of agriculture brought about the deaths by starvation of several million rural people in the Ukraine, as a deliberate act of policy (Viola 2005). The doctrine of "socialism in one country" led the Soviet-dominated Communist International to sacrifice other socialist parties (for example, during the Spanish Civil War) in favor of the interests of the Soviet system. Stalin's internal political and ideological struggles within the party led him to pursue a murderous campaign against other Communist leaders and ordinary people, resulting in show trials, summary executions, and the consignment of millions of people to remote labor camps. (See Smith 2002 for a good summary of these events.)

China's Communist Revolution was guided by Mao Zedong from its early mobilization in the 1920s, through civil war and anti-Japanese war in the 1930s and 1940s, to successful seizure of power in 1949 by the Chinese Communist Party (CCP) and the Red Army. Mao's Marxism was strongly influenced by Soviet ideology, but also incorporated the perspective of the role of the peasantry in revolution. Classical Marxism placed the proletariat at center stage as the revolutionary class, but Mao's urban proletariat strategy was destroyed in 1927 when the Republican army under Chiang Kai-shek (1887–1975) massacred the Shanghai Communist Party organization. This precipitated the Long March and Mao's regrouping around an ultimately successful peasant-based strategy for revolution. China's communist leaders too faced fateful policy choices: whether and how to implement "social ownership" of agriculture and industry, how to achieve rapid industrialization and modernization, how to create the political conditions necessary to sustain Chinese socialism and socialist identity among the Chinese population, and how to confront the capitalist world. China's history since 1949 has pivoted around these issues: the Great Leap Forward (1957), in which China underwent rapid collectivization of agriculture, and an ensuing famine that resulted in tens of millions of deaths; the Cultural Revolution (1966–1976), in which Red Guards

throughout the country persecuted and punished teachers, officials, and others for political purity; the reform of agriculture toward the Family Responsibility system in the 1980s, resulting in a surge of productivity in the farm economy; and the rapid economic growth of the 1990s into the first part of the twenty-first century. Developments since 1980 reveal a more pragmatic and market-oriented approach toward China's development on the part of CCP leadership. At the same time, the Chinese government's crackdown on the democracy movement in 1990 at Tiananmen Square demonstrated the party's determination to maintain control of China's political system.

Anticapitalist politics of the early twentieth century were influenced by several strands of activism and theory that were independent of Marx's thought, and these strands found expression in the solutions and platforms of Marxist political parties and movements. Anarchist thinkers, such as Mikhail Bakunin (1814–1876) and Peter Kropotkin (1842–1921), put forward the radical view that all forms of state power were inherently evil. Anarchism and syndicalism had significant influence on radical labor unions in Europe and North America. Revisionist socialists, such as Eduard Bernstein (1850–1932), argued that revolution by force was not a feasible path to socialism and advocated instead for gradual change from within capitalism. Democratic thinkers emphasized the ability of groups of people to govern themselves, and to press their states to undertake radical reforms of current conditions. The British Labour Party and the main European social democratic parties fall within the tradition of democratic socialism, as opposed to Marxism-Leninism. European socialist parties in the twentieth century affiliated within the loose political organizations of the Second International (1889–1916), the International Working Union of Socialist Parties, and the Socialist International (Miliband 1982).

The twentieth century witnessed several important new developments within the intellectual architecture of Marxism. Western Marxism attempted to extrapolate Marx's ideas in new ways, extending treatment of issues having to do with humanism, dialectics, history, and democracy. Critical theory was an important intellectual elaboration of some of Marx's philosophical ideas, in the hands of such thinkers as Theodor Adorno (1903–1969), Max Horkheimer (1895–1973), Hans-Georg Gadamer (1900–2002), and Jürgen Habermas (b. 1929) (Geuss 1981; Wellmer 1971). In the 1960s Western Marxism developed a distinctive political standpoint on the issues of the day under the banner of the "New Left": economic inequality within capitalist countries, inequalities within a colonialized world, and struggles for independence by countries in the developing world. Partially shaped by a growing awareness of Stalin's crimes in the 1940s and

1950s, Western Marxists developed the strand of democratic socialism into a full intellectual and political program. Particularly important were contributions by Perry Anderson (b. 1938), E. P. Thompson (1924–1993), Ralph Miliband (1924–1994), and the *New Left Review*. This body of thought retained the critical perspective of classical Marxism; it gave greater focus to the world historical importance of imperialism and colonialism; and it aligned itself with the interests of developing countries such as Cuba and India.

MARXISM AS A BODY OF RESEARCH

The other important dimension of Marxism in the contemporary world is in the area of knowledge and theory. Marx's theoretical and scientific writings are primarily expressed in his economic writings in the three volumes of *Capital* and *Theories of Surplus Value*, and in his historical writings such as *The German Ideology* and *The Eighteenth Brumaire of Louis Napoleon*. Marx's theory of historical materialism maintains that large historical change proceeds as a result of dynamic interaction between the forces and relations of production (roughly, technology and property relations) (Cohen 1978). Marx identifies the economic structure of society (the forces and relations of production) as the key factor that constrains and impels historical transformation across large historical epochs (the slave mode of production, feudalism, capitalism). And he regards other institutions, including institutions of politics and culture, as part of the superstructure of society. These "superstructural" institutions are social arrangements that serve to support and stabilize the development of the economic structure. Another important element of the framework of historical materialism is the theory of class conflict as an engine of historical change. The central conflict in every society, according to Marx, is the economic conflict between owners of property and the propertyless: masters and slaves, lords and serfs, and capitalists and proletarians. Marx also offers a theory of ideology and mystification: the view that the ideas and beliefs that people have in a class society are themselves a material product of specific social institutions, and are distorted in ways that serve the interests of the dominant classes.

Materialism implies that the economic structure of society is fundamental to its historical dynamics. How does this theory work in relation to modern society? Marx advanced a multistranded analysis of the capitalist mode of production in his most extensive work, *Capital*. This account was intended to be rigorous and scientific (Little 1986; Rosdolsky 1977). Marx hoped to succeed in penetrating beneath the surface appearances of the English economy of the nineteenth century, to discover some "laws of motion" and institutional mechanisms that

would explain its historical behavior. There are several independent strands of this analysis: a social-institutional account of the specific property relations (capital and wage labor) that defined the material and institutional context of capitalist development; a sociological description of some of the characteristics of the industrial workplace and the industrial city; a historical account of the transformations of traditional rural society that had created the foundation for the emergence of this dynamic system; and a mathematical analysis of the sources and transformation of value and surplus value within this economy. The mathematical theory based on the labor theory of value has not stood the test of time well, whereas the more sociological and institutional core of the framework continues to shed light on how a modern private-property economy functions.

There is no single answer to the question, "What is the Marxist approach to social science?" Instead, Marxist social inquiry in the twentieth and twenty-first centuries represents a chorus of many voices and insights, many of which are inconsistent with others. Rather than representing a coherent research community defined by a central paradigm and commitment to specific methodological and theoretical premises, Marxist social science in the twentieth century had a great deal of variety and diversity of perspectives. There is a wide range of thinkers whose work falls within the general category of Marxian social science and history: E. P. Thompson, Louis Althusser, Jürgen Habermas, Gerald Cohen, Robert Brenner, Nicos Poulantzas, Perry Anderson, Ralph Miliband, Nikolai Bukharin, Georg Lukàcs, Antonio Gramsci, and Michel Foucault. All these authors have made a contribution to Marxist social science, but in no way do these contributions add up to a single, coherent and focused methodology for the social sciences. Instead, there are numerous instances of substantive and methodological writings, from a variety of traditions, that have provided moments of insight and locations for possible future research.

THE TWENTY-FIRST CENTURY

Where do Marx's ideas stand in the early part of the twenty-first century? Several areas of limitation in Marx's social theories have come under scrutiny by theorists and social critics late in the twentieth century. (1) Feminist and cultural critics have argued that Marx's thought is too economistic and exclusively focused on issues of class—thereby ignoring other forms of oppression and domination that exist in modern society, including those based on gender, race, or ethnicity. (2) "Green" socialists have criticized Marx's theory of capitalist development and socialism on the ground that it is deeply pro-growth, in ways that are sometimes said to be at odds with environmental sustainability. (3) Democratic socialists have criticized

Marx's rhetoric of class politics on the ground that it gives too little validity to the demands of democracy; they have advocated for a much deeper embodiment of the importance of collective self-determination within socialist theory and practice. (4) Marx's critique of capitalist society emphasizes economic features to the neglect of cultural or ideological forms of domination. Theorists who consider the social role of communications media argue (reminiscent of Gramsci's writings) that the softer forms of oppression and domination that are associated with television, the Internet, and the instruments of public opinion are at least as profound in the contemporary world as the more visible forms of political and economic domination that Marx emphasized. Here the writings of Stuart Hall (Hall 1980, 1997) and Raymond Williams (Williams 1974, 1977) have been particularly influential.

Notwithstanding these areas of limitation in Marx's vision, the most central critical theory within Marxism is the demand for human emancipation from forms of exploitation, domination, and alienation that interfere with full, free human development. And these ideas give ample scope for twenty-first century debates and progress.

SEE ALSO *Materialism, Dialectical*

BIBLIOGRAPHY

Cohen, Gerald A. 1978. *Karl Marx's Theory of History: A Defence.* Princeton, NJ: Princeton University Press.

Geuss, Raymond. 1981. *The Idea of a Critical Theory: Habermas and the Frankfurt School.* Cambridge, U.K.: Cambridge University Press.

Hall, Stuart. 1980. *Culture, Media, Language: Working Papers in Cultural Studies, 1972–79.* London: Hutchinson.

Hall, Stuart. 1997. *Representation: Cultural Representations and Signifying Practices.* London and Thousand Oaks, CA: Sage in association with the Open University.

Kornai, Janos. 1992. *The Socialist System: The Political Economy of Communism.* Princeton, NJ: Princeton University Press.

Little, Daniel. 1986. *The Scientific Marx.* Minneapolis: University of Minnesota Press.

Miliband, Ralph. 1982. *Capitalist Democracy in Britain.* Oxford: Oxford University Press.

Newman, Michael. 2005. *Socialism: A Very Short Introduction.* Oxford and New York: Oxford University Press.

Rosdolsky, Roman. 1977. *The Making of Marx's "Capital."* London: Pluto Press.

Smith, S. A. 2002. *The Russian Revolution: A Very Short Introduction.* Oxford and New York: Oxford University Press.

Viola, Lynne. 2005. *The War Against the Peasantry, 1927–1930: The Tragedy of the Soviet Countryside.* New Haven, CT: Yale University Press.

Wellmer, Albrecht. 1971. *Critical Theory of Society.* New York: Herder and Herder.

Williams, Raymond. 1974. *Television: Technology and Cultural Form.* London: Fontana.

Williams, Raymond. 1977. *Marxism and Literature.* Oxford: Oxford University Press.

Daniel Little

MARXISM, BLACK

An examination of black Marxism—the marriage between Marxism and "black radicalism"—illuminates the theoretical gaps in the Marxist canon as it relates to non-Western movements and non-Western liberation struggles that speak in the idioms of culture, nationalism, and race. Black Marxists have grappled with the contradictions that emerge when Marxist paradigms are the medium for the articulation of a path to transformation. While theorists have noted the "anti-bourgeois tendencies in black cultures" (Duran 2005, p. 1), many of the Eurocentric assumptions that pervade Marxism are a challenge to the formulation of a black Marxist theory (see Robinson 1983). Whereas Marxism focuses heavily on the activism of a vanguard proletariat, black freedom struggles have revolved around a collective, albeit contested identity shaped by racism. In reaction, black Marxist thinkers have argued for a position that emphasizes "materialism over idealism" and acknowledges the centrality of race in the black experience (Campbell 1995, p. 420).

Marxism is a method of analysis and a theoretical critique that sees capitalism as a system which fosters social divisions. A powerful class-consciousness, specifically among the working class, is considered vital to the oppositional upsurge that Marxism contends is essential to revolution. Cedric Robinson (1983) argued against the Marxist position that the "European proletariat" is the "revolutionary subject of history" (p. 4). He criticized Marxism's "dismissal of culture" and its theoretical myopia on the issue of race (p. 78). Furthermore, as A. Sivanandan (1977) explained, "Blacks are a class apart, an underclass, a subproleteriat" (p. 339). Thus, for many black intellectuals, race, rather than being an incidental dimension of class, provides a significant subtext for the theorizing of radical change.

Collaborations between Marxists and black radicals in the United States began in the 1920s and 1930s when African Americans became a focus of organizing by the Communist Party. Early black Communists like Harry Haywood helped to elucidate the "Negro Question" and struggled against the assignment of blacks to a "subsidiary position in the revolutionary movement" (Haywood 1978, p. 234). At the Sixth World Congress of the American Communist Party in 1928, resolutions were passed on the American "Negro Question." They concluded that African Americans were an "oppressed nation which had the right to self-determination," and that the Southern "Black Belt" was prime for revolutionary activity (Haywood 1978, p. 268).

Robin Kelley (1990) charted the history of the connections between southern black resistance and the organizing of the Communist Party in 1930s Alabama. According to Kelley, historically black working-class resistance occupied the "margins of struggle," and even without a specific organizational context, southern African Americans always possessed a "rich culture of opposition" (p. 99). Communist organizers focused their recruitment on agricultural workers and sharecroppers in Birmingham, making the Communist Party in Alabama a "Southern working class black organization" (p. xii). Communists formed sharecropping unions, neighborhood relief committees, and unemployment councils for the city's poor. In Alabama, Communists "opposed race and class oppression as a totality under the banner of 'bread and freedom,' and through the newspaper, *The Southern Worker*" (Kelley 1990, p. xii).

Later, the Communist Party chose Harlem, New York, as another "concentration point" because it was the epicenter of black protest (Naison 1983, p. xvii). Early black radicalism in 1930s Harlem aligned itself with the traditions of black nationalism and black militancy. Some Communists considered "narrow nationalism" and "back to Africa" ideologies to be reactionary, although others viewed nationalism as a "legitimate trend in the Black Freedom Movement" (Haywood 229, p. 1978). Mark Naison (1983) documented Communist Party activism in Harlem and described how early black Communists were "race men and women" drawn from the ranks of nationalist organizations. In Harlem, Communists organized workers alliances, tenant unions, cultural groups, and legal defense organizations. Harlem was a rich political landscape, with organizations like the Urban League and the NAACP, and the ultranationalism of Marcus Garvey. Within Harlem, socialist ideas were spread through the work of A. Philip Randolph, president of the Brotherhood of Sleeping Car Porters union. His magazine, the *Messenger*, was accused by the U.S. government of promoting "Bolsheviki activities among Negroes" (Kornweibel 1998, p. 21). While in socialist and Communist circles the dominant view, shared by Randolph, was that "race was a strategic weapon to dissipate working class coherence," convergent race and class struggles dominated mass protests of this time (Henderson 1978, p. 148). Even at the height of the black power discourse of the 1970s, African American activists like Angela Davis—a member of the Communist Party also affiliated with the Black Panthers—continued to forge connections between class struggle and antiracism.

Within the African Diaspora, the dialectical method of Marxism proved a useful source of insights for those engaged in anticolonial and postcolonial struggles. Afro Caribbean intellectuals and activists such as Trinidadians C. L. R. James and George Padmore, Guyana native Walter Rodney, and Martinique-born Aime Cesaire merged the tenets of Pan-Africanism, nationalism, "Negritude," and Marxism. Padmore, a unionist and founder of the Pan-African Federation, remarked, "labour in white skin cannot free itself while labour in dark skin is branded" (Padmore 1945, p. 3). Cesaire, however, eventually became disillusioned and resigned from the French Communist Party, saying, "What I desire is that Marxism and communism should serve Black people, and not that Black people should serve Marxism" (Caute 1964, p. 211). C. L. R. James, a Trotskyite, lauded the independent and dynamic trajectory of black struggles in the United States. He believed that "the Negro people based on their own experiences approach the conclusions of Marxism" (Grimshaw 1992, p. 187). In the 1970s the historian Walter Rodney extolled "a working class oriented definition of Black Power" and contended that the extraction of labor from black people was a cornerstone of capitalism (Fontaine 1982, p. 16). Throughout the 1970s and 1980s, Marxism was an instrumental theory in African-based liberation movements in Angola, Mozambique, and Guinea Bissau. Amilcar Cabral, the revolutionary leader of Guinea Bissau, linked class struggle to anti-imperialism, demonstrating the necessity of "incorporating the proletarian project into the project of national liberation" (Magubane 1983, p. 25). Also, antiapartheid ideologists in South Africa adopted aspects of Marxist dictum even as they emphasized national and racial identities (see Marx 1992).

Marxism continues to inform the spectrum of black progressive politics, even as Afro-Diasporic intellectuals argue for the autonomy of black liberation struggles and their "organic political perspectives" (James 1992, p. 183). Contemporary black intellectuals urge that a tripartite analysis, stemming from "the nexus of three crucial sites of struggles, community, class and gender, be at the center of Black liberatory projects" (Marable 1997, p. 8). If they adhere to this perspective, social justice movements constituted by black people can remain "avant-garde" formations of contiguous race and class struggles (Duran 2005, p. 3).

SEE ALSO *Black Nationalism; Black Panthers; Black Power; Marx, Karl; Marxism; Politics, Black*

BIBLIOGRAPHY

Alpers, Edward A., and Pierre-Michel Fontaine, eds. 1982. *Walter Rodney, Revolutionary and Scholar: A Tribute.* Los Angeles: University of California Press.

Campbell, Horace G. 1995. C. L. R. James, Walter Rodney, and the Caribbean Intellectual. In *C. L. R. James: His Intellectual Legacies*, ed. Selwyn R. Cudjoe and William E. Cain, 405–431. Amherst: University of Massachusetts Press.

Caute, David. 1964. *Communism and the French Intellectuals, 1914–1960*. New York: Macmillan.

Duran, Jane. 2005. C. L. R. James, Social Identity, and the Black Rebellion. *Philosophia Africana* 8 (1): 1–10.

Haywood, Harry. 1978. *Black Bolshevik: Autobiography of an Afro-American Communist*. Chicago: Liberator Press.

Henderson, Jeff. 1978. A. Philip Randolph and the Dilemmas of Socialism and Black Nationalism in the United States, 1917–1941. *Race and Class* 20 (2): 143–160.

James, C. L. R. 1992 [1948]. The Revolutionary Answer to the Negro Problem in the U.S.A. In *The C. L. R. James Reader*, ed. Anna Grimshaw, 182–189. Cambridge, MA: Blackwell.

Kelley, Robin D. G. 1990. *Hammer and Hoe: Alabama Communists during the Great Depression*. Chapel Hill: University of North Carolina Press.

Kelley, Robin D. G. 1994. *Race Rebels: Culture, Politics, and the Black Working Class*. New York: Free Press.

Magubane, Bernard. 1983. Toward a Sociology of National Liberation from Colonialism: Cabral's Legacy. *Contemporary Marxism* 7 (Fall): 5–27.

Marable, Manning. 1997. Rethinking Black Liberation: Towards a New Protest Paradigm. *Race and Class* 38 (4): 1–13.

Marx, Anthony W. 1992. *Lessons of Struggle: South African Internal Opposition, 1960–1990*. New York: Oxford University Press.

Naison, Mark. 1983. *Communists in Harlem during the Depression*. Urbana: University of Illinois Press.

Padmore, George. 1945. *The Voice of Coloured Labour*. Manchester, U.K.: Panaf Service. Reprint, London: African Publication Society, 1970.

Robinson, Cedric J. 1978. The Emergent Marxism of Richard Wright's Ideology. *Race and Class* 19 (3): 221–237.

Robinson, Cedric J. 1983. *Black Marxism: The Making of the Black Radical Tradition*. London: Zed.

Sivanandan, A. 1977. The Liberation of the Black Intellectual. *Race and Class* 18 (4): 329–342.

Sayida L. Self

MARXIST COMPETITION

SEE *Competition, Marxist.*